MANAGING INFORMATION TECHNOLOGY

What Managers Need to Know

THIRD EDITION

E. Wainright Martin
Kelley School of Business, Indiana University

Carol V. Brown
Kelley School of Business, Indiana University

Daniel W. DeHayes
Kelley School of Business, Indiana University

Jeffrey A. Hoffer
School of Business Administration, University of Dayton

William C. Perkins
Kelley School of Business, Indiana University

Prentice Hall
Upper Saddle River, New Jersey 07458

Acquisitions Editor: David Alexander
Assistant Editor: Lori Cardillo
Editorial Assistant: Keith Kryszczun
Editor-in-Chief: P.J. Boardman
Marketing Manager: Nancy Evans
Production Editor: Marc Oliver
Permissions Coordinator: Monica Stipanov
Managing Editor: Dee Josephson
Manufacturing Buyer: Lisa DiMaulo
Senior Manufacturing Supervisor: Paul Smolenski
Manufacturing Manager: Vincent Scelta
Design Manager: Patricia Smythe
Interior Designers: Jill Little, Jill Yutkowitz
Cover Design: Jill Little
Cover Illustration/Photo: Doug Besser, Courtesy of SBT Accounting Systems © 1997
Composition: Monotype Composition, Inc.

Microsoft Visual Basic is a registered trademark of the Microsoft Corporation in the U.S.A. and other countries. Screen shots and icons reprinted with permission from Microsoft Corporation. This book is not sponsored or endorsed by or affiliated with the Microsoft Corporation.

Figure 4.7 reprinted with permission of MCI Telecommunications Corporation. All rights reserved. This material is based upon work supported by the National Science Foundation under Grant Number NCR9321047. Any opinions, findings and conclusions or recommendations expressed in this material are those of the author(s) and do not necessarily reflect the views of the National Science Foundation.

ISBN 0-13-011531-2
Prentice-Hall International (UK) Limited, London
Prentice-Hall of Australia Pty. Limited, Sydney
Prentice-Hall Canada, Inc., Toronto
Prentice-Hall Hispanoamericana, S.A., Mexico
Prentice-Hall of India Private Limited, New Delhi
Prentice-Hall of Japan, Inc., Tokyo
Simon & Schuster Asia Pte. Ltd., Singapore
Editora Prentice-Hall do Brasil, Ltda., Rio De Janeiro

Printed in the United States of America

10 9 8 7 6 5 4 3 2 1

BRIEF CONTENTS

CASE STUDIES

CONTENTS

PART II APPLYING INFORMATION TECHNOLOGY   180

CHAPTER 5 ORGANIZATIONAL SYSTEMS   183

PREFACE

The third edition of this widely used MBA and advanced undergraduate textbook continues the tradition of the first two editions with a focus on management topics that are illustrated by over two dozen original information technology (IT) management case studies. Every chapter has been extensively revised, and we've included a new chapter on electronic commerce. The book has been extensively reorganized to provide a stronger coverage of IT applications and greater flexibility in topic sequencing and in utilizing the case studies. The strong selection of case studies in the second edition has been expanded, with 11 new case studies and 8 updated ones. The new case studies focus on such current topics as building an infrastructure to support global operations, using the Web for electronic commerce, implementing an ERP system, security on an enterprise network, the ethical issues surrounding software piracy, the make-or-buy choice for application systems, and developing an IT infrastructure for international joint ventures.

PURPOSE

The purpose of this book is to prepare advanced management students—both undergraduate and graduate—to be effective exploiters of computer/communications technologies now and in the future. Its focus is on IT resources (computers and microelectronics, networks, software, data, and people) and alternative approaches to managing them; the opportunities and pitfalls associated with these technologies; and what the user-manager and the systems professional need to know to make effective use of these technologies. This book views IT in very broad terms, including traditional data processing and management information systems, as well as enterprise resource planning systems, electronic commerce, data warehousing and data mining, managerial support systems, groupware, artificial intelligence applications, and so forth.

The first edition of this book appeared in 1991 to fill a major gap in terms of a textbook dealing with the *management* of IT, a course newly required for all students in the Indiana University MBA program. Today most leading MBA programs include IT

management as a core course, and many undergraduate programs require a course with similar content. Earlier editions of this book have been used successfully in advanced undergraduate courses, MBA programs, executive MBA programs, and executive education courses throughout the world. This third edition builds upon the authors' experiences, along with the experiences of many others, in the use of the first and second editions in both undergraduate and MBA courses, as well as upon the authors' extensive IT experiences in teaching and the field. It also incorporates new technology advances and research findings in this rapidly changing profession. For example, the second edition had a publication date of 1994, the year that the Mosaic browser (the forerunner to Netscape Navigator) became widely used.

Our content continues to reflect a documented trend in organizations today: User-managers, as well as information systems (IS) professionals, are increasingly being relied upon to play IT leadership roles. Today's user-manager needs to be aware of the opportunities presented by IT, its limitations, and the problems involved in its use. A manager needs to understand the processes for developing or acquiring new information systems and the roles associated with effective systems implementation. A manager also must be aware of the many alternatives available in designing a system and must understand the importance of documentation, testing, and maintenance, and the need for security and controls to preserve the integrity of a system. A manager needs to understand how an organization's IT infrastructure affects its ability to use IT strategically. Finally, a manager must understand the importance of the management system for the IS organization and the organizational design tradeoffs involved.

This book, therefore, prepares the student to be a more effective IT user as well as a more effective IT manager. Managers should be prepared to exploit IT for their own work unit and career advancement, as well as for the good of an enterprise. However, managers operate in a specific organizational context, and what they can accomplish depends upon the resources provided and the constraints imposed by each of their organizations. Throughout this book we deal with both the *individual* and the *organizational* perspectives. We also emphasize the different roles of user-managers and IS professionals in exploiting information technology.

Information technology continues to change at a dizzying pace. Therefore, most organizations have a mix of new and "legacy" (old) hardware, software, systems development approaches, and other management systems. Managers must be aware that they will be operating in an imperfect, highly dynamic world. They will need to keep abreast of important developments and trends and understand what is ideally possible today and tomorrow.

ORGANIZATION AND SCOPE

This third edition is a major revision in every respect. After the stage-setting opening chapter, the book consists of four parts: "Information Technology," "Applying Information Technology," "Acquiring Information Systems," and "The Information Management System." Original, real world case studies about the management and use of IT follow the opening chapter and each of the major parts of the book. In our view and that of many other users of the previous editions of this book, these case studies provide the most effective way of demonstrating IT management issues. The scenarios in the case studies are interesting and real, and the issues encountered are important. Discussions of these case studies tend to drive home some of the complexities of managing information technology.

The opening chapter in the book stresses the enabling role of IT, which is the theme for the entire book. It is followed by an updated version of the Midsouth Chamber of Commerce case study, a classic from the first two editions that is an excellent discussion starter on the role of the user-manager in information systems.

The completely rewritten technology chapters, Chapters 2, 3, and 4, follow. These chapters have been moved to the front of the book so that they may be more easily skimmed by classes with a strong technology background. These chapters incorporate material on the rapidly evolving IT industry, the growing importance of object-oriented programming, and the emergence of organizational backbone networks linked to the world-wide Internet. Enough technology is presented in these chapters to make the manager conversant with the latest developments in IT, but the emphasis throughout the book is on the *management* of this information technology. The four

case studies at the end of Part I focus on the selection of a hardware platform, the use of object-oriented programming, the issues associated with building a global IT infrastructure, and the establishment of a telecommuting environment.

Part II on "Applying Information Technology" —Chapters 5 through 8—has been significantly expanded from the second edition. A tripartite division of the various types of IT applications provides the basis for the first three chapters in this section. Organizational systems (Chapter 5) are those designed to support the entire organization or major portions of it, such as traditional transaction processing systems, enterprise resource planning systems like SAP R/3, and groupware products like Lotus Notes. Managerial support systems (Chapter 6) are designed to support individual managers or groups of managers, such as decision support systems and executive information systems. Electronic commerce and interorganizational systems (Chapter 7) extend *outside* the traditional organizational boundaries to link the company to suppliers and customers. This latter chapter is a new one that reflects the growing importance of electronic commerce, especially via the World Wide Web. The chapter on social, ethical, and political issues (Chapter 8) highlights the context in which IT is being used (and sometimes misused) as we enter the 21st century. Eight case studies are provided at the end of Part II, including topics such as the establishment of a World Wide Web site by a traditional manufacturing company, the development of a new Web-based business by an existing firm, security on an enterprise network, the politics of information, and the implementation of a strategic information system.

Part III on "Acquiring Information Systems" begins with a fresh treatment of basic IS concepts, and continues with discussions of application development by IS professionals (using both the Systems Development Life Cycle and prototyping), purchasing systems, and systems development by users. The chapters on methodologies (Chapters 10 and 11) have been reduced and reworked from the previous edition. Chapter 12 presents a framework for assessing end-user computing management. These chapters are followed by an exceptional set of case studies covering the use of the Systems Development Life Cycle, purchasing applications software, problems in the maintenance phase of the life cycle, application development by users, the make-or-buy decision, and the use of an outside systems integration firm.

Finally, Part IV focuses on the management system required to manage information technology. Chapter 13, "Setting a Direction for Information Resources," presents the entire framework for setting a direction, beginning with the IT vision, then the creation of an appropriate IT architecture, and finally the development of both the long-run and short-run IT plans for the organization. Chapter 14 discusses the management of technology resources, focusing on the data resources of an organization. The concluding chapter on "Managing the IS Function" stresses 10 critical areas for IT management, including the role of the chief information officer, the role of the user-manager, the management of outsourcing, the development of global IS, and the importance of change management. Six additional case studies follow these Part IV chapters, focusing on IT planning, managing a small IS organization, the global implementation of an enterprise resource planning (ERP) system, and developing the IT infrastructure for international joint ventures.

BEHAVIORAL OBJECTIVES

At the completion of a course designed around this book, our intent is that students will:

- be prepared to manage IT for one or more business areas
- be able to identify ways to use IT in different areas of responsibility
- be able to choose among different ways to acquire a new system based upon the type of application and the technological and organizational environments
- be able to guide the development or purchase of a new system that is effective, reliable, secure, changeable, and consistent with business goals
- understand the need for organizations to develop an information vision, an IT architecture, and strategic and operational IT plans and be able to participate in these processes
- understand the components of an organizational IT infrastructure and be familiar with alternative approaches for providing and managing this infrastructure
- be able to effectively partner with IS specialists, both internal and external to the organization, to obtain the support needed
- anticipate the future impacts of IT on workers, organizations, and society.

TEACHING AIDS

We have found that real-world case studies are effective teaching tools and are very helpful to advanced management students in relating to this material. Therefore, we have included over two dozen original case studies at the end of the opening chapter and the four major parts of the book. Although some of the actual sites are heavily disguised, they are all faithful depictions of actual situations in specific organizations, and they have been carefully selected to illustrate major concepts in the book.

There are many lessons to be learned in each case study, often related to multiple chapters in the book. For the third edition, we felt it would provide more flexibility to group the case studies at the end of the most closely related part of the book. However, instructors may choose to use a given case study to illustrate the teaching points of chapters in a different part of the text, or an instructor may discuss a case study multiple times as the course progresses.

The *Instructor's Guide* includes syllabi for several courses (undergraduate, MBA, executive MBA) that have used this book. It also includes lecture notes on each chapter, answers to the review and discussion questions at the end of each chapter, teaching notes on the case studies, and a test bank for assistance in preparing examinations based on this book.

A new feature of the third edition is a Web site devoted to this textbook, to be found at **http://www.prenhall.com/martin.** In addition to technology updates for students, the Web site provides electronic copies of complete slide presentations (PowerPoint) for each chapter and "old favorite" case studies from the first and second editions for instructors.

ACKNOWLEDGMENTS

Our thanks go to our faculty colleagues at Indiana Univerity and elsewhere who have used one or more versions of the book and have provided valuable feedback. We are also indebted to reviewers of each of the three editions of this book. The list of these colleagues and reviewers is too long to include here—it numbers over 50—but they know who they are and so do we. Thanks! We also thank the many Indiana University MBA and undergraduate students at the Kelley School of Business who have provided suggestions.

Special thanks go to Dr. Sidney A. Davis, University of North Carolina-Greensboro, and Virginia

K. Miele who assisted with the preparation of the *Instructor's Guide*. We also recognize the significant contributions made by Lisa D. Murphy, Louisiana State University, and Andrew Urbaczewski, a Ph.D candidate at Indiana University, for drafting important sections in this book. We are particularly indebted to the organizations and individuals who served as the sources for the original cases in this book, and gratefully acknowledge the support of the Indiana University Institute for Research on the Management of Information Systems (IRMIS) for the development of some of these cases. We also thank the Massachusetts Institute of Technology and Dr. Jeanne W. Ross for permission to include the Johnson & Johnson global infrastructure case study.

Our gratitude also goes to our spouses and families who repeatedly endured the excuse: "Sorry, but I have to work on the book." Finally, each author thanks the other four for their intellect, professionalism, care, and thoughtfulness, which have made our coauthorship endeavors so worthwhile. We are all still on good speaking terms and continuing to learn from each other!

E. Wainright Martin
Carol V. Brown
Daniel W. DeHayes
Jeffrey A. Hoffer
William C. Perkins

The Enabling Role of Information Technology

In this chapter we set the context for an incredibly exciting period in the evolution of information technology and its application to business problems and opportunities. Our objective for this chapter is not so much to increase your knowledge about specific information technologies or their business applications. Rather, the primary objective here is to introduce you to the new enabling role of information technology, which is the context for managing information technology in most organizations today.

We define **information technology (IT)** to include not only computer technology (hardware and software) for processing and storing information, but also communications technology for transmitting information. Today, IT has become pervasive. Managing IT therefore includes, but doesn't end with, managing the delivery of IT applications to workers who have a personal computer on their desktop within their workplace. Managing IT today also includes managing voice mail, electronic mail, and groupware systems that enable workers to communicate and share information with members of their workteams or managers via networked computers. Managing IT also includes managing the networks that connect workers to other geographical locations, as well as perhaps to suppliers and customers via the Internet.

The technological fuel for this IT pervasiveness has not been just smaller computers that fit on a desktop, but also the "marriage" of computers and communications: the use of computers that are linked to networks. Indeed, some authors have pointed to this pervasiveness as a clear sign that we have moved from an industrial revolution to an **information revolution.** These authors have declared the beginnings of an Information Age in which information (knowledge) —not raw materials or human labor—is the most important factor of production:

> *"The emergence of the Information Age and the sudden ubiquity of information technology are among the biggest—no, they are the biggest— stories of our time."*
>
> — Thomas A. Stewart, 1997

Although the exact date of the dawning of this Information Age is a matter of opinion, there is wide agreement that an information revolution is underway. Clearly, we have entered a world in which the largest bookstore does not physically exist on terra firma, but is in cyberspace. It is also a world in which the traditional news media—printed newspapers and TV news broadcasts—provide Information Age news sources and services on the Internet (such as msnbc.com and cnn.com). It has even become a world in which the producers of hand-crafted goods—artisans such as potters and jewelry makers who sell their wares at outdoor craft fairs—distribute business cards that contain not just an address accessible via a U.S. Postal Service worker and a telephone number accessible via a long distance carrier, but also an electronic mail address accessible via the Internet—or even their own home page address on the World Wide Web, the hypertext portion of the Internet.

In the next section we illustrate this information revolution with brief descriptions of new technologies in the workplace and new ways of working that you are probably already aware of. Then we describe some marketplace trends that have been enabled (facilitated) by IT that you may or may not have already personally experienced: new ways for companies to compete and new ways for companies to organize themselves to compete in new ways.

This sets the context for our introduction to managing IT within organizations. In this textbook we use the term **Information Systems (IS) organization** to refer to the organizational unit that has the primary responsibility for managing IT. However, as we describe at the end of this chapter, IT management is also an organization-wide responsibility: there are roles not just for IS specialists, but also for non-IS specialists. As the title of our textbook suggests, our primary focus is on what business managers need to know to be effective managers in the Information Age.

INFORMATION TECHNOLOGY IN THE INFORMATION AGE

Computer Systems: Microcomputer Technology

Computer-on-a-chip (microcomputer) technology is a computer industry development dating from the 1970s that has fueled the information revolution. By the second half of the 1990s, personal computers (PCs) had become commodity products for the business or home. PCs have the processing power of a centralized computing center of the 1960s, an operating system with graphical icons understandable to the novice, and multimedia, Internet-ready capabilities. PC keyboards have been supplemented by mouse devices, touch screens, and new forms of voice and video input and output. Portable microcomputers have become so commonplace that airplane flight attendants tell passengers when the use of these ubiquitous devices is permitted. In fact, the speed of portable technology

development has been so fast that cyberpunk science fiction writer Bruce Sterling was reported as complaining: ". . . it's hard to write mind-expanding sci-fi about computers when real-world technology keeps advancing so quickly" (Deutschman, 1994).

Computer Software: Commercial Software Packages

The growth in demand for commercial software for microcomputers has been so great that one of the world's wealthiest billionaires by the mid-1990s was the chairman and founder of a software company with high name recognition: Bill Gates of Microsoft Corporation. Today, some version of Microsoft's Windows software resides on the vast majority of microcomputers in the home and office, and the company's word processing, spreadsheet, database, and presentation software packages have been bundled into an office suite that is the market leader—available for purchase by students at an attractive discounted price. Other software companies offer complete applications packages written for business functions common across companies (such as accounting or payroll), packages for business functions common within classes of industries (such as transportation logistics or materials management), or packages for a specific industry (such as healthcare or commercial lending). The software industry has seen such explosive growth that today's business school graduates in the market for jobs in the computer field are as likely to be recruited by software companies and major consulting firms as they are by manufacturing or service firms that have their own IS organizations.

Telecommunications/Networking: Increasing the Global Reach of IT

About one decade after the introduction of IBM's PC, the local area networking of desktop computers became commonplace. In contrast, it took less than a half-decade for more than 50 million users worldwide to become networked to a global Internet on which computer users of all ages can search for information, exchange e-mail messages, and buy products and services directly from companies or through new electronic intermediaries. The U.S. government has been a major player in the creation of the Internet and the

INFORMATION TECHNOLOGY MIS-PREDICTIONS

"This 'telephone' has too many shortcomings to be seriously considered as a means of communication. The device is inherently of no value to us."
–Western Union internal memo, 1876

"But what . . . is it good for?"
–Engineer at the Advanced Computing Systems Division of IBM, commenting on the microchip, 1968.

"There is no reason anyone would want a computer in their home."
–Ken Olson, president, chairman, and founder of Digital Equipment Corp., 1977

[Watson, Pitt, and Berthon, 1996]

fueling of competition in the telecommunications industry. The federal government underwrote the building of the first Internet (ARPAnet) in the late 1960s and implemented radical reforms for the U.S. telecommunications marketplace twice in the last two decades (1984 and 1996).[1] By mid-1997, television broadcasters and both TV and print advertisers regularly included a Web site address as part of their contact information, and the typical U.S. business card had an Internet e-mail address.

As we will demonstrate in Part I, the sales of IT products and services accelerated worldwide during the 1990s. Significant mis-predictions about the utility of a new information technology have been common in the past (see sidebar "Information technology mis-predictions"). This accelerating rate of change in IT products and services makes it even more difficult to accurately predict the IT "winners" of tomorrow.

The rate of change in IT also makes it difficult to predict the long-range impact on businesses and

workers. However, the information revolution has already changed the way many people work today.

WORKING IN THE INFORMATION AGE

To illustrate some of these new ways of working, we first describe what has come to be called the knowledge worker. Then we briefly describe two other major changes that have also helped mold business school degree programs in which some of our readers are enrolled: a new emphasis on teamwork and a new anytime/anywhere work environment.

Knowledge Work

A **knowledge worker** is a new category of laborer for which information and knowledge are the new raw materials of their work—and also the product of their work (Stewart, 1997). Knowledge workers certainly include those who were called white-collar (office) workers in the industrial age—but today's knowledge workers may also be found on the factory floor.

Although the above definition of a knowledge worker does not include the words "user of IT," knowledge workers that depend on information technology to do their jobs have become increasingly commonplace as the growth in microcomputers, commercial software, and networks has exploded since the 1980s. Institutions of higher education responded by introducing courses in computer literacy, which began to be prerequisites for obtaining a college degree by the early 1990s. It is now standard to note experience with personal productivity tools such as word processing, spreadsheets, and presentation software on personal resumes and job application forms. In the 1970s an elective typing course was recommended for the college-bound teenager; today, students are taught keyboard skills from computer-based tutorials in their elementary classrooms or "learning centers."

Teamwork

A related change in the way we work is a new emphasis on collaborative work, usually by teams of workers. Fueled by the publicity given to problem-solving teams in Japanese firms recognized for their high-quality

---

1 In 1984 AT&T was barred from competing in both local/regional and long-distance U.S. markets, ending an era in which companies could rely on a single supplier for their telecommunications services. In 1996 local markets were opened up to long-distance carriers, and long-distance markets were opened up to local/regional companies—like the Baby Bells that had been spun off from AT&T a decade earlier.

products, U.S. firms began in the 1980s to "empower" teams of workers to make operational decisions, recommend changes directly to top managers, and learn new ways of working from each other. By the mid-1990s, the typical U.S. knowledge worker used electronic communications (e-mail) and other personal productivity tools on a personal computer. As a result, measurable gains in workforce productivity due to the diffusion of information technology have been reported (Farrell, 1995). The U.S. workforce had gained a productivity edge over workers in other industrialized nations due to organizational investments in IT and worker training in the use of these tools.

Anytime, Anywhere

A third major change in the way we work is that many workers today can communicate with others and access organizational information anytime (24 hours a day, 7 days a week) while working essentially anywhere (from an off-site office or a home office). Remote access to corporate records and e-mail systems is still highly variable across firms of different sizes. However, by the late 1990s the majority of Fortune 500 companies had "automated" their sales forces with portable microcomputers. Many firms have implemented an infrastructure that provides managers with access to their company e-mail from a remote location over telephone lines—if not globally, then at least within U.S. borders.

The term **telecommuter** was coined in the 1980s to refer to those who "commuted" from a location outside the firm's regular offices, via telecommunications lines, in order to do their work. (A case study on implementing telecommuting at IBM can be found at the end of Part I.) In the U.S., natural disasters (like a San Francisco earthquake), disasters caused by people (like the bombing of a major city building), and environmental laws (like amendments to the Clean Air Act) have led to increased numbers of telecommuters from home offices as companies (and workers) have discovered that working at home is possible. For some workers, the anytime/anywhere way of working has meant new opportunities to find a better balance between their work and home lives (see sidebar "Telluride, Colorado"). For others, this new way of working has made it difficult to get away from work: pagers, cellular phones, and palmtop computers have become requisite pocket items.

TELLURIDE, COLORADO

Lee Taylor is huddled over his Compaq computer, poised to push a button that will zap a draft of a 40-page technical presentation to a colleague. The transmission will head east through an Internet routing center in Denver before racing over mountains and deserts to his colleague's personal computer in Santa Clara, California. . . . Once the draft is on its way, he pauses to gaze out the window of his home office to look at the mountain stream gurgling past pines and aspens. "It's better than the Dumpster I used to look at [in Silicon Valley]," says Mr. Taylor, a 37-year-old software technical writer, as he pads around his cedar-frame home in his socks with jazz wafting from his stereo. *This is telecommuting,* Telluride style, where community leaders decided in early 1993 to set up a local Internet hub, allowing telecommuters like Mr. Taylor to send data around the world with just a local phone call—just like you can from the big cities, but not in the boonies. Yet all the great technology in the world still can't solve one of the remaining drawbacks for telecommuters who need to make occasional business trips: situated at an altitude of about 9,000 feet, the town has snowfall so incessant that its airport is closed much of the winter.

[Adapted from J. Carlton, 1995]

INFORMATION TECHNOLOGY AS A STRATEGIC ENABLER

Information technology has not only changed the way people work, it has also changed the way businesses compete. Although at first computers were primarily used by businesses to gain efficiencies by automating what had been done manually before, automation is taken for granted in the Information Age. Today's firms are not just automating, but are actively seeking new ways to use IT to outperform their competitors.

New Ways to Compete

Businesses have strived to achieve a competitive advantage in the past (Porter, 1980) by competing in one of two ways:

- *By Cost,* by being a low-cost producer of a good or service

- *By Differentiation* of a product or service, by competing on customer perceptions of product quality and customer support services

Since the 1960s, when large firms began to bring computers into their accounting departments, IT has played a significant role in enabling firms to compete on low cost. Computers have been used to automate transaction processing, shorten cycle times, and provide operational data for decision-making. A flood of technology innovations in the 1980s enabled additional efficiency gains such as shortening the time to develop new products with computer-aided design tools, optimizing a shop floor process with computerized control systems that have captured a human expert's decision rules, and quickly changing a production line with planning systems that integrate research and development (R&D), production, and sales information.

During the 1980s, IT also began to play a more important role in enabling product/service differentiation. For example, firms began to develop software applications that provided a competitive advantage by providing sales personnel with information to help them better serve a specific customer, by providing materials just-in-time for business customers, and by developing new information-based services such as cash-management accounts or drug interaction information for pharmacists. Some firms developed so-called **strategic information systems** that resulted in a transformation in the way firms in their industry conduct business. One of the best known examples of competing on innovations using an interorganizational system is the SABRE reservation system of American Airlines. In Chapter 7 we describe the evolution of SABRE from an inventory system for American Airlines employees alone to an interorganizational system for airline flight reservations for American Airlines and its competitors, accessible to large and small travel agencies. By the late-1990s SABRE had also evolved into a do-it-yourself reservation system via the Internet for end consumers.

By the 1990s, applications of IT were widespread and sophisticated enough to enable firms to compete in other innovative ways. Whereas in the past firms had to choose between a low-cost or a differentiation strategy, today IT enables firms in some industries to compete on *both* low cost and product differentiation simultaneously. Further, some firms are attempting to

compete not only on both low cost and high quality, but also on the ability to make highly varied, customized products. Referred to as "mass customization," IT is used to rapidly link processes and work groups in order to produce customized products that are exactly what a customer wants (Pine, Victor, and Boynton, 1993). For example, Dell Computer uses software that captures customer orders and then translates the order into a design of needed components, which is used to "summon the right resources" needed to fulfill this order.

Advances in computer and communications technologies have also enabled firms to pursue IT investments that will help them to gain maximum advantage from their knowledge assets—to leverage the knowledge of individual employees to the benefit of other employees and the organization as a whole. This has led to a new buzzword—knowledge management—and sometimes even new organizational positions—knowledge officers—as firms have begun to look at how IT can be used to accelerate the rate of organizational learning. (Examples of these new types of organizational systems will be described in Part II.)

New Organizational Forms

Information technology has also enabled firms to compete in new ways because IT allows these firms to organize themselves in new ways. For example, today's large firms are likely to have fewer employees in middle management positions. This is because IT can facilitate expedient information sharing among larger numbers of employees, as well as support decision-making at lower levels in an organization. As a result, firms can be more efficient producers.

Advancements in IT have also enabled large and small firms to organize around processes, not functions (Keen, 1997). Fueled by the reengineering efforts of the early 1990s, many organizations are putting in place high-level positions for process executives. For example, a general manager may become responsible for a process such as order fulfillment, which requires coordinating activities performed by separate sales, manufacturing, and distribution departments. Improving the order fulfillment process means more satisfied customers.

Today's firms are also able to electronically link business units that are geographically dispersed in order to share information and expertise across the total organization. This allows firms to better coordinate activities across dispersed businesses. For example, some large firms have begun to pursue a "small but connected" strategy; divisions retain a large amount of decision-making autonomy, but teams of people from many divisions work on common problems and share "best practices." Technologies that make internal and external data accessible, including a global e-mail system and databases of electronic documents, enable this strategic objective.

The advancements in IT described at the beginning of this chapter have enabled alliances and teamwork not just across geographically dispersed work groups within the same business, but also across company boundaries (Hardwick and Bolton, 1997). By the early 1990s, electronic linkages between customers and suppliers became a standard way of doing business in many industries—including the automotive industry (Chrysler, Ford, GM) and retailing industry (KMart, Walmart). Firms in some industries even formed electronic linkages among their competitors in order to take advantage of interorganizational strengths and pooled resources. For example, when automated teller machines were being introduced to U.S. consumers, several competing banks in a large city created an alliance in order to share the costs of investing in new IT hardware and software and in the networking capabilities required for what was then an innovative service (Clemons, 1991). Within the computer industry, market leaders have formed strategic alliances to accelerate product development with potential rivals (IBM and Microsoft) and even with staunch adversaries (IBM and Apple) and to establish hardware/software technology standards (Intel and Microsoft, Sun and Netscape). IT has enabled these new kinds of alliances across businesses.

Finally, many firms have also exploited the new opportunities offered by a global marketplace. For some firms this has meant producing goods in other countries to take advantage of lower-cost human resources. For other firms, it has meant becoming a multinational corporation with a global business strategy—not just producing goods in multiple nations, but also selling to customers living on multiple continents. International IT architecture standards and large, central databases that can be accessed across national boundaries are enabling this type of global strategy.

Today's firms are implementing these new organizational forms because they can electronically link across employees, departments, and divisions, as well as across businesses and nations. According to Walter Wriston, former Chairman of Citicorp:

> *"The information revolution brings with it an explosion of new opportunities as well as new threats. . . . The corporation that understands IT capabilities will survive and prosper."*
>
> — Wriston, 1992

THE ROLE OF THE INFORMATION SYSTEMS ORGANIZATION

Just as finance and human resources departments exist in large organizations to manage the financial and people resources of an organization, an IS department typically has been given the responsibility for managing the information technology resources of a firm. Given the tremendous changes in information technologies, the way we use them, and the new ways businesses compete, the role of the IS department (IS organization) has also radically changed.

One way to view this historical evolution of the IS organization role is in the form of four eras, as identified by Rockart (Rockart, 1988) (see Figure 1.1). We summarize these four eras here, and then suggest a new, fifth era leading into the year 2000.

In the first era (1950s to early 1960s), the Accounting Era, the focus was on accounting applications, such as payroll, accounts payable, and other operations that involved processing "batches" of transactions. The IS staff was solely in charge of the development and implementation of these applica-

Accounting Era	IS Dominance
Operational Era	Line Involvement
Information Era	Individual Decision Support
Wired Society	Line Leadership in Strategic Systems

Figure 1.1 Rockart's Four IT Management Eras

tions. According to Rockart (1988), "The information systems staff swept into the department, interviewed the clerks, and designed the systems—most of which were barely understandable to anyone outside the computer hierarchy."

In the Operational Era (mid-1960s to mid-1970s), computer reliability increased and batch systems were replaced by on-line systems. (We will consider batch and on-line systems in more depth in Chapter 5). These advances enabled the development of real-time computerized systems for critical operational transactions, such as inventory updates and manufacturing scheduling. The IS staff still dominated the development and implementation of these applications. However, because these systems played critical operational support roles for the firm, business (line) managers became more involved during the development life cycle (which will be considered in depth in Part III).

The application emphasis in the third era (late 1970s to early 1980s), the Information Era, was the use of information for decision-making. Relational databases and more user-friendly, fourth-generation coding languages led to the beginning of end-user computing and the development of applications by non-IS professionals. To facilitate the adoption and continued use of these tools, the IS organization took on a new role: the support and management of end-user computing (which is our focus in Chapter 12). A partnership between the IS organization and line managers began to emerge.

In the fourth era (beginning in the mid-1980s), the Wired Society, firms began to pursue the development of systems that would give them a competitive advantage. This new strategic coupling of business strategy and IT applications required not just business manager involvement, but line management *leadership*. Senior level management support for and business manager championship of systems projects became critical for ensuring the necessary funding as well as the building of systems to support the business strategy. Many of these strategic applications exploited the vastly improved communications capabilities: firms were able to wire together geographically distributed internal units, as well as develop electronic linkages with customers, suppliers, and other business partners.

The Wired Society era is still an important characteristic of organizations in the 1990s. But we now appear to be in a fifth era: a Global Wired Society in which firms can use IT to work with multinational and multilingual business partners. In some firms, new integrated systems that provide language and currency translations are being implemented on a global basis; these systems may enable a single point of contact for global customers, as well as perhaps the opportunity to provide customized solutions. Firms are also becoming wired to the "universal dial tone" of the Internet, in order to not only support members of their dispersed workforce anytime/anywhere, but also to link directly to customers across the globe. (In Chapter 7 we will focus on these new electronic commerce opportunities.)

What Needs to be Managed

Given today's Global Wired Society, what needs to be managed? Ross, Beath, and Goodhue (1996) propose that three IT assets need to be managed well in order for IT to play a strategic role: a Technology Asset, a Human Asset, and a Relationship Asset (see Figure 1.2). Managing a firm's Technology Asset includes processing and storing data captured with desktop or shop floor tools for access by a knowledge worker. It also includes planning, building, and operating the whole computer and communications infrastructure—or information "utility"—so that computer users like yourself have information available anytime/anywhere. In other words, just like today's telephone users expect to receive a dial tone as they pick up their telephone, users of computer systems and software expect a network to be "up" and data to be accessible when needed. In fact, today's organizations have become so dependent on IT that when information systems are unavailable, whole departments can't get their work done and customers can't be fully supported.

In addition to the Technology asset, managing the Human Asset of an IS organization is critical if an organization wants to deliver, implement, and operate systems that help an organization to work "better, faster, and cheaper" than the competition can. Managing IT specialists is in many ways similar to managing specialists in other functional areas, but there also are some special differences due to the high rate of change in the IT industry and the nature of IT work. (These will be discussed in Part IV.)

The third asset, the Relationship Asset, has also become critically important as IT has come to play

IT Asset	Goal
Technology	A well-defined IT architecture and sharable IT platforms and databases
Relationship	IT and business managers share the responsibility and risks for effective application of IT
Human	High-performing IT staff due to technology skills, business understanding, and problem-solving abilities

Figure 1.2 Characteristics of Valuable IT Assets (Ross, Beath, and Goodhue, 1996).

such an important strategic role in most organizations. As described above, it is imperative for business managers to take a leadership role in decisions about IT investments and to champion the development and implementation of strategic applications in a Wired Society. However, business and IS managers have become even more dependent on each other as IT has become so pervasive in most organizations. Because of these interdependencies, business and IS managers need to build and nurture strong working partnership relationships (Brown, McLean, and Straub, 1996). Figure 1.2 emphasizes that the Relationship Asset, along with the Technology and Human Assets, has become critical for successful IT management in the Information Age.

In Part III we will describe processes and techniques for acquiring and implementing new applications that require effective relationships between IS and business managers in order to realize the benefits of an organization's IT investments. In Part IV we will extend our discussion to processes (such as service level agreements) that help ensure a strong Relationship Asset. Our view is that the management of all three IT assets should be an *organization-wide* responsibility, not just the responsibility of the IS organization.

IT Management Roles

Below we introduce several roles that are critical for the management of IT: two IS specialist roles (IS managers and IS professionals) and two roles for non-IS specialists (user-managers and end-users).

IS Managers   The label **chief information officer,** or CIO, was coined in the 1980s to signal the need for a

high level general manager who has both the technology and business leadership experience appropriate for the senior IS leadership role. Whereas firms in the 1970s needed an IS leader with more technical data processing skills, today's organizations need to have an IS leader with general management skills (see Figure 1.3). Formal and informal access to senior-level managers of a firm and its line managers is critical if IT is to play a strategic role in the organization.

Computer Sciences Corporation (CSC) annually surveys senior IS executives to identify the critical IS management issues being faced around the globe. Aligning IS organization goals and corporate goals has been a top issue for North America for eight of the past nine years of this survey (CSC, 1996). Achieving a two-way strategic alignment and developing effective relationships with line management are also at the top of a list of eight imperatives for IS organizations published by Rockart, Earl, and Ross (1996). As the list of imperatives in Figure 1.4 demonstrates, IS leaders have responsibilities that encompass not only delivering and implementing new systems but also building and managing the infrastructure, continually training the IT organization in new technologies (reskilling), and managing vendor partnerships.

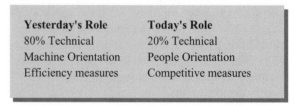

Yesterday's Role	Today's Role
80% Technical	20% Technical
Machine Orientation	People Orientation
Efficiency measures	Competitive measures

Figure 1.3 The Changing Role of the Senior IT Manager

1   Achieve two-way strategic alignment
2   Develop effective relationships with line management
3   Deliver and implement new systems
4   Build and manage infrastructure
5   Reskill the IT organization
6   Manage vendor partnerships
7   Build high performance
8   Redesign and manage the federal IT organization

Figure 1.4   Eight Imperatives for the IS Organization (Rockart, Earl, and Ross, 1996).
Reprinted from Sloan Management Review. All rights reserved.

The senior IS executive's leadership team therefore typically includes IS managers accountable for data centers, phone lines, and the human resources needed to perform all of these IT responsibilities. IS managers and IS professionals responsible for planning, delivering, and implementing strategic systems are often physically located alongside the business managers they support. In some firms, IS units with these planning, delivery, and implementation responsibilities report directly to a business manager in a federal organization design. Both large and small organizations are also increasingly turning to outside IT vendors (outsourcing) for the provisioning of some of these services. These sourcing tradeoffs and other IS organization issues will be discussed in depth in Part IV.

IS Professionals   Software engineers, systems analysts, interface designers, local area network administrators, and Webmasters all belong to the category of IS professionals. By mid-1997, the demand for IS professionals was reported to be much greater than the supply, not just within the U.S., but worldwide. A shortage of IS professionals is forecast well into the next millennium, and IS hiring managers reported paying premium prices for mainframe, client/server, and Internet skills by mid-1997 (King, 1997; Radding, 1997). For manufacturing and service firms with their own IS organizations, the demand is not just for technical skills, but for a mixture of skills that includes business knowledge and so-called soft skills (communication and interpersonal skills). Achieving business-IS alignment continues to be an IS management imperative, and IS professionals who also have a business education continue to be in high demand (Cash and Woolfe, 1992).

User-Managers   User-manager is the term we use in this textbook for business managers supported by the IS organization. User-managers are the internal customers of the IS organization. In today's Global Wired Society, the strategic uses of IT require not just business-savvy IS professionals, but also IT-savvy business managers. As described earlier, the user-managers of an organization are in the best position to identify strategic opportunities for applying IT and to successfully implement IT applications.

IT management knowledge is already being recognized by some chief executive officers (CEOs) as a critical skill for business managers in senior leadership positions. For example, in the sidebar "The CEO perspective," we provide recent quotes from two CEOs in which they share their expectations for their firm's top business managers to be IT knowledgeable. IS researchers have also provided evidence that line management's knowledge of the potential and value of IT is associated with the progressive use of IT within a firm (e.g., Boynton, Zmud, and Jacobs, 1994).

A primary objective of this textbook is to prepare our readers to be IT-knowledgeable user-managers (today or in the future). Typical examples of user-manager roles that will be described in this textbook include serving on a steering committee that approves

---

THE CEO PERSPECTIVE

"I need to understand how information technology is changing our business, and I must ensure that our organization uses technology effectively. Consequently, I spend a lot of my time trying to understand the implications of new technologies. . . . I also expect my CIO to have a rock-solid business view of technology and my line managers to demonstrate that they understand technology and are using it."

–Jonathan Newcomb, president and CEO
of Simon & Schuster

"Our CIO is a full member of my executive team, but he is by no means the only technology champion in the group. Every one of my process leaders views technology as a core asset of the business to be leveraged in almost every activity."

–Wayne Yetter, president and CEO
of Astra Merck
[Perspectives, 1995]

large IT investments, being the business sponsor or "owner" of a new systems project, serving as a process or functional expert on a project team to select a software package or develop a new system in-house, and participating in the planning and execution of the roll-out of a new IT application. In many large organizations, senior business managers may also be responsible for their own teams of IS professionals who develop applications for that business unit. (We will discuss this type of federal design for the IS organization in Part IV.)

End-Users   Although some of our readers are already user-managers, virtually all of you are already end-users of IT. (Although IS professionals are also end-users of IT, in this textbook we use the term end-user to primarily refer to non-IS specialists.) End-users also need to be IT knowledgeable. Although not every systems project team includes end-users as formal members, end-users frequently participate in application development initiatives by providing information about current work processes or procedures and by evaluating screen designs from an end-user perspective. In addition, as many innovative firms have learned, workers on the front line are closest to the customers and may be the most knowledgeable about how to improve a process or better satisfy a customer using IT. IS researchers have found that user involvement in a systems development initiative is associated with user acceptance and system usage (e.g., Hartwick and Barki, 1994). As we will highlight in Chapter 8 and the chapters in Part III, the end-user role can be critical to the effective implementation of a new computer system.

Throughout this textbook we will be providing specific examples of what it takes to perform these IS and business roles well. Some of the cases in this textbook will provide exemplars, while other cases will demonstrate some of the dysfunctional consequences when these roles are not assumed or deficiently performed.

LEARNING OBJECTIVES FOR THIS TEXTBOOK

The overall objective of this textbook is to prepare our readers to be successful participants in the management of IT in Information Age organizations.

Although some of our readers will become IS specialists, most will not; this textbook specifically targets the non-IS specialist audience. Studying and discussing the technical and management topics in this textbook will prepare you to participate in the IS-business partnership needed to manage IT resources effectively.

Part I of this text focuses on the technology asset of the IS organization: computer systems, computer software, and telecommunications/networks. In order to be an effective participant in the management of IT resources, you need to be able to communicate comfortably with IS specialists. For workers in the Information Age, this means not just gaining a fluency with IT vocabulary, but also preparing to cope with continual technology-based change. Although the specifics of computer hardware, software languages, application vendors, networking technologies, and database management systems are all moving targets, the goal is for you to become knowledgeable about some fundamental technology concepts and major industry developments from which you can continue to grow your own knowledge base.

Part II of the text focuses on applying these technology assets. An overall objective of this text is to familiarize you with ways in which IT opportunities can be exploited in a business. Here we describe different types of IT applications that can be implemented in various business areas and industries. We also introduce you to some of the social, ethical, and political issues associated with the usage of IT applications to help you better participate in the management of IT for a business area. Developing IT management skills includes gaining an understanding of how current and emerging IT capabilities can be applied to business problems and opportunities.

Part III is devoted to the topic of IT application acquisition, including the methodologies and techniques for managing the delivery and implementation of systems projects. We begin with a chapter on systems development processes and techniques in general, and we then discuss in detail the methodologies for in-house customized application development and purchasing packaged system solutions, from the viewpoint of the implementing organization. A chapter is also devoted to the management issues associated with having end-users develop their own applications using spreadsheet and other computer tools. Becoming familiar with the systems development methods and management issues in this section should greatly increase your understanding of what it takes to implement a new system not only for a for-profit business, but also for organizations in the nonprofit and public sectors.

Finally, in Part IV we devote several chapters to issues of importance for effectively managing an organization's IT resources—including developing an overall vision and strategic IT plan, building and operating an IT infrastructure, and evaluating various options for governance and sourcing of different IS responsibilities. Strategic IT capabilities require a skilled IT workforce that is responsive to business needs. For many of today's organizations, this requires at least a partial reliance on outside providers. Understanding what it takes to develop and lead an IS organization will help you to evaluate the business value created by internal and external IS specialists in your own workplace, both now and in the future.

One of the major challenges with IT education in a business curriculum is providing up-to-date material. We hope that you will visit our Web site to access new materials that will address gaps in our published text due to new technologies and industry changes. Another major challenge is providing useful and stimulating material for a readership that includes graduate and undergraduate students with broad-ranging IT-related experiences. We also hope that you will use our Web site to provide us with feedback about what aspects of this textbook helped you the most and the least, given your state of IT knowledge prior to using it.

http://www.prenhall.com/martin

Review Questions

1. Define what is included in the term "information technology."
2. What is meant by the term "information revolution"? Provide evidence of this revolution from your own personal experiences.
3. Give some examples of the "marriage" of computers and communications.
4. How has the rapid development of microcomputers, commercial software, and telecommunications networks during the past two decades changed the way workers work? How has it changed the role of the IS department?
5. Briefly describe some ways that IT is enabling new ways for businesses to compete.
6. Why has managing a Relationship Asset become so important?
7. Why has the term "knowledge worker" begun to replace the term "white-collar worker"?
8. Briefly describe the IT management responsibilities of the IS manager and the IS professional.
9. Briefly describe the IT management responsibilities of the user-manager and end-user.

Discussion Questions

1. Briefly cite some examples that show the impact the information revolution has had on a business function with which you are most familiar (e.g., marketing, production, accounting, finance, human resources). What future benefits do you envision in these areas?
2. Describe how the information revolution has affected you as a student.
3. Why do you think that achieving strategic alignment between the IS organization and the business remained a critical issue for senior IS executives for over a decade?
4. Downsizing—a major reduction in an organization's workforce—has been a common strategic tactic for firms of the 1990s. What special problems might be encountered by a user-manager requesting a new information system within an organization that is downsizing?
5. Tomorrow's user-managers will have to be more than computer literate; they will have to be information systems literate. Discuss why business managers need to have not just IT knowledge, but also IT management knowledge.
6. Virtual organizations have been defined as temporary consortia that share costs, skills, and core competencies in order to collectively offer solutions to markets that the individual members could not deliver on their own (Hardwick and Bolton, 1997). Discuss how IT can enable this new type of organizational form.

7. Why might an organization choose to rely on an outside vendor rather than an internal IS workforce for developing a new system? For administering a network? For installing new desktop machines?

REFERENCES

Boynton, Andrew C., Robert W. Zmud, and Gerry C. Jacobs. 1994. "The influence of IT management practice on IT use in large organizations." *MIS Quarterly* 17 (September): 299–318.

Brown, Carol V., Ephraim R. McLean, and Detmar W. Straub. 1996. "Partnering roles of the IS Executive." *Information Systems Management* 13 (Spring): 14–18.

Carlton, J. 1995. "Home Work." *Wall Street Journal* (Technology Supplement) (June 19): R30.

Cash, James, and Roger Woolfe. 1992. "IT gets in line." *Information Week,* September 21: 38–44.

Clemons, Eric K. 1991. "Evaluation of strategic investments in information technology." *Communications of the ACM* 34 (January): 23–36.

Computer Sciences Corporation (CSC). 1996. *Critical Issues of Information Systems Management,* North American and European Edition.

Deutschman, Alan. 1994. "Your desktop in the year 1996." *Fortune* (July 11): 86–98.

Farrell, C. 1995. "Why the numbers miss the point." *Business Week* (July 31) 78.

Hardwick, M., and R. Bolton. 1997. "The industrial virtual enterprise." *Communications of the ACM* 40 (September): 59–60.

Hartwick, Jon, and Henri Barki. 1994. "Explaining the role of user participation in information system use." *Management Science* 40 (April): 440–465.

Keen, Peter G.W. 1997. *The Process Edge.* Boston: Harvard Business School Press.

King, Julia. 1997. "IS labor drought will last past 2003." *Computer World* 31 (June 30): 1, 28.

[Perspectives.] 1995. "The end of delegation? Information technology and the CEO," *Harvard Business Review* 73 (Sept.–Oct.): 161–172.

Pine, B.J., II, B. Victor, and A.C. Boynton. 1993. "Making mass customization work." *Harvard Business Review* 71: 108–119.

Porter, Michael E. 1980. *Competitive Strategy.* New York: Free Press.

Radding, Alan. 1997. "IT careers: Skills they'd kill for." *Computer World* 31 (June 2): 93–95.

Rockart, John F. 1988. "The line takes the leadership." *Sloan Management Review* 29:4 (Summer): 57–64.

Rockart, John F., Michael J. Earl, and Jeanne W. Ross. 1996. "Eight imperatives for the new IT organization." *Sloan Management Review* 38:1 (Fall): 43–55.

Ross, Jeanne W., Cynthia Mathis Beath, and Dale L. Goodhue. 1996. "Develop long-term competitiveness through IT assets." *Sloan Management Review* 38:1 (Fall): 31–42.

Stewart, Thomas A. 1997. *Intellectual Capital: The New Wealth of Organizations.* New York: Doubleday.

Watson, Richard T., Leyland F. Pitt, and Pierre R. Berthon. 1996. "Service: The future of information technology." *DataBase* 27 (Fall): 58–67.

Wriston, Walter B. 1992. *The Twilight of Sovereignty.* New York: Macmillan.

MIDSOUTH CHAMBER OF COMMERCE: THE ROLE OF THE USER–MANAGER IN INFORMATION SYSTEMS

It was 7:30 p.m. on September 22, 1997 and Leon Lassiter, vice president of marketing with the Midsouth Chamber of Commerce (MSCC), was still in his office, reflecting on the day's frustrations. Lassiter had met with four territory managers, his marketing support supervisor, and a number of other staff representatives. All were upset about their lack of access to the new computer system and the problems they were having using the old PC systems. Lassiter had assured them that the problems were being addressed. He stressed that patience was needed during the ongoing conversion. Now, during his private moment, Lassiter was beginning to recognize the problems and complexities he faced with the system conversion. The work of his marketing staff had ground to a halt because they were unable to access the new computer system to handle their accounts. Even worse, something had happened to the data in most of the old PC systems, making it necessary to process conference registrations and complete other functions manually. These inconveniences, however, were minor compared to Lassiter's uneasy feeling that there were problems with Midsouth's whole approach to the management of information technology. Lassiter knew that time was of the essence and that he might have to step in and manage the conversion, even though he had no management information systems background. He wondered what he should do next.

Background

In the early 1900s, economic development in the Midsouth area was highly dependent on transportation systems. As a result of legislative decisions, many communities in the Midsouth area were cut off from reasonable transportation access, thus retarding business and economic development. With no one to represent their concerns to Midsouth's government, a group of powerful businesspeople formed the Midsouth Chamber of Commerce to lobby the state government on the issue of transportation.

MSCC dealt with this single issue until the 1930s, when its charter was reorganized to include a broad range of issues affecting the business community, including state banking laws, transportation, industrial development, and taxes. By the early 1980s, MSCC, under the leadership of President Jack Wallingford, became an aggressive advocacy organization for the business community.

Wallingford's shift in MSCC aggressiveness brought substantial change to the organization. In 1978 the MSCC had a staff of 14, a membership of 4,000, and an annual budget of $720,000. Over the years, the MSCC had been able to develop a reserve account of just over $1 million.

By 1986 the staff had grown to 24, the $1 million cash reserve had been drawn down to $250,000, and membership had dropped to 2,300, largely because of economic problems in the early 1980s. The reserve reduction, supported by the board of directors, had fueled considerable internal growth in terms of staff and capabilities. During this time the MSCC moved into larger offices and began the computerization of some manual processes.

By the mid-1980s the MSCC was considered to be the most powerful business advocacy organization in the Midsouth area and one of the most innovative in its approaches and techniques in dealing with problems facing the business community. The greatest problem facing MSCC was the growing concern that its aggressive growth in capabilities might have to be curtailed because it could no longer fund its annual operating budget.

Leon Lassiter

In mid-1986 Wallingford was faced with a serious dilemma. The MSCC was projecting a $330,000 deficit for the 1987 fiscal year. Wallingford realized he was going to have to cut staff and reduce the number of programs or find some way to more aggressively grow revenue in the organization. Wallingford called in his vice president of public affairs and operations, Ed Wilson, and asked him to find someone new to replace the sales manager in whom Wallingford had lost confidence.

Leon Lassiter came to MSCC in December 1987 with eight years of experience in sales management and marketing with American Brands, where he had recently turned down a promotion to regional sales manager. MSCC, he reasoned, offered more of an opportunity to have an impact than at American Brands.

Lassiter quickly began making dramatic changes. His analysis suggested that the marketing support functions were better coordinated and managed than the sales functions. Additionally, although the MSCC had purchased a personal computer for sales and marketing and had installed some custom software in 1986, the system was quite limited in capability. With these facts, Lassiter began to develop an entirely new sales and marketing system based on measurable goals, documented operating procedures, and regular training programs.

Early Computerization Activity

Ed Wilson performed a variety of duties at the MSCC. He was responsible for coordinating the legislative lobbying team, managing Midsouth's operations, and, during the time there was no vice president of marketing, managing that function as well. Wilson started with MSCC in 1975.

Beginning in 1986 Wilson began introducing MSCC to the world of microcomputers and database management. Most of the staff were fearful of the automation effort and reluctant to accept this approach. However, with the help of a consultant, Wilson determined that the MSCC's needs would best be satisfied by hiring a programmer to write custom software in each functional area. Three primary user groups were identified. One IBM PC and printer were ordered for each group.

Marketing Division

The marketing division's primary need was to track the activity and changes occurring in membership. Primary uses of its computer system included these:

- Developing a membership database
- Developing a prospective member database
- Making daily changes to both databases
- Generating a series of letters for personalized mail contact
- Generating prospect and member lists and labels by standard industrial classification (SIC) code, firm size (sales, employment), zip code, mailing designator, and other criteria
- Processing call-record activity by the territory managers
- Tracking member activities and concerns through a comment field
- Creating audit trails for reviewing changes
- Word processing

The marketing support area managed the database on the PC. They filled all requests for labels, lists, and changes from sales and marketing staff. Requested changes to the member database sometimes backed up as much as two weeks. Lassiter felt this was unacceptable and required a three-day turnaround on member-change activity.

Four territory managers, a marketing support supervisor, and two clerical people staffed the marketing division. The managers generated 75 to 80 call records per day that required database changes, letters, and invoice processing. Taking turns at the computer, both clerical people generally took a total of twelve hours to process these activities. In addition, the clerical staff processed commissions, member cancellations, and database maintenance. The clerical staff also handled special-letter requests from the territory managers and all normal secretarial duties. Soon after the installation of the first PC system, marketing staff began lobbying for additional capacity.

Operations Division

Wilson was manager of the operations division and had 14 managers and support staff. This group needed a system capable of providing financial and accounting controls because until 1986 all payment histories and financial and accounting transactions were handled on a ledger system and were tracked by hand.

Wilson and his accounting manager set out a series of needs for the information system to meet during the late 1980s. These included the following:

- General ledger system
- Fund balances
- Accrual accounting functions
- Payment history tracking
- Commission schedules
- Membership cancellation tracking
- Report generation

In addition, Wilson wanted the operations system to be able to track legislative bills from their introduction through passage or veto by the governor. This information would be processed into the system manually and updated as changes occurred. This information would be printed and sent to members on a daily basis. Soon after installing the system to handle these two functions, Wilson wished he had ordered two systems for the operations division.

Human Resources Division

The human resources division, with two managers and two support staff, was responsible for developing a conference and seminar tracking and reporting mechanism that would also have the capability of printing out badges for conference or seminar attendees. They also maintained staff records. Wilson's decision to buy a PC system for this group seemed to fit well with their needs.

From 1987 through 1991, use of the three systems grew steadily. In 1991, Wilson selected another outside consultant to review the organization's information needs and select appropriate additional hardware and software. The consultant, Ted Vassici, recommended four more IBM PCs after a careful study. In early 1992 the systems were ordered, each with HP laser printers. These systems were allocated as follows: Marketing (2), Public Finance (1), and Human Resources (1). See Exhibit 1 for the MSCC organization chart.

EXHIBIT 1-1
MSCC Organization Structure

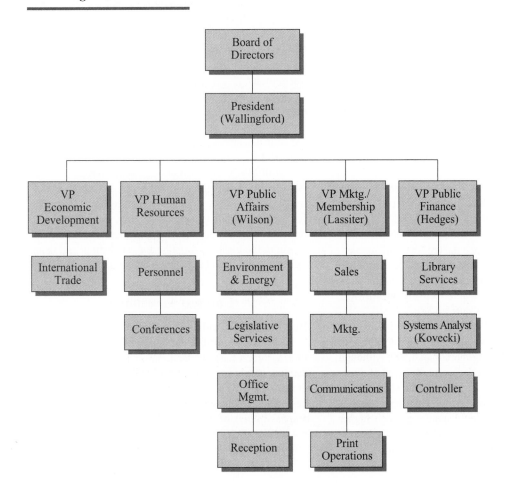

In 1991, Vassici revised and updated the custom software used by each division. He also developed MSCC's marketing software for sale to other membership-related organizations. Wilson actively promoted the software, and MSCC earned a small royalty on these sales.

Changing Times

By 1993, as a result of Lassiter's marketing and sales reorganization and Wilson's aggressive management of expenses, MSCC was experiencing solid financial growth. Although the two men were primarily responsible for the turnaround, Wilson and Lassiter clashed on numerous occasions. Lassiter felt that a large percentage of his territory managers' work and his marketing support activities could be automated to provide MSCC with much higher productivity with a significant reduction in labor and allied costs. Lassiter believed that a full-time systems analyst should be hired to meet the growing needs of MSCC.

Wilson, on the other hand, was worried about the issue of information systems cost. He felt that by maintaining the relationship with Vassici, he could control the rapidly growing demand for computer capabilities by not hiring a full-time systems analyst. He knew that, as a nonprofit agency, MSCC had limited funds for the expansion of computer capabilities. By adding a full-time systems analyst to the staff, it would be significantly more difficult to contend with growing staff demands. Continuing the relationship with Vassici provided Wilson with an ability to specify what Vassici worked on and what should be tabled until there was the time and budget to allocate to it.

Although Lassiter and Wilson continued to clash, Lassiter understood Wilson's desire to control cost in light of the limited resources of the MSCC. Lassiter knew that the slowly growing computer sophistication of the staff would "explode" once the tap was fully opened. However, Lassiter felt this was a management problem that should be allowed to manifest itself, and he felt confident that it could be dealt with effectively once MSCC determined the extent of the staff's needs.

In early 1994 Lassiter and Wilson joined forces on a concept where the MSCC would offer health insurance to its members, now numbering more than 4,500. Although the proposal was eventually rejected by the board of directors, Wilson and Lassiter, as a result of the study, determined there were many revenue-producing opportunities MSCC could pursue that would require a much higher level of information systems use. Wilson soon hired a systems analyst to increase the MSCC's capabilities.

Simon Kovecki, a young, bright, and brash computer science graduate, had no experience in a membership organization like MSCC or with accounting software and spent his first three months on the job learning the organization and its computing systems. He worked exceptionally long hours as he struggled to understand software for which there was no documentation. Calls to Vassici went unanswered because his business had closed.

Through early 1996, Wilson continued to manage the computer systems and, with the help of Kovecki, upgraded the hardware in the seven PCs and printers with faster CPUs, memory upgrades, higher-capacity hard disks, and better monitors. The software continued to work relatively well with Kovecki's constant attention. In 1995 Wilson, with Kovecki's assistance, had developed an on-line legislative information system on a PC that was considered state-of-the-art in the chamber of commerce industry. With this application and the growth in members and types of computer applications, MSCC senior management collectively felt that something had to be done. The separation of systems for membership and marketing, finance, conferences, and other applications required constant data reentry. Most of senior management felt there was a general lack of information integration.

With annual dues approaching $2.2 million and approximately 4,750 member firms, MSCC was among the largest statewide chambers in the country. By 1996 the staff had swelled to 42 and the financial reserve was nearly $2.6 million. Although Lassiter felt some satisfaction with MSCC's growth and financial strength, he was bothered with the lack of forethought as to how MSCC might develop a comprehensive plan to use information for competitive advantage. Wilson, too, was beginning to recognize the value of information systems to an organization in the business of gathering, analyzing, and using information to affect legislative outcomes.

Catalyst for Change

By 1996, MSCC had reached a point where change had to occur. Wallingford, at the urging of the board of directors, assigned Lassiter the additional areas of communications, graphic arts, and printing operations. Controller duties were assigned to Harry Taska, and Jeff Hedges, the new vice president of public finance, was assigned the responsibilities of computer operations. Wilson retained his public affairs activities and was asked to focus his effort in developing an important public affairs project.

Just after the staff changes took place, Kovecki confided to Lassiter that he was disillusioned over the changes in staff responsibility. He felt he should have been elevated to the manager of computer operations and given additional staff. Hedges, who had little computer background, was also placed in charge of the issue research area and the controller's function. Kovecki was concerned Hedges wouldn't have the time to properly manage the growing computer operations.

Although the changes took place in early 1996, Lassiter had anticipated the changes in late 1995. His concern over the continued lack of attention to the information systems area led him to send out requests for information to a number of firms servicing the software needs of organizations like MSCC. Primarily interested in sales and account tracking software, he focused on software systems from Cameo, MEI Colorado Association of Commerce and Industry, Connecticut Business and Industry Association, TelePro 2000, and Data Link. Lassiter sent the information he received to other key managers but received little interest or response. Wilson was involved in his new project, Taska was learning his new duties as controller, and Hedges showed little interest and had little time to examine the computer activities.

In August 1996, Lassiter attended a national association meeting where a session on management software led to Lassiter's discovery of a small firm called UNITRAK, which had developed a client/server software system that Lassiter was convinced would meet MSCC's needs. He based his assessment on MSCC's current and anticipated future divisional needs for computing capabilities (see Exhibit 2) that had been developed by Kovecki in 1995.

Planning the New Data Processing System

Lassiter had identified areas in UNITRAK where he felt a more powerful information system would allow MSCC to be more efficient. These improvements included the following:

- Staff members to input member information into a notes field (not available now)
- Territory managers to access all their account information from their desk rather than by going through a staff person
- Territory managers to develop letters and attachments from a PC on their desk using information in the central database rather than manually linking information contained in several separate databases
- Telemarketing scripts that would allow tree scripting based on various sales objections (not available now)
- A statistical inquiry feature that would provide quantitative analysis of sales activity figures from all marketing activities (not attempted with the separate PC systems)

The UNITRAK system, Lassiter determined, not only met his needs but was also powerful and flexible enough to provide MSCC with the room to grow over the next five years. The software also appeared to be user friendly, which Lassiter believed was the key to freeing up Kovecki's time. Lassiter explained the software to Wilson, who believed that the current accounting system should be left intact but agreed that now was the time to

EXHIBIT 1-2
MSCC Information Systems Needs

Information Systems Capabilities	Marketing	Operations	Public Affairs	Public Finance	Economic Development	Human Resources	Executive
Word Processing	X	X	X	X	X	X	X
Record Maintenance	X						
Legislative Services			X				
On-Line Publications			X			X	
List Processing	X						
Label Generation	X					X	
Database Management	X		X		X	X	
Financial Controls		X					
Conference Registration	X	X			X	X	
Seminar Registration	X	X	X			X	
Billings/Invoicing	X	X				X	
Publication Processing	X	X		X			
Data Search/Research				X			
Inventory Tracking	X	X					
Desktop Publishing	X					X	
Project Management	X	X	X		X	X	

move forward in finding a more powerful software solution to MSCC problems. Other modules in the UNI-TRAK system could be activated at a later time.

In October 1996, Lassiter contacted Greg Ozzuzo, president of the UNITRAK Software Corporation, and invited him to MSCC for a demonstration. Wilson observed about 45 minutes of the three-hour demonstration and told Lassiter, "I'll support it if you want it. It will work for my project for public affairs and free up Kovecki's time to get more involved in planning and systems development." Kovecki's comments were different. He remarked, "Yeah, the software has its strengths and weaknesses, and it probably would save some of my time. . . . But I don't like the idea of staff having access to so much data. It's not clear what they'll do with it."

The Proposal

Lassiter, surprised by Wilson's casual support, decided to move ahead quickly with a proposal to President Wallingford and the Board.

Lassiter developed simple flow charts that showed the hours it took to conduct certain activities under the current multiple-PC arrangement versus the time it would take with the new system. Lassiter knew that the Executive Committee of the Board would require considerable justification to approve an off-budget capital expenditure that would significantly reduce reserves. He had also done some calculations to show that if the new system performed as he hoped, each territory manager would be able to generate $150,000 in increased sales through an increased number of contacts. Although Lassiter knew this goal was aggressive and very difficult to justify, he wanted to be able to demonstrate a less-than-six-month payback if challenged by the Executive Committee of the Board.

Lassiter knew that UNITRAK would reduce the price of the software. The software was new, and UNITRAK had sold it to only one other statewide chamber organization, the Northern State Chamber of Commerce. Jeff Fritzly, vice-president of marketing and development of the NSCC, said, "We looked at quite a few software packages as well as writing our own custom software, but our consultant chose the A/S 400 hardware and UNITRAK software. We purchased both the hardware and software from UNITRAK and got a good discount on the hardware. They have been very helpful and supportive of our needs."

A week prior to the Executive Committee meeting, Ozzuzo and Lassiter had agreed on a price. Lassiter was elated that the price for the software was 30 percent less than Northern State had paid. With the help of Ozzuzo and a member of the Executive Committee who worked in the local branch office of IBM, Lassiter was also able to achieve an excellent discount on the A/S 400. He felt this low cost was another justification for approval of the project. Lassiter also made it a point to meet with both Wilson and Hedges to keep them abreast of the negotiation and seek their advice. He felt that by increasing the level of communication with Hedges and Wilson, he would be able to garner their interest and support, which he felt was important to the success of the project.

When the Executive Committee met in November 1996, Lassiter explained that MSCC had reached the limit of the current system design and an investment in a central system supplemented by networked PCs was needed to allow the MSCC to meet current and future opportunities for growth. During his presentation, Lassiter said this:

> "While MSCC has made significant and appropriate investments in the PC hardware necessary for MSCC to increase its operational sophistication, we have reached the limit of these smaller machines. With the spectacular growth in revenue we've enjoyed over the last six years, our requirements and demands have increased dramatically. Without an immediate investment in increased capability, MSCC's continued growth and services will be in jeopardy."

In response to challenges from the Executive Committee regarding what the new system would mean to the bottom line and MSCC's reserves, Lassiter responded, "I believe we will see a 10–15 percent increase in sales and a 20 percent increase in productivity once the new system is operational." With these assurances and a price that would consume only 10–15 percent of reserves, the Executive Committee complimented Lassiter on his work and approved the purchase of the software.

Implementation

Greg Ozzuzo of UNITRAK was ecstatic over the order and promised unlimited support at no charge to bring the new system up. Kovecki had skimmed through the software documentation and agreed that the software would be a significant enhancement to MSCC. But Kovecki continued to express concern about staff members using the new capabilities of the system:

> "I know that Lassiter expects this new software to be user friendly, but I'm uncomfortable with how strongly he feels about training the staff to use as many of the features as possible. He thinks that training the staff

on whatever they want to learn will make the MSCC more effective, but I disagree. We would be opening Pandora's box and we would lose control over what was going on. The last thing we need is for people to be getting into things they don't need to be in."

By February 1997 Lassiter had heard nothing regarding the purchase of the new system. Kovecki told Lassiter that no one had approved the purchase. Lassiter then questioned Hedges, who responded that he had heard nothing more and had been busy with research issues. "Go ahead and purchase the software," Hedges told Lassiter. "It's your system anyway." Although Lassiter tried to explain that it was not his responsibility to implement the purchase or conversion, he felt the project would not move forward without his purchasing the software. After signing the purchase order, Lassiter handed it to Kovecki and said, "You and Hedges are the project managers. I shouldn't be involved at this point. It's up to you guys to complete the project."

Around March 30 Lassiter asked Kovecki how the project was proceeding. Kovecki stated that he was busy with a project of Wilson's and didn't have time to work on the new system. Lassiter went to Wilson to inquire about the anticipated length of the project Kovecki was working on and Wilson indicated it should be finished by mid-April.

Although Lassiter felt uncomfortable about pushing Hedges and Kovecki, he was beginning to feel that he would have to use his influence to get things moving. Lassiter held a meeting with his staff, informing them that a new system had been approved that would improve operations in several areas. Several staff members were upset that they had not been consulted or informed of the idea before its approval. Specific questions were asked regarding word processing, new member recruiting, and general processing. Lassiter, anticipating that Kovecki had studied the documentation, asked Kovecki to answer the questions. Kovecki was unable to answer the questions and indicated he needed more time to study the documentation guide.

Lassiter set up an appointment with UNITRAK for training for Kovecki and himself. After a positive training visit, Lassiter asked Kovecki to spend half a day with him to set up a project flow chart and anticipate potential problems, but May and June passed with little forward progress on the conversion. Lassiter had told the Executive Committee that the project would be completed by the end of March 1997, yet little had been accomplished.

Upon Kovecki's return from a two-week vacation at the end of June, Lassiter asked Wallingford to intervene and to strongly urge Hedges and Kovecki to complete the project. Lassiter stated the following:

"It really bothered me that I had to go over Hedges' head but we were coming up on the seventh month of what should have been an easy three-month project. It's partly my fault because I didn't establish teamwork up front, nor did I make clear early in the process the responsibilities of those participating."

The Final Phase

With Hedges' agreement, Lassiter set up two days of staff training for the third week in August 1997 (see Exhibit 3). Kovecki had assured Lassiter that the system would be up by the last day of training so that the staff could immediately use the new system. Lassiter broke the training into major segments and had Kovecki set up training sites in two separate conference rooms for staff. UNITRAK sent a two-person team that would act as project managers and trainers.

The training went well with the exception of the conference and seminar segment of the software. The users brought up significant complaints that the new software servicing this area was not as functional and user friendly as the current custom-written PC software. Although Lassiter suspected that a large part of the problem was that the new software was different, he asked UNITRAK to work with the users in adapting the UNITRAK software to better meet their needs. Ozzuzo commented, "Because our software was relatively new to the market place, we were open to adjusting and changing certain aspects of the software without rewriting major portions. We feel we could learn a great deal from MSCC which would make our software more marketable."

On the final day of training, Lassiter told Kovecki to "roll over" the data in the current PC systems to the new system. Kovecki told Lassiter that he was having a few problems and would conduct the rollover after work, and it would be ready first thing in the morning. The next morning Kovecki, in responding to Lassiter's query as to why the system was not up, said, "When I attempted the rollover last night, less than 15 percent of the data rolled over into the proper assignments. With no documentation on the old software to refer to, it will probably take me a week to work out the bugs. In the meantime, the new system won't work and some of the data in our current PCs seems to have been damaged. I hope we can recover the latest backup, but some of the systems haven't been backed up for more than 3 months."

EXHIBIT 1-3
Staff Training

TO: All Staff Members
FROM: Leon Lassiter
DATE: August 12, 1997
RE: Computer Training Schedule

The following schedule has been designed to train all staff members on the new computing system:

August 18, 1997

9:30–11:30 Marketing Support
           Susan Devine
           Ann Triplett
           Dianne Hippelheuser
11:30–12:30 Lunch
12:30–2:30 Territory Managers
           Mitch Guiet
           Jim Wagner
           Gayle Roberts
           Dave Girton
2:30–3:00 Break
3:00–3:30 General Staff
      1._____
      2._____
      3._____
      4._____
      5._____
3:30–4:00 Economic Development Staff
      1._____
      2._____
      3._____
      4._____
      5._____
4:00–4:30 Public Finance Staff
      1._____
      2._____
      3._____
      4._____
      5._____

August 19, 1997

8:30–9:00 Human Resources Staff
      1._____
      2._____
      3._____
      4._____
      5._____

9:30–10:30 Conferences Staff
           Joyce Jones
           Kathy Neeb
           Carolyn Hosford
           Dianne Hippelheuser
           Gini Raymond
           Marge Price
           Amy Kerrick
10:30–11:00 Controller Staff
      1._____
      2._____
      3._____
      4._____
      5._____
11:00–11:30 General Staff
      1._____
      2._____
      3._____
      4._____
      5._____
11:30–12:30 Lunch
12:30–1:30 Legislative Services
           Darla Barnett
1:30–2:30 Doing Word Processing
           Joyce Jones
           Dianne Hippelheuser
           Gini Raymond
           Jean Wiles
           Carolyn Hosford
           Amy Kerrick
           Kathy Neeb
           Kathleen Johnson
2:30–3:00 Break
3:00–5:00 Open

Although one of the marketing division's systems had been backed up recently, the rest of MSCC's PCs were basically inoperable. Requests for lists and labels for mailings could not be fulfilled. Word processing, payment and invoice posting, changes, and list management were all inoperable or partially inoperable. UNITRAK was finding it difficult to help because Kovecki had forgotten to order a new modem that would allow UNITRAK experts access to the system.

Lassiter was finding it very difficult to gain information from Kovecki as to the progress and status of the system conversion. Kovecki, frustrated with the problems he was having and irritated with the staff coming to him to ask for assistance, was going out of his way to avoid staff. Lassiter said, "I explained to Kovecki that I wasn't trying to grill him for information, but because the staff now considered me to be the project director, I needed information with which to make decisions affecting the work flow of the staff and determine what kind of help we could request from UNITRAK." Although Lassiter knew that the staff felt he was responsible for the new system, he felt frustrated that there was little he could do in managing the conversion. Hedges remained aloof, and Kovecki did not report to Lassiter.

The Future

It was in that situation Lassiter found himself sitting in his office at 7:30 p.m. in late September. Kovecki had promised that the new system would be up on each of the last several Mondays. Each Monday brought disappointment and compounded frustration to staff. Lassiter knew that the two days of training had been wasted because the staff had long forgotten how to use the new system. Something had to be done—but what?

INFORMATION TECHNOLOGY

After the important opening chapter, which set the stage for the entire book, the next three chapters constitute the "Information Technology" portion of this book. A number of technical concepts will be introduced, and a large vocabulary of technical terms will be employed. For those of you who have a background in computer science, information systems, engineering, or one of the physical sciences, much of the material in this section of the book will be a review and an update of what you already know. For others, these chapters have been carefully written to make this initial exposure to technology as painless as possible.

Chapters 2 through 4 have been written with a particular goal in mind: To convey what you as a manager need to know about information technology and to do so in a straightforward, understandable way. (For those of you considering an information systems career, these chapters provide the essential technical background upon which much of your future course work will be based.) The intent of these chapters is to provide you with the necessary technical background for the remainder of this book and to provide you with a basic understanding of information technology on which you can build as you continue to learn during your career. These chapters give you the terminology and concepts to understand and communicate with IS professionals and to be an informed consumer of information technology. At a minimum, these chapters should enable you to be a knowledgeable reader of information technology articles in the *Wall Street Journal, Business Week, Fortune,* and similar publications.

Our overview of information technology begins with a consideration of computer systems in Chapter 2. This chapter concentrates on computer hardware, the physical pieces of a computer system, but it also introduces the all-important stored-program concept. The chapter takes a look at the information systems industry and at current technology in the hardware arena. Chapter 3 discusses computer software, the set of programs that control the operations of the computer system. As a manager, your interface with the computer system is through the software. You will work directly with easy-to-use packages such as Web browsers, spreadsheets, and word processors, and you are likely to be involved in acquiring and developing other software for your particular area of an organization. This chapter surveys the key types of software in the beginning of the 21st century—including applications software, personal productivity packages, Web software, fourth-generation languages, object-oriented and visual programming languages, and database management systems—and describes the changing nature of software.

Telecommunications and networking is the topic of Chapter 4. Virtually all medium- and large-scale computers and a rapidly growing proportion of microcomputers communicate directly with other workstations and computers by means of a variety of networks, including the world-spanning Internet. These computer networks are a major part of the current communications revolution. In fact, "the network is the computer" appears to be the key phrase of the computer industry today. Chapter 4 describes the main elements of telecommunications and networking, including transmission media, network topology, types of networks, and network protocols. It focuses on the business need for networking and the exploding role of telecommunications and networking.

Several case studies related to the "technology" side of managing information technology have been grouped at the end of Part I. The IMT Custom Machines Company, Inc., case study investigates the choice between continued reliance on a large, mainframe-based computer system and the alternative of installing a number of high-powered workstations. The Batesville Casket Company case study illustrates the use of a new programming technique, object-oriented programming, to develop a critical logistics system for this company. The focus of the Johnson & Johnson case study is on the creation of a global infrastructure to support the sales activities of this large multinational corporation. The IBM-Indiana case study describes how the entire sales and sales support work force moved to "mobility," working from home offices and their automobiles and communicating with each other and with customers via electronic mail and telephones.

CHAPTER 2

COMPUTER SYSTEMS

Chapter 1 has set the stage for the detailed study of information technology and your role in harnessing that technology. We can now take a closer look at the building blocks of information technology and the development and maintenance of information technology systems.

Our definition of information technology is a broad one, encompassing all forms of technology involved in capturing, manipulating, communicating, presenting, and using data (and data transformed into information). Thus, information technology includes computers (both the hardware and the software), peripheral devices attached to computers, communications devices and networks—clearly incorporating the Internet—photocopiers, facsimile machines, cellular telephones and related wireless devices, computer-controlled factory machines, robots, video recorders and players, and even the microchips embedded in products such as cars, airplanes, elevators, and home appliances. All of these manifestations of information technology are important, and you need to be aware of their existence and their present and potential uses in an organizational environment. There are, however, two broad categories of information technology that are critical for the manager in a modern organization: computer technology and communications technology. Both of these technologies have had and are continuing to have a gigantic impact on the structure of a modern organization, the way it does its business, the scope of the organization, and the jobs and the careers of the managers in the organization.

Perhaps the first important point to be made in this chapter is that the division between computer and communications technology is arbitrary and somewhat misleading. Historically, computer and communi-

nications technologies have been independent, but they have grown together over the years—especially in the 1980s and 1990s. Distributed systems (to be discussed in Chapter 5) exist in every industry, and these systems require the linking of computers by telecommunication lines. An increasing proportion of managers at all levels have a microcomputer on their desks that is connected by telecommunication lines to a corporate computer and often to the Internet. Often the information systems organization now has responsibility for both computing and communications. The switches used in telephone networks are computers, as are devices used to set up computer networks, such as routers and gateways. Even the historically dominant firm in the computer industry—International Business Machines (IBM)—is now a major player in the communications industry. It is still convenient for us to discuss computing technology as distinct from communications technology, but the distinctions are becoming even more blurred as time passes. In reality, computer/communications technology is being developed and marketed by the computer/communications industry.

This chapter concentrates on computer **hardware,** as distinct from computer **software.** Computer hardware refers to the physical pieces of a computer system—such as a central processing unit, a printer, and a terminal—that can be touched. Software, by contrast, is the set of programs that control the operations of the computer system. For the most part, our consideration of software will be deferred until Chapter 3, but the central idea behind today's computers—the stored-program concept—will be explored here to aid in our understanding of how a computer system works.

Evolution of Computer Systems

At present, near the beginning of the 21st century, the computer/communications industry is easily the largest industry in the world in terms of dollar volume of sales. This is a remarkable statement, given that the first large-scale electronic computer was completed in 1946. The ENIAC (Electronic Numerical Integrator And Computer), which was built by Dr. John W. Mauchly and J. Presper Eckert, Jr., at the Moore School of Electrical Engineering at the University of Pennsylvania, was composed of more than 18,000 vacuum tubes, occupied 15,000 square feet of floor space, and weighed more than 30 tons (see Figure 2.1). Its performance was impressive for its day—the ENIAC could perform 5,000 additions or 500 multiplications per minute.

First Generation of Computers

The ENIAC ushered in the so-called First Generation of Computers, extending from 1946 through 1959.

Vacuum tubes were the distinguishing characteristic of the First Generation machines. After several one-of-a-kind laboratory machines, the first production-line machines—the Sperry Rand Univac followed shortly by the IBM 701—became available in the early 1950s. But the major success story among First Generation machines was the IBM 650, introduced in 1954. The 650 was designed as a logical move upward from existing punched-card machines, and it was a hit. IBM expected to sell fifty of the 650s, but, in fact, installed more than 1,000, which helped IBM gain its position of prominence in the computer industry.

Second Generation of Computers

The invention of the transistor led to the Second Generation of Computers. Transistors were smaller, more reliable, and less expensive and gave off less heat than vacuum tubes. The Second Generation machines generally used magnetic cores (minute magnetizable washers strung on a lattice of wires) as their primary memory, compared to vacuum tubes or magnetic drums, where spots were magnetized on the

Figure 2.1 The ENIAC. (Courtesy of UPI/Bettmann)

surface of a rotating metal cylinder, that were used in the First Generation. Memory sizes were increased considerably, perhaps by a factor of 20, and execution speeds increased as well, again perhaps by a factor of 20. IBM again dominated this era, largely on the strength of the popular 7000 series large machines and the record-breaking sales of the 1400 series small machines.

Third Generation of Computers

The beginning of the Third Generation has a specific date—April 7, 1964—when IBM announced the System/360 line of computers. The System/360, as well as Third Generation machines from other vendors, was based on the use of integrated circuits rather than individual transistors. Early in the Third Generation, magnetic cores were still used as primary memory; later, cores were replaced by semiconductor memories.

Memory sizes and execution speeds continued to climb dramatically. With the Third Generation, the notion of upward compatibility was introduced, that is, when customers outgrew (ran out of capacity with) one model in a product line, they could trade up to the next model without any reworking of implemented applications. Perhaps the most drastic change was that the Third Generation machines relied on revolutionary, sophisticated operating systems (complex programs), such as IBM's OS, to actually control the actions of the computer. As one might expect, the System/360—and the System/370 that followed—were the dominant computers of the late 1960s and the 1970s (see Figure 2.2).

Fourth Generation of Computers

Unfortunately, there is no neat dividing line between the Third and Fourth generations of computers. Most

Figure 2.2 A configuration of the IBM System/360 (Courtesy of International Business Machines Corporation)

experts and vendors would agree that we are now in the Fourth Generation, but they don't agree on when this generation started or how soon we should expect the Fifth Generation. Changes since the introduction of the System/360 have tended to be evolutionary, rather than revolutionary. New models or new lines based on new technologies were announced by all major vendors on a regular basis in the 1970s, 1980s, and 1990s (although many of the players have changed). Memory sizes have continued to climb, and speeds have continued to increase. An innovation later in the Fourth Generation was to incorporate multiple processors in a single machine. The integrated circuits of the Third Generation became LSI (large-scale integration) circuits and then VLSI (very-large-scale integration) circuits. Through VLSI the entire circuitry for a computer can be put on a single silicon chip smaller than a fingernail. Communication between terminals and computers, and between computers themselves, first began during the Third Generation, but the use of this technology came of age during the Fourth. With the spread of distributed systems and various local and long-distance network arrangements, some commentators refer to communication as the distinguishing feature of the Fourth Generation.

The Development of Minicomputers

Parallel with the Third and Fourth generations, there was an important splintering within the computer industry. As IBM and the other major vendors, such as Sperry Rand, Burroughs, NCR, Honeywell, and Control Data, competed for industry leadership with more powerful, larger machines, a number of smaller, newer firms recognized a market niche for small machines aimed at smaller businesses and scientific applications. Successful firms in this minicomputer market included Digital Equipment Corporation (DEC), Data General, and Hewlett-Packard. These minicomputers were just like the larger machines (which came to be called mainframes), except that they were less powerful and less expensive. The minicomputer vendors also worked very hard at developing easy-to-use applications software. As the minicomputer market evolved, many of the mainframe vendors, such as IBM, moved into this area.

The Development of Microcomputers

Another splintering within the industry took place in the late 1970s and 1980s with the introduction and success of the microcomputer, which is based on the computer on a chip (see Figure 2.3), or microprocessor. Apple and other companies pioneered the microcomputer business, finding a market niche below the minicomputers for home use, in very small businesses, and in the public school system. Then, in late 1981, IBM entered the market with its Personal Computer, which quickly became the microcomputer standard for the workplace. In fact, the Personal Computer, or PC, became so much of a standard that most people use the terms microcomputer, Personal Computer, and PC interchangeably (and we will do so in this book, as well). Subsequent developments have included greatly increased speed and capabilities of microcomputers, as well as the introduction of a variety of IBM clones in the marketplace by other vendors. The widespread acceptance of microcomputers in the business world has placed significant computing power at the fingertips of virtually every manager. Then, in the mid- and late 1990s, the connection of all these microcomputers—as well as the larger machines —through company intranets and the world-wide Internet changed the entire face of computing. The Internet and intranets will be explored in Chapter 4 as well as in Chapter 7.

Figure 2.3 Intel Pentium II Microprocessor Chip (Courtesy of Intel Corporation)

THE MICROPROCESSOR CHIP TURNS TWENTY-FIVE

In late 1971, Intel Corporation announced the first microprocessor in a trade-magazine ad that heralded "a new era in integrated electronics." But even Intel didn't anticipate the scope of the revolution it was unleashing on business and society. Today, the world's chip population has swollen to 350 billion, including 15 billion microprocessors. At the electronics industry's COMDEX extravaganza in November 1996, Intel CEO Andrew S. Grove asserted that "we are only at the beginning of this revolution-in-progress." Ever since Intel's first microprocessor, the 4004, these chips have grown increasingly powerful in periodic leaps and bounds (see Table 2.1). Grove predicts that this inexorable march will continue for at least 15 more years, perhaps 30. By 2011, he envisions microprocessors with a billion transistors that will chew through 100,000 MIPS (millions of instructions, or operations, per second). 1996's fastest Pentium Pro chips boasted 5.5 million transistors and speeds of 400 MIPS. So that future chip will be crammed with the power of 250 Pentium Pros.

Of course, Silicon Valley-based Intel Corporation is not the only chipmaker—but it is the largest and the most important. Intel has almost a stranglehold on the all-important microprocessor chips used to power IBM and IBM-compatible microcomputers. In fact, Intel controls about 80 percent of the world's market for microcomputer processor chips. Other major players in this market include Motorola (which produces the chips used in the Apple Macintosh), Applied Micro Devices, and Cyrix Corporation (both AMD and Cyrix produce Intel-compatible chips). Whereas U.S. firms dominate the microcomputer processor market, Asian firms—particularly Samsung Semiconductors (Korea)—lead in sales of memory chips (called DRAMS, or dynamic random-access memory) used in most microcomputers. In addition to the firms mentioned above, other major chip manufacturers include Texas Instruments (who also introduced a microprocessor chip in 1971), IBM, Digital Equipment, Toshiba, Mitsubishi, and NEC.

[Adapted from Port, December 9, 1996, and Reinhardt, 1997]

Table 2.1
The Evolution of the Intel Microprocessor

Chip	Public Debut	Initial Cost	No. Transistors	Initial MIPS
4004	11/71	$200	2,300	0.06
8008	4/72	$300	3,500	0.06
8080	4/74	$300	6,000	0.6
8086	6/78	$360	29,000	0.3
8088	6/79	$360	29,000	0.3
i286	2/82	$360	134,000	0.9
i386	10/85	$299	275,000	5
i486	4/89	$950	1.2 million	20
Pentium	3/93	$878	3.1 million	100
Pentium Pro	3/95	$974	5.5 million	300
Pentium II	5/97	$775	7.5 million	500
886 (?)	2000	$1,000	15 million	1,000
1286 (?)	2011	n/a	1 billion	100,000

SOURCE: Port, *Business Week* (December 9, 1996): 150, with updates from Intel Web site, 1997.

BASIC COMPONENTS OF COMPUTER SYSTEMS

For historical completeness, we should note that there are really two distinct types of computers—digital and analog. Digital computers operate directly on numbers, or digits, just as humans do. Analog computers manipulate some analogous physical quantity, such as voltage or shaft rotation speed, which represents (to some degree of accuracy) the numbers involved in the computation. Analog computers have been most useful in engineering and process-control environments, but they have been largely replaced by digital machines even in these situations. Thus, all of our preceding discussion relates to digital computers, as does that which follows.

Underlying Structure

Today's computers vary greatly in size, speed, and details of operation—from hand-held microcomputers costing around $100 to supercomputers with price tags of more than $10 million. Fortunately, as we try to understand these machines, they all have essentially the same basic logical structure (as represented in Figure 2.4). All computers, whether they are sold by

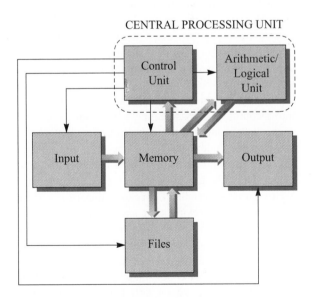

CENTRAL PROCESSING UNIT

Figure 2.4 The Logical Structure of Digital Computers

Radio Shack or by Cray (the dominant manufacturer of supercomputers), are made up of the same set of six building blocks: input, output, memory, arithmetic/logical unit, control unit, and files. (Some of the very smallest microcomputers may not have files.) Our discussion of how computers work will focus on these six blocks and their interrelationships.

In addition to the blocks themselves, Figure 2.4 also includes two types of arrows. The broad arrows represent the flows of data through the computer system, and the thin arrows indicate that each of the other components is controlled by the control unit. A dashed line encircles the control unit and the arithmetic/logical unit. These two blocks together are often referred to as the **central processing unit,** or **CPU,** or just the **processor.** (Historically, the memory was also considered part of the CPU because it was located in the same physical cabinet, but with changes in memory technologies, memory is now regarded as a separate entity from the CPU.)

Input/Output

To use a computer, we must have some means of entering data into the computer for it to use in its computations. There are a wide variety of input devices, and we mention only the most commonly used types. The input device that you as a manager are most likely to use is a keyboard on a microcomputer or a terminal. We will talk more about microcomputers (PCs) later, but they include all of the building blocks shown in Figure 2.4. A **terminal** is a simpler device than a PC; it is designed strictly for input/output and does not incorporate a processor (CPU)—or at least not a general purpose processor. Most terminals consist of a keyboard for data entry and a video display unit (a television screen) to show the user what has been entered and to display the output from the computer. The terminal is connected to a computer via some type of telecommunication line. In addition to their use by managers, terminals are widely used by clerical personnel involved in on-line transaction processing (discussed in Chapter 5). Many terminals are being replaced by microcomputers today.

Special types of terminals are also in widespread use as computer input devices. Point-of-sale terminals have largely replaced conventional cash registers in major department stores, and automatic teller machines (ATMs) are commonplace in the banking industry. These devices are simply terminals modified to serve a specific purpose. Like the standard terminals described above, these special-purpose devices serve as both input and output devices, often incorporating a small built-in printer to provide a hard copy record of the transaction.

Terminals allow users to key data directly into the computer. By contrast, some input methods require that data be recorded on a special input medium before they can be entered into the computer. Until the 1980s, the most common form of computer input involved punched cards and a punched-card reader. Users keyed in data at a punched card keypunch machine, which translated the key strokes into holes in a punched card (employing a coding scheme known as Hollerith code). Then the punched cards were carried to a punched card reader directly attached to the computer; the reader then read the cards one at a time, interpreting the holes in the cards and transmitting the data to the memory, as indicated in Figure 2.4. Until early in the 1980s, U.S. government checks, many credit card charge slips, and class enrollment cards at most universities were punched cards. Computers often had a card punch attached as an output device to produce checks, enrollment cards, and other punched card output. However, punched cards were a nuisance to handle and store, and they have disappeared because of the communications and processing developments of the past two decades.

Other input methods employing special input media have not disappeared, although their importance has shrunk. With a key-to-tape system or a key-to-disk system, data entry personnel key in data at a microcomputer or a workstation attached to a midrange computer. The computer records the data as a series of magnetized spots (using some type of coding scheme) on the surface of a magnetic tape (similar to the tape used in a home VCR) or a magnetic disk (similar in appearance to a phonograph record). After a significant quantity of data has been recorded, an output magnetic tape is created and hand-carried to the primary computer system, where it is mounted in a magnetic tape unit. This unit then reads the tape, interpreting the magnetized spots on the surface of the tape and transmitting the data to the memory.

Some input methods read an original document (such as a typed report or a check or deposit slip)

directly into the memory of the computer. Check processing is handled this way in the United States through the **magnetic ink character recognition,** or **MICR**, input method. Most checks have the account number and bank number preprinted at the bottom using strange-looking numbers and a special magnetizable ink. After a check is cashed, the amount of the check is recorded in magnetizable ink at the bottom of the check by the bank that cashed the check. A computer input device called a magnetic ink character reader magnetizes the ink, recognizes the numbers, and transmits the data to the memory of the bank's computer. **Optical character recognition,** abbreviated **OCR**, is an input method that directly scans typed, printed, or hand-printed material. A device called an optical character reader scans and recognizes the characters and then transmits the data to the system memory or records them on magnetic tape.

Imaging goes even further than optical character recognition. With imaging, any type of paper document—including business forms, reports, charts, graphs, and photographs—can be read by a scanner and translated into digital form so that it can be stored in the computer system. Then this process can be reversed, so that the digitized image stored in the computer system can be displayed on a video display unit, printed on paper, or transmitted to another computer or workstation. However, the characters in the image cannot be easily processed as individual numbers or letters. Imaging is often accomplished through a specialized image management system, which is a microcomputer-based system.

An increasingly important way of entering data into a computer is by scanning a **bar code label** on a package, a product, a routing sheet, a container, or a vehicle. Bar code systems capture data much faster and more accurately than systems in which data are keyed. Thus, the use of bar codes is very popular for high-volume supermarket checkout, department store sales, inventory tracking, time and attendance records, and health care records. They are also valuable for automated applications such as automotive assembly control and warehouse restocking. There is actually a wide variety of bar code languages, called "symbologies." Perhaps the most widely known symbology is the Universal Product Code, or UPC, used by the grocery industry.

Just as we must have a way of entering data into the computer, the computer must have a way of producing results in a usable form. We have already mentioned displaying results on a video display unit, printing a document on a small printer built into a special-purpose terminal, and punching cards. Output can also be written on a magnetic tape or a magnetic disk (such as a 3.5-inch floppy disk), which may be useful if the data will be read back later either into the same or another computer.

The dominant form of output, however, is the printed report. Computer printers come in a variety of sizes, speeds, and prices. At the lower end are serial printers, which are typically used with microcomputers. They usually employ a nonimpact process (such as an ink-jet or laser-jet process), and they normally operate in a speed range of 3 to 15 pages per minute. Printers used with larger computers may be line printers or page printers. Line printers operate at high speeds (up to 2,200 lines per minute) and print one line at a time, usually employing an impact printing mechanism in which individual hammers force the paper and ribbon against the appropriate print characters (which are embossed on a rotating band or chain). Page printers, which produce up to 800 pages per minute, print one entire page at a time, often employing an electrophotographic printing process (like a copying machine) to print an image formed by a laser beam.

In part to counteract the flood of paper that is threatening to engulf many organizations, microfilm has become an important computer output medium. The output device is a **computer output microfilm (COM)** recorder that accepts the data from memory and prepares the microfilm output at very high speeds, either as a roll of microfilm or as a sheet of film called a microfiche that contains many pages on each sheet. **Voice response units** are gaining increasing acceptance as providers of limited, tightly programmed computer output. Cable television shopping services and stock price quotation services often use voice output in conjunction with touch-tone telephone input.

The newest buzzword used to describe computer input and output is **multimedia.** A multimedia system uses a microcomputer to coordinate many types of communications media—text, graphics, sound, still images, animation, and video. The purpose of a multimedia system is to enhance the quality of and interest

VOICE INPUT TO COMPUTERS

Voice input to computers is becoming more of a reality, although we cannot converse with today's machines as easily as Starfleet officers can talk with the computer system on the U.S.S. Enterprise. But we are certainly moving in that direction! Software packages are now available to run on microcomputers operating under Windows 95 that permit users to "dictate" to the computer and have the computer produce a word-processed document. A very economical package is IBM's Voice-Type Simply Speaking, an entry level product that sells for around $50 for the U.S. English version. VoiceType Simply Speaking is also available in U.K. English, French, German, Italian, and Spanish; and both Chinese and Japanese are coming. VoiceType Simply Speaking has an initial vocabulary of 22,000 words. Most users obtain over 90-percent accuracy when they first begin using Simply Speaking, and that accuracy rate improves over time. The biggest disadvantage of Simply Speaking is that the user must pause very slightly between words for the program to recognize them. It is still possible, however, for users to "voicetype" at 70 to 100 words per minute. IBM also offers VoiceType Dictation, a more comprehensive version of the program designed for use by doctors, lawyers, and other professionals.

Other voice input products include Kurzweil VoicePad for Windows and Kurzweil Clinical Reporter, produced by Kurzweil Applied Intelligence, Inc. Kurzweil suggests that, with practice, users can obtain 97-percent or higher accuracy with their systems—but they still require slight pauses between words. Early users are quite excited by a new product from Dragon Systems, Inc., called NaturallySpeaking because it supports continuous speech. NaturallySpeaking costs a bit more (about $700) and incorporates a 30,000-word dictionary and a 230,000-word backup dictionary. In a test run, Herb Bethoney of *PC Week* Labs was able to translate his thoughts into text at a rate of 70 to 80 words per minute—after "training" the software. Immediately after installing NaturallySpeaking, he got accuracy figures in the range of 85 to 90 percent, but this increased after a week of testing to a range of 95 percent or higher.

[Adapted from Bethoney, 1997, and IBM Web site, 1997]

in a presentation, whether it is a corporate briefing, a college lecture, an elementary school lesson, or self-paced instruction. The sound and video usually come from a CD-ROM, played on CD-ROM player built into the microcomputer. Graphics or photographs used as part of the presentation may have been scanned via an imaging system, and artwork may have been created with a graphics program on the computer; these images are then stored in the computer's files. The key is that the entire multimedia presentation is controlled by the microcomputer.

To summarize, the particular input and output devices attached to a given computer will vary based on the uses of the computer. Every computer system will have at least one input device and at least one output device. On the computers you will be using as a manager, keyboards, video display units, printers, CD-ROM players, and disk drives will be the most common input/output devices.

Computer Memory

At the heart of the diagram of Figure 2.4 is the **memory,** also referred to as main memory or primary memory. All data flows are to and from memory. Data from input devices always goes into memory, output devices always receive their data from memory, two-way data flows exist between files and memory and between the arithmetic/logical unit and memory, and a special type of data flows from memory to the control unit to tell the control unit what to do next (this latter

flow is the focus of the section "The Stored-Program Concept").

In some respects, the computer memory is like human memory. Both computers and humans store data in memory in order to remember it, or use it, at a later time. But the way in which data are stored and recalled differs radically between computer memory and human memory. Computer memory is divided into cells, and a fixed amount of data can be stored in each cell. Further, each memory cell has an identifying number called an address, which never changes. A very early microcomputer, for example, might have 65,536 memory cells, each capable of storing one character of data at a time. These cells have unchanging addresses varying from 0 for the first cell up to 65535 for the last cell.

A useful analogy is to compare computer memory to a wall of post office boxes (see Figure 2.5). Each box has its own sequential identifying number printed on the door to the box, and these numbers correspond to the addresses associated with memory cells. In Figure 2.5 the address or identifying number of each memory register is shown in the upper left corner of each box. The mail stored in each box changes as mail is distributed or picked up. In computer memory, each memory cell holds some amount of data until it is changed. For example, memory cell 0 holds the characters MAY, memory cell 1 holds the

0 MAY	1 1998	2 700.00	3 4	4 OSU	5 17	6 321.16	7 3
8 C	9 OMPU	10 TER	11 32	12 0	13 MARY	14 71.3	15 L
16 27	17 18	18 103.0	19 7	20 JOHN	21 41	22 100.00	23 0
24 0	25 0	26 0	27 37	28 B	29 0	30 62	31 1

Figure 2.5 Diagram of Computer Memory

characters 1998, memory cell 2 holds the characters 700.00, and so on. The characters shown in Figure 2.5 represent the contents of memory at a particular point in time; a fraction of a second later the contents may be entirely different as the computer goes about its work. The contents of the memory cells will change as the computer works, whereas the addresses of the cells are fixed.

Computer memory is different from the post office boxes in several ways, of course. For one thing, computer memory operates on the principle of destructive read-in, nondestructive read-out, which means that as a particular piece of data is placed into a particular memory cell, either by reading it from an input device or as the result of a computation in the arithmetic/logical unit, it destroys (or erases) whatever data item was previously in the cell. By contrast, when a data item is retrieved from a cell, either to print it out or to use it in a computation, the contents of the cell are unchanged.

Another major difference between post office boxes and memory cells is in their capacity. A post office box has a variable capacity depending upon the size of the pieces of mail and how much effort is spent by postal employees in stuffing the mail in the box. A memory cell has a fixed capacity, with the capacity varying from one computer model to another. A memory cell that can store only one character of data is called a **byte,** and a memory cell that can store two or more characters of data is called a **word.** For comparability, it has become customary to describe the size of memory (and the size of direct-access files) in terms of the equivalent number of bytes, even if the cells are really words.

Leaving our post office analogy, we can note that there are several important differences between the memory of one computer model and that of another. First, the capacity of each cell may differ. In a microcomputer, each cell may hold only one digit of a number, whereas a single cell in a mainframe may hold 14 digits. Second, the number of cells making up memory may vary from several million to a few billion. Third, the time involved to transfer data from memory to another component may differ by an order of magnitude from one machine to another. The technologies employed in constructing the memories may also differ, although most memory today is based on some variation of VLSI circuits on silicon chips.

Bits and Coding Schemes   Each memory cell consists of a particular set of circuits (a small subset of the VLSI circuits on a memory chip), and each circuit can be set to either "on" or "off." Because each circuit has just two states (on and off), they are equated to 1 and 0, the two possible values of a binary number. Thus, each circuit corresponds to a *bi*nary digi*t,* or a **bit.** In order to represent the decimal digits (and the alphabetic letters and special characters) for processing by the computer, several of these bits (or circuits) must be combined to represent a single character. In most computers, eight bits (or circuits) represent a single character. And a memory cell containing a single character, we know, is called a byte. Thus, eight bits equals one byte in most machines.

Let's consider a particular example. Assume that we have a computer where each memory cell is a byte (can contain one character). Then memory cell number 327, for instance, will consist of eight circuits or bits. If these circuits are set to on-on-on-on-on-off-off-on (or, alternatively, 1111 1001), this may be defined by the coding scheme to represent the decimal digit 9. If these bits are set to 1111 0001, this may be defined as the decimal digit 1. If these bits are set to 1100 0010, this may be defined as the letter B. And so on, with each character we wish to represent having a corresponding pattern of eight bits.

There are two common coding schemes in use today. The examples given above are taken from the Extended Binary Coded Decimal Interchange Code (commonly known as EBCDIC, pronounced eb´-si-dic). EBCDIC was originally developed by IBM in the 1950s, and it is still used by IBM and other vendors. The other common code in use is the American Standard Code for Information Interchange (ASCII), which is employed in data transmission and in microcomputers. Figure 2.6 lets you compare the ASCII and EBCDIC codes for the alphabet and decimal digits. But you do not need to know these codes—only that they exist!

The bottom line is that a coding scheme of some sort is used to represent data in memory and in the other components of the computer. In memory, circuits in a particular cell are turned on and off—following the coding scheme—to enable us to store the data until a later time. It turns out that circuits are also used to represent data in the control and arithmetic/logical units. In the input, output, and files,

Char-acter	EBCDIC Binary		Char-acter	ASCII-8 Binary	
A	1100	0001	A	1010	0001
B	1100	0010	B	1010	0010
C	1100	0011	C	1010	0011
D	1100	0100	D	1010	0100
E	1100	0101	E	1010	0101
F	1100	0110	F	1010	0110
G	1100	0111	G	1010	0111
H	1100	1000	H	1010	1000
I	1100	1001	I	1010	1001
J	1101	0001	J	1010	1010
K	1101	0010	K	1010	1011
L	1101	0011	L	1010	1100
M	1101	0100	M	1010	1101
N	1101	0101	N	1010	1110
O	1101	0110	O	1010	1111
P	1101	0111	P	1011	0000
Q	1101	1000	Q	1011	0001
R	1101	1001	R	1011	0010
S	1110	0010	S	1011	0011
T	1110	0011	T	1011	0100
U	1110	0100	U	1011	0101
V	1110	0101	V	1011	0110
W	1110	0110	W	1011	0111
X	1110	0111	X	1011	1000
Y	1110	1000	Y	1011	1001
Z	1110	1001	Z	1011	1010
0	1111	0000	0	0101	0000
1	1111	0001	1	0101	0001
2	1111	0010	2	0101	0010
3	1111	0011	3	0101	0011
4	1111	0100	4	0101	0100
5	1111	0101	5	0101	0101
6	1111	0110	6	0101	0110
7	1111	0111	7	0101	0111
8	1111	1000	8	0101	1000
9	1111	1001	9	0101	1001

Figure 2.6 EBCDIC and ASCIII Computer Coding Schemes

the coding scheme is often expressed through magnetized spots (on and off) on some media, such as tape or disk. In data transmission, the coding scheme is often expressed through a series of electrical pulses or light pulses. But the coding scheme is vital to permit the storage, transmission, and manipulation of data.

Arithmetic/Logical Unit

The **arithmetic/logical unit,** like memory, usually consists of VLSI circuits on a silicon chip. In fact, the chip pictured in Figure 2.3 is the Intel Pentium II processor chip used in today's top-of-the-line microcomputers. In many respects, the arithmetic/logical unit is very simple. It has been built to carry out addition, subtraction, multiplication, and division, as well as to perform certain logical operations such as comparing two numbers for equality or finding out which number is bigger.

The broad arrows in Figure 2.4 represent the way in which the arithmetic/logical unit works. As indicated by the broad arrow from memory to the arithmetic/logical unit, the numbers to be manipulated (added, subtracted, etc.) are brought from the appropriate memory cells to the arithmetic/logical unit. Next the operation is performed, with the time required to carry out the operation varying with the computer model. The speeds involved vary from around a million operations per second up to billions of operations per second. Then, as indicated by the broad arrow from the arithmetic/logical unit to memory in Figure 2.4, the result of the operation is stored in the designated memory cell or cells.

Computer Files

As applications are being processed on a computer, the data required for the current computations must be stored in the computer memory. The capacity of memory is limited (although it may go over a billion bytes on some large machines), and there isn't enough space to keep all of the data for all of the concurrently running programs (e.g., Excel, Word, Netscape Navigator, e-mail) in memory at the same time. Adding additional memory may be possible, but memory is relatively expensive. In addition, memory is volatile—if the power goes off, everthing stored in memory is lost. To keep vast quantities of data accessible within the computer system in a nonvolatile medium but at more reasonable costs than main memory, file devices—sometimes called secondary memory or secondary storage devices—have been added to all but the tiniest computer systems. File devices include hard (or fixed) disk drives, floppy (or removable) disk drives, and CD-ROM (or optical) drives.

The broad arrows in each direction in Figure 2.4 illustrate that data can be moved from particular cells in memory to the file and that data can be retrieved from the file to particular memory cells. The disadvantage of files is that the process of storing data in the file from memory or retrieving data from the file to memory is quite slow relative to the computation speed of the computer. Depending upon the type of file, the store/retrieve time may vary from a very small fraction of a second to several minutes. Nevertheless, we are willing to live with this disadvantage to be able to store enormous quantities of data at a reasonable cost per byte.

Sequential Access Files   There are two basic ways to organize computer files: sequential access and direct access. With **sequential access files,** all of the records that make up the files are stored in sequence according to the control key of the file. For instance, a payroll file contains one record for each employee. These individual employee records are stored in sequence according to the employee identification number. There are no addresses within the file; to find a particular record, the file device must start at the beginning of the sequential file and read each record until it finds the desired one. It is apparent that this method of finding a single record might take a long time, particularly if the sequential file is long and the desired record is near the end. Thus, we would rarely try to find a single record with a sequential access file. Instead, we would accumulate a batch of transactions and process the entire batch at the same time (see the discussion of batch processing in Chapter 5).

Sequential access files are usually stored on magnetic tape. A **magnetic tape unit** or magnetic tape drive is the file device that stores (writes) data on tape and that retrieves (reads) data from tape back into memory. Even with batch processing, retrieval from magnetic tape tends to be much slower than retrieval from direct access files. Thus, if speed is of the essence, sequential access files may not be suitable. On the other hand, magnetic tapes can store vast quantities of data economically. For example, a tape cartridge which can store up to 400 million bytes of data can be purchased for under $50.

Until the mid-1980s, the magnetic tape used with computers was all of the reel-to-reel variety, like old-style home tape recorders. Then 1/2-inch tape car-

tridges were introduced, and in 1988 the sales of magnetic tape cartridge drives overtook the sales of reel-to-reel drives for the first time. The tape cartridges are rectangular and are thus easier to store than round reels, and, more importantly, the cartridges can be automatically loaded and ejected from the tape drives. With reel-to-reel, an operator must mount each individual tape; with cartridges, an operator can place an entire stack of cartridges into a hopper at one time and let the drive load and eject the individual cartridges. Thus, fewer operators are needed to handle a cartridge-based tape system.

Direct Access Files   A **direct access file,** stored on a **direct access storage device** or **DASD,** is a file from which it is possible for the computer to obtain a record immediately, without regard to where the record is located in the file. A typical DASD for a large computer consists of a continuously rotating stack of disks resembling phonograph records (see Figure 2.7). A comb-shaped access mechanism moves in and out among the disks to record on and read from hundreds of concentric tracks on each disk surface. As an example of a very large DASD, an IBM 3390 Model B9C can store up to 102 billion bytes (or, to use the

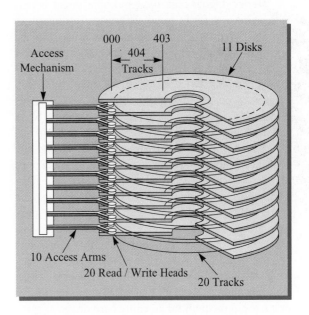

Figure 2.7 A Schematic Diagram of a Magnetic Disk Drive

shorthand notation, 102 gigabytes) on a single unit, with a data transfer rate from disk to memory of 3.9 million bytes (megabytes) per second. By combining multiple DASD units, a total on-line capacity of 544 gigabytes can be provided under control of a single disk controller. The cost of such a file is under $5 per million bytes of capacity.

The hard drives found on almost all microcomputers are another example of direct access files—in fact, they are very similar to the DASD discussed previously, but on a smaller scale. Typical hard drives in 1998 store from one to six gigabytes and cost from $200 to $1,000.

In contrast to these fixed-disk, large-capacity, fairly expensive files, direct access files can also be removable, relatively small, and quite inexpensive. For instance, a removable 3.5-inch high density disk for a microcomputer can store up to 1.44 million bytes (1.44 megabytes) of data and costs under $.50. The disk drive itself costs under $100. These 3.5-inch disks are protected by a permanent hard plastic case, but they are sometimes called floppy disks. "Floppy disk" is a misnomer for today's disks, but the name originated with their 5.25-inch predecessor disks for microcomputers, which were made of flexible plastic without sturdy cases and were in fact "floppy."

Newer, higher-capacity removable direct access storage devices for PCs include Iomega Corporation's Zip and Jaz drives. Both Zip and Jaz drives may be installed internally in a PC or attached externally. A Zip disk is slightly larger than a conventional floppy disk and about twice as thick; its capacity is 100 megabytes on a single removable disk. A Zip drive costs about $150, and each Zip disk is about $14. A Zip drive reads or writes at slightly over 1 million bits per second, which is not particularly fast, but its low cost and durability have made the Zip drive quite popular for backing up and transporting large data files. The Jaz drive occupies the high end of the removable storage market. A Jaz drive, with a capacity of 1 gigabyte (1,000 megabytes) on a single cartridge, costs about $400 for an external unit and $300 for an internal unit. The Jaz drive reads or writes on the $100 cartridge at slightly over 5 million bits per second, which makes it quite suitable as a supplementary hard drive or a backup medium for an entire hard drive.

The key to the operation of direct access files is that the physical file is divided into cells, each of which has an address. The cells are similar to memory cells, except that they are much larger—usually large enough to store several records in one cell. Because of the existence of this address, it is possible for the computer to store a record in a particular file address and then to retrieve that record by remembering the address. Thus, the computer can go directly to the file address of the desired record, rather than reading through sequentially stored records until it encounters the desired one.

How does the computer know the correct file address for a desired record? For instance, assume that an inventory control application running on the computer needs to update the record for item number 79032. That record, which is stored somewhere in DASD, must be brought into memory for processing. But where is it? At what file address? This problem of translating from the identification number of a desired record (79032) to the corresponding file address is the biggest challenge in using direct access files. Very sophisticated software, to be discussed in Chapter 3, is required to handle this translation.

On-line processing (discussed in Chapter 5) requires direct access files. Airline reservation agents, salespeople in a department store, and managers in their offices cannot afford to wait the several minutes that may be required to mount and read the appropriate magnetic tape. On the other hand, batch processing can be done with either sequential access files or DASD. Sequential access files are not going to go away, but all the trends are pushing organizations towards increased use of direct access files. First, advances in magnetic technology and manufacturing processes keep pushing the costs per byte of DASD down. Second, the newer optical disk technology (see box "Optical Disk Storage") provides drastically lower costs per byte of DASD for applications where slower data retrieval speeds are acceptable. Third, and most important, today's competitive environment is forcing organizations to focus on speed in information processing—and that means an increased emphasis on on-line processing and direct access files.

Many major computer installations today have so many DASD units that they are collectively referred to as a disk farm. It is not unusual for a large installation to have over several trillion bytes (terabytes) of disk storage on line.

OPTICAL DISK STORAGE

The newest type of file storage for computer systems is the **optical disk.** The disk is made of plastic coated with a thin reflective alloy material. Data are recorded on the disk by using a laser beam to burn microscopic pits in the reflective surface (or in some cases alter the magnetic characteristics of the surface), employing a binary coding scheme. Optical disks have a tremendous capacity advantage over magnetic disks, but they are typically much slower. There are three primary types of optical disks in use today: **CD-ROM** (compact disk, read only memory) disks, **WORM** (write once, read many) disks, and rewritable disks. Just beginning to gain acceptance are higher capacity **DVD (digital video disk,** or digital versatile disk) disks, called DVD-ROM.

CD-ROM can only be read and cannot be erased. CD-ROM is much like a phonograph record in that a master disk is originally created, and then duplicates can be mass produced for distribution. Thus, CD-ROM is particularly useful for distributing large amounts of relatively stable data (such as computer software, a book, or multimedia material) to many locations. As an example, a 4.72-inch CD-ROM can hold 680 megabytes of data.

As distinct from CD-ROM, a WORM disk can be written on by the computer—but only once! Then it can be read many times. WORM technology is appropriate for archiving documents, engineering drawings, and records of all types. Rewritable disks are the most versatile form of optical storage because the data can be altered. Writing on a rewritable disk is a three-step process: (1) Use laser heat to erase the recording surface; (2) use a combination of laser and magnetic technology to write on the recording surface; and (3) read, via laser, what has been written to verify the accuracy of the recording process. This type of optical disk may be an appropriate choice for supporting an on-line transaction processing system.

A DVD-ROM is a new type of CD-ROM that holds a minimum of 4.7 gigabytes, enough for a full-length movie, up to a potential maximum of 17 gigabytes. Some experts believe that DVD-ROMs will eventually replace CD-ROMs and VHS video cassettes, but that won't happen overnight. A significant advantage of DVD drives is that they are backward compatible with CD-ROMs, so that a DVD drive can play old CD-ROMs and video CDs as well as new DVD-ROMs. The first rewritable DVD, which can record 5.2 gigabytes of data on two sides of a disk, was announced by Hitachi in 1997.

An example of optical storage used with large computer systems, the IBM 3995 Optical Library Dataserver C-Series uses *either* rewritable or WORM 5.25-inch removable disk cartridges, with a cartridge holding up to 2.6 gigabytes of data. The total capacity per dataserver is 671 gigabytes, or 1.342 terabytes (1.342 trillion bytes) if an expansion unit is added. This unit is capable of a sustained data transfer rate of 2 to 4 megabytes per second, with a burst data transfer rate of 5 megabytes per second.

[Adapted from Hoskins, 1992; Wolfe, 1997; and IBM Web site, 1997]

Control Unit

We have considered five of the six building blocks represented in Figure 2.4. If we stopped our discussion at this point, we wouldn't have much. Thus far we have no way of controlling these various components, no way of taking advantage of the tremendous speed and capacity we have described. The **control unit** is the key. It provides the control that enables the computer to take advantage of the speed and capacity of its other components. The thin arrows in Figure 2.4 point out that each of the other five components is controlled by the control unit.

How does the control unit know what to do? Someone must tell the control unit what to do by devising a precise list of operations to be performed. This list of operations, which is called a program, is stored in the memory of the computer just like data. One item at a time from this list is moved from memory to the control unit (note the broad arrow in Figure 2.4), interpreted by the control unit, and carried out. The control unit works through the entire list of operations at electronic speed, rather than waiting for the user to tell it what to do next. What we have just described is the **stored-program concept,**which is the most important idea in all of computing.

The Stored-Program Concept

Some person must prepare a precise listing of exactly what the computer is to do. This listing must be in a form that the control unit of the computer has been built to understand. The complete listing of what is to be done for an application is called a **program,** and each individual step or operation in the program is called an **instruction.** The control unit carries out the program, one step or instruction at a time, at electronic speed.

When a particular computer model is designed, the engineers build into it (more precisely, build into its circuitry) the capability to carry out a certain set of operations. For example, a computer may be able to read a line of data keyed from a keyboard, print a line of output, add two numbers, subtract one number from another, multiply two numbers, divide one number by another, compare two numbers for equality, and perform several other operations. The control unit of the computer is built to associate each of these operations with a particular instruction type. Then the control unit is told which operations are to be done by means of a program consisting of these instructions. The form of the instructions is peculiar to a particular model of computer. Thus, each instruction in a program must be expressed in the precise form that the computer has been built to understand. This form of the program that the computer understands is called the **machine language** for the particular model of computer.

Not only will the form of the instructions vary from one computer model to another, but the number of different types of instructions will also vary. For example, a small computer may have only one add instruction, and a large computer may have a different add instruction for each of several classes of numbers (such as integer, floating point or decimal, and double precision). Thus, the instruction set on some machines may contain as few as 20 types of instructions, whereas other machines may have more than 200 instruction types.

In general, each machine language instruction consists of two parts—an operation code and one or more addresses. The operation code is a symbol (for example, A for add) that tells the control unit what operation is to be performed. The addresses refer to the specific cells in memory whose contents will be involved in the operation. As an example, for a hypothetical computer the instruction

Operation Code	Addresses	
A	470	500

means add the number found in memory cell 470 to the number found in memory cell 500, storing the result back in memory cell 500. Therefore, if the value 32.10 is originally stored in cell 470 and the value 63.00 is originally stored in cell 500, the sum, 95.10, will be stored in cell 500 after the instruction is executed. Continuing our example, assume that the next instruction in the sequence is

M	500	200

This instruction means move (M) the contents of memory cell 500 to memory cell 200. Thus, 95.10 will be placed in cell 200, erasing whatever was there before. (Because of nondestructive read-out, 95.10 will still be stored in cell 500.) The third instruction in our sequence is

P	200

which means print (P) the contents of memory cell 200 on the printer, and thus 95.10 will be printed.

Our very short example contains only three instructions and obviously represents only a small portion of a program, but these few instructions should provide the flavor of machine language programming. A complete program would consist of hundreds or thousands of instructions, all expressed in the machine language of the particular computer being used. The person preparing the program (called a programmer) has to know each operation code and has to remember what data he or she has stored in every memory cell. Obviously, machine language programming is very difficult and time-consuming. (As we will learn in Chapter 3, programs may be written in languages that are easier for us to use and then automatically translated into machine language, so almost no one programs in machine language today.)

Once the entire machine language program has been prepared, it must be entered into the computer, using one of the input methods already described, and stored in the memory of the computer. This step of entering the program in memory is called loading the program. The control unit then is told where to find the first instruction in the program. The control unit fetches this first instruction and places it in special storage cells called registers within the control unit. Using built-in circuitry, the control unit interprets the instruction (recognizes what is to be done) and causes it to be executed (carried out) by the appropriate components of the computer. For example, the control unit would interpret the add instruction above, cause the contents of memory cells 470 and 500 to be sent to the arithmetic/logical unit, cause the arithmetic/logical unit to add these two numbers, and then cause the answer to be sent back to memory cell 500.

After the first instruction has been completed, the control unit fetches the second instruction from memory. The control unit then interprets this second instruction and executes it. The control unit then fetches and executes the third instruction. The control unit proceeds with this fetch-execute cycle until the program has been completed. Usually the instruction that is fetched is the next sequential one, but machine languages incorporate one or more branching instructions that, when executed, cause the control unit to jump to a nonsequential instruction for the next fetch. The important point is that the control unit is fetching and executing at electronic speed; it is doing exactly what the programmer told it to do, but at its own rate of speed.

One of the primary measures of the power of any computer model is the number of instructions that it can execute in a given period of time. Some instructions take longer to execute than others, so any speed rating represents an average of some sort. These averages may not be representative of the speeds that the computer could sustain on the mix of jobs carried out by your organization or any other organization. Furthermore, some machines operate on two to four bytes at a time (microcomputers), while others operate on eight bytes at a time (many larger machines). Thus, the speed rating for a microcomputer is not comparable to the speed rating for a larger machine. In the 1980s, the most commonly used speed rating was **MIPS,** millions of instructions per second executed by the control unit. This measure has largely gone out of favor because of the "apples and oranges" nature of the comparisons of MIPS ratings across classes of computers.

Another speed rating used is **MegaFLOPS** or **MFLOPS**—millions of floating point operations per second. These ratings are derived by running a partic-

ular set of programs in a particular language on the machines being investigated. The ratings are therefore more meaningful than a simple MIPS rating, but they still reflect only a single problem area. In the LIN-PACK ratings, the problem area considered is the solution of dense systems of linear equations using the LINPACK software in a FORTRAN environment (Dongarra, 1992). MFLOPS ratings when solving a system of 100 linear equations (Dongarra, May 27, 1997) include 11 for a Gateway P5-90 (90Mhz Pentium), 12 for an Apple Power Macintosh 7500/100, 15 for an IBM RS/6000-930, 142 for an IBM RS/6000-R24, 164 for a DEC 8400-5/350, 479 for a Cray C90, and 1097 for a Cray T94. MFLOPS ratings when solving a system of 1,000 linear equations vary from 114 for a Pentium Pro (200 MHz), 120 for a Hewlett-Packard 9000/735, 181 for an IBM RS/6000-390, 2278 for an IBM ES/9000-982, 29360 for a Cray T932, and 31060 for a NEC SX-4/32. Of course, these LINPACK ratings are not very meaningful for applications where input/output operations are dominant, such as most business processing.

These published speed ratings may be useful as a very rough guide, but the only way to get a handle on how various machines would handle your organization's workload is **benchmarking.** Even benchmarking is quite difficult to do, but the idea is to collect a representative set of real jobs that you regularly run on your computer, and then for comparison actually run this set of jobs on various machines. The vendors involved will usually cooperate because they want to sell you a machine, but there may be severe problems in getting existing jobs to run on the target machines and in comparing the results once you get them. Computer publications often do their own benchmarking, as illustrated in Table 2.2, in which *PC World* identifies the top five computers in a class it calls "workgroup servers." *PC World* has created a representative set of applications it calls PC WorldBench 2.0 for servers, which it ran on all machines in this class.

Again, processing speeds vary across machines, but all computers use the stored-program concept. On all computers a machine language program is loaded into memory and executed by the control unit. There is a great deal more to the story of how we get the machine language program, but suffice it to say at this point that we let the computer do most of the work in creating the machine language program. Neither you

Table 2.2

Benchmarking: Top 5 Workgroup Servers

Systems	CPU	No. of drives/ individual capacity (GB)	PC WorldBench for Servers Score[a]	Total Test Times for Applications
Compaq ProLiant 800	Pentium Pro 200	3 / 2.1	100	12.5 seconds
HP NetServer LD Pro 6/180	Pentium Pro 180	3 / 2.1	76	16 seconds
Dell PowerEdge 2100/200	Pentium Pro 200	3 / 2.1	89	14 seconds
AST Manhattan D6200	Pentium Pro 200	1 / 2	70	19 seconds
Micron Vetix EL 1000	Pentium Pro 200	2 / 2.1	57	23 seconds

a A higher PC WorldBench for Servers score is better.
SOURCE: Reprinted from *PC World Magazine* (June 1997): 119.

nor programmers working for your organization will write in machine language; any programs will be written in a language much easier to understand and much more natural for humans. Chapter 3 is primarily concerned with the software, or programs, used to control computer systems.

EXTENSIONS TO THE BASIC MODEL[1]

In the previous section we considered the underlying logical structure of all digital computers, and we found that all computers are made up of the set of six building blocks shown in Figure 2.4. Now let us note that Figure 2.4 is an accurate but incomplete picture of many of today's computers. To be complete, the figure should be extended in two ways. First, today's computers (both microcomputers and larger machines) often have multiple components for each of the six blocks, rather than a single component. Machines may

---

1 The material in this section is more technical than the rest of the chapter, and it may be skipped by those readers who wish to obtain only a basic understanding of computer systems. It is included to provide a more comprehensive picture to those who are interested.

have multiple input devices, or multiple file devices, or multiple central processing units (CPUs). Second, the architecture of today's machines often includes several additional components to interconnect the basic six components. For example, magnetic disk file devices usually have a disk controller that interfaces with a data channel connected to the central processing unit. In this section, we want to extend our basic model to incorporate these additional ideas and thus present a more complete picture of today's (and tomorrow's) computer systems.

Communications Within the Computer System

Controller   As a starting point for the extended model, let us note that appropriate **controllers** are needed to link input/output devices such as terminals, direct access storage devices (DASDs), and sequential access devices to the CPU and memory of large computer systems. The exact nature of the controller varies with the vendor and the devices being linked, but the controller is usually a highly specialized microprocessor attached to the CPU (through another new component called a data channel) and to the terminals or DASDs or other devices (see Figure 2.8). The controller manages the operation of the attached devices to free up the CPU (and the data channel) from these tasks.

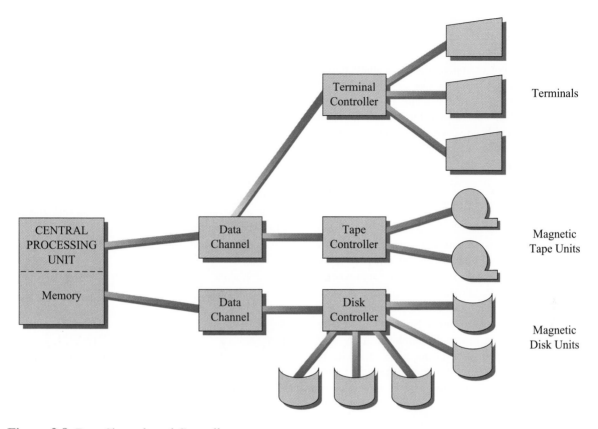

Figure 2.8 Data Channels and Controllers

For example, a DASD controller receives requests for DASD read or write activity from the data channel, translates these requests into the proper sets of operations for the disk device, sees that the operations are executed, performs any necessary error recovery, and reports any problems back to the data channel (and thus to the CPU). A communications controller has the job of managing near-simultaneous input/output from an attached set of terminals and ensuring that the messages from each terminal are properly collected and forwarded to the data channel and that responses from the data channel are properly sent to the right terminal.

Data Channel   The **data channel** is just as critical as the controller. A data channel is a specialized input/output processor (yet another computer) that takes over the function of device communication from the CPU. The role of the data channel is to correct for the significant mismatch in speeds between the very slow peripheral devices and the fast and expensive CPU. When the CPU encounters an input/output request (including requests for disk or tape reads and writes) during the execution of a program, it relays that request to the data channel connected to the device in question (the number of data channels varies with the machine). The CPU then turns to some other job while the data channel oversees input/output.

The data channel often includes some amount of buffer storage (a special type of memory), so that it may move large blocks of data into and out of main memory at one time. In this way, the data channel has to interrupt the CPU only when it is ready to move a large data block; during most of the time, the CPU can continue to process another job. The data channel, on the other hand, must wait on data transmitted from the controller as it gathers an input block, or it must wait for a block of output data to be accepted by the controller.

Another way in which the data channel may operate is by cycle stealing. In this variation, the data channel has only a small amount of buffer storage in which it receives data. For example, when this small buffer fills up during a disk read, the channel steals a cycle from the CPU and places the contents of the buffer in main memory. This operation has minimal impact on the CPU (it loses only one cycle out of thousands) and allows the data channel to employ an area of main memory as its buffer.

Cache Memory

Thus far, we have considered two (or perhaps three) levels of storage devices: main or primary memory, which is very fast and quite expensive; and secondary memory, which we can subdivide into not-so-fast and not-so-expensive direct access storage devices (DASDs) and slow and inexpensive sequential access storage devices (magnetic tapes). Now let's add **cache memory,** which was originally employed as a very high-speed, high-cost storage unit used as an intermediary between the control unit and the main memory (Grossman, 1985). The term *cache* (pronounced cash) is taken from the French word for a hidden storage place. The cache is intended to compensate for one of the speed mismatches built into computer systems—in this case, that between fetching data from main memory (to the arithmetic/logical unit or other internal registers) and executing an instruction. The CPU can execute an instruction much faster than it can fetch data (which requires electronically moving the data from memory to the arithmetic/logical unit). Thus, in a conventional architecture, the expensive CPU often waited for the completion of a data fetch.

With cache memory, an entire block of data is moved at one time into the cache, and then most data fetches take place from the higher-speed cache to the arithmetic/logical unit. The success of cache memory depends upon two characteristics of the data to be used by the CPU—locality of reference and data reuse. Locality of reference means that if a given piece of data is used, there is a high probability that a nearby piece of data will be used shortly thereafter. Data reuse means that a block of data will be kept in the cache until it has not been recently referenced; then it will be replaced by a block of data that has been requested. The use of cache memory should optimize the use of the costly CPU.

After its successful use as an intermediary between the CPU and main memory, cache memory was incorporated into DASD controllers. The basic idea is similar, except the speed mismatch is greater between the relatively slow DASD and the much faster data channel. Again, the keys to success of the cache are locality of reference and data reuse. A large block of data is moved from the DASD to the cache, and then (hopefully) most data fetches take place from the cache rather than the DASD itself. A microprocessor in the DASD controller manages the cache memory, keeping track of the frequency of reference to the data in the cache and moving blocks of data into and out of the cache in an attempt to optimize the use of the data channel (and, indirectly, the CPU). Figure 2.9

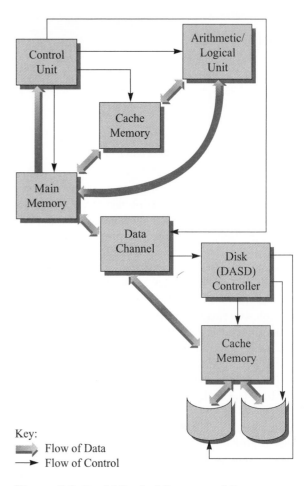

Key:
⇨ Flow of Data
→ Flow of Control

Figure 2.9 Partial Logical Structure of Computer Incorporating Cache Memory

illustrates the use of cache memory both in the CPU and in a DASD controller.

Cache memory (in the CPU and in the DASD controller) represents an important way in which the conventional storage hierarchy has been extended. Cache memory is becoming a part of many components of the hardware, including high-speed communication modules and special-purpose CPUs such as array processors. Even more layers may be added to the storage hierarchy as system designers seek to balance cost, capacity, and performance.

Multiple Processor Configurations

One of the most intriguing extensions to the basic model is the use of multiple CPUs or processors as part of a single computer system. Without using the multiple processor terminology, we actually considered such a system when we discussed the use of data channels (which are themselves processors) with a single primary CPU. Sometimes the term *front-end processor* is used instead of data channel, but in either case the additional processor (or processors) is used to offload handling of input/output from the primary CPU.

Symmetric Multiprocessors   An increasing number of computers now make use of multiple processors as a way of increasing their power (usually measured by throughput). In these cases, two, three, or more CPUs are installed as part of the same computer system. The term **symmetric multiprocessor** (SMP) refers to multiprocessor machines in which all the processors or CPUs are identical, with each processor operating independently of the others. The multiple CPUs equally share functional and timing access to and control over all other system components, including main memory and the various peripheral devices, with each CPU working in its own allotted portion of memory. One CPU might handle on-line transaction processing, while another deals with engineering calculations and a third works on a batch payroll system.

Vector Facilities   An example of an asymmetric multiprocessor is a **vector facility,** a specialized multiple processor configuration to handle calculations involving vectors. For these calculations, the same operation is to be performed on each element of the vector. By installing a number of parallel, relatively inexpensive microprocessors (operating under control of a primary

control unit and thus a single program), all these operations can be performed simultaneously. The keys to whether a vector facility is worthwhile are the percentage of the total calculations that involve vectors and the lengths of the vectors themselves. The higher the percentage and the longer the vectors, the more valuable the vector facility. For research and development activities, vector facilities are often worthwhile, but their value for most business information processing is limited.

Parallel Processors   A **parallel processor** (PP) has two major differences from a vector facility. First, there is no single primary CPU in a parallel processor, and, second, the various CPUs are not always performing the same operation at the same time. For example, a parallel processing machine may have 16, 64, 256, or more processors, each of which would work on a separate piece of the same program. In order to use a parallel processing approach, the program must somehow be divided up among the processors and the activities of the various processors must be coordinated. Many supercomputers, to be discussed later in the chapter, employ a parallel processing architecture.

The term **massively parallel processor** (MPP) is used to describe machines with some large number of parallel CPUs. There is no firm guideline to distinguish between a PP and an MPP; in general, however, 32 or more parallel CPUs would be considered an MPP if the different CPUs are capable of performing different instructions at the same time, or a thousand or more parallel CPUs would be considered an MPP if the different CPUs must all carry out the same instruction at the same time. An example of a massively parallel machine is the one-of-a-kind Intel computer located at Sandia National Laboratories in Albuquerque (Port, April 29, 1996). This machine contains 9,018 Pentium Pro chips operating in parallel and is capable of 1.8 teraflops, or 1.8 trillion floating point operations per second. This MPP computer, funded by the U.S. Department of Energy, is being used to simulate nuclear weapons to ensure their safety and effectiveness—with zero physical testing.

We are just beginning to learn how to take advantage of the incredible power of parallel processing machines. The major drawback to these machines is the lack of software to permit users to easily take advantage of the processing power. At present, users must specifically tailor their programs to utilize the parallel CPUs effectively. For the short term, parallel processors will be most useful in universities and research laboratories and in a few specialized applications that demand extensive computations, such as extremely high-volume transaction processing.

TYPES OF COMPUTER SYSTEMS

In our earlier discussion of the various generations of computers, we introduced some terminology—microcomputers, minicomputers, and mainframes—that has been applied to different types of computer systems. Now we want to expand our taxonomy of computer types to include the full range of computer systems available today. In our discussion, we will indicate the primary uses of each type of system as well as the major vendors. Our discussion must begin with a sig-

nificant caveat. While there is some agreement on the terms we will be using, there is no such agreement on the parameters defining each category or the computer models that belong in each type. Even if there were such agreement today, there would not be tomorrow as new technologies are employed and new computer models are introduced.

Generally speaking, the boundaries between the categories are defined by a combination of cost, computing power, and purpose for which a machine is built—but the *purpose* is the dominant criterion. Listed in order of generally increasing cost and power, the categories we will use are microcomputers, workstations, midrange systems, mainframes, and supercomputers (see Table 2.3). You will note that the ranges of cost and power shown in Table 2.3 are often overlapping, which reflects the differences in purpose for which the machines have been designed. Remember, also, that MFLOPS (millions of floating point operations per second) is only a very rough comparative measure of power.

Table 2.3
Types of Computer Systems

Category	Cost	MFLOPS	Primary Uses
Microcomputers	$1,000–$5,000	1–50	Personal computing Client in client/server[1] applications Small business processing
Workstations	$5,000–$100,000	50–500	Server in client/server applications Server for local area network Specific applications (CAD,[2] other graphics)
Midrange systems	$50,000–$500,000	3–1,000	Departmental computing Specific applications (office automation, CAD) Midsized business general processing Universities Server in client/server applications
Mainframes	$500,000–$10,000,000	50–2,000	Large business general processing Server in client/server applications Widest range of applications
Supercomputers	$1,000,000–$30,000,000	1,000–2,000,000	Numerically intensive scientific calculations

1 Client/server applications involve dividing the processing between a larger computer operating as a server and a smaller machine operating as a client; this idea is explored in depth in Chapter 5.
2 CAD is an abbreviation for computer-aided design, to be discussed in Chapter 5.

Please note that the category boundaries in the above table are extremely fuzzy. The boundary between microcomputers and workstations has been arbitrarily set at $5,000, but the technology employed is quite similar on both sides of this boundary. *Datamation* magazine lumps these two categories together and calls them "desktops"—both classes of machines are small enough to set on or under a desk, and both typically have a primary human user. On the other hand, the type of work done on these classes of machines is quite different, as indicated in the table, so we have chosen to separate them. The low-end midrange systems have significantly less power than workstations, but they have been designed for a much wider range of applications. Moreover, some workstations use technology similar to that of high-end midrange systems and even to low-end supercomputers—the primary difference may be the number of parallel processors. Low-end mainframes have significantly less power than high-end midrange systems, but in this case have been designed for the widest possible range of applications. *Datamation* uses the term "servers" instead of midrange systems; we disagree with this label because a wide variety of machines, including microcomputers, workstations, mainframes, and supercomputers, can and do function in a server capacity.

Microcomputers

Microcomputers, often called micros or **personal computers** or just PCs, cost from $1,000 to $5,000. They generally have less power than workstations and midrange systems, but the dividing line between these categories is faint. In general, microcomputers can be carried or moved by one person, and they usually have only a single keyboard and video display unit (which is why they are called personal computers). **Desktop PCs** are the most familiar, but PCs also come in **laptop** models in a small briefcase-like package weighing under 15 pounds, smaller **notebook** models often weighing only 5 or 6 pounds, and newer, smaller yet **hand-held** or **palmtop** models weighing in at 2 pounds or less.

By the second half of the 1980s, the most popular microcomputer for business use was the IBM Personal Computer, designed around microprocessor chips built by Intel and the PC-DOS operating system (a software package) created by Microsoft. At the end of the 1990s, IBM-compatible machines still dominate the business marketplace, but a significant portion of these machines are being sold by vendors other than IBM. Compaq has been very successful in building top-of-the-line IBM-compatible machines. Mail-order vendors like Dell and Gateway 2000 have captured significant market shares by extremely competitive pricing. In response to competitive pressures, both Compaq and IBM have lowered their prices and introduced multiple microcomputer lines.

IBM and IBM-compatible machines in the late 1990s employ predominantly Intel Pentium and Pentium Pro chips, with Pentium II chips appearing in the most advanced models. Most of these machines use some version of the Microsoft Windows operating system (either Windows 95, Windows NT, or Windows 3.1), although some use IBM's OS/2 operating system.

Another major contender in the business environment is the Apple Macintosh. Initially, the Macintosh found tough going in the business world against the entrenched IBM microcomputers, but its easy-to-use graphical interface won many converts in the late 1980s and early 1990s. Then Macintosh business sales seemed to hit a plateau, and Apple continues to struggle as we approach the year 2000. The microcomputer market is extremely competitive and should remain so for the foreseeable future.

Microcomputers have been put to a myriad of uses. In the home, they have been used for record-keeping, word processing, and games; in the public schools, for computerized exercises, educational games, and limited programming; in colleges, for word processing, spreadsheet exercises (more on this in Chapter 5), and programming; and in the corporate environment, for word processing, spreadsheets, and programming, as a terminal into a larger computer, and, more recently, as a client in a client/server application. Stand-alone microcomputers in a large organizational setting are rapidly becoming a thing of the past. For managers to do their jobs, they need microcomputers linked into the corporate computer network so that they can access data and applications wherever they exist. Microcomputers have also become important for small businesses, where they do operate as stand-alone machines or on small local area networks. The growing supply of software developed for a particular type of small business (for example, a general contractor, hardware store, or farmer), coupled with the relatively low price of microcomputers, has opened up the small business market. In the last half of the 1990s, microcomputers have also become the point of entry for all types of users into the Internet and the World Wide Web.

HAND-HELD COMPUTERS

The smallest microcomputers—hand-held machines weighing from under a pound up to two pounds and costing a few hundred dollars to two thousand dollars—appear to be versatile business tools, but they haven't caught on in a big way. Several companies, however, have equipped their field staff with these small micros to improve employee productivity and enhance communication between the field staff and the office. For example, both Hertz and Avis use hand-held computers to generate receipts and speed up car rental returns at busy locations. These devices, which hang on a strap around the agent's shoulder, include a small printer to produce the receipt right at the rental car as it is being turned in. Utility company workers use hand-held computers to read meters. Frito-Lay has provided hand-held machines to all of its 10,000 delivery people. With these computers, the delivery person enters the orders at each store and then attaches the computer to a printer in his truck to print an itemized invoice. At the end of the day, the machine generates a sales report and—via a hookup in the local warehouse—transmits the report to company headquarters.

Despite these successes, hand-held computers have not been widely adopted for general usage. Only three models (Hewlett-Packard 200LX, Psion 3A, and Sharp Wizard) have a significant number of users in the U.S. In 1996, the Palm Pilot (from U.S. Robotics) entry in this market got good reviews from analysts, such as the following: "For many mobile users, a PIM [Personal Information Manager] that fits in your shirt pocket is compelling, especially with its simple desktop data synchronization," according to Mike McGuire, senior mobile analyst at Dataquest. McGuire believes that hand-held computers will really become popular in the next few years once they integrate pagers and cellular phones.

[Adapted from Fuchsberg, 1990, and Henning, 1996]

NETWORK COMPUTERS AND NETPCs

The newest variants of the microcomputer are the **network computer** and the somewhat similar **NetPC.** With both of these machines, the basic idea is to create a stripped-down, less expensive personal computer for those users who will always be connected to a network (usually the Internet). These users don't need all the power of a typical PC; instead, they can rely on the power of the network servers.

The idea of the network computer came first: a computer with minimal memory, disk storage (perhaps no hard drive at all), and processor power, designed to connect to a network. Specifications for the network computer (specification NC-1) were jointly developed by Apple, IBM, Netscape, Oracle, and Sun. The hope was to produce NCs for about $500, but the early offerings have had price tags nearer to $1,000. Network computers have also been referred to as "Internet boxes." If the network computer is successful, it should greatly reduce the costs for businesses to provide machines for their employees and for schools to provide machines for their students.

The NetPC is a type of network computer being developed cooperatively by Microsoft and Intel. The NetPC is more powerful than the NC-1 described above; it is really a scaled-down PC that is able to execute Windows applications locally (not using the network). As you would expect, the NetPC also costs more than the NC-1. The NetPC includes features to simplify connecting it to the network and to permit remote administration (e.g., to enable the information systems organization to perform software upgrades from the network server).

Will network computers and NetPCs really save money for organizations? A study by the Gartner Group suggests that they will. The total annual operating cost for a typical PC in a corporate environment is $9,785—$7,325 for the PC itself and $2,460 for the network. Gartner estimates that for a network computer, the total annual cost will be reduced to $6,011 ($4,089 for the PC and $1,922 for the network). For a NetPC, the total annual cost is estimated at $7,267 ($5,198 for the PC and $2,071 for the network). Thus a NetPC can lower the cost per machine by 26 percent compared to a typical PC, while a network computer can lower the cost per machine by 31 percent. When multiplied by the number of PCs used in large organizations, the savings could indeed be significant!

[Adapted in part from Sager and Elstrom, 1997]

Workstations

Here is one example of the confusing terminology that abounds in the computing field. In standard industry usage, the term "workstation" means any type of computer-related device at which an individual may work. Thus, a personal computer is a workstation, and so is a terminal. But more recently, workstation has been used to describe a more powerful machine, still run by a microprocessor, which may or may not be used by a single individual. This more powerful type of workstation is the subject of our next category.

As the numbers in Table 2.3 indicate, this category of machines is very broad, with prices ranging from $5,000 to over $100,000 and an equally wide range in terms of power. **Workstations** are, in fact, grown-up, more powerful microcomputers. Workstations at the lower end of the range tend to have only one "station"—a keyboard and a high-quality video monitor—at which to "work," although this isn't necessarily true for the upper-end machines. Workstations are based on the microprocessor chip, but more powerful chips than those used in microcomputers. Workstations were originally deployed for specific applications demanding a great deal of computing power and/or high-resolution graphics, but more recently they have been used as servers in client/server applications and in network management. And, in fact, because of their very strong price-performance characteristics compared to midrange systems and mainframes (see Table 2.3), workstations are beginning to make inroads into the traditional domains of midrange systems (departmental computing, midsized business general processing) and mainframes (large business general processing).

The development of the **RISC** (reduced instruction set computing) **chip** is largely responsible for the success of this class of machines. You will recall from our earlier discussion that some computers have a large instruction set (mainframes), whereas others have a considerably smaller instruction set (microcomputers). The designers of the RISC chips based their work on already-existing microprocessor chips, not mainframe chips. By working with a reduced instruction set, they were able to create a smaller, faster chip than had been possible previously. Variations of these RISC chips power many of the machines in this category, including those produced by Hewlett-

Packard, Sun Microsystems, and Digital Equipment. IBM, the world's largest computer company, experienced serious problems during the early part of the 1990s, but one of the bright spots for IBM was the strong acceptance of its RISC System/6000 machines. In early September 1996, IBM installed its 500,000th RS/6000 workstation.

Midrange Systems

Midrange systems represent a step up in cost and power from microcomputers, ranging in price from $50,000 to $500,000. Midrange systems overlap in price and power with workstations, but tend to have less power for the same price. Midrange systems are bigger than microcomputers, and tend to be bigger than workstations as well; they are usually placed in an office or a small room. Numerous terminals or microcomputers acting as terminals (say, up to several thousand for top-end systems) can be handled by a single midrange system. Midrange systems are often used as the server in a client/server architecture, with microcomputers acting as the clients. (Chapter 5 will discuss client/server systems in more depth.) These machines are often regarded as departmental computers and may be devoted to a specific task, such as office automation or computer-aided design (CAD). Many midsized businesses use one or more midrange systems to handle their corporate data processing.

Midrange systems, as a category, tend to have an identity crisis—no one knows for sure what to call them or what machines belong in this category. Until the last few years, commentators used the label of **minicomputers** for this category (see the "Evolution of Computer Systems" section earlier in this chapter). Originally, these machines were just like the larger mainframe machines, except that they were less powerful and less expensive. For a while, the larger minicomputers were even called **superminicomputers,** which is a strange name that uses both *super* and *mini* as prefixes. Some analysts suggested that the minicomputer category would disappear, squeezed between increasingly powerful microcomputers and workstations from the bottom and entrenched mainframe systems from above, but that hasn't happened. Instead these midrange systems have often taken on the new task as server in a client/server system, in addition to their more traditional business uses. *Datamation* magazine, in fact, has renamed this category "servers" and has broadened it to include high-end workstations configured to perform the server role. But we have opted for the neutral title of midrange systems because these machines are more than servers. Midrange systems offer much better input/output capabilities than workstations, and an extensive array of easy-to-use commercial applications software has been developed for these machines. In addition, extensive specialized software has been developed by thousands of organizations to run on midrange systems, and these "legacy" systems cannot easily be converted to run on other types of hardware. Midrange systems, by whatever name, are here to stay—but their role will continue to evolve over time.

Major vendors include Hewlett-Packard, NCR, Compaq Computer, NEC, Tandem, Toshiba, Digital Equipment, and—of course—IBM. In the 1980s, IBM's System/34, System/36, and System/38 became the most popular business computers (not including microcomputers) of all time. Most of these machines have now been replaced by IBM's Application System/400, which was first introduced in 1988 and has been a major success for IBM. IBM advertises the AS/400 as "The Scalable Solution," because models are available at a price as low as $8,000 as well as at prices in the hundreds of thousands of dollars range. The newer AS/400 models employ 64-bit RISC technology—that is, they use RISC processor chips capable of handling 64 bits of data at a time.

Mainframe Computers

The **mainframes** are the "bread-and-butter" machines of information processing that are the heart of the computing systems of most major corporations and government agencies. Our earlier discussion on the evolution of computing dealt primarily with the various generations of mainframe computers. The range of mainframe power and cost is wide, with MFLOPS varying from 50 to 2,000 and cost from $500,000 to $20,000,000. Thousands of terminals (or microcomputers acting as terminals) can be handled by a mainframe, and the machine requires a good-sized computer room and a sizable professional staff of operators and programmer/analysts. The strength of mainframes is the versatility of applications they can handle—on-line and batch processing, standard business applications, engineering and scientific applica-

tions, network control, systems development, and more. They can and do operate as very large servers in a client/server environment. Because of the continuing importance of mainframes in corporate computing, a wide variety of peripheral equipment has been developed for use with these machines, as has an even wider variety of applications and systems software. This development, by the way, has been carried out by computer vendors, other equipment manufacturers, and companies that specialize in producing software, known as software houses.

Competition has been fierce in the mainframe arena because of its central role in computing. The dominant vendor has been IBM ever since the late 1950s. The current generation of IBM mainframes is the System/390 series. The newest machines in this series have been labeled the System/390 Parallel Enterprise Servers (note that IBM has positioned these large mainframes as servers!), and they vary from the single-processor Model RA4 to the 10-processor Model RX4 (see Figure 2.10). All these machines use CMOS (complementary metal oxide semiconductor) air-cooled processors. The Model RX4 can have up to 8192 megabytes of main memory. Furthermore, multiple systems, including both the newer CMOS machines and older IBM mainframes, can be combined in a Parallel Sysplex, a multisystem environment that acts like a single system. Through a combination of hardware and software, a Parallel Sysplex can incorporate up to 32 individual machines, each of which could have up to 10 processors. IBM has maintained its preeminent position in the mainframe arena through solid technical products (but not necessarily the most technologically advanced), excellent and extensive software, reliable machines, unmatched service, and aggressive marketing.

Other major players in the mainframe arena are a trio of Japanese manufacturers (Fujitsu, Hitachi, and NEC), a pair of American firms (Unisys and Amdahl), Groupe Bull (France), and Siemens Nixdorf (Germany). Amdahl and Hitachi are both interesting cases, because they have succeeded by building machines that are virtually identical to IBM's—often with slightly newer technology—and then selling them for a lower price. Unisys was formed years ago as the merger of Burroughs and Sperry (remember that Sperry built the very first production-line computer), so Unisys has been in the mainframe business a long time.

Figure 2.10 IBM S/390 Parallel Enterprise Server (Courtesy of International Business Machines Corporation)

All of the major mainframe vendors fell on hard times in the early 1990s, including IBM. Because of stronger price/performance ratios from other classes of machines, especially microcomputers and workstations, the primary focus of new systems development in the first half of the 1990s was on client/server applications designed to run on these more cost-effective platforms. But the last half of the 1990s has seen a marked movement back to mainframes! IBM and other vendors have introduced new technology (such as CMOS processors), added UNIX interfaces to proprietary operating systems,[2] and slashed prices drastically. IBM reports that it shipped 60 percent more System 390 MIPS in 1995 than in 1994, and analysts predict that gains of 40 percent to 60 percent per year will continue for the rest of the century (Pantages,

1996). Some of these sales are simply replacing older machines, but there also appears to be real growth as information systems managers are turning back to mainframes—often as a gigantic server—in new systems development efforts. The role of the mainframe will continue to evolve as we move into the twenty-first century, with more emphasis on its roles as keeper of the corporate data warehouse, as server in sophisticated client/server applications, and as controller of worldwide corporate networks (see box entitled "Mainframe Renaissance").

MAINFRAME RENAISSANCE

There are a number of reasons why the venerable mainframe computer has rebounded in the latter 1990s. First, mainframe costs are plummeting. Due largely to the introduction of CMOS technology, S/390 hardware prices (expressed as average cost per MIPS) have been dropping at the rate of 35 percent per year. Second, the cost-effectiveness of client/server computing is being questioned—some commentators describe this as the "rise and stall" of client/server computing. The long-term cost of owning a mainframe is less expensive than that of a client/server environment. According to one study, the average cost of computing on a mainframe is $2,127 per user annually, while that of a client/server network is $6,982. The average cost per transaction on a mainframe is $0.03, whereas that of a client/server environment is $0.46. Third, IBM has opened up the S/390 in a number of ways, including bundling (including in the base price) 30 software packages previously sold separately as well as providing the programming to permit the S/390 to be a part of TCP/IP networks and client/server architectures and to run UNIX and Windows NT applications.[3] Because of the complexity of client/server environments (custom coding, middleware, systems administration, and user and software-developer training), large corporations are adopting a more pragmatic approach—choosing the best platform to fit the specific job. More and more, that platform is the mainframe.

[Adapted from Simpson, April, 1997, and Depompa, 1996]

---

2 UNIX is an "open" operating system used on many workstations and midrange systems. Both open and proprietary operating systems are discussed in Chapter 3.

3 TCP/IP and Windows NT will be described more fully in subsequent chapters. TCP/IP is the networking protocol used in most local area networks and on the Internet. Windows NT is a network operating system (as well as a single microcomputer operating system) developed by Microsoft.

Supercomputers

Supercomputers are the true "number-crunchers," with MFLOPS ratings in excess of 1,000 and price tags from $1 million to $30 million. The high-end supercomputers are specifically designed to handle numerically intensive problems, most of which are generated by research scientists, such as chemists, physicists, and astronomers. Thus, most of the high-end supercomputers are located in government research laboratories or on major university campuses (even in the latter case, most of the machines are largely supported by grants from the National Science Foundation or other government agencies). Midrange supercomputers, however, have found a variety of uses in large business firms, most frequently for research and development efforts.

The acknowledged leader in the high-end super-computer arena is Cray Research, Inc., based in Minnesota. Cray Research controls roughly two-thirds of the market for large-scale supercomputers. Of the world's environmental research sites that have super-computers, 80 percent of them are Cray machines. Nearly all of the U.S. Department of Energy and Department of Defense research laboratories have at least one Cray Research system, and at least 160 universities around the world have a Cray supercomputer installed. Cray Research has maintained its dominant position by introducing machines using three primary high-performance computer architectures: parallel vector processing, massively parallel processing, and symmetric multiprocessing. All three of these multiprocessor arrangements were described in the "Extensions to the Basic Model" section earlier in this chapter. As an example, the Cray T3E can incorporate up to 2,048 parallel processors and operate at speeds up to 1.8 teraflops (1.8 trillion floating point operations per second). Most other supercomputer vendors use only one or two of these three architectures.

Other significant players, particularly in the midrange supercomputer market, include Fujitsu, Hewlett Packard-Convex (a unit of Hewlett-Packard), Hitachi, IBM, NEC, Sequent, Silicon Graphics Inc., and Digital Equipment. An interesting development in the supercomputer arena occurred in 1996 when Silicon Graphics Inc. acquired Cray Research, thus becoming the world's leading high-performance computing company. Cray Research is continuing to operate as a separate unit, focusing on large-scale

supercomputers. The focus of Silicon Graphics itself is on high-performance workstations and midrange supercomputers. The Silicon Graphics-Cray merger creates a supercomputing powerhouse!

DATA VISUALIZATION: THE FINAL FRONTIER?

It's like standing on the bridge of the Enterprise. The darkened room is circular, with a doughnut-shaped conference table of gleaming pearwood in the center and a floor-to-ceiling video wall that wraps three-quarters around. A systems engineer named Istvan Varga taps on a laptop, and the wall appears to recede, revealing a starry night. The blue earth spins tranquilly in the middle distance. Varga taps on the laptop again, and we zoom down on Tokyo, inspecting damage to company facilities from an imaginary earthquake. Web pages, news bulletins, and 3-D graphs of market activity after the quake pop up on the video wall.

Andersen Consulting calls it Pegasus. Designer Kenneth R. Straus, an Andersen manager, says Pegasus could enable better-informed, more collaborative decision-making by all of a company's executives. Andersen relied on Reuters for news feeds; CATS Software Inc. in Palo Alto, California, for historical securities data; Visible Decisions Inc. in Toronto for data visualization tools; and Silicon Graphics Inc. for the computer that runs the whole thing.

Pegasus is generating a lot of interest, Straus says. But that's all, so far, despite the Star Trek trappings. "No one," Straus concedes, "is whipping out their wallets."

[Coy, 1996]

THE INFORMATION SYSTEMS INDUSTRY

We have spent significant portions of this chapter discussing computer hardware manufacturers, providing a good start in understanding a portion of the information systems industry. The hardware vendors, however, represent only a part of a much broader information systems industry. In this section, we want to explore the global makeup of that industry and identify the major players.

The authors of this book would like to be able to provide statistics for the total computer/communications industry, but they are not readily available for such a broad industrial grouping. We have had to settle for the information systems industry, as defined by *Datamation* magazine. The *Datamation* definition of the IS industry includes information systems hardware, software, services, maintenance, and data communications, so this is a reasonable subset of our preferred broader construct. For 1996, *Datamation* estimated that the global IS revenues of the world's 100 leading IS companies (Hayashi, 1997) were $501.9 billion, up 14.3 percent over the prior year (see Figure 2.11). This sizeable 14.3-percent increase represents the combination of a year of solid growth plus numerous mergers and acquisitions among the top 100 firms. Based on estimates by Arthur D. Little, Inc., of global IS sales for all companies, the *Datamation* top 100 appear to represent more than 80 percent of the world IS industry (Hedges, 1988).

A breakdown of the total IS market in 1996 may be instructive. Computer hardware (not including data communications) constituted 53 percent of the total, with large-scale systems (including what we have called mainframes and supercomputers) accounting for 4.0 percent of the total ($20.1 billion), servers (called midrange systems) for 7.2 percent ($36.1 billion), desktops (including both microcomputers and workstations) for 21.9 percent ($109.7 billion), and peripherals (printers, disk drives, tape drives, and so on) for 19.8 percent ($99.2 billion). Data communications brings in 8.0 percent ($40.0 billion); software, 11.6 percent ($58.2 billion); and services such as consulting and maintenance, a whopping 27.6 percent ($138.4 billion).

Another way of looking at the IS industry is to check the home bases of the top 100 IS firms. Based on 1996 data (Hayashi, 1997), 70 of the top 100 are based in the United States, 13 in Japan, 4 in France, 3 in the United Kingdom, 3 in Taiwan, 2 in The Netherlands, 2 in Italy, 1 in Germany, 1 in Korea, and 1 in Sweden. Until about 1990, the number of non-U.S. companies in the top 100 was slowly rising, but now it is slowly dropping. (There were 40 non-U.S. companies in the top 100 in 1989 and 37 in the top 100 in 1992.) The IS industry is clearly global and extremely competitive, but U.S. firms are more than holding their own.

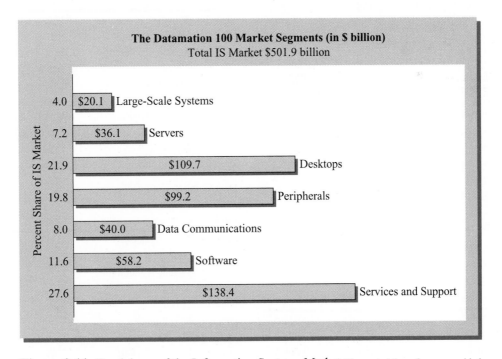

Figure 2.11 Breakdown of the Information Systems Market (Computed from figures provided by *DATAMATION,* July 1997, pp. 74–82, with permission from *DATAMATION,* © 1997, Cahners Business Information. *DATAMATION* is a trademark of Cahners Business Information. All rights reserved.

Now let us look at the top 10 firms in each of seven major market sectors—large-scale systems, servers, desktops, peripherals, data communications, software, and services. In Table 2.4, the numbers reported are the sales revenue for that firm in the particular market sector in 1996. All numbers are reported as millions of U.S. dollars. Perhaps the first thing one notices in the table is that IBM heads six of

the seven lists, but the margin over number two is not always sizeable. The second interesting fact is the presence of many non-U.S. firms in these top ten lists —six in large-scale systems, four in servers, three in desktops, four in peripherals (all from Japan!), two in data communications, four in software (three out of four from Japan), and two in services. These lists underscore once again the global nature of the IS

Table 2.4

The Top Ten Firms in Various Information Systems Market Segments

Large-Scale Systems

Rank	Company	Country	Revenue (millions)
1	IBM	U.S.	$5,316.3
2	Fujitsu	Japan	5,051.9
3	NEC	Japan	3,849.9
4	Hitachi	Japan	1,829.1
5	Unisys	U.S.	828.2
6	Silicon Graphics	U.S.	681.5
7	Siemens Nixdorf	Germany	643.2
8	Groupe Bull	France	624.0
9	Amdahl	U.S.	375.1
10	Mitsubishi	Japan	347.8

Servers

Rank	Company	Country	Revenue (millions)
1	IBM	U.S.	$7,594.7
2	Hewlett-Packard	U.S.	4,395.7
3	Compaq Computer	U.S.	3,984.0
4	NEC	Japan	2,502.4
5	Toshiba	Japan	1,967.0
6	Digital Equipment	U.S.	1,633.2
7	Tandem	U.S.	1,611.1
8	NCR	U.S.	1,495.1
9	Hitachi	Japan	1,219.4
10	Fujitsu	Japan	1,188.7

Desktops

Rank	Company	Country	Revenue (millions)
1	IBM	U.S.	$12,911.5
2	Compaq Computer	U.S.	11,227.6
3	Fujitsu	Japan	9,806.6
4	Toshiba	Japan	7,868.2
5	Packard Bell NEC	U.S.	7,500.0

Desktops (continued)

Rank	Company	Country	Revenue (millions)
6	Dell Computer	U.S.	7,488.0
7	Apple	U.S.	6,685.5
8	Hewlett-Packard	U.S.	6,593.6
9	Gateway 2000	U.S.	5,040.0
10	Acer	U.S.	4,550.0

Peripherals

Rank	Company	Country	Revenue (millions)
1	IBM	U.S.	$10,633.0
2	Hewlett-Packard	U.S.	10,361.3
3	Seagate Technology	U.S.	8,075.0
4	Canon	Japan	6,907.3
5	Quantum	U.S.	4,950.0
6	Fujitsu	Japan	4,160.4
7	Western Digital	U.S.	3,550.8
8	Toshiba	Japan	3,231.6
9	Xerox	U.S.	3,107.2
10	Matsushita	Japan	2,820.5

Data Communications

Rank	Company	Country	Revenue (millions)
1	Cisco Systems	U.S.	$5,406.4
2	IBM	U.S.	3,797.4
3	Lucent Technologies[a]	U.S.	3,400.0
4	NTT Data	Japan	3,300.0
5	3Com	U.S.	2,796.7
6	U.S. Robotics	U.S.	2,258.1
7	Bay Networks	U.S.	2,094.3
8	Hewlett-Packard	U.S.	1,569.9
9	Matsushita	Japan	1,538.5
10	Motorola	U.S.	1,446.2

Table 2.4 (continued)

Software

Rank	Company	Country	Revenue (millions)
1	IBM	U.S.	$12,911.0
2	Microsoft	U.S.	9,435.0
3	Hitachi	Japan	5,487.3
4	Fujitsu	Japan	4,754.7
5	Computer Associates	U.S.	3,156.8
6	NEC	Japan	2,309.0
7	Oracle	U.S.	2,280.4
8	SAP	Germany	1,699.7
9	Novell	U.S.	1,225.3
10	Digital Equipment	U.S.	1,224.9

Services and Support

Rank	Company	Country	Revenue (millions)
1	IBM	U.S.	$22,785.0
2	EDS	U.S.	14,441.3
3	Hewlett-Packard	U.S.	9,462.5
4	Digital Equipment	U.S.	5,988.3
5	Computer Sciences	U.S.	5,400.0
6	Andersen Consulting	U.S.	4,877.8
7	Fujitsu	Japan	4,160.4
8	Cap Gemini Sogeti	France	4,104.0
9	Unisys	U.S.	3,949.7
10	ADP	U.S.	3,567.0

a Part of AT&T in 1995.
SOURCE: *DATAMATION* 43 (July 1997): 42–82. Reproduced with permission from *DATAMATION,* © 1997 Cahners Business Information. *DATAMATION* is a trademark of Cahners Business Information. All rights reserved.

industry. A third interesting fact is that Microsoft—with all its publicity—trails IBM in software sales by nearly $3.5 billion. Microsoft has been closing the gap, however; Microsoft trailed IBM by nearly $8 billion in 1992 and by $5 billion in 1995. We will say more about this in the next chapter, because the dollar values clearly don't reflect the dominant role played by Microsoft in the software field.

Missing from these data is the true impact of information technology on those firms that are not directly a part of the IS industry. For example, these data do not reflect the growing reliance on information technology by firms who have been investing in strate-

gic information systems and electronic commerce (see Chapter 7). It does not reflect the importance of computer-integrated manufacturing and robotics to a long list of manufacturing companies. Further, these statistics do not reflect the many noncomputer products that now incorporate microprocessor chips, such as automobiles, refrigerators, stoves, and airplanes. The IS industry is not only large by itself, but it has a disproportionate impact on other industries, and that impact will continue to grow into the new millenium.

SUMMARY

There is a lot more to information technology than the digital computer, but there is no doubt that the computer is the key technological development of the twentieth century. The computer has had an astounding impact on organizations and on our lives, and it has captured our imaginations like no other recent development.

To summarize, all computer systems are made up of some combination of six basic building blocks: input, output, memory, arithmetic/logical unit, files, and control unit. All of these components are controlled by a stored program, which resides in memory and is brought into the control unit one instruction at a time, interpreted, and executed. The basic model has been extended in several directions over the years, such as by adding controllers and data channels to interface the slower peripheral devices (input, output, disks, tapes) with the much faster central processing unit. A multilevel storage system including high-speed cache memory has been adopted on many machines. To gain more power, multiple processors have been employed in a single computer system in a variety of configurations. Whatever the machine configuration, the computer system is still controlled by stored programs, or software. Chapter 3 explores computer software, concentrating on the programs that are most critical in running the computer system and the applications that you are most likely to encounter.

Let us end this chapter with the caveat that the numbers and specific details covered in the chapter will quickly become outdated, while the basic principles we presented should be valid for the foreseeable future.

REVIEW QUESTIONS

1. What are the distinguishing characteristics of the present, or Fourth Generation, computers?

2. Distinguish between microcomputers, midrange systems, mainframes, and supercomputers. Give approximate speeds (millions of floating point operations per second, or MFLOPS) and costs.

3. List the six building blocks that make up digital computers, and describe the flows of data that occur among these blocks.

4. Distinguish between the *contents* of a memory cell and the *address* of a memory cell. Distinguish between a *byte* and a *word*. Distinguish between a *bit* and a *byte*.

5. What are the advantages and disadvantages of using direct access files versus using sequential access files?

6. Explain in your own words the importance of the stored-program concept. Include the role of the control unit in your explanation.

7. Define the expressions in italics in the following sentence taken from this chapter: "In general, each *machine language* instruction consists of two parts—an *operation code* and one or more *addresses*."

8. Provide the full names for the following acronyms or abbreviations used in this chapter.

OCR	MIPS	UPC
CPU	MPP	CD-ROM
MFLOPS	DASD	PP
WORM	MICR	DVD

9. Five categories of computer systems are considered in this chapter: microcomputers, workstations, midrange systems, mainframes, and supercomputers. Provide the name of at least one prominent vendor in each of these categories (and you can only use IBM once!).

10. Describe what is meant by benchmarking. When and how would you carry out benchmarking?

11. What is cache memory? Where would it be used, and why?

12. Distinguish between a symmetric multiprocessor computer and a parallel processor computer. Which is the most important at this time for business information processing, and why?

DISCUSSION QUESTIONS

1. From the discussion in this chapter and your own knowledge from other sources, what do you think is the most important advancement in computer hardware technology in the past five years? Why?

2. Carry out library or Internet research on the latest microprocessor chips available from firms such as Intel, Cyrix, AMD, and Motorola, collecting data similar to that contained in Table 2.1. Add the new information you have discovered to Table 2.1.

3. Some writers have suggested that midrange computer systems may be squeezed out of existence in the next few years, with the incredible advances in the capabilities of microcomputers and workstations and the versatility of mainframes combining to divide up the present midrange market. What do you think? Why?

4. What are the advantages and limitations of palmtop or hand-held computers? When would you use one?

5. What are the advantages and limitations of a network computer or NetPC as compared with a traditional PC? Do you believe that the idea of a network computer or NetPC will be successful? Why or why not?

6. As this chapter has indicated, IBM has been the dominant force in the computer industry since the late 1950s. Why do you think this is the case? More specifically, why were so many large corporations seemingly committed to "Big Blue" (as IBM is affectionately known), at least until the early 1990s?

7. Building on your answer to question 6 above, why did IBM suffer serious reverses in the early 1990s? Why has IBM bounced back in the latter half of the 1990s? Do you think that IBM will retain its dominant position as we move into the twenty-first century? Why?

8. With one firm (IBM) dominating the mainframe hardware market in the United States since its inception, and with that same firm currently leading in six out of seven market segments, has the computer industry truly been competitive over the past four decades? Support your position.

9. List possible uses of a supercomputer in a business setting.

10. MIPS and MFLOPS were mentioned in this chapter as measures of the power of computer systems. If you were in charge of buying a new midrange or larger computer system (and you may be some day), what measures of power would you want to find out? How would you go about determining these measures of power?

11. The following are the *Datamation* top 10 information systems companies in the world in 1996, along with their estimated information systems revenues in millions of dollars. Either from your own knowledge or from library research, list the products and services that are primarily responsible for these companies making the top 10 list.

1996 Rank	Company	Country	1996 IS Revenue (millions)
1	IBM	U.S.	$75,947
2	Hewlett-Packard	U.S.	31,398
3	Fujitsu	Japan	29,717
4	Compaq Computer	U.S.	18,109
5	Hitachi	Japan	15,242
6	NEC	Japan	15,092
7	EDS	U.S.	14,441
8	Toshiba	Japan	14,050
9	Digital Equipment	U.S.	13,610
10	Microsoft	U.S.	9,435

12. Update the desktop portion of Table 2.4 for the most recent year for which data are available. What changes have occurred among the top 10 players, both in terms of position within the top 10 and relative total sales? Why have these changes occurred?

13. Update the table in question 11 above (top 10 information systems companies in the world) for the most recent year for which data are available. What changes have occurred among the top 10 players, both in terms of position within the top 10 and relative total sales? Why have these changes occurred?

14. For most business information processing, what do you believe are the critical or limiting characteristics of today's computing systems—CPU speed, memory capacity, DASD capacity, data channel speed, input speed, output speed, other factors, or some combination of these factors? Justify your answer.

References

1997. "Section breakout. *Datamation* 43 (July): 74–82.

1997. "Top 5 workgroup servers." *PC World.* (June): 119.

Bethoney, Herb. 1997. "Speak easy: Natural speech moves to the desktop but not to the mainstream." *PC Week* (June 2): 1, 14.

Coy, Peter. 1996. "Data visualization: The final frontier?" *Business Week* (October 28): 150.

Depompa, Barbara. 1996. "Mainframes rising from the ashes." *Information Week* (May 27): 44–50.

Dongarra, Jack J. 1992. "Performance of various computers using standard linear equations software." Computer Science Department, University of Tennessee, and Oak Ridge National Laboratory, No. CS-89-85 (December 15).

Dongarra, Jack J. 1997. "Linpack benchmark." Performance Database Server, http://performance.netlib.org/performance/html/PDStop.html (May 27).

Fuchsberg, Gilbert. 1990. "Hand-held computers help field staff cut paper work and harvest more data." *Wall Street Journal* 71 (January 30): B1, B6.

Garvey, Martin J. 1997. "Mainframes bounce back." *Information Week* (July 7): 14–15.

Gill, Philip J. 1996. "UNIX takes the high road." *Datamation* 42 (June 15): 58–60.

Grossman, C. P. 1985. "Cache-DASD storage design for improving system performance." *IBM Systems Journal* 24: 316–334.

Hayashi, Alden. 1997. "*Datamation* 100: Squeezing profits from IT." *Datamation* 43 (July): 42–47.

Hedges, Parker. 1988. "Charting the champs." *Datamation* 34 (June 15): 14–24.

Henning, Jeffrey. 1996. "Desktops: Intel in your face." *Datamation* 42 (June 15): 44–46.

Hoskins, Jim. 1992. *ES/9000: A Business Perspective.* New York: John Wiley & Sons.

IBM. 1997. "IBM VoiceType Speech Recognition Products." IBM Web site, http://www.software.ibm.com/is/voicetype (May).

Intel. 1997. "Pentium II processor." Intel Web site, http://www.intel.com/pentiumII/home.htm (May).

Mael, Susan. 1996. "*Datamation* 100: Bigger by design." *Datamation* 42 (June 15): 32–37.

Pantages, Angie. 1996. "Big iron is back." *Datamation* 42 (June 15): 66–68.

Port, Otis. 1996. "Speed gets a whole new meaning." *Business Week* (April 29): 90–91.

Port, Otis. 1996. "The silicon age? It's just dawning." *Business Week* (December 9): 148–152.

Reinhardt, Andy. 1997. "Computers & Chips." *Business Week* (January 13): 106–107.

Sager, Ira, and Peter Elstrom. 1997. "A bare-bones box for business." *Business Week* (May 26): 136.

Simpson, David. 1997. "Are mainframes cool again?" *Datamation* 43 (April): 46–53.

Simpson, David. 1997. "Big iron roars." *Datamation* 43 (July): 48–49.

Simpson, David. 1997. "New applications fuel server sales." *Datamation* 43 (July): 50.

Simpson, David. 1997. "PC management is no. 1 issue." *Datamation* 43 (July): 55.

Wolfe, Alexander. 1997. "Comdex buzz: DVD-enabled PCs set to ship." *EETimes* Web site, http://www.techweb.com/se/directlink.cgi?EET19970609S0005 (June 9).

CHAPTER 3

COMPUTER SOFTWARE

In many respects, this chapter is merely a continuation of Chapter 2, which concentrated on computer hardware, the physical pieces of a computer system. We learned that all the hardware is controlled by a stored program, which is a complete listing (in a form that the computer has been built to understand) of what the computer is to do. Such a stored program is an example of computer software, the topic of this chapter. Software is the set of programs (made up of instructions) that control the operations of the computer system. Computer hardware without software is of little value (and vice versa). Both are required for a computer system to be a useful tool for you and your organization. Thus, this chapter will explain more fully the symbiotic relationship between computer hardware and software.

As important as understanding computer hardware is, it is even more important for you as a manager to understand software. First, appropriate software is required before hardware can do anything at all. Second, most organizations spend at least twice as much money on software as they do on hardware. This ratio of software to hardware costs is rapidly increasing over time. In the late 1990s, a software company, Microsoft Corporation, is arguably the most successful and most influential company in the entire computer arena.

Third, and most personally relevant, you will be dealing directly with a number of important software packages—such as spreadsheets, word processing, and Web browsers—whereas the only hardware you are likely to interact with is a workstation (most likely a microcomputer, not one of the higher-powered workstations discussed in the previous chapter). Whatever your job within an organization, you are also likely to be involved in software development or acquisition efforts as a member of a project team or as an end-user. If your field is marketing, you may well be involved with the creation of a new sales reporting system; if your field is finance, you may develop a computer model to evaluate the impact of a possible merger; if you are an operations manager, you may participate in the development of a new inventory reporting system. (The role of the manager in software development and acquisition is discussed more fully in Chapters 10, 11, and 12.) For a variety of reasons, therefore, it is important that you understand the various types of computer software and the ways it is used within an organization.

EVOLUTION OF COMPUTER PROGRAMMING

First- and Second-Generation Languages

Computer software has, of course, been around as long as computer hardware. Initially, all software was written in machine language, as described in "The Stored-Program Concept" section of Chapter 2. Each instruction in a machine language program must be expressed in the precise form that the particular computer has been built to understand. If, for instance, we want to subtract the number found in memory cell 720 from the number found in memory cell 600 and store the result in cell 600, then the machine language instruction (for a hypothetical computer) would be

Operation Code	Addresses	
S	720	600

A complete program to carry out a particular application (e.g., compute the payroll or prepare a management report) would consist of hundreds or thousands of similar instructions expressed in the machine language of the particular computer. The programmer would have to look up (or memorize) each operation code and remember what data have been stored in every memory cell. Machine language programming was (and is) an exacting, tedious, time-consuming process, but it was the only option available on the earliest computers.

Computer software developers soon created **assembly languages** that used the computer itself to perform many of the most tedious aspects of programming. For example, easily remembered mnemonic operation codes are substituted for the machine language operation codes (e.g., SUB for S or SUB for something as unintelligible as 67 on some machines). Symbolic addresses are substituted for a memory cell address (e.g., GPAY for 600). Thus, if our single instruction above is part of a payroll program where we want to subtract deductions (DED) from gross pay (GPAY), we can write

SUB   DED   GPAY

Writing instructions such as this is much easier (and more error-free) than writing machine language instructions, particularly when we consider that there are likely to be fifty different operation codes and hundreds of memory cell addresses to remember in even a moderate-sized program.

The entire assembly language program is written using instructions similar to the one above. Then the computer, under the control of a special stored program called an **assembler,** converts these mnemonic operation codes and symbolic addresses to the machine language operation codes and memory cell addresses. The assembler program simply keeps a table of conversions for operation codes and addresses and makes the substitutions as necessary. Figure 3.1 illustrates this translation process from the assembly language program —the program containing mnemonic codes and symbolic addresses—to the machine language program. The assembly language program is also called the **source program,** and the resulting machine language program is the **object program.** Once the translation process has been completed, the outcome machine language program is loaded into memory and carried out by the control unit (as described in Chapter 2). The machine language for a particular computer is referred

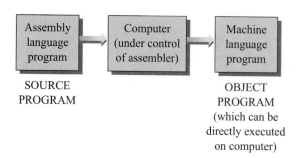

Figure 3.1 Assembler Translation Process

to as the first-generation language, or 1 GL, and the assembly language—which came along later—is called the second-generation language, or 2 GL.

Assembly language programming was popular for business applications for many years (until about 1970), and assembly language is still used by a few major firms and by some computer professionals.[1] Popular assembly languages have included SOAP (Symbolic Optimization Assembly Program), Autocoder, and BAL (Basic Assembly Language). Assembly language programming is much easier than machine language programming, but it still requires the programmer to employ the same small steps that the computer has been built to understand; it still requires one assembly language instruction for each machine language instruction.[2] Thus, even after the advent of assembly languages, efforts continued to make it easier to tell the computer what the user wanted done. The results are today's third- and fourth-generation languages (3 GLs and 4 GLs).

Third- and Fourth-Generation Languages

The third- and fourth-generation languages represent a radical departure from the first two generations. Both machine language and assembly language pro-

---

1 The primary reason for the continued use of assembly language is computer efficiency. A well-written assembly language program will require less memory and take less time to execute than a well-written third- or fourth-generation language program.

2 To be complete, assembly languages often provide for macroinstructions, where one macroinstruction may correspond to 5, 10, or more machine language instructions. A programmer writes a set of assembly language instructions that he or she expects to use repeatedly, and then gives this set a label (or a macroinstruction name). Then each time the macroinstruction is used in a program, the entire set of assembly language instructions is substituted for it.

gramming require the programmer to think like the computer in terms of the individual instructions. With 3 GLs and 4 GLs, the programmer uses a language that is relatively easy for humans to learn and use, but has no direct relationship to the machine language into which it must eventually be translated. Thus, the 3 GLs and 4 GLs are designed for humans, not computers! Typically, each 3 GL or 4 GL instruction will be translated into many machine language instructions (perhaps 10 machine language instructions per 3 GL instruction, or 100 machine language instructions per 4 GL instruction). Further, while each type of computer has its unique 2 GL, the 3 GLs and 4 GLs are largely machine independent. Thus, a program written in a 3 GL or 4 GL can be run on many different types of computers, which is often a significant advantage.

Third-generation languages are also called **procedural languages,** because they express a step-by-step procedure devised by the programmer to accomplish the desired task. The earliest procedural language was FORTRAN (an abbreviation for FORmula TRANslator), which was developed by IBM in the mid-1950s. Other popular procedural languages include COBOL (COmmon Business Oriented Language), PL/1, BASIC, PASCAL, ADA, and C. These third-generation languages—particularly BASIC, C, and COBOL—are still very important today, and a later section of this chapter will expand on these introductory remarks. Estimates vary, but it is likely that at least 75 percent of the programs in use today were written in 3 GLs.

A source program in any one of these languages must be translated into the machine language object program before it can be carried out by the computer. For 3 GLs (and for 4 GLs), the language translator is called a **compiler** if the entire program is translated into machine language before any of the program is executed, or an **interpreter** if each source program statement is executed as soon as that single statement is translated. Historically, the BASIC language was usually interpreted, while most other 3 GLs have been compiled. However, BASIC compilers now exist, and interpreted COBOL is sometimes used during program development.

Figure 3.2 depicts the process of compiling and running a compiled procedural language program, such as C, FORTRAN, or COBOL. This process is quite similar to that used for assembly language programming (see Figure 3.1), with the labels changed as

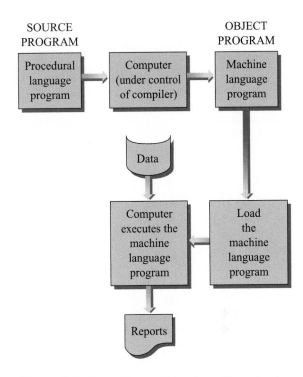

Figure 3.2 Compiling and Running a Procedural Language Program

appropriate. The key is that the entire program is translated into an object program, and then the object program is loaded and executed. Dealing with the entire program in this manner has the advantage that an efficient machine language program (one that executes rapidly) can be produced because the interrelationships among the program statements can be considered during the compilation process; dealing with the entire program has the disadvantage that the programmer does not learn about errors until the entire program has been translated.

Figure 3.3 shows the process of interpreting and running an interpretive language program, such as BASIC. With an interpreter, only one statement from the source program is considered at a time. This single statement is translated into machine language, and—if no errors are encountered—immediately executed. The process is repeated, statement after statement. This interpretive process lends itself to interactive programming, where the programmer composes the program at a workstation, keys in one statement at a time, and is almost immediately provided feedback if an error is made. If there are no errors, output is

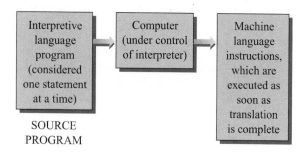

SOURCE
PROGRAM

Figure 3.3 Interpreting and Running an Interpretive Language Program

produced immediately after the last statement is entered. The machine language program resulting from the interpretive process is usually much less efficient than one resulting from compilation because only one source program statement is being considered at a time. On the other hand, program development may be speeded up because of the immediate feedback to programmers when they make an error. With an interpreter, there is often no true object program, because the machine language instructions are discarded as soon as they are executed. Further, if the program is executed repeatedly, each source statement is translated again each time it is executed, which is quite inefficient as compared with compilation.

Fourth-generation languages—also called **productivity languages** and **nonprocedural languages** —are even easier to use than the third-generation languages. To employ a 3 GL, the programmer must devise a step-by-step procedure to accomplish the desired result and express this procedure in the form of 3 GL statements. With a 4 GL, the computer user merely gives a precise statement of what he wishes to accomplish, not how to do it. Thus, the order in which statements are given in a 4 GL is usually inconsequential. Further, each 4 GL statement is usually translated into significantly more machine language instructions—sometimes by a factor of 100—than a single 3 GL statement. Thus, 4 GL programs are easier to write, shorter, and less error-prone than 3 GL programs, which in turn have these same advantages over their 2 GL predecessors. Fourth-generation languages, for the most part, use an interpreter to translate the source program into machine language. Note that the 3 GLs and 4 GLs are essentially the same from one computer model to the next, but the translation

programs (compilers and interpreters) must be specific to the particular computer model.

With these advantages, why aren't all programs written in 4 GLs today? First, some of the 4 GLs—like IFPS and SAS—are not general purpose languages and cannot be used easily for many types of programs. On the other hand, FOCUS and CA-Ramis are indeed general purpose 4 GLs. More important, many programs are not written in 4 GLs because of concern for efficient use of the computer resources of the organization. For the most part, 4 GL programs translate into longer machine language programs that take much longer to execute than the equivalent programs written in a 3 GL. (Similarly, 3 GL programs often translate into longer machine language programs that take more time to execute than the equivalent 2 GL programs.) The upshot of these arguments is that an increasing number of one-time programs or infrequently used programs (such as a decision support system or a specialized management report) are being written in 4 GLs, whereas most production programs—those that will be run every day or every week—are still written in 3 GLs. In the case of infrequently used programs, human efficiency in writing the program is more important than computer efficiency in running it; for production programs, the opposite is often the case.

In the mid- and late 1990s, new programming languages have gained popularity that are still predominantly 3 GLs, but also have some 4 GL characteristics. These languages are usually described as **object-oriented programming** or **visual programming** languages. Object-oriented programming (OOP) languages such as Smalltalk and C++ came first; these languages are built on the idea of embedding procedures (called methods) in objects, and then putting these objects together to create an application. Visual programming languages, such as Visual Basic and Java, provide a graphical programming environment and a paint metaphor for developing user interfaces. These newer entries in the programming arena, as well as 3 GL and 4 GL languages, will be described more fully later in the chapter. Overall, the programming environment in most large organizations is now more diverse than ever, with most organizations using some combination of conventional 3 GLs, 4 GLs, object-oriented programming, and visual programming. The trend is towards more object-oriented and visual programming, but there is still significant 4 GL programming and even more 3 GL programming being carried out.

KEY TYPES OF SOFTWARE

In the previous section we considered the evolution of computer programming. These programming languages—from assembly language to COBOL to FOCUS to C++ to Visual Basic—have been used over the past several decades to create an incredible array of software products, including the language translators themselves. We now want to categorize the various types of computer software that have been created and gain an understanding of how they work together.

To begin our look at the key elements of computer software, let us step back from the details and view the big picture. It is useful to divide software into two major categories:

1. Applications software
2. Support software

Applications software includes all programs written to accomplish particular tasks for computer users. In addition to our payroll computation example, applications programs would include an inventory record-keeping program, a word processing package, a spreadsheet package, a program to allocate advertising expenditures, and a program producing a summarized report for top management. Each of these programs produces output needed by users to accomplish their jobs.

By contrast, **support software** (also called **systems software**) does not directly produce output needed by users. Instead, support software provides a computing environment in which it is relatively easy and efficient for humans to work; it enables applications programs written in a variety of languages to be carried out; and it ensures that the computer hardware and software resources are used efficiently. Support software is usually obtained from computer vendors and from specialized software development companies called software houses.

The relationship between applications software and support software may be more readily understood by considering the software iceberg depicted in Figure 3.4. The above-water portion of the iceberg is analogous to applications software; both are highly visible. Applications software directly produces

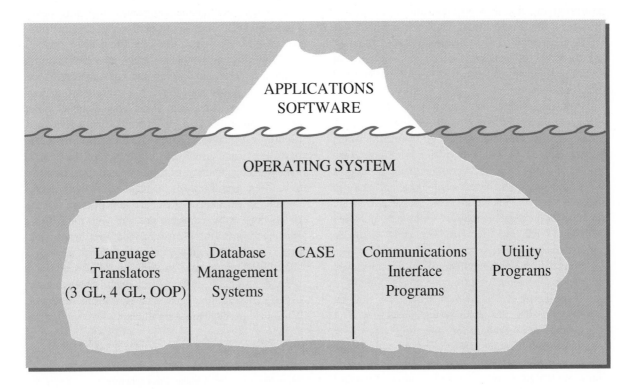

Figure 3.4 The Software Iceberg

results that you as a manager require to perform your job. But just as the underwater portion of the iceberg keeps the top of the iceberg above water, the support software is absolutely essential for the applications software to produce the desired results. (Please note that the iceberg analogy is not an accurate representation of the numbers of applications and support programs—there are usually many more applications programs than support programs.) Your concern as a manager will be primarily with the applications software—the programs that are directly relevant to your job—but you need to understand the functions of the primary types of support software to appreciate how the complete hardware/software system works.

APPLICATIONS SOFTWARE

Applications software includes all programs written to accomplish particular tasks for computer users. Portfolio management programs, general ledger accounting programs, sales forecasting programs, material requirements planning (MRP) programs, electronic mail programs, and desktop publishing packages are all examples of applications software. Each of you will be using applications software as part of your job, and many of you will be involved in developing or obtaining applications software to fulfill the needs of your organization.

Because applications software is so diverse, it is difficult to divide these programs into a few neat categories as we will do with support software later in the chapter. Instead, we will begin with a brief look at the sources of applications software, and then we will give two examples of PC-based accounting packages to illustrate the types of commercial packages that are available for purchase. Finally, we will look at personal productivity packages for handling many common applications (e.g., word processing, spreadsheets).

Where do we obtain software? Support software is almost always purchased from a hardware vendor or a software house. Only the very largest information systems organizations would even consider writing utility programs or modifying operating systems or compilers. Applications software, however, is sometimes developed within the organization and sometimes purchased from an outside source. Standard

applications packages, such as word processing, database management systems, electronic mail, and spreadsheets, are almost always purchased. Applications that are unique to the organization—a one-of-a-kind production control system, a proprietary foreign exchange trading program, a decision support system for adoption/nonadoption of a new product—are almost always developed within the organization (or by a consulting firm under contract to the organization). The vast middle ground of applications that are quite similar from one organization to the next, but may have some features peculiar to the particular organization, may be either purchased or developed.

These middle-ground applications include accounts payable, accounts receivable, general ledger, inventory control, MRP, sales analysis, and personnel reporting. Here the organization must decide whether its requirements are truly unique. Does the organization have the capability of developing this application in-house? What are the costs and benefits of developing in-house versus purchasing a package? This make-or-buy decision for applications software is an important one for almost every organization, and this topic will be addressed further in Chapter 11. Let us note at this point that the rising costs of software development tend to be pushing the balance towards more purchased software and less in-house development.

Until the mid-1980s virtually all software development done within an organization was done by the formally constituted information systems organization. The exceptions were engineers, scientists, and a few computer jocks[3] in other user departments. A revolution called end-user computing has occurred in the past decade and a half, and now much of the internal software development is done by end-users such as you. There are at least three reasons for the end-user computing revolution. First, the information systems organization was unable to keep up with the demand for new applications software, and significant backlogs of jobs developed. Second, a more knowledgeable, more computer-oriented group of users was created through the hiring of college graduates and the use of various internal and external training programs. Third, and perhaps most significant, powerful desktop

---

3 This is not meant as a term of derision. "Computer jock" is a common term used to indicate a person who spends great quantities of time and effort working with a computer.

computer systems became affordable and relatively easy-to-use tools were developed by software vendors that made it possible for interested, but not expert, users to carry out significant software development. These tools include the fourth-generation languages and the query languages associated with database management systems. This trend toward end-user computing will continue, in our view, with many of you becoming involved in software development early in your careers. Chapter 12 explores this phenomenon of user development.

Of course, not all internal software development is now or should be done by users. For the most part, information systems organizations have not shrunk because of end-user computing; they simply haven't grown as rapidly as they might have otherwise. The large, complex applications continue to be developed and maintained by the information systems organization or by consulting companies or software vendors. The IS organizations also tend to develop applications that apply to multiple areas within the organization and those applications for which efficiency is paramount, such as sales transaction processing. The IS organizations employ the same tools used by end-users, but they also do a substantial portion of their work using COBOL and other 3 GLs and, in some instances, CASE (computer-aided software engineering) tools. Chapters 10 to 12 explore the various ways in which applications systems are developed or procured.

Examples of Applications Packages

Often applications software will be purchased from an outside source. To continue our look at applications software, we will consider one category of commercially available software—PC accounting packages—as a representative of the many categories that exist. There are many microcomputer-based accounting packages available, but we will focus on only two such packages—one inexpensive package designed for small and medium-sized businesses, and one designed for larger businesses.

The package designed for smaller businesses is Peachtree Complete Accounting *Plus* Time & Billing, with a retail price of $249. This package has all the features that a small to mid-sized business needs, including time and billing, general ledger, accounts receivable, accounts payable, inventory, job project

costing, payroll and check printing, and fixed asset accounting. A screen for the accounts payable function is shown in Figure 3.5. The time and billing function, which was added in 1997, includes an easy-to-use built-in timer that tracks time spent on specific activities, such as phone calls and meeting attendance; a variety of billing types or rates that give users flexibility when invoicing clients; and an expense tracking feature that shows amounts spent on items such as copies, faxes, and telephone. *PC/Computing* magazine described an earlier version of this software as ". . . the best multiuser accounting package, but get out your CPA-to-English dictionary."

The second package—or rather an extensive set of modules that can be purchased independently—is Accpac Plus, produced by Accpac International, a division of software giant Computer Associates. Accpac Plus Accounting, and its newer cousin, Accpac for Windows, is a modular financial management system for medium and large businesses. Accpac Plus Accounting was originally developed for DOS systems, but now incorporates a Windowing System Manager module to allow Accpac Plus to function with various versions of Windows. The basic modules for Accpac were created by Accpac International, and other software firms are now developing additional modules, with the blessing of Accpac, to deal with specific industries or specific accounting needs of Accpac clients. Some of the Accpac for Windows modules that are now available include Accounts Payable, Accounts Receivable, Canadian Payroll, Cashbook for Windows, EDI Bridge (we'll find out about EDI in Chapter 7), General Ledger, General Ledger Consolidations, Inventory Control, Order Entry, Work Orders, and U. S. Payroll. An even longer list of modules is available for Accpac Plus Accounting. The prices of these modules vary, with the Windowing System Manager as low as a few hundred dollars and the EDI module priced at $2,500. The idea, of course, is for each business to select and employ the modules needed to run its business.

Personal Productivity Software

From your personal standpoint as a manager, the category of applications software that we have chosen to call personal productivity software is probably the most important of all. These are the packages that you

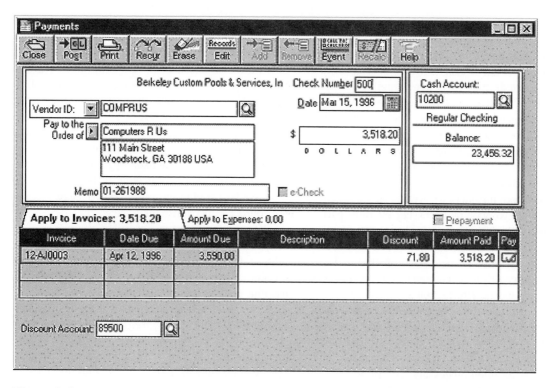

Figure 3.5 Accounts Payable Screen Shot from Peachtree Accounting *Plus* Time & Billing (Courtesy of Peachtree Software)

and your fellow managers will use on a regular basis—word processing, spreadsheets, presentation graphics, electronic mail, desktop publishing, microcomputer-based database management systems, Web browsers, statistical packages, and other similar easy-to-use and extremely useful packages. These packages are largely microcomputer-based, and they have been developed with a friendly, comfortable graphical user interface (GUI).

Exciting things are happening in the personal productivity software area. The true beginning of this area came in 1979 with the introduction of VisiCalc, the first electronic spreadsheet. With VisiCalc, microcomputers became a valuable business tool, not just a toy or a hobby. The financial success of VisiCalc convinced many individuals that there was money to be made in developing software packages that individuals and companies would buy and use. Within a few years a deluge of products appeared—a mixture of good ones and bad—that has not stopped flowing. The results have been truly marvelous for the business-

person with a willingness to experiment and a desire to become more productive. Most of the microcomputer products are quite reasonably priced (often a few hundred dollars), because the successful products can expect to reap large rewards on their volume of sales. Furthermore, a number of excellent publications have developed (such as *PC/Computing*, *Byte*, and *PC Week*), which carefully review the new products to assist us in choosing the right packages. Hardly a month goes by without the announcement of an exciting new package that may become the new VisiCalc, Lotus 1-2-3, or WordPerfect.

Word Processing   Word processing may be the most ubiquitous of the personal productivity software packages. In many organizations, the first users of microcomputers were the secretaries using early word processing packages (often WordStar). As secretaries learned the advantages of word processing—particularly the ability to make corrections in a draft without retyping the entire document—managers began to think that it might be more convenient for them, too, to have a microcomputer on their desk so that they could draft letters and reports directly at the keyboard rather than write them out longhand. There is an art to composing at the keyboard, but once a person has the hang of it, productivity (in terms of written output) can easily be doubled or tripled, as compared to writing longhand. Thus, word processing has made major inroads into the corporate world at the managerial level.

The newest versions of the popular word processing packages make it easy to get devoted to them. For example, Corel WordPerfect underlines words that might be misspelled so that you can correct them as you type, lets the user change fonts, margins, and columns easily, rewrites sentences to make them grammatically correct with the click of a mouse, links any text directly to an Internet file, and converts Web files directly to WordPerfect format, ready to use. Another popular capability is mail merge—the ability to automatically print the same letter (with the address and salutation changed, of course) to everyone on a mailing list. Other popular word processing packages include Microsoft Word for Windows and Lotus Word Pro (formerly Ami Pro). All these packages try to achieve "what you see is what you get," or WYSIWYG, and all succeed to a great extent. The idea is that the text you see on the microcomputer screen should be as close as possible to the resulting printed text. The choice of a word processor is a complex decision based on many factors in addition to WYSIWYG. Most of us tend to prefer whichever word processor we worked with first. The important thing is not which word processor, it is selecting and using any one of the better word processors in order to improve your personal productivity in writing.

Spreadsheets   Second only to word processing in popularity are electronic spreadsheet packages, the most widely used of which is Microsoft Excel for Windows. Other popular spreadsheet packages are Lotus 1-2-3 and Corel Quattro Pro. After the early success of VisiCalc, Lotus 1-2-3 became the spreadsheet standard in the early 1980s and held that leadership position for over a decade. With the growth of software suites (more on this later) and the dominance of Microsoft in the operating system arena, 1-2-3 has fallen behind Excel as the spreadsheet of choice, but

Lotus 1-2-3 is still an excellent product with a strong following.

The idea of the electronic spreadsheet is based on the accountant's spreadsheet, which is a large sheet of paper divided into many columns and rows on which the accountant can organize and present financial data. The spreadsheet approach can be used for any application that can fit into the rows and columns framework: budget summaries for several time periods, profit and loss statements for various divisions of a company, sales forecasts for the next 12 months, an instructor's gradebook, computation of various statistics for a basketball team.

The intersection of a row and a column is called a cell. Each row in the spreadsheet is given a label (1, 2, 3, etc., from the top down), as is each column (A, B, C, etc., from left to right), and a cell is identified by combining the designations of the intersecting row and column (see Figure 3.6). In a budget summary spreadsheet, for example, cell C4 might contain $32,150, the budgeted sales income for the second quarter. Similarly, cell C2 might contain the heading information "Second Quarter." To enter data into a cell, the cursor is positioned on that cell and the user merely keys in the appropriate data.

But the power of a spreadsheet program does not come from keying numeric data into particular cells, although that is certainly done. The power comes in part from the use of formulas to combine the contents of other cells, letting the program do the calculations rather than doing them by hand. For example, let us assume that cell C9 in our budget summary example is to contain the total income for the second quarter, which is the sum of cells C4, C5, C6, and C7. Rather than total C4 through C7 by hand, the user enters a formula in cell C9 that tells the program to total the contents of those four cells. One way to express that formula in Microsoft Excel is = +C4+C5+C6+C7. Then the sum is computed by the program and placed in cell C9. More importantly, if a change has to be made in one of the numerical entries—say in cell C5 —then the sum in cell C9 is automatically corrected to reflect the new number. This feature makes it very easy to modify assumptions and conduct "what if" analyses using a spreadsheet package.

Among the "big three" spreadsheet packages mentioned earlier, there is little difference in the basic approach, although the details do vary. The normal

	A	B	C	D	E	F	G
1			SECOND COMPANY PROJECTED PROFIT				
2							
3			1999	2000	2001	2002	2003
4							
5	Quantity sold		2000	2100	2205	2315	2431
6	Price		$ 50.00	$ 54.00	$ 58.32	$ 62.99	$ 68.02
7							
8	Total income		$ 100,000	$ 113,400	$ 128,596	$ 145,827	$ 165,368
9							
10							
11	Fixed costs:						
12	Rent		$ 1,000	$ 1,100	$ 1,200	$ 1,300	$ 1,400
13	Salaries		$ 20,000	$ 22,000	$ 24,200	$ 26,620	$ 29,282
14	Equipment leases		$ 4,000	$ 4,200	$ 4,410	$ 4,631	$ 4,862
15	Utilities		$ 5,000	$ 6,000	$ 7,200	$ 8,640	$ 10,368
16	Office supplies		$ 500	$ 475	$ 451	$ 429	$ 407
17							
18	Total fixed costs		$ 30,500	$ 33,775	$ 37,461	$ 41,619	$ 46,319
19							
20	Variable costs:						
21	Unit material cost		$ 8.00	$ 10.00	$ 12.00	$ 14.00	$ 16.00
22	Unit labor cost		$ 4.00	$ 4.16	$ 4.33	$ 5.11	$ 5.62
23	Unit supplies cost		$ 1.00	$ 1.00	$ 1.00	$ 1.00	$ 1.00
24							
25	Total material cost		$ 16,000	$ 21,000	$ 26,460	$ 32,414	$ 38,896
26	Total labor cost		$ 8,000	$ 8,736	$ 9,540	$ 11,820	$ 13,652
27	Total supplies cost		$ 2,000	$ 2,100	$ 2,205	$ 2,315	$ 2,431
28							
29	Total variable costs		$ 26,000	$ 31,836	$ 38,205	$ 46,548	$ 54,979
30							
31	Total costs		$ 56,500	$ 65,611	$ 75,666	$ 88,168	$ 101,298
32							
33							
34	Profit before taxes		$ 43,500	$ 47,789	$ 52,930	$ 57,660	$ 64,070

Figure 3.6 Microsoft Excel for Windows Spreadsheet

display when using Excel, for example, is a portion of the spreadsheet (a window) with a menu, icons, and a control area at the top of the screen. Using the arrow keys, the user navigates around the spreadsheet to the cell where the entry is to be made. Note that the window automatically changes to keep the cursor cell visible. As numerical or heading information is keyed in, it appears both in the control area at the top of the screen and in the desired cell. If a formula is keyed in, however, the formula appears in the control area while the resulting numerical value is placed in the cell. The various commands in Excel are accessed by the menu and icons at the top of the screen. If a particular string of commands is likely to be used repeatedly, it is possible to create a macro (a program). The user then employs a few keystrokes to call the macro rather than entering the entire string of commands.

Projecting profit for a hypothetical company will serve as a specific spreadsheet application. The Second Company wishes to project its profit for the years 1999 through 2003, given a set of assumptions about its quantity sold, selling price, fixed expenses, and variable expenses. For example, quantity sold of the only product is assumed to be 2,000 units in 1999, increasing 5 percent per year for each year thereafter. Price is assumed to be $50 per unit in 1999, increasing at 8 percent per year. Rent is $1,000 in 1999, growing at $100 per year. Similar assumptions are made for each of the other categories of fixed and variable costs. The resulting spreadsheet is shown in Figure 3.6, which indicates that the Second Company is projected to make $43,500 in profit before taxes in 1999 and $64,070 in 2003.

How were these numbers in the spreadsheet determined? Many of the numbers in the 1999 column were keyed in directly as initial assumptions. But eight of the numbers in the 1999 column and all of the numbers in the remaining columns were determined by formulas, letting the program perform the actual calculations. For instance, 2000 was actually keyed into cell C5 and 50.00 into cell C6. Cell C8, however, contains a formula to multiply quantity sold times price =+C5*C6. Figure 3.7 shows the formulas behind the numbers in Figure 3.6. If the cursor is positioned on cell C8 in the spreadsheet, the number 100,000 will appear in the spreadsheet but the formula =+C5*C6 will appear in the control area at the top. Similarly, cell C18 contains a formula to add the contents of cells C12, C13, C14, C15, and C16; one way of

expressing this formula is =SUM(C12:C16). Cell D5, the quantity sold in 2000, also contains a formula. In this case, the quantity sold in 2000 is to be 5 percent greater than the quantity sold in 1999, so the formula is =+C5*1.05. Not surprisingly, the formula in cell E5 is =+D5*1.05. Thus, any changed assumption about the quantity sold in 1999 will automatically impact both total income and profit in 1999 and quantity sold, total income, and profit in all future years. Because of this cascading effect, the impact of alternative assumptions can be easily analyzed after the original spreadsheet has been developed. This is the power of a spreadsheet package.

Database Management Systems   After word processing and spreadsheets, the next most popular category of personal productivity software is microcomputer-based database management systems. The most widely used packages are Microsoft Access for Windows and Paradox for Windows (from Borland). dBase (now from Borland), which was the desktop DBMS leader in the 1980s, also has a sizeable number of loyal users. All these packages are based on the relational data model and all meet our ease-of-use criterion. The basic ideas behind these packages are the same as those to be discussed for large machine

	A	B	C	D	E	F	G
1			SECOND COMPANY PROJECTED PROFIT				
2							
3			1999	2000	2001	2002	2003
4							
5	Quantity sold		2000	=+C5*1.05	=+D5*1.05	=+E5*1.05	=+F5*1.05
6	Price		50	=+C6*1.08	=+D6*1.08	=+E6*1.08	=+F6*1.08
7							
8	Total income		=+C5*C6	=+D5*D6	=+E5*E6	=+F5*F6	=+G5*G6
9							
10							
11	Fixed costs:						
12	Rent		1000	=+C12+100	=+D12+100	=+E12+100	=+F12+100
13	Salaries		20000	=+C13*1.1	=+D13*1.1	=+E13*1.1	=+F13*1.1
14	Equipment leases		4000	=+C14*1.05	=+D14*1.05	=+E14*1.05	=+F14*1.05
15	Utilities		5000	=+C15*1.2	=+D15*1.2	=+E15*1.2	=+F15*1.2
16	Office supplies		500	=+C16*0.95	=+D16*0.95	=+E16*0.95	=+F16*0.95
17							
18	Total fixed costs		=SUM(C12:C16)	=SUM(D12:D16)	=SUM(E12:E16)	=SUM(F12:F16)	=SUM(G12:G16)
19							
20	Variable costs:						
21	Unit material cost		8	=+C21+2	=+D21+2	=+E21+2	=+F21+2
22	Unit labor cost		4	=+C22*1.04	=+D22*1.04	=+E22*1.18	=+F22*1.1
23	Unit supplies cost		1	1	1	1	1
24							
25	Total material cost		=+C5*C21	=+D5*D21	=+E5*E21	=+F5*F21	=+G5*G21
26	Total labor cost		=+C5*C22	=+D5*D22	=+E5*E22	=+F5*F22	=+G5*G22
27	Total supplies cost		=+C5*C23	=+D5*D23	=+E5*E23	=+F5*F23	=+G5*G23
28							
29	Total variable costs		=+C25+C26+C27	=+D25+D26+D27	=+E25+E26+E27	=+F25+F26+F27	=+G25+G26+G27
30							
31	Total costs		=+C18+C29	=+D18+D29	=+E18+E29	=+F18+F29	=+G18+G29
32							
33							
34	Profit before taxes		=+C8-C31	=+D8-D31	=+E8-E31	=+F8-F31	=+G8-G31

Figure 3.7 Cell Formulas for Microsoft Excel Spreadsheet

DBMSs, but they are generally easier to use. With the aid of macros and other programming tools (such as Visual Basic for Applications in the case of Access), rather sophisticated applications can be built based on these DBMS packages.

Presentation Graphics   Presentation graphics is yet another important category of personal productivity software. Most spreadsheet packages incorporate significant graphics capabilities, but the specialized presentation graphics (sometimes called business graphics) packages have even greater capabilities. The leaders in this field are Corel Presentations and Corel-Draw, which incorporates easy-to-use tools for drawing, animating, and photo editing as well as extensive clip art; Microsoft PowerPoint for Windows, an easy-to-use package for creating presentations; and Visio, which makes it easy and quick to develop attractive business charts.

World Wide Web Browsers   A newly important type of personal productivity software is the **Web browser,** which is used by an individual to access information on the World Wide Web. The Web browser is the software that runs on the user's microcomputer, enabling him or her to look around, or "browse," on the Internet. The user's machine must be linked to the Internet via a modem connection to an Internet provider or a connection to a local area network or wide area network that is in turn connected to the Internet. The Web browser uses a hypertext-based approach to navigate the Internet. **Hypertext** is a creative way of linking objects (such as text, pictures, sound clips, and video clips) to each other. For example, when you are reading a document describing the Grand Canyon, you might click on The View from Yavapai Point to display a full-screen photograph of that view, or you might click on The Grand Canyon Suite to hear a few bars from that musical composition.

The two major Web browsers in 1998 were Netscape Corporation's Netscape Navigator and Microsoft's Internet Explorer. Netscape was available first and still has an edge in terms of number of users, but Explorer is an excellent product that is gaining in popularity. From the standpoint of the user, the interesting thing about this battle is that Explorer is free and Netscape Navigator is very economically priced. At least for the present, Netscape and Microsoft are not trying to make money by selling Web browsers; they intend to make money by selling the products needed to build and maintain Web sites and by developing applications to run on the World Wide Web.

In the newest version of Internet Explorer, Microsoft has introduced the idea of the Active Desktop, which Microsoft describes as a customizable "dashboard" for your Windows-based PC. The Active Desktop lets the user place both Windows icons (such as shortcuts to programs that you use frequently) and World Wide Web elements (such as links to Web sites that you visit frequently) on the Windows home screen. The Web elements can be dynamic, too. Users can, for example, place a Web page on the screen and have it updated by the Active Desktop at regular intervals so that the content is always current.

The Web browsers are based on the idea of **pull technology,** where the browser must request a Web page before it is sent to the desktop. **Push technology** is also important—where data are sent to the client (usually a PC) without a request from the client. E-mail is the probably the oldest and most widely used push technology. Increasingly, push technology is being used on the Internet to deliver data. Perhaps the most successful example is PointCast, which delivers customized news ticker-tape style to the user's desktop, but many additional push technology products have been developed for use within an organization over its internal network or for more broad-based use on the Internet.

Electronic Mail and Groupware   We will defer a full discussion of electronic mail (e-mail) and groupware until Chapter 6, but these clearly qualify as personal productivity software. Electronic mail has become the preferred way of communicating for managers in many businesses today—it is asynchronous (no telephone tag) and unobtrusive, easy to use and precise. Groupware incorporates electronic mail, but also much more. Groupware has the goal of helping a group become more productive and includes innovative ways of data sharing, such as Lotus Notes' threaded discussion groups.

Other Personal Productivity Packages   Desktop publishing gives the user the ability to design and print an in-house newspaper or magazine, a sales brochure, or an annual report. The more advanced word processing

PUSH TECHNOLOGY SAVES TIME AND MONEY

Push technologies are starting to live up to their hype and are finding a home in corporate America. The usefulness of the loose group of technologies that enables data to be published via Internet "channels" goes beyond the mass-audience appeal of the popular PointCast Inc. application, say corporate users.

Rather, IT managers are adopting push to automate and streamline jobs that can be time-consuming and costly, such as triggering database processes, distributing and maintaining software, and publishing sales and inventory information to business partners. The benefits are clear: savings in time and money.

"Push is not new; it's old. We've been broadcasting financial data for years," said Rich Gaiti, first vice president of advanced office systems and technology at Merrill Lynch Inc. in Princeton, N.J. "But the way we're using the technology today is enabling our consultants to be better informed, make better decisions, and as a result better service our customers and clients."

Merrill's new push application is part of a new TGA (Trusted Global Advisor) system set to be deployed this year to more than 25,000 users. Competitors Fidelity Investments Inc. and Lehman Brothers also are on the cutting edge of push technology, as are other large sites including hospitals and technology companies.

Merrill's broad TGA system provides financial consultants with client information, portfolio management, investment tools, stock market information, news reports, and historical data. Integrated into TGA is a customized version of Desktop Data Inc.'s NewsEdge online news service that provides consultants with customized news feeds about clients and companies that they track. Intermingled with the news feeds is historical analysis that is pushed out of Merrill's database on a scheduled basis.

[Moeller, 1997]

packages, such as Microsoft Word and Corel Word-Perfect, provide the capability to arrange the document in appropriate columns, import figures and tables, and use appropriate type fonts and styles. Even more powerful are popular specialized desktop publishing packages such as Microsoft Publisher and Adobe Systems PageMaker for Windows.

There are a number of other categories of personal productivity packages. Personal information managers provide an easy-to-use electronic calendar plus storage of telephone numbers, addresses, and other personal information; popular products include Lotus Organizer and Starfish Sidekick. Packages for creating and distributing electronic documents include Adobe Systems Acrobat Pro. GoldMine is an example of a contact management program to let you track past and potential customers. Project scheduling software includes Microsoft Project for Windows and Primavera Systems SureTrak Project Manager. Among the popular packages for illustration and image editing are Adobe Systems Photoshop, Adobe Systems Illustrator, and Fractal Design Painter. Valuable business and reference CD-ROMs include Rand McNally TripMaker (high-quality, zoomable street maps and precise directions), Microsoft Encarta Encyclopedia (a true multimedia encyclopedia), and Pro CD Select Phone Deluxe (looking up any telephone number in the United States).

The list of personal productivity software presented here could certainly be extended, but today's most important categories have been mentioned. New packages and new categories will most assuredly be introduced in the next few years

Application Suites   New versions of the popular personal productivity software packages have been introduced almost every year in the middle to late 1990s, but two other developments have been even more important in redefining the personal productivity software area. First, the key players have evolved over time, with some firms being purchased by others and some products being sold to a different vendor. IBM's purchase of Lotus Development Corporation in 1995 was perhaps the most significant shift among the players. The popular WordPerfect word processing package has been batted around like a ping-pong ball; first the WordPerfect Corporation was purchased by Novell, and then Novell sold the WordPerfect package to Corel. The popular packages of two or three years ago likely still exist, but they may not have the same corporate home.

Second, a very important trend is the combining of these personal productivity software packages into integrated suites of applications. With the strong popularity of Windows 95, the major software players have scrambled to introduce **application suites** that are compatible with Windows 95. Microsoft, as the developer of Windows 95, had the inside track in terms of producing Windows 95 software packages and a Windows 95 application suite. In 1998, three important application suites for Windows 95 are in the marketplace: Microsoft Office (both standard and professional editions), Lotus SmartSuite, and Corel Office Professional.

Microsoft Office (first 95, now 97) was the first suite available and has captured the largest market share, but both of the other suites have strong features and popular products. The Microsoft Office suite includes Microsoft Word (word processing), Excel (spreadsheet), PowerPoint (presentation graphics), and Outlook (contacts and scheduling) in the standard edition. The professional edition adds Microsoft Access (database management system). These individual products are all excellent applications in their own right, and they are reasonably well integrated in this suite. Lotus SmartSuite includes Word Pro (word processing), Lotus 1-2-3 (spreadsheet), Freelance Graphics (presentation graphics), Organizer (calendaring), and Approach (database management system). The newest suite entry, Corel Office Professional, includes more products than both of the other two suites combined—a total of 18. Among the products, the heavy hitters are WordPerfect (word processing), Quattro Pro (spreadsheet), Corel Presentations (presentation graphics), CorelDraw (illustrations), and Borland's Paradox (database management system), plus many more less well known applications such as Starfish Sidekick (personal information manager). Unfortunately, only the core applications are really well integrated. *PC/Computing* magazine gives all three suites a four-star rating, which is a "good" rating (five stars is "excellent"). The future of personal productivity software appears to be in application suites because of the ability to move data among the various products as needed.

Support Software

Support software has been designed to support applications software behind the scenes, rather than directly produce output of value to the user. There are several types of support software, such as the language translators that we encountered earlier in this chapter. In our discussion of the evolution of computer programming, we noted that programs written in second-, third-, and fourth-generation languages must be translated to machine language before they can be run on a computer. This translation is accomplished by support software called assemblers, compilers, and interpreters. We will now take a systematic look at the various types of support software.

The Operating System

The most important type of support software is the operating system, which originated in the mid-1960s and is now an integral part of every computer system. The **operating system** is a very complex program that controls the operation of the computer hardware and coordinates all the other software, so as to get as much work done as possible with the available resources. Users interact with the operating system, not the hardware, and the operating system in turn controls all hardware and software resources of the computer system.

Before operating systems (and this was also before PCs), computer operators had to physically load programs and start them running by pushing buttons on the computer console. Only one program could be run at a time, and the computer was often idle while waiting for an action by the operator. Now the operator's job is much easier and the computer is used more efficiently, with the operating system controlling the starting and stopping of individual programs and permitting multiple programs to be run at the same time. The operating system on a PC also helps the user by providing an easy-to-use graphical user interface (GUI).

There are two overriding purposes for an operating system—to maximize the work done by the computer system (the throughput) and to ease the work load of human computer users. In effect, the operation of the computer system has been automated through the use of this sophisticated program. Figure 3.8 illustrates some of the ways in which these purposes are advanced by the operating system. This somewhat complex diagram presents the roles of the operating system in a large computer system. To make these roles more understandable, we will concentrate on the individual elements of the diagram.

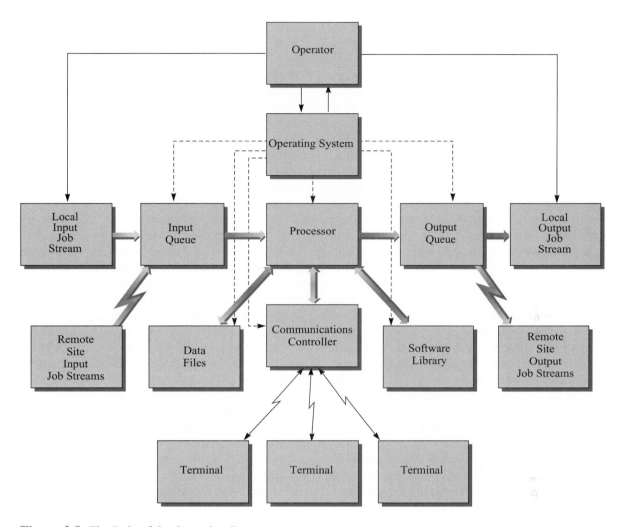

Figure 3.8 The Role of the Operating System

First, note that the human operator at the top of the diagram interfaces only with the operating system, the local input job stream, and the local output job stream. The interface with the operating system is usually by entering simple commands at an operator console (a specialized terminal); the interface with the local input job stream is usually mounting tapes or changing removable disk packs; and the interface with the local output job stream means separating and distributing printed output.

The operating system, either directly or indirectly through other support software, controls everything else that takes place in Figure 3.8. It controls the inflow and outflow of communications with the various terminals and microcomputers (often through a specialized communications interface program). Using priority rules specified by the computer center manager, the operating system decides when to initiate a particular job from among those waiting in the input queue; similarly, the operating system decides when to terminate a job (either because it has been completed, or an error has occurred, or it has run too long). The operating system decides which job to print next, again based on priority rules. It stores and retrieves data files, keeping track of where everything is stored (a function sometimes shared with a database management system). The operating system also manages the software library, keeping track of both support and applications programs.

The advantage of letting the operating system perform all the above tasks is that it can react at electronic speed to select the next job, handle multiple terminal sessions, select the appropriate software from the library, and retrieve the appropriate data file. Thus, the expensive and powerful central processing unit (CPU) can be kept as busy as possible, and the throughput from the system can be maximized. Further, the operating system can create a computing environment—in terms of what operators and other users see on their terminal screens, and what they need to key in to instruct the operating system what to do—in which it is relatively easy to work.

A microcomputer operating system, such as Windows 95 or Windows NT, performs many of the functions described above, although the scale is smaller and the complexity is reduced. It is still true that the user employs the operating system to start a program, to retrieve data, to copy files, and so on. The purpose of a microcomputer operating system is exactly the same as the purpose of a large machine operating system—to maximize the work done by the computer system, and to ease the work load of human users..

Job Control Language   As noted, it is necessary for computer users to communicate with the operating system, usually by keying in instructions at a terminal. These instructions must be expressed in the particular **job control language,** or **JCL,** that is understood by the operating system being used. This job control language varies significantly from one operating system to the next, both in terms of the types of instructions and the detailed syntax. For example, with the PC-DOS or MS-DOS operating system (used on IBM and IBM-compatible PCs before Windows became popular), to change directories, one types CD\ followed by the name of the new directory; to list the current directory, one types DIR; and to copy a file named MEMO from the A drive to the B drive, one types COPY A: MEMO B:. These are examples of the job control language. The JCL is even simpler for a Macintosh or a PC operating under Windows 95 or NT: In this case, the user may click or double-click on an icon to start an application or retrieve a file. The JCL is much more complex for a larger machine, but the ideas are the

same. To run a payroll program, for example, JCL is used to tell the operating system the name of the program to be run, the names of the data files that are needed, instructions for output of data, and the account number to be charged, among other things.

Multiprogramming or multitasking[4]   Operating systems often incorporate two important concepts—multiprogramming or multitasking, and virtual memory—in order to increase the efficiency of the computer's operations. All these concepts are concerned with the management of the memory and the CPU time of the computer system.

On larger machines, **multiprogramming** is often employed to overlap input and output operations with processing time. This is very important, because the time required for the computer to perform an input/output operation (such as reading from disk) is quite large compared to the time required to execute an arithmetic instruction. In fact, a typical computer might execute 100,000 arithmetic instructions in the time required to read a single record from a disk. Thus, it would be quite inefficient to let the CPU remain idle while input/output operations are being completed. Multiprogramming keeps the CPU busy by overlapping the input/output operations of one program with the processing time of another program.

For multiprogramming, several programs (say five to ten) must be located in memory at the same time. Then the operating system supervises the switching back and forth among these programs so that the CPU is almost always busy. When the currently executing program encounters an input/output instruction, an interrupt occurs and the operating system takes control. The operating system stores the status of the interrupted program in memory so that this information will be available when the interrupted program gets another shot at the CPU. The operating system then decides which of the waiting programs should be executed next, and it resets the computer with the status of the new program. Then the operating system gives control to the new program, which executes until it

---

4 The material in this section and the next is more technical than the rest of the chapter, and it may be omitted by those readers who only wish to obtain a basic understanding of operating systems. It is included to provide a more comprehensive picture to those who are interested.

encounters an input/output instruction. Thus, the operating system controls the switching back and forth among programs that is involved in multiprogramming.

The switching among programs in multiprogramming may be triggered by time as well as by an event (the occurrence of an input/output instruction). Time-driven multiprogramming (sometimes called **time-sharing**) is the usual mode of operation when large numbers of users are simultaneously using a computer (midrange or larger) from terminals or microcomputers serving as terminals. In this environment, each user is allocated a small slice of CPU time (e.g., a few milliseconds). When a particular user's turn arises, his program runs for those few milliseconds, carrying out thousands of instructions. Then a time interrupt occurs, and the operating system transfers control to the next user for his slice of time. Unless the number of concurrent users becomes excessively high, these bursts of available time occur so rapidly that it appears to the user that he or she is the only person who is using the computer.

On smaller computers, including microcomputers, the term **multitasking** is used to describe essentially the same function as multiprogramming on larger machines. In both cases the operating system controls the switching back and forth among programs stored in memory. There are two basic types of multitasking: *preemptive* and *cooperative*. In preemptive multitasking, the operating system allocates slices of CPU time to each program (the same as in time-driven multiprogramming). In cooperative multitasking, each program can control the CPU for as long as it needs it. In practice, multitasking means that a user can print a report at essentially the same time as he or she recalculates a spreadsheet, all the while monitoring for new electronic mail.

Virtual Memory   While multiprogramming or multitasking is primarily concerned with the management of CPU time, **virtual memory** is concerned with the management of main memory. At present, virtual memory is used only on larger computer systems. Virtual memory makes it appear to the user that he has an unlimited amount of main memory available, meaning that individual programs can be much larger than the actual number of memory cells. More importantly, virtual memory permits multiprogramming to operate more efficiently. How does this work?

The trick is the creative use of a direct access storage device (DASD), with the operating system switching portions of programs (called pages) between main memory and DASD. Unless all the programs are small, it is difficult to get enough programs stored in memory for multiprogramming to operate efficiently. For example, three large programs may occupy all of memory, and it may be common for all three programs to be processing input/output instructions at the same time. This leaves the CPU idle, which is undesirable. The cost of adding enough real memory to store ten programs at a time—to permit efficient multiprogramming—may be prohibitive. The virtual memory concept recognizes that only one segment of a large program is being executed at a time, while the bulk of the program is inactive. Therefore, with virtual memory, only a few pages of the program (perhaps only one) are kept in main memory, with the rest relegated to DASD. Because only a small portion of each program is located in memory, portions of a sufficient number of programs can be stored in memory to permit efficient multiprogramming.

Of course, it is often necessary for the operating system to bring new portions of a program (new pages) into memory so they can be executed. This swapping of pages between DASD and main memory is called paging. The size of pages varies, but each is often a few thousand bytes. When one combines the concepts of multiprogramming (switching among pages of programs already in memory) with virtual memory (requiring frequent page switches from DASD to memory), then we begin to realize the incredible complexity of tasks carried out by the operating system.

Multiprocessing   Despite the similarities between the terms, multiprocessing is quite different from multiprogramming. **Multiprocessing** refers to the processing, or work, that takes place when two or more CPUs are installed as part of the same computer system. Each CPU works on its own job or set of jobs (often using multiprogramming), with all the CPUs under control of a single operating system, which keeps track of what the various CPUs are doing. This is complexity piled on complexity! It is easy to see that today's computer systems would be much less efficient and of very limited use to us without the powerful operating systems that exist and are continually being upgraded.

Sources of Operating Systems   For the most part, operating systems are obtained from the manufacturer of the hardware—although the operating system may have been written by some other company. For example, when you buy a new microcomputer from Gateway 2000 or Dell, it likely comes equipped with Windows 95, an operating system from Microsoft. Most of the popular operating systems are **proprietary systems** that were written expressly for a particular computer system. Examples are PC-DOS and MS-DOS, which are the same operating system written by Microsoft for IBM microcomputers and IBM compatibles, respectively; Windows 95 and Windows NT, which are newer systems written for IBM-compatible microcomputers; MVS and VM, which are two alternative large machine operating systems offered by IBM; and OS/400, which is the operating system for IBM's AS/400 line of midrange systems.

In contrast to these proprietary systems, the popular UNIX operating system is an **open system.** UNIX is not tied to a particular computer system or hardware manufacturer. UNIX was originally developed by Bell Laboratories, with subsequent versions created by the University of California at Berkeley, AT&T, and a variety of hardware manufacturers. For example, Digital Equipment Corporation and IBM have developed their own versions of UNIX— ULTRIX for Digital and AIX for IBM. Many of the newer computers, such as high-powered workstations and supercomputers, run only UNIX.

UNIX is powerful and flexible, and it is portable in that it will run on virtually any computer with a C language compiler (UNIX was written in C; more on C later). Some computer professionals would like to see UNIX become the standard operating system for all computer systems. That appears unlikely to happen in the foreseeable future, but the use of UNIX will continue to spread, at least for larger machines. Some organizations have even adopted a strategy of carrying out all new applications software development in a UNIX environment and gradually moving existing applications to UNIX. In particular, many client/server applications have been designed to run on a UNIX-based server. Interestingly, IBM's OS/390 mainframe operating system, which is the newest incarnation of the MVS proprietary operating system, incorporates complete UNIX capabilities. In other words, OS/390 can run *both* MVS applications and UNIX applications. UNIX continues to move into the large computer arena, but it is unlikely to replace vendor operating systems like MVS in major corporate and government data processing centers.

At the microcomputer level, UNIX is not a serious contender in the late 1990s. For users of IBM microcomputers and IBM compatibles, the choice is among Microsoft's Windows 95 or 98, Microsoft's Windows NT, and IBM's OS/2 (which was, interestingly, originally developed by Microsoft). All 3 versions of Windows are stand-alone operating systems (as is OS/2), in contrast to the earlier versions of Windows, which operated in conjunction with PC-DOS or MS-DOS. All of these microcomputer operating systems feature a powerful **graphical user interface,** or **GUI** (pronounced goo-ey). With a GUI, the user selects an application or makes other choices by using a mouse to click on an appropriate icon or label appearing on the screen. All 3 versions of Windows and OS/2 also permit multiple "windows" to be open on the video screen, with a separate application running in each window. These operating systems are also so-called 32-bit operating systems, in that they are all designed to handle 32 bits of data at a time, in contrast to earlier operating systems, which dealt with 16 bits at a time. Because most new IBM-compatible machines come preloaded with Windows 98, it is the de facto standard for individual machines as of this writing. However, both Windows NT and OS/2 contain powerful features not included in Windows 98, and both have been adopted for critical applications in many large organizations. Windows NT is a network operating system (for a local area network consisting of microcomputers wired together in an office or a building; see box on network operating systems) as well as a single-machine operating system, and it appears to represent Microsoft's vision of the future in terms of operating systems.

In summary, all of the widely used operating systems in use today will continue to evolve over the next several years, with each becoming more complex and more powerful. Paradoxically, microcomputer operating systems will at the same time become much easier to use. It appears likely that the movement towards UNIX for larger machines and Windows for microcomputers will continue.

One of the important notions in the information technology area is that of an **IT platform,** which is

NETWORK OPERATING SYSTEMS

The network operating system (NOS) is the software that manages network resources and controls the operation of the network. Every server on your intranet[5] will have a NOS installed that supports its hardware platform. You should select a NOS based on the server software you plan on installing, because the information service is usually more important than the NOS supporting it. You have more than 50 NOSs to choose from, but only six of these are ones that you should seriously consider using on your intranet. These are Apple Open Transport, Banyan Vines, IBM OS/2 Warp Server Advanced, Microsoft Windows NT 4.0, Novell NetWare, and Solaris Internet Server.

Apple Open Transport is the modern networking and communication subsystem for the Mac OS. If you're using the Macintosh platform for one or more servers on your intranet, Open Transport is just about the only worthwhile option available. Vines is the NOS from Banyan Systems, Inc.; we recommend it only on a single server when required for specific information service server software. We recommend the OS/2 Warp Server Advanced if any of your products require this operating system (i.e., OS/2). Windows NT 4.0 is the newest server product from Microsoft. NT Server was designed for deployment in any networking environment, small or large, private or public, intranet or traditional. We highly recommend NT 4.0 as a central NOS for any intranet. NetWare has been the industry leader in the small office network market for years, and it promises to be a solid intranet solution. We recommend the Solaris Internet Server for intranets designed around UNIX-based information services.

[Tittel and Stewart, 1997]

defined as the set of hardware, software, communications, and standards an organization uses to build its information systems. Now we are in the position to point out that the operating system is usually the single most critical component of the platform. Thus, it is common to discuss an MVS (mainframe) platform, a

5 An intranet is a network with an organization that employs the TCP/IP protocol; this concept is explored more fully in Chapter 4. In reading this sidebar, think of an intranet as an internal network or a local area network.

VM (mainframe) platform, a UNIX platform, a Windows NT platform, or an OS/2 platform.

Third-Generation Languages

As illustrated in Figure 3.4, the underwater portion of the software iceberg includes support software in addition to the critical operating system. It is useful to divide this support software into five major categories: language translators, database management systems, CASE tools, communications interface software, and utility programs. Let's consider languages and language translators first.

The third-generation languages, which are more commonly called procedural or procedure-oriented languages, are and will continue to be the workhorses of the information processing field for the foreseeable future. As mentioned earlier, support software in the form of compilers and interpreters is used to translate 3 GL programs (as well as 4 GL and OOP programs) into machine language programs that can be run on a computer. The procedural languages do not enjoy the near-total dominance of a decade ago, but they are still the languages of choice for most computer professionals, scientists, and engineers. During the 1990s, 4 GLs, DBMSs, application generators, object-oriented languages, and visual languages have gained ground on the 3 GLs (in part because of the growth of end-user computing), but they will not replace the 3 GLs in the next few years. There are several reasons why the procedural languages will remain popular. First, most computer professionals are familiar with one or more procedural languages and will be reluctant to change to something new. Second, the procedural languages tend to produce more efficient machine language programs (and thus shorter execution times) than the 4 GLs and other newer alternatives. Third, new versions of the procedural languages continue to be developed, each generally more powerful and easier to use than the previous version. For example, object-oriented versions of C, COBOL, and PASCAL are now available.

Using a procedural language requires logical thinking, because the programmer must devise a detailed step-by-step procedure to accomplish the desired task. Of course, these steps in the procedure must be expressed in the particular statement types available in the given procedural language. Writing a procedural program is generally viewed as just one stage in the entire program development process. Table 3.1 provides one possible listing of the various stages in the program development process. Note that writing the program does not occur until stage four. Stage eight is debugging, which literally means to get the bugs or errors out of the program. The most difficult stages in this program development process tend to be stages one and two—the proper identification of the problem and the development of an algorithm, which is a step-by-step description (in English) of the actions necessary to perform the task. In stage three, the algorithm is converted into a structure chart, which is a pictorial representation of the algorithm, or pseudocode, which is an English-language-like version of the program. Throughout the entire process, logical thinking and a logical progression of steps are required to effectively use a procedural language.

Perhaps the most significant change in the procedural languages from their beginnings is that they are more amenable to **structured programming.** A structured program is one that is divided into modules or blocks, where each block has only one entry point and only one exit point. When a program is written in this form, the program logic is easy to follow and understand, and thus the maintenance and correction of such a program should be easier than for a non-structured program. The consequence of structured programming is that few if any transfer statements (often implemented as a GO TO statement) are required to transfer control to some other portion of the program. Therefore, structured programming is often referred to as GO TO-less programming, although the modular approach is really the central feature of a structured program. The newer versions of all the procedural languages encourage highly structured programs.

BASIC   BASIC is a good place to begin a brief look at three popular procedural languages because it is the simplest of them. BASIC, which is an acronym for Beginner's All-purpose Symbolic Instruction Code, was developed in the early 1960s by John Kemeny and Thomas Kurtz at Dartmouth College. Their purpose was to create an easy-to-learn, interactive language for college students that would let the students concentrate on the thought processes involved in programming rather than on the syntax.

The early versions of BASIC were interpreted rather than compiled, but BASIC compilers have popped up in the past decade or so. Unfortunately, there are many versions of BASIC—developed by various computer manufacturers and software houses—and they are often incompatible with one another. Attempts at standardization came too late, which is one reason why businesses have been loath to adopt it. Also BASIC has historically lacked the mathematical capabilities, data management capabilities, and control structures necessary to carry out business and scientific processing efficiently. Newer versions of BASIC have addressed these shortcomings, however, as well as added the capability of developing graphical user interfaces (more on this later). These developments promise a greater role for BASIC in the future.

To illustrate BASIC, consider the following sample problem: Write a BASIC program that will find the average of a set of numbers input by the user. Use a negative number to indicate the end of the data. A BASIC program to solve this problem is shown in Figure 3.9, together with the screen dialog that occurred when the program was run on a microcomputer using a simple data set. While the details of programming are not important, you will note that most of the instructions are quite intuitive—that is, even the uninitiated would correctly guess the meaning of most instructions.

Table 3.1

Stages in the Program Development Process

Stage 1	Problem identification
Stage 2	Algorithm development
Stage 3	Conversion of algorithm to computer-understandable logic, usually in form of structure chart or pseudocode
Stage 4	Program preparation
Stage 5	Keying program into computer
Stage 6	Program compilation
Stage 7	Execution of program with test data
Stage 8	Debugging process using test data
Stage 9	Use of program with actual data

```
BASIC PROGRAM

10        REM  THIS PROGRAM FINDS THE AVERAGE OF A SET OF NUMBERS
20        REM     INPUT BY THE USER. A NEGATIVE NUMBER IS USED
30        REM     TO INDICATE THE END OF THE DATA.
40        PRINT "ENTER AS MANY POSITIVE NUMBERS AS YOU WISH,"
50        PRINT "WITH ONE NUMBER ENTERED PER LINE."
60        PRINT "WHEN YOU HAVE ENTERED YOUR ENTIRE SET OF NUMBERS,"
70        PRINT "ENTER A NEGATIVE NUMBER TO SIGNAL THE END OF DATA."
80        LET COUNT = 0
90        LET TOTAL = 0
100       INPUT NUMBER
110       IF NUMBER < 0 GO TO 150
120       LET TOTAL = TOTAL + NUMBER
130       LET COUNT = COUNT + 1
140       GO TO 100
150       LET AVG = TOTAL / COUNT
160       PRINT "THE AVERAGE OF YOUR NUMBERS IS"; AVG
170       PRINT "YOU ENTERED"; COUNT; "NUMBERS TOTALING"; TOTAL
180       END


SCREEN DIALOG WITH ABOVE BASIC PROGRAM
(Responses keyed in by user are underlined; computer responses are not underlined.)
OK
RUN
ENTER AS MANY POSITIVE NUMBERS AS YOU WISH,
WITH ONE NUMBER ENTERED PER LINE.
WHEN YOU HAVE ENTERED YOUR ENTIRE SET OF NUMBERS,
ENTER A NEGATIVE NUMBER TO SIGNAL THE END OF DATA.
?23
?45
?1
?78.6
?-9
THE AVERAGE OF YOUR NUMBERS IS 36.9
YOU ENTERED 4 NUMBERS TOTALING 147.6
OK
```

Figure 3.9 BASIC Program and Accompanying Screen Dialog

C   For scientific and engineering programming, the most important language is C, which was written by Dennis Ritchie and Brian Kernighan in the 1970s. C is a very powerful language, but hard to use because it is less English-like and is closer to assembly language than the other procedural languages. The C programming language features flexibility of use, economy of expression, versatile data structures, modern control flow, and a rich set of operators. Because of these strengths, C is widely used in the development of microcomputer packages such as word processing, spreadsheets, and database management systems, and it is gaining on FORTRAN (more on this language later) for scientific applications. Further, C has better data management capabilities than FORTRAN and other scientific languages, so it is also being used in traditional business data processing tasks such as payroll, accounting, and sales reporting.

C was originally developed for and implemented on the UNIX operating system, and its use is growing as UNIX spreads. In fact, the UNIX operating system was written in C. C programs have a high level of portability: a C program can usually be transported from one computer system to another—even from a mainframe to a microcomputer—with only minor changes. C has been adopted as the standard language by many college computer science departments, and it is widely used on microcomputers. On large research computers, it is not unusual for C and FORTRAN to be the only languages ever used.

C's strengths are its control structures and its mathematical features. To illustrate, suppose that the result of one trial of a simulation experiment is an estimated profit for the firm for the next year. Twenty such trials have been made, each producing an estimated profit for the next year. As an example, write a C program to compute the mean and variance of the estimated profit figures, entering in the data from the keyboard, one estimated profit figure per line.

A C program to solve this problem is given in Figure 3.10. The statements beginning and ending with /* and */ are comments. The *for* statement near the top of the program is a C statement to control repeated execution of a set of instructions. Some of

```
#include<stdio.h>
/* C program to compute means and variances
of simulated profit figures */

main()
{
/* Variable declaration and initialization */
  int index;
  float sum=0.0,sumsq=0.0,trial,mean,var;
/*Control repeated execution using for statement */
  for (index = 1; index <=20; ++index)
  {
      printf("Enter a profit figure:\n");
      scanf("%f",&trial);
      sum += trial;
      sumsq += trial*trial;
}/*End control for */
  mean = sum/20.0;
  var = (sumsq/19.0) - (sum*sum)/(19.0*20.0);
  printf("Mean Value is = %f\n",mean);
  printf("Variance is = %f\n",var);
}/*End of program */
```

Figure 3.10 C Program

the mathematical statements are obvious, and some are not—but the program gets the job done.

COBOL   COBOL, which is an acronym for **CO**mmon **B**usiness-**O**riented **L**anguage, is a language specifically devised for traditional business data-processing tasks. It was developed by a computer industry committee (originally the short-range committee of the Conference on Data Systems Languages, or CODASYL; later the COBOL Committee of CODASYL) in order to provide an industry-wide common language, closely resembling ordinary English, in which business data-processing procedures could be expressed. Since its inception in 1960, COBOL has gained widespread acceptance because it is standardized, has strong data management capabilities (relative to the other 3 GLs), and is relatively easy to learn and use. COBOL is by far the most popular language for programming mainframe computers for business applications.

COBOL programs are divided into four distinct divisions. The first two divisions are usually fairly short. The IDENTIFICATION DIVISION gives the program a name and provides other identifying information, and the ENVIRONMENT DIVISION describes the computer environment in which the program will be run. The ENVIRONMENT DIVISION is also the portion of the program that has to be changed to transport the program from one computer model to another. The DATA DIVISION, which is often quite lengthy, defines the entire file structure employed in the program. The PROCEDURE DIVISION corresponds most closely to a BASIC or C program; it consists of a series of operations specified in a logical order to accomplish the desired task. The combination of all these divisions, especially the DATA DIVISION, makes COBOL programs quite long compared with other procedural languages. COBOL has been correctly described as a verbose language.

Our sample COBOL program is designed to compute and print monthly sales commissions for the salespersons of a large corporation. Each salesperson earns a 1-percent commission on the first $50,000 in sales during a month and a 2-percent commission on all sales in excess of $50,000. The data has already been keyed in and is stored as a data file on a magnetic disk. One record has been prepared for each salesperson, containing the person's name and sales for the month. The output is to be a line for each salesperson, showing the name, monthly sales, and sales commission. In addition, the program is to accumulate the total commissions for all salespersons and to print this amount after all the salespersons' records have been processed.

Figure 3.11 provides a COBOL program to accomplish this processing. Again, the details are not important, but note the four divisions of the program and the sheer length of this relatively simple program.

```
1      8   12
           IDENTIFICATION DIVISION.
           PROGRAM-ID. COMMISSIONS-COMPUTE.
           AUTHOR. JOE PROGRAMMER.
           ENVIRONMENT DIVISION.
           CONFIGURATION SECTION.
           SOURCE-COMPUTER. IBM-4381.
           OBJECT-COMPUTER. IBM-4381.
           INPUT-OUTPUT SECTION.
           FILE-CONTROL.
               SELECT SALES-FILE ASSIGN DA-3380-S-IPT.
               SELECT COMMISSIONS-FILE ASSIGN DA-3380-S-RPT.
           DATA DIVISION.
           FILE SECTION.
           FD SALES-FILE
               LABEL RECORD OMITTED
               RECORD CONTAINS 80 CHARACTERS
               DATA RECORD IS IN-RECORD.
           01  IN-RECORD                PICTURE X(80).
           FD  COMMISSIONS-FILE
               LABEL RECORD OMITTED
               RECORD CONTAINS 132 CHARACTERS
               DATA RECORD IS PRINT-RECORD.
           01  PRINT-RECORD             PICTURE X(132).
           WORKING-STORAGE SECTION.
           01  SALES-RECORD.
               05   NAME                PICTURE A(30).
               05   FILLER              PICTURE X(10).
               05   SALES               PICTURE 9(8)V99.
               05   FILLER              PICTURE X(30).
           01  COMMISSION-RECORD.
               05   FILLER              PICTURE X(10).
               05   NAME-OUT            PICTURE A(30).
               05   FILLER              PICTURE X(10).
               05   SALES-OUT           PICTURE $$$,$$$,$$$.99.
               05   FILLER              PICTURE X(10).
               05   COMMISSION          PICTURE $$$$,$$$.99.
               05   FILLER              PICTURE X(47).
           77  TEMP-COMMISSION          PICTURE 9(6)V99.
           77  TOTAL-COMMISSIONS        PICTURE 9(10)V99   VALUE 0.
           77  TOTAL-COMM-EDITED        PICTURE $$,$$$,$$$,$$$.99.
           01  MORE-DATA                PICTURE X          VALUE 'Y'.
               88   THERE-IS-MORE-DATA                      VALUE 'Y'.
               88   THERE-IS-NO-MORE-DATA                   VALUE 'N'.
```

Figure 3.11A COBOL Program

```
1        8   12
             PROCEDURE DIVISION.
             MAIN-CONTROL.
                 PERFORM INITIALIZATION.
                 PERFORM READ-PROCESS-PRINT UNTIL THERE-IS-NO-MORE-DATA.
                 PERFORM COMPLETE.
                 STOP RUN.
             INITIALIZATION.
                 OPEN INPUT SALES-FILE, OUTPUT COMMISSIONS-FILE.
                 MOVE SPACES TO COMMISSION-RECORD.
             READ-PROCESS-PRINT.
                 READ SALES-FILE INTO SALES-RECORD
                     AT END MOVE 'N' TO MORE-DATA.
                 IF THERE-IS-MORE-DATA
                     MOVE NAME TO NAME-OUT
                     MOVE SALES TO SALES-OUT
                     IF SALES GREATER 50000
                         COMPUTE TEMP-COMMISSION = .01*50000+.02* (SALES-50000)
                     ELSE
                         COMPUTE TEMP-COMMISSION = .01*SALES
                     MOVE TEMP-COMMISSION TO COMMISSION
                     WRITE PRINT-RECORD FROM COMMISSION-RECORD
                         AFTER ADVANCING 1 LINES
                     ADD TEMP-COMMISSION TO TOTAL-COMMISSIONS.
             COMPLETE.
                 MOVE TOTAL-COMMISSIONS TO TOTAL-COMM-EDITED.
                 DISPLAY 'TOTAL-COMMISSIONS ARE' TOTAL-COMM-EDITED.
                 CLOSE SALES-FILE, COMMISSIONS-FILE.
```

Figure 3.11B COBOL Program (continued)

Other Procedural Languages   There are many other procedural languages in addition to BASIC, C, and COBOL. The granddaddy of the procedural languages is FORTRAN. Originally introduced by IBM in the mid-1950s, it quickly became the standard for scientific and engineering programming. FORTRAN is still widely used today, in good part because of the significant investment made in the development of FORTRAN scientific software.

PL/1 (Programming Language One) was developed by IBM in the mid-1960s as a language to do both mathematical and business-oriented processing. IBM hoped that PL/1 would replace both FORTRAN and COBOL, but it obviously did not do so. Some companies switched from COBOL to PL/1 and have remained staunch PL/1 users, but their numbers are limited.

In the 1980s, PASCAL was often the favorite language of college computer science departments, and it was widely used on microcomputers. PASCAL has greater mathematical capabilities than BASIC, and it handles data files better than FORTRAN. However, PASCAL never caught on outside of universities except as a microcomputer language, and its popularity is now waning in favor of C.

ADA is a language developed under the direction of the U.S. Department of Defense as a potential replacement for COBOL and FORTRAN. It was first introduced in 1980 and does have strong scientific capabilities, but has not been widely adopted outside of the federal government. ADA is no longer as widely used within the Department of Defense.

Special-purpose procedural languages have also been developed. For instance, SIMSCRIPT, GPSS, and SLAM are all special-purpose languages designed to help simulate the behavior of a system, such as a production line in a factory. PERL is a special-purpose language used primarily for writing common gateway interface (CGI) scripts for World Wide Web applications. Our listing of procedural languages is incomplete, but it is sufficient for our purposes. The bottom line is that these workhorse languages are still important, because they are the primary languages used by the majority of computer professionals.

Fourth-Generation Languages

There is no generally accepted definition of a fourth-generation language, but there are certain characteristics that most 4 GLs share. They generally employ an English-like syntax, and they are predominantly nonprocedural in nature. With a 4 GL, the user merely gives a precise statement of what is to be accomplished, not how to do it (as would be done for a procedural language). For the most part, then, the order in which instructions are given in a 4 GL is unimportant. In addition, 4 GLs don't require the user to manage memory locations in the program like 3 GLs, resulting in less complex programs.

The 4 GLs employ very high-level instructions not present in 3 GLs, and thus 4 GL programs tend to require significantly fewer instructions than their 3 GL counterparts. This in turn means that 4 GL programs are shorter, easier to write, easier to modify, easier to read and understand, and more error-free than 3 GL programs. Fourth-generation languages are sometimes called very high-level languages in contrast to the high-level third-generation languages.

The roots of fourth-generation languages date back to 1967, with the introduction of RAMIS (originally developed by Mathematica, Inc., and now sold by Computer Associates as CA-Ramis). Another early entry that is still is use today is FOCUS (from Information Builders, Inc.). Initially, these products were primarily available on commercial time-sharing networks (like Telenet and Tymnet), but direct sales of the products to customers took off about 1980. By the mid-1980s, FOCUS was estimated to command about 20 percent of the market, with RAMIS following with 16 percent (Jenkins and Bordoloi, 1986).

In the late 1980s and early 1990s, the 4 GL market became even more splintered as new versions of the early 4 GLs were rolled out and a wide variety of new products entered the marketplace. The emphasis of the products appearing in the 1990s has been on *portability*: the ability of the 4 GL to work with dif-ferent hardware platforms and operating systems, the ability to work over different types of networks (see Chapter 4), and the ability to work with different database management systems (Lindholm, 1992).

Some of the 4 GL products are full-function, general purpose languages like CA-Ramis and FOCUS and have the complete functionality necessary to handle any application program. Thus, they are direct competitors with the 3 GLs. Other products are more specialized, with only limited functionality. These 4 GLs have been designed to handle a particular class of applications, such as graphics or financial modeling. For example, SAS (from SAS Institute) is a limited-purpose 4 GL which focuses on decision support and modeling. To gain a better perspective on the nature of a 4 GL, we will take a brief look at one of the most popular 4 GLs, FOCUS.

FOCUS   FOCUS is an extremely versatile general purpose 4 GL. Versions of FOCUS are available to operate under the control of all the major operating systems mentioned earlier in this chapter, including a Windows version called FOCUS Six for Windows. FOCUS consists of a large number of integrated tools and facilities, including a FOCUS database management system, a data dictionary/directory, a query language and report generator, an interactive text editor and screen painter, and a statistical analysis package. Of particular importance, FOCUS has the ability to process data managed both by its own DBMS (FOCUS files) and by an external DBMS or external file system (non-FOCUS files). We will concentrate on perhaps the most widely used of the FOCUS capabilities, the query language and report generator.

Consider the following problem situation. A telephone company wishes to prepare a report for its internal management and its regulatory body showing the difference between customer bills under two different bill computation approaches. One of these bill computation methods is the traditional flat rate based on the size of the local calling area; the other is so-called "measured service," where the customer pays a very small flat rate for a minimum number of calls and then pays so much per call ($.21 in the example) for calls above this minimum. Massive FOCUS data files already exist containing all the necessary raw data for an extended test period, with each record including customer number, area, type of service, number of calls during the time period, and the length of the time period (in months). The telephone company wants a report for present flat rate customers in area two only, showing the difference between the two billing approaches for each customer and the total difference over all flat rate customers in area two.

Figure 3.12 shows a FOCUS program (more commonly called a FOCEXEC) to produce the desired report. As with our 3 GL examples, the individual instructions are not important, but let us consider the major pieces of the program. After some initial com-

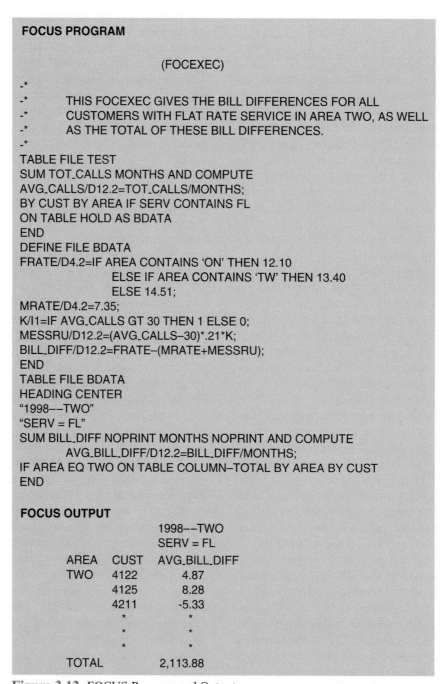

FOCUS PROGRAM

```
                       (FOCEXEC)
-*
-*         THIS FOCEXEC GIVES THE BILL DIFFERENCES FOR ALL
-*         CUSTOMERS WITH FLAT RATE SERVICE IN AREA TWO, AS WELL
-*         AS THE TOTAL OF THESE BILL DIFFERENCES.
-*
TABLE FILE TEST
SUM TOT_CALLS MONTHS AND COMPUTE
AVG_CALLS/D12.2=TOT_CALLS/MONTHS;
BY CUST BY AREA IF SERV CONTAINS FL
ON TABLE HOLD AS BDATA
END
DEFINE FILE BDATA
FRATE/D4.2=IF AREA CONTAINS 'ON' THEN 12.10
                ELSE IF AREA CONTAINS 'TW' THEN 13.40
                ELSE 14.51;
MRATE/D4.2=7.35;
K/I1=IF AVG_CALLS GT 30 THEN 1 ELSE 0;
MESSRU/D12.2=(AVG_CALLS–30)*.21*K;
BILL_DIFF/D12.2=FRATE–(MRATE+MESSRU);
END
TABLE FILE BDATA
HEADING CENTER
"1998––TWO"
"SERV = FL"
SUM BILL_DIFF NOPRINT MONTHS NOPRINT AND COMPUTE
        AVG_BILL_DIFF/D12.2=BILL_DIFF/MONTHS;
IF AREA EQ TWO ON TABLE COLUMN–TOTAL BY AREA BY CUST
END
```

FOCUS OUTPUT

		1998––TWO SERV = FL
AREA	CUST	AVG_BILL_DIFF
TWO	4122	4.87
	4125	8.28
	4211	-5.33
	*	*
	*	*
	*	*
TOTAL		2,113.88

Figure 3.12 FOCUS Program and Output

ments, the program begins with the TABLE command, which calls the query/report generator function of FOCUS. The data file is called TEST. Up to the first END, the instructions sum the variables TOT_CALLS and MONTHS for each customer in each area if the type of service is FL, then divide one sum by the other to get an average number of calls per month AVG_CALLS. The DEFINE FILE BDATA computes the rates by the two approaches as well as the difference between the two rates, storing these computed values in the temporary file BDATA. Finally, the TABLE FILE BDATA computes the average bill difference AV_BILL_DIFF and prints the report shown at the bottom of Figure 3.12.

Note that the FOCUS program is not particularly intuitive, but it is quite short for a reasonably complex problem. It is also largely nonprocedural in that the order of most statements does not make any difference. Of course, the conditional IFs and BYs must be appropriately placed.

Future Developments The fourth-generation languages are evolving even more rapidly than those in the third generation. Both large computer and microcomputer versions of the 4 GLs are continually being improved in terms of both capabilities and ease of use. Progress is also being made in terms of the efficiency of execution of 4 GL programs vis-a-vis 3 GL programs. For these reasons and others mentioned earlier (increasing computer sophistication of managers, continuing backlogs in the information systems department), the use of 4 GLs will continue to grow. The strongest element of growth will come from end-user computing, but information systems departments will also shift towards 4 GLs, especially for infrequently used applications.

Fifth-generation languages will also emerge in the next century, although it is too soon to be very specific about their form and functionality. One possibility is that the fifth-generation languages will be **natural languages,** in which users write their programs in ordinary English (or something very close to it). Users will need little or no training to program using a natural language; they simply write (or perhaps verbalize) what they want done without regard for syntax or form (other than that incorporated in ordinary English). At present, there are no true natural languages, but some restricted natural language products have been developed that can be used with a vari-

ety of database management systems and 4 GLs. Commercial developments in the natural language area have, however, been slower than expected.

For completeness, let's mention the markup languages, which are neither 3 GLs, 4 GLs, nor OOP languages. The most important of the markup languages is **HTML,** or **hypertext markup language.** HTML is used to create World Wide Web pages, and it consists of special codes inserted in the text to indicate headings, bold-faced text, italics, where images or photographs are to be placed, and links to other Web pages, among other things. VRML, or virtual reality modeling language, provides the specifications for displaying three-dimensional objects on the Web; it is the 3-D equivalent of HTML. HTML and the other markup languages are not really programming languages in the sense that we have been using this term; they are simply codes to describe the way the completed product (the Web page, the 3-D object, and so on) is to appear.

Object-Oriented Programming

In the late 1990s, the hottest programming languages (at least in terms of interest and experimentation) are not 4 GLs or natural languages, but **object-oriented programming** languages. **OOP** is not new—it dates back to the 1970s—but it has received renewed attention because of the increased power of workstations and the excellent graphical user interfaces (GUIs) that have been developed for these workstations. OOP requires more computing power than traditional languages, and a graphical interface provides a natural way to work with the OOP objects. OOP is neither a 3 GL nor a 4 GL, but an entirely new paradigm for programming with roots in both the procedural 3 GLs and the nonprocedural 4 GLs. Creating the objects in OOP is somewhat akin to 3 GL programming in that the procedures (called methods) are embedded in the objects, whereas putting the objects together to create an application is much closer to the use of a 4 GL.

The fundamentals behind OOP are to create and program various objects one time, and then store them for reuse later in the current application or in other applications. These objects may be an item used to create the user interface, like a text box or a check box, or they may represent an entity in the organization, such as Employee or Factory.

The first OOP language was Smalltalk, a language developed by researchers at Xerox to create a way that children might learn how to program. It never really took off as a children's programming tool, but was used marginally in the business world. Managers thought programming would become more efficient if programmers had to create objects only once and then were able to reuse them in later programs. This would create a "toolbox" from which programmers could just grab the tool they needed, insert it into the program, fine-tune it to meet the specific needs of the program, and be done (see Figure 3.13).

The most prominent OOP language today is C++, an object-oriented version of the original C language. It is a superset of the C language, in that any C program can also be a C++ program, but C++ introduces the power of reusable objects, or classes. Object Pascal has been created as an object-oriented version of Pascal, and Object COBOL has been developed as an object-oriented version of COBOL. Visual Basic is

usually considered a pseudo-OOP language, because it supports most but not all features of an OOP language (see below for these features).

Figure 3.14A provides an example of a simple Visual Basic program designed to compute the average, highest, and lowest grades of a college student. Figure 3.14B shows the screen layout (GUI interface) designed for this application, using the click, drag, and drop tools of Visual Basic. The user enters his or her grades in Chemistry, Calculus, English, and History, and the program computes the average, highest, and lowest grades. Note that the program itself looks very much like any 3 GL program, while the screen design becomes a much simpler task in Visual Basic (or an OOP language) than in a 3 GL.

To work with an OOP language, one must think in terms of objects. The programmer starts by defining entities that are referred to as classes. A class is the blueprint or specifications for creating an object. To work with the class, we must create an instance of the

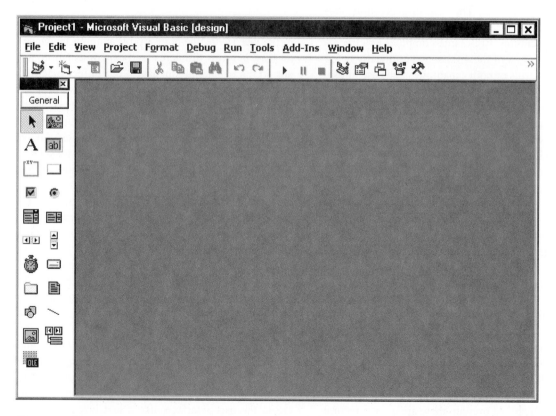

Figure 3.13 Microsoft Visual Basic Toolbox (reprinted with permission from Microsoft Corporation).

```
Private Sub btnCalculate_Click()
' Declare variables
Dim sClasses(3) As Single
Dim sMean, sHigh, sLow As Single, x As Integer
' Initialize variables
sClasses(0) = CSng (txtCalculus.Text)
sClasses(1) = CSng (txtChemistry.Text)
sClasses(2) = CSng (txtHistory.Text)
sClasses(3) = CSng (txtEnglish.Text)
sMean = 0
sHigh = 0
sLow = 100
' Do calculations
For x = 0 To 3
        sMean = sMean + sClasses (x) / 4
        If sClasses (x) > sHigh Then
                sHigh = sClasses (x)
        End If

        If sClasses (x) < sLow Then
                sLow = sClasses (x)
        End If
Next x
' Write out results
txtStatistics.Text = "Your average grade is" & sMean & vbCrLf
txtStatistics.Text = txtStatistics.Text & "Your highest grade is" & sHigh & vbCrLf
txtStatistics.Text = txtStatistics.Text & "Your lowest grade is" & sLow
End Sub
- - - - - - - - - - - - - - - - - - - -
Private Sub btnClear_Click()
' Clears the contents of the text boxes
txtChemistry.Text = " "
txtCalculus.Text = " "
txtEnglish.Text = " "
txtHistory.Text = " "
txtStatistics.Text = " "
End Sub
- - - - - - - - - - - - - - - - - - - -
Private Sub Exit_Click()
' Quits the program
End
End Sub
```

Figure 3.14A Visual Basic Program

class, which is then referred to as the object. An object has attributes, or properties, that can be set by the programmer or even by the user when the program is running if the programmer desires. An object also has methods, which are predefined actions taken by the object. Objects can also respond to events, or actions

taken upon the object. Objects, properties, methods, and events can all be a bit difficult to comprehend at first, so let's use an example which might be more familiar to you—the family dog.

We can think of a dog and identify various attributes, which programmers call properties, to

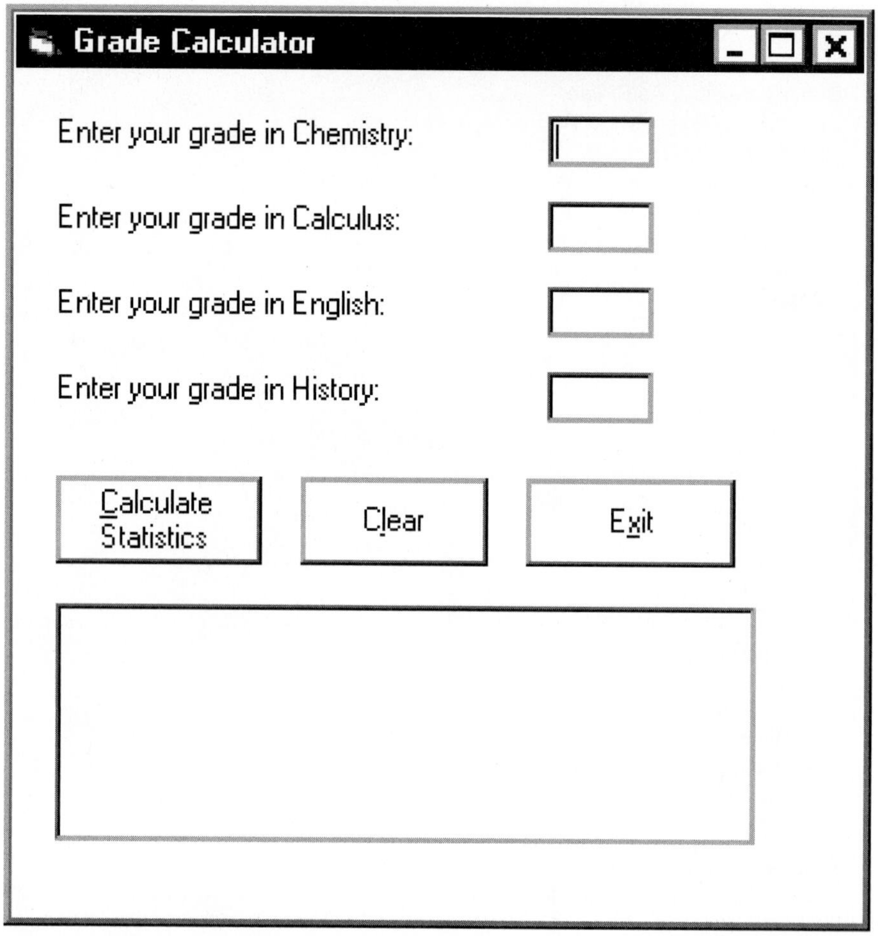

Figure 3.14B Visual Basic Screen Layout

differentiate one dog from another dog. Each dog has height, weight, color, coat thickness, eye color, snout shape, and many other features that may differ from other dogs (see Figure 3.15 left). Each of these properties thus has a value. Each dog, independent of its property values, also does several actions; programmers call these methods. Eat, sleep, run, and fetch are examples of these methods. Dogs also respond to several actions done to them—these are called events. Hearing their name called, being petted, or even being kicked are examples of events to which the dog responds (see Figure 3.15 right).

We said that objects must be instantiated, or that an instance of them must be created from a class. From our class definition of a dog, we know it has var-

ious properties, methods, and events. For a family without a pet, however, all that family has is a class definition. When the family goes to the animal shelter to rescue a furry friend, they now have an instance of the class, or an actual dog.

Objects also have two important features that make them even more useful. One of them is encapsulation. Encapsulation allows the creator of the object to hide some (or even all) of the inner workings of the object from other programmers or users. This keeps the integrity of the object very high, exposing only parts of the object that will not cause the object to crash. Let's apply this to our dog example. For a dog to survive, it needs vitamins, nutrients, proteins, and carbohydrates. These items must get into

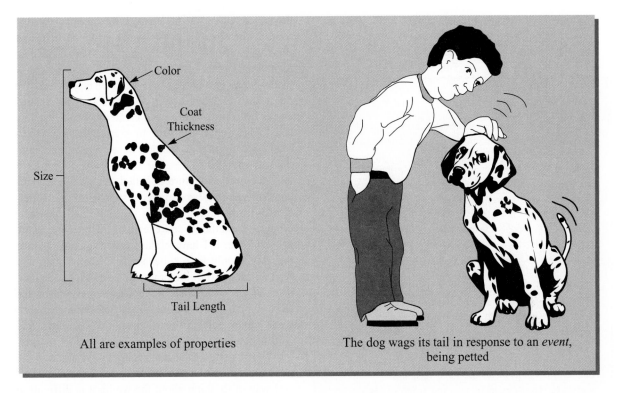

Size

Color

Coat
Thickness

Tail Length

All are examples of properties

The dog wags its tail in response to an *event*,
being petted

Figure 3.15 A Dog as an Object

WHY IS OBJECT TECHNOLOGY VALUABLE?

One reason that the term "object oriented," or "OO," is often confusing is that it is applied so widely. We hear about object-oriented user interfaces, object-oriented programming languages, object-oriented design methodologies, object-oriented databases, even object-oriented business modeling. A reasonable question might be: Is this term used because OO has become a synonym for "modern and good," or is there really some substantial common thread across all these object-oriented things?

I believe that there is such a common thread, and that it makes the object paradigm useful in all these diverse areas. Essentially it is a focus on the "thing" first and the action second. It has been described as a noun-verb way of looking at things, rather than verb-noun. At the user interface, first the object is selected, then the action to be performed on the object. At the programming language level, an object is asked to perform some action, rather than a procedure called to "do its thing" on a set of parameters. At the design level, the "things" in the application are defined, then the behavior (actions) of these things is described.

Object technology provides significant potential value in three areas, all closely related: productivity, maintainability, and paradigm consistency. We must change application development from a people-intensive discipline to an asset-intensive discipline. That is, we must encourage and make feasible the widespread reuse of software components. It is exactly in this "reusable component" arena that object technology can contribute significantly. The aspects of object technology that help in reuse are encapsulation (which allows the developer to see a component as a "black box" with specified behavior) and inheritance (which encourages the reuse of code to implement identical behavior among different kinds of objects).

[Radin, 1996]

the dog's bloodstream and be carried to the various muscles and organs that need them. However, we as dog owners don't try to inject the items directly into

---

HAVE A CUP OF JAVA

Don't burn yourself—Java is hot! Java is an object-oriented language similar to C++, but simplified to reduce the number of programming errors. Java, developed by Sun Microsystems, is a general purpose programming language well suited for use on the World Wide Web, and it has quickly gained widespread acceptance by most vendors and by programmers everywhere.

A small Java application is called an **applet** and is usually stored on a Web server. The applet can then be downloaded to a PC with a mouse click and executed by a Java-compatible Web browser such as Netscape Navigator. What can such an applet do? At the simple end of the scale, an applet can provide a Web page animation of a steaming coffee cup (the Java logo). More importantly, an applet can draw a graph of a stock portfolio and update it in real time as share prices change. An applet can be used to automatically update software on client machines in a client/server network to the most recent version of the software. Based on input received from an electronics repairman, an applet can help him focus on the appropriate components in the product needing repair.

A Java virtual machine is a self-contained operating environment—including a Java interpreter—that behaves as if it is a separate computer. Such an operating environment exists for most operating systems, including UNIX, the Macintosh OS, and Windows, and this virtual machine concept implements the "write once, run anywhere" portability that is the goal of Java. The Java virtual machine has no access to the host operating system (whatever it is), which has two advantages:

- System independence: A Java application will run exactly the same regardless of the hardware and software involved.
- Security: Because the Java virtual machine has no contact with the host operating system, there is almost no possibility of a Java application damaging other files or applications.

With Java actively endorsed by IBM and most other leading vendors, and somewhat grudgingly endorsed even by Microsoft, Java seems destined to be the primary language employed for development of World Wide Web applications.

[Adapted from van der Linden, 1997]

---

the bloodstream or the organs; we merely buy dog food at the store and set it out for our pet. He eats the food, digests it, and the nutrients are carried to their proper places. You could thus say that the digestive system of the dog has been encapsulated. We don't need to know how it works, nor in most cases do we even care. It has been created to work the way it is, although if it were to start behaving incorrectly, we might take the dog to see a programmer—the veterinarian!

The second feature is called inheritance. Inheritance means that we can create subclasses and superclasses from classes, and they then automatically have properties, methods, and events of their related class. For example, if I have a class called animal, I know that dog should be a subclass of animal. A dog is a type of animal (not the other way around) and should take on the properties, methods, and events of the class animal. Visual Basic does not support inheritance, which is the primary reason that it is not a true OOP language.

OOP is one of the most sought after skills in the job market of the late 1990s. Despite its supposed natural way of thinking about the world, it is difficult to find good object-oriented programmers. Older programmers that learned programming in structured languages like C and COBOL often don't want to be retrained, and some younger programmers don't like OOP languages because they can be very difficult to learn. It can also take longer to develop an object-oriented program than a structured program, and objects must be reused several times before any overall cost and time savings are realized.

Database Management Systems

A **database management system** is support software that is used to create, manage, and protect organizational data. A database management system works with the operating system to store and modify data and to make data accessible in a variety of meaningful and authorized ways. For most computer systems, the **DBMS** is separate from the operating system, although the trend appears to be to place some DBMS functions either in the operating system or in separate attached computer processors called database servers. The purpose of this trend is to achieve greater efficiency and security.

A DBMS adds significant data management capabilities to those provided by the operating system. The goal is to allow a computer programmer to select data from disk files by referring to the content of records, not their physical location. This makes programming easier, more productive, and less error prone. Also, this allows systems professionals responsible for database design to reorganize the physical organization of data without affecting the logic of programs, which significantly reduces maintenance requirements. These objectives are given the umbrella term *data independence.* For example, a DBMS would allow a programmer to specify retrieval of a customer record based only on knowledge of the customer's name or number. Further, once the customer record is retrieved, a DBMS would allow direct reference to any of the customer's related order or shipment records (even if these records are relocated or changed). Thus, a DBMS allows access to data based on content (e.g., customer number) as well as by association (e.g., orders for a given customer).

A **database** is a shared collection of logically related data, organized to meet the needs of an organization. The DBMS is the software that manages a database. There are several different types of DBMSs in use today:

Hierarchical: Characterized by the IBM product Information Management System (IMS)—data are arranged in a top-down organization chart fashion.

Network: A good example is Integrated Database Management System (IDMS) from Computer Associates—data are arranged like the cities on a highway system, often with several paths from one piece of data to another.

Relational: Many such products exist, including Microsoft Access, Paradox by Borland, SQL/DS and DB2 by IBM, and INGRES by Computer Associates—data are arranged into simple tables and records are related by storing common data in each of the associated tables.

Object-oriented: Among the better known products are GemStone from Gemstone Systems and ObjectStore from Object Design—data can be graphics, video, and sound as well as simpler data types; attributes (data) and methods are encapsulated in object classes, and relationships between classes can be shown by nesting one class within another.

An organization almost always purchases a DBMS, rather than developing it in-house, because of the extensive development cost and time. A DBMS is a very complex and costly software package (ranging in price from under $500 for a personal computer product to $200,000 for a DBMS on a large mainframe computer). By purchasing a DBMS, an organization is able to draw upon a larger pool of programmers and systems designers who are familiar with the package, which then reduces training costs and gives them more choices for hiring database professionals.

File Organization   The computer files are stored on the disk using the file organization provided by the operating system and special structures added by the DBMS. Although their exact details can be treated as a black box in most cases, it is useful to know some of the terminology and choices. Three general kinds of file organizations exist—sequential, direct, and indexed (see Figure 3.16).

A **sequential file organization** arranges the records so that they are physically adjacent and in order by some sort key (usually the unique key that distinguishes each record from one another). Thus, a sequential customer file would have the records arranged in order by customer name or identifier. Sequential files use very little space and are fast when the records are to be retrieved in order, but they are inefficient when searching for a particular record, because they must be scanned front to back. Also, when records are added or deleted, the whole file must be rearranged to accommodate the modifications, which can be a time-consuming task.

A **direct file organization** also uses a key for each record, but records are placed and retrieved so that an individual record can be rapidly accessed. The records are located wherever they can most quickly be retrieved, and the space from deleted records can be reused without having to rearrange the file. The most typical method employed is a hashing function. In this case, the record key, such as the customer number, is mathematically manipulated (by some algorithm) to determine the location of the record with that key. It is possible that several keys can "collide" to the same location, but such synonyms are easily resolved. Direct files are extremely fast for accessing a single record, but because the keys that exist at any point in time are usually arbitrary, sequential processing of

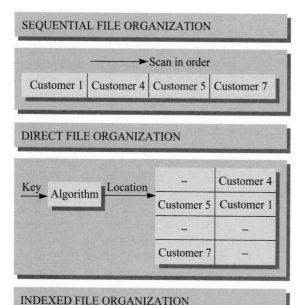

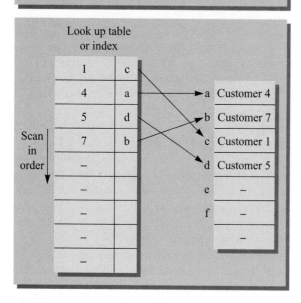

Figure 3.16 File Organizations

in the table is called a pointer). This lookup table or index is similar to a card catalog in a library, in which the author name, book title, and topics are different types of keys and the book catalog number is a pointer to its location in the library. To access the records sequentially, the table is completely scanned one entry at a time, and as each entry is encountered, its associated data record is retrieved. To access the records individually, the table is scanned until a match with the desired key is found and only the desired record is retrieved; if no match is found, an error is indicated. Because the table is quite small (just enough space for the key and location of every record, compared to possible hundreds or thousands of characters needed for the entire record—remember the analogy of the card catalog in a library), this scan can be very fast (certainly considerably faster than scanning the actual data). For a very large table, a second table can be created to access the first table (which is, of course, nothing more than a specialized file itself). Popular names for such methods of indexes on top of indexes are indexed sequential access method (ISAM) and virtual storage access method (VSAM).

Finally, because in a database we want to be able to access records based upon content (e.g., by customer number) as well as by relationship (e.g., orders for a given customer), a DBMS along with the operating system must also provide a means for access via these relationships. Record keys and location pointers are these means. For example, we could store pointers in a customer record and its associated order records to link all these related records together (see Figure 3.17). Such a scheme is called chaining or a list structure. Alternately, we could store the customer number in each of its associated order records and use tables or hashing functions to locate the related record or records in other files. This scheme is used by relational DBMSs.

direct files requires a long and tedious scan and usually sorting of the records.

Indexed file organizations provide a compromise between the sequential and direct-access capabilities. The record keys only are arranged in sequence in a separate table, along with the location of the rest of the data associated with that key (this location field

Database Programming Data processing activity with a database can be specified in either procedural programs written in a 3 GL or via special-purpose languages developed for database processing. In the case of a 3 GL program, additional and more powerful instructions are added to the vocabulary of the programming language. For example, in a customer and order database the storage of a new order record not

CHAINING

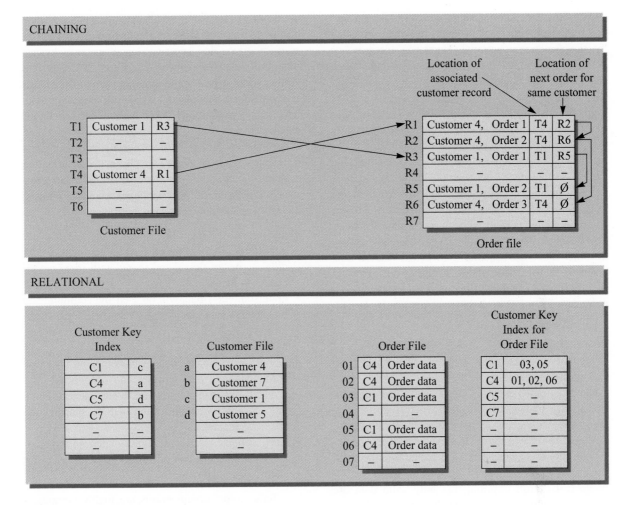

RELATIONAL

Figure 3.17 Schemes for Relationships Between Files

only necessitates storing the order data itself, but also updating various linkages that tie together a customer record with its associated order records. In a regular 3 GL program, instructions to write new data to the customer record, its index, the order record, and its indexes would have to be provided individually. With the commands available through the special enhancements to the language provided by the DBMS, only one instruction is needed in the program and all the associated indexes and records are updated automatically, which makes the programming task more productive and error free.

A DBMS also frequently provides a 4 GL, non-procedural special-purpose language for posing queries to the database. For example, the query in the SQL/DS command language

SELECT ORDER#, CUSTOMER#, CUSTNAME, ORDER-DATE FROM CUSTOMER, ORDER WHERE ORDER-DATE > '04/12/99' AND CUSTOMER.CUSTOMER# = ORDER.CUSTOMER#

is all that is required to request the display of the order number and date from each order record, plus the customer number and name from the associated customer record, for orders placed after April 12, 1999. The equivalent COBOL program might require 10 or more procedural division instructions. The popularity of such products as Access, Paradox, INGRES, and several SQL-based language products (a standard created by the American National Standards Institute, or ANSI) is due in great measure to the existence of such easy-to-use query languages.

Managing the Data Resource   A DBMS is a software tool to help an organization manage its data. Data are now recognized as a major organizational resource, to be managed like other assets such as land, labor, and capital. In fact, many observers of trends in business believe that the organizations that will excel in the next century will be those that manage data as a major resource, understand the usefulness of data for business decisions, and structure data as efficiently as they do other assets. In Chapter 14 we will discuss data resource management, and a DBMS is an important tool for this management function. From a managerial point of view, a DBMS helps manage data by providing these functions:

Data Storage, Retrieval, Update: provide a variety of commands that allow easy retrieval/presentation and modification of data.

Backup: automatically making copies of the database and the updates made to it to protect against accidental damage or deliberate sabotage.

Recovery: ability to restore the database after damage, or after inaccurate data have gotten into the database.

Integrity Control: ensuring that only valid data are entered into the database (so that, for example, data values only in a permissible range are entered).

Security Control: ensuring that only authorized use (reading and updating) is permitted on the database.

Concurrency Control: protecting the database against anomalies that can occur when two or more programs attempt to update the same data at the same time.

Transaction Control: being able to undo changes to a database when a program malfunctions, a user cancels a business transaction, or the DBMS rejects a business transaction that updates several database records.

Along with the DBMS, many organizations also use a **data dictionary/directory** or **DD/D,** which is a repository of data definitions that is shared among all the users. Such a central catalog is used by the DBMS and system users whenever the meaning, storage format, integrity rules, security clearances, and physical location of data need to be discovered. The DD/D is similar to an inventory accounting system for a parts warehouse—in this case for a data warehouse, or database. Many modern DBMSs have a built-in DD/D capability.

A DBMS and a DD/D are tools, and user-managers and database professionals in the information systems organization must use these and other tools wisely if data are to be readily accessible to all who have a need to know. The manager must:

- understand the data, the meaning of the data, and quality requirements, so that accurate definitions of data can be developed and shared with all who need access to them.
- understand how data will be used and communicate this to database designers so that efficient structures can be built to provide rapid and secure access to these data.
- recognize that data such as customer number and credit balance, part number and description, and product bill-of-materials are organizational data, the value of which is multiplied by sharing and ensuring accuracy.
- learn to make intelligent choices between developing local databases on personal computers or using central, shared databases.

Today, most organizations are highly computerized and vast databases exist. The issue often is not whether the data are available, but rather which of several alternative versions of the data to use and how to gain access to these data. A DBMS with a variety of methods to store data and easy-to-use programming and query languages is essential for such access. Although not as widely understood as spreadsheets or word processors at present, database management systems are the means for connecting a highly interrelated organization. Being able to use prewritten database processing routines and to write original database queries are necessary skills of today's general manager.

CASE Tools

It was originally predicted that CASE tools would have a major impact on computer professionals, and that has been true for some professionals in some firms. However, the growth of the use of CASE tools has been much slower than anticipated. **CASE,** an acronym for **computer-aided software engineering,** is actually a collection of software tools to help automate all phases of the software development life cycle. (The life cycle for software development is discussed in Chapters 9 and 10.) In those firms that have adopted CASE tools—and there are many of them—CASE is changing the jobs of systems analysts and programmers in radical ways. In particular, the job of the analyst or programmer involves more up-front work in clearly defining the problem and expressing it in the particular specifications required by the CASE tool. Then the tool assists in the back-end work of translating the specifications to the required output, such as a data flow diagram (see Chapter 9) or a COBOL program.

We will defer a more complete treatment of CASE software until Chapter 10, where the variety of CASE tools and their role in the systems development process will be explored. For now, note that the impact of CASE is only beginning to be felt. CASE may well change the way in which the information systems organization in your company does business, and thus CASE is indirectly important to you. CASE has the potential of providing a productivity boost to an area of the company (the IS organization) that needs such a boost.

Communications Interface Software

Communications interface software has become increasingly important with the explosion in the number of workstations attached to large computers and the advent of local area networks (LANs) and wide-area networks (WANs). Discussion of LAN and WAN software will be deferred until Chapter 4, but several other types of communications interface software will be considered now.

Communications packages on large computers have the awesome task of controlling the communications of a large number of terminals with the central computer. This software collects the messages from the terminals, processes them as necessary, and returns the responses to the proper terminals. These packages are often designed to work closely with a particular operating system. For example, IBM's CICS (Customer Information Control System) and TSO (Time Sharing Option) are communications packages

designed to work with IBM's MVS operating system. Similarly, IBM's CMS (Conversational Monitor System) is designed to work with the VM operating system. In an interesting development, IBM has created a version of CICS which works with AIX, IBM's UNIX operating system. This AIX/CICS combination makes it much easier for IBM's customers to move their applications to UNIX, and provides further evidence of the growing importance of UNIX. Microcomputer communications packages have the much simpler task of making the microcomputer act as if it were a particular type of terminal that can be handled by the large computer communications package. When paired with an appropriate program in the large computer, these microcomputer communications packages can also upload and download files between the microcomputer and the large computer.

Three additional items of communication interface software have become important in the 1990s. A Web browser, discussed in the "Personal Productivity Software" section, is software loaded on the user's PC that enables him or her to look around, or "browse," the Internet. **Telnet** is a communications interface package designed to permit a user to log onto a remote computer from whatever computer he or she is currently using, including a microcomputer. The key is that the computer currently being used must be attached to the same network as the remote computer. In some cases, this "same network" may be a local area network on a corporate or educational campus, while in other cases this network may be the worldwide Internet. The user invokes the Telnet program, identifies the remote computer he or she wishes to log onto, the connection is made, and then the user simply logs onto the remote computer as if he or she were on site. One of the authors of this textbook has taught in Europe for the past several summers, and he has a computer account at the European university where he teaches. He regularly logs onto that European computer via Telnet to carry out business there. Another valuable communications interface package is **FTP,** which is short for **file transfer protocol.** This package is designed to transfer files from one computer system to another. In effect, the user logs onto the two computer systems at the same time, and then copies files from one system to the other. The files being transferred may be programs, textual data, images, and so on.

Utility Programs

This is obviously a catch-all category, but an important one nevertheless. Utility software includes programs that load applications programs into an area of memory, link together related programs and subprograms, merge two files of data together, sort a file of data into a desired sequence (e.g., alphabetical order on a particular data item), and copy files from one place to another (e.g., from DASD to magnetic tape). Utility programs also give the user access to the software library. In most cases, the user communicates with these utility programs by means of commands in the job control language. On a microcomputer, utility programs are used to zip (compact) and unzip large files for easier transport, to reorganize the hard drive to gain disk space, to check for computer viruses, and a multitude of other tasks.

THE CHANGING NATURE OF SOFTWARE

In the process of investigating the various categories of computer software, we have noted many of the important trends in the software arena. Building upon our earlier discussions, we can explicitly identify the significant developing patterns in the software field, emphasizing those that have the most direct relevance to you as a manager. Eight key trends that we have identified are these:

1. More hardwiring of software and more microcode.
2. More complexity of hardware/software arrangements.
3. Less concern with machine efficiency.
4. More purchased applications, and more portability of these applications from one computer platform to another.
5. More programming using object-oriented and visual languages, especially Visual Basic, Java, and similar languages, in large part because of the emphasis on graphical user interfaces.
6. More emphasis on applications that run on intranets and the Internet, especially using the World Wide Web.
7. More user development.

8. More use of personal productivity software on microcomputers, especially packages with a graphical user interface (GUI).

More Hardwiring of Software and More Microcode

In their efforts to make their machines run more efficiently, hardware manufacturers will convert more and more of the present software—especially operating systems and other support software—into hardwiring and microcode. Hardwiring simply means building into the circuitry of the machine the same steps that were previously accomplished by carrying out a portion of a machine language program. Microcode accomplishes a similar function, in that the machine language instructions are permanently stored in read-only memory (ROM) microchips. In both cases, portions of key programs are removed from regular memory, freeing it for other purposes. Hardwiring also speeds up execution, because instructions do not have to be moved to the control unit and interpreted before they can be executed. This first trend has little direct impact on you as a manager; it is simply one way in which computers will be made more powerful.

More Complexity of Hardware/Software Arrangements

To a much greater extent, varying configurations of hardware will be tied together by sophisticated software packages. We discussed multiprocessing and parallel processing, which involve multiple CPUs in one machine controlled by the operating system. Another way of configuring machines is to cluster several computers together, sharing common disk devices, all under control of their separate operating systems. Increasingly, separate computers are being used as front-end communication controllers and back-end file or database servers for large mainframe computers. The coordination of these various hardware resources must be handled by the mainframe operating system and complementary software in the communications machine or database server. Even applications software is being split among machines as organizations move to client/server arrangements. More and more software is being delivered from a server rather than being directly stored on an individual workstation, and in the future much of this software may be delivered over the World Wide Web. These more complex hardware/software arrangements are yet additional ways that computers may be able to assist in the efficient and effective running of a business.

Less Concern with Machine Efficiency

The cost per instruction on computers will continue to drop dramatically, as it has for the past three decades. That is, machine cycles will continue to get cheaper. On the other hand, personnel costs—both for computer professionals and managers—will continue to climb. Thus, as time passes, we will be more concerned with human efficiency and less concerned with machine efficiency. This reduced concern for machine efficiency has both direct and indirect impacts on you as a manager. It means that software tools that improve human efficiency—such as visual and object-oriented languages, query languages, and CASE tools—will become more popular for computer professionals and, where appropriate, for managers. It also will lead to the development of executive workstations with voice and natural language interfaces—which are terribly inefficient from the machine standpoint.

More Purchased Applications

The higher personnel costs for computer professionals mean higher costs for in-house development of new applications software. In addition, the present backlogs for internal development of new applications are not going to disappear in the short run. The demand for new applications is also not going to slacken, particularly with the infusion of an increasing number of computer-literate managers into organizations. Add to this mix a healthy, growing, vigorous software industry marketing both developed packages (off-the-shelf software) and customized packages, and it is easy to predict a continuing growth in purchased software. Furthermore, more of the purchased applications will be portable from one computing platform to another, or will work with a variety of support software (especially database management systems). This gives companies more flexibility in their choice of computing platforms.

Another major reason for purchasing software is to correct internal business processes that are not working as well as they should. Most software packages designed to handle standard business tasks such as payroll, accounts payable, general ledger, and material requirements planning incorporate excellent procedures in the package, and by implementing the package the organization is required to adopt these improved procedures. Thus, the organization is forcing the "reengineering" of its processes by implementing the software package. This is particularly true for so-called enterprise resource planning packages, which we will discuss in Chapter 5. The advantage of the trend towards more purchased applications to you is that you will be able to get new applications you need implemented more quickly; the disadvantage is that the purchased software may not be able to do precisely what you want done in the way in which you want it done.

More Programming Using Object-Oriented and Visual Languages

In large part because of the emphasis on graphical user interfaces, Visual Basic, Java, and similar object-oriented and visual programming languages will gain even more widespread acceptance. These languages lend themselves to developing GUI interfaces such as those used on the World Wide Web, and they are easier to learn and use than the traditional 3 GLs. The increased use of these languages is also consistent with the lessened concern over machine efficiency noted above, because they tend to produce quite inefficient code. From the manager's perspective, the use of these languages will tend to give you the applications you need more quickly, and the GUI will make the screens more attractive and easier to use for you and your employees.

More Emphasis on Applications that Run on Intranets and the Internet

This is a very important and powerful trend, but we are somewhat premature in introducing it at this point. We will explore the idea of intranets and the Internet in the next chapter. After that discussion, this trend will be more meaningful. For the present, note that intranets are networks operating within an organization that use the same technology as the worldwide Internet, and that the Internet is a network of networks spanning the globe. More and more organizations are creating or buying applications that run on their internal intranet or the Internet because it is both easy and economical to make these applications available to everyone who needs them.

More User Development

This trend hits close to home because you and your fellow managers will carry out more software development efforts yourselves. For the most part, you will work with packages, 4 GLs, and query languages that are easy to learn and use. Why will this increase in user development occur? Because it is easier and quicker for you to develop the software than to go to the information systems organization and work with them on the development (often after an extensive wait). This will be the case for many situations where you need a one-time or infrequently used report, or a decision support system to help you with a particular decision. Managers will continue to rely on the information systems organization (or on purchased software) for major ongoing systems, such as production control, general ledger accounting, and human resource information systems. Because of its importance to you as managers, we have devoted the entirety of Chapter 12 to user application development.

More Use of Personal Productivity Software

This final trend is the most important one for most of you. The use of personal productivity software, especially a Web browser and other microcomputer-based packages, will grow for managers and other professionals. Packages with a well designed GUI will increasingly be the software of choice, because a graphical user interface makes the software easier to learn and use. Your microcomputer, linked to a local area network and the worldwide Internet (see Chapter 4), will become as indispensable as your telephone (and eventually will *become* your telephone). You will use it almost every hour of every working day—for electronic mail, Web browsing, word processing, spreadsheets, database management, presentation graphics, and other applications. In fact, most of you will find the microcomputer so essential that you will carry a notebook version or an even smaller pocket-sized computer/organizer/communicator with you when you are out of your office.

The Software Component of the Information Systems Industry

Many software products have been mentioned in this chapter, as well as many software vendors, but we lack a frame of reference in which to view the software subindustry. Some of that frame of reference was provided in "The Information Systems Industry" section of Chapter 2, but that section looked at only the giants in the software sector. The "Software" portion of Table 2.3 listed the top ten firms in the world in terms of software revenues: IBM, Microsoft, Hitachi, Fujitsu, Computer Associates, NEC, Oracle, SAP, Novell, and Digital Equipment. IBM has $12.91 billion in software revenue, Microsoft $9.44 billion, Hitachi $5.49 billion, and Fujitsu $4.75 billion—then number five on the list (Computer Associates) dropped down to $3.16 billion. Numbers six through ten ranged from $2.31 billion in software revenue down to $1.22 billion. Beyond the top ten, Lockheed Martin has $1.12 billion in software revenue (#11), Siemens Nixdorf $1.03 billion (#12), Hewlett-Packard $0.94 billion (#13), Olivetti $0.88 billion (#14), and Intel $0.83 billion (#15). Siemens Nixdorf is based in Germany, Olivetti in Italy, and the other three of these additional five companies are based in the United States (Tucker, 1997).

There are three primary groups of players in the software arena—hardware manufacturers, software houses or vendors, and consulting firms. The hardware and software vendors dominate the top fifteen list, with ten hardware vendors (hardware isn't really the main business of one of these, Lockheed Martin, and of course Intel's "hardware" is computer chips) and five software houses. The eight major hardware vendors—IBM, Digital Equipment, and Hewlett-Packard (U.S.); Hitachi, Fujitsu, and NEC (Japan); Siemens Nixdorf (Germany) and Olivetti (Italy)—all have a major presence in the mainframe/midrange computing market. In this big/midrange machine market, customers usually buy their operating systems and much of their support software from their hardware vendors, but the strength of the hardware manufacturers on this list indicates that customers must purchase a large proportion of their applications software from the hardware vendors as well.

The software houses form an interesting and competitive group, although they are increasingly dominated by a single firm. Microsoft is the largest and most influential software house, and its dominance is growing. Microsoft is based in Redmond, Washington, and is headed by Bill Gates, reportedly the richest person in the world. Microsoft's 1996 revenue jumped 27 percent to a whopping $9.44 billion on the strength of a broad range of microcomputer software products, especially Windows 95 and Windows NT. Number two among the software vendors is Computer Associates, based in Islandia, New York, with estimated 1996 revenue of $3.16 billion. Computer Associates produces a variety of mainframe and microcomputer-based software packages, with particular strength in mainframe database, job scheduling, security, and systems management software. The next largest software house is Oracle, based in Redwood Shores, California, which began by specializing in mainframe DBMSs but has now branched out into other areas, notably enterprise resource planning systems (integrated software to run a business). In 1996, Oracle's revenue was $2.28 billion. Fourth largest is SAP, a German company, which has perhaps the hottest client/server package going today—an enterprise resource planning system called R/3. Fifth is Novell Inc., based in Orem, Utah, the leader in providing local area network management software with its NetWare line. Until 1995, Lotus Development Corporation would have been listed as a major player in this group (most likely fourth largest of the software houses), but it was purchased by IBM in 1995. The hottest Lotus product, and certainly one of the big reasons for IBM's interest, is Lotus Notes, a groupware product designed to aid in information transfer and efficient communication among large groups of people. In addition to these big software houses, there are a multitude of medium-sized to small-sized software firms. Many of the smaller firms tend to rise and fall rapidly based on the success or failure of a single product, and many small firms have gone bankrupt when they attempted and failed to develop additional products.

Consulting firms constitute the third group in the software subindustry. Within this group, the leaders are the so-called "Big Five" public accounting firms, led by Andersen Consulting. For the most part, the software developed and sold by these firms has been an outgrowth of their consulting practices and thus tends to be applications software geared to particular industries in which they have consulted extensively. There are also many smaller firms in the information systems arena that are difficult to categorize as a software house or a consulting firm because they truly operate as both. Their consulting jobs often involve writing or modifying software for a particular firm, then moving to another firm within the same industry to do a similar job.

To complete the software story, we should mention that some excellent software can be obtained from noninformation systems companies that have developed software for their own use and then later decided to market the product. The software business is dominated, however, by the hardware manufacturers, software houses, and consulting firms, each having its own special niche. In Chapter 11, we will discuss the option of purchasing applications software.

SUMMARY

Both computer hardware and software are required for a computer system to perform useful work. The hardware actually does the work—adding two numbers, reading a record from disk, printing a line—but the software controls all of the actions of the hardware. Thus, an understanding of software is critical to comprehending how computer systems work. From a financial perspective, most organizations spend at least twice as much money on software as they spend on hardware. Further, managers will be directly dealing with a variety of software packages, while they rarely deal with hardware other than their own workstation. For all these reasons, the topic of software is a vital one for aspiring managers.

Figuratively speaking, software comes in a variety of shapes and sizes. Applications software consists of all programs written to accomplish particular tasks for computer users; support software establishes a relatively easy-to-use computing environment, translates programs into machine language, and ensures that the hardware and software resources are used efficiently. The most important piece of support software is the operating system that controls the operation of the hardware and coordinates all of the other software.

Other support software includes language translators, communications interface software, database management systems, and utility programs.

Applications software is often developed within the organization using third-generation procedural languages like COBOL or FORTRAN, fourth-generation nonprocedural languages like FOCUS or IFPS, or newer languages such as C++ or Java. Historically, nearly all the internal software development has been carried out by computer professionals in the information systems organization. Recently, however, more of the development has been done by end users (including managers), using 4 GLs and DBMS query languages. The trend that impacts managers even more is the growing availability and use of personal productivity software such as spreadsheets and database management systems. We anticipate that these trends toward more user development of software and more use of personal productivity packages will continue and will strengthen.

Almost all of an organization's support software and an increasing proportion of its applications software is purchased from outside the firm. The hardware manufacturers appear to supply the bulk of the support software and some of the applications programs for larger computers. Independent software houses (not associated with hardware manufacturers) are particularly important sources of mainframe applications software and microcomputer software of all types. Consulting firms are also a valuable source of applications software. When purchasing software, the organization must consider the quality and fit of the software package, and the services and stability provided by the vendor.

It is hoped that this chapter has provided you with sufficient knowledge of computer software to begin to appreciate the present and potential impact of computers on your organization and your job.

Review Questions

1. Briefly describe the four generations of computer programming languages, concentrating on the major differences among the generations. How does object-oriented programming fit into these generations? How does HTML fit into these generations?

2. List at least five categories of personal productivity software packages. Then concentrate on one of these categories and describe a representative product in that category with which you are somewhat familiar. Provide both strong points and weak points of the particular product.

3. What are the purposes of an operating system? What are the primary tasks carried out by a mainframe operating system?

4. Differentiate between multiprogramming and multiprocessing.

5. Explain the concept of virtual memory. Why is it important?

6. List the six major categories of support software.

7. Explain the concept of structured programming. Why is it important?

8. What are the primary advantages of a fourth-generation language over a third-generation language? What are the primary disadvantages?

9. What are the primary characteristics of an object-oriented language? How does an object-oriented language differ from a third-generation language or a fourth-generation language?

10. Explain the difference between push and pull technology, and give an example of each.

11. Three general types of file organizations were described in the text: sequential, direct, and indexed file organizations. In general terms, describe how each type of file organization works. It may be helpful to draw a diagram to depict each type of file organization.

12. Four different types of database management systems were described in the text: hierarchical, network, relational, and object-oriented. Briefly describe how the data are arranged in each type of database.

13. For what does the CASE acronym stand? In general, what is the purpose of CASE tools? What types of individuals are most likely to use CASE tools?

14. List at least three computer vendors that are major players in the software component of the information systems industry. List at least three independent software houses (not associated with a computer vendor) that are major players in the software component of the information systems

industry. List any software products that you regularly use and indicate the firm that developed each product.

15. Some of the acronyms used in this chapter are listed below. Provide the full names for each of these acronyms.

JCL   DD/D
4 GL   OOP
DBMS   DASD
COBOL   CASE

DISCUSSION QUESTIONS

1. From the discussion in this chapter and your own knowledge from other sources, what do you think is the most important advancement in computer software in the past five years? Why?

2. Which one category of personal productivity software is of most value to you now as a student? Why? Within this category, what is your favorite software package? Why?

3. Which one category of personal productivity software do you expect to be of most value to you in your career? Why? Is this different from the category you selected in the previous question? Why or why not?

4. Based on your own computing experience and your discussions with other computer users, which one category of personal productivity software needs the most developmental work to make it useful to managers? What type of development is needed?

5. List the pros and cons of the involvement of managers in the end-user computing revolution. What strengths and weaknesses do managers bring to the software development process? Is it appropriate for managers to be directly involved in applications software development?

6. In the mid-1980s, a movement developed within the information systems industry to "stamp out COBOL" and replace it with 4 GLs and other productivity tools. Manifestations of this movement included the slogan to "Kill the COBOL programmer" (not literally, of course) and T-shirts

bearing the word COBOL within the international symbol for not permitted (a red circle with a red line diagonally across the word COBOL). Do you think the movement will ever be successful? Why?

7. You have probably had experience with at least one procedural (3 GL) language, either in high school or college. What are the strengths and weaknesses of the particular language that you know best? Based on what you have gleaned from the text, what primary advantages would be offered by a nonprocedural 4 GL over the 3 GL that you know best? What disadvantages? What primary advantages would be offered by a natural language over the 3 GL that you know best? What disadvantages?

8. Based on your reading in this chapter and other sources, what do you believe are the primary advantages of an object-oriented language over a third-generation language or a fourth-generation language? What are the primary disadvantages?

9. The notion of a Java applet was briefly introduced in this chapter. A somewhat similar idea (but with important differences) is Microsoft's ActiveX. Research the Java applet (you may also want to check out Java Beans) and ActiveX, and identify how these concepts differ and how they are alike. *Hint: Use the Web for your research, as well as Not Just Java by Peter van der Linden.*

10. Why is the concept of a Java virtual machine important? How does running a Java applet on a Java virtual machine differ from running a Microsoft Visual Basic application on your Web browser?

11. According to the statistics quoted from *Datamation* magazine, two firms seem to dominate the worldwide software market—IBM and Microsoft. With this degree of dominance by two firms, has the software subindustry truly been competitive, particularly over the past decade? Support your position.

12. Update the software portion of Table 2.4 for the most recent year for which data are available. What changes have occurred among the top ten players, both in terms of position within the top ten and relative total sales? Why have these changes occurred?

REFERENCES

1997. "200 most valuable products of the year: Software." *PC/Computing* 10 (January): 147–167.

1997. "Accpac Online." Accpac International Web site (June), http://accpaconline.com/main.html.

Bott, Ed. 1997. "Microsoft Office 97: The incredible office upgrade." *PC/Computing* 10 (January): 87–88.

Finnie, Scott. 1997. "Lotus SmartSuite 97: Business suite smarts." *PC/Computing* 10 (January): 90–92.

Fryer, Bronwyn. 1996. "Intranet mania." *Datamation* 42 (June 15): 54–57.

Hogan, Mike. 1996. "Bean counting 101: Easy accounting for any business." *PC/Computing* 9 (July): 169–174.

Jenkins, A. Milton, and Bijoy Bordoloi. 1986. "The evolution and status of fourth-generation languages: A tutorial." Institute for Research on the Management of Information Systems (IRMIS) Working Paper #W611, Indiana University Graduate School of Business.

Leach, Norvin, and Michael Moeller. 1997. "ActiveX lags in Web race." *PC Week* 14 (June 9): 1, 14.

Lindholm, Elizabeth. 1992. "The portable 4 GL?" *Datamation* 38 (April 1): 83–85.

Mael, Susan. 1996. "*Datamation* 100: Bigger by design." *Datamation* 42 (June 15): 32–37.

Moeller, Michael. 1997. "Delivering push: Push technologies are saving corporations time and money." *PC Week* 14 (May 12): 1, 16.

Peachtree Software. 1997. "Peachtree Software introduces Peachtree Complete Accounting Plus Time & Billing." (April 28), http://www.peachtree.com/product/press/Pluspres.htm

Radin, G. 1996. "Object technology in perspective." *IBM Systems Journal* 35, 2: 124–127.

Simpson, David. 1996. "Serverwars: NT vs. OS/2." *Datamation* 42 (November): 138–140.

Simpson, David. 1996. "Win95 vs. NT Workstation: You make the call!" *Datamation* 42 (December): 110–113.

Tittel, Ed, and James Michael Stewart. 1997. "Choose the right platform and NOS for your intranet." *Datamation* 43 (January): 118–126.

Tucker, Michael Jay. 1997. "A juggling act between old and new." *Datamation* 43 (July): 61–66.

van der Linden, Peter. 1997. *Not Just Java*. Mountain View, California: Sun Microsystems Press.

White, Ron. 1996. Corel Office Professional 7: Your whole office on CD." *PC/Computing* 9 (October): 93–94.

Wohl, Amy D. 1997. "The Internet learns to push." *Beyond Computing* 6 (July/August): 14–15.

TELECOMMUNICATIONS AND NETWORKING

This chapter is the last of a trio of chapters devoted to the building blocks of information technology. If every computer were a stand-alone unit with no connections to other computers, and if there were no way of receiving input from or sending output to workstations or sites physically removed from the computer, then hardware and software would be the end of the story as far as computers are concerned. In fact, until about two decades ago, that was the end of the story. Today, however, virtually all computers of all sizes communicate directly with other computers by means of an incredible variety of networks. For computers in organizations, these networks include intraorganizational local area networks (LANs), backbone networks, and wide area networks (WANs) as well as the worldwide Internet. For home computers, the most important network is the Internet. In addition to computer (or data) communications, today's organizations also depend heavily on voice (telephone) and image (video and facsimile) communication. This chapter explores the increasingly important topic of telecommunications and networking.

The goal of this chapter is to cover only the telecommunications and networking technology that you as a user-manager need to know. You need to understand the roles and general capabilities of various types of transmission media and networks, but you do not need to know all the technical details. You certainly need to know the important terminology and concepts relating to telecommunications and networking. Most important, you need to understand the interrelationships between hardware, software, and telecommunications and networking so that you can use the full gamut of information technology to increase your personal productivity and the effectiveness of your organization.

Change is everywhere in the information technology domain, but nowhere is this change more evident and more dramatic than in the realm of telecommunications and networking. A communications revolution is taking place that is directly or indirectly affecting the job of every manager, and the primary catalyst is the Internet and the World Wide Web (an application that runs on the Internet).

The breakup of American Telephone & Telegraph (AT&T) in 1984 created an environment in which a large number of firms competed to develop and market telecommunications equipment and services. Partially because of this increased competition, innovation in the telecommunications and networking arena has been at an all-time high. Digital networks, fiber optic cabling, cellular telephones, and the ability to send both voice and data over the same wires at the same time have contributed to the revolution.

At the same time, most large American businesses have restructured internally to reduce layers of middle management and create a leaner organization (as introduced in Chapter 1). They have also tended to decentralize operations in order to respond more quickly to market opportunities and competitors' actions and have created cross-functional teams to improve business processes and carry out projects. The net result of these internal changes is that communication has become more important than ever for the remaining, often geographically dispersed, managers. They need rapid, reliable voice and data communication with other parts of the company and with suppliers and customers. Small businesses are also more dependent upon communication than ever before, and developments such as local area networks, cellular telephones, and increased functionality of the

"NETWORKS WILL CHANGE EVERYTHING"

Paul Saffo, a fellow at the Institute for the Future, has developed a fascinating set of forecasts about the effect of information technologies on the way we work, play, and conduct business in the years to come. "The short answer is that networks will change everything," says Saffo. "In the next five years, networks will be supporting a shift to business teams from individuals as the basic unit of corporate productivity. In the 10-year time frame, we'll see changing organizational structures. In 20 to 30 years, we'll see a shift so fundamental, it will mean the end of the corporation as we know it." Saffo believes that organizations have already started down the path to a pervasive interconnectivity of workstations that will result in an entirely new "virtual" corporate structure.

[Adapted from Wylie, 1993]

public wired telephone network have helped fill this need. Internal needs and external competition and innovation have combined to create a latter-twentieth-century communications revolution. The aim of this chapter is to help you become a knowledgeable participant in the communications revolution.

THE NEED FOR NETWORKING

Let us be more precise in justifying the need for networking among computers and computer-related devices such as terminals and printers. Why do managers or other professionals working at microcomputers need to be connected to a network? Why are small computers often connected to larger machines? Why are laser printers often attached to a local area network? In our judgment, there are four primary reasons for networking.

Sharing of Technology Resources

Networking permits the sharing of critical (and often expensive) technology resources among the various users (machines) on the network. For example, by putting all of the microcomputers in an office on a local area network (LAN), the users can share a variety of resources, including a single laser printer that is a part of the network or a single facsimile machine on the network. The users can also share software that is electronically stored on a file server (another microcomputer designated for that particular purpose). All these devices are connected by wiring and are able to communicate with one another under control of a LAN software package called a network operating system. When a particular user wants to print a document or send a facsimile, it is sent electronically from the user's machine to the requested device, where it is printed or dispatched.

The sharing of resources is also important for larger computers. It is quite common for mainframe or minicomputers to share magnetic disk devices and high-speed line printers or laser printers. Further, wide area networks permit the sharing of very expensive resources such as supercomputers. The National Science Foundation has funded five national supercomputer centers across the country, and researchers from other universities and research laboratories are able to share these giant machines by going through their local computer network into an evolving national network known as **vBNS (very high-speed Backbone Network Service)**.[1]

Sharing of Data

Even more important than the sharing of technology resources is the sharing of data. Either a LAN or a wide area network permits users on the network to get data (if they are authorized to do so) from other points called nodes on the network. It is very important, for example, for managers to be able to retrieve overall corporate sales forecasts from corporate databases to use in developing spreadsheets to project future activity in their departments. In order to satisfy customers, automobile dealers need to be able to locate particular vehicle models and colors with specific equipment installed. Managers at various points in a supply chain need to have accurate, up-to-date data on inventory levels and locations. Accountants at corporate headquarters need to be able to retrieve summary data on sales and expenses from each of the company's divisional computer centers. The chief executive officer,

---

1 vBNS is the successor to NSFNET, which provided the **backbone** (the underlying high-volume links of the network, to which other elements attach) for the Internet until 1995.

using an executive information system (see Chapter 6), needs to be able to access up-to-the-minute data on business trends from the corporate mainframe computer. In some instances, data may be retrieved from a commercial, public database external to the firm, such as Dow Jones News Retrieval and Mead Data Central.

Of course, the ultimate sharing of data is now occurring via the **World Wide Web** on the Internet. By conservative estimates, in 1998 there were at least 80 million users of the Web at sites around the world, and this number was growing by nearly five percent per month.[2] Each of these users has easy (and often free) access to an incredible array of information on any topic one can think of. The Web is hypertext based, so the user merely clicks on highlighted text on a page to jump to another related page of information. In short, the Web has created a new and exciting way of sharing data.

Distributed Data Processing and Client/Server Systems

With **distributed data processing,** the processing power is distributed to multiple computers at multiple sites, which are then tied together via telecommunications lines. **Client/server systems** are a variant of distributed systems in which the processing power is distributed between a central server system, such as a mainframe, minicomputer, or powerful workstation, and a number of client computers, which are usually desktop microcomputers. The two most important perceived advantages of distributed and client/server systems are reduced computing costs because of reliance on more cost-effective microcomputers and workstations and increased service and responsiveness to local users, resulting in improved local morale. On the other hand, reduced computing costs from client/server systems don't always materialize, and such systems are dependent upon high-quality telecommunications lines.

There are many examples of distributed systems. One is the use of laptop computers by a company's sales force, where orders and sales data are transmit-

ted over the telephone network to the corporate computer center. A second example is the use of a client/server application for general ledger accounting, with desktop microcomputers as the clients and a high-powered workstation as the server. In most cases, such a package is implemented over a local area network in a single building or a cluster of buildings (a "campus"). A third example, also a client/server system, involves the creation of a commercial real estate database on a server located at the real estate firm's main office. The client machines are microcomputers located in the firm's branch offices or customer offices, with the clients and server linked via the public telephone network. In any case, it is the existence of a telecommunications network that makes distributed data processing a feasible and often attractive arrangement.

Enhanced Communications

Networks enhance the communications process within an organization (and between organizations) in many important ways. The telephone network has long been a primary means of communication within and between organizations. Electronic mail over the corporate computer network has become a mainstay of communication in many major organizations in the past decade or so, and the development of the Internet has extended the reach of these electronic mail systems around the world. Electronic bulletin boards (including internal, regional, and national bulletin boards) and mass electronic mailing lists for people with common interests permit multiparty asynchronous communication on an incredible array of topics. And video communication, especially videoconferencing, provides a richer medium to permit more effective communication.

Direct data communication links between a company and its suppliers and/or customers have been successfully used to give the company a strategic advantage (this topic will be more fully explored in Chapter 7). The SABRE airline reservation system is a classic example of a strategic information system that depends upon communication provided through a network. Recent developments to be discussed later in this chapter—such as ISDN—permit both voice and data communications to occur over the same telecommunications line at the same time. Starting with "plain

---

2 In July 1997, there were 19.5 million computers on the Internet (machines with Internet addresses, or IP numbers) and 1.3 million Web servers (machines with stored Web pages).

old telephone service" (POTS) networks and continuing with today's local area and wide area networks and the Internet, networks have enhanced the communication process for individuals and organizations.

An Overview of Telecommunications and Networking

Networking—the electronic linking of geographically dispersed devices—is critical for modern organizations. To participate effectively in the ongoing communications revolution, managers need to have a rudimentary understanding of the various telecommunications and networking options available to their organizations.

The prefix *tele-* simply means operating at a distance. Therefore **telecommunications** is communications at a distance. There are a number of other terms or abbreviations that are used almost interchangeably with telecommunications: data communications, datacom, teleprocessing, telecom, and networking. We prefer telecommunications because it is the broadest of these similar terms. It includes both voice (telephone) and data communications (including text and image). Teleprocessing means the computer processing is taking place at a distance from where the data originates, which obviously requires telecommunications. Networking is the electronic linking required to accomplish telecommunications.

One might think that only a wire, or some other conduit, is needed for telecommunications, but it is much more complex than that! To begin a detailed consideration of telecommunications, first consider the primary functions performed by a telecommunications network, as listed in Table 4.1. The most obvious of these functions is the *transmission* of voice and/or data, using the network and the underlying media. The *processing* involves making sure that an error-free message or data packet gets to the right destination. Subfunctions of processing include editorial, conversion, and routing. *Editorial* involves checking for errors and putting the communication into a standardized format, and *conversion* includes any necessary changes in the coding system or the transmission speed when moving from one device on the network to

Table 4.1

Functions of a Telecommunications Network

Function	Brief Description
Transmission	Movement of voice and/or data using network and underlying media
Processing	Insuring that error-free communication gets to right destination
Editorial	Checking for errors and putting communication into standardized format
Conversion	Changing coding system or speed when moving from one device to another
Routing	Choosing most efficient path when multiple paths are available
Network control	Keeping track of status of network elements and checking to see if communications are ready to be sent
Interface	Handling interactions between users and the network

another. In networks where alternative paths are possible between the source and the destination of a communication (particularly wide area networks and the Internet), *routing*—choosing the most efficient path—is an important task. Closely related to the processing function is *network control*, which includes keeping track of the status of various elements of the system (e.g., which elements are busy or out of service) and, for some types of networks, checking each user periodically to see if the user has a communication to send. A not-so-obvious but critical function is the provision of an *interface* between the network and the user; hopefully this interface will make it easy and efficient for a manager or any other network user to send a communication. The next major section explores the variety of ways in which the functions listed in Table 4.1 can be delivered.

Key Elements of Telecommunications and Networking

We believe that you as a user-manager need to understand certain key elements about telecommunications and networking to participate effectively in the communications revolution—to know what the options are for the business systems you need. These key elements include certain underlying basic ideas, such as analog versus digital signals and switched versus private lines; the variety of transmission media available; the topology (or possible arrangements) of networks; the various types of networks, including LANs and wide area networks; and the network protocols employed on these networks. This section will be rather technical and will involve a number of difficult concepts, so it may require some effort on your part to keep sight of the big picture of telecommunications.

Analog and Digital Signals

Perhaps the most basic idea about telecommunications is that the electronic signals sent on a network may be either analog or digital, depending on the type of network. Historically, the telephone network has been an **analog network,** with voice messages sent over the network by having some physical quantity (e.g., voltage) continuously vary as a function of time. This analog signal worked fine for voice transmission because it required the significant variations provided by an analog signal (corresponding to variations in human speech characteristics) and was insensitive to minor degradations in the signal quality. On the other hand, computer data consist of a string of binary digits, or bits—a string of zeros and ones to represent the desired characters. The form of this computer data does not mesh well with analog transmission. First, only two distinct signals—representing zero and one —need to be sent, and second, the data are extremely sensitive to degradations in signal quality. Noise in a telephone line could easily cause a zero to be interpreted as a one or vice versa, and the entire message may become garbled. Because of this problem with noise, data cannot be sent directly over the analog telephone network.

Two solutions are possible to the problem of transmitting computer data. The original solution, and one that is still widely used, is to convert the data from digital form to analog form before sending it over the analog telephone network. This conversion is accomplished by a device called a **modem,** an abbreviation for a *mod*ulator/*dem*odulator (see Figure 4.1). Of course, the data must be reconverted from analog form back to digital form at the other end of the transmission line, which requires a second modem. The conversion (or modulation) carried out by the modem may be of different types. Figure 4.2 illustrates the use of amplitude modulation (two different voltage levels to represent 0 and 1), frequency modulation (two different frequencies of oscillations to represent 0 and 1), and phase modulation (the use of a phase shift to represent the change from a 0 to a 1 or vice versa). The use of modems and the analog telephone network is an acceptable way to transmit data for many applications, but it is severely limited in terms of transmission speeds and error rates.

The second and longer-term solution to the problem of transmitting computer data is to develop **digital networks** specifically designed to directly transmit zeros and ones, as in Figure 4.2 (a). Digital networks have the advantages of potentially lower error rates and higher transmission speeds, and modems are no longer necessary. Because of these advantages, the networks that have been specifically created for the purpose of linking computers and computer-related devices are digital. Furthermore, the telephone network is gradually being shifted from an analog to a digital network.

This shift of the telephone network from analog to digital is due in part to the increasing volume of data

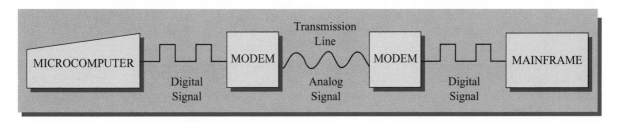

Figure 4.1 The Use of Modems in an Analog Network

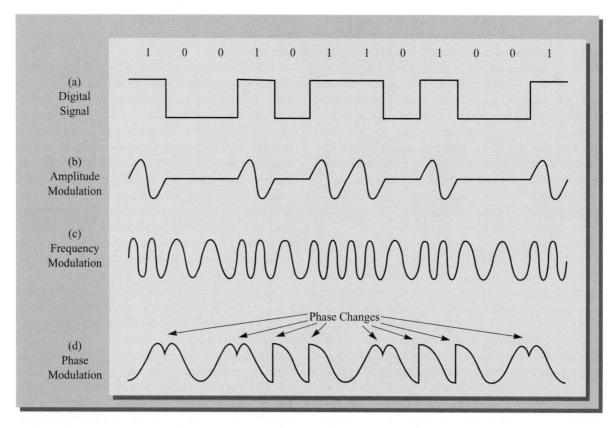

Figure 4.2 Digital and Analog Signals

being transmitted over the network, but there is also a significant advantage to transmitting voice signals over a digital network. Digital voice transmission can provide higher quality transmission—less noise on the line—just as digital recording provides higher fidelity compact disks. Most of our telephone instruments are still analog devices, so the signal sent from the instrument to the nearest switching center (which may be operated either by the telephone company or your own organization) is still an analog signal. These telephone switches, however, are rapidly being converted from analog to digital switches. When the analog voice signal arrives at a digital switch, it is converted to a digital voice signal for transmission to a digital switch somewhere else, which may be across town or across the country. Thus, an increasing proportion of the voice transmission between switching centers is digitized. In the future, our telephone instruments will

also be digital devices, so the entire telephone network will eventually become digital.

Speed of Transmission

Whether the signal is digital or analog, another basic question is the speed of transmission. Please note that by speed we *don't* mean how fast the signal travels in terms like miles per hour, but rather we are referring to the volume of data that can be transmitted per unit of time. Terms such as bandwidth, Hertz (Hz), and baud are used to describe transmission speeds, whereas a measure such as bits transmitted per second (bits per second, or bps) would be more understandable. Happily, the three terms mentioned above are all essentially the same as bits per second in many circumstances. **Bandwidth** is the difference between the highest and the lowest frequencies (cycles per second) that can be transmitted on a single medium, and it is a measure of the capacity of the medium. (Sometimes it is necessary to divide the bandwidth up into multiple channels, all carried on a single medium, to utilize the entire capacity. Thus the transmission speeds we discuss are really data rates for the one or more channels carried on the single medium.) **Hertz** is simply cycles per second, and **baud** is the number of signals sent per second. If each cycle sends one signal that transmits exactly one bit of data, which is often the case, then all these terms are identical. To minimize any possible confusion, we will talk about bits per second, or bps, in this chapter. In information technology publications, baud is often used for relatively slow speeds such as 14,400 baud (14,400 bps) or 33,600 baud (33,600 bps), while Hertz (with an appropriate prefix) is often used for higher speeds such as 133 megaHertz (133 million bps) or 500 megaHertz (500 million bps).

The notion of bandwidth, or capacity, is important for telecommunications. For example, approximately 50,000 bits (0s and 1s) are required to represent one page of data. To transmit this page using a 14,400 baud (14,400 bps) modem over an ordinary analog telephone line would take 3.5 seconds. If one were transmitting a large data file (such as customer accounts), that bandwidth or capacity would be unacceptably slow. On the other hand, to transmit this same page over a 64,000 bps (64 kbps) digital voice line would take only eight-tenths of a second. For graphics, approximately one million bits are required for one page. This would require a little over a minute for transmission at 14,400 bps over an analog telephone line, or about 16 seconds over a 64 kbps digital voice line. Full-motion video transmission requires the enormous bandwidth of 12 million bps, and thus data compression techniques must be employed to be able to send video over the existing telephone network. The bandwidth determines what types of communication—voice, data, graphics, stop-frame video, full-motion video—can reasonably be transmitted over a particular medium.

Types of Transmission Lines

Another basic distinction is between private (or dedicated) communication lines and switched lines. The public telephone network, for example, is a switched-line system. When a communication of some sort (voice or data) is sent over the telephone network, the sender has no idea what route the communication will take. The telephone company (or companies') computers make connections between switching centers to send the communication over the lines they deem appropriate, based on such factors as the length of the path, the amount of traffic on the various routes, and the capacity of the various routes. This switched-line system usually works fine for voice communications. Data communications, however, are more sensitive to the differences in line quality over different routes and to other local phenomena, such as electrical storms. Thus, a data communication sent from Minneapolis to Atlanta over the telephone network may be transmitted perfectly at 11 A.M., but another communication sent from Minneapolis to Atlanta 15 minutes later (a different connection) may be badly garbled because the communications were sent via different routes.

One way to reduce the error rate is through private lines. Most private lines are dedicated physical lines leased from a common-carrier company such as MCI, Sprint, or AT&T. A company may choose to lease a line between Minneapolis and Atlanta to ensure the quality of its data transmissions. Private lines also exist within a building or a campus. These are lines owned by the organization for the purpose of transmitting its own voice and data communications. Within-building or within-campus lines for computer telecommunications, for example, are usually private lines.

The last basic idea we wish to introduce is the difference among simplex, half-duplex, and full-duplex transmission. With **simplex transmission,** data can travel only in one direction. This one-way communication is rarely useful but might be employed from a monitoring device at a remote site (monitoring power consumption, for example) back to a computer. With **half-duplex transmission,** data can travel in both directions but not simultaneously. **Full-duplex transmission** permits data to travel in both directions at once, and, therefore, provides greater capacity and costs more than half-duplex lines. Ordinary telephone service is full-duplex because both parties can talk at once, whereas a walkie-talkie provides half-duplex service because only one party can transmit at a time. Modems often have a switch that lets the user choose between full-duplex and half-duplex operation, depending upon the type of transmission desired.

Transmission Media

A telecommunications network is made up of some physical medium (or media) over which communications are sent. There are five primary media in use today: twisted pair of wires, coaxial cable, wireless, satellite (which is a special form of wireless), and fiber optic cable.

Twisted Pair   When all uses are considered, the most common transmission medium is a **twisted pair** of wires. Most telephones are connected to the local telephone company office or the local private branch exchange (PBX) via a twisted pair. Similarly, many LANs have been implemented by using twisted pair wiring to connect the various microcomputers and related devices. A twisted pair consists of two insulated copper wires, typically about 1 millimeter thick, twisted together in a long helix. The purpose for the twisting is to reduce electrical interference from similar twisted pairs nearby. If many twisted pairs will run parallel for a significant distance—such as from a neighborhood to a telephone company office—it is common to bundle them together and enclose them in a protective sheath.

The transmission speeds attainable with twisted pairs vary considerably, depending upon such factors as thickness of the wire and the distance traveled. On the voice telephone network without modification, speeds from 14,400 to 56,000 bps are commonplace. Telephone twisted pairs can be conditioned, which means the use of testing and shielding (to minimize interference), to support speeds up to 144,000 bps for distances of several miles. Much higher speeds—16 million bps and more—can be obtained when twisted pairs are used in LANs. Shielded twisted pairs or multiple unshielded twisted pairs can support speeds up to 100 million bps when used in a Fiber Distributed Data Interface (FDDI) or Fast Ethernet local area network (more on this later). The speeds of twisted pair and other media are summarized in Table 4.2.

Coaxial Cable   **Coaxial cable,** or **coax** for short, is another common transmission medium. A coaxial cable consists of a heavy copper wire at the center, surrounded by insulating material. Around the insulating material is a cylindrical conductor, which is often a woven braided mesh. Then the cylindrical conductor is covered by an outer protective plastic covering. Figure 4.3 illustrates the construction of a coaxial cable.

Because of its construction, coaxial cable provides a good combination of relatively high transmission speeds and low noise or interference. Two kinds of coaxial cable are in widespread use—**baseband coax** used for digital transmission, and **broadband coax** used for analog transmission (Tanenbaum, 1988).

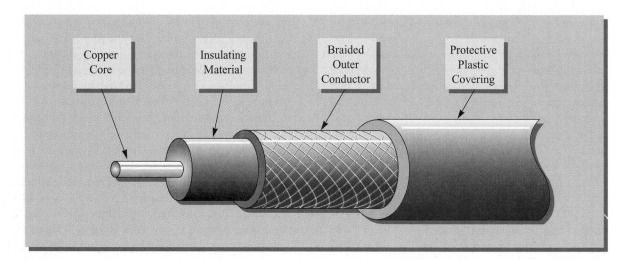

Figure 4.3 Construction of a Coaxial Cable

Table 4.2

Telecommunications Transmission Speeds

Transmission Medium	Typical Speeds
Twisted pair—voice telephone	14.4 kbps–56 kbps
Twisted pair—conditioned	56 kbps–144 kbps
Twisted pair—LAN	4 mbps–100 mbps
Coaxial cable—baseband	10 mbps–264 mbps
Coaxial cable—broadband	10 mbps–550 mbps
Radio frequency wireless LAN	2 mbps–8 mbps
Infrared light wireless LAN	4 mbps–16 mbps
Microwave	64 kbps–50 mbps
Satellite (microwave)	64 kbps–50 mbps
Fiber optic cable	100 mbps–30 gbps

KEY: bps = bits per second
     kbps = thousand bits per second, or kilo bps
     mbps = million bits per second, or mega bps
     gbps = billion bits per second, or giga bps

Baseband coax is simple to use and inexpensive to install, and the required interfaces to microcomputers or other devices are relatively inexpensive. Baseband offers a single digital transmission channel with data transmission rates ranging from 10 million bits per second (10 mbps) up to 264 mbps, depending primarily on the distances involved (longer cables mean lower data rates). Baseband coax has been widely used for LANs and for long-distance transmission within the telephone network.

Broadband coax uses analog transmission on standard cable television cabling. Higher transmission speeds are possible—up to 550 mbps—over much longer distances. Furthermore, a single broadband coax can be divided into multiple channels, so that a single cable can support simultaneous transmission of data, voice, and television. Broadband cable systems require analog amplifiers to boost the signals periodically. In general, broadband systems are more difficult to install and are considerably more expensive than baseband systems. Engineers are required to plan the cable and amplifier layout and install the system, and skilled technicians are needed to maintain the system over time. Thus, the choice between broadband and baseband hinges upon whether the additional capacity and multiple channels provided by broadband are worth the corresponding complexity and expense. Unless there are special requirements (such as the

need to transmit both video and data simultaneously), the choice is usually the less expensive baseband.

Wireless   Strictly speaking, wireless is not a transmission medium. **Wireless** is broadcast technology in which radio signals are sent out into the air. Wireless communication is being used in a variety of circumstances, including cordless telephones, cellular telephones, wireless LANs, and microwave transmission of voice and data.

A **cordless telephone** is a portable device which may be used up to about 1,000 feet from its wired telephone base unit. This permits the user to carry the telephone with him to various rooms in a house or take it outdoors on the patio. By contrast, a **cellular telephone** (installed in a car or carried in a pocket or briefcase) may be used anywhere as long as it is within range—about 8 to 10 miles—of a cellular switching station. At present, these cellular switching stations are available in all metropolitan areas of the United States and most rural areas. The switching stations are low-powered transmitter/receivers that are connected to a cellular telephone switching office by means of conventional telephone lines or microwave technology. The switching office, which is computer-controlled, coordinates the calls for its service area and links the cellular system into the local and long distance telephone network.

Wireless LANs are growing in popularity. They have the obvious advantage of being reasonably easy to plan and install. A wireless system provides networking where cable or wire installation would be extremely expensive or impractical, such as in an old building. They tend to be more expensive than a wired LAN, they are certainly less secure, and their speeds are usually slower. For example, most radio signal LANs operate in the range of 2 to 4 mbps.

Microwave has been in widespread use for long distance wireless communication for several decades. Microwave is line-of-sight transmission—there must be an unobstructed straight line between the microwave transmitter and the receiver. Because of the curvature of the earth, microwave towers (see Figure 4.4) have to be built, typically about 25 to 50 miles apart, to relay signals over long distances from the originating transmitter to the final receiver. These requirements for towers, transmitters, and receivers suggest that microwave transmission may be expensive, and it

Figure 4.4 Microwave Tower (Property of AT&T Archives.) Reprinted with permission of AT&T.

is, but long-distance microwave may still be less expensive than burying coaxial cable or fiber optic cable in a very long trench. Microwave is widely used for long distance telephone communication and for corporate voice and data networks; transmission speeds of 50 mbps or more are possible.

Other line-of-sight transmission methods exist in addition to microwave. For short distances (such as from one building to another), laser or infrared transmitters and receivers, mounted on the rooftops, are often an economical and easy way to transmit data. The fastest wireless LANs, operating at speeds from 4 to 16 mbps, use line-of-sight infrared light as their medium.

Satellite   A special variation of microwave transmission employs **satellite communication** to relay signals over very long distances. A communications satellite is simply a big microwave repeater in the sky; it contains one or more transponders that listen to a particular portion of the bandwidth, amplify the incoming signals, and retransmit back to earth. A typical satellite may have a dozen transponders, each of which can handle a 50 mbps data transmission, 800 digital voice channels of 64 kbps each, or other combinations of data channels and voice channels. Transmission via satellite is still line-of-sight transmission, so a communication would have to be relayed through several satellites to go half way around the world (see Figure 4.5).

One interesting and annoying aspect of satellite transmission is the substantial delay in receiving the signal because of the large distances involved in transmitting up to the geostationary satellite and then back down to earth. The minimum delay is about one-third of a second, which is an order of magnitude larger than on coax connections or earth-bound microwave covering the same ground distance.

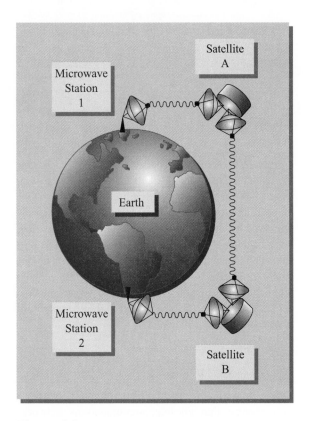

Figure 4.5 Satellite Communications

Interest in the use of satellites by corporations has been heightened in recent years by the development of KU-band satellite technology and the new very small aperture terminals (VSATs). VSATs are small satellite dishes (18 inches to 4 feet in diameter), which are much less costly than their bigger cousins. KU-band broadcasts at a higher radio frequency than the older C-band and thus can be received by a smaller antenna. VSAT data transmission rates to a satellite range from 64 kbps to 256 kbps, with rates from the satellite to the VSAT of 256 kbps to 24 mbps.

Fiber Optics   The last and newest transmission medium—**fiber optic** cabling—is a true medium, not broadcast technology. Advances in optical technology have made it possible to transmit data by pulses of light through a thin fiber of glass or fused silica. A light pulse can signal a 1 bit, while the absence of a pulse signals a 0 bit. An optical transmission system requires three components: the light source, either an LED—a light emitting diode—or a laser diode; the fiber optic cable itself; and a detector (a photodiode). The light source emits light pulses when an electrical current is applied, and the detector generates an electrical current when it is hit by light.

The speeds possible with fiber optics are much faster than the other media and the space requirements are much less because the fiber optic cable is very small in diameter. Fiber optic cables are more secure because the cables emit no radiation and thus are very difficult to tap. They are also highly reliable because they are not affected by power-line surges, electromagnetic interference, or corrosive chemicals in the air. All of these reasons are leading telephone companies to use fiber optics in virtually all of their new long distance telephone lines and lines connecting central office sites and in most of their new local lines from central office sites to terminals located in subdivisions. (The advantages of speed and security are obvious; the size is important because many of the cable ducts already installed lack room for more coax but could hold more of the thinner fiber optic cabling.) The high cost of the required equipment and the difficulty of dealing with the tiny fibers make this medium unattractive for most LANs, with the exceptions of its use as a backbone to connect multiple LANs and where very high speeds or high security needs exist.

NEW SATELLITES TO FILL THE SKY

More than a dozen projects aim to blanket the sky with satellites that could completely transform the way that telephone calls, broadcast signals, and data will dart around the earth. A staggering 1,700 or so satellites will be launched in the next 10 years—more than 10 times the 150 commercial satellites now in orbit. These new birds will be low earth orbit (LEO) satellites, orbiting at a distance of only 400 to 1,000 miles above the earth, in contrast to the present geosynchronous earth orbit (GEO) commercial satellites positioned 22,000 miles above the equator, such that they appear stationary relative to the earth's surface.

Among the major projects is Iridium, which intends to launch 66 satellites to offer mobile telephony, paging, and data communication services. Iridium investors include Motorola, Lockheed Martin, and Sprint. Similar services would be offered by Loral's Globalstar project, a 48-satellite system. Perhaps the most ambitious project is Teledesic, sponsored by Craig McCaw (who built McCaw Cellular before selling it to AT&T) and Bill Gates (Microsoft), which intends to create an 840-satellite network to provide low-cost, high-speed Internet access, corporate networking, and desktop videoconferencing.

What are the primary services these new satellites will offer?

- With the launch of Hughes Electronics' DirecTV in 1994, digital satellite television is the industry's first big hit. Satellites beam down as many as 200 crisp channels with CD-quality sound. Globally, satellite TV could draw 30 million subscribers and $12 billion in revenues by 2002.
- Loral, Motorola, and others are betting vast sums to meet expected demand for global hand-held wireless phone services. Globe-trotting executives could take a single cellular-like phone anywhere they travel as early as 1998. Phones will cost from $750 to $3,000, with charges ranging from $1 to $3 per minute. The projected market by 2005 is 7 million subscribers, $7 billion in revenues.
- Global mobile-phone providers will also use their systems to provide wireless phones to underserved rural areas in countries such as India, China, and Russia and to ease the telecommunications logjam in rapidly growing areas in Asia and Latin America. Potential market: $8 billion.
- Hughes, GE, Loral, Teledesic, and others are scurrying to buy or build satellite networks that will allow consumers to link home computers to the Internet. The two-way satellite connections promise fiber-optic-like speeds. Some plan to package satellite TV and Internet access into a single dish starting at about $1,000. With service to begin around 2000, the market could hit $10 billion by 2005.

[Adapted from Schine et al., 1997]

Transmission speeds for fiber range up to 500 mbps for large-diameter fiber (50 to 100 micron[3] core, which does not count any protective covering) to as high as 30 billion bits per second (30 giga bps or 30 gbps) for small-diameter fiber (10 microns or less). The fact that the smaller diameter fiber has much larger capacity may be surprising, but light reflections are greatly reduced with a smaller fiber—there is much less bouncing around of the light ray—which permits higher transmission speeds. The large diameter fiber is multimode, meaning that several light rays are traversing the fiber simultaneously, bouncing off the fiber walls, while the small diameter fiber is single mode, with a single light ray at a time propagated essentially in a straight line without bouncing. Single mode fiber, unfortunately, requires higher cost laser light sources and detectors than multimode fiber. One major telephone company is currently installing only one type of fiber—eight-micron single mode fiber with a transmission speed of up to 2.5 gbps. The outside diameter (including protective covering) of this single mode fiber is only 125 microns, which is about one-fiftieth the outside diameter of a typical coaxial cable. Thus, both the speed and size advantages of fiber optics are significant.

Topology of Networks

The starting point for the understanding of networks is to recognize that all telecommunications networks employ one or more of the transmission media dis-

---

3 A micron is one-millionth of a meter or one-thousandth of a millimeter.

cussed above. But what do the networks look like in terms of their configuration, or arrangement, of devices and media? The technical term for this configuration is the topology of the network. There are five basic network topologies—bus, ring, star, hierarchical or tree, and mesh (see Figure 4.6)—plus an unlimited number of variations and combinations of these five basic forms.

Bus   The simplest topology is the linear or **bus topology.** With the bus, a single length of cable (coax, fiber, or twisted pair) is shared by all network devices. One of the network devices is usually a file server with a large data storage capacity. An obvious advantage of the bus is the wiring simplicity. A disadvantage is its single point failure characteristic. If the bus fails, nodes on either side of the failure point cannot communicate with one another.

Ring   The **ring topology** is similar to the bus except that the two ends of the cable are connected. In this case, a single cable runs through every network device, including (usually) a file server. The wiring for the ring is slightly more complicated than for the bus,

but the ring is not as susceptible to failure. In particular, a single failure in the ring still permits each network device to communicate with every other device.

Star   The **star topology** has a mainframe or minicomputer, a file server (usually a microcomputer), or a PBX at its center, with cables (or media of some type) radiating from the central device to all the other network devices. This design is representative of many small-to-medium computer configurations, with all workstations and peripherals attached to the single minicomputer. It is also encountered in LANs and in networks built around a PBX (private branch exchange). Advantages of the star include ease of identifying cable failure, because each device has its own cable; ease of installation for each device, which must only be connected to the central device; and low cost for small networks where all the devices are close together. The primary disadvantage of the star is that if the central device fails, the whole network fails. A cost disadvantage may also be encountered if the network grows, for a separate cable must be run to each individual device, even if several devices are close together but far from the central device.

Tree   The fourth basic topology is the **tree,** or hierarchical. This topology is sometimes called an hierarchical star, because with some rearrangement (spreading the branches out around the central device), it looks like an extension of the star. The configuration of most large and very large computer networks is a tree, with the mainframe at the top of the tree connected (through data channels) to terminal controllers such as a multiplexer[4] and perhaps to other smaller computers. Then these terminal controllers, or smaller computers, are in turn connected to other devices such as terminals, microcomputers, and printers. Thus, the tree gets "bushy" as one traverses it from top to bottom.

The tree has the same primary disadvantage as the star. If the central device fails, the entire network goes down. On the other hand, the tree arrangement possesses a great deal of flexibility. The cost disadvantage

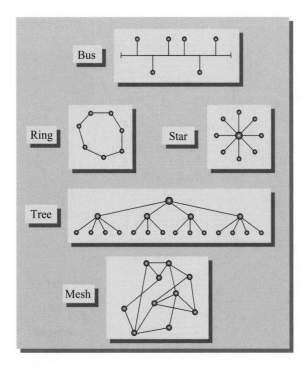

Figure 4.6 Network Topologies

---

4 A multiplexer is a device, usually located at a site remote from the mainframe, whose function is to merge ("multiplex") the data streams from multiple low-speed input devices, such as terminals and microcomputers, so that the full capacity of the transmission line to the mainframe is utilized.

of the star may not appear when devices are added to the network, for the use of intermediate devices (multiplexers, small computers) removes the necessity of connecting every device directly to the center.

Mesh   In a **mesh topology** most devices are connected to two, three, or more other devices in a seemingly irregular pattern that resembles a woven net, or a mesh. A complete mesh would have every device connected to every other device, but this is seldom done because of the cost involved. The public telephone network is an example of a mesh topology; another example is the network of networks that makes up the Internet.

The ramifications of a failure in the mesh depend upon the alternative paths or routes available in the vicinity of the failure. In a complex mesh like the telephone network, a failure is likely to have little impact except on the devices directly involved.

More Complex Networks   Now the fun begins, because the above five network topologies can be combined and modified in a bewildering assortment of networks. For example, it is quite common to attach a bus or a ring LAN to the tree mainframe computer network. Two ring LANs may be attached via a microwave channel, which is in effect a very simple bus network.

National and international networks are much more complex than those we have considered thus far, because the designers have intentionally built in a significant amount of redundancy. In this way if one transmission line goes out, there are alternative routes to almost every node or device on the network. As an example, the National Science Foundation very high-speed Backbone Network Service, or vBNS, is shown in Figure 4.7. vBNS links five National Science Foundation-supported supercomputer centers (labeled on Figure 4.7) and provides four Network Access Points

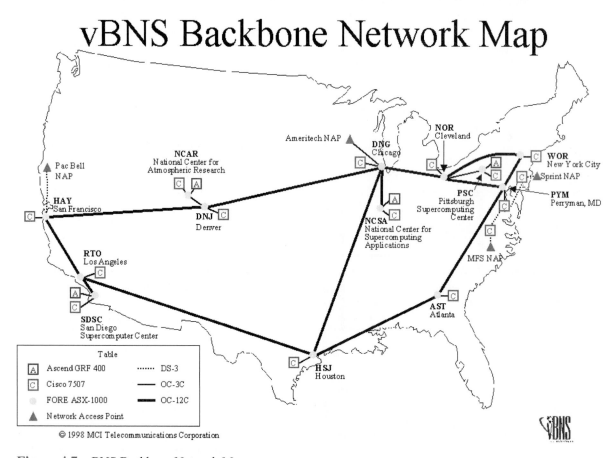

Figure 4.7 vBNS Backbone Network Map

(NAPs) where other researchers may link into vBNS from the Internet. vBNS is based upon a ring connecting the East and West Coasts, with the addition of a link from Chicago to Houston and spurs going off the ring to other sites. As another example, the long distance telephone network is a mesh topology, with numerous paths possible to connect most metropolitan areas.

Types of Networks

Thus far we have considered two key elements of telecommunications networks: the transmission media used to send the communications and the arrangement or topology of the networks. Now we turn to the categorization of networks into basic types. Please note that the categories employed here are somewhat arbitrary—but we believe extremely useful—and may differ from those used in other references. The types of networks to be described include computer telecommunications networks, private branch exchange (PBX) networks, local area networks (LANs), backbone networks, wide area networks (WANs), and the Internet.

Computer Telecommunications Networks It is almost easier to describe this initial type of network by what it is not. It is not a PBX network, a LAN, or a WAN. What we are calling a **computer telecommunications network** is the network emanating from a single medium, large, or very large computer or a group of closely linked computers. This type of network usually is arranged as a tree (see Figure 4.6) with coaxial cable and twisted pair as the media. Until the early 1980s, this was usually the only type of network (except for the telephone network) operated by an organization that did business in one building or a group of adjacent buildings (a campus). In many organizations even today the predominant communication with the central computer is through the computer telecommunications network. This type of network is controlled by the central computer, with all other devices (e.g., terminals, microcomputers, and printers) operating as "slaves" on the network. IBM's mainframe architecture was originally based on this type of network, although LANs and other network types may now be linked to a mainframe or large computer.

This is not a bad arrangement, but it puts a tremendous communications control burden on the central computer. For this reason, it is quite common to add a front-end processor or communications controller to the network—between the central computer and the rest of the network—to offload the communications work from the central computer (see Figure 4.8). A front-end processor or communications controller is another computer with specially designed hardware and software to handle all aspects of telecommunications, including error control, editing, controlling, routing, and speed and signal conversion.

PBX Networks Private branch exchanges, or PBXs, have been around for many years, but today's digital **PBXs** have extensive capabilities not possessed by their predecessors. The initial PBXs were switchboards run by human operators to operate an internal telephone system within an organization. Later PBXs worked in the same way except that electromechanical relays were used to perform the switching rather than human operators. Today's digital PBX consists of a digital switch operated by a built-in computer, and the PBX has the capability of simultaneously handling communications with internal analog telephones, digital microcomputers and terminals, mainframe computers, and the external telephone network. Figure 4.9 provides a schematic representation of a PBX.

It is obvious from Figure 4.9 that a PBX can serve as the central device in a star or a tree network. The media used are typically some combination of coax, twisted pair, and fiber (if high speeds are essential). If a mainframe computer is attached to the PBX, then the PBX can function as the front-end processor for the mainframe. In terms of the telephone network, the PBX will have to translate analog telephone signals to digital form before sending them over the digital network. Except for telephone instruments, all the devices shown in Figure 4.9 are digital, including the ISDN devices to be discussed later.

A PBX has several advantages. It can connect all, not just some, of the telecommunications devices in a building or campus; it can use existing telephone wiring, which is a major advantage; it can carry voice and data over the same network; it can connect in a transparent way to the external telephone network; and it has an incredible potential throughput of over 1 gbps. On the negative side, the maximum speed for a single channel (as distinct from overall throughput) is only 64 kbps, which is plenty for telephone and most terminal traffic but is painfully slow for shipping a

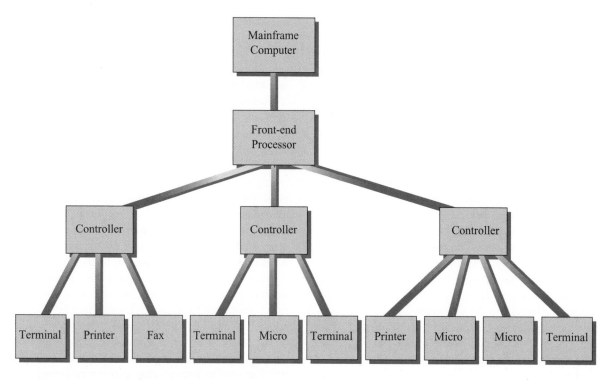

Figure 4.8 Computer Telecommunications Network

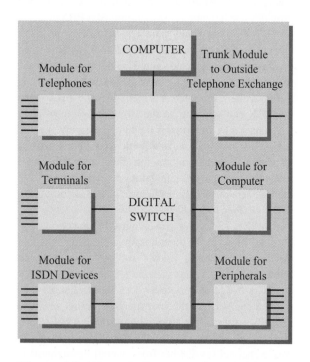

Figure 4.9 Schematic Representation of a PBX

large computer file from the mainframe to a remote disk unit. PBXs are also complex and expensive pieces of equipment.

Local Area Networks   A **local area network (LAN)** is first and foremost a *local* network—it is completely owned by a single organization and generally operates within an area no more than two or three miles in diameter. LANs are data networks that generally have a high data rate of several million bps or more.

A LAN differs from a computer telecommunications network in that a LAN contains a number of intelligent devices (usually microcomputers) capable of data processing rather than being built around a central computer that controls all processing. In other words, a LAN is based on a peer-to-peer relationship, rather than a master-slave relationship. A LAN differs from a PBX network in that a LAN handles only data, is not part of the telephone system, and requires new wiring. But a LAN does have a great deal in common with a PBX network in that both are aimed at establishing communication between a variety of devices in order to share data and resources and to facilitate office or factory automation. Thus, PBXs and LANs are often seen as competing technologies.

LANs exist in a variety of topologies, but three of these—for which standards have been developed by the Institute for Electrical and Electronic Engineers (IEEE) and subsequently adopted by both national and international standards organizations—are clearly dominant today. These three LAN standards are officially designated as IEEE 802.3 (contention bus design), IEEE 802.4 (token bus design), and IEEE 802.5 (token ring design).

The **contention bus** design was originally developed by Xerox and subsequently adopted by Digital Equipment Corporation and Novell, among others. This design is usually referred to as **Ethernet,** named after the original Xerox version of the design. The contention bus is obviously a bus topology (see Figure 4.6) and usually is implemented using coaxial cable or twisted pair wiring. The interesting feature of this design is its contention aspect—all devices must contend for the use of the cable.

With Ethernet, devices listen to the cable in order to pick off communications intended for the particular device and to see if the cable is busy. If the cable is idle, any device may transmit a message. Most of the time this works fine, but what happens if two devices start to transmit at the same time? A collision occurs and the messages become garbled. The devices must recognize that this collision has occurred, stop transmitting, wait some random period of time, and then try again. This method of operation is called a **CSMA/CD protocol,** an abbreviation for carrier sense multiple access with collision detection. In theory, collisions might continue to occur and thus there is no upper bound on the time a device might wait to send a message. In practice, a contention bus design is simple to implement and works very well as long as traffic on the network is relatively light (and thus there are few collisions).

The **token bus** design also employs a bus topology with coaxial cable or twisted pair wiring, but it does not rely on contention. Instead, a single token (a special communication or message) is passed around the bus to all devices in a specified order, and a given device can transmit only when it has the token. Thus, a particular microcomputer must wait until it receives the token before transmitting a message; when it has

completed sending the message, it sends the token on to the next device. After some deterministic period of time based on messages sent by other devices, the microcomputer will receive the token again.

The token bus design is central to **MAP (Manufacturing Automation Protocol)**, which was developed by General Motors and has been adopted by many manufacturers. MAP is a factory automation protocol (or set of standards) designed to connect robots and other machines on the assembly line by a LAN. In designing MAP, General Motors did not feel it could rely on a contention-based LAN with a probabilistic delay time before a message could be sent. An automobile assembly line moves at a fixed rate, and it can not be held up because a robot has not received the appropriate message from the LAN. Therefore, General Motors and many other manufacturers have opted for the deterministic token bus LAN design.

The third LAN standard is the **token ring,** originally developed by IBM, which combines a ring topology (see Figure 4.6) with the use of a token as described for the token bus. A device attached to the ring must seize the token and remove it from the ring before transmitting a message; when the device has completed transmitting, it releases the token back into the ring. Thus, collisions can never occur, and the maximum delay time before any station can transmit is deterministic.

The token ring is a unidirectional ring, with data flowing in only one direction around the ring. If the ring were physically implemented as suggested in Figure 4.6, a single break anywhere in the ring would disrupt communication for the entire ring. This potential problem is solved very nicely by the use of a wire center as shown in Figure 4.10, and the token ring becomes a physical star but remains a logical ring. In one implementation of a wire center, for example, up to eight individual devices are connected to the wire center using twisted pair wiring. Each twisted pair becomes an arm of the physical star, but the two wires in the pair are joined with others through the wire center to form a logical ring. Furthermore, the wire center is built to automatically bypass a nonoperative arm of the star (if, for instance, the ring breaks or the device fails).

As implied by Figure 4.10, reconfiguring a token ring is as easy as plugging in a new device or unplugging an old one. Because of the physical star arrangement, it is easy to diagnose and correct any communications problems that arise. In a very active LAN, both the

FOUR DEVICES CONNECTED VIA A WIRE CENTER

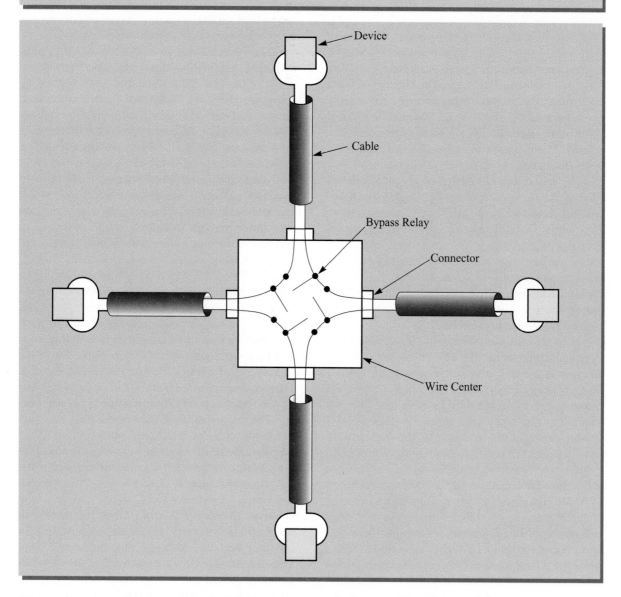

Figure 4.10 Physical Star, Logical Ring. (Andrew S. Tanenbaum, *Computer Networks*. 2nd ed. © 1988, p. 156. Reprinted by permission of Prentice Hall, Inc., Upper Saddle River, New Jersey.)

token ring and the token bus will significantly outperform the contention bus in terms of the actual data rate delivered for any potential data rate (see Figure 4.11). Thus, the token bus and ring seem to have significant factors in their favor. Nevertheless, contention bus LANs are well established and perform satisfactorily in most situations. All three types of LANs are widely used today, with token bus dominating the manufacturing scene and contention bus leading token ring in office applications.

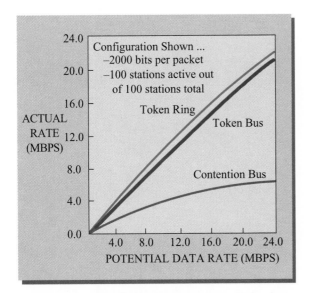

Figure 4.11 Performance Comparison of the LAN Technologies

LAN technology continues to advance in the late 1990s. The top speed of a traditional Ethernet LAN is 10 mbps, but **Fast Ethernet** operating at 100 mbps is being used in many newer LANs where greater capacity is needed. Fast Ethernet, also called 100 Base-T, uses the same CSMA/CD architecture as traditional Ethernet. The most popular implementation of Fast Ethernet uses either two pairs of unshielded twisted pair or a single shielded twisted pair (Type 1) as the medium.

Just as Fast Ethernet is sort of traditional Ethernet grown up, so is **Fiber Distributed Data Interface (FDDI)** related to a traditional token ring LAN. A traditional token ring LAN operates at a maximum speed of 16 mbps. By contrast, FDDI employs a token ring architecture to deliver 100 mbps. FDDI was originally developed to operate with fiber optic cable (hence the name), but now operates on copper media, usually shielded twisted pair. FDDI is actually a dual-ring technology, with each ring running in the opposite direction to improve fault recovery. With FDDI, the primary ring is active until a fault is detected, at which time the secondary ring is activated.

Backbone Networks   **Backbone networks** are the in-between networks—these are the middle distance net-

works that interconnect LANs in a single organization with each other and with the organization's wide area network and the Internet. For example, the corporate headquarters of a large firm may involve multiple buildings spread out over several city blocks. Each floor of a large building may have its own LAN, or a LAN may cover an entire smaller building. All these LANs must be interconnected to gain the benefits of networking described earlier—enhanced communications, the sharing of resources and data, and distributed data processing. In addition, the LANs must also be connected to the company's wide area network and, in most cases, to the Internet. A backbone network is the key to this internetworking (see Figure 4.12).

The technology involved in backbone networks is essentially the same as that described for LANs, but at the high end. Thus, the medium employed is usually either fiber optic cabling or shielded twisted pair to provide a high data transmission rate, often 100 mbps or more. The topology may be a ring (FDDI) or a bus (Fast Ethernet) or some combination. The only new terminology we need to introduce relates to the hardware devices that connect network pieces together or connect other networks to the backbone network.

A **hub** is a simple device where one section of a LAN is connected to another. Hubs forward every message they receive to other sections of the LAN, whether or not they need to go there. A **bridge** connects two LANs or LAN segments together when the LANs use the same protocol, or set of rules (more on this later); a bridge is smart enough to forward only messages that need to go to the other LAN. A **router,** or a **gateway** (which is really a sophisticated router), connects two or more LANs together and forwards only messages that need to be forwarded, but it may connect LANs that use different protocols. For example, a gateway is used to connect an organization's backbone network to the Internet. A **switch** connects more than two LANs or LAN segments that use the same protocol. Switches are very useful to connect several low-speed LANs (e.g., 16 Ethernet LANs running at 10 mbps) into a single 100 mbps backbone network (running Fast Ethernet). In this case the switch is operating very much like a multiplexer. The top vendors of these hardware devices include Cisco, Bay Networks, 3Com, and Lucent Technologies.

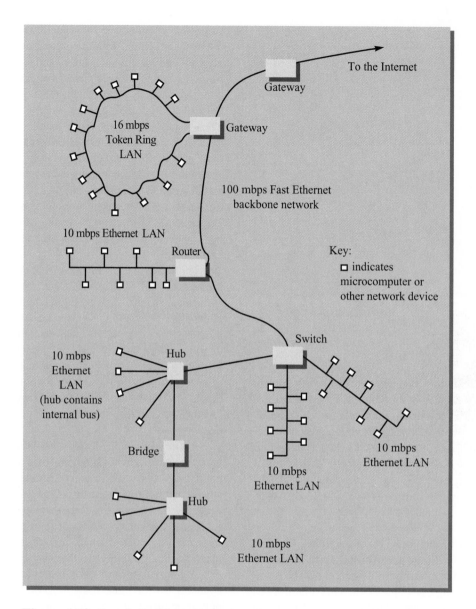

Figure 4.12 Sample Backbone Network

Wide Area Networks   Today's more complex, more widely dispersed organizations need **wide area networks (WANs)**, also called long-haul networks, to communicate both voice and data across their far-flung operations. A WAN differs from a LAN in that a WAN spans much greater distances (often entire countries or even the globe), has slower data rates (usually below 2 mbps), and is usually owned by several organizations (including both common carriers and the user organization). In addition, a WAN employs point-to-point transmission (except for satellites), whereas a LAN uses a multiaccess channel (such as the bus and ring). We will note some exceptions, but for the most part WANs rely on the public telephone network.

DDD and WATS.   The easiest way to set up a WAN is to rely on ordinary public telephone service.

Direct Distance Dialing (DDD) is available through the local telephone company and a long distance carrier—AT&T, MCI, Sprint, or others—and can be used for voice and data communications between any two spots served by the telephone network. Of course, the speed for data transmission is quite limited (up to 56 kbps, depending upon the modem), data error rates are relatively high, and the cost per hour is very expensive. **Wide Area Telephone Service (WATS)** is also available, in which the organization pays a monthly fee for (typically) unlimited long distance telephone service using the ordinary voice circuits. WATS has the same advantages and disadvantages as DDD, except that the cost per hour is somewhat lower, but the customer pays for WATS whether it is used or not, whereas DDD is paid for only when it is utilized. DDD may be appropriate for intermittent, limited-volume data transmission at relatively slow speeds, whereas WATS might be used for more nearly continuous, somewhat larger volumes of data to be transmitted at relatively slow speeds.

Leased Lines.   Another, often quite attractive, alternative is to lease dedicated communications lines from AT&T or another carrier. If a manufacturing company has three plants geographically separated from corporate headquarters (where the mainframe computer or large servers are located), it may make sense to lease lines from each of the three plants to headquarters. These leased lines are generally coaxial cables or microwave (sometimes fiber) of very high capacity, and they are less prone to data errors than ordinary voice lines. The leased lines are expensive, ranging from hundreds of dollars per month for distances of a few miles up to tens of thousands of dollars per month for cross-country lines.

The most common leased lines operate at a data transmission rate of 1.544 mbps and are referred to as **T-1 lines.** In order to effectively use this high data transmission rate, organizations must employ multiplexers at each end of a T-1 line to combine (or separate out) a number of data streams that are, individually, much less than 1.544 mbps.

Leased lines with capacities higher than T-1 are also available. Four T-1 lines are combined to create a T-2 trunk, with a capacity of 6.312 mbps, but T-2 trunks have largely been bypassed in favor of T-3 trunks (consisting of seven T-2s), with a data transmission capacity of nearly 45 mbps. T-3 links are

now available between major cities, although the costs are much higher than for T-1 lines. T-4 trunks also exist (made up of six T-3s), with a huge capacity of 274 mbps.

The newest and highest capacity leased lines (and also the most expensive) are fiber optic transmission lines, or SONET lines. **SONET,** which is an abbreviation for **Synchronous Optical Network,** is an ANSI (American National Standards Institute) approved standard for connecting fiber optic transmission systems. Data transmission rates for SONET lines are shown in Table 4.3. Note that the slowest SONET transmission rate (OC-1) of nearly 52 mbps is faster than the T-3 rate of 45 mbps. All of the primary links in the vBNS network shown in Figure 4.7 are SONET lines, although the spurs to the Network Access Points (NAPs) are T-3 lines. These SONET lines were originally OC-3 lines, but they were upgraded to OC-12 in 1997.

Satellite.   Satellite microwave communication is being used by an increasing number of organizations setting up a WAN. The satellite or satellites involved are owned by companies such as Loral and General Motors' Hughes Electronics, and the user organization leases a portion of the satellite's capacity. In addition, the user organization either provides its own ground stations or leases time on a carrier's ground stations, as well as communication lines to and from those ground stations. The use of KU-band transmission with relatively inexpensive VSAT ground stations is making satellite transmission very popular for organizations with many remote locations. Both Kmart and Walmart, for example, use VSAT networks

Table 4.3
SONET Circuits

SONET Level	Data Transmission Rate
OC-1	51.84 mbps
OC-3	155.52 mbps
OC-9	466.56 mbps
OC-12	622.08 mbps
OC-18	933.12 mbps
OC-24	1.244 gbps
OC-36	1.866 gbps
OC-48	2.488 gbps

Key: mbps = million bits per second
          gbps = billion bits per second

to link their thousands of stores with their corporate headquarters. V-Crest Systems, a member of the Volkswagen Group, runs a VSAT network for nine hundred Porsche, Audi, and Volkswagen dealerships throughout the United States. Through the VSAT network, V-Crest provides information services for order placement, warranty processing, parts and vehicle location, customer tracking, financing, insurance, accounting, inventory control, and service management.

Value Added Networks. With the WAN alternatives described above, the user organization is responsible for managing all aspects of the telecommunications function. Some pieces of the network (a T-1 line, satellite capacity) may be leased from a carrier, but the user must fit all the pieces together, including such details as the routing of communications, error checking and editing, and speed and format conversion of the data. If the organization wants someone else to handle these telecommunications management functions for it (for a fee, of course), then a **value added network,** or a **VAN,** is the way to go.

The VAN may use T-1 lines, earthbound microwave, or satellite microwave—but this is all transparent to the user. Assume, for example, that the user has computers in Seattle, Dallas, and Boston that need to communicate with one another. To use a particular VAN, connections from the computers to the VAN nodes in the three cities would be made via the local telephone network or a dedicated cable. The user does not care how these three VAN nodes communicate with one another, as long as the data are transmitted in a timely and error-free manner. The user is buying a service, or, alternatively, the VAN operating company is adding value to the basic network (which consists of some assortment of media and WANs) by managing the entire process so that it is transparent to the user.

A VAN is a data-only, private, nonregulated telecommunications network. Some VANs, like vBNS, serve a limited audience, whereas others are available to any organization that wishes to buy the networking service. This second type of VAN is called a public network; in the United States, these public networks are operated by private companies such as Infonet, AT&T, Tymnet, CompuServe, and IBM. In much of the rest of the world, these public networks were operated by government-owned postal, telephone, and telegraph companies (PTTs) until recently; now many of these PTTs and public networks have been priva-

tized. All of these VANs are computer-controlled, and they usually involve multiple media and multiple paths between points on the network.

VANs also employ **packet switching,** which is a store-and-forward data transmission technique. Communications sent over the VAN, or other packet-switched networks, are divided into packets of some fixed length, often 300 characters for a VAN. Control information is attached to the front and rear of this packet, and it is sent over a communications line in a single bundle. This is quite different from usual voice and data communications, where the entire end-to-end circuit is tied up for the duration of the session. With packet switching, the network is used more efficiently because packets from various users can be interspersed with one another. The computers controlling the network will route each individual packet along the appropriate path.

ISDN. Another way of implementing a WAN is an **Integrated Services Digital Network,** or **ISDN.** ISDN is an emerging set of international standards by which the public telephone network is offering extensive new telecommunications capabilities—including simultaneous transmission of both voice and data over the same line—to telephone users worldwide. So-called narrowband ISDN is now available in many areas of the world, with the areas served by ISDN growing every year. ISDN is digital communication, using the same twisted pairs already used in the present telephone network. Because the entire system is digital, modems are not required, but new ISDN telephone instruments are required that produce a digital rather than an analog signal.

ISDN capabilities are made possible by hardware and software at the local telephone company office and on the organization's premises (such as a digital PBX) that divide a single telephone line (twisted pair) into two different types of communication channels. The B, or bearer, channel transmits voice or data at rates of 64 kbps, faster than is possible using a modem. The D, or data, channel is used to send signal information to control the B channels and to carry packet-switched digital data.

Two narrowband ISDN services have been offered thus far. The basic rate offers two B channels and one 16 kbps D channel (a total data rate of 144 kbps) over a single twisted pair. Each basic rate line is capable of supporting two voice devices and six data devices, any two of which can be operating simultane-

MAYBE ISDN'S TIME IS FINALLY HERE!

Ultimately, there's no way ISDN could live up to the hype. If it did, the decade-old integrated data-and-voice service would be interconnecting corporate LANs, helping Internet addicts surf the Web, and bringing videoconferencing into every living room in America. Of course, it had to fall short of such unrealistic expectations.

What LAN administrators have figured out, however, is that deploying ISDN is an economical and efficient way to solve their dial-in headaches. "ISDN is the perfect niche between regular analog and T-1. T-1 was too much for us, analog was too little, but ISDN fit nicely between the two. It simply gave us a capability we didn't have before," says Tom Rose, scientific programming specialist at Chrysler Corp., Auburn Hills, Mich.

As the American workforce morphs from suit-wearing subway riders into a virtual population of bathrobe-clad telecommuters, ISDN is filling a necessary niche. At Chrysler, for example, before they started using ISDN, car designers had to send tapes with CAD (computer-aided design) drawings between satellite offices, designers' home offices, and Chrysler headquarters. "We've got about 20 suppliers who dial in on a regular basis and download files," says Rose, who manages 500 Ethernet LANs, with 40 workstations on each LAN. "The CAD files are about 10 to 20 megabytes each. Then there are people who dial in to our Cray supercomputer for injection-modeling software files and crash-test files. Those are 50 to 100 megs each. With ISDN's 128 kilobits per second [using both B channels], it works."

The simultaneous need for fast LAN connections by home and branch-office users and LAN managers' search for a dial-in solution—one that can handle both analog and digital calls seamlessly—is the major factor driving the ISDN market, says Michael Smith, analyst at Delran, N.J.-based market research company Datapro Information Services Group.

[Adapted from Tadjer, 1996]

Further, the D channel brings new capabilities to the network. For instance, the D channel can be used for telemetry, enabling remote control of machinery, heating, or air conditioning at the same time the B channels are being used for voice or data transmission. The D channel can also be used for single-button access to a variety of telephony features, such as call waiting and display of the calling party's number.

A number of innovative uses of ISDN have been implemented. In a customer service application, an incoming call from a customer comes in over one of the B channels. The D channel is used to automatically signal the file server to send the customer's record to the service representative's workstation over the second B channel. In a marketing application, a salesperson sends alternative specifications or designs to a potential buyer's video screen over one B channel while simultaneously talking to the buyer over the second B channel.

The developments in ISDN promise a bright future for the public telephone network. At present, all of the regional Bell operating companies (RBOCs) and many other local companies are providing local ISDN service as described above, and AT&T, Sprint, MCI, and other long distance carriers are providing long distance ISDN service. By 1997, ISDN service was available on well over 50% of the telephone lines in the United States, with coverage close to 100% in parts of the country. But ISDN service is still expensive. As an example, to obtain a basic rate ISDN line for home use in the Pacific Bell service area, the installation fee is $160 and the monthly line charge is $24.50. In addition, usage charges apply—a metered rate during the daytime and a flat rate in the evenings and at night. What advantages does this ISDN line provide? Pacific Bell lists its importance in telecommuting (working from home), the ability to share a computer screen display with another user, desktop videoconferencing, the ease of large data file transfer, and Internet access at 64 kbps, faster than an ordinary modem.

ATM.   The newest entry on the wide area network (WAN) as well as the local area network (LAN) scene is **ATM,** or **Asynchronous Transfer Mode.** ATM is based on the idea of **packet switching,** as described for VANs above. For ATM, each packet is rather small—a total of 53 bytes, including 48 bytes of data and 5 bytes of control information attached to the front and rear of the packet. ATM is a proposed

ously. The primary rate provides 23 B channels and one 64 kbps D channel (for a total data rate of 1.544 mbps) over two twisted pairs. Although not yet widely available, broadband ISDN—using fiber optic cabling—offers data transmission rates of over 150 mbps. Thus, ISDN provides a significant increase in capacity while still using the public telephone network.

telecommunications standard for broadband ISDN. The goal of ATM is to remove the distinction between LAN and WAN technology. By moving to ATM as a single international standard, all LANs and WANs will be able to work together (this is called "interoperability").

ATM doesn't really describe a line transmission technology, such as contention bus or token ring; it is a switching technology with line speeds from 1.544 mbps up to 622 mbps. ATM can be used with various line transmission technologies operating at various speeds. In brief, ATM is fast packet switching with short, fixed-length packets. Connectivity between devices is provided through a switch rather than through a shared bus or ring. (Of course, both buses and rings may be attached to the ATM switch.) At present, ATM LANs operating at 25.6 mbps over unshielded twisted pair are common, as well as LANs operating at 155 mbps over fiber optic cable. Many prognosticators believe that ATM represents the future for both LANs and WANs. ATM opens the door to much faster data transmission rates in the future, especially for WANs. With time, it seems likely that a national and international ISDN/ATM network will provide answers to the wide area telecommunications questions of many organizations.

Internet   Last but not least of the network types we will consider is the ubiquitous Internet itself. The Internet could be considered a gigantic WAN, but it is really much more than that. The **Internet** is a network of networks that use the TCP/IP protocol (to be discussed later in the chapter), with gateways (connections) to even more networks that do not use the TCP/IP protocol. By 1998, the Internet connected over 160,000 separate networks around the world. The number of users in the U.S. alone was estimated at 60 million. An incredible array of resources—both data and services—are available on the Internet, and they are drawing more users, which are drawing more resources, in a seemingly never-ending cycle.

The Internet has an interesting history, dating back to 1969 when ARPANET[5] was created by the U.S. Department of Defense to link a number of lead-

ing research universities. Ethernet LANs incorporating TCP/IP networking arrived in the early 1980s, and NSFNET was created in 1986 to link five supercomputer centers in the United States. NSFNET then served as the backbone (the underlying foundation of the network, to which other elements are attached) of the emerging Internet as scores of other networks connected to it. Originally, commercial traffic was not permitted on the Internet, but this barrier was broken in the late 1980s and the floodgates opened in the early 1990s. In 1995, the National Science Foundation withdrew all financial support for the Internet, and in fact began funding vBNS (see Figure 4.7)—which is sometimes referred to as Internet 2.

The Internet has no direct connection to the U.S. government or any other government. Authority rests with the Internet Society, a voluntary membership organization. The governing body of the society is the Internet Architecture Board, made up of all volunteers. Similarly, the Internet receives no government support now that NSF funding has ended. Users pay for their own piece of the Internet. For an individual, this usually means paying an Internet service provider (ISP) a monthly fee to be able to dial a local number and log into the Internet.

The Internet provides four basic functions: electronic mail, remote login, discussion groups, and the sharing of data resources (summarized in Table 4.4). Electronic mail was really the first "killer app" of the Internet—the first application that grabbed the attention of potential users and turned them into Internet converts. Electronic mail provides an easy-to-use, inexpensive, asynchronous means of communication to other Internet users anywhere in the world. Remote login permits a user in, say, Phoenix, to log into another machine on which she has an account in, say, Vienna, using a software program such as Telnet. Then she can work on the Vienna machine exactly as if she were there. Discussion groups are just that—Internet users who have gathered together to discuss some topic. **Usenet newsgroups** are the most organized of the discussion groups; they are essentially a set of huge electronic bulletin boards on which group members can read and post messages. A **listserv** is a mailing list such that members of the group can send a single e-mail message and have it delivered to everyone in the group. This usually works fine as long as users remember whether they are sending a message

---

5 ARPANET is a creation of the Advanced Research Projects Agency of the U.S. Department of Defense. Much of the pioneering work on networking is the result of ARPANET, and TCP/IP was originally developed as part of the ARPANET project.

Table 4.4

Internet Applications

Name of Application	Purpose of Application
Electronic mail, or e-mail	Easy-to-use, inexpensive, asynchronous means of communication to other Internet users
Usenet newsgroups	Internet discussion groups, which are essentially huge electronic bulletin boards on which group members can read and post messages
Listserv	Mailing list such that members of a group can send a single e-mail message and have it delivered to everyone in the group
File transfer protocol, or FTP	Permits users to send and receive files, including programs, over the Internet
Gopher	Menu-based tool that allows the user to search for publicly available data posted on the Internet by digging through a series of menus until the sought-after data are located
Archie	Allows the user to search the publicly available anonymous FTP sites to find the desired files
Veronica	Allows the user to search the publicly available Gopher sites using key words until the sought-after data are located
World Wide Web, or the Web	Hypertext-based tool that allows the user to traverse, or "surf," the Internet, by clicking on a link contained in one document to move to another document and so on; these links may also connect to video clips, recordings, photographs, and other images

to an individual in the group or to the entire group. Don't use the reply function in response to a listserv message unless you intend your reply to go to the entire group!

The sharing of data resources is another gigantic use of the Internet. **File transfer protocol,** or **FTP,** is a program that permits users to send and receive files, including other programs, over the Internet. For ordinary FTP use, the user needs to know the account name and password of the remote computer in order to log into it. Anonymous FTP sites have also been set up, however, which permit any Internet user to log in using "anonymous" as the account name. As a matter of courtesy (and to track accesses), most anonymous FTP sites ask that the user enter his e-mail address as the password. Once logged in, the user may transfer any files located at that anonymous FTP site. **Gopher** is a menu-based tool that allows the user to search for publicly available information posted on the Internet by digging (like a gopher) through a series of menus until you find what you want. **Archie** is a tool that allows the user to search the publicly available anonymous FTP sites worldwide to find files. And **Veronica** performs a similar function with Gopher sites, searching the publicly available Gopher sites using key words to identify the data you are after.

As we near the end of the 1990s, FTP is still popular, but Gopher, Archie, and Veronica have largely disappeared, subsumed by the tremendous capabilities of the **World Wide Web,** or **WWW,** or just the **Web.** The Web is a hypertext-based way of traversing, or "surfing" the Internet. With hypertext, any document can contain links to other documents. By clicking on the link with the computer mouse, the referenced document will be retrieved—whether it is stored on your own computer, one down the hall, or one on the other side of the world. More than this, the Web provides a graphical user interface (GUI) so that images, photographs, sound bytes, and full-motion video may be displayed on the user's screen as part of the document (provided your computer is appropriately equipped). All this material is delivered to the user's computer via the Internet. The World Wide Web is the second "killer app" of the Internet, and it has accelerated the already rapid telecommunications revolution.

To use the World Wide Web, the user's machine must have a Web browser program installed. This software package permits the machine to access a Web server, using either a dial-up telephone connection (with a modem) or a direct connection through a local network. The most popular browsers are Netscape Navigator and Microsoft Internet Explorer. When a user first logs into the Web, she is connected to a "home" server at her Internet service provider or her own organization. She can then surf the Web by clicking on hypertext links, or she can search for a particular topic using a Web crawler, or "search engine" program. Or, if she knows the address of the site she wishes to visit—this address is called the URL, or Universal Resource Locator—she can enter the address directly in her browser. For addresses she expects to visit frequently, she can establish "bookmarks" in her browser so that all she must do is click on the appropriate bookmark to establish the connection.

In the early days of the Web (say, 1992 to 1995), there was a great deal of factual information on the Web, but very little of commercial interest. Today, however, virtually every major organization and many lesser ones have a significant presence on the Web. The Web gives businesses a new way to provide information about their products and services, a new way to advertise, a new way to communicate with customers and suppliers and would-be customers and suppliers. With increasing frequency, the Web is actually being used to complete sales, particularly of products such as software that can be delivered via the Internet and of products such as books, CDs, and clothes that can be delivered via regular mail. (We will talk more about electronic commerce via the Web in Chapter 7.) The design of appealing Web pages has become an art—firms want to make sure that their pages convey the right image. Figures 4.13 and 4.14 show the home pages of two leaders in the information technology field, Microsoft and Hewlett-Packard.

An important spinoff from the success of the Internet has been the creation of **intranets** within many large organizations. An intranet is simply a network operating within an organization that employs the TCP/IP protocol. In most cases, an intranet consists of a backbone network with a number of connected LANs. Because the protocol is the same, the organization may use the same Web browser, Web crawler, and Web server software as it would use on the

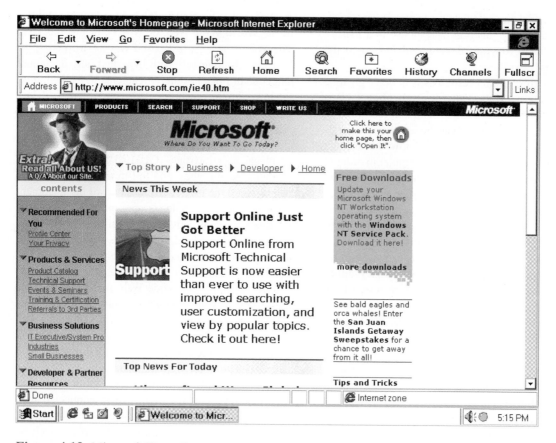

Figure 4.13 Microsoft Home Page (Reprinted with permission from Microsoft Corporation)

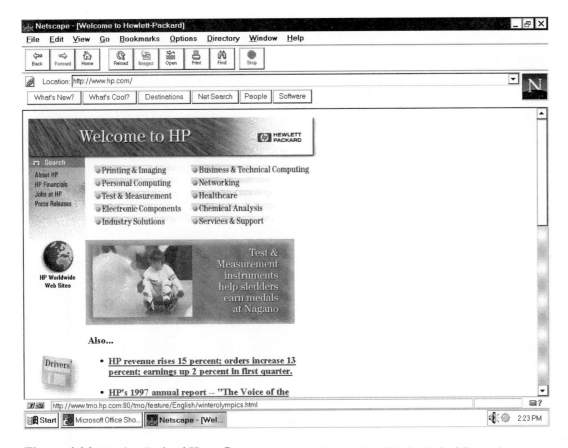

Figure 4.14 Hewlett-Packard Home Page (Reproduced with permission of Hewlett-Packard Company)

Internet; however, the intranet is not accessible from outside the organization. It may or may not be possible for people within the organization to access the Internet.

Some commentators have referred to the Internet as the "information superhighway." That is wrong, as Bill Gates, the Chief Executive Officer of Microsoft, has pointed out in his book, *The Road Ahead* (1995). The Internet is merely the precursor to the information superhighway; we are not there yet. Before we have a true information superhighway, we need gigantic increases in bandwidth, more reliability (see the box "Series of errors halts traffic on the Internet"), more security (especially for financial transactions), more accessibility by the entire population, and more applications. We are only beginning to scratch the surface of possibilities for the Internet and the information superhighway beyond.

Network Protocols

There is only one more major piece to our network puzzle. How do the various elements of these networks actually communicate with one another? The answer is by means of a **network protocol,** an agreed-upon set of rules or conventions governing communication among elements of a network, or, to be more precise, among layers or levels of a network. In order for two network elements to communicate with one another, they must both be using the same protocol. Thus, the protocol truly enables elements of the network to communicate with one another.

Without actually using the protocol label, we have already encountered several protocols. LANs, for example, have three widely accepted protocols: contention bus, token bus, and token ring. The biggest

of protocols, or rather, two sets of protocols. The International Standards Organization (ISO) has developed a model called the **OSI** or **Open Systems Interconnection Reference Model,** which deals with connecting all systems that are open for communication with other systems (i.e., systems that conform to certain minimal standards). The OSI model defines seven layers (see Figure 4.15), each of which will have its own protocol (or perhaps more than one). Happily, all major computer and telecommunications vendors—including IBM—have announced their support for the OSI model. The OSI model is only a skeleton at this point, with standard protocols in existence for some

problem with protocols is that there are too many of them (or, to look at the problem in another way, not enough acceptance of a few of them). IBM has created its own set of protocols, collectively termed Systems Network Architecture or SNA. Digital Equipment Corporation has developed DECNET as its set of protocols, and other vendors have also created their own proprietary protocols. IBM equipment and DEC equipment cannot communicate with each other unless <u>both</u> employ the same protocols—IBM's or DEC's, or perhaps another set of "open systems" protocols. The big problem involved in integrating computers and other related equipment from many vendors into a network is *standardization* so that all use the same protocols!

In the past decade, considerable progress has been made in standardization (and acceptance) of a set

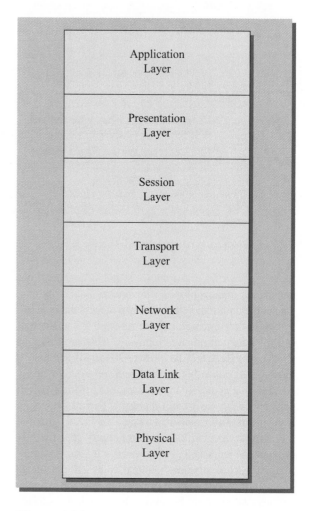

Figure 4.15 Seven Layers of the OSI Reference Model

layers (the three LAN protocols are part of the data link layer), but with only rough ideas in other layers. Thus, the OSI model is evolving, and the vendors are modifying and expanding their products to more nearly match the changing OSI model.

But the movement toward the OSI model has been slowed in the 1990s by the explosion of the role of the Internet and the creation of numerous intranets within major organizations. Both the Internet and intranets employ TCP/IP, or Transmission Control Protocol / Internet Protocol as their protocol. TCP/IP is not part of the OSI reference model, and it is a less comprehensive set of protocols than OSI, correspondingly roughly to two of the seven OSI layers. Let's briefly explore both of these important sets of protocols.

OSI Reference Model   Because of the importance of the OSI model, and because it will give us a conceptual framework to understand how communication takes place in networks, we will briefly discuss each of the layers in the OSI model and an example of how data can be transmitted using the model (see Figure 4.16). This is a very complex model because it must support many types of networks (e.g., LANs, WANs) and many types of communication (e.g., electronic mail, electronic data interchange, and executive information systems[6]).

Physical Layer.   The physical layer is concerned with transmitting bits (a string of zeros and ones) over a physical communication channel. Electrical engineers work at this level, with typical design issues involving such questions as how many volts should be used to represent a 1 and how many for a 0.

Data Link Layer.   For the data link layer to work, data must be submitted to it (by the network layer) in the form of data frames of a few hundred bytes. Then the data link adds special header and trailer data at the beginning and end of each frame, respectively, so that it can recognize the frame boundaries. The data link transmits the frames in sequence to the physical layer for actual transmittal and also processes acknowledgement frames sent back by the data link layer of the receiver and makes sure that there are no transmission errors.

Network Layer.   The network layer receives a packet of data from the transport layer and adds special header data to it to identify the route that the packet is to take to its destination. This augmented packet becomes the frame passed on to the data link layer. Thus, the primary concern of the network layer is the routing of the packets. The network layer often contains an accounting function as well in order to produce billing information.

Transport Layer   Although not illustrated by Figure 4.16, the transport layer is the first end-to-end layer encountered. In the lower layers of the OSI model, the protocols are between a sending device and its immediate neighbor, then between the neighbor and its immediate neighbor, and so on until the receiving device is reached. Starting with the transport layer and continuing through the three upper layers, the conversation is directly between the layer for the sending device and the corresponding layer for the receiving device. Thus, the upper four layers are end-to-end protocols.

The transport layer receives the communication (of whatever length) from the session layer, splits it into smaller blocks if necessary, adds special header data defining the network connection(s) to be used, passes the packet(s) to the network layer, and then checks to make sure that all the packets arrive correctly at the receiving end. If the network connection requires multiplexing for its efficient use, this is also handled by the transport layer (and in a manner transparent to the higher layers).

Session Layer.   Through the session layer, users on different machines may establish sessions between them. For most applications, the session layer is not used, but, for example, it would allow a user to log into a remote computer or to transfer a file between two computers. The session layer may provide several services to the users, including dialog control (if traffic can only move in one direction at a time) and synchronization (so that a portion of a communication received need not be retransmitted even if the network fails).

Presentation Layer.   The presentation layer, unlike the lower layers, is concerned with the information to be transmitted itself, rather than viewing it as a string of bits. The presentation layer accepts as input the communication as internally coded by the sending device and translates it into the standard

---

6 These applications and others will be explained in Chapters 5–7.

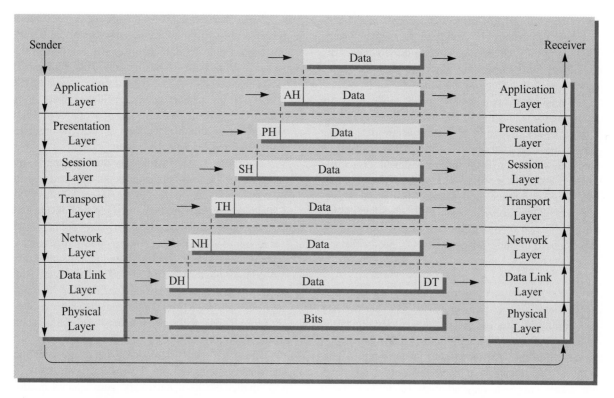

Figure 4.16 Data Transmission Based on OSI Model

representation used by the network. (The presentation layer on the receiving device reverses this process.) In addition, the data may be cryptographically encoded if it is especially sensitive. Like the layers below and above, the presentation layer adds a header to the data before sending it to the layer below.

Application Layer. The uppermost layer deals with the wide variety of communications-oriented applications that are directly visible to the user, such as electronic data interchange, file transfer, electronic mail, and factory floor control. There will always be differences across different terminals or systems, and a protocol is required for each application (usually implemented in software) to make each of these devices appear the same to the network. For a group of users to communicate using electronic mail, for example, the devices they employ must all use the same application layer/electronic mail protocol. The OSI electronic mail protocol, known as MOTIS, has gained significant acceptance.

Data Transmission Using the OSI Model. Figure 4.16 provides an illustration of data transmission based on the OSI model. The sender has some data to be transmitted to the receiver. The sender, for example, may be a manager at a workstation who wishes to transmit a query to the corporate executive information system located on a mainframe in another state. The manager types in a query, which is temporarily stored in the workstation in electronic form. When the manager hits the enter key, the query (data) is given to the application layer, which adds the application header (AH) and gives the resulting augmented data item to the presentation layer.

The presentation layer converts the item into the appropriate network code, adds a presentation header (PH), and passes it on to the session layer. The session layer may not do anything, but if it does, it will end by attaching a session header (SH) and passing the further augmented item to the transport layer. The transport layer does its work, adds a transport header, and sends the resulting packet to the network layer. The network layer in turn does its work, adds a network header (NH), and sends the resulting frame to the data link layer. The data link layer accepts the frame, adds both a header (DH) and a trailer (DT), and sends the final bit stream to the physical layer for actual transmission to the receiver.

When the bit stream reaches the receiver, the various headers (and trailer) are stripped off one at a time as the communication moves up through the seven layers until only the original query arrives at the receiver, which in our example is a mainframe computer. Perhaps the easiest way to understand this entire process is that the original data go through a multilevel translation process (which is really much more than translation), with each layer acting as if it were directly communicating with the corresponding receiving layer. Most important, the entire process should take place in a device/system independent way that is totally transparent to the user.

TCP/IP   **TCP/IP, or Transmission Control Protocol/Internet Protocol,** is not part of the OSI reference model, although it roughly corresponds to the network and transport layers. TCP/IP is used in several private VAN networks, including vBNS, as well as in many versions of the UNIX operating system and in Windows NT. Most importantly, TCP/IP is the protocol used on the worldwide Internet and on numerous intranets operating within organizations. Thus TCP/IP, not OSI, has become the *de facto* standard protocol for networking around the world. Nevertheless, TCP/IP is only a partial set of protocols, not a fully developed model. TCP/IP appears to represent only a step towards the eventual development of a worldwide accepted suite of networking protocols. Many experts believe that TCP/IP and the network and transport layers of OSI will evolve toward one another and will eventually merge.

The IP portion of the TCP/IP protocol corresponds roughly to the network layer of the seven-layer model, and the TCP portion corresponds approximately to the transport layer. TCP/IP accepts messages of any length, breaks them into pieces less than 64,000 bytes, sends the pieces to the designated receiver, and makes sure that the pieces are correctly delivered and are placed in the right order (because they may arrive out of sequence). TCP/IP does not know the path the pieces will take, and it assumes that communication will be unreliable—thus, substantial error-checking capabilities are built into TCP/IP itself to ensure reliability.

SNA   The OSI reference model and TCP/IP clearly represent the future in terms of network protocols, as indicated above. For the present, however, IBM's **Systems Network Architecture (SNA)** remains an important standard. SNA, like OSI, is really a suite or grouping of protocols. SNA was created by IBM to allow its customers to construct their own private networks. In the original 1974 version of SNA, only a simple tree topology emanating from a single mainframe was permitted. By 1985, however, arbitrary topologies of mainframes, minicomputers, and LANS were supported.

SNA is a very complicated suite of protocols because it was designed to support the incredible variety of IBM communication products, teleprocessing access methods, and data link protocols that existed before SNA. We do not need to explore the details of these protocols, but it may be useful to note that the newer OSI model was patterned after SNA in several ways: Both employ the concept of layering, have seven layers, and incorporate essentially the same functions. The contents of the two sets of layers, however, are quite different, especially in the middle three layers (called the network, transport, and session layers in OSI). Although IBM still supports SNA, it also supports both TCP/IP and elements of the OSI model under the umbrella of its decade-old **Systems Application Architecture (SAA),** which is really a philosophy rather than a set of protocols.

Other Protocols   There are a number of other network protocols, but only one of these is important enough to merit special mention. Most value added networks (VANs) employ the **X.25 protocol** for the physical, data link, and network layers of the seven-layer model. X.25 has been formally adopted by the ISO as part of the OSI model. Because VANs are based on packet switching, some sources use X.25 networks and packet-switching networks interchangeably, although there are certainly other ways to implement packet switching besides X.25.

We now have all the pieces of the network puzzle. Network protocols provide the means by which various elements of telecommunications networks can communicate with one another. Thus, networks consist of physical media, arranged according to some topology, in a particular type of network, with communication throughout the network permitted through the use of particular protocols.

THE EXPLODING ROLE OF TELECOMMUNICATIONS AND NETWORKING

We have already stressed the critical role of telecommunications and networking several times, but to make the point even stronger, we will discuss how the role of telecommunications and networking is exploding in organizations today, particularly in medium and large firms and agencies. In fact, some authorities suggest that the network (not the computer) is the most critical and most important information technology of the future. To illustrate this explosion, we will consider four areas of operation in which telecommunications networks are of critical and growing importance.

On-Line Operations

The dominant activities of many organizations have now been placed on-line to the computer via a network. For banks and other financial institutions, most teller stations (as well as automated teller machines) are now on-line. Tellers directly update your account when you cash a check or when you make a deposit. The bank does not care what branch in what city you use, because your account is always up-to-date. Not quite as obviously, insurance companies have much of their home office and branch office activities on-line. When an insurance claim is made or paid, when a premium is paid, or when a change is made to a policy, those activities are entered on-line to the insurance company computer. These and other financial institutions (such as brokerage firms and international banks) simply could not operate as they do without telecommunications networks.

The computerized reservations systems of the major airlines are another example of an indispensable use of on-line systems. Virtually all travel agencies in the United States are now on-line. Computerized reservation systems constitute the core marketing strategy of the major airlines. The major airlines introduce new versions of their reservation systems every few years, with significant new features built into each revision. For example, Delta, United, and American Airlines now provide LANs to link travel agency microcomputers to permit the agencies to integrate a wide variety of travel agency management applications with reservations processing. All this activity makes sense when one considers that the airlines make more money on their reservation systems, per dollar spent, than they make flying passengers. Historically, the airlines make 8 to 10 percent profit overall in a good quarter, while the reservation systems—through user fees and increased sales—make as much as 20 percent profit.

In the late 1990s, the airlines and private vendors have moved a step further by providing users the capabilities to make their own reservations on-line, thus bypassing travel agents entirely. United Airlines will send the user (at no charge) the disks to load its United Connection client software on the user's machine, and then the user dials into the United network to make reservations. Both American Airlines' Travelocity (actually a product of SABRE Group Holdings, which has been spun off from American) and Microsoft Expedia use the World Wide Web directly, rather than any special client software. To access Travelocity, go to http://www.travelocity.com, and to use Expedia go to http://www.expedia.com.

Connectivity

Connectivity is a very popular buzzword among major U.S. and international corporations. Many organizations now provide every managerial and professional employee with a personal workstation (usually a microcomputer), and these workstations are connected to a network structure (often an intranet) so that each of these employees has access to every person and every system with which he might conceivably need to interact.

Connectivity to persons and organizations outside the firm is also important. American Hospital Supply Corporation created a strategic advantage by providing connectivity with the hospitals it served. Chrysler Corporation has installed a system to tie its dealers to the corporation so that deviations from expected sales are spotted quickly. All the automobile manufacturers are stressing connectivity with their suppliers so that they can adjust orders efficiently. Thus, connectivity throughout the customer-manufacturer-supplier chain is a critical element.

Electronic Data Interchange and Electronic Commerce

Electronic data interchange, or **EDI,** will be covered more completely in Chapter 7, but it is certainly part of the exploding role of networking. EDI is a set of standards and hardware and software technology that permits business documents (such as purchase orders, invoices, and price lists) to be transferred electronically between computers in separate organizations. For the most part, the transmission of EDI documents takes place over public value added networks, although the Internet is also used. The automobile industry is further along in introducing EDI than most other industries, but many firms and industries are moving to implement this exciting technology.

Electronic commerce is a broad term that incorporates any use of telecommunications and networking to conduct commercial activities. EDI is part of electronic commerce, but the most explosive electronic commerce area involves commerce over the World Wide Web. Electronic commerce includes on-line catalogs, on-line ordering, on-line payment for goods and services, and sometimes on-line delivery of products. A number of virtual shopping malls have been set up on the Web, and an incredible array of products are offered. One interesting and colorful electronic commerce venture is described in the sidebar "Virtual Florist." Electronic commerce over the Web is burgeoning, and there isn't any end in sight. The authors of this book, for example, have purchased software on the Web and immediately downloaded it; registered on-line for a conference; and purchased books on the Web. Shopping on the Web is still a new experience for most of us, but it will become commonplace as we move into the 21st Century.

Marketing

In addition to electronic commerce, telecommunications is being used for many exciting projects in the

---

VIRTUAL FLORIST

The Virtual Florist is an Internet Web site operated by the Internet Florist Association, Minneapolis/St. Paul, Minnesota. The URL is http://www.virtualflorist.com. The home page for the Virtual Florist is decorated with several attractive bouquets of flowers and has three primary segments: Send a FREE Virtual Flower Bouquet, Send a REAL Flower Bouquet, and PICK UP Your Virtual Flower Bouquet. You may send anyone a virtual bouquet (as long as they have an electronic mail address), and it really is free! The user picks out the appropriate virtual bouquet from among a number of screen displays (all beautiful), and an e-mail message is sent to the lucky person who is to receive the bouquet. Then the recipient "picks up" the bouquet from the Virtual Florist Web site and it is displayed on his/her screen. After two weeks, the virtual bouquet and all records are destroyed. Of course, what the Virtual Florist wants the user to do is return to this site when a real bouquet is to be sent. Clicking on "Send a REAL Flower Bouquet" gets the user to the Internet Florist home page, and here the wide floral selection includes roses, blooming plants, fresh arrangements, and balloons as well as flowers for particular occasions such as a birthday, anniversary, or birth of a baby. The user may order on-line via the Web, or may call an 800 telephone number. In most cases, same-day delivery (excluding Sundays and holidays) is available anywhere in the U.S. or Canada if the order is submitted by 11:00 a.m. in the time zone of the delivery.

[Adapted from Virtual Florist Web site, 1997]

---

marketing area. Two examples are the use of laptop microcomputers by salespersons and the use of telecommunications for telemarketing and customer support. All business organizations sell products and services, although the distribution channels vary widely. The sales function is often performed either by sales representatives employed by the firm or by independent agents aligned with the firm (e.g., an insurance agent). In either case, telecommunications is being widely used to provide support for the sales personnel.

This sales support is not always as direct as the two examples above. Such support often takes the form of on-line information describing product or service characteristics and availability. This up-to-the-minute information makes the sales representative or agent more competitive and should increase profitability of the organization (as well as increasing the chances of retaining productive sales personnel). The importance of this instantaneous information is apparent for a St. Louis-based Merrill Lynch stockbroker talking to a client who is considering the purchase of a stock on the New York Stock Exchange, but it is almost as critical for a parts clerk at a Honda dealership in Oregon dealing with a disgruntled customer. The parts clerk can use his networked computer to check the availability of a needed part in ten Honda regional warehouses in the United States and can immediately place the order from the closest warehouse that has the part.

The Telecommunications Industry

We would like to discuss the telecommunications component of the computer/communications industry in this section, but the statistics on such a broad industrial grouping as the computer/communications industry are not readily available. In fact, statistics on the entire telecommunications industry (including both carriers and equipment vendors) are not readily available either. Estimates for the entire industry could be determined for the United States, but they would be considerably more difficult to obtain for the rest of the world, where many of the carriers are still government-owned and operated. We are forced to pursue our consideration of the telecommunications industry in a more segmented fashion.

There are three major segments of the telecommunications industry (or the telecommunications segment of the computer/communications industry): (a) carriers, who own or lease the physical plant (cabling, satellites, and so forth) and sell the service of transmitting communications from one location to another; (b) equipment vendors, who manufacture and sell a wide range of telecommunications-related equipment, including LANs, digital PBXs, multiplexers, and modems; and (c) service providers, who operate networks and deliver services through the network or provide access to or services via the Internet. This third segment includes value-added network (VAN) providers, America On-Line, Microsoft Network, and a wide variety of Internet service providers (ISPs).

As an important historical footnote, the entire complexion of the telecommunications industry changed in 1984 with the breakup of AT&T into the long-distance telephone and equipment-centered AT&T and the regional Bell operating companies (RBOCs). Although the various pieces that resulted from the divestiture were still large, there was no longer a single monolithic entity in control of most telecommunications in the United States. Just before the AT&T breakup, technological developments in long-haul communications (microwave, satellites, and fiber optics) made economically feasible the development of long distance networks to compete with those of AT&T. Thus came the rise of MCI, Sprint, and other long distance carriers. Furthermore, court decisions and management policies served to effectively split AT&T (and each of the regional operating companies) into two businesses—regulated and nonregulated. The original carrier portion of the business was still regulated, but the nonregulated portion could now compete actively in the computer/communications equipment market. AT&T, and to a lesser extent the operating companies, became major players as equipment vendors.

The 1984 AT&T divestiture also had significant managerial implications for the telecommunications function in a user organization. Prior to 1984 the telecommunications manager had a relatively easy job, dealing with AT&T for almost all of his telecommunications needs and receiving high quality, reliable service for a regulated price. After divestiture, the job got much tougher. The manager now has to deal with a variety of carriers and equipment vendors (often including AT&T), and the manager has the responsibility to make sure that all the various pieces fit together.

The last few years of the 1990s and the beginning of the next century will bring even further change, not all of it predictable, to the telecommunications industry. In much of the world, the government-owned telephone carriers are being shifted to private ownership. In the United States, the Telecommunications Reform Act of 1996 will mean increasing competition for telephone service (both voice and data). To a great extent, everything is now up for grabs: Within limits specified by the Act, the local telephone companies may enter the long distance market and perhaps the cable television market; the cable television operators may enter the local and long distance telephone markets; and the long distance telephone companies may enter the local service market and perhaps the cable television market. Furthermore, totally new players are about to enter the telephone market based on the deployment and use of a significant number of low- and medium-altitude earth satellites. For example, the Iridium system (backed by Motorola) will employ 66 satellites 400 to 700 miles above the earth. The Iridium satellites should be deployed by 1999, and Iridium expects to offer go-anywhere global phone service at rates from $1 to $3 per minute. These are exciting—and nerve-racking—times for companies in the broadly defined telecommunications industry.

To provide a rough picture of the major players in the U. S. telecommunications industry, the top telecommunications companies in sales of equipment and services, according to *Business Week*'s Corporate Scoreboard for calendar year 1997, are listed in Table 4.5. The number two company on the list, Lucent Technologies, is newly independent, having been spun off as the equipment manufacturing and sales arm of AT&T. Please note that for MCI, Sprint, and many of the other entries in this table, the services component (long distance and/or cellular) dominates the equipment component. Table 4.6 lists the top telephone companies (local service) according to *Business Week*.

Table 4.5

Top Ten Firms in Telecommunications: Equipment and Services, United States

Company	Revenue (millions)
AT&T	$51,319.0
Lucent Technologies	27,146.0
MCI Communications	19,653.0
Sprint	14,873.9
Airtouch Communications	3,594.0
DSC Communications	1,575.5
Telephone & Data Systems	1,471.5
Excel Communications	1,454.4
Scientific-Atlanta	1,213.4
Tellabs	1,203.5

SOURCE: March 2, 1998 issue of *Business Week* by special permission © 1998 McGraw-Hill Companies.

Table 4.6

Top Ten Firms in Telecommunications: Telephone Companies, United States

Company	Revenue (millions)
Bell Atlantic	$30,193.9
SBC Communications	24,856.0
GTE	23,260.0
BellSouth	20,561.0
Ameritech	15,998.0
U.S. West Communications	10,319.0
Alltel	3,263.6
Frontier	2,352.9
Southern New England Telecommunications	2,022.3
Cincinnati Bell	1,756.8

SOURCE: March 2, 1998 issue of *Business Week* by special permission © 1998 McGraw-Hill Companies.

THE TELECOM REVOLUTION

Outside the boardrooms of telecom's giants, innovation is sweeping the wired and wireless world—bubbling up from the bottom. Hundreds of alternative carriers and nimble startups are leaping head-first into the newly deregulated environment. Pioneers such as Wildfire Communications, Lucent Technologies, Dialogic, and VDONet are the new names to watch.

Their holy grail: to unite PCs, phone, e-mail, fax, and video into a seamless fabric. They are designing software that sends phone calls around the world on the Internet so cheaply it's like dialing your cousin across town. And they're offering high-quality videoconferencing systems that make it as easy to do a meeting on top of a mountain as in the company cafeteria. "Last year was year 1 of a 15-year revolution," says Joseph S. Kraemer, a vice-president at consulting group A. T. Kearney in Rosslyn, Va. "We're about to jam the equivalent of the 100-year Industrial Revolution into the next 15 years."

[Reinhardt, Elstrom, and Judge, 1997]

Neither list contains any real surprises, with the equipment and services list dominated by AT&T, Lucent Technologies, MCI, and Sprint (in that order) and the telephone companies list dominated by GTE and the RBOCs. In the hotly contested long distance market, AT&T's market share is just over 50 percent, compared to about 20 percent for second-place MCI.

For a closer look at the equipment vendor segment of the telecommunications industry, we shall rely on the statistics gathered by *Datamation* (1997).

Datamation calls the relevant category data communications, or datacom for short, and it explicitly includes the global sales of communications processors, digital PBXs, multiplexers, routers, gateways, modems, and facsimile machines but excludes central office telephone switches and analog PBXs as well as data transmission services. Thus, the *Datamation* figures are not quite as inclusive for communications equipment as we would prefer, but they should provide a reasonable overall picture of this segment of the industry.

In 1996 (the last complete year for which data are available), *Datamation* estimated the global data communications revenues of the world's top 100 information systems (IS) companies as $40.0 billion, or 8.0 percent of the total IS revenue of these 100 firms. Table 4.7 lists the top ten firms in data communications, the countries in which they are based, and their revenue in millions of dollars.

These top 10 firms are an interesting set. Eight of them are American, up from four in 1992 and only two (IBM and AT&T, the "predecessor" to Lucent Technologies) in 1989. Both NTT Data and Matsushita are based in Japan. For four of these top ten—Cisco Systems, 3Com, U.S. Robotics, and Bay Networks—data communications is their only business. By contrast, for computer vendors IBM and Hewlett-Packard data communications represents only 5 percent of their revenue. For others in the top ten, data communications varies between a low of 24 percent of revenue (Matsushita) to a high of 85 percent of revenue (Lucent Technologies). The rest of the world is accustomed to American leadership in the hardware, software, and services segment of the information systems industry, but the growing American dominance in telecommunications represents a trend in the 1990s that may be worrisome to some observers.

In addition to the three primary segments (carriers, equipment vendors, and service providers), there are other smaller but important segments of the broadly defined industry: the manufacture and sale of twisted pair, coaxial, and fiber optic cabling; the installation of cabling, microwave, and satellite stations; and the development of standards and software for telecommunications.

Table 4.7

Top Ten Firms in Data Communications Sector of Information Systems Industry, World

Company	Country	Revenue (millions)
Cisco Systems	U.S.	$5,406.4
IBM	U.S.	3,797.4
Lucent Technologies	U.S.	3,400.0
NTT Data	Japan	3,300.0
3Com	U.S.	2,796.7
U.S. Robotics	U.S.	2,258.1
Bay Networks	U.S.	2,094.3
Hewlett-Packard	U.S.	1,569.9
Matsushita	Japan	1,538.5
Motorola	U.S.	1,446.2

SOURCE: *DATAMATION* 43 (July 1997): 71.

SUMMARY

The telecommunications and networking area has existed for considerably longer than computer hardware and software, but the developments in all three areas have merged in the past several years to put more emphasis on telecommunications than ever before. The decade of the 1990s may well become known as the era of networking. Networks provide enhanced communication to organizations and individuals, as well as permit the sharing of resources and data. They are also essential to implement distributed data processing and client/server systems. The exploding role of telecommunications and networking is evident in many organizational activities, including on-line operations, EDI, and electronic commerce. There is an intense desire to improve organizational communications through universal connectivity. A communications revolution is underway, with networking—and particularly the Internet—at the heart of it.

The technology of telecommunications and networking is extremely complex, perhaps even more so than computer hardware and software. By concentrating on a number of key elements, we have attempted to develop a managerial-level understanding of networks. Communication signals may be either analog or digital. It is easier to transmit data digitally, and there is a concerted movement toward digital transmission today. Networks employ a variety of transmission media (such as coaxial and fiber optic cable) and are configured in various topologies (such as rings and trees). Major network types include computer telecommunications networks, emanating from a mainframe computer; digital PBX networks for both voice and data; local area networks for high-speed communication within a restricted area; backbone networks to connect LANs together, and possibly to connect to WANs and the Internet; wide area networks for lower-speed communication over a long haul; and the worldwide Internet. The Internet, and especially the World Wide Web, have been front-page news the past few years as the world is becoming "wired." WANs and the Internet are highly dependent upon facilities owned and operated by the telephone companies and other carriers. To enable the devices attached to any type of network to communicate with one another, protocols (or rules of operation) have to be agreed upon. Whereas the success of the Internet has led to the acceptance of TCP/IP as the *de facto* networking protocol for the present, there is also general movement towards the establishment and acceptance of a suite of protocols known as the OSI model.

This marks the end of the three-chapter technology component of this book. We have tried very hard to cover only the technology that you as a manager need to know. Whatever your personal managerial career involves, you are likely to be working both directly and indirectly with hardware, software, and telecommunications. Knowledge of information technology is essential for understanding its present and potential impact on your organization and your job.

these media has the fastest transmission speed? The slowest transmission speed?

5. Describe the similarity between the bus and the ring topology; then describe the similarity between the star and the tree topology.

6. Identify the following acronyms or initials:

   LAN   WATS   PBX
   WAN   FTP   ISDN
   VAN   FDDI   SONET

7. Explain how packet switching works. Why is packet switching important?

8. What is the Internet? What is an intranet? How are they related?

9. What is the World Wide Web, and how does it relate to the Internet?

10. In addition to the OSI model, other important protocols include TCP/IP, SNA, and X.25. In one or two sentences per protocol, tell what these names stand for (if anything) and describe the basic purposes of these three protocols.

11. Name the top firm in the world (in terms of market share) in the data communications sector of the information systems industry (as defined by *Datamation*). Also name three other firms in the top ten. In what country are the majority of the top ten firms based?

12. Considering the telecommunications industry in the U.S. as defined by *Business Week,* name three of the top firms in the equipment and services segment, and name three of the top firms in the telephone companies segment.

REVIEW QUESTIONS

1. What are the primary reasons for networking among computers and computer-related devices?

2. Explain the difference between analog and digital signals. Is the trend towards more use of (a) analog or (b) digital signals in the future?

3. What is a modem? When and why are modems necessary?

4. List the primary types of physical media in use in telecommunications networks today. Which of

DISCUSSION QUESTIONS

1. Review Question 2 refers to the trend toward more digital (rather than analog) communication. In your judgment, what are the primary causes of this trend?

2. Discuss the advantages and disadvantages of the three primary types of local area networks—contention bus, token bus, and token ring.

3. A PBX network is often viewed as an alternative to a local area network. What are the advantages

and disadvantages of a PBX network vis-a-vis a local area network?

4. As noted in the chapter, the most common transmission medium is the twisted pair. Why is this likely to continue to be true?

5. List the seven layers of the OSI reference model, and give a description of the role of each layer in one or two sentences.

6. Why is the idea of a standard network protocol, such as the OSI reference model, important? What are the advantages and disadvantages of developing a single standard protocol?

7. Has the popularity of the Internet and the related adoption of TCP/IP by many organizations and networks helped or hindered the movement towards a single standard protocol such as OSI? Why?

8. Find out what types of computer networks are used at your present organization (either the university at which you are taking this course or the company for whom you work). Does your organization have an intranet? Does your organization have one or more LANs, either operating independently or linked together? What types of LANs? Does your organization operate a WAN? Is your organization linked to the Internet? Speculate as to why your organization has developed this particular network structure.

9. Consider a large company with which you are somewhat familiar (because of your own work experience, a parent's work experience, a friend's work experience, or your study of the company). Use your imagination to suggest new ways in which the Internet could be used in this company.

10. The current status of the telecommunications industry was described near the end of this chapter. Using your personal crystal ball (and the knowledge you have picked up from reading the business news and from other classes), speculate on likely important future trends in the telecommunications industry. What firms do you think are likely to do well over the next decade? Which firms may stumble? What new developments may reshape the industry?

11. Update Table 4.5 (telecommunications equipment and services in the United States) for the most recent year for which data are available. What

changes have occurred among the top ten players, both in terms of position within the top ten and relative total sales? Why have these changes occurred?

12. Update Table 4.6 (telephone companies in the United States) for the most recent year for which data are available. What changes have occurred among the top ten players, both in terms of position within the top ten and relative total sales? Why have these changes occurred?

13. Update Table 4.7 (data communications sector of worldwide information systems industry) for the most recent year for which data are available. What changes have occurred among the top ten players, both in terms of position within the top ten and relative total sales? Why have these changes occurred?

14. Consider a particular small business with which you are familiar (as a customer, as a current or former employee, as a relative of the owner). Describe the current telecommunications employed by the business (every business uses a telephone). In what ways might telecommunications and networking be used to improve the profitability of this business? Consider, as appropriate, such ideas as the use of facsimile communication, telemarketing, enhanced communication through an in-house local area network, an Internet home page, and WATS.

REFERENCES

1998. "Corporate scoreboard." *Business Week* (March 2): 134.

Conlon, Theresa. 1990. "Mobile networks keep transportation rolling." *MIS Week* 11 (February 12): 1, 17, 20.

Fitzgerald, Jerry, and Alan Dennis. 1996. *Business Data Communications and Networking,* 5th ed. New York: John Wiley & Sons, Inc.

Gates, Bill. 1995. *The Road Ahead.* New York: Viking Penguin.

Gross, Neil. 1997. "The race to rewire corporate America." *Business Week* (April 7): 78–79.

Gross, Neil. 1997. "Netspeak for dummies." *Business Week* (April 28): 84–85.

Reinhardt, Andy, Peter Elstrom, and Paul Judge. 1997. "Zooming down the I-way." *Business Week* (April 7): 76–87.

Schine, Eric, Peter Elstrom, Amy Barrett, Gail Edmondson, and Michael Shari. 1997. "The satellite business blasts off." *Business Week* (January 27): 62–70.

Schoenung, Michelle. 1997. "IT chokes on network constraints." *Datamation* 43 (July): 71.

Tadjer, Rivka. 1996. "Remote access—dial-up darling—at long last, LAN managers and vendors are learning to love ISDN." *CKW* (March 25), Issue 602, http://www.techweb.com.

Tanenbaum, Andrew S. 1988. *Computer Networks.* 2nd ed. Englewood Cliffs, N. J.: Prentice-Hall.

Virtual Florist. 1997. "Virtual Florist" Web page, http://www.virtualflorist.com.

Washington Post. 1997. "Series of errors halts traffic on the Internet." Appeared in *The Herald-Times,* Bloomington, Indiana (July 19): C3.

Wylie, Margie. 1993. "Will networks kill the corporation?" *Network World* 10 (January 11): S9, S12.

IMT Custom Machine Company, Inc.: Selection of a Hardware Platform

From his second-story executive office, Darrin Young watched a late summer storm coming from the west across the northern Indiana cornfields. He knew how helpful the rain would be for the farmers and for his dry lawn. Turning to a growing stack of paperwork, he also thought of the dark cloud hanging over his information systems (IS) area. Something had to be done. Committee after committee had analyzed various systems needs and proposed solutions. Young's faith in his staff usually led him to approve the recommendations. But some "glitch" always seemed to pop up and put the solution on hold. "Something was missing; there is no real direction here —we don't know where we want to be or how to get there," he thought to himself. "We have to get our arms around our information systems once and for all."

Young was a vice president and division manager in a subsidiary company of International Machine and Tool—USA (IMT-USA). Building multimillion-dollar, large custom production machines for the automotive industry and delivering them on time while making a profit was the primary goal of Young's division. Young had two factories under his charge, which built about 150 machines per year. His division also included a third unit that made smaller machined parts for the two factories. A service and spare parts group within the division supported the repair and maintenance business for any custom machine, including those built by IMT's competi-

tion. The Fort Wayne, Indiana plant, where Young was located, was the largest custom machine factory in North America. As shown in Exhibit 1, Young had an executive staff and two plant managers reporting to him.

Young recognized that he had selected an unconventional strategy to get to the heart of his division's IS problems when he called Charles Browning into his office on September 3, 1996. Browning was an experienced staff engineer with an extensive scientific computing background who was finishing his MBA. Browning reported to the development engineering manager at the Fort Wayne plant. Young explained his concerns to Browning and commissioned him to "survey the big IS picture and give me three basic directional options that will satisfy our IS needs. Report your findings in six weeks. I plan to review the findings with you and incorporate one of the alternatives into my business plan for 1997." Young made it clear to Browning that he wanted the true picture. He further stated that, "there should be no limits on the type of recommendations you provide, Charlie." By using Browning, Young hoped to cut through the layers of management that may have been filtering out the root causes of IMT's IS problems.

Background

The Custom Machine Industry

Exhibit 2 summarizes the production capacity for U.S. suppliers of custom production machines for the automotive industry. The graph shows increasing production capacity additions until the 1974 Arab oil embargo, when Americans began a long-term trend toward energy conservation. Excess production capacity suddenly became a

This case was written by Christopher L. Brooks, Indiana University Executive MBA Alumnus, under the direction of Professor Daniel W. DeHayes as the basis for class discussion rather than to illustrate either effective or ineffective handling of an administrative situation. Copyright © 1997 Daniel W. DeHayes.

EXHIBIT 1
Organization Chart
IMT Custom Machine Company, Inc.

reality to the custom machine industry. Underutilized plants were targets for closing, and plans for scores of new plant additions were canceled. As the U.S.-based automobile makers' market share declined, resulting demand decreases rippled through to the U.S. custom machine industry. Annual capacity additions declined after 1974. By the 1990s, they had fallen below the level of the early 1960s.

The industry slowdown caused Williamson Machines and Engineering Corporation (WILMEC), which held about 30 percent of the market, to close its "medium horizontal"-type machine factory in Cleveland, Ohio, in 1985 and to move medium horizontal production capability to its one remaining custom machine factory in

Fort Wayne, Indiana. The Fort Wayne facility was constructed in the mid-1960s specifically to manufacture a similar, but technically different, type of custom machine called a "large vertical."

In 1990, General Engineering, Inc., which in previous years had been an equal market rival to WILMEC, abandoned its custom machine business by closing its Detroit, Michigan, plant. General Engineering (GE) sold its technology to WILMEC, and GE's production equipment was moved to WILMEC's Fort Wayne plant. The result of WILMEC's technology acquisition from GE was that a third, and very different, technology called "large horizontal" was also manufactured in Fort Wayne. At this time, WILMEC also expanded its custom

EXHIBIT 2

The U.S. Custom Machine Industry Production Capacity Additions from 1966–1995
IMT Custom Machine Company, Inc.

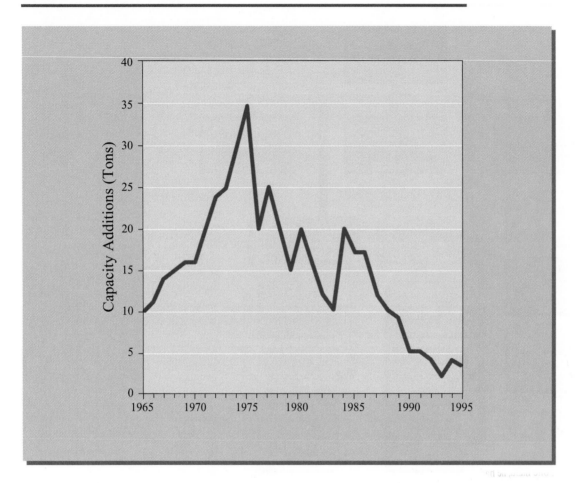

machine reconditioning operation in Chicago, Illinois, to handle the assembly of one-third of its medium horizontal machines. Fort Wayne continued to produce all three machine types: large horizontal, large vertical, and medium horizontal.

In late 1991, WILMEC refocused its strategy away from the automotive industry into various service industries. WILMEC sold all of its custom machine engineering, manufacturing, and sales operations to International Machine and Tool (IMT) of Bonn, Germany, in mid-1993. IMT was itself the result of a 1987 merger between Europe's two largest machine manufacturers—International Machine (English translation) of Germany, and Tools of Commerce (English translation) of Italy.

Numerous plant closings and shakeups had rippled through Europe as well as the U.S. in the late 1980s.

By 1995, the production capacity for custom machines in the U.S. market had nearly stabilized at the level of demand. A significant increase in demand would have caused capacity problems and resulted in delayed deliveries. Some forecasts suggested that the custom machine industry might return to a robust building program by the late 1990s.

International Machine and Tool
International Machine and Tool used a matrix style organization throughout its operations that was modeled after the structure of other large, European-based global

companies. Dr. Wilhelm Schlein, chairman of IMT, summarized the organization as "a federation of national companies with a global coordination center—a distributed organization which has many homes." Schlein's strategy for building a decentralized, multidomestic enterprise was critical to achieving IMT's goal to "Think globally, act locally."

One side of IMT's matrix organization was country-based. Each country manager (president of the national holding company) was responsible for financial targets for all products and services in that country. Country presidents coordinated synergistic relationships across IMT operations within the country (e.g., distribution and service networks). They were also responsible for maintaining relationships with national government officials.

The second side of IMT's matrix was technology-based (product classes) and reported through a separate transnational technology management group, called a business group (BG). The mission of each BG was to support shared knowledge and operations among many international factories. BG leaders served as business strategists who set global "rules of the game" and then let local managers pilot the execution.

In early 1996, IMT had eight international custom machine factories; two were located in the United States. The U.S. represented nearly one-half of IMT's global capacity. The combined capacity of the Chicago and Fort Wayne plants was larger by far than that of any of the other countries.

Darrin Young

Darrin Young reported to two managers in the matrix—the U.S. country manager and a Custom Machine BG manager. Young often felt the pressure of conflicting goals. On one hand, he had to increase return on assets to support the U.S. country manager. At the same time, he was encouraged to maintain a leading technology position by the BG head. As was true for all custom machine factories, Young's division paid about 1 percent of sales to the BG for global R&D projects.

With over thirty years of custom machine engineering experience, Young was widely known and highly respected throughout the industry. While working for WILMEC, he worked his way up through numerous engineering and manufacturing management positions. He had always been active in the industry by chairing and working on technical committees of various professional associations. Young's personal use of a computer was limited to browsing the Internet from home. He felt that his daily schedule at work had made it impossible to use the personal computer on his desk.

In 1993, Young was appointed vice president of IMT Custom Machines Company, Inc. (CMCI), the newly created IMT subsidiary in the United States. On the country side of the matrix, CMCI reported through the IMT-USA holding company in New York, which in turn reported to IMT's world headquarters in Bonn. On the BG side of the matrix, Young reported to the managing director of the Custom Machine BG. The headquarters for the business group was in Milan, Italy.

Shortly after taking the job, Young and other division managers worked with the IMT-USA president to develop mission, principles, and vision statements. The statements, applying to all IMT-USA companies, appear in Exhibit 3; they were taken from a presentation by the IMT-USA president on March 26, 1994.

The Fort Wayne Plant

The work environment at the Fort Wayne plant from 1978 to 1993 was dynamic, to say the least. The plant transitioned from a busy single-product, focused factory to a factory that was nearly closed (due to a lack of orders) and employed only a few hundred workers. It then evolved into a facility that supported three technically different products (large horizontal, large vertical, and medium horizontal custom machines), that had originated from three different factories with three different engineering design systems. In 1996, IMT's Fort Wayne facility was producing near optimal capacity and was fully staffed with about 1,200 employees.

From 1988 to 1990, all of the engineering and marketing operations for the Fort Wayne and Chicago plants were located in Cleveland, Ohio (200 miles from Fort Wayne and 350 from Chicago). In mid-1990, IMT closed the Cleveland site and transferred the engineering and marketing staffs to either Fort Wayne or Chicago.

As the Fort Wayne plant evolved to support multiple product lines, numerous informal procedures emerged to handle day-to-day situations. These undocumented processes worked despite the incompatibilities among the three different technologies, which used three separate drafting systems as well as unique manufacturing processes. Very little capital had been invested to upgrade the operations during the last several years of WILMEC's ownership. Not until IMT had completed the purchase of the technology and the factories in 1993 had a major capital upgrade program even been considered. Low margin and capital budget limits had prevented significant upgrades.

In early 1994 the plant was reorganized into three product lines. Each of the three machine types was considered a separate product line and profit center. CMCI's

EXHIBIT 3
IMT-USA Mission, Guiding Principles,
and Vision Statements
IMT Custom Machine Company, Inc.

The following was taken from a presentation given by IMT-USA President on March 26, 1994

Mission
- Serve U.S. customers to their individual needs and total satisfaction.
- Create an organizational environment that allows all IMT-USA's employees to add value.
- Promote an atmosphere of thirst and eagerness to perform, which allows delegation of responsibility to the lowest possible organizational level and attracts good people.
- Generate a sense of urgency and results orientation in the development of capital and human resources to ensure proper return for both our employees and our shareholders.
- Expand the horizon of the organization to share in and contribute to our worldwide core competencies.

Guiding Principles
- Create a sense of urgency—concentrate on priority actions rather than procedural issues.
- Promote a unifying culture: "can do—do it."
- Remove barriers to performance.
- Shift organizational focus to servicing the customers and beating competition.

Vision
- Demonstrate leadership in serving the U.S. marketplace in its transition to cleaner industry, where products are more efficiently produced, distributed, and applied.

EXHIBIT 4
Mission/Vision Statement
IMT Custom Machine Company, Inc.

The following was issued throughout the Fort Wayne plant on June 25, 1995 by Edward Fortesque, Manager of Quality Assurance.

Mission
- To be recognized as the outstanding custom machine manufacturer in the world.

Goals
- *Provide market leadership*
  - Customer satisfaction
    - Quality
    - Reliability
    - Delivery
    - Service
  - Serve the market with optional products and services
  - Be the technology leader

- *Achieve business (operational) excellence*
  - Zero failures
  - On-time performance
  - Low throughput time for orders through the factory
  - High productivity of labor
  - Return on capital employed >30% (pre-tax)
  - Revenue to total compensation growth of at least 5%/year

Vision
- To be perceived by each of our customers as superior to the best competition in the overall quality of our products and services.

mission statement appears in Exhibit 4. It was developed by the Fort Wayne plant's quality assurance manager, Edward Fortesque, and issued on June 25, 1995.

CMCI's Information System

Browning began his investigation shortly after receiving his charge from Young. By mid-September 1996, he had uncovered considerable data about the information systems at Fort Wayne and Chicago.

Organization
The support for Fort Wayne's IS was divided into two groups, an engineering systems (ES) group and a management information systems (MIS) group (see Exhibit 1). The ES group consisted of eight of the twenty-five people who reported to Dr. Michael King, Fort Wayne's development engineering manager. Dr. King was trained as an engineer and was known as an industry-wide expert on the design of automated fabrication technologies.

Twenty MIS support staff members reported directly to Bill Gears, who in turn reported to Joe O'Neil, the division MIS manager. O'Neil reported through the division controller's organization. O'Neil was a former IBM employee with extensive experience on larger mainframes and the IBM A/S 400 hardware platform. He had been the MIS manager at another IMT site before coming to Fort Wayne in 1994. Exhibit 5 summarizes O'Neil's direction and objectives for Fort Wayne's MIS group. It was taken from a memo issued to top division and plant management on July 30, 1995. In an interview, O'Neil said he did not have a formal mission for the MIS group, but offered the following: "Basically it [the mission] is to provide an adequate, responsive, and economical network structure of data processing support for all sites within the division."

The Chicago plant used Fort Wayne's mainframe, but had its own one-person MIS "group," who reported to O'Neil.

Hardware

Browning found that there was a variety of computing hardware to support the division. Exhibit 6 illustrates the various systems at CMCI.

EXHIBIT 5

Fort Wayne MIS Direction and Objectives
IMT Custom Machine Company, Inc.

The following was issued to top division and plant management on July 30, 1995 by Joe O'Neil, Division MIS Manager.

Direction
- Pursue a more structured MIS strategy with a reasonable and manageable level of risk that will be consistent with our being a leader in the custom machine industry.
- Develop and execute a plan that will continually upgrade our hardware, software, applications, database, and network environments to accomplish the above.

Objectives
- Recognize our business is designing and producing custom machines, not chasing ever-changing computer technology and theories.
- Coordinate MIS strategy with our business objectives of:
  - Zero defects
  - Low throughput time
  - ROCE of 30% (return on capital employed)
- Control our own destiny.
- Minimize risk and hidden costs.
- Work from a total systems architecture plan:
  - Develop an applications architecture
  - Select the hardware plan required to best accomplish our goals
- Maintain an integrated environment that supports the various functions of our division.

Mainframe: The division operated an IBM mainframe that could be used by anyone in the division with no direct charge. All operating and lease costs for the mainframe were covered in the division's overhead. When they joined the firm, new engineers and other professionals were "automatically" supplied with a mainframe user account, a personal computer (PC) equipped with a board to enable it to communicate with the IBM mainframe, and several PC software packages for local work. The current mainframe was an IBM model S/390, 2nd generation that had arrived in March 1996 on a five-year lease.

CMCI also had an IBM A/S 400, which it inherited from General Engineering during the acquisition. Immediately after the acquisition, MIS personnel attempted to create a facility to move data between the mainframes. Transferring data between the two systems, however, was not easily achieved. Most exchanges were done by "pulling" data from one to the other. Although a routine (called AMSERV) was available to "push" data to the other system, its use was not fully understood—or desired.

AMSERV was not used because the receiver's data file could be updated without the user's knowledge. Thus, the resolution of data security issues had slowed the practice of sharing data between systems. In sequential applications, where data was created in one system and used by another, identical data files with the same data were needed on each system.

Since 1994, the heaviest use of the mainframe was from the computer-aided drafting (CAD) and engineering users. IMT Fort Wayne used IBM's CAD product. The CAD application, along with additional engineering and drafting programs, represented about 65 percent of the current mainframe CPU use. Total usage in August 1996 was estimated at approximately 54 percent of the S/390's CPU capacity.

The 1996 mainframe upgrade had been driven by the need for improvements in CAD response time and an increasing number of users. During 1994 and 1995, 90 new users throughout the factory and front offices were

EXHIBIT 6

Computing Systems and Applications*
IMT Custom Machine Company, Inc.

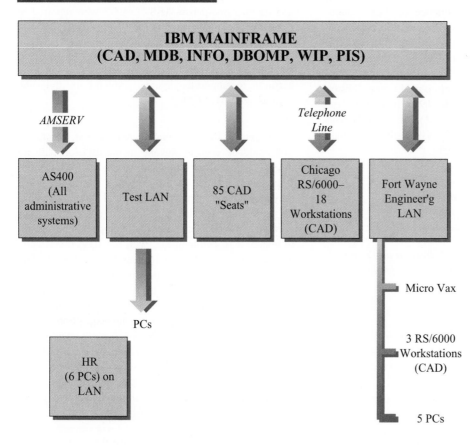

* Applications are in parentheses

connected to the mainframe as personal computing usage increased.

Personal Computers: The new policy at Fort Wayne was that anyone who needed a PC could get one. Financial justification was not necessary. PCs were considered a tool, like the necessity for a special hammer on the shop floor. Fort Wayne's standard configuration included a Pentium-based CPU with a 750MB hard disk and a printer. A spreadsheet, a word processing program, and several other popular packages were standard issue with all new PCs. PCs were obtained under a three-year lease from a local supplier. Microsoft's Windows 95 system was installed on most machines.

Many users felt that the lack of sufficient software support and development from the MIS group had been partially circumvented by the use of PCs. For example, scheduling in various major work centers in the factory was done with a spreadsheet on PCs. However, the principle use for many PCs was as a "dumb" terminal to the mainframe for database inquiry or e-mail. In addition, all personnel who performed typing used PCs, and engineers routinely used the word processor to write memos. Of the 300 users on Fort Wayne's mainframe, about 210 were accessing it through PCs. The remainder were CAD users.

Workstations: As of 1996, Fort Wayne had three RS/6000 workstations, which were used in the development engineering group for special projects but not for active production tasks. They were connected through a local area network (LAN). A Digital MicroVAX and IBM PCs had also been linked into the LAN within the past year. As of 1996, the Chicago facility used eighteen RS/6000 workstations for normal CAD production. RS/6000 workstations in Chicago used the AIX version of CAD which had a "look and feel" identical to the mainframe version of CAD used in Fort Wayne.

Drawings made in Chicago on workstations were stored on Fort Wayne's mainframe and uploaded and downloaded over a high-speed dedicated telephone line. Chicago's designers liked their CAD stations, but were having trouble with the connection between the IBM mainframe and the Chicago LAN. Tom Goodman, the MIS support person in Chicago, said the following about their AIX and network support: "I feel like we are the beta site for linking sites."

Data Flow and Functional Responsibilities

Exhibit 7 illustrates the generalized data flow among the main functional areas of the Fort Wayne operation. Of the seven functions, only human resources (HR) was not interconnected with the main flow of the information. The remaining six organizational areas participated in a continuous sequential flow of information.

Marketing
Exhibit 7 shows that the flow of business information started with the interaction between marketing and the customer. Information originated from the customer when a technical description or specification (a "spec") was sent to IMT for a new machine. The length of the spec could be from 10 pages to over an inch thick. A marketing engineer would then read the spec and enter his or her interpretation of it into a mainframe negotiation program. The negotiation program (MDB) required the input of about fifty computer screens of data and was written in COBOL.

If a marketing engineer had a question about the specs, he or she called a design engineer or another local expert. Most estimates had to be turned around in 10 working days. Because of the volume of requests and a staff of only two engineers covering all of the United States, negotiations were sometimes very hectic. Mike Rusnak, a marketing engineer, stated, "We do the best we can, but we will miss some things from time to time. Almost always after winning the order, we will go back and negotiate with the customer over what we missed."

Marketing also used Excel and Powerpoint on their PCs for presentations. Another frequently used mainframe application was a query system (called INFO) that was automatically linked to data from the negotiation program. It was used to analyze data from ongoing negotiations as well as contracts after they were won or lost.

Administration and Finance
The administration and finance group was the home for most business support systems. The purchase order, accounts payable, and accounts receivable systems were applications used by purchasing, receiving, and other groups. All three systems were custom developed by GE's MIS staff (some of whom now work at CMCI) on the A/S 400. Although wages and salaries were maintained locally, an external data service company handled payroll.

Engineering
Each machine was electrically and mechanically custom designed to a customer's exact specifications. Customization requirements, when mixed with the complexities of the economic and engineering limits, required sophisticated computer programs for modeling and design work. In 1996, Fort Wayne had three separate design systems, one for each of the three types of custom machines. Design engineers for each product line were experts on their own programs.

The first step in design engineering was to electronically receive the data previously entered into the negotiation program. The process entailed pulling the data records from the negotiation database. The engineer reread the customer's spec and decided which additional data needed to be added to the input files for the design program. The program then generated a design that the engineer reviewed in detail and often revised. Once the design was accepted by the engineer, the electronic computer file and a paper folder with completed forms were transferred to a drafting supervisor for completion.

The ES group wrote all of Fort Wayne's design systems. The number of routines that were used by each of the three systems was used as a relative measure of size and complexity of the systems. Large vertical had about 500 routines, medium horizontal had about 400 routines, and large horizontal had about 2,400 routines.

Drafting
All drafting at Fort Wayne and Chicago was performed on a CAD applications system. At Fort Wayne, the CAD application ran on the IBM mainframe, and in Chicago it ran on IBM RS/6000 workstations. There were 85 "seats" of CAD at Fort Wayne and 18 at Chicago. (A "seat" was one hardware CAD setup with a high-resolution screen,

EXHIBIT 7

Data Flow Among Functional Areas
IMT Custom Machine Company, Inc.

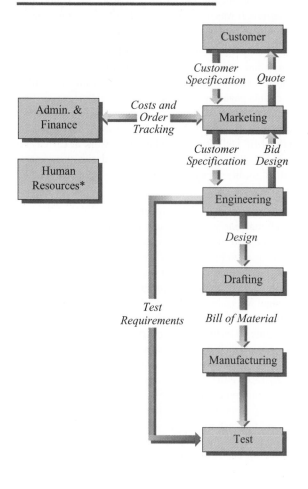

* Uses only applications supported by IMT-USA.

keyboard, function button box, and a pointing device that functioned like a mouse.) During the last five years, additional programs had been written to automatically take output from the design programs and create CAD drawings or references to drawings with standard parts. About 60 percent of the average 4,000 parts per machine were created in this way. All jobs were reduced to drawings prior to being released to the factory.

A standard part drawing included the material specification on the drawing. Assembly drawings contained the bill of material (BOM). Having CAD and the custom machine design programs on the same platform made the development of the automatic drawing programs very convenient. Jenny Velan, an engineer in the development group, said, "There are things we have been able to do with this setup that would be impossible if the jobs were split between two separate systems."

Manufacturing

When all the drawings for a custom machine were completed, the BOM was manually transferred from the drawings into the BOM database system, called DBOMP. DBOMP was originally written by IBM and extensively modified for Fort Wayne in the late 1980s to handle BOM for the vertical type machines. When production of the medium and large horizontal custom machines was transferred to Fort Wayne, DBOMP's limitations forced many "work-arounds." For example, when the General Engineering large horizontal technology was moved to Fort Wayne, it was discovered that DBOMP could not handle the longer General Engineering drawing numbers. Moreover, there was no one at Fort Wayne who knew the DBOMP code well enough to make a change.

The work-in-process (WIP) inventory tracking system for the shop floor at Fort Wayne was very limited and worked only for items required for the main aisle assembly area. It could handle only unique made-to-order parts, not stock items. The system worked by having a main aisle supervisor request a "pull" from the storeroom to get parts delivered. The tracking systems for items within feeder aisles either were manual or used custom spreadsheets. Each item's information was maintained by its respective aisle. This WIP main aisle tracking system resided on the S/390, and the data was loaded by hand from the DBOMP.

The parts inventory system (PIS) was very limited and similar to the tracking system except that it worked off all stocked inventory items for the main and all feeder aisles. It used a process identical to the WIP system.

The MIS group was backlogged in supporting the rapid changes that were occurring at the Fort Wayne plant. When a computerized system failed to provide needed functionality, paper systems were created to support the information needs.

Test

Because each custom machine was a significant investment—between $2 million and $8 million—all machines were fully tested and personally witnessed at Fort Wayne or Chicago by an employee or agent of the customer company. The test department, along with the witness, certified that every machine met the customer's test requirements set forth in the specification. Scheduling information and other test details were forwarded to the test department by hand. Test information was written on a form that was interpreted or copied from the customer specification in marketing and engineering. The biggest complaint from the test department was that sometimes the marketing department did not properly interpret the customer's test requirement specification. A failed or unnecessary test that resulted from misinterpreting a customer's specification could cost IMT well over $100,000.

The test department had several personal computers connected to a LAN. Although all PCs in the test department were thereby connected to the mainframe, this connectivity was used only occasionally. The test department was a part of the quality assurance organization at Fort Wayne, which was responsible for the data and production of the test reports sent to customers. Electronic test result data, however, remained on the test department's LAN only. The test department maintained its own LAN applications.

Human Resources

As of 1996, human resources used only standalone computers. HR had plans to install a LAN that operated customized corporate programs for handling HR functions, including benefits and pension/investment plans. There were no plans to interconnect the LAN with Fort Wayne's mainframe due to security concerns over the confidential personnel records residing on HR's computers.

Other Information

Browning discovered other information relevant to IMT's use of information technology.

Information Systems Personnel

The programmers in MIS had extensive backgrounds in COBOL and A/S 400 languages. However, none of them knew the UNIX operating system or its related programming languages. Of the 14 programmers, 4 had over 25 years of experience at Fort Wayne, 2 had about 12 years, and the remaining 8 had 3 years or less.

Engineers who supported the engineering system in the development group had significant backgrounds in scientific computing, and four had some experience in UNIX. Each engineer had more than 10 years experience with the company. One of the new programmers in the engineering systems group knew UNIX very well.

Browning heard many comments during his investigation that suggested that MIS and engineering systems

staff at Fort Wayne always made the systems work—despite the high degree of constant change.

Management Systems

Browning concluded that by employing informal systems, work-arounds, and an extraordinary amount of human effort, Fort Wayne was profitable in 1995—its first profitable year since 1990. Slowly, things were stabilizing at Fort Wayne—the informal systems were being corrected and formalized. Restructuring into three product lines helped clarify the focus and purpose of operations systems and procedures. The primary reason for progress cited by many staff was that each product line was allowed independent control and responsibility.

However, computer systems support remained an issue. The engineering systems group supported engineering, and drafting, and the MIS group supported everything else. The HR organization was not considered a local support issue because its applications were supported from the corporate MIS group in New York (IMT-USA). A small group within MIS maintained all PCs and miscellaneous computer hardware for all the functional groups across the plant.

Placement of Support for Engineering and Drafting Systems

Browning discovered that there was an ongoing debate over where the support for engineering and drafting systems should be located. Browning summarized the three alternatives that seemed to be in constant debate:

1. In the engineering support systems group: Arguments for leaving support for engineering and drafting in the development engineering line of authority were strong. The design and drafting programs produced models of the three dynamic product line technologies. The three principal people supporting these design systems were engineers with strong computer backgrounds. Two of the three had masters degrees in engineering. Support for these programs required a balance of custom machine design knowledge, creativity, and programming. By keeping program support close to the design engineers, code updates could occur more rapidly by working closer to the user engineer in the product line. As for MIS programmers taking responsibility, the engineers feared that they had little understanding of the underlying design technology. Some speculated that they might make coding changes that "would cost millions to correct once a design was committed and the parts were made."

2. In the product lines: Arguments for product line support of engineering systems included the fact that these engineers had extensive firsthand use of the system. Therefore, feedback on problems would be more obvious to those who supported the system. Ultimate control of the software should be in the hands of each of the profit centers. They should have the option to regulate the level of computer support based on their own strategy. However, if the engineering systems support responsibilities were located with the product lines, a programmer would need to be transferred from the engineering support systems group to each of the product lines.

3. In the MIS group: Arguments for MIS-based support of engineering and drafting systems included an alignment of all computer-related functions in one functional group—thus providing a common responsibility point for all computer support and integrated applications. Product line and development engineering would have to submit change requests that were more completely documented. Support through MIS would guarantee that coding changes would be better documented. If support were the responsibility of the product line engineers, MIS people argued that the end result might be "spaghetti code," which no one but the original programmer could understand.

The Move to a Common Custom Machine Design System

In early 1996, Young received instructions that his subsidiary would have to use a redeveloped set of custom machine design programs from Germany. The BG management team believed it was appropriate to institute a common custom machine design system across all factories. The BG's strategy was based on porting the German programs onto a UNIX workstation platform and then distributing and supporting it worldwide. The design system would be connected to an SAP relational database system also operating with UNIX. When the announcement was made that the German programs would be used, however, none of the programs existed under UNIX. Nor did the German developers possess more than a few years in total experience in the UNIX environment.

A New Marketing and Negotiation System

Marketing and engineering saw the existing negotiation program as inefficient and ineffective. Two years of studying how the IMT division should do business with its customers led the marketing group to propose a reengineered "Front-End Information" system. The proposed system was to include capabilities to optically scan in all customer proposals, including text. Customer specs could then be analyzed and processed more quickly.

The proposed system had an initial price tag of over $2.5 million. The original idea for the system was conceived in the marketing department, which employed two staff engineers and an independent outside consultant as its own IS expert. MIS was only recently involved with planning the system. Top division management was providing direct support for the project. The project was being led by the division strategic planning manager, which isolated the project from division MIS and engineering biases. Hardware purchases were to begin in November 1996, and the system was to be completed and operational by the end of 1997.

CMCI's Interface to Field Sales

IMT's field sales group had been planning a new system for transferring order information to the factories. The new system, called SPEC, was planned to come on line in late 1997. By mid-1997, each factory was to have installed a LAN to accommodate the data downloaded from field sales personnel. As of September 1996, SPEC had been plagued with delays because staff could not arrive at a consensus on the exact information that should be transmitted to each of the factories.

New Software Design Tools

Payments from Fort Wayne and Chicago accounted for 25 percent of the funds used for the BG's R&D development budget. IMT's MIS group felt that about 30 percent of its investment was received back in the form of useful information technologies; the remaining 70 percent benefited production hardware improvements. The BG was definitely committed to additional investments in UNIX application tools. Various software engineering and applications development tools had been mentioned, but the specific software and the number of seats that would be leased or purchased had not been finalized as of August 1996.

Bill of Material (BOM) System Replacement

The DBOMP system was nearly 15 years old and could not handle a new IMT drawing system that was to replace the three older systems. To support the new drawing system and its subsequent BOM structure, a new BOM system was required. Fort Wayne systems staff had identified a system that would run on the IBM mainframe and could be acquired at no cost. The program, called PUFR, was free because it was in the process of being made obsolete by IMT-USA's corporate MIS group. The only requirement was that Fort Wayne MIS staff had to support PUFR.

By August 1996, over 7,000 staff hours had been consumed by Fort Wayne MIS personnel trying to make PUFR operational. Projections suggested that approximately 10 percent more work had to be done in order to get PUFR in a test mode. To get this far, Fort Wayne systems had purchased additional modules that were not originally included free in the IMT corporate version of PUFR. The effort had also included converting some of the approximately 400 auxiliary programs that used the old DBOMP format. Occasional discussions of replacing PUFR "in a few years" were heard in the halls.

Browning's Options

Near the end of his investigation, Browning summarized his findings as follows: "The best way to characterize the current information systems situation at Fort Wayne is as a lot of manual points where data are transferred between a patchwork of old, semiautomatic, outdated processes. The result is that since each place where information is transferred had a probability of introducing a new error, checking and rechecking becomes necessary to ensure integrity. And since the outdated processes require constant attention with fixes and work-arounds, the newer processes never move ahead. What we really need is a clear vision to guide our decisions today, so we can be ready for tomorrow."

After his six-week study, Browning presented three potential IS options for Fort Wayne to Young. "Besides considering these alternatives," Browning told Young, "Fort Wayne needs to develop a strategy statement for its IS group which is consistent with our business objectives." Browning listed these options:

Option 1: Mainframe Computing
Commit to staying with the mainframe for all important applications, discourage the use of UNIX workstations, and eliminate the A/S 400. Maximize the use of the lower cost, energy efficient mainframe.

Commitment to the mainframe would be a long-term venture. To continue to maintain a large central mainframe and acquire new applications and full access for all users would require a systematic plan. The plan would include porting all of the major A/S 400 applications to the mainframe in order to assure central usage, support, and control. Major mainframe packages would be reviewed for upgrades that could handle Fort Wayne's current capacity and requirements. Older packages used in Fort Wayne would be phased out over the next five years.

PCs connected through LANs to the mainframe would do spreadsheet and word processing work, but most computational work would be done on the mainframe.

Option 2: Distributed Computing
Follow a strategy whereby the mainframe is phased out completely. At the same time, make significant investments in UNIX workstations, PCs, and LANs. Such an architecture would allow migration to a full client-server environment.

Plans for a long-term shift to a distributed UNIX environment would include migration of all applications to the new environment. A high-speed network would be installed to link all computers. Data and application servers would be distributed by functional area and profit centers (e.g., marketing, development engineering, human resources, test). CAD seats would be slowly transferred from the mainframe to dedicated workstations. During the transition period, the mainframe would be connected to the network and available for access from all workstations.

One database would serve the entire UNIX network system, but local databases could also exist as necessary. PCs would be linked via LANs and gateways would be installed to bridge between networks.

As CAD and other major applications were shifted off the mainframe, it would be downsized to a smaller, compatible mid-range mainframe. The process should be expected to take approximately ten years and two mainframe downgrades before all of Fort Wayne's applications would be migrated to UNIX workstations.

Option 3: Watch Carefully. Do not act yet.
Wait and see what develops; decide only as circumstances force key issues.

Following the "watch carefully" option means that each decision would be made in response to immediate demands. Decisions would be based on the lowest risk and least expensive alternative at decision time. While no long-term commitment would be made to either the mainframe or distributed strategy, only technically adequate solutions would be acceptable. As a result of incurring lower risk, faster payback was expected and additional opportunities would be available to evaluate new technology.

A Decision and Direction for IMT IS

Young's feeling was confirmed when he received Browning's report; change was going to be painful. Years of neglect, restructuring, and a growing organization had finally caught up with CMCI's information systems. Young also recognized that changes in the division's IS architecture may require organizational changes as well. A decision had to be made soon. Or did it? "Things have worked themselves out in the past," Young said to him-self. "After all, why fix something if it is at least work-ing? Our top-notch staff always finds a way to solve prob-lems when we really need it. Should I really be spending lots of money here?"

BATESVILLE CASKET COMPANY[1]

Batesville Casket Company is a subsidiary of Hillen-brand Industries, Inc., a diversified holding company headquartered in the small southern Indiana town of Batesville. Other Hillenbrand subsidiaries include American Tourister, Inc., a major U.S. luggage manufacturer; Medeco Security Locks, a leading producer of high security locks; Hill-Rom Company, the leading U.S. producer of electric hospital beds, patient room furniture, and patient handling equipment; SSI Medical Services, a leading provider of wound care and other therapy units and services; Block Medical, a leading producer of home infusion therapy products; and Forethought, an insurance company that offers specialized funeral planning products through funeral homes.

In its twenty years of operation as a publicly held company, Hillenbrand Industries has had exponential growth in revenues, cash flow, and profits. Revenues have grown from about $75 million in 1971 to almost $1.2 billion in 1991, and earnings per share have increased from about 10 cents to $1.22. Highlights of Hillenbrand Industries financial performance for 1989–1991 are presented in Exhibit 1.

Headquartered in Batesville, Indiana, Batesville Casket Company, Inc., is the world's largest producer of metal and hardwood burial caskets, having a significant percentage of the U.S. market for its products. Batesville Casket serves more than 16,000 funeral homes in the continental United States, Canada, and Puerto Rico. It operates six manufacturing plants that are specialized by product line. To provide optimum customer service, it has 66 strategically located distribution warehouses (called Customer Service Centers) from which it delivers caskets to funeral homes using its own truck fleet.

Batesville Casket's managers believe that long-term success will result from listening to their funeral director-customers and responding to their needs better than anyone else. Batesville is committed to listening to these customers in their plants, their offices, their Customer Service Centers, their sales organization—literally everywhere they do business. Another key element in Batesville Casket's strategy for achieving total customer satisfaction is to continually improve all processes and methods so that the company can serve its customers more effectively.

The MIS Department

The MIS department is responsible for providing information systems and services to Batesville Casket. As shown in Exhibit 2, applications development is basically organized functionally, with teams serving logistics, sales and marketing, and manufacturing. The Computer Aided Manufacturing group is responsible for interfacing manufacturing systems with the machines in the factories. The Data Center operates an IBM 4381 mainframe. Last year Batesville Casket spent only .73 percent of its revenue on MIS.

James J. Kuisel, who reports to the senior vice president and chief financial officer, has been director of MIS for 14 years. Until recently the MIS department has had most of the responsibility for systems projects, but it is now sharing more of this responsibility with the users. Another major thrust of the department is toward use of client/server networks rather than the mainframe. This is not just a matter of less costly processing on personal

EXHIBIT 1
Hillenbrand Industries Financial Highlights.

Dollars in thousands except per share data

Results of Operations	Fiscal Year			Percent Change	
	1991	1990	1989	1991/90	1990/89
Net revenues:					
Industrial					
Durables	$ 146,973	$ 159,872	$ 161,479	(8.1%)	(1.0%)
Health Care	592,998	523,846	469,408	13.2	11.6
Caskets	396,894	384,217	350,217	3.3	9.7
Total	1,136,865	1,067,935	981,104	6.5	8.9
Insurance	62,009	38,627	19,677	60.5	96.3
Total net revenues	1,198,874	1,106,562	1,000,781	8.3	10.6
Operating profit by segment:					
Industrial					
Durables	(2,721)	7,613	14,638	(135.7)	(48.0)
Health Care	91,883	73,453	81,143	25.1	(9.5)
Caskets	78,792	68,270	56,891	15.4	20.0
Total	167,954	149,336	152,672	12.5	(2.2)
Insurance	2,552	(1,397)	(5,009)	282.7	72.1
Total operating profit by segment	170,506	147,939	147,663	15.3	.2
Other items	(24,847)	(21,599)	(26,297)	15.0	(17.9)
Income taxes	56,472	50,662	50,048	11.5	1.2
Net income	89,197	75,678	71,318	17.9	6.1
Earnings per common share*	1.22	1.02	.96	19.6	6.3
Dividends per common share*	.29	.275	.25	5.5	10.0
Return on average equity	19.7%	18.2%	19.5%	N/A	N/A
Average shares outstanding (000's)*	72,885	73,971	74,377	(1.5)	(.5)
Shareholders	11,000	9,800	9,500	12.2	3.2
Employees	10,500	9,500	9,000	10.5	5.6

*Reflects two-for-one stock split effective February 28, 1992

computers (PCs), but it also takes advantage of the competitive environment for a whole array of software products. "Software products for the mainframe are very expensive—$250,000 for a Human Resource System," Kuisel explains. "There are only a few mainframe suppliers who have developed highly complex systems that cost an arm and a leg. But for the client/server environment there are hundreds of developers, all competing with aggressive pricing."

With the help of an outside consultant, Batesville Casket is concentrating on reducing cycle time of business processes. The MIS department is heavily involved in process mapping the company and in analyzing each process to take "non-value added" time out of it. Kuisel is the head of the "Make to Market" team that is leading this process, and many others from MIS are involved in the other teams that are working on this project.

Kuisel is proactive in the use of new technology. "We want to be leaders," he asserts, "but not heat seekers. Where we can make a tremendous gain by getting on the bleeding edge, then we will go ahead and take the risk. But when the business is not going to benefit greatly, then

EXHIBIT 2
Organization of MIS Department.

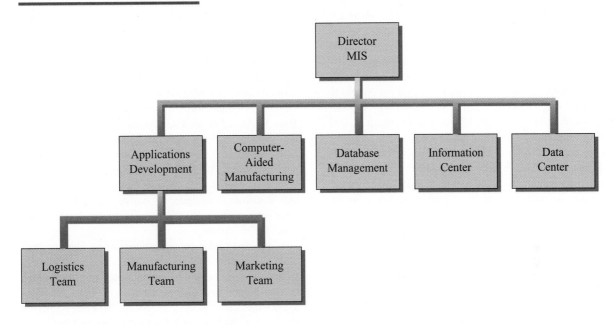

we will let the technology mature so that we do not waste resources. We want the business need, not the technology, to drive us, and we try to minimize the risk."

The Distribution System

Logistics is an important area at Batesville Casket. Caskets are bulky and heavy items, so transportation costs are significant when distributing them on a national basis. Furthermore, when a funeral director has a demand for a specific casket that he does not have in his relatively limited stock, he must have that casket in time for the family visitation and funeral, a matter of a day or two at most. So the ability to deliver a specific model quickly is essential to good customer service.

As mentioned previously, Batesville Casket distributes its products through 66 Customer Service Centers. The typical Customer Service Center has a manager and a small staff of warehouse-worker/drivers, most of whom are out of the Customer Service Center much of the time delivering caskets. Although the Batesville Casket product line includes several hundred models, the typical Customer Service Center stocks only a portion of these, depending upon the preferences of the funeral directors it serves.

In the early 1980s, Batesville Casket was a pioneer in the development of PC-based distributed systems. Working together, the MIS and logistics departments developed a PC-based system that was installed in each of the Customer Service Centers. This system served most of the operational needs of the Customer Service Center, including order entry from the customer, maintaining the Customer Service Center inventory by model and serial number, and keeping track of where each casket was located in the warehouse. It included a routing model that accepted the delivery requirements for the day, determined the route that each truck should take in order to deliver the caskets most efficiently, and printed out the routing and the sequence in which the truck should be loaded so that the first casket to be delivered was the last casket on the truck.

Through a dial-up network, each night the Customer Service Center PC transmitted that day's orders to the central computer in Batesville that handled customer billing, kept track of Customer Service Center inventory, and determined inventory replenishment schedules. The central computer then sent information on the next day's shipments back to the PC so that the Customer Service Center manager would know what was en route.

This system replaced a lot of paperwork in the Customer Service Centers, but it was justified and paid for on the basis of reducing the time to get the billing out. With the previous manual system, the Customer Service Center managers would fill out the paperwork, batch it, and mail it to Batesville, and they would receive the billing information from 3 to 10 days after the casket was delivered. With the computer system they could get the bills out the next day. Also, the system enabled the centers to respond more quickly to demand and, through centralized replenishment, reduced the probability that a desired item would not be available when needed.

This system was developed using a then-new PC development tool, called Knowledge-Man, that included a 4th-generation language and a database management system. Because some of the processing was done by the central mainframe system in Batesville and the rest was done by the PCs in the Customer Service Centers, with data transmitted back and forth at night, this was a distributed system.

When the system was installed, most of the Customer Service Center managers had never even seen a computer, did not know what a floppy disk was, and had no experience with a computer keyboard, so they were initially reluctant to become hands-on computer users. But with a lot of help and training they converted to the new system, and soon they became enthusiastic users of the new computer system.

The Decision to Replace the Customer Service Center System

The hardware for the PC-based Customer Service Center system was an early IBM PC with the 8086 chip, plus a 10-megabyte hard disk. Although the system had been enhanced over the years and was working well, by 1990 Batesville Casket had reached the limit of what could be done with this 1st-generation hardware, and there were a number of things that the logistics people wanted to do in the near future to improve Customer Service Center operations. But the major problem was that the equipment was so old and obsolete that some maintenance contractors were not willing to continue to service some of the components of the hardware. It was clear that the hardware was on its last legs.

One obvious alternative was to merely replace the old hardware with new hardware and continue to use the existing software. The functionality of the system would remain the same, but the hardware would be maintainable, and sufficient additional capacity would be available to support future enhancements of the system. Unfortunately, the Knowledge-Man software that the system was based upon had gone through several releases, and the version that Batesville Casket was using was no longer supported by the vendor. Even if Batesville Casket continued to use the existing software, they would have to change it to conform to the current version of Knowledge-Man, which would involve a substantial reprogramming effort.

In 1990 Jan Holm, a senior systems analyst, and Jerry W. Munchel, an MIS program manager, spent several months working with the logistics area to explore expectations concerning logistics developments over the next five years. "We looked at their goals and objectives, how they expected Batesville Casket's manufacturing and distribution systems to evolve, and projects they were anticipating that might impact the needs of the system," Holm reports.

One idea under consideration was to identify each casket by bar coding its model number and serial number so that the casket could be automatically tracked through the production and distribution system. Logistics managers expected to place a hand-held bar code reader on the loading dock at each Customer Service Center and connect it to the Customer Service Center PC through a radio-frequency link. Then they could automatically enter the identification of each casket into the computer as it was received into or sent out of the Customer Service Center. In order to further reduce cycle times, they wanted to send orders to the factory several times a day rather than sending them all at night. Furthermore, they wanted to replace the routing software package that was part of the system with a more powerful version.

Batesville Casket's increased emphasis on total customer satisfaction was also leading the logistics staff to plan significant additions to the system to enable them to capture data on service quality and improve customer service. For example, many funeral directors order by description rather than model number, so a Customer Service Center manager sometimes misunderstood and sent the wrong casket to the funeral home. Therefore, logistics would like to have a system that maintained a history of orders and allowed for improved identification of the models being ordered.

Therefore, in early 1991 the MIS department set up a team to investigate alternatives and recommend what should be done. Munchel headed the team, and the other members were Holm, Kenneth D. Fairchild, director of Technical Support, and Delbert Rippeltoe, manager of Database Administration. Munchel and Holm had been instrumental in the development of the old system, and Fairchild was responsible for the communications between the office and the Customer Service Centers.

Deciding What Technology to Use

The logistics study convinced the team that they needed to significantly revise the software in addition to replacing the hardware, and it also provided the basis for a number of critical decisions relating to the future technological platform. "Once we decided to replace the hardware, we had to determine how big and how fast the computers should be and what operating system to use," Fairchild explains, "and when we decided to redo the software, we had to determine what database manager and development environment to use."

The hardware and operating system decisions were relatively straightforward. The plan to place bar code readers at the loading dock and enter data from them directly into the computer determined that the new computers must be multitasking. Otherwise, the Customer Service Center manager would have to interrupt his work with the computer whenever the bar code reader was used. Another reason for multitasking was that logistics managers wanted to be able to transmit orders to Batesville during the day without interrupting computer support of normal Customer Service Center operations.

They concluded that an IBM-compatible 386-based computer would have all the processing power that the Customer Service Centers were likely to need during the next few years, and they wanted computers that could be upgraded if needs expanded even more than they planned. They chose an IBM PS/2 Model A16 with 4 megabytes of memory, a math co-processor, a color monitor, a mouse, and a 160-megabyte hard disk. They chose a Hayes 9600 Ultra external modem for communications with Batesville and an Epson LQ1170 printer. In order to minimize error and downtime problems, they decided to install an uninterruptible power supply at each site. The total hardware cost for each site was over $8,000.

The operating system had to support multitasking, and they only considered IBM's OS/2 and UNIX. Windows was not considered because its DOS base was not considered robust enough for the Customer Service Center operations. They chose OS/2 primarily because they were concerned that there would be a shortage of business software packages that operated under UNIX. In particular, they knew of no routing packages that would run under UNIX.

The database manager and development environment were related decisions, for the development environment had to support the chosen database manager. One critical issue that strongly influenced their decisions at this point was the choice of a user interface. Intuitively they felt that the new system should be based on a graphical user interface, where system functions would be controlled by using a mouse to select options by pointing and clicking on icons, buttons, decision bars, and pull-down menus. The Apple Macintosh, Microsoft Windows, and OS/2 Presentation Manager employ graphical user interfaces.

"We did not know how the Customer Service Center managers would react to using a mouse," Holm explains, "but when we looked at the interactive software packages that were becoming available, they were mouse-driven, windowing, graphical. The upgrade to our router package that logistics was considering has a mouse-driven, windowing user interface. We knew that the managers were going to have to learn how to interact with those packages anyway, so we decided that we needed to be graphical as well."

As an example of such a graphical interface, the order update screen from the new system (shown in Exhibit 3) allows a Customer Service Center manager to update an existing order. This order is from the ABC FUNERAL HOME for product number 7878. A casket, serial number WA7915, has been allocated to this order, and other information on this order is shown on the screen. The buttons along the right show the things a manager can do to this order by using the mouse to point to the button and click. The top two buttons allow him to navigate to the next and prior orders. Other buttons allow him to change data on the order, cancel the order, allocate or unallocate a specific casket to the order, assign it to a route for delivery, remove it from an assigned route, change the route, or quit the order update process.

Once they decided to use a graphical interface, the development environment had to support the easy creation (or "painting") of graphical screens. This led them to consider Object/1, a tool that Holm knew supported object-oriented programming and that claimed to allow a developer to paint dozens of graphical screens in a day. Object/1 was a product of MDBS, Inc., a small software house located in Lafayette, Indiana, which furnished the Knowledge-Man system that had been used to support the original Customer Service Center system. Because Batesville Casket had a long and favorable experience with MDBS, it was natural for the team to take a hard look at Object/1.

EXHIBIT 3

Order Update Screen.

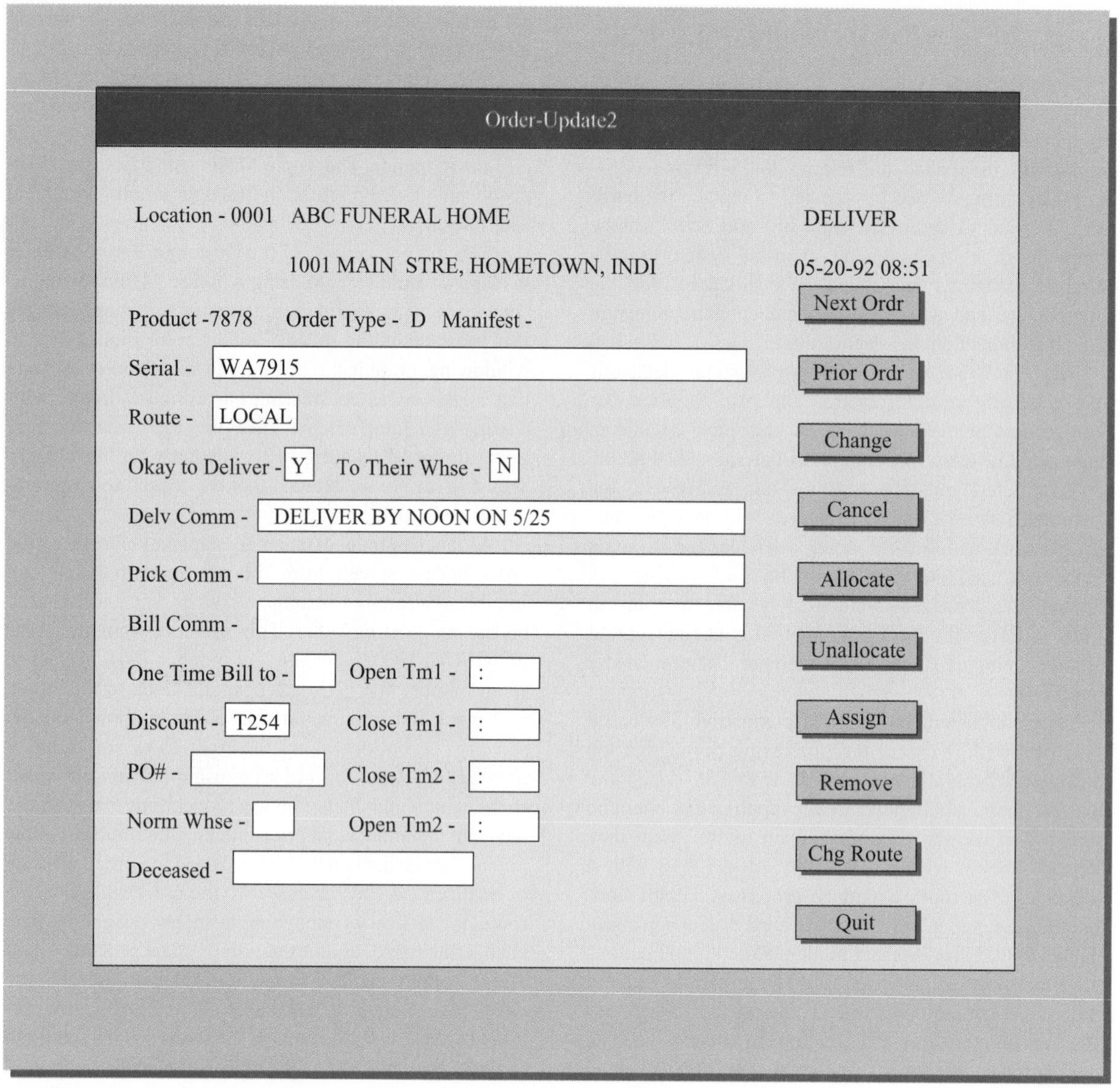

Order-Update2

Location - 0001   ABC FUNERAL HOME   DELIVER

1001 MAIN STRE, HOMETOWN, INDI   05-20-92 08:51

Product -7878   Order Type - D   Manifest -   [Next Ordr]

Serial - [WA7915]   [Prior Ordr]

Route -   [LOCAL]
                                                            [Change]
Okay to Deliver - [Y]   To Their Whse - [N]

Delv Comm - [DELIVER BY NOON ON 5/25]   [Cancel]

Pick Comm - [   ]   [Allocate]

Bill Comm - [   ]
                                                            [Unallocate]
One Time Bill to - [ ]   Open Tm1 - [:]

Discount - [T254]   Close Tm1 - [:]   [Assign]

PO# - [   ]   Close Tm2 - [:]   [Remove]

Norm Whse - [ ]   Open Tm2 - [:]
                                                            [Chg Route]
Deceased - [   ]

                                                            [Quit]

They did not know much about object-oriented programming at the time, but they were aware that it was creating a lot of excitement in the industry. Software industry gurus such as William H. Gates, Microsoft's chairman, Philippe Kahn, president of Borland International, and Steven P. Jobs, who founded Apple Computer and NeXT, were predicting that object-oriented technology would have a revolutionary impact on the future use of computers.

Object-oriented programming was extolled as a way to increase development productivity by creating programs composed of completely independent components (code modules). These building blocks are freely interchangeable among different programs, so as an organization builds up more and more such modules, new systems require the creation of less and less new code. Also, maintenance is much easier because functions are isolated in modules and thus are easy to locate, and once a module is corrected in one system, it can easily be corrected in all the other systems that use that module.

The team did not do an extensive search of development environments. "We did not have a lot of time to search," Fairchild reports, "so we looked at the products that we had in house that we had used before, and we looked at object-oriented programming and made the decision."

They chose Object/1 for a number of reasons in addition to its reputed development and maintenance efficiency. First, it would provide outstanding support for the graphical user interface approach that they wanted to use, and it could access a database manager that provided the backup and recovery capability that they needed with multitasking. Second, industry seemed to be heading that way, and keeping near the leading edge was important to them. Finally, as Holm notes, "We could have used one of our familiar tools, but there would have been no learning experience for the department, and we enjoy the challenge!"

"The team wanted to do something new and exciting, and I knew that they would dedicate themselves to making it a success," Kuisel explains. "Since we knew exactly what the system was to do, and the old system was working well in the short run, there was little risk other than the new technology. Object-oriented programming looked like it might be very important to us as we use PC platforms more extensively, so this was an investment in the future."

Learning to Use
Object-Oriented Programming

Object-oriented programming appears to be simple because there are only a few basic terms to learn: object, method, class, inheritance, and encapsulation. But it is also a new paradigm, or way of thinking about programs, and it is not easy to explain.

An *object* can represent anything of interest—a number, a date, a screen, a casket, a customer—anything that involves data. An object includes *both* the data describing the object and all of the *methods* that can operate on that object. Each method, then, is a code module that does something to or with the data of the object. *Encapsulation* refers to the binding together of the data and the methods that operate on the object; the only way that an object can be operated on is by means of its methods. Thus, the object is protected from actions performed by other parts of the program, or from actions of other programs that may use that object. Objects are the building blocks from which all programs are built, and because of encapsulation the same objects can be used by many different programs. Once the methods of an object are correct, they are correct everywhere that object is used. When one changes a method, it is changed everywhere that object is used.

"A mortgage is an example of an object," Holm explains. "There are things that you want to do against a mortgage. You might want to calculate a present value, or determine the return on investment. The mortgage has some data associated with it—interest rate, payment amount, amount owed, etc. Then there are routines that you perform against that mortgage when you ask questions about current balance or the effect on payment amount of a change in interest rate. In object-oriented terminology, these routines are called methods, and they are encapsulated in the object. So when you ask a question of an object, you don't know or care how it gets the answer. If there are ten other systems that need to ask that question, they all ask that same object. And if you decide that you want to change how you calculate the answer, you change the method in the one object and it is changed in all the systems."

The concept of a *class* is closely related to the concept of an object. A class is an abstract object that includes the characteristics (both data and methods) that are common to the objects that comprise it. For example, automobiles might be a class, and Ford Mustang and Buick Skylark might be the objects of that class. Classes are hierarchical—if vehicles were a class, then automobiles would be a subclass and trucks might be another subclass. What makes this concept powerful is *inheritance*. If one creates a new object in a class, it automatically inherits all of the properties of that class, and it is only necessary to add the data and methods that are unique to the new object.

"For example," explains Fairchild, "data might be a class, with alphanumeric data being one subclass and numeric data being another subclass. Then an integer might be a sub-subclass within that subclass of numeric data, and a decimal number might be another sub-subclass and a binary number might be another sub-subclass. Integers and decimal numbers and binary numbers would all inherit certain methods from the numeric data subclass, which would also inherit common methods from the data class."

One very powerful aspect of Object/1 is that it comes with some 300 classes and 3,000 methods already defined and ready for use. Whenever you create new objects or classes, they become available for use in all subsequent programs.

As has been previously noted, Object/1 already includes the objects necessary to create graphical screens, so they may be painted with no traditional programming. The screen painting utility displays a blank screen (called a *canvas*) along with a set of symbols denoting the various things that can be placed on a screen—buttons, list boxes, data entry boxes, display boxes, labels, etc. To create the button "Next Ordr" on the screen in Exhibit 3, for example, you would use the mouse to point and click on the symbol for push buttons. Then you use the mouse to point to the position on the screen where you want this button to appear and click again. This brings up a screen that allows you to enter the name of the push button and the method to be invoked when this button is selected. To create the entry field labeled "Serial," you would click on the symbol for entry field, point to where it should appear, and click to bring up a screen that allows you to enter the name of the field, and so forth. If you do not like where you have placed an object, the mouse can be used to "drag" it to another position. When finished, you give the screen a name, and

it becomes an object that inherits all the methods that have been created for the screen class of objects.

As an example of object-oriented programming, Exhibit 4 presents the code invoked by clicking on the *Change* button on the order update screen shown in Exhibit 3. Methods are invoked to operate on objects by the following notation:

MethodName(ObjectName, P1, P2,...)

When a pair of parentheses encloses a list of symbols separated by commas, the left-most symbol is the name of an object, and the other symbols in the list (if any) designate parameters that are used by the method. The name of the method to be applied to the object precedes the left parenthesis.

Consider line 8 of Exhibit 4:

found = returnValueOf(new(OrdrChg, self));

This nested pair of methods would execute from the inside out, so the method *new* would be applied to

EXHIBIT 4
Code for Change Button.

```
/ *  Handle change pushbutton.   */
method OrdrUpd2 : : change (self, mp1, mp2)
{
        local found ;
        show (self, false) ;
        beginTransaction (session) ;
        getCurrent (self) ;
        found  =  returnValueOf (new (OrdrChg,  self)) ;
        commitTransaction (session) ;
        if (found  != MBID_CANCEL )
          {
           get (recordHandles [0],   subString (textOf (locIdName) ,  0,  4) ) ;
           fillScreen2 (self) ;
           setText (message,  " Order  information  changed ");
          }
        else
          {
           setText (message,  "Order  information  change  bypassed") ;
          }
        nullCurrencies (session) ;
        show (self,  true) ;
        focusOn (self) ;
        return  nil ;
}
```

the object *OrdrChg* with the parameter *self.* But the object *OrdrChg* is the screen shown in Exhibit 5, which has methods that allow the manager to point to any box and enter or change the data in that box. In this example, we have typed **pick comment** in the box labeled *Pick Comm.*

When the manager is through making changes to the data shown on this screen, he or she uses the mouse to click on the *Accept* button on this screen. This button is an object, and clicking on it invokes a method that completes the change process and returns to the method *new,* which creates a new version of the object *OrdrChg* (and

completes the actions enclosed within the parentheses in line 8). Then the method *returnValueOf* is applied to this new version of the object *OrdrChg* to store a returned value into the object *found.* The result of the entire process shown in Exhibit 4 is to display the screen shown in Exhibit 6.

In the above, the object *OrdrChg* is an instance of a class that comes from Object/1, and the methods *new* and *returnValueOf* were inherited from existing objects in Object/1. All of the button objects are instances of the button class from Object/1, and all the screens are instances of a screen class from Object/1.

EXHIBIT 5
Order Change Screen.

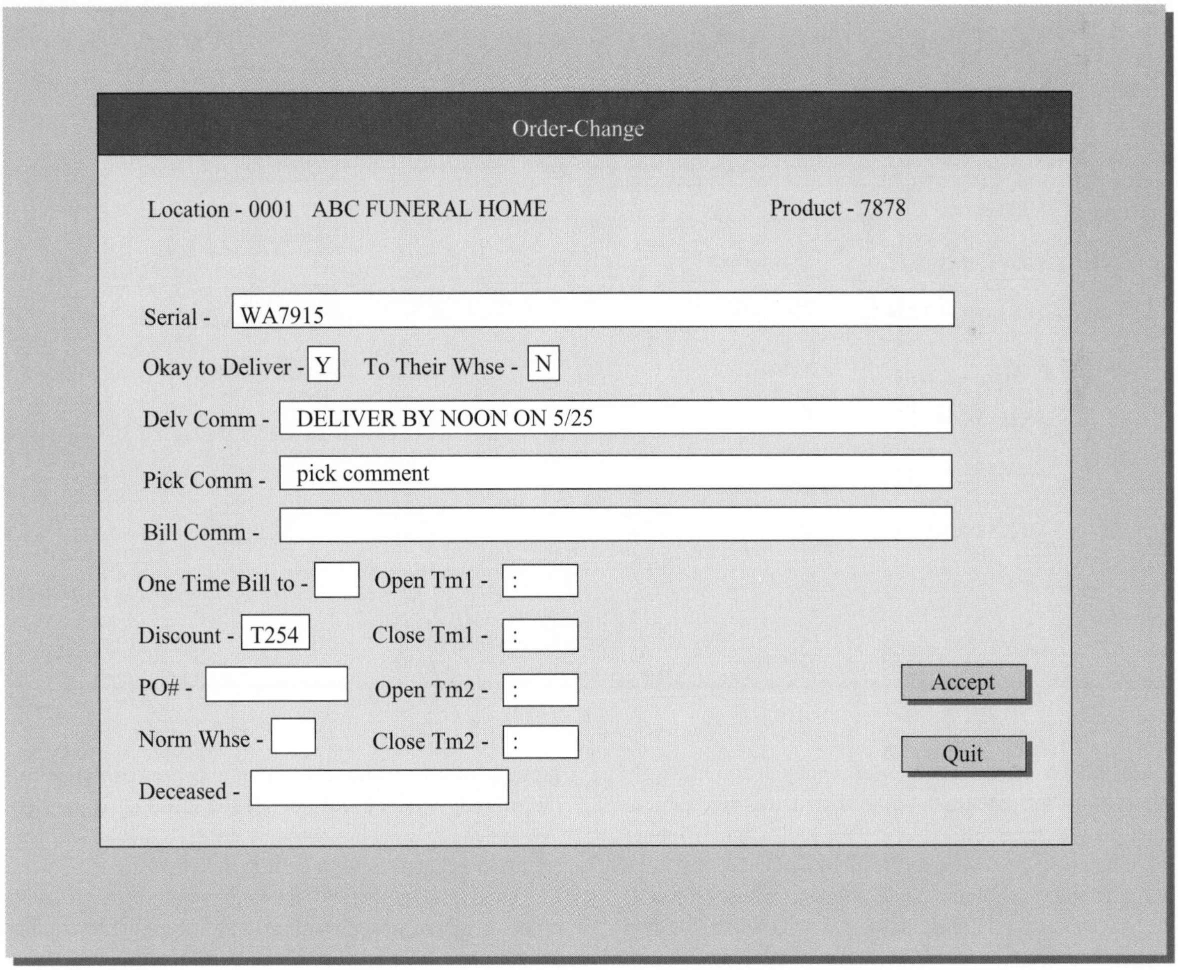

Order-Change

Location - 0001   ABC FUNERAL HOME   Product - 7878

Serial -   WA7915

Okay to Deliver - Y   To Their Whse - N

Delv Comm -   DELIVER BY NOON ON 5/25

Pick Comm -   pick comment

Bill Comm -

One Time Bill to -   Open Tm1 - :

Discount - T254   Close Tm1 - :

PO# -   Open Tm2 - :   Accept

Norm Whse -   Close Tm2 - :   Quit

Deceased -

EXHIBIT 6
Changed Order Update Screen.

```
                        Order-Update2

    Location - 0001   ABC FUNERAL HOME                    DELIVER

                      1001 MAIN  STRE, HOMETOWN, INDI     05-20-92 08:51
                                                          ┌─────────────┐
    Product -7878    Order Type -  D  Manifest -          │  Next Ordr  │
                                                          └─────────────┘
    Serial - [ WA7915                              ]      ┌─────────────┐
                                                          │  Prior Ordr │
    Route -  [ LOCAL  ]                                   └─────────────┘
                                                          ┌─────────────┐
    Okay to Deliver - [Y]  To Their Whse - [N]            │   Change    │
                                                          └─────────────┘
    Delv Comm - [ DELIVER BY NOON ON 5/25          ]      ┌─────────────┐
                                                          │   Cancel    │
    Pick Comm - [ PICK COMMENT                     ]      └─────────────┘
                                                          ┌─────────────┐
    Bill Comm - [                                  ]      │  Allocate   │
                                                          └─────────────┘
    One Time Bill to - [  ]  Open Tm1 - [ : ]             ┌─────────────┐
                                                          │  Unallocate │
    Discount - [ T254 ]      Close Tm1 - [ : ]            └─────────────┘
                                                          ┌─────────────┐
    PO# - [          ]       Open Tm2 - [ : ]             │   Assign    │
                                                          └─────────────┘
    Norm Whse - [  ]         Close Tm2 - [ : ]            ┌─────────────┐
                                                          │   Remove    │
    Deceased - [                      ]                   └─────────────┘
                                                          ┌─────────────┐
    Order information changed                             │  Chg Route  │
                                                          └─────────────┘
                                                          ┌─────────────┐
                                                          │    Quit     │
                                                          └─────────────┘
```

Although these basic concepts may seem relatively straightforward, the team found that it was not easy to learn to use them effectively. "We had a much longer learning curve than we expected," Munchel reports. "We had a training problem. When we decided on Object/1, the next vendor training class was scheduled for two months later, and we couldn't wait that long. So we brought in a consultant to do an abbreviated version of the training, and we did not get the training we needed. We ended up working through tutorials while we were trying to get started with coding the system."

This lack of formal training was critical because object-oriented programming is so different from other programming. "Object-oriented programming really is a totally different mind-set," Fairchild notes. "I couldn't find anything to relate it to in my 25 years of programming experience. In fact, my past experience often led me astray!"

"We didn't really understand the terminology," Holm explains. "It sounded like doubletalk—we laugh now. But once in a while the light would pop on and we'd think we understood. And then we would go on and find that we did not completely understand that, and we would have to go back to the beginning again. It was a highly repetitive process."

Not only did they have to learn the concepts, but they also had to learn how to use the Object/1 tool. Object/1 provides many classes and objects that one can use, but it takes some time to become familiar with what is there. "MDBS, Inc. provides a big book that contains descriptions of all these classes and methods," Fairchild explains, "and we had to learn whether to use one of theirs or write one of our own. It took us a long time to figure out what classes we were creating and maintaining. And we had to teach the other programmers (and ourselves) to look for existing methods before starting to code something new."

Object/1 supports the programmer by providing an on-line list of all the available objects and classes. When the programmer selects a class or object, a list of all the methods that apply to it appears on the screen. When a new object or method is created, it is automatically added to this on-line display. Object/1 also includes an on-line editor that enables a programmer to create code on the screen and edit it to make changes. Thus, Object/1 provides powerful assistance for on-line programming.

Developing the System

The team was scheduled to install the system in December 1991. They planned to train the Customer Service Center managers in December, when they were to be in Batesville for a national meeting, thus saving about $70,000 that it would cost to fly them in at another time. Although the team had decided on Object/1 in early June they did not produce any usable code until early September, because of their long learning curve.

By working 70-hour weeks, Holm, Fairchild, and two additional programmers were able to complete about 80 percent of the functionality of the system—the day-to-day operations necessary to run a Customer Service Center—by the training date in December, so they were able to train the Customer Service Center managers at the scheduled time. But the system was far from ready to

install—they still had to complete the remaining 20 percent of the functionality and take care of fundamental system operations like transaction logging and record locking. They also had to develop a system to convert the data files in the present system to the form required by the new system.

They also had to redo the data model of the old system. "Although about 95 percent of the data were there in the old system," Holm recalls, "the new model does not look like the model we had in the old system. We had to rethink the data in terms of object-oriented concepts."

The final system includes about 40 data objects, such as an order object, a customer object, and a casket object. There are many other objects, such as input and output screen objects. And they have created about ten "utility" classes, such as the print class that their programmers always use when printing a report. This print class includes methods that take care of the date, positioning column headers, page counts, spacing, accumulating and printing totals, and all the other things that are necessary to create a printed report.

Converting to the New System

Rather than the team going to each Customer Service Center to assist them in converting to the new system, the team devoted about two man-months to the creation of an elaborate conversion system to guide the Customer Service Center manager through the 40-odd steps necessary to install the new OS/2 operating system, load the new software on the hard disk, and convert the files from the old to the new system. It took between 6 and 12 hours to complete the conversion process at each Customer Service Center. And since there had been such a long time between the training in December and the actual installation of the system in April, the team also prepared and sent out a training version of the system in March so that the Customer Service Center managers could practice installing the system and play with it to refamiliarize themselves with the operation of the new system.

In mid-March 1992, they tested the system in the Customer Service Center in Indianapolis, and they began to convert to the new system in the rest of the Customer Service Centers in early April. When they converted the first four Customer Service Centers, they encountered a mysterious bug that set them back for a while. On rare occasions the system would mysteriously lock up, and they would have to shut it down and reload the software. With new hardware, a new operating system, the Object/1 development system, and the new application system, they were in totally unfamiliar territory and had to call in experts from IBM and the software vendor MDBS to help them diagnose and correct the problem, which turned out to be a bug in OS/2. As of June 1992, the system was successfully installed in all the Customer Service Centers.

Batesville Casket had purchased 15 of the new computers in late 1990 and installed them in Customer Service Centers early in 1991, running the old software on them. The system really flew! But the new system operates slower on the new hardware than the old system does, and the Customer Service Center managers that had used the old system on the new hardware have noticed this slowdown. The new system is slower because Object/1 programs are interpreted rather than compiled in this first generation version of the software.

Evaluation of This Experience

Although the team learned a tremendous amount about the object-oriented approach, they realize that they still have more to learn. "We need to change our approach to design as well as to writing code," Holm asserts. "We think we are in pretty good shape in object-oriented analysis, but we need to go back and work more on system and program design." Fairchild recalls that: "As part of the tool they say that a method should probably not exceed 15 to 20 lines of code, but we have some with a couple of hundred. We need to go back with what we have learned and rethink some of the things we have done."

They obviously did not meet the original December 1991 deadline for installing the system. After getting through the long learning curve, it took them about five months to code the system. "We did a lot of work in a short amount of time, even including the learning curve," Fairchild notes. "Without the Object/1 tool, I do not know how we could have produced a system with the graphical interface that we now have."

"The first system you develop using object-oriented programming may take about the same amount of time that it would using traditional approaches," Fairchild continues. "But where you are really going to make hay is on the next and succeeding systems. You don't have to go back and rewrite any of the things that you have already done. You can use the objects and methods that you have created, and they will port right into any new system. For example, we can use our print class in any new system, and there are many objects like that."

Holm notes that there are even wider implications. "One inventory control system, no matter what the industry, is much like any other. The object-oriented approach allows us to take advantage of that commonality. I would be comfortable taking this system to any company that is running a distribution warehouse, and it could be easily modified to suit its needs.

"Tools like Object/1 will eventually have an inventory control set of classes and methods that will allow any organization to easily put together an inventory control system to suit its needs. You will be able to make changes to reflect the uniqueness of your organization, while still taking advantage of all the commonality. You will be able to quickly create a working system from common objects, try it, and quickly modify it to suit your special needs."

Kuisel evaluates the project as follows: "It has taken longer than we planned, and a late project is always a disappointment. But the new system appears to be just what we wanted, and there is a lot of excitement about using it. The old system was getting to be a little shaky, but I'm confident that the new one is a solid foundation for what we want to do in the future.

"Moreover," Kuisel continues, "we have learned a lot about the object-oriented approach and how to use it. After this is over, we will evaluate this and other tools available in the marketplace and see what fits our needs best. I suspect that the object-oriented approach is going to come out ahead, but our development people will make that decision. They are the ones that must go through the very difficult learning curve to adapt to the object-oriented approach, so they must make their own commitment if we are to adopt this new technology for widespread use."

JOHNSON & JOHNSON: BUILDING AN INFRASTRUCTURE TO SUPPORT GLOBAL OPERATIONS

On January 1, 1995, Johnson and Johnson (J&J) established J&J Health Care Systems (HCS), whose mission was to provide J&J products to large managed care and provider organizations. HCS was a 1,200-person company representing the J&J U.S. pharmaceutical, diagnostic, medical/surgical and consumer companies to customers like HMOs, integrated delivery systems and hospital organizations. At the same time, it was a center of excellence defining the needs of this new breed of customer to the J&J operating companies. HCS was a response to the changing health care industry. As Dennis Longstreet, Chairman of J&J HCS, explained:

> The industry itself is reshaping and it's brought on by the desire for the payor to focus on the economics of health care. What's happened is that stand-alone hospitals and physicians, who had been our primary customers for health care products, are no longer the sole decision-makers. It's become an integrated delivery system, where the doctor and the hospital and the payor and insurance company are all becoming more connected to focus on delivering cost-effective quality health care.

© 1995 Massachusetts Institute of Technology. All rights reserved. This case was prepared by Jeanne W. Ross at the MIT Center for Information Systems Research, Sloan School of Management. The author would like to thank Mike Vitale, Jack Rockart and Debra Hofman for their helpful comments and the many Johnson & Johnson employees who contributed insights, cooperation and support.

J&J HCS was the second company that Johnson & Johnson had created to market products of existing companies to large customers. Johnson & Johnson's Customer Support Center was created in 1992 to sell J&J consumer products to large U.S. retailers like WalMart and KMart. Jim Litts, President of the Customer Support Center, noted that his efforts to work closely with six different operating companies represented a counter-cultural approach to work at J&J:

> J&J has over 100 years of history authorizing operating companies to manage all business facets to maximize their brands' P&Ls. Today, we are learning how difficult it is to break those paradigms and work together to leverage the strength of Johnson & Johnson with larger retail customers.

Whereas HCS and the Customer Support Center were different from J&J's usual independent operating company model, Longstreet and Litts felt they were representative of how J&J would operate in the future. The two executives noted that the inter-company cooperation and coordination demanded by this organizational model had significant implications for J&J's culture and for the amounts and kinds of information that would be communicated and shared across J&J operating companies.

Background

Johnson & Johnson, with 1994 sales of over $15 billion, was the world's largest manufacturer of health care products. Founded in 1886 as the first manufacturer of sterile dressings, the company had nearly doubled in size since 1987 and typically depended for one-third of its revenues on products that had been introduced within the prior five years. J&J sold products ranging from baby shampoo to treatments for leukemia and from disposable contact lenses to stents that could be inserted in arteries to improve the results of balloon angioplasty. In 1995, J&J had approximately 80,000 employees in about 160 operating companies, with markets in over 150 countries world-wide. (See Appendix A for a representative list of companies.)

Johnson & Johnson had a long history of managing its operating companies as independent businesses. Corporate executives, dating back to Robert Wood Johnson in the 1930s, embraced operating company autonomy as a path to increased flexibility, accountability and creativity. Independent analysts also credited the decentralized J&J management approach as largely responsible for the corporation's consistently strong financial performance.[1] The independence of the individual units, however, meant that J&J employees tended to view themselves as employees of a particular J&J operating company rather than of the corporation. There was rarely any movement of employees between operating companies, and operating company executives were compensated based on the performance of their company, not the corporation as a whole. Consequently, J&J companies often regarded one another more as competitors than as members of the same team.

By the early 1990s, top executives noted that J&J's autonomous operating companies were not well-positioned to service customers who were trying to limit the number of their vendor interactions. Each operating company had its own marketing and sales arm that worked directly with its customers. Matthew Martin, Vice President of Information Services for HCS, explained one consequence of this arrangement:

> Prior to the formation of Health Care Systems, each of the operating companies had a national accounts representative. Johnson & Johnson did not focus as a single corporation on its top customers. We could have up to 18 representatives from different J&J Companies calling on a customer. Eventually, we listened when the customer said, "Time out! Why can't Johnson & Johnson send me one person to deal with

to negotiate a contract. It's more efficient for me and it must be for you too!"

Over time, corporate management introduced a variety of structures to mitigate the limitations of the decentralized management approach and increase inter-company cooperation. For example, the operating companies were organized into three groups—Consumer, Pharmaceutical, and Professional—and the chairman of each group was given responsibility for identifying opportunities for leveraging services and expertise across companies in each of these markets. Franchise managers were assigned responsibility for coordinating cross-company sales of a family of products, such as the baby care products of operating companies like Johnson & Johnson Consumer in the U.S., Johnson & Johnson France, and Johnson & Johnson Pacific Pty. Ltd. in Australia. Finally, the introduction of HCS and the Customer Support Center represented radically new ways to organize work at J&J. These companies focused on working across U.S. companies to address the needs of U.S. customers, but they could eventually be expanded, or similar organizations could be introduced in other countries.

When the operating companies were completely autonomous, they had little need to share data. Most information flowed between a company and its customers, and financial data flowed from the company to corporate headquarters. Consequently, information systems, computing platforms, and data definitions grew up in J&J around individual company needs. As headquarters attempted to work across companies, management found that existing information systems and information system structures did little to facilitate those efforts. IS and business executives felt a need to build an information infrastructure that would respond to J&J's changing customer demands.

J&J's Information Technology Infrastructure

Consistent with J&J's decentralized approach to management, most information technology management responsibility was distributed to the operating companies. Each company typically had an independent information system unit responsible for systems planning, development, operations and maintenance. Operating company IT units also hired all their own IT staffs and were responsible for their compensation and professional development. Whereas historically there had been little cross-company coordination among IT professionals, Group IT Vice

---

1 See Tanouye, Elyse, "Johnson & Johnson Stays Fit by Shuffling Its Mix of Businesses," *Wall Street Journal,* December 22, 1992, p. A1, and Weber, Joseph, "A Big Company That Works," *Business Week,* May 4, 1992, pp. 124–132.

Presidents were appointed in 1993 and IT directors from the operating companies had dotted line reporting responsibility to them. (See the organization chart for the Corporate Office of Information Technology in Appendix B.)

Whereas most infrastructure support, such as LAN management, help desk, desktop support, and local computer and telecommunications operations was provided by operating company IS departments, a small centralized IT function was based in the corporate data center in New Jersey. Called Networking and Computing Services (NCS), this centralized unit was responsible for the data center, but its primary responsibility was for managing J&J's global network and providing mainframe computing services for all J&J businesses in the U.S.

J&J's global network was a traditional multiplexed T1 network providing telephone and dial-up data links between J&J headquarters, operating companies, and related facilities throughout the world. The 50 persons in the Corporate Network Services unit of NCS were responsible for contract negotiation and administration of telecommunications contracts, data network engineering and design, remote PBX and voice mail management, videoconferencing, and limited Internet support. NCS had not historically provided systems management or support for end-users and applications programmers, in part because the network environment was not conducive to centralized support. The operating companies had built a maze of subnetworks on a wide variety of computing platforms, and Network Services did not have the network management tools, the breadth of expertise, or the charter to manage those subnetworks.

Although most of J&J's operating companies received network support directly from Corporate Network Services in New Jersey, European companies (Western and Eastern Europe, Middle East, and Africa) received support from a regional center in Belgium. The European regional center managed a router-based, single transport, primarily TCP/IP network from one central location. This network was a subset of J&J's global network and supported 100 European J&J locations with a backbone of over 100 routers. More than 1,000 servers were connected to the network, and European Network Services staff managed the routers for all the local LANs to ensure that no one at a company site could configure a LAN in a manner that would jeopardize someone else. The tightly controlled nature of the network enabled a team of 11 J&J employees and 6 contractors to offer centralized support to European companies.

This team not only managed the physical part of the network (telecom lines, routers, voice multiplexers) but also increasingly emphasized deploying enterprise network applications like e-mail, groupware, executive support systems, affiliate communication, and set-up. Jos DeSmedt, Director of European Network Services, noted some implications of centralized network management:

> The design and management [of the European Network] facilitates very tight LAN and WAN integration. Since there are no subnetworks for individual companies or franchises anymore, the Network management becomes much more critical. On the other hand, we can automate the management more uniformly over the region from this central location.

The European Network Services unit had evolved from the Janssen Pharmaceutical IT unit, which serviced the largest operating company in Europe. Because many European operating companies were small, there were sometimes just a couple IT people addressing the needs of entire countries. Over time, they had purchased services from Janssen, which had resulted in many operating companies adopting Janssen standards for hardware and software. Thus, when European Network Services was formally established in July 1994, much of the service it provided had already been centralized.

Although U.S. companies were typically larger and more self-sufficient with regard to their IT needs, Bob Chaput, Vice President of Networking and Computing Services, considered the European network a model for J&J. He anticipated developing additional regional network service centers in Asia and Latin America. More immediately, he intended to upgrade the services available from the corporate facility. He created a team in his unit to evaluate and support infrastructure applications as well as a team to develop new network services. (See the Network and Computing Services organization chart in Appendix C.) He noted, however, that for these teams to fully realize their potential, the Networking and Computing Services organization would have to take a more proactive role in defining networks within the operating companies:

> We know that [centralized network support] will work because we've been successful in Europe. The difference is the companies in the U.S. are bigger and stronger. They have more people and they fight harder and longer to retain control and independence. But the businesses' applications people generally are happy to have some stability in infrastructure applications like e-mail and Notes to have something they know works and something they know is supported 24x7.

In early 1995 IT management identified four ways J&J's current infrastructure limited the company's ability to adapt to changing business conditions, particularly initiatives like HCS and the Customer Support Center. First, the amount of IS attention allocated to infrastructure management across the company was diluting the attention that could be focused on more strategic IT applications. Second, the lack of technology standards was inhibiting connectivity, aggravating attempts to service business needs, and costing too much to support. Third, the funding process for infrastructure projects was retarding efforts to build an enterprise-wide infrastructure. Finally, lack of data standards was impeding the meaningful exchange of data across companies.

Allocation of IS human resources

Bob Chaput estimated that 550 of J&J's approximately 1,500 U.S.-based IS professionals were engaged in supporting infrastructure technologies. He felt that centralizing functions such as telecommunications support, help desk, desktop and local area network management, and computer operations could cut that number in half, even if most of the staff remained physically located in operating companies. His goal was to free up IT resources to work on higher business value projects through increased centralization of infrastructure responsibilities in order to gain economies of scale and eliminate redundant work.

As a start, five major Professional Group companies in the U.S. had agreed to turn over responsibility for voice communications to Chaput's organization. In addition to its usual responsibility for working with vendors to design and install connections, Networking and Computing Services would have continuing management responsibility for telecommunications tasks such as voice mail and PBX moves, adds, and changes for the Professional Group companies. Warren Koster, Vice President of Information Technology for the Professional Group, noted that the companies expected centralized services to yield significant savings as well as some less tangible benefits:

> What we are driving to is leveraging the components of the infrastructure in Professional Group companies and driving costs out. At the same time, it's not just to drive out costs. It's to get people working on other projects that are more competitive and higher on the value chain and not worrying about the infrastructure parts.

Koster acknowledged that, despite the apparent efficiencies, there would be hesitation to move towards shared services like this, because of concerns about potential personnel shifts and decreases in service levels. The Professional Group companies were preparing to centralize their distributed systems management, and some operating company IT directors expressed concern that this responsibility should remain local because it demanded more personalized service than telecommunications, which was viewed as a commodity service. But while some IT managers were anxious about increased centralization of infrastructure responsibilities, others were enthusiastic supporters. Carolyn McQuade, Vice President of Information Technology for the Consumer Group, wanted to leverage expertise:

> We need to extend centralized management control of the infrastructure down to the desktop level. The amount of time that we all spend debugging software like WordPerfect 6.0 is just ridiculous. We all load the same software, discover the same bugs and go through the same experiences as many times as there are companies. It's a shameful waste. Some organizations have more talented people in that area than others. We really could do a much better job of leveraging what we know.

Establishing Information Technology Standards

Not surprisingly, the autonomy of the IT units at the operating companies had led to great variety in the technologies they employed. On the hardware side, there was variation in technologies like routers and bridges and small wars between MacIntosh and Windows computer users. On the software side, J&J had nine different e-mail systems, frequent debates about desktop products, and a variety of network operating systems. Jan Fields, Director of Corporate Network Services, noted that enforcing a limited set of standards was key to enabling centralization of infrastructure services:

> You can't possibly build the skills for half a dozen different kinds of routers and bridges, for example. It's foolish to do that. Managing nonstandard equipment when you have a problem, trying to sectionalize and troubleshoot it, and get the correct vendors involved—all of those kinds of things add a tremendous amount of time to solving any kind of problem.

The need to integrate different companies' systems and provide communication links for J&J HCS and the Customer Support Center highlighted the limitations of diversity in technologies. Networking and Computing Services had established standards, but operating companies were not always quick to adopt them. Nonetheless, the Customer Support Center's Jim Litts noted that he expected IT to establish standards and affiliated companies to conform to them:

> In my mind the IT community ought to come out and talk about the hardware and software to run this stuff. I think we ought to stop giving the operating companies votes. My point is, the software doesn't matter. Everybody will complain about it anyway. So let the IT guys make the economical, efficient choice, understanding, of course, what the user requirements are.

Funding Infrastructure Investments

Infrastructure development efforts by both Corporate and European Network Services were requisitioned by operating company management, who had to pay for whatever services they received. This charging mechanism sometimes acted as a deterrent to infrastructure investments. Bob Chaput provided an example:

> We'll have a franchise manager sitting in our Consumer business in New Jersey asking for manufacturing information from our plant in Singapore. Well, guess who's not connected? And so, the franchise manager will say, "Well, just go knock on their door and tell them you're here to install it." So we dutifully go out and knock on the door and say, "We're here to install your network connections at $1000 a month." And the local management says, "Time out, I don't have a thousand dollars a month."

Jan Fields noted that individual operating companies did not always see the benefit of infrastructure investments. Start-up businesses, in particular, might feel that limited funds were better spent elsewhere:

> They can say, "We can dial up for e-mail, and if we get it a day later or two days later it doesn't matter." They want to put their money where it is going to impact their customer. They may say to us "For five different countries, I expect to pay a total of no more than $2000 a month." You can't deliver service for that. But if that's what it is worth to them, then that's what it is worth.

Cross-company organizations like HCS and the Customer Support Center required that operating companies make changes for the good of J&J, even when the cost to the company seemed high. Funding processes that charged individual companies for infrastructure development could negatively impact investment levels. Chaput was trying to move discussions on infrastructure funding to higher organizational levels:

> When I go out into an operating company, I do a proposal, you react to it and we go back and forth. When you finally get the money, I get to start the project. We want to get out in advance of that. We want to build the interstate highway system. We want to be judicious about it, but we want to move towards the model of getting a congressional appropriation bill through and starting the project.

Creating Data Standards

The limitations of the existing infrastructure for addressing the changing needs of the business were exposed by the creation of the Customer Support Center and J&J HCS. When the Customer Support Center attempted to sell for national accounts, differing data definitions hindered efforts to understand how much total business any one customer did with J&J and what services J&J could offer. Jim Litts explained:

> If you go to a mass merchandiser as Johnson & Johnson, you can walk in there as the number one or number two non-food manufacturer on that account. At the same time you can bring things like pharmaceutical, professional, and pharmacy information and counsel and advice and ideas from our other J&J companies. If you do that together as J&J, you have a tremendous ability to start opening doors that you cannot do if you're one company selling sanitary protection products. You can go in there as J&J and have this story. So the guy says, "Okay, good. Give me some help." You turn around and you say, "Good grief, none of this stuff adds up." You spent an inordinate amount of time just trying to get the information together. Then you take it in there and they ask three questions, and you've got to go back and do it all over again.

Steve Piron, Vice President of Information Architecture, observed that franchise management also demanded cross-company information that was not available from existing systems:

> J&J France, for example, defined for itself the information it needed about the French Consumer business. But when we moved to worldwide franchises, like our shampoo business, we were stuck from an information point of view because we had product codes and product costs and definitions around the customer defined on a country level, and not a region [e.g., Europe] or a worldwide level. So we had apples and oranges from an information point of view.

Even where companies used common systems, they had, on occasion, abandoned common data definitions.

The Consumer companies, for example, had all adopted the same homegrown order entry system, but as Jim Litts explained, they did not all adopt the data definitions:

> Sales reporting for [Consumer] companies all comes out of the Group order entry system and is passed back in a uniform kind of format and information display. Then every company takes that and alters it. So when you try to add it back up again, or if you take the order entry system numbers and then go down and have a conversation with the company, they're different.

Building the IT Unit of the Future

To support J&J's efforts to increase cross-company cooperation and coordination, Ed Parrish, the corporation's chief information officer, identified three initiatives intended to enable easy sharing of information across companies: (1) standardizing data definitions and formats for key data elements on a world-wide basis, (2) defining and establishing the information technology infrastructure needed to share data and information electronically, and (3) developing and applying IT expertise as a corporate rather than a company function. These internal IT efforts were expected to increase the effectiveness of the IS unit and allow more time and attention for strategic applications of information technology.

Steve Piron was heading up efforts to standardize critical data definitions and the methods for communicating them. Along with a team of IT professionals who would recommend data standards to higher level IT and business managers, Piron was working to develop a data warehouse accessible, as needed, by J&J decision makers. Piron's teams would be putting a process in place that defined standard data definitions in critical areas like customer, product, competitor, supplier, and then determine which would be shared on a world-wide basis, which was a regional data item, and which was a country data item. They would also define processes to see that the standards got implemented in transaction processing systems around the world. HCS and the Customer Support Center had already specified some definitions and these would be presented to other companies.

NCS had started to define specific standards for hardware and software such as desktop office suites and LAN operating systems. Matthew Martin of HCS noted that these standards would be HCS standards and that this expectation had been communicated to all eighteen HCS companies. Executives at each company had been asked to specify needed dollar resources and time frames in order to "get up to speed." Ed Parrish noted that one company that was part of the HCS initiative had been adamantly opposed to standards, but quickly moved toward implementing them once HCS had made that commitment. Parrish said he would target 80% acceptance of standards, because by that point the other 20% would stand out and senior management would quickly bring them into line, if appropriate.

Parrish planned three efforts to position IT as a corporate function. First, he would initiate training programs in which IT staff throughout the corporation were taught what they needed to know about IT at Johnson & Johnson. Second, he would impact pay and performance by having Group Vice Presidents share their performance evaluations of IT directors with each IT director's company president. Finally, he would take over succession planning, so that when IT director positions opened up, the company president would receive a short list of candidates from which to choose a successor.

Conclusion

Johnson & Johnson had over one hundred years of experience in decentralized management practices, but the company needed to rapidly adopt processes that enabled it to share data across business units and practice cross-company cooperation. IT management identified several strategies to accelerate the process of implementing Parrish's initiatives:

- Some managers argued for adopting common systems to help implement new data definitions. Others, however, felt that common systems would not meet individual business needs and that clear definitions guiding development of translation programs were key to creating a successful data warehouse.
- Outsourcing was suggested as a means for forcing changes that consensus processes would be slow to embrace. Practices that involved personnel shifts and adoption of standards might be more easily accepted when mandated by external parties.
- Parrish noted that communicating standards and data definitions to senior management would help implementation efforts. As business executives decided they needed new kinds of information, they could enlist support for standards and force agreement on data definitions.

Johnson & Johnson would likely employ all these strategies as it attempted to adapt to dynamic business conditions.

APPENDIX A
Representative Sample of J&J Operating Companies.

Cilag—manufactures and markets products primarily discovered and/or developed by the R.W. Johnson Pharmaceutical Research Institute, includes products in areas such as fertility control, dermatology, and immunoregulatory peptides. Family of operating companies includes Cilag G.m.b.H. in Germany, Cilag-Medicamenta Limitada in Portugal, and Janssen-Cilag Pty. Ltd. in Australia.

Ethicon—develops and markets innovative products for surgeons. It produces thousands of sutures, ligatures and related products. Family of operating companies includes Ethicon, Inc. in the United States, Ethicon S.A. in France, Ethicon Endo-Surgery in Japan and Ethicon Limited in Scotland.

Janssen Pharmaceutica—produces a broad range of pharmaceutical products in areas such as allergy, anesthesiology gastroenterology, psychiatry, and cardiovascular disease. Family of companies includes Xian-Janssen Pharmaceutical Co. Ltd in China, Janssen Pharmaceutica, Limited in South Africa, Janssen Pharmaceutica S.A.C.I. in Greece and Janssen Farmaceutica, S.A. de C.V. in Mexico.

Johnson & Johnson Consumer Products, Inc.—provides wound care, baby care, oral care and skin care products. These are manufactured and sold in companies throughout the world, including Johnson & Johnson de Venezuela, S.A., Johnson & Johnson Inc. in Canada, Johnson & Johnson Limited in Zambia, and Johnson & Johnson/Gaba B.V. in The Netherlands.

Johnson & Johnson Medical Inc.—provides products for wound management and patient care, such as intravenous catheters, disposable surgical packs, latex surgical and medical gloves, and wound care sponges and dressings. Family of companies includes Johnson & Johnson Medical Thailand, Johnson & Johnson Medical in the Philippines, Johnson & Johnson Medical in Ireland and Johnson & Johnson Medical AG in Switzerland.

Johnson & Johnson Professional Inc.—develops and markets products under the CODMAN brand for the surgical treatment of central nervous systems disorders and under the J&J Orthopaedics brand for musculoskeletal system repairs. Family of companies includes Johnson & Johnson Professional Products Ltd. in England, Johnson & Johnson Professional Products in Sweden, and Johnson & Johnson Professional Products, G.m.b.H in Germany.

Ortho Diagnostic Systems Inc.—provides diagnostic reagent and instrument systems to hospital laboratories, commercial clinical laboratories and blood donor centers, such as diagnostic systems for coagulation, AIDS, hepatitis and other infectious diseases. Ortho Diagnostics is found in Canada, France, Japan, Spain and the United States.

Vistakon—produces and markets the leading disposable contact lens. This operating company is based in the United States.

APPENDIX B
Corporate Office of Information Technology.

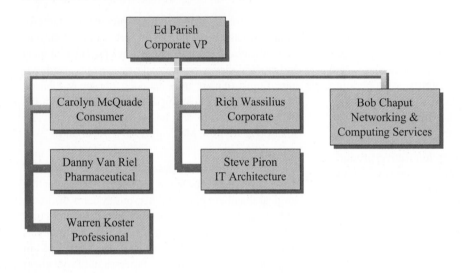

APPENDIX C
Networking and Computing Services.

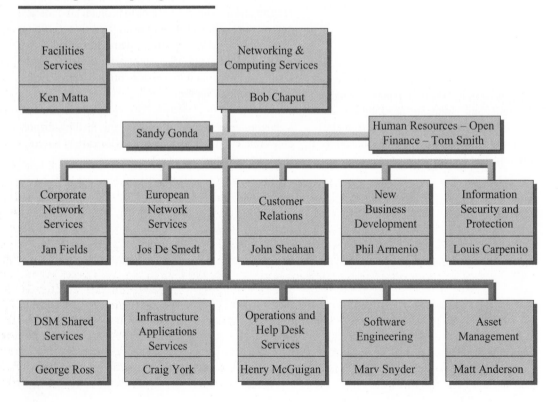

IBM–Indiana[1]

International Business Machines Corp. (IBM), a leader of the computer revolution, became one of the outstanding success stories of the second half of the 20th century. By the 1970s IBM had about 70% of the computer market and was highly respected for its progressive management and its integrity. A pioneering multinational, IBM operates worldwide and typically derives over half its revenues from outside the U.S.

Up through the early 1980s, IBM continued spectacular growth, but it also became more bureaucratic and slow-moving. Soon after career IBMer John Akers took over the helm in 1985, IBM's profit margins began to slip and it became obvious that IBM faced a troubled future. Over the years Akers downsized IBM from over 405,000 to around 300,000 employees worldwide, attempted to focus IBM more on the needs of its customers, reorganized the company twice, cut IBM's product development cycle time in half, and replaced most of the IBM product line with very competitive hardware. However, IBM continued to lose market share and profit margin and had unprecedented losses in 1991 and 1992. (See Exhibit 1.) Furthermore, IBM stock dropped from $176 in 1987 to $49 in 1992. In early 1993 Akers resigned and the IBM board decided that an outsider was required to turn IBM around.

After much speculation about possible candidates and a widely publicized search, Louis V. Gerstner was named IBM CEO. Gerstner had started his career with McKinsey & Company, joined American Express and rose to its presidency, and in 1989 he was hired as CEO by RJR Nabisco Holdings Inc. to lead a recovery after a takeover battle that saddled that company with $25 billion in debt.

Concentrating on downsizing and customer service, Gerstner targeted IBM's worldwide employment at 225,000, to be achieved by the end of 1994, and told IBM employees: "I start with the premise that our customers are looking for us to deliver solutions to their problems. So we've got to get back to delivering superior solutions to our customers."

The Telecommuting Project

In June, 1992, Michael W. Wiley became general manager of IBM's operations in the state of Indiana. Wiley was a second-generation IBMer who started as a salesman in 1980 and moved rapidly up through increasingly responsible staff and line marketing jobs to become administrative assistant to Senior Vice President George Conrades before taking over in Indiana.

During 1992, IBM continued to downsize and Indiana reduced its head count by about 30%. In 1992, IBM had its worst overall financial results ever, and word was out that Indiana faced the prospect of similar head-count reductions in 1993. In February, 1993, John F. Frank, new operations manager for the state, made his first visit to the new IBM building in Evansville that was part of his responsibility. Frank recalls:

"It was a gorgeous new building looking out over the Ohio river, and we had just moved into it in May, 1991. Although IBM did not own it, it had been built for IBM and was one of the most expensive buildings in Evansville.

That Tuesday, this beautiful building was virtually empty. I looked across a big room full of desks of marketing people, who were all out talking to customers, and I could have shot a shotgun in any direction without hurting anyone. I was shown through beautiful conference rooms and classrooms, most of which were empty. I couldn't figure out why we had all this space that must have been costing us a fortune.

1 This case was prepared by Professor E. W. Martin as the basis for class discussion rather than to illustrate either effective or ineffective handling of an administrative situation. Its development was supported by the Institute for Research on the Management of Information Systems (IRMIS), School of Business, Indiana University.

EXHIBIT 1
IBM ten-year revenues and income (in millions) and stock prices to nearest dollar).

	1992	1991	1990	1989	1988	1987	1986	1985	1984	1983
Revenue	64,523	64,792	69,018	62,710	59,681	54,217	51,250	50,056	45,937	40,180
Operating Income	8,199	9,489	15,249	13,553	12,617	11,269	11,175	14,281	14,446	13,216
Net Income	(6,865)	(564)	6,020	3,758	5,491	5,258	4,789	6,555	6,582	5,485
Stock Price (high)	101	140	123	131	130	176	162	159	129	134
Stock Price (low)	49	84	95	94	104	102	119	118	99	92

It wasn't just the real estate cost, but also the occupancy costs—the information technology, support staff, utilities, taxes—that were killing us. So I spent my time on the plane on the way back making a rough estimate of what it was costing us to run all the IBM buildings in the state of Indiana.

When I got home at 9:30 p.m., I called Mike Wiley and told him that I thought we could save a minimum of two to three million dollars in Indiana in the first year, and three to four million a year from then on, by reducing our real estate costs. After I went over my rough figures with him, Mike said, 'Let's make it happen!'"

When Frank called, Wiley was preparing for a meeting in Chicago with the Midwestern Area vice president and his counterpart general managers to talk about how many head-count reductions would be required to meet the area's profitability targets. Wiley recalls:

"With our strategy of providing value to the customer by solving problems, the last thing I wanted to do was to eliminate more people. We solve problems with highly skilled, highly specialized people, and I was convinced that we should cut everything else before reducing our competitive advantage by cutting productive people. So when John called me with his idea of saving big money by reducing facilities costs, I told him we had three days to put together a proposal to take with me to the meeting in Chicago so that I could present it as an alternative to cutting people."

They put together a team consisting of Wiley, Frank, and the chief financial and chief information people for Indiana. Frank recalls:

"We spent 36 hours straight putting the plan together. When I made the proposal I knew a little about telecommuting, but I didn't know much about the details. It was late-night trips to the library researching what other companies were doing that prepared us

to put together a rough plan. This plan called for reducing our real estate in Indiana by 65% by moving all of our client-related personnel out of the traditional office environment into offices in their homes."

IBM-Indiana's proposal to substitute telecommuting for head-count reductions was accepted by Midwestern Area management. This proposal would not affect people whose main workplace was an office. Rather, only IBM people who spent most of their time with customers and worked in their offices only 30% to 40% of the time were to telecommute. Those people whose main workplace was an office would continue to work at an IBM location.

The Telecommuting Environment

There were four important components of IBM-Indiana's telecommuting environment: home office equipment, communications facilities, shared workspace at the IBM location, and reengineered work support processes. Since the major initial motivation for telecommuting was to reduce costs, the project team did not plan to provide an *ideal* office environment, but rather to provide a *satisfactory* environment with a minimal investment.

The home office equipment provided included an IBM PS/2 computer with a standard set of software, an IBM Proprinter dot matrix printer, a desk, a chair, and a two- or four-drawer filing cabinet. The PS/2 provided was a Model 70 or 80 with a minimum of 110 MBytes of hard-drive capacity and 12 MBytes of RAM and was usually the machine that had been in the telecommuter's IBM building office. The following standard software was installed on each PC before it left the IBM location: the OS/2 Version 2 operating system, Lotus AmiPro for word processing, Lotus Freelance presentation software, Lotus 1-2-3 spreadsheet software, FaxWorks for sending and receiving FAXes, and standard telecommunications software for getting into IBM's LAN and mainframe IS facilities. The desks, chairs, and filing cabinets had been used in the IBM offices that were being phased out. An employee could opt to take a cash allowance for any piece of equipment and furnish it himself or herself, but everyone had to use the IBM-provided standard software. IBM configured the PS/2, installed the software, and moved all the equipment to the employee's home.

Good communications support would be critical to the success of telecommuting. In addition to the employee's existing telephone facilities, IBM provided two more telephone lines into the home office, one for voice and another for data. IBM also furnished a 14.4 kilobaud FAX and data modem and an AT&T 722 telephone with the following features: two lines (one personal and one IBM), speaker phone, conference between lines one and two, memories to store numbers and access codes, and hold and flash buttons. IBM paid the installation charges and monthly bills for these lines.

IBM intended that an inbound caller should never get a "no answer" or a busy signal, and the caller should be able to talk to a knowledgeable person if he or she wished. This concept was implemented as follows: Any call to the employee's IBM extension was automatically forwarded to the home office phone. If that line was busy or was not answered after three rings, the call was sent to the employee's phonemail box, where it was answered by the employee's personal message that indicated when the call would be returned. The phonemail message also instructed the caller to touch certain keys to reach a live person, and those calls were forwarded to the customer service center to be handled by the people there.

There were two types of shared workspace at the IBM office locations. First, there were small cubicles equipped with a telephone and a PS/2 computer with the standard software networked to laser printers and the IBM internal computer systems. One of these work areas was provided for every four telecommuters, and they were available on a first-come, first-served basis. A few enclosed offices were also provided that could be scheduled by managers or teams for private conferences. Although these offices also contained telephones and PS/2s, there were too few of them to allow their use as workspace, so managers were expected to use the small cubicles for everything except private conferences or team meetings.

The IBM location also included a conference room or rooms for group meetings, a mail room, a secretarial support center and an administrative support center. Each telecommuter was also provided with a file drawer near the cubicles.

IBM-Indiana also downsized its office support group and decided to use people provided by an outside con-

tractor instead of IBM employees to perform this function. In Indianapolis they established several support groups: an administrative services group that handled time cards, expense accounts, keeping publications tables up to date, and other administrative functions; a secretarial pool that scheduled the use of shared offices, set up meetings and teleconferences, and performed other secretarial duties; a word processing pool that typed letters and contracts, prepared graphics for presentations, and prepared proposal documents and meeting handouts; and a mail room crew that distributed mail and faxes, handled copying, and distributed the output sent from home offices to central office printers.

Virtually all work support processes had to be redesigned to function in this new environment. For example, how do you schedule meetings and teleconferences when no one is around the office? Does the secretary call each participant to find feasible times, and then call back to notify each person of the time chosen? Do you use e-mail for these communications? They decided to rely on the PROFS[2] calendaring function to schedule meetings and teleconferences. PROFS makes it possible for a secretary to enter a list of people and the length of the meeting, and the computer searches for a time when all the participants are available to meet. But to make this work, everyone had to maintain his or her schedule of activities on the computer, and these schedules had to be accurate and up to date. At first, some people did not keep their online calendar up to date, but the secretaries went on and scheduled meetings based on the calendars and those who missed important meetings soon learned their lesson.

The processes that had to be redesigned ranged from how to submit an expense account to how to get a proposal prepared. Not only did someone have to decide how to perform each of these activities, but they also had to provide training and written descriptions to all 300 telecommuters. The office support staff prepared a thick reference manual describing the new processes and then converted it to an online help system.

The Implementation Process

Wiley recalls setting up the team to implement telecommuting:

"We couldn't have done this without a small group of creative thinkers—visionaries like John Frank—who

---

2 IBM's Professional Office System (PROFS) is an integrated office software system that runs on a mainframe. Among its many functions, PROFs provides electronic mail, a calendaring function that keeps a person's schedule and can make it available to others, and document preparation, distribution, and retrieval capabilities.

also have the talent to organize and manage this kind of complex change.

I asked them how quickly we could implement telecommuting, and they said they thought we could do it in nine months. We couldn't wait that long, so I told them they had to get it done in 90 days. Now I wish I had told them to do it in 30 days. The faster you can get it done, the less chaos and resistance you have from your people. When they get in the new environment and see it work, they realize it makes sense, they see where they fit in, they learn what to do, and they do it."

There was a lot to do in three months. The team had to identify the needs of the telecommuters and define the specific technology to be used to meet those needs. They had to determine who would telecommute and who would not. They had to plan and schedule the activities necessary to move more than 300 telecommuters' offices to their homes. This planning and scheduling took about a month, so they had only 60 days to do the following:

- Purchase modems, software, and phone equipment
- Secure the necessary furniture
- Upgrade the local office telephone switches
- Set up each of the PS/2s with proper features and software
- Provide three days of training on the new tools for each telecommuter
- Reengineer all support processes
- Prepare homes, including new telephone lines
- Deliver the equipment to each telecommuter's home
- Vacate the freed-up office space
- Remodel remaining office space to adapt it to new uses

There were a number of issues that had to be resolved on the fly, such as the tax and liability status of the equipment being moved out into employees' homes and how to deal with security issues relating to access to IBM-confidential systems. There was a lot going on at once—for example, they had construction projects going on in six locations in the state at one time. But they got it all done and had some 300 people telecommuting, and the freed-up real estate ready for release, in 90 days!

Motivating the Change to Telecommuting

Wiley knew that the move to telecommuting was going to be a tremendous change for the people involved, and he took responsibility for leading the charge. He put a lot of effort into selling the idea and motivating those who were reluctant to telecommute, and he was one of the first people in the state to move out of his office.

Wiley sold the move to telecommuting primarily as a way to save 50 IBM jobs in the state. He also expounded other benefits of telecommuting, such as providing more effective service to customers, eliminating the time and stress of commuting into the office, eliminating parking problems, and providing more time at home with family by allowing more flexible time management. But with the history of downsizing that IBM had been through, saving jobs was the justification that most everyone accepted. According to Frank:

"When we announced the move to telecommuting, about half of the people involved were eager to go. Many who were initially reluctant were quickly convinced by Mike Wiley's explanation of why telecommuting was necessary. But the remaining group included most of our managers, who were used to private offices with secretaries answering their phones and providing plenty of one-on-one support. Wiley took the reluctant managers into a room and told them: 'I know you are uncomfortable with this. I know this is bruising your egos, because IBM has conditioned you to expect these perks. But if we don't have the guts as a management team to make radical changes in these dire circumstances, we are headed for disaster. We need to show the rest of the company what can be done. If we aren't willing to give up some perks everyone will know that management doesn't understand what is going on. So I'm asking you to fully endorse this.' Out of about twenty managers, only one transferred out."

Wiley agrees that the managers had the greatest problems coping with this change. He says:

"Those managers who had always been focused on the customer and had been out with their people helping them solve problems were eager to adopt telecommuting as a productivity enhancement. But the ones who had problems were those who were hung up on the prestige of an office and a secretary, who would come in and sign onto their electronic mail service and their phonemail service and sit in their office all day instead of being out with their customers. Not only did they have a problem with prestige, but they had a problem with what to do all day if they didn't have an office to come to. They had to ask the question: 'What marketable skills do I really have?' And if they had none, then they had to go get a skill that brings some value to our customers or there would be no reason for them to be here."

According to Frank, about 25 percent of the telecommuters went along reluctantly with the change. However, after experiencing the new environment, and after some improvements in the support technology provided, about half of this 25 percent converted to supporters of the concept. Frank notes:

> "It is kind of ironic. Many of those people who did not want to go are now the ones who are writing testimonials and volunteering to go around and talk to other employees and say: I did not want to do this; I had five kids at home; My house was too small; etc. But it works—it has advantages that compensate for the problems.
>
> Still, about 10 percent of our people will probably not be happy with telecommuting for any of a number of reasons. It could be personal in nature, or it could be that they just can't be happy changing from what they have been used to for many years."

Reactions of the Telecommuters

During the process and afterward, the team solicited feedback via e-mail from all the participants and used this feedback to identify and reduce the problems that were revealed.

Positive Reactions

The vast majority of the telecommuters agreed that telecommuting was good for IBM, and many felt that it was an improvement for them personally. Many respondents reported that they were pleased with the impact of telecommuting on their productivity and job satisfaction:

> "Telecommuting is the best idea that we have come up with in all the time I have worked with IBM. My productivity is much higher than before and, hopefully, we have saved a lot of real estate expense."

> "I can honestly say that you would have to threaten to FIRE ME to get me to go back to the traditional environment. I am almost ashamed of how much time and money I wasted in the office in my career. It has gotten to the point that I refuse to go to the office unless it is absolutely necessary because it is so unproductive."

> "This has been the greatest single boon to my productivity since I've been in IBM. I have become much more organized because I have everything I need in one place instead of in my car, on my desk, at the customer site, or at home. I also find that I do many small things at odd hours; for example, I do most of my PROFS while my kids are in the shower."

> "I am finding that I spend a lot less time at home than I imagined. Where before there was always 'the office' to go to for mail, notes, etc., I know that I can do that stuff for a short time after the kids go to bed and clear it up and get it off my mind, but still be home. I think this has let me spend more and better time with customers."

Some telecommuters were pleased that they no longer had to drive back and forth to the office:

> "My workload has increased dramatically this year, and this program has allowed me to work the extra hours I need without taking a trip downtown or walking down a dark alley to my car. The net is that I can work whenever I want, I can work safe, and I don't need to spend time traveling. That is worth a lot to me."

> "I live approximately 75 miles from the office, so telecommuting has been a real time and car saver for me."

A number of people were pleased with the improvements in their lifestyle resulting from telecommuting, especially the ability to spend more time with their children.

> "I have found that I spend less time at home than I thought I would, but I very much like the flexibility. I can eat an early dinner with the family because of special plans for the evening, then come back to my desk at 10:00 to cover just a few more things. Also, I now have the option of sitting at home in my jeans, free from traffic, suits and tall buildings, and asking myself: How can I absolutely best spend my time to get the needed results? This freedom allows more creativity in my thinking about what is needed to get the job done."

> "My typical workday has me hitting my office at 6:30, getting things done when previously I would have been starting the drive into the office. A great benefit is the ability to eat breakfast with my children, who I previously seldom saw before 6:00 p.m."

Not all the feedback was strictly serious. Someone sent in his Top Ten reasons why telecommuting should be fun:

10. Lunch is cheaper and usually resembles dinner the night before.
9. The printer is closer and isn't backed up or jammed.
8. The coffee is fresher, and the brand doesn't upset your stomach.
7. You can impress your friends because YOU have an IBM PC at home.
6. The coffee mugs don't have green fuzz in the bottom.
5. You have to keep your desk clean or your spouse will.
4. Now the neighbors really wonder what you do for a living.
3. It gives new meaning to the term "business casual."

2. The chances are better for being the ninth caller for the cash song.

AND THE NUMBER ONE REASON . . .

1. When you want something thrown out you don't have to write "Trash" on it and trip over it for three days before it disappears.

Concerns of the Telecommuters

Although most of the telecommuters ended up supporting the change to telecommuting, some of the supporters reported concerns. Several telecommuters were troubled by the lack of interaction with peers that they very much missed, and some noted that the lack of casual contact made it much more difficult to exchange information and work as a team:

"I miss the camaraderie of the branch. It's hard to get informal communication going between teams, and tracking projects is a little rougher."

"The loss of the group-work setting has been a major psychological adjustment which most people are not yet over. The interaction with peers shortened the time required to accomplish many tasks because we were able to 'group together' for many short, impromptu meetings to decide strategy, plans, etc. This is very much missing and missed."

"The grapevine thing is missing. Face it, we all like to know what's going on. We don't know what's happening out there anymore. We eat lunch alone. We don't exchange news items that concern our customers. There is no networking, no socialization, no moral support."

Wiley recognized that lack of social contact and casual communication would be problems, and he has encouraged IBM-Indiana offices to set up special occasions, such as weekly office luncheons, to provide opportunities for interaction. IBM-Indiana has also found it necessary to be intentional about communication by scheduling meetings to substitute for the informal communication that took place when everyone was in the office. They also make heavy use of teleconferencing to substitute for face-to-face meetings.

Some telecommuters noted that it was more difficult to communicate than before.

"It is almost impossible to contact someone in the branch in under eight hours. If you are in a situation where you need a resource quickly, you are in trouble."

"The one drawback seems to be playing telephone tag more often. It is a lot harder to speak with a real person unless you set up meetings or conference calls."

Some people expressed concern about never being away from the work environment:

"The only disadvantage I see is that we are working a lot more hours this way. It's just too tempting to jump on the system on weekends and during the evenings. Vacations will be forced to be 'away from home' vacations in order to really get away from it all."

"It is very hard to separate personal life from work when you can never really get away from the office. It is always just down the hall!!"

Those few who did not support telecommuting seemed to be quite frustrated by this new environment.

"I am very dissatisfied with the working environment of telecommuting and do not feel that shared workspace at the office is a workable alternative."

"Contrary to the PROFS note relating how telecommuting is a good deal, it's not. I ended up dedicating one room of my house to it. My house is not air-conditioned, and it is pretty uncomfortable sitting on a two-hour conference call in that environment. The correlation between mileage, lunch, etc., is ridiculous."

Problems with the Initial Technological Support

There were a number of significant problems with the technological support provided initially. One telecommuter reported his frustration with these problems:

"System configurations are inadequate, printing is a major league problem, the phone system does not yet support this concept, and shared workspace isn't adequate. These problems seem minor, but they add up to so much chaos and disruption that I find it difficult to get my job done."

The phone system was one of the most difficult problems, because it was very difficult to forward calls to the telephone where a person was working when in the IBM office. That meant incoming calls would end up in phonemail. Also, in some areas the phone company could not transfer a call to the IBMers' phonemail when their home phone was busy or unanswered, so all incoming calls had to go directly into phonemail to make sure that all calls were picked up. Two typical comments:

"The area that causes the most difficulty is getting my calls when I am in the downtown office. Not being able to have a customer call you back at the desk where you are sitting, but instead call your phonemail, is frustrating."

"We must get our office phones to ring at our homes and then roll over to phonemail. Our current environment of our customers not being able to reach us direct is NOT working out well, and our not being able to reach each other efficiently is greatly impacting our productivity."

One of the most common problems with the initial technology was the difficulty of getting letter-quality printing done:

"Yesterday I directed several printouts to the 3820 printer at the office. I stopped in for a few minutes this morning to pick up the printouts only to find that the printers were broken (again). So far I've spent three hours redirecting stuff to other printers. Not very productive!"

The IBM internal IS systems and the difficulty of accessing them from home offices provided many frustrations:

"Our equipment and programs are exactly what we tell our customers to move away from as quickly as possible. I am still working on a 386 with an old version of OS/2 and applications that do not work properly. Our online systems are very old and out of date. Much productivity gain could be realized by new equipment, better software, and a more up-to-date network."

"We MUST provide remote access to some of our most basic I/S tools. It boggles my mind that from my home I can pull a sales report that would be very attractive to a competitor, yet I cannot look at an on-order record to check an install date or a feature code."

One of the lessons learned from the above feedback was that success of telecommuting is heavily influenced by the supporting technology that is available. IBM-Indiana soon replaced the dot matrix printers that had been provided for the home offices with Lexmark laser printers, which greatly alleviated the printing problems. The telecommuting team also worked to upgrade the communications facilities, and Wiley has devoted a lot of effort to improving the IBM IS systems.

The Change to "Mobility"

In the fall of 1993, the IBM ThinkPad laptop was made available as an exchange for PS/2s on very favorable terms. This enabled IBM-Indiana to switch to ThinkPads that fall and to upgrade from telecommuting to "mobility." The term mobility refers to an environment in which workers can access information and perform their work anywhere and at any time. Wiley and Frank would have preferred mobility to telecommuting from the beginning, but because their first objective was major cost savings, they were initially unable to afford the technology investment required for mobility.

The technology involved in implementing mobility requires laptop computers and may also include cellular data communications, alphanumeric pagers, and dial-in LANs. In Indiana, going from telecommuting to mobility involved replacing the PS/2s with IBM ThinkPad 720M laptop computers that used a 486 chip and were about 10 times as powerful as the 386-based PS/2s they replaced. The ThinkPads deployed had 16 MBytes of memory, 160 MByte hard drives, a token ring PCMCIA card, a PCMCIA APEX 14.4 data/fax modem, a 3270 PCMCIA card, a carrying case, and batteries and charger. The ThinkPads were loaded with essentially the same operating system and applications software as the PS/2s they replaced, so it was easy for the telecommuters to convert to the use of the new machines.

IBM-Indiana also replaced the data lines to homes with dial-in access to LANs in the IBM offices. Not only was the dial-in access less expensive, but the employees could dial in from anywhere, not just their homes. In addition, alphanumeric pagers were furnished to many employees. IBM-Indiana considered cellular communications, but decided the additional cost of that technology could not be justified except in special cases. IBM-Indiana also experimented with the use of a pen-based version of the ThinkPad for some people.

Evaluation of the Results

After the telecommuting project was implemented, Wiley invited IBM to send in a financial team from outside the state to evaluate the results. This team reported that IBM had saved $3.2 million in 1993 and that they would save $5 million a year in 1994 and each year afterward, which was far better than Frank's original estimates. In addition, Wiley was convinced that the productivity of the telecommuters had been significantly enhanced. "I know that my own productivity has improved by at least 20% since I moved my office home," Wiley asserts.

Impressed with the results of telecommuting in Indiana, the Midwestern Area in late 1993 adopted the mobility concept. John Frank became the leader of the effort to extend what had been done for 300 people in Indiana to some 2,500 people throughout the Midwest.

As of March 1994, the concept of mobility was being embraced throughout IBM, although only a few locations were as far along with it as was Indiana. In addition, there has been great outside interest in this concept, and several of IBM's customers have requested help in implementing it. In response, the IBM Midwestern Area mobility implementation team has set up a consulting practice to become a total solution provider in mobile workforce deployment.

APPLYING INFORMATION TECHNOLOGY

Chapters 5 through 7 offer a comprehensive view of the applications of information technology in organizations. Rapid changes in technology, business conditions, management methods, and types of applications make it important that user-managers develop a clear understanding of how they can take advantage of the powerful capabilities of IT for themselves and their businesses. To complete the picture, Chapter 8 identifies a wide range of social, political, and ethical issues relating to the use of information technology. Managers must be aware of these issues as they consider ways in which information technology can and should be used in their organizations.

The purpose of the first three chapters of this section is to increase awareness and understanding of how information technology can be used in an organizational setting. Chapters 5 and 6 focus on IT applications *within* a particular organization: organizational systems—systems that support the entire organization or large portions of it (Chapter 5) —and managerial support systems—systems designed to provide support to a specific manager or a small group of managers (Chapter 6). Organizational systems include transaction processing, enterprise resource planning, data warehousing, office automation, groupware, intranets, and factory automation. Among the managerial support systems discussed are decision support, group support, geographic information systems, expert systems, neural networks, and virtual reality. At the beginning of Chapter 5, we introduce several concepts critical to the understanding of information technology applications, including batch vs. on-line processing and client/server systems.

The focus of Chapter 7 is applications for electronic commerce. The chapter begins with an introduction to interorganizational systems (IOS) and a classic example, the SABRE reservation system of American Airlines. Electronic data interchange (EDI), the electronic exchange of business documents using an agreed-upon set of standards, is discussed and a number of EDI applications are described. Then, building upon IOS and EDI, the primary emphasis of the chapter is on electronic commerce on the World Wide Web. Because of the widespread diffusion of Web browser software, businesses today can electronically link not only to business customers, but also to end-consumers like you. The benefits and constraints of electronic commerce via the Internet are considered along with multiple Internet applications. The Web strategies pursued by businesses are explored, as well as special management issues associated with electronic commerce.

Chapter 8 explores some social, ethical, and political issues that are raised by the use of information technology. IT impacts both our professional and our personal lives in a growing number of ways, and this chapter considers some of these impacts upon our society. Those who control IT have great power to influence the welfare of individuals and the public, and the ways in which managers use this power raises ethical issues that are explored. Further, because information is valuable to individuals as well as to organizations, political issues can be expected to arise whenever one attempts to exploit IT in an organization. Many new systems have failed because of resistance by those affected by the systems. Managers need to understand information politics and how to prevent or deal with political problems.

After studying these four chapters, you should have a more complete understanding of the scope of the use of information technology in organizations. You should also more fully comprehend how information systems management in organizations has had to change over time and how progressive user-managers are making both operational and strategic use of their computing, telecommunications, and other information technologies.

Part II concludes with a diverse set of case studies. The case study of Midstate University Business Placement Office (A) looks at the information processing system that supports the day-to-day operations of a university placement office and provides management information to the office's director and other high-level managers. The Ameritech Publishing case study provides an excellent example of the development and implementation of an organizational system to support a new vision of the business. Two case studies deal with electronic commerce applications on the World Wide Web: Batesville Casket Web Site describes the development of a Web presence for this established manufacturer, and Telamon Corporation: Creation of the Asian Mall presents the story of the development of a Web-based shopping mall for an entrepreneurial firm. Finally, a set of four short case studies emphasize political and ethical issues in the use of information technology.

CHAPTER 5

ORGANIZATIONAL SYSTEMS

Information technology is a key enabler for organizations of all sizes, both public and private. Businesses and other organizations are not the same as they were a decade ago. They are more complex but have fewer layers of management; they tend to offer more customized products and services; they are increasingly international in scope; and they are heavily dependent on the accurate and timely flow of information. And this change in organizations is accelerating, not decelerating.

As a current or future manager, you must be aware of information technology and its potential impact on your job, your career, and your organization. You cannot afford to leave consideration of information technology solely to the information systems (IS) specialists. As a user-manager, you must perform many critical roles if you and your organization are to be successful: conceptualize ways in which information technology can be used to improve performance; serve as a consultant to the IS specialists who are developing or implementing applications for your organization; manage the organizational change that accompanies new IT applications; use the technology applications and help enhance them; and help ensure the successful implementation of new IT applications.

Where do we start getting you ready for your new roles? We start with an *awareness* of how information technology is being used in a variety of organizations. Chapter 1 has already begun this process of building information technology awareness, and this chapter and the two that follow provide a systematic introduction to a wide variety of information technology applications. We think you will be impressed with the breadth of areas in which information technology is being employed to make organizations more efficient and more effective. We hope these three chapters will stimulate your thinking about potential applications in your present or future organization. Most of the obvious applications are already in place. Nearly every organization uses a computer to handle its payroll, keep inventory records, and process accounts receivable and payable; almost every organization uses a telephone system and facsimile machines. But many applications remain to be discovered, most likely by managers like you.

APPLICATION AREAS

To consider a topic as broad as information technology applications, some type of framework is needed. As a first cut, we have divided applications into those which are *interorganizational* systems and those which are *intraorganizational* systems. Electronic data interchange (EDI) and electronic commerce systems represent obvious examples of interorganizational systems—systems which span organizational boundaries. Other interorganizational systems include those that link Chrysler and Ford with their automobile dealers and the airline reservation systems (such as American Airlines' SABRE and United Airlines' Apollo) that connect a large network of independent travel agents with the major airlines' computers. In our view, the idea of interorganizational systems (and especially electronic commerce) is so important to you as a manager that we devote all of Chapter 7 to this topic.

To provide some structure to the broad range of intraorganizational systems, we have divided these

CRITICAL ISSUES OF IS MANAGEMENT

In the 10th annual survey of top IS professionals at leading manufacturing and service companies worldwide, conducted by Computer Sciences Corporation (CSC), the top concern was "aligning IS and corporate goals." As IT has become an increasingly critical component of business success, IS executives must ensure that their plans are in synch with the strategies directing the overall enterprise. Of course, all IT applications in a firm must be aimed at achieving this alignment, but enterprise resource planning systems in particular (considered later in this chapter) address this issue.

In second place in the survey is "organizing and utilizing data." A variety of IT applications, including data warehousing, data mining, groupware, decision support systems, executive information systems, and enterprise resource planning systems (topics covered in this chapter and the next), help organize and utilize data to improve the performance of the organization. Number three on the list of critical issues is "connecting to customers, suppliers, and/or partners electronically." Applications such as electronic data interchange and electronic commerce address this concern, as do electronic mail and groupware.

Tied for fourth on the list are "integrating systems" and "creating an information architecture." Once again, enterprise resource planning systems are one approach to integrating systems. Although we will defer consideration of management of the information architecture until Part IV of this book, Part I has introduced the key technologies that form the foundation for an organization's information architecture. The IT applications we discuss here are inextricably intertwined with the information architecture. Thus, the topics covered in this chapter and the next two directly relate to the top five critical issues for IS executives.

[Survey results from Computer Sciences Corporation, 1997]

the critical concept of client/server architecture. Chapter 6 deals with systems specifically designed to support managers, such as decision support systems and expert systems.

Figure 5.1 lists these two major categories of applications, along with representative application areas that fall within each category. This figure provides the primary framework for our discussion of intraorganizational IT applications in this chapter and the next. Please note that the application areas are neither unique nor exhaustive. For example, some specific applications may fall in two or more application areas (such as decision support systems and geographic information systems). Further, it is easy to argue that an application area such as groupware is both an organizational system and a managerial support system. Somewhat arbitrarily, we have chosen to discuss group support systems, which is an important subset of groupware concerned with supporting the activities of a small group in a specific task or a specific meeting, as a managerial support system while discussing the broader category of groupware as an organizational system. Despite these caveats, however, the application areas given in Figure 5.1 do encompass the overwhelming majority of specific applications, and the terminology employed generally represents standard usage.

Organizational Systems
  Transaction Processing Systems
  Enterprise Resource Planning Systems
  Data Warehousing
  Office Automation
  Groupware
  Intranets
  Factory Automation
Managerial Support Systems
  Decision Support Systems
  Data Mining
  Group Support Systems
  Geographic Information Systems
  Executive Information Systems
  Expert Systems
  Neural Networks
  Virtual Reality

Figure 5.1 Types of Application Systems

applications into two major categories: organizational systems—systems that support the entire organization or large portions of it—and managerial support systems—those designed to provide support to a specific manager or a small group of managers. The present chapter covers organizational systems, such as transaction processing systems and groupware, as well as

CRITICAL CONCEPTS

Before we turn to specific examples of the various application areas, a number of important concepts that are intertwined throughout all the applications must be considered. An understanding of these concepts is a prerequisite to an understanding of the applications.

Batch Processing versus On-line Processing

One of the fundamental distinctions for computer applications is **batch processing** versus **on-line processing.** In the early days of computers, all processing was batched. The organization accumulated a batch of transactions and then processed the entire batch at one time. For example, all inventory transactions (in and out) were recorded on paper during the day. After the close of business for the day, the transactions were keyed into some computer-readable medium, such as magnetic tape. The medium was then physically carried to the computer center, and the entire inventory was updated by processing that day's batch against the master inventory file on the computer. By the beginning of the next business day, the master inventory file was completely up to date and appropriate inventory reports were printed. Figure 5.2 represents this batch processing approach in a simplified form.

The major problem with batch processing is the time delays involved before the master file is updated. Only at the beginning of the business day, for example, will the master inventory file be up to date. At all other times, the company doesn't really know how many units of each product it has in stock.

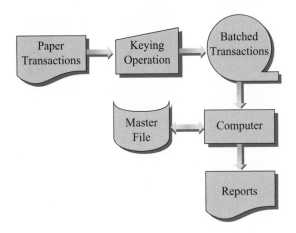

Figure 5.2 Batch Processing (simplified)

As the technology improved, on-line processing was developed to avoid the time delays in batch processing. With a fully implemented on-line system, each transaction is entered directly into the computer when it occurs. For example, in an on-line inventory system, a shipping clerk or sales clerk enters the receipt or sale of a product into a terminal (perhaps a sophisticated cash register), which is connected by a telecommunications line to the main computer, which holds the inventory master file. As soon as the entry is completed, the computer updates the master file within a fraction of a second. Thus, the company always knows how many units of each product it has in stock. Figure 5.3 depicts such an **on-line system.**

A fully implemented on-line system is also called an **interactive system,** because the user is directly interacting with the computer. The computer will provide a response to the user very quickly, usually within a second. Not all on-line systems, however, are interactive. Some systems, often called **in-line systems,** provide for on-line data entry, but the actual processing of the transaction is deferred until a batch of transactions has been accumulated.

A fully on-line system has the distinct advantage of timeliness. Why then aren't all present-day systems on-line? There are two reasons—cost and the existence of so-called natural batch applications. In most cases, batch systems are much less expensive to operate than their on-line counterparts. There are usually significant economies associated with batching both in the data-entry function and the transaction processing. But if the data-entry function can be accomplished when the original data are captured (such as with a sophisticated cash register), an on-line data entry/batch processing system may be less expensive than a straight batch system. The decision of batch versus on-line becomes a trade-off between cost and timeliness. In general, on-line costs per transaction have been decreasing and the importance of timeliness has been increasing. The result is that most applications today use on-line data entry and an increasing proportion also use on-line processing.

The exception to this movement to on-line processing has been the natural batch applications. The payroll of an organization, for example, might be run once a week or once every two weeks. There is no particular advantage to the timeliness of on-line processing; the organization knows when the payroll must be run. Even in this instance, there may be advantages to

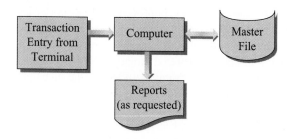

Figure 5.3 On-line Processing

on-line data entry, to permit convenient changes in employees, exemptions, deductions, and wage rates. Thus, hybrid on-line data entry/batch processing systems will continue to exist.

Functional Information Systems

Instead of considering the two major categories and associated application areas of Figure 5.1, it is possible to create a framework strictly on the basis of the primary business functions of the organization—a **functional information systems** framework. For example, consider an organization in which the primary business functions are production, marketing, accounting, personnel, and engineering. Applications may then be categorized as part of the production information system, or part of the marketing information system, or part of the accounting information system, and so on. This functional approach is simply an alternative way of classifying applications.

In this alternative view, the overall IS is composed of multiple subsystems, each providing information for various tasks within the function. In turn, each functional subsystem consists of a possibly interrelated series of subsubsystems. For example, the production information system is likely to include interrelated subsystems for sales forecasting, production planning, production scheduling, material requirements planning, capacity requirements planning, personnel requirements planning, materials purchasing, and inventory. The marketing information system may include subsystems for promotion and advertising, new product development, sales forecasting (hopefully tied into the production sales forecasting subsystem), product planning, product pricing, market research, and sales information. The accounting infor-

mation system, which is generally the oldest and most fully developed functional system, is likely to include computerized versions of the entire journal and ledger system, plus a cost or responsibility accounting system and a financial reporting system for preparing reports for stockholders and other external groups.

One of the most important trends in the last half of the 1990s is the movement toward integration of these functional information systems. Often these integration efforts have begun by focusing on a *business process*—the chain of activities required to achieve an outcome such as order fulfillment or materials acquisition—rather than functions. Such a focus on process makes it easier to recognize where formerly distinct information systems are related and thus where they should be integrated (e.g., use common data and perform an activity only once). Sometimes the development of these integrated systems has been carried out by the internal information systems department, but more often software packages called enterprise resource planning (ERP) systems have been purchased from outside vendors. We will return to these ERP systems later in the chapter.

Vertical Integration of Systems

Another important characteristic of some systems is that they operate across levels of the organization or, in some instances, across independent firms occupying different levels in an industry hierarchy, such as an automobile manufacturer and the associated independent dealers. (More on these interorganizational systems will be covered in Chapter 7.) Such a system that serves more than one vertical level in an organization or an industry is called a **vertically integrated information system.** For example, in a single firm, a vertically integrated sales information system may capture the initial sales data and produce invoices (acting as a transaction processing system), summarize these data on a weekly basis for use by middle managers in tracking slow- and fast-selling items as well as productive and unproductive salespeople (acting as a decision support system), and further analyze this data for long-term trends for use by top managers in determining strategic directions (acting as an executive information system).

In a somewhat similar way, a national fast-food chain may develop a sales information system with modules both for operating units (company stores and franchises) and for the national organization. Thus, data collected at the store level using the operating unit module are already in the appropriate form to be processed by the national organization module. These basic data are transmitted via telecommunication lines to the national organization on a periodic basis, perhaps each night. The extent of vertical integration is an important characteristic of applications.

Distributed Systems and Client/Server Systems

Distributed systems, sometimes called **distributed data processing,** refers to a mode of delivery rather than a traditional class of applications like transaction processing or decision support systems. With distributed systems, the processing power is distributed to multiple sites, which are then tied together via telecommunications lines. Local area networks (LANs) and wide area networks (WANs) are both used to support distributed systems. We should note that there are a variety of operational functions that can be distributed, including data collection and entry, data editing and error correction, file location, and processing. In our view, only the last function—processing—represents distributed systems. Whether or not the processing power is distributed, it is often appropriate to distribute data collection and entry as well as data editing and error correction to the sites at which the transactions occur (for example, the sales floor in a department store and the dock in a warehouse). File location, however, would never be distributed unless at least some processing power is also distributed.

Thus, we are defining distributed systems as systems in which computers of some size (microcomputers, minicomputers, mainframes, and so forth) are located at various physical sites at which the organization does business (headquarters, factories, stores, warehouses, office buildings), and these computers are linked by telecommunication lines of some sort in order to support some business process. The economics of distributed systems are not perfectly clear, but have tended to favor distribution. For the most part, communication and support costs go up with distributed systems, whereas computer costs go down. Placing smaller microcomputers and workstations at noncentral sites is generally less expensive than expanding the capacity of a large mainframe at the central site. Distributed systems do have disadvan-

tages, such as greater security risk because of easy accessibility, dependence on high-quality telecommunications lines, and greater required coordination across sites, but in most instances the disadvantages are outweighed by the economic advantages. The distributed mode of computing has become the norm for business firms around the world.

In the 1990s, a particular type of distributed system known as a **client/server system** has moved to center stage. With this type of system, the processing power is distributed between a central server computer, such as a minicomputer or a powerful workstation, and a number of client computers, which are usually desktop microcomputers. The split in responsibilities between the server and the client varies considerably from application to application, but the client usually provides the graphical user interface (GUI), accepts the data entry, and displays the immediate output, while the server maintains the database against which the new data are processed. The actual processing of the transaction may occur on either the client or a server. For example, in a retail client/server application, the client may be the sophisticated cash register on the sales floor, while the server is a workstation in the back office. When a credit sale is made, the data are entered at the register and transmitted to the server, the server retrieves the customer's record and updates it based on the sale, the server returns a credit authorization signal to the register, and the sales document is printed at the register. At the close of the billing cycle, the server prepares the bills for all of the customers, prints them, and produces summary reports for store management.

Now that we have a general idea about the nature of a client/server system, let's explore the three building blocks of such a system. First, the client building block, usually running on a PC, handles the user interface (perhaps using a GUI) and has the ability to access distributed services through a network. Sometimes the client also does the processing. Second, the server building block, usually running on a bigger machine (a high-end PC, workstation, minicomputer, or even a mainframe), handles the storage of data associated with the application. This associated data may be databases, groupware files (to be discussed later), Web pages, or even objects for object-oriented programs. Sometimes the server (or even another server) does the processing. The third building block is **middleware,** a rather vague term that covers all of the software needed to support interactions between clients and servers. *The Essential Client/Server Survival Guide* refers to middleware as ". . . the slash (/) component of client/server. It's the glue that lets a client obtain a service from a server."[1]

Middleware can be divided into three categories of software: network operating systems, transport software, and service-specific software. The network operating system has the task of creating a "single-system image" for all services on the network, so that the system is transparent to users and even application programmers. The user doesn't know what functions are performed where on the network—it just looks like a single system. The primary network operating systems are Novell's NetWare, Microsoft's Windows NT Server, IBM's OS/2 Warp Server, and Unix-based systems from Sun and OSF. Transport software allows communications employing certain protocols, such as TCP/IP or SNA (see Chapter 4), to be sent across the network. The network operating system often encompasses some elements of the needed transport software, but other middleware products may also be required. The service-specific software is that required to carry out a particular "service," such as electronic mail or the World Wide Web's hypertext transfer protocol.

Let's consider the split in responsibilities between the client and the server. The question is where the actual processing of the application is done. Originally, all client/server systems had only **two tiers**—a client tier and a server tier. If most of the processing is done on the client, this is called a *fat client* or *thin server* model. If most of the processing is done on the server, then it is a *thin client* or *fat server* model. For example, Web servers and groupware servers are usually fat servers (i.e., the processing is largely done on the server for Web and groupware applications), whereas database servers are usually thin servers (i.e., the processing is largely done on the client). More recently, **three-tier client/server systems** have become popular. In the most popular three-tier configuration, an application server that is separate from the database server is employed. The user interface is housed on the client, usually a PC (tier 1); the processing is performed on a midrange system or workstation operating as the applications server (tier 2); and the data are stored on a large machine (often a mainframe or midrange computer) that operates as the database server (tier 3).

The computing literature contains numerous examples of successful three-tier client/server systems. U.S. West (the regional Bell operating company in the Western U.S.) built a three-tier expense reporting system for use by its 15,000 employees. Columbia Natural Resources developed a three-tier facilities management application to improve decision-making on the maintenance of its 6,000 natural gas wells (*I/S Analyzer Case Studies,* 1995). PECO Energy, the Philadelphia-area electric utility company, used a three-tier approach to revamp its customer service system. The new system enables PECO's 450 service representatives to gain access to the multiple databases the company maintains

---

PROCESSING PRESCRIPTION DRUG CLAIMS AT LIBERTY HEALTH

Liberty Health is a supplemental health insurer based in Markham, Ontario. After a slow start in its efforts to migrate to client/server technology, Liberty Health concentrated on getting its most mission-critical system—processing claims for prescription drugs sold at more than 3,500 pharmacies across Canada—into a three-tier environment. The clients were PCs located in the pharmacies running Windows 3.1 (tier 1); the application servers were Sun workstations and Hewlett-Packard midrange systems (tier 2); and the database server was a Unisys mainframe computer (tier 3). Programmers initially used the C and C++ programming languages to develop the tier 1 and tier 3 components of the system. They used a specialized development tool, BEA Systems' Tuxedo, to develop the transaction processing component (tier 2). Some of the later development work was done using Information Advantage's DecisionSuite 3.5. The point-of-sale prescription claims system has now been operational for two years. Transaction volumes have grown substantially in that two-year period, and the system has been able to handle the increased volume without difficulty, according to Bob Jackson, Liberty Health's IT development support officer.

[Adapted from Ruber, 1997]

---

1 Orfali, Robert, Dan Harkey, and Jeri Edwards. *The Essential Client/Server Guide,* 2nd ed. (New York: John Wiley & Sons, Inc., 1996), 16.

on its 1.5 million customers. The service representatives use PCs as clients (tier 1) working through four servers that process the customer inquiries (tier 2) by accessing data from the company mainframe (tier 3) (Ruber, 1997). For a more complete description of a three-tier client/server application, see the sidebar entitled "Processing Prescription Drug Claims at Liberty Health."

TRANSACTION PROCESSING SYSTEMS

Let us begin our survey of applications with the "granddaddy" applications, the ones that started it all—**transaction processing systems.** These systems process the thousands of transactions that occur every day in most organizations, including sales; payments made and received; inventory shipped and received; hiring, firing, and paying employees; and paying a dividend. In addition to producing the documents and updated records that result from the transaction processing (such as invoices, checks, and orders), these systems produce a variety of summarized reports that are useful for upper levels of management.

Transaction processing systems are life-or-death systems for "paperwork" organizations, such as banks and insurance companies, and critical systems for the overwhelming majority of medium and large organizations. These were the first computerized systems, and they still use the majority of computing time in most organizations. For the most part, these transaction processing systems were and are justified by means of traditional cost-benefit analysis. These systems are able to process the transactions more rapidly and more economically (and certainly more accurately) than by a manual (human) system. Transaction processing systems may be mainframe-based or midrange-based, or they may be two-tier or three-tier client/server systems. Most of the newer systems being implemented are client/server systems, but there are many, many mainframe- or midrange-based transaction processing systems still in use.

As a manager, you don't need to know the details of these systems. You only need to know the general nature and importance of such systems and that they are more complex than an outsider might imagine.

Therefore, we will limit our discussion to two representative transaction processing systems—payroll and order entry.

Payroll System

The first impression of a payroll system is that it seems fairly simple. Operators input the number of hours worked for each employee (usually employing on-line data entry), and the system batch processes these transactions to produce payroll checks. While this one-sentence description is correct, it represents only the tip of the iceberg, because it involves only about 10 percent of the system. The payroll processing subsystem must keep year-to-date totals of gross income, social security income, individual deductions, various categories of taxes, and net income; it must incorporate the ability to compute federal, state, and local taxes as well as social security contributions; and it must handle both mandatory and voluntary deductions.

What other subsystems are necessary? Figure 5.4 lists the primary subsystems in most payroll systems and what these subsystems must accomplish. Thus, the payroll system is both commonplace and complex. The payroll system is usually easy to justify on a cost-benefit basis, because it would take an incredible

Subsystems to accomplish:

Payroll processing, including updating year-to-date master file

Capture hours-worked data

Add/delete employees

Change deduction information for employees

Change wage rates and salaries

Creation of initial year-to-date master file

Calculate and print payroll totals for pay period, quarter, and year

Calculate and print tax reports for pay period, quarter, and year

Calculate and print deduction reports for pay period, quarter, and year

Calculate and print W-2 forms at end of year

Interface with human resources information system

Interface with budget information system

Figure 5.4 Components of a Payroll System

number of payroll clerks to turn out a modern payroll and keep all the associated records.

Order Entry System

We will illustrate a mainframe- or midrange-based order entry system, but an order entry system could certainly employ client/server technology. The basic idea behind an on-line order entry system is simple. As orders are received (whether in person, by mail, or by telephone), the sales representative enters the information into the system. The data entry may be via a microcomputer on the person's desk, or it may be through a point-of-sale transaction recording system (a sophisticated cash register that doubles as a terminal). The computer then updates the appropriate files and prints an invoice, either at the point-of-sale terminal, the sales representative's desk, or in the computer center.

Once again, this basic idea tells only a small part of the story. Figure 5.5 provides a more complete version and shows how each transaction (each sale) interacts with as many as six different files on the computer system. In addition to the invoice itself, more than a dozen additional types of computer output may be generated. For example, the computer will check the credit status of the customer and may reject the sale if the credit limit would be exceeded. If the item ordered is in stock, a multipart shipping document is printed; if it is not in stock, a message is sent via the PC to the customer to ask if he or she wants to backorder the item. Periodically or on demand, the order entry system will print out sales reports organized by item or by customer, customer statements, inventory reports, backorder status reports, and accounts receivable reports. The system will also generate reports when exception conditions occur, such as when an item is out of stock or a customer attempts to exceed the established credit limit. In these cases, management action may be necessary. The order entry system may automatically print out purchase orders when an item is out of stock; it may also print out past-due billing notices for customers. A primary advantage of such an on-line system is that inquiries will be answered in a few seconds.

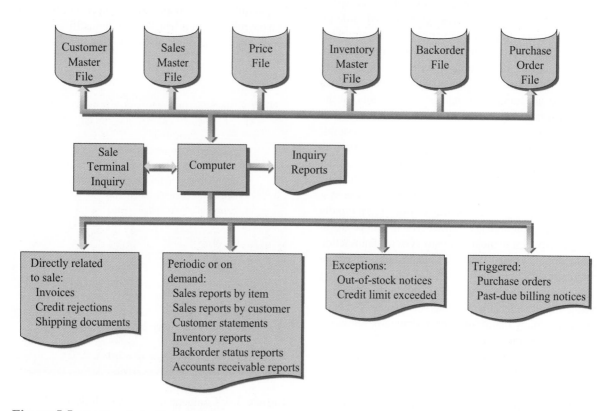

Figure 5.5 On-line Order Entry System

An important order entry system variant is an interorganizational system in which the orders are placed directly by the customer or the customer's computer (more on interorganizational systems in Chapter 7). The classic example was the American Hospital Supply Corporation's ASAP system in which order entry terminals linked to AHSC's computer were placed on the customers' (hospitals') premises, and customers placed the orders themselves by keying them in. This made placing orders much more convenient for the customers and, at the same time, greatly reduced the delays and costs associated with printing and mailing order forms. More recently, order entry has often been handled from the customer's computer to the seller's computer using electronic data interchange (EDI)—discussed in detail in Chapter 7. Order entry via the World Wide Web is another growing variation of this interorganizational approach to transaction processing (see the sidebar "Whirlwind on the Web").

WHIRLWIND ON THE WEB

Dell Computer Corporation has become an Internet phenomenon, selling $1 million worth of computers a day on its Web site. In just six months, Dell has gone from nowhere in cyberspace to being the No. 1 PC retailer on the Web—with sales growing 20 percent each month. For the Texas computer maker, electronic commerce is the perfect extension of the company's direct-sales business. Corporations and techno-savvy customers that were willing to buy over the telephone are the first ones dialing in to purchase on the Web. "The Internet," says Michael S. Dell, chairman and chief executive officer of Dell Computer, "is the ultimate direct model."

Selling PCs over the Web is one way to get more bang for the buck, for Dell needs only 30 people for its Web sales, in contrast to the 700 sales representatives that take orders over the telephone. Therefore, Dell is working furiously to stay ahead of its rivals on the Web. A planned new feature will send a digital confirmation to customers within five minutes of placing an order—Dell's way of reassuring buyers. In coming months, Dell plans to deliver "electronic commerce set-ups" to 75 companies, so that their employees will be able to order a PC and automatically receive the corporate price.

[Adapted from McWilliams, 1997]

ENTERPRISE RESOURCE PLANNING SYSTEMS

Enterprise Resource Planning (ERP) systems are also transaction processing systems (TPSs), but they go beyond traditional TPSs—and thus we think deserve treatment as a separate application area. An ERP system is a set of integrated business applications, or modules, to carry out most common business functions, including inventory control, general ledger accounting, accounts payable, accounts receivable, material requirements planning, order management, and human resources, among others. Usually these modules are purchased from a software vendor. In many cases, a company may buy only a subset of these modules from a particular vendor, mixing them with modules from other vendors and with the company's existing applications.

An ERP system differs from earlier approaches to developing or purchasing business applications in at least two ways. First, the ERP modules are integrated, primarily through a common set of definitions and a common database. As a transaction is processed in one area, such as receipt of an order, the impact of this transaction is immediately reflected in all other related areas, such as accounting, production scheduling, and purchasing. Second, the ERP modules have been designed to reflect a particular way of doing business—a particular set of business processes. Unlike a functional IS approach, ERP systems are based on a value-chain view of the business in which functional departments coordinate their work. To implement an ERP system, then, a company is committing to changing its business processes. If the company is purchasing an ERP system, the company needs to change its processes to conform to those embedded in the software package. The company must adapt to the ERP software, not vice versa.

Why has ERP become such a hot topic in the latter 1990s, with most large firms either installing ERP systems or seriously thinking about it? The answer to this question is not easy, and it clearly varies from firm to firm. In most cases, though, the companies are not happy with the old way of doing business—by separate functional departments—and they don't have the *integration* of applications to support their *decision-making* and *planning* needs. The current applications often don't talk to each other, and thus it is a time-consuming and difficult job to gather data together to present a coherent picture of what is happening in the firm, which inhibits good decision-making and planning. This situation isn't new in the latter 1990s, but previously companies didn't have packaged solutions available to them. The cost to develop a set of integrated applications internally is prohibitive; even if the company had the IS resources to perform the task, it would take years. From previous reengineering efforts, many companies *know* that their internal business processes need to be changed, and they believe that the best and easiest way to fix them is by adopting the processes built into an ERP system that can be purchased. Thus, implementing an ERP system is a way to *force* business process reengineering.

Then, to add to the demand for an ERP system, along came the year 2000 problem (more on this in Chapter 10). In 1995 or 1996, it became clear to many companies that their key application programs would cease to function correctly when dates past January 1, 2000, were used. When these programs were coded—often using COBOL—the programmers allowed for only two digits to represent the year. They didn't imagine that their programs, written in the 1970s and 1980s, would still be used when the millennium arrived. For these companies, the effort, and the cost, to change every reference to year in every program would be substantial. Adopting an ERP system, which was developed in the 1990s and correctly provided for dates beyond the year 2000, seemed to be an easy, albeit expensive, solution to the year 2000 problem. Rarely was the year 2000 problem the sole reason to implement an ERP system, but if the company wasn't very happy with its existing, nonintegrated set of applications, then the year 2000 problem may well have tipped the balance.

It should be emphasized that implementation of an ERP system is extremely difficult, because the company must change the way it does business. Further, ERP systems are very expensive. A typical large-scale ERP implementation costs tens of millions of dollars and takes a year or more.

Further, choosing the right ERP software is a difficult task. The leading vendors are SAP, Baan, J. D. Edwards, Oracle, and PeopleSoft; several smaller companies also offer ERP software. For ERP purchases, there are strong arguments for picking a single vendor, including the tight integration of applications

---

UNINTENDED CONSEQUENCES OF ERP

ERP implementations usually require people to create new work relationships, share information that once was closely guarded, and make business decisions they never were required to make. These kinds of changes are marked by resistance, confusion, redundancies, and errors—unless managed properly.

About half of ERP implementations fail to achieve hoped-for benefits because managers "significantly underestimate the efforts involved in change management," says Alfred Grunwald, CEO of Deloitte & Touche Consulting Group/ICS. "What happens in most of our engagements, to be frank, is that many clients . . . focus on the benefit: reduced inventory, shortened lead times, higher customer satisfaction. What they don't focus on is, 'Is my average employee prepared? Have I provided the educational content to my employees so they actually take full advantage of the new process?' Many organizations neglect the issue of change management. They say, 'We know how to do that.' The reality is that's not necessarily the case."

In public policy circles, this is called "unintended consequences." A manager comes up with a grand scheme to fix a systemic problem, tying together bill-of-materials, shop-floor scheduling, and other traditional manufacturing functions with the rest of the enterprise, and doesn't realize the problems the solution creates.

Unintended consequences include the emotional fallout that's left when employees suddenly are given much greater responsibilities. Managers sometimes neglect to assess not only the skills development needed by employees . . . , but also the organizational changes required of them. "The fact is that the amount of workload and the amount of human resources power in most organizations needed to run the new environment is not different," Grunwald says. "But the skills are dramatically different."

[Appleton, 1997]

---

that is possible and the standardization of common processes. On the other hand, choosing a single vendor could also reduce flexibility for the adopting company. A "best of breed" or mix-and-match approach with multiple vendors may enable the company to meet more of its needs and reduce reliance on a single vendor; conversely, such an approach is likely more time consuming to implement and will complicate system maintenance. Whichever approach is taken, it is usually essential to employ the vendor and/or another consulting firm to assist in the implementation process. For large, multidivisional firms, implementing an ERP system is a very complex, challenging task that needs the best minds and the careful attention of both internal IS and managerial people and external consultants (see the sidebar on "Unintended Consequences of ERP"). The potential payoff of an ERP system, in terms of better information for strategic and operational decision-making and planning, and greater efficiency, profitability, and growth, makes the efforts and the costs worthwhile.

An Example ERP System: SAP R/3

The most popular of the ERP systems is SAP R/3, developed by a German firm, SAP AG, headquartered in Walldorf, Germany. SAP made the top ten list of software firms (see Chapter 3) on the strength of the R/3 system, with 1996 sales of nearly $2 billion. R/3 is a client/server system employing a common, integrated database with shared application modules; SAP R/2 was a mainframe-based ERP. SAP R/3 handles both TCP/IP and SNA communication protocols. SAP developed R/3 using its own fourth generation language (4 GL) named ABAP/4, which is the key piece of SAP's ABAP/4 Development Workbench. Customers may use ABAP/4, if they wish, to modify or enhance the standard R/3 modules. However, ABAP/4 will be of primary interest to companies that wish to employ an integrated 4 GL toolkit to develop applications in addition to SAP standard modules.

SAP R/3 fits the general description of an ERP system given above. It is a tightly integrated system consisting of numerous modules (see Figure 5.6). A company may choose to implement some or all of these modules. Most importantly, implementation of R/3 requires that the company change its business processes to conform to the processes built into the software.

Let's take a closer look at SAP R/3. The R/3 modules fall into three categories that SAP calls financials, logistics, and human resources. The major strength of the SAP system lies in the logistics area, which is where SAP began. The logistics category includes

Logistics Category
> Production Planning and Control
> Project Management System
> Materials Management
> Quality Management
> Plant Maintenance
> Product Data Management
> Sales and Distribution
> Service Management

Human Resources Category
> Personnel Management
> Organizational Management
> Payroll Accounting
> Time Management
> Personnel Development

Financials Category
> Financial Accounting
> Controlling
> Investment Management
> Treasury Management
> Enterprise Controlling

Figure 5.6 SAP R/3 Modules

eight major modules, each of which is divided into a number of subcomponents (see Figure 5.6 for major modules). Five modules relate primarily to manufacturing: Production Planning and Control, Project Management System, Materials Management, Quality Management, and Plant Maintenance. The other three modules in the logistics category relate largely to sales and distribution: Product Data Management, Sales and Distribution, and Service Management. The names of these modules give us a reasonable idea of what each does; together, they provide a complete set of components to monitor and report on the entire logistics process from sourcing of materials and manufacturing through sales and service.

The modules in the human resources category provide the full set of capabilities needed to hire, manage, schedule, and pay company employees. The five primary modules include Personnel Management, Organizational Management, Payroll Accounting, Time Management, and Personnel Development. The modules in the financials category are designed to permit managers to interpret and work with company financial data effectively. The five major modules are Financial Accounting, Controlling, Investment Management, Treasury Management, and Enterprise Controlling.

Companies may choose to implement some or all of the SAP R/3 modules. Motorola's Semiconductor Products Sector, for example, chose to use the human resources modules, including Payroll Accounting. Motorola purchased the payroll module as a solution to the year 2000 problem. Motorola has implemented SAP payroll and employee recordkeeping for all 25,000 U.S.-based employees, which makes it the largest North American R/3 payroll implementation. ERP implementation is such a challenging task that most companies employ a consulting firm to assist them; in Motorola's case, Price Waterhouse served as the consultant (SAP, June 16, 1997). Pioneer New Media Technologies, which employed Hewlett-Packard as its consultant, installed four SAP modules—Financial Accounting, Controlling, Sales and Distribution, and Materials Management. Using a rapid implementation methodology proposed by Hewlett-Packard, Pioneer successfully implemented these four modules in just 5 months, and right on budget (Darling, October 1996; Callaway, 1997; Tucker, 1997).

But not all the implementation stories are this positive. Applied Materials, Inc. originally thought that deploying the financial and logistics (except manufacturing) modules of R/3 to its 2,200 global users would take about a year. Then Applied intended to implement the manufacturing modules in the U.S. After 2 years and $23 million, the financial and logistics modules have finally been installed in the U.S., but the project is far from completed. These delays were caused by system performance problems, the complexity of the project, and a lack of internal expertise with SAP. Applied originally hired Deloitte & Touche as the consultant for the logistics modules and Price Waterhouse for the financials, but when the firm reevaluated the project, it decided to go with Price Waterhouse only. Applied, however, is still committed to the project (Moad, 1996). As we near the end of the 1990s, SAP R/3 software is a very hot commodity (see sidebar "L'Oreal Is SAP's 10,000[th] R/3 Installation).

L'OREAL IS SAP'S 10,000[TH] R/3 INSTALLATION

SAP announced that L'Oreal, the leading-edge cosmetics company, is set to launch a global SAP implementation project to monitor its business activities worldwide. This large-scale R/3 project, which will be the 10,000th R/3 installation, will optimize the individual business processes of the group's 70 midsize subsidiaries, streamlining them to form a globally integrated solution. The L'Oreal group is headquartered in Clichy, France, and posted revenues for 1996 of over 60 billion francs.

Over the next two years L'Oreal will focus on implementing the R/3 components Financial Accounting, Controlling, Materials Management, Sales and Distribution, and Treasury at subsidiaries located in 59 countries. The aim of the implementation project is to standardize the group's financial processes and consolidate its vast range of activities around the world. When the implementation is complete, 3,000 users around the world will work with R/3 running under Windows NT.

L'Oreal's Chief Information Officer, Jean-Daniel Kahn, explains: "L'Oreal is made up of a large number of small and midsized subsidiaries. This means that our requirements embrace those of companies operating at both ends of the market—we're large yet small. This is why R/3 is the perfect solution for us, since it is flexible and scalable enough to meet both the needs of a small enterprise and those of a major corporate group."

[Adapted from SAP, June 11, 1997]

DATA WAREHOUSING

In order to create a data warehouse, a firm pulls data from its operational systems—the transaction processing systems we have just discussed—and puts the data in a separate "data warehouse" so that users may access and analyze the data without endangering the operational systems. Thus, **data warehousing** is the establishment and maintenance of a large data storage facility containing data on all (or at least many) aspects of the enterprise. If the data warehouse is to be useful, the data must be accurate and current and must be stored in a useable form; in addition, easy-to-use data access and analysis tools for end-users must be provided to encourage full use of the data.

Establishing a data warehouse is time-consuming and expensive. Three different types of software tools are needed: warehouse construction software, warehouse operation software, and warehouse access and analysis software (Darling, May 15, 1996). Warehouse construction software is required to extract relevant data from the operational databases, make sure the data are "clean" (free from error), transform the data into a useable form, and load the data into the data warehouse (see Figure 5.7). Software tools to construct the warehouse are available from vendors such as IBM, Information Builders, Platinum Technology, and SAS Institute. Operation software is required to store the data and manage the data warehouse. Data warehouse storage is typically accomplished by database management systems such as Computer Associates' CA-Ingres, IBM's DB2, Oracle, and Sybase; specialized warehouse management software is offered by Hewlett-Packard, IBM, Information Builders, NCR, Red Brick, and others.

The widest variety of software tools is available in the warehouse access and analysis area. Information catalog tools, such as Platinum Technology's Platinum Repository, tell the user what is in the warehouse. Reporting tools enable a user to produce customized reports from the data warehouse, perhaps on a regular basis. Information Builders' FOCUS, a 4 GL discussed in Chapter 3, is a widely used reporting tool. Query tools, such as Brio Technology's BrioQuery Enterprise, make it easy for a user to query the warehouse. For more sophisticated data analysis, specialized data mining tools, such as Thinking Machines' Darwin, are available. Visualizing the data may be important, using a tool such as SAS Institute's SAS/Insight, and presenting the data through an executive information system (EIS) can be done using

ShowBusiness Software's ShowBusiness EIS or a similar tool. We will defer further consideration of these analysis tools until the next chapter, when we consider decision support systems, data mining, and executive information systems in more detail. In our judgment, creation and maintenance of the data warehouse is an organizational system, while these end-user reporting and analysis tools are designed for management support—the topic of Chapter 6.

International Data Corporation, a market research firm, surveyed 62 organizations that had implemented a data warehouse and found that 54 of them had benefitted from their investment. Of the eight that didn't benefit, the firms had some combination of extraordinarily high costs, low usage, and a very large warehousing project (McCune, 1997).

There are plenty of positive results, too. Sears has all its sales information stored in a 1.7-terabyte warehouse, which is built on an NCR Teradata 3600 server and is accessible from 4,500 client PCs (Garcia, 1996). Within company headquarters in Hoffman Estates, Illinois, the warehouse is used by buyers, replenishers, financial analysts, and marketing employees, while 300 Sears traveling managers have dial-up access to the warehouse using various IBM laptops. Cellular One, based in Columbus, Ohio, has built a data warehouse containing summary-level telecommunications data, such as toll and long-distance charges, that is used to tailor marketing and promotional campaigns. On a smaller scale, Ingram Books, a La Verne, Tennessee, book wholesaler, has installed a data warehouse containing detailed data on customer accounts (McCune, 1997). This warehouse, which consists of four gigabytes residing on a high-end Pentium-based

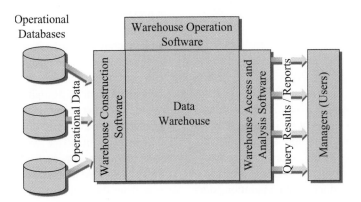

Figure 5.7 Key Elements of Data Warehousing

DATA WAREHOUSING KEEPS KARSTEN SWINGING

Now that summer is upon us, and golf season is in full swing, what will you do if you damage, or even worse, lose your golf clubs? Karsten Manufacturing, the company that has made customized Ping golf clubs for more than 30 years, has improved its profitability and efficiency by integrating information about its products and customers into a single enterprise-wide data warehouse. The data warehousing solution Karsten decided on was the NCR Teradata relational database management system, which allows Karsten to manage the production of its custom-made golf clubs, and provide anyone in the company—from customer service reps to production-line workers to shipping clerks—with access to real-time status information and history of a customer's order.

The data warehouse holds a year's worth of information about each customer's order and club specs. Each unique order, whether it be for a pro in the U.S. Open or a recreational golfer, has a serial number attached to its information. All of this data is stored in Karsten's data warehouse, so should you be on that much-needed golf trip and lose or damage your clubs, Karsten can now build an exact duplicate of your original clubs and ship them to you, often within 24 hours.

[Adapted from Greenblatt, 1997]

PC, has revolutionized decision making, according to the company's vice president. Ingram executives expect the warehouse to pay for itself in 18 months. Data warehousing has the potential to let companies understand and utilize the data that they are already collecting as they run their business.

OFFICE AUTOMATION

Office automation refers to a set of office-related applications that may or may not be integrated into a single system. The most common applications are electronic mail, word processing, voice mail, copying, desktop publishing, electronic calendaring, and document imaging, along with document preparation, storage, and sharing.

Office technology has taken major strides since World War II. Document preparation has moved from manual typewriters, to electric typewriters with a moving carriage, to the IBM Selectric typewriters with the "golf ball" typing element, to memory typewriters, to expensive terminals connected to a minicomputer, to stand-alone microcomputers, to microcomputers linked via a local area network (LAN). Copying has moved from mimeograph machines to fast photocopiers and facsimile machines. The telephone has moved from a simple instrument with no dial or keys to a dial telephone and then from a simple touch-tone telephone to a versatile touch-tone instrument with features such as automatic redial, call forwarding, call waiting, and multiparty calling. For the most part, however, these devices still do not all talk to each other today—but information technology will change that! In the office of the future, these devices and others will be connected via an integrated voice/data/image network as shown in Figure 5.8. In our discussion of the components of this figure, we will mention those connections that exist today.

Word Processing and Application Suites

A number of excellent word processing packages have been developed for microcomputers, which is the predominant workstation in offices today. Microsoft Word for Windows is the market leader in the late 1990s, and there is also strong support for Corel WordPerfect and Lotus Word Pro. As noted in Chapter 3, these packages are now usually sold as part of an application suite that includes a spreadsheet package, a presentation package, a database package, and other applications. The advantage of a suite is that is it possible to copy and paste from one application to another in the same suite; for instance, a Microsoft Office user can copy a portion of an Excel spreadsheet to the clipboard and then paste that spreadsheet directly into a Word document she is preparing. A high-quality printer may be directly connected to a PC in a small office or in an office with high print volume. It is more common, however, for the PCs to be on a local area network so that a document can be electronically sent from the preparing workstation to a high-quality printer, as depicted in Figure 5.8.

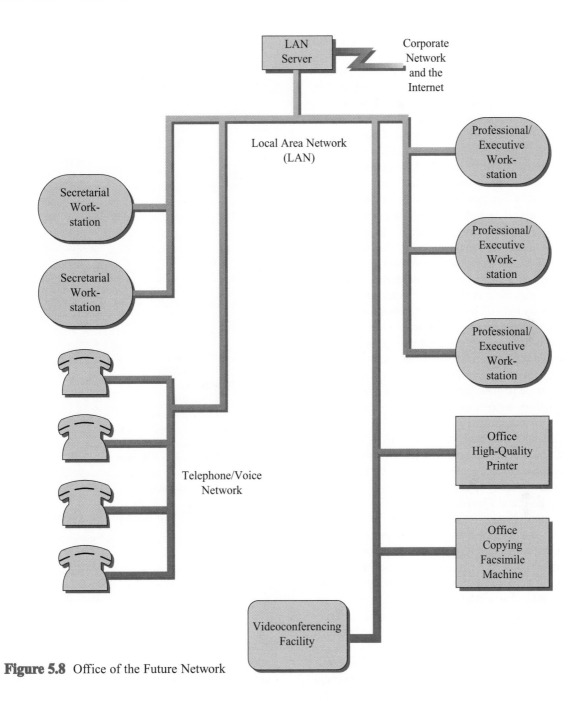

Figure 5.8 Office of the Future Network

Electronic Mail

Electronic mail systems (**e-mail**) permit rapid but asynchronous communication between workstations on a network—no more telephone tag. Most systems incorporate such features as sending a note to a distribution list, resending a note to someone else with an appended message, replying to a note without reentering the address, and filing notes in electronic file folders for later recall. All the authors of this book use electronic mail many times a day, and we feel we could not do without it.

Of course, there are potential drawbacks to e-mail communications. Because it is so easy to use, the volume of e-mail may become overwhelming, particularly standard messages sent to a distribution list. E-mail is also less personal because it is dependent on text signals alone (but see sidebar "E-mail Smileys for All Occasions"). Some people also use offensive words and phrases that they would never use in face-to-face conversation, called "flaming." Privacy issues arise because of the opportunity for electronic monitoring by supervisors. For most organizations and most users, however, these drawbacks are totally overshadowed by the advantages of rapid, asynchronous communication.

Variants of e-mail include electronic bulletin boards, listservs, computer conferencing, and chat rooms. An electronic bulletin board is a repository such as a disk on a computer on which anyone with access to the bulletin board and the computer account number can post messages and read other messages. Bulletin boards can be operated within an organization (employing the usual communication links), or they can function over the Internet. A listserv is a computerized mailing list that accepts a message sent to the listserv address and forwards it to everyone on the particular mailing list.

Computer conferencing is similar to a bulletin board, but it is set up around a particular topic. For example, a computer conference might be set up by a professional society to consider changes in its annual meeting program. The announcement of the topic and the account number on the computer on which the conference will be held are published in the society's newsletter, which may be distributed electronically via a listserv. Anyone can participate in the conference by logging into the conference, entering an opinion, and reading other participants' opinions. Chat rooms are real-time versions of computer conferencing (synchronous communication) conducted on the Internet, with an incredibly wide array of topics.

The first popular e-mail systems were mainframe or minicomputer-based, which makes sense because e-mail predated client/server systems. These systems were also designed to run under proprietary operating systems (e.g., not UNIX). Examples are Digital Equipment's VaxMail and ALL-IN-ONE and IBM's OfficeVision and PROFS (Professional Office System). The more advanced of these mainframe-based systems, such as PROFS, packaged e-mail together

---

E-MAIL SMILEYS FOR ALL OCCASIONS

As e-mail has spread through corporate America and around the world, new conventions for communication have been created. Perhaps the most humorous of these conventions is the digital smiley face and the numerous variations which have evolved from the original smiley. When you tilt your head to the left and use your imagination, the original digital smiley :-) looks like a little face with a colon for eyes and a hyphen for a nose. The use of this digital smiley at the end of an e-mail message means something like 'just kidding,' as in the following message copied from an electronic bulletin board. The subject is uncontrollable scalp flaking, and one writer is proposing a new remedy: "I find that rinsing my scalp with vinegar will cut down on it for a while, if you don't mind smelling like a salad :-)"

But the variants are even more fun. Here are some of them and their interpretations:

:-(	I'm unhappy
:-D	I'm laughing
B-)	I'm cool
:*)	I'm drunk
{(:-)	I have a toupee
}(:-(	I have a toupee and its windy
:-8	I'm talking out of both sides of my mouth
[:-)	I'm wearing a Walkman
d:-)	I'm a baseball player
:-?	I'm smoking a pipe
<<<<(:-)	I'm a hat salesman
':-)	I accidentally shaved off one eyebrow

Try creating your own smileys, and spice up your own e-mail messages!

[Adapted from Miller, 1992]

---

with electronic calendaring and other related features. In such a mainframe environment, the e-mail system is actually running on the mainframe, with the workstation being used as a terminal. In the case of PROFS, the main menu included a calendar with the current date highlighted, a clock, a message area where other users can directly communicate with this workstation, and a menu of other choices, such as process schedules (electronic calendaring), open the mail, search for documents, and prepare documents. Many of these mainframe e-mail systems are still in use in the late 1990s, although they are not as popular as they once were. This is because they do not have a GUI interface, and they don't possess the functionality of the newer groupware systems.

The second wave of e-mail systems was designed to run on UNIX servers (high-powered workstations running the UNIX operating system). Popular systems include Pine and Elm. The e-mail system is actually running on the server, with the PC being used as a terminal; again, there is no GUI interface. These systems don't have the functionality of mainframe systems like PROFS, but they are much more economical to operate on a per user or per message basis. It should come as no surprise that many colleges and universities still use these UNIX systems.

The development of POP-servers and POP-mail is an example of how PC-based "front ends" can be used to provide a more friendly interface for end-users. POP stands for post office protocol, and POP-mail is based on an analogy with post office boxes. To use POP-mail, a POP-client such as Eudora or Pegasus must be loaded on the PC. Various e-mail systems, including Pine, can be used as a POP-server. All incoming mail is kept on the POP-server until the user logs on and asks for mail to be downloaded to his or her own machine; this is analogous to traditional mail being kept in a post office box until the patron opens the box and empties it. Then the user processes the mail on his or her own machine, using the graphical user interface provided by Eudora or Pegasus. The user can read mail, throw some of it away, store some in electronic file folders, and prepare responses to some of it. When done processing the mail on the PC, the user reopens a connection to the POP-server on the host computer and uploads any outgoing messages.

The third wave of e-mail systems were LAN-based client/server software systems that incorporated well-designed GUI interfaces, complete with small inboxes, outboxes, wastebaskets, attractive fonts, color, and other GUI features. Popular packages include cc:Mail by Lotus and Microsoft Mail. If all the organization wants the package to do is e-mail, then these are excellent choices. LAN-based e-mail systems are very popular in the late 1990s.

Progressive organizations, however, are ready to move beyond simple e-mail. They want the greater functionality of the older mainframe systems plus the GUI interface of the POP-mail and LAN-based systems. They want electronic calendaring and document sharing. The answer is groupware, and we will return to groupware shortly, after we have completed our discussion of the office of the future. Groupware is, in fact, a significant step toward the office of the future.

Future Developments

Today, the telephone/voice network in most companies is totally independent of the computer/data network. In the office of the not-so-distant future, these networks will be combined into one integrated office network. Newer workstations include a voice receiver and a voice speaker and can function as a telephone. Some users are already using their workstations to make long-distance telephone calls over the Internet. At some point, when the technology has matured and the appropriate connections to the office and external networks have been made, the functions of today's telephones are likely to be totally subsumed by the workstation itself.

Almost all offices today have facsimile machines to receive electronically transmitted documents and produce a hard copy version. Faxes can also be sent and received via PC today. However, conventional copying machines are still stand-alone devices. At some point in the future, the copying machine will be integrated into the office network and will absorb the function of the stand-alone facsimile device. Single or multiple copies of a document may be printed at the copying machine, from a workstation in the same office, or from a remote site.

Document storage is another evolving area of office automation. It is not unusual today for organizations to store many of their business documents on-line to the computer, often using magnetic or optical disk technology (discussed in Chapter 2). More and more of these documents will be stored on-line in the future, particularly with the growing use of imaging technology. With imaging, any type of paper document—including reports, graphs, and photographs—can be read by a digital scanner and translated into digital form so that it can be stored in the computer system. Later this process can be reversed, so that the digitized image stored in the computer system can be printed on paper, displayed on a video display unit, or transmitted to another workstation.

A facility possessed by a limited but growing number of organizations—a videoconferencing facility—is shown at the bottom of Figure 5.8. Such facilities permit face-to-face, or, more properly, image-to-image, meetings and conferences to take place without the need for costly and time-consuming travel. By tying the videoconferencing facility into the integrated office network, computer-generated reports and graphics can also be shared during the conferences.

Whereas separate videoconferencing facilities work well for larger group meetings, desktop video-conferencing is now a reality, and as quality improves we believe it will become quite popular for one-on-one and small group conferences. The screen on a desktop PC is so small, however, that we don't think desktop videoconferencing will prove satisfactory for large group conferences. Splitting an already small screen into multiple smaller images will reduce the sense of "being there" and thus reduce the effectiveness of the conference. Thus, we believe that the office of the future will include a separate videoconferencing facility (usually a conference room) where a large group of people can participate in a conference from each location.

As an example of both group and desktop video-conferencing, let's consider the newest offerings from PictureTel Corporation, one of the leaders in this area. PictureTel's best-selling group videoconferencing units, the Concorde 4500 and System 400ZX, have list prices from $34,000 to $39,000 per unit. For an additional $7,500, one can buy a hardware acceleration option that will sustain 30 frames per second performance during motion-intensive applications using a 768 kbps transmission line. Included in these systems is a feature called LimeLight that causes the camera to dynamically locate the current speaker. LimeLight works by triangulating from the sounds received at four tiny, built-in microphones to focus on the speaker or, if several people are speaking almost at once, to zoom out and show all the people that are speaking (PictureTel, 1996). At the desktop level, PictureTel's Live 200 Series for Windows 95 lists at $1,495. Live 200 is designed to operate on an ISDN basic rate line, and the required hardware is all located on a single board to be installed in the PC. This desktop system won't provide large-system picture quality, but it does provide full-screen image and a satisfactory picture for most purposes.

In summary, the ideal office network shown in Figure 5.8 doesn't exist. Offices have the secretarial and professional/executive workstations in ever-increasing numbers, and these devices are usually linked via a LAN. Today telephony is not typically accomplished on the same network, and the facsimile machine is not on the LAN. The use of videoconferencing is increasing but still not commonplace.

As organizations have moved toward office automation, they have learned some important lessons. First, the process of office automation must be coordinated—each office unit cannot go its own way. The various islands of automation must be made compatible. In most organizations, the IS organization has been given the responsibility for corporatewide office automation. Second, the emphasis must be on the information requirements—the problems being solved—in office automation as in other information technology applications. Third, training and education of all parties involved is a necessary prerequisite for a successful system. Fourth, office automation should be an evolutionary process, moving toward the mythical office of the future, but not expecting to get there overnight. Fifth, the redefinition of the functions of the office and the restructuring of individual roles are required to achieve the maximum benefits of office automation.

GROUPWARE

Earlier in this chapter, we argued that enterprise resource planning systems deserved treatment as a separate application area because of their currency and importance, despite the fact that ERP systems are, indeed, transaction processing systems. Now we wish to make the same argument for including groupware as an application area vis-a-vis office automation. Clearly groupware is part of office automation, but it is a very critical part that deserves special attention.

Groupware is a made-up word referring to *software* designed to support *groups* by facilitating collaboration, communication, and coordination. Beyond that, there is no generally recognized definition for groupware. In choosing a groupware product, the decision-maker must decide what functions are required, and then seek a product (or a combination of

THE GROWTH OF GROUPWARE

The advantages groupware provides are well documented. Besides reducing paper flow and related costs, groupware enables users of desktop and portable computers to work more effectively because they can easily share experiences and information and collaborate on projects.

So why is groupware only now enjoying mass appeal? Some point the finger at traditional hierarchical organizations, which didn't need (or, in many cases, didn't want) individual departments or remote offices exchanging information. Today, however, the cooperation fostered by groupware is necessary in rightsized and flattened organizations.

Others attribute the groupware boom to technological maturity, which has resulted in lower prices and added functionality. And don't forget the Internet, an inexpensive and ubiquitous enabler of teams that has caused many enterprises to seriously evaluate a variety of collaborative computing solutions.

No matter what the catalyst, the number of groupware users just keeps growing. International Data Corp. (IDC), a Framingham, Mass.-based market research firm, estimates that there were 32 millions users worldwide in 1995—double the previous year's amount. By the end of the century, IDC predicts the ranks of groupware users should stand at more than a quarter of a billion people.

[McCune, 1996]

GroupWise. The third major player, and a relative newcomer in this market, is Microsoft Exchange. An interesting specialized groupware area deals with electronic meeting support systems, and we will talk more about this area in the next chapter.

Groupware, like ERP systems, is a growth area in the software industry in the late 1990s (see sidebar on "The Growth of Groupware"). As a way of gaining a greater understanding of this area, let's take a closer look at a leading groupware product, Lotus Notes.

An Example Groupware System: Lotus Notes

Lotus Development Corporation's first important product was 1-2-3, and it became the dominant spreadsheet package in the 1980s and early 1990s. The second important product was Notes, a groupware system originally featuring strong document sharing features and a reasonable e-mail package that has been growing into a more full-featured product. Notes—and Lotus' expertise in developing PC software—were important to IBM, which paid $3.5 billion to purchase Lotus in 1995. IBM was already a software powerhouse, as we noted in Chapter 3, but its strength was in large-machine software. IBM felt it needed to bolster its PC software prowess to compete with Microsoft in that market, and it also wanted the Notes groupware product. IBM has allowed Lotus to operate as a separate business unit, and so far the buyout seems to have been good for both IBM and Lotus. Notes sales jumped 57% in 1996 to 4.3 million units, and International Data Corporation, a Framingham, Mass.-based market research firm, predicts that sales will reach 6.8 million units in 1997 (Angus et al., 1997).

The main window for Lotus Notes is shown in Figure 5.9. Near the top of the screen is the menu bar containing menus used to work within Notes, and just below the menu bar is a row of icons (Lotus calls them SmartIcons) that permit the user to perform tasks quickly by clicking the mouse on an icon. Most of the screen is occupied by the workspace, which in turn contains icons representing databases. These databases are the heart of Notes; each database contains a collection of documents (of some sort) relating to the same topic. The database on the left is the mailbox, which is the entry point into the e-mail features of Notes. The other databases refer to topics of interest to

products) that provides that functionality. Among the potential groupware functions are electronic mail, electronic bulletin boards, computer conferencing, electronic calendaring, group scheduling, sharing documents, electronic whiteboards, meeting support systems, workflow routing, electronic forms, and desktop videoconferencing. None of the leading groupware packages provide all of these functions at present, but in many cases add-on packages can be purchased to fill the gaps.

One might guess that the heart of a successful general-purpose groupware product is electronic mail, and that may be right—but the key feature that put industry leader Lotus Notes in the top position is its outstanding ability to *share documents* of all types. Electronic calendaring and group scheduling are also important, and this has been a strength of Novell

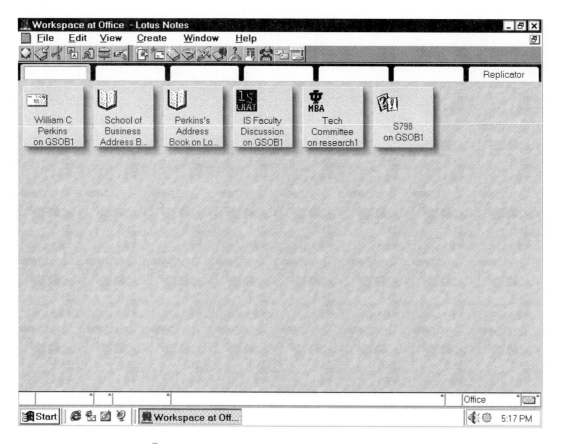

Figure 5.9 Lotus Notes® Workspace at Office © 1999 Lotus Development Corporation. Lotus Notes is a registered trademark of Lotus Development Corporation. Used with permission of Lotus Development Corporation.

this particular user, some of which are personal (such as the address book) and some of which are shared by a group (such as a group working on a particular project or all members of a college class). The user opens a database by double-clicking on the relevant database icon.

When the user opens the mailbox, for example, the Inbox view of the mailbox is displayed as shown in Figure 5.10. Again a menu bar and a SmartIcon bar appear at the top of the screen, but the entries have changed to be appropriate for e-mail. Immediately below the SmartIcon bar is a tool button bar containing tasks related to the view you are in. Then most of the screen is divided into a navigation pane on the left and an active view pane on the right. In the Inbox view, the active view pane lists the user's mail messages, tells who sent the message, the date it was sent,

and the subject assigned by the sender. To open a message to be able to read it, double-click on it. When you are reading a message, the tool buttons change to include a button to delete the message, a button to forward the message, and a button to reply to the message, among others. The navigation pane on the left lists a number of views that can be used to manage the mail. For instance, "folders and views" contains file folders in which you file messages that you want to save; "drafts" contains messages you are working on but have not yet sent; "to do" displays a task list that has been created by the user. Notes also has a valuable electronic calendaring feature that you access by clicking on "calendar" in the navigation pane. Several different calendar views are available, including a two-day view, a one-week view, and a one-month view.

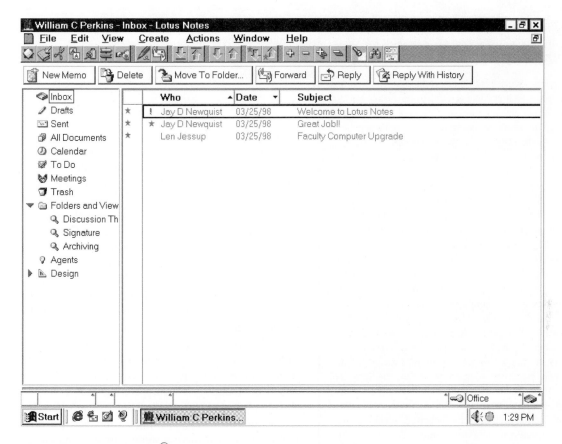

Figure 5.10 Lotus Notes® Inbox © 1999 Lotus Development Corporation. Lotus Notes is a registered trademark of Lotus Development Corporation. Used with permission of Lotus Development Corporation.

As has been mentioned, the real strength of Notes is its document-sharing abilities. This is done through the various shared databases. Some of the databases may be set up so that the user can only read documents, not modify them or add new ones; in other databases, such as discussion groups, all participants are encouraged to enter into the discussion. To open a database, double-click on its icon. The opening screen of a database looks much like Figure 5.10, with appropriate tool buttons, a navigation pane to the left, and a list of topics or documents in the view pane to the right. Double-click on a document to display it.

How does all this work? Lotus Notes is a client/server system, with the large files (databases) stored on the server, which Lotus now calls a "Domino server powered by Notes." The user may opt to have some databases stored on the PC hard drive,

but the master copies of the large corporate or departmental databases of documents are stored on the server. Corporate files are replicated from one Notes server to another on a regular basis, so that everyone across the organization has access to the same version of a document. The Lotus Notes client, operating on a PC, is used to access the server with appropriate password protection. This access may either be directly across a LAN or via a dial-up modem. More recently, Notes can be accessed by using a Web browser on the Internet. The Lotus strategy is to move both the Domino server and the Notes client squarely into the Internet camp. The new version of Domino due out in 1998 will embrace a wide variety of Internet standards, including major Internet mail and news protocols, and the new version of the Notes client will serve as a general-purpose Internet client in direct

management, health care, sales and marketing, and imaging applications.

> ### *ELI LILLY USES LOTUS NOTES TO SUPPORT ITS SALES FORCE*
>
> Eli Lilly now provides up-to-date product information to its sales representatives in the field using Lotus Notes databases. Notes also provides the link back to the office and around the world to get quick answers to specific questions. As the result, the sales team is able to get customers timely, accurate information, and customer relations is the winner.
>
> Eli Lilly & Company is a large, research-based pharmaceutical company with headquarters in Indianapolis, Indiana. Before adopting Notes, Eli Lilly relied on a traditional paper stream to keep sales representatives informed. The process was slow, constraining, unwieldy, and unfriendly. Notes has changed all that. Each sales representative has been equipped with a laptop computer, loaded with a Notes client containing product information databases. The master copies of these databases are kept on the Notes server and regularly updated, and each sales representative simply logs in and downloads the updated databases. Notes also gave sales representatives the ability to fire customer questions directly to an expert. For example, a question about feedlots in Queensland could be answered almost instantaneously by a feedlot expert in Adelaide.
>
> Eli Lilly is pleased with the increased quality of its customer service resulting from Notes. Based on that experience, Notes is now spreading across the company and is set to become the e-mail platform for Eli Lilly worldwide. "Notes has been an enabling tool," says Shaun Kerr, Project Manager in Information Technology Services at Eli Lilly. "It's like spreadsheets when they first came out. They enabled you to deliver power of analysis to people who wanted it. What we do is deliver shared information and Notes has made it happen."
>
> *[Adapted from Lotus, 1997]*

competition with Netscape's Communicator and Microsoft's Internet Explorer (Angus et al., 1997).

Finally, another strength of Lotus Notes is that it can serve as a development platform so that companies can create their own Notes applications customized for their needs. In fact, a growing number of these specialized applications are now commercially available through third-party vendors, including project management, human resources, help desk, document

INTRANETS

The notion of an intranet was introduced in Chapter 4: An **intranet** is a network operating within an organization that employs the TCP/IP protocol, the same protocol used on the Internet. In most cases, an intranet consists of a backbone network with a number of connected local area networks. Because the protocol is the same, the organization may use the same Web browser, Web crawler, and Web server software as it would use on the Internet. The intranet, however, is not accessible from outside the organization. The organization decides whether or not people within the organization have access to the Internet.

An intranet presents some incredible advantages to the organization. If an organization already has an internal network of interconnected LANs and if the organization already has an operating Web server and Web browsers on most workstations, as most organizations do, then implementing an intranet is a relatively easy task involving some programming on the Web server. With minimal effort the full functionality of a localized World Wide Web, including e-mail and document sharing, is available within the organization. The Web browser is a "universal client" that works with heterogenous platforms. Furthermore, virtually no training is needed to implement an intranet because users already know how to use a browser. Deploying a new intranet application is simple—just send an e-mail message containing the URL (address) of the new application to users.

Even if the organization does not have a Web server and Web browsers, the costs are not overwhelming. Web browsers are inexpensive or free, and a minimal Web server complete with software can be obtained for well under $10,000. Intranets are easy enough to set up that in some organizations the first intranet has been set up by end-users, such as engineers, not by the IS organization, to enable sharing of particular documents.

At Johnson Controls, a $9 billion manufacturer of automotive parts, plastics, and control systems based in Plymouth, Michigan, an intranet was the solution to the problem of keeping salespeople and technicians up to date on the company's sophisticated environmental control devices. The initial intranet at Johnson Controls provided field personnel answers to frequently asked questions about the control devices. Later, the intranet became the repository for more than 200,000 training documents—a number that is expected to grow to 500,000 documents. The intranet is also being used to distribute internal newsletters as well as to provide information on every department and individual within the firm. Johnson Controls now has 5,000 employees accessing its intranet using Netscape Navigator as their Web browser. Jim Smith, principal Web developer for Johnson Controls, says, "People really love the new system. It's truly changing the way that we communicate" (James, 1996).

AT&T had a serious problem providing 800-number service to its commercial customers. Customers calling one 800 number were frequently told by the customer service agent (CSA) to call a different 800 number, which sometimes directed them to another 800 number, and so on—in some cases requiring calls to as many as 23 different 800 numbers before a billing mistake was corrected, a new service ordered, or the needed information obtained. AT&T wanted to provide a single 800 number for its commercial customers—"one call does it all"—but this required developing a repository of information containing the shortcuts and rules-of-thumb used by the best customer service agents and making this repository easily available to all the CSAs. The solution was an intranet to permit sharing of this critical information, using Netscape Navigator on the client machines and Netscape server software on the Web server. The AT&T intranet for CSAs moved very quickly. "We went from white-board [planning] to 10,000 desktops in three months," says Mark Francis, the division manager of AT&T Customer Care Development. "And because most of the people had already used a Web browser, there was virtually no training time" (James, 1996).

In the previous section we described groupware products for office automation, such as Lotus Notes and Novell GroupWise. Note that intranets can deliver much of the functionality of groupware—and for a much smaller investment. Low cost and reduced complexity led U.S. West to choose an intranet solution rather than a groupware product. U.S. West is deploy-

> ### INTRANETS PAY OFF FAST WITH HIGH ROI
>
> International Data Corporation has released preliminary results of a study it conducted for Netscape on how quickly intranets can recover the costs associated with installing them and how high an eventual return on investment they generate. The answer? Payback in 6 to 12 weeks and an ROI [return on investment] of over 1,000%.
>
> In a relatively short period of time, intranets have become big business. Cambridge, Mass.-based Forrester Research reports that two-thirds of all midsized and large companies have either installed an intranet or are considering implementing one within the next year. The Stamford, Conn.-based Gartner Group agrees, predicting that more than 50 percent of large enterprises will have deployed an intranet by 1998.
>
> *[Adapted from Varney, 1996 and James, 1996]*

ing Netscape's Communicator to about 50,000 employees in its communications division. During a year-long process, U.S. West evaluated a variety of e-mail and groupware offerings. "Reducing complexity and giving everyone basic tools just made sense," says Barbara Bauer, senior director of corporate systems development at U.S. West. "Everyone needs a browser, and everybody needs e-mail. We don't think that every employee needs a fully integrated groupware platform" (Varney, 1996).

The Web, and intranets in particular, are certainly influencing groupware, and vice versa. A number of special software products have been developed to implement groupware-style services on an intranet. For example, SamePage from WebFlow and WebPower from Arachnid Software are packages that manage documents on an intranet. Groupware vendors have reacted to the Web phenomenon by moving quickly to support the Internet standards. We previously noted that Lotus Notes has embraced a wide variety of Internet standards, including major Internet mail and news protocols. Microsoft and Novell, the other primary groupware vendors, have taken similar steps. The reality for groupware vendors is "embrace the Internet or perish." Still, the choice between a more expensive, full service, Internet-friendly groupware product such as Lotus Notes and a less expensive, reduced services, intranet will be a difficult one for many organizations.

Factory Automation

The roots of **factory automation** lie in (1) numerically controlled machines, which use a computer program, or a tape with holes punched in it, to control the movement of tools on sophisticated machines; and in (2) **material requirements planning** (**MRP**) systems, which rely on extensive data input to produce a production schedule for the factory and a schedule of needed raw materials. The newer **computer-integrated manufacturing** (**CIM**) combines these basic ideas not only to let the computer set up the schedules (as with MRP) but to carry them out through control of the various machines involved (as with numerically controlled machines).

Computer-integrated manufacturing is one of the primary ways by which manufacturers are facing the challenges of global competition. Through the various components of CIM, manufacturers are increasing productivity and quality while simultaneously reducing the lead time from the idea stage to the marketplace for most products. A list of strong proponents of CIM reads like a who's who of manufacturing—General Motors, John Deere, Ford, Weyerhauser, FMC, and Kodak, among others.

CIM systems fall into three major categories: engineering systems, manufacturing administration, and factory operations. Table 5.1 lists the acronyms used in this section on factory automation. The engineering systems are aimed at increasing the productivity of engineers and include such systems as computer-aided design and group technology. Manufacturing administration includes systems that develop production schedules and monitor production against these schedules; these systems are usually termed manufacturing resources planning systems. Factory operations include those systems that actually control the operation of machines on the factory floor. Computer-aided manufacturing and shop floor control are examples of such systems.

Table 5.1

Abbreviations Used in Factory Automation

Acronym	Full Name
CIM	Computer-integrated manufacturing
CAD	Computer-aided design
GT	Group technology
MRP	Material requirements planning
MRP II	Manufacturing resources planning
CAM	Computer-aided manufacturing
CAE	Computer-aided engineering
CAPP	Computer-aided process planning
AGV	Automated-guided vehicle
MAP	Manufacturing automation protocol
SFC	Shop floor control

Engineering Systems

Computer-aided design (**CAD**) is perhaps the most familiar of the engineering systems. CAD involves the use of computer graphics—both two-dimensional and three-dimensional—to create and modify engineering designs. **Computer-aided engineering** (**CAE**) is a system designed to analyze the functional characteristics of a design and used to simulate the product performance under various conditions in order to reduce the need to build prototypes. CAD and CAE permit engineers to conduct a more thorough engineering analysis and to investigate a wider range of design alternatives. Advanced CAD/CAE systems store the information they generate in a database that is shared with the other components of CIM, such as CAM.

Group technology (**GT**) systems logically group parts according to physical characteristics, machine routings through the factory, and similar machine operations. On the basis of these logical groupings, GT is able to identify existing parts that engineers can use or modify rather than design new parts, simplifying the design and manufacturing processes. **Computer-aided process planning** (**CAPP**) systems plan the sequence of processes that produce or assemble a part. During the design process, the engineer retrieves the closest standard plan from a database (using the GT classification of the new part) and modifies that plan rather than starting from scratch. The resulting plans are more accurate and more consistent, thereby reducing process planning and manufacturing costs.

Manufacturing Administration

Manufacturing resource planning (MRP II) systems usually have three major components: the master production schedule, material requirements planning, and shop floor control. The master production schedule component sets the overall production goals based on forecasts of demand. The MRP component then develops a detailed production schedule to accomplish the master schedule, using parts explosion, production capacity, inventory, and lead-time data. The shop floor control component releases orders to the shop floor based on the detailed production schedule and the actual production accomplished thus far. Using the buzzwords of the 1990s, MRP II systems attempt to implement just-in-time (JIT) production. Note that MRP II does not directly control machines on the shop floor; it is an information system that tries to minimize inventory and employ the machines effectively and efficiently.

In our discussion of enterprise resource planning (ERP) systems earlier in this chapter, we noted that MRP is often one of the key modules of an ERP system. Thus, such an ERP system ties together the manufacturing production schedule with the other important aspects of running an enterprise, including sales and distribution, human resources, and financial reporting. The newest type of manufacturing administration system, however, goes beyond ERP and outside the boundaries of the firm itself: **supply-chain management systems** that are designed to deal with distribution and transportation of raw materials and finished products throughout the supply chain, and to incorporate constraints caused by the supply chain into the production scheduling process. These supply-chain management systems are often interorganizational in nature (a customer and its suppliers) and will be treated more fully in Chapter 7 for both manufacturers and retailers.

Factory Operations

Factory operations systems go a significant step further than MRP II—they control the machines. By definition, **computer-aided manufacturing (CAM)** is the use of computers to control manufacturing processes. CAM is built around a series of computer programs that control automated equipment on the shop floor. In addition to computer-controlled machines such as automated drill presses and milling machines, CAM systems employ automated guided vehicles (AGVs) to move raw materials, in-process materials, and finished products from one work station to another. AGVs are loaded using robotlike arms and then follow a computer-generated electronic signal (often a track under the floor that has been activated) to their next destination. Workers are used only to provide maintenance on the equipment and to handle problems. Because job setups (preparing a machine to work on a new part) are automated and accomplished in minimum time, CAM permits extremely high machine utilization. With the low setup time, very small batches (even as small as one) can be produced efficiently, shortening production lead times and reducing inventory levels.

As this brief description has implied, a CAM system is very sophisticated and requires a great deal of input data from other systems. Product design data would come from CAD, process design data from CAPP, and the master production schedule and material requirements from MRP II. The CAM system must also be able to communicate electronically with the machines on the shop floor.

The manufacturing communications network is likely to employ the **manufacturing automation protocol (MAP)**, pioneered by General Motors and now accepted by nearly all major manufacturers and vendors. MAP is a communications protocol (a set of rules) to ensure an open manufacturing system. With conformance to MAP by all vendors, seamless communication between all equipment on the factory floor—regardless of the vendor—will be possible. MAP is a user-driven effort, and the details of the concept are evolving over time. Nevertheless, MAP is a reality in factory automation upon which future systems will be based.

Within factory operations applications, **shop floor control (SFC)** systems are less ambitious than CAM but are still important. These systems provide on-line, real-time (immediate) control and monitoring of machines on the shop floor. For example, the SFC might recognize that a tool on a particular milling machine is getting dull (by measuring the metal that the machine is cutting per second) and signal this fact to the human operator on duty. The operator can then take corrective measures, such as instructing the SFC to change the tool or changing it himself or herself, depending on the system.

Robotics

Outside the broad area of CIM, robotics is one other aspect of factory automation that deserves mention. Robotics is, in fact, one branch of the artificial intelligence tree. (Artificial intelligence, especially expert systems and neural networks, is discussed in the next chapter.) With robotics, scientists and engineers are building machines to accomplish coordinated physical tasks in the manner of humans. Robots have been important in manufacturing for more than a decade to accomplish simple but important tasks, such as painting and welding. Robots are tireless in performing repetitive tasks, produce more consistent high-quality output than humans, and are not subject to the dangers of paint inhalation or retinal damage. Newer robots incorporate a certain amount of visual perception and thus are able to perform assembly tasks of increasing complexity. Industrial robots are very expensive, but they are becoming economically viable for a wider range of tasks as their capabilities are extended. Robots and CIM are producing a vastly different "factory of the future" based on information technology.

SUMMARY

At the end of the 20th century, virtually all large and midsized businesses and an increasing number of small businesses are dependent upon organizational IT systems. These systems support almost every function of the business, from procuring raw materials to planning the production schedule to distributing the product, from recording and summarizing sales figures to keeping track of inventory, from paying employees and suppliers to handling receivables, from maintaining the financial records of the organization to enabling employees to communicate more effectively. Modern organizations simply can-not do business today without organizational IT systems.

Transaction processing systems are central to the operations of almost every business. These workhorse systems, which were the very first IT applications installed in most businesses, process the thousands of transactions that occur every day, including sales, payments, inventory, and payroll. In recent years, many larger businesses have turned to enterprise resource planning (ERP) systems as a way to achieve an integrated set of transaction processing applications. ERP systems typically consist of a number of modules to handle the sales and distribution, manufacturing, financial reporting, and human resources areas, and the organization can buy a subset of these modules to satisfy its needs.

Transaction processing systems handle the volume of transactions generated as a firm does business, and they also produce summary reports on these transactions. They do not, however, provide this transactional data in a form that enables managers to use the data in decision-making activities—data warehousing does this. With data warehousing, organizational data are made accessible from a storage area that is distinct from that used for operational transaction processing. When combined with easy-to-use analysis tools—to be discussed in the next chapter—the data warehouse becomes a critical information resource for managers to enable strategic and operational decision-making.

Office automation systems affect every knowledge worker in a firm. Word processing, electronic calendaring, electronic mail, and many other applications are most commonly delivered via an employee's PC attached to the organization's network. Groupware is an increasingly popular way of providing office automation functionality in an integrated package. Lotus Notes, the most popular groupware package in the latter 1990s, provides an excellent document sharing capability as well as calendaring, e-mail, and other features. Intranets—networks within an organization employing Internet standards—offer an attractive, lower-cost alternative to groupware that is gaining popularity. Factory automation, especially computer-integrated manufacturing, applies information technology to the task of increasing efficiency and effectiveness in the manufacturing process.

As important as these various organizational systems are, they are certainly not the whole story in terms of IT applications. Chapter 6 focuses on managerial support systems designed to provide support to a manager or managers, and Chapter 7 explores the topic of interorganizational systems and other electronic commerce applications.

REVIEW QUESTIONS

1. Consider the organizational systems application areas listed in Figure 5.1. Which application area developed first? Which one is most common today? Which is the "hottest" application area today?

2. Describe the fundamental differences between batch processing, on-line processing, and in-line processing.

3. What is a vertically integrated information system? Give an example.

4. What is a client/server system? What is a client? What is a server? Why would an organization choose to implement a client/server system?

5. Define middleware. What are the three categories of middleware?

6. List the primary categories of modules that are likely to be included in an ERP system.

7. What companies are the primary vendors of ERP systems? Which one of these is the market leader? What are the capabilities of the package that led to this leadership position?

8. What aspects of the automated office are you most likely to encounter today? In the future, what additional features are likely to be added to the automated office?

9. What is groupware? What are the features likely to be included in a groupware product?

10. What are the primary groupware products on the market today? Which one of these is the market leader? What are the capabilities of the package that led to this leadership position?

11. Some of the most important acronyms used in the factory automation area are listed below. Provide the full names for each of these acronyms.

CIM	MAP
CAD	GT
MRP	MRP II

12. Consider again the six acronyms listed in the previous question. Give a one-sentence explanation of each term, and then describe the interrelationships among the terms.

Discussion Questions

1. Differentiate between a two-tier client/server system and a three-tier client/server system. Differentiate between a fat client and a thin client. Why would a firm choose one of these approaches over the others when implementing a client/server system?

2. In review question 5 above, you listed the three categories of middleware. In one sentence each, define the three categories. Explain the role of each category and how they interact.

3. In this chapter, payroll and order entry were used as examples of transaction processing systems. Another example with which all of us are somewhat familiar is the check-processing system employed by your bank. Consider how the check-processing system is similar to (and different from) the two examples in this chapter. Is the check-processing system likely to be batch, on-line, or some hybrid of the two? What subsystems would be required to operate the check-processing system?

4. Several reasons why firms are adopting ERP systems were given in this chapter. Review these reasons, and try to identify other reasons you think may also have been relevant. Considering the entire set of reasons, which do you think are most important and why?

5. Every large organization has large files or databases containing data used in operating the business. How does a data warehouse differ from these operational files or databases? Why are these differences important?

6. Consider an office environment with which you are somewhat familiar. What changes have occurred in the preparation of documents (such as reports and letters) over the past five years? Why do you think these changes have occurred? Have they been technology- or people-driven, or some of both?

7. Based on your reading and knowledge from other sources, in what ways has the phenomenon of the Internet influenced office automation? Hint: You may want to explore the phenomenon of intranets.

8. Many large firms have adopted groupware, and others are still using mainframe-based electronic mail systems a decade or more old. What explains this difference? Why have some firms quickly moved to groupware, whereas others are moving more slowly?

9. The terminology employed in factory automation is often confusing, in part because the names are

so similar and in part because the subareas do indeed overlap. Carefully distinguish among CIM, CAD, CAE, CAM, and CAPP, indicating any overlaps.

10. All of us come into contact with distributed systems almost every day, even if it is only while shopping at Sears or J. C. Penney. Describe a distributed system with which you have come in contact. In your view, what are the advantages and disadvantages of this system? Is the system you described a client/server system?

REFERENCES

1994. "How to deploy client/server RDBMS for operational data." *I/S Analyzer Case Studies* 33 (March): 1–20.

1994. "How middleware can be used to create enterprise and inter-enterprise applications." *I/S Analyzer Case Studies* 33 (July): 1–16.

1995. "How the 3-tier architecture enables the development of enterprise-level client/server applications." *I/S Analyzer Case Studies* 34 (May): 1–16.

Angus, Jeff, Karen M. Carrillo, Justin Hibbard, and Bruce Caldwell. 1997. "IBM and Lotus get closer." *Information Week* (July 28): 73–80.

Appleton, Elaine L. 1997. "How to survive ERP." *Datamation* 43 (March): 50–53.

Bancroft, Nancy H. 1996. *Implementing SAP R/3.* Greenwich, CT: Manning Publications Co.

Callaway, Erin. 1997. "On time, on budget." *PC Week* 14 (May 19): 135–136.

Chase, Richard B., Nicholas J. Aquilano, and F. Robert Jacobs. 1998. *Production and Operations Management: Manufacturing and Services*, 8th ed., Supplement 16 on "SAP R/3." Homewood, IL: Irwin/McGraw-Hill.

Computer Sciences Corporation. 1997. "Aligning technology and corporate goals is top I/S issue worldwide in tenth annual CSC study." Computer Sciences Corporation Web site, http://www.csc.com/about/news_stories/top_is.html (April 14).

Darling, Charles B. 1996. "How to integrate your data warehouse." *Datamation* 42 (May 15): 40–51.

Darling, Charles B. 1996. "Pioneer implements SAP R/3 with HP's help." *Datamation* 42 (October): 16–17.

Garcia, Mary Ryan. 1996. "Data warehouses grow up." *Beyond Computing* 5 (September): 24–26.

Garcia, Mary Ryan. 1997. "Taking care of your warehouse." *Beyond Computing* 6 (May): 32–36.

Greenblatt, Ellen C. 1997. "Data warehousing keeps Karsten swinging." *Datamation* 43 (July): 15.

Hecht, Bradley. 1997. "Choose the right ERP software." *Datamation* 43 (March): 56–58.

James, Geoffrey. 1996. "Intranets rescue reengineering." *Datamation* 42 (December): 38–45.

Kador, John. 1996. "Part of the family." *Beyond Computing* 5 (July/August): 50–52.

Lotus Development Corporation. 1997. "Eli Lilly enables its sales force with Lotus Notes." Lotus Development Corporation Web site, http://www2.lotus.com/Industry Spotlight.nsf (July 8).

McCarthy, Vance. 1995. "Desktop videoconferencing: still a rough cut." *Datamation* 41 (May 15): 51–55.

McCune, Jenny C. 1996. "All together now." *Beyond Computing* 5 (May): 26–31.

McCune, Jenny C. 1997. "What a difference a data warehouse makes." *Beyond Computing* 6 (May): 20–24.

McWilliams, Gary. 1997. "Whirlwind on the Web." *Business Week* (April 7): 132–136.

Miller, Michael W. 1992. "A story of the type that turns heads in computer circles." *Wall Street Journal* (September 15): A1, A8.

Moad, Jeff. 1996. "R/3: Little material gain for Applied." *PC Week* 13 (May 20): 1, 126.

Orfali, Robert, Dan Harkey, and Jeri Edwards. 1996. *The Essential Client/Server Survival Guide,* 2nd ed. New York: John Wiley & Sons, Inc.

PictureTel. 1996. "PictureTel announces enhancements to its industry-leading Concorde 4500 group videoconferencing system." PictureTel press release, PictureTel Web site, http://www.picturetel.com/conc45pr.htm (July 30).

Plumley, Sue. 1997. *10 Minute Guide to Lotus Notes 4.5.* Indianapolis, IN: Que Corporation.

Ruber, Peter. 1997. "Client/server's triple play." *Beyond Computing* 6 (March): 32–34.

SAP. 1997. "SAP announces Motorola's Semiconductor Products Sector is now live with the largest North American R/3 payroll implementation." SAP press release, SAP Web site, http://www.sap.com (June 16).

SAP. 1997. "Ten thousandth R/3 installation: L'Oreal to implement SAP software in 59 countries." SAP press release, SAP Web site, http://www.sap.com (June 11).

Stein, Tom. 1997. "Orders from chaos." *Information Week* (June 23): 44–52.

Thé, Lee. 1995. "Need groupware? Think functions, not products." *Datamation* 41 (July 15): 67–69.

Thé, Lee. 1995. "Beta not wait for groupware." *Datamation* 41 (July 15): 69–74.

Tucker, Michael J. 1997. "SAP: Two weeks from live." *Datamation* 43 (February): 21.

Varney, Sarah E. 1996. "Will intranets lay waste to groupware?" *Datamation* 42 (December): 72–80.

Wreden, Nick. 1997. "A desktop window on corporate data." *Beyond Computing* 6 (May): 26–31.

MANAGERIAL SUPPORT SYSTEMS

Managerial support systems are the topic of this second of three chapters devoted to our survey of information technology (IT) applications areas. Managerial support systems are designed to provide support to a specific manager or a small group of managers, and they include applications to support managerial decision-making such as group support systems, executive information systems, and expert systems. In contrast, the previous chapter dealt with organizational systems designed to support the entire organization or large portions of it, such as transaction processing systems, data warehousing, and groupware. Together these two chapters provide a relatively comprehensive picture of the applications of information technology within a single organization (*intraorganizational* systems). To complete the survey of IT applications, Chapter 7 will focus on *interorganizational* systems that span organizational boundaries, such as electronic data interchange (EDI) and other electronic commerce applications using the Internet. Taken as a set, these three chapters encompass the great majority of IT applications in use today.

The organizational systems discussed in the prior chapter are critical for running a business or any other type of organization, and you as a manager will be dealing with many such organizational systems, especially transaction processing systems and groupware. Nevertheless, these organizational systems have been designed to support the organization as a whole, not you in particular nor even a group of managers. Managerial support systems, in contrast, are intended to directly support you and other managers as you make strategic and tactical decisions for your organizations. For example, interactive decision support systems are designed to help managers and other professionals analyze internal and external data. By capturing the expertise of human experts, expert systems advise nonexperts in a particular decision area. Group support systems are designed to make group work, especially meetings, more productive. Executive information systems provide easy-to-navigate summary data for the top executives of an organization. This chapter will explore these and other managerial support systems that are increasingly important in running modern organizations.

DECISION SUPPORT SYSTEMS

A **decision support system (DSS)** is a computer-based system, almost always interactive, designed to assist a manager (or another decision-maker) in making decisions. A DSS incorporates both data and models to help a decision-maker solve a problem, especially a problem that is not well structured. The data are often extracted from a transaction processing system or a data warehouse, but that is not always the case. The model may be simple, such as a profit-and-loss model to calculate profit given certain assumptions, or complex, such as an optimization model to suggest loadings for each machine in a job shop. DSSs and many of the systems discussed in the following sections are not always justified by a traditional cost-benefit approach; for these systems, many of the benefits are intangible, such as faster decision-making and better understanding of the data.

Figure 6.1 points out that a decision support system requires three primary components: model management to apply the appropriate model, data

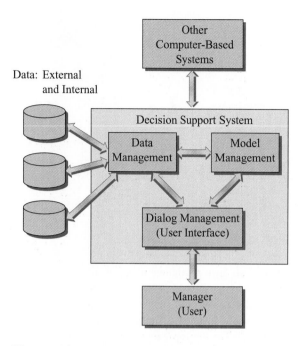

Figure 6.1 Decision Support Systems Components

management to select and handle the appropriate data, and dialog management to facilitate the user interface to the DSS. The user interacts with the DSS through the dialog management component, identifying the particular model and data set to be used, and then the DSS presents the results to the user through this same dialog management component. The model management and data management components largely act behind the scenes, and they vary from relatively simple for a typical spreadsheet model to quite complex for a mathematical programming-based scheduling model.

An extremely popular type of DSS is a pro forma financial statement generator. Using a spreadsheet package such as Lotus 1-2-3 or Microsoft Excel, a manager builds a model to project the various elements of the organization or division financial statement into the future. The data employed are historical financial figures for the organization. The initial (base) model incorporates various assumptions about future trends in income and expense categories. After viewing the results of the base model, the manager performs a series of "what-if analyses" by modifying one or more assumptions to determine their impact on the bottom line. For example, the manager might explore the impact on profitability if the sales of a new prod-

uct grew by 10 percent per year, rather than the 5 percent incorporated in the base model. Or the manager might investigate the impact of a higher-than-expected increase in the price of raw materials, such as 7 percent per year instead of 4 percent per year. This type of financial statement generator is a simple but powerful DSS for guiding financial decision-making.

An example of a DSS driven by transactions data is a police-beat allocation system used by a California city. This system enables a police officer to display a map outline and call up data by geographic zone, which shows police calls for service, types of service, and service times. The interactive graphics capability of the system permits the officer to manipulate the maps, zones, and data to consider a variety of police-beat alternatives quickly and easily and takes maximum advantage of the officer's judgment.

Other DSS examples include an interactive system for capacity planning and production scheduling in a large paper company. This system employs detailed historical data and forecasting and scheduling models to simulate overall performance of the company under differing planning assumptions. A major oil company developed a DSS to support capital investment decision-making. This system incorporates various financial routines and models for generating future plans; these plans can be displayed in either tabular or graphic form to aid in decision-making.

All the DSS examples cited are more properly called **specific DSS**. These are the actual applications that assist in the decision-making process. In contrast, a **decision support system generator** is a system that provides a set of capabilities to build a specific DSS quickly and easily (Sprague and Carlson, 1982). A DSS generator is a software package designed to run on a particular computer platform. In our pro forma financial statement example above, Microsoft Excel or Lotus 1-2-3 can be viewed as a DSS generator, whereas an Excel or 1-2-3 model to project financial statements for a particular division of a company is a specific DSS.

DATA MINING

In Chapter 5, we introduced data warehousing—the idea of a company pulling data from its operational systems and putting the data in a separate "data warehouse" so that users may access and analyze the data

A POTPOURRI OF DSS EXAMPLES

Virtually every issue of *Interfaces* contains a discussion of one or more new DSSs. To illustrate, we briefly describe four quite different decision support systems presented in the March–April 1996 and July–August 1997 issues of *Interfaces*.

"Development of a DSS for fixed-income securities using OOP" (Sodhi, 1996) describes a DSS built for an insurance company called Health Net to analyze 36 different types of fixed-income securities and derivatives such as bonds, mortgage-backed securities, commercial paper, and U.S. Treasury bills for risk and return and to manage fixed income portfolios worth $370 million. Sodhi embedded a number of sophisticated management science techniques, such as convex nonlinear programming, nonlinear regression, and stratified sampling, in the DSS. At Health Net, the portfolio manager and an assistant use the DSS for deciding on trades; analyzing securities, portfolios, and the effect of potential trades on portfolios; generating reports for the corporate board; and generating information for the accounting department.

In the same issue of *Interfaces,* Rakshit, Krishnamurthy, and Yu (1996) describe the System Operations Advisor (SOA), a real-time decision support system used by United Airlines at its operations control center to increase the effectiveness of its operational decisions. SOA is designed to help aircraft controllers deal with aircraft shortage problems that may arise at an airport because of delayed or canceled incoming flights or mechanical problems for aircraft on the ground. The DSS, which employs a network optimization modeling technique, helps controllers use spare aircraft more effectively as well as evaluate possible delay-and-swap options. Over an 18-month period, the use of SOA saved more than 27,000 minutes of potential delays, which translates into $540,000 in delay costs, and the number of flight delays charged to aircraft controllers in operations control dropped by 50 percent.

Ferrell and Hizlan (1997) employ mixed-integer programming as the primary modeling technique in their DSS for planning municipal solid waste management. Their model considers the disposition of solid waste in phases. First, all waste is processed by a recycling option, which may be either at-source separation, commingled recyclables separation, mass sorting, or convenience centers. Second, the remaining solid waste may be handled by some combination of incineration, composting, disposal at a private landfill, and disposal at a public sanitary or public inert landfill. The model minimizes the total cost of operating the solid waste management program subject to capacity constraints, conservation of mass constraints, and administrative constraints such as required minimum utilization of a particular alternative. The authors found that in order for the results of the model to be accepted, they had to allow the decision-makers to manipulate noneconomic factors and consider their impact on the results.

"An integrated spatial DSS for scheduling and routing home-health-care nurses" (Begur, Miller, and Weaver, 1997) was developed through a joint project between the University of Alabama's Productivity Center and the Visiting Nurses Association. There are currently over 10,000 organizations in the United States providing nursing-related services in patients' homes. These organizations have a continuing and challenging staff-deployment decision problem, including scheduling nurses to see patients, and specifying travel routes. The spatial DSS solves the home-health-care scheduling problem through a comprehensive system that encompasses data management of patient requirements and nurse availability, geocoding patient locations to map coordinates, establishing schedules for nurses, and visual interactive rerouting to improve the schedules. The system integrates stand-alone PC-based geographic information systems software (more on this later in the chapter) with scheduling heuristics and databases to provide a user-friendly tool that saves the nurses association travel time and schedule-preparation time and improves the balance of work among nurses.

without endangering the operational systems. In that discussion, we touched on the variety of software tools available for analysis of data in the warehouse, but deferred a more complete discussion until this chapter. Our argument was that the creation and maintenance of the data warehouse is an organizational system, in that the data warehouse supports the entire organization by making the data available to everyone, whereas the analysis of the data is performed by and/or for a single manager or a small group of managers and is therefore a management support system. Without explicitly mentioning it, we have already begun the more detailed discussion of these tools for analyzing data in the warehouse, because the decision support systems described in the previous section often pull the data they need directly from the organizations' data warehouses.

Data mining employs a variety of technologies (such as decision trees and neural networks) to search or "mine" for small "nuggets" of information from the vast quantities of data stored in an organization's data warehouse. Data mining, which is sometimes considered a subset of decision support systems, is especially useful when the organization has large volumes of transactions data in its warehouse. The concept of data mining is not new, although the name has only become popular in the latter 1990s. For at least two decades, many large organizations have used internal or external analysts, often called management scientists, to try to identify trends or patterns in massive amounts of data by using statistical, mathematical, and artificial intelligence techniques. With the development of large-scale data warehouses and the availability of inexpensive processing power, a renewed interest in what came to be called data mining arose in recent years.

Along with this renewed interest came a variety of high-powered and relatively easy-to-use commercial data mining software packages. *Datamation* describes five such packages in its July 1997 issue: Darwin from Thinking Machines, Datamind Professional Edition, IBM's Intelligent Miner, KnowledgeSeeker from Angoss Software, and Marksman from HNC Software (Freeman, 1997). These packages vary widely in cost, ranging from about $5,000 for Datamind and KnowledgeSeeker to about $150,000 for the mainframe version of Intelligent Miner. The more expensive packages incorporate a wider range of decision technologies, and generally require the use of consultants to fully utilize the capabilities of the package.

What decision techniques or approaches are used in data mining? KnowledgeSeeker uses only one technology, decision trees. A decision tree is a tree-shaped structure that is derived from the data to represent sets of decisions that result in various outcomes. When a new set of decisions is presented, such as information on a particular shopper, the decision tree then predicts the outcome. Neural networks, a branch of artificial intelligence to be discussed later in this chapter, are incorporated in Marksman, Intelligent Miner, and Darwin (the latter two also use decision trees). Other popular technologies include rule induction, the extraction of if-then rules based on statistical significance; nearest neighbor, the classification of a record based on those most similar to it in the database; and genetic algorithms, optimization techniques based on the concepts of genetic combination, mutation, and natural selection.

Of course, what can be done with data mining is more important to you as a manager than the decision technologies employed. Typical applications of data mining are outlined in Table 6.1. Whatever the nature of your business, the chances are good that several of these applications could mean increased profits for your organization. Most of these applications focus on unearthing valuable information about your customers.

The popular press is beginning to provide examples of successful data mining operations. Firstar Bank, a $20-billion bank holding company based in Milwaukee, used data mining to customize the bank's direct mailings to increase the response rate. Using the

Table 6.1

Data mining can be used for . . .

Application	Description
Market segmentation	Identifies the common characteristics of customers who buy the same products from your company
Customer churn	Predicts which customers are likely to leave your company and go to a competitor
Fraud detection	Identifies which transactions are most likely to be fraudulent
Direct marketing	Identifies which prospects should be included in a mailing list to obtain the highest response rate
Interactive marketing	Predicts what each individual accessing a Web site is most likely interested in seeing
Market basket analysis	Suggests what products or services are commonly purchased together, e.g., beer and diapers
Trend analysis	Reveals the difference between a typical customer this month versus last

SOURCE: Datamind Corp. Reproduced with permission from *DATAMATION,* © 1997 Cahners Business Information. *DATAMATION* is a trademark of Cahners Business Information. All rights reserved.

Marksman data mining package, Firstar rank-ordered customers into different groups based on the bank services they already used (such as charge cards, home equity loans, savings accounts, and investment products) and then predicted which products would be right to offer to each customer at which time. In terms of the applications in Table 6.1, Firstar used market segmentation in order to improve its direct marketing results. The results were great, according to Ted Bratanow, Firstar's director of market research and database marketing. "Direct marketers are usually pleased when they can increase response rates by a few percent," says Bratanow. "Our response rate improved by a factor of four" (Freeman, 1997).

Capital One Financial Corporation is a big believer in data mining. Capital One has created an infrastructure that mines information on 200 million consumers, permitting a mass customization approach. For example, Capital One offers 3,000 credit card variations whereas the industry norm is two, regular or gold. So far, Capital One's biggest innovation is the oft-copied teaser-rate credit card aimed at customers with low credit risk who carry a balance every month. The idea is to offer a very low interest rate (such as 6.9%) on transferred balances for some period of time, say a year, to attract new customers. Capital One is busily looking for other such innovations with continued data mining, and the company is confident that it will be successful (Morrissey, 1997).

Bank of America, based in San Francisco, was concerned about customer churn. The bank was interested in finding new ways to retain current checking-account customers while recruiting new customers. As the first step, the bank's marketing executives wanted to find out which customers tended to use which products, and they wanted to find out if a different mix of products might better serve the needs of various groups of customers. Through an extensive data mining process using various software products, Bank of America clustered its customers into smaller and more understandable groups that had similar interests and needs. "The payoff was that some customers were using the wrong product, so we set about to convert them," says Michael Koved, Bank of America's vice president of marketing. "We contacted them by mail and even phone and found the response was generally very favorable. Sometimes it meant a few dollars a

---

DATA MINING WORKS AT MERCK-MEDCO

Evan Marks, vice president for marketing at Merck-Medco, believes that the company's data mining system, named ExpeR$_x$t, "helps you ask the right questions and deliver your information even if you're not sure what patterns you're looking for." One pattern the system has uncovered is already saving Merck-Medco customers millions of dollars.

Using ExpeR$_x$t, Merck-Medco analyzed the effectiveness of certain treatments for gastric-intestinal ailments. Cost data led Merck-Medco to seek alternative treatments to the most frequently prescribed drug. The result was identification of an alternative and less costly drug that could prove effective for many patients and could even work more quickly. "Data mining didn't tell us about the new treatment," says Marks, "but it did indicate that many of our customers had high costs in this area, and that led us to look for alternatives in the medical literature."

The new drug saved one Merck-Medco client with about two million employees about $10 million in prescription drug costs. Merck-Medco has since applied the program to many other customers, helping to cut their costs by an average of 10 to 15 percent with just this one change.

Overall, ExpeR$_x$t is now being used by 400 analysts throughout Merck-Medco, and Marks expects to find similar cost-saving alternative treatments through the use of data mining.

[Adapted from McCarthy, 1997]

---

month to the bank, but the upside was that we felt those customers would feel better loyalty to a bank that was looking out for their money" (McCarthy, 1997).

Data mining *requires* a well designed and well constructed data warehouse with well maintained data in it. Before any organization even thinks about data mining, it must first be sure that it is capturing essential data and that the data are complete and accurate. For example, Merck-Medco, the prescription mail-order unit of pharmaceutical giant Merck, based in Montvale, New Jersey, had to spend 4 years working on its unwieldy database of patient and treatment records before it had a warehouse ready for data mining. At Merck-Medco, this became a major data reengineering effort to clean up the data (ensure that it is internally consistent) and align it into a meaningful framework within which data mining could be conducted. But the effort appears to be worth it at Merck-Medco, as reported in the sidebar "Data Mining Works at Merck-Medco" (McCarthy, 1997). Data mining offers exciting possibilities for learning about customers, particularly for large companies that have well established data warehouses.

GROUP SUPPORT SYSTEMS

Group support systems (GSSs) are an important variant of DSSs in which the system is designed to support a group rather than an individual. GSSs, sometimes called group decision support systems or electronic meeting systems, strive to take advantage of the power of a group to make better decisions than individuals acting alone. GSSs are a specialized type of groupware (see Chapter 5) that is specifically aimed at supporting meetings. Managers spend a significant portion of their time in group activity (meetings, committees, conferences); in fact, some researchers have estimated that middle managers spend 35 percent of their work week in meetings and that top managers spend 50 to 80 percent of their time in meetings. GSSs represent an attempt to make these group sessions more productive.

GroupSystems, developed at the University of Arizona (and now marketed by Ventana Corporation), is an excellent example of GSS software (Nunamaker et al., 1991, Ventana Corporation, 1997). GroupSystems is used by over 1200 customers, including Fortune 500 companies such as Chevron, Hewlett-Packard, IBM, and Procter and Gamble, and government organizations such as the U.S. Army, Navy, Marines, and Air Force. In a typical implementation (see Figure 6.2), a computer-supported meeting room is set up containing a microcomputer for each participant, all linked by a local area network. A large public screen facilitates common viewing of information when this is desired. GroupSystems, which is installed on each machine in the network, provides computerized support for idea generation, organizing ideas, pri-

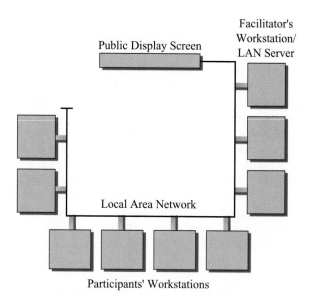

Figure 6.2 Group Support System Layout

oritizing such as voting, and policy development such as stakeholder identification.

Each participant in a group session (for example, a brainstorming session) has the opportunity to provide input anonymously and simultaneously via the microcomputer keyboard. This can encourage creative thinking, because no one can be ridiculed for a "stupid idea." Each idea or comment is evaluated on its own merits rather than in terms of the person who offered it. Similarly, in a voting session the participants will not be swayed by how someone else votes. Thus, a GSS such as GroupSystems should generate more high-quality ideas and decisions that truly represent the group.

Recent work in the GSS area has moved beyond support of the traditional group session as described above. The new focus is to support the work team in all its endeavors, whether the team is operating in a "same time, same place" traditional meeting or in a "different time, different place" mode. For instance, GroupSystems Remote allows group members to use GroupSystems over the World Wide Web as well as through a LAN. Ventana Corporation is currently developing a client/server version of GroupSystems which will permit anytime/anyplace meetings to be held over the Web or the company's intranet or a combination of the two.

GSS WORKS FOR EASTMAN CHEMICAL, CHEVRON PIPE LINE

Eastman Chemical wanted to have creative problem solving sessions to generate ideas in order to better meet customer needs, but the company found that traditional meetings were unproductive and time-consuming. Eastman installed GroupSystems, and it has paid off in a major way. In a recent GroupSystems session, 400 ideas were generated during a 2-hour session with nine people. Continuing to use the GSS in the same session, similar ideas were combined and weighted voting was employed to pick out the top ideas for implementation. Dr. Henry Gonzales, Manager of Polymer Technology at Eastman, stated, "We found that with GroupSystems, we had more unusual ideas, a richer pool to choose from, and we got to the point a lot faster. I did a study and calculated that the software saved 50 percent of people's time, and projected a cost savings of over $500,000 for the 12 people [who used the GSS] during a year's time. So we bought another license and are upgrading to another facility so more people can use the technology."

Chevron Pipe Line was establishing fourteen standardization and improvement teams to look at the company's critical business processes. The first of these teams—with the goal of analyzing procurement services—began its work with a standard manual meeting format, including flip charts and sticky pads, but by the end of the first day team members were exhausted and frustrated. The team turned to GroupSystems, and, according to a Chevron spokesperson, the group was able to complete the task in half the time and in far more detail than by manual means. The net result of the study of procurement services will be a savings of over $5 million per year, according to Chevron. Furthermore, the spokesperson indicated that the study would have been next to impossible and would have required significantly longer using traditional methods. Chevron intends to utilize the GSS to assist all of its improvement teams dealing with critical business processes, as well as within other areas of the company. The "anytime/anyplace" feature of GroupSystems proved particularly cost-effective when team members were able to continue to participate although scattered across the country.

[Adapted from Ventana Corporation, 1997]

NEGOTIATION SUPPORT SYSTEMS

Negotiation support systems (NSSs) are a special category of group support systems designed to support the activities of two or more parties in a negotiation. The core components of an NSS are an individual decision support system (DSS) for each party in the negotiation plus an electronic communication channel between the parties. To use an NSS, a negotiator in an industrial buying/selling situation enters data describing his or her understanding of the negotiation situation into a computer program, and the program then displays conclusions or suggestions about the negotiation based on the input data. These conclusions and suggestions are the output of the DSS, and they are based on whatever model of the process has been programmed into the DSS. For example, such output might include one or more suggested contract offers or an indication of the tradeoffs that the bargaining opponent might be willing to accept. The NSS also incorporates an electronic communication channel between the negotiating parties, so that a negotiator can make, receive, or accept a contract offer electronically. Thus, the NSS is a bargaining aid available to the negotiator if and when he or she chooses to use it.

One of the authors of this book has been involved in an ongoing series of laboratory experiments to assess the impact of NSS use. In these studies, which have used both students and purchasing managers as subjects, an early version of an NSS does appear to have added value to the negotiation process. Both students and managers, on average, arrived at better contracts (higher joint outcomes and more balanced contracts) when they used the NSS than when they did not use the NSS. The students took longer for the negotiation when they used the NSS, but the managers took *less* time with the NSS. As encouraging as these results are, there is a long way to go before NSSs can be of practical value in real-world negotiations.

[Adapted from Perkins, Hershauer, Foroughi, and Delaney, 1996]

GEOGRAPHIC INFORMATION SYSTEMS

Geographic information systems (GISs), spatial decision support systems (SDSSs), geodemographics, computer mapping, and automated routing are names for a family of applications based on manipulation of relationships in space. GISs capture, store, manipulate, display, and analyze data spatially referenced to the earth. As Figure 6.3 shows, GISs feature a rich user display and an interaction environment that is highly engaging to human decision-makers.

Areas as diverse as natural resource management, public administration, NASA, the military, and urban planning have used GISs for 30 years. Scientists, planners, oil and gas explorers, foresters, soldiers, and mapmakers have matured this technology, developing sophisticated capabilities for creating, displaying, and manipulating geographic information. In the 1990s, geographic technologies have come to the attention of business users as the power of desktop computing intersected with widespread access to geographic data. Today, sources such as the U.S. Census Bureau provide

high quality geographically encoded data for business to analyze and manipulate on desktop GIS software without having to digitize maps or scan photographs.

Business Adopts GISs

GISs in business were a well-kept secret for many years; the earliest business adopters of geographic technologies seldom talked about it because of its competitive value. Firms such as Arby's and McDonald's—whose ability to succeed depends on being in a better location than competitors—were some of the first to recognize the business benefits of GISs.

Whereas site location is one of the most common and powerful business uses of GISs, other applications include market analysis and planning, logistics and routing, environmental engineering, and the geographic

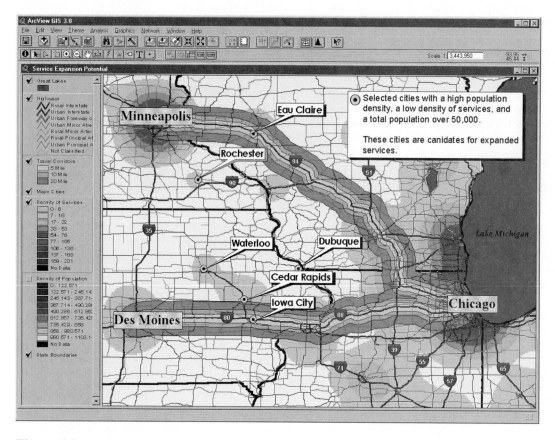

Figure 6.3 Service Expansion Potential Using GIS   (Reprinted courtesy of Environmental Systems Research Institute, Inc. Copyright © 1996 Environmental Systems Research Institute, Inc. All rights reserved.)

pattern analysis bankers must do to show that they do not "redline" areas (that is, unfairly deny loans by location).

As these examples illustrate, many functional areas in business are using GISs to recognize and manage their geographic dependencies. For example, the value of geographic tracking seems more obviously important for transportation activities (see Sears sidebar) than for health care. However, health-related applications of GISs have included analysis of patient admission rates and willingness to travel for treatment, epidemiology (study of patterns of disease), planning for location, services, and staffing at outpatient and emergency centers, long-term forecasting of health care service needs, and dispatching of ambulances. In an increasingly cost-sensitive environment, health care providers can use geographic technologies to improve service levels, identify and redeploy underutilized assets, and discover underserved markets (Davenhall, 1996/1997; Harder, 1997).

What's Behind Geographic Technologies

Two basic models for representation and analysis of spatial data have emerged: the raster approach and the vector approach. Although many of today's desktop applications can utilize both, it is helpful to understand their differences.

Raster approaches rely on dividing space into small, equal-sized cells arranged in a grid. In a GIS, these cells (rasters) can take on a range of values and are "aware" of their location relative to other cells. Pixels on a computer screen are based on the same idea. The size of the cells relative to the features in the landscape determines the precision of the data. Satellite imagery and other remote sensing applications have exploited the ability of the raster approach to identify patterns that occur across large areas.

The most familiar raster-based application of geographic technology is behind the weather report you see on your television every day. Analysis of raster data using statistical techniques and mathematical models allows meteorologists to distinguish rain from snow and foresters to identify diseased areas within a forest. Raster approaches have dominated business applications in natural resources. A recent example is called precision farming: the use of raster-based GISs with Global Positioning System (GPS) satellite

receivers to plan and deliver the specific treatment (herbicide, pesticide, fertilizer) only to the part of the field that needs it. In addition to cost savings by avoiding unneeded chemical use, precision farming can reduce environmental problems and improve overall soil quality and retention (*GPS World,* 1995).

Vector-based GIS has seen widespread use in public administration and utilities and is the most common approach used in business. Vector systems associate features in the landscape with either a point, a line, or a polygon. Points are often used to represent small features such as ATMs, customer addresses, power poles, or items in motion such as trucks. Lines are for linear features such as roads and rivers and can be connected together in networks. Polygons represent areas and surfaces such as lakes, land parcels, and regions such as sales territories, counties, and zip codes. The relationships between the vector elements are called their topology; topology determines whether features overlap or intersect. Vector systems can distinguish, for example, an island in a lake, two roads crossing, and customers within a two-mile radius of a retail site.

Most GISs utilize a "layer" concept. Different layers—also called themes and coverages—represent similar types of geographic features in the same area and are stacked on top of each other (see Figure 6.4). Like working with transparent map overlays, layers allow different geographic data to be seen together. Thus, much more so than paper maps, electronic layers facilitate geographic manipulation and analysis. Questions that geographic analysis can answer include these:

- What is adjacent to this feature?
- Which site is the nearest one?
- What is contained within this area?
- Which features does this element cross?
- How many features are within a certain distance of a site?

Infinite zoom, panning and centering, finding the distance between two points, querying and labeling features, and changing symbols and colors on demand are basic capabilities for any GIS. Desktop GISs also provide for spatial manipulation such as intersection and union, the assignment of geographic references to addresses through geocoding, and standard query language support for interacting with attribute data.

Figure 6.4 Map Layers in a GIS

Recently, advanced GIS applications have automated some very sophisticated decision support tasks such as these:

- finding shortest/fastest/safest route from A to B;
- determining if there are other locations with similar patterns; and
- grouping sales territories to minimize internal travel distance, equalize potential, or leave out the fewest prospects.

Issues for
Information Systems

Business applications of GISs often first come into a company to support a single user such as a market researcher. However, the power of GISs can't be contained, and soon it spreads within and across groups. This can create concerns for IS organizations that may not be familiar with GIS technologies, data sources, vendors, or business applications.

SEARS DELIVERS

When most of us think of Sears, we think of retail stores, not trucks. Sears, Homelife, Brand Central—these are the stores of one of the largest retailers in the U.S. Sales from these locations result in four million home deliveries each year made by thousands of trucks based at over one hundred warehouses (called Market Delivery Operations, or MDOs).

In the past, routing these trucks was a manual, time-consuming, and labor-intensive task. Daily customer orders were transmitted from stores to the MDOs where one or more individuals planned the next day's deliveries by looking up street addresses and plotting routes. Customers were then notified by phone of a four-hour "delivery window" anticipated for the following day. A customer service review of delivery performance turned up bad news: Actual deliveries during the four-hour windows happened only 78 percent of the time.

As a part of a reengineering effort, Sears sought a technological alternative to manual routing and set a goal for 90 percent delivery within a smaller two-hour window. Sears chose a geographic information system (GIS) and hired ESRI to do custom development in 1993.

Compared to other routing applications such as school buses, transit systems, or police cruisers, Sears' was a bit different. "In our case the customer might buy an appliance every ten to eighteen years," John Atkins, director of customer satisfaction explains. Without repeat patterns, the application must be very dynamic, interacting with delivery order data and real-time truck tracking collected from drivers by cellular phone.

As of April 1996, six MDOs in Southern California, Nevada, Florida, and Colorado have installed the new application based on ESRI's ArcView application. Results include: decreased miles per stop, additional stops per truck, and a better "hit rate" on the delivery window. The tool—rolled out nationwide in 1996 and 1997—will allow consolidation of Sears' routing and customer service centers from 43 to 22 over the next few years. The company is also evaluating integrating wireless communication and Global Positioning System (GPS) receivers to improve truck tracking input to the routing system.

Rarely are IS organizations in a position to develop a geographic application from scratch. Thanks to the maturity of GIS tools, this is seldom necessary. Today's desktop systems contain scripting languages and support application program interfaces with popular desktop software packages. Recently, the GIS software vendors have begun offering map object libraries (such as MapObjects from ESRI and MapX from MapInfo) and Internet-based interactive mapping application packages.

Data sources for GISs include internal sources such as customer databases and warehouse locations and external ones such as street networks and advertising media market maps purchased from data vendors. Both new users and IS personnel are often unfamiliar with cost and quality issues for geographic data. For example, although geographic files for zip codes are often included at no additional cost in packaged desktop GIS software, the U.S. Postal Service updates zip codes on an on-going basis, resulting in a decay in the accuracy of existing data stores. In addition to deciding how often to update base maps, users and analysts must learn the ins and outs of geocoding (the process of assigning a geographic reference to an address) and its importance for their firm's use.

Vendors for geographic technologies are seldom household words in IS; major players include Environmental Systems Research Institute (ESRI), MapInfo, AutoCAD, and Intergraph. Additional choices are available through specialized vendors such as Tactician and third party developers.

New directions in geographic technologies include the following:

- three-dimensional and dynamic modeling to simulate movement through time and space, such as the path of a hurricane
- map-enabled Internet sites and other customer-facing technologies such as the VISA Web site, which will identify the three nearest ATM locations to an intersection

- geographic capabilities embedded in existing applications such as spreadsheets, data warehouses, and data mining tools
- wireless technologies integrated with GPS to support real-time tracking of assets-in-motion such as trucks

EXECUTIVE INFORMATION SYSTEMS

The key concept behind an **executive information system (EIS)** is that such a system delivers on-line current information about business conditions in an aggregate form easily accessible to senior executives and other managers. An EIS is designed to be used directly by these managers without the assistance of intermediaries. An EIS uses state-of-the-art graphics, communications, and data storage methods to provide the executive easy on-line access to current information about the status of the organization.

Dating back only to the late 1980s in most cases, EISs represent the first real attempt to deliver relevant summary information to management in on-line form. Originally, most EISs were developed for only the very top executives in the firm, but today the user base in most companies has been broadened to encompass all levels of management (see the sidebar entitled "The New Role for EIS"). EISs employ transactions data that have been filtered and summarized into a form useful for the executives in the organization. In addition, many successful EISs incorporate qualitative data such as competitive information, assessments, and insights. Comshare, Inc., the vendor of Commander Decision,[1] a leading commercial product for decision support and EIS, defines an EIS as "a hands-on tool which focuses, filters, and organizes an executive's information so he or she can make more effective use of it" (Comshare, 1997).

Comshare's Commander Decision is a client/server and intranet-based software tool that enables rapid development of enterprise-wide, customized decision support applications such as performance analysis, executive information systems, and manage-

---

1 The previous version of Commander Decision was named Commander EIS. The name change reflects the broadening of the tool into decision support as well as EIS.

THE NEW ROLE FOR EIS

The purpose of an EIS is to allow nontechnical executives to access data of interest, easily create useful information from it, package the results in a clear form, then deliver it to PC monitors and printers. This report [from which this quotation was taken] analyzes the results of our research into how EIS are now being designed and used. We have found that many EIS today are effectively meeting their stated purpose, and are well-accepted tools for access to critical information, particularly in the areas of customer service and competitive action.

EIS were formerly considered to be just for the two top executive levels, but that caused many problems of data disparity between the layers of management. The most useful data are generated under the control of lower managers, dealing with customers, and they must be cognizant of what is being reported higher up. Most successful EIS today are available in consistent detail to all levels in an organization, and sometimes even to managers in customer and supplier organizations, depending upon what data is in the system.

[I/S Analyzer, January 1992]

ment reporting. Commander Decision allows business users to view information in whatever way makes sense to them, including charts, maps, exceptions, ad hoc queries and calculations, and even proactive personal alerts when a specified condition occurs. This versatile tool can be used to build traditional EIS applications for executives, as described above, or decision support systems for managers at various levels of the business. Commander Decision permits customization of a large number of easy-to-use and easy-to-interpret displays to present key information to managers. In addition, it provides exception monitoring, an intelligent "drill down" capability to identify relevant detailed information, reporting on the top or bottom ten items of a data set, an alert to important news items, and on-screen calculation of trends, ratios, and new versions of data. Examples of Commander Decision displays are shown in Figures 6.5A and B. Other leading commercial EIS products include Focus EIS from Information Builders, Decision Support Suite from Pilot Software, and Visual EIS from Synergistic Software.

Perhaps the earliest EIS described in print is the management information and decision support

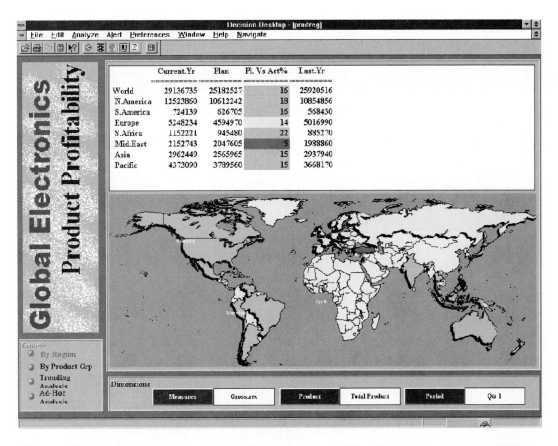

Figure 6.5A Comshare Decision Display (Screen courtesy of Comshare, Incorporated © 1998).

(MIDS) system at the Lockheed-Georgia Company (Houdeshel and Watson, 1987). The sponsor for MIDS was the Lockheed-Georgia president, and a special staff reporting to the vice-president of finance developed the system. An evolutionary approach was used in developing MIDS, with only a limited number of displays developed initially for a limited number of executives. For example, a display might show prospective customers for a particular type of aircraft or might graphically depict both forecast and actual sales over the past year.

Over time, more displays were developed and more executives were added to the system. The initial version of MIDS in 1979 had only 31 displays developed for fewer than a dozen senior executives. By 1985, 710 displays had been developed, the system was being used by 30 senior executives and 40 operating managers, and the mean number of displays viewed per user per day was up to 5.5. Many factors had to come together for MIDS to be successful, but

perhaps the most important was that the system delivered the information (based on quantitative and qualitative data) that senior executives needed for them and their company to be successful. The system provided information relevant to the critical success factors of top management.

More recently, EISs have been created and used successfully in many other large companies such as Phillips Petroleum, Dun & Bradstreet Software, Coca-Cola Company, Fisher-Price, Conoco, Inc., and CIGNA Corporation. Below we focus on two other large companies that have installed EISs in the late 1990s.

In the United Kingdom, Transco, the pipeline and storage division of BG PLC (natural gas), has employed Commander Decision to create an EIS for 150 people, from the director of the company to financial analysts and first-line managers (Comshare, 1997). The EIS incorporates cost information as well as data from supply systems and creditors. Users have easy access to the information and can drill down to

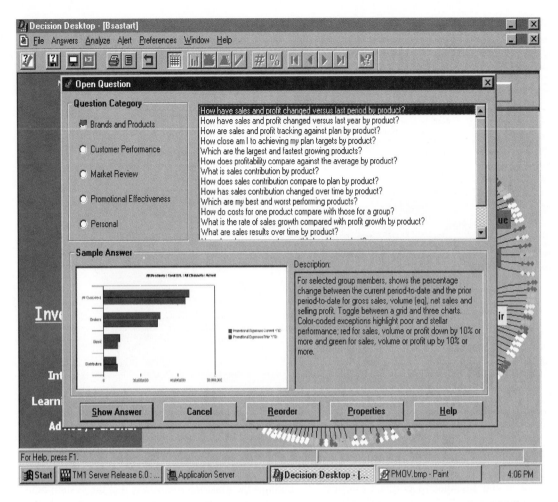

Figure 6.5B Comshare Decision Display (Screen courtesy of Comshare, Incorporated © 1998).

the level of detail they need; they can also invoke multiple views of the information and pose "what if" questions such as "What is the impact on costs if our emergency workload goes up by 5 percent?" "Commander Decision is clearly helping us make better decisions," says Colin Johnson, Manager District Operations, Hadrian District, Transco. "The application gives us a unique opportunity to work directly with our cost base so we can see the effects of decisions out in the field. This application allows us to give all of our users a single source of the truth and promotes awareness throughout the company of exactly how we're doing."

Welch Allyn is an international market-leading supplier of medical diagnostic instruments, including thermometers, ophthalmoscopes, blood pressure devices, and audiometers. As the result of growth, acquisitions, and strong international expansion, Welch Allyn decided it needed "a worldwide executive decision support system that would provide rapid access to meaningful information" (Comshare, 1997). Using Comshare software products, Welch Allyn built a financial reporting system that handles monthly consolidation and closings and currency conversion; it also provides integrated analysis capabilities for managers, analysts, and executives. The related sales analysis system allows managers to track worldwide sales by product line, region, and customer. "Our closing process is faster, and we can now drill into sales and worldwide consolidated data in a fashion that we never dreamed of," says Kevin Cahill, Welch Allyn's Vice President and Controller/Treasurer."

Welch Allyn isn't done building its EIS. "We are beginning to develop new applications using Commander Decision that will allow us to track performance versus plan and analyze prior years' results versus the current year," says Cahill. "This analytical tool will help management identify opportunities to market products where they are not selling them today."

ARTIFICIAL INTELLIGENCE

The idea of **artificial intelligence (AI)**, the study of how to make computers do things that are presently done better by people, is about 30 years old, but only recently have computers become powerful enough to make AI applications commercially attractive. AI research has evolved into five separate but related areas; these are natural languages, robotics, perceptive systems (vision and hearing), expert systems, and neural networks.

The work in natural languages, primarily in computer science departments in universities and in vendor laboratories, is aimed at producing systems that translate ordinary human instructions into a language that computers can understand and execute. Robotics was considered in the previous chapter. Perceptive systems research involves creating machines possessing a visual and/or aural perceptual ability that affects their physical behavior. In other words, this research is aimed at creating robots that can "see" or "hear" and react to what they see or hear.

The final two branches of AI are the ones most relevant for managerial support. **Expert systems** is concerned with building systems that incorporate the decision-making logic of a human expert. The newest branch of AI is **neural networks,** which is named after the study of how the human nervous system works, but in fact uses statistical analysis to recognize patterns from vast amounts of information by a process of adaptive learning.

EXPERT SYSTEMS

How does one capture the logic of an expert in a computer system? To design an expert system, a specialist known as a knowledge engineer (a specially trained systems analyst) works very closely with one or more experts in the area under study. Knowledge engineers try to learn everything they can about the way in which the expert makes decisions. If one is trying to build an expert system for estate planning, for example, the knowledge engineer works with experienced estate planners to see how they carry out their job. The knowledge gained by the knowledge engineer is then loaded into the computer system, in a specialized format, in a module called the knowledge base (see Figure 6.6). This knowledge base contains both the inference rules that are followed in decision-making and the parameters, or facts, relevant to the decision.

The other major pieces of an expert system are the inference engine and the user interface. The inference engine is a logical framework that automatically executes a line of reasoning when supplied with the inference rules and parameters involved in the decision; thus, the same inference engine can be used for many different expert systems, each with a different knowledge base. The user interface is the module used by the end-user—for example, an inexperienced estate planner. Ideally, the interface is very user-friendly. The other modules include an explanation subsystem to explain the reasoning that the system followed in arriving at a decision, a knowledge acquisition subsystem to assist the knowledge engineer in recording inference rules and parameters in the knowledge base, and a workspace for the computer to use as the decision is being made.

Obtaining an Expert System

Is it necessary to build all these pieces each time your organization wants to develop and use an expert system? Absolutely not. There are three general approaches to obtaining an expert system, and only one of them requires construction of all these pieces. First, an organization can buy a fully developed system that has been created for a specific application. For example, in the late 1980s Syntelligence, Inc., developed an expert system called Lending Advisor to assist in making commercial lending decisions for banks and other financial institutions. Lending Advisor incorporated the many factors involved in approving or rejecting a commercial loan, and it was installed in several banks. In general, however, the circumstances leading to the desire for an expert system are unique to the

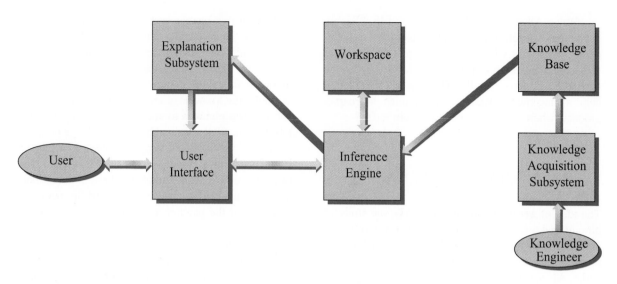

Figure 6.6 Architecture of an Expert System

organization, and in most cases this "off-the-shelf" expert system option is not viable.

Second, an organization can develop an expert system itself using an **artificial intelligence shell** (also called an **expert systems shell**). The shell, which can be purchased from a software company or a computer vendor, provides the basic framework illustrated in Figure 6.6 and a limited but user-friendly special language with which to develop the expert system. With the basic expert system functions already in place in the shell, the system builder can concentrate on the details of the business decision being modeled and the development of the knowledge base. Third, an organization can have internal or external knowledge engineers custom-build the expert system. In this case, the system is usually programmed in a special-purpose language such as Prolog or Lisp. This final approach is clearly the most expensive, and it can be justified only if the potential payoff from the expert system is quite high and no other way is possible.

Examples of Expert Systems

Perhaps the classic example of an expert system is MYCIN, which was developed at Stanford University in the mid-1970s to diagnose and prescribe treatment for meningitis and blood diseases. General Electric created an expert system called CATS-1 to diagnose mechanical problems in diesel locomotives, and

AT&T developed ACE to locate faults in telephone cables. Schlumberger, Limited, an international oil company, developed an expert system named Dipmeter to give advice when a drill bit gets stuck while drilling a well. These examples and others are concerned with diagnosing problem situations and prescribing appropriate actions, because experts are not always present when a problem occurs.

Some expert systems specialize in sifting through massive sets of rules or other data, sometimes called case-based reasoning. The Human Services Agency of Merced County, California, employs an expert system called Magic, which incorporates 6,000 government regulations relating to welfare, food stamps, medicaid, foster care, and so on. Magic determines if an applicant qualifies for benefits and then calculates the type and amount of benefits. The entire process from application to final decision now takes three days or less, whereas it used to take as long as three months. In addition, the clerks who process the applications do not require the extensive training that was formerly required—all they need to be able to do is lead applicants through a series of questions posed by the computer (Schwartz, 1992).

The United Nations has developed a somewhat similar expert system, called the Entitlements System, to interpret the complex salary regulations for all employees of the U.N. Secretariat worldwide. The pay for U.N. employees is determined by a base salary plus

tion about businesses in the apparel industry. The CCH expert system incorporates about 800 rules and cost $1 million to develop. When a subscriber calls in requesting credit information on a business, the system analyzes the payment history, financial statement, and overall strength of the business, arrives at a credit rating and recommendation, and sets a recommended credit limit in dollars (LaPlante, 1991).

Scheduling is another important area for expert systems. Expert systems currently in use include a truck routing and scheduling system that determines the sequence of stops on a route to provide the best service and a factory design system that organizes machines and operators to provide an efficient flow of materials through the factory and use the resources efficiently. American Airlines uses an expert system called MOCA (for Maintenance Operations Center Advisor), which runs on a Macintosh microcomputer, to schedule routine maintenance for all 622 planes in American's fleet. MOCA incorporates 5,000 rules that have been gleaned from 30 aircraft-routing experts. Aircraft must undergo routine maintenance at least once every 60 hours of flying time, and MOCA's job is to set up a schedule which meets this rule, covers all of American's routes, and avoids the cost of flying empty planes to regional maintenance centers. American estimates that MOCA saves the company a half million dollars a year compared to human schedulers (LaPlante, 1991; Schwartz, 1992).

In another scheduling example, General Motors created the Expert Scheduling System, or ESS, to generate viable manufacturing schedules. GM used both IntelliCorp's Knowledge Engineering Environment expert system shell and the Lisp programming language to build the system. ESS incorporates heuristics that had been developed by an experienced factory scheduler into the system, and it also links directly into GM's computer-integrated manufacturing (CIM) environment so that real-time plant information is used to generate the plant floor schedules (*I/S Analyzer,* March 1995).

entitlements, and the entitlements include benefits based on location of work plus other contractual agreements. The rules and regulations for the entitlements fill three volumes of several hundred pages each. Using PowerModel software from IntelliCorp, the U.N. has built an expert system that determines and applies entitlements automatically, employing an on-line knowledge base containing the entitlements rules. The expert system also reassesses the entitlements whenever a change to an employee's status occurs (Baum, 1996).

The Credit Clearing House (CCH) division of Dun & Bradstreet has developed an expert system to respond to requests from subscribers seeking informa-

NEURAL NETWORKS

Whereas expert systems try to capture the expertise of humans in a computer program, neural networks attempt to tease out meaningful patterns from vast

PICKING STOCKS BY NEURAL NETWORK

Bradford Lewis, the fund manager for the Fidelity Disciplined Equity Fund, gives much of the credit for the extraordinary success of his fund to the neural network programs he uses to select stocks. Fidelity Disciplined Equity Fund has beaten the Standard & Poor's 500 stock index by 2.3 to 5.6 percent in the years 1989–1991 and was doing so by 5.8 percent through 10 months of 1992. This is particularly unusual because of the nature of the Disciplined Equity Fund, which invests in the same industries and in the same proportions as does the S & P 500 index. Thus, the key for the Disciplined Equity Fund is the particular stocks picked in these industries.

Mr. Lewis' neural network program uses 11 different variables for each of 2,000 stocks as data input. It is Mr. Lewis' hope that the computer will detect patterns in stock price movements that are too subtle or too diffuse for a human to discover. If the computer can "learn" which patterns are driving the stock market, it can also find "undervalued" stocks where those patterns are not yet manifest. The neural network program tends to select little-known stocks trading at below-average multiples of earnings or book value, but with higher-than-average rates of earnings growth. The impressive performance of the fund suggests that the neural system certainly works most of the time.

[Adapted from McGough, 1992]

amounts of data. Neural networks can recognize patterns too obscure for humans to detect, and they adapt as new information is received.

The key characteristic of neural networks is that they *learn*! The neural network program is originally given a set of data consisting of many variables associated with a large number of cases, or events, in which the outcomes are known. The program analyzes the data and works out all the correlations and then selects a set of variables that are strongly correlated with particular known outcomes as the initial pattern. This initial pattern is used to try to predict the outcomes of the various cases, and these predicted results are compared to the known results. Based on this comparison, the program changes the pattern by adjusting the weights given to the variables or even by changing

the variables. The neural network program then repeats this process over and over, continuously adjusting the pattern in an attempt to improve its predictive ability. When no further improvement is possible from this iterative approach, the program is ready to make predictions for future cases.

This does not end the story. As more cases become available, these data are also fed into the neural network and the pattern is once again adjusted. The neural network learns more about cause-and-effect patterns from this additional data, and its predictive ability usually improves accordingly.

Commercial neural network programs (actually, these are shells) are available for a reasonable price, but the difficult part of building a neural network application is often the data collection and data maintenance effort. Still, a growing number of applications are being deployed. BankAmerica uses a neural network to evaluate commercial loan applications. American Express uses a neural system to read handwriting on credit card slips. The state of Wyoming uses a neural system to read hand-printed numbers of tax forms. Oil giants Arco and Texaco are using neural networks to help pinpoint oil and gas deposits below the earth's surface. As an example of data mining using neural networks, Mellon Bank is working on a system to speed up recognition of fraudulent credit card transactions by monitoring such factors as the frequency of credit card use and the size of charges relative to the credit line. In another data mining example, Spiegel, which depends on catalogs to generate sales for its mail order business, uses a neural network as a way of pruning its mailing list to eliminate those who are unlikely to order from Spiegel again (Field, 1992; Schwartz, 1992).

In the 1980s and 1990s, expert system and neural network applications received a great deal of "hype" in the popular press—these AI applications were supposedly going to solve many of the decision problems faced by managers. Near the end of the 20th century, industry has adopted a more realistic view of AI applications: AI is not a panacea, but there are a significant number of potentially valuable applications for AI techniques. Each potential application must be carefully evaluated before proceeding. The result of these "careful evaluations" has been a steady growth, but not an explosion, in the development and use of expert systems and neural networks to help businesses cope with problem situations and make better and more consistent decisions.

VIRTUAL REALITY

Virtual reality is a fascinating application area with rapidly growing importance. **Virtual reality,** or **VR,** refers to the use of computer-based systems to create an environment which seems real to one or more senses (usually including sight) of the human user or users. The ultimate example of virtual reality is the holodeck aboard the U.S.S. Enterprise on *Star Trek: The Next Generation,* where Data can be Sherlock Holmes in a realistic setting with realistic characters, and where Jean-Luc Picard can play the role of a hard-boiled private eye in the early 20th century.

Virtual reality exists today, but with nowhere near the reality of the Enterprise's holodeck. You may have played a video game where you don a head-mounted computer display and a glove to get directly into the action. The use of VR in a nonentertainment setting falls primarily into two categories, training and design. Training examples will be presented next, followed by examples of the use of VR in design.

The U.S. Army uses virtual reality to train tank crews. Through multiple large video screens and sound, the soldiers are seemingly placed inside a tank rolling across the Iraqi desert, and they have to react as if they were in a real tank battle. In a research project at the University of North Carolina, virtual reality has been used to provide a three-dimensional model of a tumor inside a patient's body. After donning special eyeglasses, a radiologist is able to get inside this model of the patient's body and adjust radiation beams so that they intersect at the heart of the tumor and yet avoid radiosensitive tissue such as the spinal cord and esophagus (Rheingold, 1992). In a related application, virtual reality is being used for surgical training. New doctors can practice surgical techniques on virtual patients in a virtual reality surgical suite. If a doctor makes a mistake, he or she can try again with no waiting—and no danger to the "patients" (Wohl, 1996).

Amoco has developed a PC-based virtual reality system, called "truck driVR," for use in training its drivers. Amoco felt that the VR system was a cost-effective way of testing how well its 12,000 drivers performed under a variety of hazardous driving conditions. This immersive VR system, which cost approximately $50,000 to develop, employs a helmet that holds the visual and auditory displays and completely immerses the user in the virtual world. To make truck driVR realistic, multiple views are provided to the user, including views of both left and right rear-view mirrors that are displayed only when the user moves his head to the left or right (*IS Analyzer,* 1997).

Duracell also employs virtual reality for training. Duracell was installing new equipment to manufacture a new line of rechargeable batteries, and the company needed to train its factory personnel on the new equipment in a safe and cost-effective manner. The Duracell system, which is nonimmersive (no helmet or special glasses), also runs on a PC and incorporates a parts familiarization module, an operations module,

EDS DETROIT VIRTUAL REALITY CENTER

A simple form of virtual reality is visualization, which shows you a scene or object that doesn't exist. For instance, a designer of home kitchens can now use inexpensive software running on a PC to create and revise elaborate room plans in simulated 3-D with realistic furnishings, floors, colors, and textures.

A professional designer might use a more robust version of such software to test whether two amateur chefs can cook comfortably in the kitchen side by side, or to adjust counter heights to accommodate people of varying stature.

The virtual kitchen is just one of the VR ideas tested by EDS at its Detroit Virtual Reality Center. The center, which partners with more than 70 hardware and software companies, universities, and government organizations, is intended to help companies leverage VR technology in commercial applications.

At the center, VR is applied to the automotive assembly and manufacturing scenario. Using computers, assembly is simulated in virtual reality before assembly lines are built. This enables methodologies to be evaluated and refined in the computer, avoiding expensive investments in technologies that don't work and resulting in increased safety and time savings.

[I/S Analyzer, 1997]

and a troubleshooting module. With this system, the user is able to completely explore the new piece of equipment within the desktop virtual world. "With the use of that special mouse [a Magellan space mouse], the user can walk around it [the equipment], they can get underneath it, they can get on top of it," says Neil Silverstein, a training manager at Duracell. "They can fly into the smallest crevices of the machine, something that you can never do in the real world because you might lose a finger." Duracell is quite pleased with the results—training is standardized and completely safe, and there is no need for on-the-job training (*IS Analyzer,* 1997).

Chrysler and IBM have developed a virtual reality system to assist in the design of automobiles. With this system, an automotive engineer—wearing special glasses and a special glove to be able to interact with the system—is able to sit in the driver's seat of a future

automobile. He turns the steering wheel and uses buttons and knobs as though he were in a real car. By letting the engineer get the feel of this future car, Chrysler hopes that problems in the dashboard and controls design can be corrected before actual—and expensive—prototypes are even built (Hamilton et al., 1992).

One intriguing and inexpensive application of virtual reality is its use for retail store layout. Using a software "walk-through" product, such as Virtus WalkThrough Pro (with a purchase price under $500) on a Macintosh or PC microcomputer, many retailers have saved time and money in designing store layouts and storefronts. WalkThrough Pro provides a three-dimensional image on the computer screen with no special glasses required. The user can, in effect, walk through the image of a store and view the layout from a variety of perspectives (see Figure 6.7). With the

Figure 6.7 Virtus Walkthrough Used for Virtual Store Layout (Courtesy of Virtus Corporation).

package, fixtures can be easily changed, the color scheme can be modified, bricks and tile can be added, and the placement of walls, doors, and windows can be moved. In related applications, one could imagine a real estate agent offering virtual walk-throughs of houses on the market or a travel agent offering virtual walk-throughs of resorts or cruise ships.

The development of virtual reality is in its infancy, and it will be a long time before anything remotely approaching the Enterprise's holodeck is possible. Nevertheless, many vendors are developing VR hardware and software, and numerous valuable VR applications are beginning to appear.

Summary

We have now completed our two-chapter survey of *intraorganizational* information technology application areas. Chapter 5 focused on application areas that support the entire organization or large portions of it, including transaction processing systems, data warehousing, and office automation. At the conclusion of that chapter, we argued that modern organizations cannot do business without these organizational IT systems. In the present chapter, we have concentrated on managerial support systems such as decision support systems, executive information systems, and neural networks. In our view, these managerial support systems are just as critical to the individual managers in a business as the organizational systems are to the firm as a whole. Modern managers simply cannot do business—they cannot manage effectively and efficiently—without managerial support IT systems.

Several types of managerial support systems are designed to support *individual* managers in their decision-making endeavors *without* the aid of artificial intelligence. Decision support systems, data mining, geographic information systems, and executive information systems all fall in this broad grouping. A decision support system is an interactive system, employing a model of some sort, to assist a manager in making decisions in a situation that is not well structured. The prototypical example of a DSS is carrying out what-if analyses on a financial model. Data mining is concerned with digging out "nuggets" of information from a data warehouse, again using a

model; thus, data mining can be considered as a subset of the broader DSS construct. A geographic information system is based on spatial relationships; many but not all GISs incorporate a model and are used as a DSS. In contrast, an executive information system does not usually involve a model. An EIS provides easy on-line access to current aggregate information about key business conditions. In general, a DSS, data mining, or a GSS provides specific information of value to a manager working on a particular problem, whereas an EIS provides aggregated information of value to a wide range of managers within the firm.

Group support systems provide support to a *group* of managers engaged in some sort of group activity, most commonly an in-person meeting. A GSS, which is a specialized type of groupware, consists of software running on a local area network that permits all meeting participants to simultaneously and anonymously make contributions to the group discussion by keying in their ideas and having them displayed on a large public screen, if desired. The software facilitates various group tasks, such as idea generation, organizing ideas, prioritizing, and policy development.

Artificial intelligence is used to support the *individual* manager in our third grouping of managerial support systems. By capturing the decision-making logic of a human expert, an expert system provides nonexperts with expert advice. A neural network teases out obscure patterns from vast amounts of data by a process of adaptive learning. In both cases, the user is led to better decisions via artificial intelligence. Closely related to AI is virtual reality, where computer-based systems create an environment that seems real to one or more human senses. Thus far, virtual reality has proved particularly useful for training and design activities.

We hope that these two chapters have convinced you of the value of these intraorganizational systems. But how does an organization, or an individual manager, acquire one of these potentially valuable systems? The complete answer to this question will have to wait until Part III of this book, entitled "Acquiring Information Systems," but we already have some clues.

The organizational systems, for example, are primarily large-scale systems that would be purchased from an outside vendor or custom-developed by the internal IS organization or an external consulting firm. In particular, enterprise resource planning, office automation, groupware, and factory automation are almost always purchased from an outside vendor—these are all massive systems that require similar functionality across a wide variety of firms. Of course, they may be customized to the organization by the internal IS department or a consultant. Data warehousing and intranets are often implemented with purchased package software, but there may also be internal or consultant development. Historically, most transaction processing systems were developed by the internal IS organization, but even these systems are likely to be purchased today, as shown in the growth of ERP systems, unless the firm's requirements are unique.

By contrast, many managerial support systems are likely to be developed by the user-manager or by a consultant (internal or external to the firm) expressly for the user-manager. In most cases, the user-manager or consultant would start with an underlying software tool (such as a DSS generator, expert systems shell, neural network program, or data mining tool) and develop a specific implementation of the tool that satisfies the need. The user-manager is unlikely, however, to develop a group support system or executive information system; these multi-user systems are more akin to organizational systems in terms of their acquisition.

All these methods of IT system acquisition—purchase of a fully-developed system, development by the internal IS organization or an external consultant, and end-user development—will be explored in detail in Part III.

REVIEW QUESTIONS

1. Describe the three primary components that make up any decision support system and describe how they interact.
2. Explain the difference between a specific decision support system (DSS) and a DSS generator. Give an example of each.
3. Describe two examples of specific DSSs that are being used to assist in decision-making. You may use examples from the textbook or other examples you have read about or heard about.
4. Negotiation support systems (NSSs) and group support systems (GSSs) are both variants of DSSs. Explain how an NSS and a GSS differ from most DSSs.

5. Explain both data warehousing and data mining. How are they related?
6. List at least two techniques (decision technologies) that are used in data mining.
7. List at least three uses of data mining.
8. What is the purpose of a group support system (GSS)? What are the potential advantages and disadvantages of using a GSS?
9. What is geocoding and why is it important?
10. Compare the raster-based and vector-based approaches to geographic information systems (GISs).
11. What are the distinguishing characteristics of an executive information system (EIS)?
12. Briefly describe the five areas of artificial intelligence (AI) research. Indicate why we in business are most interested in the expert systems and neural networks areas.
13. What are the three general approaches to obtaining an expert system? What are the pluses and minuses of each approach?
14. Describe two examples of expert systems that are being used to assist in decision-making. You may use examples from the textbook or other examples you have read about or heard about.
15. Describe two examples of the use of virtual reality in an organizational setting. You may use examples from the textbook or other examples you have read about or heard about.

DISCUSSION QUESTIONS

1. Review question 5 asked about the relationship between data warehousing and data mining. In addition to data mining, which of the other application areas discussed in this chapter may be used in conjunction with data warehousing? Explain.
2. Two of the important topics in this chapter are decision support systems (DSSs) and expert systems. Based on your reading of this chapter, you have undoubtedly noticed that these two application areas have a great deal in common. What are the primary distinctions between DSSs and expert systems?

3. Compare group support systems, as described in this chapter, with groupware, as described in the prior chapter. How do these two application areas relate to one another? Which one is most important today? Do you think this will be true in the future?

4. Several examples of geographic information systems were mentioned in the chapter. Consider an industry or a company with which you have some familiarity, and identify at least one possible application of GISs in the industry or company. Explain why you think this is a good prospect for a GIS application.

5. Explain the concept of "drilling down" as used in executive information systems (EIS). Is drilling down used in other IT applications? How do these applications relate to EIS?

6. Explain the original role that was to be played by an EIS, and then describe how this role has been modified over time. Why has this role change occurred?

7. Several examples of expert systems were mentioned in the chapter. Consider an industry or a company with which you have some familiarity, and identify at least one possible application of expert systems in the industry or company. Explain why you think this is a good prospect for an expert system application.

8. Several examples of neural networks were mentioned in the chapter. Consider an industry or a company with which you have some familiarity, and identify at least one possible application of neural networks in the industry or company. Explain why you think this is a good prospect for a neural network application.

9. Which of the application areas considered in this chapter might be of most use to a small to mid-sized business? Defend your answer.

REFERENCES

1992. "The new role for 'executive' information systems." *I/S Analyzer* 30 (January): 1–16.

1995. "How organizations are becoming more efficient using expert systems." *I/S Analyzer Case Studies* 34 (March): 1–16.

1995. "How organizations are using end-user decision support tools." *I/S Analyzer Case Studies* 34 (April): 1–16.

1995. "Precision farming's 'garden' grows in Midwest." *GPS World* (April).

1996. "GIS and Sears Roebuck and Co.: logistics and distribution moves toward 21st century." *ArcNews* (May): 1.

1997. "How businesses are cutting costs through virtual reality." *I/S Analyzer Case Studies* 36 (March): 1–16.

Baum, David. 1996. "U.N. automates payroll with AI system." *Datamation* 42 (November): 129–132.

Begur, Sachidanand V., David M. Miller, and Jerry R. Weaver. "An integrated spatial DSS for scheduling and routing home-health-care nurses." 1997. *Interfaces* 27 (July–August): 35–48.

Comshare, Inc. 1997. "Drilling for decisions: Commander Decision delivers management information for Transco," "Welch Allyn's prescription for healthy financial and sales reporting." Comshare Web site, http://www.comshare.com (September).

Darling, Charles B. 1997. "Datamining for the masses." *Datamation* 43 (February): 52–56.

Davenhall, Bill. 1996/1997. Health Care column. *Business Geographics* 4 and 5.

Ferrell, William G., Jr. and Haluk Hizlan. 1997. "South Carolina counties use a mixed-integer programming-based decision support tool for planning municipal solid waste management." *Interfaces* 27 (July–August): 23–34.

Field, Roger. 1992. "Figuring out those neural networks." *Beyond Computing* 1 (August–September): 38–42.

Freeman, Eva. 1997. "Datamining unearths dollars from data." *Datamation* 43 (July): 84–88.

Hamilton, Joan O'C., with Emily T. Smith, Gary McWilliams, Evan I. Schwartz, and John Carey. 1992. "Virtual reality: how a computer-generated world could change the real world." *Business Week* (October 5): 97–105.

Harder, Christian. 1997. *ArcView GIS Means Business.* Redlands, CA: Environmental Systems Research Institute, Inc.

Houdeshel, George, and Hugh J. Watson. 1987. "The management information and decision support (MIDS) system at Lockheed-Georgia." *MIS Quarterly* 11 (March): 127–140.

Koselka, Rita. 1997. "People - innovators: Jay Nunamaker" *Forbes* 160 (July 7): 314–315.

LaPlante, Alice. 1991. "Using your smarts." *CIO* 5 (December): 54–58.

McCarthy, Vance. 1997. "Strike it rich!" *Datamation* 43 (February): 44–50.

McGough, Robert. 1992. "Fidelity's Bradford Lewis takes aim at indexes with his 'neural network' computer program." *Wall Street Journal* 74 (October 27): C1, C19.

Morrissey, Jane. 1997. "Mining for gold." *PC Week* 14 (May 19): 137.

Nunamaker, J. F., Alan R. Dennis, Joseph S. Valacich, Douglas R. Vogel, and Joey F. George. 1991. "Electronic meeting systems to support group work." *Communications of the ACM* 34 (July): 40–61.

Perkins, William C., James C. Hershauer, Abbas Foroughi, and Michael M. Delaney. 1996. "Can a negotiation support system help a purchasing manager?" *International Journal of Purchasing and Materials Management* 32 (Spring): 37–45.

Rakshit, Ananda, Nirup Krishnamurthy, and Gang Yu. 1996. "Systems Operations Advisor: A real-time decision support system for managing airline operations at United Airlines." *Interfaces* 26 (March–April): 50–58.

Rheingold, Howard. 1992. "How real is virtual reality?" *Beyond Computing* 1 (March–April): 26–29.

Schwartz, Evan I., with James B. Treece. 1992. "Smart programs go to work." *Business Week* (March 2): 97–105.

Sodhi, ManMohan S. 1996. "Development of a DSS for fixed-income securities using OOP." *Interfaces* 26 (March–April): 22–33.

Sprague, Ralph H., Jr., and Eric D. Carlson. 1982. *Building Effective Decision Support Systems.* Englewood Cliffs, NJ: Prentice-Hall, Inc.

Ventana Corporation. 1997. "History of Ventana Corporation," "GroupSystems success story: Improving business processes," "GroupSystems success story: Problem-solving." Ventana Corporation Web site, http://www.ventana.com (September).

Wohl, Amy D. 1996. "Virtual reality is real business." *Beyond Computing* 5 (November–December): 16–19.

ELECTRONIC COMMERCE AND INTERORGANIZATIONAL SYSTEMS

Chapters 5 and 6 looked at applications of information technology within the organization that enable more efficient and effective ways of doing business within the organization. However, an organization does not exist in isolation, but instead operates in a marketplace of customers, suppliers, other business partners, competitors, and regulators. The focus of Chapter 7 is on electronic commerce applications that exploit the capabilities of both computers and communications to reach these stakeholders outside its boundaries. Our definition of **electronic commerce** is broad: Electronic commerce is the use of IT to conduct business between two or more organizations, or between an organization and one or more end-customers, via one or more computer networks.

We begin our discussion with the business-to-business electronic commerce applications, referred to as interorganizational systems (IOSs). IOSs enable firms to more effectively do business with suppliers, customers, and other strategic business partners—such as independent distributors or dealers. We first present a classic IOS example: the SABRE reservation system of American Airlines. We then focus on what has become the most common form of IOS up until the late-1990s: the use of IT to exchange business documents using a set of agreed upon standards, referred to as electronic data interchange (EDI).

Today, EDI may be conducted over a private network or over the "open" Internet.

However, the biggest electronic commerce story today is the use of the Internet to conduct commerce with the end-consumer in new ways. Using **HTTP** (hypertext transfer protocol) and the part of the Internet referred to as the **World Wide Web** (WWW), established firms have been experimenting with this new way of conducting business using IT since the mid-1990s. Our discussion of electronic commerce applications will include not only initiatives by established firms, but also those by entirely new Web-based businesses. We present the major benefits of electronic commerce via the Internet, how it works, and some of the current constraints from both a business and consumer perspective. Four business examples are then described, and we use these examples to better understand the Web strategies that today's businesses are pursuing. We then present some of the special IT management issues associated with applications based on emerging Internet technologies and interorganizational systems in general.

We close the chapter with a section on the future of electronic commerce and some of the anticipated impacts; a fuller discussion of social impacts of IT in general can be found in Chapter 8.

EXTENDING THE REACH OF INFORMATION TECHNOLOGY

Keen (1991) suggests that companies use IT for competitive advantage by extending their reach of IT. He argues that the reach of IT inside and outside a firm significantly affects the "degree of freedom a firm enjoys in its business plans." Today's technology options include establishing computer links over telecommunications lines not only across organizational boundaries, but also across national boundaries. As seen in Figure 7.1, the technologies existing by the early 1990s enable links with customers and suppliers that may be using different IT platforms, as well as "anyone, anywhere." According to Keen, the goal is IT ubiquity: IT should be able to reach anyone, anytime, with any information—with the same ease as using a telephone.

Most early electronic commerce (EC) applications were directed at automating buyer-seller transactions between businesses. One way to examine the potential benefits of EC applications is to look at them in terms of a firm's **value chain** (Porter, 1985): firm's value chain model contains the activities in the business that add value to a firm's products or services.

Figure 7.2 shows a value-chain for a hypothetical manufacturing firm. In terms of this value chain, buyer-seller transactions are involved with the sourcing of materials to be used in the manufacturing of a product and the fulfillment of customer orders. IT can therefore add value to this manufacturing firm by improving the sourcing and order fulfillment processes. A firm that implements EC applications with one or more of its suppliers is seeking to improve the logistics of its *supply chain*. A firm that implements EC applications with one or more of its customers is seeking to improve the logistics of its *product chain*. Further, for some manufacturing firms, the order fulfillment process involves an intermediary—such as an independent car dealer or an insurance agent. In addition, some manufactured products are sold to other businesses, while other manufactured products are sold directly to end-consumers.

As we will discuss in more detail below, a major benefit from extending the reach of IT to suppliers and customers is decreased transaction costs. However, IT can also be used to achieve other benefits, including increased responsiveness to customers and improved coordination with suppliers or customers. Stated differently, electronic commerce is concerned with the use of IT by a firm to optimize its "web of transactions and relationships between buyers and sellers" (Applegate et al., 1996).

Interorganizational Systems

Until the mid-1990s, the primary way to extend the reach of IT to a supplier or customer was to develop an **interorganizational system** to link a business to one or more other *businesses*. An IOS is an integrated data processing and data communications system used by two or more participant organizations. Although interorganizational systems typically link businesses that are in a customer-supplier relationship, they also may be systems that link together members of a consortium or a cooperative alliance among businesses in the same industry (such as a group of banks).

Initially, IOSs were all proprietary systems, developed by either a major industry player or a group

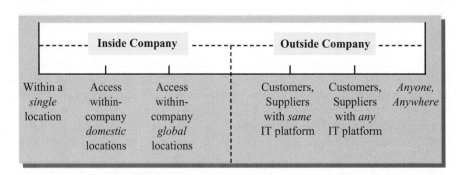

Figure 7.1 IT Reach (Adapted from Keen, 1991)

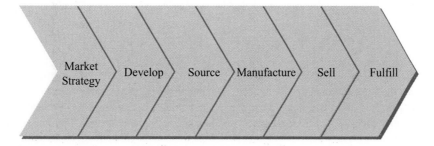

Figure 7.2 Value Chain for a Manufacturing Firm

of companies in the same industry. The costs of implementing such systems were offset by benefits such as reduced transaction costs and increased customer responsivenesss. Two of the major industries that have benefited from proprietary IOS are the automotive industry and the retailing industry. In both of these industries, IT is used to significantly reduce costs in the supply chain (i.e., the sourcing process in the value-chain), at least for the customer (see Figure 7.2). In the automotive industry, for example, the major industry manufacturers had enough buying power to demand that their suppliers implement a proprietary system that enabled just-in-time (JIT) manufacturing. Similarly, WalMart and Kmart demanded that their suppliers implement an IOS in order to replenish their store shelves based on computer-to-computer notifications of stock outages.

Once computer-to-computer links for an IOS were established, businesses also began to use them for more than just electronically transmitting order requests and confirmations. Some suppliers were given access to a customer's inventory system and essentially took on the responsibility of managing the customer's inventory. Some customers were given access to a supplier's catalog for technical specifications that were needed for manufacturing or for pricing in order to take advantage of relevant discounts. In the past, customer service meant calling a customer support desk: Application-to-application links meant that customers could answer their own questions. Because workers were no longer tied up just responding to product information inquiries, these systems also enabled some firms to develop new types of relationship manager positions responsible for managing a supplier or customer account.

In some firms, the business activities at the customer end of the value chain (sell, fulfill) are carried out by independent dealers or other intermediaries. IOS applications to add value to the sell/fulfill processes carried out by an intermediary have also been developed. One of the best known, or classic, IOS applications is the SABRE reservation system, created and operated by the parent of American Airlines (AMR Corporation).

Strategic Example: American Airlines' SABRE system[1]

The SABRE reservation system enables on-line airline reservations not only with American Airlines, but also with AA's competitors. The system is also one of the few IOS applications that has reportedly provided a sustainable competitive advantage for its creators for almost three decades. Today, SABRE is one of the largest privately owned computer systems in the world. As one of AMR Corporation's three lines of businesses (see www.amrcorp.com),[2] the SABRE group has generated sizable annual income and profits. However, as we will see, this competitive advantage has been due to continual repositioning and enhancement of the system, not continued operation of the original version of the SABRE system.

SABRE evolved from what was initially a home-grown, proprietary system for internal employees to

---

1 This account is primarily based on Applegate, McFarlan, and McKenney, 1996; Hopper, 1990; and Kettinger et al., 1995.

2 The other two groups are the Airline Group (AA and American Eagle) and a Management Services Group (aviation and related services).

manage AA's own seat inventory. In the late 1960s, it was extended to become an order-entry and transaction processing system for a select group of intermediaries: AA's major travel agencies. The system provided on-line access to AA's reservation system—saving the travel agent the time and cost of calling into an airline salesperson.

Proprietary systems such as SABRE are very expensive; this created a high entry barrier for other would-be competitors. When the airline industry was deregulated in 1978, AA was able to move quickly. It already had a major investment in SABRE and was able to extend SABRE to include airline reservations not only for the system owner (AA), but for all major airline carriers. These carriers paid a processing fee to AA for each ticket sold on their carrier. Further, SABRE was priced to be affordable to mid-sized travel agencies, not just large ones. Although an early version of this multi-carrier reservation system was reported to have an inherent bias in the reservation screen displays—such as placing AA flights at the top of the display or making electronic links to detailed data easier for AA flights than a competitor's[3]—SABRE captured an early gain in market share that it was able to maintain over the long term (Kettinger, Grover, and Segars, 1995). As early as 1986, the SABRE system was estimated by the U.S. Department of Transportation to be contributing a profit of $178 million to the parent company AMR, which was roughly 63 percent of its total net income. Its sustained competitive advantage at this time was due to the control of its distribution channels.

The next evolutionary step was to expand services beyond the airline industry. SABRE was extended into a reservation system for other travel industry businesses dependent on travel agents as intermediaries: hotels, rental cars, and other travel-related services. By the early 1990s, SABRE had also increased its reach to corporate travel departments. In the mid-1990s, the SABRE system and United Airlines' Apollo system had 75 percent of the computerized reservation system market.

AMR Corporation also began to achieve a competitive advantage from SABRE by developing systems to make use of the wealth of customer data collected by SABRE for strategic decision-making. According to the former CIO (Hopper, 1990), it took American Airlines several years to develop this capability. For example, reservation data are used to develop targeted marketing and incentive programs specific to a travel agency (Venkatraman and Christiaanse, 1996). Strategic alliances have also been formed with other businesses to increase links with end-consumers. For example, customer information is shared with Citibank so that frequent flyer credits on AA can be earned for purchases made on a Citibank credit card.

An end-consumer version of the reservation system (EasySABRE) first became accessible via on-line service companies such as America Online. This evolved to a Web-based reservation system on the Internet. During 1997, for example, AA had a special advertising campaign for discounted fares to entice end-consumers to make their own AA reservations by directly connecting to their Web site (www.americanair.com).

The SABRE system has also had a major impact on the airline industry itself. These industry impacts can be examined using the competitive forces model of Porter (Porter, 1985; Porter and Millar, 1985). As shown in Figure 7.3, successful firms develop competitive responses to five forces: supplier power, customer power, the threat of new entrants, the threat of substitute products, and within-industry retaliation

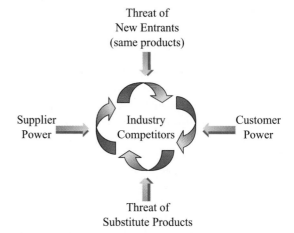

Figure 7.3 Five Competitive Forces (Adapted from Porter, 1985; Porter and Millar, 1985)

---

3 In 1984, the Civil Aeuronautics Board forced AA to remove any bias from its display screens. Its major competitor, United Airlines (Apollo system) received a similar mandate.

(competitor rivalry). The proprietary SABRE system gave AMR a competitive advantage by reducing the buying power of its customers (travel agents): the SABRE system became a major distribution channel for AA and its competitors. Since AMR owned and managed this channel, it was able to set up incentive programs for preferred travel agents.

Because SABRE was well established, the entry barriers for other airlines to develop a competing system remained high, and only a small number of SABRE competitors emerged. In addition, the threat of a substitute product—i.e., the development of a competing system by other industry players—was minimized by SABRE's incorporation of other travel-related industries. SABRE became a strategic resource that could be leveraged beyond the airline industry. AMR Corporation also leveraged the wealth of information available from this system by creating strategic decision support systems, developing other strategic alliances (Citibank), and taking advantage of new technologies or a newly deregulated industry.

Although an initial key to SABRE's success was that it gained early control over the distribution channel, sustaining its success in the 1990s has been based on leveraging its existing strategic resource (Clemons, 1991). As we have seen, the AMR Corporation has continually invested in the SABRE system in order to reposition itself. Systems enhancements have therefore been the norm, and new strategic alliances and venues have been continually exploited.

Today, however, few firms would be willing to face the risks associated with the development of a large, expensive, proprietary interorganizational system. This is because today's tools and the IT expertise available to today's organizations make it easier to imitate a competitor's proprietary application and perhaps even develop a better system with newer technologies. In fact, most firms today are developing electronic commerce applications as a competitive *imperative* (Clemons, 1991). In other words, firms are not developing new IOS applications with the expectation of developing a sustainable competitive advantage with an IOS like SABRE. Rather, the new IT applications are developed because these firms face the risk of not surviving because they didn't keep up with their competition.

Another option is to *not* "go it alone" with the development of large, strategic IOS. For example,

when automated teller machines (ATMs) were first being introduced to U.S. consumers in the 1980s, the major retail bank in the Philadelphia area established a proprietary ATM network. In response to this competitive threat, several competing banks in the Philadelphia area created a cooperative alliance that would enable them to share the high costs and risks of developing the IT infrastructure needed for this type of banking network.

A second more common option is to move away from large proprietary systems toward systems based on agreed upon standards that support EC with multiple suppliers or multiple customers. Although such systems do not usually provide a sustainable advantage to set a business apart from other industry competitors, by using standard technologies, the participating firms can achieve cost savings. The objective is to be smarter at using IT in ways that leverage an organization's existing strengths and unique capabilities, rather than taking the riskier route of being first-to-market with a proprietary system. Systems based on agreed upon standards can also lead to a competitive advantage by creating stronger linkages with suppliers or customers.

A third option, available just recently, is to develop Internet applications that reach to the end-consumer. In addition to developing business-to-business IOSs, then, today's firms are also experimenting with selling products and services directly to the end-consumer. But before looking at EC via the Internet, we will first examine today's most common type of IOS using standard technologies—electronic data interchange.

ELECTRONIC DATA INTERCHANGE

The most common type of IOS using standard technologies involves the electronic exchange of standardized business documents. **Electronic data interchange (EDI)** is a set of standards and hardware and software technology that permits computers in separate organizations to transfer business document data electronically, without manual intervention.

Typical paper business documents that are standardized include purchase orders, order acknowledgments, requests for quotations, quotes, bills of lading, shipping notices, and medical claims. EDI automates the existing paper flows between organizations: Instead of paper documents linking two or more organizations, electronic equivalents are transmitted. In order to electronically transmit documents with more than one customer or supplier, an EDI application is based on agreed-upon, structured formats for the transmission of these documents. For a given firm, these standardized formats may be industry-based, generic across industries within a nation, or even generic across industries in more than one country. Over half of the Fortune 1000 had implemented EDI applications by the early 1990s; in 1992 the annual growth rate of business users was reported to be 45 percent (Hart and Saunders, 1997).

Within the private sector, the earliest IOS examples were proprietary systems established by a single large firm for multiple customers or suppliers, or by a small set of major players in an industry. Achieving buy-in to a proprietary system, however, requires major marketplace clout, such as held by U.S. automakers in the 1970s and 1980s. By the 1990s, even firms with major market shares in the auto industry had begun to move toward the adoption of industry standards or at least EDI standards developed by a consortium within an industry.

Benefits of EDI

According to Senn (1988, 1992), computer-to-computer data transmission eliminates two important business constraints: time and distance. EDI enables a fast, reliable information exchange worldwide, in response to rapidly changing markets, products, and services. Processes like just-in-time (JIT) manufacturing, for example, have been enabled by the rapid data flows achievable with EDI. Although the EDI benefits to a given firm will vary by industry, the potential benefits fit into five categories:

- *Faster speed of doing business.* Business data is sent, received, evaluated, and processed in a fraction of the time normally associated with business processes.
- *Reduction in required working capital.* Reductions in resource commitments for both inventory and accounts receivable yield improvements in working capital.

- *Cost savings.* Purchase order processing costs are one key source of cost savings. Savings for the grocery industry, based on fifty percent implementation within the industry, were estimated to be in excess of $300 million annually. Some of these cost savings are due to the elimination of data entry errors that result from the rekeying of data as they pass from organization to organization.
- *Improved customer/supplier relationships.* Firms are increasingly dependent on each other to achieve competitive advantage, and EDI creates partnerships between customers and suppliers and other strategic partners. EDI is often the first IT link between business partners and can form the beginning of a new kind of buyer/customer relationship.
- *Enables international trade.* The primary benefits here are related to international communications networks eliminating delays in paper flows and the transit of goods and information due to geographic and national boundaries. Paper handling costs for international trade have been estimated at seven percent of the value of the product traded. Delays due to time lost in traditional paperwork channels (freight forwarders, customs and port authorities, financial intermediaries) are estimated to be as high as 70 percent of elapsed time between the shipment and arrival of an international order.

In the sidebar "EDI Implementation Benefits," we briefly summarize some of the benefits reported by U.S. businesses in the manufacturing and retailing sectors.

How EDI Works

Figure 7.4A portrays an EDI approach to an order fulfillment process. Without EDI, multiple paper documents are generated, and transported via a common carrier. With EDI, a customer sends a supplier a purchase order or release to a blanket order via a standard electronic document. There is no manual shuffling of paperwork and little if any reentering of data. The supplier's computer system checks that the message is in an acceptable format and sends an electronic acknowledgment to the customer. The electronic order then feeds the supplier's production planning and shipping systems to schedule the shipment. When the order is ready to ship, the supplier sends the customer an electronic notice of the pending shipment. The

EDI IMPLEMENTATION BENEFITS

MANUFACTURING SECTOR

Chrysler entered the 1990s with over 1600 external suppliers shipping materials to 14 car and truck assembly plants in North America. The company's EDI system supported some 17 million transactions per year with suppliers. Because JIT production was implemented in 1984, the plants had reduced on-hand inventory from 5 days to 48 hours and eliminated more than $1 billion from the inventory network.

Digital Equipment Corporation claims to have reduced order processing costs for components by more than 50 percent with EDI.

RETAILING SECTOR

Service Merchandise, a national catalog warehouse retail chain, has used EDI to reduce the time to process a purchase order from ten days to two, with faster inventory turnover and better customer service.

An EDI-based program for retail-store and catalog orders allow Sears suppliers to ship merchandise directly to customers. Instead of waiting for receipt-of-goods notifications, Sears bills the customer after receiving the EDI shipment notice.

customer's computer checks that the shipment information corresponds to the order and returns a message authorizing the shipment. The supplier then sends a message that includes the truck number, carrier, approximate arrival time, and bill of lading. The customer's computer alerts the receiving dock of the expected arrival; receiving personnel visually verify the shipment upon arrival for quality, and the shipment is accepted. Elapsed time is short, fewer errors are introduced because very little manual data entry is required, documents are not lost in transit, and the customer carries less inventory because the ordering cycle is significantly reduced by the elimination of mail and paper processing.

The acceptance of a shipment triggers a customer's accounts payable system to issue a payment. However, electronic payments require a banking partner. An IOS that involves the transfer of payments between organizations typically has an independent module (application) for payment advices and credit

and debit memos. The banking industry was a laggard in EDI adoption, however, and the typical EDI system in the early 1990s generated a physical check, not an electronic funds transfer.

Each EDI partner must sign contracts outlining each other's responsibilities and liabilities. A contract determines when an electronic order is legally binding, which could be when it is delivered, after the message is read, or after it has been checked. A contract also determines whether all messages must be acknowledged. Usually, the customer must guarantee that if it issues a correctly formatted and acknowledged order, then it is obliged to accept and pay for the requested goods. Because less time is available to correct ordering errors, an error can quickly cascade from a customer through a chain of suppliers before it is detected. It is therefore important that all parties agree to the exact point at which a message becomes binding in the electronic chain of events.

Additional uses of an EDI computer-to-computer channel can also be made by the customer or the supplier organizations. Instead of just automating the exchange of paper documents between companies, an EDI implementation can also involve integrating systems across functions to support new processes within both the customer and supplier firms. For example, an EDI application for an order fulfillment process could automate the acceptance of an order from a customer, the generation of an order for the recipient firm, the generation of an order confirmation for the requesting firm, and an automatic billing process, all as computer-to-computer transactions. In the past, a manual handling of the same purchase order typically included multiple functional departments, at both the buyer and seller organizations (see Figure 7.4B).

Standards   The technical success of EDI depends on standards. Standards for EDI are necessary because computer file formats, forms, data and transaction definitions, and the overall methods of processing data can vary considerably across companies and especially across countries. Standards provide a way to decouple the different EDI participants as much as possible, yet still facilitate data exchange.

An electronic business document is called a transaction set. Header and trailer records contain batch control information, such as the unique identifiers of the sender and receiver, a date, the number of line

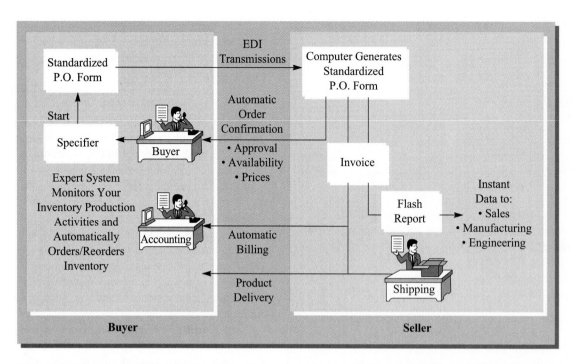

Figure 7.4A EDI Handling of a Purchase Order. (Reproduced with permission from *DATAMATION*, © 1988, Cahners Business Information. *DATAMATION* is a trademark of Cahners Business Information. All rights reserved.)

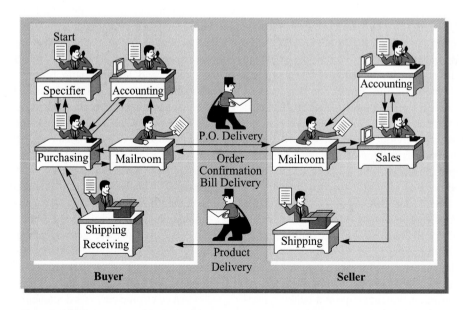

Figure 7.4B Manual Handling of a Purchase Order. (Reproduced with permission from *DATAMATION*, © 1988, Cahners Business Information. *DATAMATION* is a trademark of Cahners Business Information. All rights reserved.)

segments, and so on. Each transaction set also has a unique identification number and a time stamp. An EDI translation program converts an incoming EDI format so that it can be read by an application program, and vice versa.

The specific standard for a transaction set is established between the partners in an EDI relationship. EDI standards are of three types: proprietary formats designed for one or more organizations and their trading partners, industry-specific formats that are designed to match specific industry needs (e.g., automotive), and generic formats for use by any trading partners. In other words, in some industries a major industry player or a consortia of companies have established a standard, whereas in other industries a formal body with large representation may have established a standard. A universal standard therefore does not exist.

The American National Standards Institute has coordinated standard-setting activities in the U.S. (see ANSI X.12 following). In Japan, standards-setting efforts have been coordinated by the Ministry of International Trade and Industry (MITI). A common standard (EDIFACT) between Europe and the U.S., developed under the auspices of the United Nations' International Standards Organization, seems to be assuming the role of the dominant standard. However, no single international set of document standards exists for EDI, and some countries, such as China, are still constrained by national restrictions on data communications across borders, referred to as transborder data flows.

ANSI X.12 formats exist for standard documents in many U.S. industries—including chemicals, automotive, retail merchants, textiles, and electrical equipment. Some of these U.S. standards were developed by an industry group. For example, the Automotive Industry Action Group (AIAG) was created by Ford, General Motors, and Chrysler along with 300 large suppliers. The Transportation Data Coordinating Committee (TDCC) was created with funding from the U.S. Department of Commerce in the late 1960s. For some industries, the usage of uniform standards for product identification (product codes) is also key to EDI cost savings.

EDI is usually implemented by computer-to-computer communication between organizations. Companies typically transmit large batches of EDI standard forms over a private telecommunications network of leased lines created by one of the parties, over public telephone networks, or via a third-party intermediate processing agent—called a value-added network, or VAN (see the discussion of VANs in Chapter 4). A VAN provides the network paths between the organizations, and may also provide software to support EDI. The costs of a VAN are not inconsequential, and can contribute to perceptions that EDI can be quite expensive—especially for smaller businesses. A typical VAN charge in early 1997 was $25 to transmit 1000 characters (Radosevich, 1996–1997).

EDI Applications

Here we provide EDI examples in three different types of markets to demonstrate the widespread implementation of this type of electronic commerce application. First, we look at EDI in the manufacturing sector, focusing on 3M—a large manufacturer of diverse products. Then we look at an example from the retailing sector, focusing on grocery retailer H.E. Butt. We then briefly describe some EDI examples for trading networks that involve multiple business partners and government agencies, such as Singapore's Tradenet.

Manufacturing   In the manufacturing sector, the earliest EDI applications were usually directed at the supplier side: streamlining the *supply chain*. As mentioned previously, major players in some manufacturing industries actually mandated that their suppliers create an EDI linkage and provide just-in-time inventory. For example, in the automotive industry, many suppliers may have a single primary customer, such as General Motors or Ford. The key advantage for the manufacturer is cost savings; the key advantage for the supplier is a closer alliance with large customers. Some manufacturing firms have implemented EDI to improve not only their supply chain, but also their *product chain* (selling side).

For example, 3M is a diversified manufacturing company, noted for its innovative culture, with more than 60,000 products. 3M has implemented EDI applications to improve both supply chain and product chain logistics (Slater, 1996–1997). The company's three strategic initiatives at the end of 1996 were to accelerate new product development and commercialization, encourage supply chain excellence, and build customer loyalty. In each of the markets it serves, 3M aims to be the preferred vendor.

Over the years many of 3M's divisions have developed EDI applications, in a piecemeal fashion, to improve both supply chain and product chain logistics. By the end of 1996, EDI links had been established with over 2,000 U.S.-based trading partners. Roughly 1,100 of these trading partners are suppliers, 800 are business customers or distributors, and the remainder are financial institutions and transportation carriers. By the end of 1996 about 65 percent of 3M's purchase orders were sent to suppliers via EDI, and about 30 percent of all purchase orders from customers were received via EDI. The number of 3M's EDI partners continues to grow, and transaction volume has increased as much as 20 percent annually. The two primary benefits sought are faster speed for purchase order processing, and cost savings for the elimination of paperwork and reduced labor costs, in both its supply chain and product chain.

Because its customers and suppliers have differing levels of IT sophistication, 3M's philosophy has been to conduct EDI transactions using multiple transport methods—including VANs and direct network connections. It connects with a customer using virtually any method requested by a customer. This helps 3M build customer loyalty and customer relationships. EDI enables 3M to become a preferred supplier when it helps its customers reduce their own inventories and paperwork. EDI is also used for order status checking by customers: About 1,500 customers receive on-line order status updates. Other customers simply want a hardcopy status report waiting in their mailboxes each morning; 3M automatically faxes reports to about 3,000 customer locations.

In addition to transmitting business transactions, 3M also uses its EDI communications pipeline to transmit up-to-date product and price information to distributors and customers. One of its customers is the federal government's General Services Administration. Product information is electronically transmitted to the GSA, which maintains its own central catalog for its various departments.

Today, 3M is expanding its EC effort to include a new channel, the Internet. A description of 3M's Inter-net applications can be found in the Electronic Commerce via the Internet section below.

Retailing   EDI has also been used to streamline the supply chain in many retailing industries. In several industries in this sector, EDI applications have also enabled larger initiatives similar to the JIT initiative in manufacturing: Quick Response programs to meet the retailer's demands for fast, small, and frequent replenishment of inventory. In an industry with very low profit margins, like the grocery industry, the costs savings offered by EDI can therefore be especially significant.

A continuous replenishment initiative was the driver for EDI applications at H.E. Butt (HEB), a geographically focused grocery chain with 1992 sales of $3.2 billion. (This acccount is based on *H.E. Butt Grocery Company: A Leader in ECR Implementation,* Harvard Business School, 1994). In 1989 H.E. Butt first created an alliance with a major supplier, Procter & Gamble, to improve its supply channel efficiency: P&G would supply HEB with products based directly upon HEB's warehouse shipments to the retail stores and inventory data—rather than upon receipt of a purchase order. An EDI link was established to transmit the high volume of HEB warehouse movement transactions (for agreed upon products) to P&G on a daily basis. P&G was responsible for determining the order quantity needed, assembling the delivery, and electronically notifying HEB that the shipment was coming.

After a successful trial, EDI partnerships were established with other major suppliers including General Mills, Pillsbury, and Campbell Soup. HEB used a PC-based EDI link initially, but then began to develop a mainframe system. The plan then was to leverage the mainframe investment by converting other paper processes to EDI—including purchase orders, invoice, funds transfer, and pricing information. In 1992 there were 10 active vendors in the continuous replenishment program; during 1993, 26 new vendors were added. In addition to cost savings, the EDI implementation helped create stronger interorganizational relationships: It freed the preexisting communication channels between HEB and its suppliers so that these channels could be used to pursue other improvements for both HEB and its suppliers.

A Quick Response initiative between major vendors and major retailers in the apparel industry has also been enabled by EDI (see sidebar "Sara Lee Knit Products").

Large Trading Networks   EDI applications also play a part in the development of large, electronic trading networks sponsored by an entire industry or even a

---

SARA LEE KNIT PRODUCTS

By 1990, Quick Response had become a common term in the apparel industry for a set of business and technology improvements that targeted the relation between major retailers and their key vendors. The major goals of QR are: shorter delivery lead time, smaller delivery batch size, and increased frequency of delivery.

A key component of QR is EDI: orders, invoices, and other transactional information were exchanged between buyers and sellers via electronic communications channels according to agreed upon message formats (transaction sets) and communication protocols. EDI contributed to cutting the lead time for delivery in two ways. One was the speed of transmission. While orders mailed through the postal system could take up to several days to reach vendors, electronic orders would reach them almost instantaneously. While a telephone and FAX transmission was equally fast, EDI was the only practical way to place large numbers of orders quickly, accurately, and at low cost. The second contribution was the elimination of redundant input of data to information systems: data generated by the retailers' inventory and POS (point of sales) systems automatically generated orders that were transmitted into vendors' computers, which in turn generated production and inventory schedules automatically. For large retailers and vendors, conventional manual processing of any of these processes involved coding and keying tens of thousands of orders into computers, which could be both time consuming and inaccurate.

Before EDI it often took several weeks for sales data to be processed into purchase orders at retailers, and for purchase orders to be processed to trigger actual shipments at vendors. By 1990, many of the retailers processed their weekend's sales data Sunday night to send orders by dawn on Monday. Hanes Underwear, for example, had cut the delivery lead time to Super-Rite from two weeks to one.

[Adapted from Sara Lee Knit Products: Quick Response at Hanes, Harvard Business School, 1991]

---

government body (McCubbrey and Gricar, 1996). For example, an electronic trading network was developed for the city-state of Singapore to link government agencies (e.g., customs), financial institutions, and shippers. This trading network was developed in order to reduce the time for a vessel to clear the shipping port; the strategic intent was to help ensure that Singapore remained the port of choice in the increasingly competitive Asian marketplace (Applegate et al., 1996).

More specifically, TradeNet is an EDI system that links government agencies, traders (shippers and receivers), shipping companies (surface and air), intermediaries (freight-forwarders, carriers), and financial institutions (banks, insurance). For example, a freight forwarder completes TradeNet application forms by using a local computer system. The system translates the data into EDIFACT (an international document standard), and the EDIFACT document is transmitted to a TradeNet mainframe and then forwarded to a TradeNet database or other agency.

Launched in 1989, TradeNet supported an interchange including invoices, purchase orders, delivery orders, and debit and credit notes among the trading partners and agencies. The system also provided data on the status of a shipment and supported some electronic payments. By the end of 1989, about 45 percent of all trade documents for sea and air shipments were being handled by the network. The implementation was so successful that the date for mandatory use of TradeNet for trade transactions was moved up from 1993 to 1991 (*Singapore Tradenet: A tale of one city,* Harvard Business School, 1990).

Another EDI application spawned by the Singapore initiative is MediNet (Liang, 1992). MediNet links pharmacies, clinics, hospitals, insurance companies, and a central health care system board. The system facilitates a national exchange of various medical documents: medical records, patient bills and claims, supplier orders and invoices, and national medical research data. Similar systems have recently been called for within the U.S., but two of the major constraints are the size of the effort and the current mix of state vs. federal areas of jurisdiction.

By the 1990s, EDI had been implemented widely in many industries, especially in larger firms. Some large firms conduct as many as 80 to 90 percent of their interbusiness transactions using EDI applications

(Kavan and Van Over, 1991). EDI standards and technologies are dependable, proven, and trusted: Communications via private lines have limited exposure to the public and are therefore highly secure (Radosevich, 1996–1997). However, EDI applications also have some shortcomings: They are business-to-business systems, they are based on rigid and complex formats, and they are expensive for smaller organizations to implement. By the late 1990s, many large firms were curtailing new EDI investments in anticipation of future EDI applications via the Internet (Radosevich, 1996–1997).

Electronic Commerce Via The Internet

The biggest EC story in the late 1990s has been the explosive growth of commerce using the Internet, especially with Web technologies. As discussed in Part I, the Internet is a network of networks that use the TCP/IP protocol, with gateways to even more networks that do not use the TCP/IP protocol. No one owns the Internet; each organization or end-user pays for its piece. The World Wide Web is the hypertext, multimedia portion of the Internet, accessible via navigation software (a browser) that communicates with Web servers that store graphical pages of information. With the rapid diffusion of low-cost, user-friendly browsers, the opportunities for businesses to extend the reach of IT to end-consumers, as well as additional business customers, has become a reality.

As a new channel for EC, a global highway such as the Internet therefore holds a lot of promise. The Internet provides businesses with an open network that has a relatively cheap entry cost. It also provides connectivity not only with other organizations outside the firm but also with end-consumers, with or without an intermediary. Further, the Web offers an attractive and easy-to-use graphical user interface (GUI) that supports interactive multimedia (sound, animation, video). Compared to e-mail or the telephone, the Web is a very rich communication medium.

Whereas our discussion of EC applications has focused on business-to-business EC up to this point,

the following discussion will involve not only business-to-business EC via the Internet, but also business-to-end-consumer EC. By the late 1990s, the demographics of Web users had become more mainstream: In mid-1997, a *Business Week*/Harris poll reported the Net population to be 41 percent female (up from 23 percent two years earlier) and 45 percent aged 40 years old or older. To those of us who can now see CNN (see Figure 7.5), hunt for a book, and make our travel plans via the Web, 24 hours a day, we appear indeed to be in the midst of another revolution—what has been referred to as a business revolution. However, a more evolutionary viewpoint can also be argued: The Internet is but one of the newest transport mechanisms for electronic commerce applications.

We begin by developing an expanded list of potential EC benefits, based on the new capabilities offered by EC via the Internet. We then describe how the Internet works—including how it is governed and who enables Internet access. However, conducting EC via the Internet today also involves managing around a lot of "potholes" on the information highway. Although we expect that many of these will be overcome in the next few years, we briefly describe four current barriers: security, traffic overload, censorship difficulties, and measurement tools. Our examples include Web applications for established businesses and for new Web-based businesses.

Benefits of EC on the Internet

In the prior section on electronic commerce via EDI, we described five major benefits for computer-to-computer transactions using standardized formats:

- *faster speed of doing business*
- *reduction in required working capital*
- *cost savings*
- *improved customer/supplier relationships*
- *enables international trade*

All of these benefits are also achievable via the Internet. In fact, because of the global reach of the Internet and the relatively low cost of entry for Internet access by end-consumers (in 1998, about a $22.00 monthly fee), the cost savings and international trade benefits would appear to be even greater with Internet-based applications. These additional benefits are also emerging for Web applications:

Figure 7.5 CNN Home Page (Courtesy of CNN)

Cheaper distribution of digitized products and documents   Products that can be digitized (software, catalogs, technical reports, news services) can be both sold and delivered via the Internet. This is thus a benefit particularly accessible to firms in the software industry. For example, customers can download a purchased software product or even download a version of the software for trial basis. Every major software vendor has undoubtedly considered how it can use the Internet to distribute its products. (The potential losers here are software distributors.) For example, the Internet has become the major distribution point for small-scale software fixes via downloads using the FTP function as described in Chapter 4. On-line service vendors and browser developers offer new releases of their products via the Internet. Netscape, the vendor of the browser with the largest market share up until 1998, is but one of the computer industry players that

has greatly benefited from this new mechanism for fulfilling orders from customers. Web-based technologies have also greatly increased the possibilities for Internet distribution of documents between businesses. Large savings from distributing investor-relations materials on-line, rather than mailing quarterly printed reports, have also been reported. For example, Sun Microsystems reported an initial annual savings of $250,000 by using the Web as a communications mechanism (Settles, 1996).

New customer support capabilities   Early business payoffs have also been reported for using the Internet to handle customer service. Major software vendors provide technical support documents to help organizational members (and consultants) with customer support responsibilities; this also increases the likelihood that customers will use the Internet as a distribution channel for some products. Other support materials can take the form of frequently asked questions and troubleshooting tips, as well as targeted product catalogs. Support materials for new products and newly discovered "bugs" for products sold via other market channels need only be updated in one place: the vendor's Web page.

E-mail via the Internet also facilitates communication between businesses and end-consumers that may be using different computer platforms. Web-based communications technologies make possible interactive communications with customers. This means that customers can be asked relevant questions in response to their own inputs, which could result, for example, in obtaining a useful profile for customer support. E-mail was referred to as the first "killer app" of the Internet in Chapter 4.

Virtual user groups can also be created by electronically linking together customers with similar interests and needs: Customers of the same business can "chat" with each other, not just with the business or nonprofit organization that provides the Web home page to which they connect.

New marketing channel   The Internet is not only a cost-effective customer support channel for existing customers, but also a cost-effective new marketing channel (Himelstein, Neuborne, and Eng, 1997). To capitalize on this capability, existing businesses have been experimenting heavily with Web-based marketing. In addition, a large number of entrepreneurial start-ups have been marketing exclusively on the Web, and some have attracted major revenues very quickly. Three marketing capabilities via this new channel are described below.

1. *Attract new customers.* The low cost of entry for EC via the Internet means that new customers can be reached at a low cost. Several writers have suggested that every Web site needs to have a "freebie" to attract visitors to the site and then hopefully keep them there long enough to provide information about a product or service and perhaps attract their interest in a purchase.
2. *Single point of contact.* The Internet offers the possibility of a single point of contact for a given customer. A single marketing channel for the customer can be created for multiple products from different

divisions within the same firm, as well as for multiple products from different suppliers within the same industry.

3. *Market research.* Firms are just beginning to explore the new marketing possibilities due to the electronic collection of marketing data on customers and potential customers via Web technologies. The assumption is that end-consumers will want to provide data about their personal wants and needs so that a firm can provide them with information on only those products that might be of interest. The challenge here will be to overcome the consumers' concerns about guarding their privacy. For example, a September 1997 *Business Week*/Harris poll found that 65 percent of 1,002 adults surveyed answered "not willing at all" to the question: How willing are you to share personal and financial information about yourself so that on-line ads can be targeted to your tastes and interests? (Louis Harris & Associates, 1997).

New sales channel   As more secure methods for electronic payments become widely implemented, the number of firms conducting sales transactions over the Internet is expected to increase exponentially. For some existing firms, this new channel represents the opportunity to bypass an intermediary. The Web-based SABRE reservation system described earlier is a good example of this type of disintermediation. In other situations, this new sales channel has led to the creation of new Web-based intermediaries. On-line shopping malls are examples of Web-based businesses attempting to exploit this opportunity.

As organizations learn how to exploit the capabilities of Web technologies, the benefits that can be achieved with EC applications via the Internet will no doubt also grow. Further, as new Web technologies emerge, different types of benefits may become possible. For example, after Web users experienced Web-casting software (such as PointCast), new types of applications based on "push" technologies began to be developed (see sidebar "Push technology saves time and Money" in Chapter 3).

How the Internet Works

In Chapter 4 we introduced the network capabilities of the Internet, as well as its network protocol (TCP/

IP). In Chapter 3 we introduced some of the current Web software, including browsers, Java, and ActiveX software. From these technology sections, it should be clear that the Internet explosion during the mid-1990s is the result of a convergence of a number of new technologies.

Nevertheless, the Internet is but one of the newest transport options for applications on the EC super-highway. As shown in Figure 7.6, other current trans-port options include telecommunications lines alone, cable TV, and wireless technologies.

Between the applications themselves and the EC superhighway, there are three other infrastructure lay-ers (see Figure 7.6). The first layer includes common business *services*. Two of these services—authen-tication and encryption—ensure the security of a transmission. Authentication is concerned with estab-lishing the source of a transmission; encryption is concerned with ensuring the secure transmission of the transaction itself. A third service critical for elec-tronic commerce is electronic payments. (We describe encryption and payment methods in more detail below). The remaining two layers refer to messaging and distribution services and electronic publishing. Whereas earlier EC applications relied on e-mail and EDI standards alone, today's growth in EC is directly attributable to the multiplatform hypertext transfer protocol (HTTP) of the Web and its multimedia pub-lishing capabilities.

EC applications are also dependent on two support pillars. On the right side of Figure 7.6 is the technical support pillar—including tool standards and commu-nications protocols. Today these are being crafted by volunteer groups and predominantly the U.S. market-place. In contrast, the support pillar on the left side is highly dependent on the actions of governments, the legal system, and individuals in the global community. The support pillar therefore represents some of the major challenges for an EC transport system that is an "open highway" like today's Internet. In contrast to EDI applications implemented over private networks (including VANs), conducting EC over a highway owned by no one (or everyone) certainly poses new potential risks for businesses and consumers alike.

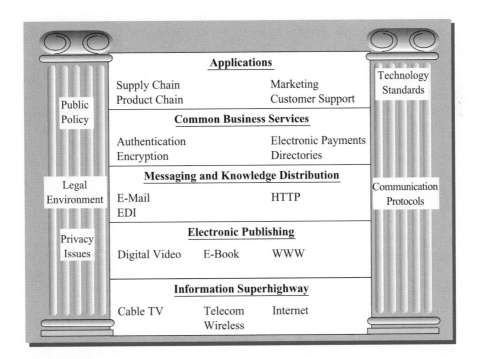

Figure 7.6 Electronic Commerce Framework (Adapted from Applegate, Holsapple, et al., 1996; Kalakota and Whinston, 1996).

The Internet today thus should be viewed as an emerging infrastructure that exists within an environment of high technical change, as well as within an environment of social, political, and legal uncertainties. As discussed in Chapter 4, many of these uncertainties are traceable to the origins of the Internet—a computer network (ARPAnet) using dedicated phone lines to link selected universities, research labs, and military bases and developed by the U.S. Department of Defense. In other words, the objective of the first version of today's Internet was to provide reliable communications and access to data distributed between a few communities in the event of a national crisis, not to support a global network for EC. Further, privacy issues are a new area of social concern; the first federal privacy legislation in the United States was passed just a few years after ARPAnet was established. As members of a democracy, as well as end-consumers, all of us need to stay attuned to developments that affect the left pillar in Figure 7.6. (See also the discussion at the end of this chapter and Chapter 8.)

Governance   The governance of the Internet is in the hands of a volunteer board, the Internet Society (ISOC), with a membership that represents multiple stakeholder groups—including users, networking professionals, and organizations in the computer industry and other businesses. Reporting to the ISOC is a board responsible for the architecture of the Internet and the setting of the standards, which is in turn supported by the Internet Engineering Task Force and its working groups. W3C is a consortium that sets standards for the Web. The members of W3C include representatives of all major software companies and individuals such as Tim Berners-Lee, the "unsung hero" who created the original standards for Web addressing and hypertext linking.

A large, informal monitoring body also exists: everyone who uses the Internet. The term netiquette has been used to refer to the accepted body of practices for communicating among users of the Internet. This term reflects the high value that many members of today's society place on the global community "ownership" of today's Internet.

A single organization that has turned out to be a key Internet governance body is Network Solutions Inc. (NSI), a Virginia-based company that was awarded the tasks of registering Internet domain names and maintaining these Net addresses in 1995. It is a contractor to the National Science Foundation (NSF), a nonprofit organization. Prior to this date the NSF was responsible for domain names. (As mentioned earlier, the NSF was also previously the sponsor for the high-speed backbone for the Internet.)

Domain Names   In the early days of the Internet, a user rarely guessed at a colleague's Internet e-mail name because it was likely to include an unmemorable machine name and even a mixture of letters and numbers for the user name. Instead, one learned of the e-mail user name and address using a nonelectronic contact with the colleague or an on-line directory for the colleague's organization. Only recently did e-mail names become more English-like and thus easier to remember. Similarly, in the early days of the Web, the URL for a business was typically retrieved from a search or some nonelectronic source (like an ad in the newspaper or on TV). However, as the EC potential of the Internet began to be recognized, existing large businesses began to take advantage of their name recognition in the marketplace and registered a domain name that reflected their company name or trademark names, such as microsoft.com, ibm.com, netscape.com (see sidebar "Domain Address").

Because domain names can be registered by anyone (for a nominal fee), domain names sometimes became hotly contested. NSI's initial policy was to register names on a first-come, first-served basis. This left open the possibility that an enterprising newcomer might register a domain name associated with a successful company before the established company did. The result was contested names, leading to some court battles, and a new NSI policy: If a plaintiff proves a legal right to a domain name registered by another, the NSI will "turn off" the domain name in question. Of the 1.2 million domain names registered by NSI between 1995 and 1997, only 26 of these names were disputed, with 22 settled out of court. (Eng, 1997). However, the NSI's monopoly on domain name assignments (and resulting profits) has come under question: an international group has proposed a world-wide registration system governed by a nonprofit association in Switzerland, with disputes moderated by the World Intellectual Property Association (Jacobs, 1997).

DOMAIN ADDRESS

The URL (Uniform Resource Locator) for a given Web site includes the Internet domain name. Each unique Internet domain name includes two parts: the organization (site) name, and a two- or three-character ending (suffix). Up until 1997, most domain names with three-character suffixes have signified U.S. organizations. The three-character suffix signals the type of organization, such as:

.com   commercial organization (business)
.edu   educational institution
.gov   government organization
.mil   military organization
.org   other noncommercial organization
.net   network provider

For organizations outside of the U.S., a two-character suffix has been used to indicate the country of origin:

.ca   Canada
.cn   China
.jp   Japan
.mx   Mexico

However, an agreement that was proposed by an international ad hoc committee and was ratified in May 1997 by eighty organizations (not including the U.S.) proposes seven new domain names, including the following:

.firm   businesses or firms
.store   businesses offering goods to purchase
.arts   arts and cultural groups
.nom   individuals

Also at issue is whether to implement a uniform system in which the U.S. would also have a country code (.us).

Network Service Providers Two types of organizations provide access to the Internet (usually via a public telephone line): Internet service providers (ISPs) that provide communications software to communicate with their computer network, which becomes a gateway to the Internet, and on-line service providers (like America Online) that offer services beyond just Internet access. On-line service providers have existed for more than a decade, although the major players have not always been the same. Some providers initially targeted only the business user (like Com-

puServe, owned by H&R Block) and had a user interface and pricing schedule based on usage and type of service appropriate for a business audience. Others initially targeted only the home user (like Prodigy, originally a joint venture between Sears and IBM), with a low flat-fee charge for basic services. The business assumption was that home users would respond to the colorful advertising banners and do on-line shopping via their service, which would in turn provide revenues for the network provider as well as the business seller.

In early 1994, only one on-line service provider offered a "ramp" to the Internet. As the growth of the Internet exploded, ISPs with low flat fees emerged, and Internet gateways became first a marketing device and then a requisite offering by on-line service providers. In 1996 Internet access also became a basic service, rather than an extra service that members had to pay a fee for. The number of vendors offering both home and business services soared. This led to a partial shake-out of the industry, as well as a major new player: Microsoft. Whereas America Online had initially used a direct mailing approach to attract new members, Microsoft began using a bundling approach: the Microsoft Network software is available on most computers with the Windows NT or 95 or later operating systems.

Electronic Payments Electronic payment systems are critical to the growth of EC. As we saw in the EDI discussion, the banking industry has lagged somewhat behind in electronic commerce in the past. The lack of well established on-line payment systems has been a bottleneck to growth in EC via the Internet well into the second half of the 1990s. However, by the mid-1990s, four general types of electronic payment methods had been implemented: electronic checking, electronic cash, smart cards (debit cards), and credit card-based payments (Kalakota and Whinston, 1996; Nash, 1997; Panurach, 1996; Zgodzinski, 1997).

Electronic checking, which has been in existence for over two decades, involves an intermediary between the buyer and seller. Also referred to as electronic funds transfer (EFT), the buyer initiates a request for a certification of payment from an intermediary (bank), and the intermediary debits the buyer's account and gives an electronic certification (like a check). The buyer then gives the certification to the seller, and the seller's account is credited when the certification notice is given to the intermediary. These transactions can occur almost instantaneously. Also, the buyer and seller don't have to have accounts with the same intermediary: the transactions can be coordinated through an authorized clearinghouse. The major drawback is that all buyer-seller transactions must pass through a banking system, which results in an audit trail.

Electronic cash is another type of token-based payment system. It differs from electronic checking in that the buyer-seller transaction is not electronically tracked by an intermediary. To be cost-effective, electronic cash systems require large numbers of consumers to want to make electronic payments and large numbers of merchants to accept them. The advantages for merchants include the instant settlement of a transaction. In early 1996, only a small number of international merchants reportedly accepted electronic cash payments. Whether these micropayment systems will be widely accepted or are a critical driver for EC is still a subject of debate. Another barrier to implementation has been the uncertainty regarding federal regulation; for example, automated teller machine (ATM) transactions fall under federal regulations, but by early 1997 there were no federal regulations for merchant's fees for electronic money.

A third token-based alternative is the smart card, or electronic purse. Cards are relatively inexpensive, can be loaded with money via an ATM or another device, and can be read by readers that combine elements of a personal computer, point-of-sale terminal, or telephone. Several European countries have had quite a few years of experience with smart cards; a joint venture (Mondex USA) between seven major U.S. banks, AT&T, and some credit card companies is expected to fuel the growth in this country.

Banks, credit card companies, and third party developers in the U.S. have also joined forces to work toward an Internet standard for electronic payment via credit card-based systems. The first new business for third-party authorization of credit card payments for Internet purchases was First Virtual (www.fv.com), which went public in 1996. That same year the first specifications for secure credit card transactions on the Web were published by a consortium that includes two major credit card players (Master Card and Visa)

and other major industry players (GTE, IBM, Microsoft, Netscape). The first version of this new standard, **Secure Electronic Transaction (SET)**, was made public in June 1997. SET is expected to become a widespread standard, because it has the backing of banks and the major credit card companies. Several major Internet vendors have now established SET-compliant-based transaction systems. It also has been predicted that this single event will fuel a large growth in buyer-seller transactions via the Internet before the year 2000. By the late 1990s, the major barrier appeared to be consumer acceptance.

Constraints to EC on the Internet

Internet applications for electronic commerce have begun to reach a take-off point. Yet many potholes still exist on this information highway. For example, several legal and regulatory issues need to be addressed, including international trade barriers, contractual issues, liability of service providers (ISPs), fraud and consumer rights, intellectual property rights, and taxes.

Our focus in this section, however, is on four other major constraints of concern to end-consumers and businesses in the late 1990s for which the technical solutions are beginning to emerge: security, traffic overload, censorship difficulties, and measurement tools. Many of today's IS managers are expecting the floodgates to open for EC via the Internet once new technical solutions to address these problems become proven.

Security   The biggest pothole, or barrier, for conducting business on the Internet has been security. As discussed earlier, the Internet was not originally designed to be a public communications utility. The security features needed to conduct commerce on the Internet were not in place in the early 1990s when the ban on commercial usage was lifted. Since then, however, there have been several advancements, and today the degree of caution exercised by the average consumer probably exceeds what is necessary with today's technology.

There are two major security issues: (1) how to control access to a computer that is physically networked to the Internet, and (2) how to ensure that the security of a given communication, including business transactions, is not violated.

The primary way to control access is via a firewall. **Firewalls** are devices that sit between the Internet and an organization's internal network in order to block intrusions from unauthorized users and hackers from remote sites. A firewall can be a router, a personal computer, a host, or a collection of hosts; routers are the simplest kind, but least secure. As seen in Figure 7.7, the firm's external Web site sits outside the firewall. Many firms also use outside vendors to host their external Web site. Unknown to the Web site user, the Web site may be on a vendor's server, not a server connected to the company's network. E-mail and other communications from the end-consumer may initially be received by a third party, not a computer (or person) internal to the company that owns the domain name.

Encryption is a primary way to ensure the security of a business transaction or other communication. Today's encryption systems are based on two decoding keys and mathematical principles for factoring a product into its two prime numbers (Gates, 1995). One decoding key is used to encipher (code) a message; a second decoding key is used to decipher it. The enciphering key makes it easy to encode a message, but deciphering requires a key only available to the intended recipient of the message.

If the enciphering key is the product of two very large prime numbers, the key is expected to have a relatively long life before being vulnerable to a hacker. For example, it took a group of 600 academics and hobbyists using computers of 1993 vintage less than one year to identify the two prime numbers for a 129-digit product. A somewhat larger product is estimated to be indecipherable within a person's lifetime.

CERT, a Computer Emergency Response Team at Carnegie-Mellon University in Pittsburgh, monitors security issues on the Internet. It helps determine who is breaking in and also devises solutions to the methods used for the break-in (Laudon and Laudon, 1996). Further, the break-in isn't publicized until a solution is found. This helps avoid public panic. It also helps avoid an escalation in criminal activity from educating the potential intruder community before having a deterrent solution in place.

Traffic Overload   Another barrier is the heavy traffic on the Internet. By 1996 the growth in the number of users on the Internet had accelerated faster than network providers could respond. Just how much corporate users depended on on-line services for Internet access alone was revealed in the summer of 1996, when America Online experienced a 19-hour blackout: six million AOL customers lost connectivity due to a bug in router software. The cost to AOL for

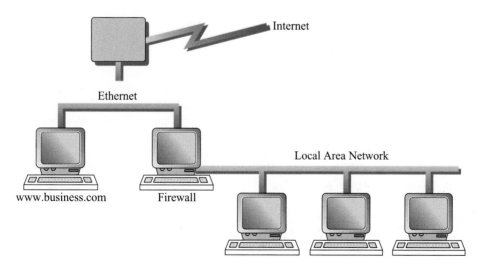

Figure 7.7 Firewall

reimbursing its customers was estimated at $3 million (*Wall Street Journal,* January 17, 1997).

An even more publicized example was the lack of capacity planning at AOL, apparently due to the lack of communication between the marketing department and the rest of the organization. In the few months leading into a holiday period in which many families would be exploring the Internet for the first time via home computers, AOL also began to introduce a flat fee pricing that encouraged users not to log off and a longer "free" trial period (50 hours versus 20 hours). The result was busy signals for customers trying to gain access to the information superhighway. Since many business organizations were using AOL as a network service provider, the company not only received repeated negative press coverage, but also court suits about breach of contract (Schiesel, 1997).

These incidents greatly increased awareness about traffic overload on the access lines of network service providers, as well as at various sites. Prior to the Web, Gopher[4] users learned to take advantage of the time zone differences in order not to get a busy signal at a popular site. Unavailable Web sites and slow response times for Web server access are also not uncommon. Some writers have suggested that for this reason alone the Internet is not a reliable network of business commerce when the speed of completing a given transaction is a critical characteristic. One proposed solution is to decrease demand by a pricing mechanism.

Censorship Difficulties   The lack of technology filters to screen out access to Web sites designated as undesirable by an overseer is also a current barrier to business use. It is well known that today's Web navigation tools lack filters for minors; assignments for elementary students that involve Web searching can frequently lead to full-screen images in the classroom that would be hidden under brown wrappers in the local drugstore. Company time spent at undesirable sites, let alone downloading images from such sites, also creates a potential problem for Web use in a business.

Several national governments have attempted to censor content accessible to its citizens, but the global

nature of the Internet makes that very difficult to do. Censorship legislation passed by the U.S. Congress in early 1996 (Communications Decency Act) has since been ruled unconstitutional (Felsenthal and Sandberg, 1997). For network service providers that also provide content services (such as AOL), the courts have also ruled that they are not responsible for Internet content, although they provide the electronic gateway.

A typical solution in businesses today is to issue a policy on Internet usage for employees, and to rely on in-person monitoring rather than technological monitoring.

Measurement Tools   New software applications are typically justified based on a cost/benefit analysis and then reassessed after implementation. For marketing initiatives via the Internet, many firms have bypassed the justification step for relatively low-cost projects; many managers have heeded the warnings in the press about the lack of a Web presence translating into a competitive disadvantage in the future and have been willing to fund start-up projects without a formal cost/benefit analysis. However, as Web site costs escalate, the demand for accountability also grows.

One of the ways that firms measure the utility of a Web application is by tracking the usage of the Web site (Young, 1996). Initial tracking tools were somewhat primitive. Just counting a "hit" (an access) doesn't tell a company much about the actual value or impact of its home page. This is because a Web surfer may not even read the content of a page, or may even terminate a page download before it is completed. Newer software captures "click-through" rates (which could measure the user's actual clicking on an ad) or cost per lead (capturing if the viewer provides e-mail information or makes a purchase). More controversial is the use of "cookies" for tracking Web site usage. Cookies store data on a user's movements within a particular Web site in a "cookie file" on the user's Web browser, unless this browser option has been disabled by the user. This enables the Web server to track return visits—a measure highly valued—as well as additional data on the surfer.

Internet Applications

Two different types of electronic commerce applications using Web technologies have emerged in the

---

4 Gopher is a menu-driven navigation tool for text documents, a predecessor to the Web; see Chapter 4.

1990s.[5] The first type is a company Web site accessible to the global Internet user, referred to as an external Web site. Within existing businesses, there has been a lot of experimentation in external Web site applications in order to achieve the potential benefits we presented earlier. This type of application will be the primary focus of this section of the chapter.

The second type, **extranets,** are Internet-based applications for key trading partners that allow linkage to a business' internal systems—to systems inside the organization's firewall. Extranets may be developed as replacements for existing EDI applications that operate over leased lines or VANs, or as new applications that take advantage of Web technologies, such as the ability to transmit graphical files. For firms (and industries) with large prior investments in EDI applications for supply-chain or product-chain logistics, an extranet may not be a viable replacement application for some time period. Another early barrier here has been that the Internet initially did not offer a reliable and secure enough infrastructure for large-volume business transactions. In the long term, however, extranets are expected to become major Internet-based applications, and pilot applications by industry consortia were already underway at the time this chapter was written.

In contrast, external Web site applications are likely to be new public relations and marketing initiatives. As Web users became more mainstream in the late 1990s, Internet advertising and Web strategies for existing traditional firms became more of an organizational priority. In addition, the new marketing and sales channel offered by the Internet has led to many Web start-up firms. Many of these start-ups have carved out new intermediary roles that link the end-customer with the service provider or product manufacturer. Among these, for example, are Web-based firms that establish virtual communities or provide a Web search tool, with strategically placed advertisements that link Web clients with Web servers.

Below we present in some detail four business examples of Web applications viewed as successful at the time this chapter was written. These examples include both existing businesses and new Web-based businesses in order to demonstrate different business

approaches to EC via the World Wide Web. However, no claims are being made about the sustainability of these strategies; history will be the judge.

Manufacturing   Earlier in this chapter we described the EDI applications at 3M and the supply-chain and product-chain benefits associated with these applications. Although EDI via private lines is still considered a vital part of 3M's business, transmission via the Internet of these standard business transactions is now being pursued in order to reduce costs, as well as take advantage of the global reach of the Internet (Slater, 1996).

3M is also exploring ways to reach the end-consumer directly for some of its products (see Figure 7.8). According to its manager of electronic commerce, Peter Jacobs, "The objective isn't to introduce electronic commerce. It's to improve the business." The firm's EC objectives have moved from a logistical EDI role to a strategic role. Its current initiatives are directed not only at streamlining the supply chain, but also at winning new customers by simplifying the buying process. For example, industrial customers are encouraged to use a Web-based order tracking application for determining when 3M shipments will reach their docks.

In addition, 3M is now providing electronic catalog information via the Internet. The Web is becoming an important platform for publishing product information because of its hypertext capabilities as well as its reach: The Web extends beyond distributors to business customers and end-consumers. In addition to the traditional EDI benefits of improved customer support and reduced costs for customer support, the Web-based product catalogs also offer the potential benefits of attracting new customers, enabling one-stop shopping and permitting the collection of marketing data on customers. According to 3M's Webmaster, Web-based publishing gives 3M a way to show off its "wildly diverse product lines" for its highly diverse customer base and it also creates an opportunity for target marketing. Company standards are in place for catalog navigation, with each of 3M's new market centers responsible for building (and updating) its own Web pages.

3M is also exploring how to use the Internet as a new channel for customer service. Customer queries are collected via e-mail from its Web site, bypassing customer phone-in lines. These queries are then

---

5 A third type of Web application, intranets, is discussed in Chapter 6.

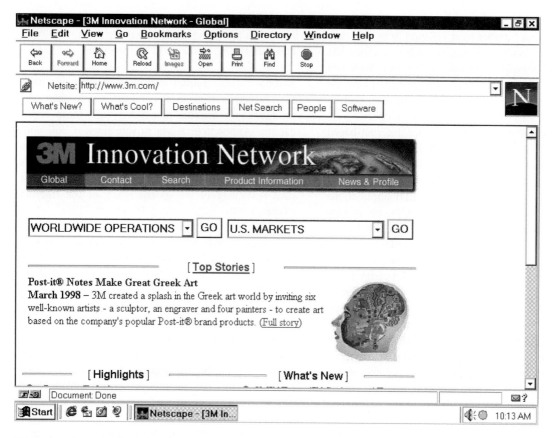

Figure 7.8 3M Home Page (Courtesy of 3M Corporation)

transferred to a Lotus Notes database, analyzed by a customer support employee, and distributed to the appropriate business unit for a response. This manual intervention step requires a delay in service; currently, a 48-hour turnaround is promised to the customer, but this is viewed as longer than desirable.

Pilot applications for direct selling via the Web were also implemented by the mid-1990s. Two computer-related products were selected for these pilots: Precise Mousing Surface and Post-it Software Notes. This was because buyers of computer-related products were expected to be less reluctant to submit credit card numbers via the Internet, even over a "secure" Netscape server, than buyers of 3M's other products would be. Increased direct-selling applications at 3M will partially depend on the firm's ability to deal with two management challenges: managing the impacts on distributors (who are a key link in 3M's value

chain) and developing cost-effective solutions for fulfilling low-volume purchases, because 3M typically distributes its products in crates or cartons.

3M is also exploring the opportunities for proactive one-to-one marketing via the Internet. Customized product catalogs for specific markets and specific customers are envisioned. For example, a repeat customer could be greeted with a short list of only those products in which he or she is interested, based on an analysis of data collected from this customer's previous Web visits and purchases.

Retailing   According to its founder Jeff Brezos, Amazon.com does things on the Web that "simply cannot be done any other way." Billed as "Earth's Biggest Bookstore," in mid-1997 it had a catalog of more than 2.5 million titles, including most of the 1.5 million English-language books currently in print and

1 million out-of-print titles. By way of comparison, its home page claims that only 170,000 titles are available via the largest chain superstore and a mere 25,000 titles in the average mall store (see Figure 7.9). (This account is partially based on Hildebrand, 1996–97. The company's website is at www.amazon.com.)

Readers can search the site by author, title, subject, keyword, and ISBN as well as by more advanced queries. There also is the option to browse for popular books by category links such as biographies and memoirs, self-help, and personal growth. Linked to book titles are book reviews posted by customers and "self-conducted interviews" posted by authors. The selection of a book title leads to a list of similar books. Amazon's actual inventory reportedly includes just some major bestsellers, but books are usually shipped within 2 to 3 days. Obscure titles may take somewhat longer.

Amazon went on-line in July 1995. It quickly became one of the most popular and well publicized business sites on the Web by providing easy consumer access to its large inventory. It has also become the leading book retailer, with 1996 sales of $15.7 million, and with projected sales of $325 million by 1999 (Hildebrand, 1996–97). Competitors such as Borders Books and Barnes & Noble are expected to increase their on-line presence, but Amazon.com has the first-mover advantage and name recognition among Web users.

Distributor Network   This third example is an application that establishes a distributor network for an apparel business, and its competitors. (This account is partially based on Radosevich, 1996. The sponsor's website is www.fruitactivewear.com.) The ActiveWear division of Fruit-of-the-Loom, with annual profits of

Figure 7.9 Amazon.com Home Page (Courtesy of Amazon.com)

$2.4 billion, makes about half of its operating profits from the manufacturing of blank shirts that are sold through distributors to thousands of small and midsize garment printers and embroiderers who decorate the shirts with logos and other designs and then sell the decorated garments to retailers. The imprinted sportswear market is in a consolidation phase, and strong customer (distributor) relationships are currently critical for their business.

Under the initial sponsorship of the vice president of marketing for the ActiveWear division, Fruit-of-the-Loom has forged an alliance with its major distributors and created a Web-based marketing and sales channel for products by Fruit-of-the-Loom as well as its major competitors (Hanes, Russell). For each of its key distributors, a customized Web site has been created that allows distributors to accept orders at all times. The typical site includes on-line access to the distributor's product catalog (including products that are competitors to ActiveWear), inventory levels, customer credit limit information, and the ability to place a bulk order. The sites were created via an alliance with a firm in the software industry (Connect Inc.), funded by Active-Wear at no charge to the distributor. The expected benefits, in addition to improved distributor relationships, are costs savings for all trading partners and the promise of attracting new customers with one-stop shopping and increased sales. The funding of the Web sites is now sponsored by the Chief Operating Officer, and the Chief Information Officer has responsibilities for the technical logistics and vendor alliances.

In return for sponsoring the Web site development, Fruit-of-the-Loom places its banner on the Web page and also controls the substitution rules for the orders. As expected, the rules favor Fruit-of-the-Loom alternatives. By sponsoring the development of Web sites for its large distributors, it has created a new marketing channel for its strategic business partners. In mid-1997, ActiveWear's managers were reporting increased revenues.

E-Communities   Our fourth example is a new type of EC application that exploits the global, distributed nature of the Internet user population: a business designed to support virtual communities of people that share a common interest. (This account is based on Hof et al., 1997, and updates from GeoCities. The company's website is at www.geocities.com.) Some

Internet surfers seek a "sense of community—the cyberspace equivalent of the bar at TV's *Cheers* where everybody knows your e-mail address." GeoCities.com is a fast-growing metropolis with a population of over 2.1 million and with thousands of new residents "arriving every day" in cyberspace. The brainchild of David Bohnett, the idea was to create on-line neighborhoods (cyberhoods) in which virtual residents who have shared interests ("homesteaders") provide the content. The company provides free personal home pages in a "themed" community and a free e-mail account (see Figure 7.10).

The site has a grassroots spirit: GeoCities provides the structure and leading-edge tools for creating and updating home pages, as well as help resources for using their utilities. The members take it from there. By 1998 GeoCities had become a top-ranked Web site, with 40 neighborhoods, each with blocks of 100 home pages each.

About 10 percent of the revenues generated from the site come from premium services to homesteaders who have created home pages at the site, such as more storage space for a home page and a personalized URL. Sales to advertisers (company sponsors) contributed 90 percent of revenues for 1997 and the first half of 1998. Company sponsors pay a monthly fee for disk space for their commercial home page, listed as an icon in a neighborhood directory. Companies can also advertise with banner ads on the home pages of consenting members—a "privilege" the virtual resident pays a premium rate for and in turn wins bonus points toward freebies such as frequent-flier miles. The 1997 revenues were $4.6 million.

The benefits for the end-consumer are free home page storage in their preferred community. The benefit for businesses is to provide a new marketing channel proven to be effective in attracting new customers who "stay put long enough to absorb their ad messages." The site sponsorships are perceived to be less intrusive to the end-consumer than typical Web ads. For example, Microsoft sponsors a Programmers Pavilion, and Visa Inc. sponsors Restaurant Row, a restaurant review area. The possibilities for collecting marketing data on members that have chosen to join a particular neighborhood for which demographics can be defined (such as residence with science fiction buffs or Silicon Valley nerds, with interest in Italian

Figure 7.10 GeoCities Home Page (GeoCities © 1995–1998. All rights reserved.)

restaurants) appears to also be a major potential benefit for these site sponsors and owners.

MANAGING STRATEGIC ELECTRONIC COMMERCE APPLICATIONS

In this section we focus on some of the key management issues associated with EC applications as they are beginning to reach their take-off point. Based on the four examples in the last section, we first discuss some of the Web strategies that have been used by these traditional existing firms and intially successful Web-based businesses, as well as some Web-based pioneers that have not yet found commercial success. Then we briefly look at some special management issues associated with developing, implementing, and operating EC applications today: developing applications with emerging versus mainstream technologies and effectively managing external business relationships associated with EC applications.

Web Strategies

In our four detailed examples of Internet Applications in the prior section, we included two examples of existing businesses and two examples of new Web-based businesses. Below we first discuss the Web strategies that we can infer from these two existing businesses. Then we compare some successfuly new business strategies with some strategies for unproven pioneers.

Existing Firms 3M and Fruit-of-the-Loom are examples of early EC applications by *existing businesses.* For existing firms, one of the key management challenges is how to integrate Web development efforts with ongoing business and application development efforts.

- 3M is pursing an *evolutionary strategy,* migrating EDI and product catalog applications from private networks to the Internet and exploring the Internet as a new channel for both direct sales and customer service.

3M is a manufacturer of diverse products and a heavy investor in EDI applications. Given its large prior investment, 3M therefore appears to be extending its earlier EC strategy, which focused on supply-chain and product-chain logistics efficiencies. By the mid-1990s, 3M had already found that applications using documents and e-mail are particularly well suited to Internet technologies.

- Fruit-of-the-Loom has created a *new marketing and sales channel* for a critical stakeholder—its *distributors;* by sponsoring the development of Web sites for its large distributors, it has created a new distribution channel under its own control.

Fruit-of-the-Loom is pursuing an approach similar to the American Airlines' SABRE reservation system described previously. Their overall goal is to achieve competitive advantage from being a "channel master." In other words, rather than initiate a strategy to replace its distributors (disintermediation), Fruit-of-the-Loom has opted to strengthen ties with its distributors. Fruit-of-the-Loom is also the first mover, with Web sites for its distributors described as state-of-the-art. One of its major competitors (Hanes) has developed a Web site of its own in partial response and reports seeing ActiveWear's early move as a potential threat to Hanes' market position (Radosevich, 1996).

Note also that the Fruit-of-the-Loom effort was spearheaded by a marketing vice president, who bankrolled the initial pilot from the marketing budget. This type of sponsorship is especially important with applications using new technologies. Sometimes a pilot is needed to find out the potential costs and benefits of a new type of application. After the initial pilot effort, however, the chief information officer was the one to demonstrate to the ActiveWear board the first Web site developed for a large distributor. This led to endorsement by top management and the bankrolling of the next wave of development (for more than 20

distributors) by the chief operating officer. At this point the Web site development effort became more of a mainstream effort, with the IS organization responsible for resolving the technology issues. In Chapters 10–12 we will see other examples of successful partnership relationships between user-managers and IS managers in order to successfully identify, develop, and implement important strategic applications.

Successful New Businesses   Amazon and GeoCities are examples of entrepreneurial businesses that take advantage of EC opportunities on the Web without being constrained by business practices of an existing firm. The first is a retailer; the second is a new kind of intermediary.

- Amazon is a *new direct retailer,* creating a new way of selling books over cyberspace that takes advantage of the electronic search and linking capabilities of the Web and third-party distribution channels.
- GeoCities is a *new intermediary* for the creation of virtual communities of people who share a common interest. The business facilitates Web site creation and electronic meetings for members of a community as well as facilitates advertising to a community by relevant companies.

Both the Amazon and GeoCities examples demonstrate that entirely new businesses can be created with a relatively low start-up cost, compared to traditional businesses. Of course, this also means that these start-ups are easily copied by competitors. Whether or not the first mover advantage noted for some of the proprietary systems of the 1980s will translate into a sustainable advantage, or even survival, in the new EC arena remains to be determined.

Both sites are also examples of successful practices for these new types of businesses by their founders: the identification of a Web-user market, designing a creative Web site that increases awareness of a company's products, and developing an electronic relationship with potential customers.

GeoCities appears to be a riskier business venture because it is an entirely new kind of business. There has been considerable debate about the long-term of e-communities, but some observers have suggested that Internet communities could be a major force for shaping the electronic marketplace (Hof et al., 1997). One of the business challenges here is that consumers appear to wield much more power in a marketplace that facilitates easily accessible price comparisons and puts large and small businesses on a much more equal footing. For businesses that choose to be a community sponsor, the potential downsides are potentially daunting. For example, advertisers in GeoCities communities have little control over community members' comments about them. These virtual residents may also move a whole community in a direction other than what was intended by the site's sponsor.

Unproven Pioneers   Not all early Web-based businesses have been successful. In some cases, the business may simply not be providing a viable product or service for the current Netizens, using the available technologies. In other cases, the EC hurdles faced by these businesses may be directly related to the newness of the Internet as an electronic commerce medium.

For example, hundreds of companies became pioneer Web publishers, but very few pioneers were able to build a lucrative electronic-publishing business (Clark, 1997; Levy, 1997). Among the new business shut-downs have been Knight-Ridder Inc.'s Viewtron (after losing $50 million) and American Cybercast's on-line soap opera "The Spot." Some Web publishers are new start-up businesses, whereas others are extensions of large media companies with deeper pockets. Many of the publishers based their business plans on subscription fees, but subscriptions have been a tougher sell than anticipated. That means revenues are dependent on advertising. In 1996 more than nine hundred companies were reportedly competing for about $300 million in ads, and the 10 biggest publishers were capturing two-thirds of these.

Some Web journalists have also complained that they are playing on an unlevel field. For example, Web journalists associated with the *New York Times* may experience few problems with gaining the same access to key informants as their print journalist counterparts, whereas journalists for an independent Web-based venture may be ignored. Further, Web journalists associated with a TV outlet may encounter difficulties not faced by journalists working for an established print medium (see sidebar "Hurdles Faced by Web Journalists"). Journalism experts point out, however, that similar hurdles were faced by TV start-up CNN before its real-time Persian Gulf War coverage catapulted the network to the top of the TV ratings. Web reporters may therefore need to patiently wait for their own public awareness coup.

Another example of an unproven Web-based business idea is the "shopping mall" concept. For example, in August 1996 IBM opened the doors to its virtual shopping mall World Avenue (www.worldavenue.com). The public Web strategy was to provide a secure shopping mall in cyberspace, developed by a world-class vendor known for reliable computer solutions, that both merchants and consumers would want to buy and sell in. However, World Avenue

---

HURDLES FACED BY WEB JOURNALISTS

ESPN SportsZone, a WWW site with nationally recognized columnists and over 250,000 readers every day, had a problem at the Atlanta Olympics: Its reporters were denied access to all events. Why was SportsZone shut out? While print reporters get easy access to the Games, TV reporters are often cut off because one network pays for the broadcast rights; and Olympic officials couldn't decide if the Web was more like print or television. Plus, "we had our own Web site," says Billy Payne, CEO of the Atlanta Committee for the Olympic Games.

Such is the fate of journalists working on the Web. Despite booming readership, Web reporters say they have had trouble getting everything from press kits to credentials for big events like the NCAA basketball tournament and the Academy Awards. Some skeptical public relations officials say they treat Web journalists as second-class citizens because they're creating second-class journalism. Many of the skeptics say they prefer to wait until journalism standards improve on the Web. Because of time pressures, some Web journalists don't check facts as thoroughly as their print counterparts. The pay and hours aren't always ideal, leading to many greener reporters on-line.

The lack of respect encountered by Web journalists is hardly surprising. After all, cable news programs weren't taken seriously by a wide audience until the Persian Gulf War, when CNN—with its constant availability and real-time coverage—became the primary source of information for the conflict. And experts say radio and television reporters had to overcome similar hurdles with the respective advent of each medium.

[Adapted from Quick, 1996]

closed its doors within one year (see sidebar "IBM Shopping Mall Closes Down"). This close-down was at least partially due to public perceptions about the lack of security for electronic payment systems available during this time period.

Special Management Issues

The overnight start-ups and shut-downs of these pioneer Web-based businesses underscore one of the key characteristics of EC applications on the Internet in the late 1990s: The initial investment can be modest, while the opportunities for learning how to successfully do business on the Internet are great. Below we discuss management issues directly related to the newness of the Internet technologies and interorganizational nature of many of these applications.

IBM SHOPPING MALL CLOSES DOWN

A shopping mall in cyberspace is about to face the wrecking ball. World Avenue, the grandly titled shopping mall on the WWW that IBM announced with much fanfare a year ago, is quietly preparing to close its doors. So what happened? When it came to shoppers, World Avenue was more like a deserted street, producing minimal revenue not only for mall tenants like department-store chain Gottschalks Inc., but also for IBM, which had planned to make money by taking a cut of every World Avenue transaction.

Visitors to the site (www.worldavenue.com) see a screen that welcomes shoppers with a simple list of stores organized by categories—not all that different from the guides found on most shopping-mall kiosks. Clicking into a "store" calls up photos and descriptions of merchandise. Shoppers add selections to an electronic "shopping basket" and then pay for them in a single on-line transaction.

The mall's untimely demise raises vexing questions about what is the right approach for on-line retailing. Should stores join on-line malls as gathering places where Internet shoppers will converge, or should they stay independent with stand-alone Web sites of their own? IBM says it will limit itself to supplying technology for shopping ventures operated by others.

[Adapted from Weber, 1997]

Emerging vs. Mainstream Technologies **Key IT** management challenges are related to the fact that Web-based technologies are still in their infancy. (It has been suggested that the World Wide Web actually stands for the Wild Wild West.) As we have seen, the activity level on the Internet has been at a frenzied pace. The risks are high, but the common perception appears to be that the risks for being on the sidelines may be even higher. As a result, many firms are conducting business transactions that are dependent on the reliability of both new products (hardware and software) and a transport highway that they essentially have no control over. The risks for an existing organization would appear to be great. Not only are there operational risks, but the adage that "nobody knows you're a dog on the Internet" doesn't appear to hold true any more (see Figure 7.11).

Many Web users also have little respect for sites that aren't updated or even that look old. The costs of keeping up with Web technology advancements (e.g., Java applets, RealAudio, RealVideo) are rising. Entirely new approaches, such as "push" technologies (Webcasting) can appear almost overnight. As we have

"On the Internet, nobody knows you're a dog."

Figure 7.11 Early Internet Cartoon (Peter Steiner
© 1993 from the New Yorker Collection. All rights reserved.)

seen in the past, a single product given away free to individual end-users can quickly result in new EC application opportunities as well as new IT management challenges. For example, Netscape's browser giveaway led to a radical increase in the demand for Internet access; PointCast's Webcasting software giveaway led to a major increase in demand for network bandwidth within organizations.

Two guidelines for managing Web development projects take into account this development context: It is better not to take a long time to develop a Web application, because there is so much change in the technology and Web population, and it is helpful to recognize that, when working in a new technology arena, some mistakes will be made (Slater, 1996–1997).

Emerging Roles   The Internet phenomenon has also led to the development of a new role—the **Webmaster.** Premium prices for Webmaster skills were being reported by the late 1990s. The demand for these skills exists not only in established companies, but also in start-up businesses (like GeoCities and Amazon) and consulting firms. Today's firms frequently rely on vendors who develop off-the-shelf software for Web site creation as well as vendors to manage Web sites. If all the needed skill sets for developing effective EC applications on the Internet were resident in one person, then a Webmaster would need to be a programmer, creative artist, and network management specialist (Nash and Hoffman, 1995).

In most IS departments in the second half of the 1990s, Internet technologies were still viewed as emerging, immature technologies. Web application development responsibilities resided within emerging technology units, and user departments. However, just as we saw in Chapter 1 that the line manager is relied on for identifying and implementing strategic applications in the Wired Society, user-managers are being relied on for the content of an external Web site. In addition, today's tools make it increasingly easy for non-IS specialists to develop home pages. Whether the Webmaster is an IS specialist or non-IS specialist, the fact that Web technologies are still emerging means additional challenges for IS managers and user-managers (see sidebar "Webmaster Role"). In Part III we will look at some of the risk/benefit tradeoffs associated with applications based on new technologies, as

---

WEBMASTER ROLE

IT executives and Webmasters are likely to butt heads on a number of different issues. The Webmaster's job is to experiment with unproven technology to develop and build internal and external Web sites. The faster a Webmaster builds a site, the faster a company can use it to grab new business opportunities. Anyone who slows down the pace is wrongheaded and obstinate. Immersed as they are in this burgeoning technical area, Web builders can also view the Web myopically as the ultimate computing solution.

"The CIO is the anchor of the IT institution and the Webmaster is a solo space explorer, off looking at way-out-in-front technology." (Harry Max, founding webmaster at Virtual Vineyards)

[Adapted from Hildebrand, 1997]

---

well as applications developed by non-IS specialists (user-developed applications).

Interorganizational versus Intraorganizational Relationships   Many of the application examples discussed earlier are interorganizational systems that require a cooperative relationship between trading partners. In the early years of EDI applications, customers often were able to coerce their suppliers into participation. Senn (1988) reports on two approaches: the carrot and the stick. In the carrot approach, the supplier may offer the customer a cash discount for electronically transmitted orders or the customer may offer the supplier an increase in the amount of business with that supplier. In the stick approach, the business partner with customer power is more likely to be sending the message "link up or lose out." For example, major automotive and retailing players, like General Motors (GM) and WalMart, basically told their suppliers that not developing EDI capabilities would lead to fewer or no orders.

The carrot approach still appears to be valid for Internet applications. However, today there appears to be an additional incentive for existing businesses to invest in Internet-based EC applications: Businesses are interested in experimenting with Web applications because of the tremendous EC potential for the future and high awareness among the U.S. public. The Fruit-of-the-Loom example also demonstrates the potential power of the Internet channel master. Here, the supplier is offering a carrot to its major customers (distributors): free development of a Web site for the distributor, in return for a buy-in to a distribution channel controlled by the supplier firm!

Managing the partnership between trading partners is also a critical success factor for EC applications. Establishing a cooperative climate in which partners trust each other has been reported to be critical for the success of business-to-business applications like EDI. Large EC applications also frequently are dependent on an external vendor to provide a wide area network, a VAN, or Internet service. Many external Web site development efforts by existing businesses involve vendor alliances in order to take advantage of scarce Internet technology expertise, as well as vendor-developed software and services. Chapter 15 is devoted to the important management issue of managing strategic relationships.

The Future of Electronic Commerce

"The Internet is the most important single development to come along since the IBM PC was introduced in 1981."—Internal Microsoft memo by Bill Gates, May 26, 1995 (Adapted from Clark and Rigdon, 1995)

The Internet has already had major impacts on organizations and individuals. However, electronic commerce on the Internet is still in its infancy. Today's Web technologies are still immature technologies. Web vendors appear and disappear overnight. The computer and communications infrastructure of the Internet is also still under construction.

The Internet of the late 1990s therefore lacks many of the characteristics of the infrastructure envisioned for the next century, but it is our closest approximation to what it will look like. Bill Gates, CEO of Microsoft, shared his vision for tomorrow's Internet infrastructure in his book *The Road Ahead*:

- Telephone lines and television cables "generalized into" a single, digital utility
- Easy-to-use information appliances, including lap desks, TV set-top boxes, wallet PCs, and e-books

- Easy-to-use navigation systems that query, filter, hyperlink, and spatially navigate under a smart agent

In the first edition of Gates' book, an implementation date close to 2005 was anticipated, based on an infrastructure investment of $120 billion.

In contrast, Vice President Al Gore's vision of a national information superhighway in the early 1990s emphasized a major national concern: the creation of an unfair advantage for a segment of the U.S. population that can not afford to access this highway. Gore's vision of a national information superhighway included the following:

- linking homes, businesses, government for information, education, and buyer/seller transactions
- using high speed transmission of multimedia (text, audio, images, video)
- ensuring costs that do not create "haves" and "have-nots"

Whatever form tomorrow's global Internet takes, most agree that the impact will be huge. The Internet as a communications vehicle has already had a major impact on the way we communicate. As discussed earlier, since the mid-1990s, many businesses have been dependent on the Internet as a communications channel, if not a vital EC channel. Consumers have also discovered the Internet as a cheap medium for information and communication. The telecommunications industry has apparently found the Internet to be a mixed blessing. Overall telecommunications demand is high, but unlimited global access via the Internet is available at the flat-rate cost of a local telephone call. As an example, for families with twenty-somethings who are geographically scattered, long-distance phonecalls for staying in touch are being replaced by local phone calls to a service provider and "free" e-mail.

For consumers, the Internet provides access to an incomparable array of information resources. Tomorrow's consumers include today's elementary and secondary school students who are learning to use browsers and search tools in order to retrieve information from this global resource. However, information retrieval via the Internet poses a new type of problem for consumers and businesses. A newspaper or book published by a major publisher has an external stamp of approval on it, and a printed report distributed by a press can be assumed to be a credible source. On the Internet, however, there is no certification process for Web site content. (As discussed earlier, there also is no universally accepted process for censorship.) The users of electronic forms of information must therefore learn new skills in order to evaluate an information source. In addition, Web sources are highly volatile: What is here today may be gone tomorrow.

Some predictions have also been made about the impacts of the Internet on industry structures. Benjamin and Wigand (1995) predict a redistribution of profits among retailers, producers, and consumers. For example, they predict that EC will lower coordination costs for producers and retailers and lower physical distribution costs. Our application examples for EC via the Internet suggest both of these benefits are being sought today. In addition, these and other authors have forecast the death of some wholesales and retailers (disintermediation) due to the option for direct buyer-seller interactions via EC on the Internet. However, the elimination of intermediaries does not appear to be a universal trend, at least not in the near future. As we saw in the application examples in this chapter, intermediary roles still exist. In fact, some of the business examples we looked at involved new intermediary roles for electronic commerce: businesses that create a new marketing niche (GeoCities) or new distributor networks (Fruit-of-the-Loom). On the other hand, we also looked at examples of disintermediation. American Airlines, 3M, and many other established firms dependent on intermediary roles in the past are indeed already experimenting with bypassing the intermediary, and direct producer-consumer sales transactions are already occurring via the Internet.

Further, during the past two decades we have seen a trend away from vertical integration, firms acquiring their own suppliers and their own distributors. During the same time, we have also witnessed a growth in IT linkages between trading partners. These two trends certainly appear complementary. IT has enabled firms to achieve some benefits across different organizations that could only be achieved within organizational boundaries in the past. In other words, improved customer and supplier relationships are being accomplished not through reporting hierarchies in the same business, but through cooperative partnering across businesses. In fact, business-to-business applications such as we saw between H.E. Butt and its primary suppliers create a kind of vertical quasi-integration (Zaheer and Venkatraman, 1994).

As we approach the new millennium, it is clear that many years will pass before the impacts of the Internet explosion on our society will be known. From our past, we can point to the enormous impact on society traceable back to the diffusion of the telephone and the automobile. These impacts are both positive and negative. For example, in the U.S., the combination of automobiles and the post-World War II interstate highway system in the U.S. has led to positive impacts on worker mobility and independence due to a lowered dependence on public transportation. However, many see the decline of public transportation as a long-term negative impact, due to the environmental destruction attributed to this same phenomenon.

There are also many controversial issues related to the societal impacts of computerization. These include potential economic and computer literacy impacts. They also include potential impacts related to work life, class divisions in society, human safety, democratization, employment, education, gender biases, military security, and health (Dunlop and Kling, 1991). Perhaps the best forecast from today's vantage point is that we expect the impacts from the rise of EC to have both negative and positive impacts. The next chapter explores some of the social, ethical, and political issues that are evident today.

Review Questions

1. Define electronic commerce.

2. What is meant by the "reach of IT"?

3. Contrast an interorganizational system with the types of systems described in Chapters 5 and 6.

4. Why haven't other airlines developed their own reservation systems?

5. What types of documents are typically transmitted in EDI applications?

6. Why were EDI standards sometimes developed by a consortia of firms within an industry?

7. What EDI benefits were achieved by 3M? H.E. Butt? TradeNet?

8. Contrast the list of benefits from EC via the Internet versus EDI.

9. What is a domain name, and how does an organization acquire one?

10. Define the term firewall.

11. Summarize the four major constraints for EC on the Internet.

12. How does an extranet differ from an external Web site?

13. What EC benefits were achieved via the Internet by 3M? Fruit-of-the-Loom?

14. What benefit to the consumer does a business like Amazon.com provide?

15. Describe the Webmaster role.

DISCUSSION QUESTIONS

1. Briefly describe the evolution of the SABRE system and the lessons that can be learned from this strategic application.

2. What additional complexities occur with inter-organizational systems that are not found with intraorganizational systems?

3. Provide an argument to either support or refute the following: In interorganizational systems, the customer holds the greatest power.

4. Identify some of the similarities between just-in-time (JIT) initiatives by manufacturers and quick response (QR) initiatives by retailers.

5. Comment on how likely it is for the U.S. to develop a TradeNet or MediNet such as exists in Singapore.

6. Briefly describe the potential of the Internet as a new marketing channel for end-consumers. Include in your answer some examples for existing businesses as well as new Web-based businesses.

7. If you have purchased goods on the Internet, describe your experiences—including your payment method.

8. Describe a range of products and services that you think end-consumers would be most likely, and least likely, to purchase via the Internet today. Justify your answers.

9. Choose three firms within an established industry that have a Web presence. Visit their Web sites, and analyze them according to the benefits discussed in the chapter.

10. Comment on the advantages and disadvantages of reading the news via a newspaper versus a Web site. Then comment on the advantages and disadvantages of news broadcasting via a TV versus Web software.

11. Summarize what Web strategies you think are most likely for large firms in an established industry.

12. Describe some of the ways the Internet has impacted the way you spend your leisure time and the way you do research for a college course.

REFERENCES

1989. *A Note on Electronic Data Interchange.* Boston: Harvard Business School, #9–190–022.

1990. *Singapore Tradenet: A tale of one city.* Boston: Harvard Business School, #9–191–009.

1991. *Chrysler Corporation: JIT and EDI (A).* Boston: Harvard Business School, #9–191–146.

1991. *Sara Lee Knit Products: Quick Response at Hanes.* Boston: Harvard Business School, #9–191–021.

1991. "Technical, organizational and managerial aspects of implementing EDI." *Gesellschft fur Mathematik und Datenverarbeitung* (September).

1994. *H.E. Butt Grocery Company: A Leader in ECR Implementation.* Boston: Harvard Business School, #9–195–125.

Applegate, Lynda M., F. Warren McFarlan, and James L. McKenney. 1996. *Corporate Information Systems Management.* Chicago: Irwin.

Applegate, Lynda M., Clyde W. Holsapple, Ravi Kalakota, Franz J. Radermacher, and Andrew B. Whinston. 1996. "Electronic commerce: Building blocks of new business opportunity." *Journal of Organization Computing and Electronic Commerce* 6 (1): 1–10.

Benjamin, Robert, and Rolf Wigand. 1995. "Electronic markets and virtual value chains on the information superhighway." *Sloan Management Review* 36 (Winter): 62–72.

Clark, Don. 1997. "Facing early losses, some Web publishers begin to pull the plug." *Wall Street Journal,* January 14: A1.

Clark, Don and Joan E. Rigdon. 1995. "Stripped-down PCs will be talk of Comdex," *Wall Street Journal,* November 10: B1.

Clemons, Eric K. 1991. "Evaluation of strategic investments in information technology." *Communications of the ACM* 34 (January): 23–36.

Dunlop, Charles, and Rob Kling. 1991. "Introduction: Social controversies about computerization," in *Computerization and Controversy,* ed. by C. Dunlop and R. Kling. Boston: Academic Press, Inc.: 1–12.

Eng, Paul M. 1997. "Get your hands off my .com." *Business Week,* July 28: 88.

Felsenthal, Edward, and Jared Sandberg. 1997. "High court strikes down Internet smut law." *Wall Street Journal,* June 27: B1.

Gates, Bill. 1995. *The Road Ahead.* New York: Viking Penguin.

Hart, Paul, and Carol Saunders. 1997. "Power and trust: Critical factors in the adoption and use of electronic data interchange." *Organization Science* 8 (January–February): 23–41.

Hildebrand, Carol. 1996–97. "Electronic commerce pioneers: Virtual companies." *CIO,* December 15, 1996–January 1, 1997: 63.

Hildebrand, Carol. 1997. "Web war." *CIO,* April 15: 74–78.

Himelstein, Linda, Ellen Neuborne, and Paul M. Eng. 1997. "Web ads start to click." *Business Week,* October 6: 128–135.

Hof, Robert D., Seanna Browder, and Peter Elstrom. 1997. "Internet communities." *Business Week,* May 5: 64–80.

Hoffman, Donna L., William D. Kalsbeek, and Thomas P. Novak. 1996. "Internet and Web use in the U.S." *Communications of the ACM* 39 (12): 36–46.

Hopper, Max D. 1990. "Rattling SABRE—New ways to compete on information." *Harvard Business Review,* May–June: 118–125.

Jacobs, Paula. 1997. "The domain name game." *ComputerWorld* 31 (September 29): 85–86.

Kalakota, Ravi, and Andrew B. Whinston. 1996. *Electronic Commerce: A Manager's Guide.* Reading, Mass.: Addison Wesley Longman, Inc.

Kavan, C. Bruce and David Van Over. 1991. "Electronic data interchange: An analysis of current adopters." University of Georgia, College of Business Administration, Department of Management, Working paper #49.

Keen, Peter G. W. 1991. *Shaping the Future: Business Design through Information Technology.* Boston: Harvard Business School Press.

Kettinger, William J., Varun Grover, and Albert H. Segars. 1995. "Do strategic systems really pay off? An analysis of classic strategic IT cases." *Information Systems Management,* Winter: 35–43.

Laudon, Kenneth C. and Jane P. Laudon. 1996. *Management Information Systems: Organization and Technology,* 4th edition. Upper Saddle River, NJ: Prentice Hall.

Levy, Steven. 1997. "What shakeout?" *Newsweek,* April 14: 82–86.

Liang, Thou-Yick. 1992. "Electronic data interchange systems in Singapore: A strategic utilization." *International Business Schools Computing Quarterly* 4 (Spring): 43–47.

[Louis Harris & Associates, Inc.] 1997. "A census in cyberspace." *Business Week,* May 5: 84–85; "A lot of looking, not much buying—yet." *Business Week,* October 6: 140.

McCubbrey, Donald J., and Joze Gricar. 1996. "The EDI Project in Slovenia: A case study and model for developing countries." *Information Technology & People* 8 (2): 6–16.

McKeown, Patrick G., and Richard T. Watson. 1997. *Metamorphosis: A Guide to the World Wide Web & Electronic Commerce,* vers. 2.0. New York: John Wiley & Sons.

Nash, Kim S. 1997. "Cybercash at risk: Money laws lacking." *ComputerWorld* 30 (December 23, 1996–January 2, 1997): 1, 16.

Nash, Kim S., and Thomas Hoffman. 1995. "Webmasters." *ComputerWorld* 29 (October 23): 1, 32–33.

Panurach, Patiwat. 1996. "Money in electronic commerce: Digital cash, electronic fund transfer, and e-cash." *Communications of the ACM* 39 (June): 45–50.

Porter, Michael E. 1985. *Competitive Advantage: Creating and Sustaining Superior Performance.* New York: Free Press.

Porter, Michael E., and Victor E. Millar. 1985. "How information gives you competitive advantage," *Harvard Business Review* 63 (July–August): 149–160.

Quick, Rebecca. 1996. "Web journalists are finding themselves out of the loop." *Wall Street Journal,* August 14: B5.

Radosevich, Lynda. 1996. "Fruits of their labors." *CIO,* November 15: 56–64.

Radosevich, Lynda. 1996–1997. "The once and future EDI." *CIO,* December 15–January 1: 66–77.

Row, Heath. 1996–1997. "The electric handshake." *CIO,* December 15–January 1: 49–63.

Schiesel, Seth. 1997. "On-line ire still directed at company." *Wall Street Journal,* January 31: C1.

Senn, James A. 1988. "Electronic data interchange: An opportunity for fundamental business alliance." *SIM Network,* September–October.

Senn, James A. 1992. "Electronic data interchange: The elements of implementation." *Information Systems Management* (Winter): 45–53.

Settles, Craig. 1996. "A dose of reality." *Internet World* (July): 63–64.

Slater, Derek. 1996–1997. "Sticking with strategy." *CIO,* December 15–January 1: 80–89.

Venkatraman, N., and Ellen Christiaanse. 1996. "Electronic channels for expertise exploitation: An empirical test of airline-travel agency relationships." *Academy of Management Best Paper Proceedings,* Fifty-sixth Annual Meeting: 318–322.

Weber, Thomas E. 1997. "IBM's electronic mall to close up shop." *Wall Street Journal,* June 10: B1.

Young, Scott. 1996. "Taking measure." *Internet World* (July): 66–67.

Zaheer, Akbar, and N. Venkatraman. 1994. "Determinants of electronic integration in the insurance industry: An empirical test." *Management Science* 40 (May): 549.

Zgodzinski, David. 1997. "Click here to pay." *Internet World,* September: 61–68.

CHAPTER 8

SOCIAL, ETHICAL, AND POLITICAL ISSUES

As we have seen, information technology is becoming a core resource for organizations in today's global economy, and is impacting, if not determining, what organizations produce and how they are managed. Anyone with a casual familiarity with today's news media knows that information technology is influencing the whole of society, not just the business arena. Information technology is rapidly changing our lives, and this process of change is ongoing. The information revolution is often compared with the industrial revolution in terms of the overall impact that the industrial revolution had upon human civilization. We are in the midst of a seismic shift, which gives rise to important issues for society, organizations, and individuals.

In this chapter we will first explore some of the impacts, both good and bad, that information technology is having on the way that humankind lives and works and upon how we view ourselves. Although many of these social concerns are beyond the control of individuals, we need to be aware of them in order to limit their impact insofar as possible. The vast diversity of these concerns is somewhat overwhelming, so we have attempted to reduce confusion by organizing them into the following groups: social benefits of IT, quasi-legal social issues, social issues involving individual rights, and long-term issues for society.

Those who control the use of information technology have immense power, and along with power comes responsibility, so managers must face ethical issues in their use of information technology. In the middle sections of this chapter we explore some of these ethical issues.

The last part of this chapter explores the internal political issues associated with the use of information technology in organizations. Because information is valuable to individuals as well as to organizations, when someone attempts to take control of information it is not uncommon to encounter fierce resistance. Many systems development efforts have failed because their sponsors did not take into account the politics of information, so it is very important that managers understand the politics of information technology. Political issues will arise again and again in the rest of this book.

SOME SOCIAL BENEFITS OF IT

Information technology has had, and continues to have, such a broad positive impact that it would require an entire book to present a comprehensive overview of its influence. We will give but a few highlights that illustrate the breadth and depth of this impact to set the stage for our discussion of the social issues raised by IT.

Economic Growth

There is wide agreement that we are in transition from an industrial to an information-based economy. Signs of this revolution are all around: supermarkets and bar codes; banks and ATM machines; FAX machines and e-mail; database marketing and just-in-time manufacturing; and on and on. In industry after industry, information technology has inspired innovations, raised efficiency, lowered prices, and increased profits.

In 1995 over half of the U.S. workforce was using computers on the job, and over 50 percent of the capital investment was in information technology. Erik Brynjolfsson and Lorin M. Hitt of Massachusetts Institute of Technology "surveyed some 400 large companies to measure the effect of investment in information technology on output per employee. They found evidence that the return on investment in information systems could exceed 50 percent and that such systems have led to improvements in product quality, product variety, and customer service" (Farrell, 1995). Since 1995 productivity growth has taken a jump, and much of this improvement is ascribed to more effective use of information technology.

The bottom line is that information technology is enabling us to compete in the worldwide economy despite the low-cost labor of the developing countries, and to expand our economy without igniting inflation.

Interconnecting People

Communications technology has exploded during recent years. We have gone from local broadcast to cable to satellite TV. The telephone network used to strain to transmit data at 1,200 bits per second, but now we do not hesitate to use 56,000 bits per second modems from our homes, and businesses can get as much bandwidth as they want to pay for. Cellular phone usage is exploding in the U.S., and underdeveloped countries are rapidly expanding telephone service by skipping the installation of expensive land lines and going directly to cellular phones. First the FAX machine and then the Internet have swept through the world like wildfire.

As a consequence of developments in communications technology, the world is rapidly becoming networked, and we recognize that the computer network is the fundamental information technology, not just the computer (See Chapter 4). Of course, the network and the computer are inseparable, for the switches and routers in the network are specialized computers, and cellular telephones and satellite transmission would be impossible without computers. Likewise, computers would be far less useful without the ability to communicate via networks.

As noted in the box "Internet U," communications technology is beginning to have an impact on higher education. Also, via the Internet, high school students are participating in sophisticated science, such as analyzing the artifacts from archaeological digs.

As noted in Chapter 1, the network revolution has made possible new organizational forms and ways of organizing and carrying out work. The virtual corporation, transnational organizations, the home office, and other forms of workforce decentralization are all enabled by the network. Not only has the Internet become a growing vehicle for transacting business, but it has also enabled the development of worldwide "virtual communities" focused around common interests

INTERNET U—NO IVY, NO WALLS, NO KEG PARTIES

Several schools, including Duke, Ohio University, and Purdue have recently launched Internet-based M.B.A. programs for far-flung execs. Other institutions have begun offering electronic graduate programs in fields from computer science to nursing, and would-be liberal arts majors can collect B.A. degrees from places like the University of Alaska without the need to invest in earmuffs. About 300 colleges and universities now offer virtual degrees, says Pam Dixon, author of the book *Virtual College.* "And in 10 years, cybercolleges will definitely be part of mainstream education," she says. Richard Staelin, director of the Duke program, is similarly optimistic. "This is a paradigm shift in education," he says. "In five years, I believe, we'll have as many applications for our [online] M.B.A. program as for our regular one."

Western Governors University (WGU) is a sort of electronic consortium of some 20 universities in 13 western states that will allow students to take classes from any of the institutions or from a combination of all of them. Some futurists go so far as to predict the demise of conventional teachers. But not even staunch proponents of on-line education believe academia's hallowed halls will disappear any time soon. Says WGU executive director Jeffery Livingston, "There's no anticipation that it's either technology or a traditional campus—this is just another alternative." And so it will likely remain, at least until they devise a way to download beer.

[Adapted from Hamilton and Miller, 1997]

of the participants (see Hoff et al., 1997). And there are some who foresee that the Internet may become the vehicle for bringing growing numbers of people from developing countries into the information age. (See box "Closing the Information Gap.")

Serving the Handicapped

Information technology has made life easier and more productive for the handicapped. For example, Stephen Hawking, renowned Cambridge physicist who is disabled by Lou Gehrig's disease, can use only a few muscles and cannot speak. He converses using a special hand-held pad to select words from a computer and construct sentences that are spoken by the computer's voice synthesizer. He also used the computer system to write the best-selling book, *A Brief History of Time,* and to publish a dozen academic papers. Hawking says he likes the synthesizer, but "the only trouble is, it gives me an American accent" (Kremer, 1993).

There exist hundreds of ingenious devices that allow the severely handicapped to interact with computers. For example, Eyegaze, a $19,000 computer system developed by LC Technologies, Inc., uses a video camera, located beneath a monitor, that takes 30 pictures per second of the user's eyeball to determine where on the monitor the person is looking. A computer keyboard can be displayed on the monitor so that a person can "type" into the computer by looking at each selected key for one-quarter of a second. Thus, someone able to move only one eye can operate a computer! Voice recognition systems also exist that allow a person to control the computer's functions and enter data into the computer via the spoken word (O'Brien, 1993).

IT allows the blind to "read" printed material without the help of a human reader by using a scanner with character recognition software to enter material into the computer and a voice synthesizer to speak the words. Screen-reading software recites on-screen text aloud through voice-synthesizing hardware. This equipment has greatly improved the quality of life for blind people, and has even allowed them to establish and run their own businesses.

Health Care

Information technology impacts both the practice of medicine and medical research. When medical records are maintained on computers, they can be analyzed to discover what treatments are most effective for a given condition so that physicians can standardize on the most effective treatments. Kaiser Permanente, the nation's largest and oldest HMO, established a computer database on the 84,000 diabetics among its 2.4 million Northern California members. Analyzing these data, Joseph Selby, Kaiser's associate director for health services research, found disturbing holes in how Kaiser was serving these patients. Although diabetes is the leading cause of blindness, Selby found that 15 percent to 20 percent of Kaiser's diabetic patients weren't getting their eyes checked routinely. Also, standard office visits weren't doing enough for patients battling complex problems such as obesity and stress, which make the disease worse. In response, Kaiser plans more aggressive eye-screening programs and more access to specialist nurses. Kaiser is leveraging its data to improve patient care and save money by preventing the need for future expensive treatment (Hamilton, 1997).

CLOSING THE INFORMATION GAP

Deep in the Amazon jungle, the remote village of Pukany struck a deal with British retailer Body Shop to sell essential oils from the rain forest. Nothing so unusual about that maybe. But then the tribal chief went on the Internet and told an "electronic conference" of 100 people all over Latin America how the deal was done. As another example, through a "virtual farmers market" on the Internet, Chilean potato farmers with a huge excess crop found willing buyers in Sao Paulo, Brazil.

These are examples of the use of an information system spanning all of Latin America that has been put together by the Rome-based International Fund for Agricultural Development. It has linked 500,000 poor households in 3,600 communities across the continent, with guidance by 5,000 technical staff members. The hope is that such projects will lead to bringing the power of information, once reserved for giants, to even the smallest players in the global economy.

[Adapted from Wysocki, 1997]

Computers are now used to monitor critically ill patients and quickly call attention to problems that develop. Without computers, modern imaging technologies such as CAT scans would be impossible. Drug companies are using supercomputers to model the structure of complex molecules and design drugs to treat specific illnesses. And the human genome project that is mapping human DNA could not progress without the use of computers.

SOCIAL ISSUES RELATED TO THE LAW

Despite all of the wonderful contributions made by information technology to the welfare of mankind, IT presents a number of troubling issues. In the following sections we will discuss some of these problem areas. In this section we will consider the growing problem of computer crime and the increasing difficulty of defining and protecting intellectual property rights in the information age.

Computer Crime

Without a doubt computer crime is a growth industry! The extensive networking of computers has made it easier for criminals and more difficult for law enforcement, because a criminal in another country can steal credit card numbers from files in the U.S. and use them to buy goods or pay for telephone calls anywhere in the world. Prosecution of such crimes is difficult because it requires cooperation by law enforcement agencies in several countries and it may be questionable where the crime occurred and which country's laws apply. Even local computer crimes may be difficult to prosecute because the laws that cover such crimes evolved before information technology became important, and they may be difficult to apply to the new electronic environment. Writing new laws is very difficult because it is not easy to precisely define what is criminal and what is not. Furthermore, the technology is advancing so rapidly that the laws lag behind.

No one knows how much is lost through computer crime, for a high percent of computer intrusions are not even detected, a small percent of those

detected are reported, and only a few of those reported are solved. But it is estimated that billions of dollars are lost from computer crime in the U.S. alone.

Computer crime takes many forms, including financial crimes, businesses stealing competitors' secrets, espionage agents stealing military intelligence, attacks on computers by terrorists, grudge attacks by disgruntled employees or ex-employees, attacks by "hackers" who invade systems for the fun of it, and use of information technology by criminals to facilitate their various activities.

Many financial crimes are old-fashioned embezzlements perpetrated by employees using company computers. For example, a person in the purchasing area may create purchase orders on fictitious suppliers, submit bills, and cash the payment checks. Life insurance company employees may create fake policies and file claims against them. Employees may transfer money to overseas banks and disappear, or steal customer files and sell them to competitors. In addition to these traditional transgressions, entirely new categories of crime are being created as increasingly sophisticated criminals are using IT to steal. (See box "**Identity Theft.**")

IDENTITY THEFT

Kathryn Rambo, a 28-year-old special-events planner from Los Gatos, Calif., was a recent victim of "identity theft." A woman impersonating her, with the help of information lifted from Rambo's employee-benefits form, had used Rambo's good credit to obtain a new $22,000 Jeep, five credit cards, an apartment, and a $3,000 loan. Straightening out the mess took months of angry phone calls, court appearances, and legal expenses.

Identity theft is an increasingly common crime committed by increasingly sophisticated swindlers. All they need is your full name or Social Security number, which they drop into Internet databases that serve up info like your address, phone number, employer or driver's license number. Then they're on their way—applying for credit using your good name. Security experts say identity theft's high profitability and low penalties could make it as common as auto theft in the coming century.

[Adapted from Gegax, 1997]

Sabotaging a crucial computer system can be an attractive way of "getting back" at a company for real or perceived transgressions. For example, an insurance company employee was fired from his IT job, but before he was fired he planted a "logic bomb" that went off after he left the firm and destroyed more than 160,000 commission records used to prepare the monthly payroll (Baase, 1997). Such sabotage is a serious potential problem, so in many companies when an IT person is fired or quits, that person's computer passwords are immediately canceled and he or she is watched while cleaning out his or her desk before being escorted off the premises. Of course, as the above example shows, when a person quits because of a grudge, such measures do not provide complete protection.

"Hackers," computer nerds who specialize in breaking into computer systems, have received a great deal of publicity in recent years. Many hackers break into systems for the challenge it presents and do no intentional harm. Those who break into systems to steal or to do intentional damage are often referred to as **"crackers."** For example, Kevin D. Mitnick broke into numerous computer networks, and (among other things) stole some 20,000 credit card numbers from NetCom, stole hundreds of programs from the home computer of a security expert at the San Diego Supercomputer Center, and wiped out some of the accounting records of an on-line service (see Cortese, 1995). For a fascinating account of the pursuit of a West German cracker who was extracting information from defense computers in Western nations and selling it to the Soviet KGB, see Cliff Stoll's *The Cuckoo's Egg* (1989).

Although Mitnick committed crimes and was arrested by FBI agents, break-ins by some hackers are more difficult to classify as criminal. Has a crime been committed when someone enters a computer, looks around at files, leaves a taunting message, and departs without taking or damaging anything? Although it is against the law to obtain unauthorized access to a computer, the hacker may in fact have done the organization a favor by pointing out a security weakness in the system. Even if the hacker downloads some data, nothing physical has been stolen, and the data are still there. The "hacker culture" maintains that information, rather than being property that someone can own, should be freely available to everyone.

CRACKER PHANTOMD

Starting in 1991, a young cracker, who called himself Phantomd, accomplished the biggest invasion of supposedly secure computers since the Internet was created. No one knows how many systems he broke into: It was at least several hundred and possibly thousands. Many were among the most sensitive—and supposedly secure—in the nation, including those of classified military sites, nuclear-weapons labs, bank ATM systems, *Fortune* 100 companies, even dam control systems.

Using cracker software available on the Internet, thousands of marginally skilled crackers could do what Phantomd did. Most computer experts agree that during this decade, Internet security has gotten worse. Personal correspondence, bank accounts, business transactions, local emergency systems, national defense—all have been jeopardized. Phantomd demonstrates how easily people can roam unconstrained on the information superhighway and, if they have a mind to, do overwhelming damage.

Like Phantomd, criminals could spend months trolling through the global network for systems worth cracking. After accumulating a list of targets, the criminals could in theory commit a rash of crimes in two minutes—and leave the country. If they were terrorists, they could bring down critical computer systems, black out power systems, open the sluice of a dam and, from a hotel room abroad, watch the resulting chaos on CNN. This may seem farfetched, but Dutch crackers stole information about troop movements and missile capabilities from 34 U.S. military sites during the Gulf War and offered it to the Iraqis.

[Adapted from Freedman and Mann, 1997]

Intellectual Property Rights

Society has long recognized the existence and value of intellectual property. Plagiarism, taking someone else's ideas and presenting them as your own, is considered dishonest. Patent and copyright laws are designed to protect intellectual property rights, but the rights associated with information—freedom of expression, freedom of information, privacy rights, and intellectual property rights—are often in conflict with one another. Balancing the public need to know against the rights of the owners of information has always been a problem for society.

Information technology has created new problems in defining and protecting intellectual property rights. Information technology separates the information from the media that contains it—one can no longer protect information by controlling the piece of paper on which it is written. An arcane example, taken from Mason (1986), relates to expert systems: Practitioners of artificial intelligence proceed by extracting knowledge from experts, workers, and the knowledgeable and then implanting it into computer software where it becomes capital in the economic sense. This process of "disemminding" knowledge from an individual, and subsequently "emminding" it into machines transfers control of this intellectual property to those who own the hardware and software. Is this exchange of property warranted?

Computer programs are undoubtedly valuable intellectual property, and they are protected by the patent and copyright laws. These laws, however, were written long before present-day information technology could even be imagined, and we are struggling with how to apply them to software.

Consider the problem of protecting the rights to a software package such as Lotus 1-2-3. Because there are many ways of doing the same thing by combining computer codes into a program, forbidding the duplication of the particular series of computer codes does not provide much protection. Several companies have produced clones of Lotus 1-2-3 that, from the standpoint of their use, are virtually identical to the original. This situation has led to a good deal of litigation over copyright protection of software, with confusing results.

Brandt, Schwartz, and Galen (1992) provide several contradictory court rulings. In one case, the court ruled that the basic structure or outline of a computer program cannot be copied. More recently, another court ruled that the basic structure of a program is not copyrightable. In *Lotus vs. Paperback* (1990), the U.S. District Court in Boston ruled that software makers cannot copy screen layouts, menu sequences, and command organization—the "look and feel" of an application. But in *Apple vs. Microsoft and Hewlett-Packard* (1992), the U.S. District Court in San Francisco ruled that only specific screen elements are copyrightable, not overall "look and feel."

U.S. copyright laws do make it illegal to copy a software package without permission of the software vendor. Although this is difficult to enforce against individuals, software vendors have become vigilant in prosecuting large companies who have (knowingly or unknowingly) allowed software to be copied. Many companies have strict policies against copying software, and they may even check periodically to make sure that an individual's office PC hard disk contains only authorized software. Nevertheless, according to a study by the Business Software Alliance and the Software Publishers Association, software piracy cost software producers $11.2 billion worldwide in 1996 (Business Software Alliance, 1997). The study showed that worldwide nearly 225 million units were pirated, which was 43 percent of the number of units that were installed in 1996. In the U.S., pirated software amounted to only 27 percent of the installed units, the lowest rate in any country, but the U.S. loss in dollars amounted to almost $2.4 billion.

Social Issues Related to Individual Rights

As the Internet makes it possible to instantly distribute ideas, pornography, and subversion throughout the world, the right to privacy and the right of society to protect itself collide. The growing collection of large databases crammed with information about individuals gives rise to horror stories concerning how the privacy of individuals can be destroyed and how inaccurate data about a person can ruin lives. In the following we explore the impact of IT on issues of freedom of speech, the invasion of privacy, and the hazards of inaccurate systems. Although these topics also involve legal issues, we have chosen to group them together because of their impact upon the individual.

Freedom of Speech

The increasingly pervasive use of the Internet and the World Wide Web has led to renewed controversy over the conflicts between our rights to privacy and freedom of speech and the right of society to protect itself against criminals and purveyors of pornography on the Web.

ELECTRONIC HATE

When junior Shawn Chen opened his e-mail the header read: "Bad Ass Mother ****er." When he read the message itself, Chen's eyes froze at the racist slurs in the text. And then it dawned on him the message wasn't just for him, but was sent to IU's Asian American Association's distribution list containing about 700 names.

When Chen reported the incident he learned that at IU there are no clear-cut policies or solutions to tame the problems in cyberspace. The first step in addressing such cases is finding out who sent the message. In this incident the sender concealed his name by hijacking another student's account, which makes tracking down the perpetrator almost impossible.

Even if the sender were to be identified, there may be little that can be done to punish that person. The courts have held that most university speech codes outlawing "hate speech" violate the First Amendment, but intentional threats are not protected by the constitution. Since the message received by Chen was not a direct threat, even if the perpetrator were to be identified all the university could do would be to take away the person's computer account for violating restrictions on the use of computer resources.

[Adapted from Yung, 1997]

While everyone recognizes that the Web is a rich educational resource for children, it is clear that the Web has become a prime distribution channel for pornography of all kinds. Parents are concerned about how they can prevent their children from being exposed to this material while at the same time allowing them freedom to explore the attractive educational resources available on the Web. Also, there have been an appalling number of instances where children have been kidnapped, raped, and murdered by men who established contact with them through Internet "chat rooms." Understandably there is a lot of pressure to legislate controls on the Internet to protect children from pornography and predators.

In 1996 congress passed the Communications Decency Act (CDA) that made it a crime to make any communication that is indecent or obscene available to anyone under 18. The CDA provided for a fine of $100,000 and two years imprisonment of those convicted of such activities. The act not only targeted the person transmitting the forbidden material, but it also made the operator of the telecommunications system transmitting the material liable to the same penalties. This placed an almost impossible burden on Internet access providers who normally have no knowledge of what is being transmitted through their facilities. In June 1977, the U.S. Supreme Court ruled that the CDA was an unconstitutional limitation of freedom of speech. This decision, of course, does not end the struggle between freedom of speech and protection against pornography on the Web.

There are alternatives to legal controls on Web content. Software, such as SurfWatch and Net Nanny, can be used to block access to pornographic Web sites

FIRST AMENDMENT LEGAL DECISIONS

DOE VS. UNIVERSITY OF MICHIGAN

In 1989, a federal district court ruled the speech codes at the University of Michigan were unconstitutional and violated a student's First Amendment freedom of speech. The court found the speech code was over-broad and vague.

SIGMA CHI VS. GEORGE MASON UNIVERSITY

In 1991, a federal district court ruled a fraternity's "Dress a Sig" contest, where fraternity brothers dressed up as caricatures of "ugly women," was protected expression under the First Amendment. The court also said no disciplinary action could be taken against the fraternity and its expression.

R.A.V. VS. CITY OF ST. PAUL, MINN.

In 1992, the U.S. Supreme Court decided a cross burning was protected expression under the First Amendment.

UNITED STATES VS. ALKHABAZ

In 1997, the 6th U.S. Circuit Court of Appeals affirmed the dismissal of all charges against Jake Baker, who was previously a student at the University of Michigan. Baker had been disciplined for sending sexually explicit messages over e-mail that were deemed to be threatening. But the court found that under any reasonable standard, the messages could not be seen to amount to a threat.

[Adapted from Yung, 1997]

THE CYBER VICE SQUAD

Sex-related material is a tiny fraction of what's available on the Internet. But it's a really, *really* conspicuous fraction, and it is as accessible to an intrepid 10-year-old as to an adult. To block access to unsuitable material parents can install one of several net filtering systems that work on the receiving PC. SurfWatch, Cyber Patrol, Net Nanny, and Cybersitter are some of the 20 or so offerings parents can choose among.

Office network managers are turning their attention to how company employees spend time and bandwidth when they use company PCs to Web-hop. One study showed that sex-related sites were not the most popular destinations—the leading sites provided news, sports, and personal finance information, but employee time and company resources were still being wasted. This new concern has given rise to still another new category of software—Internet-traffic-monitoring software—that can tell the particular Web page or newsgroup visited at any time by any company employee. Companies that announce plans to monitor Internet activity on corporate PCs have experienced immediate behavior changes. For example, a network manager at a Japanese company installed some monitoring software. He did not announce it, but left it conspicuously running on his PC. The next day, usage of the Web at the company dropped—to zero.

[Adapted from Stross, 1997]

---

or to language and files that might not be suitable for children. Such software is not perfect, but it does provide a good measure of protection, particularly when parents pay attention to what their children are doing on the Web.

Today we are faced with serious threats from criminal activity related to drug traffic. Also we are increasingly concerned about the rise of terrorism from both domestic and foreign sources. The World Trade Center and Oklahoma City bombings are graphic examples of the threats we face from terrorists.

One of the major resources used by law enforcement agencies in preventing terrorism and apprehending criminals is the ability to monitor communications between individuals and groups. In the past this monitoring has taken the form of wire-tapping telephone lines, which has been a controversial activity because it has been used to invade the privacy of those who held unpopular opinions or were political opponents of those in government. Laws permit wiretapping only after demonstrating a clear threat and obtaining a court order, but such laws have not always been obeyed by those entrusted with enforcing the law.

The Internet and other digital communication methods can defeat monitoring by encrypting the transmission so that only the intended recipient can decode the message, so law enforcement loses an important weapon against organized crime and terrorists. Providing an understanding of the various methods that are used to encrypt messages is beyond the scope of this section, but simplified discussions can be found in the Baase reference at the end of this chapter. For our purposes it is only necessary to note that **encryption** software exists that can code messages so that they are virtually impossible for anyone but the intended receiver to decode, even using the most powerful computers in existence. Using this software it is possible to ensure that communication is private despite all efforts to intercept and decode the message. Therefore the U.S. government security agencies have attempted to make the use of such encryption software illegal and ban its use or distribution.

On the other hand, there are many important areas where encryption is essential to the effective use of information technology. For example, electronic transfer of funds and transmission over the Internet of credit card numbers depend upon encryption to protect the integrity of the transactions. Although encryption is needed to protect the integrity of electronic commerce, electronic commerce does not depend upon *perfect* encryption, for methods that can be broken given powerful computers and lots of time are quite adequate to protect most electronic commerce.

U.S. government security agencies, while attempting to ban "strong" encryption software, have no objection to the use of encryption software with codes that can be broken given sufficient computing resources and time. However, "strong" encryption software is readily available, both within the U.S. and overseas, so those who want to protect the confidentiality of their communications are able to do so no matter what the U.S. laws may be.

Invasion of Privacy

What rights should a person have to keep details about his personal life and his associations from being revealed to others without his permission or even his knowledge? Information technology is making it very easy for businesses, government, and individuals to obtain great volumes of information about individuals without the knowledge of the person involved.

According to Mason, each American citizen has an average of 17 personally identifiable computer files housed in federal government agencies and several more in state and local governments. We all have other computer files in banks, credit card companies, hospitals, schools, utility companies, businesses we deal with, magazine companies, and companies with mailing lists of all kinds. It also is much easier to access the information from a computer file than from a traditional paper file. In fact, the computer makes it inexpensive as well as easy to obtain information on you from any of these files.

The privacy problem from all this computerization, however, is much more serious than just obtaining information about you from one of these files. Most of the files were created for legitimate purposes, and providing information for that purpose usually does not offend us. The problem arises when a person or organization combines the data on a person from several files and therefore obtains a very detailed picture of a person's life.

There are companies whose business is gathering data about individuals from various files, combining

---

YOU CAN RUN, BUT IT'S TOUGH TO HIDE FROM MARKETERS

For years, Lisa Tomaino kept her address secret. She and her husband Jim, a policeman, wanted to make it as hard as possible for the crooks he had put away to find out where they lived. But last year, Lisa had a baby. Within six weeks, she was inundated with junk mail aimed at new mothers. The hospital had sold her name and address to a direct marketing company, and soon she was on dozens of other lists. Efforts to get off them proved fruitless. "It was a complete violation of our right to privacy," she declared.

Names and addresses are just the beginning. In 1992, for example, General Motors Corp. joined with MasterCard to offer the GM Card. As a result, GM now has a database of 12 million GM cardholders, and it surveys them to learn what they're driving, when they next plan to buy a car or truck, and what kind of vehicle they would like. GM went into the credit card business not just to build loyalty and offer cardholders rebates on cars but also because it saw the billing process as a way to harvest reams of data about consumers.

American Express, using massively parallel processors from Thinking Machines Inc., stores every credit card transaction. Then 70 workstations at the American Express Decision Sciences center in Phoenix race through mountains of data on millions of AmEx cardmembers—the stores they shop in, the places they travel to, the restaurants they've eaten in, and even the economic conditions and weather in the areas where they live—in order to target special promotions to customers through its billing process.

[Adapted from Berry et al., 1994]

NOWHERE TO HIDE

Two influential trade groups, the American Business Conference and the National Alliance of Business, have joined with Educational Testing Service, which conducts the Scholastic Aptitude Tests, in creating a pilot program for a nationwide data base of high school records. It would give employers access to a job applicant's grades, attendance history, and the ancient evaluations of teachers. Just like Mother warned you—a ninth-grade report card could follow you for life.

[Adapted from Lacayo, 1991]

---

these data, and selling the resulting package to others. (See box "Data Collection Companies.) The danger in this use of computerized information is not so much that an individual's mailbox will be clogged with advertisements and catalogs—one can even argue that such targeting provides a valuable service to the individual as well as to the marketer. Rather, the danger is that unknown persons can use this wealth of information to make important decisions concerning someone without the person's knowledge. Such easy access to information made possible via technology presents questions for society as a whole as well as organizations.

DATA COLLECTION COMPANIES

To get a driver's license, a mortgage, or a credit card, to be admitted to a hospital or to register the warranty on a new purchase, people routinely fill out forms providing a wealth of facts about themselves. Little of it remains confidential. Personal finances, medical history, purchasing habits, and more are raked in by data companies. These firms combine the records with information drawn from other sources—for instance, from state governments that sell lists of drivers licenses or the post office lists of addresses arranged according to ZIP code—to draw a clearer picture of an individual or a household.

The repackaged data—which often include hearsay and inaccuracies—are then sold to government agencies, mortgage lenders, retailers, small businesses, marketers, and insurers. When making loan decisions, banks rely on credit bureau reports about the applicant's bill-paying history. Employers often refer to them in making hiring decisions. Marketers use information about buying habits and income to target their mail-order and telephone pitches. Even government agencies are plugging in to commercial databases to make decisions about eligibility for health care benefits and Social Security.

[Adapted from Lacayo, 1991]

Another privacy issue arises in the workplace. According to an American Management Association survey released in 1997, nearly two-thirds of employers record employee voice mail, e-mail, or phone calls, review computer files, or videotape workers. Moreover, up to a quarter of companies that spy do not tell their employees (Associated Press, 1997). In almost all cases, this is perfectly legal. The only federal law that limits employer surveillance is the 1986 Electronic Communications Privacy Act, which bans employer eavesdropping on spoken personal conversations. However, companies can listen to business phone calls and monitor all nonspoken personal communications, so e-mail messages are not private (as many have learned to their chagrin).

Also, as reported by Koepp, Pelton, and Shulman (1986), many employees who work through computer terminals are monitored by the computer, which, in addition to performing the work, records the quality and quantity of that work, even down to recording the time the employee is away from his or her workstation for breaks.

Hazards of Inaccuracy

As mentioned earlier, comprehensive data about individuals are contained in numerous large databases that are used to make important decisions that affect the individual. Unfortunately, much of this data is highly inaccurate.

There is a national computer crime network that serves local and state police by providing information on persons who have been arrested or have arrest warrants outstanding, stolen cars, and other items. Many police agencies have terminals in police cars so that when police officers stop a car for a traffic violation, they can check whether the driver is potentially dangerous or the car is stolen before an officer approaches the car. Input into this database comes from thousands of agencies all over the country. Unfortunately, there are few controls on the integrity of this input process, making the accuracy of the data quite low. There have been reports of innocent citizens being shot because they made some motion that the policeman, influenced by information from the computer indicating that the car's occupant was dangerous, interpreted as reaching for a concealed weapon. In other cases, policemen have been injured because the computer did not indicate that the car's occupant was dangerous.

Three large credit reporting services in the United States—Experian (formerly TRW), Equifax, and Trans Union—maintain huge databases of data on consumers that are used to determine the credit worthiness of individuals. These services purchase computer records from banks and retailers that detail the financial activities of most Americans, but there is little control on the accuracy of these data. In early 1991, Consumer's Union studied a sample of credit reports and found that almost half contained erroneous data and that 19 percent had errors serious enough to cause information buyers to deny credit, employment, or insurance. (See box "Credit Report Horror Stories.")

Long-Term Social Issues

A number of IT-related issues influence where we are going as a society. These include the impact of TV upon our values, the impact of IT on the quality of working life, IT's impact on the distribution of wealth, and the question of what role will be left for the human as the computer takes over more and more of what we have always considered to be brainwork.

The "Boob Tube"

Who would deny the impact that television has had on our society? By the time a child is grown, he or she typically has spent years being bombarded by images of drama, violence, history, nature, technology, sex, marketing pitches, and anything else one can think of, much of which is a gross distortion of real life. Many studies have shown that children exposed to repeated violence on TV tend to become more aggressive in their relationships with others. It is tempting to blame many of our social ills on the pervasive influence of TV on our moral development and our expectations of the "good life." Although TV obviously provides entertainment and some education, we continue to struggle with how to increase the benefits of TV and to reduce its damage while maintaining our constitutional right to free speech.

Furthermore, TV, computer, and Internet technologies are rapidly converging. Microsoft Windows 98 operating system includes software that allows people to watch TV on their PCs. Eventually TV will convert to digital signals rather than analog, and your TV set will soon provide access to the Internet. The number and variety of channels available is growing as direct satellite TV competes with cable TV. There is a rush of confusing activity as entertainment content providers, network and cable companies, software companies, and computer manufacturers merge with each other or form alliances. No one knows what the impact on our lives of this convergence will be.

Economic Impact

Despite the many benefits of the information economy and the fact that the resulting economic growth benefits all to some degree, it is clear that the gap between the haves and the have-nots is increasing. Education and information are more than ever the keys to economic security. As a part of this trend, computer literacy—access to information technology—contributes significantly to individual economic success.

Measured by MIPS per dollar, computer power is getting cheaper and cheaper, but taking advantage of this power requires that you have access to a computer and know how to use it. Sadly, access to the computer in American society is largely a privilege of the middle class, and this fact tends to widen the gap between the well-to-do and the poor. From a worldwide perspective, those in developing countries have even less access to computer power than do the American poor.

Few would doubt claims that those with computer knowledge will earn more in the future than those without it. Furthermore, those lacking minimal skills may be unable to find any suitable employment, so the richest societies on earth may be facing the prospect of a permanent underclass. This widening gap between the haves and the have-nots is a growing social problem that may someday become extremely serious.

Fortunately, there are signs that the U.S. public school system is making progress in bringing classroom access to computers to the poor, but much remains to be done to raise reading, writing, and mathematical skills to the level necessary for success in the information economy. Also, as noted previously (Wysocki, 1997), some persons see the Internet as a way to bring the economic power of information to the population of the developing world.

Impact on Quality of Working Life

What is the impact of information technology on people? As noted above, it can make a substantial contribution to one's economic success, but it can also have a negative impact on quality of working life.

Strangely, one negative aspect may be on the worker's health. People whose jobs require them to work continuously on a computer terminal often develop injuries. According to Horowitz (1992), a three-year study by the National Institute for Occupational Safety and Health found that 111 out of 518 telephone workers who used computers had repetitive stress injuries. To avoid such injuries, companies should provide ergonomic office furniture, provide variety in jobs so that keyboard use is not continuous, and train workers in how to adjust their chairs and posture and use keyboard placement in order to avoid such injuries.

The computer can also be used to monitor people, to invade their privacy, and to dehumanize their jobs. For example, according to Koepp et al. (1986), at one airline company:

> *The master computer records exactly how long the 400 reservation clerks spend on each call and how much time passes before they pick up their next one. Workers earn negative points for such infractions as repeatedly spending in excess of an average 109 seconds handling a call, and taking any more than twelve minutes in bathroom trips beyond the hour a day they are allotted for lunch and coffee breaks. Employees can lose their jobs if they rack up more than 37 points in a year.*

REPETITIVE STRESS INJURIES

As jobs in journalism go, Grant McCool's was a plum assignment. Based in Hong Kong for the Reuters news service, McCool covered breaking news throughout east Asia, traveling to South Korea, China, and Pakistan. But in 1989, after five hectic years, the native of Scotland was ready for a change. That's when his bosses transferred him to New York City to be an editor.

That's also when the trouble started. After typing on his computer keyboard for hours a day over several months, McCool developed excruciating pain in his hands; some mornings he would awake with his arms throbbing and burning. "The doctor told me to stop typing immediately," recalls McCool, 32. He hasn't written or edited a story on deadline since. Nor has he been able to clean house, carry heavy objects, or play squash. He cannot even drive a car; controlling the steering wheel with his injured hands is impossible.

McCool suffers from a severe case of cumulative trauma disorder, a syndrome that results from overusing the muscles and tendons in the fingers, hands, arms, and shoulders. The condition brings pain, numbness, weakness, and sometimes long-term disability. Such problems, more commonly known as repetitive stress injuries (RSI), now strike an estimated 185,000 U.S. office and factory workers a year. The cases account for more than half the country's occupational illnesses, compared with about 20 percent a decade ago.

[Adapted from Horowitz, 1992]

Concerning such practices, Koepp quotes Karen Nussbaum, director of 9 to 5, a national group of working women:

> *The potential for corporate abuse is staggering. It puts you under the gun in the short run and drives you crazy in the long run.*

The Information Technology Takeover

The industrial revolution replaced human and animal muscle power with machines and in the process caused painful dislocations to displaced workers. Increasingly, the information revolution results in computers replacing brainpower, and it is not clear where this process will lead or where it will end.

The computer began by taking over the calculational role of the brain in some complex operations. H. R. J. Grosch, an astronomer who became a computer pioneer, wrote his Ph.D. dissertation in the 1930s on the basis of two years of work calculating the orbits of asteroids on a desk calculator. Today these calculations would take only a moment, and we would not award a Ph.D. on the basis of such work.

Soon the computer began to take over decision-making in well-structured but complex areas, such as deciding how to formulate cattle feed from different ingredients so as to minimize the cost of the feed while meeting specified nutritional requirements. Information technology has supported the downsizing of organizations by streamlining processes and providing instant information when and where it is needed. In the military, command and control systems based on information technology have allowed humans and computers to share complex analysis and decision-making tasks, with both computers and humans doing what each does best. But it is clear that over time the computer is taking over more and more of the total task to the extent that, in some cases, the human simply has a veto power over the computer's decisions.

Today the computer is beginning to compete with humans in arenas where we always thought that human creativity was required. In May 1997, Deep Blue, an IBM supercomputer with very sophisticated software developed by a long-term IBM-sponsored research project, finally beat the current world chess champion, Garry Kasparov, in a challenge match. At one time chess was considered to require the essence of human brainpower, but now it is clear that the computer is capable of competing with any human chess player.

Although the field of artificial intelligence (AI) has advanced far slower than some predicted in its early days, it has progressed to where expert systems are commonly used in troubleshooting applications from automobile maintenance to medical diagnosis and neural networks are routinely used to sift through mountains of data and discover relationships that humans would not be able to find. As AI has improved we have had to continually revise our definition of "thinking" in order to keep it a unique quality of the human brain. However, most of the impressive things the computer has done are in very narrow fields, such as playing chess, and so far the computer has not exhibited the flexibility to generalize beyond these specialties.

WHAT WENT WRONG?

At 4 p.m. on May 11, 1997, Garry Kasparov, the world chess champion, resigned not even an hour into the final game of a tied-up six-game match against IBM's Deep Blue computer.

What went wrong? In part, hubris. Kasparov's strategy was dependent on exploiting weaknesses from which all previous computer programs had suffered. But Deep Blue's creators had openly discussed the most important piece of information its competitors should know: They had successfully corrected those vulnerabilities. Before the match, when I told Kasparov about this claim, he responded with withering derision. "This is crap!" he said. The first game seemed to prove him out. But in game two, Deep Blue unfurled a commanding—and breathtakingly human-like—attack, not only winning the game but demolishing Kasparov's psyche. Before his eyes, Deep Blue had proved that it could do what he had considered undoable. From that moment, "game two was sitting in my mind," he says, and that specter ultimately brought him down.

[Adapted from Levy, 1997]

Where will this all end? Let us explain why we cannot answer this question. The most important characteristic of the computer is that, through its software, the computer can execute over and over any procedure devised by ingenious humans, which makes it feasible to invest great resources in the creation of software. Moreover, once a software version exists, it becomes the base point for the development of an improved version, so what the computer can do gradually grows more and more impressive. For example, the first chess-playing programs could barely compete with a low-ranking player, but the present Deep Blue software is the latest in a long succession of improved versions, and it finally beat Kasparov.

It is an open question as to whether or not we will some day have machines that are smarter than their creators. However, we can say with great confidence that computers are changing our lives in ways that seem to be beyond our control, and computers will continue to take over activities that were previously the domain of humans. We will have to continue to struggle with the implications of this progress.

ETHICAL ISSUES

In the previous sections we discussed a number of social issues associated with the impact of information technology. Many of these issues present problems that information technology poses for humankind, and ethical concerns are associated with these problems. We have been concerned with what is right or wrong for society in general, something over which we as individuals have little if any control. In this section we will be concerned with ethical issues that the use of information technology poses to us as individuals, where we may have to make decisions and live with the consequences.

When we discuss ethics we are concerned with standards of right and wrong. Our ethics are the moral principles by which we are guided. Why are we discussing ethics in a book on management of information technology? First, as discussed in the previous sections, information technology has a profound and growing impact on our lives, and anything that has such powerful effects on people's lives gives rise to ethical issues. Second, managers determine how information technology is used, and therefore managers are responsible for the impacts of the use of information technology and the ethical implications of these impacts.

Although some people are intentionally evil, most of us consider ourselves to be ethical. We may come from very diverse backgrounds, but most would agree that ethical behavior is based upon integrity, honesty, competence, respect, fairness, trust, courage, and responsibility. Although we might prefer that you adhere to our particular ethical standards, this section is not intended to change your ethical make-up, for your standards of right and wrong have been determined by your life experiences from early childhood to the present and are not likely to be changed by reading and discussing a few pages from this book. Rather, the purpose of this section is to sensitize you to the ethical issues that may arise in your use of information technology so that you will apply your personal ethical standards when such situations occur.

Whatever our personal standards of right and wrong may be, it is important that we not violate them; when we violate our ethical standards we lose respect for ourselves. There is little doubt that our self-respect is one of our most valuable possessions. If we don't like someone else we can avoid that person, but we can't get away from ourselves, so if we lose our self-respect, we tend to be unhappy. Furthermore, if we don't respect ourselves it is hard to respect others, so our relations with others deteriorate and we become less effective persons.

Making Ethical Choices

In our decisions on use of information technology, most of us do far more harm by accident than we do on purpose! Therefore, we need to think about the ethical issues associated with our decisions before we take action.

The crucial first step in acting ethically is to recognize when an ethical problem has arisen. How do we identify decisions where ethical problems may arise? Because our ethical makeup lies deep within us, the most common way we recognize ethical problems is by feel—when we don't feel right about a situation there may be an ethical problem. When we suspect that there may be ethical problems, there are a number of questions that can be of help: Would I want my mother to know about this? Would I care if everyone knew about this? What would be the result if everyone did this?

If your company has a code of ethics it may provide guidance in recognizing and dealing with ethical problems. Company codes are often quite general and may not be of much help for IT-related problems, but there are specific codes that provide guidance in recognizing and dealing with ethical problems in the use of information technology. Figure 8.1 presents a section on the responsibilities of organizational leaders from the code of ethics adopted by the Association for Computing Machinery (ACM), the organization to which many computer professionals belong. Figure 8.2 presents "Ten Commandments of Computer Ethics" proposed by The Computer Ethics Institute, Loyola University (Chicago).

Once an ethical problem is recognized, many approaches have been proposed for analyzing and resolving these problems. We are familiar with absolute prohibitions such as "do not kill" and "do not steal," as well as more general rules such as "do to others as you would have them do to you." Over the ages philosophers such as Immanuel Kant and John Stuart Mill have proposed and vigorously defended their ethical frameworks. Chapter 10 of Baase (1997)

3. ORGANIZATIONAL LEADERSHIP IMPERATIVES.
As an ACM member and an organizational leader, I will . . .

3.1 Articulate social responsibilities of members of an organizational unit and encourage full acceptance of those responsibilities.

3.2 Manage personnel and resources to design and build information systems that enhance the quality of working life.

3.3 Acknowledge and support proper and authorized uses of an organization's computing and communication resources.

3.4 Ensure that users and those who will be affected by a system have their needs clearly articulated during the assessment and design of requirements; later the system must be validated to meet requirements.

3.5 Articulate and support policies that protect the dignity of users and others affected by a computing system.

3.6 Create opportunities for members of the organization to learn the principles and limitations of computer systems

[Association for Computing Machinery Council, October, 1992.]

Figure 8.1 Section 3 of the ACM Code of Ethics

provides a brief overview of some of these frameworks, and Kallman and Grillo (1996) presents a four-step analysis process for reaching defensible decision.

In order to apply your own ethical framework in the IT arena, it is often helpful to ask: *Who* will be affected by this decision and *how* will these people be affected? It is usually obvious to consider how the technology affects ourselves, our employer, and those with whom we work, but additional stakeholders may include others who use the technology in their work, fellow managers, customers, and the general public.

Choices are easy when everyone benefits from the proposed technology, but often some stakeholders will benefit while others are adversely affected. Fortunately, there are many alternatives in how information technology can be used, so if one seeks diligently it is often possible to create an option where the negative impacts are minimized without seriously reducing the benefits. The most difficult ethical dilemmas arise when there are unavoidable conflicts between the benefits to some stakeholders and the harm to others. Situations may arise where your compensation, or even your continued employment, depends upon your making a choice that violates your ethical framework. These can be wrenching decisions.

In the following sections we will discuss some areas where ethical problems may arise. Many of these problems are related to the social issues in the first part of this chapter. However, in this context we are concerned with our individual responsibility for these problems, some of which may not be obvious ethical problems until you carefully consider the total picture.

Impact on Workers

What determines the impact of information technology on the people who use it? The design of the organizational/computer system determines this impact, and managers are responsible for designing the organization and determining the requirements of the computer system.

A work system can be designed in many ways that differ significantly in how computers and people share the work. For example, most manual systems for processing insurance claims break the processing down into small steps and pass the paperwork from person to person. The individual jobs are like jobs on a production line, with each worker performing a small, dull process over and over. When a computer system for processing insurance claims is designed,

1. Thou shalt not use a computer to harm other people.
2. Thou shalt not interfere with other people's computer work.
3. Thou shalt not snoop around in other people's computer files.
4. Thou shalt not use a computer to steal.
5. Thou shalt not use a computer to bear false witness.
6. Thou shalt not copy or use proprietary software for which you have not paid (or been given authority to do so).
7. Thou shalt not use other people's computer resources without authorization or proper compensation.
8. Thou shalt not appropriate other people's intellectual output.
9. Thou shalt think about the social consequences of the program you are writing or the system you are designing.
10. Thou shalt always use a computer in ways that insure consideration and respect for your fellow humans.

[Computer Ethics Institute, June, 1992]

Figure 8.2 Ten Commandments of Computer Ethics

there are many choices. One can choose to computer-ize the manual system, keeping the work flow about the same, but combining processes and supporting them with the computer. This approach can reduce the number of people required by eliminating some manual steps and simplifying the work in others. The result is that the remaining workers' primary tasks are to input data into the computer, and the work becomes even duller and more repetitive than the manual system.

Alternatively, because the computer can provide convenient access to all the necessary information to each individual, the computer system can be designed to support a work system where each worker com-pletes all the claim processing steps. If properly designed, this approach can also reduce the number of workers required, and the remaining jobs are enriched because there is more variety to the job and each worker can see that his or her job is important to the company and to its customers. The work force can be organized into teams according to the type of policy or the geographical area served, and each team can take pride in the quality of service it provides to its group of customers.

When we determine what a new system will do and how it will be used, we may get so involved in our own ideas that we completely ignore the impact of the system on some of the people who will be affected. One way to guard against this tendency is to involve those who will use the system in its development and to challenge them to help devise a work design that will improve both the productivity of the organization and the quality of their work experience.

Even when we have considered the impact of a system on all of those who will be affected and have devised a design that minimizes negative effects, we may still have ethical concerns. Often, for example, the main objective of a computer system is to reduce costs by replacing people. How do we balance the benefits to the organization against the consequences to the people who will lose their jobs?

Privacy

In the section on social issues, we discussed how information technology can be used to invade the pri-vacy of individuals. In organizations, managers make decisions on the development and use of systems that invade privacy. For example, managers decide whether or not to monitor employee e-mail. Managers decide whether or not to sell information gathered from customer warranty forms to other organizations. And managers decide whether or not to use the computer to monitor the behavior of employees.

Do we have an ethical responsibility to protect the privacy of individuals? Is it wrong, for example, to monitor employee e-mail in order to detect and pre-vent racial or sexual harassment? Does it make any difference if this monitoring is secret or if it is announced policy? We often have the problem of weighing the benefits of monitoring against the result-ing loss of privacy.

Accuracy

As previously noted, systems are often polluted with inaccurate data that may be used inappropriately to make important decisions. What responsibility does the individual manager have for the accuracy of the data stored in a system? Managers define the require-ments for any system that is being developed, and that includes decisions on what data to include, where that

---

E-MAIL PRIVACY

Shouldn't private missives sent over a privately owned computer be sacrosanct? That's what Rhonda Hall and Bonita Bourke thought. A female supervisor heard that some of their e-mail was getting pretty steamy and began monitoring the messages. She soon discovered that the two had some disparaging things to say about her, and the women were threatened with dismissal. When Hall and Bourke filed a grievance complaining that their pri-vacy had been violated, they were fired.

One might think the two employees had a strong case for unlawful termination. But their case was dismissed. The Electronic Communications Privacy Act of 1986 prohibits "outside" interception of e-mail by a third party—the government, the police or an individual—without proper authorization (such as a search warrant). It does not, however, cover "inside" interception—sneak-ing a peek at the office gossip's e-mail, for example.

[Adapted from Elmer-DeWitt, 1993]

data can be obtained, how the data are captured, and how the data are kept up to date and accurate. These decisions set the limits on how accurate the data stored in the system can be.

Of course, the accuracy of the stored data depends upon more than the design of the system. Maintaining accurate data is not easy. Unless the people who are capturing and maintaining the data are diligent in their pursuit of accuracy, the data's accuracy quickly deteriorates. When the organization that is responsible for capturing and maintaining the data also uses that data and therefore bears the cost of any inaccuracy, the data will usually be as accurate as it needs to be. But when a group of people is capturing and maintaining data that they do not use, then accuracy problems may arise unless these people take their responsibility for the data very seriously.

When an organization considers the question of accuracy of a database, it becomes clear that the cost of complete accuracy is high. From a business perspective, it makes sense to minimize the total of the cost of maintaining a given level of accuracy and the cost incurred because of inaccurate data. As long as the company is bearing both of these costs, there is no ethical issue. Ethical issues arise, however, when the manager must balance the costs to the company of maintaining accuracy against the damage to individuals caused by inaccurate data.

Depending on its use, inaccurate data may not hurt anyone, but when it does matter, then the managers who define the system and those who are responsible for capturing and maintaining the accuracy of the data are ethically responsible for the harm caused by the inaccurate data.

Security

One may wonder why security might be considered an ethical issue. If I let someone break into my system and steal, destroy, or change data, how does this injure anyone but me? There are several answers to that question. In the first place, there may be others who use that data who could be hurt by an intrusion. Also, once a hacker has gotten into the system of a legitimate user, it may be relatively easy to invade the entire computer system, or even an entire network. Thus, the security of the entire system or network depends upon the security of each legitimate user of that system.

There are many ways that users can negate the security mechanisms designed into systems. We can set up a password that is easy to break (and computer programs are available that assist in breaking passwords). We can leave a computer terminal unattended that is signed on to a system so that anyone who comes along can sit down and play around with the system. We can write down our password so that someone can copy it. We can tell someone our password or send it to someone via e-mail. In short, unless we take seriously our responsibility for security, we can abet penetration of and perhaps destruction of the entire contents of a network.

Pirating Software

Why would someone who would never stoop to stealing anything copy software for personal use without a qualm? Why is it all right to take a software package that cost millions of dollars to develop without paying for it? Is it because there is virtually no chance that we will get caught? Is it because we figure that the software developer is not losing anything because we would never buy the software if we had to pay for it? Is it because we think that the public is being ripped off by the software industry? Whatever the reason, it is clear that many otherwise ethical individuals either do not feel that copying software for their personal use is unethical, or they simply ignore their ethical standards in this case.

THE POLITICS OF INFORMATION

It is difficult to overemphasize the importance of coping with the political difficulties involved in introducing new information systems into an organization. Historically, there has been a very high failure rate for large systems projects, and many of these failures may be blamed on opposition to new systems that might change the balance of power in the organization.

Politics is a critical element in the management of information technology. As indicated in the box "Politics of Information," serious difficulties arise when the movement toward the new information-based organization encounters the realities of organizational politics.

POLITICS OF INFORMATION

We have recently studied information management approaches in more than twenty-five companies. Many of their efforts to create information-based organizations—or even to implement significant information management initiatives—have failed or are on the path to failure. The primary reason is that the companies did not manage the politics of information. Either the initiative was inappropriate for the firm's overall political culture or politics were treated as peripheral rather than integral to the initiative. Only when information politics are viewed as a natural aspect of organizational life, and consciously managed, will true information-based organizations emerge.

Furthermore, a good argument can be made—and there is increasing evidence for it—that as information becomes the basis for organizational structure and function, politics will increasingly come into play. In the most information-oriented companies we studied, people were least likely to share information freely—as perceived by these companies' managers. As people's jobs and roles become defined by the unique information they hold, they may be less likely to share that information—viewing it as a source of power and indispensability—rather than more so. When information is the primary unit of organizational currency, we should not expect its owners to give it away.

[Adapted from Davenport, Eccles, and Prusak, 1992]

Your ability to deal with information politics may determine success or failure when you attempt to use information technology in your managerial career. While politics may not be a factor when dealing with a system that serves you alone, politics often enters the picture when dealing with a system that involves others in the organization. Political difficulties may arise when you attempt to obtain the resources required for a new system and when managing data. Political considerations may also arise when attempting to develop or implement a new system, both in dealing with other users and with the IS organization. When you sponsor a new system you are responsible for dealing with the politics of systems development, the IS organization as a political actor, and the politics of obtaining the systems resources that you need.

Therefore, it is very important that you understand the politics of information.

Politics in Organizations

Rob Kling (1980) discusses a number of models that describe how organizations function. We will not explore all of them here, but we will look at two quite different perspectives he presents—the traditional rational perspective and the political perspective. As depicted in the middle column of Figure 8.3, the traditional **rational perspective** assumes that the organization has a set of commonly accepted goals arrived at by consensus, that the predominant value that guides decision-making is the efficiency or effectiveness of the organization, and that decision-makers attempt to maximize the organizational goals by using rational analysis.

The **political perspective** conceptualizes the organization as a confederation of individuals and groups that are banded together for common ends, each contributing to the organization and each participating in the resulting benefits. The political view assumes that the various individuals in the organization have their own goals that often conflict, that the predominant value that guides decisions is the welfare of the decision-maker, and that decision-makers attempt to arrive at decisions that resolve these conflicts by bargaining and negotiation.

The political perspective does not deny that much of the decision-making in an organization may be rational and motivated by the overall success of the organization, because the organization must survive and prosper if there are to be any rewards to divide. Thus, many bottom-line decisions may follow the rational model. Decisions that affect the distribution of rewards, however, are likely to be made on a political basis and may be the result of conflict and negotiation between the groups that have interests in the decision. The tactics that they can employ are limited, of course, by the common necessity to preserve the organization from which they all receive benefits and by the fact that they have to coexist in the future.

We would not argue that the political perspective depicts the whole truth about how organizations function. Most organizations embody a mix of rational and political decision-making, the proportion of which varies from one organization to another, but we have

	Traditional Rational	Political
Goals	Organizational consensus	Individual with conflicts
Predominant values	Efficiency or effectiveness	Welfare of the decision-maker
Decision criteria	Maximize goals	Resolve the conflicts
Decision mode	Rational analysis	Bargaining and negotiation

Figure 8.3 Contrast of the Traditional Rational and the Political Perspectives of Organizations

never encountered an organization to which the political perspective did not apply to some degree.

How Information Systems Are Political

Both the rational and the political perspectives apply to the role of information systems in organizations. Rational decision-making depends upon the availability of adequate and timely information, so the development of many information systems is motivated by this need for information. At the same time, information systems may be intensely political. This is not surprising, for most of us would agree that information is power, and, therefore, that information systems affect the distribution of power in an organization.

According to M. L. Markus (1981), information systems affect organizational power for three reasons. First, individuals who control access to information used to evaluate alternatives in a decision process can influence the outcomes of decisions. Second, information systems are often used as a part of the organization's resource allocation and control system, and thus they can be used to change the behavior of individuals and of organizational units. Third, information systems provide power because they present an image of the ability to influence outcomes, and the perception of power confers power.

Because information systems often affect the distribution of power within an organization, and power is so important to everyone, the development of a new information system is likely to encounter political opposition. Markus asserts that any new information system that changes the power distribution within the organization will be resisted by those who stand to lose power.

Power is usually required to make change happen in an organization. It usually takes less power to prevent change. Not only do entities often possess veto power, but a resister may employ effective **counterimplementation** activities to disrupt, prevent, or modify the intended change. In particular, the development and implementation of a new information system is especially vulnerable to disruption by various counterimplementation tactics employed by those who may oppose it. Markus (1981, 1983) provides two detailed examples of strong and long-lasting resistance to implementation of new systems for political reasons.

INFORMATION SYSTEMS AND POLITICS

Information system development is an intensely political as well as technical process. . . . A strategy for implementation must therefore recognize and deal with the politics of data and the likelihood, even legitimacy, of counterimplementation.

[Adapted from Keen, 1981]

Resistance to information systems [is explained] as a lack of consonance between the distribution of power implied by an information system and the distribution of power existing in the organization. . . . The origins of resistance are found not in the presence or absence of any particular tactic for introducing change, but in the interaction of the substance of the change with its organizational context.

[Adapted from Markus, 1981]

Counterimplementation Tactics

Resistance to the development of a new system may be quite easy. As we will discover in the next major portion of this book, systems development is a long, complex process that is difficult to manage. If the system is complex or hard to define there is a good chance of failure, even without overt resistance. Systems development projects are often viewed by managers as costly, time-consuming, and disruptive, and therefore they may be quickly abandoned if managers come to believe that they are not going to be successful.

Resistance to a system is almost always concealed or disguised for major reasons. First, conventional corporate culture denies the legitimacy of political activity. Even in organizations where political considerations are dominant, everyone maintains the pretense that their actions are rational and are solely motivated by a concern for the welfare of the organization. Second, when opposition is recognized, it is easier to counter. Thus, some of the most effective counterimplementation strategies are concealed in the guise of support of the new system.

The resister can also take advantage of the entire systems life cycle, from initial requirements definition of what the system is to do to the final stage when the system is in operation and being changed to keep it up to date. If resistance is unsuccessful at the requirements stage, it can be continued during systems design, conversion, operations, and maintenance. Political battles may be won or lost, but the war may go on for a long, long time.

The resister's objectives can often be obtained either by preventing implementation of the system or by obtaining modifications that remove the perceived problems. The resistance tactics employed may be designed to persuade the developer to modify the system in order to avoid the possibility of failure. Thus, the resister may view systems development and implementation as a continuing process of negotiation and may use various tactics as part of this negotiating process.

A classic resistance tactic is to delay the project by raising objection after objection, each of which may be justified in the interest of producing a better system. Resisters who are participants in the process may simply be difficult to pin down on the requirements, changing their minds repeatedly. It is easy to see why organizations that try to manage data find it so difficult to obtain agreement on the definitions of the data elements involved—avoiding agreement is an easy resistance tactic when you have data that you do not want the organization to manage.

Another way to resist a project is to complicate it by expanding its size and complexity. Such a resister may pretend to be an enthusiastic supporter of the system. Also, a resister may attempt to add new participants to the process who have different (and perhaps conflicting) motivations.

Another effective resistance tactic is to withhold resources that are essential for success of the system. These resisters may profess complete support, but when the time comes to contribute the necessary resources, they just are not there in the required quantity or quality or at the right time. Often this tactic involves designating a representative on the project team who is not qualified to make the decisions that are needed.

COUNTERIMPLEMENTATION

A central lesson to be learned from examples of successful counterimplementation is that there is no need to take the risky step of overtly opposing a project. The simplest approach is to rely on social inertia and use moves based on delay and tokenism. Technical outsiders should be kept outside and their lack of awareness of organizational issues encouraged. ("Why don't you build the model and we'll deal with the people issues later; there's no need to have these interminable meetings.") If more active counterimplementation is needed, one may exploit the difficulty of getting agreement among actors with different interests by enthusiastically saying, "Great idea—but let's do it properly!" adding more people to the game and making the objectives of the venture broader and more ambitious and consequently more contentious and harder to make operational.

[Adapted from Keen, 1981]

Dealing with the Politics of Systems Development

If you are the sponsor of a new system, it is important to consider the political implications of your system from the very beginning. It is far better to avoid political problems than to become involved in trying to overcome resistance. Astute managers avoid unnecessary political battles, even those they know they can win. Politics is a long-term game, and the long-term winners are those who have the most effective network of mutually beneficial relationships—it is best to avoid alienating those whose support you may need sometime in the future.

Thus, it is wise to consider how the new system will be perceived by each person or group that it will affect. That includes the people who work for you because they may have immense power to make the system fail. Managers often make the mistake of assuming that they are the experts and that the system belongs to them alone, and they acquire systems that fail because of resistance by clerical staff.

If the system can be structured so that it will be viewed as desirable by all those it affects, then one has created a win-win situation that will be supported by all. Because it is sometimes difficult to view a system from another's perspective, one way to create win-win systems is to involve those who will be affected in the development process and to allow them to negotiate the requirements of a system that all can support.

As you analyze the political aspects of the new system, you may find that it cannot be made politically neutral without destroying its value to you—there is no win-win solution. You can then anticipate resistance and should consider how that resistance can be overcome. Do you have the necessary power? Do you want to use it for this purpose? Can you obtain the support of others with the necessary power? How can the system be structured so that you can put together a coalition with sufficient power to make it a success? Or should you just forget it and put your effort into something else?

SUMMARY

Information technology is transforming how we live and work. The world appears to be entering a new era where information is the key factor that determines economic success. The network has become the key information technology, and increasingly people and organizations around the world are being tied together electronically, with tremendous impact on organiza-

tions and those who work in them. Microchips are being incorporated into new products, and information technology is making it possible to design and manufacture products in new ways. We could go on and on, but one only needs to keep up with the daily news to be impressed with the increasing impact of information technology in our lives.

Anything with such a pervasive impact on society is bound to raise important issues, and information technology is no exception. Perhaps the most troubling question is: "With the computer taking over more and more of what was once considered the domain of the human mind, where will this all end?" We wish we could give an answer to that question, but we cannot. It is clear, however, that those who understand this technology and are able to use it for their purposes have nothing to fear, for they will reap great benefits. Other more immediate issues include the impact of TV on our children, computer crime, problems with the reliability of large systems, freedom of speech, the potential for invasion of privacy, the possible hazards of inaccurate data, protection of intellectual property rights, the growing gap between the computer literate and the poor, and the impact on our quality of working life.

In addition to the above issues facing society, information technology raises a number of ethical issues for us as individuals. Most of us consider ourselves to be ethical, and we would prefer to act ethically. Sometimes, however, we do not immediately recognize the ethical issues presented by our use of information technology. When we sponsor the development of a new system, we are responsible for the impact of that system on others, including the impact on the quality of their working lives and on their privacy. For systems we use, we often have responsibility for the accuracy of the data and for the impact on others of any preventable inaccuracy. If we do not maintain the security of our portion of a system, we may expose other people to the depredations of those who may be able to break into the system through our neglect. And, of course, there is always the temptation to copy software rather than buy it.

Dealing with politics may be the determining factor in our personal success in employing information technology in an organization. A mixture of rational and political considerations governs how most organizations function. We argue that information is inherently political, which explains why it may be difficult to obtain the resources required for a new system, implement a new system, or manage data. The manager is clearly responsible for dealing with the politics of information technology.

We do not intend to imply that the rational model of organizations is wrong or inappropriate. Quite the contrary, organizations are successful to the degree that they are able to establish appropriate objectives and motivate employees to attain them. In the long run, successful business organizations must be rationally oriented, and your long-run success in the organization will depend on how well you perform in achieving the organization's goals. Thus, although you may have employed your understanding of information politics to obtain a new system, you must make sure that the organization obtains the promised benefits.

Although many political activities, such as creating win-win solutions, are clearly ethical, other political activities may be ethically questionable. Some political activities clearly do not pass the test "Would I care if everyone knew about this?" No one ever promised that making ethical decisions would always be easy!

Review Questions

1. What is meant by the term "identity theft?" What can happen to a person who is the victim of identity theft?

2. Why is a person's Social Security number so important that someone might steal it?

3. What is encryption? Why is it needed on the Internet? Why is the U.S. government opposed to encryption?

4. Describe the services provided by a credit reporting service such as Experian, Equifax, and Trans Union. How are these services provided?

5. Describe a situation in which the accuracy of a database might raise ethical issues for the user-manager responsible for that database.

6. Computer security is an important problem for organizations. What are the responsibilities of the individual user in maintaining the security of the organization's computers?

7. Has information technology created an ethical problem for you or someone you know? Explain.

8. Contrast the rational and political views of how organizations make decisions.

9. Why is information political?

10. Give three examples of resistance tactics that might be employed by someone who feels that a proposed new information system might cause the individual to lose power.

11. If you were the sponsor of a new information system, how would you evaluate the degree to which it might encounter opposition?

12. If you were the sponsor of a new information system and you anticipated opposition to the new system, what could you do to improve the probability of success of the new system?

Discussion Questions

1. Read the box "The Cyber Vice Squad" on page 281. What would you think if Internet traffic-monitoring software were used at a company where you worked? Would your reaction be different if such software were used at a university where you were a student? Why?

2. Read the box "Electronic Hate" on page 280. Is "electronic hate" something that a university should be concerned about? Why or why not? If so, how does your university address it?

3. Many hackers claim to believe that "access to computers should be unlimited and total" and that "all information should be free." Do you agree with these statements? Why or why not?

4. In your opinion, what is the most important social issue raised by the explosion of information technology? Why? How can society best deal with this issue?

5. Should we discuss ethics in a book on managing information technology? Why or why not?

6. Do you know anyone who has copied software? How did they justify stealing the result of someone's work?

7. Although this practice may invade individual privacy, many companies use information technology

to measure the quality and quantity of an employee's work. Discuss the ethical implications of this practice.

8. Think of a specific organization with which you are familiar. In what ways does this organization operate according to the rational perspective? the political perspective?

9. You submitted a request for a new system to your IS department and were turned down by the IS steering committee. You really need this new system and are convinced that it would be quite beneficial for your company. What are the things that you would consider when deciding how to go about obtaining this system? What would you try next?

10. Consider the following statement: Sponsoring the development of an application system may be hazardous to your career. Do you agree with this statement? Why or why not?

11. If you are facing the prospect of a new system that you do not like, you can exploit the counterimplementation tactics described above to resist the system. Discuss the ethical issues, if any, involved in such resistance.

REFERENCES

Allen, Michael. 1990. "To repair bad credit, advisors give clients someone else's data." *Wall Street Journal* 71 (August 14): A1, A8.

Associated Press. 1997. "Survey: Bosses watching workers." *The Bloomington Herald-Times*. 120 (May 5): A3.

Association for Computing Machinery (ACM) Council. October 16, 1992. "ACM Code of Ethics and Professional Conduct." Section 3 (From Web Page www.acm.org/constitution/code.htm)

Baase, Sara. 1997. *A Gift of Fire—Social, Legal, and Ethical Issues in Computing*. Upper Saddle River, N.J.: Prentice Hall.

Beeman, Don R., and Thomas W. Sharkey. 1987. "The use and abuse of corporate politics." *Business Horizons* 30 (March–April): 26–30.

Berry, Jonathan, John Verity, Kathleen Kerwin and Gail DeGeorge. 1994. "Database Marketing." *Business Week* (September 5): 56–62.

Brandt, Richard, Evan Schwartz, and Michele Galen. 1992. "Bit by bit, software protection is eroding." *Time* 140 (July 20): 86–88.

Business Software Alliance. 1997. "Overview: Global Software Piracy Report: Facts and Figures, 1994–1996." (From Web Page www.bsa.org/piracy/96REPORT.HTM)

Computer Ethics Institute. June, 1992. "Ten Commandments of Computer Ethics." Loyola University Chicago. (From Web Page www.luc.edu/infotech/sae/ten-commandments.htm)

Cortese, Amy. 1995. "Warding off the cyberspace invaders." *Business Week* (March 13): 92–93.

Davenport, Thomas H., Robert B. Eccles, and Laurence Prusak. 1992. "Information politics." *Sloan Management Review* 34 (Fall): 53–65.

Elmer-Dewitt, Philip. 1993. "Who's reading your screen?" *Time* 141 (January 18): 46.

Farrell, Christopher. 1995. "Why the numbers miss the point," *Business Week* (July 31): 78.

Forester, Tom and Perry Morrison. 1990. *Computer Ethics*. Cambridge, Mass.: The MIT Press.

Freedman, David H. and Charles C. Mann. 1997. "Cracker," *U.S. News & World Report* (June 2): 56–65.

Gegax, T. Trent. 1997. "Stick 'Em Up? Not Anymore. Now It's Crime by Keyboard." *Newsweek* (July 21): 14.

Ginzberg, M. J. 1978. "Steps towards more effective implementation of MS and MIS." *Interfaces* 8 (May): 57–63.

Hamilton, Joan O' C. 1995. "Medicine's new weapon: Data." *Business Week* (March 27): 184–8.

Hamilton, Kendall, and Susan Miller. 1997. "Internet U—No Ivy, No Walls, No Keg Parties." *Newsweek* (March 10): 12.

Hoff, Robert D., Seanna Browder and Peter Elstrom. 1997. "Special Report: Internet Communities." *Business Week* (May 5): 64–80.

Horowitz, Janice M. 1992. "Crippled by Computers." *Time* 140 (October 12): 70–72.

Kallman, Ernest, and John Grillo. 1996. *Ethical Decision Making and Information Technology: An Introduction with Cases, Second Edition*. New York: McGraw-Hill.

Keen, P. G. W. 1981. "Information systems and organizational change." *Communications of the ACM* 24 (January): 24–33.

Kling, Rob. 1980. "Social analyses of computing: Theoretical perspectives in recent empirical research." *Computing Surveys* 12 (March): 61–110.

Koepp, Stephen, Charles Pelton, and Seth Shulman. 1986. "The boss that never blinks." *Time* 135 (July 28): 46–47.

Kremer, Lisa. 1993. "The Smartest Person in the World Refuses to be Trapped by Fate." *Seattle Morning News Tribune*. (July 2) (Reprinted with permission in Web page http://weber.u.washington.edu/d27/doit/press/hawking3.htm)

Lacayo, Richard. 1991. "Nowhere to hide." *Time* 139 (November 11): 34–40.

Langford, Duncan. 1995. *Practical Computer Ethics*. London: McGraw-Hill Book Company.

Levy, Steven. 1997. "Garry Sings the Blues." *Newsweek* (May 26): 84.

Markus, M. L. 1981. "Implementation politics: Top management support and user involvement." *Systems, Objectives, Solutions* 1: 203–215.

——. 1983. "Power, politics, and MIS implementation." *Communications of the ACM* 26: 430–444.

Mason, Richard O. 1986. "Four ethical issues of the information age." *MIS Quarterly* 10 (March): 5–12.

O'Brien, Timothy L. 1993. "Aided by Computers, Many of the Disabled form Own Businesses." *Wall Street Journal* 84 (October 8): A1, A8.

Stoll, Cliff. 1989. *The Cuckoo's Egg: Tracking a spy Through the Maze of Computer Espionage*. New York: Pocket Books.

Stross, Randell E. 1997. "The cyber vice squad." *U.S. News & World Report* (March 17): 45–8.

Wysocki, Bernard, Jr. 1997. "Development Strategy: Close Information Gap." *Wall Street Journal* 100 (July 7): 1.

Yung, Linda. 1997. "Electronic Hate." *Indiana Daily Student* 130 (Feb. 26): 9, 16.

MIDSTATE UNIVERSITY BUSINESS PLACEMENT OFFICE (A)

Midstate University is a major state university with about 35,000 students on its main campus. It is internationally known for its programs in the arts, sciences, music, engineering, education, business, and languages.

The Midstate University School of Business is a "national" school, ranking in the top 20 business schools in the country. It has outstanding undergraduate, MBA, doctoral, and executive programs. Its faculty is renowned for research, teaching, and service to the state and the business community.

The Business Placement Office (BPO) is among the handful of placement operations in the country that conduct over 15,000 interviews each year and has an outstanding reputation among company recruiters and other business schools. Arnold Worthy, Dean of the Midstate University School of Business, notes that the Business Placement Office (BPO) is very important to the mission of the school: "It is our marketing arm, and a very good one. We get good students at least partly because they know that they can get good jobs. Our school is in the top 20 in all the national rankings of business schools, but we rank highest where those who do the ranking are businessmen. That is quite a tribute to our BPO."

The Director of the Business Placement Office (BPO), James P. Wine, is known among his peers as an energetic and innovative director. He is a past president of the Midwest College Placement Association and is a frequent speaker at placement conventions nationwide. Wine has a degree in Electrical Engineering, an MBA in Personnel Management, and a Ph.D. in Industrial Rela-

tions. He is the author of several textbooks that are widely used in placement and career planning courses.

The primary mission of the BPO is to help Midstate University students get appropriate jobs. But, as Wine notes, "We must also serve our corporate clients, for if they don't come back year after year there won't be any jobs for our students." In 1995–1996 the BPO served about 1,700 students and over 500 employers. Over 17,000 interviews were conducted in the BPO's 34 interview rooms, an average of over 1,000 each week of the interviewing season.

In order to provide outstanding service to both students and employers, the BPO makes extensive use of sophisticated computer systems. According to Wine:

> We are rapidly becoming a paperless operation throughout the BPO. Our communication to students and employers for posting jobs, scheduling interviews, and accessing our office publications is in the user-friendly, graphical environment of the World Wide Web (WWW). With the "click" of a button, students are able to scan job listings, schedule interviews, forward resumes, and much more from personal computers located anywhere in the world. Results of the bidding process are sent from our computers to students via e-mail, and we FAX resumes directly from our computer to employers.

The Student's View of the BPO System

The BPO is not an employment agency. It does not "get" anyone a job, but it provides many services to students to assist them in obtaining a suitable job, including teaching two required courses (Career Perspectives and Career Planning and Placement), sponsoring over 600 on-campus presentations by employers each year, making available company brochures, distributing student resumes to companies not interviewing on campus, providing the opportunity to network with Midstate University alumni, and scheduling and administering on-campus interviews with over 500 companies. From the student perspective, however, the main function of the BPO is to provide on-campus interviews with companies for which the student would like to work.

The matchmaking required to schedule 1,700 students into 17,000 interviews with 500 companies so that the students talk with their desired companies and the companies interview students with the required qualifications is a very complex, high volume logistical problem. It is particularly difficult because many students want to talk with the companies offering the best jobs, but these companies may have strict requirements concerning the qualifications of the students they want to interview. Some companies have far more students seeking interviews than there are interview times available, whereas other companies' interview schedules may not be filled.

The 1,700 students submit about 65,000 requests for the 17,000 available interview opportunities. How can the BPO be fair to all in allocating these interviews to qualified students? To deal with this problem in a fair and equitable way, the Midstate University BPO uses a bidding system, where students submit "bids" for interviews with the companies of their choice. Each student is given a fixed allotment of bids with different levels of priority. A complex process (designed to be "fair" to the students given their qualifications, their time availability, when they are graduating, and the bid priority) is used to decide which students get the interview slots. Since the BPO receives up to 5,500 bids during a peak week, interview scheduling can be handled only with the aid of computers.

In order to take advantage of the BPO services a student must meet certain criteria and register at the beginning of the year. The student goes to the BPO, pays a registration fee, and is given a floppy disk containing *Resume Expert,* a DOS software system that the student uses to enter registration information such as name, identification number, e-mail address, pending degree, major(s), GPA, citizenship, etc. (See Exhibit 1.) The student then uses *Resume Expert* to construct one or more resumes that the BPO can send to companies to interest them in the student or for use during scheduled interviews. The student then brings the disk to the BPO, inserts it into one of the PCs located there, and uploads the data into the BPO computer system. By the next day the student's files will have been established and he or

she will be able to use the BPO facilities. The student keeps the *Resume Expert* disk, which can be used throughout the year to update registration data and to create or modify his or her resume.

Preparation for Bidding

All the activities involved in bidding for interviews can be done through the BPO's user-friendly WWW site, which provides information on available interview schedules and the student's bid status and allows the student to bid for available interview slots. Midstate University students are introduced to the Web in their sophomore year computer course. Since many Business School faculty communicate with their students through a class Web page, students are quite familiar with how to use the Web. All Business School students are given a computer account that provides access to network resources such as e-mail and the World Wide Web.

When entering the BPO Web site the student must provide his or her student identification number and password and is then presented with the Main Menu shown in Exhibit 2. In addition to allowing the student to enter bids, this menu provides access to much of the information needed in order to develop the student's bidding strategy. The *Career Street Journal* (*CSJ*) was formerly a printed weekly paper that contained helpful articles related to placement, announcements, and complete information on upcoming interview schedules. The weekly *CSJ* is now available on the Web by clicking on Weekly CSJ in the Main Menu.

Each student is allocated only three "A" bids, three "B" bids, three "C" bids, and 30 Regular (or "R") bids each semester and is not allowed to exceed these limits. In addition to determining the qualifications that students must meet in order to be scheduled for an interview, the companies may also establish "preference lists" of students who will get priority for interview slots. Some companies will not use preference lists, others will establish half as many preferences as there are slots available, and others may include more students on their preference list than there are slots on the company's schedule. If students are interested in a company, it is important to know whether they are on that company's preference list, and this information may be obtained by clicking on Preference Lists on the Main Menu.

The BPO provides many opportunities for students to meet with company recruiters, including company presentations, roundtable discussions, orientation programs connected with the career development classes,

EXHIBIT 1
Student registration information.

BPO Registration Information for George P. Burdell

Last Updated: 02/19/97

Current Address: 120 East 15th. St.
Midstate City
(423)345-6749

Permanent Address: 1040 Amsterdam Ave.
Atlanta, GA
(205)378-5327

Email Address:	Burdell@bluestone.
Job Targets:	1) Financial Analyst 2) Loan Officer
Current Year:	2nd
Pending Degree:	MBA
Undergraduate Major(s):	Accounting
Undergraduate GPA:	3.4
Graduate Major(s):	Finance
Graduate GPA:	3.85
Graduation Date:	5/1997
Date Available:	6/1/97
Location Preference:	No Preference - Willing to Relocate
Full-Time Work Experience: (Non-summer, non-internship)	5 years
Citizenship:	U.S. Citizen
Home Country:	USA
Authorized to Work Countries:	USA
Languages:	1) English 2) Spanish
Skills:	1) Public Speaking 2) Teaching/Training 3) Leadership
Annual Salary:	Desired: $65,000 Minimum: $50,000

and company-sponsored receptions. In addition to the information that they may obtain, students have an opportunity to meet recruiters, give them resumes, and perhaps thereby get on company preference lists. Sign-ups for these programs are handled through the bidding system, and these opportunities appear in the CSJ along with interview schedules. To sign up for these events one uses a special "Interest" or "I" bid instead of the A, B, C, and R bids used for interviews. There is no limit on the number of I-bids a student may submit. However,

EXHIBIT 2
Main menu of the BPO system.

Welcome to BPO Web Services

Main Menu

Bidding CSJ   Personal Information Calendar
Times Available
Tentative Recruiting Dates   ☐ Preference Lists
Recruiter Addresses   ☐ Review Bid History & Contacts
Placement Status   ☐ Registration Information
Behavioral/Skills Tests   ☐ Uploaded Resumé List
Weekly CSJ   ☐ Referral History
LINKS: Alumni Database   ☐ Interview Feedback Summary

Exit to the BPO Homepage

Please mail any problems or comments concerning this website.

---

attendance at these events may be limited, and the bidding system is used to determine who can attend an event if the demand exceeds capacity.

Because the data in the student's registration information file is used to determine whether or not a student meets the criteria established by the company for signing up for an interview or attending an event, the student must make sure that this information is accurate and up-to-date. This record for MBA student George P. Burdell may be viewed by clicking on Registration Information on the Main Menu (see Exhibit 2), but to change this information it is necessary to change it on the *Resume Expert* disk and upload this data again. Burdell must also provide the BPO computer information on times when he is not available for interviewing so that he will not be scheduled at such times. Clicking on Times Available on the Main Menu allows the student to view and/or change this availability information at any time.

In order to plan one's bidding strategy, it is helpful to know what companies are planning campus interviews and when they plan to be on campus. This information is obtained by clicking on Tentative Recruiting Dates on the Main Menu, which allows the student to display planned interviewing dates for a particular company, or for a particular date or date range, or by degree and major. Also, by clicking on Review Bid History & Contacts Burdell

can review his bid history and see what bids remain available (see Exhibit 3).

Submitting Bids

When ready to enter the bidding process the student clicks on Bidding CSJ and is taken to the "How to Submit Bids Using This System" screen shown in Exhibit 4. Clicking on MBA on the second line ("Sorted by Major"), the student receives the screen shown in Exhibit 5. Clicking, for example, on Finance Major, the student is given the screen shown in Exhibit 6, and choosing A.G. Edwards & Sons, Inc. provides the screen shown in Exhibit 7. The student may bid for this interview by clicking on one of the four "Select Bid" options at the bottom of the page and may also enter a code selecting the version of his or her resume to be given to the company representative before the interview.

The above process may be repeated to enter additional bids. However, none of these bids will have been submitted to the BPO until the student returns to the "How to Submit Bids Using This System" screen shown in Exhibit 4, which now shows the bids the student has tentatively selected (as shown in Exhibit 8). The student can delete or change any of these bids and when satisfied can submit them by clicking on "Submit Bids to the BPO" at the bottom of the page.

EXHIBIT 3
Review bid history.

Bid History for George P. Burdell

	A	**B**	**C**	**R**
Bids Remaining	2	1	2	11

Note: This count does not consider bids that have been used today.

Date	Company	Resumé Number	Bid Level	Bid Number
WAITLISTED	Black & Decker Corp.	00	R	015015
WAITLISTED	Transtech, Inc.	00	R	001102
WAITLISTED	American Standard Widgets Inc.	00	B	000004
01/17/97	American Standard Widgets Inc.	36	I	000006
01/17/97	American Standard Widgets Inc.	00	I	000005
01/14/97	American Standard Widgets Inc.	00	I	000005
01/13/97	American Standard Widgets Inc.	00	I	000005
01/09/97	American Standard Widgets Inc.	00	R	000005
10/06/97	Prudential/Financial Services	30	I	368702
10/06/97	Prudential/Financial Services	30	I	368701
10/06/97	Unisys Corp.	00	I	016707
WAITLISTED	Data Bank USA	00	R	069102
10/03/97	American Standard Widgets Inc.	00	R	000003
10/03/97	American Standard Widgets Inc.	30	A	000001
10/02/97	American Standard Widgets Inc.	30	B	000001

Return to the Menu

This information current as of 01/09/97

Each week of the recruiting season, the Bidding CSJ is available at 9 a.m. Friday, and the primary bidding period for its interview opportunities extends until 4 p.m. the following Monday. All of the bids received during the primary bidding period are processed together to assign students to interview slots. First, bids of students who do not meet the qualifications set by the company are rejected and the student loses that bid. If the company has established a preference list, those students are processed first in priority order (A, B, C, and R). Then the remaining students are processed in the same priority order. Finally, those students who have been selected are scheduled into time slots, taking into account the student's time availability. Students who are left over are placed on a ranked "waitlist" and will be given any time slots that become available before the interview date. Time slots do become available because some students may cancel and recruiters may add a schedule when the BPO sends them the resumes of all students on the waitlist. If a student who has submitted a priority bid is

EXHIBIT 4
Bidding CSJ initial screen.

How to Submit Bids Using This System

1. Browse the CSJ listings. The following editions are currently available:

Sorted by Job Function	MBA, Bachelors
Sorted by Major	MBA, Bachelors
Sorted by Job Type	MBA, Bachelors
Search by Bid Number	Search

2. Mark the bids you intend to submit. (bottom of each listing)
3. Review/Edit intended bids. (shown below)
4. Submit Bids to the BPO. (located at the bottom of the screen)
5. Confirm that the bids you just submitted have been received by the BPO. (located at the bottom of the screen)

Bid Summary for Submission

None Selected. Follow instructions above to build your bidding list.

EXHIBIT 5
Menu of majors from which to choose.

Career Street Journal
Graduate CRIF Summary Selection

These lists are organized by the required Majors for each job. Choose the Major you wish to view:

Accounting Major	AMID Major	Any Business Major
Any Major	CIS/Computer Science Major	Finance Major
Management Major	Marketing Major	Operations/Business Process Management Major
Non Business Majors	SPEA Major	International Business Major
Business Economics Major	Legal Studies Major	

EXHIBIT 6

Finance interview schedules.

Career Street Journal Graduate CRIF Summary

1. Browse the following listings and select your preliminary bids. This list was updated *January 9, 1997*.
2. Click on the company name to display all job listings currently listed for that company.
3. Once you've reviewed the listing, you can add it to your preliminary bidding list by selecting the desired bid level and then clicking the OK button. If you do NOT want to place a bid on that listing, simply click on the CANCEL button to return to this screen.
4. When finished, click this button to review your intended bids:

Finance Major

Company	Listing	
A. G. Edwards & Sons, Inc.	Corporate Finance Analyst	Primary
Abbott Labs	Fin./Acctg. Summer/Fall Intern	Primary
Abbott Labs	Various Summer Internships	Primary
ABN AMRO/LaSalle National Bank	Credit Analyst Program	Primary
ABN AMRO/LaSalle National Bank	Management Associate Program	Primary
ABN AMRO/LaSalle National Bank	Night Before Presentation	Primary
American Airlines	Marketing Financial Analyst	Primary
Capital One	Operations Analyst	Primary
Carson Pirie Scott & Co.	General InfoNite	Primary
Center for Entrepren/Innovation	Program Coordinator	Primary
Comerica Bank	Int'l Finance Training	Primary
Corp. & Children's Hepatitis Found.	Proposal Writing Internship	Primary
David Michael & Co., Inc.	Informational Session	Primary
Delphi/Packard Electric Systems	Accounting/Finance Intern	Primary
Disney Entertainment Career Program	1997 College Musician Audition Sites	Primary

---

waitlisted, the priority bid is returned and an "R" bid is substituted, even if the student subsequently gets on the schedule.

Bidding Results

The computer sends bid results to students via e-mail as soon as all bid processing has been completed, usually during the early morning hours on Tuesday. The bid results list the student's name, the results of each bid placed, and how many bids remain in the student's account. For each bid the following is listed: the bidding number, the employer's name, the type of bid that was taken, and the result of the bid (date, time, and place scheduled, or waitlisted). Bid results are also placed on

EXHIBIT 7
Information on a company's interview schedule.

A.G. Edwards & Sons, Inc.

Organization Profile:

A.G. Edwards & Sons, Inc. is a leader in the securities brokerage industry with over 550 retail brokerage offices in all 48 contiguous U.S. states and an investment banking division located in St. Louis. Location of Headquarters in St. Louis, MO. Number of employees is over 11,000 with sales volume of over $1.4 billion in its most recent fiscal year.

Schedule Summary: A.G. Edwards & Sons, Inc.

Mr. Frank F. Mountcastle, III, Associate V.P. — Investment Banking
One North Jefferson, St. Louis, MO 63103
(314) 955-5764 FAX: (314) 955-7387

Title: **Corporate Finance Analyst**

Corporate Finance Analyst is responsible for the generation and analysis of financial and other data relating to both proposed and active corporate finance projects. Analyses would include industry and market studies, selection and evaluation of comparable companies, development and utilization of computer models and assistance in the due diligence process. Types of projects would include equity and debt offerings (public and private), mergers, acquisitions, corporate valuations, exclusive sales, fairness opinions and other financial advisory and client service assignments. Should be familiar with computer based information retrieval, spreadsheet and word processing software packages and quantitative analysis methods. Should possess analytical and communication skills. All Corporate Finance Analyst jobs are located at our headquarters in St. Louis.

Interviewing on-campus for Full-Time Positions

Requirements:

☐ Class Status: **2nd Year**
☐ Majors: **ACCT,FIN**
☐ Graduation Dates: **05/1997–08/1997**
☐ Degree Level: **MBA**
☐ Citizenship: **C,P**
☐ Interview Date(s): 01/22
☐ Bidding **#101610** .... A.G. Edwards & Sons, Inc. .... Corporate Finance Analyst
☐ Interview Length: **30**

Select Bid: A   B   C   R
Enter Resumé:

EXHIBIT 8
Screen for submitting bids.

How to Submit Bids Using This System

1. Browse the CSJ listings. The following editions are currently available:

Sorted by Job Function	MBA, Bachelors
Sorted by Major	MBA, Bachelors
Sorted by Job Type	MBA, Bachelors
Search by Bid Number	Search

2. Mark the bids you intend to submit. (bottom of each listing)
3. Review/Edit intended bids. (shown below)
4. Submit Bids to the BPO. (located at the bottom of the screen)
5. Confirm that the bids you just submitted have been received by the BPO. (located at the bottom of the screen)

Bid Summary for Submission

Burlington Northern Santa Fe			
Business Analyst Internship	Resumé:		Remove Bid:
Bid: #016511	A	B	C R

Burlington Northern Santa Fe	
Presentation	Resumé:	Remove Bid:
Bid: #016514	I

Submit Bids to the BPO

Return to Bidding CSJ Summary

Confirm Your Bids

---

the Web so that they may be viewed at any time by clicking on the student's Personal Information Calendar or Review Bid History & Contacts.

After the results of primary bidding have been announced, there is a secondary bidding period that extends until three days before the interviews are scheduled. During this time the student may cancel a scheduled interview if necessary, although the bid that was used is lost. Also, during this time, schedules that have vacancies are shown on the Bidding CSJ, and students may bid on any such vacancies. Each day's secondary bids are processed that night, and the results are sent by e-mail the next morning. Also, if a company cancels or changes its schedule, or a student on the waitlist is scheduled for an interview, the affected students are notified immediately via e-mail. Students who are using the BPO must check their e-mail at least once a day!

The BPO has a strict policy against "no shows" for interviews. If a student does not show up for a scheduled interview, he or she is suspended from bidding until the student has made a satisfactory explanation to both the BPO and the company involved. Therefore, it is crucial that the student always know when his or her interviews are scheduled so that if something comes up, the affected interview can be canceled at least three days before the interview is scheduled. By clicking on Personal Informa-

tion Calendar on the Main Menu the student is presented with a two-week calendar of his or her scheduled events (as shown in Exhibit 9). The schedule is color coded: Gray indicates "dead days" (no longer available for bidding adjustments), white represents days still available for bidding and adjustments, and red indicates a date that has just gone "dead" but has not yet been updated with final scheduling information. More detailed information on a day's event can be obtained by clicking on that cell of the calendar.

The process of obtaining suitable employment is difficult, stressful, and crucial to the graduating student.

EXHIBIT 9
Student's personal information calendar.

George P. Burdell
January

Sunday	Monday	Tuesday	Wednesday	Thursday	Friday
26	27 WAIT American Standard Widgets, Inc.	28 12:20pm American Standard Widgets, Inc. 4:30pm American Standard Widgets, Inc. WAIT American Standard Widgets, Inc.	29 WAIT American Standard Widgets, Inc.	30	31

This information current as of 01/24/97

Review Bid History
Registration Information
Uploaded Resumé List
Return to the Main Menu

Preference Lists
Review Referral History
Times Available
Interview Feedback
Summary

Students are competing with each other (and with students from other institutions) for the jobs that are available. Recognizing that companies have strong preferences about the qualifications of students they wish to interview, that popular companies may only be willing to interview a limited number of students, and that each interview with a popular company that is taken by one student cannot be taken by another, the BPO bidding system provides each student with a fair and convenient way to schedule interviews with the companies that come to the campus.

The Employer's View of the BPO System

Employers are very pleased with the services provided to them by the Midstate University BPO, rating it among the very best placement operations in the country. This is a great advantage to Midstate University students because the number of companies that come to the campus to interview determines the number of job opportunities the students have. Therefore the BPO goes all-out to provide outstanding service to the employers, and the BPO computer system provides extensive support for most of these services.

For the employer the first step in the interview process is to schedule the dates on which to interview on campus. Whenever a company is on campus interviewing, a BPO manager attempts to set up a schedule for that company to return for interviews the next year. This tentative schedule is entered into the BPO computer system. During the summer the BPO system prepares and sends a letter to each company confirming its tentative schedule for next year. The system also produces a list of companies that have interviewed on campus in the past that are not scheduled for next year, and each of these companies is contacted by a BPO manager during the summer.

The BPO system also prepares electronic resume books that companies may order. These "books" are standard computer disks that contain the resumes of all students registered with the BPO. The disk also includes software that makes it easy to select resumes (and/or mailing labels) to print based on factors such as major, degree, GPA, geographic preference, areas of interest, skills, and graduation date. The resumes may be used by companies to determine whether or not to interview on campus, or to decide who to "preference." The mailing labels may be used to contact selected students prior to the bidding process. And companies that do not interview

on campuses may use this disk to identify students to contact directly.

Five or six weeks before a scheduled recruiting date the company must submit a *Campus Recruiting Information Form* (CRIF) that provides the information for the company's listing in the *Weekly CSJ* and the *Bidding CSJ*. This information may be mailed or FAXed, or it may be submitted directly to the system by filling out a form that is available on the Web. All of the forms that employers submit to the BPO are available on the Web for direct submission.

A few weeks before a company is scheduled to interview, the system mails (or upon request, FAXes) the company contact person a reminder notice containing the interview schedule and requesting notification of any modifications that the company wishes to make. Then, after primary bidding is completed, the system mails or FAXes updated interview schedules and waitlists to the companies, which help the recruiters prepare for their visits and sometimes leads to the last-minute addition of schedules for some of the waitlisted students. Two days before the interviews, the system prepares a packet to be given to the recruiter upon arrival that includes the final schedule and resumes for the students on the schedule.

The system also produces mailing labels for the BPO yearly report sent out in August and the *Midstate University Recruiter Newsletter* sent out twice yearly.

At the end of each season the system sends each of the companies an extensive packet of information, including a report of their recruiting activities at Midstate University. This includes a review of the past year's interview dates and a listing of next year's scheduled dates. If the company is not yet scheduled for next year, dates are suggested. The packet includes an alphabetic listing of all the students the company interviewed, accompanied by a note asking them to fill in blanks for offers and hires and return it to the BPO. The packet also includes a list of the contacts from that company along with a request to return the list after deleting the names of any persons who no longer work for the company (used to remove them from the system's database).

The BPO Managers' View of the BPO System

The BPO computer system forms an essential part of all of the critical activities of the BPO, and it would be impossible for the BPO to render the high level of services that it provides to Midstate University students and recruiting companies without this system.

During the recruiting year, the system provides Wine and other BPO managers a great deal of up-to-date information. For example, the system can highlight recruiting dates where there are rooms available or where extra rooms must be found to accommodate the scheduled interviews. It can compare the demand for the various majors and salary offers with past history. Moreover, the system provides a mechanism for collecting feedback from both students and recruiters so that common problems can be identified and corrective measures taken. Students who encounter problems are encouraged to report the problem via e-mail or to come to the BPO and talk to a consultant. Because this is an on-line system, BPO managers can search through the system to find the information necessary to investigate and resolve the problem. The BPO usually resolves student problems within 24 to 48 hours of reporting the problem.

At the end of the recruiting season the system provides comprehensive summary information on the results of the year's placement activity for the BPO Yearly Report. A small sample of tables from the undergraduate section of the report is shown in Exhibit 10. This yearly report is of great interest to the Dean and faculty of the Business School, and is avidly perused by students as they choose their major field of study. This information is also used in brochures promoting the school.

The BPO Computer System

The context diagram in Exhibit 11 summarizes the inputs to and outputs from the BPO system described above. As shown in this diagram, the system takes a variety of inputs from client companies and students and provides outputs for the companies, students, and BPO and Business School management. The system maintains a number of important databases, schedules student interviews, supports coordination with client companies, and produces a wide variety of analysis reports for management. The computer system that provides these capabilities consists of a complex combination of networks, computer hardware, systems software, applications software, and databases.

The Computer Network

The computer network on which the system runs is depicted in Exhibit 12. The Midstate University backbone network at the top of this diagram is a high speed fiber-optic network that connects all of the buildings on the five Midstate University campuses. Through this network students and faculty all over the university can access university computing resources, including the Internet, from personal computers (PCs) in computer laboratories, dormitories, libraries, and through the Internet or direct telephone lines from anywhere they may be. The University Web server (connected to the Internet), the School of Business Web server, and the BPO subnet are connected to this backbone network and are thereby connected to each other. The BPO subnet connects the BPO Unix server, printers, and various IBM-compatible PCs in the BPO waiting room and director's offices to each other and to the backbone network.

The University Web server is a DEC Alpha 1000 operating under the DEC OSF1 operating system and using NCSA Web server software; the School of Business Web server is a HP 735 operating under Unix and using NCSA Web server software; the BPO subnet Cisco router operates under Netware 3.12, and the BPO Unix server is a NCR (AT&T) System 5, Version 4, operating under Unix.

The BPO Unix server maintains the BPO databases, performs the bid processing, sends FAXes to companies, and produces management reports. The School of Business Web server presents information to students and collects data from them. Periodically a batch of data that has been collected from the students by the Web server is sent to the BPO Unix server where the data is processed, databases are updated, and a batch of results are sent back to the Web server to update its files. The students can then access these data through the Web.

The application software of this system includes some 500 programs and around 100,000 lines of code. Part of this software is dBase and C code on the BPO Unix server, and the rest is written in C and Perl on the School of Business Web server.

The Database

At the heart of this system is a comprehensive database managed by the relational DBMS dBase IV. There are about a dozen major tables (or relations) in this database, and because the BPO people refer to these tables as databases, that is what we will call them. There are over 150 tables in the BPO database, but most of the them are derived from the major tables and are used for producing reports from the system. The entire database takes up over 30 megabytes of disk space. Here we describe some of the most important of these databases, their use, and how they are maintained.

The COMPANY database, whose structure is shown in Exhibit 13, contains name and address information on

EXHIBIT 10
Summary reports from the system.

Undergraduate Recruiting Activities

Undergraduate	1992-93	1993-94	1994-95	1995-96
Number of Employers				
(on campus)	375	404	431	431
Number of Schedules	1,334	1,273	1,202	1,205
Number of Interviews	15,279	13,789	12,551	12,201
Student Registrants	1,828	1,343	1,210	1,135
Interviews per				
Active Registrant*	9.44	11.37	12.00	12.29
Assertive Registrant**	12.10	13.80	14.04	14.76

*Active registrant denotes those students who interviewed one or more times on campus.

**Assertive registrant denotes those students who interviewed six or more times on campus.

Undergraduate Registrants

Major	Registrants*	Number of Female	Male	Minority**
Business				
Accounting	250	114	136	9
Business Economics	10	3	7	1
CIS	102	33	69	5
Finance	177	46	131	4
Human Resources	13	8	5	0
International Business	5	3	2	1
Management	47	19	28	2
Marketing	235	97	138	9
Operations	5	2	3	0
Real Estate	10	0	10	0
Other Business	3	1	2	0
Subtotal	857	326	531	31
		(37%)	(62%)	(3.6%)
Non-Business				
Apparel Merchandising	21	21	0	2
Biology	3	2	1	0
Chemistry	3	1	2	0
Computer Science	1	0	1	0
Economics	22	3	19	0
English	4	4	0	0
Journalism	20	17	3	1
Psychology	11	6	5	1
SPEA	86	24	62	4
Telecommunications	20	11	9	2
All Others Combined	7	43	44	9
Subtotal	278	132	146	44
		(47%)	(53%)	(6.8%)
TOTAL Undergraduate	1,135	458	677	50
Registrants		(40%)	(60%)	(4.4%)

*The total number of business graduates is slightly higher since some students do not register for placement services.

**Total of African American, Hispanic, and Native American minority students. Excludes Asian and foreign nationals.

Undergraduate Interviews & Frequency

Major	Total Interviews	Average Interviews Per Active Registrant*
Total Undergraduate	12,201	12.29
Business		
Accounting	3,028	13.17
Business Economics	86	10.75
CIS	1,259	13.84
Finance	1,772	11.43
Human Resources	90	7.75
Management	416	11.89
Marketing	3,031	15.08
Operations	73	14.60
Real Estate	46	5.75
Other Business	22	11.00
Non-Business		
Apparel Merchandising	141	8.81
Computer Science	2	1.00
Economics	280	10.77
Journalism	40	4.00
Psychology	54	7.71
SPEA	718	9.09
Telecommunications	102	6.80

*These averages are computed using all graduation dates. Spring graduates tend to have more interviews than fall graduates since they can interview two semesters as opposed to one semester. Active registrant denotes these students who interviewed one or more times on campus.

Undergraduate Placement Salary by Major

Major	Median Annual Salary*	Salary Low	Range High
All Undergrad. Majors			
Combined	$31,000	$16,000	$100,000
Business			
All Business Majors			
Combined	$31,000	$16,000	$100,000
Accounting	31,000	16,000	39,000
CIS	35,500	23,500	45,000
Finance	32,000	20,000	100,000
Human Resources	24,000	23,000	26,000
Management	28,000	21,500	35,000
Marketing	29,000	17,000	50,000
Non-Business			
All Non-Business Majors			
Combined	$28,000	$18,000	$44,000
Apparel Merchandising	26,000	23,000	32,000
Economics	32,000	18,000	44,000
Journalism	24,000	22,000	30,000
SPEA	26,000	16,800	28,200
Telecommunications	26,000	22,000	33,000

*This column represents only those students willing to report salary information. A significant number of students are placed each year who are unwilling to report salary information.

EXHIBIT 11

Context diagram for the system.

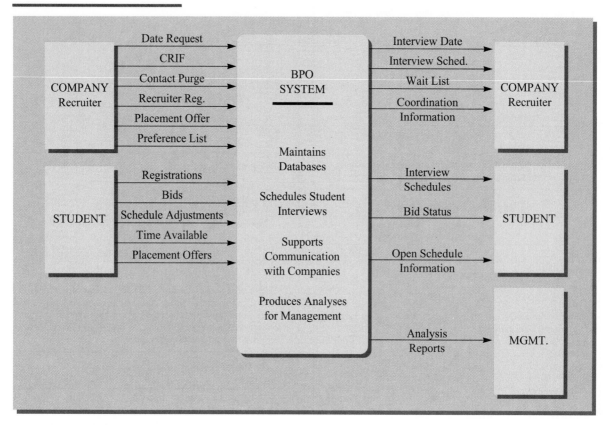

EXHIBIT 12

The computer network.

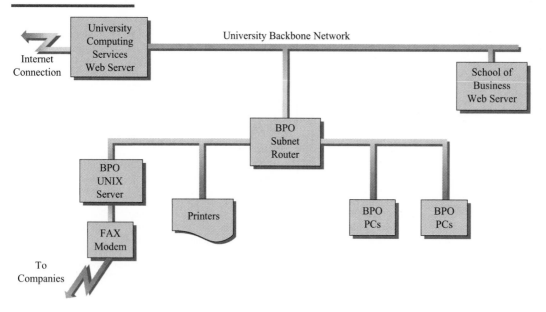

EXHIBIT 13
The Company database structure.

```
Structure for database:    /home/cris/company. dbf
Number of data records:      4730
Date of last update      :  01/23/97
Field    Field Name        Type        Width    Dec    Index
   1     COMNAME           Character      35             N
   2     COMNUM            Character       4             N
   3     ADDRESS1          Character      25             N
   4     ADDRESS2          Character      25             N
   5     CITY              Character      15             N
   6     STATE             Character       2             N
   7     ZIP               Character      10             N
   8     PHONE             Character      13             N
   9     CPCTYPE           Character       4             N
  10     UPDATE            Character       8             N
  11     DIRCODE           Character       3             N
  12     CONFCARDTY        Logical         1             N
  13     CONFCARDNY        Logical         1             N
  14     JOURNAL           Memo           10             N
  15     DESCRIPT          Memo           10             N
  16     URL               Memo           10             N
  17     LOGIN             Character      20             N
  18     _DBASELOCK        Character      16             N
 * Total **                              213
```

each of the BPO's client companies.[1] It is updated whenever BPO managers enlist a new client or when there is some change in the data on a current client. There is relatively little maintenance activity on this database.

The CONTACT database contains data on individual recruiters who have interviewed students through the BPO. It is updated with data from the registration forms that recruiters fill out when they arrive at the BPO to interview. Each summer the BPO sends a list of current contacts to each company and asks the company to return the list after crossing off the names of those who are no

longer recruiting for the company. This list is then used to purge names from the CONTACT database.

The SCHEDULE database has an entry for each planned interview schedule. Companies usually submit these data about six weeks prior to the interview date, and schedules are entered into the database when they are received. Changes to planned schedules occur, and when they are approved by the BPO manager in charge of the schedule, they are entered into the database. These data are an important input into the bid processing subsystem described below.

The CRIF database (shown in Exhibit 14) contains data describing each position offered by each company through its interview schedules and the qualifications required for a student to interview for that job. These data are provided via the Campus Recruiting Information Form (CRIF) that is submitted by the companies five or six weeks before the interview date. The CRIFs are entered into the database on a daily basis, and any

---

1 Unfortunately the data element names in the database examples are not always easy to relate to common terminology. Nevertheless, they give a fair idea of the contents of the database. The DBASELOCK data element contains a key that allows the DBMS to block access to the record unless the requester furnishes that key. Thus, for example, no other person can access a student's data.

EXHIBIT 14   *The CRIF database structure.*

Structure for database: /home/cris/crfjob.dbf
Number of data records: 9168
Date of last update: 01/23/97

Field	Field Name	Type	Width	Dec	Index
1	COMNUM	Character	4		N
2	JOBCODE	Character	2		N
3	POSITION	Character	2		N
4	DESCRIPT	Character	40		N
5	MAJORS	Character	34		N
6	DEGREE	Character	1		N
7	GRADDATE	Character	10		N
8	CITIZEN	Character	1		N
9	LISTYPE	Character	1		N
10	UPDATE	Character	8		N
11	CLASS	Character	10		N
12	GPA	Numeric	4	2	N
13	GPASCRN	Logical	1		N
14	WRKEXP	Character	4		N
15	EXPSCRN	Logical	1		N
16	SALMIN	Character	5		N
17	SALMAX	Character	6		N
18	AUTHWORK	Memo	10		N
19	FALLPRI	Logical	1		N
20	USEDATE	Character	8		N
21	JOBTYPE	Character	1		N
22	_DBASELOCK	Character	16		N
* Total **			171		

EXHIBIT 15   *The Student database structure.*

Structure for database: /home/cris/regmaste.dbf
Number of data records: 3468
Date of last update: 01/23/97

Field	Field Name	Type	Width	Dec	Index
1	REGNUM	Character	11		N
2	LASTNAME	Character	20		N
3	FIRSTNAME	Character	20		N
4	INITIAL	Character	1		N
5	MAJORS	Character	12		N
6	UDGMAJ	Character	12		N
7	DEGREE	Character	1		N
8	GRADDATE	Character	7		N
9	PAID	Logical	1		N
10	GPA	Numeric	4	2	N
11	UDGGPA	Numeric	4	2	N
12	BIRTHYR	Character	4		N
13	SEX	Character	1		N
14	RACE	Character	1		N
15	CITIZEN	Character	1		N
16	COUNTRY	Character	3		N
17	POSITIONS	Character	6		N
18	WRKEXP	Numeric	1		N
19	SKILLS	Character	14		N
20	LOCATIONS	Character	14		N
21	DATEAVAIL	Character	10		N
22	SALMIN	Numeric	5		N
23	SALMAX	Numeric	5		N
24	EMPLOYER	Character	35		N
25	EXPDATE	Character	8		N
26	NOSHOW	Character	8		N
27	BIDS	Character	10		N
28	UPDATE	Character	10		N
29	CAMPUS	Character	1		N
30	REFERRALS	Logical	1		N
31	SALUT	Character	4		N
32	OFPSTATUS	Character	1		N
33	EMAIL	Character	58		N
34	WWWREL	Logical	1		N
35	HADDRESS	Character	50		N
36	HCITY	Character	15		N
37	HSTATE	Character	2		N
38	HZIP	Character	5		N
39	HPHONE	Character	13		N
40	CADDRESS	Character	50		N
41	CCITY	Character	15		N
42	CSTATE	Character	2		N
43	CZIP	Character	5		N
44	CPHONE	Character	13		N
45	NOPRESMSG	Logical	1		N
46	WCOUNTRY	Character	9		N
47	POSEXP	Character	3		N
48	REGDATE	Character	8		N
49	JOURNAL	Memo	10		N
50	CC	Character	4		N
51	CLASS	Character	4		N
52	CYEAR	Character	2		N
53	_DBASELOCK	Character	16		N
* Total **			523		

changes to the data (such as positions available or required qualifications) are made as they occur. These data are used to establish the company's notice in the CSJ on the Web and are used by the bid processing subsystem described below.

The STUDENT database (shown in Exhibit 15) contains data on the students that are registered with the BPO. These data are uploaded from the student's Resume Expert disk, and changes during the year are also uploaded from the student's Resume Expert disk. These data are also required by the bid processing subsystem.

The BID database (shown in Exhibit 16) contains the data for each bid submitted by students via the bidding system on the Web. These data provide the most important input into the bid processing subsystem.

The INTERVIEW SCHEDULE database (shown in Exhibit 17) contains the data for a line on an interview schedule. The entries to this database are produced by the bid processing system described below. However, during

EXHIBIT 16 *The Bid database structure.*

Structure for database: /home/trnlot/bids.dbf
Number of data records: 228
Date of last update: 01/29/97

Field	Field Name	Type	Width	Dec	Index
1	REGNUM	Character	11		N
2	COMNUM	Character	4		N
3	JOBCODE	Character	2		N
4	BID	Character	1		N
5	RESNUM	Character	2		N
6	CLASS	Character	1		N
7	BIDDATE	Character	8		N
8	BIDSEQNUM	Character	5		N
* Total **			35		

EXHIBIT 17 *The Interview Schedule database structure.*

Structure for database: /home/cris/crfmaste.dbf
Number of data records: 7677
Date of last update: 01/23/97

Field	Field Name	Type	Width	Dec	Index
1	COMNUM	Character	4		N
2	CONNUM	Character	2		N
3	SCHEDNUM	Character	2		N
4	JOBCODE	Character	2		N
5	CSJCODE	Character	2		N
6	INTDATE	Character	8		N
7	NUMSCHEDS	Numeric	2		N
8	LENGTH	Character	2		N
9	START	Character	5		N
10	END	Character	5		N
11	SLOTS	Numeric	3		N
12	CBAM	Logical	1		N
13	LUN1200	Logical	1		N
14	LUN1230	Logical	1		N
15	CBPM	Logical	1		N
16	INVITE	Logical	1		N
17	UPDATE	Character	8		N
18	PROCDATE	Character	8		N
19	LISTYPE	Character	1		N
20	CRFRECVD	Logical	1		N
21	PRINTED	Character	1		N
22	LOGIN	Character	20		N
23	INPRIMBID	Logical	1		N
24	INRMDATE	Character	8		N
25	_DBASELOCK	Character	16		N
* Total **			107		

the time between when the schedule is posted on the Web and two days before the interview occurs, the student may make changes (such as canceling an interview or signing up for an open interview slot) via the Web.

The WAITLIST database contains the data for unsuccessful bids for interview slots. These data are also created by the bid processing system, and the results are provided to both the student and the company involved. However, if someone cancels an interview and a waitlisted person is given that slot, both the INTERVIEW SCHEDULE and the WAITLIST databases must be updated.

The PLACEMENT OFFERS database contains data on job offers the students have received. The students are asked to submit placement information through the Web when they receive an offer and/or accept a job, and these important data are transferred from the Web server to the database on the BPO Unix server. Also, at the end of each recruiting season each company is asked to report its hires and offers, and their replies are also used to update this database.

Changes to these databases take place quite frequently, so each of them is updated on a daily basis. BPO managers are very concerned with maintaining the accuracy of each of these databases.

Primary Bid Processing Subsystem

Because most interview schedules fill during primary bidding, the primary bid processing system is crucial to both the students and the BPO. Primary bid processing takes place on Monday evenings during the recruiting season, and results are provided to the students via e-mail and the Web by early Tuesday morning. As the following description shows, a complex process is required to process the primary bids.

A system flow chart depicting the bid processing system is shown in Exhibit 18. A system flow chart is composed of processes sandwiched between the inputs to and the outputs from those processes. Output data may be the input to another process. Each process is usually performed by a computer under control of a program. The lines indicate flows of data and are read from the top down and from left to right. Arrowheads at the end of a line indicate that the flow is up or to the right.

All of the processes in this subsystem are performed on the BPO Unix server, and the databases shown reside on that server, although the data may have been collected

EXHIBIT 18

System Flowchart of the bid processing subsystem (page 1).

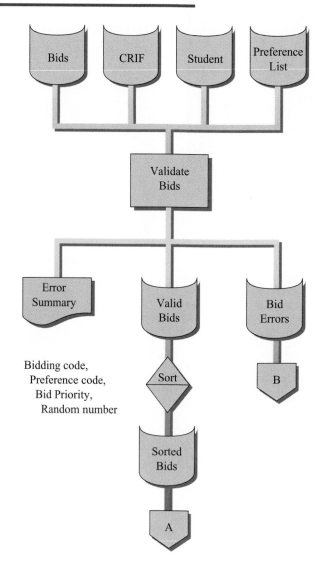

via the Web and the outputs may be transferred to the Web server for access by the student.

As shown at the top of the first page of the flow chart, the input to the bid validation process includes the batch of bids on specific jobs with specific companies from the students, the CRIF data on the requirements to bid on each job imposed by the companies, the data on the students used to determine their eligibility to bid on the job, and the preference lists. In order to validate the bids, the program first checks to see if the student has been sus-

pended for missing an interview and if he or she has the requested bid available. Then the program compares the student status from the student file with the company restrictions to determine if the student is qualified to bid on that job. If the student is on the preference list for that job, he or she is certified as qualified without checking the student's status. The program also adds two data elements to the valid bids: a preference code (1 if the student is preferenced and 2 if not) and an 8-digit number from a random number generator that is used to break

EXHIBIT 18
System Flowchart (page 2).

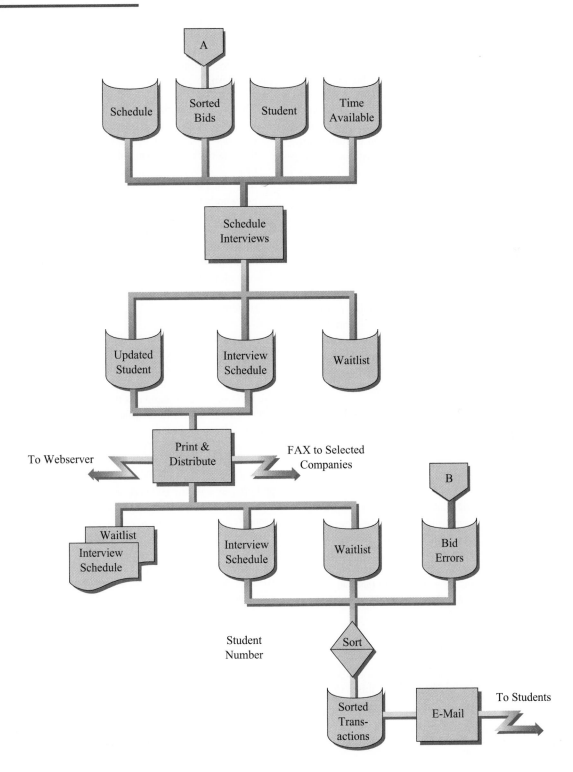

ties between students who would otherwise have equal priority. The output from this process includes valid bids, bid errors, and an error summary report summarizing the frequency of various types of errors. The bid errors file is input to a distribution process (on page 2 of the flow chart) that e-mails the notice of the error to the student and sends the bid errors file to the Web server.

The next processing step is to sort the valid bids database on the concatenation of bidding code (which is company number and job code) preference code, priority, and the tie-breaking random number. By concatenation we mean that the data elements are combined to form one long data element, starting from the left with company number, then job code, then preference code, and so on. This sorting process gets all of the bids for a company-job combination together and also arranges these bids in sequence by the complex priority scheme the BPO uses to assign bids to interview slots. Thus, if there are twelve slots available for a given company-job combination, then the first twelve bids would be given these slots.

Then (on page 2 of the flow chart) the schedule database, sorted bids, student database, and time available database are input into the interview scheduling process. As described above, the bids are sequenced so that determining which students get the interview slots is trivial, and the rest of the bids form the waitlist. But the time availability data must be used to determine which student interviews at each time slot. A complex algorithm is used to assign the selected students to time slots in such a way that all the students are scheduled to interview when they do not have other conflicts. The outputs from this process is an interview schedule database, a waitlist database, and an updated student database (whose bids available data has been updated to reflect the bids that have been used).

Next the interview schedules and waitlists are printed and sent to the Web server, and some of them are automatically FAXed to the companies who have requested this service. Finally, the interview schedule, waitlist, and bid errors databases are sorted together on student number so that all bid actions for a student are together and a single e-mail can be sent to the student that reports the results of all of his or her bids.

Conclusion

Although the Midstate University BPO has had a computerized bidding system for several years, this is the first

year that the Web has been used as the primary interface with the students. This has been a tremendous success, from both the students' and the BPO's perspective. One advantage of the Web is the ease with which changes can be made, and the BPO has been able to continuously modify this system, even on a week-by-week basis.

The system has worked so well that Wine has only one concern:

> My only worry now is security. It might be attractive to some students to get into the system and make changes so that they could get interviews to which they are not entitled. And, of course, there will always be hackers who get their kicks by causing trouble. We have built in lots of firewalls to protect this system, but who is to say that it cannot be penetrated?
>
> We do not know whether it has been by accident or on purpose, but every once in a while we have gotten a virus. Just last week a virus knocked the School of Business system down, and us with it. We are well enough protected that it doesn't take us long to clean a virus out, but it is an inconvenience to us and to the students we serve.

This concern for security has dictated how the system has been designed to operate. Although to the students the system may appear to be an on-line system, it is not. There is no on-line connection through the Web to the BPO server that maintains the files and produces the interview schedules. Rather, the Web system collects the students' input and sends it in a batch to the BPO server each night. The BPO server then updates its databases and returns a batch of changes to the students' data that is available through the Web server. Thus the databases and processes on the BPO server are protected from persons who might try to penetrate and modify the data or processes of the system.

The students, however, have a major responsibility for the security of their own data, for if a student leaves the system without exiting it properly by returning to the BPO or School of Business home page, anyone who comes to that terminal can continue to work with the student's data. Not only can this person see the student's data, but the intruder can cancel interviews, enter bids, and take other actions that may not be to the student's liking. In the manual that describes the system and explains how to use it, the BPO repeatedly cautions the reader to be sure to exit the system properly.

AMERITECH PUBLISHING, INC.

Ameritech Publishing, Inc., a subsidiary of Ameritech Corporation, publishes *Ameritech PagesPlus* telephone directories for the Ameritech Bell telephone companies in Indiana, Michigan, Ohio, and Wisconsin. Ameritech Publishing also has subsidiaries that produce 14 Ameritech Industrial Yellow Pages books covering 33 states and publish about 70 directories in 10 states outside the Ameritech area, English language directories for Tokyo and Osaka, and German, Austrian, and Swiss industrial directories. Publishing and distributing approximately 40 million copies of 484 different directories in 1990, Ameritech Publishing had $866.4 million in revenues and provided about one-fourth of Ameritech's profits in 1990.

Ameritech Publishing's primary business is publishing yellow pages telephone directories. Yellow pages advertising does not generate demand, but a person who has decided to buy something often looks in the yellow pages to decide where to buy it. Because almost everyone has access to the yellow pages, and the average person uses them about 100 times each year to decide where to obtain something he or she already wants, it can be a very productive form of advertising.

As shown in Exhibit 1, there are two different types of yellow pages advertising. The entries in the column in the upper left of Exhibit 1 are in-column ads, which vary in size and form, as described in Exhibit 2. The large ads in Exhibit 1 are display ads, and (although it is not apparent in this black-and-white reproduction) they may be

This case was prepared by Professor E. W. Martin as the basis for class discussion rather than to illustrate either effective or ineffective handling of an administrative situation. Its development was supported by the Institute for Research on the Management of Information Systems (IRMIS), School of Business, Indiana University.

black on yellow or contain several colors. For example, the elaborate border of the "Fields of Flowers" ad is green, and the name Fields of Flowers and the telephone number are bright red. Display ads are more completely described in Exhibit 3. The yearly cost of a full-page display ad is about $11,000 in a city the size of Bloomington, Indiana, but can range up to almost $30,000 in Detroit or Cleveland.

Ameritech Publishing is in a very competitive business, with other companies publishing similar directories in every one of its markets. Moreover, Ameritech Publishing must compete with newspapers, radio, television, cable TV, and direct mail for a portion of each customer's advertising budget. It has a sales force of about 700 people who are paid on a commission basis.

History of Ameritech Publishing

Ameritech Corporation was formed in 1984 as one of seven regional holding companies created from the divestiture of AT&T. Prior to divestiture, each of the Bell companies was responsible for its own telephone directories and yellow pages, but Ameritech quickly decided that there was great potential for growth in yellow pages revenues and that this potential could best be exploited by separating the directory operations from the local telephone company's responsibilities and centralizing them in a wholly owned subsidiary. Therefore, in 1984 Ameritech Publishing was formed by combining the directory publishing organizations from Indiana Bell, Michigan Bell, Ohio Bell, and Wisconsin Bell. Illinois Bell (which is part of Ameritech) was excluded because Ameritech decided to handle directory operations in Illinois through a joint venture with R. H. Donnelly. Although the telephone directory part of the Ameritech business was centralized, the five state telephone companies continued to operate as stand-alone entities.

EXHIBIT 1

Ameritech Yellow Pages In-Column and Display Ads.

Leo Egan, a general manager from Michigan Bell, was the first president of Ameritech Publishing. His mission was to build an organization while at the same time improving the profitability of the ongoing directory operations. To mold an organization out of the pieces of four previous groups, Egan organized the company functionally, with most of the field personnel reporting to publishing and sales vice presidents. He also established

EXHIBIT 2
Ameritech Yellow Pages In-Column Ad Descriptions.

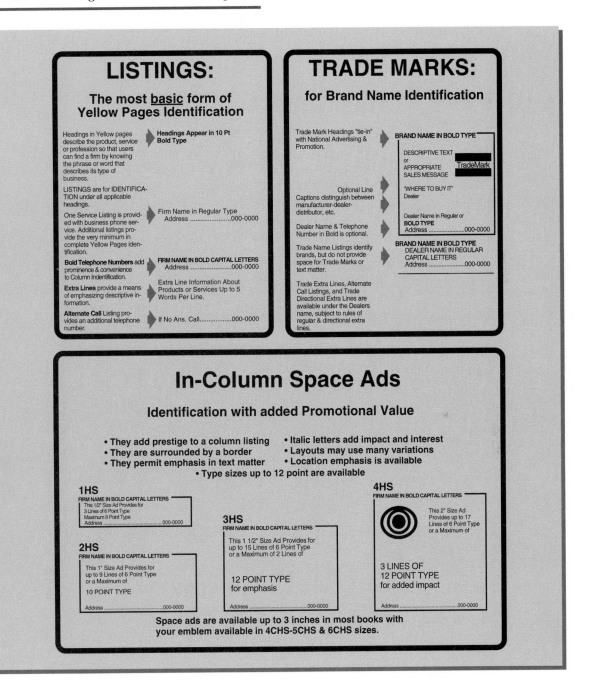

EXHIBIT 3
Ameritech Yellow Pages Display Ad Descriptions.

When you want to get

ATTENTION

this Half-Page ad size will get your business

NOTICED!

Be sure to describe all of your products, services, or special feature information for your potential customers.

Also use an attractive illustration to catch the eye! Remember that the more you tell, the more you sell.

(8QCH)

DISPLAY ADS:
The Ultimate in Yellow Pages

Advantages of Display Ads

* Complete flexibility in layout
* Pictures-speaking a universal language
* Great variety of type styles
* White space to assure interest
* Benday panels
* Selection of border styles

ANCHOR LISTING provided with each display ad. Special phrase follows address line, designed to lead column user to a more complete message in the display ad.

Firm Name in **BOLD** or Regular Type
Address 000-0000
or
000-0000
*See Advertisement This Classification

DISPLAY ADS ARE AVAILABLE IN OTHER STANDARD SIZES
IF YOU WISH TO BE CONTACTED FOR COMPLETE INFORMATION CALL (317)685-7800, INPLS. IN. OR CALL 1-800-382-1929

One Large or Several Small Illustrations May Be Used In This Size Ad

This is a Triple Half Column Display Ad

The shape and size of this ad offers designers the greater flexibility. It holds more information. Several illustrations may be used. Greater white space encourages readership. In past studies, Yellow Pages users have said that they consider the size of ad to be an indication of the size and reliability of the firm.

BOLD FIRM NAME & HEADINGS

SPECIFIC INFORMATION TO ENCOURAGE YOUR CUSTOMERS
VISIT - HOURS - MAPS

(6QCH)

staff positions in the finance, information services, human resources, and legal areas.

The four Bell companies from which the Ameritech Publishing personnel were drawn had been typical telephone companies with typical telephone company attitudes, but each had its own distinct corporate culture. Each of the Bell companies did things its own way, which carried over to the yellow pages as well. The layouts of the pages, the pricing, the contracts with advertisers, and the sales compensation plans were all different from one Bell company to another.

The new publishing vice president, Donald J. Frayer, was convinced of the need to standardize the publication of the directories. He felt that this required standard computer systems to support the publication and sales functions. Egan agreed on the need for these systems and supported their development, but his main focus was on the profitability of current operations, not on standardizing them. Having accomplished his mission of creating a new company from fragments of four Ameritech telephone companies and getting it off to a profitable start, Egan retired in 1986. He was replaced by Barry Allen, a young, energetic executive from Ameritech with marketing experience and an MBA from the Darden School at the University of Virginia.

Allen took over a young company that was going well in terms of profitability, but not much effort had been put into defining its long-range role and goals. He felt that Ameritech Publishing's culture was still essentially that of the old bureaucratic, monopolistic telephone companies from whence it came. Allen's vision for the company was that of a lean and mean, customer-focused, competitive tiger. Allen's first priority was to get the company focused on the customer and customer responsiveness. Thus, he wanted to move decision-making down so that it was very close to the customer. His second priority was to get the bureaucratic fat out of the organization. He believed that one of the best ways to remove this fat was to break down the business into many smaller pieces and to assign each piece to a manager empowered to manage that piece as if it were his own business.

Soon after he took over, Allen reorganized the company from a functional to a profit center organization (as shown in Exhibit 4). As before, there were staff positions concerned with human resources, finance, corporate planning, information services, and legal affairs. The line organization was no longer functional, but rather had a general manager for each state who was responsible for the bottom line profitability in his state. Each state manager had his or her own publishing and sales responsibil-

ities, and bottom-line responsibility was also pushed down to the district and even the office. In mid-1989, when Allen was transferred to become head of Wisconsin Bell, Ameritech Publishing had become more efficient and was even more profitable than before.

Ameritech Publishing's new president and CEO was Gary G. Drook, a dynamic executive in his mid-forties who was vice president of marketing at Ameritech. Prior to this job, Drook had been with Indiana Bell, where he had served in several assistant vice president positions in information systems and marketing. Drook found that the organization had not made as much progress toward becoming customer-focused as he desired, and that there had been little progress in replacing the individual state cultures with a unified company vision. Also, the development of the new computer systems to support the sales and publications functions had bogged down.

Drook's Vision for Ameritech Publishing

In late 1991 Drook's primary goals for Ameritech Publishing were growth and quality. He wanted continual growth in terms of market share, revenues, and profits. "Being quick and flexible is what is going to help us grow the business," Drook says. "We must be able to quickly introduce new products, new enhancements, new pricing strategies. And we must become more customer-oriented and easier to do business with."

Drook also wanted better and better quality as perceived by his customers. According to Drook, "Quality involves better and more effective products and services, but it also means a mistake-free yellow pages book where each advertisement looks exactly like the customer intended it to look."

Drook's Concerns

Even after eight years, the heritage of being a part of the old Bell System telephone companies still persisted. According to Drook:

Before divestiture the telephone companies had a tremendous internal focus—on processes, procedures, and profitability. Customers were something that they just tolerated. They sold the yellow pages more on fear and intimidation than on value and service. We still have too many traces of these old attitudes.

We are perceived as being hard to do business with. One problem is that our products are different from one state to another. Consider South Bend,

EXHIBIT 4
Ameritech Publishing 1987 Reorganization.

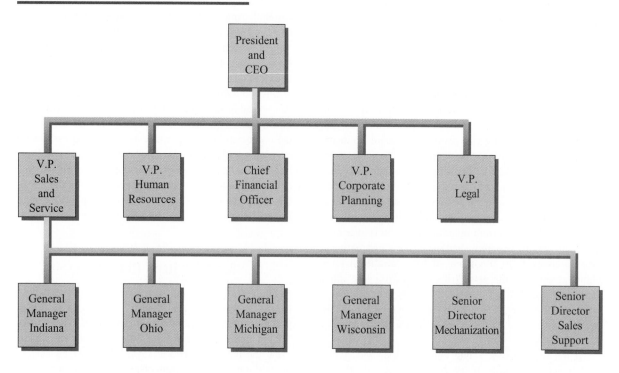

Indiana, and Niles, Michigan. These two towns are almost one town, but the state line runs down a street between them. Ads cost one thing on one side of this street and something else on the other side. Ads are vertical on one side and horizontal on the other side. It is very hard for me to explain to customers in the Niles–South Bend market why we cannot be more customer-focused.

Although the yellow pages are considered to be a local medium, we do about 12 percent of our business with national advertisers like General Motors, Ford, Chrysler, Roto Rooter, GE, and Westinghouse. The marketing department for General Motors, for example, defines and lays out all the yellow pages ads for General Motors dealers nationwide. Someone has estimated that for General Motors to place ads in our 400 directories, they need about 57 different pieces of artwork. This is partly because they have different size ads in different books, but the primary cause is that each of our states does things differently—for example, three-quarter page ads that are horizontal in Michigan are vertical in Ohio.

As a result, General Motors finds it very difficult to do business with us. They cannot just consider the market and decide which size ad they should have. Instead we have to get into long discussions about how we do our book in Detroit, and then another discussion about how we do it in Cleveland, etc. Kmart, for example, spends $300 million on advertising, but they do not advertise in the yellow pages. They, and a number of other large advertisers, have told us that we are tough to do business with, that we are expensive, that we have a lot of funny rules, that they cannot make a national buy that makes cohesive sense to them.

In order to increase business, Drook wants to be able to quickly develop, test, and introduce new products. New products may be new pricing plans, but they also include significant changes, such as the availability of colors. It is very difficult for Ameritech Publishing to introduce new products when its products are not standard across states, because it may have to have different versions of the new product in each state. Also, because other things differ so much between states, market research and customer attitude surveys on new products are suspect unless they are replicated in each state, which increases costs and slows things down tremendously.

Drook knows that the quality of his product is not what he would like it to be. One measure of quality is the number of claims that they must deal with. A claim is a request by an advertiser for compensation because there was a problem with the advertisement—the wrong phone number, a misspelled name, the wrong color of ink, and so on. "We pay out about $20 million a year in claims because of mistakes in the books," Drook notes. Today a lot of these claims go to court. "We make so many mistakes that we have to be very careful about what we give out in compensation for claims or we could bankrupt the business," Drook laments. "We want to get the claims level down to where it is much more reasonable," asserts Drook. "Then for the few customers who have a problem we could do almost anything to make them happy."

One reason there are so many mistakes today is that, because of the time pressure in preparing ads to meet publication deadlines, Ameritech Publishing is often unable to allow customers to proofread their ads before they are published.

Drook's Strategies for Improving

Drook knows that changing people's attitudes is not easy and that there is no quick fix. He is continually working to communicate his vision to everyone in the company. He designated 1991 as "The Year of the Customer" and publicized this widely within the company. Drook also has focused the attention of Ameritech Publishing on his goals by announcing and repeatedly emphasizing an "Advertiser's Bill of Rights," which states that every advertiser can expect from Ameritech Publishing:

- a simple contract that permits them to understand what we will do and how much our services and product will cost.
- the opportunity to see what their advertising will look like before the advertisement is made public.
- an account executive that is knowledgeable about OUR products and THEIR business.
- an advertisement "delivered," designed and produced as we promised.
- an accurate bill that is understandable.
- immediate, effective, and courteous resolution if a problem should arise.
- guaranteed products.

Drook has also aligned the company reward system with his customer service vision by basing 20 percent of each salesman's compensation on service performance as perceived by the salesman's customers. The company does telephone surveys that measure the customer's perception of the timeliness and accuracy of the ad, concern and helpfulness, and quality of service. The results produce a service index for each salesman on a scale of one to ten. "At the start," reports Drook, "the results were all over the map, but they have been moving up and becoming more uniform. We now have sales groups that average a nine. We are very happy with the results."

Another of Drook's strategies is to standardize Ameritech Publishing's products and operations so that they are uniform from state to state. Not only will this make them much less confusing to large customers, but it will enable the company to introduce new products much more quickly and to better control the quality of its products and services.

Finally, Drook is counting on new computer systems that are under development to provide the accuracy and flexibility that are so lacking today in the sales and publishing operations. These systems will accept orders for advertising, assist employees in creating the artwork for the ads, and store the ads in computer files. Once the ads are created and stored, the copy for a telephone book will be created by the computer and sent to the printer with no manual processes required.

New Computer Systems

The interrelated computer systems being developed to support Ameritech Publishing's sales and publishing operations are depicted in Exhibit 5.

ARIES (Ameritech Regional Information Exchange System) is a large, complex system that maintains the customer database and provides many services to the sales organization. The database contains information on customers, including their history of advertising buys and their current contract. One of its major functions is to support the salesman when he calls on the customer to sell advertising in next year's book. The system produces a report that shows the customer's past history and the contract terms for this year's products. It accepts orders and updates the database, calculates the salesman's commission, and notifies the TIGER graphics system that the ad must be included in the book. It also keeps track of claims and reflects their impact on the compensation of salesmen. The ARIES database contains the data for producing virtually any sales reports that management might desire.

EXHIBIT 5
Publication Systems.

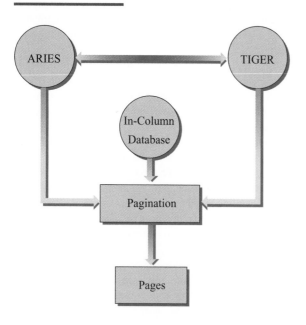

TIGER (Total Integrated Graphics Entry and Retrieval) is a large graphics and database system that can be used to create and store advertisements that will be printed in the book. The TIGER processing center is located in Troy, Michigan, and contains several rooms full of Sun workstations networked to the large VAX computer that manages the database—about $10 million worth of hardware (see Exhibit 6).

At a TIGER workstation an artist has access to a catalog of about 50,000 pieces of "clip art" that can be incorporated into any advertisement, a scanner through which images can be transferred into the computer, and a high-quality color printer for producing advertising layouts. As with most desktop publishing systems, the artist can use a mouse to draw, bring in clip art, move or rotate images, change the size of all or part of the ad, determine the color of images, modify previous versions of the ad, and store the result in the computer's digital graphical database. Thus, the artist can produce a new ad or modify last year's ad, and the result is stored in the database so that it can be used to produce the yellow pages book. The final ad can also be electronically sent to the sales office to show to the customer.

TIGER can enforce standards concerning the size and shape of ads, and it also notifies ARIES that the ad that the customer ordered has been created. If an ad is pub-

lished with a mistake, this results in a claim that is entered into ARIES. ARIES then notifies the TIGER database to tag the ad for correction before it can be used in next year's book. Thus, there should be no mistakes in the old ads that are used in the new book. Likewise, ads that require revision each year can be tagged to make sure that the required revision has been made before the ad is reused.

The in-column database has traditionally been maintained by the printer, but Ameritech Publishing has decided to bring this function in-house so that this material can be combined with the display ads to electronically produce the yellow pages.

As shown in Exhibit 5, the final component of this system is an automatic pagination system. When it is time to produce one of the telephone books, the pagination system receives the orders from ARIES, the in-column material from that database, and the display ads from the TIGER database. The pagination system then applies rules to design and create electronic page images that can be fed to a computer controlling the press to print the pages without manual intervention.

EXHIBIT 6
Using a TIGER Workstation.

Consider how the yellow pages have traditionally been produced. It all started with the canvassing function, when Ameritech Publishing's salesmen contacted customers to sell advertising in the next yellow pages directory. The creation of a new display ad was contracted out to an artist working for a local ad agency. The completed artwork was placed in a brown envelope and filed with the other ads appearing in the new book. About two and a half months before the deadline for distributing the new book, the sales office would stop selling and send these envelopes containing the hand-done artwork to the printer, along with a printout of the advertising orders from the computer. The printer would obtain the in-column information from the local telephone company, and then would lay out the pages by hand and print the book.

This process was slow, expensive, and mistake-prone. Because of the tight deadlines, there was no time to show the new ads to customers before they were sent to the printer, so errors and misunderstandings often appeared in the book. Also, when there were mistakes in the current book, someone might get confused and send the old artwork to the printer instead of the corrected version, which infuriated the advertiser.

With the new system, the display ads will be created by in-house artists using TIGER and stored in the TIGER database. Because the manual layout will be eliminated, Ameritech Publishing expects to save about $6 million of the $10 million per year that it pays the printer for these services. It also expects to save around $5 million a year on printing costs because tests indicate that the automatic pagination system is more efficient in the use of space, thus reducing the number of pages printed.

But Drook sees the main benefits of the new systems to be speed, flexibility, and accuracy. Because the company will be able to drastically compress the time required to produce a telephone book, it will be able to make sure that every ad is seen and approved by the advertiser before it appears in the book. Since the ads will have been approved by the customer (and corrected if necessary) and stored in the graphics database, there should be very few errors in the book when it is printed. Fewer errors should drastically reduce claims and enable the company to generously compensate customers for the few problems that remain. Thus, Drook is counting on these new computer systems to enable Ameritech Publishing to live up to the ideals expressed in his Advertiser's Bill of Rights.

Unfortunately, these systems, which were started in 1985, are still not completed and installed throughout Ameritech Publishing. While initial versions of components are being used in some states, and it has been demonstrated that the systems can perform adequately, the date when they will be completely operational throughout Ameritech Publishing keeps receding.

The Development of ARIES and TIGER

When Ameritech Publishing was formed in 1984, it had no information systems organization. Daniel J. Harmon, who had started out at Bell Labs as a systems analyst and worked in both information systems and the directory business at Michigan Bell, was designated to build an information services organization for Ameritech Publishing. Harmon started with a staff of two, which had grown to 160 by 1991.

Each of the Ameritech states had its own customer/contract system that was being run at that state's Bell Telephone data center. Harmon's first task was to bring them into the new Ameritech Publishing data center in Troy, Michigan, which was accomplished by the end of 1984. Ameritech Publishing management quickly decided that the company needed a single customer/contract system to serve all of Ameritech Publishing.

Management first thought that the most efficient way to get to this single system would be to take the best of the existing systems, move the other three states to that system, and then enhance it over time to include all the needed capabilities. After extensive investigation and negotiation, however, management found that each of the four existing state systems was unacceptable to the other three states. Therefore, they decided to develop a new system (ARIES) that would combine the best features of each of the existing systems.

At that time (1985), Ameritech Publishing still had a very small information services organization with little systems development capability. Therefore, the company opted to contract the development of this system to the Indiana Bell information services organization that had developed the Indiana Contract System. Ameritech Publishing planned to complete and install ARIES in the four states by the middle of 1988 at a cost of about $5 million.

During 1985, Donald J. Frayer, vice president of publishing, was developing a vision of how to run publishing in the future. He envisioned an "integrated publishing environment" that corresponds to the systems depicted in Exhibit 5 and serves the needs of both sales and publishing. Thus, the company began to envision the graphics system for producing and storing display ads that became TIGER.

The Ameritech Publishing IS organization had no experience with or capability for graphics systems, so it began to look for a system to purchase. After some investigation, Ameritech Publishing signed a system integration contract with Janus Systems to produce the TIGER system, including responsibility for both software and hardware. Development and installation of TIGER was projected to take two years and cost less than $6 million. According to Harmon, "We had originally intended to build and convert our operations to ARIES, and then schedule the graphics system to come in behind. However, the economics of TIGER were so compelling that we decided to develop the two systems in parallel, with TIGER lagging about six months behind ARIES."

The requirements analysis and system design for ARIES were almost completed when Barry Allen took over as president in 1986 and reorganized the company into profit centers. In 1987, when IS was trying to get final sign-offs on the system design so that coding could begin, it found that previously agreed upon decisions were no longer acceptable. IS could not get final agreement on the form of the contract, what the system was to provide to the salesmen, and hundreds of other standardization issues. "Our standardization committees were up against the wall because they could not get the states to agree," reports Harmon. "Each profit center was insisting that we do it their way, and since IS had no power to say no, we ended up trying to satisfy everyone." Needless to say, this resulted in a complex, unwieldy system, and in continual delays.

Indiana was to be the first state for ARIES, and management established the target date of February 1989 to begin installation, almost a year after it had originally planned to have this system operational in all four states. In order to make this deadline, whenever it got bogged down trying to make a standardization decision, the Indiana Bell IS organization had to go on and make a decision, usually based upon what was wanted by Ameritech Publishing's Indiana profit center. IS knew that these decisions would cause problems in the other states, but it had no alternative.

When Gary Drook took over as president in mid-1989, he found that Ameritech Publishing had already spent double its original $11 million development budget for ARIES and TIGER. The original plan was to install these systems throughout the company in 1988, but the company was just converting Indiana to these systems. It looked as if it would be at least three more years before the new systems would be in company-wide use.

Things were not going well in Indiana. The company had problems cleaning up the existing data and converting to ARIES. The salesmen and clerks who used the systems had to change what they did and how they did it and were not adequately trained. The Indiana profit center also was approaching its most difficult time of the year, when it was to publish its Indianapolis book. Furthermore, the other states were watching Indiana, seeing a system that was not what they wanted and increasingly questioning what the system was going to do for them.

One of Allen's last moves was to replace the user project manager, who was responsible for obtaining agreement on what the system was to do, with Walter E. Smolak, who had worked for Harmon as director of the Ameritech Publishing data center. Smolak had come from Michigan Bell, where he had run data centers and served as an internal auditing manager, and before divestiture had headed AT&T's Development and Research Center in Orlando, Florida. Given how things were going in Indiana, Smolak was very uncomfortable with the planned conversion schedule for the other states.

After reviewing the history of the ARIES and TIGER projects with Harmon and Smolak, Drook concluded that, in addition to the normal difficulties associated with developing large systems, the major problem was that Ameritech Publishing had not faced the standardization issues inherent in these systems.

"We were trying to build a car with four engines in it, one for each state," Drook recalls. "You do not see many cars with four engines because they do not work very well. Furthermore, they are expensive to build and even more expensive to maintain." Drook coined the phrase "one car, one engine" to express his determination to "standardize our products, standardize our processes, standardize our procedures, and standardize the computer systems that support these standardized processes."

To get the development of ARIES and TIGER back on track, Drook asked Smolak to make a list of the standardization issues that were holding up progress. Smolak came up with a list of 39 issues, and Drook called his state general managers together and divided these issues up among them. For example, he told the Ohio manager: "You are responsible for sales reports. You should get input from your peers, but you are going to define the sales reports that everyone is going to get." He gave another manager the responsibility for defining the standard order form, and so on.

"This was a big help," reports Smolak, "but we always had a flock of new issues coming up, so we continued to be bogged down in resolving them. Moreover, although under pressure the managers would finally agree to standardize, in their heart of hearts they really did not want to do it. They would delay as long as possible before agreeing, and then insist that it would take them two years to make the change." Progress continued to be frustratingly slow.

After finishing the Indiana conversion to ARIES and TIGER, Ameritech Publishing started converting Michigan in September 1990. Because Michigan was organized and managed differently from the other states, Michigan had even more difficulty converting to the system than Indiana.

Present Status

In August 1991, Ameritech Publishing had almost completed the Michigan conversion. The company purchased a pagination system that is very flexible in that it allows the company to insert its own rules on allocating space. Since page layout is still different in each state, however, the company is having difficulty defining these rules and has not yet started pagination in any state. Ameritech Publishing has invested several times its original $11 million development budget in these systems, and because most of the anticipated savings lie in automatic page layout, it has yet to obtain any substantial return on this investment. Furthermore, Ohio is scheduled to begin conversion soon, and the Ohio general manager is pressing to postpone it for another year.

Because these systems are essential to achieving his vision for Ameritech Publishing, Drook has been increasingly frustrated that his efforts to promote standardization and get these systems back on track have not been successful. For some time he has been considering his alternatives, and he intends to act soon.

BATESVILLE CASKET'S
WORLD WIDE WEB SITE

Batesville Casket Company is a subsidiary of Hillenbrand Industries, Inc., headquartered in the small southern Indiana town of Batesville. Batesville Casket is the world's largest producer of metal and hardwood burial caskets, having the leading position in the U.S. market. With six manufacturing plants in the U.S., one in Canada, and one in Mexico, Batesville Casket serves some 22,000 funeral homes in North America through 70 strategically located distribution warehouses.

In order to bring a spirit of entrepreneurship into Batesville Casket, in early 1996 the company reorganized from a traditional organization to a Strategic Business Unit (SBU) form. Strategic Business Units oriented around product lines include a burial urn SBU, a premium products SBU, a standard metal casket SBU, a wooden casket SBU, and an "essentials" SBU whose products are caskets made of composite materials. There are also Centers of Excellence in support functions such as finance, personnel, and sales/marketing. As a part of this reorganization, the previously centralized Batesville Casket Information Technology Department has been decentralized to better serve the needs of the SBUs and Centers of Excellence.

Batesville Casket's Market

Batesville Casket sells its products to funeral homes. The family of the deceased person chooses the casket from the selection provided by the funeral home. Typically the funeral home will have a casket selection room with a limited number of caskets that can be seen, and there may be one or more catalogues from which other models can be chosen. Because the funeral home has a rather limited stock of caskets on hand, it is critical that the casket manufacturer be able to deliver any desired casket to the funeral home within 24 to 48 hours. In order to provide the necessary level of service, Batesville Casket has some 70 service centers (warehouses), its own fleet of trucks, and a sophisticated computer system for processing orders and managing its inventory and deliveries.

Some funeral homes deal exclusively with Batesville Casket, some stock other brands of caskets as well, and some do not provide Batesville Casket's products.

During the past few years there has been a strong trend towards consolidation in the funeral home industry, with large organizations competing aggressively to buy family-owned funeral homes. According to the December 9, 1996, issue of *Time*,[1] consolidators then owned only about 10 percent of America's 23,000 funeral homes, but these homes tended to be prime properties in key markets and accounted for about 20 percent of the country's funerals and thus about 20 percent of the U. S. market for burial caskets. In late 1996 the industry leader, Service Corporation International of Houston, owned 2,832 homes and 331 cemeteries in North America, and the Lowen Group, based near Vancouver, Canada, owned 814 homes and 265 cemeteries in North America. Both organizations were expanding as rapidly as possible in order to ready themselves for the time when baby boomers begin to die in increasing numbers.

Motivation for a Web Site

Responding to the rapid changes in its market, Batesville Casket allocated more of its information technology resources to the sales and marketing areas. Accordingly,

1 Larson, Erik, "Fight to the Death," *Time,* December 9, 1996, pp. 62–67.

James J. Kuisel, former director of the centralized information technology area, is now head of the sales/marketing information technology group and reports to the vice president of sales. Kuisel explains:

> Top management thought that we could grow the business by using information technology, so they decided to concentrate IT in marketing and sales to use it for generating revenue. One of our first steps was to use the Internet to build brand preference so that we can have families asking for our product.
>
> We believe that we can offer a valuable service to families of those who are terminally ill by providing them information on the decisions that have to be made when death occurs. There are a number of things where they will be sorry for a long time if they make the wrong decision, and they can do a lot of planning in advance of the death. We hope to provide a service to the community and at the same time build brand awareness for our products.
>
> There is also a lot of negative public relations information that is out about our industry, and as the number one casket company we tend to be "picked on." We think that the Internet can give us an opportunity to present our side and counter that negative publicity.

Kuisel was concerned about the possible reactions of funeral directors to the idea of setting up a home page on the Web. Some funeral homes have used the Internet to promote cut-rate funeral services, and some critics have used the Internet to attack the funeral industry. The possibility that funeral directors would associate Batesville Casket with these negative activities on the Internet troubled Kuisel, so the first thing he did was to check out the idea with Batesville Casket's customers.

> We have an advisory council composed of representatives from 30 funeral homes nominated by our regional managers. We called each one and asked them what they thought of the idea of Batesville Casket going on the Internet, and all of the response was favorable. Incidentally, we were surprised to learn that more than half these representatives indicated that they were using the Internet!
>
> We then sent out an announcement to each of our 16,000 funeral home customers. We told them that we were attempting to promote a better understanding of the funeral process, and that we had three goals for our Web site: (1) To promote the value of the funeral and the important role of the funeral home director, (2) to educate consumers on the funeral process and

the product choices available, and (3) to make available resources that provide support in the human processes of grief. A section of questions that might be asked (with answers) was included.

Web Site Development

Development of the Batesville Casket Web site was begun in late February, 1996, and a phase one version was up and running by early May (http://www.batesville.com). The initial home page design is shown in Exhibit 1. By clicking on the buttons on the left, this home page leads to the following sections: *Decisions to Make When a Death Occurs; Grief Resource Center* (see Exhibit 2); *Funeral Products & Services* (see Exhibit 3); *Company Profile; What's New;* and *Visitor Feedback.*

Each of these section introductory pages leads to a great deal of additional information related to its topic.[2] For example, clicking on Casket Showroom on the *Funeral Products & Services* page leads to Exhibit 4. (Note: Additional casket models are shown farther down on this Web page.) Clicking on the *Classic Gold* picture in Exhibit 4 leads to the larger picture shown in Exhibit 5.

Because the Batesville Casket people had no experience in developing a Web site, Kuisel employed a Cincinnati advertising agency to do the graphics work and develop the pages. Batesville people developed an outline of the various sections to be included. For each proposed section they then collected pertinent printed material that Batesville had produced over the years. The advertising agency used the plan and this material as the basis for development of the Web site, but developing the Web pages from these materials was not a trivial matter. According to Kuisel:

> We were fortunate that we had accumulated a lot of excellent material on the grieving process over the years. We have solicited the foremost authorities in this area and have purchased exclusive rights to publishing some of their materials. However, because these materials had been written at different times and for different audiences, they had to be reworked to make a cohesive presentation. The principles associated with grieving haven't changed, but the words in which they were expressed may have changed or gone out of style. Although using the existing materials was almost as much work as starting from scratch, we felt

---

2 The reader may want to explore the current version of the Batesville Casket Web site.

EXHIBIT 1   *Batesville Casket home page.*

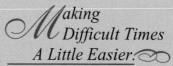

BATESVILLE:

Making Difficult Times A Little Easier.

Decisions to Make When a Death Occurs

Grief Resource Center

Funeral Products & Services

Company Profile

What's New

Visitor Feedback

It seems we never realize how important family is until we face a crisis. Difficult events like the death of a loved one or a serious illness have a way of drawing people together—to share memories, to mourn, to offer each other strength.

Your local funeral professional and the folks at Batesville understand the importance of family. We also understand how family life has changed. That's why we're here online. The information and services you'll find here are designed to help you and your family understand how your local funeral professional can help. Funeral professionals can provide assistance with the many choices and decisions that come with the death of a loved one, and can give you complete information on the topics you'll find here:

- ☐ Caskets
- ☐ Urns
- ☐ Keepsakes
- ☐ Pre-Planning Needs
- ☐ Community Services

At Batesville, we've built a tradition of working with funeral directors to help families. We take pride in manufacturing funeral products with beauty, strength and innovative features that benefit families, and we take pride in special services that honor a loved one. We're glad you stopped by our site.

If you have any questions or comments about our products or our site, we'd like to hear them. Please contact us by mail at the following address, or simply click on the "Visitor Feedback" button. Thanks for your input.

Write To Us:
Batesville Casket Company, Inc.
One Batesville Boulevard
Batesville, Indiana 47006-7798

Batesville's Site Link Statement

Contact the Batesville Webmaster
® 1996 Batesville Casket Company, Inc.

EXHIBIT 2   *Grief Resource Center page.*

Grief Resource Center

The long illness of a parent or friend. The tragic death of a young person due to an accident. The aftermath of violence. The helplessness we feel when facing our own death. No matter what the situation, grief is something that each of us must face in our lifetime.

Fortunately, many expert resources exist to help families deal with grief. Several resources are presented here, and more are available through your local funeral professional.

Whether you are helping yourself or someone else through a trying time, we hope this information gives you both practical direction and emotional comfort.

- ☐ Grief Support
- ☐ Helping Yourself with Grief
- ☐ Helping Others with Grief

Grief Support

Helping Yourself With Grief

Helping Others With Grief

VISITOR FEEDBACK

EXHIBIT 3   *Funeral Products & Services page.*

Services

Burial

Cremation

Batesville Products and Features

Frequently Asked Questions

Casket Showroom

Funeral ∞ Products and Services

Since funerals are not an everyday occurrence, most people are unaware of the many products, services and even ceremonies that are available to make a funeral a loving tribute to a friend, relative or loved one.

This section is designed to guide you through the many purchases surrounding the funeral. It details the elements of a funeral, and helps you work in partnership with your local funeral professional to create an appropriate memorial.

- ☐ Services
- ☐ Burial
- ☐ Cremation
- ☐ Batesville Products and Features
- ☐ Frequently Asked Questions
- ☐ Casket Showroom

VISITOR FEEDBACK

WHEN A DEATH OCCURS

GRIEF RESOURCE CENTER

PRODUCTS AND SERVICES

COMPANY PROFILE

WHAT'S NEW

EXHIBIT 4   *Casket Showroom page.*

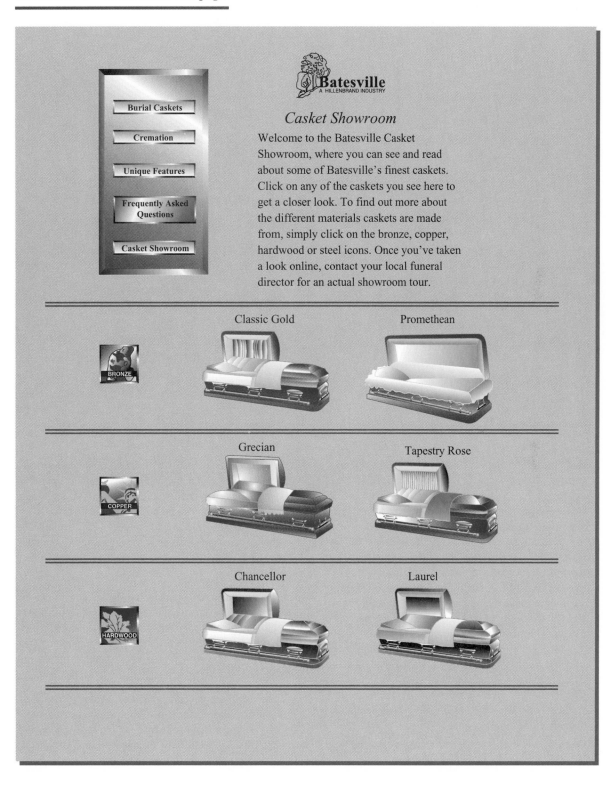

EXHIBIT 5 *Classic Gold page.*

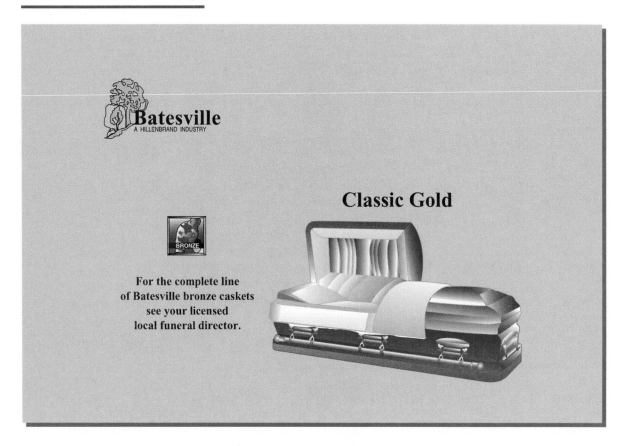

that using time-tested materials was preferable because we knew that they would not offend anyone.

Similarly, much of the content of the other sections could be compiled from existing materials, but it was much more difficult than we had expected to make sure that everything was consistent. We frequently uncovered things that did not match up. For example, we would find that on one Web page we said that Batesville Casket distributed its products from 56 warehouses, and on another Web page we said that we had 70 warehouses. This was because we had used materials from different times in our history.

We tried to be very careful in the development of the Web materials. For example, we had talked about entombment going back to the time of Christ, and one of our advisory panels suggested that we instead talk about it going back to Roman times so that we did not alienate other religious groups.

Kuisel questions their decision to develop the Web pages from previously published materials:

The documents had been written to be read sequentially, whereas on the Web everything is linked. If we had started from scratch on the Web we would probably have come up with a more effective design of how to present the material. All in all, we felt that development of most of the pages might have been easier and more effective if we had started with a clean slate.

Batesville chose the advertising agency to do the development because it had gotten a number of awards for previous Web page designs. Unfortunately, the advertising agency had farmed out most of its previous Web design work, and its in-house Web capability was minimal. Kuisel reports:

They did not understand the technology very well. The first design for our home page was a work of art—it had a beautiful white satin background with a profusion of beautifully arranged flowers. But it took about two minutes to transmit the page to the PC of someone who wanted to visit our site, so it was unusable because people would not wait that long for the home page to appear. If a visitor wanted a picture of a particular casket he might wait two minutes for it to be transmitted, but on the home page you have to get them hooked much, much quicker.

We spent a lot of time and effort with the advertising agency editing the materials, setting up linkages, and changing the site around. It was more work to undo things that they did wrong than it would have been to do them in the first place, so we feel that we would have been better off if we had done the development work ourselves.

The cost of developing the Batesville Casket Web site was in the neighborhood of $50,000, split about equally between the advertising agency and Batesville's internal costs.

Because of time pressures, possible security problems, and the capital costs involved, Batesville Casket decided to use an Indianapolis company, I-Quest, to provide the hardware and Web software for the Batesville Web site. This decision also significantly reduced the strain on Batesville Casket's relatively small information technology staff. Kuisel has been happy with this decision:

> We knew that I-Quest has a number of very successful sites, and ours has run very smoothly. I-Quest provides us with a lot of statistics on the number of people who visit the site and the number of pages that they access, and we think their prices are reasonable. There is a basic monthly fee, based upon the size of the site, that covers everything unless the number of hits exceeds a generous limit. If you exceed the hits limit you pay extra for each additional hit, but we never come close to the limit. We pay I-Quest less than $300 a month.

Early Results

In the first few weeks of operation, a number of other Web sites set up links to the new Batesville Casket home page. Batesville Casket encourages this, but with some reservations because of the possibility that a site hostile to the industry might link to this site. Therefore, the following notice appears when one clicks on the <u>link statement</u> at the bottom of the Batesville home page: "Batesville Casket Company encourages others to link to our Web site. Batesville reserves the right to discontinue the association if, in Batesville's opinion, any message or information communicated from the linked Web site is

not consistent with the goals of Batesville Casket Company." It is not clear, however, what Batesville Casket could do to "discontinue the association."

After a few months of operation, the Batesville Web site was getting around 2,000 visitors a month, with hits from all over the world. Although this was not a large number, those visiting the site seemed to be staying a long time, accessing an average of around 45 pages a visit. Those who have provided feedback are split about 50-50 between the general public and funeral industry people.

Although the feedback received has been very favorable, evaluating the success of this endeavor is a problem. According to Kuisel:

> We know our goals, but we do not know how to easily measure our goals. Our most important goal is to establish a brand preference. Also, we would like to educate consumers so that they will not be swayed by negative TV programs on the industry. We also want to increase customer satisfaction, and we think that educated customers will make a choice that they will be more satisfied with. It is easy to measure hits and to analyze the Visitor Feedback messages, but these things do not measure these goals.
>
> As far as measuring our financial success, we will probably only be able to survey our customers and ask: "Has there been any change in the number of people who have come in asking for a Batesville casket since the Web site has been operating?" That would be the bottom line, but such a survey would be quite unreliable in measuring modest changes in demand.

The Future

Kuisel is working to expand the number of people visiting the Batesville Web site:

> We are now working on getting our site to show up near the top of the list presented by the various search engines such as YAHOO and NETCRAWLER. We want to be in the top ten listings presented by each of the top five search engines, so when people query on funeral or casket or burial they will see us first.
>
> Each of the search engines uses a different algorithm to select what they show and to determine the sequence in which to present them. There are people who understand the algorithms that are used, and we are employing a consulting firm that has a good reputation in this area to help us. Although each search engine is different, our consultant knows some tricks of the trade that we think will be helpful. For example, we are considering installing a "phantom" home page

that no one will ever see, but that has the attributes that the search engines use to select the sites they present at the top of their lists.

We are also considering having some of the top search engines present an advertising banner for us whenever someone enters a search for a funeral-related topic.

Batesville is considering a number of interesting opportunities. For instance, Batesville produces custom caskets that are tailored to the interests of the deceased. The family of an avid sailor, for example, might want something incorporating sailing symbols into the burial. Because of the lead times involved, this could only be done in cases when someone is terminally ill. Normally a family would not contact a funeral home until after death has occurred, but if Batesville's Web site could make family members aware of the alternatives ahead of time, they might choose something special.

Batesville is also thinking about how to use the Internet to present product information to funeral homes. Kuisel explains:

> We depend upon our sales representatives to present product information to the potential buyer, and the Internet can provide the most up-to-date information to our funeral home customers. We have a number of large customers that our sales representatives see very frequently, and we have lots of small customers that they do not see very often. We think that it is very good to be able to supplement our sales force by getting the latest product information to our small customers and presenting it in the way the company would like to have it presented.

Kuisel sees several strategic issues to consider in Batesville's use of the Internet in the future. One issue is whether or not to list funeral homes. Kuisel explains:

> In the same city there may be a funeral home that is a 100% Batesville customer and another that is only a 30% customer. If we were to list recommended homes on our Web site, how would we deal with this disparity? If we list both homes, the 100% customer may be upset, and if we list only the 100% customer, the other customer may get upset.

Kuisel discusses other issues that Batesville is exploring:

> We were thinking about establishing an Internet mall. You would come into our page and get linkages to services and products that we do not offer, such as a vault, and you would be referred to a vault site. That raises an issue, because you might never come back to our site.
>
> Another possibility is called (in Internet terminology) planting and seeding. For example, getting insurance companies to link to our site from their sites so that when someone is thinking of insurance they might go a step further and think of funeral preplanning. And there are publications that we might like to have link to us. We also need to think of the positives and negatives of linking up with certain groups, such as various churches or cemetery organizations.

There are many opportunities and issues that Batesville Casket is considering in the use of the Web to help communicate the value of the funeral process. Therefore, the Batesville Casket Web site is likely to evolve over time.

TELAMON CORPORATION: DEVELOPMENT OF A WEB-BASED BUSINESS

Albert Chen, founder/owner of Telamon Corporation, was pleased with Kenny Chen and Paula Zhou's presentation on incorporating the Internet into Telamon's business operations. He knew these employees had reviewed all the possibilities and had recommended sound options. But his excitement about the potential for the Internet was bittersweet. It was now July 1997, and after spending two years and $250,000, he felt as if following Kenny and Paula's recommendation would mean starting at nearly the beginning again.

His immediate reaction was to hold off making any decision. But he knew he would eventually need to decide how, or if, to incorporate the Internet into Telamon's operations. He wasn't sure if there would be any benefit, or strategic advantage, to moving quickly. Besides, he was certain the move would take longer than any of them wanted. It had already taken two years and the Internet Business Group (IBG), Kenny and Paula's unit, had gone full circle. He wondered if there were any lessons to be learned from this experience.

Complicating the decision to incorporate the Internet into Telamon's business operations was the issue of what to do with the current Web site developed by IBG. Chen wondered if he should scrap it. He often thought that the amount of time and money invested in a project should not be a factor in evaluating a project's potential. At the same time, he didn't want to throw away a potential moneymaker. The site just started generating revenue, $15,000 since this spring and the number of "hits" was growing each day.

He could sell the site. One local personnel services company expressed an interest, so perhaps there was a market. But Chen wasn't certain what it would take to make the site saleable or how to assign a value. He needed to get back to the potential buyer by the end of next week. He would need to have a decision by then.

For the time being, Chen would ask IBG to minimally maintain the site, updating it every other month. He knew he would hear from Jessica Shen-Ho, the executive who had directed much of the work on the Web site but who he had recently assigned to another project. Although she was no longer officially involved, she kept up-to-date with Kenny and Paula on the project's progress. He knew she would have some thoughts on which option the company should take.

Albert Chen, Entrepreneur

After 13 years with the telecommunications giant GTE, Albert Chen found himself faced with giving termination notices to more than 200 of the 700 workers in his materials management division as a result of a corporate decision to downsize. A firm believer in the worth of individual employees and a supporter of family values, Chen was anguished by the decision. He vowed to his wife he would never be put in the position of firing employees en masse again. In late 1984, Chen left GTE to start his own business as a supplier of customized products and services to telephone companies. Befitting his business and personal philosophy, Chen named his company Telamon, a Greek word meaning "support."

Although progress wasn't always smooth, Chen had the determination to succeed. Born in Taiwan, the eldest of eight siblings, Chen received a bachelor's degree in finance law from Ching Che University. He immigrated to America in 1968 to pursue a graduate degree at Portland State University, a smaller school where Chen thought he might have more opportunity and support to improve his English. Enrolling as an MBA student, Chen quickly changed his major to computer science after attending a marketing class where he didn't understand a word of the professor's lecture. He found FORTRAN a much easier "language." Determined to finish his master's degree in three years, Chen doubled up on required courses, studying beginning and advanced calculus simultaneously.

It was at Portland State University that Chen met his future wife, Margaret. Although both are Chinese, Margaret is from Indonesia, a former Dutch colony with more of a Western influence. When Chen met Margaret, she hadn't even used chopsticks. Both were hired by GTE after graduation.

Telamon: The Early Years

After getting a couple of calls from some acquaintances at Bell Labs who had designed a new phone system, Chen found himself in business. Despite having no previous sales experience, Chen set himself up as a wholesaler/distributor to a network of about 100 dealers, with Margaret staffing the phones and translating his extemporaneous Chinese into formal business letters. After placing some ads in trade journals, Telamon sold 2,000 units in its first six months.

Then the problems started. The equipment, manufactured in Taiwan, wasn't resistant enough to static from carpets and heating units and would malfunction under certain conditions. Customers were unhappy. Chen made the painful decision to recall the product to save his reputation. Unfortunately, the recall did not revive his reputation; customers did not want to take the chance of buying a "piece of junk." Chen realized he would never be successful selling to the end consumer, at least for several years. He decided to change his customer base and his business definition.

Telamon Finds a Niche

Chen felt he turned the negative effect of downsizing into a positive by creating his own company. But he realized there was an additional positive to downsizing—leaner corporations increasingly had to rely on external suppliers to provide services previously handled in-house. Telamon became a provider of support programs between equipment manufacturers and those building and main-

taining the complex networks in telecommunications companies. Chen was careful not to classify his business as a distributor, knowing that in the long term Telamon couldn't compete directly with a major supply house.

Developing services for this market was a discovery process. Chen asked potential customers, "What's your biggest headache?" Then he would design a solution to that headache.

That process of providing custom solutions has won Telamon major customers among the Regional Bell Operating Companies (RBOCs) and other large independent telecommunications companies as well as equipment suppliers. Sales grew from $100,000 in 1984 to more than $100 million in 1996. Telamon has been recognized by *Inc.* magazine six consecutive years as one of the *Inc.* 500, a list of America's fastest growing small companies: 1991 (#368); 1992 (#228); 1993 (#259); 1994 (#297); 1995 (#397); and 1996 (#248). In mid-1997, Telamon employed more than 260 workers. In addition to its Indianapolis headquarters, Telamon maintained facilities in Chino, California, and Philadelphia, Pennsylvania.

Telamon's current mission states that "Telamon is in the business of providing customized telecommunications products and services of uncompromising quality to meet and support our customers' needs. Based on our Corporate Values, we build long-term partnerships that achieve our customers' objectives: enhancing revenues, reducing costs and delivering improved services. We will become the best small business in the telecommunications industry."

Telamon's Business Units

With 8(a) Small Business Administration and Minority/Women Business Enterprise certifications, Telamon is composed of three groups: Telamon Integrated Marketing Services (TIMS); Telamon Network Infrastructure Services (NIS); and Telamon International (TI). A corporate organization chart is in Exhibit 1. A brief description of each group follows.

Telamon Integrated Marketing Services (TIMS)
This unit designs, implements, and manages long-term programs and promotional campaigns to help telecommunications carriers and equipment suppliers sell products and services to their customers. Although each project is specific to a customer's unique requirements, TIMS has developed a set of core competencies in advertising and channel support; product sourcing and procurement; inbound/outbound call handling; database

EXHIBIT 1
Organization Structure
Telamon Corporation.

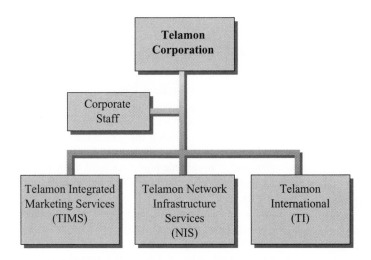

management/demographics tracking; customized fulfillment services; and repair and return processing.

An example of a TIMS service: You call your local phone company to report your home phone is not working. You subscribe to the service where, if the problem is your phone instead of your phone line, the local phone company will loan you a phone until you repair or replace the broken one. The 800 number call center, loaner phone, and the self-addressed stamped return box for when you're through using the phone are all provided by Telamon. Telamon also follows up with the customer if the loaner phone is not returned within 30 days. Customers may also purchase the loaner phone. Telamon handles that, too.

The TIMS unit generated $7 million in FY1997, or about 6% of Telamon's FY1997 revenues and employs 120, or about 40% of Telamon's workforce. Workers include customer service representatives and management who staff the call center, inventory management personnel, and project managers. All office workers have a computer connected to the corporation's local area network (LAN).

Telamon Network Infrastructure Services (NIS)
This business unit provides engineering, manufacturing, and technical assistance services to telecommunications companies and equipment suppliers. More than half the workforce is employed by this business unit, which gen-

erates about 90% of Telamon's overall revenues. The three facilities in Indianapolis, Indiana, Chino, California, and Philadelphia, Pennsylvania, provide customers with assembly of product, project materials management, cable and wire services, and engineering and installation.

For example, Telamon's Network Infrastructure Services group could assemble the complex electronics inside the outdoor cabinets that house telephone wiring for a housing subdivision. The assembly would include prewiring inside the cabinet and testing of the transmission equipment. Or, another example, Telamon's NIS group could manage the materials for a local telephone company's complex network development project. They would procure the materials, receive them at one of their facilities, and ensure delivery of all materials to the customer's site.

Telamon International (TI)
Telamon International employs 10 people, about 5% of Telamon's overall workforce. Through service offerings such as video systems and wireless communication services, Telamon International brings in about 3% of Telamon's overall revenues.

Telamon International offers planning, ordering, assembly, delivery, and support for video services enhancements such as business video conferencing, video classrooms and distance learning, continuing education programs, and specialized audio/video packaging.

TI's wireless services offering includes distributing a telecommunications system that represents the next generation in voice communication networks. This system is intended as a complement or replacement product for the licensed and unlicensed Personal Communications Services and private voice network markets.

Development of a Web Business

In September 1995, Albert Chen approached Jessica Shen-Ho, head of TI and one of his executives who was particularly adept at business plan development. Shen-Ho was accustomed to Chen's requests for the seemingly impossible. In these assignments, Chen preferred to provide very little specific direction, but she knew he expected a complete and thorough investigation.

"Albert said that we needed to do something on the Internet," Shen-Ho recalled. "Telamon already had a Web site, but Albert wanted to create a new, Web-based business." She said he had been reading everywhere about the future of commerce on the World Wide Web and that Telamon needed to develop capabilities in this area to gain new sales and take advantage of what Telamon knew how to do. When asked what he had in mind, Chen said he thought they should do "something Asian" since that was a subject they knew a great deal about. Chen also thought an on-line "mall" might be a concept for a site that would generate traffic. Similar to shopping malls, the Asian electronic mall would have "anchor" retailers that would draw the most traffic, with several other "stores" keeping customers coming back. He thought one thing that would draw traffic would be something about jobs. "Everybody's always looking for a job," he said. "Or knows someone who is. Besides, Asia is a hot area now."

Shen-Ho knew she didn't know enough about the Internet to begin to write a business plan, but she did know that Kenny Chen, a TIMS systems employee, knew a lot about computers. She enlisted his help to begin to develop a plan for the Asian on-line mall.

The Internet Business Group

Shortly thereafter, Shen-Ho formed what she called Telamon's "Internet Business Group (IBG)"—Kenny Chen, herself, and Paula Zhou, another employee borrowed from TIMS. The group envisioned the Asian mall to be just as big and as popular as Yahoo, but with the addition of developing some content (versus being solely a directory site).

With its own call center (in TIMS) and warehouse (in NIS), Telamon could provide its clients with an 800 number for customers, order processing and stock fulfillment and billing services. Overseas firms could have an immediate presence in the United States as well as the rest of the world. Shen-Ho also kept in mind Chen's idea of something job-related as an attraction for companies and Web surfers.

The group also saw other possibilities. Telamon could provide client stores without a lot of technical capability with Web page design, promotion, and maintenance services.

The Advisory Group

IBG knew they needed more help and input. They turned to their network of Asian leaders in the local community to help them further develop the concept. Five leaders were asked to participate—a phone company executive, a scientist from a worldwide pharmaceutical company, an attorney, a computer science professor, and a small business owner.

At the first Advisory Group meeting in October 1995, Albert Chen presented IBG's vision of an on-line Asian mall. All volunteers were very excited about the project and eager to begin. Each was assigned a topic or type of store to research. The group kept in constant contact, regularly sending e-mail messages about their progress. After a second meeting, the group decided they needed additional information about the Internet itself. A professor from a local university with an expertise in electronic commerce volunteered to speak to the group. After listening to the professor's two-hour presentation on the status and future of the Internet, Shen-Ho and the advisory group developed a list of 14 potential services. (See Exhibit 2.)

What's Taking So Long

It was December 1995, nearly three months since Albert Chen first approached Shen-Ho about the Asian mall, and now he was eager to see a business plan. He had been stopping by Shen-Ho's office frequently to ask for an update on the project's progress. The draft of IBG's business plan that Shen-Ho delivered to Chen (see Exhibit 3) envisioned Telamon entering the Internet in stages: first establishing a presence (a site) on the Web, then following up with Web page design and promotion for clients and finally, offering clients maintenance services. Shen-Ho also noted that the first stage would not generate revenues.

January 1996 passed, and Shen-Ho hadn't received any feedback from Chen about the business plan. But that was not unusual, given that the TIMS unit (of which Kenny Chen and Paula Zhou were still on loan) was experiencing very rapid growth and calling for more

EXHIBIT 2
Possible Topic/Service Areas
Telamon Corporation.

1. **Job Posting and Career Development Services**
   Bilingual at the minimum; multilingual preferred.

2. **Library Catalog Listing of Chinese Literature and Classic Publications**

3. **Herbal Encyclopedia and Compendium**

4. **Nick's Café**
   Cyber corner where youth can freely express, discuss and share opinions/ideas.

5. **Poet's Corner**
   Profile of Asian artists, craftsmen, writers and poets.

6. **Political Forum**
   Town hall format for debate and discussion of social, societal issues.

7. **The Magic Chef**
   Unique recipes regularly posted with the restaurant selected where the particular dish is
   actually served. Sources of ingredients are provided.

8. **The DateLine Exchange**
   Widows and widowers are the target audience.

9. **The Tivoli Square**
   A cyber bazaar where goods such as orchids and specialty items (e.g., Laotian Monk's slipper,
   Monarch butterfly wings, crocodile teeth) are bartered and exchanged between merchants.

10. **Who's Who Directory**
    Profile of Asian celebrities, stars, academicians, businessmen, and other professionals of
    considerable accomplishments and significant public recognition.

11. **Travel Guides**
    Gems of faraway and hidden spots, e.g.,
    . . . the best noodle shop
    . . . the best seamstress
    . . . the best comedy club
    . . . the most serene, scenic spot
    . . . the most trustworthy jade merchant

12. **Academics Circle**
    A scholarly exchange and collaboration among research and teaching faculty members from various
    fields of discipline.

13. **Tid Bits**
    What's New
    What's Current
    Calendar of Events

14. **Electronic Catalog**
    EuroTrade
    Other trade magazines to be added later

EXHIBIT 3
yOyee!net On-Line Business Plan
Internet Business Group, Telamon Corporation.

Menu of Services	**yOyee!net Cooking**
• Links	• Ingredients
• Shops	• Restaurants
• Resumé repository	• Cooking schools
• Magic Chef	• Recipes
• Design, promotion and maintenance services	**yOyee!net One Source**
yOyee!net Links	• Web site design
• 6 categories	▪ Web base
▪ Entertainment	▪ Web page
▪ Jobs	▪ Web site
▪ Travel	• Web site hosting
▪ News	▪ Telamon hardware
▪ Business	▪ Dedicated server
▪ Cooking	▪ Turnkey solution
• 34 Asian countries	• Web site fulfillment
yOyee!net Shop	▪ Secure access Web site
• Unique items and gift sets	▪ Client orders product
yOyee!net Jobs	▪ Telamon authentication, verification of credit card
• Repository of Résumés	▪ Order processing
▪ Stringent criteria	▪ Product pick, pack and ship
▪ Narrowly tailored population	
▪ Asian job bank	

resources and that another unit's revenues were below expectations. Shen-Ho knew Chen had his hands full.

Chen knew he should get back to Shen-Ho with some sort of feedback. But he felt overwhelmed by the scope of what the business plan proposed. In February 1996, Shen-Ho cornered Chen to ask what he thought. All he could say was, "Your plan is much too elaborate." He hadn't had time to consider the full impact of the plan. He knew Shen-Ho would proceed cautiously.

yOyee!net

Kenny, Zhou, and Shen-Ho discussed what to do next. They knew they needed to launch a site if they were to continue, so they came up with a name for the site and a shorter list of categories, including a job-related category. They chose the name "yOyee!net" for their site. "Yoyee" is a Chinese word meaning "friendship."

They set April 29, 1996, as the official launch date and hired a graphic artist to design their Web page. (See Exhibit 4.) Since they had no budget and this would be their first expense, they found a consultant (a local high school student) to design the site for minimum wage plus $2 per hour. The site was ready on the deadline date.

Shortly after April 29, IBG realized they needed to focus on generating traffic. They didn't have the budget to develop elaborate interactive attractions, so they began to swap advertising with other sites. They would advertise a site if that site in turn advertised yOyee!net.

Traffic by September 1996 was minimal, about 350 visits a month. IBG needed to invest in promotion. Infoseek, an on-line search site, offered to provide them with a keyword for six months for $10,000. Whenever an Infoseek user typed in a word to search for sites on that topic, a listing of all sites with that keyword would appear, including the IBG site.

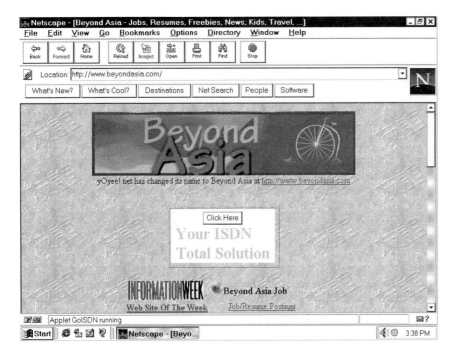

EXHIBIT 4 (top)
Beyondasia.net Home Page Telamon Corporation.

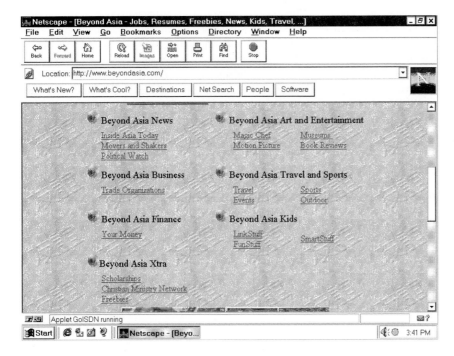

EXHIBIT 4 (bottom)

IBG proceeded and chose "Chicago Bulls" as their keyword due to the popularity of that basketball team. Before Shen-Ho received Chen's final approval he added, "One other thing. Yoyee is not a memorable enough name. You need something more universal so people will remember it." Shen-Ho knew he had thought a great deal about it, so she asked, "Did you have a name in mind?" Chen answered, "How about 'beyondasia?'"

Their investment in Infoseek did not yield the traffic they had anticipated. Beyondasia.net did not get one visit as a result of the Infoseek investment. Shen-Ho, Kenny, and Zhou were more than disappointed; they were disheartened. After hearing the results for three months, Albert Chen no longer thought the Asian mall concept was viable. He approached Shen-Ho and they discussed the next steps.

Chen said he thought the site would be more successful if they first concentrated on one area where there is the greatest need/demand. Shen-Ho agreed. As they looked over the current Web offerings, Chen stated, "People are always looking for jobs. Perhaps we could concentrate on job-related items."

Shen-Ho cringed. She knew little about job placement. She said IBG would further discuss narrowing the focus to one category.

When IBG next met in late December 1996, they looked over demand for the categories. The three topics receiving the most traffic were Sports, Magic Chef (a page on cooking), and Jobs. Shen-Ho, Kenny, and Zhou all agreed that the job-related page had the clearest need. Currently, the job page had about 50 to 60 hot links to open jobs at corporations. But they didn't have any resumés. In addition to Asians, they felt they should target the Caucasian mainstream who had Asian skills.

In January 1997, Shen-Ho was pulled from IBG to develop Telamon's entry into the wireless market. Albert Chen asked Vincent Liu, Information Systems Director, to take over IBG when he assumed additional responsibilities in TIMS in February 1997. Shen-Ho offered to keep up-to-date with IBG, knowing that Liu, new to the company, would have other more pressing priorities. Chen agreed.

By March 1997, Kenny and Zhou had contacted universities with Asian studies and Asian student clubs to collect more than 100 resumés. (See a partial list in Exhibit 5.) They also had 500 job postings. (See Exhibit 6 for a partial list.) In addition, they began generating revenues for beyondasia from companies posting jobs and asking for Web page design and promotion.

Their great success prompted Shen-Ho to contact a local provider of personnel services for more help in developing the site. Kenny developed a demonstration for an April 1997 meeting with Jeffrey Buhner, President of Organizational Development & Management, Inc. In the meeting, Buhner shared that the future in his business required more sophisticated development of technology and that his corporation was looking to establish an international focus. He was very much interested in beyondasia and offered to further discuss four options: an investment by his firm, a partnership arrangement, a joint venture, or an outright purchase. Shen-Ho, Kenny, and Zhou were excited about the meeting. They hadn't anticipated such interest. They told Buhner they would contact him after evaluating what they wanted to do.

Albert Chen Must Decide

Buhner had arranged for his staff to view the demonstration last week (mid-July 1997) and now Kenny and Zhou had just presented their vision of the future of the Internet at Telamon. They wanted to continue to develop the mall beyond just a job-matching site and significantly build the site as another business segment for Telamon. They also wanted to use the skills they had developed to help other Telamon units—giving customers services like electronic ordering and tracking ability. Telamon's customers were clamoring for these on-line capabilities. Chen could have them develop a bigger mall site or more fully develop the current jobs site and then operate it or sell it to Buhner or someone else. Or he could ask Kenny and Zhou to use the skills they developed for other groups in Telamon. But he knew that he couldn't do all three. He needed to have an answer soon—he was to meet with Buhner next week.

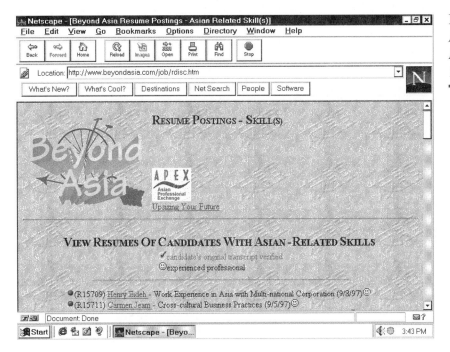

EXHIBIT 5 (top)
Partial Resumé List
Beyondasia.net
Telamon Corporation.

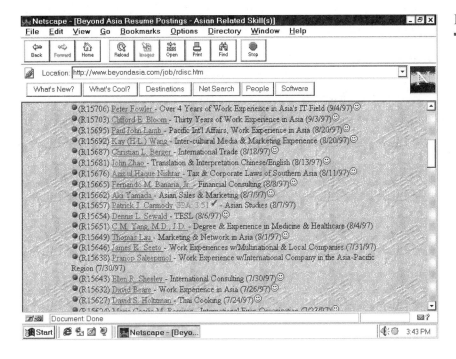

EXHIBIT 5 (bottom)

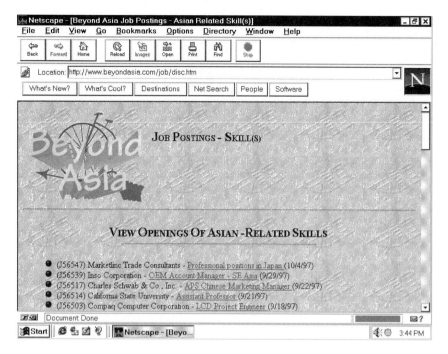

EXHIBIT 6 (top)
Partial Job Postings
Beyondasia.net
Telamon Corporation.

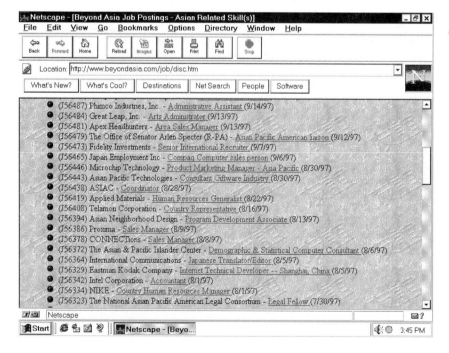

EXHIBIT 6 (bottom)

HARNETT & SERVICE, INC.

Five years ago, when Eugene (Gene) Picard became marketing manager for a small division of consumer goods manufacturer Harnett & Service, Inc., the first thing he did was to examine his strategic position. He found that his division was viewed as a small cash cow with a mature but profitable product. The division was facing increasing competition, and he anticipated declining sales in the future if they did not do something to counter this competition.

Picard decided that they could improve their market position by providing quicker service on orders and by targeting their promotional efforts more precisely. Both of these strategies depended upon computer systems that would handle orders more quickly, manage distribution more effectively, and gather information about their consumers that would enable him to analyze the impact of his promotional efforts. Unfortunately there was little computer support available when he took over the job.

Believing that computer systems were strategically important to his marketing efforts, Picard laid out a five-year strategic computerization plan for the marketing area. First he stated his long-term plan to increase their market position and counter competition. Then he described his proposed computer systems and explained how these computer systems related to the marketing plan.

Working Into the Power Structure

Picard knew what systems he needed and could define what they should do, but his problem was getting the resources to develop those systems. It took him almost a

year to figure out the political network that allocated the Information Services development resources and to get himself wired into that network. As Picard recalls, "It was a nightmare trying to identify what the structure was and where the power lay!"

He found that Information Services development hours were allocated by the corporate IS Advisory Committee, composed of representatives from the different user areas and from the IS Department. There were a limited number of development hours available, and the different units of the organization competed for those hours. Because a lot more hours were requested than were available, the competition was tough.

George Householder, Picard's boss, was the division's representative on the IS Advisory Committee. Householder wasn't particularly interested in computer systems, and he was bored and frustrated during the long committee meetings. So when Picard volunteered to take his place on the committee, Householder was delighted.

For the first few committee meetings that he attended, Picard just sat back and tried to figure out what was going on. He identified the big hitters on the committee and analyzed what their motivations were and what was important to them. And he worked to gain their confidence and to develop good relationships with them.

To initiate a system development project, it was necessary to submit a Systems Development Order (SDO) to the IS department. They would analyze the SDOs, determine how many hours of effort each would take, and bring a batch of them to the IS Advisory committee for action at each meeting. The IS representative would indicate how many development hours were available for allocation and comment on each request.

It was obvious that the IS representative had a lot of power on the committee—it was difficult to get a system approved without his support. Picard was very concerned because of a history of cool relationships between IS and his division caused by some poor development experiences several years before.

In his previous job with another company, Picard had been very successful in developing outstanding computer systems. He was quite knowledgeable about computer technology, and he knew how to work with IS in developing systems. So Picard worked hard to develop good relations with IS people and to convince them that he could work successfully with them to develop good systems. He also discovered that IS had recently decided to move in the direction of on-line systems and away from their traditional batch systems.

After determining the lay of the land, Picard decided that his next step would be to develop SDOs for all the systems he needed. Together those SDOs required extensive development hours, and he was requesting more hours than anyone else in the company. "We wanted to let them know that we had a long-term strategic plan," Picard reports. "Also, we knew that if we requested a lot of hours we probably would get a percentage of them, which would give us more hours than we would otherwise get."

So Picard worked closely with an analyst from Information Services to develop those SDOs. He was careful to make sure that these systems would be on-line systems and thus would be attractive to the IS representative on the IS Advisory committee.

With the support of the IS representative, Picard was able to obtain enough hours to get started developing his highest priority system. And by getting to know the major players on the committee and supporting their requests, Picard was quickly accepted into the group of heavy users who controlled the committee. They would get together informally with the IS representative before each committee meeting, discuss their needs, and negotiate the distribution of most of the hours.

Picard packaged his requests to fit the situation—sometimes asking for several small projects and sometimes requesting big ones. "I weigh and balance who is coming in with projects and how many hours I'm asking for," Picard reveals. "And I negotiate. I've been able to get some pretty hefty projects approved by trading off some of the lower priority projects that I had submitted for bargaining purposes."

Changing Directions

For two years Picard made excellent progress in developing and installing the computer systems that he needed. But when he got to the last major system that would enable him to evaluate the impact of his promotional activities, he knew that he could not get the IS resources

to develop that system within the next three years—there were just too many high-priority systems being requested by other divisions that were more strategically important to Harnett & Service, Inc.

Because he couldn't afford to wait three years for this crucial system, Picard decided that he would develop a basic PC system that he could use until he could get the resources to develop the mainframe system he needed. This would be a very big and complicated system for PCs, so he had to get the resources—PCs, software, and people—required to develop and operate it. This presented a different problem—these resources had to come from his division.

Ever since he became marketing manager, Picard had been trying to convince Householder that they were facing increasing competition in the marketplace and that they were going to be in trouble if they didn't do something. But the total market for their product was growing slowly, and this growth concealed their gradual loss of market share to increasing competition. Householder's attitude was that they had a good product, a secure market position, and "if it ain't broke, don't fix it!"

So Picard spent two months doing a thorough study of the market, collecting data on the size of the market, the firms competing in the market, and how the number of competitors and their market shares had been changing over the past five years. He prepared a 15-page report with graphs showing the trends and presented it to Householder, and 2 weeks later he was given all the resources he needed to develop the PC system.

During the next nine months he developed the PC system, and for the past year it has been very helpful to him, but it isn't what he really needs. It is too slow, it can't do some things he needs, and it is awkward to combine data from the PC system with the data from his mainframe systems for important analyses.

The Uncertain Future

Now it looks like some IS development resources may be available next year, so Picard has prepared an SDO to replace his PC system with a mainframe system. But he is really worried. Harnett & Service, Inc. has a new president, several top managers are retiring, and the Director of IS has recently been eased out. The membership on the IS Advisory Committee is changing. "It's very frustrating because of the new membership and new leadership," Picard reports. "It's very difficult for me to know who to communicate with and who to try to influence right now. This week I've made five phone calls trying to influence people, and I don't know whether they're major players or what's important to them. I'm really not sure which people to contact and what buttons to push. And I'm afraid that I'm in jeopardy because of that!"

Furthermore, it is rumored that the new president may change how system development resources are allocated. Today the hours are allocated by the IS Advisory Committee, and the cost of development is treated as overhead. They are talking about charging the user departments for systems development—they would have to pay real money from their budgets for the IS hours.

That would be a radical change for Picard—he would have to make some hard decisions about whether he could get more for his money by developing systems for himself or by paying IS to develop them for him. "It is very expensive to do a project through IS," Picard muses. "We don't mind that now because it's not our money. But it takes them 200 hours to write a screen, and we can do it in three days. So I may be faced with the necessity of building my own systems support group."

He would have to justify those costs to Householder, who is a hard-nosed, bottom-line-oriented guy, and that could be a problem. "I've never experienced a computer system that reduced the cost of what we had been doing," Picard explains. "If we just look at what we did with paper, to do the same thing with the computer costs more. The payoff from the computer system lies in doing things that weren't even in the realm of possibility with a paper system. They're things we couldn't imagine doing when we were planning the computer systems, and we're **making** lots of money because of those things!"

Building his own systems group will be difficult to justify on a dollars and cents basis ahead of time, but fortunately Picard understands what motivates Householder, so he is confident that he can develop a successful justification of what he needs.

INDIANA UNIVERSITY COMPUTER NETWORK

On Wednesday, March 12, 1997, over 2,000 Indiana University (IU) faculty received the following e-mail message: "Are you aware that Indiana University put your privacy at risk? Have they contacted you about it?"

The sender of this message was Glen Roberts of Oil City, Pennsylvania, who describes himself on his Web home page as a talk show host, privacy advocate, and Internet entrepreneur. Searching the Internet, Roberts located an IU file containing the names of 2,760 IU faculty, along with their Social Security numbers, addresses, and phone numbers, which Roberts had downloaded and posted on his Web site. The file had been created by the University Graduate School to provide information on the research interests of the faculty members so that they could be notified of funding opportunities that might be of interest to them.

All IU information on the Web is supposed to be protected by a "safeword card." According to Norma Holland, director of university computing services: "We have what is called a 'firewall,' an Internet term that essentially prevents access to data which are not public. The safeword card allows only authorized and authenticated users to get to those data." But this sensitive file apparently was not protected. According to Jeffrey Alberts, associate dean, this was an obsolete file that escaped unnoticed when the system was being upgraded to make it more secure. The university immediately removed the file and disabled the old gateway service.

The situation was called "an eye-opener" by IU Vice President for Public Affairs Christopher Simpson: "It

was fortunate that more sensitive data was not compromised. Although we are very sensitive to the release of information like this, this is vastly different from having individual access to the university's most sensitive proprietary information. This is a good wake-up call. That is exactly how we are viewing it."

But Roberts posed a question of other potential security problems. "You must remember that even though my page may have brought this to your attention in an unpleasant manner, the real danger lies in those who may have silently obtained the information from your site with no one the wiser," he wrote in a Web page dialogue with Mark S. Bruhn, IU information security officer.

Roberts claims the Privacy Act of 1974 "forbids such agencies (as IU) from even asking for Social Security numbers in other than specifically enumerated situations. That the SSN is included in any such faculty Internet research database is outrageous," Roberts wrote on his Web conversation with Bruhn. "Even if the files are not meant to be available to the public, the wholesale collection of such information in an 'Internet database' demonstrates a clear failure to understand even the most basic precepts of personal privacy."

Roberts' Justification

Roberts was described by people at two Pennsylvania newspapers as "an interesting fellow and a computer whiz-bang." According to the *Erie Times,* which did a profile on Roberts several months prior to this incident, he came to Oil City from the Chicago area, where he published a paper that dealt with privacy issues. He has done a short-wave radio program and now does a radio program on the Internet. Also, he has been a network television consultant and appeared on local talk shows. Roberts also publishes several Web pages and works as a computer consultant.

Roberts said he came across the IU file during a check of his own domain. By typing "SSN" into the Infoseek search engine, Roberts said, he called up a list of entries that showed a name and Social Security number. By opening that file, he found the IU research database.

Roberts said he has been involved in publicizing privacy issues for about 15 years. His interest began, he said, by using the Freedom of Information Act and obtaining copies of government documents. He said he was surprised at the amount of information available of which people aren't usually aware. He has been particularly interested in the seemingly widespread availability of individuals' Social Security numbers, which are pathways to other information and whose disclosure raises the potential of unauthorized use of a person's identity.

Roberts states that the issue is this: "Should the university be collecting this information and putting it in data bases, with maybe not the intent to pass it out all over the world but with intent that a fair number of people may be accessing that information?"

Roberts said he published the IU list because the privacy issue doesn't usually become tangible to people until they experience an invasion themselves. "The bottom line is privacy is an extremely important issue but it is only important when you see it affect yourself firsthand," he said. "That's what I have done with other Web pages. People can experience it firsthand, and with that experience can be more public debate and action on the issues."

He added that he is disturbed that people are unhappy with him for posting names and Social Security numbers where they can be obtained free, but no one seems concerned that the same kind of information is being sold all over the country. "The same outrage should apply to companies for however long they've been selling this kind of information," Roberts said. "Unless it is in your face, it doesn't seem to matter."

Faculty Reaction

Many of the IU faculty members on the published list disagree with Roberts' tactics. They were primarily concerned that their Social Security numbers were made easily available for the obvious reasons, and over a hundred faculty e-mailed protests to Roberts.

"I go to Roberts and say 'I like people who are watchdogs, but do you need to post this information in a convenient location to make your point?'" said Kurt Zorn, of the IU School of Public and Environmental Affairs. "I think he might have done more damage by

doing this than the university did in its oversight. There might have been more effective ways of calling attention to the problem."

Law professor Ed Greenebaum added that he believes Roberts made a judgment about the university without any information, which is unfair. "The impact is to expose us to a danger he says he is trying to prevent, and it's much more than it otherwise would have been," Greenebaum said. "My concern is not with the university's intent but why this individual feels the need, inconsistently in my view, to facilitate the distribution of our Social Security numbers."

With IU threatening to take legal action and the heavy volume of protests from IU faculty, Roberts removed the IU file from his Web page and said he has no intention of posting the names and Social Security numbers again.

The Consequences

On March 27, religious studies professor James Ackerman said he recently has been billed for phone lines, Internet access, and credit card accounts that are not his own. Although it has not been verified, he believes someone picked up his name and Social Security number from Roberts' Web page.

Within two weeks of the posting, Ackerman received a bill for a month's Internet time, had a call from AT&T saying it was ready with a conference call he didn't order, got an inquiry from Ameritech asking if he made a call from Germany to Portland, Oregon, and discovered there were calling card accounts opened in his name.

William Boone, an education professor, said his wife received an inquiry from MCI's fraud department about calls originating from Germany using the Boones' calling card number. Although there has been no proof that Roberts' Web page was the source of the information used in the fraud, Boone and others believe the incidents are more than a coincidence. "What are the chances two IU professors are getting unauthorized calls from Germany? What are the chances this is not related to the World Wide Web issue?" Boone said.

Boone's wife said the issue is unsettling. "It feels like such a violation," she said. "You feel like someone knows you but you don't know them. That is very uncomfortable."

The situation has been frustrating to Ackerman, who said the credit card companies told him they could not put a block on his Social Security number. He was told he could contact three credit agencies, which many banks use to check a person's credit, and they could put a hold on his records.

Ackerman also contacted the office of IU's legal counsel, which was unable to offer much assistance. "At this point, we don't even know if his experience relates in any way to Roberts' Web page," said Michael Klein, associate university counsel. "There are some timing coincidences, but you just don't know." However, the uni-versity is exploring whether there is any legal liability Roberts might incur if faculty members are damaged, financially or otherwise.

Klein added that the university is reviewing the issue of using Social Security numbers in its course of running the school. "As an institution, we are taking a look in-ward to determine if there are some alternatives," he said.

MARY MORRISON'S DILEMMA

Mary Morrison, a second-semester sophomore business major at Big State University, was unpacking the new PC that her mother had given her for Christmas when she discovered that, except for the *Windows 95* operating system, no software was included with the machine. Although the new PC was an adequate computer, it was a stripped-down off-brand machine, and one way that the store kept the price low was to not include software. Mary was upset, because she knew she would need a good word processor, a spreadsheet program, and some presentation software, and she had expected that this software would be included with the computer.

According to her friends, *Microsoft Office Professional* was the recommended suite of software for business students. Mary quickly checked around the university and found that she could buy *Microsoft Office Professional* at the special price of $199, or she could get some shareware software that would have the basic capabilities that she needed for only $25. Knowing that she could not afford the $199 for *Microsoft Office Professional*, Mary was about to buy the shareware when a friend, Frank Taylor, offered to let her copy his *Microsoft Office Professional* onto the new machine. Mary was tempted, but she was also uneasy about accepting Frank's offer because she had learned from her computer literacy class that copying his software was tantamount to stealing it. She told him that she needed to think about it. Frank couldn't understand her hesitation. "Everybody does it," he explained.

Mary's Background

Mary's mother, Caroline Morrison, grew up on a farm near Minifee, Arkansas, the second of eight children of a hard-working but poor black sharecropper couple. Although her parents had only a fourth-grade education, Caroline graduated from the local all-black high school with outstanding grades. Seeing little future beyond sharecropping in Minifee, after her graduation Caroline left for St. Louis, where she found work as a janitor in a nursing home.

Caroline soon met and married James Morrison, also from the South, who had a job driving a local delivery truck. They had four children, Mary being the oldest. Things went well for them for a few years, but James developed a drinking problem, and was fired from his job as a driver; and when Mary was nine, he abandoned his family and left town. Caroline had four children aged 3, 5, 7, and 9 to feed, clothe, and take care of, so she was forced to go on welfare.

Caroline hated being on welfare, so when her youngest child entered school she got a job as a nurse's aide on the night shift at a nearby hospital. Working at night, she could get the children off to school in the morning and be home to greet them in the afternoon. In a few years the hospital sponsored Caroline in a part-time training program to become a Licensed Practical Nurse (LPN), which she completed in two years. Thus, she became a LPN at the hospital, still a low-paying job, but better than her previous pay. She also worked part-time as a cleaning lady in addition to her night work at the hospital.

Mary grew up to be an excellent, highly-motivated student and graduated from high school near the top of her class despite working at a succession of part-time jobs to augment the family finances. Knowing that her mother could not afford to send her to college, Mary applied for scholarships at several colleges and universities. She was accepted by all the schools that she applied to and was offered a full-ride scholarship—tuition, room, and board—at Big State. The scholarship was for four years, subject to maintaining good grades.

Because her mother could not help her financially, Mary worked at a part-time minimum-wage job 20 hours a week so that she would have money for books and clothes. Despite this, and despite the handicap of coming from an inner-city high school, Mary had been able to maintain her grades and keep her scholarship.

Mary's Analysis

Mary couldn't imagine how her mother had gotten the $1,000 to purchase the PC that she had given her for Christmas, so she knew that Caroline could not help her buy *Microsoft Office Professional*. Mary was barely keeping her head above water with her expenses, so she could not possibly afford $199 for this software. Therefore, her choices were to accept Frank's offer to copy his *Microsoft Office* or to obtain the shareware software.

Mary considered the following rationale for accepting Frank's offer:

- Although it was illegal, there was no chance that she would get caught.
- Although it would be stealing in a sense, it would be a victimless crime—it would not cost Frank anything, and, because she could never buy the software, Microsoft would not be losing any revenue.
- Even if Microsoft were losing revenue, it would go to Bill Gates, who already had more millions than Mary's whole family had tens of dollars.

Mary's arguments against copying Frank's software were:

- She knew that copying Frank's software was stealing the product of someone's effort. She viewed herself as an honest person. She had never stolen anything and she knew that she would never consider shoplifting something worth $199 from a store, even if she knew she would not get caught. In fact, if she had found a wallet containing $200 in cash she would go to great lengths to return the wallet and its contents to its owner.
- She could get by using the shareware software.

After carefully considering her analysis, Mary picked up the phone to call Frank and tell him her decision.

STATE ECONOMIC DEVELOPMENT AGENCY

The State Economic Development Agency (SEDA) was established by the state legislature with the mission of fostering economic development throughout the state by supporting the state's existing industry, developing new business enterprises, and attracting new industries to the state.

David Prince, director of SEDA, felt that it would be difficult to assess the economic health of the state and assist in economic development when no one knew what businesses existed, where they were located, what goods and services they provided, how many people they employed, and so on. Therefore, one of Prince's first decisions was to develop a State Enterprise Database (SED) containing data helpful to those interested in economic development in the state.

Rather than building his own data processing department, Prince decided to contract with the State University Center for Business and Economic Research (CBER) to explore the development of the SED. Robert Mixon, SED project director for CBER, began the project in June 1990 with a needs analysis. CBER asked economic developers throughout the state what they needed to know and how they would use that data. CBER found that (among other things) economic developers wanted detailed data on the existing businesses in the state, and they wanted it by location. They wanted the name and address of each business with more than eight employees, the products and services it provides, historical employment by quarter, wage data by quarter, sales data by quarter, whether the business imports or exports, standard industrial classification, and often a product description. They needed an actual local address in addition to a

legal mailing address, which might be the home office rather than the local address.

It quickly became clear that such a database for the entire state would be so massive that they needed to narrow the scope of this initial project. Therefore, Prince and Mixon decided to restrict the initial SED project to Washington county, a typical county in the state that had about 1,800 businesses of interest.

Because it was impractical to collect the needed data directly from the businesses, they began to search for sources that might already collect the data they needed. The Internal Revenue Service (IRS) collects financial data from businesses, but access to this data is heavily restricted by law. They considered the state Department of Revenue, the state Employment Security Department, the state Department of Commerce, the chambers of commerce in the state, and also such business organizations as Dun and Bradstreet.

During this investigation they found that the state Employment Security Department collected much of the data that they needed. So Mixon assigned his senior systems analyst, Ruth Blair, the task of determining what data Employment Security collected and how the data on the businesses in Washington county might be obtained. In early January 1991, Mixon arranged a meeting with James Hogan, executive director of Employment Security, in which he explained the purpose of the SED project, introduced Blair, and requested permission for her to work with Employment Security people to explore what data might be available and how they could be obtained. Hogan was quite agreeable and suggested that Blair start with Jean McAnally, deputy director for Statistical Services.

The mission of the state Employment Security Department is to collect unemployment insurance taxes from businesses in the state and to distribute unemployment benefits to workers who have been laid off. Because the tax rate for a business depends upon its past layoff history, Employment Security must collect and maintain detailed quarterly employment data for each business. Ruth found that Employment Security has highly complex computerized systems that support collecting unemployment insurance taxes and distributing unemployment benefits.

McAnally's Statistical Services unit analyzes some of the data, but this analysis is not the central focus of Employment Security. The systems for supporting operations and for statistical services are quite separate, and just a small part of the data collected for operations goes to statistical services. One reason for this separation is that Employment Security is legally required to protect the confidentiality of the data it collects, and therefore the organization is very security conscious. Upon being hired each employee is required to sign a disclosure form stating that he or she understands that unauthorized disclosure of data is grounds for dismissal and that violators will be prosecuted to the full extent of the law. The law pertaining to Employment Security states in part:

> Information obtained or obtained from any person pursuant to the administration of this article and the records of the department relating to the unemployment tax or the payment of benefits shall be confidential and shall not be published nor be open to public inspection, in any manner, revealing the individual's or the employing unit's identity, except in obedience to an order of a court.
>
> A claimant at a hearing before a referee or the review board shall be supplied with information from such records to the extent necessary for the proper presentation of the subject matter of the appearance, and the director may make such information available to any other agency of the United States or of the state.

Despite this emphasis on confidentiality, Blair was pleased to note that "the director may make such information available to any other agency . . . of the state."

In early February 1991, Blair started working with the Statistical Services unit to determine what data it could provide on businesses in Washington county and to define reports containing that data. During February and March, they negotiated a price and developed a contract between Employment Security and SEDA to produce the desired reports. Blair received the results of the first run at the end of April. It was full of mistakes caused by programming errors, and Blair requested a rerun, which was completed around the first of June 1991.

As Blair began to work with the data in this report, it became obvious that the data had some severe limitations for the SED. In the first place, there was no unique identifier for each record. For example, if there were two McDonald's restaurants in a county, there would be two records that could only be distinguished by their quantitative data, such as number of employees. Second, she did not understand the meaning of some of the data elements. For example, employment data by quarter was collected, but she didn't know whether this was an average, or at the end of the quarter, or what. Finally, she suspected that there was other data in the Employment Security system that might be quite useful for economic development if she knew what was there. Therefore, Mixon suggested that Blair find out more about the data in the Employment Security operational systems.

Starting the middle of June 1991, Blair began trying to find out details about the data in the Employment Security operational systems. It took two weeks for her to obtain a data dictionary, and when she got it she found that it was a brief programmer's data dictionary that didn't contain the user's data definitions that she needed. It did, however, give her enough hints about the contents of the Employment Security files to indicate that they might contain much useful data for economic development. For example, there was a "foreign ownership code" that might be of tremendous interest. She wasn't sure what it meant, however, because many state departments define foreign ownership to mean that the business is not incorporated in the state.

It took Blair several weeks to locate people who could answer some of her questions about the data in the programmer's data dictionary. These people were very helpful, and she eliminated some possibilities and highlighted others that might turn out to be important. During these discussions Blair found that Employment Security was in the process of adding an ad hoc reporting system to its software. Based on this, she questioned whether SEDA ought to be developing the SED. Perhaps SEDA should simply use the existing Employment Security system to serve the needs of the economic development community.

When Blair suggested this possibility to the Employment Security people that she was working with, they responded positively and invited her to a training session on the new system. After this introduction to the ad hoc reporting system, Blair was even more interested in determining whether the Employment Security system might eliminate the need for much of the proposed SED system.

Blair asked Employment Security to have someone work with her to evaluate the economic development needs and determine whether the Employment Security system could serve some or all of them. Employment Security could not make anyone available to perform that evaluation, so in early October 1991, Blair suggested that perhaps she could perform that evaluation herself. The programmer she had been working with thought that was a good idea. He introduced Blair to a supervisor of data entry who could assign her to a clerk who could walk her through the system, but there was a problem. According to the supervisor, she could not see the system without having a "sign-on" (which was a user number, password, and security authorization to access the system). Blair did not need to access the system; she merely wanted to know in detail what data it contained and how it worked. But the supervisor was adamant that she must have a sign-on to look at the system.

After several weeks of frustration trying to find out how she could get a read-only sign-on, Blair and Mixon decided that she was getting nowhere, and they set up a meeting on November 23, 1991, with Prince and Hogan. In this meeting Mixon explained the objectives of the SED project, the possibility of using the Employment Security system instead, and the difficulties that Blair was experiencing. He asked for Hogan's assistance and support. Hogan assured them of his support and promised that he would facilitate getting a sign-on for Blair. Hogan's memo to Frank Hall, automation project manager of Employment Security, is shown in Exhibit 1.

Exhibit 2 on page 354 shows Hall's reply to Hogan's memo. As suggested, Blair contacted Harvey Moore and set up a meeting with him on December 11 to discuss her needs and how they could be met. When she arrived at Moore's office for the discussion with him, he told her that he had set up a conference room for the meeting because he had invited a few more people to join them. When she was ushered into the conference room, she found that all the deputy directors of the Employment Security Department were waiting for her.

As soon as the meeting began, it became obvious that the attendees intended to stop Blair from getting her

EXHIBIT 1
Memo to Hall.

DEPARTMENT OF EMPLOYMENT SECURITY

TO: Frank Hall
FROM: James Hogan, Executive Director
DATE: November 27, 1991
SUBJECT: Sign-On Capabilities for Ruth Blair

Please check with DP Security and complete all pertinent forms necessary to give Ruth Blair sign-on capabilities which will allow Ms. Blair to inquire into the new tax system. It would also be a good idea for you to give Ms. Blair a quick review of the new tax system.

Also, please process request forms authorizing Ms. Blair a sign-on for CQS so that she may have access to employment data.

Ms. Blair is aware that she will have access to confidential data and understands the limitations of informed consent.

Thank you for your assistance in this matter.

JH:bj
cc: Ruth Blair

EXHIBIT 2
Hall's Reply.

DEPARTMENT OF EMPLOYMENT SECURITY

TO: James Hogan, Executive Director
FROM: Frank Hall, Automation Project Manager
DATE: December 5, 1991
SUBJECT: Sign-on for Ruth Blair

The following is in regard to your memorandum on November 27, 1991, requesting that I provide Ruth Blair sign-ons for the new tax system and CQS.

CQS sign-ons are comprised of two basic parts. One, identifying the user (Ms. Blair) and two, identifying the data accesses. The first is very simple. The second is more complex. Both are needed to have a CQS sign-on.

I talked to Ms. Blair on 11/30/91 to find out what data records or files she needed access to and she informed me that she did not know what records or files she needed. She indicated that she wanted to see the tax inquiry system so that she could determine:

(a) if there was any data she could use
(b) if she would need access to the tax inquiry
(c) if she needed a CQS access.

I have referred her to Harvey Moore so that she can sit down and go through the tax inquiry screens with Mr. Moore and/or a qualified tax employee. I made sure that she understood that I would do everything in my power to get her access to tax inquiry and/or CQS as soon as she could tell me which she needed and in the case of CQS what data she needed.

I did talk to Mr. Moore personally, so that he is aware of the situation. I talked to Ms. Blair on 12/4/91 so that she could schedule a meeting with Mr. Moore as soon as convenient.

cc: H. Moore
     R. Blair

sign-on. They questioned her need for a sign-on, and she explained that she didn't really want a sign-on, just to obtain sufficient understanding of their system and its data to determine whether or not it could be used to support economic development in the state. Pointing out their legal concerns and constraints, they questioned whether Blair should even be allowed to see their system, much less to access it. Blair felt that the meeting was a disaster, and at the end she suggested that they delay processing her request for a sign-on.

After the meeting Blair sent the conciliatory letter shown in Exhibit 3 on page 355 to Moore, but she was very discouraged. After almost a year of effort working with Employment Security to get access to its data, it seemed that she had made very little progress. And the contract between the CBER and SEDA was coming up for renewal soon.

EXHIBIT 3
Letter from Blair.

December 19, 1991

Harvey Moore
Department of Employment Security
Street Address
Capital City, State

Dear Harvey,

We discussed several important issues in Monday's meeting. We decided to put a hold on the processing of a sign-on for me. I understand the need for timely consideration of such a precedent setting move.

As I indicated, the purpose of the sign-on request was to facilitate data analysis. It is most likely that the analysis can be accomplished using the existing system documentation, training manuals, and most important, the expertise of those who know the data. I will appreciate your help in providing access to these materials and the expertise, as appropriate.

The ultimate objective of this endeavor is to provide a more efficient and effective system to make information collected by one state agency (Department of Employment Security) available for use by another state agency (Economic Development Agency). It is my understanding that the law permits such interagency sharing and a policy that promotes and facilitates such sharing is critical. I hope that those who were in attendance at Monday's meeting will continue to think strategically toward such an objective.

Sincerely,

Ruth Blair

Ruth Blair

cc: Robert Mixon
    David Prince
    James Hogan

ACQUIRING INFORMATION SYSTEMS

Obtaining and successfully implementing a new information system is far from trivial. Acquiring large application systems involves a substantial commitment of organizational resources as well as potential risks. Thus, it is very important for user-managers to know how to be successful in obtaining and implementing a new information system, as well as providing effective end-user computing support.

In Chapter 9 we focus on basic information systems concepts on which modern systems are designed, built, and implemented. In Chapters 10 and 11 we describe alternative approaches that organizations use to acquire and implement information systems. In Chapter 12 we discuss application development by end-users.

Chapter 9 presents some fundamental systems principles on which information systems are built. We introduce some good design practices, characteristics of systems, and characteristics of humans as information processors. In this chapter, we also describe how systems thinking underlies business process reengineering and present an overall life cycle process for systems development. A variety of structured techniques, both procedurally-oriented and object-oriented, are presented. The chapter concludes with a discussion of information system controls.

Chapter 10 focuses on the process of developing customized applications by IS professionals. Two approaches are described in detail: the traditional systems development life cycle (SDLC) and an evolutionary prototyping approach. After presenting the steps for each methodology, we discuss the user and IS roles, some key management challenges, and highlight the advantages and disadvantages of each approach. We conclude the chapter with a brief survey of some new techniques.

In Chapter 11 we present a life cycle process for purchasing large packaged systems. Many organizations today are purchasing systems whenever it is feasible and cost beneficial to do so. We discuss some of the advantages and disadvantages of this approach, as well as the user and IS roles. At the end of the chapter we discuss factors that may influence the decision to make versus buy an information system.

Application development by people who are not IS professionals is the focus of Chapter 12. User application development has been common in some organizations for more than a decade. In fact, user developed applications are frequently used not only by the developer, but also by entire workgroups or departments. The chapter focuses on what it takes to have high quality user developed systems, as well as on the role of the IS organization in facilitating end-user computing activities. Our focus is on how organizations can effectively leverage end-user computing resources while effectively managing the risks.

Eight outstanding case studies accompany Part III. The SouthWest University Financial Information Systems case study was originally developed as part of the EDS Challenge competition at Indiana University and may be used in a role playing mode. This case study considers whether a new client/server financial system should be developed with the aid of an external consultant.

The Baxter Manufacturing Company case study is concerned with the make-or-buy decision for a critical piece of software. The Consumer and Industrial Products, Inc. case study describes the roles of user-managers and IS professionals when using the systems development life cycle (SDLC) approach in the development of a complex system. The American Foods Company case study illustrates some of the problems involved in operating and maintaining application systems. Jefferson County Schools provides an example of the pitfalls involved in purchasing and installing an application system, while Methodist Hospital of Indiana illustrates a prototyping-based approach—with the aid of external consultants—to a large system integration project.

Finally, the Grandma Studor's Bakery and Midstate University Business Placement Office (B) case studies consider the opportunities and problems of user application development. Midstate University (B) presents the history of development of the BPO system for managing the student interviewing process and the problems encountered. Grandma Studor's Bakery describes the problems encountered when a small, personal Lotus 1-2-3 spreadsheet system evolved into a complex system that was critical to the organization.

BASIC
INFORMATION
SYSTEMS CONCEPTS

"It's the SYSTEM's fault."
"I have a SYSTEM that can't lose!"
"Don't buck the SYSTEM."
"The SYSTEM is down."

Part I of this textbook focused on the three major technology components of information systems—hardware, software, and telecommunications. However, familiar phrases such as those above remind us that systems are much more than information technology. In this chapter we will present a systems view of organizations in which technology is depicted as but one of four major elements.

At least two problems arise with this universal nature of systems: We need to identify the scope of a system and describe systems in the abstract versus the physical. This requires some concepts that will help us to take a systems perspective, to develop representations of existing and envisioned systems, and to diagnose system deficiencies. The purpose of this chapter is to present these concepts.

Although mastery of systems principles is requisite for the IS profession, why is it important for business managers to also be familiar with them? First, overall systems concepts help us to understand the intricate networks of related business activities and events so that we can make positive changes to the business. The ability to view organizations as systems and to illustrate their processes is an essential skill of an effective business manager. Second, today's user-managers frequently develop their own personal information systems and supervise people who build

information systems for end-user workgroups. To build quality systems, you will need to apply some of these same principles. Third, today's business managers are increasingly asked to take major roles in project teams for evaluating and developing information systems. You may be asked to work on project teams with internal information system professionals or outside consultants to analyze, design, and build customized systems or purchase packages that have the requisite capabilities for your business. An understanding of systems concepts will help you communicate your needs and ensure that an envisioned system design will address them. Finally, this chapter will also familiarize you with some of the specific methods and techniques that are used by application developers.

In sum, many of the systems concepts introduced in this chapter can be applied to a wide variety of business situations, not just IS-related situations.

THE SYSTEMS VIEW

We have titled this section "The Systems View" because in this section we provide some templates for analyzing, describing, and redesigning systems. Although our intent is to discuss systems concepts in general, we naturally use many information systems examples.

What Is a System?

A **system** is a set of interrelated components that must work together to achieve some common purpose.

Even when each component is well-designed, efficient, and simple, the system will malfunction if the components do not work together. Further, a change in one component may affect other components. For example, suppose marketing (one component of the system that is the organization) sells more than expected of some product, then production (another component) would have to special-order materials or pay overtime to produce more than the planned amount. The likely result would be a rise in the costs of goods sold and the company might actually lose money from this apparently successful selling spree.

An **information system** (**IS**) is the collection of computer hardware and software, procedures, docu-

mentation, forms, and people responsible for the capture, movement, management, and distribution of data and information. As with any system, it is crucial that the components of an IS work together. The components must be consistent, minimally redundant, complete, and well connected with each other.

An example of what happens when system components do not work together appears in Figure 9.1. This house has all the components necessary for a functioning home, but the rooms, plumbing, electrical wiring, and other components just do not fit together. The functional relationships among these components are simply not right. For example, front steps exist, but not where needed.

Figure 9.1 Poorly Designed House

Key System Characteristics

Systems share the seven general system elements briefly defined as follows:

1. **Boundary:** the delineation of which elements (such as components and storage) are within the system being analyzed and which are outside; it is assumed that elements within the boundary are more easily changed and controlled than those outside.
2. **Environment:** everything outside the system; the environment provides assumptions, constraints, and inputs to the system.
3. **Inputs:** the resources (data, materials, supplies, energy) from the environment that are consumed and manipulated within the system.
4. **Outputs:** the resources or products (information, reports, documents, screen displays, materials) provided to the environment by the activities within the system.
5. **Components:** the activities or processes within the system that transform inputs into intermediate forms or that generate system outputs; components

may also be considered as systems themselves, in which case they are called subsystems, or modules.

6. **Interfaces:** the place where two components or the system and its environment meet or interact; systems may need special subcomponents at interfaces to filter, translate, store, and correct whatever flows through the interface.
7. **Storage:** holding areas used for the temporary and permanent storage of information, energy, materials, and so on; storage provides a buffer between system components to allow them to work at different rates or at different times and to allow different components to share the same data resources. Storage is especially important in IS because data are not consumed with usage; the organization of storage is crucial to handle the potentially large volume of data maintained there.

Figure 9.2 graphically illustrates how these seven components interrelate in a system.

These elements can also be used to describe computer applications. For example, in Figure 9.3, a payroll application and a sales tracking application are

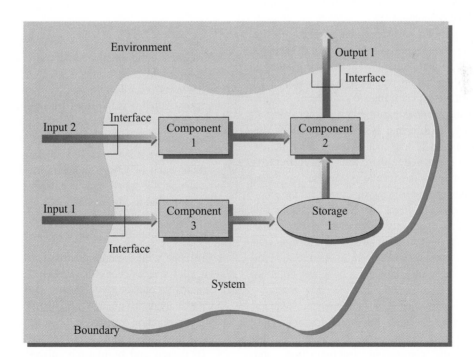

Figure 9.2 General Structure of a System

System:	Payroll	Sales Tracking
Inputs	Time cards Vouchers	Customer orders Customer returns of goods
Outputs	Paychecks	Monthly sales by product
	W-2 forms	Monthly sales by territory
Components	Calculate total pay Subtract deduc- tions	Accumulate sales by product and compare to forecast
Interfaces	Match time cards to employees Sort paychecks by department	Translate cus- tomer zip code into territory code
Storage	Employee benefits Pay rates	Product list Sales history Sales forecasts

Figure 9.3 Examples of Systems

described in terms of five system elements, excluding boundary and environment.

Another important system characteristic is the difference between **formal** versus **informal systems** within organizational contexts. The *formal system* is the way an organization was designed to work. By contrast, when workers continue to reference a bill-of-materials listing that has handwritten changes posted over the years, an informal system has replaced the formal information system that prints a materials list for each shop order. When there are flaws in the formal system, or when the formal system has not been adapted to changes in business situations, an *informal system* develops. The "real" system is actually the informal system, or some combination of the formal and informal system. Recognizing that an organization's formal system may not be equivalent to the real system is crucial when analyzing a business situation or process.

Now we expand further on three system characteristics that are especially important for analyzing and designing information systems: determining the system boundary, component decomposition, and designing system interfaces.

System Boundary   As mentioned previously, the system **boundary** delineates what is inside and what is outside of a system. A boundary segregates the environment from the system, or delineates subsystems from each other. A boundary in the systems world is often arbitrary, and, we can often choose to include or exclude any component in the system. The choice of where to draw the boundary depends on the following three factors:

What can be controlled.   Usually, elements outside of project team control are part of the environment. What is in the environment also can place a constraint on the system. For example, if a preexisting billing system is treated as part of the environment of a new product management system, the product management system may be limited to devising products that can be priced and billed in ways now supported.

What is manageable.   Large, unwieldy systems may take so long to analyze or redesign that the need for the analysis or change may have passed by the time the analysis is complete.

The purpose.   We can choose to concentrate on just those aspects of the system that require analysis and redesign.

Component Decomposition   A system is a set of interrelated components. What principles influence these groupings? A component of a system that is itself viewed as a system (set of interrelated components) is called a **subsystem (module).** The components of a subsystem can be further broken down (or decomposed) into more subsystems. The process of breaking down a system into successive levels of subsystems, each of which shows more detail, is called hierarchical (or functional) decomposition. An example is provided in Figure 9.4.

Hierarchical decomposition of a system helps us to accomplish five important goals:

1. To cope with the complexity of a system, because it allows us to break the system down into understandable pieces.
2. To analyze or change only part of the system; decomposition results in specific components at just the right level of detail for the job.
3. To design and build each subsystem at different times, as business needs and resources permit.

(a) SALES SUMMARY SYSTEM

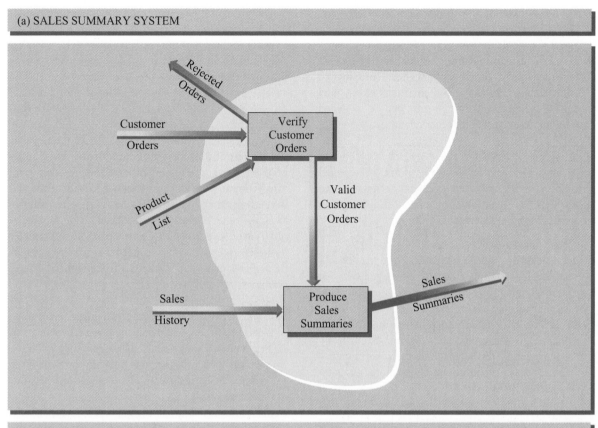

(b) PRODUCE SALES SUMMARY SUBSYSTEM

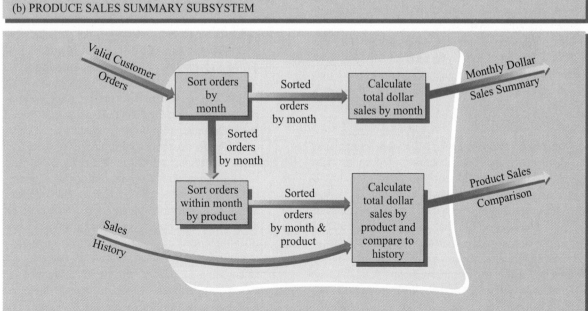

Figure 9.4 Sales Summary Reporting System and Subsystem

4. To direct attention only to the components of interest of a certain target audience, without forgetting about the whole system.

5. To allow systems to operate, as much as is possible, as independent components; hence, complicated coordination can be avoided, problems in one area can be isolated, and components can be switched with minimal impact on other components.

Interfaces   An interface is the point of contact between a system and its environment or between two subsystems. In an information system, the functions of an interface are generally as follows:

Filtering: disposing of useless data (or noise).

Coding/decoding: translating data in one format into another (for example, switching between two part numbering schemes, one used by marketing and another used in engineering).

Error detection and correction: checking for compliance to standards and for consistency; by isolating this task in interfaces, other components can concentrate on their more essential responsibilities.

Buffer: allowing two subsystems to work together without being tightly synchronized, as by having the interface collect data until the next component is ready to accept the data.

Security: rejecting unauthorized requests for data and providing other protection mechanisms.

Summarizing: condensing a large volume of input into aggregate statistics or even mathematical parameters to reduce the amount of work needed by subsequent subsystems.

Interfaces also can be built between preexisting independent systems. For example, a company may contract with an outside organization (possibly a bank) to process payroll checks or with a market research firm to capture competitor sales data. In each case, an interface is built that will allow the external system to communicate with the company's internal systems. Different formats for data, different identifications for customers or employees, and various other differences in definitions and coding need to be translated to support this type of interface. Sometimes these interfaces are called bridges because they connect two "island" systems.

Bridge programs are relatively common. Bridges are an expedient way to accomplish the goal of expanding the capabilities of any one system. Rather than take the time to redesign two systems into one (for example, to reduce redundant steps, to share common data, and to discontinue duplicate processing and calculations), the two systems are simply interfaced.

Another important purpose of an interface is the **decoupling of system components.** Two highly coupled system components require frequent and rapid communication, thus creating a dependence and bottleneck in the system. If one of the components fails, the other cannot function; if one is modified, the other may also have to be modified. Appropriately designed interfaces help to decouple system components. The principal methods of decoupling system components are these:

Slack and flexible resources: providing alternative paths to follow when one component breaks down or slows down, such as having an interface reroute data transmissions to public carriers, if the company's private data communications network becomes busy.

Buffers: storing data in a temporary location as a buffer or waiting line that can be depleted as the data can be handled by the next component, as in collecting customer orders over the complete day and allowing an order-filling batch program to allocate scarce inventory to highest-need jobs.

Sharing resources: creating shared data stores with only one program (part of the interface component) maintaining the data, thus avoiding the need to synchronize multiple step updating or to operate with inconsistent multiple copies of data.

Standards: enforcing standards that reduce the need for two components to communicate, as in adopting a business policy that requires all interunit transfer of information about customers to be done using the company standard customer identification code.

Decoupling allows one subsystem to remain relatively stable while other subsystems change. By clustering components into subsystems and by applying various decoupling techniques, the amount of design and maintenance effort can be significantly reduced.

Because business is constantly changing, decoupling can significantly reduce an organization's systems maintenance burdens.

Organizations as Systems

Several useful frameworks exist to conceptualize how information systems fit into organizational systems. The framework in Figure 9.5 graphically depicts four fundamental components in an organization—people, technology, task/procedure, and organization structure—that must work in concert for the whole organization to be effective.

What can we learn from this systems view of an organization? Figure 9.5 suggests that if a technology change is made in an organization—such as the introduction of a new software application—this change is likely to impact the other three components. For example, people may have to be retrained, methods of work (task/procedure) may have to be redesigned, and old reporting relationships (structure) may have to be modified. The important principle here is this:

Each time we change characteristics of one or more of these four components, we must consider compensating changes in the others.

This raises an interesting question: With which of the four components do we start? There is no universal answer to this question, and issues of organizational politics can play a role (see Chapter 8). For example, organization theorists have argued that changes in technology can create organizational changes (techno-

logical imperative); that organizational factors can drive changes in technology (organizational imperative); and that changes are difficult to predict because of variations in purpose, processes, and organizational settings (Markus and Robey, 1988).

In a later section we discuss a change process adopted by many organizations in the past decade: business process redesign, or reengineering. As we will see, information technology is being used as a key enabler for significant process changes that affect multiple units and individuals within an organization.

THE HUMAN ELEMENT

In today's organizational systems, humans are the providers and consumers of information, as well as the designers of information systems. How people interact with systems is an important consideration in the design of any system. The designers of these systems are also humans who have their own information processing and problem-solving preferences, as described below.

Humans as Information Processors

Humans constantly receive stimuli from all of our operating senses. We take these stimuli, or input, digest them, compare them to what we know and remember, and produce some type of response. Newell and Simon (1972) outlined this in their model of human information processing, which has four components: reception of stimuli, effecting actions, processing, and memory. This is also the basis for the IPO model of an information system: Input, Process, Output (including storage).

Human memory is an important component of human information processing. Newell and Simon's experiments have shown that humans use three different memories, or storage systems:

1. *Short-term memory:* a limited amount of space (possibly with five to nine pieces of data at a time) where the brain manipulates data.
2. *Long-term memory:* a vast storehouse of facts and relationships contained in the human brain.
3. *External memory:* notepapers, printouts, computer displays, and so on, which extend the capacity of long- and short-term memory.

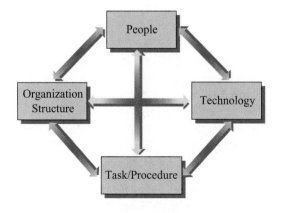

Figure 9.5 Fundamental Components of an Organization

Computer systems can be used to extend the information-processing capabilities of a human, and are used frequently as memory aids.

Besides the limitations of a human's short-term memory, other characteristics of human information processing have been identified:

- Just Noticeable Differences: The ability of a given person to identify variations and errors is in the same proportions for different situations, so larger differences are needed in situations involving larger numbers. For example, an individual who can identify a budget variance when there is a $10,000 variation in a $100,000 line item will need a $100,000 variation for a $1 million line item.
- Deficiencies in Handling Probabilities: Humans are poor at understanding causation, integrating and synthesizing data, and dealing with sample size and variance.
- Recency Effect: The most recent data we have heard, felt, tasted, or seen carries far more weight than does other data in forming our opinions.
- Bounded Rationality: Humans are, because of limited capacities, able to cope with only so much data before they become overloaded—thus we have a tendency to restrict problems and the way we view the world to a manageable size; we do this by eliminating some data or some possible actions, and we seek satisfying, not optimal, solutions.
- Cognitive Style: Different individuals use different processes for organizing and changing data during decision-making and other tasks; some are more analytical, others are more intuitive, some concentrate on details, and others focus on the big picture.
- Left Brain-Right Brain: The brain contains two hemispheres and each person appears to have a dominant hemisphere; the left brain is analytical, sequential, realistic, and highly organized, and the right brain is intuitive, simultaneous, imaginative, and impulsive.
- Individual Differences: Concepts of dogmatism, risk-taking propensity, tolerance for ambiguity, quantitative and verbal abilities, age, gender, experience, and position in the organization all influence the way people process data or the way data contributed by one person are perceived by others who interpret that data.

These human characteristics plus many more interact to determine the information-processing style and capabilities of an individual. In order to support humans in information tasks, information systems need to be designed to tolerate such individual differences, to help people overcome their information processing biases, and to complement and supplement an individual's natural capabilities. Some research has shown there may be significant enough variations in information-processing styles among people in the same or similar jobs that effective systems must take into account these human factor differences. For example, today's personal productivity software packages typically accommodate different information-processing styles by designing into a package multiple ways to accomplish tasks and easy mechanisms for the user to change parameters, such as the type of statistical data display (tables of data versus bar charts, 2-D versus 3-D charts, etc.)

Software houses in the U.S. and large manufacturing and service organizations with their own internal IS staffs typically employ human factors experts as system design team members. These specialists assess the amount of information presented, its format, the effects of color and graphics on understanding data, consistency in screen and report layouts, and compliance with sound principles of report and screen designs. Most large organizations have general guidelines for designing system interfaces with which all new systems are expected to comply. Human factors researchers have also developed guidelines related to computer user health and safety, including the ergonomics of computer workstations, such as keyboard design, video display height and tilt, and mouse location and design.

Humans as Decision-Makers

Because decision-making is such a common managerial task, there has been considerable study of the processes that people use to make decisions in organizations. Understanding the decision-making process for a specific set of tasks is, of course, critical for designing managerial support systems as described in Chapter 6.

Decision-making involves far more than making choices. The model in Figure 9.6 depicts the decision-making process as a six-phase cycle, with feedback (the inner loop). Information systems can be designed to support human decision-makers in any one or more of these phases:

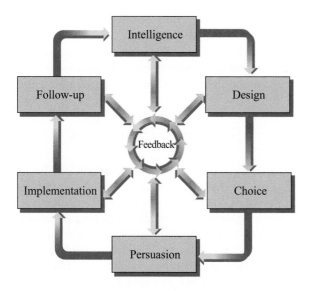

Figure 9.6 Decision-Making Process

- Intelligence: searching the environment for conditions that suggest the need to make a decision, and the collection of relevant data.
- Design: developing and finding alternative solutions or actions, and testing the feasibility of these solutions/actions.
- Choice: selecting among the alternatives the one that best (or at least satisfactorily) addresses the problem.
- Persuasion: influencing others who are involved in the implementation of the decision so that they accept and follow the chosen solution.
- Implementation: managing the installation of the new solution so that it is done in a timely and efficient manner.
- Follow-up: monitoring the solution to be sure it works as expected and modifying or refining the solution.

Humans as Problem Analysts

A major process used in developing a new information system is called **systems analysis and design (SA&D)**. SA&D processes are based on a systems approach to problem solving. Here we describe several fundamental principles associated with good SA&D that stem from the key system characteristics described previously.

The first two principles are these:

- Choose an appropriate scope: selecting the boundary for the information system greatly influences the complexity and potential success of an IS project.
- Logical before physical: you must know *what* an information system is to do before you can specify *how* a system is to operate.

1: System Scope   Often the fatal flaw in conceiving and designing a system centers on choosing an inappropriate system scope. Apparently the designer of the house in Figure 9.1 outlined each component separately, keeping the boundaries narrow and manageable, and did not see all the necessary interrelationships among the components. Turning to a business situation, when a salesperson sells a cheaper version of a product to underbid a competitor, that salesperson has focused only on this one sale. However, the costs of handling customer complaints about inadequacy of the product, repeated trips to install upgrades, and other possible problems make this scope inadequate.

The system boundary indicates the system scope. Defining the boundary is crucial to designing any system or solving any problem. Too narrow a scope may cause you to miss a really good solution to a problem. Too wide a scope may be too complex to handle. Choosing an appropriate scope is difficult but crucial in problem-solving in general and in information systems projects in particular.

2: Logical before Physical   Any description of a system is abstract because the description is not the system itself, but different system descriptions can emphasize different aspects of the system. Two important general kinds of system descriptions are logical and physical descriptions. Logical descriptions concentrate on *what* the system does, and physical descriptions concentrate on *how* the system operates. Another way to say this is "function before form."

Let's return to our example of a house as a system. As an architect knows, function precedes form with the design of a new house. Before the house is designed, we must determine how many people will live in it, how each room will be used, the lifestyle of the family, and so on. These requirements comprise a functional, or logical, specification for the house. It would be premature to choose the type of materials, color of plumbing fixtures, and other physical characteristics before we determine the purpose of these aspects.

We are often anxious to hurry into designing the physical form before we determine the needed functionality. The penalty for violating the function before form principle is increased costs—the cost and efforts to fix a functional specification error grows exponentially as you progress to the physical. We must get the logical or functional specifications right to understand how to choose among alternate physical implementations.

As an example of the difference between a logical and a physical information system, consider a class registration system. A **logical system** description would show such steps as submitting a request for classes, checking class requests against degree requirements and prerequisites, and generating class registration lists. A **physical system** description would show whether the submission of a request for classes is via a computer terminal or a touch-tone telephone, whether the prerequisite checking is done manually or by electronic comparison of transcript with course descriptions, and so on.

Problem-Solving Steps   The three following principles, or problem-solving steps, have also been associated with good SA&D processes. In fact, they are recommended as good principles for problem-solvers in general.

- A problem (or system) is actually a set of problems; thus, an appropriate strategy is to keep breaking a problem down into smaller and smaller problems, which are more manageable than the whole problem.
- A single solution to a problem is not usually obvious to all interested parties, so alternative solutions representing different perspectives should be generated and compared before a final solution is selected.
- The problem and your understanding of it may change while you are analyzing it, so you should take a staged approach that incorporates reassessments; this allows an incremental commitment to a particular solution, with a "go" or "no-go" decision after each stage.

Later in this chapter we will introduce a generic life cycle process for developing new systems, as well

as some specific techniques used by SA&D professionals. First, however, let's develop a shared understanding of the "what" that is driving many IS development and implementation projects today: systems to support cross-functional business processes.

BUSINESS PROCESSES

Over the past decade, many organizations have begun to take a process-oriented view of their organizations in pursuit of competitiveness in the Information Age. Organizing work and work structures around business processes—rather than business functions or business products—has required a new mindset in which basic assumptions are challenged and change is embraced. Systems thinking has played a key role in moving managers to a process-oriented view.

According to Peter Senge (1990), systems thinking is:

- a discipline for seeing wholes
- a framework for seeing interrelationships rather than things
- an antidote to the sense of helplessness when confronted with complexity

No one would disagree that organizations and the environments they compete in have become more complex since the 1980s. Nor would they disagree that environments are changing faster. Senge and other management gurus have therefore argued that more holistic, systems thinking is needed to enable organizations to more quickly adapt to complex environments.

Identifying Business Processes

In our discussion of electronic commerce and interorganizational systems in Chapter 7, we introduced a value chain for a manufacturing firm that included six core processes: market strategy, develop, source, manufacture, sell, and fulfill. According to Keen (1997), the identification of a firm's core processes is a key analytical task. A firm's core processes should not just be viewed as its workflows. Rather, these business processes should be viewed as the firm's assets and liabilities. By evaluating the worth of a process to a firm's competitiveness, managers should be able to identify a small number of processes that need their attention the most.

Figure 9.7 presents one way that managers can evaluate the importance of a given business process. Folklore processes are those processes that are carried out only because they have been in the past; they are often difficult to identify because they are so embedded in an organization's tasks. When they are identified, they should be abandoned because they create no economic value. Keen also warns that the salience or importance of a given process is not necessarily the same in different companies in the same industry or even in the same company under different circumstances.

Business Process Redesign

Over the past decade, many organizations have undertaken major business process redesign projects in an effort to move from a functional "silo" approach to business operations, to a more process-oriented approach. Current thinking is that the most significant payoffs from redesigning business processes come from processes that focus on the firm's customers. For many organizations, this requires taking a "clean slate" approach in order to radically change the organization's business processes. The term **business process reengineering (BPR)** has been used to describe radical business redesign initiatives that attempt to achieve dramatic improvements in business processes by questioning the assumptions, or business rules, that underlie the organization's structures and procedures, some of which may have been in place for decades.

Simple questions like "why," "what if," "who says so," and "what do our customers think," can lead to breakthrough insights that result in totally new business processes. The goal is to achieve an order of magnitude improvement, rather than incremental gains. According to reengineering guru Michael Hammer (1990): "Don't automate; obliterate!"

The origins of the business process redesign trend are in manufacturing. Innovations such as concurrent

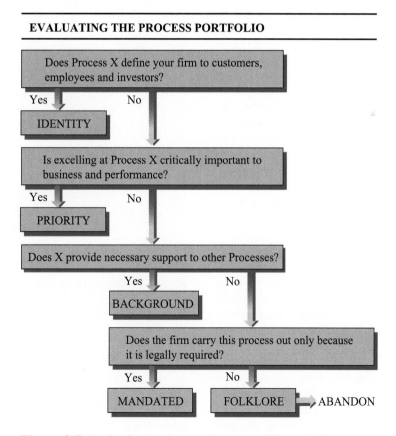

Figure 9.7 Evaluating Businesses Processes (Keen, 1997)

engineering and just-in-time inventory controls created profound changes in manufacturing management. Activities previously handled by separate departments became integrated, resulting in new processes that cross functional boundaries.

Two widely cited examples of business process reengineering success stories are described next (Hammer, 1990).

Accounts Payable at Ford Motor Company   During an initial redesign of its accounts payable process, Ford concluded that it could reduce the number of employees needed in this department by 20 percent. The initial solution was to develop a new accounts payable system to help clerks resolve document mismatches. This solution was based on the assumption that problems with coordinating purchase orders, shipment documents, and invoices are inevitable. The proposed new system would help prevent the document mismatches.

Ford's managers were reasonably proud of their plans until the designers discovered that Mazda accomplished the same function with just five people. The difference was that Ford based their initial system solution on the old business assumptions. In particular, Ford had not questioned its assumption that it could not pay a vendor without an invoice. When Ford questioned its assumptions, a truly reengineered solution was identified, as follows: capture the receipt of goods at the loading dock using computer scanners, and use the negotiated price to pay the vendor based on a validated receipt of goods instead of an invoice. When Ford took a "clean slate" approach, they achieved a 75 percent improvement gain—not the original projected 20 percent.

Mutual Benefit Life Insurance   Mutual Benefit Life's old insurance application processing was a thirty-step process that involved 19 people in five different departments. Rather than automating the old workflows across multiple people in multiple departments, the process was radically redesigned. Under the reengineered process, an individual case manager is empowered to handle the entire loan application process. This was accomplished by supporting the case manager with an advanced PC-based workstation, expert system software, and access to a range of automated systems. Time to issue a policy dropped from 3 weeks to about 3 hours.

In both of these examples, information technology played a key role as an enabler of radical business process redesign. Hammer and Champy (1993) encourage managers to go through exercises that help them think about how IT can be used to "break" old assumptions and rules. Three of their generic examples of rule-breaking IT are provided in Figure 9.8.

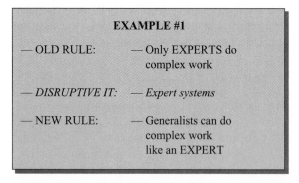

EXAMPLE #1

— OLD RULE: — Only EXPERTS do complex work

— *DISRUPTIVE IT:*   — *Expert systems*

— NEW RULE: — Generalists can do complex work like an EXPERT

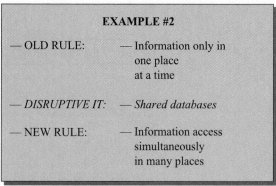

EXAMPLE #2

— OLD RULE: — Information only in one place at a time

— *DISRUPTIVE IT:*   — *Shared databases*

— NEW RULE: — Information access simultaneously in many places

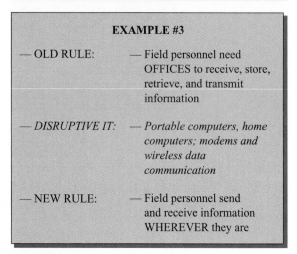

EXAMPLE #3

— OLD RULE: — Field personnel need OFFICES to receive, store, retrieve, and transmit information

— *DISRUPTIVE IT:*   — *Portable computers, home computers; modems and wireless data communication*

— NEW RULE: — Field personnel send and receive information WHEREVER they are

Figure 9.8 Examples of Rule-Breaking IT (based on Hammer and Champy, 1993)

Hammer (1990) advocates the use of key principles for redesigning business processes. A consolidated list of six principles is presented below:

1. *Organize business processes around outcomes, not tasks.* This principle implies that one person should perform all the steps in a given process, as in the case of Mutual Benefit Life, where one manager handles the whole application approval process. Information technology is used to bring together all the information and decision-making resources needed by this one person. Often this principle also means organizing processes around customer needs, not the product.

2. *Assign those who use the output to perform the process.* The intent of this principle is to make those most interested in a result accountable for the production of that result. For example, Hammer reports the case of an electronics equipment manufacturer that reengineered its field service function to have customers perform simple repairs themselves. This principle causes a reduction in nonproductive overhead jobs, including liaison positions. Principles 1 and 2 yield a compression of linear steps into one step, greatly reducing delays, miscommunication, and wasted coordination efforts. Information technologies, like expert systems and databases, allow every manager to perform functions traditionally done by specialty managers.

3. *Integrate information processing into the work that produces the information.* This principle states that information should be processed at its source. For example, at Ford this means that the receiving department, which produces information on goods received, should also enter this data, rather than send it to accounts payable for processing. This puts data capture closest to the place where data entry errors can be detected and corrected, thus minimizing extra reconciliation steps. This principle also implies that data should be captured once at the primary source, thus avoiding transmittal and transcription errors. All who need these data work from a common and consistent source. For example, the true power of electronic data interchange (discussed in Chapter 7) comes when all information processing related to an EDI transaction works from a common, integrated database.

4. *Create a virtual enterprise by treating geographically distributed resources as though they were centralized.* This principle implies that the distinction between centralization and decentralization is artificial with information technology. Technologies such as teleconferencing, group support systems, and e-mail can create an information processing environment in which time and space are compressed. Hammer reports on the experience of Hewlett-Packard, which treats the purchasing departments of 50 manufacturing units as if they were one giant department by using a shared database on vendor and purchase orders. The result is 50 percent to 150 percent improvement in key performance variables for the purchasing function.

5. *Link parallel activities instead of integrating their results.* This principle says that related activities should be constantly coordinated rather than waiting until a final step to ensure consistency. For example, Hammer suggests that different kinds of credit functions in a financial institution could share common databases, use communication networks, and employ teleconferencing to constantly coordinate their operations. This would ensure, for example, that a customer is not extended a full line of credit from each unit.

6. *Have the people who do the work make all the decisions, and let controls built into the system monitor the process.* The result of this principle is the drastic reduction of layers of management, the empowerment of employees, and the shortcutting of bureaucracy. This principle emphasizes the importance of building controls into a system from the start, rather than as an afterthought (see section on IS Controls later in this chapter).

However, not all business process redesign projects are successes. In fact, Keen (1997) points out that Mutual Benefit Life, whose radical reengineering effort was described previously, was taken over by regulators due to insolvency about the time it was lauded as a success story. Many other reengineering project failures have also been reported in the trade press. In some situations the organization failed to recognize that redesigned processes require new integrative systems, not modifications to old, single-function systems. In fact, the need for large-scale, integrative systems changes to support business process reengineering outcomes has fueled the growth of vendors of packaged enterprise resource planning systems (such as SAP and PeopleSoft—see Chapter 5).

INFORMATION SYSTEMS PROCESSES

We turn now to an overview of the process of developing information systems, some of the techniques employed by IS professionals who develop software applications, and a discussion of information systems controls. For IS professionals, these are bread-and-butter topics. Semester-long courses on systems analysis and design processes are typically offered for undergraduate and graduate students interested in IS careers. Our intent here is not mastery, but familiarity with key methods and techniques that are part of the toolkits of system professionals. Our emphasis will be on topics of use to business managers who are asked to participate in or lead systems projects.

The Information Systems Life Cycle

In the remaining chapters in Part III of this textbook (Chapters 10, 11, and 12) we will discuss in detail the major methodologies for customized system development, purchasing system packages, and application development by end-users. All of these methodologies follow a variation on a general **life cycle** for systems development that has been used for decades. Although there are many descriptions of life cycle approaches—each involving a different number of phases and stages and using different names for them—there is general agreement in the field on the generic activities that are involved.

Figure 9.9 presents the generic systems life cycle model in terms of three phases: Definition, Construction, and Implementation. The analysis and design of a business problem and IS solution to the problem is reviewed after each phase and often after each stage within these three phases. The systems life cycle also follows the principles of logical before physical (function before form) and component decomposition.

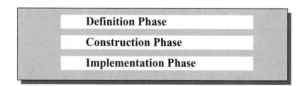

Figure 9.9 Generic Systems Life Cycle

In the *Definition* phase, end-users and systems analysts conduct a multistep analysis of the current business operations and the information system or systems in the area of concern. Current operations and systems are described via both process- and data-oriented notations. Process-oriented analysis concentrates on the flow, use, and transformation of data. Data-oriented analysis focuses on the kinds of data needed in a system and the business relationships between these data. Problems with current operations and opportunities for achieving business value through new IT capabilities are identified. A business case is made for the feasibility of new systems, and one solution is chosen. This solution is detailed in a requirements statement agreed to by all parties. If a software vendor has already developed a "packaged" system that meets these requirements, this phase also includes steps to identify and select the best packaged solution. The Definition phase of the life cycle is very much a cooperative effort between business and systems professionals. Doing this phase right can have significant impact on the competitive use of IT.

The *Construction* phase entails the designing, building, and testing of a system that satisfies the requirements developed in the Definition phase. The system first is logically described, and then its physical design is specified. Programs and computer files are designed, and computer technology is chosen. Inputs such as business forms and computer screens are designed, as well as outputs such as reports. After the physical design is accepted as feasible (technically, economically, and operationally), the computer software is programmed and tested. Users play a major role in acceptance testing to verify that the system requirements have been met.

In the *Implementation* phase, business managers and IS professionals work together to install the new system, which often involves converting data and procedures from an old system. The installation of a new system can occur in a variety of ways, such as in parallel with operation of the old system or in a total and clean cutover. The implementation phase also includes the operation and continued maintenance of the system. Maintenance is typically the longest stage of the systems life cycle and incurs the greatest costs. It includes system changes resulting from flaws in the original design, from changing business needs or regulations, and from incorporating new technologies.

Just as architects use blueprints as abstract representations of a house, IS professionals have developed techniques for representing system requirements and designs. In the next section we describe some of these techniques.

Structured Techniques for Life Cycle Development

Today, IS development projects range in size from a single-user application for a desktop machine to one that will be used by thousands of people in a large organization. The scope of today's large development projects has brought system builders up against both cognitive and practical limitations: the scale and complexity of these projects exceed the capacity of one developer or even a single team of manageable size. Effective large system development requires more systematic approaches that allow partitioning of the problem so that many developers can be working on the project simultaneously. Increasing the scale also increases the number of parties involved. Systems today may exceed a single manager's responsibilities or perhaps go beyond a single organization (such as interorganizational systems discussed in Chapter 7). System builders must be able to communicate with other IS professionals about what system modules do and how they do what they do. IS project managers must be able to coordinate and monitor progress and understand the commitments they are asking business managers and IS project team members to make.

A body of tools has emerged to document system needs and requirements, functional features and dependencies, and design decisions. Called **structured techniques,** these techniques exist for all phases of the systems development process, and many variations have emerged. Additionally, the techniques may be embodied within a larger approach called a **system development methodology.** A methodology is a framework consisting of guidelines, tools, and techniques for managing the application of knowledge and skills to address all or part of a business issue. A systems development methodology, then, consists of processes, tools, and techniques for developing systems. In addition to the types of structured tools discussed below, these methodologies prescribe who should participate and their roles, the development stages and decision points, and specific formats for system documentation.

This section will provide a conceptual introduction to the most common structured techniques in a general life cycle development framework. Two major approaches to systems building have emerged: procedural-oriented and object-oriented. Procedural-oriented systems have historically been the most common as they appropriately represent a large class of business activities. They include data-oriented as well as sequential, process-oriented activities such as tabulating time cards and printing paychecks, inventory handling, and accounts payable. Object-oriented (O-O) techniques are a newer approach to systems development. Considered by some to be revolutionary and by others to be evolutionary, O-O techniques are better suited to the development of graphical user interfaces and multimedia applications, but require an entirely new way of thinking for veteran IS professionals.

Procedural-Oriented Techniques

In the past, the vast majority of IS development projects have involved automating an existing paper-oriented business process or updating and expanding an existing automated or partially automated business process. This reality is reflected in the fundamental procedural approach to systems development: describe what you have, define what you want, and describe how you will make it so.

As shown in Figure 9.10, this approach involves documenting the existing system (the As-Is model), creating a model of the desired future system (the Logical To-Be model), and then interpreting the logical future model as a physical system design (the Physical To-Be model). The motivation for following such a process derives in part from human nature. Most people find it easier to imagine the future by conceiving of how it is different from today. A systematic effort to document the existing system can also yield important insights about its deficiencies and worker ideas about improvements.

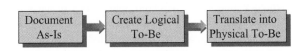

Figure 9.10 As-Is, Logical To-Be, Physical To-Be Modeling Approach

This sequential approach is also effective when a new business process is being put into place at the same time that a new IS is; it helps ensure that the new process will work in concert with the new IS, not against it. As described previously, business process redesign has become increasingly common during the 1990s.

Describing the three models in Figure 9.10 requires a significant amount of effort prior to building the software. User-managers are often surprised at the demands placed on them to support this definition phase. The objective of this process is to have a thorough description of what the construction phase for the system will entail, so that the project risks can be assessed and planned for with some level of confidence or the decision can be made to abandon the project. In fact, actual software coding during the construction phase typically represents less than one-quarter of the entire systems development effort (Page-Jones, 1988).

The *As-Is* model provides a baseline for the system: why build a new one if it will not do more than the old one, do it faster, or avoid existing problems? The As-Is model typically includes both logical and physical models.

Although developing the As-Is model can be user-intense, the majority of the effort is typically involved with developing the second model: abstracting the As-Is model into the *Logical To-Be.* Logical To-Be modeling involves a critical appraisal of existing work processes in order to:

- identify major subprocesses, entities, and their interactions
- separate processing from the flow of data
- capture relationships between data elements
- determine those entities and processes within the project scope, and those that are not.

Creation of the *Physical To-Be* model is a task dominated by IS specialists, as it requires technology expertise to map the logical requirements to available technology. Although information systems are implemented with specific hardware and software, participants in systems development efforts are cautioned to resist the urge to make decisions related to design and implementation until as late as possible in the project. Premature fixation on a particular technology has often led to unsatisfactory outcomes because it may

cause important aspects of the system to go undiscovered or put undue emphasis on *how* to do something before there is certainty about *what* needs to be done. In reality, while no IS project is truly "clean slate," delaying judgment until the Physical To-Be stage is the recommended strategy.

After a new system has been implemented and is operational, a diagram like that in Figure 9.11 would be used to show a physical model of the key system components and their relationships. It uses the following symbols:

Boxes	for	Major modules
Cylinders	for	Databases
Arrows	for	Flow of data

Note, however, that this diagram makes no references to details such as what type of computer hosts the software or what language it is written in. Instead, the Physical To-Be model is a high-level model. It communicates how the new system will work and helps identify any dependencies that might lead to downstream impacts, such as data integrity problems or inadequate process definitions.

Distinct tools are used at each stage of procedural-oriented development. The output from one stage serves as the input for the next. As firms gain experience with systems development, they may develop a preference for certain tools or adopt variations in the notation. The following section introduces some of the most common tools, concepts, and terminology using widely recognized notation. The tools will be presented with the model (As-Is, Logical To-Be, Physical To-Be) with which they are most closely associated using a common business example throughout: accounts payable. An accounts payable example is useful because accounts payable activities interact with other business activities (such as purchasing and receiving), are familiar to most managers and business students, and are common across industries.

Tools for the As-Is Model

Whether a system is entirely manual or very automated, the functions and flows of the existing business activity must be captured. Knowledge of a business process is rarely entirely in the possession of one person, and there may be disagreement as to the actual or preferred processes. Procedures, policies, manuals,

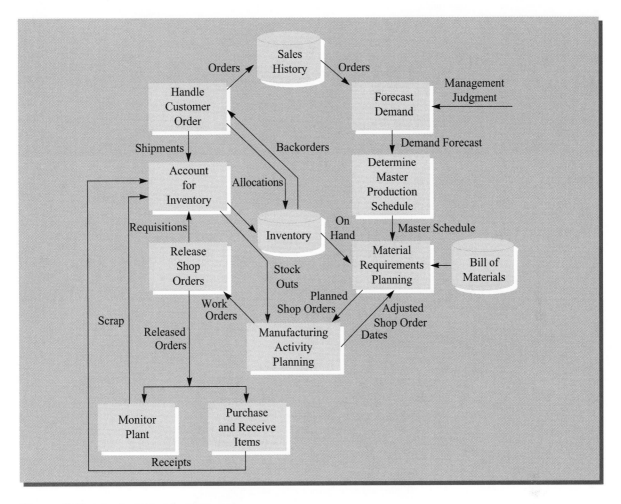

Figure 9.11 Physical Model of a System

forms, reports, and other documentation are used along with individual and group interviews to identify existing processes, external participants such as vendors and other functional departments, other databases or applications, and the inputs and outputs of the activities concerned.

A **context diagram** positions the system as a whole with regard to the other entities and activities with which it interacts. This provides a common frame of reference for project participants and helps define the project scope. Figure 9.12 illustrates a context diagram for an accounts payable system. We can see from this diagram that the accounts payable function both receives input from vendors and sends output to them. Other accounting functions receive sum-

mary information about payables activities, whereas purchasing provides the input needed to process payables. Vendors, accounting, and purchasing are all considered to be outside the project scope for this development effort.

Another common tool for documenting the As-Is system is a work process flow diagram, as shown in Figure 9.13. This flow chart identifies the existing information sources (purchase order file, receipts file), information sources that are updated (changes to payables), the order in which steps occur (approvals before checks are printed), and some of the dependencies (need to know whether vendor is new or not). The way in which exceptions are handled should also be captured (e.g., what happens to invoices not

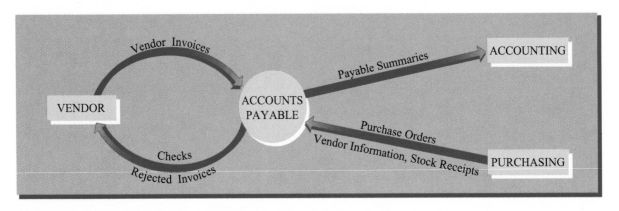

Figure 9.12 Accounts Payable Context Diagram

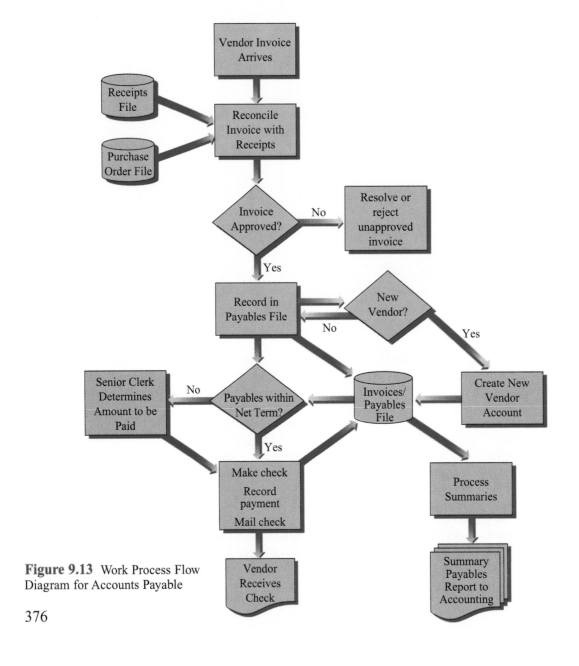

Figure 9.13 Work Process Flow Diagram for Accounts Payable

approved). No two workflow diagrams are identical, because they capture the unique patterns and procedures—formal and informal—of a company.

The work process flow diagram and other As-Is tools serve to point out where the existing system does and does not perform as desired. Common problems include repeated handling of the same document, excessive wait times, processes with no outputs, bottlenecks, and extra review steps. This shows how systems development efforts are closely associated with business process redesign efforts.

Tools for the Logical To-Be Model

In this step, systems developers build a high-level model of a nonexistent system: the system that the users and managers would like to have to replace the one they have now. The Logical To-Be model is an abstraction that identifies the processes and data required for the desired system *without* reference to who does an activity, where it is accomplished, or the type of computer or software used. The model describes the "what," rather than the "how." Stated differently, it separates the information that moves through the business process from the mechanisms that move it (e.g., forms, reports, routing slips). This is important because IT enables information to be in more than one place at the same time; paper does not possess this attribute. By leaving physical barriers behind, the analyst can better determine how to exploit IT. This abstraction step can be difficult for first-time business participants because it appears to ignore issues crucial to their daily work (e.g., specific forms, reports, routing slips). Understanding that the Logical To-Be model encompasses information flows, rather than physical flows (paper, money, products), is the key.

The Logical To-Be model is most closely associated with the **data flow diagram** or **DFD** (see Kozar, 1989, for a thorough discussion of DFDs). The DFD notation itself is technology independent; the symbols have no association to the type of equipment or the humans that might perform the process activities or store the data. DFD creation typically involves groups of people and is accomplished through multiple iterations.

Four types of symbols are used in Data Flow Diagrams:

External Entity: A square indicates some element in the environment of the system that sends or receives data. External entities may not directly access data in the system, but must get data from processing components of the system. No data flows between external entities are shown. External entities have noun labels.

Data Flow: Arrows indicate data in motion, that is, data moving between external entities and system processes, between system processes, or between processes and data stores. Timing and volume of data are not shown. Data flows have noun labels. Because data flow labels often sound similar, and there may be hundreds of distinct data flows in a project, numbers may also be assigned.

Process: Circles represent processing components of the system. Each process has to have both input and output (whereas an external entity may have either input, output, or both). Processes have verb-phrase labels as well as a numerical identifier.

Data Store: Open rectangles depict data at rest; that is, data temporarily or permanently held for repeated reference by one or more processes. Use of a data store implies there is a delay in the flow of data between two or more processes or a need for long-term storage. Each data store contained within the system must have both input and output (that is, be populated and be used) within the system. Data stores that are outside the system may provide only input or only output. Data stores have noun labels and a unique identifier.

The process of creating data flow diagrams:

- identifies the entities that supply or use system information
- distinguishes processes from the data that they use or produce
- explicates business rules that affect the transformation of data to information
- identifies logical relationships
- pinpoints duplicate storage and movements of data

In Figure 9.14(a), a "top level" DFD for the Accounts Payable system is shown. Consistent with the context diagram of Figure 9.12, the dashed line delineates the system boundary. The system includes four processes (circles). Data stores internal to this

(a) TOP-LEVEL DFD

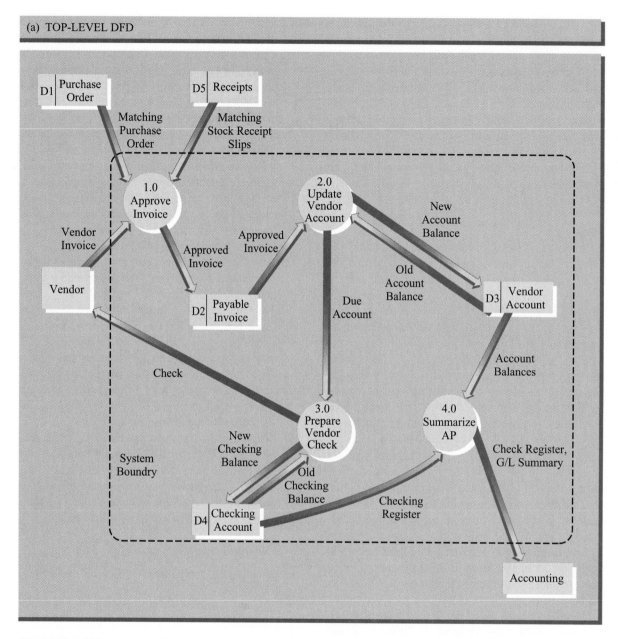

Figure 9.14(a) Accounts Payable System Data Flow Diagram (Top Level)

system (D2, D3, and D4) serve as buffers between the process components (e.g., to compensate for different processing rates of the components or to permit batch processing of transactions), as well as semipermanent storage for auditing purposes. Because this is a top-level DFD, or macro view, processing details are not depicted. For example, this top-level diagram does not show what happens to exceptions—such as what the process does to deal with invoices that do not match purchase orders or shipment receipt records.

A key to the effectiveness of DFD modeling is the enforcement of strict hierarchical relationships. Each

(b) SECOND-LEVEL DFD FOR PROCESS 1.0 IN TOP-LEVEL

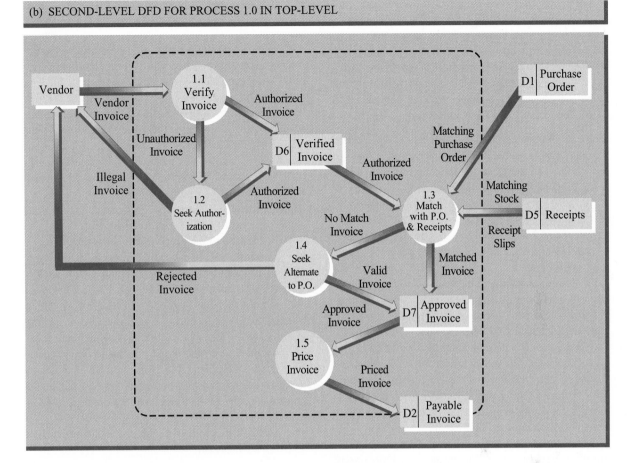

Figure 9.14(b) Accounts Payable System Data Flow Diagram (Second Level)

process (circle) on the top-level DFD has a lower-level DFD that documents the subprocesses, data stores, and data flows needed to accomplish the process task. This "explosion" continues for each subprocess until no further subprocesses are needed to describe the function. A process at the lowest level in the model must be definable by a few descriptive sentences. Figure 9.14(b) is the next-lower-level explosion DFD for Process 1.0 (Approve Invoice) in Figure 9.14(a). The process decomposition relationship is shown by the process numbering scheme (1.1, 1.2, etc.).

The lower-level DFDs may result in the identification of additional data stores and data flows as well as subprocesses, but the exploded DFDs must balance with their higher-level counterparts. All data flows

identified in a lower-level DFD must be accounted for in the description, source, and destination of data flows at the higher level. During the Logical To-Be defining process, external entities and data flows may need to be added to higher-level DFDs to assure completeness. It is not uncommon for business systems to have four or five levels of DFDs before exhausting all subprocesses.

When complete, DFDs tell a story about the business process that does not depend upon specific forms or technology. The rigor imposed by the explosion, aggregation, balancing, and documentation of DFDs results in more than simple circle-and-arrow diagrams. For example, from reviewing the accounts payable DFDs, we see:

1. Purchase orders and shipment receipt records are produced by systems outside the accounts payable system (because they are shown as inputs from the environment, i.e., outside the system boundary).
2. The payable invoice data store temporarily stores and groups invoices after invoice approval and before subsequent vendor account updating and check writing (data flows into and out of D2).

These statements describe two aspects of the accounts payable organizational data flows as we want them to be without implying computerization or any other form of new system implementation.

In addition to diagrams such as in Figures 9.14, each external entity, process, data flow, and data store is documented as to its content. The documentation also shows how the components are related; for example, the description for the Vendor entity would include both inbound and outbound data flows. Similarly, the data store documentation includes the individual data elements that are input into the store, and matches them to output descriptions.

The accuracy and completeness of a DFD model is crucial for the process of converting the Logical To-Be model into the Physical To-Be design. However, prior to commencing this physical design step, additional logical modeling is required to define the system's data elements and relationships.

Data modeling is the process of logically defining the necessary and sufficient relationships among system data. The specialized terminology for the four levels of data modeling is provided here:

Data elements are the lowest unit of data. These represent individual types of data such as "purchase order number," "vendor name," or "quantity received."

Entity instances are groupings of related data elements that correspond to a single entity in the world. For example, an entity instance would be all the different data elements needed to represent an invoice.

Entities (or data entities) are groups of entity instances. As such, all the instances have the same structure because they all have the same data elements. This entity then represents a collection of like items such as all invoices or the transactions that make up a checking account.

Data stores (or databases) are groups of entities that have a relationship. This highest level captures

the relationship between entities such as how invoices can be associated with a purchase order.

The most common approach to defining data elements in a DFD is to create a **data dictionary.** The goal of the data dictionary entry is to describe the data element as completely as possible; these entries should err on the side of too much information, rather than too little. This is also the place to capture whether elements are calculated, how many decimal places are required, and how an element may be referred to in external systems that reference it. Figure 9.15 shows a typical data dictionary entry for the data element Purchase Order (PO) Number. The data dictionary concept is more fully described in Chapter 14.

In addition to the detail at the data-element level, the relationships between entities must be determined. A tool for capturing this information is the **entity-relationship diagram,** or the E-R diagram. Figure 9.16 shows that the data entity "Vendor Invoice" is related to the data entity "Purchase Order" by the relation type "includes." Further, the numerals next to the data entities show that a many-to-one relationship has been defined. This means that one invoice can refer to only one purchase order number, but that a purchase order number can have many invoices associated with it.

The E-R diagram in Figure 9.16 thus reflects an existing business rule:

Vendor invoices cannot include items from more than one purchase order.

The motivation for such a business rule may lie in difficulties related to manual paper processing. However, IT may be used to "break" this rule by eliminating the problems of manually reconciling invoices to multiple purchase orders. If this decision rule is changed, the E-R diagram would be changed to reflect a new many-to-many relationship desired in the Logical To-Be system.

In summary, creating a Logical To-Be model requires the abstraction of existing business processes from the As-Is model into representations that separate data flows from processes and entities, accurately identify business rules, and capture the relationships among data. Though a demanding effort, the creation of a complete To-Be model for complex systems is our best assurance that the new system will improve upon the existing one.

Accounts Payable Project Data Dictionary Entry for PO Number

Label	PO Number
Alternate Names	Purchase Order Number. PO Number. PO#
Definition	Unique identifier for an individual purchase order: alpha character designates the division. The five digit number is assigned in sequential order at the time of creation.
Example	C07321
Field Name	PO_Num
Input Format	A##### (single alpha followed by five integers, no spaces or symbols allowed)
Output Format	Same as input format
Edit Rules	No values below 1000 allowed in numeric portion: currently using A-E as division code indicators.
Additional Notes	At conversion to the former system in 1991, numbers below 1000 were discontinued. Each division writes about 700–1,000 purchase orders per year. PO Numbers cannot be re-used.
Storage Type	Alphanumeric, no decimals
Default Value	None
Required	Each purchase order must have one PO Number.

Prepared by: JDAustin	Date: 8/27/97	Version No.: 1

Figure 9.15 Data Dictionary Sample Entry

Figure 9.16 Entity-Relationship Diagram for Invoice and PO

The next step is to develop a physical model based on the Logical To-Be model—including all the decisions necessary to determine how the logical requirements can be met. In preparation for our Physical To-Be model discussion below, Figure 9.17 identifies relational database terminology (as used in a physical model) that corresponds to the various logical E-R model terms. For each pair of terms, a corresponding example from the accounts payable system is also provided.

Tools for Documenting the Physical To-Be System

The end deliverables from the Logical To-Be modeling process are called the **system requirements.** Any proposed system design must address the need for each requirement, provide a substitute, or justify its exclusion. Of course, the objective is to meet as many of the requirements as possible without jeopardizing project scheduling and budget constraints.

Making the Logical To-Be model "physical" requires additional analysis and a host of decisions. Tools for physical design include those that represent how processes and data stores will be partitioned, how program control will be handled, and how the database will be organized.

One of these tools is called a **program structure chart.** Figure 9.18 shows the program structure chart for a subsystem called "Handle Customer Order." Boxes represent subprocess modules, and arrows

Logical Data Modeling Terms	Physical Data Terms	Example from Figure 9.14
Data Store	Database	Accounts Payable Database
Entity	File or Table	Purchase Orders (D1)
Entity Instance	Record or Row	All information on purchase order number A07321
Data Element	Field	PO Number

Figure 9.17 Key Terms for Logical Data Modeling

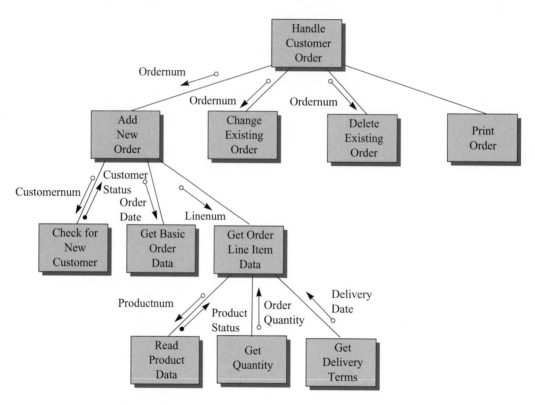

Figure 9.18 Program Structure Chart

represent the flow of control during program execution. The diagram is read from top to bottom starting from the left and moving to the right. Flags (arrows with circles) come in two forms: data couples (open circle) and control flags (filled circle). Both flags direct the program modules to take action. Data couples cause action to be taken based on the data passed to the module, whereas control flags causes program execution based on the result of another module's processing. The module at the top controls all these processes and is the only means by which other program modules can interact with any of the subprocesses.

Program structure charts have rules for determining when they are complete by evaluating design factors such as cohesion and coupling (Page-Jones, 1988). Cohesion requires that each component within the system has a well-defined function and that all components cooperate to achieve an overall system goal. As discussed above (see "Key System Characteristics"), coupling refers to the degree to which components are dependent on each other. Similar to DFDs, a complex system will have many program structure charts organized in a hierarchy of greater to lesser detail.

Data design issues must also be resolved for a specific database and application architecture. The number, content, and relationship of data tables and their elements must be defined. For example, a closer look at the accounts payable system reveals that purchase orders, receipts, and invoices may contain several similar data elements. An Item Master table is created into which data about all invoice items must be entered. Figure 9.19 shows the Item Master table and its relationship to other tables in the accounts payable database. The creation of this table greatly facilitates the reconciliation of receipts and purchase orders to invoices.

Our final example for the Physical To-Be model is layouts for system interfaces with end-users. The most common interfaces are on-line screen layouts and report layouts. In the Logical To-Be modeling, the need for an interface was identified, as well as its frequency of use and information content. In the Physical To-Be modeling, the specific interface design is addressed.

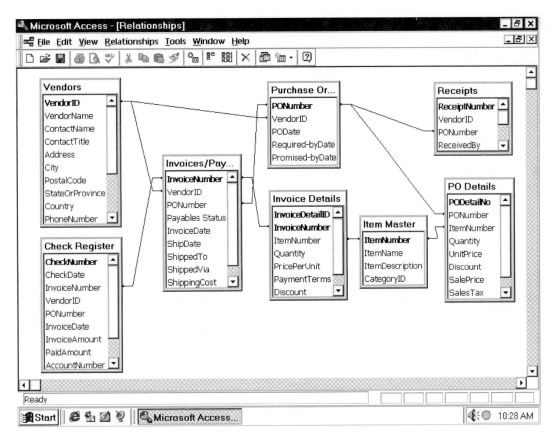

Figure 9.19 Relationships for Data Elements in Accounts Payable Tables (Access Implementation).
Screen shot reprinted with permission from Microsoft Corporation.

Figures 9.20 and 9.21 show draft layouts for an input screen and a report for the accounts payable system. Layouts such as these are often developed in close consultation between systems designers and the end-users who will be directly working with a computer display. Today's system building tools allow for easy prototyping of such interfaces by end-users before the system itself is actually built. Systems today are also frequently built with some flexibility, so that the user can directly control design options for reports and data entry forms in order to adapt to changing needs of the business or the end-consumer of the report.

You have now considered some of the tools used to capture system needs, document business rules, and uncover hidden dependencies and relationships as part of the process of developing a new computer system using procedural-oriented techniques.

Object-Oriented Techniques

Object-oriented (O-O) techniques are touted by some as a distinct alternative to the procedurally oriented techniques discussed above. Other authors emphasize that there are several points of similarity. Nevertheless, there is consensus in the field that the level of abstraction required for object-oriented analysis and design requires new skills on the part of the seasoned IS professional. Moving to an O-O approach can be a difficult transition for those with well-honed skills in procedural techniques. The IS professional must learn new concepts, new development methodologies, and new programming tools.

Unfortunately, O-O techniques have also been portrayed as a "silver bullet" for software engineering deficiencies of the past decades. For example, a 1991 *Business Week* cover story article entitled "Software

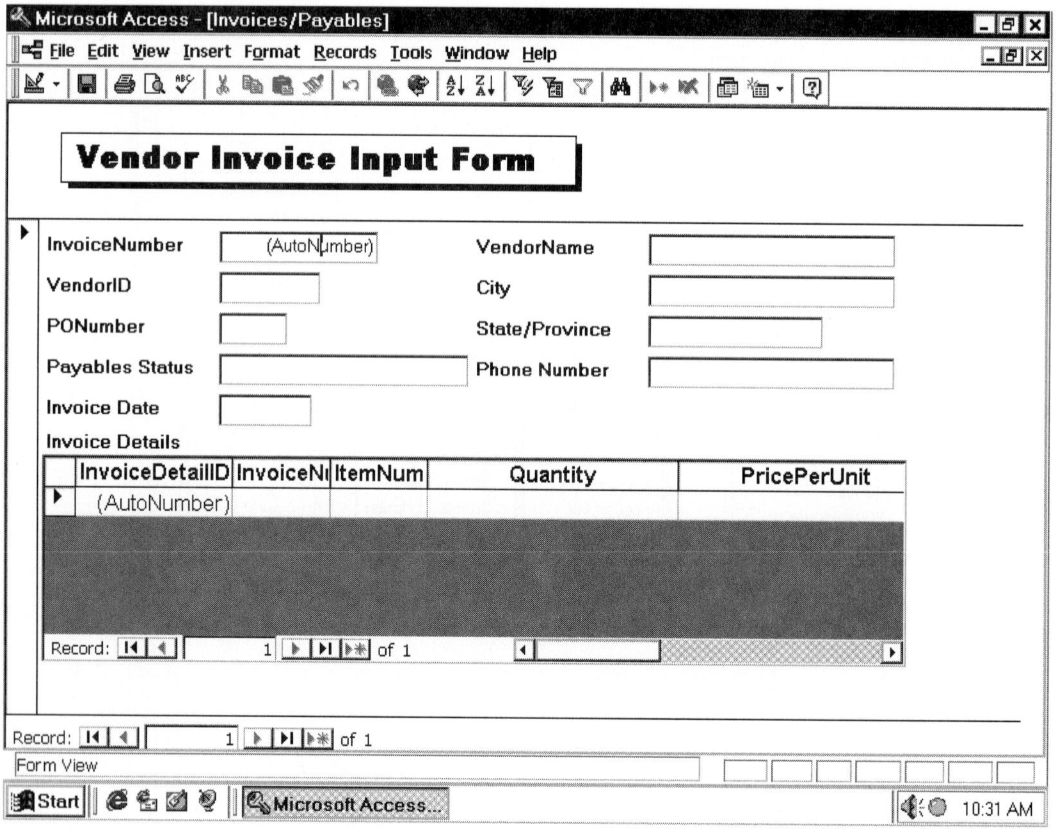

Figure 9.20 Input Form Layout for Vendor Invoice.
Screen shot reprinted with permission from Microsoft Corporation.

Check Register

Account Number 2936

CheckNumber	CheckDate	InvoiceNumber	VendorID	PONumber	InvoiceDate	InvoiceAmount	PaidAmount
482441	8/3/98	C1523	178	A00702	7/20/98	1,925.50	1,925.50
482442	8/3/98	1398752	52	C00321	7/24/98	408.92	408.92
482443	8/3/98	E17982	104	E00052	7/23/98	1,500.00	1,200.00
482444	8/3/98	175632	89	C00323	7/24/98	10,328.72	10,328.72
TOTAL						14,163.14	13,863.14
482445	8/4/98	R1689	13	B00824	7/27/98	505.17	505.17
482446	8/4/98	M568930	97	B00825	7/28/98	12,327.18	11,094.46
482447	8/4/98	897532	152	A00704	7/28/98	765.15	765.15
482448	8/4/98	C1527	178	D00376	7/30/98	1,534.83	1,534.83
TOTAL						15,132.33	13,899.61
MONTHLY TOTAL						29,295.47	27,762.75

Figure 9.21 Check Register Report Layout with Sample Data

385

Made Simple" pictured a baby at the computer keyboard! A summary of the *Business Week* description of the differences between "old-style" approaches with third-generation languages and O-O approaches using Smalltalk is captured in Figure 9.22.

This figure clarifies two potential O-O advantages from an IS management perspective: the ability to reuse objects programmed by others and the ability to quickly mock-up a prototype application. A third benefit is easier maintenance after an application has been implemented, due to the nature of the objects.

In this section we will present the core concepts of the O-O approach, as well as some of the modeling techniques for O-O analysis.

Core Concepts

The key terminology to describe the O-O approach to software engineering is summarized in Figure 9.23. According to Fichman and Kemerer (1993), the "essence" of the approach can be captured in two principles:

- Storing data and related operations together within objects (encapsulation)
- Sharing commonalities between classes of objects (inheritance)

The attributes of an object and its methods are *hidden* inside the object. This means that one object does not need to know the details about the attributes and methods of another object. This lack of interdependency across objects means that systems developed using O-O techniques have loosely coupled modules. Each object is therefore independent and can be interlocked with other objects. This means that systems developed using O-O techniques are more flexible from the perspective of system development and maintenance. It also means that an entire system could be created from preexisting objects. In today's fast-

---

PROCEDURAL APPROACH

Defining the Task
A team of business managers prepare a detailed document specifying, as precisely as it can, just what the program should do.

The Process
The document is used to prepare a design of the program. Programmers divide up the design and write thousands of lines of program from scratch. If all goes well, the pieces work together as planned and the system fulfills the original requirements—which may be out of date by then.

Elapsed Time
Months. And if the application needs major modifications, it may have to be rewritten extensively.

OBJECT-ORIENTED APPROACH

Defining the Task
The O-O programmer searches a library of objects (prefabricated chunks of software) looking for those that may be useful to the task.

The Process
Within days, a few objects have been slapped together to create a bare-bones prototype. The customer gets to "test-drive" the prototype and provide critical feedback. By repeatedly refining and retesting the prototype this way, it develops into just what the customer needs.

Elapsed Time
Weeks. And the program is always ready for future changes, using the same procedure.

Figure 9.22   Comparison of Procedural and Object-Oriented Approaches [Verity and Schwartz, 1991]

Class	An abstract definition or template for a collection of objects that share identical structure and behavior.
Encapsulation	Enclosing a data structure and all operations that access the structure inside a "capsule" or object, which prevents direct access to the data by means other than those operations.
Information Hiding	A design principle that states that the internal structure of a given module should be a black box that stays hidden from other modules. Information hiding insulates other modules from changes that affect a given module's internal representation but not its external interface.
Inheritance	A mechanism that allows objects from different but related classes to share common characteristics (variable and method definitions) by placing those common characteristics in higher-level classes and creating links to those classes.
Message Passing	The practice of using explicit messages sent from one object to another as the only form of object communication. A message consists of an object identifier, a method name, and a set of arguments.
Method	A small program associated with an object that performs an atomic and cohesive operation, usually on that object's data.
Object	An abstraction of a real-world object that encapsulates a set of variables and methods corresponding to the real-world object's attributes and behaviors.

Figure 9.23 Object-Oriented Terminology [Fichman and Kemerer, 1993].
Reprinted from *Sloan Management Review.* All rights reserved.

changing business environments, this ability to react more quickly to changing business needs is a major driver for implementing an O-O approach.

O-O Analysis Modeling

O-O modeling involves static models and dynamic models (Hoffer, George, and Valacich, 1996). Static models represent three kinds of relationships, or connections, between classes and objects, as shown in Figure 9.24:

- *Gen-Spec:* Generalization-Specialization connections indicate relationships between a generalized class and one or more specialized classes. Similar to E-R modeling, it is an "is-a" relationship. Specialization subclasses inherit all of the properties of their superclasses. For example, on the left side of

Figure 9.24, a Campus Course is a Course; a Correspondence Course is also a course. A specialized subclass can also add (or "override") properties.

- *Whole-Part:* Whole-Part connections show the details of the object, which are aggregated over one or more components. For example, on the right side of Figure 9.24, the Exam and Book objects are components of the Course object; the Course object is composed of the Exam and Book objects. (Note: The cardinality symbols show that an exam is a part of exactly one course, but a course may have zero or many exams as part of it.)

- *Instance:* Instance connections show additional relationships between objects, similar to relational data modeling. (Note: The cardinalities are as follows—an Instructor object is mandatory for each Course, but each Instructor object may have zero to many Course objects.)

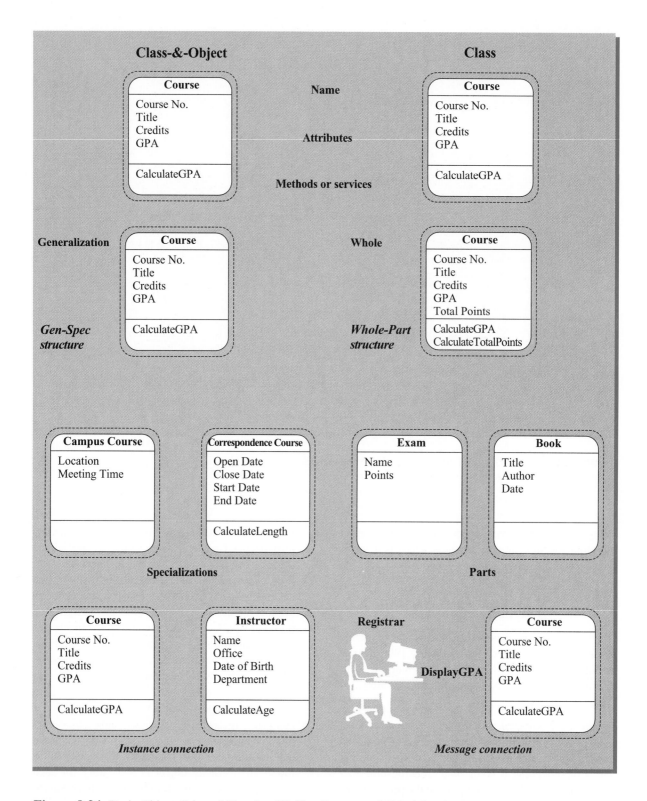

Figure 9.24 Basic Object-Oriented Notation [Hoffer, George, and Valacich, 1996]

O-O models also can represent dynamic states in terms of message passing and methods (also called services). Methods are specific functions that an object can exhibit, and are classified into three types: simple, complex, and monitoring/triggering. Simple methods are mandatory methods that exist in all classes, and include these:

Add an object
Delete an object
Connect with another object
Display the attributes of an object

Complex methods include mathematical functions (both statistical and logical). Monitoring/triggering methods alert users about events due to processing another method, such as an exception value, or due to user-initiated actions, such as the use of a button on a graphical user interface.

Two dynamic modelling techniques include message connections and state-transition diagrams (also a procedural technique). As shown in Figure 9.24, message connections show which objects call upon the services of other objects; here, a user interface object calls for the display of the GPA attribute. A state-transition diagram of a Spell Checker is shown in Figure 9.25. The Spell Checker object has three possible states. When it is in an Open but Idle state, it can be requested to move to the Open and Checking state, move to the Closed state, or be left in the Open but Idle state.

In summary, O-O analysis requires the following overall steps (*I/S Analyzer,* 1995):

- Creating object classes and class hierararchies reflecting inherited commonalities
- Modeling class relationships
- Modeling object attributes, which become the data the object encapsulates
- Modeling behaviors, which become the encapsulated methods to access the data

As can be seen from the above examples, the distinction between data analysis and process analysis in the procedurally-oriented methods does not exist with object analysis; O-O analysis encompasses both data and analysis. According to industry observers, successful O-O analysis can produce big payoffs in object reusability and therefore productivity. Yet objects developed for individual applications are not necessarily reusable; to be widely reusable, object classes must be broad enough to be scalable. Several methodologies have emerged to help IS professionals move to this new paradigm, including those by Booch, Coad and Yourdan, Rumbaugh, and Taylor (see Hoffer et al., 1996, and *I/S Analyzer,* 1995). Successful O-O analysis has also been associated with business process redesign (see sidebar "O-O Analysis for Business Process Redesign").

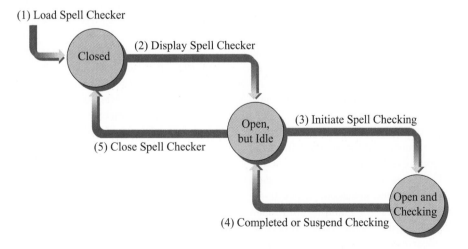

Figure 9.25 State-Transition Diagram [Hoffer, George, and Valacich, 1996]

O-O ANALYSIS FOR BUSINESS PROCESS REDESIGN

According to a manager at CableData, a leading provider of subscriber systems to cable companies, "One of the things we strive for is getting our programmers to work at a higher level. If a person can think about a customer object, what it knows and how it behaves, they are focusing on the business problem, not the infrastructure."

[IS Analyzer, 1995]

INFORMATION SYSTEMS CONTROLS

Suppose you and your spouse or a friend with whom you have a joint savings account separately go to the bank one day to withdraw the same $500 in savings. Or suppose a trainee forgets to include the decimal point in a new billing rate scheme. Or suppose an inventory clerk enters a wrong part number to record the issue of an item from the storeroom; this results in an out-of-stock status, which automatically generates a purchase order to a vendor, who then begins production, and so on. These situations illustrate just some of the ways in which potential human errors can arise in information systems. These also suggest possible wasted work, customer and employee confusion, and added expenses. For the integrity of the organization, control mechanisms need to be implemented for detection, prevention, and correction.

However, risks due to human error are only a small part of the potential risks that are associated with the use of IT. For example, Bashein, Markus, and Finley (1997) have identified IT-related risks that go far beyond risks due to human error, as shown in Figure 9.26. Organizations need to protect against these risks as well as risks due to human error.

Control mechanisms include management policies, operating procedures, and the auditing function. Some aspects of control can be built-in to an information system itself, whereas others are the result of day-to-day business practices and management decisions. Information system controls, for example, are needed to maintain data integrity, allow only authorized access, ensure proper system operation, and protect against malfunctions, power outages and disasters.

Some controls are appropriately implemented during the Definition and Construction phases of the systems life cycle, and others are part of the Implementation phase, which includes operations. Figure 9.27 shows a few control approaches usually employed in the indicated phases of the systems life cycle.

Security controls related to the technology infrastructure—such as backup power supplies, network access control, and firewall protection—are typically the purview of the IS organization. In addition, IS developers will include some standard controls in all applications. However, specifying checks and balances to ensure accurate data entry and handling is a user-manager responsibility. Managers must carefully identify what are valid data, what errors might be made while handling data, what nontechnical security risks are present, and what potential business losses could result from inaccurate or lost data. Because the identification of potential IS controls is to a large extent a user-manager responsibility, we provide a detailed discussion of some of these controls in this chapter.

It is during the systems analysis and design process that the needs for specific controls are identified and control mechanisms are developed to address these needs. Some mechanisms are implemented during the system design, coding, or implementation. Others become part of the routine operation of the system, such as backups and authorization security, and still others involve the use of manual business practices and management policies, such as formal system audits.

Newer technologies, such as advanced software tools for system testing, have in some cases improved an organization's control processes, whereas in other cases the technologies have introduced new potential risks. In particular, the emergence of distributed computing has increased our reliance on network transmission of data and software—which requires additional technical and managerial controls (Hart and Rosenberg, 1995). Here we discuss some of the most common control mechanisms that apply to a wide range of application development situations.

Controls in the Definition and Construction Phases

In the initial two phases of the systems life cycle, the accurate and reliable performance of the system can be assured by the use of standards, embedded controls, and thorough testing.

Competitive risk occurs when a company is unable to achieve business value from its investments in information technology, either because it has misperceived what would be required to give competitive advantage or because competitors have responded more swiftly than expected.

Control design risk is associated with errors built into the technology or with error-checking features omitted from the technology; for instance, program trading systems without self-correcting feedback loops, weak or absent automated checking for fraudulent usage of telephone networks, or software failures caused by the year 2000 date change.

Development risk occurs when the technology is not available on schedule. The implementation project may be delayed for various reasons, such as personnel issues, budget overruns, or vendor delays.

External fraud, theft, or crime risk occurs when unknown outsiders perpetrate willful damage on or through technology; for example, hackers who steal computer time, information, and funds or who propagate computer viruses, as well as organized criminals who steal access to the telephone network.

Extraordinary event risk is associated with accidents and natural disasters; for example, a flood destroying a data center or a car accidentally driving into a power box and bringing down a network.

Internal abuse risk is associated with trusted people (employees and business partners) intentionally using technology in ways contrary to the organization's interests; for example, employees who misappropriate confidential client data for personal gain or business partners who use electronic networks to divert funds into their own accounts.

Nonuse and unintentional misuse risk is associated with people not using the technology in ways intended by the organization or unintentionally using the technology in ways that are contrary to the organization's goals; for example, the business partner who will not transmit orders via electronic data interchange, or who makes unacceptable errors in doing so, or the poorly trained user who accidentally crashes the network.

Personnel and expertise risk occurs when employees who know the technology leave, and new employees with equivalent expertise are not readily available. This risk is associated with new technologies such as enterprise client/server systems; for example, a company that provides extensive client/server training to employees, only to have them lured away by offers of higher salaries.

Reputation risk occurs when the public at large or key stakeholders have negative reactions to a company's information technology initiatives; for example, negative reaction from mortgage brokers to a financial institution's proposed automated mortgage loan origination system.

Technical risk is inherent in the underlying information technology or support arrangements; for example, computing hardware or software that does not work reliably when needed, or a vendor who fails to support the technology acceptably.

Figure 9.26 Sources and Consequences of IT-related Risks [Bashein, Markus, and Finley, 1997]

Methodology Standards   The reliable performance of a system depends upon how well it was designed and constructed. No amount of automated checks can override errors in the software itself.

One way to avoid errors is to develop standard, repeatable, and possibly reusable methods and techniques for system developers. The use of standard programming languages and equipment means that systems developers will be more familiar with the tools and will be less likely to make mistakes. A common method is to create a library of frequently used functions (such as calculation of net present value or a sales forecasting model) that can be used by many different information systems. Such functions can then be developed and tested with great care and reused as needed, saving development time and reducing the likelihood of design and programming flaws. Most organizations also have standards for designing user interfaces, such as screen and report layout rules and guidelines.

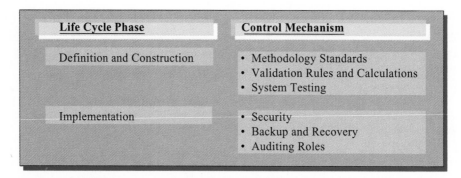

Life Cycle Phase	Control Mechanism
Definition and Construction	• Methodology Standards • Validation Rules and Calculations • System Testing
Implementation	• Security • Backup and Recovery • Auditing Roles

Figure 9.27   Pre- and Post-Installation Controls

The importance of standards also extends to the documentation of the system during construction and the following period of maintenance and upgrades. If future programmers do not have access to systems documentation that is complete and accurate, they may be unaware of prior changes. Documentation for the system's users also needs to be complete and accurate so that system inputs are not incorrectly captured and system outputs are not incorrectly used.

Validation Rules and Calculations   Each time a data element is updated, the new value can be checked against a legitimate set or range of values permitted for that data. This check can be performed in each application program where these data can be changed (for example, in a payables adjustment program that modifies previously entered vendor invoices) and in the database where they are stored. Edit rules are also used to ensure that data are not missing, that data are of a valid size and type, and that data match with other stored values.

Simply visually displaying associated data can be a very useful edit check. For example, when a vendor number is entered, the program can display the associated name and address. The person inputting or modifying data can then visually verify the vendor information. Edit rules can also ensure that only numbers are entered for numeric data, that only feasible codes are entered, or that some calculation based on a modified data value is valid. These edit checks are integrity rules that control the validity of data.

Various calculations can be performed to validate processing. Batch totals that calculate the sum of cer-

tain data in a batch of transactions can be computed both manually before processing and by the computer during processing; discrepancies suggest the occurrence of data entry errors such as transposition of digits. Though they are not foolproof, such approaches, along with automated edits, go a long way toward assuring valid input.

A **check digit** can be appended to critical identifying numbers such as general ledger account numbers or vendor numbers; the value of this check digit is based on the other digits in the number. This can be used to quickly verify that at least a valid, if not correct, code has been entered, and it can catch most common errors.

User-managers and their staff are responsible for defining the legitimate values for data and where control calculations would be important as a part of the information captured in the data dictionary. Further, business managers must set policy to specify if checks can be overridden and who can authorize overrides. Validation rules should permit business growth and expansion, yet reduce the likelihood of erroneous data.

System Testing   Certainly the most common and effective of all IS controls is complete system testing. Each program must be tested individually and in combination with the other programs in the application. Managers develop test data that have known results. Programs are run with typical and atypical data, correct and erroneous data, and the actual results are compared to what should be produced. Testing occurs not only when systems are initially developed, but also when systems are modified. (See Chapter 10 for an additional description of the user role in system testing.)

Controls in the Implementation Phase

Not all the elements necessary to assure proper systems operation can be built into an application. Avoiding and detecting inappropriate access or use, providing data backups and system recovery capabilities, and formally auditing the system are all ongoing control mechanisms. As mentioned earlier, many application-level controls work in concert with managerial controls. User-managers are responsible for being familiar with any firm-wide control mechanisms and identifying when additional ones are needed for a specific application.

Security   The unauthorized use of data can result in a material loss, such as the embezzlement of funds, or in harder to measure losses, such as the disclosure of sensitive data. In any case, the security of data and computers is necessary so that employees, customers, shareholders, and others can be confident that their interactions with the organization are confidential and the assets of the business are safe.

Security measures are concerned with both logical and physical access. Logical access controls are concerned with whether or not users can run an application, whether they can read a file or change it, and whether they can change the access that others have. Managers work with the systems personnel to identify and maintain appropriate authorization levels based on work roles and business needs. Two mechanisms for controlling logical access are authentication and authorization (Hart and Rosenberg, 1995). Authentication involves establishing that the person requesting access is who he or she appears to be. Authorization involves determining whether or not authenticated users have access to the requested resources. Authentication is usually handled by the use of a unique user identifier and a private password. Authorization involves the identification of allowed access to resources.

Encryption techniques are used to encode data that is transmitted across organizational boundaries. Data may be stored in an encrypted form and then decrypted by the application. Unless a user knows the decryption algorithm, an encrypted file will be unreadable.

The physical security of specific computers and data processing centers must also be established. Badge readers, voice, fingerprint, and retina recognition, or combination locks are common. Formal company statements about computer ethics raise awareness to the sensitivity of data privacy and the need to protect organizational data. When combined with knowledge of the use of transaction or activity logs which record the user ID, network location, time-stamp, and function or data accessed, many security violations may be discouraged.

Because no security system is foolproof, detection methods to identify security breaches are also needed. Administrative practices to help deter computer security abuses have been compiled by Hoffer and Straub (1989). Detection methods include these:

- hiding special instructions in sensitive programs that log identifying data about users
- analysis of the amount of computer time used by individuals
- analysis of system activity logs for unusual patterns of use

With the rise of end-user computing and use of the Internet, additional risks due to inappropriate behaviors while using these tools have emerged, as well as issue stemming from work-related use of home PCs. Some specific end-user computing risks and controls are discussed in Chapter 12. Today, organizations are developing similar controls to manage intranets and access to external Web sites from intranets.

In the sidebar "An Integrated Approach to Security Risks," Bashein, Markus, and Finley describe a comprehensive approach that involves tight, loose, and flexible (variable) mechanisms, based on case studies of five large firms.

Backup and Recovery   The ultimate protection against many system failures is to have a backup copy. Periodically a file can be copied and saved in a separate location such as a bank vault. Then, when a file becomes contaminated or destroyed, the most recent version can be restored. Of course, any changes since the last copy was made will not appear. Thus, organizations often also keep transaction logs (a chronological history of changes to each file), so these changes

AN INTEGRATED APPROACH TO SECURITY RISKS

Controls are expensive, can reduce business flexibility, and can have negative side effects. Therefore, managers must be concerned not only with providing enough control but also with not imposing too much.

For major risks involving core business activities, the companies investigated in the case studies always installed a first line of controls that were relatively loose. That is, they imposed minimal restrictions on the free flow of normal business operations. So, for example, USAA customer service representatives with valid passwords were enabled to access virtually all data about a customer, because this level of flexibility was needed in USAA's business model. Similarly, virtually all associates with valid passwords at Microsoft could make purchases of up to $1,000 from any vendor for anything, because this flexibility was deemed appropriate given the nature of Microsoft's business.

However, because these first lines of control create too much potential for control violations, the case study companies installed one or more additional layers of backup safety nets. In some cases, the backup layers had tighter weaves than the first, so that they could deter, prevent, or detect certain types of inappropriate behavior. For example, USAA disciplined the people whom monitoring showed had broken data access rules (e.g., the prohibition against accessing their own account data). In other cases, one or more backup layers had variable weaves, to permit the exercise of judgment in the application of controls. So, for example, budgets were used to ensure that Microsoft's generous purchase policy did not get out of hand, and data ownership authority was used to enable legitimate ad hoc access to databases that would otherwise be off limits to particular categories of users. Since managers can tighten or loosen budgetary controls and data access authorizations easily on a case-by-case basis through the normal course of business, they provide extremely flexible controls without the expense of a dedicated control apparatus.

[Adapted from Bashein, Markus, and Finley, 1997]

can be automatically applied to a backup copy to bring the file up to current status.

A common flaw in backup plans is storing the file backup in the same location as the master file. If stored in the same location, a backup is no more likely to survive a fire, flood, or earthquake than its source file. A secure, off-site location for the backup must be provided, along with a foolproof tracking system.

Some organizations can operate only if their online computer systems are working (such as airlines, banks, and telephone networks). One approach is to provide redundant systems and operations that "mirror" the production system and data located at a distant facility. This improves the chances of an effective recovery due to a widespread power or network outage or a natural disaster. If data recovery processing via another location is immediately available, these locations are known as "hot sites."

Information systems and computer equipment are now distributed throughout business departments and in small businesses where IS professionals are not present. Thus, making backups is becoming more of a user-manager responsibility. Further, user-managers and IS professionals together need to determine how frequently backup copies are needed, the business cost of recovering files from backup copies, and how much should be spent on specialized backup resources. As with any security procedure, the ongoing backup and recovery costs need to be in line with the potential organizational risks.

Auditing Roles Critical business processes are subject to periodic formal audits to assure that the processes operate within parameters. As more and more organizations have become dependent on information systems in order to operate their busines, the importance of IS auditing has increased. IS auditing is frequently referred to as **EDP auditing**—a name chosen when the term electronic data processing was used to refer to computer operations. EDP auditors use a variety of methods to ensure the correct processing of data, including compliance tests, statistical sampling, and embedded auditing methods.

Compliance tests check that systems builders use high-quality systems development procedures that lead to properly functioning systems. Statistical sampling of a portion of databases can identify abnormalities that indicate systematic problems or security breaches. Embedded auditing methods include reporting triggers programmed into a system that are activated by certain processing events. The flagged records are then analyzed to determine if errors or security breaches are occurring in the system.

The most commonly used EDP auditing technique in the past has been an **audit trail.** Audit trails trace transactions from the time of input through all the processes and reports in which the transaction data are used. Audit trail records typically include program names, user name or user ID, input location and date/time stamps, as well as the transaction itself. An audit trail can help identify where errors are introduced or where security breaches might have occurred.

Managers need to participate in the identification of elements that should be captured in the audit trail to detect errors and assure compliance with all relevant laws and regulations. Further, the frequency and extent of formal information system auditing is a management decision that should take into account the breadth and role of the system, its relationship to other business processes, and the potential risks to the firm.

Summary

This chapter presents some basic information systems concepts on which modern information systems are designed, built, and implemented. Systems analysis and design is based upon systems principles and good design practices. Three systems characteristics especially important for IS work are determination of the system boundary, component decomposition, and system interface design.

Understanding the human element is also important for system designers. Your own experiences and human information processing characteristics will impact the way you interact with a system. Systems analysts are trained in design principles such as the distinction between logical and physical systems and the consideration of human factors in system design.

In this chapter we also provide a discussion of the application of system principles in the reengineering of an organization. This section shows the significant impact systems thinking can have on a business and how information technology can be an enabler of business process redesign.

This chapter also introduces you to the overall life cycle process for systems development, as well as some specific techniques used by IS professionals. A variety of structured techniques are presented so that you as a user-manager can unambiguously communicate your

information needs and understand the graphical representations of these systems provided by an analyst.

The chapter concludes with a discussion of IS controls to improve the likelihood that systems operate correctly and securely.

Review Questions

1. Define the term *system.* Give an example of a business system and identify for this example the boundary, environment, inputs, and outputs.
2. Define the term *subsystem.* Give an example of a business subsystem and identify the other subsystems with which it relates.
3. What are the six phases of the decision-making process?
4. Define the term *business process reengineering.*
5. Contrast the logical and physical representations of a To-Be system.
6. Outline the factors to consider when choosing a system boundary.
7. What are the functions of an interface component of a system?
8. Define the term decoupling. Grocery and other retail stores have decoupled pricing from the display of products in the store. Why?
9. Contrast the use and content of data flow diagrams.
10. What is a data dictionary?
11. Briefly describe why O-O approaches result in reusable components.
12. List and briefly explain two types of controls commonly introduced in the Definition and Construction phases of the system life cycle.
13. List and briefly explain two types of controls commonly introduced in the Implementation phase of the system life cycle.
14. What is an audit trail? How is an audit trail used for controlling an information system?

Discussion Questions

1. Explain and give an example that supports the following statement: "Each time we change

characteristics of one or more of the components of the organization (organization structure, people, task/procedure, and technology), we must consider compensating changes in the other components."

2. Explain the function of hierarchical decomposition in systems analysis and design and discuss the reasons for viewing and analyzing systems in this way.

3. Why do informal systems arise? Why should systems analysts be aware of them?

4. For each of the six phases of the human decision-making process, give examples of information system capabilities that would help or support a manager.

5. Describe a situation in which the Recency Effect played a role in your processing of information.

6. Some observers have characterized business process reengineering as evolutionary, others as revolutionary. Explain why you think this discrepancy exists.

7. Describe why analysts begin with the As-Is system, rather than the To-Be system.

8. Explain why a logical model of the To-Be system is done before the physical model.

9. Explain the differences between a context diagram, a top-level DFD, and a lower-level DFD.

10. Study the processes followed at your university for registering for classes. Represent this as a context diagram and a top-level DFD.

11. Define the encapsulation principle for O-O approaches and the benefits that result from it.

REFERENCES

1995. "How companies benefit from object-oriented analysis." *I/S Analyzer* 34:8 (August).

Bashein, Barbara J., M. Lynne Markus, and Jane B. Finley. 1997. *Safety Nets: Secrets of Effective Information Technology Controls.* Morristown, N.J.: Financial Executives Research Foundation.

Fichman, Robert G., and Chris F. Kemerer. 1993. "Adoption of software engineering process innovations: The case of object orientation," *Sloan Management Review* 34 (Winter): 7–22.

Fitzgerald, Jerry, and Alan Dennis. 1996. *Business Data Communications and Networking,* Fifth Edition. New York, NY: John Wiley & Sons, Inc.

Hammer, Michael. 1990. "Reengineering work: Don't automate, obliterate." *Harvard Business Review* 68 (July-August): 104–112.

Hammer, Michael. 1996. *Beyond Reengineering.* New York: HarperCollins.

Hammer, Michael, and James Champy. 1993. *Reengineering the Corporation.* New York: HarperCollins.

Hart, Johnson M., and Barry Rosenberg. 1995. *Client/Server Computing for Technical Professionals: Concepts and Solutions.* Reading, MA: Addison-Wesley Publishing Company.

Hoffer, Jeffrey A., Joey F. George, and Joseph S. Valacich. 1996. *Modern Systems Analysis and Design.* Reading, Mass.: Benjamin/Cummings Publishing.

Hoffer, Jeffrey A., and Detmar W. Straub, Jr. 1989. "The 9 to 5 underground: Are you policing computer crimes?" *Sloan Management Review* 30 (Summer): 35–43.

Keen, Peter G.W. 1997. *The Process Edge.* Boston: Harvard University Press.

Kozar, Kenneth A. 1989. *Humanized Information Systems Analysis and Design.* New York: McGraw-Hill Book Company.

Markus, M. Lynne, and Daniel Robey. 1988. "Information technology and organizational change: Causal structure in theory and research." *Management Science* 34 (5): 583–598.

McFadden, Fred R., and Jeffrey A. Hoffer. 1998. *Modern Database Management.* Menlo Park, Calif.: Benjamin Cummings Publishing Company.

Newell, Allen, and Herbert A. Simon. 1972. *Human Problem Solving.* Englewood Cliffs, N.J.: Prentice-Hall.

Page-Jones, Meilir. 1988. *The Practical Guide to Structured Systems Design,* Second Edition. Englewood Cliffs, NJ: Yourdon Press.

Senge, Peter M. 1990. *The Fifth Discipline.* New York: Doubleday.

Verity, John W., and Evan I. Schwartz. 1991. "Software made simple," *Business Week,* September 30.

APPLICATION DEVELOPMENT BY INFORMATION SYSTEMS PROFESSIONALS

In Part II we introduced three types of information technology applications: organizational systems, managerial support systems, and electronic commerce applications, including interorganizational systems. Until the late 1980s, most business applications such as these were software applications customized for a specific firm. If an organization had its own information systems (IS) professionals, these custom applications were most likely developed in-house by these IS specialists. If an organization did not have the resources or IS expertise to develop custom applications, an outside vendor would be employed to either provide IS contract personnel on a temporary basis or to completely develop the customized application for the organization.

Our focus for this chapter is the process of developing customized applications in-house by IS professionals. We describe two overall approaches: the traditional systems development life cycle (SDLC) approach and an evolutionary prototyping approach. Many characteristics of these two approaches to system development, and the newer techniques described in this chapter, also hold true for application development approaches used within software houses. A key difference is that with customized application development for a specific business, users must play a key role in both the Definition and Construction phases of the development cycle. In Chapter 11 we will focus on the process for purchasing systems.

SYSTEMS DEVELOPMENT LIFE CYCLE METHODOLOGY

We turn now to a detailed discussion of the systems life cycle for in-house application development by IS professionals. The traditional life cycle process for developing customized applications is referred to as the **systems development life cycle (SDLC)**. As discussed in Chapter 9, the life cycle concept recognizes that large systems are major IT investments and the development of a system may continue even after it is implemented. Although systems built in the 1980s can still be found in today's organizations, the typical system over a decade old has been modified multiple times in order to keep current with the changing needs of the organization. The SDLC process therefore includes a maintenance step.

The SDLC approach is but one of several alternative approaches to developing systems. We have chosen to focus on this approach first for three reasons.

First, the SDLC approach provides a baseline for understanding what is involved in developing an application system, whether by IS professionals in your organization, by IS professionals in a software firm, or by some combination of in-house and vendor IS specialists. Even if you purchase the system (see Chapter 11) or develop it yourself (see Chapter 12), you need to understand the elements of the traditional approach and both the user-manager and end-user roles in that approach. The SDLC approach includes not only process steps, but a framework for project management. Second, this traditional approach is often the primary approach for a large strategic system. Because your competitors can quickly implement the same purchased solution that you do, purchased systems are unlikely to provide a sustainable competitive advantage. However, customized applications that exploit a particular strategic strength are much more difficult for either a competitor or a vendor to develop. Large organizations today still rely on their IS staffs to both develop and support strategic applications that have become an organization's key means for survival.

Third, as described in Chapter 1, the responsibilities for identifying the need for new applications and effectively implementing them are in the hands of today's user-managers. Line managers are responsible for determining what systems to develop, for making the business case that justifies the cost of the system, for helping to specify what the system will do and how it will enable organizational processes, for managing the changes involved in implementing the new system, and for making sure that it is used to achieve the envisioned benefits for the organization. Recent research has shown that the IT management knowledge of line managers is related to the progressive use of IT within an organization (Boynton, Zmud, and Jacobs, 1994). Further, as we will see in Part IV, in many large organizations the IS managers and professionals who develop and support business applications actually report to senior managers who are line managers, rather than to a senior IS manager.

The SDLC Steps

In Chapter 9 we introduced the three phases of the systems life cycle process: Definition, Construction, Implementation. This basic life cycle approach is sim-

ple in concept, but there is substantial complexity in using it to develop a high-quality, customized application. Over the past three decades, SDLC methodologies have evolved that describe in detail the activities required for each phase. Each SDLC-based methodology specifies the modeling tools to be used at each stage of the process, and IS professionals are trained in the use of these tools. Several of these tools—data flow diagrams, structure charts, E-R models, data dictionaries—were introduced and illustrated in Chapter 9.

In this chapter we will describe a generic SDLC methodology that includes three phases and eight steps. This template is shown in Figure 10.1. The SDLC is also referred to as the "waterfall" model (Boehm, 1981): The outputs from one step are inputs to the next step.

However, the reader should be warned that the initial approval/prioritization process and the specific labeled steps in Figure 10.1 typically vary across organizations. Your organization may have a total of five steps or ten steps, and the SDLC or "waterfall" methodology may also have its own unique name. Nevertheless, an organization's internally developed SDLC methodology should essentially map into the steps for each of the three phases in Figure 10.1, and our discussion below will provide you with a useful template for the SDLC process.

The overall thrusts of the three phases of the SDLC are quite straightforward. For customized application development, the Definition phase is critical: It defines precisely what the system must do in

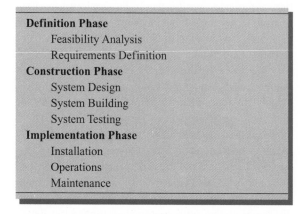

Definition Phase
    Feasibility Analysis
    Requirements Definition
Construction Phase
    System Design
    System Building
    System Testing
Implementation Phase
    Installation
    Operations
    Maintenance

Figure 10.1 The Systems Development Life Cycle

sufficient detail for IS specialists to build the right system. In the Construction phase, the IS specialists produce a working system according to the specifications set forth in the earlier phase. This is where many of the structured techniques and IS controls discussed in Chapter 9 become critical for ensuring a quality application. The completion of each of the first two phases represents a major milestone in the development of the system. In the Implementation phase, the new system is installed, becomes operational within the organization, and is maintained (modified) as needed so that it continues to satisfy the changing needs of the organization.

In Figure 10.2 a typical cost breakdown is presented for these three phases for a medium-sized project with a total development cost of $1 million. (Note: Training and other business costs absorbed by the business unit are not included.) As can be seen from this hypothetical example, the requirements definition is the most costly step. The reasons why will become clear in the following pages.

The SDLC approach also typically requires extensive formal reviews by IS and user management before the next step or phase is begun. Most SDLC methodologies are documentation-based in that until code is produced, the outputs produced by each task

Development Activities	Percentage of Total Cost	Dollar Cost
Definition Phase		
Feasibility analysis	5	$ 50,000
Requirements definition	25	250,000
Construction Phase		
System design	15	150,000
Coding and initial testing	15	150,000
System testing	13	130,000
Documentation and procedures	12	120,000
Implementation Phase		
Installation planning, data cleanup, and conversion	15	150,000
Total	100%	$1,000,000

Figure 10.2 Cost Breakdown for $1 million SDLC Project

are written materials. The specific deliverables from each step are written materials that are specified by the organization's chosen methodology. An SDLC step is not complete until a formal review of this documentation takes place.

The first documentation actually may be developed before a formal feasibility analysis is conducted. This initial request process is briefly described below, followed by a description of the eight steps in our SDLC template of Figure 10.1.

Initiating New Application Investments   There are a number of approaches that organizations use to decide which new applications to invest in. Most organizations today require that an initial application system request be initiated by an executive sponsor. This request is processed differently, depending on the anticipated size of the capital investment. Large system projects typically must be tied to the strategic plan of the overall organization or the requesting unit. For projects of a certain size, an annual approval and prioritization process by a **steering committee** of user representatives may be required. Very large, high-budget projects may require approval by a corporation's top management executive committee or a board of directors for the organization. Projects of relatively small dollar investment (for the organization) may be approved on a much more frequent basis and typically involve a simpler approval process and fewer participants.

In most organizations, the development of a new business application begins with the submission of a formal request by a user department. Some large organizations require that initial proposals first be reviewed and prioritized by a committee at the department or division level, before the SDLC formally begins. However, in order to evaluate these requests, typically an IS professional needs to be included in the evaluation of the proposed system requests.

At a minimum, a document that presents the proposed application need and outlines the potential benefits that the application will provide to the organization is prepared by the user-manager. Frequently, an IS manager that has a close relationship with the requesting business unit will also participate in the development of this document

Once the proposal has received initial approval by a committee or manager responsible for this initial process, IS resources are assigned to the project and the formal SDLC process begins. For large projects, the initial approval may only be an endorsement to proceed with a **feasibility analysis.** The documents for the feasibility analysis then become the basis for a decision on whether or not to make that capital investment.

Definition Phase

Feasibility Analysis. For this first step of the SDLC process, a project manager and one or more systems analysts are typically assigned to work with business managers to prepare a thorough analysis of the feasibility of the proposed system. Three different types of feasibility will be assessed: *economic, operational,* and *technical* feasibility.

The IS analysts work closely with the sponsoring manager who proposed the system, and/or other business managers, to define in some detail what the new system will do, what outputs it will produce, what inputs it will accept, how the input data might be obtained, and what databases might be required. An important activity is to define the scope or boundaries of the system—precisely who would it serve, what it would do, as well as what it would not do—and what data processing would and would not be included. The IS analyst is primarily responsible for assessing the technical feasibility of the system, based on a knowledge of current and emerging technological solutions, the IT expertise of in-house personnel, and the anticipated infrastructure needed to both develop and support the proposed system. The business manager is primarily responsible for assessing the operational feasibility of the system. In some organizations business analysts who are knowledgeable about IT but are not IT professionals play a lead role in this process.

Both business managers and IS analysts work together to prepare a cost/benefit analysis of the proposed system to determine the economic feasibility. Typical benefits include costs to be avoided such as cost savings from personnel, space, and inventory reductions; new revenues to be created; and other ways the system could contribute business value overall. However, for many applications today, some or all of the major benefits may be intangible benefits; they are hard to measure in dollars. Examples of intangible benefits include better customer service, more accurate or more comprehensive information for decision-

making, quicker processing, or better employee morale. (See the "Managing an SDLC Project" section later in this chapter for a further discussion of system justification.)

The IS analyst takes primary responsibility for establishing the development costs for the project. This requires the development of a project plan that includes an estimated schedule in work-weeks or months for each step in the development process and an overall budget estimate through the installation of the project. Estimating these project costs and schedules is especially difficult when new technologies and large system modules are involved. (Note that these costs usually do not include user department costs, which may be substantial during both the Definition and Implementation phases.)

The deliverable of the feasibility analysis step is a document of typically 10 to 20 pages that includes a short executive overview and summary of recommendations, a description of what the system would do and how it would operate, an analysis of the costs and benefits of the proposed system, and a plan for the development of the system. Sometimes referred to as a systems proposal document, this document is typically first discussed and agreed to by both the executive sponsor and the IS project manager and then reviewed by a management committee that has authority for system approvals and prioritization.

Before additional steps are undertaken, both IS and user-managers need to carefully consider whether to commit the resources required to develop the proposed system. The project costs up to this point have typically been modest in relation to the total project costs, so the project can be abandoned at this stage without having spent much money or expended much effort. As described above, the approval of a large system request may not actually occur until after the completion of a formal feasibility analysis. For large projects, the executive sponsor of the application is typically responsible for the presentation of a business case for the system before the approving body.

Requirements Definition. If the document produced from the feasibility analysis receives the necessary organizational approvals, the requirements definition step is begun. Both the development of the "right system" and developing the "system right" are highly dependent on how well the organization conducts this step in the SDLC process. This requires heavy participation on the part of user management. If this step is not done well, the wrong system may be designed or even built, leading to both disruptive and costly changes later in the process.

Although in the past new systems often automated what had been done manually, most of today's systems are developed to do new things and/or to do old things in entirely new ways. While the executive sponsor plays a key role in envisioning how IT can be used to enable change in what her people do and how they do it, the sponsor is often not the manager who helps to define the requirements of the new system. Rather, the sponsoring manager must make sure that those who will use the system and those managers responsible for the use of the new system are involved in defining its detailed requirements.

Also referred to as systems analysis or logical design, the requirements definition focuses on processes, data flows, and data interrelationships rather than a specific physical implementation. The systems analyst(s) is responsible for making sure these requirements are elicited in sufficient detail to pass on to those who will build the system. It may appear easy to define what a system is to do at the level of detail with which systems are often described by system users. However, it is quite difficult to define what the new system is to do in the detail necessary to write the computer code for the system. Many business applications are incredibly complex, supporting different functions for many people or processes that cross multiple business units or geographic locations. Although each detail may be known by someone, no one person may know what a new system should do in the detail necessary to describe it. This step can therefore be very time-consuming and requires analysts who are skilled in asking the right questions to the right people and in conceptual system design techniques. In addition, there may be significant disagreements among the business managers about the nature of the application requirements. It is then the responsibility of the IS project manager and analysts to help the relevant user community reach a consensus. Sometimes outside consultants are used to facilitate this process.

Further, some new applications are intended to provide decision support for tasks that are ill-structured. In these situations, managers often find it difficult to define precisely what information they need and how the application will be used by them to support their decision-making. Their information needs may also be highly variable and dynamic over time. As noted in Chapter 9, many of today's large systems development projects may also arise in conjunction with reengineering an organization's business processes. Redesign of the organization, its work processes, and the development of a new computer system may be going on in parallel. The ideal is to first redesign the process, but even then the work processes are seldom defined at the level of detail required for a new business application.

Because defining the requirements for a system is such a difficult and a crucial task, analysts rely on a number of techniques and approaches. Examples of these were described in detail in Chapter 9. Later in this chapter we also describe an evolutionary prototyping approach that can be used to help define systems requirements—in particular for the user interface.

The deliverable for the requirements definition step is a comprehensive *system requirements document* that contains detailed descriptions of the system inputs and outputs, and the processes used to convert the input data into these outputs. It typically includes several hundred pages with formal diagrams and output layouts, such as shown in Chapter 9. This document also includes a revised cost/benefit analysis of the defined system and a revised plan for the remainder of the development project.

The system requirements document is the major deliverable of the Definition phase of the SDLC. Although IS analysts are typically responsible for drafting and revising the requirements specifications document, business managers are responsible for making sure that the written requirements are correct and complete. Thus, all relevant participants need to carefully read and critique this document for inaccuracies and omissions. Case studies have shown that when key user representatives do not give enough attention to this step, systems deficiencies are likely to be the result.

The deliverable from this step is typically subject to approval by business managers for whom the system is being built as well as by appropriate IS managers. Once formal approvals have been received, the system requirements are considered to be fixed. Any changes to the requirements typically must go through a formal approval process, requiring similar sign-offs and new systems project estimates. All key participants therefore usually spend considerable time reviewing these documents for accuracy and completeness.

Construction Phase

System Design. In this step, IS specialists design the physical system, based on the conceptual requirements document from the Definition phase. System design involves deciding what hardware and systems software will be used to operate the system, designing the structure and content of the databases that the system will use, and defining the processing modules (programs) that will comprise the system and their interrelationships. A good system design is a critical contribution, because the technical quality of the system must be designed into the system—it cannot be added later during the build process.

As shown in Figure 10.3, a quality system includes adequate controls to ensure that its data are accurate and that it provides accurate outputs. It provides an audit trail that allows one to trace transactions from their source and confirm that they were correctly handled. A quality system is highly reliable; when something goes wrong, the capability to recover and resume operation without lost data or excessive effort is planned for. It is also robust—insensitive to minor variations in its inputs and environment. It provides for interfaces with related systems so that common data can be passed back and forth. It is highly efficient, providing fast response, efficient input and output, efficient storage of data, and efficient use of computer resources. A quality system is also flexible and well documented for both users and IS specialists. It includes options for inputs and outputs compatible with its hardware and software environment, and can be easily changed or maintained. Finally, it is user friendly: easy to learn and easy to use, and it never makes the user feel stupid or abandoned.

Accurate	Reliable
Auditable	Robust
Changeable	Secure
Efficient	User friendly
Flexible	Well documented

Figure 10.3 Characteristics of High Quality Systems

To ensure that the new system design is accurate and complete, IS specialists often "walk through" the design first with their colleagues and then with knowledgeable user-managers and end-users, using graphical models such as described in Chapter 9. This type of technique can help the users understand what new work procedures may need to be developed in order to implement the new system.

The major deliverable of the system design step is a detailed design document that will be given to programmers. Models created by various development tools, such as diagrams of the physical structure of the system, are also an important part of the deliverable. The documentation of the system will also include detailed descriptions of all databases and detailed specifications for each program in the system. Also included are a plan for the remaining steps in the Construction phase. Again, this document is typically approved by both user and IS managers before the system is actually built.

System Building. There are two activities involved in building the system—producing the computer programs and developing the databases and files to be used by the system. These activities are performed by IS specialists. The major involvement of users is to answer questions of omission or help interpret requirements and design documents. The procurement of any new hardware and support software (including the database management system selection) is also part of this step, which entails consultation with IS planners and operations personnel.

System Testing. Testing is a major effort that may require as much time as writing the code for the system. This step involves testing first by IS specialists, followed by user testing. First, each module of code must be tested. Then the modules are assembled into subsystems and tested. Finally, the subsystems are combined and the entire system is integration tested. Problems may be detected at any level of testing, but correction of the problems becomes more difficult as more components are integrated together, so experienced project managers build plenty of time into the project schedule to allow for problems during integration testing. The IS specialists are responsible for producing a high quality system that also performs efficiently.

The users of the system are also responsible for a critical type of testing—user acceptance testing. The objective here is to make sure that the system performs reliably and does what it is supposed to do in a user environment. This means that users must devise test data and procedures that completely test the system, and then they must carry out this extensive testing process. Plans for this part of the application testing should begin after the requirements definition phase. Case studies have shown that end-user participation in the testing phase can contribute to end-user commitment to the new system, as well as provide the basis for initial end-user training.

Both user and IS management must sign off on the system, accepting it for production use, before it can be installed. **Documentation** of the system is also a major mechanism of communication among the various members of the project team during the development process: Information systems are simply too complex to understand by verbally describing them.

Once the users sign off on this part of the testing, any further changes typically need to be budgeted outside of the formal development project—that is, they become maintenance requests.

Implementation Phase   Strong IS/business relationships are essential for successful implementation efforts. In fact, potential political problems (such as described in Chapter 8) need to be anticipated and dealt with before the Implementation phase.

Installation.   Both IS specialists and users play critical roles in the installation step, which includes building the files and databases and converting relevant data from old systems to the new system. Depending on the extent to which the data already exists within the organization, some of the data conversion burden may also fall on users. In particular, data in older systems may be inaccurate and incomplete, and considerable user effort may be required to "clean it up." The clean-up process, including the entering of revised data, can be a major effort for user departments. Sometimes the clean-up effort can be accomplished in advance. In other situations, however, the data clean-up is done as part of the new system implementation. This means users have a lot of data verifications to check and conversion edits to resolve, sometimes without the benefit of additional staff, as they also learn the new system.

Another crucial installation activity is training the system's end-users, as well as training other users impacted by the new system. If this involves motivat-ing people to make major changes to their behavior patterns, planning for this motivation process needs to start well before the Implementation phase. User participation in the earlier phases can also help the users prepare for this crucial step. Similarly, user training needs to be planned and carefully scheduled so that people are prepared to use the system when it is installed, but not trained so far in advance of the installation that what they learned is forgotten. If user resistance to proposed changes is anticipated (see Chapter 8), this potential situation needs to be addressed during training or earlier.

Installing the hardware and software is the responsibility of the IS organization. This can be a challenge when the new system involves technology that is new to the IS organization, especially if the technology is on the "bleeding edge." The major problems in system installation, however, usually lie in adapting the organization to the new system—changing how people do their work.

Converting to the new system may be a difficult process for the users because the new system must be integrated into the activities of the organization. The users must not only learn how to use the new system, but also change the way that they perform their work. Even if the software is technically perfect, the system will likely be a failure if people do not want it to work or do not know how to use it. The **conversion** process therefore may require attitudinal changes. It is often a mistake to assume that people will change their behavior in the desired or expected way. On the other hand, not all user reactions can be planned for; some may require improvisatory responses by management as the unexpected is encountered (Orlikowski and Hofman, 1997).

Several strategies for transitioning users from an old system to a new one are commonly used (see Figure 10.4). This is a critical choice for the effective implementation of the system and needs to be chosen well in advance of the Implementation phase by a decision-making process that includes both IS and user-managers. Good management understanding of the options and tradeoffs for the implementation strategies discussed below can reap both short-term and long-term implementation benefits.

In the *parallel* strategy, the organization continues to operate the old system in parallel with the new system until the new one is working sufficiently well to

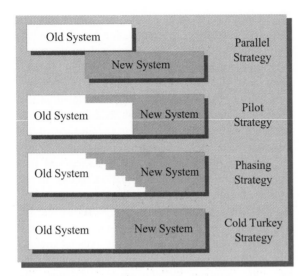

Figure 10.4 Implementation Strategies

discontinue the old. This is a conservative conversion strategy, because it allows the organization to continue using the old system if there are problems with the new. However, it can also be a difficult strategy to manage because workers typically must operate both the old system and the new while also comparing the results of the two systems to make sure that the new system is working properly. When discrepancies are found, the source of the problem must be identified and corrections initiated. Parallel conversion can therefore be very stressful. A parallel strategy also may not even be feasible due to changes in hardware and software associated with the new system.

The *pilot* strategy is an attractive option when it is possible to introduce the new system in only one part of the organization. The objective is to solve as many implementation problems as possible before implementing the system in the rest of the organization. For example, in a company with many branch offices, it might be feasible to convert to the new system in only one branch office and gain experience solving data conversion and procedural problems before installing the system companywide. If major problems are encountered, companywide implementation can be delayed until they are solved. Pilot approaches are especially useful when there are potentially high technological or organizational risks associated with the project.

For a large, complex system, a *phased* conversion strategy may be the best approach. For example, with a large order processing and inventory control system, the firm might first convert order entry and simply enter customer orders and print them out on the company forms. Then it might convert the warehouse inventory control system to the computer. Finally, it might link the order entry system to the inventory system and produce shipping documents and update the inventory records automatically. The downside to this approach is that it results in a lengthy implementation period. Extra development work to interface new and old system components is also typically required. On the other hand, a phasing strategy enables the firm to begin to achieve some benefits from the new system more rapidly than under other strategies.

In the *cold turkey* (or cutover) strategy the organization totally abandons the old system when it implements the new. In some industries, this can be accomplished over holiday weekends in order to allow for a third day for returning to the old system in the event of a major failure. The cold turkey strategy has greater inherent risks, but it is attractive when it is very difficult to operate both the old and new systems simultaneously. Some also argue that the total "pain is the same" for a system implementation, whether implemented cold turkey or not, and this strategy moves the organization to the new operating environment faster.

Combinations of the above four strategies are also possible. For example, when implementing system modules via a phased conversion strategy, one still has the option of a parallel or cold turkey approach for converting each phase of the system. Similarly, a pilot strategy could include a parallel strategy at the pilot site.

Operations. The second step of the Implementation phase is to operate the new application in "production mode." In the operations step, the IS responsibility for the application is turned over to computer operations and technical support personnel. The project team is typically disbanded, although one or more members may be assigned to a support team.

New applications are typically not moved into production status unless adequate **documentation** has been provided by the project manager. Implementing a large complex system without documentation is highly risky. Documentation comes in at least two flavors: system documentation for IS specialists who operate and maintain the computer system and user documentation for those who use the system.

Successful operation of an application system requires that people and computers work together. If the hardware or software fails or people falter, system operation may be unsatisfactory. In a large complex system there are thousands of things that can go wrong, and most companies operate many such systems simultaneously. It takes excellent management of computer operations to make sure that everything works well consistently and to contain and repair the damage when things do go wrong.

In Part IV we consider what it takes to successfully schedule and run large applications on a large computer system in what is typically referred to as a data center.

Maintenance. **Maintenance** refers to the process of making changes to a system after it has been put into production mode, i.e., after the operations stage of its life cycle. The most obvious reason for maintenance is to correct errors in the software that were not discovered and corrected prior to its initial implementation. Usually a number of bugs in a system do elude the testing process, and for a large complex system it may take many months, or even years, to discover them. Changes may also be required to adapt the system to changes in the environment— the organization, other systems, new hardware and systems software, and government regulations. Another major cause for maintenance is the desire to enhance the system. After some experience with a new system, managers typically have a number of ideas on how to improve it, ranging from minor changes to entirely new modules. The small changes are usually treated as maintenance, but large-scale additions may need approval as a new development request.

Because both business and technology environments change rapidly, periodic changes to large systems are typical. In fact, the total costs over a typical system's life cycle have been estimated to be about 80 percent on maintenance, and only 20 percent on the original development of the application. As a result, many IS organizations have to allocate a significant number of their IS specialists to maintaining systems, rather than developing new ones. In the early 1990s, maintenance resources were consuming as high as 75 percent of the total systems development resources in many large organizations (see Figure 10.5). The IS

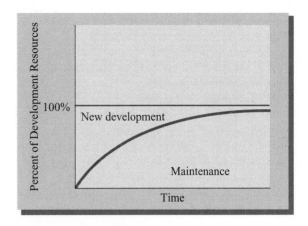

Figure 10.5 Percent of Development Resources Devoted to Maintenance

organization is responsible for making the required changes in the system throughout its life, as well as for eliminating any bugs that are identified prior to starting to use the new system in a production mode.

To make a change in a system, the maintenance programmer must first determine what program(s) must be changed and then what specific parts of each program need to be changed. The programmer must also understand the logic of the part of the code that is being changed. In other words, one must understand the system in some detail in order to change it.

Because systems can be very complex, the system documentation is critical in providing the necessary level of understanding. This brings up another difficulty—the documentation must be changed when the system is changed or the documentation will provide misleading information about the system rather than assistance in understanding it. Most programmers are primarily interested in programming and are not rewarded for updating the documentation, so in many IS organizations the documentation of old systems becomes outdated and includes inaccuracies.

Further, when changes are made in complex systems, a **ripple effect** may be encountered such that the change has an unanticipated impact on some other part of the system. For example, a change in a program can affect another program that uses the output from the first program. A change to a line of code can affect the results of another line of code in an entirely different part of that program. Another change must be made to correct those problems and that change may cause unanticipated problems elsewhere.

Another major problem with maintenance is that most IS professionals prefer to work on new systems using new technologies, rather than maintain old systems. Maintenance is therefore often perceived as low-status work, although it is critical to the business. Maintenance is often the first assignment of a newly hired programmer, and most organizations do not have mechanisms in place to ensure that really good maintenance people are rewarded well.

From the perspective of the user-manager, the major problems with maintenance are getting it done when it is needed and dealing with the problems caused by new system problems introduced as part of the maintenance process. A high proportion of operational problems are caused by errors introduced when making maintenance changes. Changes to production systems need to be carefully managed. Maintenance changes are typically made to a copy of the production system and then fully tested before they are implemented. An effective change management process for changing from an older to a newer version of the system is critical to avoid introducing large numbers of new problems when maintaining operational systems.

If adequate numbers of IS specialists are not available for systems maintenance projects, the manager often must suffer long delays before needed changes are made. Figure 10.6 graphically displays the widening gap that can occur between the organization's needs and the system's performance over time. Also, as a system gets older and is repeatedly patched, the probability of performance problems becomes even greater and reengineering or replacement solutions may be required. (These are discussed in more detail in Part IV.)

At the end of this chapter we address a special maintenance issue that is requiring large capital investments and creating even more of a shortage of IS professionals at the end of the 1990s: the Year 2000 maintenance problem.

The SDLC Roles

Most application systems are developed by a temporary project team. When the system project is completed, the team is disbanded. Most project teams include representatives from both the IS organization

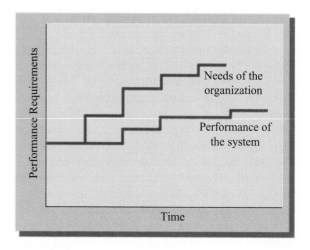

Figure 10.6
The Widening Gap Between the Organization's Needs and the System's Performance

and relevant user departments. If the system will be used by several organizational units or by several levels of people within a unit, the project team may include representatives from each of these organizations and levels. In addition to an IS project leader and at least one systems analyst, IS team members include programmers, data administration specialists, telecommunications specialists, and others.

The project team also may vary in membership during the systems life cycle: A few members may be assigned full-time to the project for its entirety, whereas others may join the project team only temporarily as their specific knowledge or skills are required. As described at the beginning of the chapter, it is also not unusual for IS specialists from outside firms who specialize in furnishing contract analysts or programmers to work on development project teams alongside the client firm's IS personnel.

In this section we describe in some detail four different roles that are critical to the success of an SDLC project. Two of these roles are user management roles: the user sponsor and the user champion. Two other roles require IS skills: the project manager and the systems analyst.

Historically, the **project manager** was an IS manager. Today, however, a user-manager with IT management skills may be the project manager, or a project may have two project managers: a user-manager responsible for all user activities and managing the change processes and an IS manager who is the technical director of the project, responsible for the activities of all IS specialists.

Whether or not this role is shared, the project manager is held responsible for the success of the project—for delivering a quality system, on time, and within budget. Managing a systems project typically involves coordinating the efforts of many persons from different organizational units, some of whom work for the project only on a part-time or temporary basis. Some guidelines for whether the manager of a specific project should come from the IS organization, user organization, or both, are provided in the "Choosing the Project Manager(s)" sidebar.

The project manager must plan the project, determine the SDLC tasks that must be carried out and the skills required for each task, and estimate how long each will take. The tasks then must be sequenced and people assigned to each in order to meet the project schedule. The project manager is also responsible for obtaining the necessary personnel to carry out the project plan; the quality and skills of the people are just as important as their numbers for producing a high quality system, on time, and within budget. Today's project manager also typically relies on project management tools to monitor and control progress on the project. The system documentation produced at each step of the project also provides a major tool for communication across team members and for assessing the quality of the development effort throughout the life cycle.

Because an IS project manager may have no authority over users assigned to the project team, as well as some of the IS specialists, the project leader needs to be skilled not only as a project manager, but also as a team leader, communicator, effective motivator, and negotiator. Frequently, the project manager must also build a cohesive team out of people from many backgrounds and several different organizational units. If there has been a history of conflict and distrust between the IS organization and the user community or between different user departments involved, the project manager may have to devote substantial effort to team-building activities and reaching consensus.

Most organizations require that systems for which an SDLC process is appropriate have an executive **sponsor** of the new system. The sponsor participates in the justification of the system, funds the approved project, and plays a role in seeing that the promised benefits of the system are achieved after it is installed. The sponsor also typically takes responsibility for ensuring that the appropriate user-manager representatives are assigned to the project team. The user representatives on the project team must be knowledgeable about their business unit's system needs and must have the authority needed to make decisions for the business unit they represent; achieving effective user participation is absolutely critical. Because the most capable representatives often cannot be easily spared by the business unit, the system sponsor needs to take an active role in arranging for the best user representatives possible to be freed up enough from their normal duties to participate on the project team.

Another critical user-manager role is the user **champion.** The SDLC process is long and expensive, subject to many hazards. In addition, user participation on a systems project team is also a temporary assignment, and often only a part-time one. Users who have other full-time responsibilities must often make time for the project by ignoring other daily responsibilities. Problems may arise that require exceptional efforts or additional resources to overcome. Without an effective champion who pushes the project forward,

---

CHOOSING THE PROJECT MANAGER(S)

If the project involves new and advanced technology,
   Then it should be managed by someone from the IS department.
If the project's impact would force critical changes in the business,
   Then it should be managed by someone from the business unit.
If the project is extremely large and complex,
   Then it should be managed by a specialist in project management.
If a project shares all of the above characteristics,
   Then senior management should consider multiple project leaders.

[Radding, 1992, based on Applegate]

helps remove obstacles, and never lags in enthusiasm, the development project is unlikely to be successfully completed. In some situations the executive who sponsors the system also serves as its champion. However, when the executive sponsor is too far removed from the activities impacted by the system or from the end-users of the system, the champion role may not receive enough attention if left to the sponsor.

Systems analysts, who are usually members of an IS organization, work with user-managers and end-users to determine the feasibility of the new system and to develop the system requirements. During the Construction phase, they work with other IS specialists in designing the system, and they supervise the writing of the computer code. A good systems analyst has problem-solving skills, a knowledge of IT capabilities, and an understanding of the business. The role of the systems analyst needs to be played well in order for multiple user perspectives to be taken into account and for conflicts between different managers to be resolved without any supervisory authority to do so. Sometimes the systems analyst also helps to serve as a check and balance for IS specialists eager to work with new, but unproven, technologies.

Managing an SDLC Project

SDLC project success is typically measured by three primary criteria: system quality, time-to-completion, and project cost. Below we first discuss five characteristics of SDLC projects that have been associated with successful customized development projects: manageable project size, justification methods that go beyond traditional financial analysis, accurate requirements definition, obtaining and keeping user buy-in, and change management. Then we briefly describe efforts directed at software quality improvement by the Software Engineering Institute.

Manageable Project Size   Experience has shown convincingly that huge projects requiring hundreds of work-years of development effort are almost never successful. On the other hand, projects that take a few technical people a year or less to complete are manageable and are quite likely to be successful. Thus, large systems must be broken down into relatively independent modules, each of which provides its own benefits and stands on its own merits. The overall system can then be built as a sequence of small, manageable projects, rather than as a single monster project.

Justification Methods   New application projects need to be justified as capital investments. A simplified example of a traditional justification approach is presented in Figure 10.7. Here the costs and benefits of systems are projected as cash flows in order to analyze the return on investment and payback period. In this example, the payback period to recoup a projected $550,000 development investment is a little over four years. The net present value at a discount rate of 15 percent is $71,000 over a six-year time period, and the return on investment (the interest rate that makes the present value equal zero over this time period) is 20.6 percent.

Traditional financial justification works best for systems that improve the efficiency of operations. Today, however, companies are investing in new applications intended to improve the effectiveness of individuals, groups, departments, and entire organizations, and these traditional economic measures do not work well (*I/S Analyzer,* 1987). In particular, when potentially large intangible benefits are involved, traditional financial analysis becomes much less suitable.

Managers and IS researchers have therefore developed alternatives to techniques such as Return on Investment (ROI) calculations for evaluating new application development efforts as capital investments. One approach to dealing with intangibles is to assign relative weights to impacts (positive weights) and risks (negative weights) of the proposed system (Parker and Benson, 1987 and Pastore, 1992). An example of a scoring system using this approach, in which traditional financial measures account for only 25 out of the 100 positive points available, is provided in the sidebar "A Scoring System for Project Goals and Risks." Several approaches for evaluating strategic IT investments, in particular, have been recommended by Clemons (1991). These range from ranking alternatives without ROI to taking into account competitor reactions.

Accurate Requirements Definition   The SDLC "waterfall" process is based on the premise that requirements for a new system can be defined in detail at the beginning of the process. The downside is that if the requirements are not well defined, then there may

	1999	2000	2001	2002	2003	2004
Investment						
System design	$ 200					
Programming	100					
Testing	100					
Installation	50					
Hardware	100					
Total	550					
Operating Cost						
Computer processing		$ 100	$ 100	$ 100	$ 100	$ 100
Data entry		100	105	110	116	122
Supplies		50	52	54	56	58
Total		250	257	264	272	280
Yearly Savings						
Clerical		250	263	276	289	304
Inventory		150	165	182	200	220
Total		400	428	457	489	523
Net Yearly Savings	(550)	150	171	193	217	243
Cumulative Savings	(550)	(400)	(230)	(37)	180	424
Net Present Value at 15%	71					
Internal Rate of Return	0.206					

Figure 10.7 Simplified Financial Analysis Example (in thousands of dollars)

A SCORING SYSTEM FOR PROJECT GOALS AND RISKS

At Cincinnati Bell Telephone, projects receive positive and negative points based on their level of impact on the following goals and risk categories.

BUSINESS OBJECTIVE SCORES

1. Economic cost impact: Up to 25 points
2. Strategic business direction: 20 points
   Projects receive a full 20 points if they impact any one objective in four strategic direction subcategories:
   a. Corporate goals (e.g., expanding beyond current market area)
   b. Network goals (e.g., enhancing the network infrastructure)
   c. Employee goals (e.g., reducing impact from employee retirements)
   d. Customer goals (e.g., allowing customer to more easily do business with company 24 hours a day)
3. Competitive advantage: 0 to 15 points
4. Management decision support: 0 to 5 points
5. Other intangible benefits: 0 to 5 points
6. Support for new technology: 0 to 15 points

RISK SCORES

1. Competitive response: 0 to 15 points
   Based on the competitive risks of not undertaking a project.
2. Project/organizational risk: 0 to –5 points
3. Definitional uncertainty: 0 to –10 points
   Based on how well the sponsor has defined his or her project's objectives, scope and requirements.
4. Technical uncertainty: 0 to –5 points
   Based on how much the project relies on IS's current versus new technical skills.
5. Infrastructure risk: 0 to –10 points
   Based on degree to which projects are aligned with IS architecture trends.

[Pastore, 1992]

be large cost overruns, and the system may be unsatisfactory. Early studies have shown that about half of the total number of requirements errors (or omissions) are typically detected in the Requirements Definition step. Further, as shown in Figure 10.8, experience at IBM, GTE, and TRW indicates that an error detected in the Implementation phase costs about 150 times as much to fix as an error detected in the Definition phase. Every effort must therefore be put into obtaining as accurate a requirements definition document as possible. This requires systems analysts skilled in eliciting requirements, as well as skilled in process and data representation techniques. It also requires access to business users knowledgable about both current business operations and the envisioned system.

User Buy-in   Both user-managers and end-users need to understand the potential benefits of the proposed system and be dedicated to contributing first to the development effort and then to sustained usage of the new system. As described above, user management needs to be committed to funding as well as to devoting significant amounts of time and effort to the development project. Sometimes managers are assigned full-time to the project team, but usually their work on the project is in addition to regular responsibilities. Although not every project team has end-users as formal team members, end-users frequently participate by providing information about current work processes or procedures, and evaluating screen designs from an end-user perspective. IS researchers have found that user involvement is associated with user acceptance and system usage (e.g., Hartwick and Barki, 1994). Case studies have also shown that end-user buy-in can be critical to the initial implementation of a new computer system.

Beath and Orlikowski (1994) have pointed out that systems development managers also need to recognize that assumptions about IS-user relationships are embedded in systems development methodologies. For example, the ETHICS method and the Soft Systems Methodology are specifically designed to facilitate more user involvement.

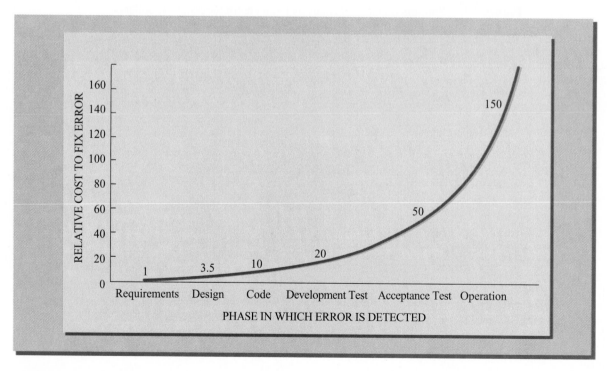

Figure 10.8 Costs of Error Correction by SDLC Step [Adapted from Boehm, 1976]

Change Management At the end of the Definition phase, most organizations institute a strict change process for any modifications to the original requirements document. Although this helps ensure a high-quality system and keeps the development effort on schedule, this process becomes dysfunctional if it results in the installation of a system that is obsolete. A process to identify and evaluate proposed system changes during the course of the SDLC project is therefore critical to its success.

Each proposed change must be evaluated in terms of how it impacts the system under development and how it will affect the project schedule and budget. Most changes will add to the project time and cost, so making changes either involves trade-offs or the project budget and completion date may need to be renegotiated. Managing change means having a mechanism in place that involves the right organizational members to make good decisions about whether to make the change or postpone it until the maintenance step of the life cycle. Of course, system implementation also requires managing organizational changes. Because managing change in general is an important capability of all IS organizations, we delay its discussion until Part IV.

Improving the Software Process A framework that describes the key elements of an effective software process, as well as an evolutionary path for organizations to move from an ad hoc, immature process to a mature, disciplined one has been developed by the Software Engineering Institute (SEI) (see Figure 10.9). The inability of firms to manage the systems development process has been identified as a major contributing factor to poor software quality. In a mature software organization, roles and responsibilities within the process are clear, participants understand the value of consistently following a disciplined process, and there is a broad-scale, active involvement in software quality improvement activities. The key principle is to improve quality by preventing problems, not just reacting to them (Bollinger and McGowan, 1991).

SDLC Advantages and Disadvantages

The SDLC process is a highly disciplined approach to the development of large, complex applications for one or more business units. A summary of the advantages and disadvantages of the SDLC approach is provided in Figure 10.10 and is discussed below.

In the hands of competent IS specialists and knowledgeable user-managers, the SDLC process sets up formal steps with clear IS and user roles, formal checkpoints, and tools for development and project management. The tools and rigorous discipline associated with an SDLC methodology help project leaders produce a well-engineered system on time and within budget.

Level 1: "Initial" processes
- Includes nearly all "unprepared" organizations
- No entry requirements, so skills may vary greatly

Level 2: "Repeatable" processes
- Focus on management and tight project control
- Focus on collecting various types of "trend" data

Level 3: "Defined" processes
- Focus on software design skills, design tracking
- Focus on various types of traceability

Level 4: "Managed" processes
- Focus on technology management and insertion
- Focus on estimates/actuals, error-cause analysis

Level 5: "Optimizing" processes
- Focus on rapid technology updating, replacement
- Focus on process optimization to reduce errors

Figure 10.9 The SEI Process-Maturity Framework [Bollinger and McGowan, 1991]. © 1991 IEEE.

- **Advantages**
  Provides steps for IS project management
  Produces high quality systems
    Well defined, designed, constructed
    Secure, with controls
- **Disadvantages**
  Dependent on accurate and complete Requirements Definition
  Full cost/benefit justification difficult (due to intangibles)
  Time-consuming (and costly) process
  Top-down commitment required

Figure 10.10 SDLC Advantages and Disadvantages

The major disadvantages are inherent in the methodology. First, the success of the project is dependent on the accurate and complete specification of detailed requirements at the beginning of the development process (Definition phase). There are several serious problems with this dependency. For example, many new systems are conceived in response to perceived problems, and, because the managers involved may have only an incomplete understanding of what an information system must do to alleviate these problems, it may be necessary to try several approaches before discovering an effective one. New types of decision support systems, for example, often are directed at providing support for ill-structured problems. Another problem is that the business environment is changing so rapidly that there will be significant differences in business needs between the time the requirements are specified and the time the system is installed.

Second, the SDLC process as described previously is a time-consuming process and therefore a costly process. In the 1980s, the typical systems project took more than a year; many took several years. Third, a strong commitment from top management is required. This is because the SDLC process is both lengthy and costly and requires a significant level of participation on the part of user-management. Fourth, the SDLC process requires that a full cost/benefit analysis be developed based on a conceptual Definition phase. When it is difficult to specify the system requirements or many of the benefits are intangible, the justification process can be difficult to accomplish using traditional approaches such as ROI calculations. When new technologies are involved, it is often difficult to estimate the project costs and to adequately assess the technical and operational feasibility.

In the next section we will look at an alternative approach to systems development that addresses some of these disadvantages.

PROTOTYPING METHODOLOGY

Traditional life cycle development using an SDLC process is based on the fundamental premise that system design and programming are so expensive and time-consuming that efforts in these areas must be minimized. Thus, the system requirements must be completely specified in detail before the Construction phase is begun. Once the requirements have been agreed upon, changing them leads to significant project delays and costs.

In the second half of the 1980s, the growing availability of fourth-generation nonprocedural languages and relational database management systems offered an alternative approach. These tools make it possible to more quickly build a system and then change or redo the system after users have tried it out and discovered its inadequacies. Thus, rather than first defining the system and then building it, the system can evolve based upon the user's experience and understanding gained from the previous versions. This approach is very powerful because, while most people find it very difficult to specify in great detail exactly what they need from a new system, it is quite easy for them to point out what they like or do not like about a system they can try out and use.

This general approach is most commonly known as **evolutionary development,** or **prototyping.** However, the prototyping concept can be applied to a process in which only a "toy" system is developed for the user to try out, as well as to a real system that employs actual data. In addition, sometimes only a part of a real system is prototyped. For example, prototype input and output screens are often developed for users to work with as part of the requirements definition or detailed design steps.

Below we first discuss prototyping as an evolutionary methodology that is an alternative to the traditional SDLC methodology: its steps, the roles, project management considerations, and its overall advantages and disadvantages. This approach is particularly attractive when the requirements are hard to define, when a critical system is needed quickly, or when the system will be used infrequently (or even only once)—so that operating efficiency is not a major consideration. These are characteristics that often apply to new types of managerial support systems. Prototyping also provides a practical way for organizations to experiment with systems where the probability of success is unclear but the rewards of a successful system appear to be quite high.

At the end of this section, we will also describe two ways in which prototyping can be used *within* an SDLC process to increase the likelihood that the system requirements are well defined.

The Prototyping Steps

Figure 10.11 presents the steps for an evolutionary methodology for developing a new, working system. The process begins with the identification of the *basic* requirements of the initial version of the system (step 1). The analyst/builder(s) and user(s) meet together and agree on the inputs, the data processing, and the system outputs. These are not complete detailed requirements; rather, this is a starting point for the system. If several builders and users are involved, a joint application design (JAD) session may be used to determine requirements (see JAD description under "Newer Approaches" section below).

In step 2 the system builders produce an initial prototype system according to the basic requirements agreed on in step 1. The system builders select the software tools, locate the necessary data and make these data accessible to the system, and construct the system using higher level languages. This step should take from a few days to a few weeks, depending on the size and complexity of the system.

When the initial prototype is completed, it is given to the user with instructions similar to the following: "Here is the initial prototype. I know that it is not what you really need, but it's a beginning point. Try it and write down everything about it that you do not like or that needs to be added to the system. When you get a good list, we will make the changes you suggest."

Step 3 is the user's responsibility. He or she works with the system, notes the things that need to be improved, and then meets with the analyst/builder to discuss the changes. In step 4 the builder modifies the system to incorporate the desired changes. In order to keep everyone actively involved, speed is important. Sometimes the builder can sit down with the user and make the changes immediately; for larger systems, the changes may take several weeks. Steps 3 and 4 are repeated until the user is satisfied with the current version of the system. These are *iterative steps* within the prototyping process. When the user is satisfied that the prototype has been sufficiently developed, step 5 begins.

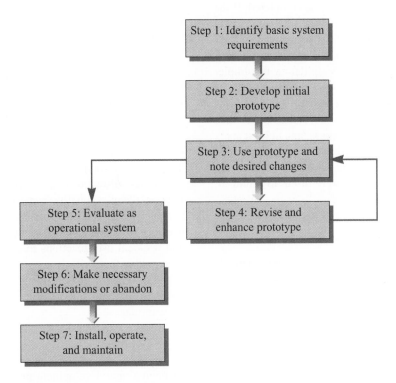

Figure 10.11 The Prototyping Life Cycle

Step 5 involves evaluating the final prototype as an operational system. It should be noted, however, that not all prototypes become operational systems. That is, it may be decided that the prototype system should simply be thrown away. For example, it may be decided that no additional costs should be devoted to the application because a system could not be developed that solved the original problem. That is, the prototyping process helped the organization decide that the system benefits do not outweigh the additional development and/or operational costs or that the expense of developing an operationally efficient system is too high. At this point it could also be decided that the system will be implemented, but that the system needs to be built using different tools in order to achieve performance efficiencies.

If the prototype is to become an operational system, in step 6 the builder completes the Construction phase by making any changes necessary to improve operational efficiency and to interface the new application with the operational systems that provide it with data. This is also the step in which all necessary controls, backup and recovery procedures, and the necessary documentation need to be completed. If the prototype is only slightly modified, this step differs from the end of the Construction phase of an SDLC methodology in that most (or all) of the system has already been tested. Step 7 is similar to the Implementation phase of the SDLC: The new system is installed and moved into operational status. This is likely to be a much easier Implementation phase than under the traditional SDLC process, and at least some of the intended users are already experienced users. Step 7 also includes maintenance. Because of the advanced tools that likely were used to build it, changes may be easier to make.

The Prototyping Roles

The same four roles described for the SDLC methodology are relevant for an evolutionary methodology, and there are new roles. An executive **sponsor** is still responsible for justifying the system and acquiring the necessary resources to develop the system. However, because the initial development costs for a prototype are usually substantially less than for a fully constructed system, justification may be easier. When small systems are involved, prototyping may reduce these costs to the point where they come within the

normal discretionary spending authority of lower level managers, so a high-level executive sponsor may not even be required.

The user **champion** role differs in that the prototype can be used to "sell" the system to other users. Different versions of the prototype can be used by one or more users. Because there is continuous user involvement with the various versions of the system, the champion's role as a change agent begins much earlier in the development process; it is quite different in the SDLC process, where users must be prepared for changes involving a new system that they have not yet seen.

Managing an evolutionary development process is clearly a joint IS and user management responsibility. Whether the **project leader** role is carried out by IS alone, by user-managers, or by both IS and user-managers, both IS and user management need to jointly determine when to continue to request revisions to a prototype and when to end the iterative try-out-and-revise steps. The user-manager needs to determine whether or not a satisfactory solution has been developed, and the IS manager needs to determine whether or not all relevant technology capabilities have been explored.

Because only basic requirements are being defined, the **systems analyst** and **prototype builder** (which may be one and the same) need to have some skills different from those required for the SDLC process. Techniques to elicit abstract requirements and an emphasis on detailed documentation under the SDLC process are replaced by a heavy reliance on skills to build systems quickly using advanced tools. The initial prototypes are assessed more in terms of their look-and-feel from a user perspective and less in terms of technical quality from a systems performance perspective. Interactions between IS specialists and users center around creative development solutions and personal user reactions to concrete system interfaces and outputs.

If different from the champion, the **user** who tries out the prototype and suggests changes also plays a critical role.

Managing a Prototyping Project

Managing new development projects with a methodology based on an iterative or evolutionary process requires a different mindset than managing projects using an SDLC methodology based on a highly structured development approach. IS project managers and system builders need to approach the project differently: The objective is to respond quickly to user requests with a "good enough" prototype multiple times, rather than produce a tightly engineered actual system at the outset of the project. This may require some cultural changes within the IS organization. IS professionals who have built their careers on skills and attitudes required by an SDLC approach may need to acquire new skills for prototyping approaches.

IS managers also find managing prototyping projects more problematic because it is difficult to plan how long it will take, how many iterations will be required, or exactly when the system builders will be working on the system. Project managers need to have sufficient IS resources available for system building in order to quickly respond to user requests for system changes within an agreed-upon timetable. Users who will be trying out each prototype version must be committed to the process and must be willing and able to devote the time and effort required to test each prototype version in a timely fashion. IS managers may rightfully feel that they have less control over the scope of the project. One of the potential hazards of prototyping is that the iterative steps will go on and on and that the project costs will keep accumulating. Good working relationships between IS personnel and users responsible for the project are required to move to the prototype evaluation step (step 5) at the optimal time. Joint IS-user accountability would appear to be a key to success for these types of projects.

Depending on the software tools used to build the prototype, the operational efficiency of a prototype that is evaluated in step 5 may be significantly inferior to systems developed using the traditional SDLC methodology. Technical standards established by the organization also may not be rigorously followed, and the documentation may be inadequate. A substantial investment in CASE tools (see below), database management tools, and IS specialist training may be required before an IS organization can successfully implement the end-prototype as the final system.

Prototyping Advantages and Disadvantages

The advantages of the evolutionary development methodology address the disadvantages inherent in the SDLC methodology. First, only *basic* system requirements are needed at the front end of the project. This means that systems can be built using an evolutionary approach that would be impossible to develop via an SDLC methodology. Further, prototyping can be used to build systems that radically change how work is done, such as when work processes are being redesigned or a totally new type of managerial support tool has been envisioned but never seen. It is virtually impossible to define requirements for these kinds of systems at the beginning of a systems development process. Prototyping also allows firms to explore the use of newer technologies, because the expectations under an evolutionary methodology are that the builders will get it right over multiple iterations, rather than the first time.

Second, an initial working system is available for user testing much more quickly. In some cases a working prototype may actually be used by user-managers to respond in some way to a current problem or at least to quickly learn that a given systems approach will not be the best solution. Although the complete process may take several months, users may have a working prototype in a few weeks or months that allows them to respond to a problem that exists now and is growing in importance; often a user-manager cannot wait many months, let alone years, for a particular system to be built.

Third, because of the more interactive nature of the process, with hands-on use of working system models, strong top-down commitment based on a well-substantiated justification process may be less necessary at the outset of the project. Instead, the costs and benefits of the system can be derived after experience with an initial prototype.

Fourth, user acceptance of an application developed with an evolutionary process is likely to be higher than with an SDLC process. The final version of the system is more likely to meet the needs of the business, and the evolutionary process results in more active involvement and joint control of the process on the part of the user.

The disadvantages of an evolutionary methodology are related to the evolutionary build process. The end-prototype typically lacks some of the security and control features found in a system developed with an SDLC process. It also does not undergo the same type of rigorous testing. Documentation is typically also less complete because of the iterative nature of the process. In the past the operational inefficiencies of fourth-generation tools also contributed to the inadequacies of end-prototypes. However, with recent advancements in hardware and software tools for developers and end-users, these issues have become much less important than implementing a system that meets user needs. As described previously, these potential deficiencies are assessed in step 5 and corrected in step 6 of the evolutionary methodology in Figure 10.11.

The only other potential disadvantage is related to managing user expectations. Frequently, a prototype system appears to be so useful that users are reluctant to wait for a well-functioning, well-documented operational system. It is easy to see how users can become impatient with lengthy IS development processes that require lots of preliminary conceptual work once they have been exposed to evolutionary methodologies. As described in the next section, this is why prototyping *within* an SDLC process has become a common practice.

Prototyping within an SDLC Process

As fourth-generation tools have become commonplace, the incorporation of a few steps of an evolutionary process into an SDLC methodology has also become common. Here we describe two ways that prototyping is commonly incorporated into an SDLC process.

First, a prototype is used to help users define the system requirements for user interfaces in the Definition phase of an SDLC process. As shown in Figure 10.12, the SDLC process still begins with a feasibility analysis. But for the requirements definition step (step 2), IS specialists use screen painting tools to produce initial versions of screens and reports that users can experiment with. This is an example of a toy system prototype in which the screen designs are not connected to a live database. After the requirements have been determined with the help of the prototype, the remainder of the steps in the SDLC process remain the same. However, the system builders can also make use of the screens during the design and build steps and may actually use computer code generated by the prototyping tools in the final system.

The second way prototyping is used is more complex and includes a pilot implementation of a working prototype. This type of pilot differs from the pilot con-

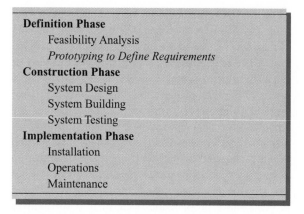

Figure 10.12　SDLC with Prototyping to Define Requirements

version strategies discussed for the Implementation phase of the SDLC process. Rather, the intent here is to use a scaled-down prototype in only a minimal number of locations within the organization in order to assess its feasibility in an operational setting. As shown in Figure 10.13, the Definition phase of the SDLC process is replaced by three steps of an evolutionary approach. After basic requirements are determined (step 1), a working prototype is developed (step 2). The initial prototype may not use "live" data, but is sufficiently developed to demonstrate a technical solution using hardware and software components that has not been used before in a real-world setting by the

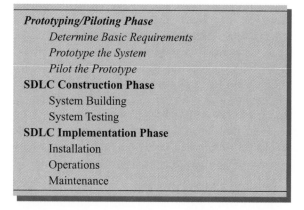

Figure 10.13　Combination Prototyping and SDLC Life Cycle

developers and users. In step 3 the prototype is extended to become a working prototype that can be piloted with a subset of the targeted users.

This combination prototyping/piloting approach is especially useful for large, risky projects that involve technological and/or organizational risks. For example, one major objective may be to demonstrate the basic capabilities or provide a proof-of-concept test of a technical solution. A second major objective may be to get buy-in to the proposed system by executive sponsors. By working with a prototype with live data, user-managers can evaluate the potential benefits and risks of the new application in an operational setting. The expectation is that this prototype, developed at minimal cost, will be changed significantly if an operational system is built. For example, changes in functionality based on using the pilot, as well as changes in the technology, are anticipated before the final system will be implemented at all locations. The prototype is used to help "sell" the system to key users and to those who have budgeting authority.

If the pilot is successful, a formal SDLC process begins with step 4. What was learned in the step 3 pilot using the system prototype becomes the system design specifications for building the actual system. The learning from the pilot step also helps users prepare for the organizational changes needed to implement the full system. The remaining steps match the typical SDLC process.

Newer Approaches

The demands for speedier development of new application systems have steadily increased over the past decade. In this section we briefly discuss four examples of approaches that have been shown to result in faster development of high-quality customized applications.

Joint application design (JAD) is a technique in which a team of users and IS specialists engage in an intense and structured process to develop system requirements or review a major system design deliverable. A JAD session could last several hours or could be held over several consecutive days. It is often held at a location removed from the participants' usual workplace so they can concentrate on this task without interruption. The technique is used within an SDLC methodology as well as within an evolutionary methodology. It is also one of several techniques and tools associated with rapid application development and may involve the use of a computer-assisted software engineering tool.

The primary objective of the JAD technique is to minimize the total time required for information gathering from multiple participants. It provides a forum for user representatives to work through areas of disagreement; this is especially important when cross-functional systems are being developed. The JAD session is led by a facilitator who is not only skilled in systems analysis and design techniques, but is also skilled in managing group interactions. A person outside the organization is sometimes used in this facilitator role in order to have a neutral third party who can resolve conflicts and keep the group focused on the JAD session outcomes. An additional benefit associated with the use of this technique, then, is the achievement of a shared understanding among user-managers and IS specialists.

Computer-assisted software engineering (CASE) refers to a collection of software tools used to automate some or all phases of an SDLC process. Most CASE tools are designed to support one or more structured development methodologies (see Chapter 9) and have a pricetag anywhere from $5,000 to $15,000 per workstation (*I/S Analyzer,* 1993).

Not all CASE tools have the same functionality. Some are only front-end analysis tools (upper-CASE) that support the Definition and system design steps of the SDLC. For example, an early entry in the front-end CASE marketplace was Excelerator by Intersolv. Excelerator provided a set of integrated tools to support the development of system specifications, production of the system documentation, and management of the project. In addition to screen and report generators, it has an intelligent drawing tool to support the development of diagrams for process and data modeling. The CASE tool maintains a comprehensive database (repository) of all diagrams, data element specifications, processing logic, and other documentation associated with the project and makes it electronically accessible to all members of the project team with the appropriate security levels. For example, a data dictionary entry is automatically generated for each data flow and each data store in a data flow diagram (process model). CASE systems also include various design analyzers that check for violations of system decomposition rules and other consistency checks. CASE systems often include interfaces to fourth-generation languages to make it easier to build a prototype system.

Lower-CASE tools are back-end code generators that automate some of the building steps of the SDLC by generating computer code from high-level specifications. These tools can also be used to automate maintenance: Changes in computer code can be generated from changes in system designs. There are also full-cycle CASE systems called Integrated-CASE or I-CASE tools that combine front-end and back-end functions to produce a working system. In the sidebar "Life-Cycle Software Development Tools," we describe a tool based on the methodology of IS guru James Martin, marketed by Sterling Software.

CASE tools have been reported to have a major impact on system development productivity—including faster development and improved system quality during the initial development process. In the early 1990s, for example, there were reports of development times cut to one-third of the time required for traditional methods (*I/S Analyzer,* 1992). However, the initial introduction of CASE tools into an organization requires a major commitment by management to a structured development methodology that is embedded within the CASE tool. The start-up costs are also high due to the need for substantial IS specialist training costs.

Early users have reported that it may take several years before the benefits of CASE implementation outweigh its costs. If an organization is changing its methodology as it introduces a CASE tool, the cultural changes for an IS professional can be significant. Orlikowski (1989) has found that IS specialists interested in a technical career may be more resistant to CASE tool implementation than those on a managerial career path. This appears to be due to the lack of flexibility of many of the tools. A lack of compatibility across CASE tools has also been an implementation barrier. Although the adoption of CASE tools within U.S. companies has been slower than originally expected, a high penetration has been forecast for the end of the 1990s.

Rapid application development (RAD) is a methodology based upon the use of JAD, prototyping, and Integrated-CASE (I-CASE) tools with the objec-

---

LIFE-CYCLE SOFTWARE DEVELOPMENT TOOLS

COOL:Gen supports model-based application development over the full life cycle of a software application. Known as Composer, this tool was originally developed by Texas Instruments as part of a fully integrated suite of tools for automating the entire IS development life cycle. The entire set of tools, named the Information Engineering Facility, is based on the Information Engineering methodology pioneered by James Martin. The full IEF product architecture covers all phases of systems development: information strategy planning through systems analysis, design, code generation, maintenance, and documentation.

COOL:Gen supports multi-user development of model-driven applications. Graphical logical models, independent of the underlying technology, can be used to generate code for both clients and servers for major mainframe and microcomputer platforms. The modeling and checking capabilities of the development tool aid in the analysis of an entire information architecture and its decomposition into manageable project components. Applications developed with a COOL:Gen environment typically serve as the backbone for major business processes, whether they be batch, high-volume transaction processing, or interactive managerial support applications at the desktop.

[Adapted from www.sterling.com and www.ti.com]

---

tive of rapidly producing a high quality system. The RAD methodology includes the three life cycle phases, combining the SDLC sequence with an iterative, continuous improvement approach. I-CASE tools are used to support rapid prototyping, and JAD sessions are used for design reviews. Unlike the evolutionary methodology discussed in this chapter, the end-prototype becomes the actual system.

RAD is a methodology that works well in a business environment characterized by rapid change. The smaller design teams and shorter development times associated with RAD also can lead to lower development costs. Some organizations adopting RAD approaches require that all projects fit within a short timebox—such as six months (Clark et al., 1997). However, an accelerated approach also has its downsides. For example, programming and formatting standards may be sacrificed, and the system components may need further development to be reusable.

Object-Oriented (O-O) methods also hold great promise for producing better systems at less cost, and tools to support this approach are becoming more readily available. However, the learning curve associated with the adoption of object-oriented technology is even greater than the learning curve associated with CASE tools. Nevertheless, by the second half of the 1990s, success stories of large-scale systems using O-O approaches began to appear (LaBoda and Ross, 1997). As discussed in Chapter 9, the productivity gains associated with O-O technologies are primarily due to the reusability of the system components. However, O-O analysis requires that analysts learn new concepts, terminology, and representation methods, and the development of reusable objects requires considerable expertise. By the end of the decade, companies are expected to be purchasing libraries of objects from vendors and using these objects to quickly develop applications that are more customized than is feasible with the typical purchased package.

SPECIAL ISSUE: YEAR 2000 MAINTENANCE

The turn of the century has created significant challenges for systems development managers and an unanticipated demand for IS programmers skilled in older languages such as COBOL. This is because more than two decades ago, when computer systems had much less memory and storage space than they have today, information systems were designed to use a two-character format for calendar year fields. More specifically, dates were stored in a six-digit date field, such as MMDDYY, in order to conserve on processing and storage.

Why did this convention become a major maintenance problem as we approached the Year 2000? Dates are used in calculations for a wide variety of business processes. Because only a two-digit year field is stored, calculations involving the year 2000 (and beyond) involve only the stored two digits. For example, in 1999 the difference from 1995 will be calculated as 4 (99 minus 95), whereas in 2000 the difference will be calculated as –95 (00 minus 95). This means that, for example, when a credit card

expiration date, retirement benefit, or product delivery date is calculated for the year 2000, an error will occur. Unfortunately, easy technological solutions (referred to in the field as "silver bullets") are not available. Instead, date-based calculations and logic statements within old applications must be identified, rewritten, and tested, and the revised system must be implemented before the date error becomes a problem for the business process supported by that application.

Why wasn't this obvious problem corrected sooner? IS specialists have of course known there was a potential problem for some time. However, many of the systems that need to be revised were developed well over a decade ago. Until organizations got closer to the calendar dates when Year 2000 calculations would become a problem, it was difficult to get organizational funding for the clean-up effort. Significant maintenance dollars are required just for the organization to maintain the status quo; the ROI for Year 2K projects is measured in terms of business survival, not growth in business revenues (Williamson, 1996). Further, some of these older applications are being replaced by new applications that are "Year 2K compliant." Major software vendors such as SAP began to include the avoidance of the year 2K problem in their software advertisements by the mid-1990s.

> *"It's not even as satisfying as fixing a roof. We get absolutely nothing out of it. We get to stay in business, that's all."*
> —John Lutz, president of Mason Shoe,
> *New York Times,* April 7, 1997

Public awareness of the Year 2K maintenance problem increased dramatically in the mid-1990s. For example, the average business employee of 1998 knew that the date problem affects both computer hardware and software, including ATM machines, air traffic systems, and software programs that calculate credit card payments (see sidebar "Year 2000 Predictions"). Estimates for 1997 global costs for Year 2K fixes range from $300 billion to twice that amount, and actual costs are expected to be even higher due to litigation costs for Year 2K glitches. One can safely predict that not all tested changes will be fault-free; that's why some enterprising firms are selling Year 2K insurance.

By early 1998, some IS-related impacts of the Year 2K problem were already observable. Software

YEAR 2000 PREDICTIONS

Ideally, the millennium bug will have had a minimal effect on the average person by the time Jan. 1, 2000 arrives. But if the debuggers were not diligent enough, the bug could intrude into everyday life in ways like these.

- **Your telephone service** is terminated because of errors in date calculations.
- **Your driver's license** expires because the motor vehicle department systems cannot recognize dates after Dec. 31, 1999.
- **Your broker** miscalculates your capital gains, bond payments and other transactions because of faulty dates.
- **Your department store** rejects your credit card because your payment is 100 years overdue.
- **Your bank's automated teller** swallows your card, thinking it has expired.
- **Your Social Security payments** are cut off because the agency's computers miscalculate your age.
- **Your tax payments** are erroneously billed as overdue by the I.R.S.
- **Your mortgage payment** arrives late because the bank's computers fail to note the century change.
- **Your home VCR** fails to record a show because it mistakes the year.
- **Your car's dashboard** "Service Engine Now" light falsely indicates that the car is due for a tune-up.
- **Your pharmacy** refuses to refill your prescription because the computer says it has expired.

While elsewhere. . . .

- **Bank vaults** refuse to open.
- **Building security systems** fail, refusing to read coded cards or keys.
- **Production schedules** at all kinds of manufacturing facilities are corrupted by improper date-coding.
- **Automatic elevator programs** crash, freezing high-rise elevators.
- **Airline flight schedules** are thrown into disarray because of flaws in the air traffic control system computers.

[Broder and Zuckerman, 1997]

10%	Inventorying the systems that need correction
20–25%	Coding the changes
10%	Moving fixed systems into production
60%	Testing

Figure 10.14 Typical Workload for Large Year 2K Projects

fits. CIO's were being warned to also assess Year 2K compliance of their suppliers, customers, and other business partners (Kirsner, 1998). Retired COBOL programmers had reportedly come out of retirement as a result of the lure of short-term jobs with big paychecks. Major consulting firms also reported turning down requests for Year 2K maintenance projects by client firms because of their lack of skilled IS resources to assign to these types of projects. Class-action suits against technology vendors have already been filed in anticipation of software problems (Gunn, 1998).

In addition to contributing to a global shortage of IS professionals, what are some of the other anticipated IS management impacts of the Year 2000 crisis? Because 60 percent of the typical effort of a Year 2K project is directed at testing the changes in production systems (see Figure 10.14), organizations have reported greatly improving their testing processes. In general, there has also been a greater endorsement of a standard methodology and a repeatable process (Williamson, 1996). A likely outcome, then, is both improved processes and better project management skills within IS organizations.

SUMMARY

System development by the IS department using the life cycle methodology is the traditional way to obtain new computer systems and to maintain them. Development by the IS organization using some or all of the SDLC methodology steps is still the most viable approach when the system is large, complex, and serves multiple organizational units and when suitable packaged software is not available. Development by

houses were advertising Year 2K "ready" applications that could not only help a firm avoid fixing an old legacy system, but also could help achieve new benethe IS organization using some or all of the evolutionary methodology steps is a more effective approach when multiple versions of a prototype system can be used to help users and IS specialists move cost effectively from a set of basic requirements to a fully functional system design. Today, a prototyping approach is often incorporated into an SDLC process to exploit the system definition strengths of the evolutionary approach and the system construction and implementation strengths of the SDLC approach. A combination prototyping/piloting approach is especially useful when the systems project is characterized by major technological and/or organizational risks. New methodologies that exploit the advantages of both the SDLC and prototyping are also being pursued by today's organizations.

Whether traditional SDLC, prototyping, or some combination of the two is used, it is the responsibility of both user-managers and IS specialists to ensure that the system that is installed meets the needs of the business at the time of installation. IS specialists typically hold primary responsibility for all system building and the conduct of the project on a day-to-day basis, while sharing the overall responsibility for managing the project with user management. User-managers are relied on to sponsor the system and champion its development and implementation, and to participate actively in the development process. If the user sponsor and user champion roles are not played well, users will suffer on a day-to-day basis as they attempt to achieve the envisioned benefits with a suboptimal system.

The responsibilities of user sponsors, user champions, and user representatives for customized application development projects include the following:

- conceptualizing how a new system can benefit the business
- justifying the new system to the organization, including establishing a business value for potential intangible benefits
- championing the new system throughout the development process and assigning user-managers and end-users to participate
- participating in the definition of a system's requirements and either reviewing all formal written requirements specifications to ensure they are complete and accurate or testing system prototypes to

ensure they are functional system solutions that match the business needs
- adopting joint project leadership roles as necessary
- conducting rigorous user acceptance testing
- redesigning the organization to take advantage of the new system and managing the organizational changes before, during, and after implementation
- overseeing effective use of the new system over its life, including the timely initiation of maintenance requests

Review Questions

1. Describe the steps in the systems development life cycle (SDLC) as presented in this chapter.
2. Describe the user-manager roles in each step of the SDLC.
3. Describe the role of the IS specialists in each step of the SDLC.
4. Describe how the SDLC methodology is also a project management tool.
5. What are the characteristics of a high-quality application system?
6. Describe the role of documentation in the SDLC methodology.
7. Describe the four different strategies for conversion to a new application system.
8. Why is an accurate requirements definition a critical success factor when using the SDLC approach?
9. Describe the steps of an evolutionary methodology when prototyping is used as part of the development process. How does this differ from the SDLC process described in Question 1?
10. Describe the disadvantages of an SDLC process. Which disadvantages are addressed by a prototyping approach?
11. Describe two ways that a prototyping approach is used within the traditional SDLC methodology.
12. Define JAD and CASE, and comment on how they can be used in projects developed with either the traditional SDLC process or the evolutionary method.
13. Describe what was meant by references to a Year 2K problem prior to the end of 1999.

DISCUSSION QUESTIONS

1. Discuss the strengths and weaknesses of the SDLC methodology for developing application systems.

2. Your IS department believes that it is responsible for making sure the requirements of the system are properly defined, but in this chapter the user-manager's responsibility for defining requirements is emphasized. How can you reconcile these two points of view?

3. There have been many failures in the development of application systems using the traditional SDLC. Discuss what might be some of the primary reasons for this high failure rate.

4. Discuss some of the approaches that can be used to justify an application system when most of its benefits are intangible.

5. Describe the role of the systems analyst in the development of an application system using the SDLC. Then compare it to the role of the systems analyst for a prototyping approach.

6. Some IS specialists contend that end-prototypes are poor technical solutions. Comment on why this may be true.

7. Discuss why an application might be built using prototyping as part of the SDLC methodology, rather than by an evolutionary methodology alone.

8. Discuss the roles of the executive sponsor and user champion in the in-house development of a customized application. Under what situations might these roles be played by the same or different persons?

9. Discuss the role of the project manager in the in-house development of a customized application. Under what situations might IS managers and user-managers serve as co-leaders of a project?

10. In many companies there is a history of a lack of trust between the IS department and the user community. Pretend that you are a user champion for a new system in an organization with such a history. What can you do to help overcome this lack of trust and help IS specialists work well with users so that this system development project is a success?

11. It has been said that a system without good documentation is worthless. Provide support for this statement. Then comment on how today's advanced tools may avoid this problem.

12. Discuss how some modern tools (such as CASE), techniques (such as JAD), and methods (such as RAD) help today's IS organizations overcome the disadvantages of the traditional SDLC methodology.

13. According to some observers, Year 2K projects resulted in better project management and systems testing skills within the IS professional community. Explain why this may be true.

REFERENCES

1987. "The new economics of computing." *I/S Analyzer* 25 (September): 10.

1992. "From application development to software engineering." *I/S Analyzer* 30 (July): 7.

Beath, Cynthia M., and Wanda J. Orlikowski. 1994. "The contradictory structure of systems development methodologies: Deconstructing the IS-user relationship in information engineering." *Information Systems Research* 5 (December): 350–377

Boehm, Barry. 1976. "Software engineering." *IEEE Transactions on Computers* C-25 (December): 1226–1241.

Boehm, Barry. 1981. *Software Engineering Economics.* Englewood Cliffs, N.J.: Prentice-Hall.

Bollinger, Terry B. and Clement McGowan. 1991. "A critical look at software capability evaluations." *IEEE Software* (July 1): 25–46.

Boynton, Andrew C., Robert W. Zmud, and Gerry C. Jacobs. 1994. "The influence of IT management practice on IT use in large organizations." *MIS Quarterly* 18 (September): 299–318.

Broder, John M., and Laurence Zuckerman. 1997. "Computers are the future but remain unready for it." *New York Times* (April 7): 1, 11.

Clark, Charles E., Nancy C. Cavanaugh, Carol V. Brown, and V. Sambamurthy. 1997. "Building change-readiness capabilities in the IS organization: Insights from the Bell Atlantic experience." *MIS Quarterly* 21 (December): 425–455.

Clemons, Eric. 1991. "Evaluation of strategic investments in information technology." *Communications of the ACM* 34 (1): 23–36.

Colter, Mel A. 1984. "A comparative examination of systems analysis techniques." *MIS Quarterly* 8 (March): 51–66.

Davis, Gordon B. 1982. "Strategies for information requirements determination." *IBM Systems Journal* 21:4–30.

DeMarco, Tom. 1982. *Controlling Software Projects.* New York: Yourdon Press, Inc.

Fedorowicz, Jane, and Janis Gogan. 1997. "Metropolitan Transportation Authority: On track with the year 2000 project?" PH Case Series for *Management Information Systems.* Edited by Joyce Elam, Prentice-Hall. (www.prenhall.com/elam)

Gane, Chris, and Trish Sarson. 1979. *Structured Systems Analysis: Tools and Techniques.* Englewood Cliffs, N.J.: Prentice-Hall, Inc.

Gunn, Eileen P. 1998. A new legal target: The millennium bug. *Fortune* 137 (April 27): 438.

Hartwick, Jon, and Henri Barki. 1994. "Measuring user participation, user involvement, and user attitude." *MIS Quarterly* 18 (March): 59–79.

Kirsner, Scott. 1998. "The Ripple Effect." *CIO* 11 (April 1): 28–32.

LaBoda, Douglas M., and Jeanne W. Ross. 1997. "Travelers Property Casualty Corporation: Building an object environment for greater competitiveness." Center for Information Systems Research, Sloan School of Management, MIT, WP No. 301.

Orlikowski, Wanda J. 1989. "Division among the ranks: The social implications of CASE tools for system developers." *Proceedings of the Tenth International Conference on Information Systems:* 199–210.

Orlikowski, Wanda J., and Debra J. Hofman. 1997. "An improvisational model for change management: The case of groupware technologies." *Sloan Management Review* 38 (Winter): 11–22.

Pastore, Richard. 1992. "Many happy returns." *CIO* 5 (June 15): 66–74.

Radding, Alan. 1992. "When non-IS managers take control." *Datamation* 38 (July 1): 55–58.

Robey, Daniel. 1987. "Implementation and the organizational impacts of information systems." *Interfaces* 17 (May–June): 72–84.

Sterling Software. Web site at http://www.sterling.com.

Texas Instruments. Web site at http://www.ti.com.

Williamson, Miryam. 1996. "Will your systems survive the year 2000?" *CIO* 9 (September 15): 53f.

CHAPTER 11

ALTERNATIVE APPROACH: PURCHASING SYSTEMS

In Chapter 10 we discussed two alternative approaches for the development of customized applications by in-house IS professionals: a traditional SDLC approach and a newer evolutionary approach using prototyping. At the end of Chapter 10 we described a methodology that combines the best of both of these approaches plus newer tools and methods to more quickly produce a high quality system: rapid application development (RAD). All of these approaches are in use not only within manufacturing and service firms that have their own IS specialists, but also in the software industry itself.

In this chapter we focus on a life cycle process for purchasing large packaged systems. Today, many organizations purchase system packages whenever it is cost beneficial to do so. The process we describe is a life cycle process for selecting, modifying, and implementing packaged systems. At the end of the chapter we will identify some factors important for choosing a customized solution versus a packaged solution, referred to as the "make or buy" decision. A discussion of outsourcing alternatives will be postponed until Part IV.

Note that our focus here is on what has been referred to as a "dedicated" package that offers a solution to a particular business problem. (Many organizations also use a project team to select general productivity tools, such as the Microsoft Office or Corel WordPerfect suites. As discussed in Chapter 12, selecting a standard personal productivity suite helps the organization provide training and consulting support for users.) Successfully implementing a dedicated package typically requires a major commitment on the part of user-managers to changing an organization's processes and procedures in order to exploit the capabilities of the purchased solution.

PURCHASING METHODOLOGY

In many industries today, the standard way to acquire application systems is to purchase software packages. Of course, many small businesses buy all their systems because they have no one capable of building their own. In contrast, larger organizations are choosing purchased system solutions over in-house developed solutions whenever it is feasible and cost beneficial to do so. As discussed in Chapter 3, thousands of applications software packages are available from a growing, global software industry. Systems that can be used across industries vary from generalized accounting and payroll systems for PC platforms to large, complex Enterprise Resource Planning (ERP) systems on client/server platforms with integrated modules for order entry, production and logistics, and human resources activities. In addition, there are industry-specific systems such as sales and inventory management systems for retailers, commercial loan systems for banks, claim processing systems for insurance companies, and patient admission systems for health care providers. Wherever there is a sizable market for a standard system, vendors are likely to be selling software packages.

In the next section we begin with a presentation of the purchasing process steps, followed by a discussion of the purchasing roles, managing a purchased system project, and the advantages and disadvantages of purchasing systems. The reader should note that our discussion below focuses on organizations with their own IS specialists. Organizations that have no IS specialists will need to rely on their own user-managers and on outside consultants to play these IS specialist roles and provide the necessary IS expertise.

The Purchasing Steps

Although at first glance it appears relatively easy to purchase packaged software, there have been many instances of systems implementation problems because the organization simply did not understand what was involved in acquiring and installing an application package. Our description below assumes that an initial approval has been received for a system purchase and that the purchase being considered is of sufficient size to merit a full purchasing process. As we will discuss, the package selection should be a joint decision between business managers who can assess the organizational benefits and risks and IS professionals who can help assess the benefits and risks from an IT implementation perspective.

The steps for purchasing application packages fit into the three life cycle phases introduced in Chapter 9: Definition, Construction, and Implementation. In the SDLC methodology, detailed systems specifications of what the system is to do are documented in the Definition phase; the system is built in the Construction phase; and the system is installed, operated, and maintained in the Implementation phase. For system purchases to be successful, adequate attention needs to be given to the Definition phase. Here an organization defines its system needs and then uses this set of requirements to identify and evaluate potential packaged (off-the-shelf) application solutions. The Construction phase is radically reduced, because the vendor has already designed, built, and tested the

application. The steps in the Implementation phase remain essentially the same, except that maintenance by the vendor is usually part of the purchase contract.

The reduction in time required to obtain a purchased system may be an important factor in the decision to purchase a system. Instead of taking 18 to 24 months to be developed, a purchased system might be operational in half that time. A custom-developed system could take even longer if a queue of systems projects are awaiting in-house IS resources to work on them.

The template for the purchasing process steps is shown in Figure 11.1. In the following section, we discuss the life cycle process for purchased systems in detail. Because customized application development using an SDLC process came first in larger, older organizations, this process is also referred to as a modified SDLC approach for software purchases.

Initiating the Purchasing Process   Similar to the decision for customized application investments, there are a number of approaches that organizations use to decide whether to invest in a purchased system. Some organizations do not require a detailed formal request to begin an investigation of a possible system purchase because there is an assumption that fewer IS resources are needed. At a minimum, the user-manager prepares

Definition Phase
    Feasibility Analysis
    Requirements Definition
    Create Short List of Packages
    Establish Evaluation Criteria
    Develop and Distribute RFP
    Choose Package
    Negotiate Contract
Construction Phase
    System Design (for package modifications)
    System Building (for package modifications)
    System Testing
Implementation Phase
    Installation
    Operations
    Maintenance

Figure 11.1 The Purchasing Process

a document that briefly describes the proposed application needs and outlines the potential benefits that the application will provide to the organization.

As when building the system using the SDLC, a project team should be established and given the responsibility for acquiring the software. The team should include representatives from the business units that will implement the system, IS analysts, and other IS specialists who will operate and support the packaged system and other systems that will interface with the package.

Definition Phase   The Definition phase begins with the same two steps as in the SDLC process. However, there are also five addititional steps specific to the purchasing process.

Feasibility Analysis.   Similar to the SDLC, the objective of this step is to determine whether the proposed system is economically, technically, and operationally feasible. When purchasing a system, the feasibility of purchasing rather than building a system solution is also being considered. This step would therefore include a preliminary investigation of the availability of packaged systems that might be suitable candidates, including a high-level investigation of the software features and capabilities provided by the vendors.

Helpful resources for this preliminary investigation include lists of software recommended by hardware vendors, user groups, or professional associations and software catalogs published by third parties (such as Auerbach). Software vendor advertisements in technical and trade publications, as well as vendor booths at professional conferences, are also good sources of information. Managers also may learn of packages in use at similar organizations through interpersonal networks.

The deliverable for this step is a high-level proposal that includes a description of the overall system needed, a cost/benefit analysis based on the assumption that the system will be purchased, and a plan for obtaining, implementing, and maintaining a suitable package.

The cost/benefit analysis of the proposed system should be developed with both business manager and IS analyst input. Determining the system costs involves much more than identifying the purchase costs of candidate packages. Figure 11.2 compares the costs for a $1 million in-house developed system (a midsized system) with the costs for selecting and purchasing a packaged system with the same overall functionality. The total cost of purchasing ($650,000) is about two-thirds of the total cost of building the system in-house. Note that the purchase price of the

Stages	Cost of Building System	Cost of Buying System
Definition Phase		
Feasibility Analysis	$ 50,000	$ 50,000
Requirements Definition	250,000	200,000
Construction Phase		
System Design	150,000	—
Coding and Testing	150,000	—
System Testing	130,000	100,000
Documentation and Procedures	120,000	25,000
Implementation Phase		
Installation Planning, Data Clean-up, and Conversion	150,000	175,000
Software Purchase Price	—	100,000
Total	$1,000,000	$ 650,000

Figure 11.2   Comparison of Costs of Building versus Purchasing a System

package is less than one-sixth of the total costs for defining, selecting, and implementing the package.

Looking in more detail at Figure 11.2, the costs of the Definition phase for both alternatives are comparable. Although the requirements analysis will be less detailed when purchasing, the entire process of searching for and evaluating packages is included in this phase. For the Construction phase, we have assumed that no modifications to the package or to the company's other systems are required. In this situation, there are considerable cost savings. The systems testing and documentation costs, in addition to the purchase price itself, are less than half as costly as the Construction costs for the customized solution. This $350,000 difference between the cost of building the system in-house and the cost of purchasing the package may quickly vanish if the assumption of no system modifications does not hold true. Costs due to system modifications can also be hard to predict. Keen (1991) has reported that the total life cycle costs of both customized systems and purchased systems were frequently underestimated and warns managers that the total life cycle cost for a purchased system can be up to seven times the original estimate.

Requirements Definition. The requirements definition is a critical step in the SDLC approach. The SDLC deliverable is a detailed specification of what the system must do in terms of the inputs it must accept, the data it must store, the processes it must perform, the outputs it must produce, and the performance requirements that must be satisfied. It must be accurate, complete, and detailed because it is used to design and program the system and because it determines the quality of the resulting system.

When purchasing the system, this step is equally critical. In order to select the best software package, one must first have at least a high-level conceptual understanding of the system requirements. Here, however, the focus is on defining the functional requirements of the system to the degree needed for developing a *request for proposal (RFP)* from a short list of vendors. The requirements need to be more fully developed than the basic requirements used to build a prototype, but less detailed than the requirements elicited under an SDLC process when they are used to design the actual system. Research has shown that uncertainty about an organization's needs is a significant barrier to packaged software adoption.

Create Short List of Suitable Packages. In this step, the organization's requirements are used to eliminate all but a few of the most promising candidate packages that were identified in the feasibility analysis step. For example, packages should be eliminated if they do not have particular required features or will not work with existing hardware, operating system and database management software, or networks. Further research on the vendor's capabilities can be undertaken to eliminate vendors due to problems experienced with other users of the package, an inadequate track record or firm size of the vendor, or other concerns about long-term viability. Independent consultants with expertise on specific types of applications or specializing in a given industry can also be key resources here and may be able to help the project team eliminate inappropriate candidates.

Establish Criteria for Selection. In this step, both business and IS team members need to work together to determine relevant criteria about the candidate packages and vendors in order to choose the best one. Some criteria can be categorized as mandatory requirements, whereas others may be categorized as desirable features.

Some areas in which detailed criteria should be developed are shown in Figure 11.3. For example, the business characteristics of the vendor category may include items such as how long the vendor has been in the software business, the number of employees, financial reports over the past five years, its principal products, its yearly software sales revenue, and the location of its sales and support offices. The functional capabilities of the packaged system should include the degree to which the package allows for multiple options and the ease with which it can be tailored to fit company needs using parameters or other approaches that do not require system coding.

Business characteristics of the vendor firm
Functional capabilities of the packaged system
Technical requirements the software must satisfy
Amount and quality of documentation provided
Vendor support of the package—initial and ongoing

Figure 11.3 Criteria for Purchased Software Decision

The technical requirements to be evaluated include the hardware and system software required to run the system and the package's software and database architectures. This information allows one to evaluate how well the package will conform to current organizational standards for hardware, software, and networks. The types, amount, and quality of the documentation provided should also be evaluated, as well as the quality and amount of vendor support available, including training, consulting, and system maintenance.

In addition to detailing the evaluation criteria, consideration should be given to the measures that will be used in the evaluation process. It is not uncommon to evaluate packages using a scale with numbers (such as 1 through 10) or qualitative labels (such as outstanding, good, average, fair, or poor). If a scale with numbers is used, each criterion can be assigned an importance weight, and a weighted score can be computed for each evaluation category for each package. Although quantitative scores may not be the sole means for selection, they help to quantify differences among the candidate packages.

Develop and Distribute the RFP. An RFP is a formal document sent to potential vendors, inviting them to submit a proposal describing their software package and how it would meet the company's needs. In organizations with prior experience purchasing software, a template for the RFP may already have been developed, although the requirements will be highly dependent on the type of package and the end-users. A sample table of contents is shown in Figure 11.4.

The criteria for selection are used by the project team to develop the RFP. The RFP provides the vendors with information about the objectives and requirements of the system, the environment in which the system will be used, the general criteria that will be used to evaluate the proposals, and the conditions for submitting proposals. Specific questions may need to be developed to capture performance characteristics of the system, whether source code is provided, and

	Page		Page
I. Introduction		**III. Requirements**	
A. Structure and Scope of the RFP	3	A. Vendor Information	12
B. Objective of RFP	3	B. Vendor Support/Training	13
C. Company Background and Philosophy	3	C. Documentation	15
D. Hardware/Software Environment	4	D. Package Hardware and System	
E. Current Business Environment	5	Software Environment	17
		E. Application and Database Architecture	21
		F. Tuning and Measurement	26
		G. Functional Requirements	28
II. Guidelines for Vendor Response		**IV. Costs**	
A. Guidelines	6	A. Summary	33
B. Vendor Response	8	B. Non-Recurring	35
C. General Evaluation Process	10	C. Recurring	37
		D. Price Guarantee	39
		E. Maintenance Agreement	40
		F. New Releases	41
		V. Signature Page	42

Figure 11.4 Sample RFP Table of Contents

whether the purchasing organization is allowed to modify the package without voiding the vendor warranty. In addition to pricing information for the package itself, any additional costs for training and consulting need to be ascertained. The RFP can also be used to capture historical information about the package, such as the date of the first release, the date of its last revision, and a list of companies in which the package has been implemented—including contact information to obtain references from these companies.

This step ends when the RFP is sent to the short list of qualified vendors.

Evaluate Vendor Responses to RFP and Choose Package. In this step, the vendor responses to the RFP are evaluated and additional actions are taken to evaluate the candidate packages and their vendors. The overall objective of the evaluation process is to determine the extent of any discrepancies between the company's needs as specified by the requirements and the weighting system and the capabilities of the proposed application packages. Aggregate evaluations (scores) need to be calculated for each set of criteria and for the overall package. These figures are then used by the team to discuss the major strengths and weaknesses of the candidate packages. This can be a large data collection and analysis task and may involve independent evaluations by all project team members. Both IS and business team members may need to confer not only with other project team members, but also with other members of their departments.

In addition to evaluating the vendors' responses from the formal RFP process, two other types of data collection are commonly pursued, at least for the leading candidate packages. First, demonstrations of the leading packages can usually be arranged. Sometimes it is feasible for the vendor to set up a demo on-site at your organization; at other times, another location is required—either at a vendor location or at another company that has installed the package. Detailed requirements for software demos should be provided to the vendors to ensure equitable conditions for demonstrating system performance, because response times and other characteristics of system performance can vary greatly depending on the hardware and system software being used to run the package. An example of demo specifications for a financial modeling package, and a form for evaluating the demo specified, are provided in Figure 11.5.

Presentation Directions

The format must follow the outline provided.

The mainframe to which the PC is connected for this presentation must be an IBM running under MVS. If your MVS is not exactly like ours (as outlined in the RFP) you must provide a written explanation of how the differences (i.e., response time, color, etc.) affect the demonstration.

The presentation is limited to 2 hours, including 30 minutes for questions at the end. You will be given 30 minutes to set up.

With the data and formulas provided create a relational database so that the following Profit and Loss (P&L) statements can be modeled and reported.

Fiscal 1997 Plan:

Item P&L: by month with total year at the right.
Control Unit P&L: by item with total at the right.
Business Unit P&L: by Control Unit with total at the right.

Fiscal 1998 Projection:

Business Unit P&L: by Control Unit with total at the right.

Combined Fiscal 1997 & Fiscal 1998:

Control Unit Change Analysis: by item for total Fiscal 1997 vs. proj. Fiscal 1998.
Business Unit Change Analysis: by Control Unit for total Fiscal 1997 vs. proj. Fiscal 1998.

Provide a listing of the populated database relations and/or tables.

Provide an example listing of the programs/models and report format files for each type of P&L and Change Analysis above.

Figure 11.5(A) Vendor Demonstration Requirements

Second, references from users of the software package in other companies are usually obtained. Each vendor may be asked to provide a reference list as part of the RFP. One especially effective technique is to require the vendor to provide the names of users

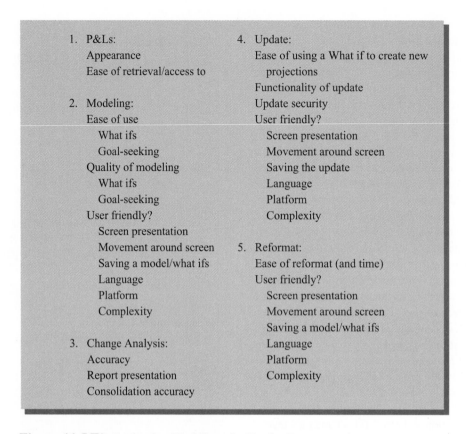

1. P&Ls:
   Appearance
   Ease of retrieval/access to

2. Modeling:
   Ease of use
     What ifs
     Goal-seeking
   Quality of modeling
     What ifs
     Goal-seeking
   User friendly?
     Screen presentation
     Movement around screen
     Saving a model/what ifs
     Language
     Platform
     Complexity

3. Change Analysis:
   Accuracy
   Report presentation
   Consolidation accuracy

4. Update:
   Ease of using a What if to create new
     projections
   Functionality of update
   Update security
   User friendly?
     Screen presentation
     Movement around screen
     Saving the update
     Language
     Platform
     Complexity

5. Reformat:
   Ease of reformat (and time)
   User friendly?
     Screen presentation
     Movement around screen
     Saving a model/what ifs
     Language
     Platform
     Complexity

Figure 11.5(B) Evaluation Worksheet for Vendor Demonstration

as well as IS specialists for each customer organization on their reference list. Task force members can then divide up the names with, for example, IS specialists contacting their counterparts in companies that have already implemented the package. Site visits to one or more of these companies may also be possible. Evaluations of the vendor's consulting and training services can also be obtained from these sources.

Based on all of the above information sources, the project team needs to assess how well the needs of the company match with the capabilities of the available packages (see Figure 11.6). Sometimes it is better for a company to change its procedures to conform to the way the software package works than to try to change the purchased system. A company may even find that the procedures incorporated in the package are better than those initially specified by the project team; the developers of the package may have worked with one or more leading organizations in order to develop best-in-class solutions.

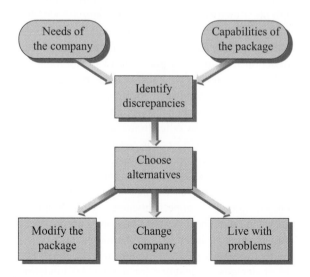

Figure 11.6 Process for Matching Company Needs with Capabilities of the Package

Once the discrepancies are identified, the team needs to decide the best way to deal with these discrepancies for the top candidate packages. As shown in Figure 11.6, the company can change its procedures to fit the package, do nothing and live with the limitations, or make plans to modify the package. An important factor in this decision process is the additional development effort that may be required to tailor the system to the company's needs or to integrate it into the company's environment. These decisions need to be made in cooperation with internal IS specialists and the vendors of the top candidate packages in order to identify the extent of the discrepancies as well as the feasibility and advisability of modifying a given package. If system modifications are being considered, plans for who will do the modifications and what they will cost need to be taken into consideration.

The decision to purchase a system is therefore not only a commitment to purchase the best of the available systems, but also a commitment to whatever organizational compromises need to be made in order to implement the system. Packaged software is a vendor's solution to a problem that is perceived to exist in a significant number of firms. Thus, it is likely that discrepancies between the needs of the organization and the package capabilities will exist. Before finalizing the purchase decision, the project team should ensure that the relevant user-managers support the decision to buy the selected package and agree that they will do whatever is necessary to successfully implement it. Similarly, the project team should ensure that the IS specialists agree that the system can operate in the current environment and that they can satisfactorily support it in-house as required.

Negotiate Contract. The deliverables from this stage are a legal contract with the vendor of the selected software package and a detailed plan for the remainder of the life cycle steps. The contract with the software vendor specifies not only the software price and payment schedule, but also functional specifications, acceptance-testing procedures, a timetable of the delivery process, protection of trade secrets, repair and maintenance responsibilities, liabilities due to failures, required documentation, and options to terminate the agreement (Gurbaxani and Whang, 1991).

Contract negotiations should therefore be an integral part of the purchase process. When working with vendors to determine how to reduce the discrepancies between the company's needs and the capabilities of the packages, one is actually prenegotiating a contract with the selected vendor. Uncertainty about package modification time and cost and about vendor viability are reported to be key obstacles to package adoption (Lucas, Walton, and Ginzberg, 1988).

Many organizations have software purchasing specialists who assist in the contract writing and negotiation steps. Because the contract will be the only recourse if the system or the vendor does not perform as specified, legal assistance may be needed. Gurbaxani and Whang suggest that the use of an attorney is required to reduce the probability of future legal wrangling or a loss of rightful claims. Purchasing software therefore involves contractual costs that are avoided with in-house software development.

Construction Phase In the SDLC process, the construction phase includes three steps: system design, system building, and system testing. With purchasing, the extent to which the first two steps are needed depends on whether or not the purchased package is modified.

If no modifications to the system are to be made, the firm can move to the system testing step after the purchase contract is signed. Many off-the-shelf packages, such as accounting applications, are often not modified because the business practices they support are quite standardized and the package was not developed by the vendor with modifications in mind (Rockart and Hofman, 1992). Packaged systems have typically been beta-tested in companies in the targeted industry before they are sold on the open market. Despite the fact that the package may have been thoroughly tested and already used in other organizations, user acceptance testing still needs to be conducted to ensure that the system works properly with your data, using hardware and system software that already exists in your organization. This may require significant time and effort because no one in your organization is familiar with the system's detailed design. The vendor provides user documentation for those who will use the system and technical systems documentation for those who install the system and operate it. However, new procedures for end-users may need to be developed to fit your own organizational implementation.

If modifications to the system need to be made, a significant investment in time and money may be required. There are three options to sourcing the modifications to an application package: contract with the vendor to make the changes, contract with a third party, or modify the software in-house. Many vendors routinely contract to make the desired modifications. If a vendor will furnish only the machine-language code of the system—not the source code in which the program was written—the only alternative may be to contract with the vendor to make the modifications.

If the purchased system is being modified by the purchaser, then the system design and building stages of the SDLC are implemented just as they would be in traditional development. Because your staff must devote substantial effort to understanding the details of the design and structure of the software package in order to modify it, more effort may be required in these stages than one might initially estimate. If object-oriented approaches are used, it may be easier to tailor the package to the special needs of a firm.

Large ERP system packages can entail multiple years of work by in-house IS specialists as well as outside consultants in order to initially implement these integrated systems. This is because these systems may include many parameters that need to be set in order to tailor some aspects of the system to fit the organization. The systems also require significant changes in day-to-day business processes. In these and other large system purchases, the total effort required to modify and install the package becomes comparable to a large, in-house development project.

Often it is also necessary to modify existing company systems to integrate them with the new package. Creating these interface programs can be difficult and costly, and integration testing is typically a time-consuming process.

If the modifications are made by the vendor, the system changes need to be tested by both the vendor and the purchaser. Acceptance testing is especially important if the package has been modified by the vendor and typically requires significant time and effort. The revised user and system documentation also need to be reviewed.

Implementation Phase   The implementation phase of the SDLC involves installation, operations, and main-

tenance. As seen in Figure 11.1, these are all major activities in the system purchasing life cycle.

Installation.   The installation stage in the SDLC involves installation planning, training, data cleanup, and conversion. The installation of a packaged system also includes all these activities. A key obstacle to implementation success is the quality of vendor support in the installation of the package (Lucas et al., 1988).

Special attention needs to be given to the training needs for a purchased system, because the users may be asked to make significant changes in how they do their jobs in order to conform to the characteristics of the package. Under these circumstances, there also may be more user resistance to be overcome. User-managers must be actively involved in these activities and committed to devoting the time necessary to anticipate such problems, and resolve any problems that arise.

Operations.   Operations are similar whether the company purchases the system or builds it using the SDLC. A key to success in the initial days of operation may be good lines of communication with the vendor in order to quickly resolve any problems. Long-term success depends on the degree to which the organization has successfully integrated the system into the company's ongoing operations.

Maintenance.   As described above, it is common for package maintenance to be the vendor's responsibility, as detailed in the purchase contract. This can lead to considerable cost avoidance to a firm over the life of the system. On the other hand, the purchaser is dependent upon the vendor for future system changes. Because the vendor must balance the desires and needs of all the organizations who use the system, your company may not get all the changes it wants, and it may even have to accept some changes it does not want. The worst case here is that the purchased system has a significantly shorter useful life than originally intended.

If the original package was modified, the installation of a vendor's new version of the package may not be the optimal solution for the purchasing organization. With the help of the vendor, the company needs to evaluate the functionality of the new version of the package with its current modified version and then decide the best way to deal with these discrepancies. The choices are similar to those shown in Figure 11.6, except the "do nothing" choice means that the organization may be left operating a version of the package that the vendor may or may not continue to support. If the organization modified the original package in-house or built extensive interfaces to the earlier version of the package, the implementation of a new version of the package can result in considerable maintenance costs for the organization.

The Purchasing Roles

Several roles are critical to the success of a package purchase. Similar to the SDLC process, user-managers need to play the sponsor and champion roles for the project. The **sponsor** participates in the justification of the system and typically takes responsibility for ensuring that the appropriate user-manager representatives participate in the selection process. The **champion** helps push the project forward and is responsible for implementing the new system in the organization. To the degree that company operations must be adapted to the characteristics of the package, implementation may require considerable organizational changes, and thus may present a challenge even greater than implementing a custom system.

Also as in the SDLC process, the **project manager** is responsible for the success of the project. The project manager role is more likely to be played by a user-manager when a package is being purchased, but IS expertise is still required in order to assess the technical quality of the candidate packages. Small organizations that have no IS specialists will need to rely on their own user-managers, as well as outside consultants, to provide the necessary IS expertise.

Unlike software developed in-house, purchased software also entails an external role: the **vendor.** The vendor initially provides information on the package capabilities via a proposal in response to an RFP. Vendors of leading packages may then be asked to provide a demonstration, and to consult with the purchaser about potential system modifications in order to reduce mismatches between the packaged system's capabilities and the organization's needs. The vendor may also be contracted to provide system modifications prior to implementation as well as ongoing maintenance support for the purchasing organization, including the periodic issuance of new releases.

Because of this dependence on an external vendor, one or more other internal roles are also important: **purchasing specialists** and external **contract specialists.** Persons with both types of expertise should be involved in the purchasing process and may even be formal members of the project team. For example, if an RFP is sent to vendors, a purchasing specialist may help determine its content. Firms with prior software purchasing experience may have developed boilerplate sections for the RFP. As described above under the Negotiate Contract step, attorneys should oversee the writing and approval of the external contract in order to reduce uncertainties and vulnerability to the vendor.

Managing a Purchased System Project

Purchased system projects are successful when the organization has selected a product and a vendor that is able to satisfy the firm's current and future system needs. This requires an effective project team with representative members committed to the project goals at the outset. Unlike the traditional SDLC process, where a long Construction phase buffers the Definition phase from the Implementation phase, large system purchases can be decided on within a few months. The right business managers, users, and IS specialists need to be a part of the project team to ensure that the best vendor is contracted and that both IS and business problems with the package implementation have been considered.

A typical problem with managing the life cycle of a purchased system project is ensuring that adequate attention is given to the initial Definition phase steps. A common mistake is that user-managers become aware of a single package and begin negotiations with a vendor without adequate attention to the functional requirements definition step. Project teams that don't do a good job identifying their requirements will not be able to do a good job assessing the discrepancies between the company's needs and the capabilities of candidate packages. The contract with the vendor developed at the end of the Definition phase is typically even less flexible than the sign-offs between users and IS developers at the end of the Definition phase under a traditional SDLC process. It is therefore critical that the Definition phase be performed well.

The success of the Implementation phase also depends on how well the Definition phase was performed, because this is where the team members assessed the organizational changes needed to successfully implement the purchased system. As discussed above, users of the packaged system may be asked to make significant changes in how they do their jobs in order to conform to the characteristics of a package. This requires a well-planned installation step under the leadership of committed user-managers who are very knowledgeable about the needed changes.

In addition, purchased system projects introduce several new types of risks. First, the success of the project is highly dependent on the performance of a third party. The quality of the purchased system will depend on the software engineering capabilities of the vendor, as well as the vendor's training and installation capabilities. As discussed above, a key aspect of the vendor selection process is the accurate assessment of the vendor's capabilities, not just an evaluation of the current software package.

Second, the initial success of the project, as well as the long-term effectiveness of the system being installed, is highly dependent on the contract negotiation process. In most situations, system implementation does not simply involve "turning the key." Vendor expertise may be required to install the package, build interfaces to existing systems, and perhaps modify the package itself to better match the needs of the purchasing organization. Service expectations between the purchaser and vendor need to be a part of the contract developed at the end of the Definition phase. The contract will be the only recourse for the purchaser if the system modifications, vendor training, or the implementation of the package do not go well.

Purchasing Small Systems The discussion in this chapter has focused on the purchasing process for large, complex systems. If a smaller, simpler system is being considered, the time and effort put into the process can, of course, be scaled back. However, a small system can still be a major investment for a small business. Unfortunately, many small businesses have limited experience with and knowledge of evaluating and installing such systems. The hardware vendor, a local software supplier, and/or consultants may need to be relied on in these situations.

Purchasing Advantages and Disadvantages

The modified SDLC approach is a disciplined approach to purchasing a preexisting (packaged) system. A summary of the advantages and disadvantages of this approach is provided in Figure 11.7.

The primary advantage of purchasing a package is that it reduces the time to implement the system as compared to customized application development. Nevertheless, for midsized systems, the entire process will still require several months. For large organizational system packages (such as ERP systems), the process can take several years.

A second major advantage is that packaged systems are very attractive from an economic standpoint. For example, a small business can obtain a complete accounting system for less than $10,000, which is very low compared to the cost of developing a comparable customized application. Assuming that the vendor has more than 10,000 installations of this package, this represents about $100 million in revenues, so the vendor can afford to spend millions of dollars developing and improving this package. Everyone comes out a winner because each purchaser has cost avoidance from purchasing a package, and the vendor makes a large enough profit to stay in business and provide upgrades and other support on an ongoing basis. As shown previously in Figure 11.2, the purchase price of a software package may be a relatively small fraction of the total cost of acquiring and installing the system, although there usually are

Advantages
    Reduced time to implement
    Lower acquisition costs
    Potential application quality
    Infusion of external expertise
    Freed-up internal IS specialists
Disadvantages
    Increased risks due to package and
      organizational changes
    Initial and ongoing dependence on vendor

Figure 11.7 Advantages and Disadvantages of Purchased Packages

substantial savings compared to the costs of developing a customized application.

A third advantage is that the quality of an application package may be substantially better than that of a custom system. The vendor can afford to spend much more time and effort developing the system than an individual company. Further, a package is usually thoroughly tested through its use in other organizations, and new releases of the package may incorporate the experience and desires of many companies that are using the system. The documentation may also be much better than the typical custom system's documentation.

Fourth, a packaged solution is a quick way to infuse new expertise—both IT expertise and business expertise—into the organization. Given the pace of change of new technology developments, most organizations today find it difficult to develop and keep IS personnel with expertise on new, emerging technologies. Software vendors have the funds and motivation to develop new systems using newer technologies. Packaged solutions for a particular industry, or large ERP systems, may also be purchased in order to take advantage of best-in-class processes and procedures. In other words, business expertise is embedded in the software that is purchased.

A final advantage is that purchasing packages for relatively common processes that provide no specific strategic advantage for a firm will free in-house IS specialists to work on mission-critical applications that could provide the firm a competitive advantage.

The primary disadvantage associated with purchasing an application package is that a package rarely meets exactly the needs of a given organization. The decision to purchase a package, rather than pursue a customized solution, partially depends on the extent to which modifications can be made to resolve these discrepancies and on their estimated costs. As described earlier (see Figure 11.6), one can change the package, change the company's procedures to match the package, decide to live with a system that does not match the company's procedures well, or decide that purchasing an application package is not viable and explore other alternatives for acquiring the system. This critical decision requires that knowledgeable business managers and skilled IS specialists be significantly involved during the Definition phase of the project.

Another potential disadvantage is that modifying a software package involves greater risks than in-house maintenance of a custom-developed application. There have been numerous examples where organizations have made the mistake of attempting to modify a package that did not meet their needs well; after several years of effort and millions of dollars of expense, they abandoned the effort. The expertise of in-house IS specialists and the vendor are needed to ensure that these risks are minimized. When you purchase a packaged system, you are also buying vendor expertise.

Similarly, because of an organization's relative unfamiliarity with the system and the need to change operations to conform to the processes embedded in a purchased system, it may be much more difficult to install a purchased system and integrate it into a company's operations than to implement a customized application solution. Significant training beyond system training may be required, and there may be more user resistance due to the extent of changes associated with a packaged solution. When a customized application is developed, user-managers and end-users help to define, design, and test a system, which can result in greater buy-in to the changes required.

A final related disadvantage is that purchasing a system leads to dependence on a vendor. In many situations, this becomes a long-term relationship, with the vendor company responsible for ongoing system support and maintenance. Although in many cases this may result in a strategic alliance of value to both the vendor and purchaser, the coordination costs associated with managing the vendor relationship may not be fully anticipated by the purchaser. In addition, of course, there is the risk that the vendor will go out of business or be unresponsive to the needs of the purchasing firm.

THE MAKE-OR-BUY DECISION

In Chapters 10 and 11, we have discussed three important approaches to obtaining a new application system: the traditional systems development life cycle (SDLC), prototyping, and purchasing packaged software as an alternative to customized application development. The choice between the first two approaches for developing a customized application is essentially an IS management decision: The question is which acquisition approach best fulfills the business vision for the system, taking into account the advantages of the SDLC, newer evolutionary approaches, or both. Key factors include the degree to which requirements can be easily determined, the functionality of the application, and application size and complexity. As discussed in Chapter 10, most of today's IS organizations have competencies with a portfolio of methodological approaches.

In contrast, the *make-or-buy decision*—that is, the choice between customized application development and purchasing a system—is a decision that should be jointly made by business managers needing the application and IS professionals who can assess the organizational benefits and risks. The most obvious advantages of purchasing include economic benefits and speed of implementation. The downside is that a purchased system seldom exactly fits a company's needs: Users need to change processes and procedures to match the package and/or change the package to fit the company. This means that the organization's managers must make some tough decisions about the degree to which a package needs to be modified in order to successfully exploit it. As more software applications are based upon object-oriented approaches in the future, managers can expect it to become easier, and less risky, to tailor the package to the special needs of an organization.

For organizations with IS resources, there are also other important considerations in this make-or-buy decision. One of these is the opportunity cost of devoting the organization's scarce IS specialist resources to the development of a system that could be purchased, rather than another system that cannot be purchased and may provide the organization with a greater competitive advantage. Another consideration is that purchased systems can in some cases provide more advanced technological solutions to a given organization than could be achieved with in-house personnel alone.

For small businesses that do not have IS resources, the make-or-buy decision may be simple. Purchasing a package has both economic and technological advantages, and it avoids activities for which the business has no particular expertise. The "buy" option for a small business has clear advantages over

the "make" option, which would mean contracting with an outside vendor to develop a customized application.

Purchasing packaged software is an alternative approach to customized application development that has been increasingly pursued by organizations of all sizes over the past decade. As business environments have become more dynamic, many organizations have chosen to modify their organizational practices in order to implement a system solution more quickly. This has been especially true as organizations have taken a more process-oriented view and found that their current customized applications cannot be easily modified to support cross-functional processes. Another alternative, outsourcing the development of the system, may be attractive to organizations that have their own IS organization when the resources needed—IS specialists, new IT skills, and/or time— are not available to build it internally. Outsourcing takes many forms, from using contract programmers on a project team alongside in-house personnel to contracting with an external systems integrator to build the system entirely. As found with the system purchase option, however, dependence on a third-party vendor can be an advantage or a disadvantage. The outsourcing alternative in general will be discussed in more detail in Part IV.

SUMMARY

Whether an organization develops a custom application in-house or purchases a packaged application solution, the process for acquiring the application is based on the systems life cycle introduced in Chapter 9, which includes three phases: Definition, Construction, and Implementation. Even if an application is purchased, an organization first must define its basic system needs before attempting to identify potential prepackaged, or off-the-shelf, application solutions. The Definition phase also includes the development of an RFP to be sent to vendors of candidate packaged systems. If successful, the Definition phase ends with the development of a vendor contract.

The Construction phase is considerably shorter than the Construction phase in an SDLC process. This is because the application has already been designed and built by the vendor, and the typical purchased system has already been beta-tested in companies in the vendor's targeted market before it is sold to other companies. The importance of the Construction phase varies based on whether any modifications are made to the package, as opposed to being a "turnkey" solution. If there are no or few modifications, the organization can quickly prepare for user acceptance testing.

The Implementation phase can be more difficult for user-managers and IS specialists than in a customized application due to lack of familiarity with the details of how the package operates. The last step, maintenance, typically differs from the SDLC in that the vendor is usually under contract for all system maintenance and will be relied on to provide system upgrades for the life of the application. Establishing the vendor's responsibilities is an important part of the purchasing contract; this is especially important if the packaged system has been modified and these modifications may not be incorporated into a future release of the package by the vendor.

Similar to a customized application process, user-managers must sponsor the system and champion its implementation. If the champion role is not played well, user acceptance of the system can be jeopardized due to the likelihood that organizational changes will be required in order to implement a pre-existing, packaged solution. Even if no modifications are made to the packaged system, IS specialists need to be involved in the process to ensure that the system is compatible with existing systems and to help negotiate a favorable solution with the vendor. If system modifications are to be made, considerable IS expertise may be required to define the needed changes and to avoid creating undue risks for the organization over the life of the package.

The fact that packaged solutions can be implemented more quickly than custom-developed solutions is a major advantage. In addition, if the purchased application fits the organization's requirements well, there may be considerable cost savings. Purchasing also allows the purchasing organization to take advantage of the IT expertise of external software vendors and the "best-in-class" processes often embedded in the purchased application. Disadvantages include increased implementation risks due to dependence on a vendor and a package that may not be fully understood until after it is purchased.

Recent trends suggest that the more technical IS work will increasingly be performed by vendors outside user organizations. Successful management of the packaged system purchasing process by user and IS managers is thus expected to become increasingly important for the effective use of IT. Expertise in the implementation of packaged systems and change management is becoming a critical internal competency (Markus and Benjamin, 1997). The change agent role of the IS organization will be considered in Part IV.

REVIEW QUESTIONS

1. List the phases and steps of the modified SDLC approach for software purchases.
2. Describe the additional steps included in the Definition phase for purchasing a system that are not included when building a system in-house with an SDLC process.
3. What is an RFP? Describe the role that an RFP plays in purchasing a major application system.
4. What is the role of the sponsor in purchasing? the champion? the project manager?
5. What are the major advantages of purchasing an application system?
6. Describe the different alternatives available for modifying a package. In your answer, explain why making a lot of modifications to a packaged system is considered risky.
7. Describe the role of the vendor in terms of each purchasing life cycle phase.
8. Summarize the key tradeoffs that need to be considered in a make-or-buy decision.
9. Describe how purchasing a small system differs from purchasing a large system.

DISCUSSION QUESTIONS

1. Critique the following analysis: It would cost us $800,000 to build this system, but we can purchase an equivalent package for $125,000. Therefore, we can save $675,000 by purchasing the software package.

2. Discuss the options an organization needs to choose from when the best packaged system solution is not a perfect fit with the needs of the organization.

3. You run a small business. You have no IS specialists on your staff and plan to purchase all of your software. What would be your three most important concerns, and how would you deal with them?

4. You are a manager in a company that has a lot of in-house IS expertise. What would be your key decision rules for when to purchase a system versus when to develop it in-house?

5. Discuss why an assessment of the financial stability of the vendor can be an important consideration.

6. Comment on what you see as the three to five critical success factors for successfully implementing a large packaged system that also requires the organization to adopt new cross-functional processes.

7. By the end of 1997, many large U.S.-based firms had made major investments in the implementation of large ERP system packages, such as SAP and PeopleSoft. Comment on what you think may be particularly important parts of the decision process when assessing this type of package. (You may wish to refer to the description of ERP systems in Chapter 5.)

REFERENCES

Gurbaxani, Vijay, and Seungjin Whang. 1991. "The impact of information systems on organizations and markets." *Communications of the ACM* 34 (January): 59–73.

Keen, Peter G. W. 1991. "Chapter 6: Managing the economics of information capital." In *Shaping the Future: Business Design Through Information Technology*. Boston: Harvard Business School Press.

Lucas, Henry C., Jr., Eric J. Walton, and Michael J. Ginzberg. 1988. "Implementing packaged software." *MIS Quarterly* 12 (December): 525–549.

Markus, M. Lynne, and Robert I. Benjamin. 1997. "The magic bullet theory in IT-enabled transformations." *Sloan Management Review* (Winter): 55–68.

Martin. E.W. 1988. "Halsted, Inc."

Rockart, John F., and J. Debra Hofman. 1992. "Systems delivery: Evolving new strategies." *Sloan Management Review* (Summer): 21–31.

Weston, Rusty, and Clinton Wilder. 1993. "Partners in profit." *Corporate Computing* 2 (March): SR 3–SR 36.

Wreden, Nick. 1992. "Custom-developed software: You bought it, but do you own it?" *Beyond Computing* 1 (October/November): 39–42.

CHAPTER 12

SYSTEMS DEVELOPMENT BY USERS

This chapter focuses on the development of application systems by people who are not IS specialists. We will use the term **user application development** to refer to the use of computer tools to develop business applications by workers who are not IS specialists. User application development (UAD) is not a totally new phenomenon: Even before the advent of microcomputer technology and personal productivity software, workers in accounting, finance, operations, research and development, and marketing have used mainframe tools for analysis and to generate reports. In the Information Age, however, the development of applications by the people who use them directly in their work has become ubiquitous.

Another characteristic of UAD today is that applications developed by an end-user are not necessarily only used by the developer of the application. User-developed applications are often used by entire workgroups or departments. In many small organizations, of course, there may be no employees at all who are IS specialists; packaged solutions and user-developed systems are their primary alternatives, unless an outside IS contractor is used. In both these smaller organizations and larger ones, it is common for a non-IS specialist to become a first line of support for other end-users, a kind of resident expert.

The overall objective of this chapter is to prepare you to be a knowledgeable manager of systems development by users, as well as an end-user knowledgeable about the benefit/risk tradeoffs associated with end-user computing in general. We define **end-user computing** as hands-on use of computer resources by employees throughout the organization to enter data, make inquiries, release orders into production, prepare reports, communicate, perform statistical analysis, analyze problems, design products, and perform a myriad of other tasks.

Although query and report generator tools for end-user development first became available for mainframe platforms, today's end-users typically develop applications on microcomputer platforms using spreadsheet, database management, financial modeling, statistical modeling software, and fourth-generation languages (4GLs). In fact, many managerial support applications (discussed in Chapter 6) typically involve some development activities by professionals, managers, and even senior managers. Today, a user-developed application is also increasingly likely to be part of a client/server system that interacts with databases stored on a mainframe or other large servers.

How to effectively leverage end-user computing resources—both people and technology—continues to be a difficult management issue for IS managers and user-managers alike. Many senior managers are concerned about the ongoing costs of supporting end-users. For example, in 1994 the Gartner Group estimated the five-year cost of a desktop personal computer to be $40,000. Only 15 percent of these costs were hardware and software; the bulk of the remaining costs were for initial and ongoing support services.

In the next section we discuss some of the drivers for the UAD phenomenon as well as the range of user-developed applications in today's organizations. We then look at the tradeoffs involved with user-developed versus IS-developed systems. First we discuss the advantages and disadvantages of this development alternative, and then we present a list of factors that should be considered by business managers as they assess the tradeoffs. In the next section we describe a methodology (process) for systems development by end-users that maximizes the strengths and minimizes the weaknesses of the user development approach.

The remainder of the chapter is devoted to a discussion of what actions IS and non-IS managers can take to leverage end-user computing in general. We first present a framework to help managers think through alternative strategies and tactics for managing end-user computing in organizations. The underlying theme of our discussion is that in order for end-user computing to be effectively leveraged, IS and business unit managers must both take responsibility for its management. In many of today's organizations, end-user computing has become institutionalized, which means that it is being managed as an integral part of the mainstream computing environment within the organization.

THE EMERGENCE OF USER APPLICATION DEVELOPMENT

To those readers who were in secondary schools less than a decade ago, systems development by users may appear to be an obvious first choice for data capture, retrieval, and analysis. Just as calculators have become standard tools for secondary school and college students for mathematical calculations, computers are the most important productivity tools for today's knowledge workers.

However, to the typical IS manager of the early 1980s, end-user computing using a microcomputer may have seemed like a trivial, temporary phenomenon. After all, the first microcomputers were distributed by mail order to hobbyists as electronic toys with limited processing and storage capabilities compared to the mainframe and minicomputers being used in the business world. In fact, IS managers had already begun to invest in end-user tools for these much more reliable computer platforms by the early 1980s. However, the IS manager's perceptions began to change

when IBM introduced its first desktop microcomputer in late 1981: the personal computer, or PC. At that time, IBM was the premier source of computer systems and services for the Fortune 500. The fact that IBM thought microcomputers could play a significant business role became a wake-up call for the more progressive IS manager.

Driving Forces

The growth of end-user computing was primarily an end-user "pull" phenomenon. Well into the mid-1980s, business managers in some organizations were purchasing PCs on office equipment budgets with the knowledge or support of IS professionals. Other IS managers viewed IBM's early desktop PCs—with less than 640K RAM and only floppy disk storage devices—as similar to business calculators; they were aware of PC purchases but took a hands-off approach. Much less typical was the firm in which the IS organization "pushed" for the purchase of microcomputers by business managers.

Despite this lack of IS push, there was a widespread diffusion of microcomputers into businesses within the first decade after IBM's first personal computer was introduced. Kaiser (1993) has identified four primary causes for this phenomenon (see Figure 12.1):

The first causal force, the proliferation of low-cost microcomputers for desktops, is a characteristic of the Information Age described in Chapter 1. The second cause refers to advances in nonprocedural languages (4GLs like FOCUS, query languages like SQL) that end-users can learn to use well after only a two-day workshop. Some of today's user-friendly database tools have query-by-example interfaces that don't even require the user to know SQL. The third cause was also mentioned in Chapter 1: an increased

1. Availability of low-cost microcomputers
2. High-level languages for end-users
3. Computer literacy among college graduates and professionals
4. Increase in systems development backlog

Figure 12.1 Four Driving Forces for End-User Computing. (Adapted from Kaiser, 1993)

computer literacy among college graduates and professionals. Kaiser points out that whereas in the 1960s only engineers typically received computer training, by the 1990s the typical college-bound high school senior already had some basic computer skills. Further, by the early 1990s literally every business school had invested in microcomputer labs and undergraduate courses that included education in spreadsheet tools at a minimum. This tremendous rise in computer literacy of the U.S. workforce continues to fuel the growth of jobs in business requiring computer skills.

The fourth cause—an increase in the systems development backlog—may be less intuitively obvious to you. The term **systems backlog** is used by IS professionals to refer to systems development requests by business users that are not currently being worked on by members of the IS organization. By the early 1980s, the organizations that had their own IS specialists also typically had two types of systems development backlogs: a visible backlog and an invisible backlog (Gremillion and Pyburn, 1983). The so-called visible backlog included systems project requests (usually with initial estimates for IS resources required) that were on the organization's formal to-do list. When and if IS resources became available, the projects on the backlog would become active projects. However, the business manager knew that many of the projects on the formal backlog list would never be worked on; these projects hadn't received a high enough priority ranking for the current budget year, and next year's new project requests might also be ranked ahead of this year's projects on the growing backlog.

Because of this typically large visible backlog of systems requests, there was also an invisible backlog: systems projects desired by business management, but not even formally requested by them due to the expectation that they would receive too low a priority ranking to be worked on and/or would not be completed in time to be useful. This imbalance between the business demand for IS resources and the IS organization's supply of resources caused some tensions between the two groups. It also sometimes resulted in highly political maneuverings by members of the cross-functional committees (often called steering committees) that determined the systems project priorities on a periodic basis. As user demands grew in the 1980s, the visible and invisible backlogs also grew. According to Kaiser, this unmet demand helped to fuel the desire for micro-computers and application development tools for end-users so that small applications and reports could be developed quickly, as needed, without IS specialists.

According to Kaiser, the four conditions listed in Figure 12.1 also created an environment that challenged the traditional model of organizational computing in which the IS organization alone had the IT expertise with which to support the naïve user. Computer-literate user-managers began to demand the capabilities to support their own data access, reporting, and decision analysis needs. In time, the organizational experts in the use of the new productivity tools (such as spreadsheets on a microcomputer) were typically not found in an IS organization, but in a business department.

Nevertheless, although the typical reader of this textbook is likely to be a regular user of personal productivity software, not every worker is an eager end-user of microcomputers. Not every employee finds today's office suites—with graphical user interfaces that may have dozens of icons—"user friendly" at all. Further, because of the newness of this phenomenon, a large number of managers and other end-users in today's organizations are self-taught end-users or are users who have had only minimal formal education in computer literacy or tool training. In fact, many of today's senior managers have only rudimentary keyboarding skills and may rely heavily on clerical support staff. Some of these managers and other employees even opt not to be end-users of computers at all. For example, some senior managers may choose not be direct users of their e-mail, but instead use their support staff as "chauffeurs." When there are other ways to accomplish the same task, there may be some very good reasons for a potential end-user to refuse to voluntarily adopt computing tools. Although not all employees can refuse to adopt a computing tool, some may wish to take a stance as strong as one writer (see sidebar "Why I Am Not Going to Buy a Computer").

Types of User-Developed Applications

Let's look now at what types of business applications are being developed by end-users. We will describe these applications according to three dimensions: the business activity being supported by the application, the application scope or level at which it is being used within the organization, and the degree to which an

WHY I AM NOT GOING TO BUY A COMPUTER

I am a writer. A number of people have told me that I could greatly improve things by buying a computer. My answer is that I am not going to do it. I have several reasons, and they are good ones.

The first one is I would hate to think that my work as a writer could not be done without a direct dependence on strip-mined coal [used by energy corporations]. How could I write conscientiously against the rape of nature if I were, in the act of writing, implicated in the rape?

The second one is I do not admire the computer manufacturers a great deal more than I admire energy industries. I have seen their advertisements, attempting to seduce struggling or failing farmers into the belief that they can solve their problems by buying yet another piece of expensive equipment. I do not see that computers are bringing us one step nearer to anything that does matter to me: peace, economic justice, ecological health, political honesty, family and community stability, good work.

My final and perhaps my best reason for not owning a computer is that I do not wish to fool myself. I disbelieve, and therefore strongly resent, the assertion that I or anybody else could write better or more easily with a computer than with a pencil. I do not see why I should not be as scientific about this as the next fellow: when somebody has used a computer to write work that is demonstrably better than Dante's, and when this better is demonstrably attributable to the use of a computer, then I will speak of computers with a more respectful tone of voice, though I still will not buy one.

[Adapted from Berry, 1990]

---

end-user developed application is integrated to mainstream applications (interconnectedness).

Business Activity In the earlier chapters, we introduced several kinds of managerial support tasks for which end-users typically develop applications, including information queries, reporting, model building and analysis, statistical data analysis, and expert systems. In a recent survey of end-user computing in the grocery industry, applications associated with computer-aided design, computer-aided instruction, and process control were also included. User developers are therefore not found just in administrative

offices, but also on the plant floor or even at a remote customer site.

In the mid-1990s, a new type of user-developed application emerged: Web home pages. By using special Web technologies or new versions of word processors to generate HTML code, end-users are developing home pages for either intracompany use (intranets) or for access by anyone traversing the World Wide Web.

Application Scope As discussed above, many user-developed applications are used for personal decision-making only, but some user-developed applications are used by workers throughout a business department or even by workers in multiple departments. This difference in application scope is important to recognize when making decisions about how to manage end-user computing. For example, the following definitions are based on Pyburn (1986–1987):

- *Personal applications* are developed and used (operated) by the primary user for personal decision-making, often replacing work formerly done manually.
- *Departmental applications* may be developed by a single user but are operated and used (and may be enhanced) by multiple users in a department. Often departmental applications evolve from applications originally developed for personal use.
- *Corporate applications* are used by multiple users across a number of departments.

Pyburn also points out that the risks associated with user-developed applications are not the same across these three types. Personal applications typically have the least risk, whereas organizational applications have the greatest. Although the organizational exposure, or risk, due to the use of an end-user developed application also depends on other factors (which will be discussed below), control policies and procedures for end-user computing should be designed to take into account the scope of the application and the level at which the application is being used. For example, some firms make the distinction between applications that are developed for personal use only and those used by more than one person.

Home pages that are part of an external Web site for a manufacturing or service organization, for example, typically are reviewed by an individual or council within the organization; a firm's communications, public relations, and legal departments in particular may be concerned about both the content and overall image conveyed. Similar concerns may exist for more traditional applications.

Interconnectedness   The interconnectedness of an end-user application also varies. As shown in Figure 12.2, the interconnectedness dimension helps distinguish early end-user applications from today's client/server applications (Huff, Munro, and Martin, 1988). The stage one, early microcomputer applications were typically spreadsheets developed by accounting and financial professionals to replace manual methods. These applications were typically run on **stand-alone** microcomputers; spreadsheet templates and data therefore couldn't be shared with others over a network. These spreadsheets may also have made use of data from other computerized applications, but there was no electronic link with these sources; instead, data were manually rekeyed by the user into the application.

The first stage of application integration was accomplished via the so-called "sneaker network" (files stored on hand-carried diskettes). The next stage of integration was to electronically connect with corporate databases. Prior to the diffusion of reliable local area networks at the end of the 1980s, file transfers via a mainframe or minicomputer network were common enhancements to stand-alone applications. The final stage of integration, distributed integration, is becoming more of a reality today as organizations implement client/server environments. Data can be accessed from multiple distributed servers throughout the organization, including mainframe database servers.

The above three dimensions—business activity, application scope, and interconnectedness—are ways that managers can characterize their organization's existing portfolio of user-developed applications. Our discussion of the different types of user-developed applications also highlights the fact that most organizations have a diverse range of end-user computing activities. This suggests that a totally centralized, "one-size-fits-all" approach to end-user computing management may not be the best approach in most organizations. We will return to this topic later in this chapter.

Stage	Extent of Interconnectedness
1. Isolation	Little or no exchange of data or programs with other applications.
2. Stand-alone	Applications operate in a stand-alone fashion; data entered into an application is keyed in manually.
3. Manual Integration	Data is transferred from application to application by manual interchange, such as hand-carried diskette (the sneaker network) or manually controlled file transfers over an electronic network.
4. Automated Integration	Applications connect with one or more corporate databases and routinely transfer data between microcomputer workstations and mainframe databases using automated processes designed into the applications.
5. Distributed Integration	Applications are part of a network that accesses data distributed throughout the organization; distinctions concerning the location of data (e.g., whether on a microcomputer or mainframe) disappear.

Figure 12.2 Stages of Connectedness. (Huff, Munro, and Martin, 1988)

THE USER–DEVELOPED VERSUS IS–DEVELOPED DECISION

As we have seen for each of the other alternative methods for acquiring new systems—SDLC, prototype, and package purchase—systems development by non-IS specialists involves some organizational trade-offs. Here we first discuss the potential advantages and potential disadvantages for systems development by users (see Figure 12.3). Based on this discussion, we then present a list of factors that should be considered by managers faced with the choice of user-developed versus IS-developed solutions for a given information need.

Advantages

User application development presents the opportunity for users to have total control over the initial development of the application, as well as any ongoing maintenance. Rivard and Huff (1988) found that this independence from the IS department was perceived by user-managers to be a key advantage. First, it meant that the users did not have to wait for IS resources to be available to work on their project; the business manager could determine when the development effort would be initiated. Second, it meant users did not have to explain their information requirements to someone who may not understand the business problem; typically, users are able to communicate more easily among themselves than with an IS specialist—especially if that IS specialist has only minimal knowledge about the area of business for which the application will be used. Third, it meant that the

users had total control over the systems budget. This increased flexibility was very attractive to the business manager: There is no cost chargeback from an internal IS organization or contractual obligations with an outside vendor if the manager's own employees develop the application. Fourth, for managers in organizations where a cross-functional committee determined priorities for systems projects for multiple business units, it meant that they could avoid the risk of having their systems request turned down or delayed because it was not given a high enough priority. In other words, user-manager control over the development of a new system produces a more timely response to business unit needs.

Another advantage associated with user developed systems is the possibility of greater user acceptance of the application solution. User-developed systems typically entail no IS involvement in the systems effort. End-users tend to be more involved throughout the process because they may be physically near the user developer. User-developed systems are also typically smaller systems and may be developed using a prototyping process, which involves significant end-user involvement. Because the application is totally "owned" by the business unit, user application development also eliminates the possibility of "we-they" finger-pointing.

The last two advantages shown in Figure 12.3 are clearly benefits for the organization as a whole. When an application can be developed by non-IS professionals and IS expertise is a scarce resource, then it is advantageous to free up IS resources to work on projects within the business that require higher levels of IS skills. This advantage was recognized by the prolific IS guru James Martin at the time of the introduc-

ADVANTAGES
Increased user control over systems development project
Increased user acceptance of systems solution
Frees up IS resources (and may reduce development backlog)
Increased IT management knowledge of users

DISADVANTAGES
Loss of quality controls
Increased operational risks due to developer turnover
Potential labor/time inefficiencies
Loss of integration opportunities/capabilities

Figure 12.3 Advantages and Disadvantages

tion of the IBM microcomputer. In his book entitled *Application Development Without Programmers* (1982), he shocked many IS professionals by advocating a large number of powerful software products for end users—including fourth-generation languages and report writers. McLean (1979) also was an early predictor of the rise of application development by non-IS professionals. The costs of end-user computing via a mainframe computer platform had become low enough to provide a compelling business case for user-developed applications.

> *The continuing drop in cost of computers has now passed the point at which computers have become cheaper than people."*
>
> —James Martin, 1982

The last advantage listed in Figure 12.3 is also a motivator for a textbook, such as this one, that focuses on what managers need to know about IT management. As mentioned in Chapter 1, information technology (IT) is increasingly being recognized as a strategic resource for most organizations. Recent research has shown a correlation between the IT management knowledge of key *user-managers* and the progressive use of IT within that firm (Boynton, Zmud, and Jacobs, 1994). That is, in order to leverage IT for strategic advantage, organizations need IT-savvy business managers. User-managers become more knowledgeable about IT when they are business sponsors of a new systems project, a major participant in a systems project effort, or the user developer of a system. Every organization should be striving to increase the IT management knowledge of its users, and user application development is an experience that can contribute to this long-range goal.

Disadvantages

The first disadvantage shown in Figure 12.3 should be a major concern for user-managers as well as IS managers: the potential loss of quality controls. By virtue of their training, IS professionals are aware of the potential pitfalls in designing an information system. For example, IS professionals are trained to think about input controls, output controls, and processing controls. As in any profession, applications developed by those with less training and experience will, on the average, be of lower quality. Undetected bugs in processing logic, the lack of audit trails, inadequate

backup and security procedures, and undocumented systems are much more common among user-developed systems than those developed by a trained IS professional (Schultheis and Sumner, 1991). According to a Price Waterhouse study, about one-third of spreadsheets may contain errors (Panko, 1996). These shortcomings support the worst fears of the IS community and obviously should be of concern to the user-manager as well (see sidebar "Errors in Spreadsheets" later in this chapter).

In addition to quality concerns about the application design, user-developed systems also involve increased operational risks. In other words, user-developed applications that are used on an ongoing basis are "production systems" from the IS perspective. However, the responsibilities for operations and continued maintenance of a user-developed application typically belong to the business unit that owns it. This becomes an especially important consideration when the application is being used as a decision support tool for decisions with high impact or as a transaction processing and reporting system at the workgroup or department level. The loss of the original user developer due to transfer or promotion can occur with little advance notice, which can result in a crisis situation for the business unit. For database applications in particular, the loss of the original user developer often results in abandoned user-developed systems due to the lack of resident operational and systems maintenance expertise within the business unit (Klepper and Sumner, 1990).

Of course, the user-manager needs to assess the potential inefficiencies due to systems being developed by users with little or no IS training. First, depending on the type and size of the application, there is an organizational cost associated with having users spend considerable amounts of time on what may be much more efficiently achieved by an IS professional. There is a learning curve associated with end-user development. Second, when systems are developed outside of a centralized IS organization, the likelihood of "reinventing the wheel" is considerable. Duplicated efforts within the same department, let alone across business units within an organization, are well documented. A similar problem is faced by organizations with decentralized IS units that do not have mechanisms in place to identify duplicated efforts. This type of organizational inefficiency is exacerbated at the end-user level.

Another potentially serious problem for a business unit and the organization as a whole is the possible proliferation of unit-specific solutions that inhibit information access and sharing in the future. When business units throughout an organization independently develop applications using software and data definitions of their own choosing, the result is dozens or hundreds of isolated islands of automation with unsharable data and with potentially conflicting information reports based on the same transaction data. (Incompatibilities across departmental systems are also a problem faced by organizations when business units have the authority to independently purchase systems packages.) Organizational risks increase considerably when user-developed solutions are allowed to proliferate without adequate coordination.

The challenge in managing user application development is to find the best combination of tradeoffs: to maximize the potential advantages without creating unacceptable levels of risk associated with the disadvantages. Finding the right balance requires good partnering relationships between IS and business management, as well as knowledgeable user-managers.

Key Decision Factors

Given this list of advantages and disadvantages, let's turn now to the issue of when an application should be developed by users who are not IS professionals. Managers can consider the factors listed below in order to assess the feasibility and potential effectiveness of a user-developed solution for a specific application need (see Figure 12.4). Although this list works best for assessing the tradeoffs within organizations that have their own IS professionals, smaller organizations and other organizations who do not have their own IS resources can use this list for assessing the tradeoffs between user-developed systems and contracting with an outside vendor with IT expertise.

Several overall characteristics of the application to be developed should be considered. The scope, size, and usage of the application should be assessed first. In many situations, these will become key factors. For example, if the application is being developed for personal use for a one-time decision by a marketing analyst, a user-developed solution may be the optimal choice. However, if the application is to be used by more than one department on a regular or perhaps daily basis, the application may be a poor candidate for end-user development.

The potential impact of the intended application, including the potential risk exposure for the business unit and the organization as a whole, can also be a dominant factor. In some situations, the potential importance is hard to assess before the application is developed and actually used. Nevertheless, the organizational risks are greater when high-impact applications are developed, operated, and maintained without the benefit of IS professional expertise. In fact, assessing the risk exposure of a user-developed application

Application Characteristics
Scope (personal, departmental, organizational)
Criticality/Impact (risk exposure)
Size and usage (one-time, periodic, ongoing)
System complexity:
    Commonality of the problem
    Problem structure
    Interconnectedness
    Tool sophistication

Individual and Organizational Characteristics
Skills, experience, and availability of user developers
Skills, experience, and availability of IS professional developers
Status of support and control for user application development

Figure 12.4 Decision Factors: User-Developed versus IS-Developed Systems

should not be just a one-time activity that occurs when deciding whether or not to develop an application without IS specialists. Rather, the assessment of application impact must be an ongoing management responsibility.

The remaining application characteristic, system complexity, has several dimensions. The commonality of the problem can be used to determine the likelihood that a packaged system solution may already exist. If the application requires integration with other applications and/or involves the use of more complex and sophisticated technologies, an IS-developed solution may be the only suitable long-term solution. However, a stand-alone user-developed application might be developed first and then subsequently used as a prototype for further development by IS specialists.

Less clear is the best solution for a difficult-to-explain (ill-structured) business problem that requires decision support on a periodic or ongoing basis. For the ill-structured problem, a combination of business and IS professional expertise may be the best solution. On the other hand, if simple end-user tools can be used, it may be more effective for the system to be entirely user developed. In addition to the other dimensions of system complexity, the size of the application could be a key determinant for the methodology choice (also see the next section).

Individual and organizational characteristics need to be assessed along with application characteristics. These factors involve assessing the tradeoffs in terms of the skills and experience of both the potential user developers and the potential IS human resources that could be assigned to the project. Another consideration is the availability of these human resources for work on the application, in relation to the time constraints faced by the users. As discussed previously, reduced dependence on IS professionals can be a considerable advantage if user developers have or can be trained to have the skills required for a given application. Many non-IS professionals have considerable IT-related expertise and may also even have some training in IS development methodologies. The difficulty is that sometimes the user-manager may not have the knowledge to adequately assess the skills needed before the application is developed or to assess the current skill levels of his/her own employees. Consultation with IS experts inside or outside the organization may be required to adequately assess these factors.

The final factor, the status of the support and control available to an organization's user developers, will be better understood after we discuss the range of support services and control policies and procedures that may or may not be available in today's organizations (see "Strategies and Tactics for Managing End-User Computing" section later in this chapter).

USER DEVELOPMENT METHODOLOGY

When systems are developed by IS specialists, the methodology used to develop the application is defined by the IS organization. One of the responsibilities of the IS project leader is to monitor the status of the project according to the agreed-upon process steps appropriate for the application being developed.

For user-developed systems, the user developer (or user-manager) typically decides the process to be used and is responsible for executing that process. In large user-developed system efforts, a project team may be established with users playing all of the user and IS roles we saw being used for the Systems Development Life Cycle (SDLC) and prototype approaches for IS-developed applications.

Panko (1988) suggests that the most appropriate methodology for a user-developed application depends upon the size and complexity of the application, as well as the target users (see Figure 12.5). Small and simple applications that will be used only by the developer should be developed with a straightforward, but "collapsed" life cycle approach. When the application is for personal use, but is somewhat larger and more complex, a more disciplined approach needs to be taken. However, this need not be entirely sequential. The Definition phase would involve thinking through what you want the system to do (inputs, processing, outputs) and then constructing it and testing it. It could be tried out and then modified by the developer (who is also the user) as needed. However, a disciplined approach should be taken to ensure that modifications are adequately tested.

If the application is for a workgroup or department, other users should be involved in all three phases, with or without a formal project team. If a large, complex system is to be developed for multiple

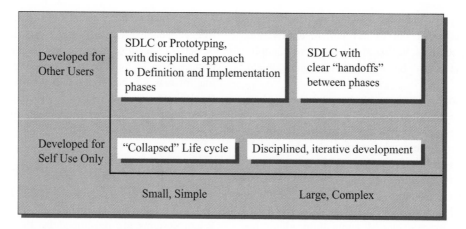

Figure 12.5 Guidelines for Choosing the Development Process. (Based on Panko, 1989)

users, it should be developed using a full SDLC process, with clear user and developer roles to ensure a high-quality application. The initial phase should also include an assessment of whether the project should be user developed or IS developed, using the factors discussed here (see Figure 12.4). This assumes, however, that the user developers are knowledgeable about the SDLC methodology and have the systems and project management skills to ensure the development of a high-quality application.

Prototyping is especially well suited for user-developed systems because the end-users may be close by, the requirements may not be totally clear, and the application may be small. Today's end-user development tools support prototyping well. As described in Chapter 10, a basic set of requirements should first be defined in order to develop the prototype. Multiple users should try out the prototype and suggest changes, and the prototype should be modified until there is agreement that the application meets the business users' needs.

In the sidebar "Tales of User Developers," three user developers describe the processes they followed for their first multi-user applications.

A key learning point for most first-time user developers is not to move to the Construction phase, or building of the prototype, too soon. User developers are likely to underestimate what it takes to define a system's requirements, especially if multiple users are involved in the process. (The IS professional is typi-

cally trained in systems analysis techniques and is in a better position to determine the level of basic system requirements needed before proceeding to build a prototype.) The larger and more complex the system, the more critical the need to devote effort to the up-front analysis (definition) in general. In the Construction phase, the major components need to be identified, as well as how they fit together. A good design should also be easy to change and should take into account security features such as application backup and recovery controls.

Whatever approach you use, IS professionals have learned that a simple system that works reliably is much more useful than an elaborate failure. It is therefore often a good idea to start with a limited version of the system and then to expand it after some experience with this initial version. Indeed, user-developed systems can stimulate ideas for larger systems for competitive advantage that may be developed by IS professionals.

Guidelines for User Developers

Figure 12.6 lists a number of important questions that can be used as a guide for user developers, especially when developing larger systems that may include transaction processing. The first four items are questions to be answered when defining the requirements of the system. High-level answers to the next two questions are also an important part of the definition

TALES OF USER DEVELOPERS

CONTACT MANAGEMENT SYSTEM

This program was designed to better manage the contacts each member of the C workgroup has with external contacts, in order to help improve the efficiency and productivity of all members. The Contact Management System stores information about employees in the C workgroup, contacts at various sites, and the sites themselves. Contacts with other sites are captured and categorized according to their contact method. Information about a contact includes the parties involved, the time and date, the subjects discussed, and a synopsis of the communication. Reports include all contacts by individuals within a given time period, contacts on a specific topic, and contacts regarding a specific project. Visual Basic and Access were the primary tools used for this application.

The methodology used was a modified software development life cycle approach using prototyping. I discussed the requirements of the program with several competent peers who had a desire to be a player in the development of the system. We met and discussed potential uses for the system and discussed requirements for expansion of the system to meet future goals. We utilized Visual Basic's rapid development environment to "test drive" possible screen layouts. This worked quite well, as the others were able to actually see rather than just listen to ideas and concepts for the user interface. As with most projects, this one did not progress as rapidly as predicted; the current version lacks some of the overly ambitious original goals. These will be implemented in the near future in a later release. There is a high level of anticipation for a fully functional product among the users who are currently using the program to enter the data to create the database. Their use of the product at this time is helping to finalize the interface for the final release.

TRACKING DATABASE

This application is a Lotus Notes project tracking database for my workgroup. It is used to track activities between my workgroup in the parent company related to current and prospective customers. In my workgroup, projects are segmented by customer. The process starts with a customer inquiry, followed by actual work done, and concluding with problem resolution. With the current version of this application, my group can track different kinds of activities with a customer: action items, call reports, incoming correspondence, internal correspondence, outgoing correspondence, meeting reports, and miscellaneous activity. The database was tailored from a template provided with Lotus Notes to meet the needs of my workgroup.

I employed the prototyping methodology. Before beginning the project, my manager and I discussed the tracking system I envisioned; I convinced him that this application would help us manage our work more effectively. In the requirements definition phase, a colleague and I developed a list of the requirements for our tracking database. During this phase, we reviewed the Lotus Notes tracking database template to verify the compatibility of our requirements with those of the template. Many of the requirements we desired, like check boxes for project type and technology type, and activities such as internal e-mail, were not a part of the Notes template. However, many of the structural needs of our system were included in the template.

I spent most of the first couple of days working with the Lotus Notes tool to become proficient as a user before diving into the developer world. I wanted to be sure I fully understood *how* Lotus Notes worked, how users interfaced with it, and what its capabilities were. The Notes tool is very intuitive and, after only a couple of days, I began work on the tailored project tracking database. My goal was to have a usable prototype as quickly as possible so I could take it to three key users: my manager and two colleagues. I chose one colleague who was very computer literate and one that seems to merely know where the "ON" switch is on his workstation. I had a usable prototype in three days.

As expected, the majority of my effort was *after* the working prototype was rolled out to key users. While using the new tracking system, the key users were able to identify several items they now wanted in the system and also found a few bugs. The bugs were corrected quickly but the changes/additions to the system required several iterations. Within a few weeks, we had a fully operational system.

As with any application where the developer resides within the department, new iterations, though minor, continue. Tweaking the tracking system in this manner has allowed us to reach a point where the application is so useful that our entire department depends heavily on it for up-to-the minute information on projects.

[Evening MBA students, Indiana University]

DEFINITION PHASE

What outputs should the system produce?
What processes are necessary to produce the needed outputs?
What should the system be able to do?
What input data are needed?
  How can data best be obtained?
  How can data accuracy, completeness, and timeliness be assured?

CONSTRUCTION PHASE

What data must be stored in the system?
  How should data be organized?
  How can data be maintained?
How can this system be decomposed into modules?
  How do these modules relate to each other?
  In what sequence should the modules be executed?
How can the system be recovered if anything happens?
Is an audit trail necessary?
What level of documentation is necessary?

Figure 12.6 Questions to Guide User Developers

process: determination of how the data can best be obtained and how data accuracy, completeness, and timeliness can be assured. Can the needed data be obtained from another system, or will the data have to be collected and keyed into this system? If the data must be keyed into the system, how can accuracy and completeness be controlled? If the data are to be extracted from other systems, separate modules may need to be constructed in order to perform this function. Some way of coordinating the processing across these applications must also be considered; for example, today's office suites allow for automatic linking of database tables to spreadsheets that use these data for decision analysis. The data flow diagrams and other analysis tools discussed in Chapter 9 may prove helpful in these definition tasks.

Figure 12.6 also provides questions for the Construction phase. Designing the data to be stored in the system is a critical activity. One must decide what different files or tables are required and what data elements will be stored in each record. Designing a database structure is one of the most difficult, and least understood, tasks for novice user developers. The discussion on relational database design and data modeling techniques in Chapter 14 should prove useful for these tasks. However, this is an area where access to IS consultants or a user developer experienced in database applications can help avoid a costly reworking of a poorly designed system.

How each record is to be maintained must also be planned—how new data are to be entered, how obsolete data are to be removed, and how necessary changes to the data will be made. Today's PC-based database software packages (see Chapter 3) make these tasks relatively easy for the end-user. For example, for a customer name-and-address file, the database software provides a user-friendly interface for entering new customers, removing (deleting) the records of former customers, and changing data (such as customer address) when necessary. Data entry "forms" can be developed to facilitate these tasks when the tables are large. A frequent error of a new user developer is to use a spreadsheet program for an application that requires data-management functions only available with a database management system.

It is also important to consider how to recover the system if a file is destroyed; if the application is stored on a server and a multi-user version of the system is being used, some backup and recovery procedures should already be in place. The user developer needs to assess whether or not these are sufficient. An audit trail is a way of tracing activity through the system to make sure that it has handled each transaction appropriately, according to organizational and accounting rules. This is closely related to the recovery process, and the provisions made for recovery may provide a basic audit trail.

Significant time should be devoted to system testing to make sure an application does what it should. In particular, one needs to design a rigorous test process. The lack of adequate testing for decision support applications can lead to serious consequences for a business. Errors in spreadsheets, for example, are known to have caused losses of hundreds of thousands to millions of dollars (Galletta et al., 1996). Although spreadsheet audit programs and features are more

prevalent today, research shows that organizations need to devote much more attention to spreadsheet error detection: Some consultants have claimed that one-third of spreadsheet models contain errors (Panko, 1996). An IS professional typically does extensive planning before coding and engages in extensive debugging of programs. In contrast, the spreadsheet developer typically has little training in debugging techniques and may rely wholly on self-testing. The sidebar "Errors in Spreadsheets" describes the types of errors that are typical in spreadsheets, and some reasons why they are so common.

ERRORS IN SPREADSHEETS

End-users produce countless spreadsheet models each year, often to guide mission-critical decisions. In recent years, several cases of spreadsheet errors have been reported. Given the reluctance of organizations to publicize embarrassments, these few cases may be only the tip of the iceberg. Some consultants have claimed something like a third of all operational spreadsheet models contain errors. One Price Waterhouse consultant reported auditing four large spreadsheet models for a client and finding 128 errors.

Several academic researchers have done experiments to identify the different types of errors contained in spreadsheets. Even in relatively simple spreadsheets that do not require specialized business area knowledge, laboratory subjects made errors in 38% of their models. In a debugging phase, only 16% of the subjects who had made spreadsheet errors were able to identify and fix all their errors. Every research study known to us that looked for errors in user-developed systems has found them, and found them in abundance.

Spreadsheet errors can be of two types: quantitative and qualitative. Most researchers have looked at quantitative errors, which include the following:

- Mechanical errors: typing errors, pointing errors, and other simple slips. Mechanical errors can be frequent, but they have a high chance of being caught by the person making the error.
- Logic errors: incorrect formulas due to choosing the wrong algorithm or creating the wrong formulas to implement the algorithm. Pure logic errors result from a lapse in logic, whereas domain logic errors occur because the developer lacks the required business area knowledge. Some logic errors are also easier to

identify than others: easy-to-proof errors have been called Eureka errors, and difficult-to-proof errors have been called Cassandra errors.
- Omission errors: things left out of the model that should be there. They often result from a misinterpretation of the situation. Human factors research has shown that omission errors have low detection rates.

Qualitative errors are flaws that do not produce immediate quantitative errors. Some qualitative errors lead to quantitative errors during later "what if" analyses or when updates are made to a spreadsheet model. Other qualitative errors make debugging difficult, may cause users to misinterpret the model's results, or make maintenance difficult, leading to increased development costs.

The spreadsheet developer's pattern of work practices appears to be a major cause of application errors. Mandated programming practices for IS professionals—such as preplanning and post-development debugging—are not that common among user developers. Even such simple things as using cell protection are far from universal. Many spreadsheet developers apparently do not attempt to reduce their spreadsheet errors systematically; it also is not a common practice to have others check their programs. Because research on IS professionals has found that spotting errors by inspection is difficult for the original programmer, user developers should regularly involve others in debugging their applications.

To err is human. We do not make mistakes all the time, but we consistently make a certain number, even when we are being careful. To reduce error rates requires aggressive techniques—similar to the discipline followed by developers of more complex applications.

[Adapted from Panko, 1996, and Panko and Halverson, 1996]

Complex, modular systems also require more planning and coordination for testing, installation, and training. As seen in earlier chapters, organizational changes often accompany the implementation of new department-wide systems; as with larger, more complex systems, user-manager attention to implementation planning is important for system acceptance and usage. If the system is to be implemented in multiple releases, choosing the modules to include in the initial version is also a critical planning and design task.

The documentation that is necessary for a user-developed application depends upon the characteristics of the application. Personal systems frequently have little or no formal documentation; however, if this is a system that a successor to the current user developer will also be expected to use, formal documentation should be provided and kept up-to-date; it should also include documentation that is not embedded in the application itself, in the event of a system crash. The documentation for a multi-user system, operated by people in different workgroups, may require the same level of documentation as a system produced by IS specialists. If the user-developed system will be audited, it is obviously a good idea to consult with these auditors while defining and constructing the system to ensure that the organization's auditing concerns are adequately addressed.

Even with education in IS development methodologies, the user developer typically undergoes a significant learning curve. This learning involves both tool learning and process learning. In the sidebar "Lessons Learned" the same knowledge workers who described their processes in the sidebar "Tales of User Developers" share the lessons that they learned while developing their first multi-user applications. In both instances, the user developers were also developing applications in which they were using an end-user development tool that was new to them.

The Development Roles

In systems development by users, the IS organization typically plays no more than a consultant role. The importance of the consultant role depends on some of the factors shown in Figure 12.4: characteristics of the application being developed, as well as the skills and experience of the user developer(s) involved. In large organizations in the early 1980s it was not uncommon for no one in the IS organization to be an expert in an

---

LESSONS LEARNED

CONTACT MANAGEMENT SYSTEM

During the development of this project, a number of important lessons were learned. Most important was the need to stay in touch with the end-users of the product throughout the development cycle. Not only does this assure that their needs are being met and the program will be useful to their productivity, but it also entices excitement which is vital to the acceptance of the final product. Even with rapid development tools, the several months required to develop a quality product can be enough of a lapse in the anticipation of the end-users such that acceptance of the product is less than enthusiastic. Another valuable lesson learned was that when the program gets close to being completed is always when the intricate, hard-to-find bugs seem to be seen.

TRACKING DATABASE

One key lesson I learned in developing this system overshadows all others. I learned that managing user expectation is paramount to user satisfaction early in a project. My "key users" believed that since I had a prototype with the user screens developed very rapidly, that the workable system with "everything they wanted" would follow equally as fast. Another lesson I learned is the value of the prototyping methodology: It enabled our group to develop a powerful system with little time and little money invested.

[Evening MBA students, Indiana University]

---

end-user tool like a spreadsheet; in some organizations today, this situation may still exist. However, for database management systems, the skills needed are conceptual (e.g., understanding relational database concepts) as well as technological (e.g., knowing how a given tool works). Although an IS consultant may have little experience with a specific PC-based database tool, IS consultants may be very useful for developing a rigorous and flexible database design.

The roles of the user developer and user-manager are clearer: Essentially all of the roles described for IS-developed methodologies need to be played by the users alone. This means that technological expertise, as well as project management expertise, are requisite skills for the user organization. For many business users, project management is already a well-honed skill. However, user-managers and developers also need to be familiar with the basic steps of a life cycle process, both the advantages and pitfalls of alternative processes such as an iterative methodology, and some good models for documentation and recovery/auditing procedures.

Depending on the organizational context, it may also be the role of an IS organization and/or an internal auditing department to ensure that user-developed applications do not expose the organization to unacceptable levels of risk. We began this chapter by stating that in order for end-user computing to be effective at the individual, departmental, and overall organization levels, IS and business unit managers must develop a shared set of responsibilities that is appropriate for their organizational context. In the next section we present a framework to describe what some of these responsibilities might entail.

STRATEGIES AND TACTICS FOR MANAGING END–USER COMPUTING

Effective management of end-user computing requires an understanding of the diversity of application types being developed with today's microcomputer tools,

the perceived benefit/risk tradeoffs for systems development activities by user developers, and the knowledge to assess the skills of potential user developers. In addition, effective management of end-user computing requires management actions to support not only user developers, but also the end-users of all computer systems within the organization. Figure 12.7 presents a framework that can be used by managers to assess their strategic and tactical choices for leveraging end-user computing from an IS/business partnership perspective (Brancheau and Brown, 1993).

The individual-level box in Figure 12.7 lists four factors that characterize an individual application. All of these factors were addressed earlier in this chapter:

User developer:	the IT-related skills and application development experience
Task:	the business activities and scope of the problem being addressed
Tool:	the end-user tools accessible to the user developer, and their perceived characteristics
Development Process:	the application development methods and techniques used by the user developer

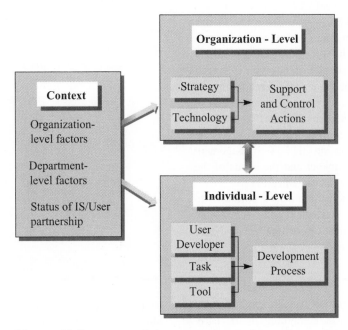

Figure 12.7 Framework for Leveraging End-user Computing. (Based on Brancheau and Brown, 1993)

The organization-level box in Figure 12.7 has three factors that are the responsibility of an organization's management—both IS and business managers. These organization-level factors are our focus in the remainder of this chapter:

Strategy: the strategic objectives and overall approach to end-user computing

Technology: the range and accessibility of end-user tools

Support and Control Actions: support services and control policies and procedures

The two-headed arrow between the organization-level and individual-level boxes in Figure 12.7 graphically portrays one of the key learning points here: There is no one best way to manage end-user computing. An organization's strategy and tactics for end-user computing need to take into account factors at the individual level. In addition, as indicated by the arrow from the context box, an organization's strategy and tactics need to take into account context characteristics, such as the way the IS department is organized, special characteristics of a given user department, and relationships between these two groups.

For example, if systems development groups have been decentralized to business unit control, there is a greater likelihood that "local" IS professionals will have a high degree of business-specific knowledge and may be more heavily relied on for consulting with user developers. Similarly, if a given user department is headed by a highly computer literate user-manager, there is a greater likelihood that a large amount of user application development activity will be occurring in that department. Whether or not that department should seek a high degree of independence from the IS organization depends on the IT management knowledge of the user-manager and the status of the IS/user partnership within the organization.

With this framework in mind, let's now turn to a discussion of some strategies and tactics that have been used by organizations to leverage end-user computing.

Strategies

Many IS organizations did not have an explicit strategy for managing end-user computing in the early 1980s (Benson, 1983; Rockart and Flannery, 1983).

At that time, both mainframe and microcomputer tools were being used for user application development, but end-user training and support for the mainframe tools was much more likely to be in place than end-user training for microcomputer tools. There were also few policies and procedures in place. In fact, many IS managers took a laissez-faire approach to end-user computing with desktop computers: IS managers may have signed-off on user requests to purchase some tools, but end-users were typically left on their own to install the equipment, learn the software, and manually enter their own data into a stand-alone application.

Expansion versus Control Philosophy   Today, most organizations have a strategy for managing end-user computing, but the specific strategy varies widely across organizations—even in those that have implemented a centralized support unit. Munro et al. (1987–1988) have documented four different management approaches being utilized in large organizations, based on two strategic levers: the degree to which the organization wants to expand end-user computing activities and the degree to which the organization wants to control these activities. Their 2-by-2 matrix can be found in Figure 12.8.

The *Laissez-faire* cell (low expansion, low control) was reported to be a common starting place for organizations in the 1980s. This was partly because end-user computing using microcomputers was a new phenomenon; as we discussed at the outset of this

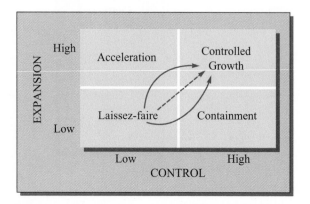

Figure 12.8 Expansion/Control Matrix. (Based on Munro et al., 1987–1988; Brancheau and Amoroso, 1990)

chapter, some IS managers initially viewed micro-computers as inexpensive tools similar to calculators. However, as end-user computing expanded, these firms then moved to either the Acceleration cell (high expansion, low control) or the Containment cell (high control, low expansion).

Firms in the *Acceleration* cell provide abundant central resources for end-user computing, with little concern about central controls. The objective is to enable each user to have the best possible opportunity to make his or her own decisions about end-user computing solutions to address business problems.

Firms in the *Containment* cell have opted to develop end-user computing slowly and carefully. The objective is to expand end-user computing activities within an established set of narrow growth boundaries. Very specific controls are put into place and users are required to carry out their computing activities within the range of choices permitted.

The *Controlled Growth* cell (high expansion, high control) is perceived to be the most advanced or mature approach. As shown in Figure 12.8, firms that begin in an Acceleration cell gradually add high levels of control as end-user computing becomes mainstream—institutionalized as another type of organizational computing. Similarly, firms that begin in a Containment cell gradually increase the level of support for end-user activities after the organization has learned how best to do so without increasing organizational risks.

Other researchers (Brancheau and Amoroso, 1990) have found evidence that some organizations actually take a middle ground or balanced approach. In Figure 12.8 we have added a dotted line to represent this alternative approach. This *Balanced* strategy involves starting with small amounts of resources and few controls and then increasing both resources and controls as the number of end-users and end-user applications increases.

Similar strategies to those in Figure 12.8 are being pursued by firms today for the management of Web applications developed by end-users. Some firms are applying significant resources and few controls (Acceleration), whereas others are taking a Containment approach. When Web technologies become mainstream and when the organization knows more about the pitfalls associated with developing this type of application, firms are expected to pursue a more

mature approach similar to a Controlled Growth approach.

Information Center Approach Beginning in the 1980s, many firms also implemented what became known as an **Information Center** strategy: the establishment of an independent support unit for managing end-user computing activities. Actually, the term Information Center (IC) was coined well before the utilization of microcomputers for user-developed business applications. The term was initially used to refer to an additional mainframe computer on which was loaded a full copy, or extract, of one or more production databases as well as software tools for end-users to develop queries, generate reports, and build decision models. According to a widely disseminated description of the IBM-Canada IC installation (Hammond, 1982), a typical ratio for IC/user staffing was one IC staff member for each 100 workstations.

However, by the late 1980s, the IC term was commonly used for any centralized support unit, often reporting to an IS organization, with a mandate to support end-user computing. ICs also typically are charged with implementing appropriate control policies and procedures to help ensure high-quality user-developed applications and low organizational exposure to risks.

A critical success factor for the effectiveness of an IC is its staffing. End-users value IC support staff that have not only technical competence, but also the following characteristics: the ability to relate well to users, good communication skills, and advocates of user developer self-sufficiency (Magal and Carr, 1988). The ability to provide quick turnaround time in response to user requests for help is also a key performance measure. Many IS managers also found that among the best sources for IC support staff who could provide skilled consulting and troubleshooting support were experienced developers in their own business units.

Alternatives to the Information Center Approach Other researchers (Gerrity and Rockart, 1986) have characterized the typical Information Center approach as IS-dominated and centralized, with too narrow a focus. These authors argue that organizations need to adopt a more comprehensive approach that takes a more distributed, shared philosophy about end-user computing management. They propose a "managed free economy" approach with five components:

1. A stated strategy	an explicit support and control philosophy
2. A user/IS working partnership	management responsibilities shared among IS and business managers
3. An integrated end-user support organization	instead of an independent centralized support unit separate from other IS units, the support organization should be integrated with other IS groups, especially systems development units
4. Targeting of critical end-user applications	support efforts should be focused on high impact applications that leverage the business expertise of end-users
5. Emphasis on end-user education	both IS and business managers should accept the responsibility for educating end-users in IS development processes, including quality controls; training on hardware and software tools alone is insufficient

Other authors have argued that a centralized support structure such as an Information Center is still a relevant vehicle for facilitating end-user computing, but that the managers of this support unit need to focus more on mainstream business concerns. For example, Karten (1990) argues for an IS/user partnership, but with a focus on high-payoff applications. Overall, IS managers with IC responsibilities need to take a more proactive focus in order to better leverage both scarce end-user support resources and increasing

numbers of business users with sophisticated IT knowledge and powerful end-user tools. Figure 12.9 summarizes Karten's descriptions of the older Stage One IC role versus its Stage Two role.

Whether or not an organization has a strategy that involves a centralized support structure such as an IC, all organizations need to establish an end-user computing environment that reflects its overall strategy. The major tactics for establishing this environment are described below.

Tactics

Two major categories of tactics are associated with implementing an end-user computing strategy: support services and control policies and procedures. After discussing these two categories of end-user computing management actions, we will discuss a third tactic: decisions about the locus of responsibility for support and control.

Support Services   A list of typical support services is provided in Figure 12.10. These services can be provided via a centralized support structure like an IC or via a more distributed approach, such as the managed free economy alternative described in the prior section.

Based on a survey of firms in the grocery industry (McLean, Kappelman, and Thompson, 1993), troubleshooting (hot-line support), consulting, training, and assistance in tool selection, maintenance, and upgrading were services offered by more than three-quarters of large firms by the early 1990s. Our list distinguishes between tool training and IS education; training refers to learning to use a specific tool,

STAGE ONE	STAGE TWO
Reactive services	Proactive services
Individual solutions, quick-and-dirty	Departmental solutions, in-depth
Product training	Business problem-solving
All needs supported	High-payoff needs supported
Computer literacy training	Information literacy education
One-way relationships	Alliance; IS/user partnerships

Figure 12.9 Evolution to a Stage Two Information Center Approach

- *Troubleshooting:* a hot line or help desk round-the-clock service
- *Consulting:* one-on-one application development consulting
- *Training:* technology (tool) training in classroom setting as well as self-paced delivery options
- *IS education:* development methodology education, backup procedures, etc.
- *Product research and evaluation:* investigating end-user tools and recommending products for purchase
- *Information sharing:* formalizing communications between support unit personnel and end-users, and across end-users. Typical content includes evaluations of new tools by IS or end-users, development "tips." Typical delivery mechanisms include newsletters, home pages on an intranet, and "user groups" that periodically meet.
- *Tool selection and purchasing:* hardware, software, local area networks
- *Tool installation, maintenance, & upgrading:* hardware, software, local area networks

Figure 12.10 Common Support Services

whereas what we refer to as IS education is not tied to a specific tool. Many firms in the 1990s also provided some IS education in their tool training classes. In the 1980s, the information sharing service was frequently delivered in a newsletter format; in the 1990s, the information sharing service is more likely to be an on-line service, perhaps via an intranet.

To save costs and keep focused on core services, several of these end-user support services may be outsourced. For example, many organizations have outsourced hardware installation and maintenance services, as well as the administration of local area networks (LANs). The outsourcing of classroom training has also become more popular as firms have begun to standardize on office suites of productivity tools. However, it should be noted that by turning over classroom training to an outside firm, an end-user support organization may lose a valuable opportunity for education on company-specific IS issues as well as the opportunity for establishing a support relationship with end-users. In other words, cost efficiencies alone should not be the only criterion for choosing whether to provide a service in-house or via a third-party supplier. Other firms have attempted to reduce classroom training costs by providing self-paced training alternatives, including just in time training (see following discussion).

Another frequently outsourced service is **help desk** (hot line) support. Some firms have contracted

with the software vendors themselves to provide support by telephone. However, the difficulties in staffing and supporting customer service desks in general are also faced by the software vendors. Like other business units with help desks, many IS organizations have implemented expert system applications to help their support personnel respond to telephone inquiries from end-users. One of the implementation problems with such systems is, of course, keeping them up-to-date. Some organizations use help desk positions as an initial training ground for entry-level IS positions; in a very short period of time, the new employee gains a first-hand appreciation for the difficulties faced by the organization's end-users.

Another trend that has impacted the provisioning of support services has been the embedding of support within the technology itself. For example, today's network administrators have an array of tools to help them troubleshoot hardware at a remote site from a central location. Other firms have invested in electronic support systems for just in time (JIT) training of workers in organizational procedures and uniform work practices associated with spreadsheet or other productivity tools (see sidebar on "JIT Training").

In addition, the software industry has made great strides in improving on-line support for the end-user. For example, tools with graphical user interfaces have more sophisticated help functions that include searching by key words as well as context-specific

JIT TRAINING

Developers of computer-based training (CBT) are hoping to learn something from electronic performance support systems (EPSSs). Applied most commonly in large customer-support applications, the concept is quite simple. Rather than relying on expensive classroom training or videos and typical CBT systems that remove learners from the real tasks they're trying to accomplish, EPSSs integrate training right into work by presenting support electronically and interactively on a worker's desktop computer. When workers need help with a problem or encounter new situations, they can, with a click on an icon, get as much or as little instruction as necessary. Vendors of client-based development tools and network management software are piloting integration of CBT directly into their products.

[Adapted from Moad, 1994]

help functions. The vendors of office suites have developed various types of on-line "assistants"—including wizards that help users create graphs in spreadsheet programs, create tables for common entities in database management programs, and format text, spreadsheets, data entry forms, and reports. In recent versions, vendors have provided cartoon characters that pop up to offer help to the user. "Tips" change based on recent keystrokes by the end-user using a particular application, and animated examples help to train end-users in a specific task. The trend is toward the development of autonomous agents, developed using artificial intelligence technologies, that become effective personal assistants that collaborate with the user (see sidebar "Personal Assistants").

Control Policies and Procedures   Management actions directed at controlling end-user computing typically take the form of policies or procedures. A list of common policies and procedures for end-user computing is provided in Figure 12.11. Many organizations place the primary responsibility for developing these policies and procedures in the hands of a centralized unit, such as an information center or other IS unit. In some organizations, a steering committee is responsible for establishing policies, including standards, whereas a centralized unit has the primary

responsibility for monitoring compliance with these standards. In other organizations, user-managers have considerable latitude in standard-setting and enforcement.

McLean, Kappelman, and Thompson (1993) found that more than three-quarters of the organizations they sampled had control policies and procedures for approvals for product acquisitions, keeping product (hardware) inventories, and guidelines for backups. Only about half of the organizations sampled reported having policies and procedures for inventory-

PERSONAL ASSISTANTS

Techniques from the field of AI, in particular so-called "autonomous agents," can be used to implement a complementary style of interaction. Instead of user-initiated interaction via commands and/or direct manipulation, the user is engaged in a cooperative process in which human and computer agents both initiate communication, monitor events, and perform tasks. The metaphor used is that of a *personal assistant* who is *collaborating with the user* in the same work environment. The assistant becomes gradually more effective as it learns the user's interests, habits, and preferences (as well as those of his or her community). Notice that the agent is not necessarily an interface between the computer and user. In fact, the most successful interface agents are those that do not prohibit the user from taking actions and fulfilling tasks personally.

Agents assist users in a range of different ways: they hide the complexity of difficult tasks, they perform tasks on the user's behalf, they can train or teach the user, they help different users collaborate, and they monitor events and procedures.

The set of tasks or applications an agent can assist in is virtually unlimited: information filtering, information retrieval, mail management, meeting scheduling, selection of books, movies, music, and so forth.

Two main problems have to be solved when building software agents. The first problem is that of *competence:* how does an agent acquire the knowledge it needs to decide when to help the user, what to help the user with, and how to help the user? The second problem is that of *trust:* how can we guarantee the user feels comfortable delegating tasks to an agent?

[Maes, 1994]

Specified (or recommended) product standards (hardware and software)
Guidelines (recommendations) for workstation ergonomics
Approval process for product purchases
Requirements for product inventorying
Upgrade procedures

Application quality review process
Guidelines to identify critical applications and data
Policies for corporate data access
Guidelines for program and data backup procedures
Requirements for audit trails
Documentation standards

Policies to control unauthorized access
Policies for unauthorized software copying
Virus protection procedures

Figure 12.11 Common Policies and Procedures

ing software, guidelines for identifying critical applications and data, and security controls. The degree to which organizational policies are mandates versus guidelines and the manner in which they are enforced can vary widely across organizations and even across different departments within the same organization (Speier and Brown, 1997).

The communication of standards to end-users is also an ongoing management issue. It is not unusual for an organization to do a better job of communicating end-user computing policies and procedures to its new workers than to its existing employees. This is because orientation programs for new employees are periodic events that provide a forum for communicating these policies. For existing employees, other communication channels need to be devised, and the use of periodic newsletters and printed guidelines in booklet form have met with mixed success. Today, electronic methods of communication about end-user computing policies and procedures are becoming more common. Control policies and procedural deadlines can be broadcast to all end-users via electronic mail, and current policies and approval or review forms can be accessible via a Web browser linked to an intranet.

Software copyright compliance has been a weak area of end-user computing control. Although enforcing control policies for software copyrights is less dif-

ficult in a networked environment, software vendors are still losing significant revenues due to software copyright violations. To put pressure on IS organizations and IS managers to take a more proactive role in monitoring copyrights and software licensing agreements, an association of vendors became active in the 1990s: the Software Publishers Association (SPA). One of their tactics is to do on-site compliance checks. Another tactic has been to increase end-user awareness of copyright issues by placing notices in popular periodicals; for example, a recent SPA advertisement in *PC/Computing* featured a multi-colored cartoon figure in a full-page ad to capture the attention of the reader. The number of organizations with formal procedures in place to monitor software licenses and to inventory software on all desktop machines is clearly much higher today than when the SPA began its awareness and enforcement campaigns. Organizational compliance with copyrights and licensing agreements is usually the responsibility of the senior IS manager.

In summary, today's network technologies make it easier to provide some support services and to enforce some control policies and procedures from a centralized site. In particular, the increasing use of networks has made the tasks of product inventorying, upgrading, and the enforcement of security controls and procedures easier because these tasks are in the hands of a trained network administrator rather than an individual end-user. The overall trend has been to embed more support and control in the technology itself.

Locus of Responsibility for Support and Control

As we discussed above, a centralized support unit such as an IC can be an effective delivery structure for end-user computing management. IC managers in many firms are responsible for providing support services, as well as implementing control policies and procedures. In firms with a centralized support structure, a steering committee of both users and other IS managers can be used to help integrate end-user computing with other organizational computing. Other firms may accomplish this integration via a reporting structure—such as having an IS manager accountable for both systems development by IS specialists and end-user computing support. Supporting end-users in today's networked environment also involves coordination with IS units responsible for planning and operating the overall IT infrastructure. For example, new releases of an end-user tool may require not only retraining of end-users, but also refitting end-user workstations with more memory or disk storage space to support the new software. Also, as reported in the April 1995 issue of the *I/S Analyzer*, to support users who are navigating through databases and generating queries on their own, IS staff should monitor their queries in order to fine-tune the structure of the databases to optimize the performance of the tools. IS expertise is also required to help make choices between traditional relational database and newer multidimensional tools.

Even in firms with a centralized support unit, however, end-user computing support and control is increasingly being recognized as a shared, organization-wide responsibility. In some organizations, managers of user developers are explicitly responsible for adherence to organizational policies and procedures, as well as for the management of any risks associated with any user-developed application being used by workers in their units. Incentives can be used to help establish a norm in which user developers take the time to appropriately plan for and systematically test applications in order to eliminate errors. User-managers, therefore, can play a critical role in establishing and rewarding behaviors that decrease

organizational risks, such as described in the sidebar "Risky Behaviors."

In some large firms, a centralized IC unit may provide some services, and local support units and personnel provide others. Many business areas have end-users who are not IS specialists but have become recognized as "power users," or local experts, within their business workgroups or departments, providing front-line training and consulting. In some organizations these support roles are formalized: The local expert takes on a type of IS coordinator role and is the primary liaison between the IS organization and the workgroup or department. However, in many organizations the local support roles are not formalized. In some situations, not formalizing these roles can result in considerable role ambiguity and frustration for the end-user who is informally assisting other co-workers.

Sources of support outside the IS organization may also be used by end-users. These include direct contacts with hardware and software vendors, IS professionals that report to a business unit, and colleagues inside and outside the workplace. User-managers frequently rely on outside vendors to help

---

RISKY BEHAVIORS

In a recent survey, spreadsheet developers were found to exhibit a high level of risk in their development practices. The applications in the study were of significant status. Most applications were characterized as of large size, and of moderate or high impact. The majority involved corporate rather than purely private data, and the output of nearly one-third was distributed beyond the organization where it was developed. Yet most of these applications were developed in relatively uncontrolled environments—with little managerial, IS department, or auditor control. Few of the developers surveyed were aware of a spreadsheet control policy within their organizations, and even less had a documented copy available. When asked whether they used specific controls, more developers responded that they "should have" used a specific control than that they "did" use one. This survey does not inspire confidence that end-users are currently succeeding in controlling all their spreadsheets optimally.

[Adapted from Hall, 1996]

with a user developed system—either at the outset of a project or after a key user developer has left their unit. It is also common knowledge that older managers who are beginning computer users themselves often are introduced to computer basics by their own family members—typically children who are using Web tools, on-line services, and/or interactive CD-ROM programs.

Summary

The development of applications by workers who are not IS specialists has become commonplace. The pervasiveness of user-developed applications is partly due to the clear advantages associated with the use of these systems. However, user-managers should carefully consider the potential disadvantages associated with user-developed applications when the scope, criticality, size, usage, and complexity of a new application suggest that the organizational risks may outweigh the benefits. User developers should also use a development methodology that is appropriate for the specific application and their own skills. Consultation with IS professionals and auditing personnel should be encouraged, as appropriate.

Effective management of end-user computing in organizations requires strategies and tactics that take into account the range and maturity of user development activities within the specific organization. IS and user managers need to approach end-user computing management as a user/IS working partnership that promotes the integration of development activities by IS professionals and user developers. A centralized support unit may be an effective delivery mechanism for support services and control policies and procedures for all knowledge workers. However, user-managers play a critical role in establishing the workgroup "norms" under which applications are developed outside of an IS organization. Today's end-user technologies also allow for more support and control to be embedded in the computer and network tools themselves.

Lessons learned from managing user-developed applications in the past can be applied today to develop effective strategies and tactics for managing applications developed by end-users using emerging technologies, such as Web technologies.

Review Questions

1. What is meant by user application development? Relate your definition to the bigger issue of end-user computing management.
2. Describe some of the forces that fueled the proliferation of end-user computing in the 1980s.
3. Contrast the advantages and disadvantages associated with user-developed applications.
4. Describe the application and organizational factors that should be considered by user-managers in the decision to sponsor the development of an application without IT specialists.
5. What is meant by the term "information center"?
6. Contrast the Managed Free Economy approach with the Information Center approach.
7. What support services are commonly provided in organizations today?
8. Describe some control policies and procedures that organizations should consider developing in order to minimize the risks of end-user computing.
9. What are the common types of spreadsheet errors?
10. Provide some examples of end-user support and controls that can be embedded in today's end-user technologies.
11. Comment on why today's organizations are more vigilant about enforcing copyright laws.

Discussion Questions

1. From the perspective of the organization as a whole, discuss the risk/benefit tradeoffs for user application development.
2. Describe a situation in which one of the advantages of user-developed applications might be (a) more or (b) less important to a user-manager than an IS manager.
3. Using the factors shown in Figure 12.4, describe a scenario in which you think a user-manager should endorse (sponsor) a user-developed application. Then describe a scenario in which you think a user-manager should *not* endorse a user-developed application.

4. Comment on how typical you think the user developers' remarks are in the sidebars "Tales of User Developers" and "Lessons Learned."

5. Describe the degree to which the support services in Figure 12.10 are available in an organization familiar to you.

6. Develop some guidelines for spreadsheet developers to help prevent spreadsheet errors.

7. Comment on the three "paths" followed by organizations in the 1980s that are shown as arrows in Figure 12.8. Then comment on the relevance of this figure for managing user-developed Web pages in today's organizations.

8. Describe situations in which you think a centralized support unit, such as an information center, is an appropriate delivery mechanism for support services and for implementing control policies and procedures.

9. Comment on what end-user computing management responsibilities you think should be *shared* by IS and user management.

10. More and more workers are telecommuting—working in home offices or on the road with computers that can access organizational computers. Describe how providing support for these teleworkers may differ from providing support for desktop computing in a regular office.

References

1995. Case studies. *I/S Analyzer.* 34 (April).

Benson, D.H. 1983. "A field study of end user computing: findings and issues." *MIS Quarterly* 7 (4): 35–45.

Berry, Walter. 1990. "Why I am not going to buy a computer," in *What Are People For,* North Point Press, 1990, as reprinted in C. Dunlop and R. Kling, *Computerization and Controversy,* Academic Press, 1991.

Boynton, Andrew C., Robert W. Zmud, and Gerald C. Jacobs. 1994. "The influence of IT management practice on IT use in large organizations." *MIS Quarterly* 17 (March): 299–318.

Brancheau, James C., and Donald L. Amoroso. 1990. "An empirical test of the expansion-control model for managing end-user computing." *Proceedings of the 11th International Conference on Information Systems:* 291–303.

Brancheau, James C., and Carol V. Brown. 1993. "The management of end-user computing: status and directions." *Computing Surveys* 25 (December): 437–482.

Galletta, Dennis F., K. S. Hartzel, S. Johnson, J. Joseph, and S. Rustagi. 1996. "An experimental study of spreadsheet presentation and error detection,." *Proceedings of the 29th Hawaii International Conference on System Sciences:* 336–345.

Gerrity, T. P., and John F. Rockart. 1986. "End-user computing: Are you a leader or a laggard?" *Sloan Management Review* 27 (Summer): 25–34.

Gremillion, Lee L., and Philip Pyburn. 1983. "Breaking the systems development bottleneck." *Harvard Business Review* 61 (March–April): 130–137.

Hall, M.J.J. 1996. "A risk and control oriented study of the practices of spreadsheet application developers," in *Proceedings of the 29th Hawaii International Conference on System Sciences:* 364–373.

Hammond, L.W. 1982. "Management considerations for an information centre." *IBM Systems Journal* 21 (2): 131–161.

Huff, Sid L., Malcolm C. Munro, and Barbara H. Martin. 1988. "Growth stages of end-user computing." *Communications of the ACM* 31 (May): 542–550.

Kaiser, Kate M. 1993. "End-User Computing," in *Encyclopedia of Computer Science and Technology.*

Karten, Naomi. 1990. "The two stages of end-user computing," in *Mind Your Business: Strategies for Managing End-User Computing.* Wellesley, Massachusetts: QED Information Sciences, Inc.: 3–24.

Klepper, Robert, and Mary Sumner. 1990. "Continuity and change in user developed systems." *Desktop Information Technology,* K. M. Kaiser and J. J. Oppelland (Eds.), Amsterdam: North-Holland, 209–222.

Maes, Pattie. 1994. "Agents that reduce word and information overload." *Communications of the ACM* 37 (July): 31–40.

Magal, S. R., and Houston H. Carr. 1988. "An investigation of the effects of age, size, and hardware option on the critical success factors applicable to information centers." *Journal of Management Information Systems* 4 (4): 60–76.

Martin, James. 1982. *Application Development Without Programmers.* Englewood Cliffs, N.J.: Prentice-Hall.

McLean, Ephraim R. 1979. "End users as application developers." *MIS Quarterly* 3 (4): 37–46.

McLean, Ephram R., L.A. Kappelman, and J.P. Thompson. 1993. "Converging end-user and corporate computing." *Communications of the ACM* 36 (December): 79–92.

Moad, J. 1994. "The training crisis: school's out!" *Datamation* (August 1): 46–48.

Munro, Malcolm C., Sid L. Huff, and G.C. Moore. 1987–1988. "Expansion and control of end user computing." *Journal of Management Information Systems* 4 (Winter): 5–27.

Panko, Ralph R. 1988. *End User Computing: Management, Applications, and Technology.* New York: Wiley.

Panko, Ralph R. 1996. "Minitrack on risks in end-user computing." *Proceedings of the 29th Hawaii International Conference on System Sciences.*

Panko, Ralph R., and R.P. Halverson, Jr. 1996. "Spreadsheets on trial: A survey of research on spreadsheet risks." *Proceedings of the 29th Hawaii International Conference on System Sciences:* 326–335.

Pyburn, Philip J. 1986–1987. "Managing personal computer use: The role of corporate management information systems." *Journal of Management Information Systems* 3 (3): 49–70.

Rivard, Suzanne, and Sid L. Huff. 1988. "Factors of success for end-user computing." *Communications of the ACM* 31 (5): 552–561.

Rockart, John F., and L.S. Flannery. 1983. "The management of end-user computing." *Communications of the ACM* 26 (10): 776–784.

Schultheis, Robert A., and Mary Sumner. 1991. "The relationship of application risks to application controls: A study of microcomputer-based database applications." *Computer Personnel* 13 (3): 50–59.

Speier, Cheri S., and Carol V. Brown. 1997. "Differences in end-user computing support and control across user departments." *Information & Management* 32 (February 15): 85–99.

SouthWest University Financial Information System

SouthWest University (SWU) is a large state university located in the U.S. Southwest. With more than 70,000 students and almost 4,000 faculty, last year's SWU budget was about $1.8 billion. In addition to over 800 undergraduate and graduate degree programs, SWU runs 75 research centers and institutes, has a large school of medicine, and operates a major complex of hospitals and medical research centers. In addition to its main campus in the state capital, SWU has four satellite campuses that offer undergraduate and graduate programs in the four corners of the state.

The Need for a New Financial Information System

SWU's computerized financial systems are old and obsolete. These systems were developed in the 1960s, when SWU had less than 30,000 students and finances were centrally managed. Based upon 1960s hardware and software technology, these systems are managed and operated by the Financial Services unit of SWU central administration.

Two years ago, new SWU President M. R. Snoddy decided to distribute fiscal responsibility throughout the University by instituting "Activity Center Management," under which many financial decisions were decentralized to schools, departments, institutes, hospitals, support services, and auxiliary enterprises. Under Activity Cen-

ter Management, each entity is required to live within its own revenues rather than negotiating its budget with central administration. A school, for example, gets its own income from tuition, state support, and grants, but must in turn pay its own expenses, such as salaries, rent, and fees for library use and computer services.

The existing financial systems do not cope well with the demands of Activity Center Management. The old systems do not deal with revenue, only with expenses. They were designed primarily for central administration's needs in conforming to the requirements of state government auditors and were never intended to serve the needs of decentralized managers. They are batch systems in which transactions are recorded on paper, sent through an approval process, and then sent on to Financial Services, where they are entered into the mainframe computer through dumb terminals. After transactions are entered into the computer, they are edited in a batch process, and an error list is produced and returned to the user to make necessary corrections. Reports are not available until two weeks after the end of the month, and thus some of the information they contain may be more than six weeks old.

Understandably, each entity keeps its own "shadow system" set of books, and a good deal of effort goes into reconciling the official reports with these local books. These local systems are somewhat different, but all are based on PC local area networks (LANs) or stand-alone PCs. Some were built using packages such as Excel or Microsoft Access, and some use accounting software packages.

In addition to the above inadequacies, SWU managers are increasingly concerned about being charged their share of the cost of the central financial systems in addition to the cost of their shadow systems.

This case was prepared for the 1996 EDS Challenge at Indiana University. It is intended to be used as the basis for class discussion rather than to illustrate either effective or ineffective handling of an administrative situation.

The Financial Services Proposal

The Financial Services organization has proposed to replace the existing financial systems with a new financial information system (FIS) designed to support the needs of SWU managers under the decentralized approach of Activity Center Management. Lou Hanson, Director of Financial Services, explains:

> Our present system is based upon obsolete mainframe technology, COBOL programs, and flat files. We will replace it with a modern client/server based system so that users throughout the University can use their own PCs with the Windows graphical user interface to interact with the system. They will enter their own data, which will be edited on-line so they can be confident of its accuracy and timeliness. And they can interrogate the database and generate their own reports at any time rather than waiting until two weeks after the end of the month to obtain their reports. (Exhibit 1, prepared by Financial Services, describes this FIS.)

At present many transactions have to go through a cumbersome approval process before Financial Services can enter them into the computer. Some personnel actions, for example, must get as many as a dozen

EXHIBIT 1
The Proposed FIS.

In the new FIS, electronic documents initiated on a personal computer will be processed by the Transaction Processing component. This component will electronically route the "documents" through an approval process and then pass them to the university's financial data repository, called the General Ledger. A third component, Decision Support, will provide each organization (whether department, activity center, or campus) with access to those data for its reporting and analysis needs. Data from the FIS can be passed down into departmental systems upon request. The following is a simple depiction of these main components of the new FIS.

This will be a client/server system operating through an existing fiber-optic backbone network that connects all the buildings on the main campus and the satellite campuses. The server, a Hewlett-Packard G60 operating under Unix, will maintain the general ledger database and contain some of the processing logic. The client IBM-compatible PCs will be at least 33 megahertz 486s with 8 megabytes of memory and 100 megabyte hard drives and will operate under the Windows operating system. The client will perform the data capture and much of the routine reporting based on data retrieved from the server database.

The new FIS has many advantages. It will:

- reduce paper trails
- allow for faster turnaround
- allow for decisions to be made based upon up-to-date information
- reduce mistakes and the need to correct errors, since checks and balances will be built into the system
- give more control and management flexibility to departments
- create more appropriate data and permanent computer records
- support activity center management

The new FIS will be composed of a number of separate but interrelated subsystems:

1. The **Chart of Accounts** will be the set of controlling tables which defines the financial information. In the present accounting system the campus code, fund group, and department are all part of the account

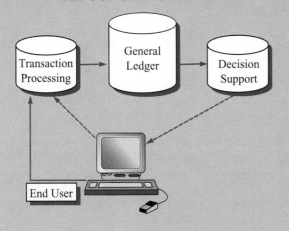

FIS CONCEPTUAL MODEL

Transaction Processing → General Ledger → Decision Support

End User

EXHIBIT 1 (continued)

number. In the new system the account number will be arbitrarily assigned and these and other attributes will be maintained in tables within the system for use in input editing, reporting, and analysis. Each account will have an attribute, Object Code, which will map the account into the university income, expense, and balance sheet items for both accounting and budgeting purposes. Each account may have subaccounts and subobject codes, defined by the account manager, so that organizational units will be able to set up their own more detailed account breakdowns.

2. The **General Ledger** will be the repository of all financial and budget information for the university. It will be composed of three databases: one for accounting and budget balances by month for four years, one for the detailed transactions that update the balances, and one for open encumbrances. The General Ledger will be interfaced with the following systems to automatically receive data from them: Payroll, Accounts Payable, Bursar Accounts Receivable, and Interdepartmental Billings.

3. **Transaction Processing** will allow account managers and organizations to transact financial business through their computers, rather than using the paper forms as they do at present. There will be "electronic forms" to replace each of the paper documents that are currently used. The system will be able to route these documents electronically, and locate and display a document while it is in the approval process as well as after it has been approved and processed.

4. **Decision Support** will be a new environment which allows account managers and others to access financial information and will provide tools to assist in the analysis of the financial information. It will produce standard reports on a scheduled basis, run predefined queries on an ad hoc basis, extract detail information and download it to local systems, and drill down through levels of detail.

5. **Labor Distribution** will tie together the position budgeting with the payroll and accounting process to provide better and more timely information.

6. **Capital Assets Management** will be used to track and account for all capital assets of the university, including moveable equipment, land, and buildings.

7. **Accounts Receivable** will provide all departments a nonstudent revenue receivable system that formats bills or invoices and processes payments while performing all of the accounting work. It will also provide reports stating the current status of a department's receivables.

8. **Contracts and Grants** will track research proposals and resulting grants for all areas within the university. It will be linked to the FIS so it can reflect the budgets and expenditures of the grants as well.

approval signatures. This process goes very slowly as the paperwork winds its way across desk after desk, so it may take six weeks or more before the action is entered into the computer. According to Hanson,

> President Snoddy was flabbergasted to learn how long it takes for personnel actions to be approved, and has mandated that this process be drastically improved. Accordingly, the new system will eliminate all paperwork and the electronic transactions will be automatically routed to those who must see them. Moreover, a transaction will be approved and go into the computer database as soon as the account manager, and his or her superior, have approved it. We will still route the information to the other people who have to sign off

today, but only for information purposes. Incidentally, this new process has been enthusiastically approved by the state auditor.

The existing financial systems being based on a single chart of accounts has led to a very cumbersome account structure. Hanson explains the problem:

> To the academic units, supplies and expenses are just that, and they are not interested in much more detail. But to campus foods, supplies and expenses involves excruciating detail—chocolate ice cream, vanilla ice cream, strawberry ice cream, and so forth. With a single chart of accounts, the schools have to cope with thousands of codes within supplies and expenses that

have no meaning for them, while the service units have to deal with academic-related codes that do not affect them.

To tailor the system to each user, in the new FIS we propose nine charts of accounts—one for each campus and university hospitals, buildings and grounds, food services, and student housing. They will all map upward into a central administration chart of accounts, but each unit will have its own accounting system at its level. This will allow the users to dispense with their ad hoc shadow systems.

The existing financial system is huge. It includes major applications systems such as accounts payable, accounts receivable, general ledger, budget development, budget control, and payroll. There are hundreds of thousands of lines of COBOL code that must be replaced. Financial Services estimates that it would cost at least $10 million to develop a new Financial Information System to replace these current systems.

Realizing that SWU cannot afford to develop a new FIS, Hanson has negotiated a special deal with Academic Information Services, a major supplier of applications software for universities, to produce SWU's new FIS. Under a tentative agreement, SWU's Financial Services will produce the detailed requirements for the new system and assign two high-ranking people to work with Academic Information Services during the development process, and Academic Information Services will produce the new FIS software for a fixed price of $3 million. Academic Information Services will own the rights to distribute the new software and expects to recoup its expenses and make a profit selling this software to other universities.

The timing for the new system is critical. Financial Services will produce the detailed requirements in three months, and Academic Information Services will then have the new system ready for installation in June, two years from this year. However, since SWU cannot convert to the new system in the middle of its fiscal year, if this schedule slips the new system cannot be installed until June a year later. Therefore a go/no-go decision must be made within the next two weeks or the new system will be delayed for a full year.

Although SWU Vice President for Finance P. K. Johnson has always insisted that systems development investments produce an internal rate of return (IRR) of at least 15 percent over a seven-year period, Hanson feels that the new FIS must be obtained whether or not it meets this criterion. However, Hanson is confident that the sav-

ings from eliminating the data entry group in Financial Services and replacing the shadow systems in the user organizations will easily justify the cost of the new FIS. (Financial Services estimates of these savings are presented in Exhibit 2 on page 468.)

Reactions to the Financial Services Proposal

Although some SWU managers welcome the proposal for a new financial information system, this proposal has generated controversy. The users of this system realize that, under Activity Center Management, they will pay for this development, and they are concerned with this cost.

Also, several users oppose the Financial Services proposal because they are getting along reasonably well with their local systems that supplement the existing financial systems, and some are reluctant to give up these local systems. Some also believe that there will be significant additional costs to the users that are not included in the costs of the proposed development contract with Academic Information Services. Some have questioned whether the proposed time schedule for defining the detailed system requirements is realistic, and others have questioned the claimed savings.

Tracy Russ, University Director of Information Systems, has just recently learned about this proposal and has some serious concerns. Russ believes that the IS organization should develop the system requirements and manage any outside development contract. Also, Russ thinks that it might be more cost effective to upgrade and augment the existing systems rather than replacing them.

Your Role

In light of the above controversy President Snoddy of SWU has engaged your team of outside consultants to do a quick study and make a recommendation concerning what to do about SWU's financial systems. Specifically, you will:

1. Interview the following SWU managers to obtain additional information about the present financial systems, the proposed FIS, the costs of various alternatives, the needs, attitudes, and opinions of SWU managers, etc.

Lou Hanson, Director of Financial Services
Tracy Russ, Director of the Information Systems Department

EXHIBIT 2

Anticipated Annual Personnel Savings from FIS.

Organization	Positions	Dollars
Financial Services	9.0	$132,000
Main Campus Administration	2.0	51,000
Campus B Admin	1.0	26,000
Campus C Admin	0.8	18,000
Campus D Admin	1.0	25,000
Campus E Admin	1.0	25,000
Buildings & Grounds	1.0	20,000
Student Housing	1.0	22,000
Food Services	1.0	23,000
Research Administration	1.5	40,000
University Hospitals	1.5	35,000
Libraries	1.0	21,000
School of Humanities	1.6	39,000
School of Sciences	1.0	25,000
School of Agriculture	1.4	33,000
School of Business	1.0	25,000
School of Medicine	1.5	41,000
School of Music	1.0	20,000
School of Education	1.0	22,000
School of Law	1.0	26,000
School of Public Administration	1.8	42,000
School of Physical Education	1.0	20,000
Department of English	1.0	22,000
Department of Languages	1.0	22,000
Department of Mathematics	1.0	24,000
Department of Biology	1.0	23,000
Department of Chemistry	1.0	24,000
Department of Psychology	1.0	23,000
Department of Sociology	1.0	22,000
Department of History	0.5	11,000
Department of Computer Science	1.4	33,000
TOTAL	43.0	$935,000

Lee Morrison, Finance Officer of the School of Medicine
Jerry Anderson, Business Manager of the School of Sciences

2. Make a formal oral and/or written presentation to President Snoddy and SWU senior managers stating and defending your recommendations concerning how to deal with the proposed FIS and the problems that led to this proposal. Your presentation should:

- Identify the issues that should be considered in this situation.

- Analyze the proposal by Financial Services to produce a new FIS. This analysis should include both the advantages and disadvantages of this proposal as well as a financial analysis that shows whether or not the 15 percent IRR hurdle is met.

- Recommend what SWU should do about its financial systems problem and discuss why this recommendation should be adopted. A time schedule for implementation of this recommendation should be included.

CONSUMER AND INDUSTRIAL PRODUCTS, INC.

Late Friday afternoon, T. N. (Ted) Anderson, director of disbursements for Consumer and Industrial Products, Inc. (CIPI), sat staring out the wide window of his twelfth-floor corner office, but his mind was elsewhere. Anderson was thinking about the tragic accident that had nearly killed Linda Watkins, project director for the Payables Audit Systems (PAS) development project. Thursday night, when she was on her way home from a movie, a drunken driver had hit her car head on. She would survive, but it would be months before she would be back to work.

The PAS system was a critical component of a group of interrelated systems intended to support fundamental changes in how billing and accounts payable at CIPI were handled. Without Watkins, it was in deep trouble. Deeply committed to the success of these new approaches, Anderson did not know exactly what he could do, but he knew he had to take drastic action. He picked up his phone and told his secretary, "Please get me an appointment with IS Director Charles Bunke for the first thing Monday morning." Anderson would have the weekend to decide what to do.

The Origin of the PAS Project

Consumer and Industrial Products, Inc. is a Fortune 100 manufacturer of a large variety of well-known products for both individuals and industry. Headquartered in the United States, CIPI is an international company with facilities in Europe, Asia, and North and South America.

The PAS project was one of several interrelated projects that resulted from a fundamental reevaluation of CIPI's accounts payable process that was part of CIPI's company-wide emphasis on total quality management (TQM). Anderson recalls:

In late 1991 we began to look at what we were doing, how we were doing it, the costs involved, and the value we were adding to the company. We realized that, even with our computer systems, we were very labor intensive, and that there ought to be things we could do to increase our productivity and our value added. So we decided to completely rethink what we were currently doing and how we were doing it.

Since we were a part of the procurement process, we needed to understand that total process and where accounts payable fit into it. We found that procurement was a three-part process—purchasing the goods, receiving them, and finally paying for them. And we concluded that our role was pretty extensive for someone who was just supposed to be paying the bills. We were spending a lot of effort trying to match purchase orders with receiving reports and invoices to make sure that everyone else had done their job properly. We typically had about 15,000 suspended items that we were holding up payment on because of some question that arose in our examination of these three pieces of information. Many of these items spent 30 to 60 days in suspense before we got them corrected, and the vast majority of the problems were not the vendor's fault but rather the result of mistakes within CIPI. For some of our small vendors for whom we were a dominant customer, this could result in severe cash flow problems, and even bankruptcy. With today's emphasis upon strategic partnerships with our vendors, this was intolerable.

We finally recognized that the fundamental responsibility for procurement rests with purchasing, and once they have ordered the goods, the next thing that is needed is some proof that the goods were received, and we are outside that process also. We concluded that our role was to pay the resulting bills, and that we should not be holding the other departments' hands to make sure that their processes did not break down. And we certainly should not be placing unfair burdens upon our vendors.

So we decided to make some fundamental changes in what we did and how we did it. We told the people in our organization what we wanted to do and why we wanted to do it and gave them the charge to make the necessary changes. After about nine months we discovered that we were getting nowhere—it was just not moving. Obviously we could not just top-down it and get the results we wanted. With the help of a consultant we went back to the drawing board and studied how to drive this thing from the ground up rather than from the top down. We discovered that our people were very provincial—they saw everything in terms of accounts payable and had little perspective on the overall procurement process. We had to change this mindset, so we spent almost a year putting our people through training courses designed to expand their perspective.

Our mindset in accounts payable changed so that we began to get a lot of ideas and a lot of change coming from the floor. There began to be a lot of challenging of what was going on and many suggestions for how we could reach our strategic vision. In cooperation with the other departments involved, the accounts payable people decided to make some fundamental changes in their role and operations. Instead of thoroughly investigating each discrepancy, no matter how insignificant, before paying the bill, we decided to go ahead and pay all invoices that are within a reasonable tolerance. We will adopt a quality control approach and keep a history of all transactions for each vendor so that we can evaluate the vendor's performance over time and eliminate vendors that

cause significant problems. Not only will this result in a significant reduction in work that is not adding much value, but it will also provide much better service to our vendors.

We also decided to install a PC-based document imaging system and move toward a paperless environment. We are developing a Document Control System (DCS) through which most documents that come into our mail room will be identified, indexed, and entered through document readers into the imaging system. Then the documents themselves will be filed and their images will be placed into the appropriate processing queues for the work that they require. The Document Control System will allow you to add notes to the document, route it from one computer system to another, and keep track of what has been done to the document. This will radically change the way we do business in the department. Things that used to take 18 steps, going from one clerk to another, will take only 1 or 2 steps because all the required information will be available through the computer. Not only will this improve our service, but it will drastically reduce our processing costs. It will also require that all of our processing systems be integrated with the Document Control System.

In addition to developing the new Document Control System, this new accounts payable approach required CIPI to replace or extensively modify five major systems: the Freight Audit System (FAST); the Computerized Invoice Matching System (CIMS), which audited invoices; the Corporate Approval System (CAS), which checked to assure that vouchers were approved by authorized persons; the vendor database mentioned above; and the system that dealt with transactions that were not on computer-generated purchase orders. The PAS project was originally intended to modify the CIMS system.

Systems Development at CIPI

Systems development at CIPI is both centralized and decentralized. There is a large corporate IS group that has responsibility for corporate databases and systems. Also, there are about 30 divisional systems groups. A division may develop systems on its own, but if a corporate database is affected, then corporate IS must be involved in the development. Corporate IS also sells services to the divisions. For example, corporate IS will contract to manage a project and/or to provide all or some of the technical staff for a project, and the time of these people will be billed to the division at standard hourly rates.

Similarly, computer operations are both centralized and decentralized. There is a corporate data center operated by corporate IS, but there are also computers and LANs that are operated by the divisions and even by departments. Corporate IS sets standards for this hardware and the LANs, and will contract to provide technical support for the LANs.

Because the accounts payable systems affected corporate financial databases, Anderson had to involve corporate IS in the development of most of these systems. The Document Control System (DCS), however, did not directly affect corporate databases, so Anderson decided to use his own systems group to develop this imaging system.

Corporate IS had just begun the use of a structured development methodology called Stradis. This methodology divides the development into eight phases: initial study, detailed study, draft requirements study, outline physical design, total requirements statement, system design, coding and testing, and installation. This methodology provides detailed documentation of what should be done in each phase. At the end of each phase detailed planning of the next phase is done, and cost and time estimates for the remainder of the project are revised. Each phase produces a document that must be approved by both user and IS management before proceeding with the next phase. Stradis also includes a postimplementation review performed several months after the system has been installed.

Roles in the PAS Project

The Stradis methodology defined a number of roles to be filled in a development project: Anderson was the executive sponsor, Peter Shaw was the project manager, and Linda Watkins was the project director.

Executive Sponsor

Ted Anderson, director of disbursements, is responsible for all CIPI disbursements, including both payroll and accounts payable. Starting with CIPI in 1966 in the general accounting area, Anderson had a long history of working as the user-manager on systems development projects, including projects in payroll, human resources, and accounting. He spent a year doing acquisitions work for CIPI and in 1978 served a stint in Europe as area treasurer. He has made steady progress up the CIPI management ladder.

In the Stradis methodology the executive sponsor has budgetary responsibility and must approve all of the expenditures of the project. He or she must sign off at the end of each phase and authorize the team to proceed with the next phase.

According to Watkins, Anderson was a very active executive sponsor:

Ted was determined that this project would produce a quality system and get done on time and that his people would commit themselves to the project. He not only talked about these priorities, but he also led by example by attending working sessions where lower level people were being interviewed and participating in data modeling sessions. By visibly spending a lot of his personal time on the project, he showed his people that it was important for them to spend their time.

"The area manager has to take an active role in the development of systems," Anderson asserts,

particularly when you are trying to reengineer the processes. If you do not have leadership from the manager to set the vision of where you are going, your people tend to automate what they have been doing rather than concentrating on what really adds value and eliminating everything else, so I took a fairly active role in this project. I wanted to make sure that we were staying on track with our vision and on schedule with the project.

User Project Manager

Peter Shaw was the user project manager. He had worked for CIPI for eighteen years, starting as a part-time employee working nights while going to college. Over his career he had worked in payroll, accounting, and human resources, part of the time in systems work and part in supervisory positions. For the past three years, he had been a supervisor in accounts payable.

The user project manager is responsible for making sure that the system meets the user department's business needs and that the system is completed on time. He or she manages the user department effort on the project, making sure that the proper people are identified and made available as needed. He or she is also responsible for representing the user view whenever issues arise and for making sure that any political problems are recognized and dealt with.

The user project manager and the project director work closely together to manage the project and are jointly responsible for its success. Shaw also served in the role of business analyst on this project.

Project Director

Linda Watkins, senior analyst in the corporate IS department, was the project director. Watkins, who had recently joined CIPI, had an MBA in MIS and seven years of experience as an analyst and project manager with a Fortune 500 company and a financial software consultant. She had experience using Stradis to manage projects, which was one of the reasons she had been hired by CIPI. Because they were being charged for her time, Watkins viewed the disbursement department managers as clients for whom she was working as a consultant.

The project director was responsible for managing the IS people on the project. "My job resembled that of the general contractor on a construction project who has to deal with all the subcontractors and manage the budget and schedule," Watkins explains.[1] She developed the project plans, determined what each phase would cost, managed the budget, involved the necessary technical people at the right time, and worked through Shaw to make sure that the proper client people were available when needed to be interviewed or make decisions.

"I felt like I was ultimately responsible for the success of the project," Watkins reports, "because if things fell apart I would be the one that would take the blame, both from IS management and client management. Therefore my major concern was to look ahead and foresee problems and make sure that they were solved before they impacted the success of the project." "That is what I look for in a project manager," Ted Anderson asserts. "Most of the day-to-day work just happens if you have good people, but the crucial thing is to anticipate potential problems so that you are preventing them rather than just reacting."

Watkins also tried to make her clients aware of what was possible with computer technology so that they would not simply automate what they had been doing. "I tried to help them think about why they were doing things instead of just how they were doing them," Watkins says. "Because I was not an expert in accounts payable, I could ask the dumb question that might lead to a new perspective."

Another important part of Watkins' job was communication. "I tried to make sure that the client managers knew what was going on at all times and that they knew all the options when there were decisions to be made. I trusted them to make the right decisions if they had the information they needed." Anderson found that to be a refreshing change from his past experience. "Previously IS has not told its customers any more than it had to. But Linda was very open and we felt that we could trust her."

That trust was very important to Watkins, for her ultimate responsibility was to ensure that everyone worked together effectively on the project. She devoted a lot of effort to selecting technical people who had good communications skills and could interact positively with her clients.

IS Management

Henry Carter, IS supervisor of disbursements systems, was Watkins' supervisor. He was responsible for integrating all the projects in the disbursements area and for allocating IS people to these projects. His role included advising and coaching the project directors, reviewing their project plans, and making sure that they got the technical assistance they needed from the IS organization.

Carter had been responsible for maintenance of the Disbursement Department's systems for many years. When the new development projects were initiated Carter became responsible for them also, but he had little experience with systems development and was of little help to Watkins.

Carter reported to Clark Mason, IS manager of financial systems, who was aware of some of Carter's limitations but who valued him for his knowledge of the existing systems. To compensate for Carter's weaknesses, Mason had tried to get the best available project managers, and he told them to come directly to him when they had strategic questions or problems with client relationships.

Steering Group

The steering group was chaired by Anderson and included three accounts payable supervisors whose areas were affected by the project, Shaw, and the manager of the disbursements systems group, Tom Hill. Watkins and Carter were ex-officio members of this group. The role of the steering group was to approve budgets, determine the business direction of the project, and make any necessary decisions.

The steering group met on alternate Wednesdays at 3:30 P.M. The agenda and a project status report were distributed at least 24 hours before each meeting. Exhibit 1 shows the Project Status Report distributed at the October 6, 1993, steering group meeting. Under the **Recap Hours/Dollars** section, the "Original" column refers to the original plan, and the "Forecast" column

---

1 The interviews for this case were conducted while Watkins was recovering from her accident, a few months after the events described.

EXHIBIT 1

PAS PROJECT STATUS REPORT As of October 1, 1993.

Recap Hours/Dollars	Original	Forecast	Variance	Actual-to-Date
Initial Study:				
Hours	577	448	129	434
Dollars	$20,000	17,000	3,000	16,667
Detailed Study:				
Hours	1,350	1,337	13	1,165
Dollars	$45,000	47,927	–2,927	42,050
Total:				
Hours	1,927	1,785	142	1,599
Dollars	$65,000	64,927	73	58,717

Milestone Dates	Original	Revised	Completed
Complete Context DFD—Current	8/3		8/4
Complete Level 0 DFD—Current	8/6		8/13
Complete Level 1 DFD—Current	8/22	9/12	9/14
Complete Level 0 DFD—Proposed	9/17	9/21	9/21
Map System Enhancements to DFD	9/17	9/21	9/24
Complete Data Model (key-based)	10/2	10/11	
Complete Detailed Study Report	10/8	10/15	

Accomplishments This Week:

Project Team:
    Completed the documentation library for the current system.
Lucy Robbins:
    Completed the PAS system's Business & System Objectives.
    Documented the PAS system's constraints.
    Started compiling the Detailed Study Report (DSR).
    Completed the documentation library for the current system.
Arnold Johnson:
    Completed the documentation library for the current system.
Linda Watkins:
    Reviewed the estimates and work plan for the three enhancements.
    Drafted the authorization for the enhancements.
    Initiated the Draft Requirements Statement (DRS) work plan.
Peter Shaw:
    Identified the new system's Business & System Objectives.
Carol Hemminger and Paul Brown:
    Completed the documentation of the workshop findings.
    Refined the ERM diagram.

Plans for Next Week:
    Finish and distribute the draft DSR.
    Finish the data modeling workshop documentation.
    Complete the DRS work plan.
    Distribute the finalized Initial Study Report (ISR).

Problems That May Affect the Project Status:

1. The DSR will not be finalized until the documentation from the data modeling workshops is completed.
2. Two walkthroughs are still outstanding, the key-based data model workshop and current system task force. Both will be completed when client schedules allow.

Issues:
1. Due to delays in scheduling interviews with AP, Robbins' time has not been utilized as well as possible. If this continues it may cause delays.

gives the current estimated hours and cost. The "Variance" column is the original plan minus the current estimate, whereas the "Actual-to-Date" column shows the hours and cost incurred up to October 5. A major function of the steering group was to deal with problems and issues. Problems require immediate attention, and issues are potential problems that will move up to the problem category if they are not dealt with.

At the start of each steering group meeting, Anderson would ask whether or not everyone had made themselves available when they were needed, and if not he would talk to them afterward. According to Watkins, "Ted was very vocal with his opinions, but he was not autocratic. When there were differences of opinion within the steering group, he would subtly hint at the direction he wanted to go, but it was still up to the interested parties to work out their own resolution of the problem. On the other hand, if he thought the project was getting off the track, he would put his foot down hard!"

Shaw was knowledgeable about the political climate, and he and Watkins would meet to plan the steering group meetings. They would discuss the issues that might come up and decide who would present them and how. If there were significant decisions to be made, Watkins and Shaw would discuss them with Anderson ahead of time to see where he stood and work out an alternative that he could support. Watkins did not try to force a recommendation on the committee; rather, she presented the problems in business terms along with a number of possible alternatives. Because the agenda was well organized and all the information was in the hands of participants ahead of time, the steering group meetings were quite effective, usually ending before the scheduled hour was up.

Several of the steering group members were the sponsors of other projects, and after the PAS steering group meetings were finished they would stay around and discuss these projects and their departmental problems with Watkins. She was pleased that she was viewed as a Disbursements Department colleague and not as an outsider.

Project Planning

The Stradis methodology requires that the project director estimate two costs at the end of each phase of the project: the cost of completing the rest of the project and the cost of the next phase. At the beginning, estimating the cost of the project was mostly a matter of judgment and experience. Watkins looked at it from several perspectives. First, she considered projects in her past experience that were of similar size and complexity and used their costs to estimate what the PAS system would cost. Then

she broke the PAS project down into its phases, did her best to estimate each phase, and totaled up these costs. When she compared these two estimates, they came out to be pretty close. Finally, she went over the project and her reasoning with several experienced project managers whose judgment she respected. This initial estimate was not too meaningful, however, because the scope of the project changed radically during the early stages.

Estimating the cost of the next phase requires that the project director plan that phase in detail, and then that plan is used to set the budget and to control the project. According to Watkins,

> The Stradis methodology provides an outline of all the steps that you go through to produce the deliverables of a stage. I would go through each step and break it down into activities and then break down each activity into tasks that I could assign to people. I would estimate the time that would be required for each task, consider the riskiness of that task, and multiply my estimate by a suitable factor to take the uncertainty into account. I would also ask the people who were assigned the task what kind of effort they felt it would require and would consult with experienced people in the IS area. Finally, by multiplying my final time estimate by the hourly rate for the person assigned to the task I would get a cost estimate for each task and add them all up to get a total cost for the phase. Again I would go over this with experienced project managers, and with Peter and Ted, before making final adjustments.

> Then I could start scheduling the tasks. I always included the tasks assigned to user department people, although I did not need them for controlling my budget and many other project managers did not bother with them. I wanted Peter and Ted and their people to see where they fit into the project and how their activities impacted the project schedule.

To help with the scheduling, Watkins used a tool called Project Manager's Workbench that included a PERT module and a Gantt Chart module. With the possibility of time constraints and different staffing levels, she often had to develop several different schedules for discussion with Shaw and Anderson, and for presentation to the steering group.

Staffing the Project

In addition to Watkins, Arnold Johnson was assigned to the project at the beginning. Johnson had worked for Carter as a maintenance programmer for many years.

Carter valued him highly as a maintenance programmer and therefore only assigned about 20 percent of Johnson's time to the PAS project. According to Watkins,

> Arnold did not see any urgency in anything he did, and being primarily assigned to maintenance, he never had any commitment to our deadlines, and he would not even warn me when he was going to miss a deadline. When you are on a project plan that has tasks that have to be done by specific times, every person must be fully committed to the project, so the project plan was always in flux if we depended on him to get anything done.

Johnson had a detailed knowledge of the existing CIMS system, and Watkins had planned for him to document the logical flow of the 14,000 lines of spaghetti code in the main program of the CIMS system. Watkins reported,

> He knew where things were done in the existing program, but he never knew why they were being done. He would never write anything down, so the only way to get information from him was verbally. We eventually decided that the only way to use him on the project was as a consultant and that we would have an analyst interview him to document the existing system.

A few weeks after the start of the project, Watkins obtained Lucy Robbins from a contractor firm to be her lead analyst. Robbins had managed a maintenance area at a medium-sized company and had also led a good-sized development project. She could program, but her main strength was in supervising programmers and communicating with the technical specialists in IS. Watkins was able to delegate much of the day-to-day supervision to Robbins so that she could concentrate on the strategic aspects of the project.

The Stradis methodology required the use of a CASE tool, and Robbins became the CASE tool "gatekeeper" who made sure that the critical project information stored therein was not corrupted. She said,

> We used the CASE tool to keep our logical data dictionary, data flow diagrams, and entity/relationship data models. The CASE tool keeps your data repository, and then uses that repository to populate your data flows, data stores, and entity/relationship models. It also assists in balancing the diagrams to make sure that everything that goes into a diagram is necessary, and everything that is necessary goes in.

Because IS had far more projects under way than it had good people to staff them, Watkins was never able to convince Henry Carter or Clark Mason to assign a qualified CIPI person to the project full time, so she had to staff the project with temporary employees from outside contractors:

> After I determined what resources I could get from CIPI, I would look at the tasks the project team had to perform and then try to find the best persons I could that fit our needs. I took as much care hiring a contractor as I would in hiring a permanent CIPI person. I tried to get people who were overqualified and keep them challenged by delegating as much responsibility to them as they could take. My people had to have excellent technical skills, but I was also concerned that their personalities fit in well with the team and with our clients.

Watkins hired two contractor analysts who had skills that the team lacked. One was a very good analyst who had experience with CIPI's standard programming language and database management system and had been a liaison with the database people on several projects. The second contractor analyst had a lot of experience in testing.

The project got excellent part-time help from database specialists in the CIPI IS department. Watkins recalls,

> We used IS database people to facilitate data modeling workshops and to do the modeling. We also used a data analyst to find a logical attribute in the current databases or set it up in the data dictionary if it was new. There were also database administrators who worked with the data modelers to translate the logical data model into physical databases that were optimized to make sure we could get the response time we needed.

Watkins also used consultants from the IS developmental methodologies group:

> Because my supervisor was not experienced in development, I used people from the methodologies group to look at my project plans and see if they were reasonable. We also used people from this group as facilitators for meetings and to moderate walkthroughs, where not being a member of the team can be a real advantage. Also, when we needed to have a major technical review, the methodologies group would advise me on who should be in attendance.

Carrying Out the Project

This project began in mid-June 1993 as the CIMS Replacement Project. The Computerized Invoice Matching System (CIMS) was an old, patched-up system that matched invoices to computer-issued purchase orders and receiving reports, paid those invoices where everything agreed, and suspended payment on invoices where there was disagreement.

The Initial Study

Because of strategic changes in how the department intended to operate in the future, a number of significant changes to the system were necessary. The project team concluded that it was impractical to modify the CIMS system to include several of these important enhancements. Therefore, Shaw and Watkins recommended that a new system be developed instead of attempting to enhance the existing CIMS system. They also suggested that the scope of this system be increased to include the manual purchase order and some transactions that did not involve purchase orders, which effectively collapsed two of the planned development projects into one. At its meeting on August 8, 1993, the steering group accepted this recommendation and authorized the team to base the Initial Study Report on the development of a new system that they named the Payables Audit System (PAS).

The Initial Study Report is a high-level presentation of the business objectives of the new system and how this system will further those business objectives. A 17-page document released on September 21, 1993, it discussed two major problems with the old system and described five major improvements that the new system would provide. The estimated yearly savings were $85,000 in personnel costs and $50,000 in system maintenance, for a total of $135,000. On October 9, 1993, the Initial Study Report was approved by Anderson, and the team was authorized to proceed with the Detailed Study.

The Detailed Study Report

The Detailed Study Report begins with an investigation of the current system, production of level 1 and level 2 data flow diagrams, and an entity/relationship diagram of the existing system. Then, given the business objectives of the new system, the project team considers how the current system can be improved and prepares data flow diagrams and entity/relationship diagrams for the proposed system. Much work on the Detailed Study Report had been done before it was formally authorized, and this report was issued on October 26, 1993. This report was a 30-page document, with another 55 pages of attachments.

The major activities in this stage were initial data modeling workshops whose results were stored in the CASE tool logical data dictionary. Most of the attachments to the Detailed Study Report were printouts of data from this logical data dictionary providing information on the data flow diagrams and the entity/relationship models that were included in the report.

The body of this report was mainly an elaboration of the Initial Study Report. It included the following business objectives of the new system:

- Reduce the cost of voucher processing over the next three years to be less than the current cost.
- Reduce the staff required for processing vouchers by 50 percent over the next five years.
- Significantly reduce the time required to pay vouchers.
- Provide systematic information for the purpose of measuring quality of vendor and accounts payable performance.
- Support systematic integration with transportation/logistics, purchasing, and accounts payable to better facilitate changes due to shifts in business procedures.

Among the constraints on the PAS system cited in the Detailed Study Report were that it must be operational no later than September 30, 1994; that it would be limited to the IBM mainframe hardware platform; and that it must interface with six systems (Purchase Order Control, Supplier Master, Front-End Document Control, Electronic Data Interchange, Corporate Approval, and Payment). Four of these systems were under development at that time, and it was recognized that alternative data sources might need to be temporarily incorporated into PAS.

The estimated savings from the new system remained at $135,000 per year, and the cost of developing the system was estimated to be between $250,000 and $350,000. It was estimated that the next phase of the project would require 1,250 hours over 2.5 months and cost $40,000. The Detailed Study Report was approved on October 31, 1993, and the team was authorized to proceed with the Draft Requirements Study.

The Draft Requirements Study

As the Draft Requirements Study began, Watkins was concerned about three risks that might impact the PAS project:

First, so many interrelated systems were changing at the same time that our requirements were a moving target. In particular, the imaging Document Control System that was our major interface had not been physically implemented and the technology was completely new to CIPI. Second, the schedule called for three other new systems to be installed at the same time as PAS, and conversion and testing would take so much user time that there simply are not enough hours in the day for the accounts payable people to get that done.

Finally, I was the only full-time person from the CIPI IS department. Although the contractors were excellent people, they would go away after the project was over and there would be little carryover within CIPI.

Watkins discussed her concerns with Carter and Mason and with Anderson and the steering group. They all told her that, at least for the present, the project must proceed as scheduled.

The Draft Requirements Study produces detailed information on the inputs, outputs, processes, and data of the new system. In addition to producing level 3 data flow diagrams, the project team describes each process and produces data definitions for the data flows and data stores in these data flow diagrams, and describes the data content (though not the format) of all input and output screens and reports of the new system. The project team was involved in much interviewing and conducted a number of detailed data-modeling workshops to produce this detail. The major problem encountered was the inability to schedule activities with Disbursements Department people when they were needed. For example, in early December, Anderson came to Watkins and told her that his people would be fully occupied with year-end closing activities for the last two weeks of December and the first two weeks of January and that they would not be available for work on the PAS project. He was very unhappy with this situation and apologized for delaying the project. Watkins told him that she understood that the business came first and that she would reschedule activities and do what she could to reduce the impact on the schedule. This potential problem had been brought up at the steering group meeting in early November, but the group had decided to go ahead with the planned schedule.

The PAS Draft Requirements Statement (DRS) was completed on March 21, 1994, four weeks behind schedule, but only $5,000 over budget. The DRS filled two thick loose-leaf binders with detailed documentation of the processes and the data content of the inputs, outputs, data flows, and data stores in the new system. Preparation of the Outline Physical Design was projected to require 600 hours over six weeks at a cost of $25,000. The DRS was approved on April 3, 1994, and the Outline Physical Design phase was begun.

The Outline Physical Design

In the Outline Physical Design phase the IS technical people become involved for the first time. They look at the logical system and consider alternatives as to how it can be implemented with hardware and new manual procedures. The approach in this phase is to map the processes in the logical data flow diagrams and the data models to manual processes and hardware and to make sure that this proposed hardware can be supplied and supported by the organization. Programming languages and utilities are also considered, so at the end of this phase the project team knows what kind of programming specifications and technical capabilities will be required.

The PAS system was originally planned to run on the IBM mainframe, but given the use of a LAN for the Document Control System, the technical people decided to move as much of the PAS system to the LAN as possible. This was a radical change that increased the estimated development cost substantially.

Watkins' new estimate of the total cost of the PAS system was $560,000. This was a substantial increase from the previous estimate of $250,000 to $350,000, and it caused some concern in CIPI management. Peter Shaw asserted:

> The company treasurer doesn't care a bit about the PAS project. All he cares about is how many dollars are going to be spent and in which year. When the cost went up so that we were substantially over budget for this year, that got his attention. If the increase were for next year it would not be a major problem because he would have time to plan for it—to get it into his budget. But this year his budget is set, so Linda and I have to figure out how we can stay within our budget and still get a usable system this year as version 1 and upgrade it to what we really need next year.

On June 27, just as the Outline Physical Design report was being completed, Watkins was seriously injured in a car accident and would not be back to work for months.

Anderson's Concerns

Watkins' accident focused Anderson's attention on some long-standing concerns. He was worried because among the five projects he was sponsoring, Watkins was the best project director that he had. All of his other projects were behind schedule and in trouble, and now he did not know what would happen to the PAS project.

Anderson was fully committed to his strategic direction for the disbursements area, and he felt that his reputation would be at risk if the systems necessary to support his planned changes could not be completed successfully. He was convinced that he had to take decisive action to get things back on track. He needed a plan of attack to present to IS Director Charles Bunke at tomorrow's meeting.

THE AMERICAN
FOODS COMPANY

On October 5, 1996, Wendell T. Johnston, vice president of information services, was reading his mail and messages in his office in the American Foods headquarters building when his telephone rang. His secretary announced that William C. Monroe, vice president for materials management, wanted to speak to him. "Oh, oh," Wendell thought to himself. "Here it comes again!" He was right.

"Hello, Bill," Wendell said. "What can I do for you this morning?"

"Well, for starters you could get your damn IS organization to quit fouling up the entire company operations!" Monroe answered belligerently.

"You sound upset," Wendell replied in a conciliatory tone. "What's the problem?"

"You know damn well what the problem is!" shouted Monroe. "It's the same problem we've had for the past two weeks. The order processing system is still producing garbage by the ton! This is the second time in a row that my people have had to work all weekend to get the orders that got lost in the system processed so that we can ship some product to those customers. You do realize, don't you, that if we don't ship product we're out of business?"

"My people worked all weekend, too," Wendell retorted. "We're doing everything we can to get things straightened out. But it's a very frustrating thing—when we solve one problem, two more seem to spring up. I thought that by now things would be much better."

"Better? They're getting worse and worse! My people are ready to take all our data entry away from that new company you farmed it out to and hire a competent vendor who can do the job right!" threatened Monroe. "You ought to have known better than to go with the lowest bidder!"

"It's just not that simple," Wendell heatedly replied. "The vendor contends that most of the problems have been caused by your people not recording the data right in the first place, or delivering it to them late, or writing illegibly! The people I've had working on it believe that your people are causing a lot of the problems."

"Bullbleep!" shouted Monroe. "You better get your act together or we're going to take matters into our own hands!"

Background

The American Foods Company makes and sells well-known brands of breakfast cereals, baking mixes, flour, prepared dough, frozen and canned vegetables, ice cream, and frozen foods, such as fish, pizza, and gourmet meals. Its industrial foods division sells a wide range of biscuit, doughnut, and other dough mixes, several types of specialty flours to bread and cereal makers, and various commodities and feed ingredients. In 1996 American Foods made after-tax profits of $145 million on sales of $2.8 billion.

The American Foods order entry system, composed of some 700 programs, accepts orders for all their products, manages finished-goods inventories and distribution, and prepares shipping notices and invoices. It is crucial to American Foods operations.

The system is a batch system that was developed 20 years ago, when American Foods was basically a breakfast cereal company. As new companies with new product lines were acquired, their order processing systems were grafted onto the American Foods system. Therefore, the order processing system became more complex and unwieldy every year.

This case was prepared by Professor E. W. Martin as the basis for class discussion rather than to illustrate either effective or ineffective handling of an administrative situation.

Copyright © 1997 (revised) by E. W. Martin.

In March 1996 the American Foods Information Services Division (ISD) made the strategic decision to gradually convert its old batch systems to on-line data entry. Consequently, in early 1996 ISD also decided to subcontract most of its batch data entry to a local data entry contractor and eliminate American Foods' in-house data entry department.

ISD people spent April and May planning the change and training the batch users. ISD managers knew that user training was important because within their own data entry department everyone was used to working together, ISD people were familiar with the applications and the forms used, and ISD people were accustomed to resolving problems either face-to-face or on the phone. With an outside vendor they knew that things would be more formal.

During June and July a pilot test was conducted with the prepared dough product line. Users in this area were trained well and did an excellent job of documenting everything. The pilot test went well, and it was felt that the few problems encountered had been ironed out. The cutover of the rest of the system was made during August and September. The following month Bill Monroe made his heated call to Wendell Johnston.

The Investigation

Immediately after his conversation with Monroe, Johnston called in his director of data services, Harold Crawford, and asked him for a report on the problems.

"We really don't know for sure what is causing the problems," Crawford admitted. "Some of my people say it's mainly a problem with the telecom between here and the vendor. Others say it's the new data entry vendor, others are blaming it on the users, and others think it might be the result of the new customer profile modifications. Everyone is pointing fingers and claiming that it's not their fault."

"What a mess!" exclaimed Johnston. "We've got to do something to straighten this out, and do it in a hurry. The credibility of the IS organization is at stake. You've got to get this straightened out quickly or heads will roll!"

Crawford immediately assigned Carol Morgan, the new supervisor of problem management, to tracking down and eliminating the problems on a full-time basis. She began the next day, and by the end of October, she had identified the causes of most of the problems and put temporary fixes in place. Most of the month-end reports were run without trouble, but it was well into December before the order processing system was back to normal and Morgan had developed a plan for long-term solutions.

"Most people thought the data entry vendor was causing the problems," Morgan related, "but they were causing only about 5 percent of the problems—about what you would expect with a new organization taking over data entry. About 35 percent of the problems were due to poor execution of the transfer of the data entry responsibilities on the part of American Foods, and the remaining 60 percent were due to the changes we had made in the order processing system when we converted to the customer profile invoicing during September."

Problems with the Transfer of Data Entry

Although the six-week pilot test of the cutover to the data entry vendor had gone well—American Foods had done the needed training and documentation—from then on things were very slipshod. The transfer of the remaining 80 percent of the work was done in three weeks, and the people doing the documentation and user training were being phased out toward the end of the cutover. As Morgan said, "They just shoved it out of the door. Under the circumstances they didn't have much motivation to kill themselves to do it right."

Morgan also found that the data entry had been a mess all along, but over the years the in-house data entry group had adapted to the users' peculiarities. Each group made zeros differently and the way they indicated negative amounts varied—some put the minus sign on the left, others put it on the right, and others enclosed the number in brackets. Handwriting was sloppy, and people often did not use the proper forms.

Further, users would hand in work after the deadline and someone would sneak it into the processing. The vendor, however, did not know when it was critical to do this and just followed the rules. These problems, caused by inadequate user training and documentation, accounted for about a third of the difficulties.

Problems Caused by Changes to the System

Previously, American Foods had four different invoicing systems that operated on different cycles. A customer would receive four different bills from American Foods —one for the products of each of their major acquisitions. To compound the problem, some of the invoicing systems used different codes to identify customers. The customer profile modification to the system was intended to rationalize this situation and provide a single invoice for each customer.

The customer profile modification was installed in September, about the time that data entry was transferred to the outside vendor. Because the customer profile modification was mainly to the output of the system rather than the input, and because the people responsible for the modifications vehemently denied that they had made any changes that could cause the problems they were experiencing, no one suspected that this was causing most of the problems.

It took Morgan about two weeks to realize what was going on. She would show a programmer what was happening on one of the data entry forms, and the programmer would say: "That isn't anything that we could be causing." The next day the problem would disappear. That happened five or six times before Morgan caught onto what was going on. The programmers would figure out what had happened and fix the problem, but would not admit that they had changed anything.

When Morgan met with the supervisor of that maintenance group, she found that he was unaware of what had been going on. After that meeting the rest of the problems caused by the modification were quickly cleared up. Morgan found that they had changed the definitions of some data elements to make the different invoicing systems compatible, but they did not realize that these changes would affect other parts of the system. Further, they had changed the processing cycles of some of the databases, which caused unforeseen problems in other parts of the system.

These problems were caused by the condition of the order processing system rather than the programmers' competence. It was mostly a manifestation of the ripple effect, where a change in one part of a poorly designed system causes unforeseeable problems with another part. The American Foods system was in dreadful shape—it had no reliable documentation, data elements had different names in different parts of the system, and there were 25 different databases being used without a data dictionary.

They had thoroughly tested those parts of the system that they were working with, but they had not done adequate testing of the entire system before installing the customer profile modification in September.

Morgan found other problems with the data entry system, the communication system, and the management of the process, but by the middle of December the crisis was over, and she had prepared a plan describing the steps that should be taken to eliminate the problems they had identified.

Johnston's Dilemma

After discussing Morgan's report with her, Wendell Johnston was relieved that the crisis appeared to be over, but he knew that the problems would continue. From 200 to 400 changes to the order processing and other crucial operational support systems were being made each month just to keep them going, and he knew that any of those hundreds of changes could cause another collapse of one of the systems.

Johnston believes that the solution to these problems is to replace several old systems, but replacing the order processing system alone would take five years and cost roughly $5 million. Even if the money to replace these systems were available, he would not have the necessary manpower because he has to build a long list of new systems that senior management has identified to be of strategic importance to American Foods.

JEFFERSON COUNTY SCHOOL SYSTEM

The Jefferson County School System (JCSS) educates about 10,000 students in 14 elementary schools, two middle schools, and two high schools. It serves a diverse community consisting of a county seat of 80,000 with a substantial industrial base and a major state university, and the surrounding rural area.

Central High School and Roosevelt High School, located on the eastern edge of town, are spirited athletic rivals whose attendance districts split the county into approximately equal areas, with each district including about 1,450 city and rural patrons. The two middle schools each have about 750 pupils in the seventh and eighth grades and also serve diversified areas. The elementary schools are located throughout the county and range in size from rural schools with about 250 students up to almost 700 students for the largest city school.

History of Administrative Computing in JCSS

Administrative computing at JCSS began in the early 1970s when computing resources at the university were leased to do scheduling and grade reporting and to keep student enrollment data. In 1976 the school corporation purchased a DEC PDP 11/34 computer, and the student management applications were converted from the university computer. Over the next few years, financial applications were added and more student management applications were developed. In 1984 a PDP 11/44 was acquired and located in the JCSS Administration Building next to Central High. The PDP 11/34 was moved to Roosevelt High, where it was used for student manage-

ment applications at Roosevelt and a nearby middle school. The payroll processing was farmed out to the data processing subsidiary of a local bank.

All of these applications, both financial and student management, were custom developed by the longtime director of data processing, David Meyer, and the two programmers on his staff. The users of these systems were satisfied with them, and when they wanted changes and improvements, Meyer and his programmers would make them. All of the systems were written in BASIC, and there was no end-user capability—if anyone needed a special report, a program to produce it was written in BASIC by one of the programmers. In 1986 the two PDP computers were replaced by two PRIME 2755 computers, and the BASIC programs were converted to run on the new machines.

In late 1993, however, the JCSS director of finance, Harvey Greene, became concerned with problems he saw developing in the data processing area. First, it was apparent that the JCSS computers were becoming overloaded, and these old machines were becoming more and more difficult to maintain. Additional capacity was going to be needed soon, but the PRIME line of computers were no longer in production, so any replacement would involve incompatible hardware and software. Mr. Greene was very concerned because he felt that converting the old custom systems to a new hardware/software environment would be time-consuming and a waste of money.

Therefore, early in 1994 the JCSS administration set up a small task force of administrators to evaluate the JCSS data processing systems and to recommend directions for the future. This task force recommended that:

- The PRIME hardware should be replaced.
- Because JCSS could not afford the time or money to convert its current systems, the JCSS systems should be replaced with purchased software packages.

This case was prepared by Professor E. W. Martin as the basis for class discussion, rather than to illustrate either effective or ineffective handling of an administrative situation.

Copyright © 1997 (Revised) by E. W. Martin.

- The new systems should utilize an integrated database and report-generation software so that people could share data from various applications.
- JCSS should contract with a vendor who would accept total responsibility for both the hardware and software.
- Because JCSS would no longer be doing custom development, the programming staff of the data processing department could be reduced.

Soon after the recommendations were accepted by the JCSS administration, Meyer resigned as data processing director. In July 1994 he was replaced by Carol Andrews, who had 13 years experience as an applications programmer, systems programmer, and systems analyst with a nearby federal government installation.

Purchasing the New System

After spending several months getting acclimated to the JCSS and her new job, Andrews set about the task of selecting a vendor to provide the hardware and software to replace the current administrative computing applications at JCSS. In late November 1994 a computer selection committee was appointed to evaluate available systems and recommend a vendor to the JCSS School Board. This 14-member committee included representatives of most of the major users of the system—assistant principals who did scheduling and were responsible for student records; deans who were responsible for attendance and student discipline; counselors; teachers; the personnel director; and the chief accountant. It also included representatives of the different levels of schools in the system and from each of the larger school locations.

By late March 1995 Andrews and the committee had prepared a 71-page request for proposal (RFP) that was sent to 23 possible vendors, asking that proposals be submitted by May 4, 1995. The RFP stated that "The proposals will be evaluated on functional requirements, support services, and a five-year life cycle cost." The table of contents of the RFP is included as Exhibit 1. Appendices A through E listed in the contents were in the form of fill-in-the-blank questionnaires that defined the information that JCSS desired from the vendors.

The RFP was sent to vendors that would contract to accept responsibility for all the hardware, software, and support and training services required to install and maintain the new system. The RFP specified the number and location of the terminals and printers that were to be connected to the system in Part III-D and Appendix C. The desired requirements for the applications software were described in Appendix D in the form of characteristics that could be checked off as included or not. The applications specifications for the attendance accounting and student scheduling systems from Appendix D are included as Exhibit 2.

The requirements for terminals and printers in the various buildings were determined by Andrews in consultation with someone on the selection committee who was familiar with each school. Although members of the selection committee made suggestions, Andrews determined most of the requirements for the application systems by examining what the existing systems did and talking with people throughout the JCSS.

Seven proposals were submitted in response to the RFP. Andrews was able to winnow them down easily to three serious contenders that were evaluated in detail. Each of the three finalists was invited to demonstrate its system to the selection committee. The vendors were not told in detail what to show, but they were asked to demonstrate the operation of several of the major systems. The three vendors brought in their own small computers for the demonstration, and all of the demonstrations were quite satisfactory to the committee.

The committee originally intended to visit a school that used each vendor's system, but because of time and money constraints they were only able to visit two sites—one Data Systems, Inc. installation and one Scholastic Systems Corporation installation. Andrews and Dr. Paul Faris, assistant principal at Roosevelt High, spent one day at each of these locations observing their systems in action and talking with users. In addition, members of the committee made telephone calls to their counterparts at other schools that used each vendors' systems without unearthing any major problems or concerns. Everyone seemed quite positive about all three vendors and their products.

The committee had a difficult time deciding between the three finalists. Each of the vendors proposed software packages in all the areas that JCSS had asked for, but none of these systems did exactly what they wanted in exactly the way the current systems did things. The committee finally chose Data Systems, Inc. (DSI) because the members felt they could work well with the DSI people and they felt that DSI proposal was best on balance, as indicated in Exhibit 3, which was presented to the JCSS School Board. This table rates seven factors on a scale from 1 to 5, with a total rating for each of the finalist vendors at the bottom. The "cost of ownership" includes the purchase price of the hardware and software, installation, training, and five years of hardware and software mainte-

EXHIBIT 1
Jefferson County School System Request for Proposal.

Table of Contents

nance and support. The "bid exceptions" rating refers to how well the proposed software fits the JCSS specifications and thus a high rating indicates that little modification of the software would be needed.

The JCSS School Board awarded the contract to DSI in June 1995, which included the following systems: financial, payroll/personnel, fixed assets, warehouse inventory, registration, scheduling, grades/transcripts, attendance, book bills, office assistant, electronic mail, and special education. These systems utilize a standard relational database management system that includes a query language called INFORM that generates ad hoc reports.

DSI agreed to make specific changes in the software packages where the committee had indicated that the packages did not meet the JCSS specifications. The contract also provided that DSI would devote up to 100 hours of programming time to making other modifications (not yet specified) in its software. Any additional changes requested by JCSS would be billed at $100 per programmer hour. JCSS also purchased DSI's standard software maintenance contract.

The operating system for the IBM RS/6000 is AIX, IBM's version of UNIX. The Administration Center and each of the 18 schools are connected via an existing

EXHIBIT 2
Application Specifications
Appendix D.

Student Administration System
Attendance Accounting

Included		
Yes	**No**	
_____	_____	1. Provide for interactive CRT entry and correction of daily attendance information.
_____	_____	2. Provide for interactive entry and correction of YTD attendance information.
_____	_____	3. Provide for interactive entry of period by period, and half or whole day attendance.
_____	_____	4. Capable of input of attendance by CRT entry or optional scanning device(s).
_____	_____	5. Provide CRT access to student attendance records by date or course, showing period by period attendance and reason for absence for any date.
_____	_____	6. Provide "user defined" definition of ADA and ADM calculation requirements.
_____	_____	7. Provide for entry of absence reason codes by exception.
_____	_____	8. Provide for multiple attendance periods with "user defined" number of days in each.
_____	_____	9. Provide for entry of entire year school calendar.
_____	_____	10. Provide for student registers.
_____	_____	11. Provide for entry and withdrawal. Provide for student withdrawal, which retains all student information and tracks the withdrawn student's attendance as "not enrolled;" in the event the student returns to the district and reenrolls all attendance calculations will automatically be current and up-to-date.

Included		
Yes	**No**	
_____	_____	12. Daily absence worksheet phone list.
_____	_____	13. Daily absence report.
_____	_____	14. Absence report by reason.
_____	_____	15. Student Attendance Register Report. List by class and section.
_____	_____	16. Student Absence by Reason listing.
_____	_____	17. School Absence by Reason listing.
_____	_____	18. Provide attendance reports with ADA and ADM calculations from any beginning date through any ending date.
_____	_____	19. Provide attendance reports by: Student
_____	_____	Absence and Absence reason(s)
_____	_____	Sex
_____	_____	Grade level
_____	_____	Course and section
_____	_____	Multiple combinations of the preceding requirements
_____	_____	20. Provide ADA and ADM calculation reports, with any "from" and "through" dates for the following:
_____	_____	Any and all schools
_____	_____	The entire district
_____	_____	Each attendance register
_____	_____	21. Provide M–F absence reports by any "from" and "through" dates, also by student, grade, sex, course and section, and/or absence reason code.
_____	_____	22. Provide daily entry and withdrawal reports.

EXHIBIT 2 (continued)

Student Administration System
Student Scheduling

Included		
Yes	**No**	
_____	_____	1. Provide for interactive CRT entry and correction of student course requests and master schedule data.
_____	_____	2. Automatically process student course requests against the master schedule to produce class schedules for each student.
_____	_____	3. Provide for Arena Scheduling.
_____	_____	4. Provide for interactive CRT drop/add of students from classes after initial schedules are established, at any time.
_____	_____	5. Scheduling data must interface with student records.
_____	_____	6. Provide for course restrictions by grade level and/or sex.
_____	_____	7. Allow for addition of new courses and sections at any time.
_____	_____	8. Provide current enrollment summary of each course and section via CRT and report.
_____	_____	9. Provide for mass adds, deletes or changes based on grade, sex, etc.
_____	_____	10. On-line editing of valid course number requests during CRT entry is required.
_____	_____	11. Provide for scheduling retries without erasing previous scheduling runs.
_____	_____	12. Provide for override of maximum enrollment.

Included		
Yes	**No**	
_____	_____	13. Provide for each student a year-long schedule, with up to 20 different courses (excluding lunch and study hall).
_____	_____	14. Provide for "prioritizing" scheduling runs by grade level and/or student number.
_____	_____	15. Provide master schedule by teacher listing.
_____	_____	16. Preregistration "by student" course request report.
_____	_____	17. Preregistration "by course" request listing.
_____	_____	18. Provide course request tally report.
_____	_____	19. Provide potential conflict matrix.
_____	_____	20. Provide student conflict report.
_____	_____	21. Provide student schedules.
_____	_____	22. Provide course and section status summary.
_____	_____	23. Provide course rosters by teacher.
_____	_____	24. Provide room utilization report with conflict alert.
_____	_____	25. Provide teacher utilization report with conflict alert.
_____	_____	26. Provide schedule exception listing showing student and open periods (by either closed or conflict status), also show all filled periods.
_____	_____	27. Provide scheduling by quarter, semester, year-long, or trimester options.

TCP/IP wide area network, so each school has access to the system. The system is character-based, using existing PCs emulating DEC VT 220 terminals for input and output.

Implementation of the Systems

The hardware arrived and the RS/6000 was installed in the Administration Center in October 1995. After the hardware was checked out, Andrews and her staff began to install the software and phase in some of the systems. They encountered their fair share of problems, and as of February 1997 they had not been able to transfer all of the old systems from the PRIMEs to the RS/6000.

Although they have had some problems with the financial systems, they have successfully installed most of them. But they have had major problems in installing and using the student management systems.

EXHIBIT 3
Evaluation of Bids.

Selection Criteria	Data Systems	Scholastic Systems	Orian Computer Systems
1. Vendor Profile	5	5	3
2. Vendor Services	5	4	3
3. Hardware (Rating)	IBM RS/6000 4	DEC ALPHA 5	HP 9000 3
4. Application Software	5	4	3
5. 5 yr. Cost of Ownership (Rating)	$698,600 4	$874,730 3	$495,060 5
6. Software support	5	4	3
7. Bid Exceptions	5	4	3
TOTAL RATING	33	29	23

Andrews planned to follow the cycle of the academic year when implementing the student systems. First, they would transfer all the student demographic information from the present system to the new system's database. Then they would complete the students' fall class schedules by the end of the spring semester, as they had been doing with the old system, so the students' schedules would be on the new system and ready to go in the fall. During the summer they would pick up the attendance accounting on the new system so it would be ready for the fall. Then they would implement grade reporting so it would be ready for use at the end of the first six-week grading period in the fall. Finally, they would convert the student transcript information from the old system so that fall-semester grades could be transferred to the transcripts at the end of the semester.

They successfully transferred the student demographic information from the old system to the new in February 1996. Then they started to work on student scheduling. Things did not go well. The training provided by DSI for the scheduling officers was a disaster. Then, after entering the student class requests and the available faculty data, they started the first scheduling run. After it had run all day without completing the schedules, they decided that there was something definitely wrong. Andrews still has not completely resolved this problem with DSI's experts. DSI claims that it was caused by how the scheduling officer set up the scheduling system—the various parameters that the system uses. Andrews is still convinced that there is some sort of bug in the scheduling program.

DSI did make some minor modifications to the program, and they sent some people out to consult with Andrews and her staff on how to set up the schedule, but they were unable to get the schedules done by the end of the spring semester as planned. This caused severe problems because the assistant principals who are in charge of scheduling are not on the payroll during the summer. Fortunately, Paul Faris, the scheduling officer at Roosevelt, was working summer school, and with his assistance they were just able to get all the schedules done two weeks before school started.

Preparation for the fall was also hindered by the fact that neither the school secretaries, who entered much of the data for the attendance module, nor the counselors, who had to work with the scheduling of new students in the system and changes to schedules of continuing students, were on the payroll during the summer. The administration would not spend the money to pay these people to come in during the summer for training on the system, so all training was delayed until the week before school started, when everyone reported back to work. The training was rushed, and again DSI did a poor job with it.

When school started in the fall, the system was a total disaster. The people who were working with the system did not understand it or know what they were doing with it. When the counselors tried to schedule a new student into his classes, the system might take 20 minutes to produce his new schedule. Needless to say, there were long lines of students waiting in the halls, and the students, their parents, the counselors, teachers, and administrators were upset and terribly frustrated.

Also, the attendance officers did not know what they were doing and could not make the system work for the first few weeks of the semester. Things were so bad that at the end of the first grading period Andrews decided that, although the grade reporting system was working all right, it was not feasible to have the teachers enter their grades directly into the system as had been planned. Instead, she hired several outside clerical people to enter the grades from forms the teachers filled out. After some well-executed training, the teachers successfully entered their grades at the end of the semester.

By the end of the fall semester most of those working with the student systems had learned enough to make them work adequately, and a few of them were beginning to recognize that the new systems had some significant advantages over the old ones. They did get the second semester under way without major problems, and in early February 1997, they were getting ready to bring up the transcript system and start the scheduling process for the fall.

Perspectives of the Participants

Given everything that had transpired in acquiring and implementing the new system to this stage, it is not surprising that there are many different opinions on the problems that have been encountered, whether or not the new system is satisfactory, and what the future holds. The following presents the perspectives of a number of those who have been involved with the new system.

Dr. Harold Whitney, Assistant Principal, Central High School

Dr. Whitney believes that the previous system was an excellent system that really did the job for them. "It was fast, efficient, and effective. And when we needed something, rather than having to call DSI in Virginia to get it done, our own people would do it for us in a matter of two or three days. However, the study committee (that probably didn't have enough good school people on it) decided on the new system, and we were told that we would start with the new scheduling software package early in 1996."

The first acquaintance that Whitney had with the new system was in early February when DSI sent someone in to train four or five of the scheduling people on how to use the new system to construct a master schedule. Whitney recalls:

> Over a three-day period we took fifty students and tried to construct a master schedule. And at the end of the three days, we still hadn't been able to do it. It was apparent that the lady they sent out to train us, while she may have known the software, had no idea of what we wanted in a master schedule, and had never experienced the master schedule building process in a large high school.

> The master schedule is the class schedule of all of the courses that we offer—when and where they will be taught, and by whom. In the past, I would take the course requests from our students and summarize them to determine the demand for each course, and then I would develop a master schedule that assigned our available teachers to the courses that they could best teach while meeting the student demand as well as possible. I had to take into account the fact that, among all the teachers that are certified to teach mathematics, some are more effective teaching algebra and geometry than they are in calculus, and similarly for other subject areas. Also, we have 15 or so teachers that are part-time in our school and therefore can only teach here during the morning (or the afternoon). Furthermore, we need to lock our two-semester courses so that a student will have the same teacher for both semesters.

> With the new system we were supposed to input our teachers and their certifications and the student requests for courses, and the DSI software would

generate the ideal master schedule to satisfy that demand. But we had to place quite a number of restrictions on what and when the teachers could teach and into what sections a student could be scheduled. When we tried to run the software, it just ran and ran, but it never produced a satisfactory schedule.

DSI sent one of its top executives out to talk with Whitney about these problems. The executive told Whitney that "the reason that you're unhappy is that you're placing too many restrictions on the schedule." Whitney replied, "All well and good. But are you telling me that your software package should dictate our curriculum? That it should dictate who teaches calculus, who teaches general math, who teaches advanced and who teaches beginning grammar? That's hardly sound educationally!"

Whitney ended up doing the schedule by hand, as he had done before, and the students were scheduled by the end of the spring semester. Some of the other schools continued to try to use the full system, and they had a hard time getting the schedules out by the start of school.

Whitney had a very bad impression of the system until the end of 1996, but he now thinks that things are improving some. DSI people are beginning to listen to him, and so he is more receptive. "I've always been able to see that somewhere down the road the new system will have capabilities that improve on our old system."

Dr. Paul Faris, Assistant Principal, Roosevelt High School

Dr. Faris, an active member of the computer study committee that chose the new system, is responsible for class scheduling at Roosevelt High, and, unlike Harold Whitney at Central High, he used the system as it was intended to be used both to develop the master schedule and to schedule the students into their classes. He had a struggle with the system at first and had not completed the master schedule by the end of spring. However, he was on the payroll during the summer and was able to complete the master schedule a few weeks before the beginning of school in fall 1996.

In doing so he learned a great deal about how the scheduling system worked.

The way your master schedule is set up and the search patterns you establish determine how the system performs. The individual principals have control over many aspects of the process, and there is a lot of leeway—whether you set up for one semester or two, whether you strictly enforce class sizes, whether or not you have alternatives to search for with specific courses, and so on. We set it up for double semester,

which is the hard one, but I had generous limits on my class size and we had limited search for alternatives, which kicked the difficult ones out of the system to handle on a manual basis. And I limited certain courses to seniors, or sophomores, et cetera, and that restricted the search pattern somewhat.

Paul knew that the beginning of the fall semester would be crunch time, when lots of work would have to be done with the new system in a limited amount of time. So he prepared his people for the transition ahead of time. Paul's secretary was skilled on the old system. Early in the spring Paul told her: "We are going to change over our entire system in four months. And week by week I want you to tell me what files have to be changed over, and you and I are going to do it." Again, it was a matter of making sure things were done in a nonpressure situation where they could learn what they had to know.

Paul and his counselors still had many problems during the first few weeks of school in the fall, but nothing that they couldn't cope with. Things are going well in Paul's area now. They recently started the second semester, which was a crunch time again. The counselors got along fine with schedule changes, and they completed the new schedules faster than they had with the old system.

Paul believes that the new system is a substantial improvement over the old one.

I can follow through and find the kids' attendance, current program, grades, past history and transcripts, and probably have everything I need in two or three minutes. Before the new system I could barely walk to the filing cabinet and find his folder in that time. And then I'd still have to go to the counseling office and get the current schedule, and then to the attendance office and get the attendance record.

I'm really pleased with the new file structures. And Carol's programmer is starting to add back some of the custom things that we had in the old system. I'm looking forward to being trained on the report generator so that I can produce my own special reports without getting a programmer involved.

Dr. Ruth Gosser, Assistant Principal, Central High School

Dr. Gosser is the attendance and disciplinary officer at Central High and was a member of the computer selection committee. Ruth recalls:

We looked at about four different companies. Several had very good packages, although I will admit that by the time you sit through four or five different presentations, they all tend to run into one another.

My participation in specifying the requirements and evaluating the proposed systems was minimal. It was a big committee, and I was busy with other things, so I didn't even read the materials very carefully. I disliked spending the time that I did, and I was really turned off by the details, especially the technical details. I remember thinking: Ugh! I'm sick of this. Just go ahead and buy something!

She and her people had only two days of training on the system before the start of school, and Gosser thought the training provided was pretty useless. "They weren't very well organized, and they spent too much time on the technical aspects of the system. I just wanted to know how to use the system, but they tried to give me a lot more and it really confused me and made me angry."

When school started in the fall, it was a disaster. Ruth remembers it vividly:

It was awful! Awful! I didn't get home till after 6:30 for weeks. Just getting the information in and out was a nightmare. We had a terrible time trying to change the unexcused to excused, and doing all the little things that go with that. It was so bad that we seriously considered abandoning the system and trying to do it by hand. It was horrible!

But we've just gone through second semester class changes, and I haven't heard anyone weeping and wailing about what a crummy system this is. We're beginning to recognize that we've got the new system, and we're going to have it for a long time. They're not going to junk a system that we have paid all that money for, so we'd better work to make the very best out of it that we can. And I can see that there are some really good things about the new system that the old system didn't have, and never could have.

Looking back, I don't think that the computer selection committee did a very good job. If I had known then what I know now I'd have put a lot more effort into it than I did. Since most of us didn't put in the effort to get down to the details of exactly what we needed, Carol pretty much had to do it herself. Unfortunately, we only gave her enough information to get her off our backs. Like "I need something that will chart attendance for me." That wasn't much help. Every system we considered would chart attendance, so we had no basis for deciding which system would have been best for us.

Dr. Helen Davis, Assistant Principal, Roosevelt High

Dr. Davis is the attendance and disciplinary officer at Roosevelt High School. She was not a member of the computer selection committee, and she doesn't think it did a very good job.

The committee looked at a lot of different kinds of things, but they didn't communicate. Even though we all were supposed to have representatives on the committee, we didn't know what they were doing, nor did we have the opportunity to discuss any of the systems that they were looking at and whether those systems would help us or satisfy our needs.

When the new system was put in last fall a lot of us had no training, no information, and didn't know what was going on. My secretary had a day and a half training in August, but I had no training at all. Some training was offered to me in August, but I had already made arrangements to be out of town, and no flexibility was provided as to when the training would be available. Furthermore, there are no user-friendly manuals for the system—the manual they gave me is written in computerese. So I've had to learn the system by bitter experience, and I still don't know what it offers me. I could go through a hundred menus and not find what I want because I don't know what they are for.

Last fall when school opened my blood pressure probably went to 300 about every day! We couldn't do attendance—it wouldn't work. We couldn't print an absence list for the teachers. We couldn't put out an unexcused list. We couldn't get an excessive absence report, so it was mid-semester before I could start sending letters to parents whose kids weren't attending regularly. That really impedes the work of trying to keep kids in school.

The thing that frustrates Helen the most is that she resents being controlled by the software system.

The system is dictating what we can do with kids and their records. It needs to be the opposite way. We ought to be driving that machine to service what we need to do as easily as possible. But the machine is driving us, and I'm really displeased with that.

We're stuck with DSI and their software because we've got so much money invested in it. In time Carol will be able to make this system as compatible with our needs as it can be, but it will never be as suitable as it should be. And it will take a long, long time before we get all the things that we need.

Catherine Smith, Counselor at
Central High School

Catherine Smith has been a counselor at Central High School for 20 years, but she had no experience with the computer before the training session that was held the Thursday and Friday before school started. According to Catherine:

> The first day of school was just unbelievable! It took two hours to schedule one new student. Everyone was running up and down the halls asking each other questions. No one knew what was going on.
>
> The first two days I had absolutely no control over that computer! It would bleep, and you didn't know why. But by Wednesday morning I began to get control. I knew that if I pushed this button, this would happen. And I knew how to make it do some of the things I wanted it to do.
>
> Now that I've worked with it for a semester, I'm happy with it. The system contains a tremendous amount of information that I need to help the students. The thing I like most about the system is that when I want to put a kid in a class and it's full, I can find out instantly how many kids are in each section, and I can usually find a place for the kid. I can even override it if the section is closed. Despite the fact that we almost died during that first week, now that I have control over it I think it's tremendous!

Murphey Ford, English Teacher
at Roosevelt High School

Murphey has taught English at Roosevelt for twelve years, and he has had no experience with a computer beyond entering his grades into the old system.

> This new computer has been a disaster from the word go. Last fall they didn't produce a class schedule until two weeks before classes were to start, so I had no time to prepare to teach a class I hadn't taught for five years! And I wasn't even asked if I would be willing to teach it—the computer just assigned me to it.
>
> Then they relaxed the limits on class size. We ended up having some classes with 30 students and others with 40. That's not fair to either the students or the teachers. And it was a zoo around here at the beginning of the fall. It was three weeks before they got all the new students into their classes and things settled down a little.
>
> In this community we have very high expectations for the education system, but we never have enough money to provide the special programs we want, or

get adequate supplies, or pay decent salaries. It really burns me up that we spent almost a million dollars on this new computer that doesn't work anything like as well as the old one.

Carol Andrews,
Director of Data Processing

The 15 months since the new hardware arrived have been very difficult and stressful for Carol:

> I often wonder what it was that caused things to have gotten so difficult and to have raised so much negative reaction to the new system. One explanation is that we have a history of custom developed systems, so anything that users wanted got done exactly the way they wanted it. Now we have a set of generic software that is meant to serve many school systems and it doesn't do exactly what they want in exactly the way they want it.
>
> It was hard to get effective participation from the members of the computer selection committee. Coming from the government our RFP wasn't very big to me, but when I passed it around to the committee they couldn't believe it. I couldn't even get the people to really read the RFP, let alone the responses. Actually, it should have been even more detailed. It was the lack of detail that really caused us most of our problems, because it has been the details that have determined whether or not the systems were suitable to our people.
>
> We should have paid a lot more attention to training. DSI hasn't had much experience with training, and they just didn't do a good job with it. They left me, a new user, with too much responsibility for setting up the training and making sure that everything in the system was ready for it. And they didn't provide me with the training that I needed.
>
> Money is a big constraint to the JCSS. I needed a lot more programming help in-house, and someone from DSI—a week here and a week there—to fill in for our lack of knowledge in being able to support our users.
>
> Looking back at it, 15 months seems like an extremely long time to implement a new system. But it might have been better to take even more time to do it. Maybe we should have piloted the system at one school for a year and worked the bugs out of it before installing it system wide.
>
> Where do we go from here? How do we handle the negative reaction that has been generated from all the stumbles and falls? How do we get things turned around to take advantage of some of the things that

are really positive for the school system now that we have access to all this information? I'm beginning to see little pockets here and there where people are starting to use the capabilities of the new system and are developing positive attitudes. I hope that we're getting over the hump!

If we had it to do over again, would we make the decision to go with DSI? That's a question I ask myself every day! Could we have done better? Would we have had fewer problems? I don't know.

METHODIST HOSPITAL OF INDIANA

Before Clarian Health was formed in January 1997 through the merger of Methodist Hospital of Indiana with Indiana University Hospitals, Methodist Hospital was a stand-alone 1,200-bed tertiary care teaching hospital that was nationally known for its organ transplant program and its Emergency Medicine and Trauma Center. The main hospital complex was located just northwest of downtown Indianapolis, and the hospital had established outpatient clinics throughout central Indiana. In 1990 when the events described below began, Methodist Hospital had about 43,000 patient admissions, served 250,000 outpatients, and received about 80,000 visits to its emergency room. In the year ending February 28, 1991, Methodist Hospital had a net income of over $23 million on total operating revenue of over $416 million.

In 1988 the longtime head of Methodist Hospital retired, and William J. Loveday was hired away from Long Beach California Memorial Hospital to become the new CEO. Loveday quickly brought in a new management team, including John Fox as chief financial officer. The Information Services (IS) department reported to Fox, and it did not take Fox long to discover that Methodist Hospital had a stagnant IS department. To revitalize IS, Fox brought in Walter C. Zerrenner with the title of chief information officer (CIO). Prior to joining Methodist Hospital, Zerrenner was vice president of information systems for Evangelical Health Systems of Oak Brook, Illinois, a regional health care system managing five hospitals and an extensive managed care network in the Chicago area.

This case was prepared by Professor E. W. Martin as the basis for class discussion, rather than to illustrate either effective or ineffective handling of an administrative situation. Its development was supported by the Institute for Research on the Management of Information Systems (IRMIS), School of Business, Indiana University.

Copyright © 1997 (Revised) by E. W. Martin.

Information Systems at Methodist Hospital

Zerrenner found that the IS department was living in the past. In the mid-1970s Methodist Hospital had spent about $20 million to install a then state-of-the-art proprietary patient management system called TDS that maintained the medical records of admitted hospital patients. TDS allowed the physician to order laboratory tests, X-rays, and other procedures through TDS terminals and to have the results reported through these terminals. This mainframe system also captured admitting information and produced billing information upon discharge of patients from the hospital. Over 500 dumb terminals located throughout the hospital were attached to the TDS system. After that big investment in the mid-1970s, however, the hospital had made only very minimal capital expenditures within the IS department, whose efforts had been primarily devoted to keeping the TDS system working and maintaining other mainframe administrative systems.

When Zerrenner talked to doctors, nurses, and administrators throughout the hospital, he found that almost everyone was dissatisfied with the services provided by the IS department. As a consequence of this poor reputation, the departments and laboratories of the hospital had been acquiring their own systems, and 40 percent of Methodist Hospital's information technology expenditures were outside the IS department.

Thus, in addition to a large IBM mainframe, Methodist Hospital had some 700 PCs, about a dozen local area networks, and 13 minicomputers scattered throughout the institution. These departmental minicomputer systems were the best systems available when they were purchased, and they served the departmental needs very well, but, with a few exceptions, none of these systems was capable of communicating with any of the others. Methodist Hospital's data on patients were trapped in these separate systems and could not be obtained by those who needed the data unless they had access to the particular system where the needed data were stored.

The one major exception to this inability to share data was the TDS patient care system, but this system had serious limitations. First, it only maintained data on current admitted patients, so it could not be used for the growing long-term requirements of the hospital's outpatients. Second, it did not connect to systems in nuclear medicine, respiratory therapy, sports medicine, occupational health, medical research, marketing, and the operating room. Third, it could only be accessed from terminals located in the hospital, so doctors could not use it from the clinics or their offices. Finally, the patient's record was no longer available as soon as the patient was billed, so if a discharged patient had unforeseen complications, his hospital records were only available in the paper medical records files.

Zerrenner found that the users were unhappy with the isolated systems that made it impossible for doctors and nurses to obtain data on patients. Surgeons recounted frustrating incidents when patients were already on the operating table, but they could not start the operation because they could not get lab results. Physicians in the clinics found it very difficult to obtain information on test results, diagnoses, or procedures performed in other clinics or the hospital. And nurses were concerned because it was very difficult to care for the patients when they lacked information on certain procedures ordered by doctors.

The various clinics and departments did not have a standard way to identify patients, which also caused problems. Some of their systems had seven-digit identifiers, some had eight digits, some had alphanumeric identifiers, and so on. In addition, the filing system in medical records did not use the patient numbering system from the registration process. Therefore, when physicians needed information on a patient's history, they could not get it from the various computers because the patient was identified differently in each of them. This drove both doctors and patients crazy, because they sometimes had to repeat tests on a patient when they could not find the previous result. This was costly, wasteful, and sometimes painful, and it also delayed treatment.

Patients also were inconvenienced by the lack of integration in the systems. Outpatients had to register at each clinic, and it was not uncommon for patients to have to answer the same questions four or five times in a day as they visited different clinics and hospital departments.

Moreover, patients were irritated because one clinic did not have access to medical records from other clinics or departments. "My son had a problem that was difficult to diagnose," reported one mother, "and I spent several months going from one Methodist Hospital clinic to another. I soon discovered that they had no access to records, so I had to maintain his record myself. I carried a big folder with me, and made sure that I got copies of everything that was done at each visit and put them in the folder. Then I would give the folder to the next doctor that we visited. It was so frustrating—the only reason that I put up with Methodist Hospital was that they had the best doctors!"

Developing an IS Vision

When Zerrenner arrived at Methodist Hospital he found three IS strategic plans sitting on the shelf gathering dust. These plans had been developed, without user input, by his predecessors. "I do not intend to develop another massive document," Zerrenner told CEO Loveday. "Instead, we are going to develop a vision of where we need to go, and then we are going to follow that vision!" This IS vision was driven by the Methodist Hospital Strategic Vision depicted in Exhibit 1.

At Zerrenner's suggestion, Loveday appointed a 25-member IS planning committee, a short-term task force that would be disbanded after developing an IS vision. This committee had at least one person from every caregiving department in the hospital, with heavy representation from physicians and nurses and relatively few administrators. It met ten times in the summer and fall of 1990 to formulate its recommendations.

The planning committee recognized that each of the stand-alone departmental computer systems was outstanding in its field and that these systems contained a lot of useful information. The problem was that this information was not accessible for use where it was needed. The clinics and departments needed to integrate their existing systems so that everyone could share access to the information contained in each computer. The planning committee also recognized that it was not enough to share this information within the confines of the hospital—they needed to provide access to this data from locations outside the hospital.

Dr. Douglas J. Moeller, an internal medicine specialist with the Aegis Medical Clinic, was an active member of the planning committee and the elected chairman of the 200-physician internal medicine section of the hospital staff. "Our vision," Moeller reports, "is that our

EXHIBIT 1   *Methodist Hospital Strategic Vision.*

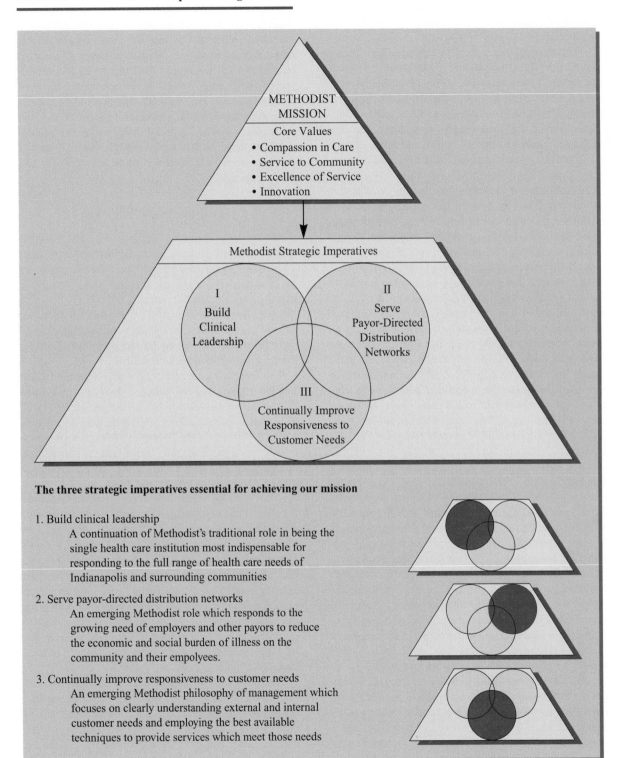

METHODIST
MISSION

Core Values
• Compassion in Care
• Service to Community
• Excellence of Service
• Innovation

Methodist Strategic Imperatives

I
Build
Clinical
Leadership

II
Serve
Payor-Directed
Distribution
Networks

III
Continually Improve
Responsiveness to
Customer Needs

The three strategic imperatives essential for achieving our mission

1. Build clinical leadership
    A continuation of Methodist's traditional role in being the
    single health care institution most indispensable for
    responding to the full range of health care needs of
    Indianapolis and surrounding communities

2. Serve payor-directed distribution networks
    An emerging Methodist role which responds to the
    growing need of employers and other payors to reduce
    the economic and social burden of illness on the
    community and their empolyees.

3. Continually improve responsiveness to customer needs
    An emerging Methodist philosophy of management which
    focuses on clearly understanding external and internal
    customer needs and employing the best available
    techniques to provide services which meet those needs

information system will contain complete medical record data for admitted patients, outpatients, and clinical patients. Furthermore, every Methodist Hospital staff physician can have a PC in his office, or even his home, that will provide user-friendly, convenient access to the medical records of patients and allow the physician to enter orders for patient treatment through the system. We would also like to provide limited access to the system to physicians outside of our immediate medical staff, so that they can have access to data on patients they have referred to Methodist Hospital."

Having determined the vision and set the direction for the future, the question of how to provide the desired integration and access became paramount. "What we proposed to do," Zerrenner explains, "was to keep our present systems and technology and to integrate them by means of an intelligent network that will connect them with the various users and also do the translating necessary to allow them to communicate with each other." This architecture, which is depicted in Exhibit 2, made sense to CEO Loveday, and the development of this Information Exchange Platform (IXP) was endorsed by the Methodist Hospital board and included in the Methodist Hospital foundation strategies, shown in Exhibit 3. The IXP also supports the "enhance physician/hospital collaboration" foundation strategy.

EXHIBIT 2
Methodist Hospital IS Architecture Strategy.

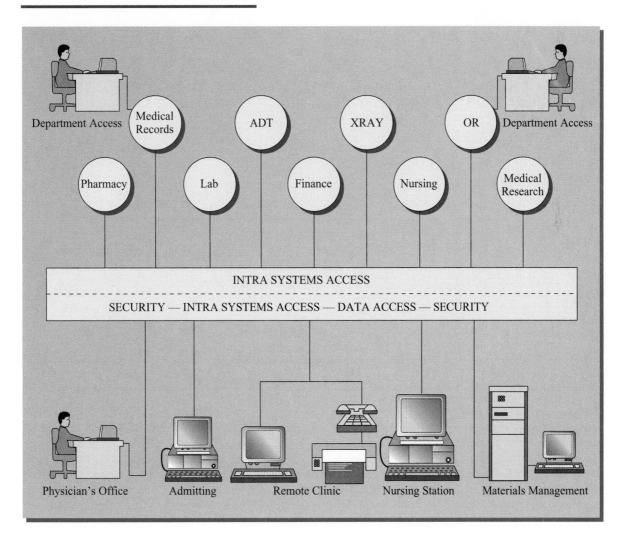

EXHIBIT 3
Methodist Hospital Overall Strategy.

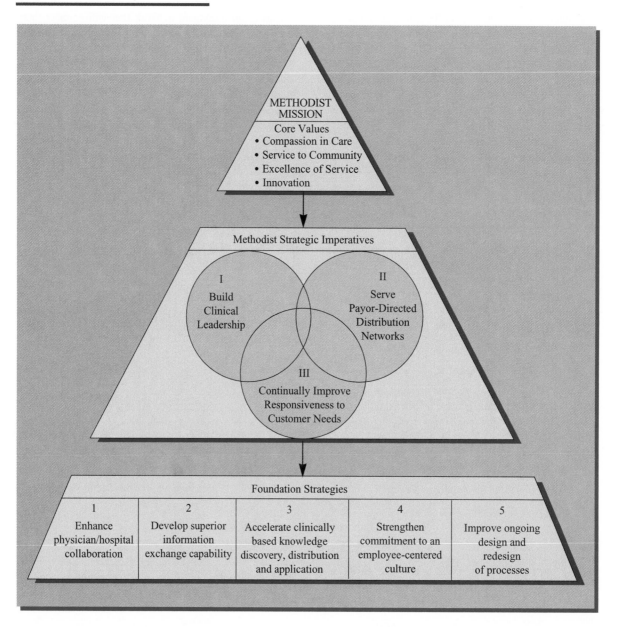

Having completed its mission, the planning committee was disbanded in the fall of 1990. It was replaced by a ten-person IS steering committee whose mission was to provide policy direction, approve the IS plan, allocate IS resources, and oversee the development of the IXP. Because the medical staff had the most clout with hospital top management, Zerrenner stacked the IS steering committee with physicians, including the president of the medical staff, the director of quality assurance, and Moeller as its chairman. Chief Financial Officer Fox and Zerrenner were also members of the steering committee. This committee quickly exerted its influence on information technology spending throughout Methodist Hospital, and most systems purchased since then by the departments have been approved by the committee to make sure that they conform to the IXP architecture.

The IXP Project

Zerrenner decided to use a four-stage approach to develop the IXP:

1. Define the basic objectives and scope of the system.
2. Build a prototype to prove the concept and get buy-in from the organization.
3. Build a pilot system and use it to demonstrate the feasibility of the concept.
4. Use the pilot to refine the system and upgrade it to full production status.

Zerrenner had been introduced to this approach by John Donovan of the Cambridge Technology Group and had used it with great success when he was at Evangelical Health Systems.

The Methodist Hospital IS department did not have the skills required to exploit leading-edge technology, so Zerrenner set out to find a systems integrator to help develop this system. "One nice thing about our four-stage approach," Zerrenner noted, " is that each stage can stand alone, so we can change our systems integrator or bring the project in-house at the end of any stage." After evaluating about a dozen candidates, in the spring of 1991 he chose IBM Consulting Services to be the hospital's systems integrator. A project team composed of individuals from Methodist Hospital and IBM was formed to develop the prototype IXP.

Zerrenner and the development team also decided to begin with a very basic system that only provided access to data from admitting, the laboratory, radiology, and the TDS patient management system. This basic system provided access to data on the patient, but did not allow doctors to enter orders for patient care. It included outpatients as well as admitted patients, and it provided physicians with access to patient data from the clinics and from remote locations. They planned to enhance this system incrementally, with each enhancement going through the definition, prototyping, piloting, and rollout process.

Development of the Prototype

Because support from the medical staff was crucial to success of the IXP project, the team decided to demonstrate what could be offered through a physician's PC workstation. Because he was actively involved and a willing participant, Dr. Moeller played the user role in the prototyping process.

The team that developed the prototype included four persons from IBM and several people from the Methodist Hospital IS department. Computer specialists from the laboratory and radiology departments also helped out. Starting in May 1990, prototype development was scheduled to be completed in four weeks, but it ended up taking five. The prototype cost about $170,000, evenly split between hardware and consulting services.

Although it would not be suitable for the production system, for rapid screen development they used Easel, a screen painting tool that the IBM people had used before. They used a PS/2 with the OS/2 operating system as the server on a small token ring network.

Moeller reported:

> We had to consider issues related to networking, the database, and the physicians' workstation. We did not attempt to create a production network, but only tried to explore some of the issues we would encounter. Most of our technical problems were in the communications area. Before we were done we had six different architectural layouts of how we would do the communications. Although our networking was fairly primitive, we did demonstrate the ability to access all of the systems and to be interactive with a couple of them.
>
> We agreed to use a graphical user interface and to use a client/server architecture, locating as much of the functionality as possible in the workstation, with a network database server providing data. This allows us to customize the application for different users.

Moeller demonstrated the completed prototype to more than 150 people, including top hospital management, top physician leadership, and people from the various service areas. "We had overwhelming acceptance of the capabilities of the prototype," Moeller reports. "Some people were absolutely flabbergasted at what we had been able to do." With this positive response from the hospital power structure, the team was quickly authorized to proceed with the piloting phase of the IXP project.

Development of the Pilot

The purpose of the piloting process was to prove the feasibility of the concept that was demonstrated by the prototype. With the technical problems in integrating the diverse systems that existed at Methodist Hospital, there was a significant question as to whether the proposed system would work.

The pilot system was a limited production system using real data, including data from all of the 200-odd registrations that take place each day in the hospital and in the clinics served by the pilot. For these patients it also included data on laboratory and radiology procedures ordered and the test results. The database was large enough to hold up to six months of data on the patients served. It had ten workstations supporting about 30 users at six different locations, including some at nurses' stations in the hospital, some in clinics, and 1 in a physician's office several miles away.

The permanent staff on this project was 10 people, 4 from Methodist Hospital IS and 6 from IBM, and IBM specialists from other localities were brought in as needed. In addition to their roles in development, IBM personnel trained Methodist Hospital personnel on the technologies being employed, such as the UNIX operating system and the C++ object-oriented programming language.

The development team used the information engineering methodology to develop the pilot and supported it with the Bachman CASE tool. This development process includes the following stages: requirements definition, external design, internal design, coding, testing, and installation.

They started work on the pilot in June 1991, and it was scheduled to be installed by April 1, 1992. The pilot project was budgeted at about $1.2 million, including hardware, the fees to IBM, and the cost of Methodist Hospital IS personnel.

The JAD Sessions

In October 1991, the project team refined and augmented the initial set of functional requirements defined by the prototype by using joint application design (JAD) sessions. The JAD approach brings together a carefully selected group of users and systems people, with a facilitator to run the meetings. There is a recorder who captures data on what took place, and technical people and facilities are available to prototype screens in response to suggestions from the group.

Dr. Moeller participated in all three of the JAD groups. "The facilitator must be able to unobtrusively manage the group and prompt active and dynamic input from all the people involved," Moeller reported. "Our facilitator, who was brought in from Pennsylvania by IBM, was outstanding."

The first JAD group consisted of three physicians—a pediatrician, a surgeon, and an internist (Dr. Moeller). The purpose was to refine the procedures and screens of the prototype system to produce the requirements of the initial patient care application that would be used by the doctors in the pilot. They met with project personnel for five four-hour sessions in which they discussed what information they needed and how they would prefer to control its presentation. At the end, the facilitator told Moeller: "That was extremely useful, but I have never been in such an intense session. You guys were beating each other up right and left!" Moeller's response was: "That was mellow. I thought we were pretty darn cordial—we weren't even fighting."

"What had happened," Moeller explained, "was that we had deliberately chosen three physicians from different specialties so that they would represent the diverse population of physicians within the hospital. They were chosen because they had different perspectives on how to practice medicine, were leaders in their respective areas, and were committed to developing a system that would enable them to provide improved care of their patients."

The second JAD group consisted of user representatives from the emergency room, patient accounts, admitting, operating room services, radiology services, the pharmacy, the laboratory, and Dr. Moeller. They met for five four-hour sessions in early November 1991 to define the data and screens for the Master Patient Index (MPI) subsystem. This subsystem matches a client with a unique client identifier (ID) and enables users to access all the records for that client, no matter where or when the patient had been served.

According to Moeller, Methodist Hospital had a problem of interdepartmental communication:

> With some 7,500 employees, we had some aspects of a stove-pipe organization where huge departments did not interact effectively with each other. The people at the top were supportive of the system, but the people several layers down who were really doing the work did not see the need to share their information. So one of our objectives was to get them to see the need for a common vision.
>
> On the first day most of the participants were wondering what they were doing there, but by the end of the fourth day these people had arrived at a common vision and realized that there were uses of the information generated in their departments that they had never even conceived of. They understood that

when this project is successful they will have a tremendously enhanced way to deliver their department's data to their users.

In this JAD session the participants discovered that the admitting office was entering the data on patients into the medical records system, but that the medical records office was responsible for the accuracy of these records. The hospital was depending on medical records to correct any input errors, and there was no feedback to the admitting office, so the people entering the data had no accountability for the data's accuracy. "We were all startled when we realized the implications of that," Moeller reported, "and both the medical records and admitting groups agreed to make admitting responsible for entering and maintaining the Master Patient Index information."

The third JAD session brought together the computer specialists from the labs and departments whose computers were to be interfaced with the network, together with the IS and IBM people on the project. The purpose was to clarify the technical issues in the project. This session, which was held in mid-November 1991, was only half as long as the other two had been. "We made the assumption that we would not need as much time to obtain consensus among the technical people," Moeller explained, "but in retrospect this has come back to haunt us because of incomplete buy-in from the IS technical people. If we were to do it again we would make the technical JAD session at least as long as the others."

In addition to developing process definitions and defining all the input and output screens, another result of the JAD sessions was a revision of the data model that was created in the prototyping process. The entity-relationship diagram from the data model is presented in Exhibit 4, but the data model also includes a table of the business rules that apply to each entity and relationship and a description of the attributes associated with each entity.

"The data model forced us to adopt a broader point of view," asserted Moeller. "When there are a lot of arrows into a box, you have to come to grips with all the different functions that use it. And it also gave me a radically different way of understanding what is occurring. For example, taking an X-ray film of a patient is a procedure. Understanding that an office visit, an X-ray, a blood draw, and a physical therapy appointment are all examples of procedures that are all handled in the identical fashion in the data model was quite interesting. It was quite a different way of thinking for me."

The Design of the Pilot System

Based on the prototype and the JAD sessions, the team designed the IXP pilot system. This pilot system had two components—a computer and communications "platform" to support access to the different computer systems at Methodist Hospital, and the initial applications to be delivered by this platform.

The IXP Platform

According to a design document produced by the team,

The objective of the IXP is to provide the user a single point of access to data that originates on several incompatible systems. Access to the data must be transparent to the user and presented in a readable and meaningful format across applications in the Methodist Health Care System (MHCS).

The IXP will achieve this objective by providing an integrating platform of hardware, software, and network components. The IXP will provide functions which will ultimately interface to systems both internal and external to MHCS, will provide database and network services to client applications on a local area network (LAN), and will provide a control point for IXP LAN management and maintaining system integrity.

The pilot platform configuration is shown in Exhibit 5. An Ethernet protocol over untwisted shielded pair was selected as the backbone network, partly because Ethernet skills were already available in the IS department. The software running the Communications Server was PICSTalk. According to Zerrenner, "At 30-second intervals the Communications Server polled each of the systems, providing data and reading any new data they had generated. PICSTalk performed the translations required to translate the data from each system into standard form for transmission to the SYBASE relational database in the Database Server. PICSTalk also screened this data to eliminate any data not required for our system. For example, the name of the technologist who did a test is generated by the lab system, but it is not of interest to the physicians, so it is eliminated before the data is sent to the IXP database."

The SYBASE software in the Database Server was a relational database management system with which some members of the design team were already familiar. The primary function of the Database Server was to provide data, because most of the application software resided in the Applications Server. Applications were run directly on the Applications Server or downloaded into the workstations

EXHIBIT 4 *IXP Pilot Data Model.*

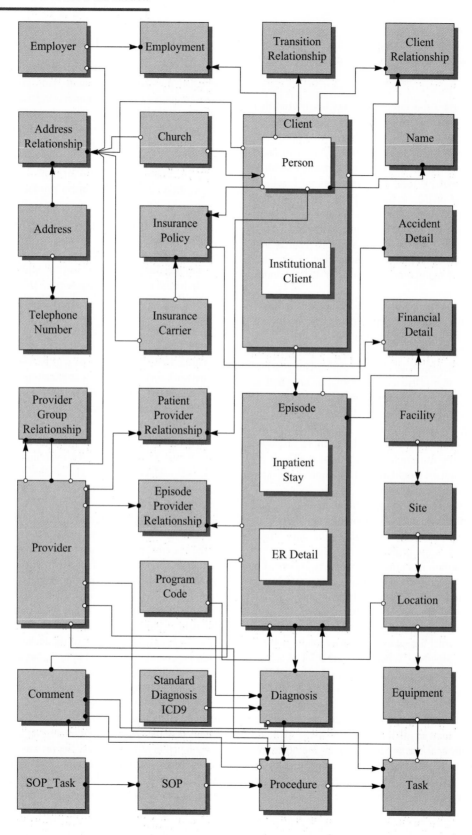

EXHIBIT 5   *IXP Pilot Platform Configuration.*

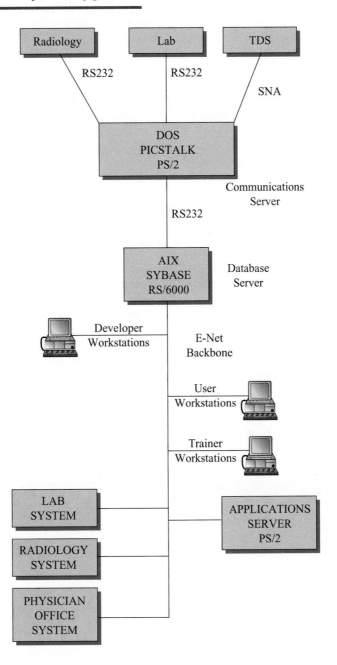

for execution. Because the network architecture provided for modularity, other types of workstations and additional servers could be easily added to the system.

The RS/6000 had the power to run both PICSTalk and SYBASE at the same time, but PICSTalk did not run under the UNIX/AIX operating system when the pilot was being designed. Therefore, the team was forced to use a PS/2 to run PICSTalk until a version of PICSTalk that ran under UNIX/AIX became available. Unfortunately, such compatibility problems are not uncommon.

The Pilot Applications

The major application provided through the pilot system was the Patient Care Application that provided physicians with information on their patients. The pilot system also provided a purchased electronic mail system and WordPerfect word processing software. Another application emulated the dedicated terminals of the laboratory computer system, the radiology computer system, and the physician office system on the IXP's PC workstations. This emulation allowed a person to access these three systems from an IXP workstation, but did not change the look or feel of these systems, and the person still had to have an authorized password to access these systems. Because of its size and complexity, the team decided not to include the Master Patient Index application in the initial pilot.

The data for the Patient Care Application were created as a result of procedures performed for a patient and were originally stored in ancillary or departmental systems, such as the laboratory or radiology. This application extracted these data from the various computers and made the data available to physicians on intelligent workstations in several formats, such as reports and/or graphs.

As shown in Exhibit 6, the Patient Care Application employed a graphical user interface. By double clicking on the In-Patients icon, a physician obtained a list of all his or her patients in the hospital, as shown in Exhibit 7.

Information on patient ROBERTSON is contained in four folders that are available by double-clicking on Robertson's name to obtain the Patient Care Results window shown in Exhibit 8. Clicking on the Laboratory icon displays a list of all the available lab procedures for patient Robertson in notebook format as shown in Exhibit 9, with tabs shown for each department that has performed tests on her. By clicking on the Hematology tab, we obtain the spreadsheet display of hematology tests shown in Exhibit 10. By pointing to the MCHC line, the physician could obtain detailed data from that test or cause the data to be displayed in graphical form as shown in Exhibit 11. The above example is representative of many options from which the physician could choose.

Installation of the Pilot System

As mentioned previously, the pilot was scheduled to be delivered to users on April 1, 1992. But problems arose with project staffing and management, and there were delays in installing a new laboratory computer and in moving the multiplexer room, both of which caused delays in this project. In August 1992, the pilot system was installed and user training began.

When the pilot system was installed and used by a diverse group of about 30 people, it became clear that the

EXHIBIT 6
Patient Care Main Menu.

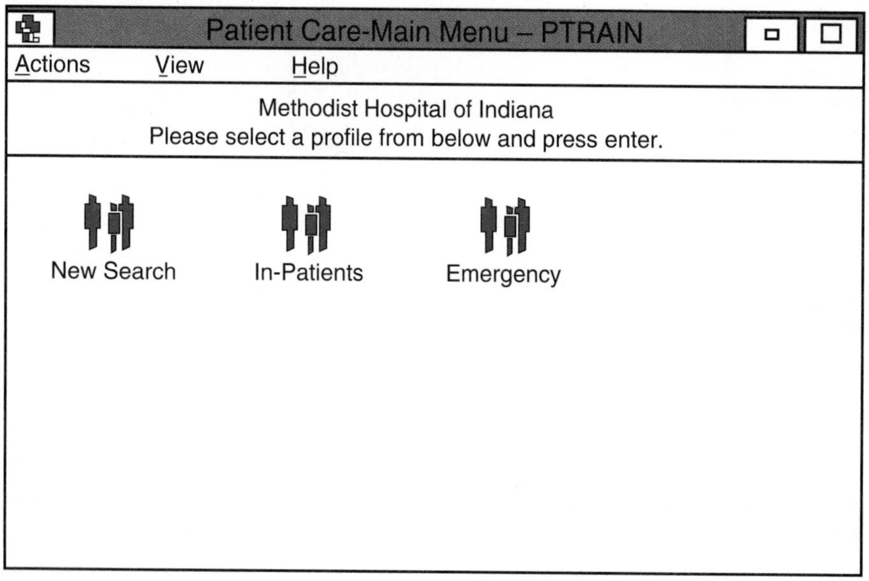

Patient Care-Main Menu – PTRAIN

Actions   View   Help

Methodist Hospital of Indiana
Please select a profile from below and press enter.

New Search   In-Patients   Emergency

EXHIBIT 7
Patient Search Results.

Patient Search Results for Profile In-Patients			
Actions View Help			
Methodist Hospital of Indiana 6 patient records found.			
Last, First, Middle	Patient ID	Patient Type	Attendin
PANGALLO, EMERG	67891234	In-patient	SMITH
RICHARDS, RALPH	70044252	In-patient	JONES
ROBERTSON, ANGELA K	70218338	In-patient	SMITH
WORTHINGTON, PATRICK	67891235	In-patient	SMITH

EXHIBIT 8
Patient Care Results Window.

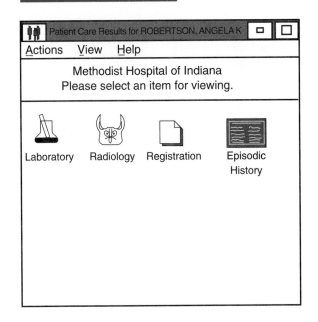

software and hardware would not support a full deployment of the system. According to Zerrenner,

> The PICSTalk system for interfacing all our various computers with the system could not handle the load. Furthermore, OS/2 would not allow us to make a software change on our workstations from a central location—we had to physically change each workstation, which was not acceptable when we were planning to deploy a thousand workstations.

The failure of the pilot was a major setback in the development of the IXP in both time and dollars, but it was not fatal. Methodist Hospital lost about a year, but according to Zerrenner:

> We had invested about $2 million at that point, but we were able to salvage all the hardware and the system design work, so we only lost the $700,000 we spent on writing code. But this was a tremendous educational experience for my staff and made us a much better software purchaser.

At that point Methodist management had to decide whether or not to continue the IXP effort. Zerrenner went to CEO William J. Loveday and explained:

> This was unfortunate, but it proves the value of the incremental prototype-pilot-deploy approach. Instead of risking a $20 million failure with a contract for a complete system, we are only out $700,000, have learned a lot from the experience, and have not been seriously embarrassed.

Continuation of the Project

Loveday might have shut down the IXP project and waited until the technology was more mature, but he agreed with Zerrenner's analysis and authorized the continuation of the project.

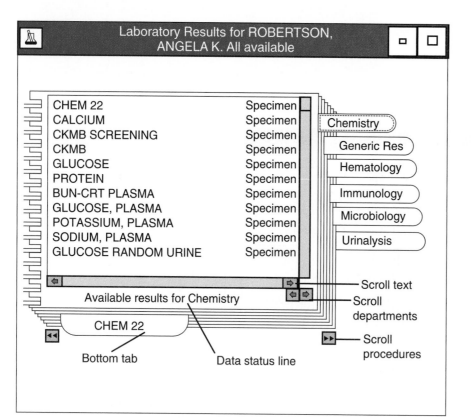

EXHIBIT 9
*Laboratory Results
Window.*

Laboratory Results for ROBERTSON, ANGELA K. All available

CHEM 22	Specimen
CALCIUM	Specimen
CKMB SCREENING	Specimen
CKMB	Specimen
GLUCOSE	Specimen
PROTEIN	Specimen
BUN-CRT PLASMA	Specimen
GLUCOSE, PLASMA	Specimen
POTASSIUM, PLASMA	Specimen
SODIUM, PLASMA	Specimen
GLUCOSE RANDOM URINE	Specimen

Chemistry
Generic Res
Hematology
Immunology
Microbiology
Urinalysis

Available results for Chemistry

CHEM 22

Bottom tab

Data status line

Scroll text
Scroll departments
Scroll procedures

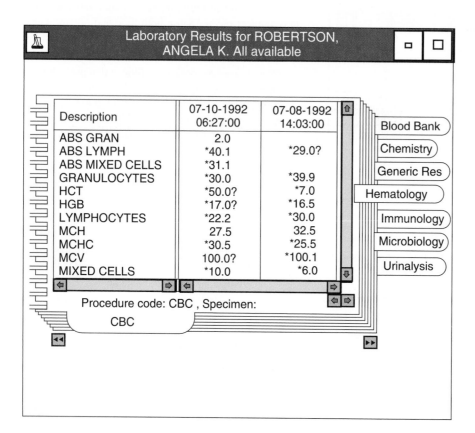

EXHIBIT 10
*Results from
Hematology Lab.*

Laboratory Results for ROBERTSON, ANGELA K. All available

Description	07-10-1992 06:27:00	07-08-1992 14:03:00
ABS GRAN	2.0	
ABS LYMPH	*40.1	*29.0?
ABS MIXED CELLS	*31.1	
GRANULOCYTES	*30.0	*39.9
HCT	*50.0?	*7.0
HGB	*17.0?	*16.5
LYMPHOCYTES	*22.2	*30.0
MCH	27.5	32.5
MCHC	*30.5	*25.5
MCV	100.0?	*100.1
MIXED CELLS	*10.0	*6.0

Blood Bank
Chemistry
Generic Res
Hematology
Immunology
Microbiology
Urinalysis

Procedure code: CBC , Specimen:

CBC

504

EXHIBIT 11
Graph of MCHC Tests.

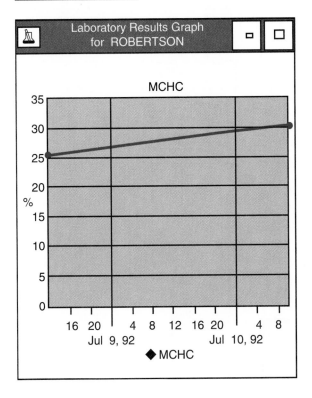

In late 1992 Methodist Hospital sought another systems integrator to assist with the project. In April of 1993 Ameritech Health Connections (AHC), a subsidiary of Ameritech, was chosen to continue the project. According to Zerrenner,

> Ameritech Health Connections (AHC) had two efforts underway at that time—development of community health information networks, and building the repository for electronic patient records. These fit in with what we were trying to do in the IXP, and my staff felt that the AHC approach best fit our needs. It was also very "open," with a standard interface engine and a standard database; nothing was proprietary.

Using AHC's network technology, Methodist was able to rapidly upgrade the IXP network by replacing the pilot IXP's hardware and software. The PS/2 communications server running PICSTalk in Exhibit 5 was replaced with a Sun SparCenter 1000 computer running Datagate software under UNIX (called the data integration hub in Exhibit 12), and the RS/6000 database server was replaced with the SUN SparCenter 2000 replica-

tion server as shown in Exhibit 12. In mid-1993 Methodist began to put applications on this upgraded IXP network and to add workstations and locations to the network.

In mid-1993 Methodist also negotiated a fixed-cost $600,000 contract with AHC to provide the repository for Methodist patient records. The repository was to be delivered in March of 1994, but that date proved to be unrealistic. Zerrenner explained:

> Unfortunately the AHC software was not as far along as we had thought. We started out Beta testing, soon went back to Alpha testing, and finally got back to quality assurance testing of the system. Then we went back through Alpha testing and Beta testing with AHC before AHC finally had a product we could use and AHC could sell. That took an extra year, so we did not begin to install the production system until May 1995.
>
> Although it has been frustrating, the process has also been rewarding both for us and for AHC. AHC has been totally committed to the project and has poured resources into it far beyond what we paid for. Four or five major health centers around the country have already bought the system, so AHC will get its money back selling the system to other hospitals.
>
> We now have a clinical repository that contains the information to satisfy about 80 percent of the requests for patient record information within a few seconds. The data in this repository is obtained through the IXP from other systems serving the laboratory, radiology, and patient registration. Even dictated reports such as Post-Operative Reports and Discharge Summaries are captured from the medical transcription system that is on the IXP.

During the period from 1993 to 1995—while the repository was under development—Methodist installed over 30 applications on the IXP network. For example, the materials management system allowed users to order all supplies and medicines from any location in the Methodist Health Care System. Methodist also installed the Pyxis automatic drug dispensing system at the nursing units. This system was linked through the network to the materials management system so that inventories are updated and replenishment of medicines at the various stations is automatically scheduled.

The nurses' staffing and scheduling system was interfaced to the patient registration system as well as a time and attendance system. This combination allowed Methodist to better utilize its nursing staff by immediately shifting nurses from an overstaffed unit to a unit

506

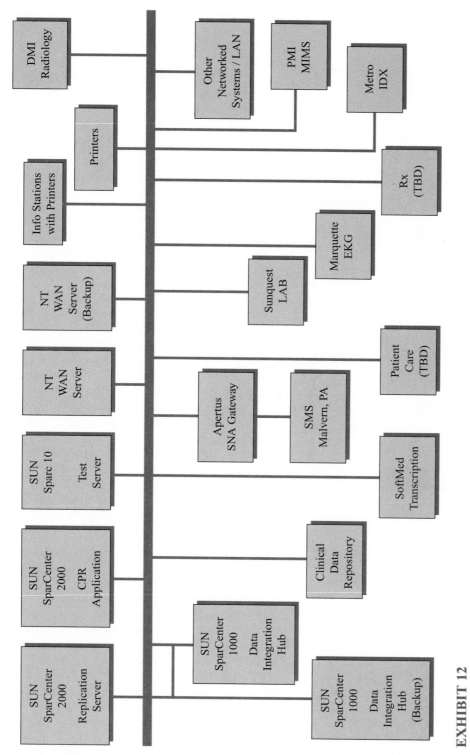

EXHIBIT 12
IXP Technology Architecture–September 1995.

that was understaffed based on current patient demand at each unit. The nurses' staffing and scheduling system was also interfaced to the payroll system that calculates each nurse's pay based upon the rates of the various units within which the nurse has worked. Previously the unit managers had to do these complex payroll calculations manually, so this interface eliminated some 1,200 hours a month of effort by the 30 unit managers.

Status in September 1995

By September 1995, some 300 workstations at the main Methodist Hospital campus and some 18 remote locations were being served through the IXP, and the patient record system was operational. When a patient showed up at the Emergency Room, the staff could immediately bring up his record on the computer instead of waiting 45 minutes for a paper record to be manually retrieved from medical records storage. Dr. Moeller's vision that patients' medical records be available through the system from every physician's office and every Methodist Health Care location was becoming a reality.

When Zerrenner took over in 1991, there were 98 people with six layers of management in the Methodist IS department. The main function of these people was to support the TDS system on the mainframe. In September 1995 there were only 58 people in the central IS department. Seven of these people were directors reporting to Zerrenner, and everyone else was a knowledge worker.

The main function of the IS department had become supporting the IXP network and writing the interface code between purchased systems and Datagate rather than developing new systems. Most of the IS staff have become telecommunications people, database people, or systems integrators. As was true before the development of the IXP, other computer specialists continued to work for the various laboratories supporting minicomputers and systems that make data available via the IXP.

Zerrenner emphasized that the system was still quite basic:

> Now that the physicians have access to all this information, they also want two-way communication so that they can order lab tests and X-rays through the system. Then they will want to place medication orders, so we will need to get the hospital pharmacy system hooked in, and perhaps even include major drugstore pharmacy systems. Each time we add capability to the system we will prototype it and pilot it before rolling it out.

According to Moeller,

> The current system only retains information on a patient for a few months. With our modular system, it should not be too difficult to add a mass storage component for medical records so that we can make all the history of a patient available, although it may take a minute or so rather than a few milliseconds to retrieve it.
>
> We have not even touched the research potential of having medical records in electronic form. We need to be able to analyze the effectiveness of patient care for a diagnosis-related group. For example, recently we had to do a very expensive chart-by-chart review of coronary bypass patients in order to bid on a Medicare project. The cardiologists were shocked at some of the sources of error that they discovered when they systematically analyzed the data on a large number of patients. We have radically improved our success rate by modifying our coronary bypass process, and I am sure that we will greatly improve many of the other things we do when we can obtain the necessary data.

Dr. Moeller's Role and Perspective

Dr. Moeller was on the original planning committee and has chaired the IS steering committee since its inception. Although there have been a number of physicians on the hospital staff who have been strong supporters of the IXP project, Dr. Moeller has provided extraordinary leadership in a number of roles.

According to Zerrenner:

> As much as Doug enjoyed playing with the IXP and computers, he was still a physician first. He truly understood the value of information at the point of care. And he was empathetic with the other physicians' problems, whether they were specialists, primary-care physicians, or whatever.
>
> Doug has been an effective voice for the IXP vision to the power structure of the hospital. He was on the executive committee of the Medical Staff Council, one of the most powerful policy bodies in the hospital, and he constantly talked about the value of the information exchange platform to the council. Doug was also on the Methodist Hospital delivery system board that was formed to enhance relations between the hospital and physicians. This board is very key in building our referral business and our managed care business, and in networking between physicians, HMOs, and hospitals all across the state.

Doug has been an enthusiastic and effective salesman. Not only did he design the prototype system, but he gave about 50 demonstrations to over 150 people. And every time he did a presentation he was just as enthusiastic as the first time! If a physician was looking at the screen he would talk in physician language, and when he was demonstrating to nurses he would talk in nursing terms. Because he understood their problems and could talk their language, they could all visualize how they could solve some of their information problems with this platform.

Finally, as an influential physician, he was able to keep some of the players honest. Everyone understands that the physicians are the true customers of the hospital. Doug was able to defuse turf battles by being very vocal in keeping people focused on the hospital's true business rather than on how the system affected their individual departments.

Moeller reminisced:

When I started out I knew very little about the technology, but Walt gave me some books to read and took me to some conferences, and I have worked hard to educate myself. The hardest part was learning the terminology, not only computerese but also understanding business terms.

I have found that the discipline involved in the design and analysis process is quite similar to the analysis I do if you come to me as a patient. A human can be viewed to be a system of components—liver, heart, kidneys—with very complex relationships and communications between these components. My definition of a complex system is one in which multiple measures exist for each component, and if you simply pick one and fail to measure others you can come to the wrong conclusions by reducing the system to something simpler than it actually is. That is why information is so important to medical care. This exposure to the systems approach has radically changed the way I do almost everything that I do, including my medical practice.

Physicians have always been trained to be independent decision-makers, and they tend to function as independent units. The transition that health care needs to make is to go from a craft-based specialty organization to a team-based production facility, where there is interdependency and shared resources. If the internetworking that can occur in our IXP system is successful then we will have made a major advance in supporting health care requirements.

GRANDMA STUDOR'S BAKERY, INC.

Grandma Studor's Bakery, Inc. (GSB), is a major national supplier of bread, sweet rolls, cakes, and other bakery products. In addition to its bakery products, Grandma Studor's makes and sells well-known brands of baking mixes, flour, prepared dough, and frozen pizza. GSB's industrial foods division sells a wide range of biscuit, doughnut, and other dough mixes, several types of specialty flours to bread and cereal makers, and various commodities and feed ingredients. In 1996 GSB made after-tax profits of $92 million on sales of about $1.5 billion.

Materials Management

The GSB materials management area purchased about $200 million of ingredients and commodities during 1996. One of GSB's most important commodities and ingredients is flour. GSB treats flour as a commodity that is used as an important raw material but also sells flour to others and deals in flour and wheat futures to reduce risk related to price fluctuations. In 1996 one of the senior buyers, David Prince, managed about $90 million in transactions relating to flour and wheat.

GSB uses many different kinds of flour in its various products. GSB manufactures flour as well as buying it on the open market, and since GSB produces several different kinds of flour, GSB must buy several different varieties of wheat. Prince attempts to minimize the final cost of a hundredweight of flour, which is a complicated task because there are so many variables involved, and they are changing all the time. The costs of flour, flour futures,

---

milling flour, transporting flour, wheat, wheat futures, transporting wheat—all of these factors may affect the cost of a hundredweight of flour.

The Flour Commodity Report System

To manage the acquisition of the flour that GSB needs each year and to control the risk and minimize the cost of this important material, Prince needs a great deal of information in order to analyze alternatives. Since things are always changing, timing is very important when buying and selling flour, wheat, and futures contracts for both. For this information Prince depends upon the flour commodity report system that is operated by his assistant, Donna Hornibrook, on her PC.

The flour commodity report system is a LOTUS 1-2-3 application consisting of seven large spreadsheets, several of which contain mostly LOTUS macros. This system requires manual input of data from at least three of GSB's mainframe systems that forecast future requirements for different kinds of flour and provide current cost factors for manufacturing flour, price data from several markets, reports of actions in buying and selling, and other information. It produces histories of daily flour costs by product group and location for the past month, summaries of the days of coverage of each type of flour that GSB uses, comparisons of anticipated costs of each flour based upon their inventories and futures contracts for flour and wheat, and futures contracts outstanding, among other reports. Also, someone who understands the system can use it to explore the impact of changes in the various cost factors on the future costs of the different kinds of flour.

In January 1996, Hornibrook told Prince that her husband was being transferred to the West Coast and that she would be leaving in about a month. That precipitated a crisis for Prince and the materials management area, because she was the only person in the organization who had any idea of how to run the flour commodity report system. This system is highly manual in that Hornibrook enters data from various sources and invokes many macros to process the data and produce the reports used to manage the flour and wheat positions. Neither the LOTUS spreadsheets nor the procedures Hornibrook used were documented. Even Hornibrook does not completely understand how the system works, and she does not think she could teach it to someone else.

History of the System

The system was begun in 1990 by Anthony Pizzo, who was in Prince's position as senior buyer for flour and wheat. Pizzo had used LOTUS 1-2-3 and thought that a spreadsheet would be helpful in keeping track of his flour and wheat requirements and commitments, so he developed the first spreadsheet. Over the next year he expanded the spreadsheet and found it useful enough that when his assistant left, he decided that he would replace him with someone who knew the computer and was skillful with spreadsheet software.

He hired Elmer Smith, an enthusiastic spreadsheet jockey who began to work with Pizzo to expand the system. A year later Pizzo was promoted to a better position within GSB and was replaced by Prince, who continued to work to expand the system. Prince was not a knowledgeable PC user and was content to have Smith operate the system and enhance it from time to time as they saw opportunities to improve it. By the time that Smith left for a better job in early 1994, the system included five spreadsheets, three of which were primarily composed of macros.

Hornibrook replaced Smith, and although she was competent in entering data into a 1-2-3 template, she had little prior proficiency in macros. However, before Smith left, he taught Hornibrook how to use the system, and she was able to take over its operation. During the drought in the summer of 1995, Prince began to worry about possible wheat shortages if the drought continued, so Hornibrook added two more spreadsheets to the system to provide more information to help Prince track things more closely.

Hornibrook had trouble in making some of the system changes that Prince requested. She also occasionally got results from the system that did not make sense. The system was unwieldy in that it often took a long time to recalculate its values when a change was made in one or more of the input parameters. Hornibrook felt that the system was extremely precarious and was secretly relieved to be leaving.

The IS Department Response

When Prince learned that Hornibrook was leaving, he immediately called Roy Morgan, director of the IS materials management systems group, and asked him for help. Despite the fact that the IS Department has had nothing to do with this system (and did not even know of its existence), Morgan agreed to provide all possible assistance in resolving this crisis situation.

Because Microsoft Excel was the spreadsheet package supported by IS, Morgan did not have anyone available with the depth of expertise in LOTUS 1-2-3 required to analyze this system and correct its problems. The IS group was planning to develop a corporate wide material requirements planning (MRP) system starting in 1998 that would include a component that would serve the needs of flour and other commodity buyers, but that would be far too late to solve Prince's problem.

Therefore, Morgan suggested that the Gamma Consulting Group, which provides LOTUS training and consulting, be employed to analyze the system, redesign it, and rebuild it using LOTUS 1-2-3 and/or other PC software.

The Consultant's Preliminary Report

Tully Shaw, the Gamma consultant assigned to this project, spent several days working with Hornibrook and Prince and prepared the following preliminary report on the problem:

During January I met with David Prince and Donna Hornibrook to review the existing PC-based system and to discuss revising it into a new easier-to-use system for tracking flour and wheat usage, flour and wheat costs, and to assist in the buying and selling of futures at three exchanges. The existing system does not track all flours being used in all GSB products.

The existing system is made up of several LOTUS 1-2-3 spreadsheets. Other than the disk files containing these spreadsheets, there is no documentation for this system. The spreadsheets making up this system were authored by several different persons and are driven by macros written in a format that makes them difficult to edit.

Because the existing system is in such bad shape, I do not believe the existing system should be upgraded and reused. Rather, a new system should be built. Although the ranges currently being printed from these spreadsheets can be helpful as a basis for designing the new system, a major task in developing this system will be to create a specification from the existing spreadsheets with the assistance of GSB staff.

Preliminary cost and time estimates are as follows:

System Design	30 days	$60/hour	$14,400
Programming	25 days	$50/hour	10,000
Procedure Manual	5 days	$50/hour	2,000
TOTAL (estimate)			$26,400

These estimates for design allow for approximately three days for each major section of the system. This a minimal amount of time for specification for a system of this complexity, and it could easily require more time. I estimate that the project will require at least 3.5 calendar months to complete.

This is not a fixed-cost bid for this project. In view of the uncertainties involved, we would only contract for this project on an hourly basis with the costs per hour specified above.

MIDSTATE UNIVERSITY BUSINESS PLACEMENT OFFICE (B): DEVELOPMENT OF THE SYSTEM

Starting in the early 1970s there was a nationwide explosion in the number of college students majoring in Business Administration. At Midstate University, undergraduate enrollment in the Business School grew from about 2,500 in 1973–74 to almost 4,500 in 1979–80.

Increasing numbers of business students began to graduate and seek jobs, which exerted tremendous pressure on the Business Placement Office (BPO). The number of students served grew from around 1,200 in 1974–75 to 2,100 in 1979–80, and the number of interviews conducted more that doubled during the same period (from around 10,000 to 22,000 per year). As the article from the January 23, 1979, *Midstate University Student Observer* illustrates (see Exhibit 1), the BPO was being overwhelmed!

James P. Wine, Director of the Business Placement Office (BPO), was as frustrated as the students. "I had what ought to have been an ideal situation," he recalls. "My business was growing by leaps and bounds. We had lots of companies that wanted our students, and we had lots of students who wanted to interview with them, but we couldn't cope with the problem of getting 2,000 students together with 500 companies for over 20,000 interviews."

This case was prepared by Professor E. W. Martin as the basis for class discussion rather than to illustrate either effective or ineffective handling of an administrative situation.

Copyright © 1997 (revised) by E. W. Martin.

The interview sign-up process BPO used was a simple one that gave priority to the students who wanted the interviews the most and thus were willing to stand in line the longest. At 7:45 A.M. on Monday the doors to the BPO were opened and the students in line were allowed to sign their names on a preliminary list. Then, beginning at 9:00 A.M. placement assistants started calling off names from the preliminary list, starting from the top. As their names were called, students were allowed to come to the counter and sign up for up to three interviews on the schedules that had available slots. Students whose names were low on the preliminary list often found slim pickings!

First Attempts to Use the Computer

Jim Wine was convinced that with so many students, the only practical way to solve the interview scheduling problem without long lines was through the use of the computer. So in the fall of 1978 he submitted a formal request to the University Data Processing Department describing his problem and requesting the development of a computer system to equitably schedule students into interviews. This request was reviewed by the Data Processing Advisory Committee, composed of representatives of the various university administrative offices. Jim Wine was told that his request would be put in the queue, but that the earliest that they could possibly start work on it would be in three years. The Data Processing Department system development group was overwhelmed with work on a student financial aid system, a new university

EXHIBIT 1
January 23, 1979 newspaper article.

NEAR RIOT OUTSIDE BUSINESS BUILDING

Campus Police were called to the front entrance of the Business Building at 7:45 Monday morning to quell fights that had broken out between students waiting to sign up for job interviews.

"We'd been freezing in line all night long," said Marketing major Julie Sterbenz, "and this bunch of creeps came along just as the doors opened and tried to push in from the side! There was a lot of pushing and shoving, and then all the guys began slugging. It's a wonder someone wasn't hurt badly!"

Campus Police Chief Harold Deckard noted that there has been trouble at the Business School all year. "We've had problems with students trying to hide in the building restrooms when the building closed and even breaking into the building at night so that they could get to the Placement Office first in the morning. And there's been a lot of rowdyism and partying in the line at times."

Business school seniors and MBAs are disgusted with the situation. "After working hard for four years to get my degree, I really resent having to spend hours and hours in line just to sign up for job interviews," complained Decision Sciences major Mike Turner. "You'd think that a school that claims to teach management could figure out a better way to handle interviewing than by making you spend half your senior year in lines!"

payroll system, and the student records system. Besides that, there was no one on the advisory committee that represented the interests of the Business School, so Wine had no one to fight for a higher priority.

Because he couldn't wait for over three years for a solution to his problem, Jim Wine decided to try an end run. He had a faculty account on the Control Data Corporation (CDC) mainframe at the Academic Computing Center, and he and a couple of graduate assistants programmed a simple lottery system to produce a preliminary sign-up list in which the sequence of names was determined by chance. All business students had to take a FORTRAN programming course at that time, and there were plenty of punched card keypunches available, so punched cards were used as input to the system.

In 1979–80 the BPO used the computer for the first time. The students submitted requests for a place on the sign-up list by key-punching an IBM card and dropping it in a box outside the BPO by Friday afternoon. Over the weekend, these request cards were transmitted to the

CDC computer and it assigned a random number to each request. Then the requests were sorted in sequence by these random numbers, and the sign-up list was printed. Monday morning the sign-up list was posted, and the students could go to the BPO counter and sign up for interviews in sign-up list order just as they had the previous year. The difference was that the students didn't have to wait in line to get on the sign-up list.

This was an improvement over the old system in reducing the lines, but it didn't give the students any control over their destinies—they couldn't influence the probability of getting an interview even if they were willing to stand in line all night. Moreover, when the Academic Computer Center caught on to what was going on, the Academic Computing Policy Committee told Jim Wine that, although they were quite sympathetic to his problem, he couldn't use the academic computer for administrative data processing after that recruiting season. Because there was so much accumulated demand for administrative data processing that was not being satisfied by the University Data Processing Department, they had to make that ruling or all the Academic Computing resources would have been eaten up.

But during that year Jim Wine had a graduate assistant, Bob Rivers, who had used an Apple computer with accounting software while working for a small public accounting firm. Being an electrical engineering undergraduate, Wine had programmed the computer and used the research computer on campus. He'd even used the early IBM 1401 computer that only had 4,000 bytes of memory, so he felt that he knew what could be done with a small computer. Jim and Bob figured that the placement job could be done on the Apple, and, because Wine knew his days on the CDC were numbered and he still was faced with his problem, Wine decided to get an Apple and see what they could do.

First Attempt at a Microcomputer System

He had sufficient money in his budget, so Wine submitted a Purchase Request for an Apple to the Purchasing Department. But the University Data Processing Director, Larry Easterly, had established an equipment committee that had to approve any purchases of computers, and they would not approve any Apples. (At that time most computer professionals thought that micros were toys that had no place in data processing.) Wine was stymied again.

But Wine still had another alternative—he could go to some companies who had used the BPO to hire Midstate University graduates and see if they would help him out. Wine explained his problem to a friend who was a partner in a small public accounting firm. This strong supporter of the BPO had his firm purchase an Apple computer with a printer and two floppy disk drives and give it to the BPO. Wine quickly filled up all of its expansion slots with an 80-column video card, added memory chips to the maximum 64K bytes, and so on.

Once he had a computer, Wine had to decide how to use it to schedule student interviews. He had always thought that the fairest way to allocate the interviews would be to get all the students together in a big room and hold an auction where each student would have a fixed number of "points" that he could use to bid for interview slots. When a student had used up all his points obtaining interviews, he would be through for the semester. In such a system each interview slot would go to the student who was willing to spend the most of his or her limited supply of points for it.

It wasn't practical to get the all students together at one time, but Wine wanted to use the computer to get as close as possible to this ideal. Wine spent a lot of time batting ideas around with Bob Rivers and finally came up with the idea of a "blind" auction, where each student who wanted to bid on a schedule would submit a written bid specifying the schedule number, his or her student number, and the number of points he or she would spend. The computer would check to see if the student had that many points left, and if so would allocate the slots to the highest bidders and reduce the winners' available points by the amount of their bids.

Bob Rivers and two other graduate assistants programmed this system in BASIC for the Apple. The system had a student file with the student's name, number, and available points and a file containing the schedule data. The bids were entered into a floppy disk file through the Apple keyboard. The system first indexed the student bids by schedule number, which was a major task for the Apple. Then the first schedule was read into the Apple's memory and the bids for that schedule were processed to determine who was to be allowed to sign up on that schedule. The program was simple—it didn't even check to see if the students were qualified to be on that schedule. "We had told the students we were checking," says Wine, "but it was just a head fake!" For each schedule the computer produced a list of the successful bidders that was posted to notify them to come in and sign up for the interview. Because the bids didn't contain the student's time availability, occasionally some of the selected students could not be scheduled because of time conflicts.

This system was ready to use for the 1980–81 recruiting year. But it was a first-class flop! When the students submitted their bids they were told that the results would be posted by the beginning of the week before the interviews were scheduled so that they could come in and sign up for their interview times. But they could never get the results out of the Apple on time—the system just wasn't able to handle the volume of input data and processing that was involved.

By superhuman effort over unreasonably long hours, the BPO staff managed to complete the schedules by hand to get students into interviews most of the time, but it was a terrible mess, both for the BPO and the students. Before the end of the first semester they were forced to give up and go back to the previous punched card lottery system, which the Academic Computing Policy Committee graciously allowed them to do.

There were three major problems with the system. In the first place, Wine and Rivers hadn't understood how much activity was taking place at the BPO counter, and they didn't realize how much extra activity would be generated by a bidding system, so the system was overwhelmed by input data—they just couldn't get it all entered in time through the Apple keyboard.

Second, the Apple wasn't designed for that kind of heavy usage. They were pushing the machine to the limits with add-on components, and the Apple's power supply and cooling system weren't up to the task. The early model dot-matrix printers weren't too reliable either; they weren't designed for printing the high volumes of output from the system. They quickly got a back-up Apple and another printer, but machine failures still added significantly to their problems in meeting schedules.

Finally, they really didn't do a very good job of designing, writing, and debugging the programs. The long runs were not checkpointed, for example, so if a failure occurred in the middle of the run, the whole thing had to be started over. "Our problems weren't all the Apple's fault," Wine noted, "it was partly our inability to anticipate all the logical possibilities that could exist."

Needless to say, Jim Wine's incompetence was the subject of a lot of gossip around the campus spread by the data processing people who were upset about Wine's getting the Apple in the first place. He heard a lot of "We told you so—you should have taken our advice and waited for a real system!" And his reputation as a manager took quite a beating!

The Second Apple System

Despite his embarrassment at the failure of the system, Wine knew that the BPO's problems weren't going to go away—he still desperately needed a system. Because he still could not get any help from the University Data Processing Department, he had no choice but to press on.

Both Wine and Rivers learned a lot from that year's experience. They had started out thinking that the key to success would be how they wrote the programs, but they found that the key was the up-front design of the system as a whole. "After that fiasco we knew that all the parts of the system—manual procedures, input processes, data files, computer processing—have to be considered, and getting a sound design is critical," noted Wine.

They knew that the system required more muscle than they had. Wine had discovered that he could get any reasonable help he needed from his client companies, so he raised the money to get a 10-megabyte Corvis hard disk, three more Apples, several more printers, and a Corvis Omninet local area network to connect them all together.

And they also knew that they had to solve the input problem. With the help of a consultant, Greg Mather, who worked for the local computer store that supplied a lot of their equipment, they found out about and obtained a Mountain Computer optical card reader that reads pencil marks from cards.

Also, Bob Rivers was a MIS major, and he took a Systems Analysis and Design class and a Database class that first year, so he was better prepared to do a good job of system development. Furthermore, Rivers realized that their major problem—other than scheduling the interviews—was handling files and writing reports, and he recommended that they switch from BASIC to a new microcomputer database management system (DBMS) called dBASE. In the long run, that was a very wise decision, but in the short run it caused a lot of problems. That first version of dBASE was quite limited in its capabilities, and it was full of bugs. Bob had to help the dBASE people debug their DBMS, and that caused many problems for the BPO system.

With both the significant hardware changes and the switch to dBASE, they had a major redevelopment project on their hands. Wine spent a lot of time with Rivers defining the databases and structuring the data. Rivers did the technical part, but Wine spent hours answering questions such as "What data elements in the *Campus Recruiting Information Form* (CRIF) relate to the student?" and "How will you want to use that information?" and "How will you want to put these things together in analysis reports?" Wine recalls: "Bob really pressured me—there were a lot of nights when we were up till three or four o'clock trying to hash through some of those points. And that was very important to the long-run success of the system."

Rivers and some graduate students handled the reprogramming in dBASE and the extensive programming changes necessary to convert to the new hardware environment. Wine gives a lot of credit to Rivers: "He was brilliant, and he would work all the time. The guy never slept—he literally worked all night. I came in a couple of times early in the morning and caught him in a sleeping bag. He had been watching the Corvis disk all night long, not because I'd asked him to, but because he was so involved with the system. I don't know how he managed to keep up with his classes."

Unfortunately, Larry Easterly, the Data Processing Director, was still tightly controlling the use of microcomputers for administrative work. All Wine's requests for equipment now had to go through his office. Because Wine had outside money and his dean's approval,

Easterly was forced to approve them, but he took a long time to do it. "I would send through a purchase requisition, Purchasing would send it to Easterly, and he would sit on it," Wine recalls. "That was terribly frustrating for me because I was under such intense time pressure to get the system ready to use for the upcoming recruiting season!"

They also had some problems making the various components from different manufacturers work together successfully. Corvis technical people helped and they got a lot of help from Greg Mather, the local computer store's consultant. "Greg and Bob worked a lot of long nights eliminating hardware bugs," remembers Wine.

Although there were still a lot of problems, that system did work and was used during the 1981–82 recruiting year. By using several Apples at the same time for data entry, they were able to get the student and the company data in very quickly, so they had the beginnings of a reasonable database. The optical card reader solved the bid input problem, so most of the time they were able to get the interview schedules back to the students on time.

The weak part of the system was the scheduling program—it took hours on the Apple. When hardware problems occurred, and problems happened rather frequently, they had to do a lot of scheduling by hand. Keeping that invisible to the students put tremendous pressure on the BPO staff; they were working hours and hours of unscheduled overtime. Recalls Wine: "It was computer assisted scheduling, not computerized scheduling."

Finally, in mid-February, the sprinkling system opened up overnight and soaked the hard disk, and they had to send it back to California for two weeks to get it fixed. "We just announced to the students that the computer had crashed and burned," recalls Wine, "and we completed the remaining part of the semester with manual sign-ups, which meant going back to the long lines." So Wine had egg on his face again!

Success at Last!

About the time the hard disk got soaked, Wine got a memo from University Data Processing Director Larry Easterly saying: "That request of yours that we've had in our queue for the past three years is now at the top, and we can allocate some hours to you for development. What do you want us to do?"

That was the answer to Wine's prayer because it enabled him to get the scheduling process that was too much for the Apple onto the IBM mainframe where it belonged. Wine immediately filled out Data Processing's standard request form describing the interview schedul-

ing process used on the Apple and requesting that the same process be programmed for the IBM mainframe (with suitable arrangements for transferring the data back and forth from the BPO to the Data Processing Center).

The development of that part of the system was quite an experience, both for Wine and the Data Processing Department. Wine was under difficult time pressure because he needed to have the new system available by the start of the 1982–83 recruiting season. In the spring of 1982, Bob Rivers had graduated and Wine badly missed Rivers' expertise and experience with the system. Also, this was the first time that Wine had worked with a professional data processing group, and he was not accustomed to how they operated.

Stan Brown, the Data Processing Department programmer assigned to the project, was both brilliant and a workaholic. But Brown was very difficult for Wine to work with. Wine recalls: "He would listen to me and I would think that I had told him exactly what I wanted, but what I said and what came out in the program were not always the same thing." Brown's response was: "This is what you need, no matter what you told me you wanted." Wine was not happy with that: "He made decisions for me on what he thought would be best way to run the BPO, and I found that difficult to deal with. For example, in the way we did the lottery to assign students to interviews, he decided that it would be fairer to students if it was done another way. But I didn't want to be that fair—there were some other factors that I had to take into consideration that he didn't understand."

But Wine acknowledges that "Stan was really dedicated, working maybe a hundred hours many weeks on this project just to get it completed in time. I'd come in the office at 7 A.M. and he'd be waiting for me—he'd been up all night! He got involved in it to the point that he neglected many of his other responsibilities to carry this project through."

Paul Abernathy, Director of Systems Development at Data Processing, recalls that Wine had a hard time adapting to their development methodology. Wine was used to working closely with Bob Rivers, and when the program didn't do what Wine wanted, Rivers would work all night to change it. Thus Wine didn't have to carefully specify requirements at the start—he and Rivers developed them by trial and error. But Data Processing expected the request for service to define the requirements, and when Wine found that it didn't, he wanted to change things right in the middle of programming. That caused a good deal of conflict—Wine was upset and the Data Processing people didn't like the idea of "finding out about the specifications after the programming was completed." It took Wine a while to catch onto the fact that he had to put a lot of effort into preparing his request for service: "If it wasn't in the request they weren't going to do it, at least not on that request! I had a lot of problems dealing with that way of operating."

Getting into the IBM mainframe from the Apple was really a big deal, both for BPO and for University Data Processing. Larry Easterly had been vigorously enforcing a policy that allowed only IBM-compatible terminals to be attached to his network. Wine had to exert every pressure he could muster to get Easterly to agree to allow access from the Apple, even through a modem for uploading and downloading files.

Wine and Easterly had never gotten along very well. Wine felt that Easterly was opposed to him from the start, and that he never gave BPO any more resources than he absolutely had to. But once Easterly allocated some resources to a project, Wine felt that the Data Processing systems development people who worked on it really wanted to do a good job.

Despite the problems between Data Processing and BPO, the deadlines were met and they were able to use the new system during the 1982–83 year. The students submitted their bids by marking on cards (see Exhibit 2) that were read by the optical card reader. The bid files were built on floppy disks and once a week they were transmitted to the data processing center by modem from an Apple. Then the IBM mainframe produced the schedule and they downloaded everything back to the BPO Apple via the modem.

BPO updated its databases and could do everything else it needed to do on the local network of Apples. They printed updated interview schedules, student notifications, and any analyses of placements, offers, and interviews that were needed. And BPO vastly improved its services to the companies that interview at M.U.—when a company called BPO people could tell them how many students were signed up for interviews, how many were on the waiting list, what dates were open for them to come to campus, and so on.

With the huge scheduling processing load off the Apples, the system stability improved significantly. The dBASE software had also been upgraded and most of the bugs were out of it. They still had lots of hardware problems with the Apples, and hardware and capacity problems with the hard disk. But the system worked well enough that, for the first time in years, the placement operations ran smoothly without a tremendous overtime effort by BPO personnel.

Replacement of the Apples

In the fall of 1983 the NCR Corporation, who had hired a lot of students from the Midstate University Business School over the years, gave the BPO a substantial grant of NCR hardware. "It was like God had opened up to us!" said Wine. The NCR gift included an NCR Modus fileserver with a 60-megabyte hard disk and 18 NCR DecisionMate 5 PCs, one with 512K of memory and a 10-megabyte hard disk.

They converted to the new hardware during the 1983–84 recruiting year. By the 1984–85 year they had replaced everything except the Omninet LAN and one Apple that was used to upload to and download from the mainframe (because Easterly would not give them permission to replace it). This new hardware eliminated the problems they had with the old Apples and the hard disk capacity and reliability problems. Since the fall of 1984 the BPO computer system has been flying high, but Wine commented:

> I consider myself to be a really gung ho, effective manager—when I make a decision I really go at it. I can't believe that it took me seven years of turmoil to get to where I really felt comfortable with what we were doing—but it did!

Continued Enhancement

Since 1985 Wine has continually improved the system by upgrading the hardware and software and working to improve the student interface with the BPO system. One of his major problems in dealing with this process of continual change was the glacial pace of the University Data Processing Department in responding to Wine's need to change his system. Wine recalls:

> We needed to change things on the fly, but we had to give them the complete specifications six to nine months in advance. By then I would need changes to those changes. And they did not seem to understand that I had to have everything ready to go at the start of recruiting season each year.

Wine found that the Modus was powerful enough to handle the bid processing that was on the University Data Processing mainframe, so he had his programmers rewrite that system in dBASE. After debugging this system and running it in parallel with the mainframe system for a while, Wine switched to his Modus for bid processing and was free from the constraints and aggravations of depending upon Easterly and the University Data Processing Department. Incidentally, Easterly left Midstate

EXHIBIT 2
BPO Bid/Transaction Card.

Bid/Transaction Card

A sample bid/transaction card is shown here. The same form is used for both bids and transactions, although some fields of the card are used only for bids or only for transactions (see below). The major portion of the information required is completed by filling out the blank spaces along the top of the card and filling in the spaces below by darkening the circle within the appropriate square. When filling in the boxes, please note:

—Use a number 2 pencil. Anything else will not be read by the computer.

—Darken the circle only in each square indicated. DO NOT fill in the complete box. Your pencil markings should not touch the lines forming the box.

—Complete the additional information in the lower right portion of the card by writing in your name, the company name, and the other information requested.

BPO NUMBER	SCHED NO	BID SUF	POS	SCHED TIME	A C	TIMES AVAILABLE

(form with darkened-circle matrix for BPO NUMBER, SCHED NO, BID SUF, POS, SCHED TIME, AC columns with digits 0–9 and letters; TIMES AVAILABLE with times 8:00, 8:30, 9:00, 9:30, 10:00, 10:30, 11:00, 11:30, 12:00, 12:30, 1:00, 1:30, 2:00, 2:30, 3:00, 3:30, 4:00, 4:30 marked Y/N; ADD/CANCEL column)

NAME _____

COMPANY _____

CITIZENSHIP _____

MAJOR _____

DEGREE _____

GRAD. DATE _____

When using the card for bidding, DO NOT put anything in the columns marked SCHED TIME or AC. These fields are used for counter transactions only. At the counter, the graduate assistant will add the time scheduled, and you will note whether you are adding to or canceling from a schedule in the "AC" column.

When using the card for transactions, DO NOT complete the "Times Available" section. As you complete the transaction at the BPO counter, you will then complete the "BID SUF" section.

University shortly thereafter and the University's central data processing unit has become much more service-oriented and responsive to the needs of University managers like Jim Wine.

Although the BPO system was a vast improvement over past approaches to handling the difficult job of scheduling students into interviews, this system had a major weakness. Having the students mark their bids on cards that could be rapidly read into the system was efficient in getting the data into the computer, but the task of marking the bids on cards was difficult and rife with errors. Each week the bid processing system created a large error list (see Exhibit 3) in which many entries represented students who were frustrated because the opportunity to bid for a desired interview had been lost.

The On-Line System

In the late 1980s the main campus of Midstate University made a commitment to computer literacy for its students and began to expand and upgrade its computer network and to issue computer accounts to all students. In addition, University Data Processing and the Academic Computing Center were merged into a single organization, so the old restrictions on how computers could be used crumbled. In 1988 all School of Business students were given computer accounts that allowed them access to e-mail and to the VAX cluster of on-line computers, and the BPO set out to replace the cumbersome marked cards with an on-line approach to entering bid transactions into the system.

This new system allowed the student to sign on to the BPO bidding system through hundreds of microcomputers located all over the campus, including over a hundred in the School of Business. Through a menu or by entering a command, the student entered the BPO system and was asked for student number and password to verify that he or she was registered with the BPO. A menu then appeared that allowed the student to choose to enter bids, cancel an interview or a position on a waitlist, or enter time availability information.

To enter bids the student first consulted the printed *Career Street Journal* to find the exact six-digit bidding number for the desired interview schedule, and then typed this number into the computer. The computer verified that this was a valid bidding number and asked the student to enter the desired bid level and the number identifying one of the four different resumés the student could have on the computer file. The student could repeat this process to enter additional bids. None of the bids

were submitted until the end of the process when the student was asked to verify his or her bids and given the opportunity to cancel them if desired. Submitted bids were processed as in the system described in the *"Midstate University Business Placement Office (A)"* case study, and the results were returned to the student via e-mail.

The **Resumé Expert** system for capturing student registration data and preparing student resumés was implemented at the same time as the above on-line bidding system, so the student resumés could be printed from the system and provided to interviewers when they arrived on campus.

This on-line system was very convenient and significantly reduced the number of bidding errors. Despite some irritation when the computers would go down or when the response time would be slow, this system was a big improvement over the marked card system it replaced.

Development of the Web System

During the 1990s students became more and more addicted to the Windows' "point and click" environment and less patient with the restrictions of the character-based interface of the BPO bidding system. Also, the students became more knowledgeable about technology —not only were they "surfing the Web," but some of them had set up their own Web home pages. Many students began using the Web to look for job opportunities, and they were coming to Wine and suggesting that he put the *Career Street Journal* on the Web. So Wine began to think about the Web, and soon realized that he could make the entire bidding system more convenient and easy to use by putting it on the Web.

In late 1995 the BPO began to develop and test a Web-based version of the bidding system which they tried out on a few students in the spring of 1996. It worked so well that Wine decided to switch to the Web-based system in the fall of 1996. The first version of the Web-based bidding system was a straightforward conversion of what had been done on the on-line computer system. Wine relates what happened then:

> Our students are so technically savvy nowadays that they would come in and say: "I understand what you are doing, but why are you doing it that way?" We were doing it that way because we had to do it that way on the older technology. The students were very helpful in reminding us that, now that we no longer faced some of the old constraints, we should free up our thinking and look at new possibilities.

EXHIBIT 3   *The first page of a long error list.*

BPO BID ERROR LISTING FOR BID WEEK STARTING ON: 01/25/88

If you submitted a bid, your name should appear on one of 3 lists: 1) ALPHABETICAL LIST 2) BPO BID ERROR LIST 3) BID ERROR LIST from Information Services. 'P' bids will not appear on the alpha or either error list. A P bid error list will be posted at a later date. If your name is not on that list, it has been forwarded to the company.

If your name does not appear on any list, the card reader was unable to read your card. Your only recourse is manual transactions.

If this happens two times, there is a chance that your SDS is invalid or a more serious problem exists. Submit a trouble log request at the counter. We will check out your situation and contact you.

ERROR EXPLANATION: If there is a duplicate bid, the computer picks the last one and processes it. If there is an invalid position code (or more), the computer randomly assigns a valid code, but it may or may not be one for which you are qualified. Invalid bid levels (or missing bid levels) are automatically assigned an 'R' bid level. All of these bids are then processed so your name will appear on the Alpha List.

STUDENT NUMBER	SCHEDULE NO.	PROBLEM
011-76-0687	38251	INVALID OR MISSING POSITION CODE
025-62-3244	88551	INVALID OR MISSING POSITION CODE
040-58-2093	65451	INVALID OR MISSING BID
040-58-2093	65451	ALL TIMES ARE AVAILABLE
042-46-1754	26654	INVALID OR MISSING POSITION CODE
045-62-3876	94551	ALL TIMES ARE AVAILABLE
045-62-3876	97251	ALL TIMES ARE AVAILABLE
048-46-9107	57650	INCORRECT SCHEDULE NUMBER
048-46-9107	75051	INVALID OR MISSING BID
049-58-9993	75051	ALL TIMES ARE AVAILABLE
060-64-4926	59951	INVALID OR MISSING POSITION CODE
062-48-1312	42554	INVALID OR MISSING BID
079-56-6182	75051	INVALID OR MISSING BID
080-64-4664	38251	INVALID OR MISSING POSITION CODE
087-50-1006	28855	DUPLICATE BID
101-60-1022	52657	INVALID OR MISSING POSITION CODE
106-60-2869	75051	INVALID OR MISSING BID
121-52-1828	42554	INVALID OR MISSING POSITION CODE
121-52-1828	42554	DUPLICATE BID
138-66-1654	17651	ALL TIMES ARE AVAILABLE
138-66-1654	26953	ALL TIMES ARE AVAILABLE
138-66-1654	38251	ALL TIMES ARE AVAILABLE
141-50-6964	59950	INCORRECT SCHEDULE NUMBER
145-48-1526	17552	INVALID OR MISSING POSITION CODE
145-64-9937	25355	ALL TIMES ARE AVAILABLE
146-72-2776	26954	INVALID OR MISSING POSITION CODE
148-58-7670	49352	ALL TIMES ARE AVAILABLE
148-66-7618	28851	INVALID OR MISSING POSITION CODE

An example is the way we handle the companies' preference lists. We used to notify the students by e-mail, and then the student would have to keep track of that preference until the bidding schedule came up for that interview, which was confusing. After we went to the Web system the students asked why we couldn't put preferencing information on the Web. So now each student can see a list of the companies who have preferenced him or her, with the ones that are up for bidding at the top of the list in red. Then students can go right from there and enter their bids.

Because it is so easy to make changes to the Web system it is possible to quickly evolve into an improved system. In the past it took months to make a change to the system, so the BPO only made changes during the summer and students would be graduated before their suggestions for change would be implemented. Today the BPO can make changes in a few days and the students can see the results and react via e-mail, so the feedback loop is quick and effective. It is an exciting environment in which to work!

Future Developments

Although the present BPO system keeps the Midstate University Business Placement Office well ahead of its competitors, Wine has ambitious plans for enhancements. The BPO is beta-testing a Web-based system for the students to enter their resumes, which will eliminate the present DOS-based Resumé Expert system that the students dislike. If all goes as planned, the old Resumé Expert will be replaced for the 1997–98 recruiting season and all student input will be through the Web.

The next major push is to give the employers access to their recruitment information through the Web. The *Career Street Journal* information for a company will be available to that company through the Web, and recruiters will be able to make changes to their job listings before bidding begins if they wish. After primary bidding the recruiters will also have direct access to their interview schedules and waitlists, and they may set up additional interview schedules through the Web. All of this will appear to be on-line, but for security reasons the changes submitted will be gathered and batched, the files will be updated at night, and the changes will be available to the students the next day. Wine explains the motivation for these changes:

Today we have a high volume of calls from companies seeking information or wanting to make changes. This is a pain to us and to them, for we may not be available when they call, and when we call back they are not available, and the phone tag goes on and on. Any of that load that can be handled through the Web will make life easier for recruiters and free up our time to concentrate on better service to students and companies.

We know that many of our customer companies will not be on the Web for a while, if ever. We have customer companies that do not have e-mail, some that do not have FAX, as well as many who do not have access to the Web. With the students we could insist that they have e-mail and Web accounts, but you cannot do that with companies. Therefore we will continue to provide multiple ways to serve our company customers, which means that we will have to provide multiple systems to fit each of their needs, and that is one of our greatest challenges.

BAXTER MANUFACTURING COMPANY

It is late Friday afternoon, and Kyle Baxter, President of Baxter Manufacturing Company, Inc., and his sister, Sue Barkley, Vice President for Customer Relations, are discussing whether or not to purchase the Effective Management Systems manufacturing software package proposed by manufacturing Vice President Lucas Moore.

"I'm really fearful of buying such a large, complex software package given our past experience," Baxter exclaims. "What do you think?"

"I really don't know," Barkley replies. "We do need manufacturing software, and there are some obvious advantages to purchasing this software. We have had bad experiences in past attempts to buy such software, but we have learned from some of our mistakes, so we might be successful this time. But I have been impressed by the success that MIS has had in building new systems for us, so I am in a quandry right now."

"We're going to have to decide before long," Baxter notes, "but we need to talk with some of our people first."

Baxter Manufacturing Company Background

Baxter Manufacturing Company (BMC), located in a small Midwestern town, is a leading manufacturer of deep drawn stampings, particularly for electric motor housings. (Exhibit 1 shows a few of BMC's products.) The company was founded in 1978 by its chairman, Walter R. Baxter, as a supplier of tools and dies, but it soon expanded into the stamping business. BMC is a

closely held corporation, with the family of the founder holding most of the stock.

BMC's engineers have implemented some of the most complex stamping concepts in the industry as the company has established its niche as a quality supplier of deep drawn stampings to the automotive (85 percent of sales) and appliance (15 percent of sales) industries. BMC's major customers include Ford, General Motors, Honda of America, General Electric, Whirlpool, Amana, and Maytag. BMC puts great emphasis on quality and has achieved Q-1 status from Ford, a QSP Award from G. M., and Quality awards from Honda, and is recognized as a world-class supplier within its niche.

EXHIBIT 1
Some of BMC's stamped parts.

This case was prepared by Professor E. W. Martin as the basis for class discussion, rather than to illustrate either effective or ineffective handling of an administrative situation.

Producing a deep drawn part is a complex process requiring repeated stampings, each with a different male/female die pair. This process is performed on a heavy press, using a very complex die that consists of perhaps ten individual dies assembled together in a line. A coil of steel of the proper width and thickness is fed into one end of the press. After each stamping cycle a precision transport mechanism moves the material forward exactly the right distance so that a part that has completed one stage is positioned correctly at the next stage to be struck by the next die on the next cycle of the press. Thus each cycle of the press performs a different forming operation on each of ten parts, and a finished part comes off the machine at the end of each cycle. (Exhibit 2 shows the different stages of a motor housing stamping.)

BMC's strength lies in its ability to efficiently produce large volumes of high-quality complex stampings. It may take 6 to 8 hours to install the dies and set up the huge stamping presses for a production run, so BMC cannot efficiently produce short runs and therefore does not serve the replacement market well.

BMC uses state of the art equipment to develop and manufacture the necessary tooling for the needs of its customers. With the use of wire Electrical Discharge Machines (EDM), Computer Numerical Control (CNC) vertical machining centers, and CNC horizontal lathes, it is able to produce quality tooling efficiently. For the life of a part, BMC's computerized equipment can reproduce identical die components for replacement of worn or damaged dies.

BMC's 140,000-square-foot manufacturing facility is one of the best in the country, with 39 presses that range from 50-ton to 600-ton capacity. Every press is equipped with accessory items such as feeds, reels, and electronic detection systems. In addition to the presses, BMC has recently added the capacity to weld, drill, tap, and assemble stampings into more complex parts to suit the needs and desires of its customers.

BMC employs about 420 people and is non-union. Management believes that these employees are BMC's greatest asset. According to Chairman Walter Baxter:

> We have a great group of people! We are fortunate to be located in a farming area where the people have a strong work ethic and a "do whatever it takes" attitude. We started out as a family company and we have a lot of families—husbands and wives, their children, aunts and uncles—working here. My son, Kyle, is now President, and my daughter Sue is Vice President for Customer Relations. We cherish our family atmosphere.

Over its 19-year history, BMC has grown at about 20 percent a year. The last five years of sales have been as follows:

1992	$32,000,000	1995	$61,976,000
1993	$37,292,000	1996	$74,130,000
1994	$49,900,000		

This rapid growth has caused problems at times. For example, in 1990 its sales were so close to BMC's production capacity that, even when running its production

EXHIBIT 2

The stages of a motor housing stamping.

24 hours a day seven days a week, it became almost impossible to meet promised delivery schedules. According to Sue Barkley:

> In 1991 we had to turn down business from existing customers who wanted to give us new parts to make. For almost a year we did not accept any new business. That was the most difficult thing we ever did because we were fearful that customers who had to go to our competitors might never come back. We told our customers that we hated to refuse their business, but we had to because if we took more business we couldn't handle it—we would be late and couldn't provide the level of service that we are committed to providing. Most of our customers understood. They were not happy about it, but they respected us for being up front about it. We did lose some good orders because we weren't accepting business when they came out, but I don't think that there are any customers who haven't come back to us with more business.

By 1992 BMC had made the large investment necessary to significantly increase capacity and was back on its historical growth track.

In the late 1980s BMC's automotive customers started to go to a "just in time" (JIT) philosophy in which they carry minimal inventories of raw materials and parts. Rather than sending an order for a month's parts at a time as they used to do, the customers now tell BMC today what to ship tomorrow. They give BMC a blanket order for planning, but reserve the right to change the amounts at the last minute.

Including the time to procure the raw materials, run them through the presses to make the parts, clean and pack them, and ship them out, BMC's production process requires at least two weeks if things go well. Thus the automotive companies are forcing their suppliers to maintain their inventories for them, which places great pressure on BMC to reduce its cycle times. Because of its two-week production cycle and long set-up times, BMC is often forced to maintain finished goods inventory that is substantially above its target of a three-day supply.

About five years ago its automotive customers began to pressure BMC to convert to Electronic Data Interchange (EDI), where all paper document flows between customer and supplier are replaced by electronic flows directly between the customer's computer and BMC's computer. Thus BMC receives all purchase orders and shipping schedules electronically and sends out electronic shipping notices and bills. EDI has the potential to be quicker and more efficient for both parties, but BMC's factory computer systems were incomplete and fragmented, so for several years BMC accepted the data electronically, printed it out, and then rekeyed the data into those relevant systems that existed. The IS department is now building interfaces to enter the EDI data directly into some of BMC's systems. One reason for this delay was that their automobile customers use one EDI standard while their appliance customers use another, and each customer has its own variation on the standard it uses. BMC has had to build a separate subsystem to handle each of its customers.

Information Systems at BMC

BMC's managers have been very receptive to the introduction of new technology. They were early adopters of CAD/CAM, and are at the forefront of stamping technology. However, they have had little experience with the use of computers in business applications and have limited understanding of what the technology can do for them.

BMC got its first PCs in 1987 and a few managers started experimenting with Lotus spreadsheets. One of the first applications they set up was a spreadsheet for generating customer quotes by calculating what price to charge for a part based on estimates of raw material cost, tooling costs, the costs of stamping, and the expected quantity to be produced. Another early use of the PC was a scheduling spreadsheet developed by the company president, Kyle Baxter, when serving as Vice President for Manufacturing. This spreadsheet, which is still used today, contains data for each part, including the machine used, the number produced per hour, and the setup time. The quantity required and the delivery date are entered and the spreadsheet determines when each part should be started into production and generates a schedule of what should be run when on each machine group. If the schedule is not feasible (e.g., some parts must be started last week), the scheduler can make manual adjustments in due date, quantity required, overtime, and other factors to produce a feasible schedule.

Realizing that they needed someone to lead and educate them in the use of computers, in 1989 BMC management set up an MIS department and hired an MIS manager, Nancy Shaw. BMC installed a Data General MV minicomputer, and the first application was interoffice e-mail. This was a great way to start because it demonstrated how helpful the computer could be in sharing information. According to Sue Barkley:

E-mail was very well received because we were growing so rapidly and the need to communicate within the plant was so important. It wasn't until we got on e-mail that we realized how much time we had been spending running around the plant trying to find somebody and leaving little notes on their desk. We really became dependent on our e-mail system.

During the next two years Shaw led the purchase and successful installation of a package of financial applications, including payroll, accounts payable and receivable, and general ledger. Also, in 1989 BMC was beginning to encounter problems in production because of its growing capacity problems and its customers' switch to JIT. When customers changed their requirements the production schedule had to be changed, which forced changes in the schedules of other parts, and production people seemed to be spending all their time rescheduling things. Because demand was so near to capacity it was difficult to get all the orders done on time and there was a lot of expediting going on, which again led to the need to reschedule. Although there was no computer support for manufacturing other than the spreadsheet used for scheduling, BMC's management decided that if scheduling could be speeded up the problems would be alleviated. Consequently, the decision was made to purchase a software package for scheduling.

Sue Barkley, who was involved in the process, remembers:

Our MIS manager, Nancy Shaw, did some research and selected four packages from which we tried to choose the best one. That was my first exposure to software, and it was a terrible experience. Each vendor claimed that his software would do anything you wanted to do, and there were so many questions we should have asked but didn't.

Vendors all offered integrated packages that included production scheduling, but you also got sales, inventory, purchasing, shipping, etc. We made our selection and paid about $120,000 for the system, including both hardware and software, which was a large expenditure for us at the time.

Then we started to load the data and implement the scheduling package. The training the vendor provided was poor, the manual was full of errors, and support from the vendor was minimal. We worked and worked, and finally became so frustrated by our inability to get the system to do what we wanted it to that we just gave up. On top of everything else the vendor went bankrupt. It was a total disaster—$120,000 down the tube!

As mentioned previously, by 1991 the problems in meeting shipping schedules had gotten so bad that BMC began to have to turn down new business. Management again decided that they had to do something about machine scheduling, so again they decided to purchase a scheduling package. Sue Barkley remembers:

This time things went better. Nancy Shaw and I got more people involved in the decision on what package to buy. This vendor provided some in-depth training to our MIS people, and vendor people came down here for two weeks to help us load the data and get the production scheduling module working. Again, we found that the manual was full of errors and that the vendor people did not fully understand the logic that the system was using. But we got the system up and working and taught the production scheduling people how to use it.

The problem was that whenever we had to expedite something—give it top priority because it had to be shipped quickly—the schedule had to be regenerated, and that took two hours. Then we had to take the schedule for each machine and examine it to see what the impact on its schedule was and change what it was going to do. Because we were always expediting something, we were constantly churning.

After about a month the production scheduler came to me and said, "I'm not getting anything done. It takes me two hours to regenerate a schedule. I look at it and I then have to change five or six machines because of what the system did. Then it takes me two more hours to generate a new schedule and I have to change another five machines, and I have to go through the cycle again. It's just a continuous process of change, change, change!"

We tried for another month to make the system work for us, but we were in such bad shape with our capacity that we just couldn't take the time to try to cope with the system anymore. So we abandoned it and went back to our Lotus spreadsheet. The $150,000 that we had spent for that system was down the drain!

The Present MIS Department

In 1994 Shaw left and BMC hired Don Collins to replace her as MIS manager. Collins had 20 years of experience as a lead systems analyst with a large manufacturer and broad experience with manufacturing systems. In 1996, Collins has a programming staff of four. The 1996 capital budget for hardware, software, and other information technology items was about $200,000. The MIS expense budget for payroll, supplies, and education was about $350,000.

The MIS department is using a development tool called Cyber Query Cyber Screen (CQCS) from Cyber Science, but Collins is giving some thought to what BMC's development environment of the future should be. The Data General MV computer is becoming obsolete and is reaching capacity, so BMC will have to obtain additional capacity soon.

In order to plan a production schedule you need to know what you have in inventory, so the MIS group has created systems to track raw material, in process, and finished goods inventories. MIS has also developed a minicomputer system that accepts EDI orders from customers and allows the customer service group to create a shipping schedule on the computer. Collins believes that within two more years the MIS group can build and install a set of manufacturing systems that will satisfy BMC's basic needs and provide quite satisfactory EDI service to customers.

This success in building new systems opened BMC managers' eyes to the possibilities for using the computer, and they have generated so many requests for new systems that an MIS steering committee has been established to approve projects and set systems development priorities. The members of the MIS steering committee are President Kyle Baxter, Controller Lou Wilcox, Sue Barkley, and Don Collins.

The New Proposal

In late 1996 Lucas Moore, Vice President of Manufacturing, suggested that BMC purchase and install an integrated package of manufacturing software sold by Effective Management Systems, Inc. (EMS). Moore had worked as an engineer with the company for seven years and then took a leave for two years to get an MBA. The Vice President of Manufacturing retired soon after Moore returned, and Moore was promoted to that management position.

Moore supports the proposal that BMC install the EMS Time Critical Manufacturing package consisting of eight modules: Shop Floor Control, EDI Integration, Inventory Management, Factory Data Collection, Standard Routings, Labor Collection, Engineered Product Configurator, and General Ledger. The purchase price

of this software package is $220,000, including documentation, training by EMS, and consulting help during installation of the software. The cost of a software maintenance contract is $55,000 a year, and EMS will make limited changes requested by BMC at a cost of $60 per hour.

The EMS software will run on several minicomputers, including BMC's Data General MV. However, additional computer capacity will be needed whether BMC purchases the EMS package or builds its own manufacturing systems.

Moore's Views

Moore is relatively new to the manufacturing area, having taken over that area about a year ago, and was not involved in the past attempts to purchase scheduling software. Moore explained to Baxter that BMC should purchase the EMS package because:

> We are still fudging our EDI and still scheduling with a Lotus spreadsheet. The entire industry has passed us by in our use of the computer in manufacturing and we are in danger of losing our reputation as a world-class parts manufacturer. Both my MBA studies and our experience with the new inventory systems that Don has installed have convinced me that computer systems can significantly enhance our efficiency and improve our service to our customers, but we can't wait another two years to complete home-grown manufacturing systems that will still need to be upgraded before they are really first class.
>
> I have had extensive discussions with EMS manufacturing specialists, read their literature, and seen the proposed systems demonstrated, and am convinced that the proposed system will do everything that we will ever want to do. EMS has assured me that there will be no problem integrating these manufacturing modules with our existing financial systems, and that we can be up and running with the entire system in six months.

"Given that our MIS group is doing a good job developing new systems," Baxter asked, "why should we purchase the EMS package rather than building manufacturing systems in-house? Moore's reply was:

> The time and cost differences between purchasing and building are too significant to ignore: six months to install this advanced system versus two years to build our own basic system, and a firm $220,000 to purchase this system versus over $400,000 to build our

own. These costs do not include new hardware, but we will need to increase our capacity whether we purchase or build our new systems.

Furthermore, we will get a high quality state-of-the-art system instead of a simple "first try" system. EMS has sold this system to hundreds of manufacturers, and thus has been able to spend much more time and money developing it than we could possibly afford. EMS has a large staff of more creative and sophisticated programmers than we can get, and EMS has gone through several cycles of improvement of this system based upon the experience of hundreds of users of the earlier versions of the system.

It is true that the EMS system will not always do things the way we currently do them. But is the way we do them better than the way that is based on the experience of hundreds of manufacturers? We are always making changes in how we do things, so it will not be difficult for us to make some changes to conform to this new software, and I expect that these changes will improve our operations.

"We have not been successful in two tries to use purchased software packages in the manufacturing area," Baxter noted. "What makes you think that we would be successful this time?" Moore replied:

There are a number of important differences this time. First, in the past there was little ownership of the new system by the factory people, but this time I am the champion of the new system and my people will make it work. Second, in the past the conversion strategy was flawed—BMC tried to install scheduling without having inventory data under control, but this time we will go at it a module at a time in the sequence that EMS has been very successful with in many previous installations. Third, during the previous attempts we were pushing capacity and no scheduling system was going to work when we were having to expedite everything, but today capacity is not a major problem and things are reasonably calm in our factory so we can devote our energy to making the new system successful.

Collins' Views

Baxter also talked with Collins, who argued that BMC should continue its process of building the manufacturing systems that it needs. He estimates that the needed systems could be completed in about two years at a cost of around $420,000—$220,000 for outside help (includ-

ing training his people in new development tools) and $200,000 in internal costs.

When Baxter asked Collins why BMC should not purchase the EMS software, Collins replied:

First, the EMS software is far more complicated than we need. For most general manufacturers each part may require six operations on six different types of machines, and each part has a routing that is different than other parts. Then several parts may be assembled into a subassembly, so you have two- or three-level bills of material. We typically take a coil of steel, stamp out the part, clean it, box it, and ship it out, so both our routings and our bills of material are very simple, as is our production process. The EMS system is designed for much more complex manufacturing.

Second, we have had little or no experience with computerized production systems. Does it make sense for us to try to jump to a very complex and sophisticated system like the EMS proposal? Lucas has a very superficial understanding of this software package, and he doesn't know any of the details of how it will work. Therefore, he has no idea of the difficulties that his people will run into in adapting to this complex package. It will require them to do many tasks that they have never done, or even considered doing. And they don't need this complexity. Wouldn't it be better to build our own systems that correspond to where we are on the learning curve and plan to upgrade them as we progress in our understanding of our systems needs?

Third, it is likely that the system does not fit the way we are running the business. Do we change the system or do we change how we run our business? We probably can't change a purchased system, so we would have to change the way we run the business. Do we really want to do this?

Fourth, we are constantly changing our manufacturing facilities and processes, and they may be unique to our business. If you purchase a package you are at the mercy of the vendor to make changes in it. He may or may not make the changes that you want, and in fact he may make some changes that you do not want. If you do not expect the system to change and it is a common system, you probably should purchase it. For example, one general ledger system is just like any other, and they haven't changed in 20 years, so you should purchase this application. But we are continually changing things out in the shop, and if we build our own systems we can change them when we need to.

Finally, we have demonstrated that we can build and successfully install our own systems, but our record with purchasing and installing manufacturing systems is dismal. The EMS proposal may fulfill our needs, but then again it may not. We failed twice in the past because the system we purchased did not fit our needs. Why take that chance again?

"You seem very concerned that the EMS system might not suit our needs or that our needs might change," Baxter replied. "Could we modify this system if it does not suit our needs?"

Because we will not have a source-code version of the software, it will not be feasible for our programmers to modify the functionality of this system. However, we can write interface software to change the form of the system's input and output.

When Baxter noted the cost and time differences between purchasing and building the system as estimated by Moore, Collins replied:

The figures Lucas quotes are very misleading. The purchase price is but a part of the total cost of buying, installing, and maintaining the software. To be sure you are choosing software that truly meets your needs, you must put a substantial effort into defining your needs and evaluating each candidate package against those needs. One of the major weaknesses of the present proposal is that this process of defining needs and evaluating possible packages has been completely ignored. In my opinion we must go through this process before buying any packaged software, and this will affect both the proposed cost and how long it will take to install the system.

Another cost of purchasing a system is the cost of modifying your existing systems so that they can feed data to or receive data from the purchased package. If the systems that must be interfaced with the purchased systems are also purchased systems that you cannot modify, you may have to create additional systems to translate from one packaged system to the other packaged system. In addition there will be costs of training the users, data conversion, and the changeover to the new system. A good rule of thumb for the total cost of installing a purchased package would be twice the purchase price of the software, which in this case would be $440,000. I doubt that we could do it for any less, and that compares with about $420,000 to build our own systems (which

includes all the costs involved, such as training, conversion, and defining the needs of our manufacturing people).

It will take at least a year to properly evaluate and install a purchased system. This is less than the two years we will need to complete our own system, but we will be installing and using components of the new system as we complete them, so the time advantage is not that great.

When asked what it would take to do a more complete evaluation of the proposal to purchase the EMS system, Collins replied:

We would need to spend about six months studying our manufacturing area to determine what we are doing now and what the new systems should do. Then we would take some time to explore the many packages that are available, and winnow them down to the three or four most suitable. Then we would invite the chosen vendors to submit proposals so we could study and evaluate each of these proposals in detail and pick the best one. Meantime, we would prepare a proposal for building the new system that would describe the proposed system in detail and include a plan for its development including schedules of both time and dollars. Finally, we would compare the best proposal with the plan for building the system ourselves and decide which to do. That would take at least a year and cost between $50,000 and $90,000.

Decision Time

After his discussions with Moore and Collins, Baxter sat down with his sister, Sue Barkley, to discuss what to do about Moore's proposal. "Sue," Baxter began, "you were able to get the second manufacturing software system we bought up and running, but conditions in the shop were so chaotic that we abandoned trying to use it. Why don't we go back and try it again?" Sue replied:

We recently considered trying again to use this system, but the special computer we bought to run it died and the software vendor has gone out of business, so we were out of luck.

"Lucas claims that BMC is losing its reputation as a world-class parts manufacturer because its systems are inadequate, and therefore BMC must purchase a system without delay," Baxter says. "Do you believe that it is critical that we get these new systems immediately?" Sue thought a while before replying:

> I don't think that our customers care about our systems as long as we provide high quality products at a good price and deliver them when they are needed, which we are doing. From their perspective, we are already interacting with them via EDI, so that is a problem for us rather than for them. It would be great to have the proposed systems as soon as possible, but we have been getting along without them for a long time.

"Well, Sue," Baxter says, "I still don't know what we should do. What do you think?"

PART IV

THE INFORMATION MANAGEMENT SYSTEM

Every user-manager is responsible for managing information resources. Like other resources (such as people, capital, and facilities), information assets require planning, directing, and controlling. This section lays out a model system for managing information resources—one where the user-manager plays a critical role. A vision shared by information systems (IS) professionals and user-managers for the role of information in the business is required. IS direction must be linked to the direction of the business. All technology assets must be managed as critical corporate resources. Difficult choices must be made on how to structure the IS organization, what role it should have, and where to place it within the organization.

This part of the book opens with Chapter 13, "Setting a Direction for Information Resources," which lays the critical groundwork for the management system by outlining the process for setting a direction for an organizational information resource. An overall scheme for IS planning is presented that includes assessment, visioning, and plan construction steps. The idea of information vision and architecture is presented to be comprehensive, covering both technology and human assets. The chapter demonstrates the need for a vision and the benefits of having an information technology architecture. The chapter covers planning tools such as critical success factors and reviews methods for identifying strategic applications. The chapter also discusses various types of IS plans and outlines the contents of both the strategic and operational IS plans. The chapter concentrates on the role that a user-manager must play in IS planning.

Chapter 14, "Managing Technology Resources," and Chapter 15, "Managing the Information Systems Function," outline issues and suggestions for managing IT assets. Chapter 14 focuses on the three major elements of the technology component of an IT system: data, the physical infrastructure, and the applications portfolio. Information systems collect, manage, and distribute data; thus, the effective management of the data resource is central to all systems issues. Chapter 14 demonstrates that data must be considered as a resource separate from the software applications that capture and manipulate data. Individual user-managers are seen as stewards of the data they use. The chapter presents a variety of tools that can improve data administration. Critical issues in the management of all three technological assets are outlined. User-manager input is called for in each area.

Chapter 15 looks at the human aspects of the IT management system and discusses the user-manager's relationship with the IS professionals in the organization. A central theme of this chapter is the partnership between IS and user-managers that is needed to manage information resources. This chapter outlines ten critical areas for successful management, such as alternative structures and reporting channels for IS units.

Part IV closes with six case studies, the latter three of which are related. The Clarion School for Boys case study provides an opportunity to review a past IS planning effort and to assess the current state of information resource management in an organization. The Midstate University Business Placement Office (C) case study concentrates on how this organization developed its own capability to manage the operation and maintenance of its crucial computer systems. The Advantage 2000 case study details the approach used as Owens Corning reengineered its business and installed an extensive enterprise resource planning (ERP) system. Finally, the Cummins/Komatsu/TELCO joint ventures case studies describe the information systems coordination necessary to create global information systems for a series of joint ventures between Cummins Engine Company, a multinational organization based in Columbia, Indiana, and its foreign partners. Part A provides the background for these joint ventures, Part B explores the pair of joint ventures between Cummins Engine and Komatsu (Japan), and Part C describes the joint venture between Cummins Engine and TELCO (India).

CHAPTER 13

SETTING A DIRECTION FOR INFORMATION RESOURCES

In previous chapters, the technical and operational groundwork crucial to an understanding of the management of the information resources in an organization has been established. The reader should now be familiar with many of the issues of computing hardware and software, telecommunications and networking, the variety of information technology (IT) applications, and the development and maintenance of application software systems. The successful management of an organization's information resources in the next century must combine this knowledge with a thorough understanding of business strategy to guide the development of information resources for the firm.

This chapter deals with one of three fundamental components of effectively managing information technology in an organization—setting a direction. The development of an overall management system for the information resources in an organization is not complete without a clear understanding by information systems (IS) professionals and user-managers about *how* the information resources of the organization will be developed.

This chapter asserts that a system of information resource planning must include (1) an assessment of current information resources, (2) the establishment of an information vision and the information technology architecture, and (3) the strategic and operational IS plans needed to move an organization's information resources from their current status toward the desired architecture. It would not be appropriate here to outline detailed instructions for a specific planning system because planning needs and styles differ greatly from organization to organization and many approaches seem to work, but the basic issues and concepts for an effective information resources planning effort are addressed in this chapter.

Likewise, the exact organization structure for IS varies widely among firms. Many organizations have multiple IS departments, but they are treated as a single organization here. Although some parts of the detailed planning process are typically internal to the IS organization, it is helpful for the user-manager to understand and be involved in the overall process. Therefore, this chapter structures the entire IS planning process in rather broad terms. The focus is on those areas where the user-manager should be involved. Examples are used from a variety of organizations to explain the concepts.

This chapter points out some of the reasons companies should set an IS direction, defines some terms, explains the planning process and each of the steps in the process, and focuses on the issues that should be addressed. The chapter ends with some guidelines for developing an information resources plan and outlines the benefits to user-managers and IS professionals of having a clear direction for the development of the total organization's information resources.

WHY SET A DIRECTION FOR INFORMATION RESOURCES?

Organizations need a plan for the development of their information resources for several reasons. In some firms, the management of all the diverse applications of information technology are not, and never will be, organized under a single person. Yet most firms want to share information within the firm and sometimes outside and use that information for strategic or operational advantage. Discussion and agreement on a common structure or architecture, as defined later in this chapter, for the varied applications of information technology in an organization can provide a shared understanding among IS professionals and user-managers of how the company can make best use of its information resources.

Developing a plan for a company's information resources helps communicate the future to others and provides a consistent rationale for making individual decisions. Sometimes an information resources plan is created because user-managers have expressed concern about whether there is some grand scheme within which to make individual decisions. The plan for information resources development provides this grand scheme. The decentralization of IS decisions and information resources makes the establishment of a well-understood overall information resources direction critical to making consistent, timely decisions by both user-managers and IS professionals.

Planning discussions often help user-managers and IS professionals in making basic decisions about how the "business" of information systems will be conducted—defining the basic style and values of the organization. Such discussions may be part of comprehensive programs that attempt to define or refine the culture of the overall company. In 1997, for example, a growing medical device manufacturing company felt it necessary to instill a greater awareness about the concept of quality in the entire business to compete more effectively in the global marketplace. The effort led the IS director of that company to consider more precisely the quality-related values to be embraced by the IS organization. For the first time, the IS organization began to consider the role of quality in the shared beliefs of people within the IS organization. Discussion focused on various IS quality issues such as excessive rework in the design of major systems.

Traumatic incidents sometimes create the need for an information resources direction-setting process. In early 1995, telecommunications network redundancy was a significant architecture discussion topic among some IS directors within the financial services industry. A tornado had destroyed much of a critical switching center of a telecommunications company in a major money center. The extensive damage reduced data and voice circuit availability for several days. As a result, banks and other organizations that depend on the constant availability of the public telephone network for certain operations, such as automatic teller machines (ATMs), were forced to reexamine contingency plans associated with the non-availability of telecommunications service. Some organizations realized that IS management had not thought seriously about what to do when faced with such a loss. The result in many firms was an extended set of discussions on network architecture and network plans.

BUSINESS DRIVERS?
SURE, WHERE ARE WE GOING?

According to a 1996 survey by the research wing of the American Management Association, 600 senior executives reported that many of the divisions in their companies understood the company's mission, vision, and values "poorly or not at all." And no division ranked higher than 61 percent for truly understanding the company's raison d'etre.

IS came up comparatively clueless next to marketing and sales.

How Well Do You Understand Your Company's Mission?

Department	Very Well	Poorly/ Not At All
Human Resources	51%	10%
Information Systems	35%	20%
Marketing	61%	4%
Research & Development	37%	21%
Sales	53%	8%

[Adapted from CIO, September 15, 1996, p. 26.]

UNDERSTANDING
THE OUTPUTS

Although IS managers have developed plans and budgets for years, the task of formally developing and communicating an overall information resources plan, with an *explicit* information vision and architecture, is relatively new to most organizations. Most have only a few years experience in developing such outputs formally. As a result, the deliverables at each step in the process take on somewhat different meanings from organization to organization. It therefore makes sense to define each output or deliverable in the planning process.

Information Resources Assessment

As outlined in Chapter 1, any organization has a set of information resources—both technological and human—with which user-managers conduct the business of the organization. An **information resources assessment** includes the following:

> *Inventorying and critically evaluating these resources in terms of how well they are meeting the business needs of the organization.*

An information resources assessment includes reviewing the quality and quantity of the technological resources—the hardware, software, networks, and data components of an information resources system. The human asset portion of an information resources assessment includes a review of the quantity and training/experience level of both users and IS professionals as well as the management systems and values that drive IS decisions in the organization.

Information Vision and Architecture

At a recent meeting of IS directors, the following ideas emerged about the meaning of the information vision and architecture concept. Some executives described the term as a "shared understanding of how computing and telecommunications technology will be used and managed in the business." Others reported that they generate a "comprehensive statement about our future information resources that is part philosophy and part blueprint." The group felt that a vision and architecture statement must be "specific enough to

guide planning and decision-making but flexible enough to avoid restatement each time a new information system is developed." Finally, several in the group felt that a "vision and architecture statement should provide the long-term goal for the IS planning effort"—the vision and architecture statement represents the overall design target.

Several ideas common in these descriptions suggest a definition. First, the information vision and architecture statement is an **ideal** view of the future and not the plan on how to get there (the information resources plan is discussed later). Second, the vision and architecture statement must be flexible enough to provide policy guidelines for individual decisions but more than just fluff. Third, deliberation about both vision and architecture must focus on the long term, but usually exact dates are not specified. Finally, there is some difference between a vision and an architecture, although some firms combine the two concepts into a single statement.

With these ideas in mind, the terms may be defined as follows:

> ***Information vision*** *is a written expression of the desired future for information use and management in the organization.*

> *The **information technology architecture** depicts the way an organization's information resources should be deployed to deliver that vision.*

Much like the design of a future complex aircraft or a skyscraper, an information vision and an information technology architecture together translate a mental image of the desired future state of information use and management into a comprehensive set of written guidelines, policies, pictures, or mandates within which an organization should operate and make decisions. Either the vision or the architecture may take the form of a set of doctrinal requirements or rules. Other organizations create architectural diagrams or blueprints much like a building architect uses a diagram to represent his/her mental image of the future. As is true for a business vision, the information vision and architecture may also be a written statement. For example, one organization found it sufficient to define its information vision by stating, "We must provide quality data and computing products and services that meet our clients' needs in a timely and cost-effective manner." Regardless of the form, statements about vision and architecture should provide the business, managerial, and technical platform for planning and executing IS operations in the firm.

Information Resources Plans

The information resources planning process should generate two major plan outputs—the strategic IS plan and the operational IS plan. The **strategic IS plan** contains:

A set of longer range goals that document movement toward the information vision and technology architecture and the associated major initiatives that must be undertaken to achieve these goals.

At the strategic level, these initiatives are not typically defined precisely enough to be IS projects. Instead, the IS strategic plan lists the major changes that must be made in the deployment of an organization's information resources over some time period.

The **operational IS plan** can be defined as follows:

A precise set of projects that will be executed by the IS department and by user-managers in support of the strategic IS plan.

The operational IS plan also incorporates the precise goals that will be accomplished and often the budgets for each project identified in the plan. The operational plan crystallizes the strategic plan into a series of defined projects.

The process of generating each of these outputs and how they are linked together is discussed in more detail in the next section.

THE PROCESS OF SETTING DIRECTION

IS and Business Planning

Earlier chapters have argued that IS decisions must be tightly related to the direction of the business. Such a maxim exists whether for the design of a particular application system or for the overall direction of the organization's information resources. Figure 13.1 depicts the relationship between setting the direction for the business as a whole and setting the overall direction for information use and management in that business. This process may be applied for the entire company, a division, or an individual user-manager's department. On the left side of the chart are the general steps required to set direction for the business. On the right are the required planning steps for the organization's information resources. Note the myriad of arrows depicting how the output of a step impacts both the next step on the same side (left or right) of the figure as well as steps on the other side of the figure. This chart provides the outline for the rest of the chapter.

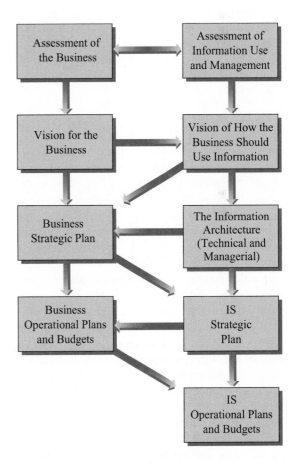

Figure 13.1 The Information Resources Planning Process

Assessment

Any organizational planning process starts with an assessment step, both for the business and for information use and management. Current performance is compared to a previous plan or set of objectives. Operating data are collected. Surveys are often conducted to measure customer attitudes on performance. Competing organizations are benchmarked to determine both what is possible and what is being achieved at other organizations. Both a business and information use and management assessment should be conducted. More on the information assessment step is discussed later in this chapter.

Vision

The second basic step in any planning process should be to envision an ideal state at some distant point in the future. This step defines what the organization wants to become or to create. It does *not* define how to achieve this vision. For the IS area, a technology architecture is added to the information vision for an organization.

Strategic Planning

Strategic planning is the third step and should be conducted for both the business and its information resources. **Strategic planning** may be defined as the process of constructing a viable fit between the organization's objectives and resources, and its changing market and technological opportunities. The aim of any strategic planning effort is to shape the company's resources and products so that they combine to produce needed results. Strategic *business* planning sets the basic course for the use of all resources, usually over an extended time period. It is designed to be general in nature and typically does not set forth precise budgets, schedules, or operating details. Instead, it translates the organization's vision into a set of major initiatives that describes how to accomplish the organization's vision of its future. Review of the strategic plan is exercised by regularly examining the status of the major initiatives contained in the plan.

In parallel with the business plan, a strategic IS plan should be built considering the vision for the use of information and the overall management of information technology in the company, as well as the role for the IS department. The strategic IS plan outlines the results desired for a specified time period and the necessary major initiatives.

Operational Planning

Operational planning lays out the major actions the organization needs to carry out in order to activate its strategic initiatives. It typically includes a portfolio of projects that will be implemented during some time frame in order of priority or urgency. Specific, measurable goals are established, and general estimates of costs and benefits are prepared. Quite often, capital expenditures are identified and justified. Responsibility for achievement of the objectives, actions, and projects is also specified in this plan. Review of the operational plan is more precise, often on a time-and-cost basis at the project level. Specific details, responsibilities, and dates of projects that move to the implementation stage are identified in the budget, listing staffing requirements, facility scheduling, specific demand and usage forecasts, and detailed expense estimates. Once set in motion, the operational plan is naturally less flexible than the strategic plan. The operational plan relies heavily on the operating budget for control purposes. Quite often, companies develop both long-term (three to five years) as well as short-term (one year) operational business plans.

The operational IS plan, although usually coinciding in length with the business operational plan, is likely even more project-specific than its business plan counterpart. This difference is a natural result of the operational plan's purpose—to translate the general information resources direction, as defined in the strategic IS plan, into specific systems development projects or other efforts for the IS department (such as a capacity upgrade) that also meet specific initiatives for the business. In addition to defining methods by which the IS department plans to complete projects for other units in the organization, the operational IS plan should also list internal projects designed to enable the IS department to better meet the needs of its users.

The operational IS plan should identify specific accomplishments on multiyear application systems development projects. Suggestions should be made for improvements in IS department operating procedures and increasing infrastructure capacity. Specific goals, actions, due dates, and budgets should be proposed for software purchases. Professional IS staff should be allocated to systems development projects.

Traditional Planning in the IS Organization

In many IS organizations, the process of overall information resources planning has not been structured in the same way as the business planning process. Instead, the majority of IS planning emphasis was on major application systems internal development project planning rather than on overall organizational planning. Because of this emphasis on internal development projects, many IS organizations adopted a bottom-up, needs-based approach to information resources planning, referred to as **needs-based IS planning.** When a specific, urgent business need called for a new information system, some form of formal project planning process was invoked to address the situation.

Over time, this **project-oriented IS planning** process was found to be largely reactive in nature and often did not ensure that the proposed system meshed well with the overall business plan of the organization. In some cases, not enough consideration was given to the potential impact that one proposed system might have on another proposed or existing system. This orientation toward IS planning, although practical from the perspective of the IS department and perhaps the individual user-manager, often resulted in lost strategic business opportunities, incompatible systems and databases, unacceptable implementation time frames, and a host of other problems. The needs-based IS planning approach often failed to give adequate consideration to the total information requirements of the organization across operating units, possible economies of scale, and avoidance of duplication of efforts. As demand for information to be shared across functional organizational lines increased and the distinction between classes of information technology blurred, the shortcomings of the needs-based approach to planning have led many companies to seek better ways to set a direction for their information resources. Thus, the concept of developing a strategic IS plan, driven by the business strategic plan and seeking to conform to an agreed upon information vision and technology architecture for the organization, began to be used more extensively.

While both the business planning and information resources planning processes are important, the next five sections of the chapter deal in detail only with the steps on the right-hand side of Figure 13.1.

ASSESSING CURRENT RESOURCES

The information resources planning process should begin with an assessment of the use of information and information technology in the entire organization and an assessment of the IS organization itself. The information resources assessment step is usually conducted by a committee of user-managers and IS professionals, perhaps with the aid of outside expertise. Outside facilitators can bring needed objectivity and experience to the process, but their value must be weighed against the added cost. Alternatively, the assessment may be conducted totally by an outside organization and presented to top business and IS department management. As with all such outside studies, however, there is the distinct possibility that this approach will result in resentment by the IS organization and some user-managers. If carefully orchestrated, however, an outside information resources assessment can be very successful, as demonstrated at Methodist Hospital in Indianapolis (Palmer, 1993) and the Methodist Hospital of Indiana case study in this book.

Measuring IS Use and Attitudes

The information resources assessment, however it is conducted, should measure current levels of information resources use within the organization and compare it to a set of standards. These standards can be derived from past performance in the organization, technical benchmarks, industry norms, and "best of class" estimates obtained from other companies. In addition to use measures, the attitudes of users and staff of the IS organization are important. Opinions about the performance of the IS organization in relating to the business must be measured. Likewise, a technical assessment of the IT infrastructure should be conducted. Figure 13.2 contains a portion of an information resources assessment conducted in late 1996

- **A *single* information system does not exist in our organization.**
  A variety of disconnected information systems exists throughout our organization. Some systems are contained in isolated PCs, some on isolated mainframes/minis. Such disintegration causes needless effort on the part of staff.

- **Substantial potential exists for "cleaning up" the automation of existing work processes.**
  Significant manual processing of information currently occurs in such areas as the compilation of statistics, reporting, billing information given to finance, typing, and administrative functions. There are several work steps that our software doesn't treat, and there are steps where the software has a different set of requirements than is practiced at our company. Consequently, staff must override the software or supplement it manually.

  Our organization maintains several paper-based "shadow" systems created to fill in where information systems don't connect. These paper systems are costing our organization a significant loss in time.

- **Significant gaps exist in automation of the "value-added" process in our company.**
  Many of the steps involved in the value-added process are conducted either manually or, if the computer is used, operate from old data. Automating and integrating these steps will offer a significant strategic advantage for our company.

- **There is a perception that the IS organization is not a company-wide support organization.**
  The staff feels that IS seems to focus almost exclusively on the order processing function. IS has not been seen as a source of leadership for solving problems that are in other functions and PC-based. Staff associated with the distributing function seem to receive better service on their information requests and have software upgrades made more easily.

- **Except for the last year and a half, IS appears to have been a "stepchild" of senior management.**
  The staff questions whether senior management is really committed to making IS an integral part of our company. Senior management is still seen by some staff as too distant from information resource management. Active participation by senior management will be required if leadership is expected from IS.

- **There is a significant perception among the user population that IS is not particularly responsive to their needs.**
  Turnover of personnel in the PC support positions has been high, resulting in staff not understanding its role.

  There seems to be a general lack of trust between the user community and the IS organization. Requests for new software are denied with little explanation. Many people feel standards are enforced in situations that should not be subject to arbitrary standards.

- **IS personnel seem dedicated to IS and the company.**
  A strong team spirit exists in IS to operate in the current adverse situation (i.e., without a director).

- **The level of user training and support is substantially below needs and expectations.**
  Training on software is inconsistent. There is a strong feeling among staff that "tunnel training" exists (only taught enough to perform specific job). Opportunities to use software to extract data and be creative do not exist.

  Past PC training also seems inconsistent, but a PC training function has been budgeted for 1996. Very little of that budget has been spent through September 1996.

- **Although the workload in IS is heavy at times, current staffing levels should be sufficient to meet current expectations.**
  Current IS staff are performing their regular duties consistently without a director, but nonroutine functions, many of which were previously performed by the director, are not being done. Personnel seem willing, but have not been trained in these functions, many of which require a high level of system knowledge.

  There are a number of users within our organization who would like to see IS take on a much more active role. Such a role will increase human resource requirements, both in numbers and skill levels.

Figure 13.2 Example Information Resources Assessment

for a Michigan-based food products company. The assessment was initiated by the company president after the IS director was terminated. The assessment was undertaken by a team of user-managers and IS personnel facilitated by an outside consultant. As should be clear by reading the example, the assessment will likely lead to substantial changes in overall information resources direction at this organization.

Reviewing the IS Organizational Mission

Another important part of the assessment step is a review of the IS department's mission. The IS mission statement should set forth the fundamental rationale (reason to exist) for the activities of the IS department. The activities of the IS department must be assessed in light of this mission.

Sinclair (1986) suggests that a mission can best be defined by clearly delineating the reasons—from the total organization's perspective—for having an IS function. Each reason given may be classified under one of three categories, which he labeled as domains—efficiency, effectiveness, and competitiveness. The performance of the IS organization should in turn be assessed compared to expected roles in each domain. The following questions should be asked during the mission assessment process:

Efficiency:	Is the IS organization helping the organization do what it does with minimum resources?
Effectiveness:	Is the IS organization helping the user-managers in the organization spend their time doing the right things?
Competitiveness:	Is the IS organization engaging in projects that will ensure the organization's competitive position in the future?

It is not unusual in the assessment process to find an imbalance of performance in these three areas. Traditional needs-based planning approaches often do not address the requirements of all three domains. Instead, the domain of efficiency usually receives the majority of the planners' attention. Unfortunately, satisfying needs of one domain may contribute little to the needs of the others. Involving user-managers in the assessment exercise is one way to ensure that the IS mission statement defines the most appropriate role of the IS department. This involvement also allows user-managers throughout the organization to understand better why the IS department needs a mission statement and a strategic plan.

It is often useful to involve both user-managers and IS professionals in the mission assessment process, especially when there is not a well-defined mission statement for the IS organization. Figure 13.3 contains a mission statement for the IS organization of a West Coast machinery manufacturer developed by people in the IS organization in 1995 and based on what they thought users wanted from the organization. The identified roles include an emphasis on secure data storage for the official records of the organization, maintaining processing capacity, managing the data network, and offering systems development capability. Whereas all these are important technical functions, this "inside-out" view of the IS organization's mission may not match a statement developed from a user-based perspective.

Figure 13.4 provides a mission statement for the same IS organization developed by some of its users —in this case, the nine officers of the corporation. The second paragraph in particular makes it clear that these users, who are senior managers, see the IS organization as not being in the computing business at all, but as the provider of "management tools" to increase effectiveness and the developer of the information infrastructure and services needed to improve

---

RELATIONSHIP MATTERS

International Data Corporation has found "a strong correlation between the effectiveness of the IS organization and the relationship between the CIO and the CEO," notes the study, which surveyed 283 top executives across three vertical industries: finance, manufacturing, and retail/wholesale. "We suspect that this relationship, if it is close, permits the CIO to develop the IS organization into a service that delivers competitive advantage for the company, thus enhancing the careers of every IS professional in the organization." In other words, you don't have to be regular golfing buddies, but a certain amount of mutual esteem will help IS function as a business partner.

[Selected from CIO, August 1997, p. 34.]

Information Services is responsible for a wide variety of computing systems and services for the people of our corporation.

In this role, the department:

- Provides a secure location for housing and accessing the official electronic data records of the company.
- Maintains computer processing capacity and support for file maintenance and information reporting.
- Manages a corporate data network that delivers services to departmental and individual workstations linked to its data center.
- Provides integrated IS development for departments in order to advance organizational strategies (systems development services are available for mainframe, local area network, workstations, and supply chain applications).

Figure 13.3 IS-Prepared Mission Statement Example

decision-making in the business. Operating an IS department with this latter mission statement would clearly require a major reconsideration of the basic activities of the IS organization as represented in the first statement. Indeed, some assessments reveal that an outdated mission statement is the root cause of user concern about the IS department.

Assessing Performance versus Goals

The traditional goal of many IS applications was to reduce cost by increasing the operating efficiencies of structured, repetitive tasks, e.g., the automation of the payroll function. The scope of IS applications has expanded dramatically in recent years to include sys-

tems to assist in the decision-making process for unstructured problem situations and in providing competitive advantage for the organization. This broader scope in the uses of information technology has required IS and user-managers to assess the IS organization based on objectives in addition to reducing cost.

Table 13.1 shows the objectives of an IS organization at a regional bank in the Midwest. Eight objectives for 1996 were identified in an earlier planning process, and data were collected during late September 1996 to estimate actual performance for the year. The assessment report noted that on some measures, such as the number of users and network availability, actual performance during the year exceeded expectations.

In order to meet the challenges outlined within the company Vision Statement and support the strategic objectives and values of our company, the mission of Information Services is to provide reliable information, data, and computing services to all clients, both within and, where appropriate, outside of the company.

To accomplish this role, it will be necessary to exercise leadership in identifying new management tools based on evolving information technology that enables management to increase their effectiveness in operating and managing the business. The department's ultimate objective is the development of an integrated information infrastructure and associated services required to facilitate the decision-making process.

Figure 13.4 User-Prepared Mission Statement Example

Table 13.1

Example Objectives for the IS Department

Achievement Area	1996 Objectives	1996 Performance	2001 Objectives
Percent user satisfaction with applications development services	80%	71%	85%
Number of employees with central computer account or networked workstation	1,000	1,250	1,400
Percent of scheduled hours data network is available to users	99%	99%	99%
IS personnel turnover	12%	14%	8%
Percent of departmental computing equipment purchases that comply with the supported equipment list	85%	88%	85%
Percent of total organization computing resource capacity connected to data network	80%	85%	85%
Cost per transaction on common systems	$.025	$.0285	$.02
Percent of targeted systems converted to client/server architecture	55%	42%	75%

On other measures, notably user satisfaction with certain services and conversion to a client/server architecture for certain systems, actual results were far short of the goal. These conclusions and a new set of objectives for the year 2001 were used as input to later steps in the information resources planning process shown in Figure 13.1.

CREATING AN INFORMATION VISION

After assessing the current use and management of an organization's information resources, the shared business and IS leadership expectations of how information will be used in the business should be specified. Developing these expectations requires both an understanding of the future of the business or organization and an understanding of the role information can play in competing in the future.

Vision creation starts with speculation as to how the competitive environment of the business will change in the future and how the company should take advantage of it. Once this business vision is specified and written, the information use implications of how a firm wants to operate in the future should be clear. The information vision for the organization may then be written.

An example may be useful to explain the process. A $35 million printing company in Atlanta was taken over by new management in early 1997 as the result of an acquisition. After four off-site, full-day discussion sessions to create a new vision and direction for the company, the group came to a set of basic specifications for the company as it entered the next century:

- We will compete in five major market segments, each supplied by distinct business units.
- We will have revenues of at least $100 million and be known for our quality and leading-edge technology.
- We will be a leading "national player" in the printing industry.
- We will exploit new business lines or market niches via acquisition or joint ventures or by spinning off existing operations.
- Our centralized administrative units (personnel, accounting, purchasing, etc.) will operate in support of all business units.
- We will achieve strategic advantage in each market via our "information-based" decisions.
- Our profit margins will exceed 10 percent.

These fundamental propositions about the company in the future led to some basic business strategy decisions leading into the new century:

- We must improve gross margins and lower overhead costs while achieving moderate sales growth.

- We must increase the productivity of every person in the company.
- We must shorten the job fulfillment cycle time (from customer order to delivery).
- We must strive toward "zero defects" in all we do (quality objectives and monitoring systems will exist).
- We must be able to receive jobs electronically from all our customers.
- We must improve companywide internal management systems (e.g., budgeting, personnel evaluation).

These business priorities were then reviewed along with the business vision by senior management and senior professionals in the IS department. After several sessions, they jointly arrived at a shared vision for information use and management in the company. They chose to represent this vision via a set of bullet points:

- Our corporate network will be able to service a large number of remote nodes at high speed.
- User demand on our information system each year will experience:
  1. Medium growth in transaction volume on existing common systems.
  2. High growth in ad hoc requests for information on all shared and personal systems.
  3. High growth in transaction volume from new applications on shared and personal systems.
- New data fields will be defined and managed each year.
- The entire job acquisition and fulfillment cycle will be supported by an integrated, comprehensive, and accurate database.
- Our corporate network will be able to send and receive large files from customers at high speed.
- User-managers will know how to use information to make decisions and how to use the capabilities of our information resources effectively.
- Each business unit and functional department will manage its information resources within an overall information technology architecture.
- All existing business support processes (e.g., purchase order processing) will be automated via expert systems to free up time of critical human resources.
- Users will have workstation tools to make all information easily accessible.

Taken together, these statements represent a specification of how senior management wants information to be used and managed in the future. These statements are not a plan—how the IS department working with user-managers will create this environment must still be determined. Instead, these statements represent a vision of what is desired. The architectural decisions on how to deploy the company's data, software, people, and other IS assets are also not all specified. That is the next step.

DESIGNING THE ARCHITECTURE

Now that a vision for future information use in the organization has been formulated, the IS organization, often in cooperation with user-managers, must design an information technology architecture. This architecture specifies how the technological and human assets available to users and the IS organization should be deployed in the future to meet the information vision. The plan for migrating the organization's current information resources to the deployment specified in the architecture is developed later.

Components of Architecture

Several models have been developed that define the elements that make up an architecture for information technology. Traditionally, the treatment takes on a very technical definition of an IT architecture. Later models have expanded the dimensions to include more managerial, less technical aspects of information resources. One balanced explanation is provided by Seger and Stoddard (1993).

In keeping with the classification of IS assets outlined in Chapter 1, it makes sense to structure an information technology architecture into its technological and human components. Each component in turn contains several elements. Figure 13.5 contains a list of the elements of each component.

The **technological assets** component of the IT architecture contains desired specifications about future hardware and operating systems, network, data and data management systems, and applications software. Some of the tradeoffs and issues in developing the specifications about these elements are dealt with in more detail in Chapter 14. Figure 13.6 contains an example of the technology elements of an IT architecture developed by the IS department of a rapidly growing, privately held

TECHNOLOGICAL COMPONENT
- Hardware
- Software
- Network
- Data

HUMAN COMPONENT
- Personnel
- Values/Culture
- Management System

Figure 13.5 Elements of an Information Technology Architecture

- An effective IT architecture is dependent on a high quality process by which data are collected and transformed into information.

- The company's process for information creation will apply regardless of the diverse source of data, the division, or location.

- The process of transforming our data into information will be carefully designed.

- Our core data are always stored in a secure place.

- The entire information creation process must be supported by an excellent technical IT infrastructure.

- All company staff will be attached to a high-speed electronic network that provides easy access to a variety of data and computing resources.

- Small, ad hoc reporting systems created to access existing core data are not covered by these specifications.

- All information systems that contain or use core data will be available on the electronic network.

- All information systems that contain or use core data will be of an "open" design.

- All systems development processes will follow the protocol developed by the Systems Development Policy Committee.

- All data management systems in the company will be relational and be selected from a list of supported data management software maintained by the Information Services organization and approved by the Data Committee.

- The Information Services organization will maintain a list of supported word processing, spreadsheet, statistical, and e-mail software.

- The Data Committee will regularly publish a list of data collection and data maintenance standards.

- A corporate data model for our core data will be developed and regularly maintained by the Data Committee, using outside consultants.

- Each manager in the company will be held responsible for the integrity of the core data maintained by his/her organization.

- Information Services will provide support for a set of hardware/operating system platforms that are approved by the Information Resources Management Committee.

- Data analysis methodologies will be regularly reviewed by the Data Committee.

- The standards called for in this document applicable for 1998–2000 will be issued by September 30, 1997.

Figure 13.6 Example Technology Component of an IT Architecture

personnel outsourcing company in Ohio in 1997. By carefully examining this part of an architecture, you should be able to picture the technical IT system being designed.

The **human assets** component of an IT architecture outlines the ideal state of the personnel, **values,** and **management system** aspects of an IT system. Together, these elements specify how the "business" parts of managing the IS department will be accomplished, how user-managers will be involved, and how IS decisions will be made. These areas are dealt with in more detail in Chapter 15. Figure 13.7 shows the companion human assets component of the Ohio outsourcing firm's IT architecture developed in 1997. By carefully reviewing this part of an architecture, the reader should be able to understand the future culture, organizational structure, and management system for this organization's information resources.

- Trained customers may access either the information or the data stored in our systems.

- The entire information creation process must be supported by a responsive management system.

- The Data Committee will exercise overall responsibility for the quality and cost of using data and information in carrying out the mission of our company.

- The Information Resources Management Committee will be responsible for insuring that the infrastructural components of individual systems comply with the architecture.

- The Systems Development Policy Committee will develop and maintain policies relating to information systems development.

- The Data Committee will oversee and update the company's data architecture.

- The Information Resources Management Committee will approve an information systems funding system.

- The head of the Information Services organization (i.e., the CIO) will lead and support the development and maintenance of an enterprise-wide information system for the organization.

- The Director of Network Services will be responsible for maintaining and improving the technical infrastructure.

- The Director of Customer Development will provide for longer-term user development and support.

- The Director of Data Quality will support the improvement of data integrity throughout the company.

- The Information Systems Director will be responsible for maintaining and improving existing information systems.

- Support for the development of new application systems and the maintenance/upgrade of existing systems will be housed in the Information Services organization.

- Each manager in our company will be responsible for budgeting and executing a data/systems training plan that meets our data training requirements.

- Each Vice President will insure that each department within the organization has developed its own information systems plan.

- A plan for the migration of each information system in the company to be compatible with this architecture will be established by the Data Committee and approved by the Executive Staff.

- Each member of the staff will take at least 24 hours of IT training each year.

Figure 13.7   Example Human Component of an IT Architecture

THE STRATEGIC IS PLAN

According to Figure 13.1, the next two IS planning steps involve creating plans for the development of an organization's information resources. After assessing the current information resources situation and establishing a vision and architecture, the first plan that should be developed for an organization's information resources is the strategic IS plan. The strategic IS plan is a statement of the major initiatives, not yet defined precisely enough to be projects, that the IS organization and user-managers must accomplish over some time period to move the company toward the information vision and fit the business strategic plan. The plan should also contain a set of measurable results (goals) to be achieved during this time period in order to act as benchmarks for assessing progress toward the vision. The plan may also contain the results of an internal and external strategic analysis performed as part of the strategic IS planning process.

The Strategic IS Planning Process

The development of the IS strategic plan is accomplished in four basic steps—setting objectives or goals, conducting an external analysis, conducting an internal analysis, and establishing strategic initiatives. Although they are treated here in sequence, most planning processes involve iterations through these four steps.

Setting Objectives   The setting of IS objectives is done in much the same way as strategic objectives are specified for any business or functional organization. Measures are identified for each of the key result areas for the organization. IS objectives are often established in the areas of IS department service image, IS personnel productivity, and the appropriateness of technology applications. Goals relating to increased effectiveness and breadth of user-manager involvement in IS applications are also possible.

A sample of strategic IS objectives for a regional bank in the Midwest was shown in Table 13.1. This organization included goals in the areas of user satisfaction, breadth of coverage, data network performance, personnel turnover, supported equipment list acceptance, pervasiveness of the data network, cost per transaction, and client/server conversion progress. Whereas the choice of results will vary by the organi-

zation's circumstances, each objective should provide some clear benchmark toward achieving the vision and architecture for information technology.

Conducting Internal and External Analyses   The second step in the development of a strategic IS plan is a review of the external environment within which the organization's information resources must be developed over the planning period, say three to five years. This step should include reviews of the strategic business plan of the company as well as an information technology forecast. Quite often, the result of this process is a series of statements called opportunities, or areas in which new systems should be created or where the IS organization could take some action to the company's long-term advantage, and threats, those performance areas that must be corrected or for which some countermeasure must be developed. Along with the external analysis, a review of the internal strengths and weaknesses of the IS department and in the role of user-managers in the entire IT process is also conducted. These four statements together make up a **SWOT** (strengths, weaknesses, opportunities, and threats) strategic situation analysis. The internal analysis parts of this step are often conducted during the assessment phase of the planning process described earlier in this chapter.

A sample SWOT analysis for the Ohio outsourcing company mentioned earlier that was input into its strategic IS plan is shown in Figure 13.8. Note that the company (via a working group of user-managers and IS managers) identified seven strengths related to the organization's information resources. Most relate to technical skills of IS professionals and the quality of their transaction processing systems. Five weaknesses in the use or management of information are listed, ranging from personnel issues within the IS organization to limited departmental applications beyond routine transaction processing. These strengths and weaknesses act as either leverage points (strengths) or as limiting factors (weaknesses) for new strategic initiatives. The threats and opportunities lists contain both factual and attitudinal issues that must be dealt with in the plan. Both user and technology issues should be mentioned in the opportunities and threats sections.

Establishing Strategic Initiatives   Figure 13.9 contains eight strategic initiatives resulting from a 1995 strategic information resources planning effort for a

Strengths

- Major transaction control systems are relatively new, functionally adequate, well-documented, maintainable, and operationally efficient.

- The IS department has demonstrated effectiveness in adding new technologies (e.g., client/server systems).

- The IS department has demonstrated competence and effectiveness in applications development in group decision support.

- There is a stable, competent professional IS staff with expertise in designing and programming transaction processing systems.

- Our outsourcing partner seems to manage a reliable, cost-effective data center.

- There is a substantial in-house electronic mail operation, frequented by most managers in the company.

- There is substantial user-manager computing expertise in both line and staff organizations.

Weaknesses

- A single point of IS contact for end-user operational problem diagnosis and resolution has not been established.

- There are limited data center performance measurement systems.

- There has been only limited transaction-based systems development productivity.

- There is a high degree of technology specialization (narrowness) among IS professional staff and a limited degree of business orientation.

- There is limited departmental use of information technology beyond simple decision support and participation in common transaction processing systems

Opportunities.

- The IS department enjoys a high degree of credibility among the large and growing user commuinity.

- The user-manager concept has been institutionalized, facilitating ease of future system implementation.

- There is a growing base of users who understand a wide range of information technologies and want to use IT for their business.

Threats

- The IS department's effectiveness is threatened by pockets of user negativism, especially among top management..

- End-users are developing a high degree of technical competence, which they may employ in a non-integrated fashion.

- The accelerating pace of technological change and proliferation of information technologies pose risks of control loss, obsolescence, and difficulty in maintaining IS professional staff competence.

- The extensive internal communication networks and user accessibility to external databases pose security risks to our data.

- The IS department is still not an integral part of company's business planning process.

Figure 13.8 Example SWOT Analysis

Management wants the Information Services and Systems department to develop its own long-range plan utilizing the vision, mission, values, and principles of operation outlined previously. The following is a listing of initiatives we feel should be undertaken in the ultimate formulation of this plan:

1. Manage development and operations of network architecture and security in accordance with business and end-user requirements.

2. Help departments build individual information plans, utilizing Information Services and Systems departmental expertise and knowledge of overall company system requirements.

3. Create and maintain a short list of approved hardware and software that can be efficiently utilized within the designed network to meet end-user requirements.

4. Coordinate with other departments in the evaluation and design of telecommunication and data communication systems that meet the company's strategic and business needs.

5. Encourage active client participation in network utilization through training programs and user help sessions that increase the efficiency and effectiveness of the overall company decision-making process.

6. Restructure the departmental organization to accomplish better the mission of the department.

7. Develop a structured timetable and system of application backlog reductions.

8. Formulate a written standardization process for application development.

Figure 13.9 Sample Strategy Agenda

medium-sized energy company. Each statement represents an important initiative needed to enhance the role of information technology at this corporation. Some of these initiatives will require substantial investment and create new operating costs for implementation. Yet none of the initiatives is spelled out well enough to be immediately translated into action. The operational planning step is required to translate these eight initiatives into actual projects.

Tools for Identifying IT Strategic Opportunities

While building the strategic IS plan, organizations often seek help in identifying ways by which IT can provide strategic advantage for the firm. Several tools for finding new strategic insights have proven useful.

None of the tools discussed here explicitly considers how an opportunity, once identified, can be translated into a comprehensive IS plan for the organization. The tools, however, have proven of value in finding specific opportunities for IT applications and showing the role that IT may play in achieving certain business objectives. Because the use of these tools may result in IT applications during the operational planning process that help change the strategic direction of the firm, their use is most important to effective strategic IS planning.

Critical Success Factors   One well-known method for identifying strategic IT opportunities is to define information needs and processes critical to the success of a business function like sales or to the entire organization, called **critical success factors** (CSFs). Any recent text on strategic management should contain a fuller discussion of CSFs. Generally, however, CSFs define a limited number of areas, usually four to six, that, if executed satisfactorily, will contribute most to the success of the overall performance of the firm or function. Many CSFs have either short-term or long-term impact on the use of IT. Once identified, the factors can be stated as opportunities for the application of IT. An analysis may then be conducted to determine more precisely how IT can be used to accomplish the needed task.

Analysis of Competitive Forces   It is generally accepted that competitive advantage can come about by changing the balance of power between a business and the other actors in the industry. As seen from the strategic systems examples in earlier chapters, a company interested in finding a strategic initiative can:

- Inhibit the entry of new competitors by raising the stakes for competing in the market or by redefining the basis for competition in at least one dimension (price, image, customer service, product features).
- Slow the application of substitute products/services by providing difficult-to-duplicate features.
- Make products/services more desirable than those of current competitors by providing unique product features or customer services or by shifting some customer product selection criterion (for example, by being a low-cost provider).
- More strongly link with customers by making it easy for them to do business with the company and difficult to switch to a competitor.
- More strongly link with suppliers to obtain lower-cost, higher-quality materials.

An analysis of these competitive sources can identify ways by which competitive advantage can be achieved through information technology. But where exactly might opportunities exist? Figure 13.10 lists various questions that IS strategic planners can ask about suppliers, customers, and competitors to identify opportunities for the strategic use of information technology. An individual manager can also study these questions and use them to stimulate discussion in a brainstorming session aimed at suggesting possible applications of IT.

Value Chain Analysis   Another technique frequently used to suggest strategic IS initiatives is the **value chain analysis** method described by Porter and Millar (1985). As depicted in Figure 13.11, the value chain includes five primary and four support activities within an organization that can each add value for the customer in the process of producing, delivering, and servicing a product or service.

Information technology can be used in each activity to capture, manipulate, and distribute the data necessary to support that activity and its linkages to other activities. To be of strategic or competitive importance, automating an activity in this chain must, for instance, make the process run more efficiently or lead to differentiation of the product or service.

For example, an organization's goal of market differentiation by a high level of on-time delivery of products requires that operations, outbound logistics, and service activities such as installation be highly coordinated, and the whole process may need to be reengineered. Thus, automated information systems in support of such coordination could have significant strategic value. In automotive manufacturing, for example, systems that facilitate sharing of design specifications among design, engineering, and manufacturing, which may be widely separated geographically, can greatly reduce new vehicle development time and cost. Significant advantage also can be gained at the interfaces between the activities, where incompatibility in departmental objectives and technologies can slow the transition process or provide misinformation between major activities.

From a broader perspective, the value chain of an organization is actually part of a larger system of value creation, called a supply chain, that flows from suppliers, through the firm, to other firms providing distribution, and ultimately to the end-customer. Opportunities for improvement in the supply chain could thus be intercompany, such as automating the automobile ordering process from dealers to manufacturers. As a result, electronic data interchange (EDI) has been of strategic importance in several industries. It is also important to remember that activities in a value chain are not necessarily sequential because many activities can occur in parallel. In fact, significant competitive advantage can occur by using IT to allow these activities to be done in parallel, thereby developing or delivering products sooner. Thus,

Suppliers

- Can we use IT to gain leverage over our suppliers?
    - Improve our bargaining power?
    - Reduce their bargaining power?

- Can we use IT to reduce purchasing costs?
    - Reduce our order processing costs?
    - Reduce supplier's billing costs?

- Can we use IT to identify alternative supply sources?
    - Locate substitute products?
    - Identify lower-price suppliers?

- Can we use IT to improve the quality of products and services we receive from suppliers?
    - Reduce order lead time?
    - Monitor quality?
    - Leverage supplier service data for better service to our customers?

- Can we use IT to give us access to vital information about our suppliers that will help us reduce our costs?
    - Select the most appropriate products?
    - Negotiate price breaks?
    - Monitor work progress and readjust our schedules?
    - Assess quality control?

- Can we use IT to give our suppliers information inportant to them that will in turn yield a cost, quality, or service reliability advantage to us?
    - Conduct electronic exchange of data to reduce their costs?
    - Provide master production schedule changes?

Customers

- Can we use IT to reduce our customers' costs of doing business with us?
    - Reduce paperwork for ordering or paying?
    - Provide status information more rapidly?
    - By reducing our costs and prices?

- Can we provide some unique information to our customers that will make them buy our products/services?
    - Billing or account status data?
    - Options to switch to higher-value substitutes?
    - By being first with an easy-to-duplicate feature that will simply provide value by being first?

Figure 13.10 Questions to Identify Opportunities for Strategic Information Technology Applications (continued on next page)

competitive advantage can result from improvements in either the internal value chain or the interorganizational supply chain.

A series of idea-generation and action-planning sessions are often used to generate possible strategic applications of IT for the organization. The idea-generation sessions typically include example strategic applications from other organizations (to stimulate ideas by analogy). Small groups then brainstorm on possible strategic opportunities that address the

Customers (continued)

- Can we use IT to increase our customers' costs of switching to a new supplier?
    - By providing proprietary hardware or software?
    - By making them dependent upon us for their data?
    - By making our customer service more personalized?

- Can we use external database sources to learn more about our customers and discover possible market niches?
    - By relating buyer behavior from us to buying other products?
    - By analyzing customer interactions and questions to us to develop customized products/services or methods of responding to customer needs?

- Can we use IT to help our customers increase their revenues?
    - By providing proprietary market data to them?
    - By supporting their access to their markets through our channels?

Competitors

- Can we use IT to raise the entry barriers of new competitors into our markets?
    - By redefining product features around IT components?
    - By providing customer services through IT?

- Can we use IT to differentiate our products/services?
    - By highlighting existing differentiators?
    - By creating new differentiators?

- Can we use IT to make a preemptive move over our competition?
    - By offering something new because we have proprietary data?

- Can we use IT to provide substitutes?
    - By simulating other products?
    - By enhancing our existing products?

- Can we use IT to match an existing competitor's offerings?
    - Are competitor products/services based on unique IT capabilities or technologies and capabilities generally available?

Figure 13.10 (Continued from previous page)

competitive assessment. Questions such as those in Figure 13.10 can be used to stimulate ideas for IT application. A critical element of this brainstorming process is that criticism and negative comments about new ideas are prohibited.

Subsequent evaluation of these ideas involves the degree of competitive advantage expected, cost to implement, technical and resource feasibility, and risk.

Based upon these criteria, ideas are then grouped into ranked categories. Top-priority ideas are identified and used in the strategic IS planning process.

The constructs and opportunity identification techniques discussed here are nothing more than tools for creating a strategic IS plan. Like any tools, they can be misused or misinterpreted to the detriment of the information resources planning process and

SUPPORT ACTIVITIES	Firm infrastructure	Planning models				
	Human resource management	Automated personnel scheduling				
	Technology development	Computer-aided design			Electronic market research	
	Procurement	On-line procurement of parts				
PRIMARY ACTIVITIES		Inbound logistics	Operations	Outbound logistics	Marketing and sales	Service
	Examples of IT application	Automated warehouse	Flexible manufacturing	Automated order processing	Telemarketing Remote terminals for sales representatives	Remote servicing of equipment Computer scheduling and routing of repair trucks

Figure 13.11 Strategic Information Systems Opportunities in the Value Chain

ultimately the organization. While tools and concepts help, the key to the development of a viable strategic IS plan is clearly the ability of the IS department and user-managers to work together.

THE OPERATIONAL IS PLAN

After the strategic IS plan has been developed, the initiatives identified in it must be translated into a set of more defined IS projects with precise expected results, due dates, priorities, and responsibilities.

The Long-Term Operational IS Plan

Operational planning differs from strategic planning in its focus, its linkage to the business, and in the specificity with which IS projects are defined and addressed (see Figure 13.1 on page 535). The long-term IS operational plan is generally developed for a three- to five-year time period and focuses on project definition, selection, and prioritization. Resource allocation among projects and tools for providing continuity among ongoing projects are also components of the long-term plan.

The first step in preparing the long-term operational IS plan is to define long-term IS operating objectives. Key changes in the business direction should be identified and an assessment made of their possible impact on IS activities. The inventory of available information resources is then reviewed to determine what needs can be met over the planning period. Alternatives to new systems are developed in light of the constraints identified by the information resource inventory process conducted earlier.

IS development or acquisition projects must next be defined and selected. The criteria for evaluating projects include availability of resources, degree of risk, and potential of the project to contribute value to the objectives of the organization. Clearly, politics often play a significant role in the final project selection process.

Many IS planners have taken a cue from financial analysts by adopting a portfolio view of the IS long-term operational plan. They attempt to select new systems to be developed or purchased based on their association with and impact on other projects in the current systems development portfolio. Factors to consider include, but are not limited to, the level of risk of the various projects in the portfolio, the expected time until completion, their interrelation with other projects, their nature, such as being transaction processing-oriented, and the amount of resources required. IS planners then seek to balance the projects in the portfolio.

Firms that ignore portfolio balance and concentrate solely on implementing lower risk transaction processing systems, for example, may lose the opportunity to develop higher risk systems offering potential competitive advantage. Conversely, a project portfolio of nothing but risky applications with unknown chances for success and uncertain economic benefits may place the firm itself in financial jeopardy. Table 13.2 shows a portion of the systems development and enhancement project portfolio developed for the Ohio-based outsourcing company referred to earlier in the chapter.

Each IS project in the portfolio must then be subjected to a more detailed project planning process as described in Chapter 10. The IS and other information resources enhancement projects are portrayed in the form of a budget for review by management. Once the long-term operational IS plan has been approved, it should be publicized throughout the organization. Publication of the plan will help instill a sense of commitment on the part of the organization that will hopefully have a positive impact on users. As with all business functions, the IS plan should be reviewed and updated as necessary, at least annually.

Table 13.2
IS Long-Range Operational Plan Project Portfolio

System/Project	1998	1999	2000	New (N) or Replacement (R)	Make (M) or Buy (B)	Risk Assessment	Project Size	Comments
Executive & retiree personal income tax assistance		X		N	B	Low	Small	Manual assistance currently provided.
Fixed assets accounting		X	X	R	B	Med	Lrg	Improved asset mgmt. and ability to respond to tax law changes.
Corporate competitive database	X	X		N	M	High	Med	Improved analytical capabilities, access.
Common tactical sales information system		X	X	N	M/B	High	Lrg	An ongoing series of installations of capabilities to enhance the effectiveness of the sales organization.
Order entry by field organization	X			N	M	Med	Sml	Provide more timely processing of customer orders

The Short-Term Operational IS Plan

The short-term operational IS plan is usually one year in length. Its focus is on specific tasks to be completed on projects that are currently underway or ready to be started. It is linked to the business priorities of the firm by the annual budget. Immediate hardware, software, and staffing needs, scheduled maintenance, and other operational factors are highlighted in detail in the short-term plan.

Sometimes the long-term and short-term operational plans are combined into a single document. Figure 13.12 contains an annotated outline of a combined plan document.

GUIDELINES FOR EFFECTIVE PLANNING

Planning for the development of an organization's information resources can be a very complex, time-consuming process. Planning efforts attempt to make provisions for the rapid rate of change in IT and capture the often hazy definition of exactly what a strategic system is supposed to do. The first step in developing an organizational planning focus, as opposed to only a project focus, is to change the way in which the IS organization's professionals view their jobs. These changes include adoption of a service

I. Mission
Briefly describes the mission of the IS department within the firm.

II. Environment of IS
Provides a summary of the information needs of the various user groups and of the corporation as a whole.

III. Objectives of IS Department
Describes the direction in which the IS department is heading. While it may later be revised, it represents IS' current best estimate of its overall goals.

IV. Constraints on IS Department
Briefly describes the limitations imposed by technology and the state-of-the-art of systems in general. It also describes the constraints imposed by the current level of resources within the company—financial, technological, and personnel.

V. Long-term Systems Needs
Presents a summary of the overall portfolio of systems needed within the company and the set of long-range IS projects chosen by the IS Planning Committee to fill the needs.

VI. The Short-range Plan
Shows a detailed inventory of present projects and systems, and a detailed plan of projects to be developed or advanced during the current year.

VII. Contingencies
Contains likely but not-yet-certain events that may affect the plan, an inventory of business change elements as presently known, and a description of their estimated impact on the plan.

Figure 13.12 Outline of an Operational IS Plan

orientation by the IS staff in order to view users as partners. Change must also be viewed by IS professionals as a constant process to be exploited, not just an intermittent disturbance to be controlled.

User-managers can take certain actions to increase the likelihood of adoption of the proposed mindset. By taking these actions, they also increase the likelihood of the successful creation and implementation of an IS plan.

1. Early clarification of the purpose of the planning process is essential. The IS planning group must know what they are being called upon to perform prior to their work. IS professionals and user-managers will not adopt the shared vision necessary for success of the direction-setting process if they do not understand the purpose of the effort, its scope, and its relevance to their individual efforts.
2. The information resources planning effort should be developed in an iterative—not serial—process. An extended planning process that generates reams of paper that are left untouched will not be as effective as a short process that generates a plan that is reviewed and modified periodically to reflect the new realities facing the organization. Many IS plans have lengthy implementation periods. Needs and situations may change, calling for the revision of the original plan before it is implemented.
3. The plan should reflect realistic expectations. IS application development managers have received much bad press over the years, not all of it undeserved, for "promising the sky" and delivering something far short of that. User-managers must believe that objectives are attainable or they simply will not internalize them.
4. The process of setting realistic expectations should involve user-management. Input into the planning process by user-managers can result in much more feasible plans, greater probability of acceptance, and systems that more closely resemble those envisioned by the user.
5. The resulting plans should integrate all applications of IT if possible. The boundaries between technical computing, business computing, networking, video conferencing, and other information technology application areas are increasingly blurred. Separate plans for each of these areas will result in duplication of effort, lack of integration,

lost opportunities, and lower economies of scale. IS planners should seek to integrate these various applications at every possible chance. Integration of these various activities will result in the adoption of one overall strategy that will eliminate the sending of confusing messages to users. For example, a very confusing message is sent when telecommunications is centrally planned and is a free service while scientific computing is treated as a scarce resource and charged for by the use-unit.
6. An effective IS plan will also take into consideration the barriers and constraints facing all organizations. Very important, but often overlooked, is simple human resistance to change. The best-planned, most technically well-designed systems often meet with resistance and even defeat if adequate consideration is not given to how people will react to them on both an individual and group basis.

BENEFITS OF INFORMATION RESOURCES PLANNING

The cost of developing an IS plan can be substantial, especially in terms of IS leadership and user-management time, but companies have found that there can be significant benefits from such endeavors. Both the resulting documents and the processes used to create the assessment, vision and architecture, and strategic and operational plans contribute to these benefits.

Better IS Resource Allocation

A good plan provides the basis for more specific IS resource allocation. In most organizations, IS management is charged with creating budgets that reflect business priorities for the IS organization over the next several years. A planning process that contains a vision answers "what" the group should be trying to create. Likewise, a good plan answers "how" the organization will get there. Budget requests then make a lot more sense to those outside the IS department.

Communicating with Top Management

Top management insists on a rationale for major capital or staffing investments in the information technology arena. Many IS directors often request significant operating or capital budget increases—well above that available to other departments. A solid IS plan, clearly linked to the direction of the business, can help explain the need for such expenditures by showing a nontechnical context for priorities.

Helping Vendors

Having an IT architecture and plan also helps those from whom the IS organization buys products and services. Most hardware, software, and communications vendors have a defined range of products built around their own definitions or conclusions on the future architecture their customers will want. An explicit information technology architecture and plan is an effective way for the IS director to communicate with vendors on the need for certain capabilities in future products.

Creating a Context for Decisions

Another important function of an information resources plan is to create a clear context within which user-managers and IS professionals can make individual decisions. In many organizations, it is possible to come to work every day, moving from one meeting to another and from one project to another, not really understanding the overall direction of the organization. It is critical to communicate the overall direction of information use and management widely throughout the firm so everyone can understand that the organization is focused on the same defined target in the future.

Achieving Integration and Decentralization

Most IS organizations are focused on achieving tighter integration of their common systems and networks while simultaneously decentralizing the technology and operational activities. Developing an overall information resources plan forces discussion on how exactly to go about achieving these seemingly opposite objectives. The issues can then be discussed in much more detail, often without the emotion that arguments surrounding a specific decision would provide. Such intense discussions may promote a greater understanding of the trade-offs between autonomy and integration and result in a commitment to a particular course of action. In this way, later specific issue discussions are more focused and efficient.

Evaluating Options

The range of architecture options for IT applications is broad and growing. Microcomputer-based, client/server, and mainframe-based solutions to problems may all seem feasible and appropriate. Moreover, the number of IT vendors is growing rapidly. A clear IS plan can provide guidance in selecting one vendor over another. It allows an organization to take advantage of a range of options and see how they best fit into some overall architecture for the future. Otherwise, the organization runs the risk of being vendor-driven, as well as responding only to current needs rather than designing long-term solutions to major future business problems.

Meeting Expectations of Management

Today, senior management in most organizations has higher expectations than ever before on what IT can do strategically for the company. Company executives are looking for new sources of competitive advantage. In a global competitive arena, where many organizations have excellent scientists, design engineers, and new product development specialists, company leaders want to use information technology as another source of distinction in the market. The development of an explicit vision and architecture for information technology generates discussion on the role of this critical resource in meeting the objectives of the firm.

ROLES IN THE INFORMATION RESOURCES PLANNING PROCESS

Both user-managers and IS professionals have crucial roles to play if the IS plan is to be linked to the business direction and contain creative IS applications.

Role of the User-Manager

It should be clear that active participation in the information resources planning process on the part of the user-manager is integral to the successful development of a comprehensive, realistic IS plan that is well-linked to the business plan of the organization. Because user-managers typically have a better understanding of the true nature of the business activities of the organization, they should be charged with the responsibility of sharing their visions of what the need for information technology will be in the organization. Architectures, strategies, and specific plans will then all evolve from these visions.

Vision, of course, is not enough. User-manager vision must be articulated in such a manner that it can be successfully communicated to others. Employee understanding of a well-communicated, clear vision of the firm is a prerequisite to the planning process. Once this understanding of the vision is achieved, it then becomes possible to develop an IS plan that is truly consistent with the needs of the organization.

User-managers must also accept most of the responsibility for identifying specific projects that might contribute to the realization of the vision. Responsibility does not cease with the identification of an information technology opportunity. Successful planning and implementation of any plan is an iterative process, containing built-in review and feedback mechanisms. As a possessor of vision and a representative of the business, the user-manager must stay involved in the planning and system development activities in order to provide the feedback and input necessary to ensure that work is proceeding on course with the needs of the organization. Failure to do so can be disastrous. Remember, IS professionals are not mind readers, even though they are often asked to be.

Role of the IS Professional

The changing use of information technology in organizations has caused a dramatic change in the responsibilities of IS professionals. In the formative years of IT, the IS professional was typically technically oriented and rewarded for writing code that made the most effective use of the available information technology resources. Needs of the user sometimes had to be sacrificed in order to achieve desired hardware and software efficiencies. The data processing department had a certain mystique about it that caused most people not to question the programming wizard. Because only they knew the capabilities of the computer, the IS professionals were the ones who did most IS planning. The result was sometimes a piecemeal approach not in line with future business needs.

Times, of course, have changed. In their day-to-day activities, many IS professionals now act more in

a consulting and planning role than in a programming one. They must assist the user-manager to understand how his or her ideas for competitive advantage can get built into a new information system. They must be able to create a project plan for acquiring the new system.

The increased sophistication of user-managers and the recognition that the IS function of the firm should be afforded the same strategic status as such functions as marketing, finance, and manufacturing have also changed the role of the IS professional in the information resources planning process. IS professionals must be able to combine their technical skills with a sharp understanding of planning and how the organization works and should work to accomplish its goals.

This chapter provides only a brief summary of the duties of the parties involved in the information resources planning process. The message of the chapter, however, should be clear: User-managers and IS professionals must work together from start to finish in setting the direction for the development of an organization's information resources. Frequent review and feedback must occur.

Summary

To ensure that information technology is effectively utilized in today's competitive, rapidly changing world, the organization must engage in a proactive, future-based information resources planning process. To develop a meaningful IS plan, the firm must have a clear understanding of both the technology and the information resources planning process. The process must begin with a thorough assessment of the current situation. The IS mission, goal accomplishment, information use intensity, and user-manager attitudes must all be reviewed.

The definition and development of an information vision and architecture is a difficult conceptual task. Yet the value of an explicit vision and architecture statement, over a period of time, usually exceeds the creation and maintenance costs. Often organizations create visions or architectures that explicitly deal with only some of the issues mentioned in this chapter. It is not always possible to deal with all critical issues in a short period of time. Therefore, it is important to revisit a vision/architecture statement regularly to resolve issues not dealt with earlier and to determine if the information vision still meets the needs of the business. In any case, attention to architecture decisions is critical for the user-manager and IS organization leadership.

Planners must have an understanding of the environment in which they make their plans. Such understanding includes not only knowledge of the competitive marketplace in which the company operates, but also of the strengths and weaknesses of their own IS department, its relative maturity, and the ways by which the IS plan will be linked to the business plan.

The information resources planning process should be documented and controlled. Documentation ranges from the broad objectives stated in the strategic IS plan to the detailed staffing requirements and expense forecasts made in the short-term operational IS plan. The overall IS plan should provide a well-documented road map from which the firm may navigate. The IS plan should mirror and be clearly linked to the business plan.

A number of tools exist for the development of an IS plan. The methodology most appropriate for the organization should be determined as the result of a conscious thought process. A number of tools can be used to identify strategic opportunities to be assimilated into the IS plan. As firms continue to realize the increased importance of information resources planning, greater emphasis will be placed on comprehensive planning methodologies.

REVIEW QUESTIONS

1. How does the information technology architecture differ from an information vision?

2. List the critical information technology issues about which Figure 13.2 makes an explicit statement. Why do you think these particular areas were specified?

3. What important issues does Figure 13.2 *not* address that would normally be part of a complete information resources assessment? Why do you think these issues were not addressed?

4. How would you respond to the criticism that a particular architecture is not feasible based on today's technology?

5. What are the benefits of stating an architecture via a picture rather than a text statement? What are the problems?

6. Consider the objectives for the IS department shown in Table 13.1. What other functions or responsibilities normally assigned to the IS organization should have objectives?

7. Describe the basic steps in the development of the IS strategic plan.

8. Contrast the critical success factors (CSFs) and Strengths, Opportunities, Weaknesses, and Threats (SWOT) approaches to strategic planning.

DISCUSSION QUESTIONS

1. In addition to the reasons listed in the chapter, what other issues or events may cause an organization to recognize the need for an information resources plan?

2. What are the major implications for the user-manager if a review of current practices indicates substantial inconsistency in the information vision and architecture for the company? for the IS director?

3. How might the human assets architecture described in Figure 13.7 have an impact on the company's technological assets architecture?

4. What are the user implications of the technological assets architecture shown in Figure 13.6?

5. What are some of the most important problems that would likely be encountered in working toward the architectures in Figures 13.6 and 13.7?

6. Through which media can an information vision and architecture be represented? What are the advantages of each approach?

7. Making assumptions where necessary, construct an information technology architecture that is consistent with the Atlanta printing company's information vision explained in the "Creating an Information Vision" section of this chapter.

8. Compare and contrast the mission statements contained in Figures 13.3 and 13.4.

9. Given the rapid rate of change in information technology capabilities, do you believe that strategic IS planning efforts are worthwhile? realistic? Why or why not?

10. As information technologies continue to advance, is it reasonable to assert that in many instances the strategic IS plan will drive the business strategic plan instead of being driven by it? Why or why not? Can you think of an example where this might be the case?

11. Do you believe that strategic advantages obtained by the effective use of information technology are sustainable? Why?

12. In what phases of the IS planning process is the user-manager most likely to be involved? What are his or her responsibilities likely to be during each of the stages?

13. What role do you envision the user-manager playing in plan justification as the benefits of proposed systems become increasingly difficult to quantify?

REFERENCES

1991. "The good, the bad, and the fired." *CIO* 4 (May): 15.

Allen, Brandt R., and Andrew C. Boynton. 1991. "Information architecture: In search of efficient flexibility." *MIS Quarterly* 16 (December): 435–445.

Coleman, Kevin G. 1996. "Strategic information asset management." *Database Advisor* 6 (November): 90–93.

Davenport, Thomas H. 1994. "Saving IT's soul: human centered information management." *Harvard Business Review* 75 (March-April): 119–131.

Drucker, Peter. 1995. "The information executives truly need." *Harvard Business Review* 74 (January–February): 54–62.

Gage, Glen. 1991. "IS architecture artistry." *Computerworld* 23 (July 29):67–68.

Goodhue, Dale L. et al. 1992. "Strategic data planning: Lessons from the field." *MIS Quarterly* 17 (March): 11–34.

Keen, Peter G. W. 1991. *Shaping the Future: Business Design through Information Technology.* Boston: Harvard Business School Press.

Keim, Robert T. 1992. "Apple's VITAL statistics for enterprise architecture." *Corporate Computing* 1 (October): 173–177.

Koch, Christopher. 1996. "Beating a bad gap." *CIO* 10 (September 15): 28–30.

Mechling, Jerry. 1995. "The benefits of strategic computing." *Governing* 17 (March): 56.

Newman, David. 1996. "Data warehouse architecture." *Data Management Review* 19 (October): 34–39.

Palmer, Scott D. 1993. "A plan that cured chaos." *Datamation* 39 (March 1): 77, 78.

Parker, Marilyn M., and Robert J. Benson. 1989. "Enterprisewide information management: State-of-the-art strategic planning." *Journal of Information Systems Management* 6 (Summer): 14–23.

Porter, Michael E., and Victor E. Millar. 1985. "How information gives you competitive advantage." *Harvard Business Review* 63 (July–August): 149–160.

Rechtin, Eberhardt, and Mark Maier. 1997. *The Art of Systems Architecting.* Boca Raton, FL: CRC Press.

Row, Heath. 1997. "Taking care of business." *CIO* 11 (April 1): 62–72.

Seger, Katherine, and Donna B. Stoddard. 1993. "Managing information: the IT architecture." *Harvard Business School* #9-193-059.

Sinclair, Stuart W. 1986. "The three domains of information systems planning." *Journal of Information Systems Management* 3 (Spring): 8–16.

Swanborg, Richard W., Jr., and Paul S. Myers. 1997. "Wise investments." *CIO* 11 (October 15): 28–30.

Williamson, Miryam. 1997. "Weighing the no's and con's." *CIO* 11 (April 15): 49–57.

CHAPTER 14

MANAGING TECHNOLOGY RESOURCES

In addition to setting an architecture and overall plan for the future deployment of an organization's information resources, information system (IS) leaders must actively manage the technology and human resources that comprise the organization's information resources. Laying out an IS plan for reaching the information vision is only part of the task. Success is reached only by actively implementing that plan via projects, daily tasks, and an overall management system.

Managing the technology assets in an information technology system (data, the physical infrastructure, and the applications portfolio) requires an understanding of each of these three areas as well as an awareness of critical management issues or trade-offs that must be addressed. This chapter explains the key issues involved in managing each of these technical resources of the information technology (IT) system.

Many IS leaders argue that the data element of the technology component in the IT architecture is the most important one. They argue that data architecture should reflect the inherent nature of the organization, which should stay relatively unchanged over time. For example, where the organization operates, how business processes are conducted, and the forces that drive the IS department's activities are constantly changing. These changes cause computer hardware, software, networks, and the management system to adjust, often radically. By contrast, as long as the basic concept of the organization (e.g., a financial institution, a manufacturer, or a human services agency) does not change, the nature of the organization's data will remain relatively constant. The data area is also the part of the technology infrastructure where user-managers must be most involved, whether managing information resources themselves or helping a professional IS manager with the task. It is for this reason that most of this chapter is devoted to managing the data resource.

It is also important for IS leadership and user-managers to cooperate in making basic decisions about the other two elements of the technology component of an IT system: the physical infrastructure (hardware and networks), and the applications portfolio. In both these areas difficult technological trade-offs must be considered and key decisions must be made. Most importantly, these decisions can have a major impact on the business. For example, a policy to buy rather than build software (popular in most organizations) usually has a positive impact on the speed with which a new system can be up and running. However, using a packaged software product can severely restrict the ways by which the business can be run and perhaps even limit the ability of the business to grow. It is for these potential types of impacts that user-managers need to be involved (at least to some level) in decisions about how the technological resources of the organization will be managed. The key issues/trade-offs in determining the physical infrastructure and the applications portfolio follow the data discussion.

Finally, the chapter concludes with a summary of the role of the user-manager in helping to manage these technological assets.

559

THE DATA RESOURCE

Data are now recognized as a major organizational resource, to be managed like other assets, such as facilities, labor, and capital. In fact, many observers of trends in business believe that the organizations that will excel in the early 21st century will be those that manage data as a strategic resource, understand the usefulness of data for business decisions, and structure data as efficiently as they do other assets.

Of course, data can be an asset only if they are available when needed, and this can not occur unless an organization purposely organizes and manages its data. Financial resources are available to build a new plant or to buy raw materials only if a financial manager and other business managers have planned for enough funds to cover the associated cash requirements. A new product can be designed only if engineering and personnel managers have anticipated the needs for certain skills in the work force. A business certainly would not ever think about *not* planning and managing facilities, labor, and capital. Similarly, data must be planned and managed.

The effort to manage organizational data is the responsibility of every user-manager. In addition, a special management unit, often called data administration, usually provides organizational leadership. Every manager in an organization has some financial, personnel, equipment, and facilities/space responsibilities. Today, often data must be added to this list of managed assets.

Why Manage Data?

One way to view the importance of managing the data resource is to consider the following questions:

- What would your company do if its critical business data, such as customer orders, product prices, account balances, or patient history, were destroyed? Could the organization still function? for how long?
- What costs would your company incur if its database was damaged? Are the data irreplaceable? How would business operations change without the computerized data?
- How much time does your organization spend reconciling inconsistent data? Do account balances in your department agree with those in central

accounting? What happens when these figures do not agree? Do marketing and engineering use the same product identifiers? Are there problems with providing custom products because of different specifications by sales and engineering? Can you track a customer order all the way from receipt through production to shipping and billing in a consistent and unconfused way?
- How difficult is it to determine what data are stored about the part of the business you manage? What data exist about customer sales in a particular market? In what databases do these data reside? What is the meaning of these data (for example, do the data include lost sales, blanket orders, special orders, private label sales)? How can you gain access to these data?

Although managing data as a resource has many general business dimensions, it is also important for the cost-effective development and operation of information systems. Poor systems development productivity is frequently due to a lack of data management, and some methods, such as prototyping, cannot work unless the source of data is clear and the data are present. Systems development is enhanced by the reuse of data and programs as new applications are designed and built. Unless data are cataloged, named in standard ways, protected but accessible by those with a need to know, and maintained at a high quality, the data and the programs that capture and maintain them cannot be reused.

A key element in the effective management of data is an overall map for business data—a **data model.** A manufacturing company would never think about building a new product without developing a detailed design and using common components and parts from existing products where appropriate. The same is true for data. Data entities, such as customer, order, product, vendor, market, and employee are analogous to the components of a detailed design for a product. Just as the detailed blueprint for a product shows the relationships among components, the data model shows the relationships among the data entities.

Although there are many technical issues regarding the technology used to manage data, the issues to be emphasized in this section are managerial. How to plan for data, to control data integrity, to secure access to and use data, and to make data accessible are important to the user-manager. As with any business resource, quality sources for data must be identified and the data acquired; enough space must be available for data storage; obsolete data must be identified, disposed of, or archived; and usage of data must be accounted for, and, if appropriate, usage fees should be charged to those utilizing the data. These are not just technical issues—the user-manager should as well be equipped to deal with these issues.

Key Concepts in Managing Data

Successful management of the data resource is dependent on understanding certain key ideas:

1. The Permanence of Data. Any organization has customers or clients, whether these are other organizations, individual consumers, or patients. No matter whether a company makes to stock or to order, there are vendors or suppliers, orders or reservations, products or services, and employees. Further, irrespective of how accounting, selling, billing, or any other management activity is performed, there still will be data about customers, vendors, orders, products, and employees. Data values may change, new customers may be added, products discontinued, and employees hired and retired, but a company will always have customers, products, and employees about which it needs to keep current data. Occurrences of data are volatile, but the existence of data is persistent and the need for data is constant.

Business processes change, and so must information systems. If the company decides to change a sales forecasting method, programs will have to be rewritten, but customer, order, and general economic condition data are still needed. In fact, if data are well-managed, the databases will remain relatively unchanged when an organization decides to change the way it does business. At the same time, the programs that analyze, process, and report information may change drastically.

Thus, data are fundamental to the business. Data remain over time and need to be managed over time.

2. The Data Pyramid. Although the business retains vast amounts of data, there may be relatively few basic classes of data on which to base most information. One way to organize data is called the data pyramid, as depicted in Figure 14.1. Although new data can enter this pyramid at any level, most new data

are captured in the base of the pyramid in operational databases. These databases contain the business transaction history of customer orders, purchases from suppliers, internal work orders, changes to the general ledger, personnel transfers, and other day-to-day business activities. Managerial control and strategic databases are typically subsets, summaries, or aggregations of operational databases, with key external data as supplements. For example, a database for sales forecasting, a managerial function, may contain past monthly summaries of sales by product family or geographical area derived from customer orders and product data. These data might be supplemented with economic indicators and sales force judgments to produce sales estimates needed for production planning and scheduling.

When managerial databases are constructed from sources other than internal, shared operational databases, there can be significant inconsistencies. For example, a marketing department might track customer sales in a local database before passing these on to order entry. If they use these figures for forecasting final sales, they may not consider canceled orders, orders rejected due to insufficient credit, returned goods, or sales not met because of inadequate production capacity. These information items may not be considered because they enter the business at other points of contact with the customer. A well-run organization must coordinate all customer contacts through a common understanding of the customer.

Developing an understanding of the relationships between data in various databases is a critical element of managing the data resource. Ideally, aggregate data will be derived from operational data, not collected separately (and, hence, inconsistently), and different databases will receive data transferred from a common source. The systems that populate these databases, move data, and produce reports are described later in this chapter.

3. Information Processing and Application Independence. One goal of data management is **application independence,** the separation, or decoupling, of data from applications systems. This concept, embodied in Figure 14.1, is further illustrated in Figure 14.2.

In this figure, the processing of data into information is viewed like the processing of the raw and component material resources into final products in a

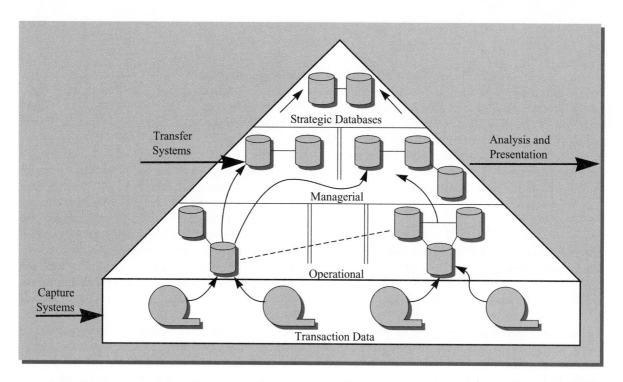

Figure 14.1 The Data Pyramid

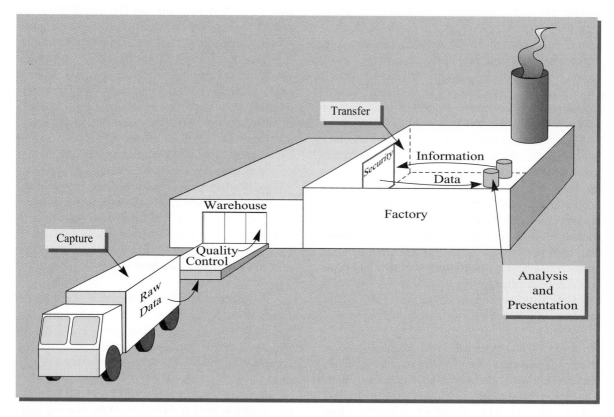

Figure 14.2 Categories of Information Processing with Application Independence

562

manufacturing company. Raw data are captured or received, inspected for quality, and stored in the warehouse. Data in storage are used in the production of any authorized information product. Data are retrieved from the warehouse when needed but, unlike raw materials, are not consumed when used. As data become obsolete, they are replaced with new data. Data are transferred to other parts of the organization or other organizations when authorized. As data are processed into information, this information is added to the warehouse, similar to the entry of products into finished goods storage. The raw material warehouse is used by all information production operations and work centers to produce information products (e.g., reports), but individual work centers (applications) have their own work-in-process inventory of data and receive a few kinds of data that are not shared among other applications. Thus, data are cataloged, managed, and, at least conceptually, stored centrally, where they can be kept safe and uncontaminated for use throughout the business.

The central point of Figure 14.2 is that data and applications must be managed as separate entities. When treated separately, data are not locked inside applications, where their meaning and structure are hidden from other applications that also require these data.

4. The Data to Information Cycle. The concept of application independence suggests that different data processing applications can be classified into three groups, based upon their role in managing data: capture, transfer, and analysis and presentation as shown in Figure 14.1.

The process of transforming data into information useful for transaction management or higher level decision-making includes data capture, data transfer, and data analysis and presentation.

Data capture applications gather data and populate databases. They store and maintain data as shown in the data pyramid of Figure 14.1. Ideally, each datum is captured once and fully tested for accuracy and completeness. Responsibility for ensuring the quality of data capture systems might be distributed across the organization. Localized data capture applications are developed for data with an isolated use or data for which coordination across units is not required. Still, because localized data might eventually be useful somewhere else in the organization, an inventory (kept

in the data dictionary) must be maintained of all database contents.

Data transfer applications move data from one database to another. These applications are often called bridges or interfaces because they connect related databases. Once raw data are captured, they may be copied to various databases, where they are stored for specific purposes. For example, customer order data may be stored in multiple subject or target area databases supporting production scheduling, billing, and customer service. Also, this kind of application extracts and summarizes data, as well as distributes copies of original data. Ideally, this transfer would be event triggered; that is, if new basic data are captured or changed in value, messages are sent as needed to all other databases that build on these data to alert these databases that changes have occurred.

Data analysis and presentation applications provide data and information to authorized persons. Data might be summarized, compared to history, reformulated into graphs, or inserted into documents being developed using a word processor. Data might be input to a decision support system or executive information system. Data analysis and presentation applications can draw upon any and all data from databases the user-manager receiving the presentation is authorized to see. Data are independent from the way they are presented, and those who determine the format for presentation do not necessarily control the location and format for capture and storage of data.

5. Disposable Systems. A significant result of application independence is the creation of **disposable systems.** In many organizations, older systems cannot be eliminated or easily rewritten because applications and data are so intertwined. When the presentation capabilities of an application system become obsolete, an inefficient system may have to be kept alive if the application also maintains data essential to the business. With application independence, a company can replace the capture, transfer, and presentation modules separately when necessary. Presentation systems are often the most volatile types of application, and these types of systems provide management with business value. In addition, with modern programming languages and system generators, user-managers can customize their own presentation and analysis systems to meet personal needs.

6. Capturing Data Once. Another implication of the separation of data from applications is that data should be captured at one source and, even when not shared from one common database, synchronized across different databases. It is simply too costly for an organization to capture the same data multiple times and reconcile differences across applications. For example, not long ago, a university discovered during a review of its applications systems that 17 different systems captured a student's home address. The redundant data management cost was estimated at several hundred thousand dollars per year. Thus, an IT architecture based on application independence permits a more responsive, flexible, and beneficial approach for managing the data resource.

Figure 14.1 is another way to view the data architecture discussed in Chapter 13. The **data architecture** of an organization should contain an inventory of the uses of data across the business units. The architecture also includes a plan to distribute data to various databases to support the analysis and presentation needs of different user groups. The same data may be stored in multiple databases because that is the most efficient architecture to deliver data to users. To ensure that data are current, accurate, and synchronized across the organization, however, key business data are captured once and transferred between databases as needed.

7. Data Standards. Because the same and similar data are used in various application systems, data must be clearly identified and defined so that all users know exactly what data they are manipulating. Further, shared databases and data transfer systems require that database contents be unambiguously defined and described. The central responsibility in managing the data resource is to develop a clear and useful way to uniquely identify every instance of data and to give unambiguous business meaning to all data. For example, an organization must be able to distinguish data about one customer from data about another. Further, the meaning of such data as product description and product specification must be clear and distinct.

Figure 14.3 lists the five types of **data standards** that must be established for a business: identifiers, naming, definition, integrity rules, and usage rights. User-managers, not IS managers, have the knowledge necessary to set these standards and therefore should actively participate in the standards-setting process.

Identifier. The identifier is a characteristic of a business object or event (a data entity) that uniquely distinguishes one instance of this entity from every other instance. For example, an employee number is a distinctive feature of each employee, and a unique bill of lading number clearly identifies each shipment. It is not uncommon to find applications in different units of a business using different identifiers for the same entity. As long as there is a one-for-one match of identifier values (e.g., part numbers) across the various systems, there is not a problem, but often there is no such compatibility. The ideal identifier is one that is guaranteed to be unique and is stable for a long time. For example, a hospital may wish to use a social security number to identify a patient. Also, identifiers related to meaningful data tend not to be desirable because they are not stable. For example, a customer identification number based on geographical region and standard industrial classification (SIC) code will no longer be valid if a customer moves or changes

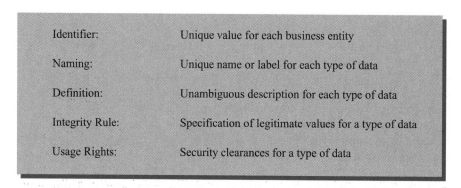

Identifier:	Unique value for each business entity
Naming:	Unique name or label for each type of data
Definition:	Unambiguous description for each type of data
Integrity Rule:	Specification of legitimate values for a type of data
Usage Rights:	Security clearances for a type of data

Figure 14.3 Types of Data Standards

primary businesses. Thus, it is wise to design a non-descriptive, sequential assigned code as the identifier and to use such data as geographical location and SIC code as descriptive data.

Naming. Distinct and meaningful names must be given to each kind of data retained in organizational databases. If two data elements have the same name, their true meaning will be confusing to users. If the same data element is referred to by different names that are never associated, user-managers will think that these are different pieces of data. Many organizations develop a naming scheme or template for constructing all data names, with common terms to be used for different elements of the scheme. For example, a data name of employee-monthly-pay indicates which entity, which time period, and which type of data. Each of the three components of this data name would be limited to a restricted vocabulary; for example, the time period would have values such as daily and weekly, and abbreviations for each could be assigned. Standard names make naming new data elements easier and give a user a quick start on knowing what data are on a report or in a certain database.

Definition. Each data entity and element is given a description that clarifies its meaning. The definition applies to all business circumstances and users. Surprisingly, terms such as customer, employee, and product may not have universal meaning. For example, does customer refer to someone who has bought from you or any potential consumer of your products or services? Over the years, different parts of the business may have developed their own interpretation of such terms, so definitions must be constructed through review by a broad range of organizational units.

Integrity Rules. The permissible range or set of values must be clear for each data element. These integrity rules add to the meaning of data conveyed by data definitions and names. For example, a data element of region is probably limited to some set of valid values based upon sales territories or some other artificial construct. In addition, an established standard for valid values can be used by those developing all data capture applications to detect mistakes. Also, because exceptions may be permitted, the integrity rules may specify who can authorize deviations or under what circumstances values outside of the valid set can be authorized.

Usage Rights. These standards prescribe who can do what and when to each type of data. Such security standards state the permissible uses for every type of data (e.g., whole databases, individual files in a database, particular records, or data elements in a file). For example, a user-manager might be restricted to retrieving only the employee-monthly-pay data element, only during regular business hours, only from an authorized terminal, and only about herself and those people he or she supervises.

These data standards should be retained in a standards database called a data dictionary/directory (see Chapter 3). This central repository of data about data helps users learn more about organizational databases. It should also be used by database management systems to access and authorize use of data.

The Data Management Process

A manager of real estate, personnel, or finances is familiar with the basic but essential functions necessary to manage effectively those resources. Figure 14.4 lists the generic functions for managing any business resource. This section overviews each of these functions within the context of data management. An important point to note is that as with other resources, every user-manager should be involved, in some way, in every one of these functions for data.

- Plan

- Source

- Acquire and Maintain

- Define/Describe and Inventory

- Organize and Make Accessible

- Control Quality and Integrity

- Protect and Secure

- Account for Use

- Recover/Restore and Upgrade

- Determine Retention and Dispose

- Train and Consult for Effective Use

Figure 14.4 Asset Management Functions

1. Plan. Data resource planning develops a blueprint for data and the relationships between data across business units and functions. As with most plans, there will be a macro-level data plan, typically called an enterprise data model, to identify data entities and relationships and more detailed plans to define schedules for the implementation of databases for different parts of this blueprint. The plan identifies which data are required, where they are used in the business, how they will be used (that is, what they will be used to produce), and how much data are expected. This plan must then be communicated to all business functions that are involved in aspects of data resource management. For example, system capacity planning must be informed of this schedule, along with data and processing volumes, so that adequate computer and network technology can be in place to operate and access these databases.

2. Source. Decisions must be made about the most timely and highest quality source for each data element required. For example, should customer sales data be collected at point of sale or entered later? Concerns over error rates, frequency of changes, chance of lost paper documents, technology costs, training requirements, and many other factors will influence this decision. For data to be acquired from sources external to the organization, the quality, cost, and timeliness of these sources need to be considered. For example, different market research organizations may collect competitive sales data from retail outlets or telephone surveys. The original source, the reliability of the data, the timing of when the data are needed and when they were collected, the precision and detail collected, and other factors should be checked in selecting an external data source.

3. Acquire and Maintain. Once the best sources for data are identified and selected, data capture systems may be built to acquire and maintain these data. Changes in data need to be broadcast to all databases that store these data. Users of the data need to know when the data are updated and possibly automatically informed of exceptional conditions (such as inventory stockout, stock price below a critical level, or receipt of an especially large customer order). Appropriate systems need to be built to track data acquisition and transfer. For example, suppose mag-

netic tapes of customer list data are sent to telemarketing vendors for a promotional campaign, and results are returned by magnetic tape. A system is needed to confirm that all tapes were sent and received, that all customers on the list were called, and that a status is received on each.

4. Define/Describe. A basic step in managing any resource is defining what is being managed. For a real estate manager, each property must be described, standards and scales must be set to define the size and shape of each building and land parcel, and terminology must be defined to refer to different pieces of each building. Similarly, in managing data, each data entity, data element, and relationship must be defined, a format for storage and reporting must be set up, and the organization of the data must be described so users can know how to access the data. As mentioned earlier, a data inventory catalog must be maintained, usually in a data dictionary/directory, where all data definitions and descriptions are kept, volume statistics on data are maintained, and other data about data (such as access rights and integrity rules) are stored. All users can go to the data dictionary to find out what data exist and what the data mean.

5. Organize and Make Accessible. Databases need to be designed in a way that allows data to be retrieved and reported efficiently in the format required by user-managers. Data should be arranged and stored so that information can be produced easily. Although most of the work here is technical, this physical arrangement of data cannot be done unless potential uses of the data are well-defined, and this task is best done by user-managers. Two aspects of data usage need to be known for proper organization—what data are required and how the data are to be selected. For example, database designers need to know if customer data are to be selected by their unique name or code or if customer data will be selected by markets, geographical regions, what products they have bought, which sales staff they buy from, or other criteria. Orders of magnitude improvements in processing speed can be achieved when the data organization is well-tuned to the processing requirements. Of course, significant reductions in the cost to maintain data and to process data can similarly be achieved by wise choices for database designs.

TURNING DATA INTO DOLLARS

Information exhaust needn't be limited to internal uses. MasterCard International Inc. is pursuing a different path: making data available to its member banks in order to add value to MasterCard's product offerings and win member loyalty. The company does not offer credit cards; its customers are banks that provide the cards under the MasterCard brand. MasterCard's data warehouse helps its member banks identify the behaviors of various consumer segments. (For example: "Dual-income urban dwellers spend heavily on entertainment, meals and travel.") The banks in turn use the data for marketing purposes, often by marrying it to data from other sources, says Ann Grim, senior vice president of global information services for MasterCard in Purchase, N.Y. MasterCard's member banks typically have the same data already in their possession but don't store it in a way that is easy to access and understand, Grim says. In many cases, MasterCard must work closely with external member banks to make sure they can get the maximum value from data. That assistance gives the banks a boost and in turn makes MasterCard a more attractive business partner.

[Slater, 1997]

tems, each containing data difficult to extract, but needed by other units in the company. Likewise, because of the way data were organized, it was difficult to analyze the data residing in these application systems. A data warehouse was proposed whereby certain data from each existing system and new ones to be built would be extracted on a regular basis and put in the "operational store." In this facility, the data would be cleansed and organized for analysis (e.g., by product versus by order) and transferred to the data warehouse. Analysts would have data available from each plant and for all product lines. Improvements in forecasting ability and reductions in lost analyst time were estimated to generate a 31 percent return on investment.

6. Control Quality and Integrity. As with employee certification, audits of financial records, and tests for hazardous materials or structural defects in buildings, quality and integrity controls must be placed on the data resource. The concept of application independence implies that such controls must be stored as part of the data definitions and enforced during data capture and maintenance. In addition, periodic checks of databases should be made as part of the audit of financial records.

7. Protect and Secure. The rights each manager has to each type of data must be defined. Privileges for use of data might include definition, retrieval, insertion, deletion, update, and retrieval of the datum by itself or in combination with other values. For example, a user-manager might be permitted

One highly popular method for making data accessible to many people in an organization is the **data warehouse** (also see Chapter 5). Figure 14.5 depicts how a large division of a furniture manufacturer planned to implement a data warehouse in 1998. The company operated several legacy application sys-

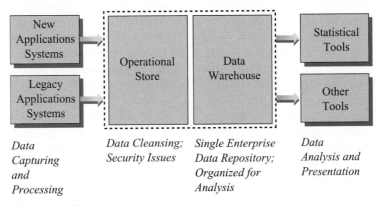

Figure 14.5   The Data Warehouse

DATA WAREHOUSE DOLLAR DATA

In late 1995 and early 1996, Stephen Graham, vice president of software research at International Data Corp. (Canada) Ltd., evaluated 62 organizations that had had a data warehouse up and running for at least six months. Excluding 17 exceptional cases, or what statisticians call "outliers," for which the ROI (return on investment) was either negative or above 2,000 percent, the average ROI for implementing a data warehouse over a three-year period was 401 percent. Including outliers incorporates an astonishing high ROI of 16,000 percent and a miserable low of −1,857 percent. More than 90 percent of those organizations in the statistically meaningful range reported a three-year ROI in excess of 40 percent, half reported returns of more than 160 percent and one-quarter reported ROI above 600 percent. The average three-year cost was $2.3 million; the median payback period was 1.7 years.

[Baatz, 1996]

to see the salaries of everyone in his department, but might not be able to match names with salaries. Privileges might be assigned to programs, databases, files, individual records or data elements, terminals, and workstations. Use of other equipment, data, and programs might be limited by time of day or days of the week. In determining rights on a system, there is a delicate balance between the need to protect the quality and integrity of data by protecting a valuable asset from damage or theft and the right of individuals to have easy access to the data they need in their jobs. Because security is so important and can be dysfunctional if done improperly, security should be considered when databases and application systems are originally built and not considered as an afterthought.

8. Account for Use. Because there is considerable cost to capture, maintain, and report data, these costs must be identified and an accounting system must be developed to report them. Further, an organization may choose to distribute the costs to appropriate responsibility centers. Two conditions make accounting for the use of data especially difficult as compared to other information resources. First, frequently the organizational unit responsible for

acquiring data is not the primary user of the data. Second, usage is shared because data are not consumed from usage. The actual costs of computer disk storage and computer processing time can be captured by the operating system and database management system. The real issue is to develop a fair **chargeback** scheme that promotes good management of data but does not deter beneficial use. Because the value of data is so elusive, the linkage of readily identifiable costs to value is difficult. At a minimum, the costs for data storage and processing and a reliable list of users of particular data can be determined. Of course, how to charge to recover these costs is a separate and more difficult issue.

9. Recover/Restore and Upgrade. When a property becomes old or damaged, it is often renovated and put back into operation. When an employee's skills become obsolete because of new technology or methods, the employee is trained for the new environment. The same process is true with organizational data. When a database is damaged because of a hardware or software malfunction, procedures must be in place to restore the database to its original condition. Usually, periodic backup copies of the database are made and a computer-based log is kept regarding updates to the database, so the restoration can happen quickly. The user-manager must anticipate what actions should be taken when a database is not accessible because of a recovery or upgrading that temporarily takes the database out of action. In addition, the user-manager must be able to determine what wrong actions or decisions might have been taken from the bad data and correct them before they cause excess costs or other problems for the business. For example, if an inventory file has been inaccurately changed and inventory replenishment orders have been written, an inventory control manager should immediately determine whether work, purchase, or expedited orders should be recalled.

10. Determine Retention and Dispose. Data are not useful forever, and user-managers must decide, on legal and other grounds, how much data history needs to be kept. Some data need to be kept in active databases, whereas other data may be archived to magnetic tape to be used only when needed. Eventually, data should be summarized and/or eliminated.

Keeping data too long is costly in terms of storage space, and the use of out-of-date information can also bias forecasts and other analyses.

11. Train and Consult for Effective Use.   Just because data exist, they will not necessarily be effectively used. What data are stored in databases, what they mean, what presentation systems report these data, and how they can be accessed all have to be explained to user-managers who might want to use the data. This training might include review of the contents of the corporate data dictionary, with an emphasis on a particular user group (for example, consumer marketing), or the training might be on how to use a statistical package (like SAS) to access a database for decision support.

Data Management Policies

The implementation of these concepts and processes for data management occurs differently in each organization. However, policies should be developed in several areas.

1. Data Ownership.   User-managers can become very possessive of data, for both business and personal reasons:

- The need to protect personal privacy.
- The need to protect trade secrets.
- The requirement to allow only those with a need to know to see sensitive business plans.
- The desire to promote internal competition and to justify the use of scarce resources.
- The desire to show commitment to one's job and ownership of the data needed to carry out one's job.
- The desire to use information as power for political gain.

This protectiveness is both good and bad. A commitment to quality data, cost control of data management, and use of data for strategic advantage are essential for obtaining the greatest benefits from managing the data resource. On the other hand, a possessiveness about data can stifle data sharing, which can limit access to data, reduce the ability to answer important business questions, and increase data processing costs for the whole enterprise. The culture about data must be managed as part of data resource management.

A **corporate information policy** is the foundation for managing the ownership of data. Figure 14.6 contains a data access policy statement developed in late 1997 for a large Midwestern manufacturer of truck parts. The President and the CIO (chief information officer) developed this policy after it was clear that many managers were not sharing data useful to others in the corporation. The new policy was communicated to all managers through a series of written announcements and staff meetings. This policy states that each manager has responsibility for managing data as a resource for the good of the whole enterprise, not just the gain of his area. Some policies will distinguish among classes of data—such as personal, departmental, and organizational—although the trend is to make all data organizational.

As organizations and the markets they serve become more global, issues of international regulations, standards, and cultures relating to data ownership can have major impacts on data management. One specific issue is relevant in the discussion of data ownership—regulation of the flow of data across international boundaries.

Transborder data flows are electronic movements of data that cross a country's national boundary for processing, storage, or retrieval of that data in a foreign country. Data are subject to the laws of the exporting country. Legislation to control transborder data flows varies widely from country to country. These laws are justified by these perceived needs:

- Prevention of economic and cultural imperialism, including preventing the change of social values (a kind of antipropaganda mentality) and preventing the usurpation of local decisions by multinational headquarters outside the country.
- Protection of domestic industry, including protecting the local computer hardware, software, and services industry.
- Protection of individual privacy, including protecting individual citizens against storage of personal health, employment, and political affiliation data in databases held in foreign countries.
- Fostering international trade, including measures to make the flow of data easy during desirable international trade and to promote the exporting of information technology and services.

Data is a corporate resource. Much of our corporate data is stored electronically. Excellence in data management is key to achieving many of our business goals.

The following statements constitute our electronic data access policy:

- Corporate data will be shared internally. Data are not owned by a particular individual or organization, but by the whole organization.

- Data will be managed as a corporate resource. Data organization and structure will be planned at the appropriate levels and in an integrated fashion.

- Data quality will be actively managed. Explicit criteria for data accuracy, availability, accessibility, and ease of use will be written by the IS department.

- Data will be safeguarded. As a corporate asset, data will be protected from deliberate or unintentional alteration, destruction, or inappropriate disclosure.

- Data will be defined explicitly. Standards will be developed for data representation.

- Databases will be logically designed to satisfy broad business functions.

Figure 14.6 Example Data Access Policy

Mechanisms to control transborder data flows include tariffs, ministries of telecommunication and trade to formulate and implement policies, and formal application processes for conducting data processing activities in the country. Often no one administrative body has overall authority, and there is very little similarity of mechanisms from country to country. International standards bodies on data communications, programming languages, and electronics help to reduce many operational problems, but policy matters still have to be negotiated, often separately with each country.

2. Data Administration. To better manage data, many organizations have created a unit to lead the efforts in data management. Typically, this group is called **data administration,** although other terms may be used. This group often reports as a staff unit to the IS director, although other structures are possible. In any case, the company should have a policy that outlines the role of the data administration group and the role of user-managers in data administration.

Typically policies that assign the data administration group both operational and limited planning responsibilities work best. Data administration helps design databases to make them efficient for the processing requirements. The group works with systems analysts, designers, and users to identify future databases and database technology requirements. Members of the data administration group should include both technical and managerial staff, often with extensive experience and with considerable respect throughout the business and within IS management.

The data administration group should be a high-level function with responsibility for determining or coordinating data management from policy to implementation. A purely technical group, geared only to the optimization of database structures, may be insufficient to deal with the range of issues in data management.

Key functions of the data administration group should include the following:

- Promote and control data sharing. The group should encourage all business units to define data and to increase the use of common sources of data for different application systems. The group should work to determine the appropriate ownership for each kind of data and the responsibilities data owners should have.

- Analyze the impact of changes to application systems when data definitions change. The application independence concept is usually not fully implemented, so evolution and change to databases may require programming modifications. A schedule of which systems to be changed must be developed considering the needs of all database users.
- Maintain the data dictionary. When a data dictionary is started, data administration must clean up existing data definitions and write definitions for those that do not exist. As new data are added or when unclear definitions or insufficient formats are identified, the dictionary needs to be changed.
- Reduce redundant data and processing. The group should encourage not only dropping unnecessary copies of data and programs that maintain them, but also helping to synchronize purposefully redundant copies and managing data distributed across the various computer systems within the organization, ranging from mainframe to desktop.
- Reduce system maintenance costs and improve systems development productivity. Data administration should work to create database organizations that are easy to use, select database technology that reduces the amount of programming, and train database analysts and programmers in the most current methods. These efforts should improve the development and maintenance of application systems.
- Improve quality and security of data. The group should take leadership in this area, helping user-managers to define data quality standards, set security clearances, and work with data center operations to implement these guidelines.

Within the overall data administration function, two distinct roles have emerged—database administration and data stewardship. A **database administrator** (or **DBA**) is responsible for the management of computerized databases and may be placed in the technical unit that supports various system software and hardware. A DBA is concerned with the following:

- Tuning database management systems.
- Selection and evaluation of and training on database technology.
- Physical database design.
- Design of methods to recover from damage to databases.

- Physical placement of databases on specific computers and storage devices.
- The interface of databases with telecommunications and other technologies.

A **data steward** is a user-manager who, in addition to his normal duties, is responsible for and held accountable for the quality and viability of a particular data entity or subject area (for example, customer, product, bill, or employee) and the data associated with it. The data architecture of an organization (see Chapter 13) should outline the major data entities, and a separate data steward should be assigned for each. A data steward coordinates all database and program changes that deal with the entity for which he is responsible, and a data steward initiates quality improvement programs for this data entity. However, a data steward is not the data's owner; the owner is the enterprise. A typical policy for establishing the role of the data steward is found in Figure 14.7. This policy was developed in 1997 for a large Midwestern truck parts manufacturer. More information on the job of a data steward may be found in "The Role of the User-Manager" section later in this chapter.

Tools for Managing Data

This section provides an overview of the most common tools used by data stewards, database administrators, and systems analysts for describing and managing data. As responsibilities for managing the data resource are distributed to the business units, these topics become important to all managers.

1. Data Modeling. Data modeling involves both a methodology and a notation. The methodology involves the steps that are followed to identify and describe organizational data entities, and the notation is a way to show these findings, usually graphically. Several possible methodologies are introduced below, but the reader is referred to texts on database management for a discussion of data modeling notations.

The role of data modeling as part of IS planning was outlined in Chapter 13. In practice, two rather different approaches are followed—one top-down, called enterprise modeling, and one bottom-up, called view integration. Many organizations choose to do both approaches because they are complementary methods that emphasize different aspects of data and, hence, check and balance each other.

Data stewards are responsible for assessing corporate-wide information needs and promoting organizational data sharing. Data stewards shall be at the director level or higher. In consultation with a committee of interested users of the data entity and a representative of the IS Department, the steward is responsible for:

- Establishing procedures governing both initial definition and change of the data elements within the assigned data entity.

- Establishing access authorization procedures at information services for the data entity to facilitate access and ensure data security.

- Determining the most reliable sources of data and regularly evaluating the quality of the data entity.

- Providing the intellectual content of a data dictionary so that all data users may know what shareable data are available, what the data mean, and how to access the data.

- Planning the content of the assigned data entity by identifying gaps and redundancies in the data and, to the extent possible, ensuring that only needed versions of each data element exist.

- Developing procedures to ensure that any use of the data contains the most appropriate version.

- Determining responsibilities for data maintenance to ensure data integrity.

- Resolving the issues that may arise concerning the assigned portion of the shareable data.

- Consulting with users on the use of electronic data.

Figure 14.7 Example Data Stewardship Policy

The **enterprise modeling** approach involves describing the organization and its data requirements at a very high level, independent of particular reports, screens, or detailed descriptions of data processing requirements. First, the work of the organization is divided into its major functions (such as selling, billing, manufacturing, and servicing). Each of these functions is then further divided into processes, and each process is divided into activities. An activity is usually described at a rather high level (e.g., "forecast sales for next quarter"). This three-level decomposition of the business is depicted in Figure 14.8.

Given a rough understanding of each activity, a list of data entities is then assigned to each. For example, quarterly forecasting activity might have the entities product, customer order history, and work center associated with it. The lists of entities are then checked to make sure that consistent names are used and the meaning of each entity is clear. Finally, based on general business policies and rules of operation, relationships between the entities are identified and a database chart, called a **corporate data model,** is drawn. Priorities are set for what parts of the corporate data model are in need of greatest improvement, and more detailed work assignments, often for the data

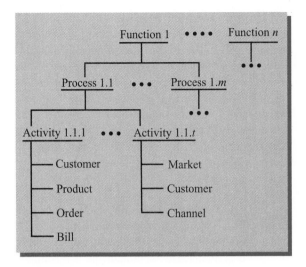

Figure 14.8 Enterprise Decomposition for Data Modeling

stewards, are defined to describe these more clearly and to revise databases accordingly.

Enterprise modeling has the advantage of not being biased by a lot of details, by current databases and files, or by how the business actually operates today. It is future-oriented and should identify a comprehensive set of generic data requirements. On the other hand, it can be incomplete or inaccurate because it may ignore some important details. This is where the view integration approach can help.

In **view integration,** each report, computer screen, form, and document to be produced from organizational databases is identified (usually starting from what is done today). Each of these is called a user view. The data elements in each user view are identified and put into a basic structure called normal form. The normal form is a set of rules that yields a data model that is very stable and useful across many different requirements. In fact, using a normal form rids data of troublesome anomalies, and databases can evolve with very few changes to the parts that have already been developed and populated.

After each user view has been normalized, they are all combined (or integrated) into one comprehensive description. Ideally, this integrated set of entities from normalization will match those from enterprise modeling. In practice, however, this is often not the case because of the different focuses (top-down and bottom-up) of the two approaches. Therefore, the enterprise and view-integrated data models are reconciled and a final data model is developed.

Data modeling methods are neither simple nor inexpensive to conduct. They require considerable time, organizational commitment, and the assignment of very knowledgeable managers and data specialists. In order to deal with these concerns, certain guidelines have been developed.

- Objective: The modeling effort must be justified by some clear overriding need, such as coordination of operational data processing, flexibility to access data, or effectiveness of data systems. The less clear the goal, the higher the chance for failure.
- Scope: The coverage for a data model must be carefully considered. Generally, the broader the scope, the higher the chances for failure. Scope choices include corporate-wide, division, areas with particular high-impact needs, and a particularly important or willing business function (for example, sales).
- Outcome: Choices here include a subject area database definition (for example, all data about customers), identification of common data capture systems to be shared by several departments (replacing separate current databases), managerial and strategic databases (see Figure 14.1) and access services to support the information needs of these levels of management, and a more nebulous architecture for future databases. The more uncertain the outcome, the lower the chances for success.
- Timing: Few organizations can put all systems development on hold while a complete data model is developed. It is possible, for example, to do only a high-level data model with just major data categories and then fill in details as major systems projects are undertaken. This evolutionary approach may be more practical, but it must be done within the context of an initial overall, general enterprise data model.

Regardless of the approach, data modeling represents a radical change to the more traditional approach of making short-term fixes to systems. A user-manager often simply wants access to needed data and is not interested in waiting for an entire data model to be built. Unless an overall data management approach is taken, however, the inconsistencies and excessive costs of poorly managed data will consume the integrity and viability of the data resource.

It should be clear that data modeling is not an issue of centralized versus decentralized control. In fact, the data administration approach with database administrators and data stewards emphasizes placing decision-making power in the hands of those most knowledgeable about data. However, some managers, both users and IS, will resist data planning and modeling because they sense a loss of influence.

2. Database Management Systems. Database management systems (DBMSs) were described in Chapter 3, but a few additional points related to data management need to be discussed.

Today the most popular type of DBMS used to develop new systems is relational. A relational DBMS allows each entity of the data model to be viewed as a simple table, with the columns as the data elements and the rows as different instances of the entity. Also, high-level relational query languages make programming much simpler than with other types of DBMSs (which often use third-generation programming languages). The real power of these systems comes from being able to retrieve related data from multiple tables easily.

Not all relational systems are identical, so there has been considerable effort to standardize with one style, allowing each DBMS vendor to concentrate on extra features beyond the standard and on performance issues. SQL, developed by the independent American National Standards Institute (ANSI), is a standard query language prevalent in both mainframe and personal computer DBMSs. Some relational DBMSs have been designed from this standard; others permit users to work either with SQL commands or the native set of commands designed for that system. This standard allows an organization to transfer training, experience, and programs more easily between DBMSs, to more easily convert from one DBMS to another, and to make it easier to have a mix of DBMSs without duplicating support groups.

A relatively recent trend is to make the DBMS (using SQL as the standard) a kind of engine on which other support software is built. This can be done by putting the DBMS into a separate computer processor, called a **database machine** or **database server,** or by

having system and application software refer to a software DBMS using SQL. Some operating systems now include an SQL-based **DBMS engine** that handles the manipulation of data, so DBMS and other software vendors can concentrate on issues of user interface, not data management. This standardization of data management functions should make it easier to share data across different applications and decision support system generators (see Chapter 6) because they will all use the same database structures and processing logic from the engine.

3. Data Dictionary/Directory. The **data dictionary/directory,** or **DD/D,** is a central encyclopedia of data definitions and important usage descriptions. The DD/D is a database about data and is a common source for data definitions for database software, system developers, and user-managers.

The DD/D contains a definition of each entity, relationship, and data element of a database. It also retains descriptions of the display format, integrity rules, security restrictions, volume and sizes, and physical location, as well as a list of the application systems that use these data.

The DD/D is invaluable to database analysts and user-managers. For example, a marketing user-manager could query the DD/D to find out what kinds of data are kept in a database about customer market segmentation. By using key words that were assigned to each data definition and by scanning data descriptions, the DD/D would develop a list of data elements that deal with this topic. User-managers can then determine which of these are most relevant to their needs and develop queries or report requests to the proper databases to retrieve these data. In a sense, the DD/D acts as a card catalog to the data library. The DD/D is also valuable to assess the impact of planned changes to databases. For example, if an organization was considering changing the meaning of a data element, it would be useful to know which databases need to be modified to reflect the change. Physical database designers can also use the DD/D to find statistics about data volume, size, and usage needs in order to design efficient data organizations.

Ideally, an organization would develop the DD/D before or at the same time as its first DBMS, but this is not usually the case. As mentioned earlier, many of the responsibilities of database administrators and data stewards can be facilitated by a DD/D. In fact, not having a DD/D makes it so difficult to coordinate the evolution of databases that it is more likely that independent and inconsistent databases will arise when no DD/D is used. The DD/D is one of the soundest investments that can be made toward achieving the goals of data management.

THE PHYSICAL INFRASTRUCTURE

In addition to managing data as a valuable asset, user-managers and IS professionals must develop policies and procedures to manage the physical assets of an IT system—the computer hardware and the data network—on a global basis. These assets have always represented a high capitalized value. As hardware costs have decreased and PCs have proliferated, many user-managers have forgotten that the aggregate monetary value of network and hardware assets is now higher than ever—even in a smaller organization.

The Importance of Managing the Infrastructure

There was a day when failure of the computer network affected only a few administrative workers. Today, employees at all levels in the organization all around the world interact with the computer network for essential aspects of their work. Thus, network or computer failure now has a high degree of visibility—it may disrupt plant managers, division heads, vice presidents, and even sometimes the CEO. Computer power is like electrical power—if it goes out, everything comes to a halt until service is restored.

Furthermore, with the advent of strategic application systems, the impact of infrastructure management is no longer restricted to company employees. Poor infrastructure management may have a direct impact on the company's customers. For example, problems with a bank's network directly affect those customers who enter transactions into the bank's ATM system. Problems with an airline's reservations system may affect travel agents worldwide. In today's world, most people are dependent every day on the successful management of one or more IT networks.

The same basic functions that must be performed to manage any asset successfully should be applied to the IT global physical infrastructure. It must be planned, acquired, and made available (see Figure 14.4). Because of the high degree of specialized skill/training required to perform these functions, however, most user-managers outsource the management of the infrastructure to either the organization's IS department or to an outside vendor. For this reason, the focus here is on infrastructure management policy issues where user-managers will be most affected. More information on the elements in a physical infrastructure may be found in earlier chapters.

Infrastructure Management Issues

The following are some of the issues that must be resolved in an infrastructure management system, typically through policy statements:

1. Location.   Clearly, most organizations today operate in a distributed computing environment. However, the physical location of the hardware on a network can be a critical issue from cost, control, and security standpoints. Physically distributing equipment, other than microcomputers, can create additional costs for managing the hardware and safeguarding data. Many computers and telecommunications switches benefit significantly from being housed in a secure, environmentally controlled location. Quite often, however, physical location connotes a sense of control to many user-managers. A division general manager may be comforted by locating the division's servers in a room on divisional premises rather than in the IS data center in corporate headquarters a few blocks away. Likewise, some countries may be better hosts than others for location of complex data centers.

2. The Workstation.   Policies on the future design and role of the IT workstation should be determined. Which workstations should have independent intelligence and which should be a network device slaved to some central server? (For more on network PCs, see Chapter 2.) Should the telephone and computer components of the workstation be physically integrated? Should video conferencing capability be integrated into the user-manager workstation? What is the most appropriate location of each type of computing work? At the workstation? At a central server? At a remote hardware resource? On a local area network? Or at some departmental server? What level of access should the workstation have to outside resources such as the Internet? In answering all these questions, cost, convenience, and security tradeoffs must be made.

3. Supported Operating Systems.   Many vendors of technology hardware still offer a proprietary operating system, although more commonality exists now than in the past. How many and which operating systems will the organization support? Each different operating system creates more difficulty in sustaining a seamless network, and support costs increase rapidly as new operating systems are added. Confining the company to one computing vendor, however, reduces bargaining power, limits access to the best software, and makes the organization more dependent on a particular vendor. For example, if all workstations are required to operate with the latest version of a particular company's software, the company's future partially depends on that software company's success.

Some policy agreement on these standards should be established to allow for the needed flexibility and the required integration level and cost control. Some organizations implement this policy through a supported equipment list, containing the operating systems the IS organization will support through training, connectivity, repair, and other services.

4. Redundancy.   Because organizations are so dependent today on their networks, many user-managers want full redundancy of the key nodes and paths in the IT network. Yet full redundancy can be very expensive. How much redundancy should there be in the design of the network? Should there be full redundancy only for major nodes and high-volume pathways? The cost for full path redundancy can be very expensive because there must be at least two different paths to every node in the network from every other node. Likewise, "hot" backup sites that allow failed critical nodes to return to operation quickly are also expensive. The lack of redundancy, however, can be very expensive in terms of lost user time if the network or a critical node is not available for some period. User-managers need to express their views on the tradeoff between the cost of downtime due to network unavailability and the cost to provide continuous access.

5. Supported Communications Protocols.   As with operating systems, many hardware vendors support their own proprietary communications protocols as well as some mix of standard communications protocols. For example, most vendors support the ASCII file transfer protocol, the Ethernet protocol for local area networks, and the TCP/IP protocol for use of the Internet. However, there are many other protocols to be considered. (See Chapter 4 for a discussion of protocols.) Although the selection process is complex, some set of communications protocols should be established as standards in the firm.

6. Bandwidth.   What bandwidth, or transmission capacity, should be provided between hardware nodes in the network? The decision is, of course, dependent on the applications to be used. Image and graphical applications require much greater transmission rates for effective use than do text-only applications. However, how much bandwidth can a company afford on a global basis? Should a company provide excess capacity to allow users to try new applications? Or should the network be designed to meet only current needs? Specifications about the desired technical infrastructure to meet the vision for information use are critical to help drive individual decisions. User-managers should make their views known on this issue.

7. Response Time on the Network.   Response time was not a big issue when most application systems processed data in batches and there was a planned delay of hours, or even days, between the time a user submitted data and the time results were to be returned. With on-line systems, however, hundreds of users are simultaneously interacting with the network, and each of them is directly affected by the response time of the system—the delay between when the return key is pressed and when the response from the system appears on the screen. If this delay is reasonable and consistent, the system is satisfactory. If the delay is excessively long—3 or 4 seconds when one is used to subsecond responses—it can be frustrating and can significantly hamper use of the system. Yet the costs needed to reduce response delays tend to increase exponentially below some level, so input from user-managers is critical in making this decision.

8. Security versus Ease of Access.   If steps are taken to make the network and its nodes more secure, quite often the result is to reduce ease of access to data for users. In a number of companies, for example, user-managers cannot dial in directly to the data center from home because of security concerns. Instead, the user-manager calls the data center, and an operator calls the user back after verification. In other organizations, systems can be much more easily accessed from the desk, from home, or from a hotel room in another part of the world. Some trade-off between security and access ease is being made by either procedure. Organizations should make an explicit decision to operate somewhere along the spectrum between maximum ease of access and maximum security. User-managers should provide input to the decision.

9. Breadth of Network Access.   How ubiquitous should access to the network be? Should everyone in the organization have access to all corporate data? Or should access be restricted to those who have a "need to know?" Some organizations have gone on record as striving for access by all personnel. As soon as such a commitment is made, however, training and other support requirements increase significantly. User-managers should provide input to this policy decision.

10. Access to External Data Services.   What should be the range of data services that a user-manager may receive via the network? Should access to customer and supplier databases be allowed? How active will the company be in electronic data interchange with customers and suppliers? Should the network provide access to personal data services? At some firms, viewing the results of athletic events or even the events themselves is permitted from the workstation at the desk. Others restrict even external e-mail. Some organizations provide broad access to a variety of commercial services. Some prohibit such access. User-managers must clearly state their need for such access.

Figure 14.9 shows a policy statement that addresses many of the above issues for a multi-divisional company in the medical device industry. The statement

An information technology infrastructure through which video, voice, data, image, and text information may be created, accessed, manipulated, and transmitted electronically will allow our company to enhance its position in the industry. The continued enhancement of such an integrated network must be a key priority into the next century and requires policies.

The policies are as follows:

- A standard workstation shall be used uniformly in offices, laboratories, meeting rooms, and all other facilities.

- Every shareable node on the network will operate with UNIX as one of its operating systems.

- A common set of physical distribution facilities (servers and LANs) shall be used throughout the company.

- Each physical distribution subsystem shall be designed in such a way that it can be replaced or modified without affecting the performance of the other subsystems.

Figure 14.9 The Infrastructure of the Information Technology Network
(continued on next page)

- Each divisional chief executive shall designate the organization responsible for the design, operation , maintenance, and allocation of the appropriate physical distribution facilities.

- Strong consideration shall be given to the installation of adequate pathways and substantial reserve transmission capacity when new physical distribution facilities are installed or existing ones enhanced.

- The public network will be used among locations for voice, data, and video and a private data network will be developed at each site.

Figure 14.9 (Continued from previous page)

was the result of an assessment conducted by a major IS consulting firm in 1996 that criticized the organization for not having policies for the use of the IT physical infrastructure.

THE APPLICATIONS PORTFOLIO

The third and final IT technology resource that should be managed as an asset is the applications portfolio. Earlier chapters in this book have discussed alternative methods for the acquisition of individual applications. However, user-managers and the IS department need to manage a bundle of applications as a critical organizational asset.

Managing the Software Portfolio as an Asset

In contrast to the physical infrastructure, too often the software portfolio is not managed as an asset. Frequently, the focus of the user-manager is on an individual application, and applications development and maintenance costs are treated as a current expense. Unlike equipment and facilities, software is not depreciated to recognize that it has a limited useful life. Consequently, software, and particularly software maintenance, is treated as an expense to be minimized rather than as an essential activity that preserves or enhances the value of a critical asset.

Most organizations with a long history of computer use have a substantial investment in their software portfolio. Some have hundreds of systems, thousands of programs, and millions of lines of code that are the result of investing hundreds of millions of dollars in thousands of staff-years of system development. These applications are critical assets without which the company could not operate, but many companies have never seriously thought about managing these programs as costly and critical assets. Some companies do not even know what software resources they possess. They may not know the condition of their application systems, and some companies have no plan for replacement or renovation of critical obsolete systems.

Treating software as an asset changes how the portfolio is viewed and managed. A company should know what software it owns, where it is located, what it does, how effective it is, and what condition it is in. Companies should treat maintenance of software just as they treat plant maintenance—as an activity that is necessary to preserve the value of the asset. Software managers are obligated to evaluate the effectiveness of the software inventory and to plan, organize, and control this inventory to maximize the return it provides to the company. In particular, the company should allocate adequate resources on a yearly basis to rehabilitate and upgrade existing systems so that they never get close to the crisis stage.

When a company with several obsolete systems decides to manage its software portfolio as an asset, it should evaluate all its systems and develop a long-range plan that prioritizes the needs and allocates the resources required to bring them up to standard within a target time frame.

Applications Portfolio Management Issues

The development and maintenance of IS applications should be subject to a set of policy guidelines derived from the organization's IT architecture. Figure 14.10 contains a statement developed in early 1997 that makes a set of conclusions about how applications should be developed in a distributed computing environment at a major personnel services company. The statements impose a standard set of management controls on company-critical, computer-based applications being developed and supported by all company business units. These guidelines, developed by a committee representing the organization's central IS department, business unit IS groups, and users, define controls that must be applied to critical applications.

Other issues that applications portfolio policies should deal with include the following.

1. Assumed User. For any applications system, some assumption is made about who will use the application. Data entry operators were assumed to be the users of many transaction processing systems. As more individuals inside and outside the company become potential users and the technology skills of people grow, some clarity about likely IS users is required. What is the training level required? Should all help facilities be resident in the system? How deep into the applications system can external users get? The design requirements for the user interface and associated security are thereby likely to change and should be made explicit. User-managers must provide input to this policy issue.

2. Application Location. With the immense popularity of PCs, many PC applications have been developed which would work much better on a more centralized resource. Where (at what network node)

- Information systems development in departments is best done on distributed computers when the object of the analysis (e.g., an asset type or set of transactions): (a) is local and self-contained; (b) has sufficient commitment in the department for funding systems development and operations over the life of the system; (c) has little likelihood to be needed outside the department; and (d) has total life cycle development and operational cost less than on a central resource.
- Support for the development of distributed information systems is available on a coordinated basis at each division. Support participants include the local IS organization and corporate IS personnel.
- Distributed information systems development is normally expected to have been identified as a priority in an approved departmental information resources plan.
- Support software standards for information systems should be used. The list of supported software is determined at the local site in cooperation with the corporate IS organization.
- The department should be prepared to commit approximately 25 percent of the initial hardware, software, and personnel investment associated with systems development each year for the ongoing support of the system.
- Documentation standards for all application systems are published on a regular basis by the corporate IS organization. These standards may be supplemented by standards published by the local IS organization.
- The hardware on which the system is developed should be supported by the local IS organization and/or the corporate IS organization and should be attached to either the local network or to the company-wide network or both.
- Units engaging in information systms development activity should review their internal policies and procedures to bring them into compliance with these policies.

Figure 14.10 Example Distributed Applications Development Policy

should a particular type of application be performed? For example, where in the network should word processing normally be done? For most organizations, that decision seems clear. Users find it convenient to do word processing on their personal computers. On the other hand, some organizations encourage users to save files on department servers, citing the improved ability to share and back up files. There are also many other issues as to where certain applications should be performed in the network. Guidelines need to be developed with user-manager input to assign applications to places in the network.

3. Process-Driven or Data-Driven Design. It must also be determined whether future applications development is going to be data-driven or **process-driven.** Most past systems have been designed to represent a process and to collect and manipulate only the data necessary to operate the particular process. For example, under the process approach, the job classification information system would be designed to mirror the job of the personnel analyst, who must review a particular job description and make a decision on rank classification. The system would require collection of the necessary information to help make that decision. The process approach is efficient for that one particular application.

There are, however, other decisions that require much of the same data, such as hiring. The hiring information system would collect some of the same data, add more data, and store the data in that system. Now there are two different representations of several data fields, each collected for a particular process. The alternative **data-driven** approach is to concentrate on all the data needed in an area or department and to collect these data into a database. Each application would be designed to access this common database and extract only the needed information.

4. Evaluation Criteria for New Applications Systems. What should the requirements be for justifying new systems? Should a return on investment analysis be required? Should a risk assessment be performed on every application? Most organizations attempt to adopt some decision rules, such as expected return on investment, risk analysis, cost/benefit analysis, or expected payback period. These methods may prove to be beneficial when systems with benefits that

are not easily quantifiable are considered for implementation. User-managers should actively participate in the process to determine how systems will be evaluated.

THE ROLE OF THE USER-MANAGER

Some user-managers, especially those in smaller organizations, may have direct responsibility for managing a significant portion of the information assets they use. Given today's distributed IT environment, it is highly likely that user-managers control parts of the three technical components of an IT system: data, the physical infrastructure, and the applications portfolio. Clearly, the user-manager should review the tradeoffs and issues posed in this chapter and develop written policies that will provide for the effective management of those assets under his/her control.

Yet most user-managers do not have or want direct control over all the IT assets they use. In these cases, the following suggestions apply.

1. Make your position clear on critical infrastructure management issues. Too often, decisions are made on a particular system that impact future decisions. It is the responsibility of IS leadership to consider the issues and trade-offs including those outlined here and develop policy statements that guide decisions on individual systems. Likewise, the user-manager must see it as his or her duty to provide input to these decisions using business needs as the basis for such an opinion.

2. Take an active role in data stewardship. As a data steward, the user-manager can play a major role in setting up data integrity rules, data names and definitions, and security guidelines. A data steward may also lead the effort to create so-called subject area databases around each entity. For example, the customer data steward might organize a managerial or strategic database useful in tracking customer demographics, buying behavior, sales contacts, and service/repair history.

Although there are different types of data stewards, according to English (1993), typical data stewards carry out the following tasks:

- Develop or review data models for their subject areas.
- Establish data quality standards in their areas.
- Grant access rights to data under their authority.
- Maintain official tables of codes (product, region, customer type) used with data in their areas.

The goal is to anticipate organizational needs for data and to promote sharing of critical data. Usually a data steward comes from a business unit that is the source for or is the primary user of the data, and the data steward has the best organizational understanding of the meaning and uses of the data.

Data stewardship is a challenging role, in part because it is a significant departure from the processing control of data and systems of the past. IS leadership must ensure that data center operations, programmers, systems designers, database administrators, and data stewards all work together. Each must have a clear and recognized role. Each must work at being sensitive to the objectives and backgrounds of the others.

3. Take responsibility for operating in line with the organization's policies on information resources. User-managers must take responsibility for those problems under their control. Many problems are caused by mistakes made by people in the business units, and these problems might be prevented by better training or supervision. User-managers should also be supportive of change management efforts initiated by IS leadership even when the initial impact on the manager's area may not be positive.

4. Be active in demanding quality asset management by the IS organization. The organization's information assets can be managed in such a way as to provide quality services. User-managers should expect no less from the IS department.

Summary

This chapter illustrated that organizational data can be described unambiguously in business terms using a blueprint, called a data model. Personal, departmental, and organizational data can all be described using this type of graphical model. User-managers should ensure that such a model exists for their organization.

An important distinction has been made between three types of data management systems: those that capture, transfer, or present data. This separation of data management functions leads to greater flexibility, longer life for some systems and the ability to easily dispose of others, and the benefits of greater sharing of data.

Although data management is critical, this chapter also points out the need to manage the physical infrastructure of an IT system. Computers and networks represent a major financial investment for most firms and require careful, thoughtful policies. Many issues must be addressed in this management process.

Finally, policies must be developed for the software or applications portfolio to insure that it is treated as a critical asset. User-managers should take an active role in all three areas of technology resource management.

The technology resources of an IT system are an organizational asset that must be explicitly and professionally managed as other assets are managed. This management requires a combination of efforts by IS professionals and user-managers. The next chapter discusses how organizations should manage the other resources in an IT system. Technology resource management is only one part of this total management system—but a very important part.

Review Questions

1. What is a data model? What does it contain?
2. Why do organizations often have several databases?
3. Define application independence.
4. Who is a data steward, and what does this person do?
5. What are the basic functions of managing the data resource?
6. Briefly outline some international issues related to data management.
7. What are the objectives of data administration?
8. Why are relational database management systems so popular?

9. Explain the significance of "disposable systems" as described in this chapter.

10. What are the arguments against broad access to external databases from the desktop?

11. Should applications ever be process driven? Why? When?

12. What needed policies regarding the physical infrastructure are not addressed in Figure 14.9?

Discussion Questions

1. Why do some user-managers resist managing technical IT assets as organizational resources? What does an individual manager have to gain or lose from IT resource management?

2. By distinguishing between data capture, transfer, and analysis and presentation systems, what are the major implications for systems development?

3. What are the different kinds of data standards and why are these an essential part of data management?

4. Consider an organization with which you are familiar. Develop a policy for managing the applications portfolio.

5. Discuss the advantages and disadvantages for an organization in setting the types of data standards listed in Figure 14.3.

6. As a manager of a major business unit (division), what would you do to implement a corporate infrastructure policy, such as the one in Figure 14.9?

7. What are the major differences between the two approaches to data planning and modeling outlined in this chapter—enterprise modeling and view integration? Why do these two methodologies usually yield different results?

8. Discuss the problems or pitfalls of doing data planning and modeling. How can these be alleviated?

9. What objections by user-managers would likely arise from the distributed applications development policy shown in Figure 14.10?

References

Baatz, E.B. 1996. "What's it all about?" *CIO* 9 (October 1): 28–34.

Betts, Mitch. 1990. "Romancing the segment of one." *Computerworld* 24 (March 5): 63–65.

Bresnahan, Jennifer. 1997. "Blueprint for success." *CIO* 10 (March 15): 56–66.

Celko, Joe, and Jackie McDonald. 1995. "Don't warehouse dirty data." *Datamation* 31 (October 15): 42–52.

Crafts, Steven. 1997. *Data Warehousing: What Works?* Volume 4. New York: The Data Warehousing Institute.

Davenport, Thomas H. 1994. "Saving IT's soul: Human-centered information management." *Harvard Business Review* 61 (March–April): 119–131.

Edwards, John. 1996. "Data scrubbing." *CIO* 9 (October 1): 108–114.

English, Larry P. 1993. "Accountability to the rescue." *Database Programming & Design* 6 (June): 54–59.

Hurwitz, Judith. 1994. *Second-Generation Client/Server Computing.* Watertown, Mass.: Hurwitz Consulting Group, Inc.

Koch, Christopher. 1997. "A tough sell." *CIO* 10 (May 1): 74–86.

Mayor, Tracy. 1997. "Ensured stability." *CIO* 10 (August): 62–68.

McWilliams, Gary. 1995. "Small fry go online." *Business Week* 86 (November 20): 158–164.

Novak, Janet. 1996. "The data miners." *Forbes* 158 (February 12): 96–97

Percy, Tony. 1988. "Unfreezing the vital corporate asset—information." *CIO* 1 (Summer): 38–40.

Slater, Derek. 1997. "The data game." *CIO* 10 (May 1): 90–96.

Sullivan-Trainer, Michael. 1989. "Sharing the wealth: Data becomes community property." *Computerworld* 23 (May 22): 71–76.

Williamson, Miryam. 1997. "Weighing the no's and con's." *CIO* 10 (April 15): 49–57.

MANAGING THE INFORMATION SYSTEMS FUNCTION

In many organizations, the information systems (IS) function has undergone a sequence of frequent and significant changes since 1980 in response to rapid changes in technology and user-manager expectations. As was mentioned in the introduction to Part IV, the job of IS leadership starts with helping set a vision for how the organization should use information, an architecture for the deployment of information resources to support that vision, and a plan to achieve the architecture (see Chapter 13). IS leadership must as well manage the technology assets—data, the physical infrastructure, and the applications portfolio. The concepts and issues regarding these technology assets that have the most impact on the user-manager were covered in Chapter 14. This final chapter of the book focuses on the human and organizational aspects of managing the IS function in an organization. As was pointed out in Chapter 1, IS leadership must insure that its human and organizational assets are as fully developed as the technology assets. The user-manager must be an active participant in this process.

Many organizations are making dramatic changes in their IS management system. Some organizations are switching from either highly centralized or highly decentralized IS organizations to a more cooperative, client/server-type structure to parallel the latest trend in information technology (IT) architecture. IS organizations, like other functions, suffered through the downsizing of the early 1990s as companies tried to become more globally competitive for customers and shareholders. Also common is the outsourcing of a portion of the IS department to an independent organization.

This organization may be a subsidiary of the corporation, but usually is a separate service company in the business of running data centers, telecommunication networks, or systems development groups. Another major theme in IS management today is helping the organization participate in a global marketplace. As noted in this chapter, managing global systems raises unique factors and issues for an organization.

As information systems become more pervasive throughout organizations, user-managers have demanded more IS support and guidance as they use and develop systems. The important topic of management of end-user development was addressed in Chapter 12 and is not repeated here. It is nevertheless a critical part of the entire IS management system.

These and many more developments serve to make it difficult for IS professionals and their customers (the user-managers) to determine how best to manage the IS function. Complicating this confusion is the fact that in today's (and tomorrow's) business environment, the way in which the IS function is managed and its contribution to the organization as a whole are critical success factors for the whole organization. Today, information technology is pervasive and requires attention by every organizational unit and every user-manager. Ensuring payback from IT investment, being able to respond quickly to changing requirements, and leveraging technology for increased business value are now basic to conducting a successful business or other organization.

This chapter introduces some of the challenges faced by IS leadership and outlines the ten elements of a management system for the IS function that studies and experience have shown lead to success. The user-manager must understand and actively participate in each of these elements.

THE CHALLENGES OF IS LEADERSHIP

Since 1980, major external developments have required the IS function to undergo significant changes in the basic definition of its mission and the way it carries out its role. Why has IS management evolved from highly centralized in a low-level management unit, to a mixture of centralization and decentralization across all units and levels? Basically, the changes reflect trends in technology, applications, and data; an increased understanding of information technology by managers; and changes in environmental factors. These have been treated throughout the book. A few of the more critical influences are reviewed here as a basis for the suggestions in this chapter.

Rapid Technological Change

Small and inexpensive electronic technologies have made it possible for each user-manager, department, and small business to acquire sophisticated computer and communications equipment. In fact, many managers today have more data on their hard drive than in their file cabinets. With this distribution of technology comes a need for local responsibility for operations, backup and recovery, security, development, education, and planning. Even with these needs to manage the distributed technology, there is still the need to ensure that desktop and departmental technologies do not become isolated islands of automation. A central IS group usually coordinates, standardizes, and inventories distributed technology and the applications and data managed by them.

Exploding Applications and Data

To give business units and user-managers greater control over information support and the allocation of IS and other expenditures, applications and database development have often been distributed. In response to this fragmentation, the central IS organization has often become a support and training group. Currently, an important part of a centralized IS unit mission is to facilitate this distributed development for the good of the whole organization. Frequently, the IS organization has been broken apart, with much of the systems analysis and design activities reporting to business units. Along with this reorganization, user-managers have had to take more direct roles in systems development, managing systems professionals, and negotiating with other managers over system interfaces.

Growth in User-Management Understanding

There is now a greater technology awareness and skill level among those who are not systems specialists, which creates higher and more diverse expectations for new and improved systems and greater confidence that user-managers can develop and run systems themselves. More use and development of systems by user-managers stimulates the need for additional systems, because the more one knows, the more one wants. Many of these systems, because they are common across business units or link data across subunits, are natural for a central IS organization to develop and manage. In fact, many IS organizations are evolving into a data warehousing or utility function in which their primary role is the management and transfer of data between data suppliers and consumers within the organization. Although their role has changed considerably, many IS organizations are busier than ever and still in critical need of qualified technical and managerial personnel. It seems clear that the IS organization will continue to change, often more so than its counterparts in finance, marketing, and production.

Frequent External Shocks

External developments have caused major changes in the IS organization. For example, the deregulation and resulting greater competition of the telecommunications industry has forced organizations to manage aspects of data and voice communications previously entrusted to the vendor. International regulations on transborder data flow and vast differences in labor rates have caused organizations to reconsider where systems will be built and operated and where data entry is most economical. The shortage of highly qualified IS professionals has encouraged organizations to expect greater productivity from existing IS staff and resulted in the distribution of more systems work to non-IS professionals. Organizations are also relying more on purchased software from the growing application software industry (see Chapter 11). The exploding growth of the Internet has challenged IS to redefine the interface between the company and its customers—not to mention dealing with a massive increase in traffic to and from external data sources.

THE SUCCESSFUL INFORMATION TECHNOLOGY MANAGEMENT SYSTEM

Faced with these challenges and changes, how can IS leadership and user-managers partner in designing a successful IT management system? What are the areas that most need attention? Figure 15.1 lists ten decision areas that the authors believe contribute to designing a successful management system for information technology. Each area is explained in the sections that follow.

1. An Agreed-Upon Role for the IS Organization

The role of the IS organization is changing, but often it is not clear where the function is headed. How IT is best managed depends on how the senior management of the organization sees information and IT as a part of the overall business vision. Therefore, there must also be a clear, shared understanding of what the IS department's mission is.

What mission or role the IS organization takes on, how it performs these duties, and how it organizes to get its job done will vary from organization to organization. Two sample IS department mission statements may be found in Chapter 13. As a general trend, however, business managers expect a future-oriented IS organization that can anticipate their needs and meet today's requirements. This means that senior business management expects the IS unit to align its activities with the overall business mission. IS must exercise business leadership while also providing technical support. More specifically, these expectations mean:

- Demonstrating an understanding of the business, through an awareness of business plans and strategies and close communication with business managers.
- Responding quickly with systems to meet changing business conditions (not waiting years for a strategically important system to be built).
- Helping to reengineer business processes to be more responsive to customers, to bring product to market faster, or to improve business process quality.
- Keeping the final customer, not just internal operations, in mind.
- Building systems that provide direct and identifiable benefits to the final customer, thus building stronger customer relationships.

- An agreed-upon role for the IS organization
- A leader whose position, skills, and personality fits business management's expectations
- A clearly defined, active role for the user-manager, resulting in an IS/customer partnership
- A rationale for outsourcing IS functions that is based on economic and strategic factors
- An equitable financing system
- A consistent development effort for both IS professionals and users
- Development of global information systems
- IS organization design in line with mission
- Regular performance measurement
- A change management system

Figure 15.1 Critical Areas of the IT Management System

- Helping managers make better decisions with information.
- Using information technology for sustainable competitive advantage and increased market share.

It is important to note that the traditional dominant expectation of the IS function—saving money through cost efficiencies such as work-force reduction due to automation—is not included in this set. Although such short-term tangible benefits are still important (yet often difficult to attribute solely to an information system), expectations today are more comprehensive and complex than merely reducing cost.

It is not unusual to find that most CEOs and other senior executives are skeptical that they are getting the most from their investment in information systems. At the same time, these leaders admit that information systems significantly change the way their organizations operate and compete and that good systems are critical to the organization's success. It is therefore clear that effort must be expended to develop a shared understanding of what the IS organization's role should be.

In general, the role of the IS organization (both central and distributed units) is to be the steward of the information and IT resources of the organization, much as the finance organization is the steward for financial resources. More specific roles are to:

- Deploy IT resources throughout the organization.
- Facilitate the productive and effective use of these resources today, not just in the future.
- Lead the development of a vision and an architecture for information technology that will support the rapid deployment of new and improved systems (through both original software development and packaged products).
- Communicate this vision and architecture to the entire organization in business terms.
- Maintain managerial control and integrity over important information resources.
- Administer corporate data and the movement of data between systems.
- Make current and new information technology available at the lowest possible cost.
- Help user-managers become comfortable with information technologies and knowledgeable about their effective use.
- Develop a partnership with user-managers to exploit technology for business value and to influence the products and services offered by the organization.

Cooperative efforts between IS leadership and senior user-managers have often proven useful in clarifying how information technology is to be exploited in the firm and what the role of the IS function should be. Figure 15.2 shows an example statement of values and beliefs about information technology that was drafted by a joint IS leadership/senior business management task force. The statement was developed at a $350 million manufacturer of industrial painting systems in late 1996.

The need for stating these shared beliefs came from an assessment of the company's IT management system. It revealed that the expectations of senior business management and IS leadership differed widely. Indeed, the statement in Figure 15.2 took several months of discussion to develop due to these different perceptions of the participants. The first item listed in Figure 15.2 was derived from user-management's belief that the IS organization spent more time generating ideas on the possible use of IT than it did delivering systems that worked. The second item was needed because IS management felt regional managers and product managers in the company were developing systems in a haphazard, uncoordinated way. The interaction in developing this statement served to "clear the air" on these views. The statement later provided the basis for more specific policies.

2. IS Leadership

The second key factor in determining the success of the IT management system and the IS function is, not unsurprisingly, the leader. The leader's level of authority in the organization and his or her business skills, personality, and leadership style are all important. Most important, however, is that the leader and his attributes fit the mission and expectations laid out for the IS function.

In most organizations, someone can be identified as the manager or executive to whom all centralized IT management activities report. In some enterprises, this person may be the IS department manager, director, or vice president; in other organizations, this person might be a finance or administrative executive. Since the mid-1980s, organizations have created the role of **chief information officer** (**CIO**) to lead IT management. A true CIO is part of the officer team of the organization. He or she is one of those executives responsible for the strategic decisions for the whole organization. The

1. **We stress implementation of ideas.** We have generated many new ideas and concepts which will help us develop our systems. We must refine these concepts and implement these ideas. Good ideas without implementation are insufficient.

2. **We believe in a planned, coordinated approach.** Individual decisions will be based on a well-developed and communicated information technology plan within each regional and corporate staff area. Each area will explicitly recognize information needs in the annual plan. Because many good ideas have been thought of or are being used by areas of our operations, we stress the importance of communicating these ideas to other individuals and operating units. Planning will take place at the regional level; planning and coordination will take place at the corporate staff level.

3. **Information technology will be made a valuable resource in our jobs.** We will make information technology services valuable to everyone in the organization. We recognize the change that is required. We will encourage the responsible use of this important asset throughout the organization. We will help all users of information understand the effective and responsible use of the technology.

4. **We welcome the organizational impacts of information technology advances.** Improving technology will provide the potential to increase service to our clients and reduce our overall cost. These changes will create opportunities to reconsider organizational span of control, reporting lines, and communication paths. We will assess potential improvements on a regular basis and implement those changes that demonstrate enhancements to accomplish our mission.

5. **Data will be shared.** Data are not "owned" by a particular individual or department, but belong to the whole organization. Data will be made easily accessible to all authorized users. Each individual within our company should be able to access appropriate information based on her or his responsibility. Policy guidelines will be established for data to be shared.

6. **We encourage innovation in the use of information.** We are committed to the creative use of information to identify and respond to basic changes in the company's environment. We will challenge the status quo in how we use information to do our jobs. We will encourage our people to apply information technology in new ways so as to benefit our clients and owners.

Figure 15.2 Example Values Statement

CIO focuses on information technology. This section addresses this senior general business manager role.

It is clear that some mix of business and technical skills and duties is required for IS leadership—regardless of the title. Figure 15.3 is a fictitious advertisement for a CIO. It makes clear the challenges inherent in many senior IS leadership positions. The role defined for the CIO says much about what an organization can expect from its IS organization.

The Job of Senior IS Leadership   Above all, the CIO is responsible for guiding and unifying the entire organization's information technology resources—data processing, office automation, telecommunications,

and possibly guiding the reengineering efforts for examining business processes. Although different divisions, lines of business, or subsidiaries may have their own information executives, central IS leadership is charged with coordinating all the resources. The CIO is usually a staff function, not a line function in the whole organization. Likewise, the CIO usually does not have responsibilities for day-to-day IS operations.

Clearly, CIOs should be business, not technical, managers. They are, however, expected to bridge the gulf between the IS organization and general business managers. Traditional IS managers spent most of their time interacting with other IS professionals and users,

> Wanted
>
> Bright, versatile, industrious individual to lead the effort in determining the information vision for the company, creating partnerships with internal customers, and ensuring that IT delivers business value. Person must be able to understand how to apply information technology to corporate strategy. Must be able to work well under pressure and have strong analytical capabilities. Outstanding interpersonal and communication skills are required because the individual will interact with all information suppliers and customers inside and outside the company. Must add value as a member of the senior management team.

Figure 15.3 Example of a CIO Job Advertisement

focusing on specific user needs. In contrast, CIOs spend the greatest percentage of time interacting with peer general managers as part of managing the business as a whole. CIOs need to be able to see the advantage of technology and where to apply it broadly in the business. This role is suited for men and women who can explain what IT is accomplishing in business terms.

Although the idea is now a reality, the role of the CIO is still emerging. In some cases, therefore, the CIO may not yet have the authority he or she needs for carrying out the responsibilities of the position. Not all CIOs report directly to the CEO or president. Few small or medium-sized companies have a full time CIO. Usually, organizations on the frontier of information management have a true CIO—such information-intensive enterprises as banks, insurance companies, and airlines—although more and more manufacturing and retailing firms have created the position and are effectively implementing the concept.

Senior IS Management Issues   Various studies in recent years have tracked the major concerns of senior IS executives, including the CIO. While the exact list and ranking of issues vary from year to year, some general patterns have emerged. These following concerns represent a good summary of the kinds of expectations the business has for IS management.

- Improving information and IT planning, especially linking IS to the business: With rapidly changing businesses and technologies (e.g., selling over the Internet), such planning is not easy, but it is essential to anticipate information needs and manage resources prudently.

- Gaining business value through IT: Systems that enable the organization to achieve competitive advantage give the IS organization visibility and attention that can help to make many other changes in IT management possible.

- Facilitating organizational learning about and through information technology: This issue is consistent with the evolution of the IS organization into an enabling role rather than exclusively a doing

---

THE ELUSIVE VALUE OF IT

Just as the accounting system hides many aspects of the costs of IT, it overlooks many of the ways in which IT contributes to business units' performance. The most important contribution IT can make is in avoiding costs. For example, by adding IT costs in Year X, a firm might avoid increased business costs in Year X+5. Looking just at financial records, the user-manager sees a growth in IT expenditure and a reduction in business cost growth. IT is now 12 percent of the company's total cost base versus 8 percent previously, whereas the business units have managed to reduce labor costs as a percentage of sales by 30 percent. What's going on? The user-manager's likely conclusion: "IT is out of control!" But what may be going on is that the IT investment generated the labor cost savings by ensuring that the firm could handle larger volumes without adding staff. The accounting system will never tell! Possibly a better measure of the impact of IT investment would be sales per employee, which captures the changes in both benefits and costs.

[Adapted from Keen, 1991]

role. In particular, training on how to use information to make better decisions can now be an important function of senior IS leadership.

- Refining the IS unit's role and position: CIOs are concerned about the IS organization's ability to be proactive and what responsibilities should be distributed to achieve the greatest payoff for the whole enterprise.
- Guiding end-user development: The development of systems by end-users directly or by IS staff in line organizations is now a major alternative way to have systems built. Determining the proper standards for programming languages, systems justification procedures, documentation, database management, and the like is a difficult policy challenge for the CIO.
- Managing data as a resource: This issue has been rising in the list of top concerns for the CIO (see Chapter 14).
- Measuring IS effectiveness: Frequently the strategic and decision support systems being introduced today are difficult to justify with hard benefit numbers. Further, it is difficult to show the contribution of information and IT planning and architecture work. Thus, IT resources may be cut in hard times unless the real contributions can be shown.
- Integrating information technologies: Often the primary role of the CIO is the unification of IS services and technologies. The history of isolated islands of automation, each with strong and protective organizational homes, usually makes integration a difficult political as well as technical problem.
- Managing systems personnel: Finding and retaining staff knowledgeable in such strategic technologies as enterprise resource planning systems and global telecommunications networks are of special concern. Motivating systems personnel to be productive and aware of business needs is also of high concern to the CIO and other IS managers.

3. Active Role for User-Managers

If the CIO is truly an officer of the business, then he or she is not the only person at that level concerned with managing IT issues for the business. In many organizations, issues at the officer level are issues for all officers. Cross-functional management, where problems are addressed in partnership among peers, is more and more the culture of business. Even when a strong consensus or collaborative culture is not present, senior IS leadership cannot address the above concerns alone.

It is essential for the CIO as well as other senior IS managers to build strong working relationships with other top managers. This result cannot be achieved unless the senior IS person is a peer in authority and responsibility, the IS department's mission and vision are clearly communicated, and other user-managers view IT as an area that cannot be managed by delegation to lower-level personnel.

A partnership, a cooperative relationship, must be defined. User-managers must welcome such partnerships and explicitly communicate this receptivity to their peers and subordinates. The CIO and other senior IS managers must be committed to working on non-IT issues. In many organizations, one senior user-manager, recognizing the power of such an alliance, has championed the partnership concept.

Defining a Partnership   **Partnership** is a critical strategy for IS management. It is based on sustaining a long-term relationship between IS and business management. Partners share key common goals. Partners seek benefits not possible to each party individually. Partnership is based on mutual trust as well as shared benefits, responsibilities, and risks. Its goal is to achieve a greater contribution for IT to the benefit of the organization. Each partner understands and appreciates the critical stakeholders and business processes that influence the performance of the organization. A partner respects the distinctive resources and competencies of other partners. More on partnerships may be found in Henderson (1990).

Implementing Partnerships   Whereas these attributes of a true partnership are the goal, partnership sometimes starts by clearly defining the authority of the partners. Figure 15.4 contains an example of a statement developed in mid-1997 that defines the authority of both user departments and the IS department. In this mid-size manufacturer of electric motors, relations between IS and several business departments had deteriorated to the point where such a statement was needed prior to building a better relationship.

The statement in Figure 15.4 created the IS Policy Committee that is now the focal point for the developing partnership. Although working IS/business partnerships can be implemented in several ways, by far

1. All user departments will be fully accountable for their use of information resources, including the skill level of people using information technology resources.
2. User departments will pay an annual fee to the IS Department for workstations to include capital, software, and maintenance costs.
3. The IS Department will set and enforce standards for user workstation hardware, software, and network connections.
4. User departments will pay for use of shareable information technology resources through a fair division of overhead.
5. Senior management will be kept engaged in information technology issues via regular communications by IS staff.
6. The IS Department will actively initiate communication with all user departments.
7. The IS Department will build its plan and budget with full knowledge of company business plans.
8. Members of the IS Department will serve as internal business process improvement consultants.
9. The IS Department will be represented on issue-oriented or business planning teams where information definition and/or collection is crucial.
10. Policy affecting users will be determined by the IS Policy Committee, chaired by a senior business executive.

Figure 15.4 Expectations/Responsibilities Statement

the most frequent is the steering committee for IS management. An **IS steering committee,** issue forum, or advisory board can be used to ensure frequent interaction. Much discussion of such groups has centered on how they have been misused or abused. Inadequate authority, narrow perspectives, uninformed or inappropriate membership, and a host of other problems can hamper these committees. When properly set up, however, such groups can be used effectively to:

- Set priorities for systems development and IS direction.
- Check progress against an established direction.
- Allocate scarce resources, especially IS staff, to achieve business objectives.
- Communicate concerns, issues, and possible remedies.
- Provide education and the development of shared mind-sets.
- Develop shared responsibility and ownership of actions.

Such groups are not a substitute for a good CIO and IS management. Instead, they work best when there is responsive management for IS already in place. Partnership means cooperation, dealing with problems jointly, and managing the business, not managing empires. A good steering committee, along with professional IS leadership, can be an effective part of the management system for information technology exploitation in the business.

4. Strategic and Economic Rationale for Outsourcing

A sizable number of medium to large organizations have hired outside professional IS services organizations to run part of their IS operations. This approach to IT management is commonly called **outsourcing.** For many companies, internal computer operations have never held a monopoly position. Public data banks, market research data processing firms, and time-sharing and other computing services with special software and data have been around for decades. With the cost-cutting emphasis since the mid-1980s, there has been renewed interest in outsourcing data center operations, sometimes called IS facilities management, to external service organizations. Besides the data center, an organization may outsource the management of telecommunications or traditional transaction processing systems programming.

In the early years of computing in businesses, some banks and other aggressive adopters of computer technology performed data processing for other organizations. For example, banks often provided total automation for payroll, receivables, and payables processing under contract for their regular commercial banking customers. As the price of computer equipment fell and the availability of programming talent improved, however, most organizations chose to bring these operations in-house.

The Economic Value of Outsourcing

Much of the outsourcing craze in the 1990s was driven by the need to downsize and to respond to other significant organizational changes taking place (mergers, acquisitions, and divestitures). With these changes often come sudden shifts in demands for computing power. Moad (1993) claims that the major benefit of the First Fidelity Bancorporation (FFB)–EDS outsourcing deal was the speed and efficiency with which FFB could integrate acquired institutions (approximately two to three months). Also, some companies report cost savings of 10 to 20 percent from the economies of scale and competitive rather than captive pricing provided by the data center suppliers.

Outsourcing allows a company with greatly fluctuating computer processing demands to pay for only what it uses, rather than build a data center for peak load and letting it sit underutilized during other periods. Companies can invest the savings in identifying and developing high-impact IS applications. The trend toward outsourcing may also be related to the establishment of a CIO, who is not tied emotionally to the existing data center and does not feel that the IS function has to manage hardware to prove its value to the firm. A CIO may view data processing much as a manufacturing operation, which is a candidate for outsourcing when demand is highly variable.

Some firms have chosen to outsource IS operations because it is difficult to keep pace with technological change and to hire and retain highly skilled IS staff, especially outside urban areas. Others simply believe that a large outsourcing supplier, with experience in many organizations, can cut costs and provide better service. Other senior executives were not satisfied with the service being delivered by in-house staff.

Making the Right Decision

The decision to outsource must be viewed as both a remedy for service failures or cost issues and as a strategic choice. Likewise, outsourcing must be done selectively. In the early 1990s, Eastman Kodak outsourced its data centers to IBM, its telecommunications to Digital Equipment Corporation, and its microcomputer systems to Businessland, Inc. Kodak did not see these areas as core to its vision for information technology or as a significant strength for competitive advantage. The savings from outsourcing could be used in other parts of the business, where Kodak felt a greater return on investment could be achieved. Other organizations, however, have outsourced critical strategic IS functions in response to short-term emergencies and subsequently have lost the competitive advantage its prior investment in IS staff had brought.

As discussed in earlier chapters, outsourcing systems development and integration is also possible and popular. Contracted systems development and programming as well as purchasing of system and applications software, both common today, are a form of outsourcing. Because the bulk of IS costs are in personnel and because most IS personnel are in systems development, major cost-reduction benefits may come from outsourcing if the outsourcing partner is able to bring improved productivity tools to the process.

When information technology has strategic value to the firm, stable and healthy organizations should not see outsourcing as a viable option, especially of sensitive development and planning activities. Security and privacy issues and the strategic value of some data may mean that certain applications should not be developed or run outside the organization. For example, systems in support of research and development may be considered too sensitive to outsource. Further, it may be quite difficult to bring systems development or operations back in-house if prices for outsourcing services increase or there is a change in the need for strategic control of these system functions or for technical know-how. Hiring staff and familiarizing them with company operations, building data centers, and setting methods and procedures cannot be done quickly. Organizations with highly variable needs for computing power, however, are increasingly considering the outsourcing option.

Outsourcing arrangements that work over time are usually those whose participants (the company and the outsourcer) see the arrangement as a partnership.

The outsourcer should know and care about the business as much as client executives do. Sometimes an outsourcer will specialize in particular industries (such as retail or health care) to gain a depth of knowledge. In such instances, care should be taken to ensure that the outsourcer does not leak out competitive information. An outsourcer can also help the firm make sound technology decisions, not just solutions convenient for the outsourcer. The outsourcing contract should accommodate growth and expansion in the business. Finally, the firm should select an outsourcer who can operate as geographically dispersed as the company's operations.

Several key factors in selecting an outsourcing vendor are:

- Vendor reputation, which includes understanding the business and technology standards.
- Quality of service, which means a clear comparative advantage over in-house services.
- Flexible pricing, which means cost effectiveness because, as processing volume increases or new services are added, costs can escalate.

5. An Equitable Financing System

Information technology services cost a lot. IT systems are complex and IS personnel are among the best-paid employees in the company. At the same time, the value of IS services is not always clear. Systems often take years to build and are sometimes over budget. The direct business impacts (e.g., reduced personnel costs) of new systems are not as evident as they were in the past. More and more systems are being built in order to compete better—and the impact on sales increases is not always easy to predict.

An effective IT management system must carefully measure IT costs, enable the understanding of the financial impacts of new and existing systems, and find a way to fund IS operations and new systems. Measuring the organization's investment in IT and calculating the impact of this investment on the organization's performance are still not well understood activities. Most benefits are indirect or confounded by other organization changes.

Managing IT Costs   The typical measures used for tracking IT costs are as follows:

- Total IT budget as a percentage of total organization revenues, income, premiums, deposits, or other indicators of overall financial activity of the organization.
- Total IT budget as a percentage of total organization budget.
- IS personnel costs as a percentage of total organization professional personnel salaries and wages.
- The ratio of hardware and software costs to IS personnel costs.
- The costs for IT hardware and software per managerial or knowledge worker.

No one of these measures is by itself perfect or complete, and most organizations should track several of them. Sizable changes in these measures might be more significant than the absolute values. Further, high or low values are not by themselves necessarily bad or good. All of these measures require interpretation, matching them with IS and business directions. Organizations that try to be pioneers and leaders should expect, for example, to have higher values on many of these measures than less aggressive firms.

Even in combination, these measures must be used cautiously because of various definitional and measurement problems:

- Some IT costs are hidden because of the highly distributed nature of information processing in most organizations. Not all costs appear as IS department budget items, and certainly not all are spent in the IS organization. Personal computer hardware, software, training, and services can be purchased as general office expenses or from petty cash—costs that are difficult to track.
- No relationship to benefits is directly included in these measures. Costs without benefits give a very incomplete picture.
- Benefits happen after many of the development costs occur, and the lag is not considered in these measures. Direct benefits can occur quickly, but secondary benefits of technology diffusion and new ways of doing business may not emerge for years.

Measuring Benefits   There is no simple, reliable way to measure the value-added benefits of information technology. IT costs are easier to see; IT value is typically much more intangible. Organizations must capture and track measures of IS performance over time to best utilize such indicators, so that values can be interpreted, changes explained, and reasonably helpful comparisons made. Some organizations now treat investment in IT like research. No matter how IT investments are valued, it is the job of the user-manager, not the IS manager, to justify the investment.

Controlling IS Costs   A primary mechanism for financial control of IT is the IS organization's budget. One way to divide costs creates four primary groups—personnel, equipment and software, outside services, and overhead. But not all organizations use these areas. Furthermore, statistics from studies on IS budgets vary widely across industries. Because of these reporting and measurement issues, some individual statistics can be misleading, but some general observations appear to be valid:

- The most common measure, IT expenditures as a percent of revenue or assets, varies widely by industry and size of firm. Information- and technology-intensive industries spend the highest percentage on IT. Smaller firms suffer from a lack of economies of scale and typically spend a higher percentage (all else being equal).
- Personnel costs are the largest piece of the IT budget, typically more than 50 percent (depending on the industry) of the total. Although increased productivity aids have helped to keep this percentage from growing faster, the demand for new systems along with the stiff competition for qualified people makes reduction of IS development staff budget difficult.

Obviously, the IS budget depends on the demand for new systems. As the application portfolio increases, greater budget pressures occur due to enhancement and maintenance requirements. Keen (1991) estimated that every $1 of development causes $4 of ongoing costs over the following five years. Without sizable productivity gains, it is easy to incur double-digit annual IS department budget increases.

Chargeback Systems   Some senior business managers believe that the best way to hold IS and line organizations accountable for the impact of systems on the organization is to have the IS unit operate as a business within a business. In this instance, the IS unit would be a profit center, with a flexible budget and an agreed-upon transfer pricing scheme. This design places control of IS spending in the hands of those who use such services. Control changes from a vague annual negotiation process of capital expenditures approvals and cost allocations into forcing the IS head or CIO to manage the department in order to make a profit.

For user-managers, the business unit or organization is affected directly by an IS chargeback process. If done well, a chargeback system can be a way to better understand true costs. Certainly there are many positive aspects to charging for IS services, but, as with any profit-center and transfer-pricing scheme, short- and long-term costs and benefits become difficult to balance. User-managers adapt behavior to take advantage of the pricing structure. For example, discounts for overnight processing might cause a user-manager to rely less on on-line reporting. Thus, it is important for every user-manager to understand why chargeback schemes are put in place and what characterizes a good process.

Organizations usually adopt a chargeback process for IS services for one or more of the following reasons:

- To assign costs clearly to those who consume and benefit from IT.
- To control wasteful use of IT resources by encouraging users to compare the benefits with the costs and eliminate unprofitable use.
- To overcome the belief that IT costs may be unnecessarily high.
- To provide incentives by subsidizing the price of certain services or innovative uses of technologies.
- To change the IS department's budgeting process to be more business driven, thus rewarding the IS organization for improved service and greater efficiency rather than technological change for its own sake.
- To encourage line managers to be knowledgeable consumers of IS because they must directly pay for such support.

A major problem in any chargeback system is that many IT costs are joint costs, not easily attributed to one single organization, such as the cost to store and maintain a shared database. Further, some costs are essentially fixed, such as systems software and many components of a data center complex. Thus, calculating costs and reducing expenditures as demand varies may not be as easy as one would wish.

Also, in applications in which the benefits of IT may be difficult to determine, as in education, research, and customer service, chargeback can limit creative uses of technology.

Transfer prices can be developed for a broad and comprehensive range of IS activities, including charges for:

- Personnel time.
- Computer usage or wall-clock time (or computer cycles used).
- Disk file space.
- Number of transactions processed.
- Amount of computer main memory used (per unit of time).
- Number of screens accessed.

Charges might be cost-based (to recover all costs) or market-based (to be comparable to market alternatives). A combination of clearly identifiable direct costs plus an allocation of other overhead costs (space, administrative staff, and so on) might be used.

Chargeback systems for IT activities can be a great source of irritation between the IS organization and user-managers unless a mutually agreed-upon structure for charging can be developed. A successful chargeback system should incorporate the following characteristics:

- Understandable: An understandable chargeback system reports use in business terms that user-managers can relate to their own activities, not just computer operations. For example, charges per customer order, invoice, or report relate more to business activity than does the number of computer input/output operations performed or machine cycles used.
- Prompt and regular feedback: Charges should be reported soon after the activity to which they are related so that use and cost can be closely linked and total costs can be accurately monitored by those who can control the costs.
- Controllable: The activity for which user-managers are charged must be something they can control (for example, charges for rerun computer jobs because of operator errors would not be controllable). Further, users must have a choice to use alternative services or to substitute one kind of usage with another (for example, switching between two alternative database management systems or trading computer time for data storage).

- Accountable: Managers responsible for generating IS activity must be identifiable and must be held accountable for their charges. Otherwise the charges are meaningless and useless.
- Relate to benefits: Managers must see a link between costs and benefits so they can balance the value of the IS services against what is being spent.
- Consistent with IS and organizational goals: Charges should be designed to achieve the goals set for the business and the goals of the IS organization. Thus, charges should encourage use of important information technology services, efficient use of scarce technology and services, the desired balance of internal and external sourcing of IS services, and development of systems that comply with accepted architectural standards.

Chargeback systems must be periodically evaluated to check that the desired results are being achieved. In any case, the chargeback or funding mechanism for the IS organization is one of the keys to having an effective IT management system.

6. IS Staff/User Development

An effective IT management system will allocate significant resources to the continuing development of both IS personnel and users. In an environment of rapid change in technology and business demand, significant effort in technology training is required. The IS field is diverse and traditionally specialized. Although senior IS executives are more and more becoming general business managers, most IS professionals, whether based in the IS organization or in business units, have specific duties and require specialized training. With product life cycles for software shortening, it is not uncommon for organizations to have technology training under way all the time.

Table 15.1 lists generic job titles and a brief description for many possible IS management positions in a typical IS organization. Depending on the IS department structure, these positions may reside in a business unit, in a divisional group, or in the corporate IS unit. All of these roles are essential for the high-quality operation of the systems in the organization. This list does not include the programmers, analysts, computer operators, trainers, and consultants. Each of these professionals have substantial training requirements as well.

Table 15.1

Selected IS Management Positions

CIO

Most-senior executive responsible for leading in the introduction of information technology across the whole organization.

IS Director

Responsible for the day-to-day operations of all aspects of IS for the whole organization.

IS Executive

Responsible for the day-to-day operations of all aspects of IS in one division, plant, or unit of the business; usually a general manager of that business unit, not the central IS group.

Information Center Manager or Manager of End-User Computing

Oversees the operation of computer hot line and user help desks; training on user development tools and fourth-generation languages; and personal computer installation and support.

Systems Development Manager

Coordinates all new systems development projects, allocates systems analysts and project managers to projects, schedules development work.

Systems Maintenance Manager

Coordinates all systems maintenance projects, allocates systems analysts and project managers to projects, schedules maintenance work; depending on organization structure, development and maintenance manager may be one person or several people responsible for different segments of the business.

IS Planning Manager

Analyzes business and develops an architecture for hardware and software to support systems in the future; may also forecast technology trends.

Data Center Manager

Supervises the day-to-day operations of data centers and possibly also data entry, data network, computer file library, and systems hardware and software maintenance staff; schedules computer jobs, manages downtime, and plans computer system capacity.

Programming Manager

Coordinates all application programming efforts: allocates and organizes staff into project teams, acquires tools and languages to improve programmer productivity.

Manager of Emerging Technologies

Evaluates new technologies, fosters experimental projects to test new technologies in the organization, consults with users on appropriate application of new technologies, and approves new technologies for use in the organization.

Telecommunications Manager

Plans, designs, and coordinates the operation of the corporate data and voice network.

(continued on next page)

Table 15.1   *(continued from previous page)*

Systems Programming Manager

Responsible for support and maintenance of systems software such as operating system, utilities, programming language compilers; interacts with vendors to install updates and request changes; may overlap duties with Telecommunications Manager and Database Administrator.

Database Administrator

Plans databases and coordinates use of data management software (duties outlined in Chapter 14).

Project Manager

Supervisor of analysts and programmers working on the development or maintenance of an application system and coordination with customers of the system.

Quality Assurance Manager

Coordinates activities that set standards and checks compliance with standards to improve the quality and accuracy of systems.

Computer Security Manager

Develops procedures and policies and installs and monitors software to ensure the authorized use of computing resources.

The user-manager community and IS leaders share in the responsibility of providing IT training for all users. Table 15.2 shows the IT training requirements for employees in a major metropolitan healthcare organization. In 1995, senior management committed the organization to a policy that all employees should have at least 24 hours of IT training each year. The required courses had to be taken in the first year of employment.

7. Global Information Systems Development

A more recent requirement for an effective IT management system is building global information systems. While some large multinational corporations have had global systems in place for some time, the growing importance of global business and the Internet as a basis for electronic commerce now makes this feature a required part of the IT management system for most firms. There are, of course, some businesses—those involved in local services—that may not need a global IS, but the need for global thinking about information systems applies more broadly than might be thought. A 1997 survey of small, Midwestern businesses conducted by one of the authors found that more than 40 percent see themselves competing

on a global scale. These firms now or in the near future will have a need for a global information system.

Reasons for Global Systems   Ives and Jarvenpaa (1991) suggest that there are ten reasons why user-managers are requesting the creation of global systems:

1. **Global Customer Requirements.** Global customers include travelers who require consistent service worldwide and customers that demand common worldwide services to support their integrated international business operations.
2. **Global Products.** Worldwide marketing and distribution programs require a global perspective on supporting information systems.
3. **Rationalized Operations.** IT is used to coordinate worldwide manufacturing processes.
4. **Flexible Operations.** Businesses want to be able to move operations between countries as labor rates or skills, raw material availability, laws, trade agreements, and other factors dictate.
5. **Joint Resources.** National subsidiaries may share facilities, people, or materials (for example, oil tankers, warehouses, or consultants).
6. **Duplicate Facilities.** The company may operate similar manufacturing plants, refineries, or sales

Table 15.2

IS Training Architecture

Required courses:

Hourly	Professional	Executive
OfficeVision	OfficeVision	OfficeVision
Windows Basic	Windows Basic	Windows Basic
Basic Network Navigation	Basic Network Navigation	Basic Network Navigation
Microsoft Office	Microsoft Office	Microsoft Office
MS Word—Basics	MS Word—Basics	MS Word—Basics
MS Word—Advanced	MS Word—Advanced	MS Word—Advanced
Excel—Basics	Excel—Basics	Excel—Basics
	Excel—Advanced	Excel—Advanced
	Windows Advanced	FoxPro or Access
	FoxPro or Access	Microsoft Project
		Excel Charts and Graphs

Electives:

Windows		UNIX	Miscellaneous
MS-Access Basic	Lotus 1-2-3 Basic	ArcView	Internet training
MS-Access	Lotus 1-2-3 Advanced	UNIX Basic	
Intermediate	PCAnywhere	UNIX Advanced	
MS-Access Advanced	MS-PowerPoint Basic		
MS-Excel Basic	MS-PowerPoint		
MS-Excel	Advanced		
Intermediate	MS-Project Basic		
MS-Excel Advanced	MS-Project Advanced		
FoxPro Basic	MS-Word Basic		
FoxPro Intermediate	MS-Word Advanced		
FoxPro Advanced			

offices in different countries, so common software can be used to support all of these sites.

7. **Scarce Resources.** A unit of the firm may need to use a unique resource or materials that cannot be made available economically at all sites, and careful coordination of use is required through integrated materials movement systems.

8. **Risk Reduction.** Care must be taken to account properly for currency conversions, international sourcing of raw materials, or bidding on international projects. A global system is necessary to guarantee that any international site can equally participate without fear of inaccuracy.

9. **Legal Requirements.** A subsidiary that sells in or uses products from multiple countries requires a system that handles laws and accounting practices in all countries involved.

10. **Economies of Scale.** Consolidated data centers and systems can reduce costs, increase reliability and consistency, and ease maintenance and evolution of systems.

Organizing for Global Systems   The choice of how to manage IT internationally is contingent on how the organization as a whole is managed globally. Strong divisional or headquarters control will influence the stance on international IT management. The degree of interdependence between international units will suggest the requirements for tight or loose information flows in different functional and staff areas. The size and location of business operations will also influence the decision. Large groups that are geographically close would suggest a common IS organization, whereas numerous small and highly scattered units would be more difficult to service from one central IS group.

According to Roche (1992), U.S. business has tended to adopt a decentralized strategy for managing IT on a global basis. This tendency was driven by the difficulty of dealing with international differences and the unavailability or lack of uniform quality of the technology components worldwide. Consequently, only a few truly global applications have been developed. Instead, organizations have deployed systems according to old organization structures. Thus, IT deployment has tended to follow, not lead, the corporation. Roche cites the case of Ford Motor Company as an example in which global business and IS strategy are meshing, although IS strategy is responding to business direction, not leading the business. As part of Ford's efforts to implement the "world car" concept, Ford IS units have installed a second data communications network dedicated to computer-aided design workstations worldwide. Ford insists on common systems in this area and places the burden of proof on local units for justifying unique systems for a particular engineering center or manufacturing facility. In contrast, because there is no driving business reason to globalize dealers, such systems as order processing are localized.

IS has the same basic options as does the corporation for organizing itself on a global scale—imperialistic, multidomestic, and global (Reck, 1989). Each has different implications for IS management. The imperialistic strategy tightly controls international operations, making them simply extensions of headquarters. In such firms IS management would usually be centralized, there would be a common architecture for IT, computing activities would be concentrated in one or a few data centers, planning and funding of systems would be centralized, and a strict hierarchical IS organization structure would be used.

A multidomestic IS style is highly decentralized with only necessary financial ties between subsidiaries and headquarters. In a sense, a multidomestic company is not truly global, but a federation of different companies. Thus, IS management and operations are localized.

A global IS strategy promotes a high degree of integration, but also a high degree of local control. Teamwork best describes this style. IS in a global firm will integrate a few key technologies and resources as part of the IT architecture, such as data and telecommunications, with dispersal of most planning and control. The IS organization usually follows a matrix structure. Of course, many companies follow a mixed strategy, such as employing an imperialistic strategy for financial systems, multidomestic strategy for sales systems, and global strategy for manufacturing systems.

Barriers to Global IT Management   There are various characteristics of the countries in which an organization operates that influence decisions on global IT management:

- Language, character set, and currency differences influence how easily a central systems development group and common or shared systems can satisfy user needs. Local accounting and securities practices directly affect the nature of financial systems. The ability and willingness of clerical staff to use systems based in a foreign language or currency must be considered. Fluctuations in exchange rates can drastically affect the cost of distributed IS operations.
- The support of operations across many time zones may not be possible from one central staff and from centralized systems. For example, central systems have to be shut down occasionally for maintenance and upgrade, and such scheduling becomes difficult across various time zones, working hours, holidays, and vacation schedules. On the other hand, a wide geographical telecommunications network can shift work between data centers, order entry offices, telemarketing facilities, and user help desks so that operations can proceed outside of normal local business hours and on local holidays.
- Regulations and tariffs for transporting data across international boundaries dictate the economics of processing and integration (see Chapter 14 for further discussion of this topic). Laws exist in some parts of the world that require programming and operations to be done locally, thus ensuring that national data resources are not abused by foreign companies. Import restrictions or tariffs may make the use of standard (foreign-developed) software and hardware prohibitively expensive in certain

international units. A company must also protect its intellectual property rights for such assets as computer software. Although several international efforts have tried to standardize the process of intellectual property protection, companies still suffer substantial copyright losses. Losses from U.S. commercial software companies alone are estimated in the billions of dollars annually.

- The cultures and professional practices of different countries influence the systems development process (for example, in some European countries IS personnel are unionized) and suggest whether one staff or several staffs are needed. Also, differences in accounting practices, tax calculations, and regulations make the deployment of standard application systems for business operations difficult because such systems must support local practices as well as organization standards.

- Computer industry standards for computer and telecommunications equipment influence to what degree operations in different locations can be tightly linked. The existence or strength of computer vendors or representatives to support and maintain local equipment and staff affects the ability to have common technology and, hence, common systems in all countries. Even the availability of quality electrical power affects the ability to have local operations.

- The cost and availability of reliable voice and data telecommunications networks influence the ability to share systems, to transfer data electronically without rekeying, and to build on-line systems in foreign sites. The difficulties of getting telephone lines installed and maintained can significantly increase the costs for on-line systems. The quality of circuits and of telecommunication services varies enormously around the world. Rates for the same services can vary by as much as ten times, depending on the country. Although there have been many improvements in recent years, there are still some limitations on using the same telecommunications equipment in several countries, and it still may be a challenge to work with highly bureaucratic postal telephone and telegraph authorities.

- Information technology platforms and systems development approaches vary worldwide. Although many of the same technologies exist around the world, IS professionals may prefer to use home-grown brands for performance, support, and familiarity. A country-specific IS unit in a multinational corporation frequently prefers to use its national software development standard method to simplify training, for compatibility with older systems, and for reasons of national pride. The deployment of standard application software can be deterred by such differences.

- The availability and cost of trained local IS professionals and consultants to provide local management expertise and the costs to relocate your personnel to a foreign site are important. The education level, absenteeism, and other characteristics of the general labor force also affect the nature of systems that can be developed or used effectively. Labor rates for IS professionals across the world also vary considerably. Today, some U.S. firms are taking programming assignments offshore to take advantage of these labor rate differences.

Planning for Global Systems   As in other areas of the business, the extension of IS management to other countries should be carefully planned. When considering international mergers or acquisitions, IS management issues should be researched. In fact, the proper conduct of IS management is crucial to the success of global firms, because IS links units across space and time.

Roche (1992) outlines eight elements of a successful global IS plan for a tightly integrated multinational corporation. Although some of these elements are debatable, they suggest a need for comprehensive policies to make global systems successful.

1. **Informatize strategic alliances.** Value chain linkages (see Chapter 13) are common practice in global firms to enhance international competitiveness. Improved information and telecommunication services between alliance partners (such as international EDI) make the coordination between global partners easier. A shared international database, containing, for example, sales referrals or vendor data, can provide valuable business intelligence.

2. **Develop international systems development skills.** Systems development staff must have a global view of the business, and they must be able to work with foreign cultures and different management styles in different countries. Management of international projects requires a sensitivity to international politics within a foreign unit and within its

local business environment. Standards of IS practice vary across countries, and a champion with global influence may be necessary for successful systems deployment.

3. Build an anticipative infrastructure. It is necessary to build for the future because global systems generally take longer to deploy than single country systems. A goal to build transportable systems requires careful coordination of technology throughout all international operations. Key elements of this strategy are common telecommunications, consistent hardware and software platforms, and global management of data definitions.

4. Tear down the national model. Totally independent or semiautonomous data centers and systems will never allow a truly global firm to adequately link business operations worldwide. The tearing down of the national model begins with the hardware and system software standards of strategy 3 above. The second stage is consolidation of application systems to facilitate international workflow automation, such as in production scheduling, inventory control, and order processing.

5. Capture residual value. The heart of this strategy is eliminating duplicate facilities and staff and then using the cost savings to invest in improving other international operations. Thus, IT becomes a contributor to international growth of the global firm. Business process redesign may be necessary for a thorough capture of residual value. As is typical of such projects, the driving force for consolidation of international IS functions may be customer demands for seamless interaction with the global business.

6. Exploit the coming liberalization in international telecommunications. The monopolistic dominance of national telephone organizations is slowly but inevitably disappearing. Several nationalized telephone systems were privatized in the mid-1990s. Similar to the example of the Bell System divestiture in the United States, a global firm must be ready to take advantage of opportunities that will result (such as lower costs, higher quality and more modern services, faster installation). These changes are especially dramatic in Asia and Eastern Europe, where countries may leapfrog technology stages by installing wireless telecommunications systems as part of economic revitalization efforts. On the other hand, the lack of qualified people and sufficient capital to support this infrastructure will require considerable investment by the governments and the private sector.

7. Homogenize data structures. Data elements that are needed to manage the global business must be standardized. National pools of key data make this global management of data as a resource (see Chapter 14) a difficult but necessary task. Without such standards, it is impossible to obtain a global view of an organization (for example, international sales comparisons require common product-class distinctions, units of measure, time units, back-order handling, and booked versus billed designations).

8. Globalize human resources. Most IS employees take a national and not a global view of systems, which is caused by a lack of training, country-specific experience, and reward systems. Worldwide promotions and relocations can help overcome such narrow mindsets. Special IS skills found in certain countries can be globalized by focused training programs, careful project team selection to maximize exposure to diverse expertise, language education, and a thorough international IS skills inventory.

As organizations become more global, user-managers must consider how to design and deliver information services to all international operations. User-managers should communicate plans for globalization to the IS department and work with IS professionals to evolve the IT architecture to accommodate the global nature of future business.

8. Appropriate IS Organization Design

Just as the IS leader must be selected to fulfill the expectations for IT in the total organization, the IS organization itself must be designed to fit the information vision as well. A wide variety of IS organization structures may be found in small to large organizations and in all kinds of industries. The options are almost endless. Several structures are presented here that demonstrate the range of structures used. Regardless of the design, an effective IT management system must align the IS organization with its mission.

The major organizational elements of an IS function are operations, systems development and maintenance, technical services, and administration. These elements or pieces can be arranged in many ways and located throughout the organization. Although the trend is clearly toward the distributed IS organization, many hybrids, including federal type structures, exist.

Operations include data entry, centralized machine operation, tape and disk file library management, hardware/network maintenance, and job scheduling. Systems development includes analysis and design, programming, package acquisition, system installation and conversion, training, and application software maintenance. Technical services is responsible for system software maintenance, technology assessment, and data administration. Administration includes capacity and systems planning, budgeting, personnel management and training, and development of standards and procedures.

Other important IS activities, such as end-user support (for example, the information center) and electronic data processing (EDP) auditing, are often separate units and may report outside the central IS organization. The function of research and development, which is responsible for researching new technologies, forecasting trends in technology, and diffusing their use throughout the organization, is very important in many organizations. This group may have 15 to 20 employees in a large company that takes an aggressive stance with information technology. The R&D group may become involved in pilot or demonstration projects. Once this group proves that a given technology is viable and has potential uses, further development is turned over to other systems or user groups.

Figure 15.5 illustrates four different generic structures for the IS organization. Each shows a different arrangement for the IS functions and the specific division of responsibility for IT between IS and user-managers. These four structures are certainly not inclusive of all possible schemes. For example, many IS organization structures decentralize systems development but centralize operations. However, the four options highlight some of the structures that are possible in organizing the IS function. An organization may also have several of these structures, with different operating units organizing their own systems organization in different ways. For example, one division could be running a centralized internal IS organization handling all its IS activities, and another division could work within a service structure. Further, these organization designs are presented and explained in the extreme, to highlight the salient features of such arrangements. Most organizations are a blend of these options.

Classic IS   The classic IS organization of Figure 15.5(A) is a highly centralized and task-oriented structure. The IS director is a manager of technical personnel, not a general business manager. A pool of analysts and programmers is used interchangeably as new systems and maintenance projects are approved. Operations, whether physically centralized or distributed, is managed by the central IS group. Systems programmers maintain language compilers, the operating systems, telecom software, and other system utilities. Data center and network staff operate and maintain the facilities. Batch data entry is performed in-house or by outsourcing to vendors; in this design, the operations group could even handle a telephone order processing center.

The focus of the classic IS organization is on efficiency (low cost) of systems development and operations and on skill specialization. IS careers follow through various levels of project administration and lateral moves. There are typically few job transfers in and out of the IS organization. This type of organization can be duplicated, on a smaller scale, in autonomous divisions of a large organization or in a medium-sized business. In smaller businesses, the IS director and head of systems development and maintenance could be the same person, with a computer operator/programmer reporting to him or her. As the name implies, many IS organizations started with this structure, and some still use it.

Functional IS   The functional area IS organization of Figure 15.5(B) is a precursor to the distributed IS organizations found in many companies today. Here, the central IS staff is broken into separate development groups for different line units, such as marketing systems and production systems, and staff units such as support services. Particular staff members in the development group and/or in user groups are appointed to liaison roles with their counterparts in IS or business functions. Business students with a concentration in IS are prime candidates for these liaison roles because they have the skills to bridge the technical and business

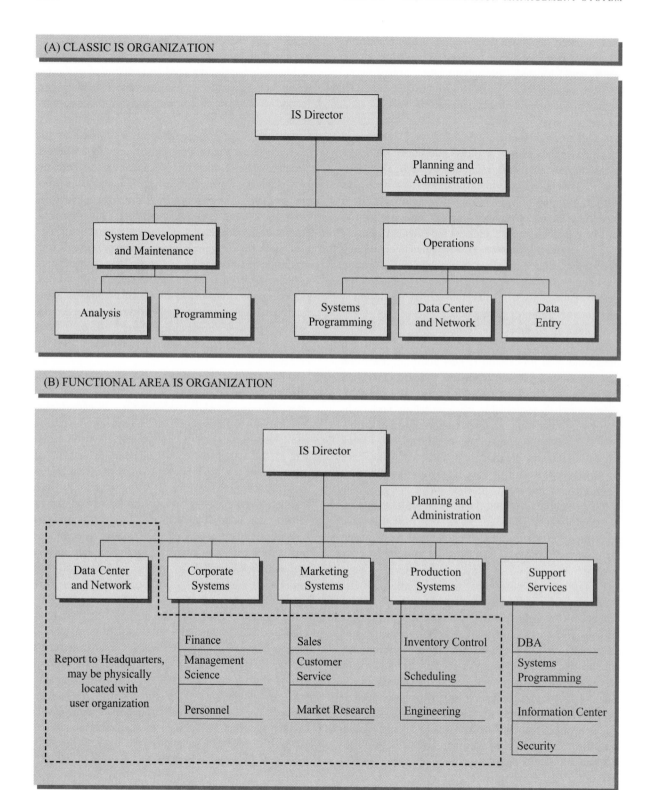

Figure 15.5 Alternative IS Organization Structures

(C) SERVICE-ORIENTED IS ORGANIZATION

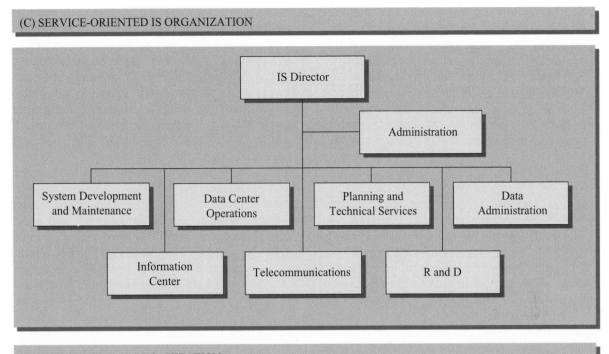

(D) DISTRIBUTED IS ORGANIZATION

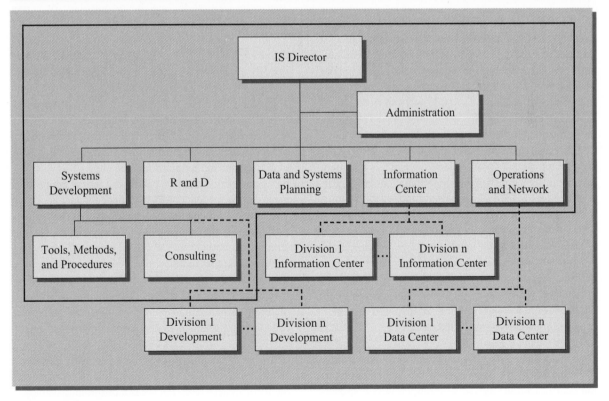

Figure 15.5 *(continued)*

areas. Distributed technology may be used, with specialized equipment and software for different user groups, but IS professionals and the other information resources may not be distributed in the same way.

The focus of the functional area IS organization is to serve the needs of particular client groups, often at the expense of the overall organization. Considerable negotiation occurs between user-managers and IS professionals when resources allocated to IS are insufficient to handle all the required work. A steering committee is often used to allocate resources. Transfer in and out of the IS organization occurs through the business units. Frequently, IS project management might actually be done by a business manager on assignment to the IS line organization. Corporate IS support is similarly handled by a corporate functional group.

An extreme case of the functional IS approach is a totally decentralized strategy in which each business unit has a complete IS organization. Such styles are used in some holding companies or other organizations that encompass unrelated lines of business, emphasize strong local autonomy, or actively change by acquisition, merger, or divestiture.

Service IS   The service-oriented IS organization of Figure 15.5(C) recognizes the growing importance of the functions of data administration and telecommunications management. The research and development group scans emerging technologies, evaluates alternative products, and sets standards and approved equipment for all of IS and user computing. The information center supports users with personal computers or those using fourth-generation tools on centralized equipment. In this organization, systems development and operations are typically centralized, although personal computers are actively used for decision support systems and report generation.

The focus of the service-oriented IS organization is responsiveness to the needs for major systems, management of a corporate data and systems architecture, and the support of users doing their own small-scale computing. Transfer of personnel between systems development, the information center, and business organizations is reasonably frequent.

Distributed IS   The fully distributed IS organization of Figure 15.5(D) is characterized by the staff nature of the central IS unit. Systems development is responsi-

ble for evaluating, acquiring, developing, and training activities concerning tools, methods, and procedures used in systems analysis, design, and programming. Systems building is usually done in line division units, with consulting help from the IS group. The IS group may also act as a hired contractor, often in competition with external consulting firms, when the divisional group does not have the capacity or qualifications for parts of projects. Technology is highly distributed, with the central IS group possibly responsible for management of the backbone network, systems security and auditing policies, and technology transfer to the divisions. In the early 1990s, organizations began to consolidate decentralized data centers, while still maintaining distributed IS staff. These structure types came to be known as federal organizations. Client/server technology makes such a hybrid approach easier to deploy.

The focus of the typical distributed IS organization is to develop and manage the corporate plan for IS and to assist the divisions in making the best use of information technology. IS organization staff may move between the central and divisional groups and may assume an IS specialist role or a business manager role. Central IS may be responsible for career planning of all IS professionals.

The IS Subsidiary   Some organizations have adopted the strategy of making the IS organization a wholly owned subsidiary, responsible for its own financial and market survival. In this structure, IS is treated like a vendor by the business units with separate cost and revenue accounting. Sometimes, creating a subsidiary is a test to determine if contracting out IS is more cost-effective than keeping an internal unit.

Such a subsidiary is usually put into a competitive position. The parent company units are free to contract with other suppliers for IS services, and the subsidiary is allowed to provide services to noncompetitors. This strategy is another method for managing IT more efficiently and for making the IS organization more responsive to user needs. Typically, systems development and operations are moved into the subsidiary; planning, data administration, and other infrastructure functions are retained by the parent company.

Selecting the Right Organization Structure   The above IS organization structures illustrate several arrangements of IS activities. Each has a different distribution of IT management functions between a central IS group, distributed IS groups in business organizations, and user-managers themselves.

The nature of distributed IS operations and some of the operational reasons for such systems were covered in earlier chapters. Not only can the IS operations of data collection and processing power be distributed, but the systems development staff and managerial control of IS can also be distributed. It is important to note that the decision on how to distribute IS operations is separate from the decision on how to distribute IT management. When these decisions are mixed together, confusion and unproductive discussions can occur. The purpose here is to consider factors affecting the location of the management of the IS function, not the economies of locating data processing operations close to the suppliers and users of data. As noted previously, IS management centralization and decentralization should not be considered absolutes; most organizations today have a hybrid approach.

Several key factors affect the structure and location of IS organization functions:

- Business characteristics, such as number and size of products or market divisions and their locations.
- Level within the organization of the most senior IS manager or officer.
- How the rest of the enterprise is organized, including global operations.
- Types of technologies managed by IS.
- The role of IS in the organization.
- The organizational philosophy on the responsibility of business managers for IT.

The following IT management functions are almost always (to some degree) centralized:

- Support, consulting, and training.
- Direction and standards setting and architecture development.
- Development and/or purchase of common systems that serve the entire organization (e.g., order entry, personnel, and accounting systems).
- Operation of the corporate data center and backbone or wide area telecommunications network.
- Integration of related but separate systems and technologies.
- Research and development into new information technology.

- Leadership in exploiting information technology for competitive gain.
- IS professional career path management.

Even these central functions are undertaken with considerable input from distributed IS groups.

Beyond these core functions, there is no generally accepted rule on when IT management (and what parts of it) should be centralized, decentralized, or mixed in some way. Most important is the organizational fit, that is, the management structure for IT should in great measure parallel the general organization structure, mission, strategy, and objectives for IS.

Boynton, Jacobs, and Zmud (1992) have outlined key questions that can be used for developing the most appropriate IT management structure (see Figure 15.6). The challenge is to evaluate these questions in a particular organizational situation and to consider what the answers indicate about the best structure. Not surprisingly, it is common to find frequent reorganizations of IS functions as the answers to these questions inevitably change. Structural shifts occur because of technology, business unit success and failure, a desire to make systems have more strategic value, turnover in key business leaders and hence business direction, and a tendency to become too central or too autonomous. As the story goes, a good IS organizational consultant only needs two file folders. One contains the boilerplate of the report that recommends centralized IS management to the client, and the other folder contains the skeleton of the decentralization plan. When the one report is submitted, the consultant simply puts a tickler note on his calendar to call the client in about three years. The other report will be needed then to undo the problems of following the first solution in the extreme.

9. Regular Performance Measurement

Another key element in a modern IT management system is the regular evaluation of the IS organization by its internal customers. Many user-managers are not sure they are getting their money's worth from the IS function, even after many years of investment. More importantly, many organizations simply do not know what the impact of IT investments has been. Often, huge cost savings were never realized, project budgets were exceeded, head count was not reduced or personnel were simply moved to more sophisticated jobs,

Networking Resources

- To what degree do our business units require networking capabilities?
- Do we need to transport information in the form of data, voice, video, text, graphics, and/or images? Internally or externally?
- Do we need to connect business units internally for electronic mail, access to data, and so forth?
- Do the business units need to connect externally with business partners (i.e., via electronic data interchange)?
- Do we need to reduce costs by sharing networking resources?

Shared Data

- To what extent are data (e.g., product, marketing, and supplier data) shared across any of our business units?
- Do we need standardized subject databases?
- Do the functional areas need to share more than financial data (e.g., customer, market, product, and services data)?
- Do the business units need to share data with customers, suppliers, or buyers?

Common Application Systems

- To what extent do the business units have common application system requirements?
- Do we need consistent application architecture (e.g., consistent office automation or electronic mail) across the firm?
- Should we have a standardized presence or image with customers or suppliers?
- Do the functional areas need high levels of integration and coordination?
- Do the functional areas need process integration (e.g., order entry, billing, or customer service)?

Human Resources

- To what extent are the people required to run critical systems becoming more difficult to find and more expensive to hire and retain?
- Do we need to increase productivity in building information systems?
- Do we need to maximize critical skills?
- Do we need to support remote operations or provide remote technical support?
- Are critical skills in short supply? Should we have backup people with these skills?

(Boynton, Jacobs, and Zmud, 1992)

Figure 15.6 Questions for Initiating Management Dialogue on IT Management Structure

and the important benefits could not be directly attributed to the use of IT. By contrast, certain general impacts are clear. Many organizations have become very dependent on IT, and IT is often being used for competitive advantage. In these instances, systems are critical to the success of the organization.

Organizations and individual managers need agreed-upon and measurable criteria by which to judge the health and contribution of the IS organization and the systems it manages. IS organizations also need metrics to judge the quality of their work. We concentrate in this section, however, on the measures of most interest to the user-manager.

Measures of IS Unit Success   Traditional productivity measurement approaches, such as cost-benefit analysis and return on investment, can be used to justify and evaluate individual systems, as discussed in Chapter 10. A wide variety of other criteria for evaluating the IS organization are possible, many of which are outlined in Figure 15.7. These criteria are used in combination; no one or two measures adequately provide the complete picture of the contribution of the IS department.

The IS evaluation criteria of Figure 15.7 require specific measures to be useful, some of which will be subjective. For example, the "Meeting business objectives" criterion could be measured by an opinion survey involving such questions as:

- Does the IS plan support the corporate strategic plan?
- Would the organization be out of business without the IS unit?

- Meeting business objectives: This means increasing business effectiveness and developing systems that support annual and long-term business goals and directions.
- Responding rapidly and economically to new needs: Reducing the cycle from product idea generation to its market introduction can have tremendous value in cost reduction, personnel time, earlier revenue generation, and competitive advantage.
- Expanding business or services: Reaching new markets, adding features (often information-based) to existing products or services, or improving product service quality can be used for differentiation and revenue generation.
- Developing an architecture and plan: An architecture allows line managers to access easily the data now contained in data storage systems and supports the more rapid development and deployment of new systems.
- Operating reliable and efficient technology resources: Reliable and efficient operation of both internal systems and external services (such as order entry, reservations, and point-of-sale) is essential for the business to succeed.
- Focusing on the customer: Better customer support helps the organization to retain customers, gain new customers, and increase sales; the goal is to make it easy for the customer to do business with us and for us to know as much about the customer as he expects us to know.
- Providing quality IS staff: Indicators such as a high level of education, low turnover rate, and a large number of employees outplaced to line management jobs all suggest an IS organization of productive and useful people.
- Reducing size of backlog: Although a backlog of work indicates a strong demand for IS services, a large backlog can be a source of considerable frustration and unmet business opportunities; with a proper mix of end-user development, use of fourth-generation languages, and purchasing package software, this backlog should be reduced to a manageable and reasonable level.
- Satisfying users: In the spirit of the business focusing on a satisfied customer, the IS organization can be measured by how satisfied line managers are with the technology, systems, and support services provided to them.

Figure 15.7 IS Evaluation Criteria

Other criteria can be assessed by more quantitative and objective measures. For example, the "Operating reliable and efficient technology resources" criterion could be measured by:

- On-line response time.
- Computer up-time as a percentage of total time.
- Number of system crashes.

As with any measurement system, an organization should measure only what is important, what needs improvement, and what is meaningful to some audience. Typically, measures of time, money, and defects are the most useful. Kaplan and Norton (1992) call for using a set of measures that "balance" various assessment categories, including financial measures as well as the drivers of future performance:

- Customer satisfaction (such measures as on-time delivery of new systems, number of defects in a system).
- Internal processes (for IS, this could be the productivity of computer system developers, often measured by an industry standard of number of function points per month).
- Innovation and learning (education level of IS staff and user-managers).

Service Level Agreements The IS organization can be evaluated through a **service level agreement** similar to one that would be written with an external supplier. This agreement makes expectations—from both IS and user-management—explicit and defines agreed-upon criteria for a successful system and quality service.

User Satisfaction Measures If IS is viewed as a service organization, then user satisfaction is a very important measure of IS success. Such measures are an excellent way for managers to communicate their assessment of IS to senior officers and IS executives. Although not economic in nature and not related directly to business impacts such as reduced inventory, increased customer satisfaction, or improved product quality, user satisfaction measures can be captured easily and compared over time. User attitudes about systems and the IS department affect a user-manager's willingness to work with IS professionals in the kinds of partnerships discussed earlier.

Typically, an annual survey would be conducted for each major system, systems that may have problems, IS support organizations such as the information center, or any area of IS that is receiving criticism; that is, a user satisfaction survey can be conducted on an application system or on an IS unit. Different levels of managers should be surveyed separately, because their different systems perspectives and roles (for example, direct user, source of funding, supervisor) can affect their evaluation.

Figure 15.8 lists some criteria that can appear on user satisfaction surveys for a specific system and other criteria that could be customized to particular IS units, such as systems development or end-user support. The survey would ask the respondent to rate the individual system or unit on, for example, a one-to-ten scale (low to high performance) or ask customers to respond on a scale of strongly disagree to strongly agree concerning various statements involving the criteria in Figure 15.8. The survey might also ask the user-manager to indicate how important each criterion is, so that a weighted assessment can be derived. The survey may include some open-ended questions that ask for problems, complaints, praise, particular system features to add or delete, and what the customer likes best or least about the system or IS unit.

10. A Change Management System

There is no other organization in a business that initiates more change for others than does the IS organization. New systems, new technologies, and new ways to operate the business or communicate with colleagues emanate from the IS department on a regular

---

THE DIFFICULTY OF CHANGE

Let it be noted that there is no more delicate matter to take in hand, nor more dangerous to conduct, nor more doubtful in its success, than to set up as a leader in the introduction of changes. For he who innovates will have for his enemies all those who are well off under the existing order, and only lukewarm supporters in those who might be better off under the new.

[Machiavelli, 1513]

USER SATISFACTION CRITERIA FOR INDIVIDUAL SYSTEMS

- Accuracy of outputs
- Quality/readability of output format
- Completeness of outputs
- Relevance of outputs
- Completeness of or accessibility to database
- Currency of database
- Response time (or other measure of work completed)
- Availability
- Mean time between failures
- Downtime or malfunction recovery time
- Charges/costs
- Quality of system documentation
- Number and severity of security breaches
- Ease of operation
- Ease of making changes
- Increased confidence in decisions and actions taken due to system
- Extent of achieving expected benefits

USER SATISFACTION CRITERIA FOR IS UNITS

- Quality of system specification documents
- Size of request backlog or workload
- Projects completed on time and within budget
- Speed at which requested system changes are made
- Professionalism of IS staff
- Nature of relationships with IS staff
- Business knowledge of IS staff
- Quality of user training
- User feeling of involvement in systems management

Figure 15.8 Criteria for User Satisfaction Surveys

basis. As a result, an effective IT management system must include a **change management** system.

In order to design a change management system, some basics about change and the adoption of innovation must be understood. First, when introducing change into an organization, one cannot assume that people will change just because they are told to change. Second, one cannot assume that people will change their behavior in the desired or expected way—they often change in ways that are unintended and unexpected.

The remainder of this section introduces some basic ideas that are helpful in managing the behavioral change involved in implementing new systems. Because the ability to manage change is essential for success as an IS professional or user-manager, it is hoped that the reader explores this topic more thoroughly through other avenues.

Attitudes Toward Change According to Student (1978), people do not resist change as much as they resist being changed. Thus, acceptance of change is more likely if those who must change have influence in determining the nature of the new state. People tend to support what they help create, and meaningful participation provides both comfort with the change and a sense of responsibility for the success of the new system.

Contrary to the common saying, familiarity breeds comfort and acceptance, not contempt. Changes in feelings and attitudes do not take place instantaneously—they always take time. Student cites several studies that show that mere exposure to a person, thing, or concept changes attitudes from aversion to acceptance and attachment. Thus, those implementing change need to allow plenty of time to overcome initial resistance and for attitudes to change, and provide opportunities—such as pilot testing—for people to become familiar with a new system before acceptance is required.

Student notes that participants often test the soundness of a new system and the degree of support that it has from other important participants. Those implementing change must anticipate some skepticism toward a new system and expect people to test to see if the system is beneficial to them. Furthermore, people often will take some time before accepting a new system to determine whether the organization is serious about the new system or whether it will be sabotaged by a little foot-dragging. It is obvious that omissions and bugs in the new system can create great problems during this psychological testing process and encourage resistance to change. This resistance is one of the reasons why it is so important to thoroughly test new systems before they are installed.

Student also describes a stress factor associated with change. Facing the unknown consequences of change may challenge an individual's sense of adequacy and may seriously threaten self-esteem. Not only do individuals experience stress during change, but organizational units may be under significant tension associated with the resulting individual stress.

There is a relationship between the type of change required by a new system and the difficulty involved in accomplishing the change. Changes in procedures and practices usually involve relatively little stress, but changing role expectations involves more stress, and changing basic orientation and values involves even greater stress. Those implementing change must be aware that systems that involve changing role expecta-

tions are likely to encounter substantial resistance, and systems that require different orientations and values may be quite difficult to implement.

The Lewin/Schein Change Model The classic **Lewin/Schein change model** depicted in Figure 15.9 describes planned change in an organization as consisting of three stages—unfreezing, moving, and refreezing (Lewin, 1947; Schein, 1987). This perspective is very helpful in planning and managing change due to information systems.

The unfreezing stage includes two aspects. First, a felt need for change must be established in those who will be changing or there is no motivation for changing. Second, because change tends to be viewed as risky, it is helpful to create an atmosphere in which change is safe. Those who will be changing must be convinced that they will not be hurt by giving up the old, safe behavior.

The moving stage also involves two aspects. The first is the provision of the information needed to bring about the changes in attitudes and behavior. Until the knowledge and skills required by the changed roles are available, change cannot take place. This information not only must be available, but it must be assimilated by those who must change, which means that time, motivation, and assistance in learning new skills and attitudes may be required.

The refreezing stage fixes the new behavior as the accepted routine. It involves integrating the new behavior into the larger, ongoing behavior, rather than viewing it as something new and special. Refreezing frequently requires diffusing the change throughout the relevant social system, which may be much larger than the directly involved group of individuals.

- Unfreezing
  - Establish a felt need
  - Create a safe atmosphere
- Moving
  - Provide necessary information
  - Assimilate knowledge and develop skills
- Refreezing

Figure 15.9 The Lewin/Schein Change Model

The Innovation Adoption Perspective   An innovation is an idea or methodology that is perceived as new by an individual. Adoption is a decision to use an innovation. Many of the most important applications of information technology cannot be mandated by the organization; instead, they must be adopted by those who are to use them. Decision support systems, office automation systems, and executive information systems must be adopted by their users because the managers must use them to support their ongoing activities—they do not replace these activities. Strategic systems that serve customers or suppliers cannot be mandated. Many conventional information systems have failed because they were installed but never adopted. Thus, if you want to manage the changes that are involved in using information technology, viewing these changes as innovations that must be adopted provides a valuable perspective.

Everett M. Rogers (1962), a rural sociologist, studied hundreds of research studies on the diffusion of innovations, and produced a general model of the adoption process (see Figure 15.10), which views the adoption process as taking place in five stages. If one is interested in encouraging the adoption of an innovation, it is helpful to understand this process that individuals go through in adopting an innovation.

1. Awareness. Here individuals are exposed to the innovation, but lack complete information about it and are not yet motivated to seek further information.
2. Interest. At this stage, individuals become interested in the innovation and seek additional information. Although the individuals are favorably disposed to seek further information, they have not yet judged its personal value. The function of this stage is to increase the potential adopters' information about the innovation.

Figure 15.10 Rogers' Stages of the Adoption Process

3. Evaluation. Here individuals mentally try out the innovation, evaluate whether or not it is beneficial, and decide whether or not to try it. At this stage individuals are teetering on the brink and may need reinforcement or advice from someone they trust and respect before deciding to try the innovation.
4. Trial. At this stage, individuals tentatively use the innovation, on a small scale if possible, in order to evaluate its value in their own situations. They may need and obtain more information about how to use the innovation at this stage. The individuals are not committed to adoption until they have evaluated the results of the trial. The ease of using and learning to use the innovation is crucial here, because if potential adopters find the trial to be difficult and get discouraged, the innovation is likely to be rejected.
5. Adoption. At this stage the individuals have favorably evaluated the results of the trial and decide to continue full use of the innovation.

Rogers' five-stage process describes a successful adoption, but an innovation may be rejected at any of these stages. The potential adopter may never become aware of the innovation, may never develop interest in it, may lose interest after evaluation, or may reject it after some trial. Furthermore, rejection of an innovation can occur after adoption. Rogers examined many case histories and found a relatively high rate of discontinuance after initial adoption. This seems to relate to the third stage of the Lewin/Schein model—for some reason the refreezing stage failed.

Rogers also presented five characteristics of an innovation that affect its ease of adoption. In dealing with information technology, it may be important to define the system so that it has characteristics that make it easy to adopt.

1. Relative advantage is the degree to which an innovation is superior to ideas it supersedes. The perception of relative advantage is more important than the reality in adoption decisions. As marketing people know, this perception may be altered by information dissemination, education, and promotion programs.
2. Compatibility is the degree to which the innovation is consistent with the existing values, attitudes, opinions, and past experiences of the potential adopters. It may be possible to design a new system to obtain its major benefits without requiring major

changes in the existing values, attitudes, and opinions of its users.

3. **Complexity** is the degree to which the innovation is difficult to understand and use. Again, perceived complexity is more important than actual complexity, so a system should appear simple to its users.
4. **Divisibility** is the degree to which an innovation can be tried on a limited basis. It is easier to make the decision to try an innovation if it can be tried without much investment of time or expense.
5. **Communicability** is the degree to which the results of the innovation can be observed by potential adopters or the ease with which the results can be explained to them.

As an example of how the ease-of-adoption criteria can be useful, consider corporate data modeling as discussed in Chapter 14. If corporate data modeling is viewed as an innovation that must be adopted and we examine the above characteristics that affect its ease of adoption, it would seem to fare poorly. Although it may have substantial long-term payoff for the organization, its relative advantage is usually several years in the future, and the benefits to the individual manager are not compelling. It is not compatible with existing values and attitudes because people are used to owning their own data, and most of them prefer not to give up this ownership. It is not easy to understand and use and is often perceived as complex. Its results are not easily observed or explained. No wonder corporate data modeling has been difficult to implement in many organizations.

Diffusion of an Innovation   In many cases, one is concerned with the diffusion of an innovation throughout an organization rather than in an adoption of the innovation by any one individual. The diffusion of an innovation throughout a group or an organization is very much a social process. Rogers reported that diffusion over time usually follows a bell-shaped curve, and this observation allowed him to categorize individuals in terms of how quickly they adopt an innovation. He called the first 2.5 percent the innovators and the next 13.5 percent the early adopters; these two groups are critical to success in diffusing an innovation through an organization.

The innovators tend to be quite adventuresome and have more cosmopolitan social relationships and

a wider set of sources of information. They are risk-takers who have the ability to understand and apply the technical knowledge required to use the innovation, but they are not usually opinion leaders in the organization or social group because they tend to be viewed as outsiders who are not in tune with the social norms of the group.

The early adopters, on the other hand, tend to be opinion leaders in their groups. Opinion leaders are very important in the diffusion of an innovation because they are looked up to as role models by others in the organization. If they reject the innovation, it may get no further in the group, but when they adopt it, most of the rest of the group will go along. It is important in sponsoring a new system to locate opinion leaders and do everything possible to help them to be successful early adopters.

Finally, the chances of success of an innovation are greatly improved if it has a **champion.** The champion probably has a stake in the success of the system and should be an opinion leader in the organization. A user-manager who is sponsoring a new system that must be diffused through an organization should do everything possible to identify opinion leaders and assist them in adopting the system.

SUMMARY

The nature of how organizations manage information systems and technologies is changing. Increasingly, IT is managed like other business units, with expectations for contribution to the organization and with shared responsibilities for all managers.

Although some IS professionals initially resisted management system changes such as end-user development and distributed IT management, the partnership of IS and business managers is now strong in most organizations. A business unit now typically manages the development of systems that primarily support that unit, and the unit is held accountable for the contribution of its systems to its success. The central IS unit acts as a technology transfer function, as a consultant to distributed IS units, and as an architect that provides the framework in which other units utilize information technology.

The importance of IT is reflected in many organizations by the establishment of a chief information officer or other senior IS executive responsible for linking the IT and business plans. A diverse set of other IS management positions exists in central IS departments as well as in line organizations. Career opportunities in IS are plentiful, challenging, and increasingly similar to other general management careers in possible long-term responsibilities and the essentials for success.

Organizations have not settled on one best way to organize the IS unit. The globalization of companies makes structuring this function even more difficult. Although history suggests that the IS function has periodically shifted between centralization and decentralization, today many organizations have very distributed IS functions. At some point early in the 21st century, if history repeats, organizations will decide that they are not achieving some of the advantages of a more centrally managed IT infrastructure, and some functions will be reeled in to headquarters. Thus, the function of the IS unit to develop and communicate a future vision for IT is extremely important. These efforts ease the pain of periodic moves to centralize and distribute responsibilities for IS operations, development, and management.

These issues and more must be dealt with in the design of an effective management system for IT. Only when combined with direction setting (setting a vision, an architecture, and an IS plan) and excellent management of the technology assets can an IS organization perform most effectively.

Review Questions

1. Why have IT management and structure changed in the past ten years? That is, what changes in IT or the business have caused the IS unit to be restructured or to take on a new mission?

2. How have the perspectives of IS professionals changed in the past 10 to 15 years?

3. Why are strictly financial measures like return on investment and cost-benefit analysis insufficient for evaluating information systems?

4. What are the major responsibilities of the chief information officer? How are these different from the traditional IS director?

5. Name and outline the essential characteristics of the four major generic IS organization structures discussed in this chapter.

6. What is IT outsourcing? Is it good or bad?

7. What is the largest cost in the IS budget today?

8. What are the characteristics of a good IS charge-back system?

9. What are some unique issues concerning IT management that arise in multinational firms or firms doing business in many countries?

10. What should be the nature of the partnership between IT and business managers?

Discussion Questions

1. If you were to write an IS department mission statement, what key words would you have used 10 years ago compared to the words you would use today?

2. What financial measures can be used to assess the contribution the IS organization makes to the business? What are the caveats involved with these measures?

3. What type of person in an organization should be considered for a chief information officer position? That is, what type of individual would be a prime candidate for such a job?

4. This chapter emphasizes the need for a partnership between IS and user-managers for managing IT. Define your concept of a management partnership and relate this to making people accountable for business operations and functions.

5. Review the various pros and cons of distributing the systems development organization between central IS and line management organizations.

6. What type of organization would benefit most from creating an IS subsidiary? What type of organization would benefit most from outsourcing IS operations?

7. Under what circumstances would you recommend an organization to adopt a direct chargeback scheme for IS services?

8. As the manager of a statewide ATM network, how would you evaluate the quality of the IS

organization serving you? If you were director of consumer marketing for a major appliance manufacturer, how would you evaluate the quality of the IS services you receive?

9. What arguments would you use to justify a career in IS management as a way to senior management in an organization?

REFERENCES

1993. "The changing role of the mainframe." *I/S Analyzer* 31 (January): 1–14.

1997. "The decade of the CIO." *CIO* 10 (September 15): 26–27.

Boynton, Andrew C., Gerry C. Jacobs, and Robert W. Zmud. 1992. "Whose responsibility is IT management?" *Sloan Management Review* 33 (Summer): 32–38.

Brown, Carol V. 1997. "Examining the emergence of hybrid IS governance solutions: Evidence from a single case site." *Information Systems Research* 8 (March): 69–94.

Brown, Carol V., and Sharon L. Magill. 1994. "Alignment of IS functions with the enterprise: toward a model of antecedents." *MIS Quarterly* 18 (December): 371–403.

Byrne, John A. 1996. "Has outsourcing gone too far?" *Business Week* (April 1):26–28.

Daily, John C. 1995. "What it takes to be CIO." *Datamation* 40 (November 1): 61–62.

Deans, P. Candace, and Michael J. Kane. 1992. *International Dimensions of Information Systems and Technology.* Boston: PWS-Kent Publishing Company.

Guez, Jean-Claude. 1992. "Systems integration for the international company." *The Journal of European Business* 4 (November/December): 10–14.

Henderson, John C. 1990. "Plugging into strategic partnerships: The critical IS connection." *Sloan Management Review* 31 (Spring): 7–18.

Ives, Blake, and Sirkka Jarvenpaa. 1991. "Applications of global information technology: Key issues for management." *MIS Quarterly* 15 (March): 33–49.

Kaplan, Robert S., and David P. Norton. 1992. "The balanced scorecard—measures that drive performance." *Harvard Business Review* 70 (January–February): 71–79.

Keen, Peter G. W. 1991. *Shaping the Future: Business Design through Information Technology.* Boston: Harvard Business School Press.

Laud, Robert L., and Peter K. Thies. 1997. "Great expectations: Structuring IT organizations that really deliver." *Business Horizons* 29 (July–August):25–35.

Lee, Louise. 1994. "Information chiefs get plaudits but rarely promotions." *Wall Street Journal* 77 (November 10): B1 and B11.

Lewin, Kurt. 1947. "Frontiers in group dynamics." *Human Relations* 1: 5–41.

Machiavelli, Niccolo. ca. 1513. *The Prince.* Translation by Hill Thompson (1988). Palm Springs, CA: ETC Publications.

Madnick, Stuart E. 1995. "Integrating information from global systems: Dealing with the 'on- and off-ramps' of the information superhighway." *Journal of Organizational Computing* 5 (2): 69–82.

Moad, Jeff. 1993. "Inside an outsourcing deal." *Datamation* 39 (February 15): 20–27.

Parker, Marilyn M., and Robert J. Benson. 1988. *Information Economics: Linking Business Performance to Information Technology.* Englewood Cliffs, NJ: Prentice Hall, Inc.

Reck, Robert H. 1989. "The shock of going global." *Datamation* 35 (August 1): 67–70.

Roche, Edward M. 1992. *Managing Information Technology in Multinational Corporations.* New York: Macmillan Publishing Company.

Rogers, Everett M. 1962. *Diffusion of Innovation.* New York: The Free Press.

Ross, Jeanne W., Cynthia M. Beath, and Dale L. Goodhue. 1996. "Develop long-term competitiveness through IT assets." *Sloan Management Review* 21 (Fall): 31–42.

Saviano, James P. 1997. "Are we there yet?" *CIO* 11 (June 1): 86-96.

Schein, Edgar H. 1987. *Process Consultation,* Volume II. Reading, Massachusetts: Addison-Wesley.

Schifrin, Matthew. 1997. "The new enablers—chief information officers." *Forbes* 158 (June 2): 138–143.

Slater, Derek. 1996. "More power to you." *CIO* 9 (October 15): 28.

Smith, Sheila, and Mary Silva Doctor. 1997. "Change channelers." *CIO* 10 (September 1): 32–36.

Student, K. R. 1978. "Managing change: A psychologist's perspective." *Business Horizons* 21 (December): 28–33.

Tractinsky, Noam, and Sirkka L. Jarvenpaa. 1995. "Information systems design decisions in a global versus domestic context." *MIS Quarterly* 19 (December 1995): 507–534.

THE CLARION SCHOOL FOR BOYS: EVALUATING INFORMATION SYSTEMS INVESTMENTS

John Young, business manager of the Clarion School for Boys, hung up the telephone as the school bell signaled the end of another day's classes. Young's conversation with Sean McHardey, the long-time superintendent of Clarion, was short and to the point. McHardey had called to confirm that Young would be prepared to present his long-range information systems (IS) plan at the quarterly Board of Trustees meeting scheduled for next week (June 18, 1996).

As an MBA student, Young had learned about the importance of an overall information systems strategy. McHardey's request, however, required Young to formalize a full plan, complete with projects and budgets. As business manager, Young knew that the Board of Trustees also wanted to hear that Clarion's current investment in information technology was paying off. Since 1993, when the board had approved a sizable investment in hardware and software, there had been little monitoring of the system's benefit.

Young had joined the Clarion School for Boys in August 1992. His previous job had been as an assistant to the controller at American Chemical Company in Chicago, a position he held for five years after receiving his MBA in finance from a well-known Midwestern business school.

After five years, Young had his fill of big companies and decided to move into a position with broader respon-

sibility. However, most of his days at Clarion had been spent "fighting fires" rather than planning business strategy. Although his position was quite different from what he had expected, he felt that the intangible rewards surpassed those at American Chemical. Young had developed several good friends at Clarion and enjoyed his daily routine.

The Clarion School

The Clarion School for Boys was founded in 1921 as "a refuge for wayward boys" through sponsorship of the Wisconsin Kiwanis Clubs. The school soon outgrew its only building on a farm near Milwaukee. Two large building projects were subsequently completed with the support of the Kiwanis. Construction of these two new dormitories marked a period of rapid expansion that was soon followed by a time of serious financial distress. Nearing bankruptcy in the 1930s, Clarion was placed under the administration of the Kiwanis International. During the next 50 years, Clarion established a diverse program of care that relied on the dedication and the community devotion of this fraternal organization.

Financial problems in the late 1960s and early 1970s, largely brought on by rising costs and declining support, influenced the Board of Trustees' decision to separate Clarion from financial dependence on the Kiwanis and rely more on per diem charges paid by government agencies and families and on fund drives as primary sources of funding for the school.

As involvement of the Kiwanis declined during the 1970s, additional paid staff were hired to replace the volunteers. Functional specialization increased as new staff positions were added. New programs which focused on specific student needs gave impetus to greater departmental independence.

The Clarion School for Boys was classified as a private, not-for-profit residential treatment facility for delinquent boys between the ages of 10 and 18. In 1996, there were 128 full- and part-time employees who provided care and treatment to 120 students. Of the 29 private, not-for-profit, residential child-care facilities operating in Wisconsin, Clarion was the second largest in terms of enrollment and the third most expensive in per diem charges. Unlike Clarion, most other child-care facilities were not designed to help children who were exhibiting severe behavioral problems. As a result, Clarion often functioned as a "last resort" before a child was placed in a mental hospital or state correctional institution.

Clarion's ability to manage difficult cases was largely the result of its comprehensive treatment program. The treatment effort was supported by a faculty-managed school program plus modern crisis-management facilities and tracking devices. Clarion's strategy to differentiate itself from its competitors emphasized the importance of using modern information technology in combination with a caring staff attitude. Because the school typically dealt with potentially dangerous students, the ability to contact support staff and access student records quickly was considered essential to effective performance.

As operational expenses and capital requirements continued to rise, the school became more dependent on increased per diem charges and higher enrollments to balance the budget. During the 1995–96 school year (ending June 30, 1996), Clarion charged placement agencies or families $90.50 per day for each student enrolled in the regular treatment program and $152.00 per day for students enrolled in the ISIS program (a premium care/rehabilitation facility opened in 1994 for students whose next option was a juvenile delinquency institution). Total per diem revenue for 1995–96 was budgeted to be $3,691,000, but enrollments had been running well ahead of projections. In addition, there was considerable interest in expanding the school's capacity in 1996–97.

All capital expenditures were allocated from the Capital Assets Fund of the school. The three major projects scheduled for 1996–97 were 12 more PCs and a hardware upgrade for the IBM AS/400 computing system, remodeling of a living unit to expand the ISIS program, and construction of a cottage that would accommodate ten additional students for the regular program. Young would have responsibility for managing each of these major capital projects. All capital projects exceeding $25,000 had to be approved by the Board.

Information Systems Planning

With labor costs representing 68 percent of the school's operating budget, Young considered computerization one way to increase staff effectiveness in accessing information and to improve communications among the staff. He did not put an emphasis on using automation to reduce cost directly (e.g., by reducing staff). On the recommendation of Young in January 1993, the Board of Trustees approved the purchase of an IBM AS/400 computer and associated applications software. Because Clarion was a not-for-profit institution, Young knew that capital expenditures for computers were considered difficult to justify, especially if they were not connected directly to a new revenue stream. Nevertheless, members of the Board of Trustees exhibited interest in the new information systems project even before the approval in 1993. As Young began to describe the capabilities of the system in detail, the Board's interest rose even further. Likewise, staff from all treatment programs and support areas expressed enthusiasm for the proposed benefits. Based especially on the treatment staff's support, the Board approved the project.

The stated objective of the hardware and software investment was to save staff time by using electronic communications, accelerate routine tasks, and provide easier, faster access to student data held in the computer. Critical functions at the time were considered to be electronic mail, student database access, and appointment/room scheduling. Applications software was purchased for each of these functions as well as support packages for accounting and human resources. This system supplemented the 32 personal computers using MS-DOS, which had been purchased from 1983 to 1993.

In order to synchronize implementation of the 1993 computer acquisition project with the needs of all departments, the Board of Trustees had also approved a long-range organization plan for Clarion. A joint effort between board members and staff from all levels had led to the adoption of the school's first five-year plan. This comprehensive plan focused on both administrative and treatment issues and was also approved in January 1993.

Clarion School's Computer System

While no longer state-of-the-art (i.e., not a client/server system), Clarion's computer network was custom-designed for its application needs in 1993. The distributed system was networked campus-wide and in 1996 included 37 linked personal computers (that acted as "dumb" terminals when interacting with the central system) and attached laser printers. Each personal computer was provided with word processing and spreadsheet software. According to the IBM sales representative, the network architecture allowed for 40 to 50 more personal computers to be added over time. Additional AS/400 computers could also be networked to provide peer-to-peer communications if additional central computing power was needed at the school.

Clarion's AS/400 computer was located in the front office building, where eight personal computers were also located (see Exhibit 1). The primary system console—used for initial program loads and file backups by Jean Baker, the senior bookkeeper who worked for Young—and Clarion's PBX unit (for the telephone system) were also located in the front office. The "White House," where the offices of the assistant to the superintendent and the business manager were located, housed 10 personal computers.

The Education Center contained all of Clarion's classrooms and was by far the largest building on campus. Twelve PCs (password protected) were available in a pool in the staff lounge of the Center for teachers and the education supervisor, who shared these systems with personnel who worked under the supervisor of services and others who worked in the east wing of the Center.

The ISIS treatment program was located in Sherer Hall. Seven PCs were available in a community cubicle office environment for shared use by treatment and support staff. Knight, Gibson, and Kunkler Halls, dormitories that could house up to 45 students each, were not equipped with computers, nor were the maintenance facilities.

Evaluating the Current System

After being installed for about two years, Young thought that the new computing system should be evaluated. During a staff meeting in November 1995, Young commented that he thought the decentralized campus-wide IS architecture was "leading-edge" for schools like Clarion. He viewed the network as an advantage Clarion had over other schools providing similar services. Young also mentioned the pride with which the Board of Trustees still spoke when discussing the system.

Following his comments, Young raised the question, "What are your opinions of the system?" A sampling of the answers follows (the organizations these people belong to are described in Exhibit 2).

EXHIBIT 1
Campus Computing Network.

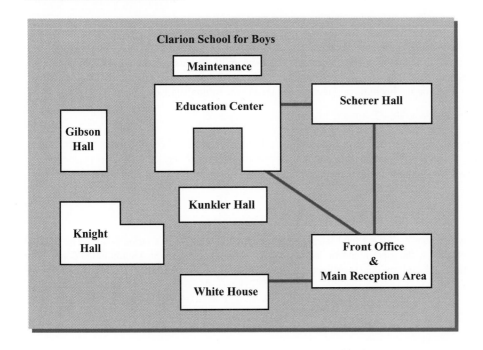

EXHIBIT 2

Responsibilities for Each Functional Unit and Organizational Chart.
Clarion School for Boys.

Social Services Department

The Social Services Department was responsible for ensuring that those under care received the appropriate clinical treatment. Because of the involvement of this department with the boys, their placing agencies, and various treatments, access to the treatment files, telecommunications, mail routing, and dictation was extremely important. The supervisor of social services functioned as department head and was a member of the Administrative Council. She was also a member of the Institutional Treatment Team.

Social services counselors handled direct counseling and casework functions, entered various progress data, and served as members of the Institutional Treatment Team and Unit Treatment Teams. Most of the documents and reports that were the responsibility of the Unit Treatment Teams required user data entry and report generation on the part of counselors.

Program Department

The Program Department was responsible for the group living aspects, crisis intervention, recreation, and special events of the treatment program. Staff in this department supervised other employees within their treatment area (child care workers, recreation workers, and program aides). One lead program supervisor functioned as the primary department head and needed access to computer treatment data and all other information resources. Five associate program supervisors shared direct supervisory responsibility for the child care and recreation data.

Education Department

The Education Department was responsible for the operation of Clarion's comprehensive year-round education program. Because the Education Department coordinated its activities with the Program Department, effective communication between these departments was critical. The education supervisor functioned in the role of principal for the school. She was a member of the Administrative Council and the Institutional Treatment Team. Sixteen teachers provided instruction to the boys in a regular classroom environment. Some teachers had telephones, and others did not. Assisted by teachers' aides, most communication was through direct contact and written memos.

Transition Department

The Transition Department was responsible for the treatment and care of twenty boys enrolled in Clarion's "transitional living" program. In most respects, the transition program was a separate treatment entity with its own supervisory, counseling, and care staff, but most supplementary functions were still performed by main campus personnel. The transition supervisor served as the department head and was on the Institutional Treatment Team and the Administrative Council.

ISIS Department

The ISIS Department was created in response to the development of the ISIS rehabilitation program. The ISIS Department reported to the supervisor of social services but had its own program supervisor. ISIS social service counselors performed some of the same functions as their counterparts in the regular program. Certain treatment needs required computer access to specialized treatment data.

Development Department

The Development Department was responsible for the fund-raising efforts and public relations of Clarion School. The development director also served as assistant to the superintendent. Development had direct access to the AS/400-based donor data, telecommunications, dictation, and mail routing. The director was a member of the Administrative Council.

EXHIBIT 2 (continued)

Business Department

The Business Department performed accounting, purchasing, and financial control functions as well as most personnel functions. The business manager, who also assumed overall responsibilities for personnel and finance, led the department. The head bookkeeper reported to the business manager and spent about one-quarter of her time performing system operator responsibilities. Typical daily tasks included answering users' questions and performing file backups for the AS/400. The business manager was also responsible for the Housekeeping and Maintenance Departments. Neither department was tied into the computer network.

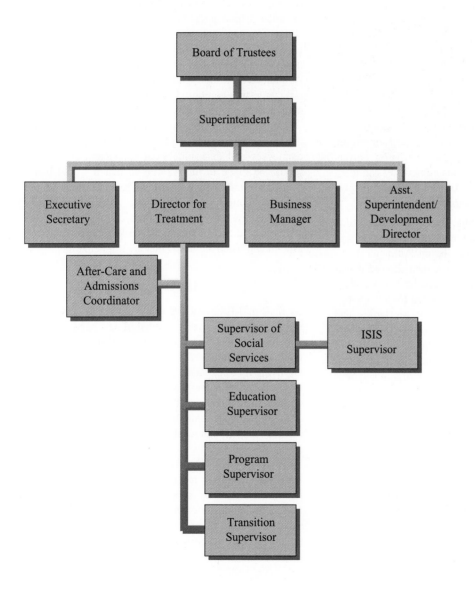

"I can't wait to learn e-mail so I can use it to distribute weekly teaching plans to our aides."—Teacher

"I could see us putting the whole report card process on the system. Each teacher could input grades from a terminal—it would save a lot of time if the cards didn't have to go to each instructor individually."—Education Supervisor

"I recently talked with an old classmate of mine who is using a computerized database to store addresses for frequent mailings. He addresses envelopes through the printer in a fraction of the time it used to take. I send a lot of mail to local businesses every month. Can we do that on the system?"—Executive Secretary

"We had two programmers working for us at my last job. They would ask us about our needs in Admissions and customize software that we licensed. I enjoyed using the system since I helped design the applications. Why don't we have that kind of help?"—After-Care and Admissions Coordinator

"Since I just joined the Clarion staff about a month-and-a-half ago, I'm not sure what is available on the system. We used computers extensively at my university. Are there training sessions offered so I can learn more about the system?"—Associate Program Supervisor for Activities and Honor Jobs

Following the staff meeting, Young spent some time trying to determine if he could prove that the current system really was an advantage at Clarion. Although it was clear that the system had potential, data showed it was not getting much use. Young realized he faced a challenge in convincing his boss of the need for any change in the current system. Superintendent McHardey had always been hesitant to incorporate any new technology into the school's operations. Young once overheard McHardey mention to a board member that he felt that "computer technology and the treatment of troubled boys just don't mesh."

A New Long-Range IS Plan

In December 1995, McHardey called Young into his office. "John," he began, "I'm hearing that you're asking questions about the computer system. Your inquiry matches my concern about the way we are managing our information system—or should I say *not* managing it? From what I can tell, no one on Clarion's staff fully understands how our current systems are functioning. Furthermore, we have only sketchy ideas of what our IS

objectives should be over the next few years—and most of those are probably only in your head." Young nodded in agreement, as if he truly had a vision of Clarion's IS strategy. McHardey continued, "We've also got to get a handle on the cost situation. Are you aware that we have spent more than $100,000 on hardware and software maintenance agreements alone in the last 12 months? I want you to really dig into the IS area so you can include a long-range information systems plan along with your regular business plan and budget presentation to the Board of Trustees next June. Can you do it?"

In mid-January 1996, Young formed the Information Systems (IS) Task Force to help develop the long-range IS plan. Besides Young, the six-member task force included Christopher Larson, director for treatment; Brian Thomas, assistant to the superintendent; Ann Lyman, supervisor of social services; Lara Kirk, education supervisor; and Michael Todd, program supervisor. As indicated on the organization chart in Exhibit 2, the task force was composed primarily of department-level management.

At its first meeting, Young defined the objectives of the IS Task Force—to explore the IS needs of Clarion employees and determine what enhancements (if any) should be made to the AS/400 so that it would better fulfill the staff's mission-critical requirements. At the meeting, Young suggested that task force responsibilities would require only minimal time commitment by the staff. He told the group simply "to keep your ear to the ground and listen for needs that are not being met."

An IS Assessment

By their mid-February 1996 meeting, the IS Task Force members had not developed a list of new needs. Instead, they reported that they had received substantial informal input from staff indicating that the current system was not living up to expectations. In an effort to identify the root causes of these disappointments, the task force decided to conduct a staff survey with the goal of understanding the most common complaint—the lack of communications throughout the organization and the failure of the AS/400 to remedy the situation. The survey was distributed by Young's office during March 1996. Some responses were not received until a full month later. Results of the survey are shown in Exhibit 3.

An initial review of the results of the IS Task Force's survey indicated that personal contact was perceived as the most important form of communication among staff at Clarion. Second was the telephone system. Third on

EXHIBIT 3
Information Systems Survey.
Clarion School for Boys.

Background

A questionnaire was distributed to all full-time employees except for janitorial and temporary services personnel. A one-week turnaround time was requested. Although the employees were not required to identify themselves on the form, department names were noted on each questionnaire before it was distributed. The overall survey response rate was 71 percent. Lower return rates were apparent in the Education and Services Departments. No surveys were returned from the Maintenance Department. Some returned surveys contained questions that were not answered.

Findings

The following summary of the information resources survey has three main sections: Mechanisms for Verbal Communication, Mechanisms for Written Communication, and a Summary of Detailed Data Analysis.

Mechanisms for Verbal Communications

Type	Frequency
Large formal staff gatherings	
• General staff meetings	One per year, or when there was a major crisis
• Convocations	Three per year
• Institutional Treatment Team meetings	1–2 hours, once per week
• In-service training sessions	One per month
Large informal staff gatherings	
• Weekday lunches	Most staff were required to eat with the students
• Holiday parties and banquets	Five per year
Small formal staff gatherings	
• Unit treatment team meetings	One or two per week
• Administrative Council meetings	One per week
• Departmental meetings	One per week
• Teachers' meetings	Every weekday morning
• Supervisory sessions	Approximately one per month
• Performance reviews	Annual, with supervisor
• Scheduled one-on-one meetings	Various
• Long-range planning committee meetings	Four per year

Other informal staff gatherings

- Teachers' lounge discussions
- Work space area conversations by coffee machine and mailboxes
- Service staff's break room conversations
- Unscheduled one-on-one meetings
- "Parking lot" conversations

Mechanisms for Written Communication

- Scrap notes: notes of all shapes and sizes, no format
- Memos: a standard 4-copy form, many per day
- Weekly treatment services calendar: 4 to 6 pages

EXHIBIT 3 (continued)

- Special request forms: various requests
- Minutes of formal meetings and supervisory sessions: 1 to 6 pages
- *The Clarion Record*: 5 to 10 page quarterly internal report
- Semester calendar: 20 to 26 pages biannually
- Financial statements: 6 pages issued monthly
- Departmental one-year goals: 2 to 6 pages annually
- Annual audit: 10 to 12 pages annually
- Five-year plan: 80 to 120 pages, updated annually

Summary of Detailed Data Analysis

For each of the following questions, the survey question (as it appeared on the questionnaire) precedes the summary analyses.

Question: What information sources do you rely on most to accomplish your daily job tasks?

	Direct	*Telephone*	*Written*	*Computer*	*Other*	*Total*
Responses	32	11	6	8	0	57
Percent (rounded)	56%	19%	11%	14%	0%	100%

Data from the above question displayed by job classification (percent rounded):

	Direct	*Telephone*	*Written*	*Computer*	*Total*
Treatment	65%	16%	10%	10%	100%
Management/Administration	67%	11%	11%	11%	100%
Secretarial	20%	20%	0%	60%	100%
Clerical	0%	100%	0%	0%	100%
Services	100%	0%	0%	0%	100%

Question: Which of the following information resources would you most like to use more?

	Direct	*Telephone*	*Written*	*Computer*	*Other*	*Total*
Responses	8	5	5	19	0	37
Percent (rounded)	22%	14%	14%	51%	0%	100%

Data from the above question displayed by job classification (percent rounded):

	Direct	*Telephone*	*Written*	*Computer*	*Total*
Treatment	24%	24%	24%	29%	100%
Management/Administration	10%	0%	10%	80%	100%
Secretarial	50%	0%	0%	50%	100%
Clerical	0%	25%	0%	75%	100%
Services	0%	0%	50%	50%	100%

EXHIBIT 3 (continued)

Question: Which of the following computing functions have you used? (Select more than one if necessary.)

"Percent of respondents" designates percent of respondents who indicated the specific answer for this question if they indicated at least one answer for this question. "Percent of all" indicates the percent of responses as a portion of all Clarion employees.

	E-mail	Database Entry	Database Query	Calendaring	Spreadsheet	Accounting
Responses	36	32	23	7	3	10
Percent of respondents (rounded)	80%	71%	51%	16%	7%	22%
Percent of all (rounded)	28%	25%	18%	5%	2%	8%

Question: How much formal training have you had on the computer system?

"Percent of respondents" designates percent of respondents who indicated the specific answer for this question if they indicated an answer for this question. "Percent of all" indicates the percent of responses as a portion of all Clarion employees.

	None	Demo	1–3 hr.	4–7 hr.	8–16 hr.	17–32 hr.	32+ hr.
Responses	2	5	11	7	7	6	7
Percent of respondents (rounded)	4%	11%	24%	16%	16%	13%	16%
Percent of all (rounded)	2%	4%	9%	5%	5%	5%	5%

Question: Circle either I am satisfied or dissatisfied with the amount of training I have received.

"Percent of respondents" designates percent of respondents who indicated the specific answer for this question if they indicated an answer for this question. "Percent of all" indicates the percent of responses as a portion of all Clarion employees.

	Satisfied	Dissatisfied
Responses	18	25
Percent of respondents (rounded)	42%	58%
Percent of all (rounded)	14%	20%

Question: How much time do you spend working on a PC or the central system on the average each day?

(For this question, answers were compiled only by job classification.)

	None	<1 hr.	1–2 hr.	3–4 hr.	>4 hr.
Treatment	0%	50%	27%	14%	5%
Management/Administration	0%	31%	38%	15%	15%
Secretarial	0%	0%	0%	20%	80%
Clerical	0%	0%	67%	33%	0%
Services	0%	0%	0%	0%	0%

the staff's list was AS/400 electronic mail. Almost every staff member was aware of the communications software products available on the AS/400, but most were not using them. Further down the list were reports. Although hundreds of different paper reports were processed regularly, the importance of these types of written communication was perceived as "low."

The task force considered the possibility that the AS/400 had not paid off simply because it was not being used by staff. By checking the system logs (an automatic record of system usage generated by the operating system), it was determined that while an employee might have been logged on to the system for most of the day, he or she was actively using it for less than 30 minutes each day. The task force members were not sure why the system was not being used as expected.

In addition to conducting the survey, IS Task Force members allotted time at their own departmental meetings in March 1996 and during one-on-one conversations to solicit responses from the units for which they had primary responsibility. Discussion of these issues was awkward for some of the task force members because they were not well educated in the area of information systems.

Task Force Interviews

Highlights from IS Task Force personal interviews helped better define the attitudes of Clarion's staff. One task force member, Lara Kirk, reported to the committee at its late-March 1996 meeting that she had conducted a group interview with instructors who had used the system for electronic mail. She recalled one teacher saying, "It was great during the first month or two when we could actually find a PC available, but after that, they got so crowded. I don't have time to wait in line." Another added, "I have found PCs available early in the morning, say between eight o'clock and nine, but whenever I try to log on, I get a message telling me the system is not available. I think it says something about backups—whatever that is."

When Kirk pursued these problems, she learned from Jean Baker (Young's lead bookkeeper) that the system backup schedule took place each morning between 8:00 and 9:30. When Baker was backing up the system, she specified that no other users could log on.

Christopher Larson also relayed comments from one of his sessions. "We have found that it is easier to use our old file card system to look up student records rather than walk all the way down the hall to the nearest PC to use the system. But I heard the same information is actually available on-line. I just haven't had time to figure out how to use the system yet."

Michael Todd reported that although he had thought the secretaries were using the calendaring software product on the AS/400 to help his associate program supervisors with room scheduling and personal calendar services, they were actually using the functions very infrequently. When he questioned the secretaries, they told him that "the associate program supervisors like to keep their own calendars and they never give us enough time to schedule activities ahead of time. We usually end up rushing around trying to find an open classroom or conference room for their needs at the last minute."

Brian Thomas discovered that his assistant and the director of planned giving were using the system less than he had thought as well. "To make a long story short," he said, "no one ever told me what value I would get from the new computer system. As a matter of fact, for a start, I could use a better phone system so I could hold conference calls among potential donors. I'm sure I could raise more money if I could put them in contact with each other one-on-one. I have heard that we spent a lot of money on the AS/400. Who is using it?"

Young also heard reports that staff members at Clarion found themselves in a defensive position when faced by what they perceived as an "interrogation" by their supervisors on the IS Task Force. It was obvious that some employees were sugar-coating their answers while others simply avoided giving their opinions.

Obtaining Outside Help

One important result of the task force assessment survey and individual interviews was the conclusion that the task force needed additional assistance from an objective source. At the special request of the task force, Clarion's Board of Trustees approved funding in late April 1996 for Young to hire a consulting firm to assist with his plan.

In a hurried search for a consulting firm to assist at Clarion, the IS Task Force selected LTM Consultants, Inc., from among three companies that submitted proposals, largely because LTM had a local office in Milwaukee and had done some work for Clarion two years ago.

LTM was a growing firm of 92 professionals and 30 support staff based in Chicago. The firm had offices in eight states, and its expertise included accounting, information technology, and general management consulting. It was Young's opinion that LTM would provide the best value to Clarion for the fees it charged. The final engagement letter from LTM is included as Exhibit 4. Young

EXHIBIT 4
Engagement Letter from LTM Consultants, Inc.

LTM Consultants
765 Corporate Circle
Milwaukee, WI 51744

April 20, 1996

John F. Young
Business Manager
Clarion School for Boys
Post Office Box 2217
Milwaukee, WI 51740-2217

Dear John:

LTM appreciates the opportunity to work with the Clarion School for Boys in identifying critical issues related to its future information systems environment and determining its future systems strategy. The primary objectives of our engagement are to:

- Evaluate the current strengths and weaknesses of Clarion's information systems
- Determine the information systems strategy required to achieve Clarion's short-term and long-term business goals.

In consideration of the importance of this engagement, we have combined the unique talents of LTM consultants from three of our offices. A three-person team of consultants from LTM's Information Technology Group in Milwaukee, Human Factors Group in Indianapolis, and Strategy Group in Chicago will ensure that this engagement is approached from both a business and technical solution perspective.

One critical success factor of this project is to quickly gain an in-depth understanding of the needs, issues, and constraints related to the Clarion School's information systems environment. Only then can we convert the present functional needs into a broad set of systems requirements and a subsequent strategy.

We estimate this analysis will require approximately four weeks to complete at an estimated cost for Professional Services of $30,000. Costs for travel and lodging expenses will be billed as incurred. An initial invoice of $20,000 will be issued fifteen days after start-up and a reconciling invoice will be submitted upon completion of the engagement.

John, we look forward to working with you and the Clarion School on this important assignment. I can assure you that we will bring the value that will make a difference to Clarion in the future.

Sincerely,

C. J. VanZant

Carl John VanZant
Vice President

Approved: _John F. Young_____   ___4/23/96_____
                Clarion School for Boys   Date

expected LTM to deliver an IS strategic plan by the first week of June 1996. Although Young would assume ultimate responsibility for the recommendations he would deliver to the Board of Trustees, he considered an outside set of recommendations as well as the task force work critical to his success with the trustees in June.

Young spent a full day briefing the three LTM consultants on the history of Clarion's IS situation, including the recent IS Task Force survey. In his position as business manager, Young explained that he was responsible for making sure that major capital investments were paying off. He wanted to know why the system was not filling the information needs at Clarion and which long-term improvements should be made. He also pointed out organizational change issues to LTM that he thought might have affected system usage. For example, Clarion had grown in three years from 90 to 120 students. A number of new positions had been created to take on the extra load. Full- and part-time staff had increased by almost 30 percent, and turnover and absenteeism was very low.

"I'm not sure," Young told the LTM team, "but my biggest challenge may be in selling McHardey that I can make the system work for Clarion." He went on to describe a brief communication he had with McHardey when they bumped into each other on the way to the parking lot one evening. "When I asked Sean's opinion of the AS/400, he said that he hadn't found any practical use for computers so far besides the word-processing software on his PC (he uses it for his daily 'to-do' lists)." Young recalled McHardey's words, "I don't use e-mail, I just make a phone call or walk over to someone's office." McHardey continued, as he headed for his car,

"Sometimes I wonder if our investment was worthwhile, John. I know the Board of Trustees is counting on you to make sure that Clarion is getting full value from the system."

Regarding his own concern about the current system's usage, Young remembered that his own department had a difficult time with specialized billing needs. Most of the billing was done directly through the system's accounting software, but about 10 percent was first done by hand and then manually entered into the invoicing system as adjustments at the end of a period. Young admitted to the consultants, "If I can't get invoicing to work consistently for my own staff, how can I expect others to be excited about other applications?"

Decision Time

It was 4:35 p.m. on June 11, 1996—one week before his presentation. Knowing he would have to work with his IS Task Force to finalize the report next week, Young poured himself a cup of coffee and flipped open the consultants' findings, which he had received earlier that day (the report's text is included as Exhibit 5). He read LTM's report with the vigor of a graduate student, hoping the findings would be a panacea for Clarion's information systems problems.

Young had intended to make LTM's report the basis of his own report to the Board of Trustees. Now that he had read it, he thought it included some good ideas and suggestions, but it seemed lacking as a long-range IS plan. Young was unsure exactly what he needed to do, but he knew he would be burning a lot of midnight oil during the next few days.

EXHIBIT 5
LTM's Consulting Report.

LTM Consultants
765 Corporate Circle
Milwaukee, WI 51744

June 7, 1996

John F. Young
Clarion School for Boys
Post Office Box 2217
Milwaukee, WI 51744-2217

Dear John:

LTM has completed our study at Clarion and we submit the enclosed written report per our agreement. As I mentioned to you during our telephone conversation, we would be happy to present our findings to Clarion's Board of Trustees if you wish.

Please note the four main sections of the report. First, a sampling of comments from Clarion's staff characterize the general attitude toward information systems (IS). Strengths and weaknesses of the current IS are highlighted. Finally, specific recommendations are presented for improving Clarion School's information system.

As I am sure you will agree, there are many opportunities to improve Clarion's daily IS operations. We would like to meet with you soon to discuss how LTM can assist you in making our recommendations operational.

Sincerely,

C. J. VanZant

Carl John VanZant
Vice President

Long-Range IS Plan Final Report

Findings in this report are a result of analysis during the last week of April and the first three weeks of May 1996. Fifteen person-days were spent on site at the Clarion School for Boys. LTM consultants began with a kickoff meeting that included six department supervisors, three directors, and the superintendent. In this meeting, the scope and purpose of LTM's engagement was defined: to identify critical issues related to Clarion's future information system (IS) environment with the goal of defining Clarion's future IS strategy.

Included in this report is a selection of comments made by Clarion staff during both formal and informal interactions with LTM consultants. The following six questions were used as a starting point for each interview. A majority of the interview time was devoted to exploring responses to initial questions using follow-up questions.

EXHIBIT 5 (continued)

1. Are there any recommendations you would like to make regarding how the Clarion School handles information—written, computer, telephone, or direct (face-to-face)?
2. What is the most useful form of information you receive?
3. In what ways do you feel this form of information is vital to your work objectives?
4. What could be done to make Clarion's information system even more beneficial to your work?
5. Summarize the strengths of the current information system.
6. Are there any additional comments you would like to make regarding future enhancements to Clarion's information system?

The following interviews were conducted during the first three weeks of the study:

- Six two-hour two-on-one interviews with department supervisors (two LTM consultants and one supervisor)
- Six one-hour interviews with the three directors
- Twenty-three one-hour two-on-one interviews with nonsupervisory staff

LTM consultants attended the following meetings during the last three weeks of the study:

- Two weekly Administrative Council meetings (comprised of the nine supervisors and the superintendent)
- One weekly Institutional Treatment Team meeting (comprised of the superintendent, director of Treatment Services, deputy director of Treatment Services, supervisor of the Program Department, associate program supervisors, supervisor of Social Services, social service counselors, Education Department supervisor, and Transition Department supervisor)
- Two scheduled department meetings and four impromptu department meetings
- Five daily teachers' meetings
- One weekly Unit Treatment Team meeting (comprised of one teacher, two members of the child-care workers staff, and a member of the social service staff)

LTM consultants randomly queried seventeen Clarion employees in the halls of the school and in the parking lot by asking questions about their uses of current IS resources at Clarion. Staff comments were recorded during both formal and informal conversations.

The remainder of this report is divided into four main sections: A Sampling of Staff's Comments, Strengths of Clarion's Information System, Weaknesses of Clarion's Information System, and Information System Strategy.

A Sampling of Staff's Comments

"I have been trying to finish this month's books for the last two days, but I am having the same problems as last month. The accounts receivable software program is still giving me difficulties. I think I'll just do them by hand again this month."

—Bookkeeper

"I use the scheduling module all the time for my scheduling since most of the work I do runs in biweekly cycles. The automatic messages remind me when I have something due."—Clerical Worker

"There was a lot of initial excitement about e-mail, but I haven't heard much about it since then. I know I've been too busy to learn it myself, and I missed the training ses-

EXHIBIT 5 (continued)

sions because of other meetings. The only thing I've heard is that a few of the teachers sent out e-mail to others, but never got a reply. Maybe the interest died down because everyone didn't get training right away."—Education Supervisor

"I'll be honest with you. Although I have been using the system for almost a year now, it is not easy to use. I think my daughter's Mac is much easier."

—Development Staff Member

"I remember someone mentioning that there is an inventory management software package we might use for our kitchen supplies, but I haven't checked into it yet."

—Kitchen Manager

"In my last job, we used a program on our computer to monitor the progress of our students. It was a custom package written for us by a consulting group. Although it took about ten months to complete the software, it worked very well for our special needs."—Transition Counselor

"It would help us if we had a reliable system for keeping the students' medical records. Sometimes the note cards get misplaced, and you don't know about it until you really need one."—Nurse

"I just bypass the menu system since it slows me down . . . especially since I have set up generic templates for all of the common reports." —Secretary

"I am responsible for producing the weekly treatment services calendar. Because I am continually making updates, my biggest complaint is that I have to walk down the hall whenever I want to get a printed copy."—Associate Program Supervisor

Strengths of Clarion's Information System

Hardware and Software

1. Dictation equipment is used extensively by treatment personnel. This use increases efficiency for both treatment staff and the secretarial staff who transcribe the dictations.
2. Personal computers are used by the business manager and the director of development to generate overhead slides for presentations.
3. Software application programs are flexible enough to be useful for both beginners and advanced users.
4. Adequate software documentation manuals are available for users.
5. The AS/400 file transfer product allows data transfer between PC and mainframe units. It allows flexibility for those who use PCs a lot.
6. The AS/400 is expandable in case additional workstations or processors are needed.

Policy and Procedures

1. System backups are done on a daily basis and are well organized.
2. Quarterly preventive maintenance schedules coordinated through IBM representatives are effective.

Staff Perceptions

In general, interviews revealed that most of the staff, although not totally satisfied with Clarion's information system, felt that the system was likely better than what existed in

EXHIBIT 5 (continued)

comparable facilities. Most frequently noted comparisons were with a local mental health facility that is experiencing severe system difficulties.

Weaknesses of Clarion's Information System

Hardware and Software

1. Resultant quality of dictated memos is largely dependent on the level of experience of the secretary.
2. Some needed software is not available on the AS/400, necessitating use of personal computers for some reporting functions.
3. Self-paced tutorial software is not available for users.
4. A number of users stated that PCs were not available when they needed them late in the day. PCs are used heavily from 3:00 to 5:00 p.m.

Policy and Procedures

1. At least 90 minutes each day of the senior bookkeeper's time is spent running system backups and initial program loads (IPLs). Consequently, others cannot use the system during that time, and Ms. Baker is not available to perform her regular supervisory functions.
2. Requests for report changes are routed through department supervisors to either John Young or Jean Baker. Once each month they are reviewed and reprioritized by Baker and Young. Baker then works on requests according to priority, as time permits. Day-to-day operations require Young or Baker to answer user questions as they come up, which reduces the time they have for their primary responsibilities.
3. Only two individuals have attended college-level computer courses. A formal training schedule does not exist.

Staff Perceptions

1. Administrative Council members were given very limited opportunities to provide input for the original computerization project in 1993. Thus, they perceive the current system as incapable of providing for their needs.
2. Direct personal communication has become more difficult as staff size has increased and departmental specialization has evolved.
3. Many of Clarion's would-be IS users have decided not to use the system because they find it difficult to find an open PC.
4. Secretarial staff use the AS/400 application software more than any other personnel. The AS/400 is regarded by many as only a tool for performing reporting tasks.
5. Staff who use accounting applications have a sense that they are "the shoemaker's children" whose applications receive lowest priority.

Information System Strategy

The following recommendations are arranged in general categories, with more specific suggestions offered in the conclusion:

1. **Establish a permanent staff position for IS management.** It is difficult for a key staff member to handle an information system project as a temporary assignment when he/she has a multitude of other responsibilities and projects to oversee at the

EXHIBIT 5 (continued)

same time. For this reason, a staff position should be created with primary responsibility to manage Clarion's information system (including computing networks, personal computers, and telephone systems). Additional responsibility should include evaluation and implementation of IS training needs. The new IS manager should report directly to the superintendent and have permanent membership on the Long-Range Planning Committee. The individual selected for the IS manager position should have extensive computer science background and information systems experience.

2. **Establish a team approach to planning.** Planning should initially be conducted by a small team with strong leadership, making sure that feedback is obtained from the various user groups in each of the departments. A feedback process should be used to motivate staff toward cooperation and support of IS projects. This feedback can be done by soliciting their input and explaining system benefits so they will develop a sense of ownership. Potential stakeholders should also be identified; this facilitates reduction of barriers to change.

3. **Involve and evaluate the entire system when considering all IS projects.** Telecommunications, central computer, and PC decisions should not be made in a vacuum. When IS-related decisions need to be made, Clarion's entire IS must be considered. The new IS manager's responsibilities should include researching high-impact issues. This procedure should be regarded as an integral part of Clarion's information system evolution. Overall evaluation should include input from experts within each department.

   A formal impact assessment methodology should be established to ensure a comprehensive and consistent evaluation. The methodology should include consideration of the following:

   - What are the attitudes of employees regarding the introduction and use of the new system?
   - Will Clarion's business practices change as a result of the new system?
   - Should organizational restructuring occur, including changes, additions, or eliminations of staff positions?
   - How much experience does Clarion have in this particular area?
   - What other current projects or strategic issues could compete with this project?

   Use of a formal impact assessment methodology will allow identification of opportunities with low, medium, and high risk that can be considered when appraising the response to future change. Furthermore, in concert with evaluation of the entire information system, this technique facilitates development of a rolling, long-range IS plan.

4. **Install a formal approach to IS planning.** There are a variety of techniques that can be used in matters of IS planning. "Critical success factors" and "investment strategy analysis" are common frameworks. Elements of several of these techniques should be combined in structuring planning activities. It is also vital for the superintendent and the Board of Trustees to have proposals that can be judged according to the same criteria in the process of decision-making. Although the formal process will undoubtedly be time-consuming, our experience with IS projects suggests that this practice will benefit the school in the long term by reducing the likelihood of inappropriate projects being implemented. A specific planning framework should include the following features:

EXHIBIT 5 (continued)

   A. **Master IS Plan.** A Master IS Plan involves identification of the school's strategic issues and the development of the planning infrastructure for the future. The master plan is based on an examination of Clarion's formal mission statement with respect to current strategic emphases. Workshops should be held for staff with the goals of educating them as to the strategic process of IS planning and providing an understanding of broad IS management objectives. All employees at Clarion should be aware of the necessity to manage all information—including text documents, voice messages, diagrams, and statistics—as valuable corporate assets. Staff should understand that computers, software, written documents, and telephones are not "theirs." Decisions and procedures regarding these assets will be based on the treatment of these elements as "Clarion" resources addressed within the master plan. Staff should also be instructed to identify "critical success factors" vital for accomplishing Clarion's objectives. This process will link specific task activities to the Master IS Plan.

   B. **Top Management Involvement.** Primary attention should be given to techniques that facilitate top management involvement and support. The superintendent, along with the new IS manager, should play a critical role in long-range IS planning. All future IS planning decisions should also include substantial input from members of the Administrative Council.

   C. **Systems Life Methodology.** A "systems life" methodology is recommended for use on each specific application systems. It is also useful for establishing requirements definitions and project timetables. When evaluating new application systems, consideration should be given to the life-cycle stage of each component. Avoid decisions that lead to purchase of an application just prior to the release of a new option. A formal system should be developed that facilitates identification of a software product's evolutionary position with respect to Clarion's current technology. Only after application systems are characterized within the spectrum of "cutting edge" to "nearing obsolescence," and compared to the Clarion School's ability to manage new technology, should tactical decisions be made.

   D. **Rolling Timetable.** The Master IS Plan should include a rolling timetable in order to coordinate various project efforts and make effective IS investment decisions.

5. **Incorporate IS requirements in proposed long-range planning objectives.** Long-range planning (LRP) objectives must include information regarding a standard set of topics relevant to information systems. Each LRP objective should address its potential impact on Clarion's information system and specifically identify any additional requirements. It is because of the highly integrated nature of IS planning and other long-range planning that the new IS manager will have to work closely with Clarion's business manager.

6. **Establish IS objectives within Clarion's five-year plan.** As Clarion's IS planning requirements become more complex, it will be imperative to continually seek out new ways to make strategic decisions. For this reason, Clarion should include ongoing evaluation of computer-based methodologies, which would increase planning efficiency and integrity, as part of the long-range planning process. The role of IS management must be evaluated and redefined in light of technological changes.

MIDSTATE UNIVERSITY BUSINESS PLACEMENT OFFICE (C): MANAGEMENT OF THE COMPUTER SYSTEM

The Midstate University Business Placement Office (BPO) computer system is an integral part of the BPO operations, without which the BPO could not function. Not only is the computer system essential, but it also is somewhat complex, and the computer processing and the activities of the BPO staff are intimately interrelated. Furthermore, the BPO system has been created, and is continuously being improved, by the BPO staff. Thus Jim Wine, Director of the BPO, is the de facto manager of a small information systems department, and his success as BPO manager depends upon how well he manages his information systems function.

The BPO Staff

Jim Wine, Director of the BPO, is also Assistant Dean for Company Relations of the School of Business. Although he is ultimately responsible for all BPO operations, Jim cannot devote all his time to running the BPO on a day-by-day basis, so the BPO has a very professional management team.

Elliott Gordon, Senior Associate Director, manages the day-by-day operations of the BPO. Gordon is in charge of all office operations, the student counseling program, staff training and development, and administration of the BPO facilities.

This case was prepared by Professor E. W. Martin as the basis for discussion rather than to illustrate either effective or ineffective handling of an administrative situation.

Copyright © 1997 (Revised) by E. W. Martin.

Margaret Brown, Associate Director, is responsible for recruiting operations, new employer development, external marketing, and operations documentation.

Stanley Russ, Associate Director, is responsible for career placement counseling for MBAs, MBA placement, international programs, and special projects.

Bill Alcorn, Associate Director, directs all BPO computer operations, including technical support, systems design, programming, and management.

In addition to the above managers, the BPO has several Assistant Directors, a small staff of computer professionals, and some clerical workers.

The BPO Computer Organization

The organization of the BPO computer group is shown in Exhibit 1. Bill Alcorn, Associate Director, Systems Technology, has his undergraduate degree in Psychology and an MS in Instructional Systems Technology where he had a good deal of training on and experience with computers. He has also had prior experience in evaluating, purchasing, and installing computer hardware and software.

Dick Greene, Computer Operations Supervisor, is responsible for the day-by-day operations in the back room. Greene has put a lot of effort into organizing the processing and getting the system documentation in good shape. Greene also does some programming, mostly making changes to existing programs.

Greene supervises Mary Parsons, Technical Assistant, whose duty is to manage the data flows between the Unix server and the Web server and to get data into the system and distribute the reports from the system.

EXHIBIT 1
BPO Computer Group Organization Chart.

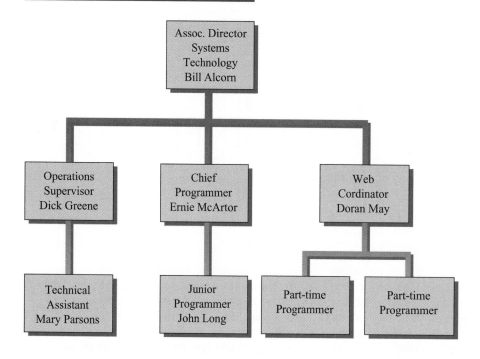

Parsons also processes the high volume of e-mail that comes into the BPO—she scans it, answers the routine questions, and forwards the rest to the proper person to handle it. Students are encouraged to report problems via e-mail, and the BPO strives to resolve these problems within 24 hours.

Ernie McArtor, the chief programmer, is responsible for the continual changes and additions to the system. He is skilled in several programming languages and does most of the database programming, C programming, and UNIX administration. McArtor also supervises John Long, Junior Programmer, who researches and debugs problems, handles some program maintenance, and works on projects assigned by McArtor.

Doran May, Web Coordinator, is a recent addition to the BPO computer staff. When Wine and Alcorn decided to convert to a Web-based system they realized that they had to acquire some new talents, so they hired May, who gained experience in system administration, Web programming, and UNIX systems while working for University Computing Services (UCS) at Midstate University. May's connections at UCS are helpful in preventing the BPO from going off in directions that conflict

with where the rest of the University is headed. May supervises the two part-time Web-based programmers who are programming in HTML, C, Perl, and Java.

Development of the Computer Organization

When Bob Rivers, the brilliant and dedicated MBA half-timer who had helped Wine develop the initial Apple-based system, graduated and left in the spring of 1982, Wine replaced him with another half-time MBA, Roger Snider. Within a few months both Snider and Wine realized that the job was beyond Snider's capability—there was no way that in 20 hours a week Snider could do what Bob had been doing. Of course, as brilliant as he was, Bob hadn't been doing the job in 20 hours a week either—he would work 40 or 50 hours a week if necessary to get the job done. Snider didn't see it that way, and he was extremely resentful when Wine expected him to work as much as necessary to get the job done, even if he was only being paid for 20 hours a week and trying to complete a heavy load of MBA classes at the same time.

So in January 1983, while Wine was under lots of pressure to get the scheduling process transferred to the IBM mainframe, Snider abruptly resigned. "That was the straw that broke the camel's back and convinced me that I couldn't handle the computer system with part-time temporary people," recalls Wine. From then on he set out to develop a full-time professional computer staff.

That was a problem—he didn't have authorization to hire people at the level he needed. So Wine took some of his clerical positions and gradually upgraded them. He would hire someone for $10,000 a year in a clerical position, teach them programming, and then go to the University Personnel Department and get the position upgraded to correspond to what the present occupant was doing.

Until Wine realized that he needed a different type of person in these jobs, he had a lot of turnover. "People were being burned out very quickly by the magnitude of the job and the chaotic conditions caused by the fact that we had to be ready to bid on Monday, whether the computer worked or not," Wine recalls. After Bob Rivers left Wine had a succession of two or three people in that job until he got Julia Workman, who was a stabilizing force.

> Julia was not a workaholic—she did what she could in the eight to nine hours a day that she would give us, and then she was done. But that really was a good thing, because she began to get some things routinized that should have been routinized. She convinced me that we had to have an adequate number of people and that they had to be organized and managed.

The first computer staff people that Wine hired were Greene and McArtor, neither of whom had computer training when they were hired. Greene had a BA in English, but no formal computer background beyond a FORTRAN programming course many years before. He got involved with the computer as a hobby, buying an early kit and constructing a small (4K memory) machine. He quickly outgrew that and added an additional 16K of memory, learned to program in machine language, and was always experimenting with how he could make the machine do more than it reasonably ought to do. This was his first computer job, and he didn't really apply for it— Wine hired him as the result of a casual conversation at a party with a mutual friend. McArtor was a musician who played in a rock band and got interested in amplifiers and electronics that way and finally drifted into computers.

When Workman left, Wine made Jane Meyer the BPO Assistant Director responsible for the computer system in addition to her responsibility for alumni placement and coordinating company presentations on campus. Before that Meyer had worked as a graduate assistant at the BPO for a year as a practicum for her master's degree in college counseling. Other than an undergraduate course in FORTRAN programming, Meyer had no experience with computers before joining the BPO staff.

Meyer was the intermediary between the other BPO managers and the computer staff—she explained new projects to the programmers, made sure that they stayed on the course that the other directors wanted, and tried to see that the projects got done on time.

As a novice with computers, supervising the programmers was a frustrating experience for Meyer. "It seemed so simple to me," Meyer reported. "I'd just tell them to fix this simple problem. A month later it wouldn't be done, I'd ask them why, and they'd explain that they'd had these problems. I'd been used to telling a human: Don't do that any more! And they wouldn't do it any more. But I've had to recognize that with a computer it's a lot more complicated!"

When Meyer finished her graduate degree in college counseling and left for a job in that field, Wine placed Alcorn in charge of the computer systems, without Meyer's other responsibilities. Because of Meyer's lack of computer experience and knowledge, she had never been able to take over all of the responsibility for directing the programmers when developing new systems, so Wine had to be involved in managing the programmers. But with his experience and training in computers, Alcorn has been able to take over most of the system development responsibility. Wine is still the main conceptualizer and remains the major "idea man," but Alcorn and the computer staff can be depended upon to implement these ideas without Wine's participation.

The recent conversion to the Web has required the BPO to acquire people with new skills. Yet because the basic processing system has not changed the old skills are still critical. In the new system a great deal of interaction is required between the old systems and the new Web systems, and developing the required teamwork between the old and new people has required Alcorn's attention.

Managing System Operations

We have already mentioned the "back room" computer organization. There is also a "front office" operation where the computer system interacts with the BPO staff, the students, and company recruiters.

The Back Room Operations

As mentioned above, during the recruiting season the system is driven by inflexible deadlines set by the bidding process. The bids are accepted from Friday through Monday, and the results of the bidding have to be available for students on Tuesday morning. Thus, the databases used in the bid processing must be up-to-date and the bidding file must be complete to process the bids on Monday night.

Because a lot of things have to be completed in a specified sequence and by a number of different people, considerable organization and discipline are required. If someone forgets something, or does it wrong, it can cause a lot of problems.

Dick Greene is responsible for the day-by-day processing and has developed a set of forms to control the processing—a different form for each day of the week that shows every computer program that must be run in the proper sequence. The form has a blank to fill in the time of completion of each program. He also has a set of forms for end-of-month, end-of-semester, and end of the recruiting year.

Greene has also put a good deal of effort into documentation of the system. In addition to his forms for controlling processing, the BPO has a "run book" that tells how to run each program, with suggestions as to what to do when anything goes wrong. The BPO also has a listing showing the databases and index files that each of the programs uses and a manual describing the databases and the procedures for initializing them at the beginning of the recruiting year. Thus, the operational aspects of the system are well documented.

However, the BPO has little system level documentation—the system descriptions in the (A) case were created from scratch by the case writer. And the BPO has very little documentation of the individual programs beyond that provided by dBASE. When Greene was revising a program recently, he spent a lot of time creating a program flow chart in order to get an understanding of how the program worked.

The BPO also uses a form for controlling backups to the database. The BPO staff learned about the importance of backing up the database soon after they got their first hard disk. Wine remembers:

A secretary was working with dBASE and accidentally entered a command that cleaned off the entire hard disk—almost 10 megabytes of data. She knew the second she had done it what she had done, but there wasn't a thing she could do to stop it. She came out of that office bawling, and it was a tearful day for everybody in the office because we had to go back and repeat almost a week of data entry work! Ever since then we have done daily backups.

The design of the present system provides automatic backup for many of the databases. The master copy of the database resides on the BPO UNIX server, but a copy of many of the databases also resides on the BPO Web server to furnish information to the students. During the day transactions are accumulated, but the databases are not updated. At the end of the day that day's transactions are sent to the BPO server to update the master database and print a transaction log for control purposes. Then the updated databases are sent to the BPO Web server so it is ready for the next day's processing. Thus, the Web server database is also a backup for much of the master database. The entire master database is independently backed up each night after the database is updated. Also, all source documents are filed for reference in case there are problems.

The "Front Office" Operations

The BPO staff continually interacts with the BPO computer system, both to obtain information from the database and to enter or modify the data maintained by the system. Whenever the students or the companies encounter problems, the staff consults the data maintained by the system to diagnose and resolve the problem. Whenever the companies set up an interview date, establish or modify an interview schedule, establish a preference list, request resumés, and so on, the staff must enter information into the system. Clearly the computer database is central to the BPO's operations, and the accuracy and integrity of the database is crucial.

Back in 1984 when the first successful version of the system was new, there were some problems with the integrity and accuracy of the database. There were occasions when data would not get entered, would be entered twice, or would be entered erroneously because the responsibility for the accuracy and completeness of the database had not been defined. So Wine assigned the responsibility for maintaining each of the databases to a specific director. Margaret Brown was assigned responsibility for the COMPANY, COMPANY SCHEDULE, CONTACT, and CRIF databases; Jane Meyer was in charge of the STUDENT and PLACEMENT OFFERS databases, and so on. The directors did not personally enter all the data, but they did closely supervise their data entry personnel.

Funneling all the changes to each database through one person virtually eliminated the accuracy problems, but it created bottlenecks for companies who needed to make changes to their schedules or preference lists because only one person could handle these requests over the phone, and if that person was busy the telephone tag game came into play. Therefore the restrictions on updating databases have been relaxed so that several managers are authorized to update some of the databases. The system has been modified, however, so that each update automatically logs the time and who made the change, and the manager doing the update can also enter the name of the person at the company who requested the change. This approach is working well, both in terms of service to the companies and the integrity of the database.

As noted previously, students who have problems with the bidding system are encouraged to report them via e-mail. The routine problems are dealt with by the person who screens the e-mail, and the difficult problems are forwarded to the appropriate manager who usually uses the system to obtain the information necessary to resolve the problems.

Managing Change

Over the 15 years since Wine began trying to use the computer, technology has progressed rapidly, from the early Apple computer and million-dollar mainframes to the Pentium PC, inexpensive but powerful UNIX servers, fiber-optics communication networks, and the Web. These changes have been very beneficial, but it has not been easy to exploit them. Wine has found that many of the difficulties in exploiting these changes have been political and bureaucratic rather than technical in nature.

Political Opposition

Change was particularly hard to cope with during the early years, when Larry Easterly was University Director of Data Processing. Easterly was a traditional, conservative data processing manager, very concerned with controlling the university's computer resources and protecting his department's territory.

For example, in 1983 when NCR gave the BPO the MODUS file server and the DecisionMate PCs, Easterly was trying to control acquisition of all microcomputers that might be used for data processing. Every purchase of micro components had to be approved by Easterly's office. Although Wine did not have to purchase the NCR equipment, he did have to buy some additional components to make the overall system work, and Easterly would not approve those purchases on the grounds that Wine's equipment was not compatible with the microcomputer standards that Data Processing had set.

Dean Worthy and Wine called Easterly over to discuss the matter, and the issue of who really had control

got laid out on the table. Easterly finally agreed to let the purchases go through because Dean Worthy got tough with him, asking, "Who are you to tell the Business School how we run our business and who we get our resources from?" Easterly's reply was: "I'll let this through as an exception because of the NCR grant, but in the future I expect Jim to quit circumventing the established University rules and procedures."

A few years later, the University administration realized that the computer should be a strategic asset in higher education, and Easterly left. Since then the central computing organization has been very supportive, and Wine has not been impeded by political factors in his efforts to improve the BPO systems.

Personnel Department Problems

Although Wine has managed to obtain the necessary technical people, getting them into appropriate slots in the University position structure has been a serious problem. As mentioned above, when Wine realized he needed a professional staff he was unable to get approval for appropriate positions for them, so he cannibalized some clerical positions, hired the technical people he needed, and worked hard to get the pay up to a reasonable level. But the positions are still "clerical/technical" positions rather than "professional" positions, which means that the fringe benefits and salary levels are not appropriate to the duties that they perform. Wine explains:

> These guys are programming now in C++, Java, assembly language, dBASE and Foxpro, and they are still not classified as professional employees. There are people in the School of Business Computer Center who are professional employees making much more than my people, but are doing work that requires much less technical ability.
>
> The University has just completed a reclassification study, and everyone agrees that the duties and skills of my people justify them being in professional positions. But the Personnel Department will not reclassify my people into professional positions because we now have a clerical/technical union, and the personnel people do not want to get in trouble with the union by moving unionizable people into nonunionizable jobs.
>
> It appears that we are going to have to write new job descriptions for professional positions and then promote my people into them and not fill their old jobs. So we are still playing games because of the subterfuge we had to employ to get into the technology in the first place.

Technological Challenges

Managing the changes in the technology has not always been easy. The BPO has been through several generations of computer upgrades, and each has caused problems. Each of the hardware changes required a change in operating systems, with consequent retraining of people and conversion of the system. Also, each change in operating systems forced a conversion of the system from one database management system to another. Fortunately, the database management systems were quite similar, so the conversions were not particularly difficult, but they took time and effort and caused disruption.

The Future

When Jim Wine looks back over the history of his systems, he is amazed at the changes that have taken place:

> During the early years what we did was determined by limitations imposed upon us by hardware, politics, limited technical skills, and cost. But the Apple computers have given way to powerful Pentium PCs, and for about $20,000 we will be installing a server that is more powerful than the University mainframe that we once used for bid processing. Larry Easterly, with his focus on control of resources, is long gone, and now the central University computing organization provides a powerful computer network that we can use as we see fit. And we have our own staff of highly skilled technical people. So today what we are doing is driven by the needs of our customers, both our students and the companies who hire them.

Wine sees changes in how his system will be supported:

> Our younger managers have grown up with word processing, spreadsheets, databases, and Windows, so they sit there and fly away with multiple windows open, which wouldn't have been dreamed of just a few years ago. Today they locate the data they need, download it to their PCs, massage the data, get the results they need, and dispose of the results without help from anyone. In the future, programming may become more object-oriented, the coding will be a less demanding task, and my managers may be able to do a lot of their own work in developing or modifying our system rather than having highly technical support people do it for them.

There are three software vendors who are now offering software based upon what the Midstate University BPO has done. Their systems are roughly equivalent to Wine's system before he adopted the Web-based approach. Wine thinks that in a few years they will have caught up and he will have to consider whether to continue to develop and maintain his own system or to purchase one of these packaged systems:

> In the next three to five years we will probably have to face the issue of whether to replace our system with a software package. The tradeoff will be the cost of the people we have maintaining our software versus the cost of buying the package. Maintaining it yourself gives you great flexibility because the vendors only upgrade once a year and you have to conform to their schedule. But I expect that they will be offering excellent systems and we may not be able to justify the extra costs of having our own unique system. On the other hand, we would be giving up the competitive advantage that our system has provided to our students in attracting recruiters and keeping them coming back.

Wine's Role

In the early years of the system, Wine was continuously involved in both the development and operation of the system. Wine is aware of the huge opportunity cost of the time and effort that he has put into the BPO computer system over the years:

> A person at my level shouldn't be spending so much time working on internal operations and monkeying around with the computer system. I would be more valuable to the school if I were out visiting more companies to get them to recruit our students or soliciting gifts from them. But getting the things done that needed to get done required my leadership, vision, and technical knowledge.

Today Wine's role has changed substantially, and he is only involved when there are major operational problems and in exploring new enhancements to the system. But Wine continues to skim the articles in *PC World, PC Week,* and *Infoworld,* although he no longer reads them from cover to cover. Wine explains:

> I read these technical publications because I want to see what the major corporations are doing, and I want to know what is happening out there on the fringes where I'm going to have to be in five years. I don't have to know the details of how the technology works. I don't even have to know what it won't do, for there are lots of people who will point that out. But I want to know enough to visualize how we can use the continuing flood of new developments to improve our service to our student and company customers.

Wine is always impatient with his rate of progress in improving the system. "There are three constraints that hold you back," he explains. "First, you've got to overcome your budget constraints to get the resources you need. Second, you've got to bring your people up to where they can cope with the changing technology. Finally, you can only move so fast because your organization can only cope with a limited amount of change in a period of time."

ADVANTAGE 2000 AT OWENS CORNING

By March 1997, almost 100 weeks after the launch of Advantage 2000, Owens Corning was well on its way toward meeting its goal of implementing common, simple, global processes. It would also be one of the first U.S.-based companies to have SAP R/3[1] globally installed. In fact, Advantage 2000 had brought the company some bottom-line gains ahead of schedule:

> A key benefit of SAP is the integration of our businesses into a common global system. This increases our purchasing leverage, and we expect to save more than $17 million over the next three years. SAP also gives us a powerful tool to analyze our spending. We expect to reduce material inventories by 50 percent by the year 2000.
>
> Chief Procurement Officer, Global Sourcing

> The financial benefits already are appearing, and I believe they will exceed our expectations. With these systems we expect to perform our monthly closings in just two days by next year and in a day by the year 2000. SAP alone will give our business a full percentage point gain in productivity.
>
> Chief Financial Officer

Copyright © 1998 by Carol V. Brown. This case was prepared by Professor Carol V. Brown as the basis for class discussion, rather than to illustrate either effective or ineffective handling of an administrative situation. The author is indebted to Michael D. Radcliff, David Johns, and Robert Heinaman, who generously shared their time and insights, as well as all of the other Owens Corning managers who were interviewed by the author over a period of several years.

1 Founded in 1972, SAP AG is based in Walldorf, Germany. R/3 is SAP's enterprise-level software solution for a client/server platform that includes modules for Accounting/Finance, Materials Management, Manufacturing/Operations, Sales and Distribution, and Human Resources processes.

The Advantage 2000 project had also played an important role in the company's 1996 launch of System Thinking™, a growth strategy that shifts the market focus from individual products to system-driven solutions. This strategy leverages the company's brand and distribution strengths by offering whole-project solutions to consumers and industrial customers. For example, a Roofing System solution not only fends off outside elements, but also lets moisture out from the inside and comes with a warranty. This solution requires not just shingles products, but a full system solution of underlayment and ventilation materials as well as shingles. In the future, even Owens Corning's small building materials customers could have one-stop shopping: With a single phone call, they could order all the construction materials they needed—not just roofing materials, but eventually exterior siding, insulation, doors, windows, and pipes as well. According to CEO Hiner:

> The System Thinking concept calls for an integrated focus, a common resolve, a new way of doing business, and a sense of team that is always at the heart of success. It is a mandate for the way we think. It spells out how we approach our markets. It is the path of growth, and no one else in our industry can lay claim to this position.
>
> Glen Hiner, CEO

Advantage 2000 had also enabled the company to move towards a more process-oriented structure. Process executive roles for Finance and Sourcing were held by the CFO and Chief Procurement Officer. In early 1997, a new process executive position for Customer Fulfillment had been filled with a former business unit president. This appointment sent a clear signal that the process executives were on equal footing with the business unit presidents under a matrixed, process-oriented structure.

The key to our new process organization is the ability of Advantage 2000 systems to deliver data. With the data it provides across our businesses, the opportunities for process improvement are tremendous. Our customer fulfillment process, which spans all of our business units and business regions, will deliver more than $30 million in cost savings over the next two years through gains in productivity in each part of our process.

Process Executive, Customer Fulfillment

Yet Hiner's management team knew that when they took the industry lead with a project as large as Advantage 2000, they would make some mistakes. There was no defined path for the organization to follow in pursuit of its vision of common, simple, global processes. But that's what industry leadership is all about: pushing forward with what you believe to be the best path, and not being afraid to make a few mistakes along the way.

The Owens Corning Turnaround

Owens Corning's history began in 1935, when it was formed as a joint venture of Corning Glass and Owens-Illinois Glass to exploit a new technology: glass fiberization. By the mid-1990s, it was a world leader in building material systems and a leading producer of advanced composites and glass fiber insulation. Its 1995 sales of $3.6 billion were primarily from five businesses that produced and marketed more than 25,000 separate products, including glass fiber and foam insulation; roofing materials; doors, windows, and outdoor vinyl siding; large industrial pipes made of reinforced glass; and glass fibers and resins for synthetic yarns and composite products. Headquartered in downtown Toledo, Ohio, in early 1996 it had 11 business units, 17,000 employees in 30 countries, a 45-percent market share in the composites materials market, and the leading market position in glass fiber insulation.

However, the company was heavily in debt when Glen H. Hiner took over as CEO of Owens-Corning Fiberglas in January 1992, after a 35-year career with General Electric Company. Its successful defense against a takeover bid in the mid-1980s had required major cash and stock payouts to shareholders, and it was faced with a slew of litigation related to an insulation product that contained asbestos, a product it manufactured for 14 years from 1958 to 1972. During the next three years, Hiner infused his management team with outside talent, including a strategic planner, a new CFO from Honeywell, a new vice president of procurement, and two other new vice presidents he had worked with at General Electric (Research & Development, and Human Resources).

Under its new management team, Owens Corning began to make its customers its first priority and renewed its focus on R&D. Non-core businesses were sold, and new plants were built in Europe, Latin America, and Asia. In mid-1996, the company's New York Stock Exchange ticker symbol was changed from OCF to OWC to reflect its name change from Owens-Corning Fiberglas to Owens Corning. By July 1996, its earnings per share had more than quadrupled and its first dividend in a decade had been declared. Its trademarked pink color and Pink Panther logo had begun to be leveraged in the new System Thinking™ campaign.

Vision 2000

By early 1994, CEO Hiner had established ambitious financial, business, and workplace goals for the Year 2000, driven by three core values: customer satisfaction, individual dignity, and shareholder value (see Exhibit 1). To achieve these outcomes, the company would have to change the way it did business. The intent was to "commoditize" what didn't deliver value to the customer. This would allow the company to focus on the things that did make a difference to its customers and to make its aggressive growth goals a reality.

Hiner's Vision 2000 also included a new way of working, as summarized in Exhibit 2. These eight qualities drove his design for a new world headquarters building that became a visible symbol for the abandonment of an old hierarchical culture for the new, more entrepreneurial way of working. Completed in fall 1996, the new 3-story building replaced the 28-story tower in downtown Toledo, a few blocks away from the new site on the city's riverfront. The new headquarters is of modular design and has walls of glass with views of the Maumee River. Teamwork is supported by open workspace "pods," an abundance of formal meeting rooms, and lots of informal gathering places.

EXHIBIT 1
Year 2000 Goals.

Sales:	$5 billion in sales
Globalization:	40% sales outside the U.S.
Earnings per share:	2 × sales growth
Workforce:	Diverse
Productivity:	6% improvement each year
Workplace:	Preferred place of employment

EXHIBIT 2
Guiding Principles.

Three Core Values:

Customer Satisfaction

• World-wide product availability, pricing, delivery commitments and accurate order status at *anytime*

Individual Dignity . . . for everyone

• Global, diverse, world-class work environment with real-time information at the fingertips of *anyone* in the company who needs it *anywhere*

Shareholder Value . . . improve productivity

• Improve pre-tax earnings *by more than 1%* of sales

Workplace Vision:	
global	team-oriented
mobile	learning-based
paper-free	customer-focused
integrated	technology-enabled

We want to leverage the breadth and depth of the organization by engaging as many people as possible in problem-solving. Our focus is on decision-making closer to the customer and a culture that is more diverse and entrepreneurial.

Process Executive, Customer Fulfillment

As a first step toward achieving Vision 2000, three business process reengineering (BPR) projects were initiated by Hiner in early 1994: reengineering of the logistics and customer service processes and consolidating the finance function. Deloitte & Touche Consulting Group (CG) was engaged to work with these BPR teams. It didn't take long for the teams to conclude that the company's existing information systems would not be able to support the envisioned new processes. Information technology would therefore need to play a critical role in this companywide transformation.

New Role for the Information Systems Organization

Information systems at Owens Corning (OC) had been custom-developed in the past in order to support separate businesses and single functions. Computer interfaces were written to move data across separate functional systems and to consolidate business unit data for corporate information systems. In some cases, the old computer systems couldn't talk to each other, so inventory or production numbers had to be manually reentered. It was often impossible for a salesperson to know the availability of a product or to research an invoice problem for a major account. By 1994, the company had a complex, incompatible, and highly redundant set of more than 200 legacy systems. Due to different data definitions and years of maintenance, some of these systems now also had reliability problems.

A string of business managers had been at the helm of the Information Systems (IS) organization since the mid-1980s; a career manufacturing executive had most recently been the IS head. When the reduction of overall IS costs became a business priority in 1993, all IS units that had been reporting to business managers throughout North America were recentralized. The IS heads and their systems development teams were relocated to Toledo and began reporting to corporate IS. At the time of the reengineering projects, about 75 percent of the IS budget was directed at legacy systems enhancement and support. New development was done only on a limited basis.

In May 1994 Michael Radcliff was brought on board as the company's Chief Information Officer. Radcliff and OC's Chief Financial Officer had been executives at Honeywell at the same time. Radcliff's selection signaled top management's decision to hire a career IS executive with a significant track record who could also work well with the top management team. He arrived with a clear mandate: to help move the company into the next century by strategically aligning the IS organization to the ambitious vision for Year 2000 and to significantly cut IS operational costs worldwide.

Prior to Radcliff's coming on board, top management had assumed that the newly centralized IS group would build systems to support the new processes being designed by the BPR teams. In the past the IS organization had primarily been an order-taker, rather than a key participant in exploring alternative systems solutions to meet business needs. There was no significant IS management involvement on the BPR projects.

By June 1994, Radcliff had reoriented the logistics and customer service reengineering teams to focus on global, enterprisewide BPR and common processes that could be supported with integrated systems. A global supply-chain view of the enterprise (see Exhibit 3) was developed with the Deloitte & Touche CG consultant team as part of the enterprise process modeling over that summer.

EXHIBIT 3
Original Supply-Chain Model.

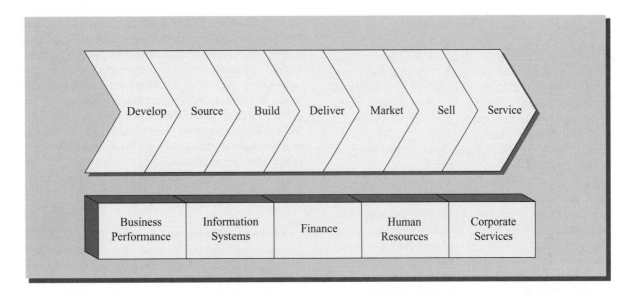

After there was a buy-in to an enterprisewide integrated systems solution, the organization sought to identify an off-the-shelf enterprise resource planning (ERP) system that could simplify the support of common, global business processes and enable OC managers to do the following:

- *access worldwide information in real time* (for inventory, production, pricing, and distribution information)
- *customize responses to meet customer needs* (for pricing, production and delivery schedules, purchasing forecasts)
- *make fully informed decisions*
- *communicate paperfree* (internal and external in-person communications and business transactions)

Radcliff also asked for and received an early management buy-in to an open systems client/server solution. This would mean migrating from an older mainframe architecture to a UNIX-based platform and a centralized relational database. Terminals connected to mainframes would be replaced with standard desktop technologies.

> Making fact-based decisions in real time is the new playing field. But you have to take care to avoid multiple images of an SAP or Oracle database or you may not get this benefit and you won't have a standard template to bring in an acquisition.
>
> Mike Radcliff, CIO

In parallel with the selection for an ERP system, an outsourcing vendor for Owens Corning's legacy systems was also sought. Outsourcing would enable the company to move from fixed cost to variable cost funding for mainframe data center operations and legacy system maintenance until the systems were replaced. An estimated $30 million in legacy system costs would be redirected toward the funding of the ERP project.

In late fall 1994, the BPR teams were brought into a lab for a hands-on investigation of SAP R/3. The feasibility of an enterprise process model and global systems solution for Owens Corning was validated. SAP's R/3 client/server enterprise system was chosen as the foundation package, and a contract was signed in December. The contract with SAP represented an enterprisewide commitment to a global initiative that would involve the redesign of most of the company's supply chain processes and the replacement of virtually all of its major systems. It also meant a large number of business users would need to be trained on Windows and personal productivity tools, including many factory floor workers who had never used computers before.

For the first time, the IS organization would be partnering with business management on a project that would radically transform the business. The new IS role was not to be an order-taker, but to "lead the parade" by managing the project teams responsible for enterprisewide implementation of common, simple, global business process redesign and systems integration. A key challenge for the IS organization was to transform itself to be in "planetary alignment" with the business transformation.

> The company has said that we'll all use the same processes. Information systems is leading the parade here because we have told the businesses that "they will" have common processes. This is a macro systems change that takes the right mix of consultants, IS, and business folks. After this implementation, the process owners will have the tool they need to drive it to best-in-the-business.
>
> VP of Global Sourcing and Logistics

In January 1995, more than 200 legacy systems were outsourced to Hewlett-Packard for operations and support. The contract included the selling of data center assets to HP and the transfer of over 50 IS personnel, who remained in the Toledo area. Outsourcing the legacy systems sent a clear signal to the whole company that the old systems were "ships to be burned" as the new systems came on-line. There was no turning back.

The "fencing off" of legacy system support via an outsourcing contract was also considered critical for another reason. It allowed IS managers to focus on acquiring the new skillsets that were needed for the ERP initiative—coined Advantage 2000.

The SAP Implementation Plan

A senior executive steering committee for the Advantage 2000 project was formed by the end of 1994. The members of the steering committee included the CFO, three business unit heads, a VP of corporate Human Resources, and two other functional VPs. The makeup of the committee clearly reflected the top-down leadership support that would be needed for a multiyear initiative with an estimated $100 million pricetag.

By early 1995, a 100-week implementation plan had been agreed on for reengineering the company's global business processes and replacing about 200 of its legacy systems with SAP's client/server system. The 100-week schedule also helped both IS and business managers have an end in sight. However, OC's top managers also believed that no other company was trying to do an implementation of this scope so fast.

> Advantage 2000 is a bold move for Owens Corning. We're replacing 200 legacy systems across the company with a handful of systems using SAP as the backbone.
>
> Chief Financial Officer

An aggressive timetable was a critical decision. The intent was to minimize the likelihood that a key senior business executive would "jump ship" or cease to support the project goals before it was completed. Top management was sure that the pain would be considerable, but the pain to achieve integration would be the same whether an aggressive schedule was followed or not. Full support and leadership at the top executive level was the only way a project of this magnitude could succeed. Some thought that the longer a project dragged on, the greater the risk that midlevel managers would design ways to protect the status quo. Weekly goals of 1 percent progress were identified and reported on each week to the project steering committee.

> We decided to learn not by studying it and then training on it, but by doing it.
>
> Mike Radcliff, CIO

> The longer you take, the harder it is: managers change and the business requirements change. We have been very careful not to delay unless it was absolutely necessary. In the old Owens Corning we would have changed this schedule fifty times for all different reasons. Today we plow through.
>
> Global Development Leader, Sales Advantage

The two-year schedule for a global implementation also meant that "good enough" process reengineering would be the initial focus. Achieving an integrated process solution was the initial implementation outcome, not achieving best-in-class processes. Multiple project teams would work in parallel to identify and gain buy-in to simple, common, global process solutions across its business units. Variations would be driven by customer and product differences, not business unit differences. A perfection mentality would not work under this plan —initially there would be no bells and whistles. Instead, successive waves of process-driven change would be directed at achieving world class outcomes by the Year 2000.

> We told the Division Presidents we're going to piss off a lot of people, but it is more important that systems work for the whole company than to have all the bells and whistles everyone wants.
>
> Mike Radcliff, CIO[2]

The development process basically had four steps. First the business team members would design the global process. Then the business and IS team members would

---

[2] Based on a quote reported in the June 19, 1995 issue of *Forbes*.

look at SAP, identify the gaps, and work through them. A prototype was built, and then the system configuration was finalized.

Multiple SAP releases were planned over the 100-week period. The release concept entailed "shrink wrapping" several products—new processes and new systems—into a single release. This avoided the problem of business units having to contend with multiple delivery dates by multiple project teams. The number of releases was intentionally small. At a given point in time, then, the SAP global teams would be engaged in different project phases for a given release.

The release plan in effect in early 1996 is shown in Exhibit 4. Release 1 targeted a single corporate function (finance), which was one of the original reengineering projects and had computer-savvy leaders. Release 2 included a full set of manufacturing and distribution modules using version 2.2 of SAP R/3 for a major business unit outside the U.S. (Building Materials Europe), as well as several fabrication plants in North America. Release 3 implemented a standard client/server infrastructure in about 100 North American locations. It entailed installing wide area networks, local area networks, and about 5000 new desktops (hardware and software) that would be able to access the centralized Oracle database in Toledo. Release 4 would begin to exploit the multinational and multilingual capabilities of a new R/3 version (3.0) that would be implemented over several waves. By 1997, the scope had grown to more than 140 locations and more than 10,000 end-users.

The 4-release plan was also designed to take advantage of organizational learning from earlier releases. Release 1 would require learning the package and development tools as well as a new systems integration methodology by the project teams. It also needed to be an

EXHIBIT 4
100-Week 4-Release Plan as of March 1996.

1995			1996				1997	
Q2	Q3	Q4	Q1	Q2	Q3	Q4	Q1	Q2

R1
R2
R3
R4

"early win." Release 2 would be the pilot for implementing a full global supply chain set of modules within a single business unit and would serve as a pilot for change management and end-user training. Release 4 would have multiple waves so that mistakes made in the first business unit implementation could be corrected before the next wave. In the literature this became known as a "slow burn" type of a "big bang strategy."[3]

At the time of the formal Advantage 2000 launch in April 1995, Radcliff didn't have an IS workforce with the capabilities needed to manage this megaproject, let alone a workforce skilled in client/server technologies and global IS-business partnering. To be successful, the IS organization would also have to take the lead in learning to work in new ways.

Creating a High Performance IS Organization

Radcliff knew when he arrived in Toledo that he would need to transform the IS organization from a maintenance and support mindset to a high performance mindset. But he didn't yet know how to design a high performing IS organization or exactly what it would take to get there. His ideas began to crystallize as he became familiar with Hiner's vision for the new world headquarters and worked with that planning group. At a two-day retreat with his IS management team a few months after his arrival, Radcliff shared his overall vision for a high performance, project-based IS organization focused on rapid systems delivery. Moving to an integrated, cross-functional systems environment was a paradigm shift for this IS organization. So were the "stretch" project goals and highly visible milestones of Advantage 2000.

One of the outcomes of the IS team's discussions about what high performance really meant was a set of six values (see Exhibit 5). The first three values emphasized work changes critical to the 100-week schedule: invention, fast tracking, partnership. The other three values were slogans that characterized a team-based project environment: IS employees in the new IS organization would have to be encouraged to challenge the status quo, initiate bold changes, and learn, but to also work fast and be a team player. The "attitude wins" value was intended to help set up an environment in which an individual was free to fail.

---

3 For example, see Christopher Koch, "Flipping the Switch," *CIO,* June 15, 1996, pp. 43–66.

EXHIBIT 5

Six Values for the IS Organization.

Invention	*Invent the future; continuously challenge the status quo*
Fast Tracking	*Performance: start now, deliver soon, learn quick*
Partnership	*Collaborate for results; harness diversity*
Everything is a Project	*Achieve your goals by: aim high, set directions, plan milestones*
We All Contribute	*World Class organizations are built by world class people; competitive advantage from personal growth*
Attitude Wins	*Integrity, pride, and enthusiasm count*

We needed to create an environment for the new playing field, but this was a big change. Our strategy was to be an easy, friendly, desirable company to do business with, and we needed the best, happiest, empowered people to do this. But empowering people to do their jobs—so that they don't have to ask permission to make good decisions—had a much broader range of personal reactions than we thought. Some people gravitated to it and jumped across to lead in the new way right away. Others went through a "feeling bad" stage, then confusion until they found a ladder or a rope that helped them figure it out. Then there's a "not so bad" stage before the final stage in which you can see some advantages from the change.

Mike Radcliff, CIO

Deloitte & Touche CG (D&T) was the consulting company engaged by OC's top management prior to Radcliff's arrival due to their expertise in organization design, BPR, and change management. In consultation with D&T, the new IS organization was graphically designed as three primary structures, linked to each other and to the business units (see Exhibit 6). First, Global Development Teams of IS employees and business representatives were responsible for delivering the four releases over the 100-week project. Second, IS Consultants would serve as account managers for each business unit (or region). They would not only ensure ongoing IS service levels (by the outsourcing vendor) during the transition period, but would also help prepare the business units for SAP deployment. Third, IS Capability teams would be established to diffuse new methods, build new skillsets, and integrate initiatives across the IS organization.

By early 1995, some of the Advantage 2000 project teams started to be formed and people began to be identified for the IS and business roles on these teams. Once the Advantage 2000 project was launched, an average of 50 to 75 consultants (including consultants from SAP AG) worked side-by-side with OC's IS managers as IS Capability leaders, global development subteam leaders, and technology trainers as well as in other development and implementation roles. Full-time D&T consultants were relied on for their systems integration and project management expertise.

Two "IS transformation" workshops were held in order to communicate to the entire IS community the new high performance environment (HPE) objectives. The June 1995 workshop focused on the vision and values of IS, and the October 1995 workshop focused on how the IS organization would be organized to do it. How to juggle three balls at once was a skill taught to all IS employees as a metaphor for learning how to manage a complex megaproject, as well as learning how to help each other.

Juggling is a great metaphor for what we are doing, which is getting everybody involved, mastering their competencies, and learning by doing. We all have a responsibility to ourselves for individual transforma-

EXHIBIT 6
The High Performance Environment.

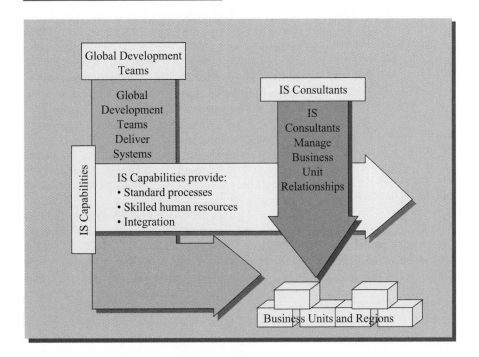

tion, but we also have a collective responsibility to help everyone on the team make the transformation as well. We are not done until everybody can juggle.

Mike Radcliff, CIO[4]

We needed to move people from a Comfort zone to an Awkward zone, but not get people in a Fear zone where they'd be paralyzed. You can't learn to juggle three balls at once. You have to learn to juggle one, learn to juggle two and then learn to juggle three. We also made it fun; it broke up the day.

Bob Heinaman, IS Director

During the fall of 1995, the new HPE design began to "all come together" for those in the new IS leadership positions. At its peak, a total of about 250 internal employees were assigned full-time to the Advantage 2000 project, including approximately 120 IS, 115 business, and 12 full-time Human Resources personnel. Having about half of the team members come from the

business side meant that the focus was on achieving the business outcomes.

The Human Resources employees included 10 to 12 change management, organization design, and training employees who were dedicated to Advantage 2000 from the outset of the project. HR staff worked closely with the BPR teams, doing a lot of benchmarking. They also worked alongside the Deloitte & Touche CG/ICS experts to develop and deliver training to the project teams on process simplification. The HR unit had a contractual arrangement with DDS, one of SAP AG's partners, for the development of end-user training materials, including language translations (e.g., French). Change management was critical for the project to succeed, and the HR component of the Advantage 2000 project was viewed as an integral piece.

The HR staff also helped design two financial incentive plans to help retain employees critical to the project. The first incentive plan took advantage of a preexisting incentive structure at OC: a year-end bonus. OC employees already a part of this plan were eligible for a bonus of 15 to 40 percent of one year's salary; employees not on this plan were eligible for a bonus up to 15 percent. The

---

4 A juggling CIO Mike Radcliff was featured on *Computer World's* cover for their June 1996 "The 100 Best Places to Work" issue.

second incentive plan was unique to the Advantage 2000 project: a project completion bonus in the form of stock options at 20 percent of the employee's annual salary (or higher). The plans were put in place at the time of the Advantage 2000 launch.

Finding the right mix of consultants and internal employees was an ongoing challenge. Top management knew they needed external expertise for this scope and type of organizational change. However, if the external consultants were relied on to lead project teams, then project management skills and SAP knowledge might not be transferred to OC's workforce as quickly. By early 1996, each D&T consultant was paired with two OC managers—one with a business focus, one with a technology focus—as part of a plan to transition out the consultants. By the fall of 1996, all full-time consultants had been transferred out of the IS organization.

> We were clear up front that we were hiring expertise for knowledge transfer. Determine what you want the consultants to do and have that as an agreement in the consultant contract. Don't hand the project over to an outside integrator.
>
> David Johns, Director of Global Development

More detailed descriptions of the groups and roles represented by the three arrows in Exhibit 6 are provided below.

Global Development Teams

A Global Development Team of IS and business representatives was created for each of the global processes in the revised business process model (see Exhibit 7). The primary objective of each global team was to develop and deliver process and systems solutions on time. Five teams were given responsibility for the supply-chain processes (product development, sourcing, manufacturing, sales, and customer service). Each global development team also had subteams. For example, the Sales Advantage Team had three subteams: Field Sales Automation, Pricing, and Demand Forecasting. Two additional teams were responsible for enterprise support.

A third enterprise support team (Workplace Technology) was initially charged with selecting standard desktop tools and rolling them out to every link in the value chain. However, after release 2 it was decided that these tasks could be better achieved if these team members were integrated into the other global development teams. Except for a small subset of team members who were

EXHIBIT 7
Global Development Teams.

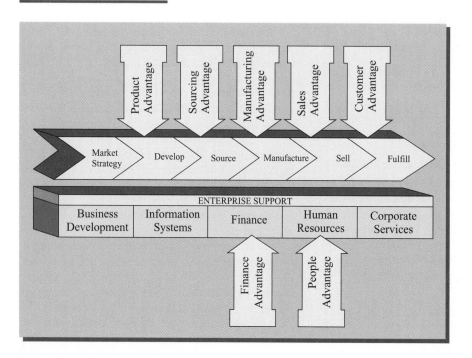

responsible for the technology for the new headquarters building scheduled to open in fall 1996, the Workplace Technology team was disbanded and its members were reassigned.

A standard report format was used to keep the Steering Committee members informed. Three "vital signs" were reported on by each project team on a weekly basis: Scope, Schedule, and Budget. For each vital sign, there was a color code:

Red	External intervention required ("In trouble")
Yellow	Behind, but recoverable ("Caution")
Green	On track (a "Go")

For any vital sign not coded Green, a plan "to get to Green" was part of the report.

Each team had a **Global Development Leader** (GDL) who was responsible for project planning and making sure the team was "on course" in terms of both schedule and budget. Each GDL was a full-time OC employee, although some consultants were assigned to be leaders of subteams. Initially, some GDLs had responsibility for more than one project team, but as the project teams became established and the project work was launched, each project team had its own GDL.

Most of the GDLs had previously been systems development managers reporting to business unit heads a few years earlier. This meant that the typical GDL had already established extensive working relationships with key members of the business community. This IS leadership experience came to be recognized as a major workforce asset for the Advantage 2000 project.

> All GDLs have experience in the business units, many in multiple businesses. That means they are credible on the business side and have a huge informal network.
>
> Global Development Leader, Sales Advantage

The only external IS hire for a GDL position was David Johns who had worked with CIO Radcliff at Honeywell. Johns originally headed up both the Finance and Sourcing Advantage project teams when he arrived in Fall 1994, and then he became the GDL for Finance alone. But in July 1995, it became clear that integration across the supply chain project teams needed to be focused on by someone on a weekly and daily basis, and Johns moved into the new Director of Global Development position.

> The integration of SAP is one of its biggest benefits, but also the most difficult part of it. Everything has touchpoints. Each team wants to focus on their own project, but complete integration is needed across the development teams. A Director position is the best approach to fit a very aggressive timeframe. This was a big lesson learned.
>
> David Johns, Director of Global Development

Multiday, intensive workshops with GDLs and other IS managers were held in order to plan a new release. When major issues arose among business executives, Johns and Radcliff helped provide "air cover" for the GDLs and their team members so that they could stay focused on the release deadlines.

Success in a GDL position required a mixture of solid technology, business, and leadership experience. They needed to be comfortable with learning new technologies, as well as leading a cross-functional team with business managers and IS professionals. GDLs also needed excellent interpersonal skills as they sometimes had to make some unpopular decisions. They also had to get comfortable with and trust the business leaders on their teams, as the success of the project relied heavily on the process knowledge and negotiation skills of these team members.

GDLs also needed to be able to help create a work environment based on the new IS organization values in which it was all right to take risks and make some mistakes. The aggressive schedule often meant that they themselves had to believe in the Advantage 2000 project goals, even though they might not yet know how they would achieve them.

Business Roles on the Global Development Teams

A co-leadership role with the GDL was played by **Business Process Leaders** (BPLs) who had primary responsibility for business process reengineering. BPLs were senior managers or other high achievers from a function or business unit who were typically assigned to an Advantage 2000 project team full-time.[5] They were the primary business interface for their team during the life of the project. Having a high-level business manager assigned full-time to an IS project was new at OC, so the BPL role was a highly visible sign that Advantage 2000 was a strategic business initiative.

For example, the Manufacturing Advantage team had four BPLs who were responsible for business process innovation across four major business units (Insulation-North America, Composites, Roofing & Asphalt, Building

---

5 Some compromise arrangements were made for those from Europe: not all were full-time.

Materials), two smaller business units (Windows, Foam), and the VP of Engineering. One BPL was assigned to each of the three global manufacturing processes (product definition, manufacturing planning and execution, plant maintenance), and the fourth BPL was a "floater."

All business team members were physically located ("co-located") with the IS team members at the Toledo headquarters. For example, all four of the Manufacturing BPLs had relocated to Toledo in order to take this Advantage 2000 assignment. Team members saw each other daily, and OC's top management team shared the same building.

The BPLs were responsible for taking global business process redesign to the point of buy-in from the process owners in each affected business unit and corporate function. The business process owners were typically at the VP level within a function or business unit; in a few cases the BPL on a project team was also a process owner. In the past, business units did not regularly confer with each other; they were "stovepiped." The BPL's job thus entailed getting buy-in to common processes across constituencies that had not been required to work together before. The BPL was responsible for ensuring that all process owners endorsed the new common, global processes and enterprisewide systems products that the project team was preparing to configure and deliver. Because business process redesign was required for every release, this was a critical role.

Accepting a BPL position involved some career risks. A BPL sometimes needed to convince high-level business managers of the value of a new process design that could be significantly different from the old way of doing things. Sometimes a BPL had to persuade old bosses to accept a suboptimization of an existing business process within their own former business unit in order to optimize a given process for the good of the enterprise. A customized legacy system solution may have offered more functionality than would be provided by an SAP module. Getting buy-in to common processes therefore often required giving up a former business allegiance or personal loyalty. BPLs needed to be open and candid communicators and persuasive negotiators.

There were also some risks on the part of the business units. A business unit may have given up one of their best-and-brightest to the Advantage 2000 project in order to increase the likelihood that a new global process would be closer to world class during the initial SAP implementation. Business unit heads also had to decide whether or not to "backfill" a BPL's job in the business unit. In most cases, the business units couldn't afford to leave a business unit position open for the duration of the project and did replace the manager. They also had to resist pulling off one of their prized managers from the Advantage 2000 project as time went on, although the vast majority of BPLs were expected to return to a business unit assignment after the release 4 rollout. Management also had to figure out ways to keep their key business representatives informed of important business changes. Many BPLs had a high-level mentor to help them stay current; those from international sites tried to arrange in-person visits to the home unit.

In addition to the BPLs, other business personnel were full-time members on the development teams as business process experts and analysts. Managers at lower levels than the BPLs were relied on for their detailed knowledge of old business processes and their ability to learn how to script the new processes for SAP. For many of these business managers, there was also considerable personal sacrifice: Relocation to Toledo was required, and for some this meant an international move (from Europe, Latin America, or Asia). Some business personnel were transitioned back to a business or corporate unit prior to a release in order to become a resident process expert and business champion.

The IS Consultant Role

Under the prior IS organization structure, each North American business unit had its own IS head and systems development teams that serviced its needs with considerable autonomy. In recent years IS developers had often performed heroic systems maintenance efforts for them as their legacy systems became unwieldy. This relationship changed in 1993, when North American IS units were centralized into a corporate IS group as part of the company's overall recentralization strategy.

> There was a tremendous sense of loss. Business managers were asking "who is my IS guy?" They needed a senior person who was an IS spokesperson, who could help match their systems plan with the business plan.
>
> Mike Radcliff, CIO

Under Radcliff, the former IS units heads continued to be the senior IS strategists for their business units. Similar to an account manager in a consultant organization, they would sit on the leadership team of their business unit and often were treated as if they continued to report to the business unit head, rather than to the new CIO. However, as the IS leadership team began to identify what management skills were needed for the Advantage 2000 projects during the initial months of planning in 1995, essentially all of these recentralized IS unit heads were tapped for global project team roles due to their business process knowledge and project management experience.

Other IS managers were therefore selected for the new account manager roles represented by the rightmost vertical arrow in Exhibit 6. These IS Consultants became the business unit's new primary point-of-contact and spokesperson for corporate IS. Key attributes were really understanding the business and having an interest in partnering with senior business managers; acquiring hot technology skillsets was not the key focus of this role. Two IS Consultants also had larger operational roles for non-U.S. regions: one for the U.K and Europe and the other for Asia (including China).

Because legacy systems operations and support in North America were outsourced to Hewlett-Packard, a primary IS Consultant responsibility was to serve as the business unit's liaison with HP to ensure satisfactory service levels. The goal was to decrease legacy spending, but to keep the old mainframe systems operational until the new systems were implemented. Managing the IS outsourcing costs became a key concern as the Advantage 2000 project costs increased. The IS Consultant helped plan the business unit's budget for any legacy systems maintenance during the transition period. Only changes that were absolutely necessary were to be contracted for—such as changes dictated by a regulatory agency or other competitive conditions.

All IS Consultants also played a key role in helping to plan for the Advantage 2000 releases. For release 3 they inventoried existing desktop tools, helped the IS organization understand the business unit's end-user computing needs, and oversaw the local implementation of the standard networked desktop. For release 4 they worked with business unit management to get business resources assigned to the local deployment teams. By early 1997 the relatively free-standing IS Consultants were given an even stronger accountability to corporate IS by assigning them to the Sourcing & Alliances Capability; the intent was to improve the management of contracts and relationships with legacy system and desktop support vendors.

Developing New IS Capabilities

The implementation of cross-functional global project teams for systems integration and IS Consultants for single-point-of-contact roles for business managers are organization designs that can be found in many other organizations. However, the design and implementation

of the new IS Capabilities represented by the horizontal arrow in Exhibit 6 was a much bigger challenge for Radcliff's management team. The objectives weren't the problem. It was clear that new capabilities needed to be developed to ensure both speed and quality—hallmarks of a high performance work environment. What wasn't clear was what kind of structure should be developed in order to provide new standard processes and methods, new supporting tools, and human resources skilled in these methods and tools. Another unknown was the range of capabilities that would be needed.

As a result, the needed IS Capabilities continued to evolve over the 100-week implementation plan. For example, Exhibit 8 shows the eleven capabilities in place in March 1996. The first four were related to the systems integration life cycle—Planning & Project Management, Process Innovation, Technology Applications (development work, including SAP configuration and scripting), and Release Management. Three other capabilities were related to ongoing IT infrastructure planning and systems support: Architecture, Service Operations, and Sourcing & Alliances. The last four capabilities provide ongoing support to project teams, the IS leadership team, and sometimes the IS organization as a whole: Communications (including the intranet), Resource Development, Finance, and Administration.

EXHIBIT 8
IS Capabilities.

System Integration	Planning & Project Management
	Process Innovation
	Technology Applications
	Release Management
Architecture & Alliances	Architecture
	Service Operations
	Sourcing & Alliances
Intranet/Communications	
Resource Development	
Finance	
Administration	

Each capability had a **Capability Leader** who was accountable for the processes, methods, and tools of the capability, as well as the development of the skillsets for the people assigned to the capability. Usually reporting to each Leader was one or more **Capability Experts** who concentrated on the identification and transfer of best practices for the capability. Most capabilities also had a **Capability Council** that served as the training center for the capability.

Each member of a Global Development Team was assigned to a capability, and each team had at least one representative on the Capability Council. Subteams within the Councils worked on special initiatives. Initially, the capability assignments were made for each project team member based on their old job duties. Eventually, all IS assignment (job) descriptions included not only project team responsibilities, but also capability responsibilities.

Each project team member was responsible for balancing their time between global team project tasks and tasks to enhance an IS Capability. However, the tie-breaker for an individual team member was clearly the project: The primary allegiance was to the project team. This was a paradigm shift for the IS employees, because in the past, an individual had considered himself or herself to be a database person or a telecommunications person first. A key Capability Leader role, then, was to help an individual negotiate the best balance when project team and individual capability objectives were in conflict.

When Advantage 2000 was launched, some of the Capability Leaders for the systems integration life cycle were Deloitte & Touche CG/ICS consultants. For example, the **Planning & Project Management Capability** had a D&T leader after the project was underway in order to leverage the consultants' expertise in managing this type and scope of project. As the Advantage 2000 project plans progressed, more focus was placed on transferring project management skills. David Johns became the Director of the five supply chain teams in late 1995. Several months later he moved into the Capability Leader position and formed a Council of GDLs that began to meet weekly. By late summer 1996, all other Capability Leader positions were also held by Owens Corning staff.

The **Release Management Capability** was responsible for product deployment, which includes two primary tasks: release preparation, including the "cleansing" and converting of data and infrastructure work; and actual deployment and coordination of post-installation support. Deploying a product release required coordination across multiple project teams, HR personnel responsible

for training, and local business unit managers. For releases 1 and 2, the primary responsibility for deployment was in the hands of the GDLs and their team members assigned to this capability. For the desktop implementation in release 3, the Capability Leader took the lead role because the focus was on infrastructure rather than system development. This meant that the global development team leaders could stay tightly focused on getting the release 4 products ready for on-time delivery.

Another capability closely tied to the GDLs was the **Intranet/Communications Capability.** Initially part of the Planning and Project Management Capability, it became a separate capability after it became clear that communications and information sharing would be key success factors for the Advantage 2000 project. Each global development team had at least one member assigned to the Communications Capability, which was responsible for communications across global project teams and the rest of the IS community as well as for communications between the IS organization and the rest of the company. Each capability member was responsible for providing monthly reports and sharing best practices for their project team. After the implementation of a standard desktop technology (Windows 95 platform) in release 3, the emphasis shifted from hardcopy reports to intranet communications. Progress reports from the project teams and new procedures could be posted on a single Web server, and documents could be quickly and easily shared across geographic distances.

Another capability that did not initially exist was the **Sourcing & Alliances Capability,** responsible for managing vendor relationships for the IS organization. At the start of the project, there was only one major outsourcing partner (Hewlett-Packard for legacy systems operation and support), and the management of the outsourcing relationship was dispersed across the IS Consultants (described previously). This plan made sense because in the past systems had been custom developed for the business units. However, under this dispersed structure, the execution of the outsourcing contract with HP turned out to be a very bumpy ride. The legacy system costs continued to be a larger organizational expense than expected.

The Sourcing & Alliances Capability set up a superstructure for coordinating contacts across the IS Consultants who previously had acted on behalf of their business managers, not on behalf of the enterprise as a whole. Giving the responsibility for managing this strategic alliance to a high-level capability manager meant that the rest of the IS leadership team could stay focused on the systems integration goals. The Capability Leader position was given a dual reporting arrangement—reporting not only to the CIO, but also to the VP of Sourcing—in order to establish high-level accountability to the senior business managers. As business units encountered problems with service levels provided by the outsourcing vendor—e.g., help desk services—the IS Consultants worked with the Capability Leader to identify the scope of the problem and to provide input to enterprise-level solutions.

An external hire who had previously worked with Radcliff at Honeywell was brought in to lead the Sourcing & Alliances Capability, and the scope of his responsibilities expanded as new vendor contracts were established. For example, HP was also contracted for wide area network support and help desk support for the new systems, and Vanstar was engaged to provide LAN and desktop support.

The transformation of the IS organization to a high performance environment required a whole new structure for the IS organization as well as a whole new set of human resource practices and processes. Radcliff originally planned to rely heavily on OC's HR department, and a corporate HR staff member was assigned to the IS organization. However, after a few months it became apparent that the "care and feeding" of the IS people was receiving inadequate attention. With the blessing of the new senior vice president of HR, a **Resource Development Capability** was established within the IS organization in August 1995, and Bob Heinaman was designated the Capability Leader. The establishment of this capability was a clear signal to the IS workforce that the new IS organization was committed to developing a high-performance workforce.

Several reasons surfaced to explain why the original plan for an HR partnership did not work. Some felt that the assigned HR employee was not in a senior enough position to expeditiously implement all of the changes needed to move an entire unit from job-based work to project-based assignments and from manager-initiated to employee-initiated career development. Others pointed out that the Global Development Leaders and some of the other Capability Leaders had aggressive project milestones, and their attention was supposed to be focused on project demands, not the people side. Their incentives were directed at short-term results, not long-term development of internal human resources.

Several major HR initiatives were championed by Heinaman (see Exhibit 9). For example, a new six-level broadband compensation scheme that was competency-based was initiated in the first quarter of 1996. Each project team role was assigned a competency level and an IS

EXHIBIT 9
Processes and Subprocesses for IS Human Resources.

Capability assignment. Within each level there were three sublevels to ensure that IS employees would help each other: *learning, can do,* and *can teach.* Another early initiative was the implementation of an employee-led appraisal process with 360-degree feedback: Employees solicit evaluations from up to 10 people of their choice who are in positions below, above, and beside their own, or some other relevant sampling.

> We tried to stay aligned with the resource development of OC as a whole and act as a pilot. We didn't want to look as if we were on attack. We focused on what was IS-specific and identified individual skillsets and stretch goals for their development.
>
> Bob Heinaman, Resource Capability Leader

By early December 1996, after new processes and structures had been successfully implemented for the IS organization, it was decided to "turn back the keys" to HR for these initiatives. The separate IS Capability was terminated, and Heinaman moved on to the People Advantage GDL assignment responsible for HR systems.

Learning from the Early SAP Releases

Release 1: Finance Consolidation

Release 1 involved implementing SAP as part of the consolidating of financial operations, including the centralization of accounts payable, expense and travel accounts, and payroll systems. The reengineering project for Finance was one of the early ones, and the process reengineering began an entire year before Radcliff's arrival. By late 1994, these functions had pretty much been consolidated, one North American factory at a time, and operations were being run out of headquarters and out of an accounting center set up in West Virginia. The SAP R/3 system replacement was scheduled for release 1 because it would provide an SAP project experience for a corporate function that had already been heavily reengineered.

Release 1 was scheduled for October 1995 and was completed on time. This was an early, visible win for the project and bolstered confidence that the 100-week plan was on target.

> You need to do everything you can to make the first cycle happen as quickly as possible. We focused on speed. The consultants brought to the plate an understanding of SAP. Having the project teams live together and work together also helped.
>
> Global Development Leader, Sourcing Advantage

That doesn't mean there weren't some implementation problems. For example, a software glitch that delayed the printing of payroll checks was highlighted in an article published in *Forbes.*[6]

Release 2: Supply Chain Processes Pilot

Release 2 was scheduled for early 1996 and involved rolling out SAP R/3 version 2.2E at eight fabrication plants in North America, five plants in the United Kingdom (Building Materials Europe division), and in the corporate research and engineering function. Release 2 was viewed as critical for finding out what it took to deploy new processes and systems within a business unit release, including SAP training and change management. This would allow for adjustments to be made to the deployment plans before release 4, when a newer SAP version would be rolled out to all business units, including sites in Latin America and the Asia Pacific.

Building Materials Europe (BME), an organization with a total of 750 employees in the United Kingdom, served as a business unit pilot.[7] Because BME had been developed, in large part, with acquisitions from 1994 to 1996, its management had inherited multiple systems that did not provide the information they needed to run the business. The BME president and his leadership team were all willing to risk the problems associated with being first, because it would mean a major step forward toward system integration and process improvements.

BME's legacy systems were outsourced to HP shortly after a new IS manager came on board at the end of 1994 as the business unit's IS head and new corporate IS manager for all of Europe. The intent was to do only "good enough reengineering" as part of the release. The six values put together by the IS leadership team in 1994 helped serve as "navigation instruments" for this IS team, which was working in a different culture with different work habits.

> The values are all the more important for me since I'm not in Toledo. We have a laminated card that gives us three- to four-word sentences about what high performance means.
>
> IS Consultant for BME and Service
> Capability Leader for Europe

The release 2 deployment was driven by the global development teams, along with corporate HR. BME didn't have the advantage of being able to learn from

---

6 Neil Weinberg. "Think globally, act incrementally," *Forbes,* June 19, 1995, pp. 88–89.

7 In January 1998, BME's organizational name was changed to International Building Materials Systems.

other business units in the U.K. or any other OC business units. In fact, most companies in Europe were implementing SAP module by module, rather than in the "big bang" approach being used at OC.

One of the biggest surprises from release 2 was that the resources needed for deployment preparation and for actual deployment had been significantly underestimated. The training programs were expanded to include not just basic PC navigation skills, but also process training. This would mean a lot more business involvement in the training. Deployments also began to be planned much further in advance, and the training was timed to be as close to actual deployment as possible. The training and deployment cost estimates for 1995 to 1997 were increased to $35 million, with a projected total project cost of $110 million.

Release 2 had also significantly increased the confidence of the project team members; the consultants were gone, and the release was successful. They also had learned a lot about each other: The business process leaders better understood the trials and tribulations faced by IS managers, and the IS people learned to appreciate how changes in business executives and business processes affected the work of the business process leaders. Co-locating the project team members had helped create a learning environment. While still housed in the glass tower in downtown Toledo, the global team members worked in four-person pods alongside the consultants and global team leaders. Some building walls were even physically removed, and the CIO and his Director of the SAP project worked without walls between their key administrative assistants and their own desks. The first end-of-year bonus for the global development teams also had worked well in terms of the systems release schedule and proved to be "battery-recharging."

Releases 3: Developing a Global Infrastructure
Like many large organizations, OC had multiple e-mail systems and network standards as well as many different PC platforms and desktop software applications across its business units. The objective of release 3 was to implement a simple, common, global infrastructure solution that would enable reliable desktop access to the Toledo headquarters worldwide as well as lower global support costs. Initially about 80 geographic locations were involved, but the scope and complexity of the project grew over the life of the 100-week project due to acquisition activity and other growth initiatives. By the time of deployment, release 3 entailed installing wide area networks, local area networks, and about 5000 standard desktop setups for more than 10,000 end-users at more than 140 locations.

The responsibility for selecting the new standards and planning the infrastructure upgrades initially resided in an independent enterprise support team—a Workplace Technology team. Microsoft was selected as the vendor standard for microcomputer operating systems (Windows 95 and NT) and personal productivity software (Microsoft Office). In order to support the global implementation of a client/server application such as SAP, the network implementation included upgrading "by orders of magnitude" to a cost-effective solution capable of handling the anticipated increase in global communications traffic (via frame relay). At the time of release 3 deployment, most of the original team members had been reassigned and a core technology team oversaw the global implementation, including the new world headquarters.

Release 3 was therefore the first Advantage 2000 implementation that involved widespread technology change across the company. It also was on the critical path for release 4 because it established both the client/server infrastructure and the basic end-user computing skills required for the effective SAP R/3 deployment at OC's largest business units. The HR members of the Advantage 2000 project partnered with an outside vendor to deliver end-user training. The IS Consultants played a key role in inventorying the pre-existing desktop tools; the knowledge they gained about end-user computing in these business units was used in the selection of local deployment teams for release 4.

Release 4: Global R/3 Implementation
The primary systems objective of release 4 was to get all of the business running on a common platform. SAP was to be deployed in successive waves—a mini "big bang," one business unit at a time. In the original 100-week plan, deployment would begin in the summer of 1996. The plan was initially revised to roll out the new SAP version at BME and the three major business units (Composites, Roofing & Asphalt, Insulation North America) during the first quarter of 1997.[8] Sometime later it was determined that the company wouldn't be able to sustain the successive 30-day deployments at these major business units,

---

8 In a January 1998 reorganization, BME became International Building Materials Systems, the Composites division became Composites Systems Business, and the other North American divisions were reorganized under an umbrella organization: North American Building Materials Systems, encompassing Roofing Systems Business, Insulating Systems Business, Exterior Systems Business, and System Thinking Sales and Distribution.

and the plan was changed to allow 60 days between waves. The deployment of a field sales automation tool would follow four to six weeks after a business unit switched over to SAP.

The holiday window at the end of December 1996 was used to upgrade the release 2 sites to version 3.0d of SAP R/3. This wave involved not only a new R/3 version, but also new configurations due to process changes as well as new functionality. December 25 was the only day the project teams weren't working. The first new business unit implementation (Roofing & Asphalt) was scheduled for March 1997, with the Insulation division to follow 60 days later, followed by Composites.

> We've become experts in system testing and very good at understanding what SAP integration means. The release deployment was changed because we had significantly increased the scope. We now have 140 locations, instead of about 80 as originally planned, because of acquisitions. The scope has also increased as we have turned over the rocks; we have increased the functionality and have additional bolt-ons. We also need time to pay attention to the lessons learned from what other business units did.
>
> David Johns, Director of Global Development

> The delays were greeted with mixed emotions. This is an intense project, and we wanted to be done. But the people had been giving as much as they could, and they didn't want to jeopardize the success of the project. Still, it was tough to have an installation over the holidays.
>
> Global Development Leader, Sourcing Advantage

Several learnings from release 2 were incorporated into the release 4 deployment. First, more accountability for deployment activities was given to the Release Management Capability and less to the GDLs. This separation of development and deployment responsibilities meant that the project team leaders could stay focused on getting the products ready to deploy, while the Capability Leader could begin release planning and communications way ahead of the rollout date. For example, the local business people responsible for leading the release 4 implementation were identified one year in advance.

Another learning from release 2 was to increase the training time on the new business processes. Once the first major business unit was brought on-line, it would also be possible to use a "play with sand in the sandbox" training approach: Actual production data could be used to train on different business scenarios. The business process owners would also be more involved in and have greater accountability for the deployment.

The number of business employees that would receive training at corporate headquarters was also significantly increased. Instead of the 500 "champions" in the original plan, more than 900 people were identified and trained to become the on-site trainers and support personnel at the local sites. This resulted in a champion/employee ratio of 1:7 instead of 1:10 or 1:15 in some plants. The typical-sized plant would have multiple champions trained for each process.

The March 1997 Roofing & Asphalt Rollout

Domenico Cecere had been Corporate Controller and a member of the original steering committee for Advantage 2000 during the release 1 financial accounting rollout. As President of Roofing & Asphalt, he opted to be the first major North American business unit to go live with release 4. Cecere told his plant managers that SAP R/3 would free them up to visit their large customers, to come up with new product ideas, and to move the business forward. All their paperwork would be done for them at headquarters beginning with the release 4 implementation.

The Roofing & Asphalt implementation involved 32 plants. Fifteen of these were shingle plants with an average of 100 workers. The 17 asphalt plants had about 13 workers per plant. Logistics for this division involved 700 to 900 trucks a day.

Process consolidation and simplification to improve profitability were the major release 4 goals for Roofing & Asphalt. The division didn't have enough business leader resources to fully populate the project teams, so it was decided to have some of the Insulation division's business leaders represent Roofing & Asphalt's interests. The teams looked at every piece of their business in order to identify inefficiencies that had evolved over the past 20 years and to rewrite their business rules. In the past, sales transactions could be informal and inefficient, with special deals made to please a customer without knowing the ramifications for the business. Beginning with release 4, the ordering process would be consolidated and operated out of Toledo.

> I told the plants "we're the best," so we'll be the first to do it. We'll show everybody else how to do it. The project forced us to look at every piece of our business and find out how many dumb practices we had. We rewrote our business rules.
>
> Dom Cecere, President, Roofing & Asphalt

Cecere looked forward to when he could begin each day by pulling up a few screens to learn how well his more than 30 plants had done the day before and to check the month-to-date totals—by plant, by product, and by customer. He could even get the information over a cup of coffee at home, before leaving for the office. If he had questions, he could just call his plant manager, and they could look at the numbers together because the managers could see everything he could see.

Several implementation risks were identified just prior to the decision date for turning the switch. First, only about 60 percent of the workers had been certified close to the "go live" date. A contributing factor here was that one person might play multiple roles in many of the asphalt plants—production scheduler, production ordering, inventory management, stock checking, sourcing—because of their small size. This factor alone significantly increased the training complexity. Also, the original training plan hadn't been designed to allow enough time for a single individual to come up to speed that quickly for multiple processes.

We only had about a 60 percent certification level. One-third of the Roofing & Asphalt sites were flawless. Another third needed help—they weren't comfortable yet but were getting there. Another third were struggling. We had to decide: Do we learn from that and go live, or do we minimize the risk and then go live. We got the certification level up to 70 percent and accepted this level of risk to support the go live date.

Director, Human Resource Development

The switchover to the new system took place in early March 1997. Beginning that day, all order processing would be handled at the Toledo headquarters. This meant that new trainees would be talking with customers as they switched over to SAP. Everyone on the project knew that changing processes and systems at the same time increased the project risks, but going live with the change to consolidated ordering and logistics was rockier than hoped. As CEO Hiner was quoted as saying on a front page story in the March 14, 1997, *Wall Street Journal,* "The pain is about a 6 or a 7 on a scale where 10 is a hurricane."

The implementation problems were analyzed according to five categories: system, data, people, process, and organizational. The system problems included about 60 bugs in the new SAP version. Some of the people problems were the function of the size of the plants. Others were due to consolidating the customer service function.

Customer Service was changed from 32 systems to 1 at the same time as we went live with Advantage 2000. It was a big mistake. There was so much change and so many variables it was very difficult to understand and fix.

David Johns, Director of Global Development

It was a complete nightmare. Everything that could go wrong, did. Some of our mistakes were also visible to our customers.

Dom Cecere, President, Roofing & Asphalt

What To Do Next

Despite two years of aggressive milestones, bought-out vacations, and well-honed SAP skillsets, it looked like the implementation schedule was once again in jeopardy. The time between the release 4 waves had already been extended from 30 to 60 days to better prepare for the next business unit deployment. The question was whether to delay even longer before going live with Insulation, given the rocky Roofing & Asphalt implementation. Changing business processes at the same time as completely replacing the systems to support them proved to be even more difficult than anticipated.

Turning the switch for Roofing & Asphalt with only a 70-percent certification level had been a risky move. When a factory floor worker enters a shipment into the computer, SAP generates a general ledger entry. That's how tightly integrated the software is: everything drives everything else.

How much time should they spend incorporating what they learned before implementing the next wave for the Insulation business? Could they delay the training of the Insulation plant workers, even though the training vendor was already on-site? Could the business leaders on the SAP project teams be asked again to delay their return to the business units? What would be the impact on morale?

Radcliff was also unsure how long he could ask his IS workforce to stay in an overdrive mode. His IS employee turnover was still about what it had been before—only 8 percent. This was partly because many of his workers had lived in the region all their lives. Would another schedule delay increase the risks of losing IS project team members before release 4 was completed? Could he ask his leaders once again to not take vacations? Advantage 2000 was clearly the best game in town, and not too many had jumped ship so far, but he knew that their newly acquired SAP skillsets would be highly valued outside of Toledo.

Another concern was the end-of-project bonus. It had already been delayed 6 months from the original plan. Would top management stick to the November timetable for issuing the end-of-project bonuses if the rollout was incomplete?

Some folks have been pirated by the consulting craze; all the best are looking here. At some point the organization will need to just "declare victory."

Mike Radcliff, CIO

CUMMINS/KOMATSU/ TELCO JOINT VENTURES (A)

In 1993 Cummins Engine Company established major joint ventures to manufacture Cummins-designed diesel engines with Komatsu in Japan and with Tata Locomotive and Engineering Company (TELCO) in India. As these joint ventures were developed from the agreement stage to operating organizations, a number of issues came to the fore. The following explores the problem of interfacing Cummins' information systems with these new organizations. Part A explores the needs of both joint ventures, Part B continues with Cummins' experience with Komatsu, and Part C relates Cummins' experience with TELCO. Part A must precede either of the other two parts, but **either** Part B **or** Part C (or both) may follow.

Cummins Engine Company

Cummins Engine Company, Inc., is a leading worldwide designer and manufacturer of fuel-efficient diesel engines and related products for trucks and other equipment. The company was founded in 1919 in Columbus, Indiana, where its corporate headquarters and largest engine manufacturing facility are located. Ranking 121st in sales among the Fortune 500, in 1993 Cummins reported net sales of $4.25 billion and had approximately 23,600 employees worldwide.

Cummins sells directly to original equipment manufacturers and to 33 distributors operating through approximately 200 locations in North America and to 110 distributors at approximately 300 locations in 130

countries outside North America. In addition, there are approximately 3,500 dealer locations in North America and a total of 5,000 worldwide at which Cummins-trained service personnel and Cummins parts are available to repair and maintain engines. Cummins has a worldwide reputation for providing outstanding service on its engines.

For the past decade Cummins has had a strong emphasis on "Customer-led Quality" which focuses on providing a comparative advantage to customers. This emphasis, supported by extensive training programs, has resulted in improved product quality with significantly reduced warranty expense to Cummins, better work processes emphasizing cross-functional teams, and smoother product introductions. Cummins' management believes that this quality emphasis is largely responsible for Cummins' improving financial performance. Cummins' ten-year consolidated financial summary is presented in Exhibit 1.

Products

Cummins' diesel engines, ranging from 76 to 2000 horsepower, power a wide variety of equipment in its six key markets: heavy-duty and mid-range trucks, power generation, industrial products, bus and light commercial vehicles, government products, and marine products. In addition to diesel engines, Cummins products include generator sets and alternators, electronic control systems, remanufactured engines, filters, turbochargers, and heat transfer systems.

Cummins' diesel engine product line had evolved slowly over the years until 1981, when Cummins decided to design new heavy-duty truck engines that are smaller and lighter and also to develop a new line of "B- and C-series" engines for medium- and light-duty trucks and

---

This case was prepared by Professor E. W. Martin as the basis for class discussion rather than to illustrate either effective or ineffective handling of an administrative situation.

Copyright © 1997 by E. W. Martin.

Summary of Consolidated Financial Information for 10 Years
Cummins Engine Company, Inc., and Subsidiaries

$ Millions, except per share amounts	1993	1992	1991	1990	1989	1988	1987	1986	1985	1984
Results of operations:										
Net sales	$4,247.9	$3,749.2	$3,405.5	$3,461.8	$3,519.5	$3,309.9	$2,767.4	$2,303.7	$2,146.3	$2,325.8
Cost of goods sold	3,211.0	2,906.7	2,776.7	2,857.1	2,856.9	2,669.8	2,071.4	1,757.5	1,577.5	1,595.6
Gross profit	1,036.9	842.5	628.8	604.7	662.6	640.1	696.0	546.2	568.8	730.2
Selling, administrative, research and engineering expenses	788.8	712.0	619.3	631.7	607.4	579.8	617.0	541.4	458.1	437.2
Interest expense	36.3	41.0	42.5	43.9	51.8	51.7	51.7	44.8	28.1	31.6
Other expense (income), net	6.8	13.1	12.7	8.4	(17.2)	6.6	(7.0)	(18.0)	(18.1)	(12.6)
Unusual charges				62.9		49.0		134.9	39.7	29.6
Earnings (loss) before income taxes	205.0	76.4	(45.7)	(142.2)	20.6	(47.0)	34.3	(156.9)	61.0	244.4
Provision (credit) for income taxes	22.3	8.9	16.9	25.0	22.2	13.5	15.6	(52.5)	10.6	56.5
Minority interest	.1	.4	3.0	(2.1)	4.5	2.9	4.8	2.9	—	—
Earnings (loss) before extraordinary items and cumulative effect of accounting changes	182.6	67.1	(65.6)	(165.1)	(6.1)	(63.4)	13.9	(107.3)	50.4	187.9
Extraordinary items	(5.5)	(5.5)	—	27.4	—	—	—	—	—	—
Cumulative effect of accounting changes	—	(251.1)	51.5	—	—	—	—	—	—	—
Net earnings (loss)	**177.1**	**(189.5)**	**(14.1)**	**(137.7)**	**(6.1)**	**(63.4)**	**13.9**	**107.3**	**50.4**	**187.9**
Preferred and preference stock dividends	8.0	8.0	8.0	13.7	9.8	8.1	8.1	.8	—	—
Earnings (loss) available for common shares	**$ 169.1**	**$ (197.5)**	**$ (22.1)**	**$ (151.4)**	**$ (15.9)**	**$ (71.5)**	**$ 5.8**	**$ (108.1)**	**$ 50.4**	**$ 187.9**
Per common share:										
Earnings (loss) before extraordinary items and cumulative effect of accounting changes:										
Primary	$4.95	1.77	$ (2.48)	(7.23)	$ (.76)	$ (3.35)	.27	$ (5.23)	$ 2.64	$ 9.88
Fully diluted	4.77	1.77	(2.48)	(7.23)	(.76)	(3.35)	.27	(5.23)	2.61	9.69
Net earnings (loss):										
Primary	4.79	(6.01)	(.75)	(6.13)	(.76)	(3.35)	.27	(5.23)	2.64	9.88
Fully diluted	4.63	(6.01)	(.75)	(6.13)	(.76)	(3.35)	.27	(5.23)	2.61	9.69
Cash dividends	.20	.10	.35	1.10	1.10	1.10	1.10	1.10	1.10	1.03
Common shareholders' investment	18.40	11.21	17.14	18.69	19.89	27.51	32.50	30.94	37.14	34.31
Average number of common shares (millions):										
Primary	35.3	32.9	29.7	24.7	20.9	21.3	21.2	20.7	19.0	19.0
Fully diluted	38.3	32.9	29.7	24.7	20.9	21.3	21.2	20.7	19.4	19.4
Operating percentages:										
Gross profit	24.4%	22.5%	18.5%	17.5%	18.8%	19.3%	25.1%	23.7%	26.5%	31.4%
Return on net sales	4.2	(5.0)	(.4)	(4.0)	(.2)	(1.9)	.5	(4.7)	2.3	8.1
Financial data:										
Working capital	$ 371.4	$ 271.4	$ 219.2	$ 263.4	$ 224.2	$ 306.0	$ 239.2	$ 285.0	$ 339.7	$ 370.9
Property, plant and equipment, net	958.2	928.7	953.0	921.2	890.1	911.2	909.7	840.6	702.0	567.4
Total assets	2,390.6	2,230.5	2,041.2	2,086.3	2,030.8	2,064.0	2,019.4	1,989.9	1,705.1	1,505.5
Long-term debt and redeemable preferred stock	189.6	412.4	443.2	411.4	473.7	408.8	332.6	319.9	234.0	222.4
Shareholders' investment	821.1	501.1	623.8	669.3	559.2	701.5	807.3	770.3	711.6	648.2
Supplemental data:										
Property, plant and equipment expenditures	$ 174.2	$ 139.3	$ 123.9	$ 147.0	$ 137.9	$ 150.8	$ 133.1	$ 213.1	$ 198.2	$ 109.1
Depreciation and amortization	125.1	122.5	127.2	143.4	135.0	131.8	119.4	106.6	79.2	72.2
Common shareholders of record	4,400	4,800	5,900	5,900	5,700	5,700	5,400	5,500	5,900	5,900
Number of employees	23,600	23,400	22,900	24,900	25,100	26,100	24,500	23,400	19,600	21,000

EXHIBIT 1 *Cummins' Ten-year Consolidated Financial Summary.*

industrial equipment. The B-series is now Cummins' highest-volume engine, used in both Ford and Dodge trucks. This product line introduction required an investment of around $1 billion. In 1988, Cummins introduced a line of cleaner, heavy duty engines and soon thereafter introduced electronic fuel injection, which improved fuel efficiency and reduced truck operating costs.

With growing pressures throughout the world for reduced pollution and increased fuel efficiency, diesel engine technology is being forced to evolve rapidly, and thus there is a growing emphasis upon research and development in this industry. Being the world's highest volume diesel engine producer above 2,000 hp, Cummins is well positioned to respond to these pressures. Cummins has Research and Development facilities in the U.S., the United Kingdom, Brazil, and India. Cummins' research and engineering investments over the past 10 years are shown in Exhibit 2.

Exhibit 3 presents an overview from a sales brochure of Cummins' current line of on-highway engines. Information on the B-series engine from a sales brochure is shown in Exhibit 4.

International Activities

Since 1956 Cummins has been a multinational business, and Cummins' operations include plants, joint ventures, or license agreements in the United Kingdom, India, Mexico, Brazil, Japan, South Korea, China, Russia, Zimbabwe, Pakistan, and Turkey, as well as in the United States. A distribution of Cummins' U.S. and international net sales over the past 10 years is depicted in Exhibit 5.

Cummins has license agreements under which two Chinese plants produce Cummins engines, and in recent years sales of these engines have doubled each year. The Chongqing Automotive Engine Plant makes heavy duty diesel engines for work boats, electrical generator sets, and many other types of equipment, and Dong Feng Motors makes Cummins' midsized truck engines. In early 1994 Cummins was negotiating to turn these license agreements into joint ventures under which Cummins would invest additional money and technology in China. Cummins was also working on similar arrangements in Korea.

In early 1994 Cummins was engaged in two activities in the international arena that were of major importance. In late 1993 Cummins and Komatsu Ltd. announced a joint venture to manufacture Cummins' B-series engines at a Komatsu plant in Oyama, Japan, and another joint venture to manufacture Komatsu's 30-liter engines at a Cummins plant in Seymour, Indiana. Production in Japan is scheduled to begin in 1996 and is expected to produce around 40,000 engines a year by the end of the decade.

Also in 1993 Cummins and TELCO, a member of the huge Tata group in India, formed a joint venture to manufacture Cummins B-series engines in India. Starting in early 1994, they are building a factory in India that they expect to be one of the most efficient diesel engine factories in the world.

EXHIBIT 2
Cummin's Ten-Year Research and Engineering Investments.

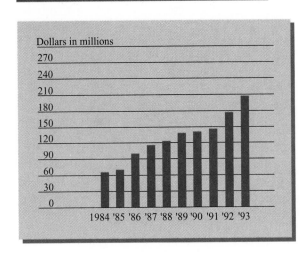

Information Systems in Joint Ventures

Information systems (IS) are a critical part of Cummins operations and are central to design, manufacturing, and service of Cummins' engines throughout the world. Joint ventures combine the resources of two companies, which involves combining or at least interfacing their information systems. John L. Becker, Director of Business Development, who has been involved in the development of several Cummins' joint ventures, explains:

> We establish an operating joint venture in two phases: First we negotiate a contract between the two organizations, and then we implement this agreement and set up a functioning business. In the negotiation phase there are so many things to deal with and so much uncertainty that we do not get all the important operating functions involved. I am currently involved in the implementation phase of both the TELCO and the

EXHIBIT 3
Cummins' On-Highway Engines.

Power that's right for you.

For over-the-road power, there's a hardworking Cummins diesel that is just your style. From 105 to 460 horsepower, Cummins is the world leader in designing and manufacturing diesel engines that deliver the fuel efficiency, performance, reliability and durability you're looking for.

Because Cummins leads the way in diesel technology, you can count on your Cummins diesel to always be on the cutting edge.

N14
If you're looking for big power, the N14 has what it takes. The power to get the big loads up the big hills… and with Cummins C Brake™ as an option, you get strong braking power to slow you on the way down.

L10
The perfect combination of strength and fuel efficiency, the L10 has the technology to pass up every competitive diesel engine on the market today. The proven lightweight leader, the fuel-efficient L10 is one of the most popular fleet engines on the road today.

CELECT™ electronics.
N14 and L10 engines are available with CELECT, Cummins totally integrated electronic control system. Through CELECT technology, you get the benefits of integrated electronic controls engineered and built to put you in total command of fuel efficiency, performance, and more.

C8.3
The C8.3 is smaller and over 600 pounds lighter than its nearest heavy-duty competitor. The C8.3's lighter weight adds up to higher payloads…and higher profits for you. Even though it's compact in size, the Cummins C8.3 has heavy-duty big bore design features and is built to last.

B5.9/B3.9
With over 750,000 in operation, Cummins B engines are proving they really deliver. Advanced design and modern manufacturing techniques have given Cummins B engines "big bore" engine durability in a smaller-size engine.

Power your way.
Whatever your application, there's a Cummins engine right for the job. Designed, built and backed better than any other diesels on the road today.

Choose the one that's right for you and then see your Cummins distributor or dealer, or call 1-800-DIESELS for more information.

Engine Model	Power	Torque
B3.9-105	105 hp @ 2500 rpm	265 lb-ft @ 1700 rpm
B3.9-120	120 hp @ 2500 rpm	300 lb-ft @ 1700 rpm
B5.9-160	160 hp @ 2500 rpm	400 lb-ft @ 1700 rpm
B5.9-190	190 hp @ 2500 rpm	475 lb-ft @ 1600 rpm
B5.9-210	210 hp @ 2500 rpm	520 lb-ft @ 1600 rpm
B5.9-230	230 hp @ 2500 rpm	605 lb-ft @ 1600 rpm

Engine Model	Power	Range	Torque
C8.3-210	210	1300-2400 rpm	605 lb-ft @ 1300 rpm
C8.3-250	250	1300-2400 rpm	660 lb-ft @ 1300 rpm
C8.3-250	250	1300-2200 rpm	800 lb-ft @ 1300 rpm
C8.3-275	275	1300-2200 rpm	800 lb-ft @ 1300 rpm
C8.3-275	275	1300-2000 rpm	860 lb-ft @ 1300 rpm
C8.3-300	300	1300-2400 rpm	820 lb-ft @ 1300 rpm
L10-260	260	1200-1800 rpm	975 lb-ft @ 1200 rpm
L10-260	260	1200-1950 rpm	975 lb-ft @ 1200 rpm
L10-280	280	1200-1800 rpm	1050 lb-ft @ 1200 rpm
L10-280	280	1200-1950 rpm	1050 lb-ft @ 1200 rpm
L10-280E	280	1200-1800 rpm	1050 lb-ft @ 1200 rpm
L10-300	300	1200-1950 rpm	1150 lb-ft @ 1200 rpm
L10-310	310	1200-1800 rpm	1150 lb-ft @ 1200 rpm
L10-310E	310	1200-1800 rpm	1150 lb-ft @ 1200 rpm
L10-310E	310	1200-2000 rpm	1150 lb-ft @ 1200 rpm
L10-330E	330	1200-1800 rpm	1250 lb-ft @ 1200 rpm
L10-330E	330	1200-2000 rpm	1250 lb-ft @ 1200 rpm
L10-350E	350	1200-1800 rpm	1250 lb-ft @ 1200 rpm
N14-310P	310	1100-1700 rpm	1250 lb-ft @ 1100 rpm
N14-330P	330	1100-1700 rpm	1350 lb-ft @ 1100 rpm
N14-330	330	1100-1950 rpm	1350 lb-ft @ 1100 rpm
N14-350P	350	1100-1700 rpm	1400 lb-ft @ 1100 rpm
N14-350	350	1100-1950 rpm	1350 lb-ft @ 1100 rpm
N14-370	370	1200-1800 rpm	1400 lb-ft @ 1200 rpm
N14-370	370	1200-1950 rpm	1400 lb-ft @ 1200 rpm
N14-410	410	1200-1800 rpm	1450 lb-ft @ 1200 rpm
N14-410	410	1200-1950 rpm	1450 lb-ft @ 1200 rpm
N14-430	430	1200-1800 rpm	1450 lb-ft @ 1200 rpm
N14-310E	310	1100-1800 rpm	1250 lb-ft @ 1100 rpm
N14-330E	330	1100-1800 rpm	1350 lb-ft @ 1100 rpm
N14-330E	330	1100-2100 rpm	1350 lb-ft @ 1100 rpm
N14-350E	350	1100-1800 rpm	1400 lb-ft @ 1100 rpm
N14-370E	370	1200-1800 rpm	1400 lb-ft @ 1200 rpm
N14-370E	370	1200-2100 rpm	1400 lb-ft @ 1200 rpm
N14-410E	410	1200-2100 rpm	1450 lb-ft @ 1200 rpm
N14-430E	430	1200-1800 rpm	1450 lb-ft @ 1200 rpm
N14-430E	430	1200-2100 rpm	1450 lb-ft @ 1200 rpm
N14-430E	430	1200-2100 rpm	1550 lb-ft @ 1200 rpm
N14-460E	460	1200-2100 rpm	1550 lb-ft @ 1200 rpm

Cummins Engine Company, Inc.
Box 3005
Columbus, IN 47202-3005
USA

EXHIBIT 4
Cummins' B-Series Engines.

SPECIFICATIONS

PERFORMANCE

Performance at SAE standard J1995 conditions of 300 ft. (90m) altitude (29.61 inches Hg[100 kPa] barometic pressure), 77°F (25°C) air intake temperature, and 0.30 inches Hg (1 kPa) water vapor pressure with No. 2 diesel fuel will be within 5% of that shown at the time of engine shipment. Actual peformance may vary with different ambient conditions.

Curves represent performance of the engine with fuel system, water pump, lubrication oil pump, air compressor (unloaded), and with 10 in. H_2O (250mm) inlet air restriction and with 2.0 inches Hg (50mm) exhaust restriction; not included are alternator, fan, optional equipment and driven components.

The BSFC curve shown is at full load conditions. This is not a true indicator of fuel tank mileage due to the fact that the engine spends only a portion of time operating on the full load curve. A significant amount of time is spent at various part load conditions. Therefore, full load BSFC curves should not be used as an indicator of fuel tank mileage.

SPECIFICATIONS

Maximum Horsepower	160 bhp	(119 kW)
Peak Torque (1200 rpm)	400 lb.-ft.	(542 N•m)
Governed Speed (Vocational)	2500 rpm	(2500 rpm)
Number of Cylinders	6	(6)
Bore and Stroke	4.02×4.72 in.	(102x120 mm)
Engine Displacement	359.0 cu.in.	(5.9 L)
Compression Ratio	17.5:1	(17.5:1)
Operating Cycles	4	(4)
Oil System Capacity	17.3 U.S. gals	(16.4 L)
Coolant Capacity (Engine Only)	10.5 U.S. qts.	(9.9 L)
Net Weight with Std. Accessories, Dry	942 lbs.	(428 kg)
Installation Diagram Number	3626286	

EXHIBIT 5

Cummins' U.S. and International Sales.

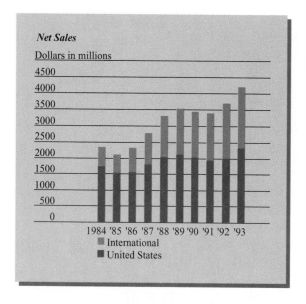

Net Sales

Dollars in millions

1984 '85 '86 '87 '88 '89 '90 '91 '92 '93
■ International
■ United States

Komatsu joint ventures. In the process of business planning and bringing the functional areas of the company into these projects, we encountered a number of IS issues that should have been considered in the negotiation phase.

In early 1993 M. D. (Maury) Lankford, Business Systems Consultant in the Cummins Management Systems Department, was assigned responsibility for leading the effort to identify and deal with the information systems issues involved in Cummins' joint ventures. Lankford, who had 30 years of varied experience in Management Systems at Cummins, explains how he started:

> My first challenge was to obtain an understanding of the systems and information requirements for a joint venture with an international corporation. This presents some real problems, when you start to think about how much information has to be exchanged between the two parents and the joint venture and what kind of systems support has to be in place so that the joint venture will be successful. Then we have to figure out how to provide this systems support.

In March 1994, the Joint Ventures Support Group was formed when Diane Chu and Jerry Pennington began to work with Lankford. Chu had been with Cummins for 13 years in Management Systems and in the after-market service area, and Pennington had 17 years of experience working in plant support and was part of the start-up

team for the new B-series engine plant in Columbus that was completed in 1991.

After some initial investigation of the problem, Lankford recognized that there are a number of obvious considerations that affect the systems support that will be required. First, there will be significant differences between the required systems support, depending upon the joint venture. In India, for example, they will be building a new plant, so they have a free hand in the systems to be employed. In the Komatsu joint venture, however, the engines will be produced in existing plants in Japan and the United States, so one would presume that the local plants' systems would be used to support manufacturing.

Cummins' Information Systems Environment

The Cummins Management Systems (IS) Department reports to Wynne W. Gulden, Jr, Vice President—Information Processes and Technology. Management Systems is responsible for systems development and maintenance, but not mainframe operations because the Columbus data center has been outsourced to Electronic Data Systems (EDS).

All of Cummins' engine plants in the U.S. and the U.K. operate with a set of systems referred to as "Cummins Common Systems" for manufacturing and logistical support. These systems are based on 1970s software technology—COBOL and IMS—operating on IBM 3090-type mainframes in the Columbus data center. Although they are strategically important to Cummins, these systems are old and difficult to change and are based on obsolete technology.

As an example of how difficult it is to implement these systems for a new plant, when the new B-series engine plant in Columbus was started in 1991, 25 people and $750,000 of effort were required to set up the Cummins Common Systems for that plant. Because the systems for the new plant operate on the same computer as the systems for the old plants, each database in the system must be renamed to make it refer to the new plant, and each database reference in every program of the system must be changed to conform to the new name of that database. Also, if a program is changed, it must be tested. All of the above has to be done not only for routine parts of the system, but also for each special report, weekly summary, monthly report, and so on.

The Management Systems Department has recognized the problems with these technologically obsolete common systems and in 1993 established a project team to plan how to replace these systems with more modern technology. Cummins now plans to move to distributed processing and relational databases in a UNIX environment. Cummins is purchasing Avalon software packages that can provide 50 percent to 60 percent of the functionality needed and will modify these packages to satisfy Cummins' special needs. A pilot project is under way to install the Avalon software in the engine assembly plant in Brazil, and Cummins' subsidiary Holset Engineering has also signed a contract to install this software. After three to five years and several million dollars, Cummins should have a set of common systems that can be easily replicated throughout the world.

Systems Needs of All Joint Ventures

After talking with representatives of both TELCO and Komatsu and conferring with many others at Cummins, the Joint Ventures Support Group found that there was little agreement on the IS support that would be needed

by the joint ventures. To get a better understanding of the support required, the group decided to analyze the role of information systems in Cummins' manufacturing operations. They started by determining the business processes that are necessary for a Cummins plant to operate. A high-level diagram of the result of their analysis depicts both corporate and plant level business functions, the databases that support them, and the relationships between these functions (Exhibit 6).

At a more detailed level, they identified some 70 business functions. Then they were able to identify the information systems that are necessary to support each of these business functions. These 70 business functions also provided the basis for a responsibility chart for each joint venture that suggests who (the joint venture team, the joint venture, Cummins, the other parent) should be responsible for each of these business functions. Exhibit 7 is the first page of this proposed responsibility chart for the joint venture with TELCO.

EXHIBIT 6
Cummins Engine Manufacturing Business Systems Overview.

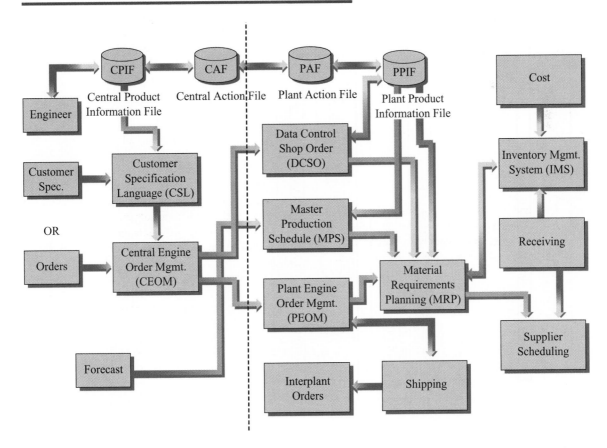

TATA CUMMINS LIMITED
TCL

	A	B	C	D	E	F
		JV TEAM	TCL	TELCO	CUM	
1	FUNCTIONS BY LEVEL					NOTES
2						
3	CORPORATE BUSINESS FUNCTIONS					
4	• DESIGN CONTROL	X			X	USE CUMMINS CHANGE CONTROL
5	• ELECTRONIC VAULT DRAWING ACCESS	X	X	X	X	AS PRACTICAL & COST-EFFECTIVE
6	• ENGINE EMISSION CERTIFICATION	X			X	USE CUMMINS RIL/DCSO
7	• CSL/CEOM-ORDER MANAGEMENT	X			X	USE CUMMINS SYSTEMS
8	• APPLICATIONS ENGINEERING			X	X	PERFORMED BY PARENTS
9	• ENGINE HISTORY/WARRANTY- AFTERMARKET SUPPORT	X	X	X	X	REQUIRES DATA FROM PLANT
10	• DUTY DRAWBACK (INDIA?)		X	X	X	REQUIREMENTS?
11	• WARRANTY/CLAIMS PROCESSING		?	X	X	PERFORMED BY PARENTS
12	• SERVICE MANAGEMENT		?	X	X	PERFORMED BY PARENTS
13	• FAILURE & COST ANALYSIS		X	X	X	PERFORMED BY PARENTS
14						
15	PLANT BUSINESS FUNCTIONS					
16	• LOGISTICS MANAGEMENT	X				TELCO SYSTEM INADEQUATE (OPPORTUNITY FOR AVALON)
17	—MATERIAL REQUIREMENTS PLANNING (MRP)		X		X	TELCO SYSTEM INADEQUATE
18	—INVENTORY (INCLUDING CHARGE-OFF)		X		X	
19	—PURCHASING		X		X	
20	—SUPPLIER MASTER MAINTENANCE		X		X	
21	—BILL-OF-MATERIAL (BOM)		X		X	
22	—RECEIVING/INSPECTION		X		X	
23	—SUPPLIER QUALITY ASSURANCE		X		X	
24	—MATERIAL/ORDER RELEASES/SUPPLIER SCHEDULING		X		X	EDI ORDER TO CUMMINS
25	—SHIPPING (BILL-OF-LADING?)		X		X	
26	—MASTER PRODUCTION SCHEDULING (MPS) (FORECASTING?)		X		X	TELCO DOES NOT HAVE
27						
28	• CUSTOMER/ORDER MANAGEMENT	X				
29	—CUSTOMER MASTER MAINTENANCE ("BILL-TO"/"SHIP-TO")		X		X	
30	—PLANT ORDER MANAGEMENT/ORDER SCHEDULE		X		X	INTERFACE TO CUMMINS CEOM
31						
32	• MANUFACTURING PRODUCT MANAGEMENT	X				
33	—PLANT CHANGE CONTROL		X		X	CUMMINS CHANGE CONTROL
34	—ORDER CONTENT (BUILD DOCUMENT/DATA PLATE)		X		X	CUMMINS DCSO PROCESS

EXHIBIT 7
Proposed Responsibility Chart.

Based on the above business process analysis and much discussion with Cummins' management, the Joint Ventures Support Group has also defined the following six crucial interfaces that usually must exist between Cummins and any joint venture.

Engineering Change Control

Any joint venture plant must use the Cummins Engineering Change Control/Engineering Release Process, including maintaining a Plant Product Information File, if any of the following conditions hold:

- Cummins controls the product design.
- The joint venture plant will be a source of parts for other Cummins plants.
- The products will be resold to Cummins' customers.
- Cummins' distribution channel will be responsible for aftermarket support.

Cummins retains control of the B-series engine design in both the Komatsu and TELCO joint ventures. According to Lankford,

> We have complete authority on all design changes and control on the B-series engine worldwide, and that is managed out of our Mid-range Engine Technical Center (METC) in Columbus, Indiana. This means we have to link the joint ventures in Japan and India with our product definition system to deal with all the configuration management, change control management, and the engineering releases that take place.

> There will be some local product engineering in Japan and India, primarily to deal with add-on parts to customize the engines for specific equipment installation requirements. These joint ventures will also initiate some engineering changes, both in the product and in the manufacturing process, leading to improvements that we will want to utilize worldwide. In any case, the final design authority remains in Columbus, so the joint ventures will be putting in requests for changes that will be processed in Columbus and fed back to them.

Engine Certification

Emissions control is a very important aspect of diesel engine technology today. The United States, Australia, the European Community, and California all have emissions standards for on-highway engines, and most of the world is adopting such standards. The United States and other countries will also mandate emissions controls for off-highway engines in the near future. One of the primary motivations for TELCO and Komatsu to partner with Cummins is to avoid the high engineering cost of redesigning their engines to meet these emissions standards.

Each engine sold in a country with emissions controls must be certified to assure that it meets the specified standards. Certification is a complicated process in which the engines are run in a test cell and the emissions are measured and compared with the applicable standards. Certification is not just by engine model, but rather by a list of part numbers that make up the certified engine, so if a part that affects emissions (e.g. piston, fuel pump, fuel pump setting) is changed in any way, that is a new engine for certification purposes. Several countries require that a manufacturer keep certification information on line so that inspectors can visit the plant and examine this information in real time. Inspectors may also randomly pick engines off the line and set them aside for testing to make sure that they still meet certification standards.

All certified engines sold by Cummins must be validated by using Cummins' Regulatory Item List and Certification Compilation Process computer systems. Therefore, all joint venture plants that furnish engines for sale by Cummins must use these systems.

Original Engine Parts List

For each engine produced in a Cummins factory, Cummins maintains an original engine parts list (OEPL) record that lists the parts in the original engine and maintains that engine's service history. This information is provided to Cummins distributors worldwide so that any service facility can determine exactly what part is required when a replacement is needed.

Joint venture partners may be competing with each other for the very profitable aftermarket support business. For example, Cummins and Komatsu often have dealerships in the same cities throughout the world, and a Cummins engine in a Komatsu bulldozer might be repaired by either company's dealer. Because OEPL data makes it easier to service an engine, having this data provides a competitive advantage to a distributor. Therefore, the ownership of this OEPL data for particular engines may be a sensitive issue with the joint venture partners. Cummins' statement on the required interfaces with Cummins systems specifies that the joint venture must feed the necessary data to the Cummins OEPL file *for all engines that are sold through the Cummins distribution system and/or supported by the Cummins aftermarket group*. But Cummins does not require the OEPL data on engines sold by and supported by the joint venture or the joint venture partner.

This may present a problem when Cummins engines are being produced by many organizations. Lankford elaborates:

> I can imagine a major construction project, say in Brazil, having Komatsu equipment with Komatsu-built Cummins engines, construction equipment from other manufacturers with Cummins engines, trucks from India with TELCO-built Cummins engines, and trucks with Cummins engines built in Brazil or the U.S. or the U.K. All of this equipment would be on the same site, and the owner may recognize that they are all Cummins engines and take them to the local Cummins dealer when repairs are needed. But the Cummins dealer would not have OEPL data on some of these engines.

Cummins Order-Entry System

Cummins has an on-line order-entry system that is used worldwide by customers to order engines from any of Cummins factories. Each engine model may have many variations, and this system guides the person entering the order through the process of specifying exactly what the engine is to include, while checking to assure that the specified configuration is feasible, that it conforms to the current engine design, and that it meets certification requirements. Then the system produces a list of the parts required that the plant can use to build the engine. Although Cummins does not require that joint ventures use this system, some such system will be needed to enter orders. Because such order-entry systems are quite complex, joint ventures may decide to use the Cummins order-entry system rather than developing their own. But if a joint venture develops its own order-entry system and Cummins sells engines from the joint venture, then the Cummins order-entry system will have to feed Cummins-generated orders into the joint venture's order-entry system.

EDI Standards

Any engine parts or components that the joint venture procures from Cummins must be ordered via EDI using the UN/EDIFACT standard. In the long run, a joint venture may produce all the engine parts itself, but during start-up of the factory most joint ventures will procure some parts or components from Cummins. Therefore this interface will usually be necessary, but it may be temporary.

Financial Reports

In addition to the normal financial reporting from a joint venture to the parents, product cost information must be provided in order to determine transfer prices that conform to government tax regulations.

Lankford believes that most people in the companies involved do not understand the implications of the above required interfaces:

> It is so easy to say that they must use the Cummins product definition system, but that means a lot more than what it says! In addition to engineering change control, it implies a great deal about manufacturing management, starting with capturing an accurate customer order, checking it to make sure it meets the design control and certification requirements, providing a parts list to the MRP system and the shop order processing system, and so on. It is all very complicated and everything is interrelated.

While the Joint Ventures Support Group was developing the principles described above that apply to most joint ventures, Lankford was simultaneously working with Komatsu and TELCO to develop a shared understanding of the information systems support needed by their joint ventures. Part B describes the Cummins/Komatsu joint venture and Lankford's interactions with Komatsu. Part C describes the Cummins/TELCO joint venture and Lankford's interactions with TELCO.

CUMMINS/KOMATSU /TELCO JOINT VENTURES (B)

Part A of this case should be read before the following discussion of the relationships between Cummins and Komatsu, Ltd.

Komatsu Ltd. is a Japanese worldwide manufacturer and marketer of heavy construction equipment and industrial machinery, and is also involved in civil engineering projects. Komatsu has over 55 subsidiaries and affiliates located worldwide, with many in Japan, several in the U.S., and others in Brazil, Mexico, Belgium, Canada, Singapore, France, Germany, the U.K., Australia, and Indonesia. Exhibit 1 shows a breakdown of Komatsu's 1993 sales and a five-year summary of sales and net income (all in millions of yen).

Komatsu's construction equipment products include bulldozers, excavators, loaders, graders, dump trucks, cranes, compactors, pipe layers, coal haulers, tunnel boring machines, amphibious bulldozers, underwater rubble leveling robots, and construction robots. Komatsu's industrial machinery products include many types of sheet metal and forging presses, laser cutting machines, fine plasma cutting machinery, band sawmills, multiplex machine tools, crankshaft millers, robot systems, semiconductor manufacturing equipment, and plastics injection molding machinery. Other Komatsu products include diesel engines, marine engines, power units, gas engines, engine-driven heat pumps, compressors, diesel generator sets, cogeneration systems, hydraulic equipment, torque converters, steel castings, intelligent panels, vehicular controllers, vision recognition systems, armored vehicles, and ammunition.

This case was prepared by Professor E. W. Martin as the basis for class discussion rather than to illustrate either effective or ineffective handling of an administrative situation.

Copyright © 1997 (revised) by E. W. Martin.

The largest of the two joint ventures between Cummins and Komatsu, Komatsu Cummins Engine Company (KCEC), will produce the Cummins-designed B-series engine on an assembly line located in Komatsu's engine plant in Oyama, Japan. Production is scheduled to begin in 1996. At least 40,000 engines per year will be produced, with 30,000 slated to power Komatsu equipment and 10,000 to be sold by Cummins in the Japanese and Northern Pacific markets.

The other joint venture, Cummins Komatsu Engine Company (CKEC), will produce Komatsu-designed 30-liter engines in an existing Cummins plant in Seymour, Indiana. The 30-liter engine volumes will be low relative to the B-series volumes, with about 2,000 engines produced annually.

The Komatsu/Cummins joint ventures were announced in October, 1993, but Lankford got involved in April, 1993, when he visited Komatsu in Japan to begin conversations about systems for the proposed joint ventures. Lankford recalls:

> There were two people from Komatsu corporate and five systems people from the Oyama factory across the table from me. They had not thought about the problem and had not discussed the issues among themselves, so they were not ready to discuss anything substantive. I suspect that the Japanese did not want to talk about the systems issues until all the business issues had been completed and the contract signed. At any rate, it turned out to be a typical first meeting with the Japanese where we each talked about who we were and what kind of things we were interested in and agreed to meet later.

During this trip Lankford visited one of the Komatsu data processing centers. He recalls the experience:

EXHIBIT 1
Komatsu Sales and Net Income.

1993 SALES IN MILLIONS OF YEN

Construction Equipment	549,198
Civil Engineering Works	100,076
Industrial Machinery	64,710
Electronic Equipment	50,165
Other	105,779
	869,928

FIVE YEAR SUMMARY IN MILLIONS OF YEN

DATE	SALES	NET INCOME
1993	869,928	5,199
1992	919,753	13,105
1991	988,897	33,477
1990	887,108	28,447
1989	792,809	22,016

Source: *Moody's Investors*

The data center director who took me on the tour spoke no English. His card did not even have English on the back. The interpreter spoke English well, but she did not understand the technical terms of the computer area. I could not ask any meaningful questions because she could not translate them into Japanese, nor could she translate answers back into English. Fortunately, it was an IBM shop, and I could tell a lot by just looking at the numbers on the computer components.

Most of the Japanese I have encountered understand some English, so if you speak slowly they will understand most of what you say. Not many of them speak English well enough to be easily understood, so communicating precisely is very difficult.

In early 1994, after the contract had been signed, Lankford went back to Japan to attend a meeting on aftermarket support issues. He also spent a day with the systems people at the Komatsu corporate office in Tokyo. He recalls:

> The Komatsu systems people I have encountered are below average in their English language skills and must always have an interpreter. Many of the concepts we deal with in the systems world are very complex and are difficult to explain even to other English speaking people, which makes it very difficult to communicate well with the Japanese systems people. It is slow and frustrating to explain something, have it interpreted, and wait five minutes while the Japanese discuss it among themselves before they ask a question about it that you cannot understand. After several tries you give up and assume that you have communicated.

Lankford also found a number of cultural differences between Japanese and U.S. organizations:

> The hierarchy is a lot stronger than it is here, and it is not accepted for a person to reach outside his level. In Japanese organizations they avoid any appearance of conflict and strive to reach consensus. When dealing with them on a problem they will say that they have to get back to you on it, and it usually takes them two weeks to discuss it with everyone and come up with a consensus. In the U.S. we might have someone write down his or her recommendation and circulate it for comments before rewriting it. But when the Japanese write something down it is a commitment, so they do not do much writing when they go through their consensus process. Also, the use of electronic mail is not a part of the Japanese culture.
>
> In the U.S. we do not value age. We use bright young MBAs and put them in situations that will challenge them. In Japan they come from a totally different cultural background. Age and experience is highly valued and respected, so when I go to Japan I wear my 30-year pin and it means a lot to them.

Komatsu wants Cummins to send a team of six people over to meet with them—three systems people, a materials person from the Rocky Mount engine plant, an engineer, and a business leader. It will be very expensive to send such a team to Japan, but Lankford believes that it is necessary:

> The Japanese feel some loss of face if we are only willing to send one person over to meet with them and they have six to nine people spending the day with

him. We need to understand their feelings and get the right people there to get things done, and that means both systems people and business people.

The Komatsu Cummins Engine Company (KCEC)

Due to the dynamics of the industries in which they compete, there are important differences in how Komatsu and Cummins build engines. The Komatsu factory where KCEC will build its engines produces engines mainly to power Komatsu construction equipment, and they have stable production schedules and relatively long lead times with a standard product that has few engineering changes. Cummins primarily sells loose engines in a very competitive market where there are many different customers with diverse requirements and lots of engineering changes and where response time is critical, so production is very dynamic. For example, Komatsu runs its Manufacturing Requirements Planning (MRP) system monthly, and Cummins runs its MRP weekly and often runs a daily net change MRP. Cummins will be selling 25 percent of the KCEC production in the dynamic loose engine market, and Komatsu will be using the rest of the engines in its construction equipment, so there may be different expectations from the two parent companies.

In June 1994, three Komatsu Cummins Engine Company people came to Columbus to learn about Cummins systems. They spent a week in corporate headquarters and a week at the B-series engine plant at Rocky Mount, North Carolina, that is a joint venture with Tenneco. The original presumption was that KCEC would use mostly Komatsu systems because the production line would be located in an existing Komatsu plant. However, Lankford believes that the Komatsu systems are inadequate to support Cummins' business of selling loose engines, and the visiting KCEC systems people returned to Japan very impressed with the functionality of the Cummins systems. Consequently, the decision as to what systems to use is up in the air. Komatsu is amply equipped with IBM mainframes and uses the same operating systems and communications software as Cummins, so Komatsu could use the Cummins Standard Systems. Alternatively, Komatsu could run these systems remotely via a high-speed communications link to the Cummins Columbus Data Center as does the Cummins B-series engine plant in Darlington, England.

Because the KCEC engines will be built in the existing Komatsu factory, Komatsu will assign its own part numbers to the engine parts and assemblies to use throughout the manufacturing process. This means that Komatsu part numbers will be used when the data on the engines Cummins sells is reported to Cummins for the Original Engines Parts List (OEPL) system that Cummins uses to support its aftermarket. Komatsu will provide a cross-reference list that can be used to translate from the Komatsu part numbers to the corresponding Cummins part numbers.

Both Komatsu and Cummins are very protective of their aftermarket business, and they have agreed that Komatsu will service the engines it sells, Cummins will service the engines it sells, and neither will take any overt action to interfere with this arrangement. The consequence of this agreement is that the cross-reference list for translating from Komatsu part numbers to Cummins part numbers cannot be provided to either Cummins or Komatsu distributors. However, this cross-reference list can be used at Cummins corporate headquarters to translate the part numbers of the KCEC engines Cummins sells from Komatsu numbers to Cummins numbers, and this OEPL can be provided to Cummins distributors. In our example of the construction site in Brazil with a mixture of Komatsu-sold and Cummins-sold engines, neither the Cummins nor the Komatsu distributor will have the parts list for the KCEC engines sold by the other company. This will be an inconvenience, but does not mean that the Cummins distributor cannot repair Komatsu-sold Cummins engines, for the parts manager should be able to recognize a Cummins part when he sees it.

The Cummins Komatsu Engine Company (CKEC)

The 30-liter engine production by CKEC will take place in the existing Cummins plant in Seymour, Indiana. The existing Cummins systems and Cummins part numbers will be used, and Cummins has some of the problems facing Komatsu in the KCEC venture. First, when Cummins procures parts from Komatsu, the Komatsu part numbers must be used to order them and Cummins purchase orders must conform to the requirements of the Komatsu EDI system. And for Komatsu-sold engines produced by CKEC, Cummins must provide Komatsu with the build data and a cross-reference list to translate from Cummins to Komatsu part numbers. Also, Cummins must provide cost data to Komatsu for any CKEC engines that Komatsu sells. At the beginning, however, it is expected that all the CKEC output will be sold by Cummins.

Finally, for any parts purchased by CKEC the Komatsu invoice will be in yen, and Komatsu expects to be paid in yen, which will be a challenge for the Cummins accounts payable system.

Current Status

Lankford and the Joint Ventures Support Group have accomplished a great deal during the past year. They have defined the crucial systems interfaces that must exist between Cummins and any joint venture. They have also developed a standard responsibility chart that can be used to determine who should be responsible for each of the seventy business functions that are required for a joint venture to produce Cummins engines. In addition to the Komatsu and TELCO joint ventures, Cummins is involved in the development of several other similar ventures throughout the world, and these accomplishments will make the implementation of future joint ventures much easier.

Through this experience Lankford has also recognized how important flexible systems have become to a modern business:

> Today most business functions are supported by a systems function, and a business function can only be as flexible and responsive as the system that is supporting it. In today's environment, a business must be able to change its business rules to react to competition, and it is a lot easier to change the business rules than it is to change the systems that support those business rules. That is why many of our systems need to be rearchitected so that they are easier to change.

Current Issues

The Joint Ventures Support Group has identified and resolved many issues, but a number remain. One such issue is data security. According to Lankford:

> We need to come to a consensus on what we want to do about data security. The contracts have nondisclo-

sure provisions that apply to both companies, and that may be perfectly adequate, but we need to address this issue and make sure we get closure on it.

Komatsu has not responded to Lankford's responsibility chart suggesting who is responsible for the systems supporting each business function. Also, Lankford's recommendation that Cummins' systems be used is still under discussion. A meeting between systems and business people from Komatsu and Cummins to come to some conclusions about what systems to use for KCEC has been postponed from May to June, and now to August, as the Komatsu people rethink what the needs might be. The Komatsu people have been very impressed with the functionality of the Cummins systems, and there are rumors that they may want to use some Cummins systems, not just for the B-series line, but throughout the Oyama plant. According to Lankford, this would raise some touchy issues:

> Our systems really define our culture and our processes for doing business, and Cummins management is not sure how much of that we are willing to share.

Another issue yet to be faced is that Cummins is going to have to have some sort of regional order management system for Japan. Lankford notes:

> Our existing Japanese regional office is going to have to accept orders for B-series engines, and, rather than forwarding those orders to Columbus or Darlington, they will have to send some of them to the Oyama plant. There is no agreement yet on roles and responsibilities on that, but it puts Japan in a new role in the Cummins organization.

In late 1994 the Cummins/Komatsu joint ventures were far from being completely implemented. According to Lankford:

> We have resolved a number of issues. But as we settle one issue a new one arises, so we continue to face plenty of challenges.

Cummins/Komatsu /Telco Joint Ventures (C)

Part A of this case should be read before reading the following description of the relationships between Cummins and TELCO.

Tata Cummins Limited (TCL) is a joint venture between Cummins and the Tata Engineering and Locomotive Company (TELCO), one of the largest companies in the huge Tata group. The largest truck manufacturer in India, TELCO manufactures a wide range of diesel-powered commercial vehicles and excavators and makes the diesel engines for this equipment. TELCO produces its own machine tools, processing equipment, and heavy dies and also has a subsidiary that sells CASE software. Selected TELCO sales and income data are shown in Exhibit 1.

With the opening of India's economy, TELCO recognizes that it must compete with foreign producers, both inside and outside the country. Thus, TELCO intends to produce a world-class truck with a world-class engine. Instead of making the large investment required to develop a world-class engine, TELCO has chosen to form TCL and use Cummins-designed engines.

In the past TELCO has had little competition within India and so it has produced essentially the same products with very little technological change. Consequently, TELCO's engine production environment has been very static, with little product change and long runs with stable schedules. TELCO's information systems reflect this stable environment and are not well suited to the complex, changing conditions that Cummins faces in the loose engine market. TCL is expected to produce around

60,000 B-series engines a year, primarily for use in TELCO vehicles, but a small part of the production will be sold by Cummins through its existing Indian joint venture, Kirloskar Cummins Ltd.

Cummins is responsible for designing the new TCL factory and its production equipment. Scheduled to begin production in July 1995, this factory is expected to be among the most efficient diesel engine producers in the world. The TCL factory is being built within the TELCO truck factory complex in Jamshedpur, about 200 miles west of Calcutta, where TELCO employs some 78,000 people in several factories.

There is no commercial air service into Jamshedpur, and it is a 5- to 6-hour train ride from Calcutta to Jamshedpur. The telephone lines into Jamshedpur are very bad—it took Lankford five days to get a FAX from the U.S. through to Jamshedpur.

TELCO is quite sophisticated in the information systems area. As mentioned previously, TELCO has a subsidiary that sells CASE software developed by the TELCO IS group, and another Tata subsidiary, Tata Consulting, has a large contract programming business, with 1,200 contract programmer/analysts working in the U.S. alone. In the past few years, the TELCO IS group has converted many TELCO systems from the mainframe to a client/server architecture using Silicon Graphics RISC processors running UNIX with Oracle relational databases. The data center in Jamshedpur is connected to all the TELCO plants via a fiber optic network.

The TCL Initial Business Plan

Lankford was the first systems person from either TELCO or Cummins to get involved with the TCL joint venture. He began in the fall of 1993 by providing Becker

---

This case was prepared by Professor E. W. Martin as the basis for class discussion rather than to illustrate either effective or ineffective handling of an administrative situation.

Copyright © 1997 (revised) by E. W. Martin.

EXHIBIT 1
TELCO Sales and Net Income.

1993 SALES IN MILLIONS OF RUPEES	
Trucks and Buses	26,897
Excavators	1,451
Software Services	46
Marine Engines	6
Other	358
TOTAL	28,758

FIVE-YEAR SUMMARY IN MILLIONS OF RUPEES		
DATE	SALES	NET INCOME
1991	20,990	1,421
1990	16,171	1,025
1989	13,829	700
1988	11,633	270
1987	9,398	29

Source: 1994 CFARbase

with a quick analysis of the systems issues inherent in the recently signed TCL Enterprise Agreement, License Agreement, and Initial Business Plan. The Initial Business Plan contains a section on systems that includes the following:

The Systems Plan supports the other elements of the Business Plan and is key to their effective integration. This plan shall include means to develop consistent data and see that it is maintained in formats that shall drive other systems that are linked to attain maximum efficiency. The MANAGEMENT shall assure that proper systems are in place prior to putting any business function in operation.

Systems are supported by computer hardware and software, but are much broader and deeper in scope than either of these. Systems span the entire process of organizing and managing the work and flows of information that are required to successfully operate a business. The MANAGEMENT shall, in the preparation of the Systems Plan, identify and specify the total scope of the systems to be utilized within TCL.

Lankford's analysis of this section noted:

This is a difficult task because the senior executives will be coming to TCL with expectations based upon differing experiences with systems at TELCO and Cummins. Also, systems development, training, and implementation will likely be on the critical path in many business function start-ups.

As soon as possible joint meetings must be held with the systems manager, each senior TCL executive, and systems representatives from Cummins and TELCO to assure that all develop common expectations on systems support required from TELCO, Cummins, and TCL.

Lankford also observed that, although there were many systems implications in these documents, they were quite vague on details, so he provided Becker a two-page list of the systems that would probably be needed (see Exhibit 2, where a question mark indicates systems that may not be required).

The Initial Business Plan also specified which senior executives of TCL would come from each parent. Cummins was to provide the managing director, engineering manager, quality manager, manufacturing engineering manager, and aftermarket support manager. TELCO was to provide the operations manager, materials manager, finance manager, systems manager, and company secretary/personnel manager. Ron Moore, who had managed the start-up of the Columbus B-series engine plant in 1991, was named as TCL managing director.

First Visit to Jamshedpur

Lankford sat in on a meeting in Columbus with some of the TELCO planning people in late November 1993, but they did not discuss systems problems. Just before Christmas Lankford received a note from Moore requesting him to be in Jamshedpur for meetings starting January 7. It was quite a scramble for Lankford to get his immunizations—polio, tetanus, smallpox vaccination, gamma globulin, and oral vaccine for typhoid—start taking malaria pills, and get ready to leave by then.

There was an additional complication in making travel arrangements. Although many controls on the

EXHIBIT 2
Needed Systems.

Plant Operating Systems Plan
  Assembly Management System
  • Line Scheduling
  • Line Sequencing
  • Component Serial Number Entry
  • Fail-Safing
  • Quality Data Collection
  • Test Data Collection
  • Paint Interface/Management
  • Charge-off
  Engine Order Management
  Parts Order Management
  Shop Floor Control (Machining)
  Forecasting
  Capacity Resource Planning
  Master Production Scheduling
  Plant Change Control
  • Plant Action File (PAF)
  • Plant Product Information File (PPIF)
  Date Controlled Shop Order (DCSO)
  Bill-of-Materials
  Material Requirements Planning
  Purchasing
  Supplier Quality Assurance
  Supplier Scheduling
  Receiving
  Inventory Management
  Shipping/Bill-of-Lading
  Skid Tracking/Management
  Tool Management
  Machine Maintenance
  Master Summary Bill of Material
  Process Documentation
  • Routings
  • Assembly Instructions
  FPEPS (Fuel Pump Engine Performance Specifications)

Personnel Systems Plan
  Personnel Records
  • Personal Data
  • Skills
  • Training
  Time & Attendance
  Employee Benefits
  • Life Insurance
  • Health Insurance
  • Retirement
  • Savings
  • Bonus/Profit/Incentive Programs
  Payroll Tax Management

Financial Systems Plan
  General Accounting
  • Budgeting
  • Forecasting
  • Tax Accounting
  • Travel (Expense Report)
  • Petty Cash
  • Internal Auditing
  General Ledger
  Payroll
  Pricing
  • Price Development
  • Price Application
  Accounts Receivable
  • Customer Master Maintenance
  Accounts Payable
  • Supplier Master Maintenance
  Invoicing
  Cost Accounting
  • Activity Based Costing?
  Direct Engine Sales Analysis (DESA)?
  Financial Reporting

Product Engineering Support Plan
  Engineering Activity File (EAF) Access?
  Electronic Vault Drawing Access?
  Application Engineering Support
  Customer Specifications Language (CSL) Support

Aftermarket Support Plan
  Warranty Administration
  Claims Processing
  Failure Analysis
  Cost Analysis
  Original Equipment Parts List (OEPL)
  Engine History Database
  Warehouse Management (?)
  Service Management

General Support Plan
  Electronic Data Interchange (EDI)
  Local Area Network (LAN) Management
  • Account Administration
  • Training
  • Security
  • File Backup
  • Software Installation/Maintenance
  IMS Training & Support
  TOSS Administration, Training, & Support
  Personal Productivity Software Support
  • Spreadsheet
  • Word Processing
  • Presentation Graphics
  • Desktop Publishing
  • Project Management
  • CASE Tools

Indian economy have been relaxed, the Government will not allow TCL to fund international travel in dollars. Therefore, to charge Lankford's travel to TCL it was necessary for TCL to make the reservations, buy the tickets in rupees, and send everything to Columbus before the trip. According to Lankford:

The Indian Government will allow dollars to be spent to import physical things like manufacturing machinery that are important to India, but it makes it very difficult to pay for any sort of intellectual services such as consulting or planning.

Lankford's flight from Europe arrived in Calcutta about 3 A.M., after which he had the 5-hour train ride to Jamshedpur. Lankford had strong impressions of India:

India is a country of extremes: extremely rich and extremely poor. Some parts of the cities are like any big city with fancy high-rise buildings, and other parts are shacks and tents, and people are squatting on public ground living in filth.

In addition to the few very rich, there are about 200 million that are lower middle class and about 700 million living in poverty. The middle class is highly educated, but by U.S. standards barely getting by economically. For example, a graduate engineer earns between $120 and $210 dollars per month. It is no wonder that so many educated Indians want to come to the U.S. where they can live very well and still send home more money than they could earn in India.

The TELCO corporate structure is very hierarchical. There is little discussion up and down—whatever the boss says is the final word. I had a systems person tell me that he knew they were making a bad decision, but he could not tell his boss.

Jamshedpur is very much a company town, and social position corresponds with the company hierarchy. As you go up the ladder you get better housing and you start having servants—first a house servant, then a driver, then a cook, and so on.

That part of India has a very hot climate, with temperatures typically exceeding 110 degrees in the summer. The TCL plant will be the first air-conditioned factory in that part of the country. That may be a problem because the electrical service is quite unreliable, so computers must be run off of motor-generators.

Lankford spent a week in Jamshedpur talking with TELCO systems people and was able to get a pretty good feel for TELCO systems during that time.

When he returned to the U.S., Lankford felt that it was very important for some TELCO systems people to visit Columbus as soon as possible to get them exposed to the Cummins culture, processes, and systems. The newly designated TCL systems manager made a three-week visit to the U.S., but it took three months to get a temporary visa for him, and this was much quicker than normal. It typically takes six months to get visas for India nationals to come to the U.S. for training, which has been a major problem in getting TCL under way. The American embassy has caused most of the problems, but the India government has also slowed things down.

Lankford's Recommendations

After visiting India and talking with many people at TELCO and within Cummins, Lankford believes that the TELCO systems are inadequate for TCL. Using Cummins Common Systems through a high-speed data link to the Columbus data center, as does the Cummins engine plant in Darlington, England, is not feasible due to communications costs and reliability problems. Also, TELCO's mainframe computers in Jamshedpur are not capable of running these systems, and installing an IBM 3090 in Jamshedpur is not a viable alternative. Therefore, Lankford recommends that TCL not use the Cummins Common Systems, except those required for design control and certification.

Instead Lankford recommends that TCL install the Avalon systems that are being modified to replace Cummins Common Systems throughout the world. The problem with this is that modification of these systems will not have been completed by the time the TCL factory begins production, so skeleton versions of these systems would have to be used initially. Because the Avalon systems should have the required interfaces with Cummins corporate systems by then and TCL start-up will be slow, Lankford believes that this approach is viable.

The TELCO systems people agree that TELCO systems are not adequate for TCL, but they would prefer to start out by using basic PC software readily available in the U.S. while they develop the systems for long-term use. Excellent analysts and programmers are quite inexpensive in India and TELCO has a very capable systems group that would like the challenge of developing these systems.

No matter what happens, TCL must interchange a lot of data with Cummins data center in Columbus, so there must be a high-speed data link between Jamshedpur and Columbus. Although this will probably be a satellite link, the local telephone company must be involved, and approval by three different governmental organizations must be obtained.

Current Status

Lankford and the Joint Ventures Support Group have accomplished a great deal during the past year. They have defined the crucial systems interfaces that must exist between Cummins and any joint venture. And they have developed a standard responsibility chart that can be used to determine who should be responsible for each of the seventy business functions that are required for a joint venture to produce Cummins engines. In addition to the Komatsu and TELCO joint ventures, Cummins is involved in the development of several other similar ventures throughout the world, and these accomplishments will make the implementation of future joint ventures much easier.

Through this experience Lankford has also recognized how important flexible systems have become to a modern business:

> Today most business functions are supported by a systems function, and a business function can only be as flexible and responsive as the system that is supporting it. In today's environment a business must be able to change its business rules to react to competition, and it is a lot easier to change the business rules than it is to change the systems that support those business rules. That is why many of our systems need to be rearchitected so that they are easier to change.

Current Issues

The joint ventures systems support group has identified and resolved many issues, but a number of issues remain. One such issue is data security. According to Lankford:

> We need to come to a consensus on what we want to do about data security. The contracts have non-disclosure provisions that apply to both companies, and that may be perfectly adequate, but we need to address this issue and make sure we get closure on it.

TELCO has not responded to Lankford's responsibility chart suggesting who is responsible for the systems supporting each business function.

The issue of whether to use the Avalon software or allow TELCO's systems group to develop systems for TCL has become very political. Lankford has discussed it with TCL managing director Moore, and Jerry Pennington of the Joint Ventures Support Group will soon spend two weeks in Jamshedpur to try to help Moore sell the TELCO people on using the Avalon software.

If TCL decides to use the Avalon software, then the Cummins systems group will have to make sure that the necessary additions to this software are available and work properly. At a minimum there must be interfaces with the Cummins product definition systems, electronic data interchange (EDI), and the original equipment parts list (OEPL) data collection process. There will also be some installation and training issues to be faced.

Another issue is the support from the Cummins engine plant at Columbus that is required to start up the TCL plant. Cummins is responsible for designing and sourcing the assembly line, getting all the equipment on order, and working with the suppliers. According to Lankford:

> The TCL plant will have an assembly management system exactly like the one in the Columbus Midrange Engine Plant (CMEP), which means that someone must interface between the assembly management software and the plant business systems and between the assembly management software and the program logic controllers that make the assembly line go. This software is the responsibility of plant-level people, and the Cummins Management Systems group does not have the expertise to deal with these problems. But CMEP does not have qualified people that can be spared to work on this, so this problem will have to be kicked upstairs.

Finally, they still have been unsuccessful in getting the high-speed data link established between Jamshedpur and Columbus. The Cummins telecommunications people are working on this, but so far they have not made much progress.

In late 1994, the Cummins/TELCO joint venture is far from complete implementation. Lankford summarizes:

> We have resolved a number of issues. But as we settle one issue a new one arises, so we continue to face plenty of challenges.

GLOSSARY

AI: *See* Artificial intelligence, Expert systems shell.

American National Standards Institute (ANSI): The United States standard-setting body for many IT standards.

Analog network: The electronic linking of devices, where messages are sent over the links by having some analogous physical quantity (e.g., voltage) continuously vary as a function of time. Historically, the telephone network has been an analog network.

ANSI: *See* American National Standards Institute.

Applet: An application written in the Java object-oriented programming language; usually stored on a Web server and downloaded to a microcomputer with a mouse click and executed by a Java-compatible Web browser. A major advantage of a Java applet is that it can be run on virtually any IT platform. *See also* Web browser, IT platform.

Application independence: The separation, or decoupling, of data from application systems. Application independence means that applications are built separate from the databases from which applications draw their data; application independence results in lower long term costs for systems development.

Application suite: The name given to a collection of personal productivity software packages (e.g., word processing, spreadsheet, presentation graphics, database management system) that are integrated to some extent and marketed as a set. In the late 1990s, the three primary suites in the marketplace are Microsoft Office, Lotus SmartSuite, and Corel Office Professional.

Application system: *See* information system.

Applications architecture: That part of an IT architecture that defines the process for applications development and management.

Applications software: All programs written to accomplish particular tasks for computer users. Examples include programs for payroll computation, inventory record-keeping, word processing, and producing a summarized report for top management.

Archie: An Internet application, or tool, that allows the user to search the publicly available anonymous file transfer protocol (FTP) sites to find the desired computer files. *See also* File transfer protocol.

Architecture: *See* Information technology architecture.

Arithmetic/logical unit: The portion of a computer system in which arithmetic operations (such as addition and multiplication) and logical operations (such as comparing two numbers for equality) are carried out.

Artificial intelligence (AI): The study of how to make computers do things that are presently done better by people. AI research includes five separate but related areas: natural languages, robotics, perceptive systems (vision and hearing), expert systems, and neural networks.

Artificial intelligence (AI) shell: *See* Expert systems shell.

Assembler: A program (software) that translates an assembly language program—a program containing mnemonic operation codes and symbolic addresses—into an equivalent machine language program.

Assembly language: Second-generation computer language in which the programmer uses easily remembered mnemonic operation codes instead of machine language operation codes and symbolic addresses instead of memory cell addresses. Such a language is considerably easier to use than machine language, but it still requires the programmer to employ the same small steps that the computer has been built to understand.

Asynchronous Transfer Mode (ATM): An approach to implementing a local area network or a wide area network based on high-speed switching technology to accomplish fast packet switching with short, fixed-length packets. With ATM, connectivity between devices is provided through a switch rather than through a shared bus or ring, with line speeds of over 600 million bits per second possible. *See also* Packet switching, Bus topology, Ring topology.

ATM: *See* Asynchronous transfer mode.

Audit trail: An EDP auditing technique that allows a business transaction to be traced from the time of input through all the processes and reports in which the transaction data are used. An audit trail is used to identify where errors are introduced or security breaches may have occurred.

Backbone: In a telecommunications network, the underlying foundation to which the other elements attach. For example, NSFNET served as the backbone for the Internet until 1995 by providing the underlying high-volume links of the Internet to which other elements attached. *See also* Backbone network.

Backbone network: A middle-distance network that interconnects local area networks in a single organization with each other and with the organization's wide area network and the Internet. The technology employed is at the high end of that used for local area networks, such as FDDI, Fast Ethernet, or ATM running over fiber optic cabling or shielded twisted pair. *See also* Asynchronous Transfer Mode, Fast Ethernet, Fiber Distributed Data Interface.

Backlog: *See* Systems backlog.

Bandwidth: The difference between the highest and the lowest frequencies (cycles per second) that can be transmitted on a single medium. Bandwidth is important because it is a measure of the capacity of the transmission medium.

Bar code label: A label consisting of a series of bars used to identify an item; by scanning the bar code, the data can be entered into a computer. There are a variety of bar code languages, the most widely known of which is the Universal Product Code, or UPC, used by the grocery industry. The use of bar codes is very popular for high-volume supermarket checkout, department store sales, inventory tracking, time and attendance records, and health care records.

Baseband coax: A simple-to-use and inexpensive-to-install type of coaxial cable that offers a single digital transmission channel with maximum transmission speeds ranging from 10 million bits per second (mbps) up to 264 mbps. Baseband coax has been widely used for local area networks and telephone long-distance transmission.

Batch processing: A mode of transaction processing in which a group or "batch" of transactions (of a particular type) is accumulated and then processed as a single batch at one time. For example, all sales for a firm would be accumulated during the day and then processed as a single batch at night.

Batch total: The sum of values in a specific field across all transactions in a group.

Baud: Number of signals sent per second; one measure of data transmission speed. Baud is usually equivalent to Hertz (another measure of transmission speed) and to bits per second.

Benchmarking: A procedure to compare the capabilities of various computers in a particular organizational setting by running a representative set of real jobs (jobs regularly run on the organization's existing computer) on each of the machines and comparing the resulting elapsed times.

Bit: Widely used abbreviation for a *bi*nary digi*t*, i.e., a 0 or a 1. Coding schemes used in computer systems employ particular sequences of bits to represent the decimal numbers, alphabetic characters, and special characters.

Boundary: Identifies the scope of a system. A boundary segregates the system from its environment.

BPR: *See* Business process reengineering.

Bridge: A hardware device employed in a telecommunications network to connect two local area networks (LANs) or LAN segments together when the LANs use the same protocols, or set of rules. A bridge is smart enough to forward only messages that need to go to the other LAN.

Broadband coax: A type of coaxial cable—more expensive and harder to use than baseband coax—that uses analog transmission; can be divided into multiple channels, and can achieve transmission speeds up to 550 million bits per second.

Browser: *See* Web browser.

Bus topology: A network topology in which a single length of cable (coax, fiber optic, or twisted pair)—not connected at the ends—is shared by all network devices; also called a linear topology.

Business process reengineering (BPR): The radical redesign of business processes to achieve dramatic improvements by taking advantage of information technology. Also referred to as business process redesign.

Byte: A memory cell that can store only one character of data. *See also* Memory.

Cache memory: A very high-speed storage unit used as an intermediary between elements of a computer system that have a significant mismatch in speeds (e.g., the very fast data channel and relatively slow direct access storage device). An entire block of data is moved from the slower element to cache memory, so that most requests for data from the faster element can be satisfied directly from the very high-speed cache memory.

CAD: *See* Computer-aided design.

CAE: *See* Computer-aided engineering.

CAM: *See* Computer-aided manufacturing.

CAPP: *See* Computer-aided process planning.

CASE: *See* Computer-aided software engineering.

CD-ROM: An abbreviation for compact disk-read only memory; the most common type of optical disk, it can only be read and cannot be erased. CD-ROM is particularly useful for distributing large amounts of relatively stable data to many locations.

Cellular telephone: A telephone instrument that can be installed in a car or carried in a pocket or briefcase; this instrument can be used anywhere as long as it is within the range of 8 to 10 miles from a cellular switching station.

Central processing unit (CPU): The name given to the combination of the control unit, which controls all other components of a computer, and the arithmetic/logical unit, in which computations and logical comparisons are carried out; also referred to as the processor.

Champion: A business manager who has the motivation and/or power to push a systems project through to successful implementation by helping to remove obstacles and by motivating users to accept the system. Under special circumstances, an IS manager can also play this role.

Change management: A process approach to managing change; includes changes to information systems under development or undergoing maintenance, as well as changes to organizations as a part of systems implementation.

Chargeback: The process that is used to internally charge client units for IS services provided. These internal charges may be established to recover costs or may represent market prices.

Check digit: One or more digits appended to a critical value; the check digit has some mathematical relationship to the other digits in the number.

Chief information officer (CIO): The most senior manager responsible for information systems and information technology at the corporate level. The CIO is a high-level manager responsible for IS leadership, similar to a chief financial officer responsible for the finance function. Sometimes CIOs have no operating responsibilities because the organization has decentralized these responsibilities to division heads.

CIM: *See* Computer-integrated manufacturing.

Client/server system: A particular type of distributed system in which the processing power is distributed between a central server computer, such as a minicomputer or a powerful workstation, and a number of client computers, which are usually desktop microcomputers. The split in responsibilities between the server and the client varies considerably between applications, but the client often handles data entry and the immediate output, whereas the server maintains the larger database against which the new data are processed. *See also* Distributed systems.

Coaxial cable (coax): A common transmission medium that consists of a heavy copper wire at the center surrounded by insulating material, then a cylindrical conductor such as a woven braided mesh, and finally an outer protective plastic covering. The two kinds of coaxial cable in widespread use are baseband coax for digital transmission and broadband coax for analog transmission.

Code generator: *See* Computer-aided software engineering.

COM: *See* Computer output microfilm.

Commercial software package: *See* Software package.

Compiler: A program (software) that translates a third- or fourth-generation language program into an equivalent machine language program, translating the entire program into machine language before any of the program is executed.

Computer-aided design (CAD): The use of computer graphics (both two-dimensional and three-dimensional) and a database to create and modify engineering designs.

Computer-aided engineering (CAE): The analysis of the functional characteristics of an engineering design by simulating the product performance under various conditions.

Computer-aided manufacturing (CAM): The use of computers to plan and control manufacturing processes. CAM incorporates computer programs to control automated equipment on the shop floor, automated guided vehicles to move material, and a communications network to link all the pieces.

Computer-aided process planning (CAPP): A computer-based system that plans the sequence of processes that produce or assemble a part. During the design process, the engineer retrieves the closest standard plan from a database and modifies that plan rather than starting from scratch.

Computer-aided software engineering (CASE): A set of integrated software tools used by IS specialists to automate some or all phases of an SDLC process. Upper-CASE tools support project management, the Definition phase, and the initial steps of the Construction phase, including the creation of a DD/D. Lower-CASE tools are back-end code generators (usually COBOL code) and maintenance support tools. *See also* Integrated-CASE.

Computer-integrated manufacturing (CIM): A broad term that encompasses many uses of the computer to help manufacturers operate more effectively and efficiently. CIM systems fall into three major categories: engineering systems, which are aimed at increasing the productivity of engineers; manufacturing administration, which includes systems that develop production schedules and monitor production; and factory operations, which include those systems that actually control the operation of machines on the factory floor.

Computer output microfilm (COM): A computer output method using microfilm or microfiche (a sheet of film) as the output medium. A computer output device called a COM recorder accepts the data from memory and prepares the microfilm output at very high speeds.

Computer telecommunications network: The type of network emanating from a single medium-sized, large, or very large computer or a group of closely linked computers; usually arranged in a tree topology.

Computer virus: A small unit of code that invades a computer program, and, when the invaded program is executed, the virus makes copies of itself that are released to attack other computer programs. Hundreds of virus programs have been created, some of which are intended as jokes that do little harm; however, some of them degrade performance by using up computer memory, and others wipe out memory or destroy files.

Contention bus: A design standard for a local area network based on a bus topology and contention for the use of the bus by all devices on the network, i.e., any device may transmit a message if the bus is idle, but if two devices start to transmit at the same time, a collision will occur and both messages will be lost. *See also* CSMA/CD protocol.

Context diagram: A logical model that identifies the entities with which a system must interface. *See also* Data flow diagram.

Control unit: The component of a computer system that controls all the remaining components. The control unit brings instructions (operations to be performed) from memory one at a time, interprets each instruction, and carries it out—all at electronic speed. *See also* Central processing unit, Stored-program concept.

Controller: A hardware unit to link input/output or file devices to the CPU and memory of large computer systems (through the data channel). The controller is a highly specialized microprocessor that manages the operation of its attached devices to free the CPU from these tasks (e.g., a DASD controller handles direct access devices, and a communications controller handles multiple terminals).

Conversion: The process of changing to a new system, such as with a pilot or cutover (cold turkey) conversion strategy.

Cordless telephone: A portable telephone instrument that can be used up to about 1,000 feet from its wired telephone base unit; this permits the user to carry the instrument to various rooms in a house or take it outdoors on the patio.

Corporate data model: A chart that describes all the data requirements of a given organization. This chart shows what data entities and relationships between the entities are important for the organization.

Corporate information policy: The foundation for managing the ownership of data.

Counterimplementation: Actions taken to resist or prevent the successful implementation of a new system.

CPU: *See* Central processing unit.

Critical success factor (CSF): One of a few organizational activities that, if done well, should result in the strategic success of an organization.

CSF: *See* Critical success factor.

CSMA/CD protocol: An abbreviation for Carrier Sense Multiple Access with Collision Detection, the protocol used in the contention bus design for a local area network. With this protocol, any device may transmit a message if the bus is idle. However, if two devices start to transmit at the same time, a collision will occur and the messages will become garbled. Both devices must recognize that this collision has occurred, stop transmitting, wait for some random period of time, and then try again.

DASD: *See* Direct access storage device.

Data administration: The organizational unit that leads the efforts to plan, control, define, justify, and account for organizational data as a resource. Data administration has both managerial and technical interests in data and databases. *See also* Database administrator.

Data analysis and presentation application: An application that manipulates data and then distributes information to authorized users. These applications concentrate on creating useful information from established data sources and, because they are separate from data capture and transfer systems, can be individually changed without having to modify the more costly to change data capture and transfer systems.

Data architecture: *See* Data model.

Data capture application: An application that gathers data and populates databases. These applications allow the simplification of all other applications that then transfer or report data and information.

Data center: A large mainframe computer installation that stores, maintains, and provides access to vast quantities of data; includes computer hardware, communications facilities, system software, and technical support and operations staff.

Data channel: A specialized input/output processor (hardware) that takes over the function of device communication from the CPU. The data channel corrects for the significant speed mismatch between the slow input/output and file devices and the fast and expensive CPU.

Data dictionary/directory (DD/D): Support software that provides a repository of metadata for each data element in a system—including the meaning, alternative names, storage format, integrity rules, security clearances, and physical location of data—that is used by the DBMS and system users.

Data-driven design: An approach to systems development that concentrates on the ideal and natural organization of data, independent of how or where data are used. *See also* Process-driven design.

Data flow diagram (DFD): A common diagrammatic technique for logical As-Is and To-Be models. Symbols are used to represent the movement, storage, and processing of data in a system and both inputs from and outputs to the environment. Each process in a top-level DFD is decomposed to a lower level, and so on.

Data mining: Searching or "mining" for small "nuggets" of information from the vast quantities of data stored in an organization's data warehouse, employing a variety of technologies such as decision trees and neural networks. *See also* Data warehousing.

Data model: A map or blueprint for organizational data. A data model shows the data entities and relationships that are important to an organization. Data modeling is the process of defining a data model.

Data standards: A clear and useful way to uniquely identify every instance of data and to give unambiguous business meaning to all data. Types of standards include identifiers, naming, definition, integrity rules, and usage rights.

Data steward: A business manager responsible for the quality and viability of a particular data entity (like customer, product, or employee).

Data transfer application: An application that moves data from one database to another. These applications permit one source of data to serve many localized systems within an organization.

Data warehousing: The establishment and maintenance of a large data storage facility containing data on all or at least many aspects of the enterprise; less formally, a popular method for making data accessible to many people in an organization. To create a data warehouse, a firm pulls data from its operational transaction processing systems and puts the data in a separate "data warehouse" so that users may access and analyze the data without endangering the operational systems. *See also* Data mining.

Database: A shared collection of files and associations between these files. A database reduces redundancy and inconsistency compared to file processing, but this lack of natural redundancy can cause risks from loss of data or breaches of authorized data access or manipulation.

Database administrator (DBA): The person in the data administration unit who is responsible for computerized databases. A DBA is concerned with efficiency, integrity, and security of database processing.

Database management system (DBMS): Support software that is used to create, manage, and protect organizational data. A DBMS is the software that manages a database; it works with the operating system to store and modify data and to make data accessible in a variety of meaningful and authorized ways.

Database machine: *See* Database server.

Database server: A separate computer, attached to another computer, that is responsible for only processing database queries and updates. A database server is usually part of a local area network and serves the database needs of all the personal and larger computers on this network.

DBA: *See* Database administrator.

DBMS: *See* Database management system.

DBMS engine: A computer program that handles the detailed retrieving and updating of data for a wide variety of other DBMSs, electronic spreadsheets, and other software. Use of a DBMS engine allows the other software to concentrate on providing a convenient user interface while the DBMS engine handles the common database access functions.

DDD: *See* Direct Distance Dialing.

DD/D: *See* Data dictionary/directory.

Decision analysis: A requirements definition approach in which analysts identify the key decisions made by those who will use the system, formulate models that describe how these decisions are or should be made, and thus determine what information is needed to improve the decision-making process.

Decision support system (DSS): A computer-based system, almost always interactive, designed to assist managers in making decisions. A DSS incorporates both data and models and is usually intended to assist in the solution of semi-structured or unstructured problems. An actual application that assists in the decision-making process is properly called a specific DSS; examples of specific DSSs include a police-beat allocation system, a capacity planning and production scheduling system, and a capital investment decision system.

Decision support system (DSS) generator: Computer software that provides a set of capabilities to build a specific DSS quickly and easily. For example, Microsoft Excel, a spreadsheet package, can be used as a DSS generator to construct specific financial models that can be used in decision-making.

Decoupling of system components: Reducing the need to coordinate two system components. Decoupling is accomplished by creating slack and flexible resources, buffers, sharing resources, and standards.

Desktop personal computer: The most common type of personal computer, which is a personal computer large enough that it can not be moved around easily on a regular basis. The monitor and the keyboard, and sometimes the case containing the rest of the computer, set on a table or "desktop." If the case containing the rest of the computer sets on the floor under the table or desk, it is called a "tower" unit, but this configuration is still regarded as a desktop personal computer.

DFD: *See* Data flow diagram.

Digital network: The electronic linking of devices, where messages are sent over the links by directly transmitting the zeros and ones used by computers and other digital devices. Computer telecommunications networks are digital networks, and the telephone network is gradually being shifted from an analog to a digital network.

Digital video disk (DVD): A new type of CD-ROM that holds much more data than a conventional CD-ROM—up to 17 gigabytes. Also called a digital versatile disk. *See also* CD-ROM, Optical disk.

Direct access file: A basic type of computer file from which it is possible for the computer to obtain a record immediately, without regard to where the record is located on the file; usually stored on magnetic disk. Computer files, also called secondary memory or secondary storage, are added to a computer system to keep vast quantities of data accessible within the computer system at more reasonable costs than main memory.

Direct access storage device (DASD): The device on which direct access files are stored. *See also* Direct access file.

Direct Distance Dialing (DDD): The normal way of using the long-distance telephone network in the United States in which the user directly dials the number with which he or she wishes to communicate and pays for the service based on the duration of the call and the geographical distance; may be used for voice and data communications between any two locations served by the telephone network.

Direct file organization: *See* Direct access file.

Disposable system: A system that can be discarded when it becomes obsolete without affecting the operation of any other information system.

Distributed data processing: *See* Distributed systems.

Distributed database: A database that is physically located across several computer systems. A goal of managing a distributed database is to give the impression to all database programmers and users that the database is actually in one location.

Distributed systems: Application systems in which the processing power is distributed to multiple sites, which are then tied together via telecommunications lines. Distributed systems have computers of possibly varying sizes located at various physical sites at which the organization does business, and these computers are linked by telecommunications lines in order to support some business process.

Documentation: Written descriptions produced during the systems development process for those who use the system (user documentation) and for IS specialists who operate and maintain the system (system documentation).

Downsizing: A term that usually means making something smaller. When referring to computer hardware, downsizing refers to the substitution of minicomputers, workstations, or PC networks for mainframes as the platform to support applications.

DSS: *See* Decision support system.

DVD: *See* Digital video disk.

EDI: *See* Electronic data interchange.

EDP auditing: A variety of methods used by trained auditors to ensure the correct processing of data. EDP auditing combines data processing controls with classical accounting auditing methods.

EIS: *See* Executive information system.

Electronic commerce: The use of information technology to conduct business between two or more organizations or between an organization and one or more end-customers via one or more computer networks. Beginning in the mid-1990s, the World Wide Web and other Internet technologies became major platforms for conducting electronic commerce.

Electronic data interchange (EDI): A set of standards and hardware and software technology that enable computers in independent organizations to exchange business documents electronically. Typical transactions include purchase orders, order acknowledgments, invoices, price quotes, shipping notices, and insurance claims, but any document can potentially be exchanged using EDI. The transaction standards are typically established by an industry consortium or a national or international standards body (such as ANSI).

Electronic mail: A system whereby users send and receive messages electronically at their workstations, which are usually microcomputers connected to a local area network or to a minicomputer or mainframe computer. Electronic mail, or e-mail, can help telephone tag and usually incorporates such features as sending a message to a distribution list, resending a message to someone else with an appended note, and filing messages in electronic file folders for later recall.

E-mail: *See* Electronic mail.

Encryption: Conversion, or encoding, from the original form in which a communication is expressed into another form that will be difficult or even impossible for anyone else except the intended receiver to decode.

End-user computing: Hands-on use of computer resources by employees throughout the organization to enter data, make inquiries, release orders into production, prepare reports, communicate, perform statistical analysis, analyze problems, design products, and so forth.

Enterprise data planning and modeling: A top-down approach to detailing the data requirements of an organization. Enterprise modeling describes data at a very general level and indicates how data relates to various business activities.

Enterprise resource planning (ERP) system: A set of integrated business applications, or modules, to carry out most common business functions, including inventory control, general ledger accounting, accounts payable, accounts receivable, material requirements planning, order management, and human resources. ERP modules are integrated, primarily through a common set of definitions and a common database, and the modules have been designed to reflect a particular way of doing business, i.e., a particular set of business processes. The leading ERP vendors are SAP, Baan, J. D. Edwards, Oracle, and PeopleSoft.

Entity-relationship (ER) diagram: A common notation for modeling organizational data requirements. ER diagramming uses specific symbols to represent data entities, relationships, and elements.

ERP system: *See* Enterprise resource planning system.

Ethernet: The name of the original Xerox version of a contention bus local area network design, which has come to be used as a synonym for a contention bus design. *See also* Local area network, Contention bus.

Evolutionary development: Any development approach that does not depend upon defining the final requirements early in the development process, but, like prototyping, evolves the system by building successive versions that eventually result in a system that is acceptable. *See also* Prototyping, Rapid application development.

Executive information system (EIS): A computer application designed to be used directly by top managers, without the assistance of intermediaries, to provide the executive easy on-line access to current information about the status of the organization and its environment. Such information includes filtered and summarized internal transactions data and also "soft" data such as assessments, rumors, opinions, and ideas.

Expert systems: The branch of artificial intelligence concerned with building systems that incorporate the decision-making logic of a human expert. Expert systems can diagnose and prescribe treatment for diseases, analyze proposed bank loans, and determine the optimal sequence of stops on a truck route.

Expert systems shell: Computer software that provides the basic framework of an expert system and a limited but user-friendly special language to develop the expert system. With the purchase of such a shell, the organization's system builder can concentrate on the details of the business decision being modeled and the development of the knowledge base.

Factory automation: The use of information technology to automate various aspects of factory operations. Factory automation includes numerically controlled machines, material requirements planning (MRP) systems, computer-integrated manufacturing (CIM), and computer-controlled robots.

Fast Ethernet: A relatively new approach to implementing a high-speed local area network, operating at 100 million bits per second (mbps). Fast Ethernet, also called 100 Base-T, uses the same CSMA/CD architecture as traditional Ethernet and is usually implemented using either two pairs of unshielded twisted pair or a single shielded twisted pair as the medium. *See also* Contention bus, CSMA/CD protocol, Ethernet, Twisted pair.

FDDI: *See* Fiber Distributed Data Interface.

Feasibility analysis: An analysis step in the systems development life cycle in which the economic, operational, and technical feasibility of a proposed system is assessed.

Fiber Distributed Data Interface (FDDI): An American National Standards Institute (ANSI) standard for building a local area network that offers a transmission speed of 100 million bits per second and fault tolerance because of its double-ring architecture; FDDI utilizes either fiber optic cabling or shielded twisted pair wiring.

Fiber optics: A transmission medium in which data are transmitted by sending pulses of light through a thin fiber of glass or fused silica. Although expensive to install and difficult to work with, the high transmission speeds possible with fiber optic cabling—100 million bits per second (bps) to 30 billion bps—are leading to its use in most new long distance telephone lines.

File processing: An approach to managing data in which each application system separately maintains its own set of computer files. File processing permits different systems to remain independent of one another, but redundant and inconsistent data across systems can cause costly problems.

File transfer protocol (FTP): An Internet application, or tool, that allows users to send and receive files, including programs, from one computer system to another over the Internet. The user logs onto the two computer systems at the same time and then copies files from one system to the other.

Firewall: An electronic device, such as a router, personal computer, or workstation, that inhibits access to an organization's internal network from the Internet.

A firewall is the primary approach to security used by firms with Web sites on servers accessible to the public; external Web sites sit outside the organization's firewall.

Formal system: The way an organization was designed to work. *See also* Informal system.

Fourth-generation language: A computer language in which the user gives a precise statement of what is to be accomplished, not how to do it. No procedure is necessary; the order of statements is usually inconsequential. Examples include IFPS, SAS, FOCUS, and NOMAD.

FTP: *See* File transfer protocol.

Full-duplex transmission: A type of data transmission in which data can travel in both directions at once over the communication line.

Functional information system: An information system, usually composed of multiple interrelated subsystems, that provides the information necessary to accomplish various tasks within a specific functional area of the business, such as production, marketing, accounting, personnel, or engineering. For example, the marketing information system may include subsystems for promotion and advertising, new product development, sales forecasting, product planning, product pricing, market research, and sales information.

Gateway: A hardware device employed in a telecommunications network to connect two or more local area networks (LANs) or to connect two different types of networks, such as a backbone network and the Internet, where the networks may use different protocols. The gateway, which is really a sophisticated router, forwards only those messages that need to be forwarded from one network to another. *See also* Router.

Geographic information system (GIS): A computer-based system designed to capture, store, manipulate, display, and analyze data spatially referenced to the earth; a GIS links data to maps so that the spatial characteristics of the data can be easily comprehended.

GIS: *See* Geographic information system.

Gopher: A menu-driven Internet application, or tool, that allows the user to search for publicly available data posted on the Internet by digging like a gopher through a series of menus until the sought-after data are located. Gopher has largely disappeared, subsumed by the greater capabilities of the World Wide Web.

Graphical user interface (GUI): An interface between a computer and a human user based on graphical screen images, such as icons. With a GUI (pronounced gooey), the user selects an application or makes other choices by using a mouse to click on an appropriate icon or label appearing on the screen. Windows 95/98, Windows NT, and the OS/2 operating system employ a GUI.

Group support system (GSS): A variant of a decision support system (DSS) in which the system is designed to support a group rather than an individual. The purpose of a GSS is to make group sessions more productive by supporting such group activities as brainstorming, issue structuring, voting, and conflict resolution.

Group technology (GT): A computer-based system that logically groups parts according to physical characteristics, machine routings through the factory, and similar machine operations. Based on these logical groupings, GT is able to identify existing parts that engineers can use or modify rather than design new parts.

Groupware: A made-up word referring to soft*ware* designed to support *groups* by facilitating collaboration, communication, and coordination. The functionality of groupware products varies considerably, but potentially may include electronic mail, electronic bulletin boards, computer conferencing, electronic calendaring, group scheduling, sharing documents, electronic whiteboards, meeting support systems, workflow routing, electronic forms, and desktop videoconferencing.

GSS: *See* Group support system.

GT: *See* Group technology.

GUI: *See* Graphical user interface.

Half-duplex transmission: A type of data transmission in which data can travel in both directions over the communication line, but not simultaneously.

Hand-held personal computer: The smallest type of personal computer, weighing from under a pound up to two pounds, which can easily be held in one hand while using the other hand to enter instructions or data; also called palmtop computers.

Hardware: The physical pieces of a computer or telecommunications system, such as a central processing unit, a printer, and a terminal.

Help desk: A support service for the users of IT that can be accessed via phone or e-mail. The service is provided by IS specialists within the organization that owns, operates, or develops the resource, or it is provided by IS specialists external to the organization that have been contracted to provide this service (an outsourcing vendor).

Hertz: Cycles per second; one measure of data transmission speed. Hertz is usually equivalent to baud (another measure of transmission speed) and to bits per second.

Hierarchical decomposition: The process of breaking down a system into successive levels of subsystems. This recursive decomposition allows a system to be described at various levels of detail, each appropriate for a different kind of analysis or for a different audience.

HTML: *See* Hypertext markup language.

Hub: A simple hardware device employed in a telecommunications network to connect one section of a local area network (LAN) to another. A hub forwards every message it receives to the other section of the LAN, whether or not the messages need to go there.

Human assets: A component of the IT architecture outlining the ideal state of the personnel, values, and management systems aspects of an IT system.

Hypertext: A creative way of linking objects, such as text, pictures, sound clips, and video clips, to each other so that by clicking on highlighted text or a small icon, the user is taken to the related object. As used on the World Wide Web, when users are reading a Web page describing the Grand Canyon, they might click on The View from Yavapai Point to display a full-screen photograph of that view or click on The Grand Canyon Suite to hear a few bars from that musical composition.

Hypertext markup language (HTML): A specialized language to "mark up" pages to be viewed on the World Wide Web. The "mark ups" consist of special codes inserted in the text to indicate headings, bold-faced text, italics, where images or photographs are to be placed, and links to other Web pages, among other things.

I-CASE: *See* Integrated-CASE.

IC: *See* Information center.

Imaging: A computer input/output method by which any type of paper document—including business forms, reports, charts, graphs, and photographs—can be read by a scanner and translated into digital form so that it can be stored in the computer system; this process can also be reversed so that the digitized image stored in the computer system can be displayed on a video display unit, printed on paper, or transmitted to another computer or workstation.

In-line system: A computer system in which data entry is accomplished on-line (i.e., a transaction is entered directly into the computer via some input device) but the processing is deferred until a suitable batch of transactions has been accumulated.

Indexed file organization: A method of organizing a computer file or database in which the control keys only are arranged in sequence in a separate table, along with a pointer to the complete records associated with each key. The records themselves can then be arranged in any order.

Informal system: The way the organization actually works. *See also* Formal system.

Information: Data (usually processed data) that are useful to a decision-maker.

Information center (IC): An organizational unit whose mission is to support end-user computing by providing services such as education and training, application consulting, assistance in selecting hardware and software, facilitating access to computerized data, and so forth. An IC may also be responsible for policy-setting for end-user computing, including the selection of standards for PC tools.

Information resources assessment: Taking inventory and critically evaluating technological and human resources in terms of how well they meet the business needs of the organization.

Information revolution: A radical economic reorientation in the late twentieth century in which information and knowledge in combination with communication have replaced natural resources and physical labor as the fundamental sources of wealth. This new economy has been referred to as the Information Age.

Information system (IS): The collection of computer programs, hardware, people, procedures, documentation, forms, inputs, and outputs used in or generated by handling business data. An information system consists of these components and their interrelationships.

Information systems (IS) organization: An organizational unit responsible for managing information technology. Traditional IS organization functions include computer operations and systems development. These have now been expanded to include other functions such as telecommunications operations and end-user computing support. Also referred to as the IS department.

Information technology (IT): All forms of technology involved in capturing, manipulating, communicating, presenting, and using data (and data transformed into information).

Information technology architecture: A written set of guidelines for a company's desired future for information technology within which people can make individual decisions that will be compatible with that desired future; should include components relating to beliefs or values, data, the technology infrastructure, applications, and the management system for information technology.

Information vision: A written expression of the desired future for information use and management in an organization.

Infrastructure architecture: A structure that describes the technical components of the IS infrastructure and the relationships between these components. The technical architecture is concerned with such things as the types of computer hardware, telecommunications network topologies, communications protocols, and requirements for interfacing local equipment with the network.

Innovation adoption: The process followed by an individual or organization to use a new idea, method, system, or technology.

Instruction: An individual step or operation in a program, particularly in a machine language program. *See also* Machine language, Program.

Integrated-CASE (I-CASE): A set of full-cycle, integrated CASE tools, in which system specifications supported by the front-end tools can be converted into computer code by the back-end tools included in the system. *See also* Computer-aided software engineering.

Integrated Services Digital Network (ISDN): An emerging set of international standards by which the public telephone network will offer extensive new telecommunications capabilities—including simultaneous transmission of both voice and data over the same line—to telephone users worldwide.

Interactive system: A computer system in which the user directly interacts with the computer. In such a system, the user would enter data into the computer via some type of input device and the computer would provide a response almost immediately, as in an airline reservation system. An interactive system is an on-line system in which the computer provides an immediate response to the user.

Interface: The point of contact where the environment meets a system or where two subsystems meet. Special functions such as filtering, coding/decoding, error detection and correction, buffering, security, and summarizing occur at an interface, which allows compatibility between the environment and system or two subsystems. *See also* Graphical user interface.

Internet: A network of networks that use the TCP/IP protocol, with gateways (connections) to even more networks that do not use the TCP/IP protocol. The Internet connects over 150,000 separate networks around the world, and the number of Internet users in the U.S. alone is over 40 million. The two primary applications on the Internet are electronic mail and the World Wide

Web. *See also* Electronic mail, Transmission Control Protocol/Internet Protocol (TCP/IP), World Wide Web.

Interorganizational system (IOS): An information system used by two or more independent organizations. An IOS typically links customers and suppliers or other strategic business partners in order to replace the manual handling of data and other paperwork with electronic transactions.

Interpreter: A software program that translates a third- or fourth-generation language program into an equivalent machine language program, executing each source program statement as soon as that single statement is translated.

Intranet: A network operating within an organization that employs the TCP/IP protocol. Because the protocol is the same, the organization may use the same Web browser, Web crawler, and Web server software as it would use on the Internet; however, the intranet is not accessible from outside the organization.

Invisible queue: Those systems development requests that are not formally submitted because their sponsors are discouraged by the pool of projects that are already approved and awaiting development or because the sponsors doubt that they would be approved if submitted. These requests are in addition to the official backlog of work.

IOS: *See* Interorganizational system.

IS: *See* Information system.

IS coordinator: A position in a user organization whose role is to serve as a liaison between the organization and the IS organization. The IS coordinator must understand the business and the user organization, but must also understand the technology and the IS organization's perspective.

IS mission: The reason(s) for the existence of the IS organization. Typical reasons include reducing the costs of the organization, creating an effective information technology system, and exercising leadership in creating competitive advantage for the organization.

IS operational plan: Part of the IS plan that focuses on IS project selection and prioritizing.

IS plan: A statement of the objectives and initiatives that relate information systems to business priorities. The plan can be divided into a strategic plan, a long-term plan, and a short-term plan and budget.

IS steering committee: A committee of business managers whose function is to advise the head of IS on policy matters and often to decide which proposed systems will be developed by IS.

IS strategic planning process: Setting objectives, conducting internal and external analyses, and establishing strategic initiatives.

ISDN: *See* Integrated Services Digital Network.

IT platform: The set of hardware, software, and standards an organization uses to build its information systems.

JAD: *See* Joint application design.

JCL: *See* Job control language.

Job control language (JCL): The specialized computer language by which computer users communicate with the operating system. The term JCL is used primarily in the context of IBM mainframe computers.

Joint application design (JAD): A technique in which system requirements are defined by a team of users and IS specialists during an intensive effort led by a trained facilitator. JAD sessions are often held at special facilities with CASE tool support.

Knowledge worker: A typical worker in the Information Age, whose performance depends on how well he or she utilizes information and knowledge to create value for the organization.

LAN: *See* Local area network.

Laptop personal computer: The type of personal computer that can easily be carried with the user. A laptop PC occupies a small briefcase-like package weighing under 15 pounds. The terms "laptop" and "notebook" PC are now used almost interchangeably, although the notebook PC originally was a smaller machine than a laptop.

Lewin/Schein change model: Describes planned change in an organization as consisting of three stages: unfreezing, moving, and refreezing.

Life cycle process: The process for defining, building, and implementing a customized application or selecting, modifying, and implementing software packages. *See also* SDLC.

Listserv: An Internet application, or tool, which is essentially a mailing list such that members of a group can send a single electronic mail message and have it delivered to everyone in the group.

Local area network (LAN): A local data-only network, usually within a single organization and generally operating within an area no more than two or three miles in diameter, that contains a number of intelligent devices (usually microcomputers) capable of data processing. LANs are usually arranged in one of three topologies: contention bus, token bus, and token ring. *See also* Contention bus, Token bus, Token ring.

Local support: People and services that support end-user computing and are located within the user's own department or division.

Logical system, or model: A depiction of the function and purpose of a system without reference to or implications for how the system is implemented; includes both As-Is and To-Be models. *See also* Physical system, or model.

Lower-CASE: *See* Computer-aided software engineering.

Machine language: The form of a computer program that the control unit of the computer has been built to understand. In general, each machine language instruction consists of an operation code that tells the control unit what basic machine function is to be performed and one or more addresses that identify the specific memory cells whose contents will be involved in the operation.

Magnetic ink character recognition (MICR): A computer input method used for check processing in the United States. Identifying information and the amount are recorded in magnetizable ink at the bottom of the check; a computer input device called a magnetic ink character reader magnetizes the ink, recognizes the numbers, and transmits the data to the memory of the bank's computer to permit the check to be processed.

Magnetic tape unit: A computer file device that stores (writes) data on magnetic tape and retrieves (reads) data from tape back into memory; the usual device on which sequential access files are stored. *See also* Sequential access file.

Mainframes: The type of computer system that is used as the main central computing system of most major corporations and government agencies, ranging in cost from $500,000 to $10,000,000 or more, and in power from 50 to 2000 MFLOPS; used for large business general processing, as the server in client/server applications, and for a wide range of other applications.

Maintenance: The process of making changes to a system after it has been placed in operation, including changes required to correct errors, to adapt the system to changes in the environment, and to enhance the functionality of the system. Vendors of a purchased system may be contracted for maintenance as part of the purchase contract.

Make-or-buy decision: Within the context of systems development, the choice between customized application development and purchasing a software package.

Management system architecture: The portion of an information technology architecture that specifies the management process for IS in an organization.

Manufacturing automation protocol (MAP): A communications protocol (a set of rules) for communicating between automated equipment on a factory floor. MAP, which was pioneered by General Motors and has now been accepted by most major IT manufacturers and vendors, ensures an open manufacturing system in which communication between equipment from various vendors is possible.

Manufacturing resources planning (MRP II): A computer-based manufacturing administration system that usually incorporates three major components—the master production schedule, which sets the overall production goals; material requirements planning, which develops the detailed production schedule; and shop floor control, which releases orders to the shop floor based on the detailed schedule and actual production to date.

MAP: *See* Manufacturing automation protocol.

Massively parallel processor (MPP): A parallel processor computer with some large number of parallel CPUs; in general, 32 or more parallel CPUs is considered an MPP if the different CPUs are capable of performing different instructions at the same time, or a thousand or more parallel CPUs is considered an MPP if the different CPUs must all carry out the same instruction at the same time. *See also* Parallel processor.

Material requirements planning (MRP): A computer-based system that accepts the master production schedule for a factory as input and then develops a detailed production schedule, using parts explosion, production capacity, inventory, and lead time data; usually a component of a manufacturing resources planning (MRP II) system.

MegaFLOPS (MFLOPS): Shorthand for millions of floating point operations per second, a commonly used speed rating for computers. MegaFLOPS ratings are derived by running a particular set of programs in a particular language on the machines being investigated.

Memory: The primary area for storage of data in a computer system; also referred to as main memory or primary memory. All data flows in a computer system are to and from memory. Memory is divided into cells, and a fixed amount of data can be stored in each cell.

Mesh topology: A network topology in which most devices are connected to two, three, or more other devices in a seemingly irregular pattern that resembles a woven net, or a mesh. Examples of a mesh topology include the public telephone network and the network of networks that makes up the Internet.

MFLOPS: *See* MegaFLOPS.

MICR: *See* Magnetic ink character recognition.

Microcomputers: The category of computers with the lowest cost ($1,000 to $5,000) and the least power (1 to 50 MFLOPS), generally used for personal computing, small business processing, and as the client in client/server applications; also called micros or personal computers.

Microwave: Considered a transmission medium, although strictly speaking it is line-of-sight broadcast technology in which radio signals are sent out into the air. With transmission speeds of 56 thousand bits per second (bps) to 50 million bps, microwave is widely used for long distance telephone communication and for corporate voice and data networks.

Middleware: A term that covers all of the software needed to support interactions between clients and servers in client/server systems. Middleware usually includes three categories of software: network operating systems to create a single-system image for all services on the network; transport software to allow communications employing a standard protocol to be sent across the network; and service-specific software to carry out specific services such as electronic mail.

Midrange systems: The category of computers that can be viewed as "small mainframes" in that their technical architecture is derived from mainframe architecture; formerly called minicomputers or superminicomputers. Midrange systems represent a step above microcomputers in terms of both cost ($50,000 to $500,000) and power (3 to 1000 MFLOPS), but they overlap with workstations in both cost and power; they are generally used for departmental computing, specific applications such as CAD or office automation, and midsized business general processing, and they function as the server in client/server applications.

Minicomputers: *See* Midrange systems.

MIPS: An acronym for millions of instructions per second executed by the control unit of a computer, a commonly used maximum speed rating for computers.

Modem: An abbreviation for modulator/demodulator, a device that converts data from digital form to analog form so that it can be sent over the analog telephone network and reconverts data from analog to digital form after it has been transmitted.

Module: A self-contained unit of software that performs one or more functions. Ideally it has well-defined interfaces with the other modules in the program so that changes in a module only affect the rest of the program through the outputs from that module. *See also* Subsystem.

MRP: *See* Material requirements planning.

MRP II: *See* Manufacturing resources planning.

Multimedia: The use of a microcomputer system to coordinate many types of communication media—text, graphics, sound, still images, animations, and video. The purpose of a multimedia system is to enhance the quality of and interest in a presentation, whether it is a corporate briefing or a school lesson.

Multiprocessing: The method of processing when two or more CPUs are installed as part of the same computer system. Each CPU works on its own job or set of jobs (often using multiprogramming), with all the CPUs under control of a single operating system.

Multiprocessor: A computer configuration in which multiple processors (CPUs) are installed as part of the same computer system, with each processor or CPU operating independently of the others. *See* Multiprocessing, Symmetric multiprocessor.

Multiprogramming: A procedure by which the operating system switches back and forth among a number of programs, all located in memory at the same time, to keep the CPU busy while input/output operations are taking place; more specifically, this is called event-driven multiprogramming.

Multitasking: The terminology used for microcomputers to describe essentially the same function as multiprogramming on larger machines. In preemptive multitasking, the operating system allocates slices of CPU time to each program as in time-driven multiprogramming; in cooperative multitasking, each program can control the CPU for as long as it needs it, as in event-driven multiprogramming. *See also* Multiprogramming, Time-sharing.

Natural language: A computer language (often termed a fifth-generation language) in which the user writes a program in ordinary English or something very close to it. Little or no training is required to use a natural language.

Needs-based IS planning: The process of assembling the IS plan by addressing only the stated needs of users.

Negotiation support system (NSS): A special type of group support system designed to support the activities of two or more parties in a negotiation. The core components of an NSS are an individual decision support system for each party in the negotiation plus an electronic communication channel between the parties.

NetPC: A somewhat stripped-down, less expensive variation of a personal computer being developed by Microsoft and Intel for those users who will almost always be connected to a network (usually the Internet). The NetPC is more powerful than the network computer and is able to execute Windows applications locally. *See also* Network computer.

Network computer: A stripped-down, less expensive variation of a personal computer being developed by Apple, IBM, Netscape, Oracle, and Sun for those users who will always be connected to a network (usually the Internet). The network computer is less powerful, and thus less expensive, than the NetPC and must be connected to the network to accomplish useful work. *See also* NetPC.

Network operating system (NOS): Support software, installed on the network server, that manages network resources and controls the operation of the network. The primary network operating systems are Novell's NetWare, Microsoft's Windows NT Server, IBM's OS/2 Warp Server, and Unix-based systems from Sun and OSF.

Network protocol: An agreed-upon set of rules or conventions governing communication among elements of a network, or, more specifically, among layers or levels of a network.

Networking: The electronic linking of geographically dispersed devices.

Neural networks: The branch of artificial intelligence concerned with recognizing patterns from vast amounts of data by a process of adaptive learning; named after the study of how the human nervous system works, but in fact uses extensive statistical analysis to identify meaningful patterns from the data.

Nonprocedural language: *See* Fourth-generation language.

NOS: *See* Network operating system.

Notebook personal computers: The type of personal computer that can easily be carried with the user; this type of PC is similar in size to a student's notebook and typically weighs no more than 5 or 6 pounds. The terms "laptop" and "notebook" PC are now used almost interchangeably, although the notebook PC originally was a smaller machine than a laptop.

NSS: *See* Negotiation support system.

Object-oriented programming (OOP): A type of computer programming based on the creation and use of a set of objects (each object is a chunk of program code) and the development of relationships among the objects. The most popular OOP languages are C++ and Smalltalk.

Object-oriented technology: A broader term than object-oriented programming that includes object-oriented analysis and design as well as programming.

Object program: The machine language program that is the result of translating a second-, third-, or fourth-generation source program.

OCR: *See* Optical character recognition.

Office automation: The use of information technology to automate various aspects of office operations. Office automation involves a set of office-related functions that may or may not be integrated in a single system, including electronic mail, word processing, photocopying, document preparation, voice mail, desktop publishing, personal databases, and electronic calendaring.

On-line processing: A mode of transaction processing in which each transaction is entered directly into the computer when it occurs, and the associated processing is carried out immediately. For example, sales would be entered into the computer (probably via a microcomputer) as soon as they occurred, and sales records would be updated immediately.

On-line system: *See* On-line processing.

OOP: *See* Object-oriented programming.

Open systems: Systems (usually operating systems) that are not tied to a particular computer system or hardware manufacturer. An example is the UNIX operating system, with versions available for a wide variety of hardware platforms.

Open Systems Interconnection (OSI) Reference Model: An evolving set of network protocols developed by the International Standards Organization (ISO), which deals with connecting all systems that are open for communication with other systems (i.e., systems that conform to certain minimal standards) by defining seven layers, each of which will have one or more protocols.

Operating system: Very complex software that controls the operation of the computer hardware and coordinates all the other software. The purpose of an operating system is to get as much work done as possible with the available resources and to be convenient to use.

Optical character recognition (OCR): A computer input method that directly scans typed, printed, or handprinted material. A computer input device called an optical character reader scans and recognizes the characters and then transmits the data to the memory or records them on magnetic tape.

Optical disk: A relatively new medium upon which computer files can be stored. Data are recorded on an optical disk by using a laser to burn microscopic pits on its surface. Optical disks have a much greater capacity than magnetic disks but are typically much slower.

OSI: *See* Open Systems Interconnection Reference Model.

Outsourcing: The elimination of part of the internal IS organization by hiring an outside organization to perform these functions. Outsourcing has most often involved the operation of data centers, but may include applications system design or programming and data communications network management. Outsourcing is done to achieve economies of scale by combining the functions of several organizations into one highly-qualified professional staff. IS employees impacted by outsourcing are often transferred to the outsourcing organization.

Packaged system: *See* Software package.

Packet switching: A method of operating a digital telecommunications network (especially a value-added network) in which information is divided into packets of some fixed length that are then sent over the network separately. Rather than tying up an entire end-to-end circuit for the duration of the session, the packets from various users can be interspersed with one another to permit more efficient use of the network.

Palmtop personal computers: *See* Hand-held personal computers.

Parallel processor (PP): A multiprocessor configuration of multiple CPUs installed as part of the same computer system, designed to give a separate piece of the same program to each of the processors so that work on the program can proceed in parallel on the separate pieces.

Partnership: A coordinating strategy for IS management. Partnership creates strong working relationships between IS personnel and peer managers in business functions and often results in more effective information systems and IS management.

PBX network: The type of network emanating from a *p*rivate *b*ranch *e*xchange, or PBX, which is a digital switch operated by a built-in computer with the capability of simultaneously handling communications with internal analog telephones, digital microcomputers and terminals, mainframe computers, and the external telephone network; usually arranged in a star or a tree topology.

Personal computers: *See* Microcomputers.

Physical system, or model: A depiction that shows the physical form (the how) in which a system operates. *See also* Logical system, or model.

Political perspective: The view that decisions in organizations are influenced by political considerations

rather than always being entirely rational. It holds that the interests of the decision-makers, rather than just what is best for the organization, influence the outcomes of decisions. *See also* Rational perspective.

Procedural language: *See* Third-generation language.

Procedurally-oriented techniques: *See* Structured techniques.

Process-driven design: An approach to systems development that concentrates on the flow, use, and transformation of information. *See also* Data-driven design.

Processor: *See* Central processing unit.

Productivity language: Another name for a fourth-generation language. This type of language tends to make the programmer or user more productive, which explains the name.

Program: A complete listing of what the computer is to do for a particular application, expressed in a form that the control unit of the computer has been built to understand or that can be translated into such a form. A program is made up of a sequence of individual steps or operations called instructions.

Program structure chart: A common diagrammatic technique for showing the flow of control for a computer program.

Project-oriented IS planning: An approach to building the IS plan that assembles the IS plan from individual projects.

Proprietary systems: Systems (usually operating systems) that were written expressly for a particular computer system. Examples are Windows 95, Windows 98, and Windows NT, which are Microsoft's current operating systems for personal computers, and MVS and VM, which are the two alternative large machine operating systems offered by IBM.

Prototyping: An approach to systems development in which an initial version of the system is built very quickly using fourth-generation tools; it is then tried out by users to determine its weaknesses, an improved version is built, and this process of trial and improvement is continued (reiterated) until the result is accepted. *See also* Rapid application development.

Pull technology: Refers to the mode of operation on the Internet where the client must request data before the data are sent to the client. For example, a Web browser represents pull technology in that the browser must request a Web page before it is sent to the user's screen. *See also* Push technology.

Push technology: Refers to the mode of operation on the Internet where data are sent to the client without the client requesting the data. Examples of push technology include electronic mail and PointCast, which delivers customized news ticker-tape style to the user's screen. *See also* Pull technology.

Query language: Fourth-generation software that allows one to produce reports without writing procedural programs by specifying their contents and format.

Rapid application development (RAD): A systems development methodology based upon a combination of prototyping, JAD, and I-CASE tools, in which the end-prototype becomes the actual system. *See also* Prototyping, JAD, I-CASE.

Raster-based GIS: One of two basic approaches for representation and analysis of spatial data in which space is divided into small, equal-sized cells arranged in a grid; these cells (or rasters) can take on a range of values and are "aware" of their location relative to other cells. Weather forecasting employs a raster-based approach.

Rational perspective: A traditional view of how organizations function, with decision-making based upon maximizing organizational objectives using rational analysis. *See also* Political perspective.

Reengineering: *See* Business process reengineering, Software reengineering.

Relational database: *See* Relational DBMS.

Relational DBMS: A particular style of database management system (DBMS) that views each data entity as a simple table, with the columns as data elements and the rows as different instances of the entity. Relational DBMSs are the most popular type of DBMS today, especially for data analysis and presentation systems.

Request for proposal (RFP): A document that is sent to potential vendors inviting them to submit a proposal for a system purchase. It provides the objectives and requirements of the desired system, including the technical environment in which it must operate; specifies what the vendor must provide as input to the selection process; and explains the conditions for submitting proposals and the general criteria that will be used to evaluate them.

Response time: The elapsed time between when a user presses a key to send data to a computer and when the response from the computer appears on the terminal screen.

Reverse engineering: A term used to describe the generation of program specifications by starting with the existing source program code.

RFP: *See* Request for proposal.

Rightsizing: A term that means choosing the right number of something or the right components. When referring to computer hardware, rightsizing means fitting computer technology to the diverse needs within an organization. Rightsizing typically involves use of a combination of mainframes, intelligent workstations, and client/server software that blends aspects of centralized and decentralized computing.

Ring topology: A network topology in which a single length of cable—with the ends of the cable connected to form a ring—is shared by all network devices.

Ripple effect: When a change in one part of a program or system causes unanticipated problems in a different part of the program or system. Then changes necessary to correct that problem may cause problems somewhere else, and so on.

RISC chip: Very fast processor chip based on the idea of reduced instruction set computing, or RISC; originally developed for use in high-powered workstations, but now used in other machines, especially midrange systems.

Router: A hardware device employed in a telecommunications network to connect two or more local area networks (LANs), where the networks may use different protocols. The router forwards only those messages that need to be forwarded from one network to another. *See also* Gateway.

SA&D: *See* System analysis and design.

SAA: *See* Systems Application Architecture.

Satellite communications: A variation of microwave transmission in which a communications satellite is used to relay microwave signals over long distances.

SDLC: *See* System development life cycle.

Sequential access file: A basic type of computer file in which all of the records that make up the file are stored in sequence according to the control key of the file (e.g., a payroll file will contain individual employee records stored in sequence according to the employee identification number); usually stored on magnetic tape. Computer files, also called secondary memory or secondary storage, are added to a computer system to keep vast quantities of data accessible within the computer system at more reasonable costs than main memory.

Sequential file organization: *See* Sequential access file.

Service level agreement: An agreement between IS and a client that specifies a set of services to be provided, the amount of those services to be provided, the quality or these services and how it is to be measured, and the price to be charged for these services.

SFC: *See* Shop floor control.

Shop floor control (SFC): A computer-based system which releases orders to the shop floor based on the detailed production schedule and the actual production accomplished thus far; usually a component of a manufacturing resources planning (MRP II) system.

Simplex transmission: A type of data transmission in which data can travel only in one direction over the communication line. Simplex transmission might be used from a monitoring device at a remote site back to a central computer.

SIS: *See* Strategic information system.

SNA: *See* Systems Network Architecture.

Software: The set of programs (made up of instructions) that control the operations of the computer system.

Software package: Computer software that is sold as a self-contained "package" so that it may be distributed widely. In addition to the computer programs, a package may include comprehensive documentation of the system, assistance in installing the system, training, a hotline consulting service for dealing with problems, and even maintenance of the system.

Software reengineering: Upgrading an existing system to improve its functionality and changeability by evaluating the structure and components of the system to create a new structure if necessary, continuing to use those components that are satisfactory, rehabilitating those components that can be modified to be satisfactory, replacing those components that cannot be rehabilitated, and adding components that are needed to enhance the functionality of the system.

SONET: *See* Synchronous Optical Network.

Source program: A program written in a second-, third-, or fourth-generation language.

Spaghetti code: Programs with complex logic, where the flow of control may take many intertwined paths through the various parts of the program. Logically, it resembles a plate of spaghetti where the many strands are tangled in a confusing jumble. The opposite of structured code.

Specific DSS: *See* Decision support system.

Sponsor: The business executive who is responsible for funding a new system and ensuring that the necessary resources are available to a systems project team. Also called sponsoring manager.

SQL: A standard query and data definition language for relational DBMSs. This standard, endorsed by the American National Standards Institute (ANSI), is used in many personal computer, minicomputer, and mainframe computer DBMSs.

Stages of growth: A framework for viewing the management of technology that assumes that organizations go through an organizational learning curve that can be described in terms of stages such as initiation, contagion, control, and maturity.

Standalone: Used to describe hardware that is not networked to other computers, or a software application that is accessible only to the user of the computer where the application is physically stored.

Star topology: A network topology that has some primary device at its center with cables radiating from the primary device to all the other network devices.

Steering committee: *See* IS steering committee.

Stored-program concept: The concept of preparing a precise list of exactly what the computer is to do (a program), loading or storing this program in the memory of the computer, and then letting the control unit carry out the program at electronic speed. The listing or program must be in a form that the control unit of the computer has been built to understand.

Strategic information system (SIS): The use of information, information processing, and/or communications for implementing business strategy or obtaining a competitive advantage. An information system is strategic if it changes an organization's product or service or the way a firm competes in its industry. An SIS often is a system that links an organization to its customers or suppliers. *See also* Interorganizational system (IOS).

Structure chart: A tree-structured diagram that shows the logic (flow of information and control) within one computer program.

Structured programming: A technique of writing programs so that each program is divided into modules or blocks, where each block has only one entry point and one exit point. In this form, the program logic is easy to follow and understand, and thus the maintenance and correction of such a program should be easier than for a nonstructured program.

Structured techniques: A body of structured approaches and tools to document system needs and requirements, functional features and dependencies, and design decisions. Also referred to as procedurally oriented techniques. *See also* Structured programming.

Subsystem: A component of a system that is itself viewed as a set of interrelated components. A subsystem has a well-defined purpose that must contribute to the purpose of the system as a whole. *See also* Module, Hierarchical decomposition.

Supercomputers: The most expensive and most powerful category of computers, ranging in cost from $1,000,000 to $30,000,000 and in power from 1000 to 2,000,000 MFLOPS; used for numerically intensive computing.

Superminicomputers: Large minicomputers; the upper end of the minicomputer or midrange systems category. *See also* Midrange systems.

Supply-chain management system: A computer-based manufacturing administration system designed to deal with distribution and transportation of raw materials and finished products throughout the supply chain and to incorporate constraints caused by the supply chain into the production scheduling process.

Support software: Programs that do not directly produce output needed by users, but instead support other applications software in producing the needed output. Support software provides a computing environment in which it is relatively easy and efficient for humans to work, enables applications programs written in a variety of languages to be carried out, and ensures that computer hardware and software resources are used efficiently. Support software includes operating systems, language compilers, and sort utilities.

Switch: A hardware device employed in a telecommunications network to connect more than two local area networks (LANs) or LAN segments that use the same protocols. For example, a switch might connect several low speed LANs (16 Ethernet LANs running at 10 mbps) into a single 100 mbps backbone network running Fast Ethernet.

SWOT analysis: Part of IS planning, referring to strengths, weaknesses, opportunities, and threats.

Symmetric multiprocessor (SMP): A multiprocessor computer configuration in which all the processors (CPUs) are identical, with each processor acting independently of the others. The multiple CPUs equally share functional and timing access to and control over all other system components, including memory and the various peripheral devices, with each CPU working in its own allotted portion of memory.

Synchronous Optical Network (SONET): ANSI (American National Standards Institute)-approved standard for connecting fiber optic transmission systems; this standard is employed in a range of high-capacity leased lines varying from the OC-1 level of 52 mbps to the OC-48 level of 2488 mbps.

System: A set of interrelated components that work together to achieve some common purpose.

System development methodology: A framework of guidelines, tools, and techniques for developing computer systems. *See also* Systems development life cycle, Prototyping.

System flow chart: A diagram which shows the relationship between major system components, not detailed logic.

System release: An distinct version of a software system. Maintenance and other changes to the current release (say release 4.2) are combined to produce the next version (release 4.3), which is "released" to replace the previous version.

Systems analysis and design (SA&D): The process used to develop a system. *See also* Systems development life cycle.

Systems analyst: IS specialist who works with users to develop systems requirements and help plan implementations, and works with systems designers, programmers, and other information technology specialists to construct systems based on the user requirements.

Systems Application Architecture (SAA): An evolving set of specifications, under development by IBM, defining programming, communications, and a common end-user interface that will allow applications to be created and moved among the full range of IBM computers. IBM has stated its intention of supporting both SNA and OSI protocols in its future efforts under the SAA umbrella.

Systems backlog: Refers to the number of requests for new systems development and/or maintenance requests that have not yet been assigned IS resources to work on them. An "invisible backlog" refers to systems requests not even formally submitted by users due to the size of the existing "visible" backlog.

Systems development life cycle (SDLC): The traditional methodology used by IS professionals to develop a new computer application that includes three general phases: Definition, Construction, and Implementation. Also referred to as a "waterfall" process because of its sequential steps. The SDLC methodology defines the activities necessary for these three phases, as well as a framework for planning and managing a development project. Operations and maintenance are included in the Implementation phase. A modified SDLC approach is used to purchase packaged systems.

Systems development portfolio: The mix of IS development projects arrayed by risk and return.

Systems integrator: A firm that will take overall responsibility for managing the development or integration of large, complex systems involving the use of components from a number of different vendors.

Systems Network Architecture (SNA): A set of network protocols created by IBM to allow its customers to construct their own private networks using the wide variety of IBM communication products, teleprocessing access methods, and data link protocols. SNA was first created in 1974 and is still in widespread use.

Systems package: *See* Software package.

Systems software: *See* Support software.

T-1 lines: The most common leased communication lines, operating at a data transmission rate of 1.544 million bits per second. These lines, which may be leased from AT&T or another long distance carrier, often provide the basis for a wide area network (WAN).

TCP/IP: *See* Transmission Control Protocol/Internet Protocol.

Technological assets: A component of the IT architecture that contains desired specifications about future hardware and operating systems, network, data and data management systems, and applications software.

Telecommunications: Communications at a distance, including voice (telephone) and data (text/image) communications. Other similar terms used almost interchangeably with telecommunications include data communications, datacom, teleprocessing, telecom, and networking.

Telecommuter: A person who works at home or at other locations that are not owned by the organization the person works for and who uses computers and communications to connect to resources inside the organization's physical facilities.

Telemarketing: The use of the telephone, customer databases, direct mail, and data processing to market and support a product or service. Telemarketing is used by many organizations as a strategic information system.

Telnet: An Internet application, or tool, that allows a user to log onto a remote computer from whatever computer he/she is now using, as long as both computers are attached to the Internet.

Terminal: A computer input/output device, usually incorporating a keyboard for input and a video display unit for output; does not incorporate a processor (CPU) and thus operates as a "slave" to a "master" computer, usually a minicomputer or a mainframe.

Third-generation language: A programming language in which the programmer expresses a step-by-step procedure to accomplish the desired task. Examples include FORTRAN, COBOL, BASIC, PASCAL, and C.

Three-tier client/server system: A variation of a client/server system in which the processing is split across three tiers, the client and two servers. In the most popular three-tier system, the user interface is housed on the client, usually a PC (tier 1); the processing is performed on a midrange system or workstation operating as the applications server (tier 2); and the data is stored on a large machine (often a mainframe or midrange system) that operates as the database server (tier 3).

Time-sharing: A procedure by which the operating system switches among a number of programs, all stored in memory at the same time, giving each program a small slice of CPU time before moving on to the next program; this is also called time-driven multiprogramming.

Token bus: A design standard for a local area network based on a bus topology and the passing of a token around the bus to all devices in a specified order. In this design, a given device can only transmit when it has the token and thus collisions can never occur. The token bus design is central to the Manufacturing Automation Protocol, or MAP.

Token ring: A design standard for a local area network based on a ring topology and the passing of a token around the ring to all devices in a specified order. In this design, a given device can only transmit when it has the token and thus collisions can never occur.

Transaction processing system: A very common type of computer application in which transactions (of a particular type) are processed in order to provide desired output. Examples include the processing of employee work records (transactions) to produce payroll checks and accompanying reports and the processing of orders (transactions) to produce invoices and associated reports. Transaction processing systems may be batch, on-line, or in-line.

Transborder data flow: Electronic movement of data across a country's national boundary. Such data flows may be restricted by laws that protect a country's economic, political, or personal privacy interests.

Transmission Control Protocol/Internet Protocol (TCP/IP): A popular network protocol used in many versions of the UNIX operating system, many value-added networks, the Internet, and intranets operating within organizations. Although not part of the OSI model, TCP/IP corresponds roughly to the network and transport layers of the seven-layer model.

Tree topology: A network topology that has some primary device at the top of the tree, with cables radiating from this primary device to devices further down the tree that, in turn, may have cables radiating from them to other devices still further down the tree, and so on; also called hierarchical topology.

Twisted pair: The most common transmission medium, with two insulated copper wires (about 1 millimeter thick) twisted together in a long helix. Data transmission speeds of 14,400 to 56,000 bits per second (bps) are possible with twisted pairs on the voice telephone network, with higher speeds up to 144,000 bps attainable on conditioned lines or up to 100 million bps on local area networks.

Two-tier client/server system: The original implementation of a client/server system in which the processing is split between the client (usually a PC) and the server (workstation, midrange system, or mainframe). If most of the processing is done on the client, this is called a fat client or thin server model; if most of the processing is done on the server, this is called a thin client or fat server model.

UAD: *See* User application development.

Upper-CASE: *See* Computer-aided software engineering.

Usenet newsgroups: An Internet application, or tool, setting up discussion groups, which are essentially huge electronic bulletin boards on which group members can read and post messages.

User application development (UAD): Development of business applications by people who are not IS professionals, but rather are primarily in traditional business roles such as accountants, financial analysts, production schedulers, engineers, and brand managers. In most but not all instances, the people who develop the applications also directly use them in their work.

User-developers: *See* User application development.

User friendly: A perceptual measure of how easy it is to navigate and use particular hardware or software from the perspective of a person who is not an IS specialist.

User interface: That part of a system through which the user interacts with the system. As examples, it may use a mouse, a touch-screen, menus, commands, voice recognition, a telephone keypad, output screens, voice response, and printed reports. *See also* Graphical user interface.

Value added network (VAN): A data-only, private, nonregulated telecommunications network that uses packet switching. An organization may choose to buy the services of a VAN provider to implement its wide area network (WAN).

Value chain analysis: A method developed by Michael E. Porter to identify possible strategic uses of information technology. A firm's value chain contains the activities in the business that add value to a firm's products or services.

Values architecture: That part of an IT architecture that specified the basic beliefs of the people about IT in the organization.

VAN: *See* Value added network.

vBNS: *See* very high-speed Backbone Network Service.

Vector-based GIS: One of two basic approaches for representation and analysis of spatial data in which features in the landscape are associated with either a point (e.g., customer address, power pole), a line (road, river), or a polygon (lake, county, zip code area). The vector-based approach is in widespread use in public administration, public utilities, and business.

Vector facility: A specialized multiprocessor configuration (multiple CPUs installed as part of the same computer system) to handle calculations involving vectors. The same operation is performed simultaneously on each element of the vector by parallel microprocessors. A vector facility can be attached to a mainframe or superminicomputer to handle numeric- or compute-intensive parts of programs.

Veronica: An Internet application, or tool, that allows the user to search publicly available Gopher sites using key words until the sought-after data are located. Veronica, like Gopher, has largely disappeared, with both subsumed by the greater capabilities of the World Wide Web.

Vertically integrated information system: An information system that serves more than one vertical level in an organization or an industry, such as a system designed to be used by an automobile manufacturer and the associated independent dealers.

very high-speed Backbone Network Service (vBNS): The National Science Foundation backbone network linking five NSF-supported supercomputer centers in the United States with access points where other researchers may link into vBNS from the Internet; the successor to NSFNET.

View integration: A bottom-up approach to detailing the data requirements of an organization. View integration analyzes each report, screen, form, and document in the organization and combines each of these views into one consolidated and consistent picture of all organizational data.

Virtual memory: A procedure by which the operating system switches portions of programs (called pages) between main memory and DASD so that portions of enough programs are stored in main memory to enable efficient multiprogramming. To the user, it appears as though he or she has an unlimited amount of main memory available, whereas in fact most of each program is stored in DASD.

Virtual reality (VR): The use of computer-based systems to create an environment that seems real to one or more more senses (usually including sight) of the human user or users. Examples of practical uses of virtual reality include the training of tank crews for the U.S. Army, the design of an automobile dashboard and controls, and retail store layout.

Virus: *See* Computer virus.

Visual programming: A type of computer programming built around a graphical programming environment and a paint metaphor for developing user interfaces. The most popular visual programming languages are Visual Basic and Java.

Voice response unit: A computer output method using the spoken voice to provide a response to the user. This output method is gaining increasing acceptance as a provider of limited, tightly programmed computer output, often in conjunction with touch-tone telephone input.

VR: *See* Virtual reality.

WAN: *See* Wide area network.

WATS: *See* Wide Area Telephone Service.

Web: Shorthand for World Wide Web. *See* World Wide Web.

Web browser: Personal productivity software that runs on the user's microcomputer, enabling him/her to look around, or "browse" the Internet, as long as the user's machine is linked to the Internet via a modem or a connection to a local area network. The Web browser uses a hypertext-based approach to navigate the Internet. *See* Hypertext.

Wide area network (WAN): A type of network over which both voice and data for a single organization are communicated among the multiple locations (often far apart) where the organization operates, usually employing point-to-point transmission over facilities owned by several organizations, including the public telephone network; also called a long-haul network.

Wide Area Telephone Service (WATS): A service available from the telephone company in which an organization pays a monthly fee for unlimited long distance telephone service using ordinary voice circuits. WATS is an easy way to set up a wide area network (WAN) and costs less per hour than standard Direct Distance Dialing (DDD).

Wireless: Considered as a transmission medium, although strictly speaking it is broadcast technology in which radio signals are sent out into the air. Wireless transmission speeds vary from 2 million bits per second (bps) to 50 million bps. Examples are cordless telephone, cellular telephone, wireless LAN, and microwave.

Wireless LAN: A local area network employing wireless communication between the various devices in the network. Compared to a wired LAN, a wireless LAN is easier to plan and install, generally more expensive, less secure, and usually slower, with transmission speeds from 2 million bits per second (bps) to 8 million bps for a radio signal LAN.

Word: A memory cell that can store two or more characters of data (see memory); alternatively, the amount of data handled by the central processing unit (CPU) as a single unit.

Workstations: Generally, any computer-related device at which an individual may work, such as a personal computer or a terminal. Specifically, the category of computers based on powerful microprocessor chips, with costs from $5,000 to $100,000 and with power ranging from 50 to 500 MFLOPS; generally used as the server in client/server applications, the server for a local area network, or for specific applications such as computer-aided design or graphics.

World Wide Web: An Internet application, or tool, that uses a hypertext-based approach to traverse, or "surf," the Internet, by clicking on a link contained in one document to move to another document; these links may also connect to video clips, recordings, photographs, and other images.

WORM disk: An abbreviation for write once, read many disk, a type of optical disk that can be written on by the user once and then can be read many times. WORM technology is appropriate for archiving documents, engineering drawings, and records of all types.

WWW: An abbreviation for World Wide Web.

X.25 protocol: A network protocol, formally adopted as part of the OSI model, employed to handle the packet switching in many value-added networks (VANs). X.25 encompasses the physical, data link, and network layers of the seven-layer OSI model.

INDEX